International Economics

International Economics
A Heterodox Approach

SECOND EDITION

Hendrik Van den Berg

M.E.Sharpe
Armonk, New York
London, England

Library of Congress Cataloging-in-Publication Data

Van den Berg, Hendrik, 1949–
International economics : a heterodox approach / Hendrik Van den Berg. — 2nd ed.
    p. cm.
  Includes bibliographical references and index.
  ISBN 978-0-7656-2544-1 (pbk. : alk. paper)
  1. International trade. 2. Protectionism. 3. Investments, Foreign. 4. International finance. 5. International economic relations.
  6. Emigration and immigration. I. Title.

HF1379.V36 2011
337—dc22
                                                                                    2010054103

Printed in the United States of America

The paper used in this publication meets the minimum requirements of
American National Standard for Information Sciences
Permanence of Paper for Printed Library Materials,
ANSI Z 39.48-1984.

∞

SP (p)   10   9   8   7   6   5   4   3   2   1

Contents

Author's Note

"The composition of this book has been for the author a long struggle of escape, and so must the reading of it be for most readers if the author's assault upon them is to be successful—a struggle of escape from habitual modes of thought and expression. The ideas which are here expressed so laboriously are extremely simple and should be obvious. The difficulty lies, not in the new ideas, but in escaping from the old ones, which ramify, for those of us brought up as most of us have been, into every corner of our minds."

—John Maynard Keynes, in the Preface to his *General Theory of Employment, Interest, and Money* (1936, p. viii)

This new edition of *International Economics* marks a significant advance in my thinking since the first edition was published in 2003. In this edition I have consciously adopted a multiparadigmatic approach that draws from neoclassical models along with models and ideas from other schools of economics—as well as sociology, political science, ecology, psychology, neuroscience, and history—in a concerted effort to clarify the causes and consequences of international economic integration. If a paradigm is like a language, then heterodoxy effectively enables an economist to become multilingual. This edition's interdisciplinary and heterodox approach places international trade, international investment, international finance, and immigration in a much more exciting holistic framework that links the economic, social, and natural spheres of human existence. It should broaden the view of economics majors and build bridges to students majoring in international relations, business, and other social science fields.

I am certain that, as one person, I have not come close to capturing all the relevant knowledge related to the many issues of international economics; but my hope is that this book will play a role in furthering the discussion of how international economic integration can best advance the well-being of humanity and Earth.

Many people played important roles in bringing this book to publication. First of all, I want to thank everyone at M.E. Sharpe for their efforts in making this project a reality. They have made me sound much better than my own writing, and they were a pleasure to work with throughout this project. Of course, I take full responsibility for any remaining errors.

I want to thank my teachers. At the State University of New York at Albany, I must mention Fred Dickey, who taught me principles of economics and inspired me to major in economics; Helen Horowitz, who inspired me to become a teacher of economics; and Franklin Walker and Pong Lee, who introduced me to the cutting edge of economic thinking at the time. At the University of Wisconsin–Madison, I owe special debts to Arthur Goldberger, who taught me to be critical of technical approaches to economics. His courses in econometrics demanded critical thinking and a heavy dose of skepticism. I must also thank the professors I worked with most closely at the University of Wisconsin: Robert Baldwin, J. David Richardson, Rachel McCullough, and Kenneth Rogoff. While I have now embraced heterodoxy in place of the orthodox neoclassical analysis they taught, they introduced me to many broad perspectives that prepared me well for my growth as an economist. Their endless energy in research and teaching made it clear that we never stop learning and revising our thinking.

Among my colleagues here at the University of Nebraska, I above all thank Greg Hayden and Ann Mari May, who never hesitated to challenge me as I struggled with the neoclassical paradigm. They also provided insight into heterodoxy, institutional economics, and feminist economics. And, of course, I thank all my students who asked difficult questions and wrote unconventional answers to my conventional questions. The insight I gain from students convinces me that academia's focus on research should not be allowed to diminish the importance of teaching; we do not know how good a new idea is until we try to teach someone.

My wife, Barbara, provided the most comprehensive editing throughout the many, many stages of development of this new edition. She added many ideas and perspectives from her reading and experience as a community activist. I also want to thank our three sons, Paulo, Matthew, and Tom, who continually challenged my reasoning. Matthew, who now also teaches economics, provided many detailed ideas, concepts, and additions that substantially expanded the book's heterodoxy. Paulo has always provided timely advice that kept my feet on the ground. And Tom and his trombone provide the jazz that reminds us of the importance of improvisation and art: despite what orthodox neoclassical economics contends, we humans cannot survive on GDP alone.

Hendrik Van den Berg
Lincoln, Nebraska
September 7, 2011

PART ONE

INTRODUCTION TO INTERNATIONAL ECONOMICS

CHAPTER 1

Interdependence!

[T]he sea brought Greeks the vine from India, from Greece transmitted the use of grain across the sea, from Phoenicia imported letters as a memorial against forgetfulness, thus preventing the greater part of mankind from being wineless, grainless, and unlettered.

—Plutarch, 100 A.D.

China's rapid economic growth in terms of gross domestic product (GDP) per capita has been widely described as a major economic development success of the last twenty-five years. China has, since the late 1970s, achieved annual growth rates of over 8 percent. The power of compounding led per capita income to double in less than ten years and quadruple in less than one generation. China contains one-fifth of the world's population; its rapid growth in material output means that a very large percentage of the world's poor people have experienced improvements in their standards of living.

The economic development of the Chinese economy cannot be fully described by the simple compounding of annual growth rates of GDP, however. The process of economic development is much more complex than that. For example, the town of Jinfeng, situated along the lower Yangtze River in China, illustrates the complexities of recent Chinese economic growth.[1] At the start of the twenty-first century, every morning more than thirty thousand of Jinfeng's workers walked or bicycled to an array of industries paying wages equal to about US$0.50 per hour. Compared to working on small farms in their villages, these wages constituted a substantial increase in real income, which is why so many workers flocked to cities like Jinfeng. Among Jinfeng's many industrial firms is the Shagang steel mill, which opened in 2002 after being transported, piece by piece, from the Ruhr Valley of Germany. The Ruhr Valley was until recently the center of Germany's powerful steel industry.

In the early 2000s, the German steel conglomerate ThyssenKrupp faced strong foreign competition and tightened environmental regulations. It therefore began selling off many of its ageing steel manufacturing plants. But it did not sell the plants to new owners who would continue operating them in Germany. Rather, the plants were sold to bargain-hunting Chinese entrepreneurs who sent work crews to dismantle the equipment and pack it off to China, where labor costs were a tiny fraction of Germany's. ThyssenKrupp had estimated it would take three years to dismantle the plant. The Chinese work crews sent to Dortmund by Shagang finished the dismantling in one year. They worked seven days a week for many more hours per day than German labor law allowed but, somehow, the German government looked the other way. Today, the plant produces steel at much lower cost in Jinfeng, and this steel is used to produce many Chinese products that are shipped all over the world, including to the wealthy German market. Because of the relocated steel plant in Jinfeng and dozens more like it throughout the country, China is now the world's biggest steel producer, well ahead of the once-dominant German steel industry.

The example of Jinfeng suggests that international trade and accompanying international investment are an intimate part of Chinese economic development. Indeed, many economists position international trade as an important generator of economic growth. But further information suggests that the Jinfeng plant is not necessarily a positive development for China or the world. Before we jump to conclusions, we must recognize that China's steel mills, and the coal-fired power plants that provide their electric power, have also produced the massive **greenhouse gas (GHG) emissions** that helped China overtake the United States in 2007 as the largest emitter of the GHGs that cause global warming. China was also releasing into its air more than 26 million tons of sulfur, the pollutant that causes respiratory problems for humans, and acid rain, which contaminates water supplies—about two and one-half times as much sulfur as the United States emitted in 2005. In the case of Jinfeng, German GHG and sulfur emissions were simply transferred to China. While Germany proudly confirmed that it was on schedule to reduce its greenhouse gas emissions by 40 percent by 2020, its former steel mills were increasing China's emissions. One study attributes four hundred thousand premature deaths in China to air pollution. Evidence shows that China's sulfur emissions and other pollutants also travel across the Pacific Ocean and now account for nearly 15 percent of California's air particles allowable under U.S. environmental laws.[2] We clearly live in an integrated international economy, in which one country's economic activity affects the well-being of people in other countries in a variety of ways.

The rest of the world has felt the effects of China's industrial growth. The $0.50-per-hour wages paid in Shinfeng may be attractive for workers with few options in China's rural communities, but in the integrated global economy the low Chinese wages and poor working conditions have put severe downward pressure on wages and working conditions in other countries. According to the British-based Catholic Agency for Overseas Development (CAFOD), Chinese workers producing high-tech computer products often work 16-hour days in factories with unclean air, high noise levels, and dangerous machinery. Workers also often live in company dormitories, and they do little more than work and sleep for months on end.

The interdependence among economies that trade and invest is much more complex than the example of Jinfeng suggests at first glance. For one thing, all firms in the international market must compete with these Chinese manufacturers and their low labor costs. For example, Mexican factories producing for the U.S. market compete directly with Chinese factories. This is why a Mexican labor activist complained that "[l]ast year, the average pay for production line workers was a not very generous 500 pesos [about US$45 a week]. This year, most people are being offered 450 pesos."[3] She claimed that Mexican working conditions are deteriorating because workers are threatened with dismissal by firms that have the option of **outsourcing** part or all of their manufacturing to subsidiary and third-party manufacturers in China. According to a psychologist who worked for one of the employment agencies used by manufacturers in the Guadalajara region, firms seek workers with little self-esteem or aspiration. The applications of workers involved with labor unions, with relatives in government, or with work experience in the United States are rejected out of hand. Prospective workers are sometimes required to strip naked so they can be checked for tattoos (a sign of rebelliousness), and they are often given pregnancy tests. Such pre-employment tests are illegal under Mexican labor laws, but the law is routinely ignored. In practice, complaining immediately disqualifies a job applicant. Workers continue to apply for any available jobs because Chinese competition means there are many more workers than jobs in Mexico.

The interdependence is even more complex when we take into consideration that most workers in Mexican manufacturing plants come from small towns and villages, where agricultural jobs have been lost as a result of the 1994 **North American Free Trade Agreement (NAFTA)**. NAFTA opened the Mexican market to subsidized U.S. grain exports. Because small Mexican farmers have neither the capital nor the technology to compete with the capital-intensive and subsidized U.S. agricultural producers, most have given up farming. Without local employment opportunities, unemployed workers from rural towns and villages accept whatever Mexican manufacturers offer. For many young displaced Mexican workers, a more attractive alternative is to migrate illegally to the United States. Thus, NAFTA not only has caused some jobs to be shifted to Mexico, but it has encouraged immigrant workers to compete directly with U.S. workers in the U.S. labor market. The recently enacted **Central American Free Trade Agreement (CAFTA)** will likely have the same effect. The vicious anti-immigrant rhetoric in the United States conveniently ignores the role of U.S. agricultural subsidies and NAFTA in expanding illegal immigration to the United States, probably because it is more difficult to assess blame for illegal immigration once the complexity of interdependence is understood.

The full costs and benefits of international trade such as the export of Chinese products made with Jinfeng's steel are even more difficult to assess once the social consequences are added to the standard economic gains from trade that economists like to focus on. For example, the social implications of the human migration from Mexico to the United States are substantial. Mexican families are split up, children are not cared for, and rural communities have been reduced to populations consisting disproportionately of children and the grandparents left behind to care for them. In the United States, illegal status subjects Mexican immigrants to abuse, exploitation, insecurity, and effectively second-class social status not unlike the bottom rungs of a rigid caste system. Many U.S. employers exploit illegal workers because, similar to insecure workers in Mexican plants, illegal workers are unlikely to complain or join a union. Many people question whether such expansion of international trade, investment, and migration has really led to an improvement in human welfare in each individual country and the world as a whole.

There is also the growing income inequality that threatens China's social and political orders. China's rapid growth has not provided all 1.3 billion Chinese with comparable improvements in well-being. Some regions have grown faster than others, and some people in each region have captured greater income gains than others. China's income is now much less equally distributed than before its recent growth spurt began three decades ago. The willingness to work long hours in Jinfeng's dirty industries for low wages reflects the decline in job opportunities in the Chinese countryside.

International interdependence also has macroeconomic consequences. For example, China's rapid economic growth slowed in late 2008 and 2009 because the world economy, where the Jinfeng steel plant and all of China's many industries sold their products, fell into a deep recession. The recession seems to have started in the United States, where a bubble in housing prices burst and sharply reduced the value of mortgage securities and other derivative securities based on those mortgages. The collapse of U.S. housing prices affected the rest of the world because the derivative assets based on the underlying mortgages had been acquired in other countries. As the default rate on U.S. mortgages shot up and the mortgage securities proved to be worth much less than their inaccurate AAA ratings had suggested, balance sheets deteriorated and bankruptcies spread across the economies of Europe, Asia, and other continents. At the start of 2009, it was estimated that 20 million workers in Jinfeng and elsewhere in China had lost their jobs and were returning to the countryside. The Chinese government quickly expanded domestic infrastructure expenditures to offset the drop in foreign demand for its products, and it appears that this fiscal stimulus may have spared China from being adversely affected by the rest of the world's economic recession.

In short, the international economic activities normally studied in the field of international economics, such as international trade, international investment, international finance, and immigration, are interrelated and have broad economic, social, and environmental consequences. The interdependencies created among countries by trade, investment, finance, and migration imply that countries are no longer in complete control of their own destinies, and the effects of economic change in one country inevitably spill over into other economies. The purpose of this textbook is to extend the traditional analysis of international economics in order to recognize the complexity of international economic activity, provide the perspectives from which we can make sense of these complexities, and arrive at more accurate assessments of how international economic activity affects human well-being.

THE BIGGER PICTURE

Fundamentally, international economic integration implies an increase in human interactions over greater distances, across more borders, and between more and different countries. Humans, like all living creatures, have struggled with the choice between expanding or limiting contact with other members of their species. Throughout nearly all of their existence to date, humans lived in small groups and dealt almost exclusively with people they knew well and interacted with on a regular basis. Humans evolved as social animals, but their societies were small.

However, as the economic historian Paul Seabright (2010) describes in his aptly entitled book *The Company of Strangers,* ten thousand years ago humans transformed their existence with the invention of agriculture:

> [O]ne of the most aggressive and elusive bandit species in the entire animal kingdom began to settle down. . . . [N]ow, instead of ranging in search of food, it began to keep herds and grow crops, storing them in settlements that limited the ape's mobility and exposed it to the attentions of the very strangers it had hitherto fought or fled. Within a few hundred generations—barely a pause for breath in evolutionary time—it had formed social organizations of startling complexity. Not just village settlements but cities, armies, empires, corporations, nation states, political movements, humanitarian organizations, even internet communities.[4]

Seabright also describes why the expansion of human interaction beyond the immediate family or social group to a more widely dispersed population of complete strangers is inherently problematic. Human behavior largely reflects biological success before the social complexity of current human existence, and this evolved and hardwired individual behavior is not optimal for dealing with to-day's complexities. In today's very integrated world, humans still have mixed feelings about dealing with strangers. Yet, humans have grasped that there is the potential to gain from migrating to areas inhabited by strangers, engaging strangers in trade, borrowing from them or lending to them, and purchasing their property and assets.

The Gains from Dealing with Strangers

There are many reasons why humans are better off when they cooperate with strangers than when they isolate themselves into small groups. Seabright (2010) points to three fundamental advantages of expanding the number of people that humans interact with:

- Higher levels of **specialization**
- Reduced **uncertainty** and **risks** from unpredictable adverse outcomes
- Faster accumulation of knowledge and **technological change**

Later chapters of this textbook will detail these, and many more, benefits of dealing with strangers.

The gain from specialization that Seabright mentions was described long ago, in 1776, by Adam Smith in his *An Inquiry into the Nature and Causes of the Wealth of Nations:*

> The greatest improvements in the productive powers of labour, and the greater part of the skill, dexterity, and judgement with which it is any where directed, or applied, seem to have been the effects of the division of labour.[5]

That is, by splitting tasks among people within a society, the total product is increased. In his analysis of the Industrial Revolution, which was gaining momentum in Britain and his native Scotland at the time of his writing, Smith also recognized the phenomenon that we now call **economies of scale**. He observed large differences in productivity between the traditional cottage system of production and the *factory system* that characterized the Industrial Revolution. He explained that such improvements in productivity required large-scale factories; they could not be achieved by simply multiplying the number of cottage industries. He also noted that large-scale production requires people to exchange products over greater distances with people engaged in other types of specialized large-scale production, people they almost certainly do not know personally. Economies of scale required more impersonal transactions.

Seabright's second stated advantage of expanding economic interaction to more people is that wider human interactions reduce individual risk and uncertainty. What he means is that when people face risks and uncertain outcomes that are, at least in part, specific to them rather than to all of society, cooperation with a variety of others can reduce the individual's risks and uncertainty. For example, if an isolated individual's crops fail, starvation is the likely outcome. It should be obvious that people located over a larger geographic area can spread localized risks among more people. For example, geographically dispersed groups of people could agree that when one group's crops fail, others will feed them, and when the others' crops fail, the former will help the latter. People who engage in such cooperation are likely to survive longer than they could in isolation.

Modern societies have developed a great variety of institutions, markets, and organizations that effectively enable distrustful individuals to cooperate in order to deal with misfortune. For example, we have insurance companies that compensate people for a variety of disasters, bond markets where accumulated wealth can be quickly converted to cash when needed, private charities that extend personal assistance beyond traditional family units, foreign trade networks that make goods and services available anywhere on earth, and international organizations that directly assist people in dealing with misfortune.

Seabright's third advantage of dealing with strangers is that the expansion of human interaction accelerates technological change. Since the source of knowledge is the human capacity to think and reason, the rate of technological change depends directly on the number of people who think, experiment, and develop new ideas. Two heads are better than one. Or, according to the seventeenth-century writer William Petty, "it is more likely that one ingenious curious man may rather be found among 4 million than among 400 persons."[6] Also, since new knowledge builds on existing knowledge, the greater the diversity of the people who share their ideas, the more knowledge will be created. That is, interaction with different people is more likely to expand knowledge than interaction with people who closely share your own experiences and knowledge.

The accumulation of knowledge also depends on how quickly new knowledge is passed from the person(s) who originated it to others. When people are willing to communicate and deal with strangers, their accumulated knowledge can be passed on to many more people than just those who happen to live close to those who originally developed the knowledge. It is no coincidence that throughout history the most advanced societies were those that had the most contact with other societies, and the most backward regions have generally been those most isolated from the rest of the world. Isolated societies literally have to reinvent the wheel. In an integrated world, only one person has to invent something for the innovation to become available to everyone. Plutarch's nearly two-thousand-year-old quote at the head of this chapter shows that this third gain from dealing with strangers has been recognized for some time.

The Three Benefits of Human Interaction Are Intertwined

The three benefits of human interdependence are related. For example, Adam Smith saw a close relationship between specialization, or what he referred to as the "division of labour," and the creation of knowledge:

[T]he invention of all those machines by which labour is so much facilitated and abridged, seems to have been originally owing to the division of labour. Men are much more likely to discover easier and readier methods of attaining any object, when the whole attention of their minds is directed towards the single object, than when it is dissipated among a great variety of things.[7]

Smith describes a concept that we now refer to as **learning by doing**. That is, when people concentrate on a specific task, they gain experience faster and have a stronger incentive to learn to perform the task more efficiently. Thus, exchange among a greater number of strangers promotes specialization, and specialization, in turn, promotes learning and the accumulation of knowledge.

There is also, potentially, a positive relationship between knowledge creation and risk reduction. If people are less likely to die during any given year of their lives, as would happen if people reduced the chance of starvation by expanding trade with strangers, they are likely to take a longer-term view of life. A longer time perspective enhances investment, innovation, and learning, all activities that require some form of short-run sacrifice in exchange for potential future gains. In short, Seabright's three advantages of larger societies interact to enhance each of the advantages of dealing with strangers.

Dependence on Strangers Is Inherently Problematic

Interaction with strangers also has its costs and dangers, however. First of all, cooperating with others forces people to adjust their own behavior to that of others. At the personal level, humans still struggle with the fact that working with someone else means that you cannot do everything exactly the way you are used to doing things. At the national level, countries struggle with foreign affairs and relations with other governments. Economically, people become interdependent. For example, participating in an international monetary system imposes restrictions on national policy makers and impacts a nation's overall economic outcomes. Also, international economic activity and frequent contacts with foreigners may undermine the authority of national leaders. International trade opens domestic producers and consumers to foreign competition. Interaction with foreigners may cause cultural clashes and conflicts among institutions. And historians have estimated that after European explorers arrived in the Western Hemisphere five hundred years ago, as many as 80 percent of the original Western Hemisphere residents eventually died because of diseases carried by the European explorers. This health disaster came in addition to the blatant theft of resources on the part of the European invaders and the introduction of African slaves to replace the deceased labor force. In fact, the predominance of slavery and oppression throughout history suggests that it was often advantageous to force others to do the least desirable work. History shows that individuals, groups, and entire nations often have incentives to exploit, oppress, rob, pillage, and murder. In short, strangers not only enable trade, reduce risk, and expand knowledge, they may take your job or they may even kill you. Human survival has always depended on a careful balance between closer interaction and keeping one's distance.

The Crucial Role of Institutions

Because interaction with others was mostly limited to family, clan, and other small groupings during nearly all of human history and the history of humans' immediate ancestors, Seabright (2010) interprets today's growth of economic and social interaction between strangers as an indication that humans have found ways to control their inherent propensity to exploit, steal, and kill when they are not restricted to their immediate social circumstances:

To manage the hazards imposed on us by the actions of strangers has required us to deploy a different skill bequeathed to us by evolution for quite different purposes, the capacity for abstract symbolic thought.[8]

This is a very important point: Humans' exceptional capacity to engage in **abstract reasoning** has enabled them to design social and economic institutions that effectively enable strangers to behave in a cooperative manner despite their instinctive fears of exploitation or personal harm. **Institutions** are the cultural norms, social customs, formal laws, and explicit government regulations that shape individual human behavior. Institutions are needed because hardwired human behavioral instincts, evolved when social and natural environments were different, are not appropriate for dealing with the complexity of modern societies. The cruel and deadly Crusades, the Inquisition's severe oppression of human thought, the Atlantic slave trade, World War I, the Holocaust, World War II, the Soviet Gulags, and a long list of other atrocities right up through the wars and social conflicts of our present-day global society all serve to remind us that humans often do not manage their complex society very well. The noted economic historian Douglass C. North (2005) reminds us that the very real improvement in the human existence "has been a trial and error process of change with lots of errors, endless losers, and no guarantee that we will continue to get it right in spite of the enormous accretion of knowledge over those centuries."[9]

Our knowledge of our natural and social environments is woefully incomplete, and this means that our ability to accurately apply our capacity for reason and abstract thought is limited as well. Again in the words of North:

> Throughout human history there has always been a large residual that defied rational explanation—a residual to be explained partly by non-rational explanations embodied in witchcraft, magic, religions; but partly by more prosaic non-rational behavior characterized by dogmas, prejudices, "half-baked" theories. Indeed despite the . . . assertion by eminent theorists that it is not possible to theorize in the face of uncertainty, humans do it all the time; their efforts range from ad hoc assertions and loosely structured beliefs such as those encompassed in the labels "conservative" and "liberal" to elegant systematic ideologies such as Marxism or organized religions.[10]

Sociologists would classify these "ad hoc assertions and loosely structured beliefs" as part of human **culture**, the symbolic structures that humans create to give their activities significance and importance. In sum, humans must deal with life in their complex social and natural environments with the help of their evolved instincts, a small amount of rationally acquired knowledge, and a whole set of nonrational beliefs we can best describe as culture.

Institutions Evolve Slowly and Unevenly

All institutions, because they are human-made, are subject to revision and change. But circumstances, economic activity, and institutions never change in unison. Deepak Lal (1998) argues that culture inevitably lags behind the ever-changing realities of our natural and social environments. These differences in the rates of change of reality, knowledge, formal legal institutions, culture, and human instinct almost guarantee that when economic and social environments change more rapidly, humans' culture and evolutionary hardwired behavioral systems fall further behind. Historical evidence shows how exceptional episodes of expanding international economic integration, or what we have referred to as the expansion of interactions with strangers, are often reversed because institutional support is not sufficient to prevent human interaction from deteriorating into exploitation, theft, and fraud.

In fact, all episodes of rising international economic integration and the expansion of cooperation with strangers were eventually reversed, at least in part. For example, after people from three continents increasingly traded with each other and migrated to each other's territories during the time of the Roman Empire, the world again broke up into more isolated regions. Europe entered a period that we now refer to as the Dark Ages. China was the most advanced economy of the world in the year 1000, when it traded with other countries throughout the Far East and the Asian subcontinent. But its economy stagnated during the last millennium when its leaders opted to isolate the country from foreign influences. More recently, the nineteenth century's **globalization** was substantially reversed after the political turmoil of World War I and the economic turmoil of the Great Depression.

International economic activity is also greatly hampered by differences in institutions across countries. International trade, international investment, international financial transactions, and **international migration** involve complex forms of human interaction. When cultures, rules, laws, and traditions differ, people have trouble carrying out international trade, international investment, long-term lending and borrowing, and absorbing foreign immigrants. An interesting example of how seemingly straightforward interaction with strangers can go awry is the Dutch West India Company's settlement of the Hudson Valley in what is today New York State. The Dutch first established Fort Orange far up the river near present-day Albany and settled thirty Dutch families. A war with the Native Americans soon followed, as the native residents of the Hudson Valley did not take kindly to new settlers occupying what they saw as their land. The Dutch thus sought a more secure location, and they settled at the tip of Manhattan Island in what is today New York City. In order to avoid future conflicts with the local natives, the Dutch offered to buy the island. This seemed like a perfectly reasonable approach to the commercially minded Dutch.

In 1626, the Dutch gave the Native Americans trinkets and other items worth 60 Dutch guilders. Such a sum would be about US$400 today.[11] The problem with this transaction was that the natives did not think they were selling the island. The Dutch concept of land ownership was unknown in native societies of the Western Hemisphere, and the native residents of Manhattan thought they were merely letting the Dutch use the land. This misunderstanding is readily apparent in the writing of one of the "patroons," as the early Dutch landowners in New York were called: "It was [the Indians'] custom, when a new governor came . . . that there should be a gratuity given them, thereby to continue the friendship between ye Indians and our nation."[12] The Native Americans saw their consent to let the Dutch inhabit certain areas of New York as a friendship that had to be continually nurtured with gifts, a type of rental rather than ownership. The Dutch officials in New Amsterdam, on the other hand, saw the 60 guilders as payment for the permanent transfer of ownership. In sum, because Dutch and Native American cultures did not view property rights from the same perspective, it was difficult for the natives to engage in exchanges with the newly arrived European settlers. Ultimately, the Dutch used force and established themselves in the region without the cooperation of the natives. A mutually agreed-to exchange was not possible given the inconsistencies between the Native American and Dutch cultures.

The disconnect between the Dutch and the natives on Manhattan Island may be an extreme case of cultural inconsistencies, but when people, firms, and governments engage in international trade, investment, finance, or migration, there are almost always cultural clashes of some sort. Humans and their capacity for abstract reasoning have not consistently been able to build the new institutions needed to support the complexity of changing social environments. International economic interdependence is a complex phenomenon, and human society has struggled to deal with it. The important lesson of the past is that human interactions between strangers have not, and still do not, always turn out to be mutually beneficial for all involved.

THE EVOLUTION OF INTERNATIONAL ECONOMIC INTEGRATION

The purpose of this textbook is to advance the understanding of international economics for both economics students and the general public. International economics has, traditionally, focused on four different components of **international economic integration**:

- International trade
- International investment
- International finance
- International migration

Therefore, the chapters that follow explain the traditional models economists use to explain international trade, international investment, international finance, and international migration. We will use the term **international economic integration** to describe the expansion of some combination of these different types of economic activities that cross national borders.

Because mainstream economics has traditionally addressed each of these components of international integration in isolation, many students of economics come away with the impression that these four types of international economic activity are separate issues that can be analyzed in isolation and addressed by separate policies. However, the many different international economic activities are closely linked, albeit in ways that are often difficult to distinguish clearly. The introduction to this chapter showed how all four components of international economic integration are potentially related: the investment by a Chinese firm in acquiring a German steel plant involved trade, investment, financing, and the temporary migration of workers.

This textbook confronts this complexity by extending the discussion of international economic integration beyond the mainstream, or orthodox, models from the field of international economics. This textbook adopts a heterodox approach that actively employs different models, recognizes complex relationships, and seeks multiple perspectives in order to provide a more realistic explanation of the rapid growth of international economic activity over the past several centuries.

The Growth of International Trade

Over the last two hundred years, a period equal to just one-tenth of 1 percent of our existence as a species, humans have experienced high rates of population growth, technological progress, and increases in standards of living. The world's population has grown sixfold, per person material output has increased about tenfold, and we live, on average, three times as long as people did two hundred years ago. What has caught the eye of economists, social scientists, and all keen observers of human society is that this unprecedented growth in human economic activity has been accompanied by the expansion of international economic activity. Humans have become increasingly interdependent, to the point where most people today could not survive were it not for jobs performed, goods produced, and income spent in other parts of the world.

Table 1.1 presents Angus Maddison's estimates for international trade and per capita real GDP throughout the world since 1820. Clearly, economies have grown larger and they have also become much more open to trade over the past two hundred years. On average, international trade has grown much faster than overall economic activity. In 1820, only 1 percent of the total value of world output was exported beyond individual countries' borders. By 1870, the advent of railroads and steamships as well as the reduction of tariffs and other trade restrictions by many countries had increased trade to where nearly 5 percent of the world's output was destined for foreign markets. In 1929, the year before the world began its descent into the Great Depression, exports reached 9 percent of world GDP. In 1950, exports had fallen to less than 5.5 percent of world GDP, battered by protectionist trade policies during the 1920s, the economic stagnation during the Great Depression, and the disruption of World War II. Since 1950, world GDP has increased more than sixfold while world exports have increased nearly twentyfold. In short, international economic integration expanded to unprecedented levels in the second half of the twentieth century.

Data from the World Bank show that total exports of goods and services exceeded US$17.0 trillion in 2007, which was over 25 percent of the world's gross domestic product. That is, on average, countries export over one-fourth of everything they produce, which means they also import over one-fourth of all the goods and services sold in their economies. The percentage of trade relative to the size of the economy varies greatly from one country to another, and larger countries generally trade less than small economies. Trade data for individual countries show that the percentage of national output traded increased for all countries over the past half century, regardless of their size.

Table 1.1

World Exports and Per Capita Gross Domestic Product: 1820–2007

Year	World Exports (millions 1990$)	World GDP (millions 1990$)	Exports as % of World GDP	Per Capita GDP (1990$)
1820	$7,255	$694,442	1.0	$667
1870	50,345	1,101,369	4.6	867
1913	212,425	2,704,782	7.9	1,510
1929	334,408	3,696,156	9.0	1,806
1950	295,621	5,336,101	5.5	2,114
1973	1,690,648	16,059,180	10.5	4,104
1990	3,456,762	27,076,007	12.8	5,154
2007	17,170,533	54,273,887	31.6	7,000

Source: Data for all years except 1820, 1929, and 2007 are from Angus Maddison (2001), *The World Economy: A Millennial Perspective*, Paris: OECD, Tables F-3, F-5, and C5-b. The figures for 1820 and 1929 are from Angus Maddison (1995), *Monitoring the World Economy 1820–1992*, Paris: OECD, Tables E-2, p. 211, and I-4, p. 239. The 2007 figures are from UNCTAD's *Handbook of Statistics 2008*, New York: United Nations.

Some economists suggest that the growth of trade and the growth of per capita real GDP are related. When international trade grew rapidly in the nineteenth century, economic growth also reached new highs. When governments intentionally cut off trade during the 1930s, economic growth slowed or stopped altogether. After 1950, unprecedented rates of economic growth were matched by equally unprecedented growth of trade. Correlation does not imply causation, however. Broader measures of economic development, such as education, people's satisfaction with life, and health, are not as neatly correlated with the growth of exports and imports of goods.

The Growth of International Investment and Finance

International investment, which is the acquisition of real assets located in one country by citizens, firms, or governments of another country, has grown rapidly over the past two centuries. Also, international borrowing and lending, or what we call international financial flows, have grown rapidly as well. But unlike trade, which has occurred for millennia, only over the past two or three centuries have banks lent and borrowed and have people from throughout countries' populations and a wide range of private businesses purchased and sold other assets across borders on a regular basis. One reason for the late blooming of international investment and finance is that the overall level of wealth in the world was very small before the surge in economic growth during the past two hundred years; there simply was not much wealth to store in available assets or to lend to others, either within or across borders. Another reason international investment and finance have only recently grown is that the institutions required for complex asset exchanges, such as banks, stock markets, bond markets, legal systems, accounting practices, and financial rules, have been developed only within the past two hundred years in most countries. For people to invest in assets, contracts must be enforced and legal recourse must be available. There must be markets or other channels through which assets can be exchanged.

International investment first grew rapidly at the end of the nineteenth century. In fact, when measured as a proportion of GDP, capital flows between some countries were larger toward the end of the 1800s than they were even during "globalization," as the rapid international economic integration of the 1990s was called. For example, over the period 1880–1914, financial outflows averaged about 5 percent of GDP in the United Kingdom, reaching 9 percent in 1913. The United

Kingdom exported nearly half of its total savings as British citizens purchased large amounts of foreign bonds and indirectly made loans to foreign governments and firms through their banks. The largest importers of foreign savings were the rapidly growing immigrant countries Australia, Canada, the United States, and New Zealand.

This surge in international investment came to an end in 1914 when, first, World War I disrupted all international transactions and, later, the slow economic recovery after the war further reduced the incentives for international investment. The Great Depression and widespread isolationist economic policies in many countries essentially ended all international investment during the 1930s. International investment resumed only gradually after World War II, and fifty years later, by the mid-1990s, cross-border sales of assets again reached the levels, relative to GDP, of one hundred years earlier. Of course, the world is much wealthier today than it was a century ago, and the total value of international investment is many times larger than it was then. Also, the variety of international investment is much greater today. Before World War I, about 90 percent of international investment consisted of purchases of bonds issued by foreign governments and large private railroad and other infrastructure ventures.[13] There was little direct investment by transnational firms, but today the growth of transnational firms represents the single largest category of international investment.

The growth of international investment and finance has not been a smooth process, by any means. In fact, repeated financial crises over the past several decades make it clear that the modern financial industry still has trouble sustaining international financial flows. And international investment by private firms and corporations has been often erratic and occasionally quickly reversed.

International Migration

The fourth component of international economic integration is the movement of people across borders, or what we commonly refer to as **immigration**. People have always moved across the face of the earth. International migration is probably the oldest form of international economic integration; hunters and gatherers continually walked to new regions that were more fertile or where there was less competition from other humans. The massive movement of people from labor-abundant and land-scarce Europe to the labor-scarce and land-abundant Western Hemisphere between 1500 and the present stands out as one of the greatest mass migrations. It is estimated that about 75 million Europeans left their native countries and migrated to what are now Canada, the United States, Argentina, Brazil, and many smaller countries in Latin America and the Caribbean. Over 10 million Africans were carried against their will as slaves to the Western Hemisphere between 1500 and 1850.

International migration slowed drastically during the Great Depression of the 1930s, just as international trade and international investment did. But, after World War II, the international movement of people began growing again, and it reached unprecedented proportions by the end of the twentieth century. In 2000, for example, over 10 percent of the U.S. population was foreign born, compared to just under 5 percent as recently as 1960. Today, nearly all high-income countries receive immigrants from low-income developing economies who are attracted by higher wages. Continued government barriers to immigration have not been able to stem the tide; the barriers have simply led more and more people to seek work in other countries illegally. The number of foreigners living and working in the United States illegally probably exceeded 10 million in 2010. More than 5 million illegal immigrants were working in various European countries.

The flows of immigrants have changed in the late twentieth century compared to earlier periods of migration. Beginning around 1960, a number of countries in Western Europe, the region that was the source of the 75 million migrants to the rest of the world after 1500, began receiving large inflows of immigrants from elsewhere in Europe and North Africa. The United States and Canada, which received immigrants mostly from Europe in the nineteenth century, now receive immigrants predominantly from Asia and Latin America.

Immigrants have large economic, social, and political impacts on communities. For example, in the 1980s the small city of Lexington, Nebraska, was suffering the fate of many cities on the high plains of the American Midwest: It was losing population because the U.S. agricultural industry's switch to large-scale industrial farming reduced its need for labor inputs. Lexington was characterized by abandoned homes, and many downtown businesses were boarded up. Lexington's population had declined from ten thousand in 1960 to just over six thousand in the late 1980s. Then, in 1990, a large meat packer was attracted by various tax benefits and subsidies to set up operations in Lexington. Almost immediately, many Mexican and other Hispanic immigrants arrived to work in the new packing plant. How many were legal immigrants and how many were undocumented is not known. Several other industries moved to vacant facilities in Lexington, more immigrants arrived, and the population grew to over ten thousand. The economy grew, but the ethnic makeup of the population changed, and today one out of every two Lexingtonians is Hispanic.[14]

High rates of immigration sometimes cause strong negative reactions. There have been racial and ethnic tensions in countries whose previously homogenous cultures have been upset by substantial inflows of foreign workers and their families. There have been, for example, race riots in Britain in 2001, a string of fire bombings of the homes of Turkish immigrants in Germany, and the passage of a law in Switzerland banning minarets on mosques. In Lexington, Nebraska, a number of residents moved to other communities after Hispanic immigrants repopulated the declining town. On the other hand, the economic decline of the community was reversed. As will become apparent in later chapters, immigrants have a variety of positive and negative effects on the economies where they settle and work.

International Economic Integration Is Far from Complete

Only a little more than 3 percent of the world's people live outside their country of birth. That is a historically high percentage, but it is still very low if you consider how much people move around within countries. Political borders are still formidable barriers to the movement of people. Studies that have compared the levels of trade between cities within countries and cities located on opposite sides of a national border have found that borders keep international trade at just a small percentage of domestic trade. For example, Charles Engel and John Rogers (1996) compared trade within Canada and the United States to trade between Canada and the United States, and they estimated that the political border between the United States and Canada had the same effect on the volume of trade between Canadian and U.S. cities that a distance of seventy-five thousand miles would have in the absence of national borders. International trade is still a small percentage of most economies' aggregate activity. Major economies such as Japan and the United States export only about 10 percent of their production. This means that 90 percent of everything produced is for their domestic markets. In a paper entitled "The Myth of Economic Globalisation," Alfred Kleinknecht and Jan ter Wengel (1998) showed that Europe as a whole had not increased its trade with the rest of the world at all over the previous thirty-five years. The rapidly increasing international trade by European economies was entirely with other European economies; trade between European and non-European countries, as a percentage of total GDP, had not grown at all.

Jeffrey Frankel (1999) points out that if the world were truly "borderless" and "completely integrated," as some writers claim is the case today, then the United States should be trading about eight times as much as it does now. Frankel's reasoning is simple: "The U.S. economy accounts for 24 percent of gross world production. If it were, in fact, true that firms trade with the other side of the globe as easily as with the other side of town, the share of trade in U.S. GDP would be the same as the share of non-U.S. output in gross world product."[15] Since the share of trade in the U.S. GDP is about 10 percent now, Frankel concludes that "we have traveled only one-eighth of the way to complete integration." Many countries trade higher proportions of their GDPs than does the United

States, but still in no country is the ratio of trade to total production anywhere close to what its share in world output would suggest.

It is clear, therefore, that international economic integration can continue to progress for quite some time before reaching levels compatible with a truly integrated world economy. But that does not make the continued expansion of international trade, international investment, and immigration inevitable. There are people who do not want to see further international economic integration. It is not clear that those who favor continued international economic integration will continue to carry the day over those who oppose international economic integration, either out of self-interest or a simple fear of the unknown. As noted earlier, international economic integration has in fact been stopped or reversed many times throughout history. Trade liberalization inevitably creates new competition for domestic producers, and that obviously generates opposition to trade. Depending on domestic producers' political connections and clout, trade liberalization often seems to have generated new protectionist trade policies. The immigration of foreigners into a country sometimes results in ethnic strife and the closing of borders to foreigners. Cycles of liberalization and isolation can last for centuries, and they can be easily distinguished by even a casual reading of history.

The twentieth century provides the best-documented example of how quickly international economic integration can be reversed. The world was highly integrated economically by means of international trade, investment, and migration in the latter half of the nineteenth century. The noted British macroeconomist John Maynard Keynes quite accurately described the period just before World War I:

> What an extraordinary episode in the economic progress of man that age was which came to an end in August, 1914! . . . The inhabitant of London could order by telephone, sipping his morning tea in bed, the various products of the whole earth. . . . [H]e could at the same moment and by the same means adventure his wealth in the natural resources and new enterprises of any quarter of the world. . . . But, most important of all, he regarded this state of affairs as normal, certain, and permanent, except in the direction of further improvement, and any deviation from it as aberrant, scandalous, and avoidable.[16]

Yet, despite most people's apparent confidence that international economic integration had become the "normal" state of affairs, policy makers in the world's major nations made political and economic decisions that completely reversed the course of economic activity after World War I. Joseph Stalin led the Soviet Union into economic isolation in order to separate its economy from international capitalism, and Adolf Hitler isolated Germany when he focused entirely on domestic economic growth and the interests of the national state. Democracies like France, Britain, and the United States also shifted national policies almost entirely toward domestic priorities after experiencing the devastation of World War I and, later, very high levels of unemployment during the Great Depression.

The reversal of international economic integration after World War I was itself reversed after World War II, in large part because it had become obvious that increased economic isolation had reduced economic welfare and contributed to the animosities and political events that precipitated the Second World War. Once technology and population growth made it impossible for countries to avoid each other, attempts at isolation and inward-looking economic and social policies ended up spilling over into open warfare.

New Concerns about International Economic Integration

In the first decade of the twenty-first century, after decades of unprecedented growth of international trade, investment, financial integration, and immigration, there is still strong opposition to international economic integration. Organized labor in most developed economies has seen its membership dwindle as manufacturing employment is shifted to other countries. Those unions that remain often resist further **outsourcing** of production to overseas factories. Firms routinely lobby for protection from what they claim is unfair foreign competition. The international integration of financial markets and the consolidation of finance into a small number of very large transnational financial firms ended up transforming the failure of mortgage securities that originated in one country, the United States, into a massive global economic recession in 2008. Many policy makers and even some mainstream economists have asked whether international economic integration has gone too far.

Critics of international economic integration fear that transnational corporations will come to dominate production and distribution of goods and services throughout the world, overwhelming national governments' and countries' ability to control their own social and economic destinies. Environmentalists note that the growth binge in the latter half of the twentieth century and the international integration of economic activity has already done lasting damage to the earth's ecological systems. They fear that global economic competition will make it difficult to reach an international consensus on how to reverse the environmental deterioration.

THE FIELD OF INTERNATIONAL ECONOMICS

The arguments for and against international economic integration will no doubt be part of the political discussions in most countries in the future, as they have been throughout the past. Unfortunately, mainstream international economics does not provide an unbiased framework of analysis with which to address the issues that seem to be driving current opposition to international trade, investment, finance, or immigration. Most economists continue to advocate free trade, unrestricted financial flows, and open borders for workers in large part because the culture of mainstream economics, which many international economists embrace, seems to generate a pro-globalization bias.

The Bias of Mainstream Economic Analysis

Beginning with Adam Smith and David Ricardo two centuries ago, economists have developed *economic models* that support the general hypothesis that there is a positive relationship between international economic integration and human welfare. Textbooks in international economics frame their analysis around these models, which we will refer to as mainstream, or orthodox, international economics.

It is important to remember that even though mainstream textbooks give students the impression that international economic integration is a sign of economic progress and largely beneficial for human well-being, the benefits of increased international trade, investment, finance, or migration were not convincing enough, for example, to prevent governments from implementing policies in the 1920s and 1930s that completely reversed the rapid international economic integration of the nineteenth century. And, despite the impressions still recounted by economists, in recent decades the accelerated growth of international trade, investment, financial flows, and migration has coincided with slowing GDP growth and rising unemployment in many countries.

Many people remain unconvinced by economists' theoretical arguments because they, correctly as we will see in later chapters, view some of the changes that accompany the integration of their national economies into a single international economy as a threat to their well-being. The noted international economist Dani Rodrik describes the popular beliefs, that "in a fully integrated world economy, wages would be set in Shenzen [China], the price of capital determined in New York, and tax rates legislated in the Cayman Islands."[17] Surveys consistently confirm the general public's skepticism about the merits of international trade. For example, a late 1990s survey reported that nine out of ten economists favor further international agreements to liberalize trade, but only about half of the U.S. public thought that further agreements to liberalize trade would be "good for the

Figure 1.1 The Economy's Position in Society and the Natural Environment

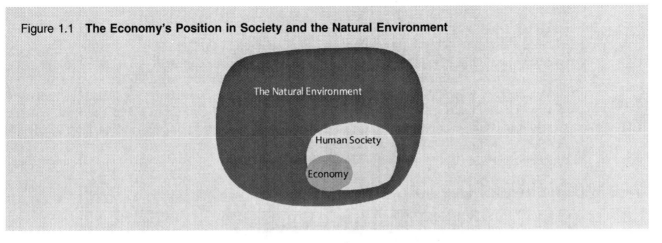

economy."[18] And not only Americans are skeptical of the process that is effectively spreading U.S.-based corporations and their corporate culture throughout the rest of the world's economies. Many foreigners are not comfortable with the American business culture that is changing consumption patterns, labor markets, and government policies in their countries.

Of course, some of the opinions on international trade, international investment, international finance, and immigration reflect the self-interest of people, firms, and organizations. Business leaders often call for "protection" from foreign competition that places their firms at a disadvantage, and labor unions in high-income countries complain that international trade, investment, and migration undermine their wages. But, the large gap between most economists' active advocacy of policies to promote international economic integration and the general public's distrust of "globalization" is also driven by different perceptions of how international economic integration affects human society. This gap has not been well addressed by mainstream economics. This textbook, therefore, addresses the complexity of the process of international economic integration by expanding our analysis beyond the familiar economic relationships studied by orthodox international economics.

The Spheres of Human Existence

Economics has traditionally recognized that in an economy "everything depends on everything else," although economists have usually limited the scope of their analysis and their published studies to economic relationships. For example, the field of macroeconomics claims to look at the whole economic system as the aggregate outcome of the individual markets, firms, and households that make up the economy. The environmental economist Herman Daly (1999) reminds us, however, that "the macroeconomy is not the relevant whole, but is itself a subsystem, a part of the ecosystem, the larger economy of nature."[19] Daly argues that the strategy of focusing on economic variables and conveniently assuming that everything else remains the same implies that **orthodox economics** generates inherently biased conclusions about economic phenomena.

From his perspective as an environmental economist, Daly links the economy to the earth's ecological system, or **ecosystem**. In this textbook, we go a step further by first placing the economy within human society, which we then link to the earth's ecosystem and the universe beyond. Figure 1.1 provides a suggestive depiction of the position of the human economy within human society and nature. The economic sphere is linked to the social sphere in many complex ways, and human society, in turn, interacts with the natural environment, or the natural sphere, in many more complex ways. In Figure 1.1 we draw the economy as mostly contained within human society, but note that it also partially interacts directly with nature. Similarly, human society directly touches the natural sphere without first going through the economy.

Once we recognize that economic activity does not occur in an isolated bubble free from social and natural constraints and influences and, at the same time, that economic activity has very substantial social and natural consequences, it becomes clear that we have to approach the study of international economics from a much broader perspective. This textbook, therefore, takes a heterodox approach to international economics, which rejects the conventional mainstream, or orthodox, notion that social and natural events are noneconomic phenomena that can be modeled as exogenous shocks, or influences, in our models of international economics. The next chapter explains exactly how **heterodox economics** addresses Daly's multiple spheres, how they are related, and how they interact to produce specific observed outcomes we want to study in international economics.

The Natural Environment

Earth's ecosystem is under severe pressure from the past and present growth of the human population and it's expanding environmental footprint. It is well understood that humanity is using up exhaustible natural resources, such as oil, minerals, and coal, at a pace that cannot be sustained. But there is also vast evidence that humanity's exploitation of the earth's renewable natural services—such as oxygen, clean water, wind power, soil nutrients, rainfall, climate, pollination, and the like—that humanity depends on for its existence now exceeds the earth's capacity to sustain those natural services in the long run. A study by Mathis Wackernagel and a group of associates (2002) estimates that humanity's exploitation of the earth's **renewable resources** corresponded to 70 percent of capacity in 1961, but grew to 120 percent in 1999. The World Wildlife Fund (WWF) (2008) estimates that in 2005, "humanity's demand on the planet's living resources . . . now exceeds the planet's regenerative capacity by about 30 percent."[20]

The WWF defines humanity's global **ecological footprint** in terms of global hectares (gha). The latter is the average capacity of one hectare of the earth's surface to produce services and absorb waste, and the former is effectively the sum of (1) all forest, grazing land, cropland, and fishing grounds required to produce the food, fiber, and timber humanity consumes; (2) all land and water to absorb the wastes emitted when humans use energy; and (3) all land and water required for humanity's living space, production, transportation, and storage. According to the WWF (2008), the total productive area of the earth is equal to 13.6 billion gha, or 2.1 gha per person in 2005. In that year, however, the global ecological footprint was estimated to be 17.5 billion gha, or 2.7 gha per person. Hence the WWF's conclusion that exploitation of the earth's resources exceeded the planet's regenerative capacity by about 30 percent. Figure 1.2 illustrates the estimated path of ecological sustainability since 1960. It was during the 1980s that the human population began using the earth's renewable resources at a rate that exceeded the capacity of the ecosystem to replenish itself.

Perhaps most discomforting is the realization that humanity's efforts to compensate for the stress on nature's renewable resources as well as the depletion of nonrenewable (exhaustible) resources have often made things worse. The so-called **Green Revolution** that increased the amount of food produced per acre during the latter half of the twentieth century has caused numerous stresses in the social and natural spheres. For example, the rapid introduction of machines, chemicals, and an industrial-model organization to agriculture has destroyed traditional rural communities and displaced hundreds of millions of people. The consequences show up in the form of growing urban slums, mass illegal immigration, broken family structures, and greater income inequality. It has also become clear that the Green Revolution has caused massive environmental damage. Modern agriculture, among all sectors of the economy, is the single largest contributor to global warming, even larger than transportation or power generation. The growth of **monoculture**, the large-scale, capital-intensive production of single crops covering vast territories formerly devoted to much

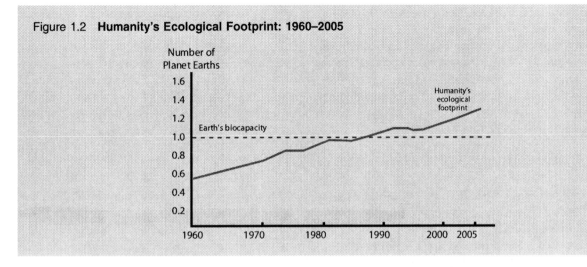

Figure 1.2 **Humanity's Ecological Footprint: 1960–2005**

more varied agricultural production, is the main contributor to species depletion and the loss of biodiversity. Monoculture is motivated by economies of scale, which are derived from the substitution of large equipment for labor, the heavy application of chemical fertilizers and insecticides in place of more labor-intensive and varied exploitation of the land, and industrial food-processing operations in which machinery and assembly-line methods require uniform products. In short, once all spheres are taken into consideration, it is not obvious that the technological change induced by population growth and the need to use nature's land more efficiently is sufficient for sustaining economic growth in the long term.

The close relationship between the economic and natural spheres is also apparent in the earlier example of Jinfeng, China, where the transported German steel plant not only produced steel, but also contributed to an acceleration of greenhouse gas (GHG) emissions. In 2007, China overtook the United States as the largest emitter of the GHGs. In effect, German GHG emissions were transferred to China. While Germany proudly confirmed that it was on schedule to reduce its greenhouse gas emissions by 40 percent by 2020, its former steel mills were now increasing China's emissions. International trade further contributed to GHG emissions with the transport of iron ore to China, the shipment of the steel around the world, and the generation of electricity to power the steel mill using China's dirty coal in poorly regulated power plants. In sum, before we can conclude that international economic integration stimulates real sustainable economic development, we need to analyze not only the direct costs and benefits of international trade, investment, finance, and migration, but also the environmental costs.

Social Stress

The growth and international integration of economic activity has also caused severe social conflicts and oppression. The growing demand for material output has in recent years triggered wars over oil supplies in Kuwait, Iraq, and Georgia, and repeated threats of war by petroleum importers such as the United States against oil producers like Iran, Venezuela, and Ecuador. There have also been lengthy civil wars in more than a dozen African countries for control of assorted natural resources. The continuing violence in the oil-rich Niger delta in Nigeria is driven by the extreme poverty that exists side by side with the oil industry. Large countries such as China, the United States, Russia, and others are actively engaged in a military arms race in order to expand and maintain their control over the world's scarce resources. Several countries, among them Iran,

Pakistan, and North Korea, have developed or are seeking to develop nuclear weapons to protect themselves and their resources.

International economic integration has disrupted traditional societies and their customary economic relationships. The consequences of NAFTA were described earlier in this chapter. Economically driven social stresses manifest themselves in many ways, including the long-distance international migration of millions of people, rising income inequalities within most of the world's countries, and hunger for one billion of the world's seven billion people despite enough global agricultural production to feed nine billion people.

HOW ECONOMISTS DEAL WITH COMPLEXITY

Social scientists must develop hypotheses that are simplified representations of our world, because of its overwhelming complexity. In economics, we refer to such simple hypotheses as **models**. We will often describe and use models in this textbook because many of them help us understand the process of international economic integration. It is useful, therefore, to review what models are, why we use them, and how they help us understand complex phenomena.

Economic Models

Without realizing it, people use models all the time in order to make decisions. For example, suppose you and two friends are waiting at the clubhouse to begin a round of golf. A fourth friend, Mary, has not yet arrived, which leads one of your other friends to comment: "Mary is not going to show up, because it is raining." This seemingly straightforward statement effectively reflects the application of a model of a specific aspect of Mary's behavior, namely that she dislikes rain more than she likes to play golf with her three friends. Perhaps this model was inspired by the fact that Mary did not show up for golf the last few times it rained. In this case we say that the model of Mary's behavior is supported by **empirical evidence**, that is, observations of Mary's behavior. Or, perhaps the statement is based on logical reasoning and observations of Mary's reactions to rain under similar circumstances. Perhaps Mary failed to show up at a company picnic when it rained; in this case your friend is hypothesizing that Mary will treat the picnic and golf similarly. There is no guarantee that the hypothesized model of Mary's behavior is correct, of course. Mary could falsify the hypothesis by walking in the door with her golf clubs. The important point here, though, is that whether we refer to them as rules of thumb, common sense, heuristics, or models, we normally deal with complexity by focusing on what we think are the relevant relationships by which we can predict or explain some phenomenon of interest.

By definition, a model is a simplification of reality that explicitly highlights key relationships that we deem important to understanding and analyzing certain economic issues while omitting many details deemed to be less relevant to the problem at hand. The term *model* can apply to both the hypotheses that we make about economic phenomena and the confirmed theories that remain after we systematically confront the hypotheses with real world evidence.

The Dangers Lurking behind Economic Models

Economic modeling should follow the scientific method. This means that when an economic model is hypothesized, economists must confront the model with unbiased observations or carefully designed objective tests. In practice, economists often use statistical data to test models, which means models must be represented in mathematical forms that can be tested using statistical methods.

Suppose that we want to test the relationship between Y, the economy's per capita gross domestic product (GDP), and X, the proportion of a country's production that is exported. Specifically, we want to test the hypothesis that economies that engage in more international trade have higher standards of living than economies that trade less, all other things equal. Suppose, also, that we have three observations of GDP and exports, which are shown as three points in Figure 1.3. Such observations could be from one country at different times, in which case the statistical data is called **time-series data**, or from three different countries at the same point in time, in which case we have **cross-section data**. Since the three points all lie right on a single line, we will be tempted to hypothesize a linear relationship between exports and per capita income represented by an equation of a line: $Y = a + bX$, where a is the Y-intercept and b is the slope of the line. The three observations shown in Figure 1.3, say for three different countries in the year 2010, suggest that there is a negative relationship between international trade and per capita GDP. The greater a country's exports, the lower its per capita GDP.

Suppose that another researcher gathers data for additional countries, and this larger sample of observations is shown in Figure 1.4. It appears that the relationship between GDP and international trade is not exactly the linear model represented by the line in Figure 1.3. Using a standard least squares regression to fit a line to the scatter of points in Figure 1.4 results in an upward-sloping line. This suggests that the greater the proportion of its output a country exports, the higher its per capita GDP! The simple matter of adding some observations thus completely changes the conclusion about how international trade affects the economy. The evidence on trade goes from confirming it as a negative factor to confirming it as a positive factor.

This example suggests that economic models based on a small number of observations or even more formal statistical regressions using larger data sets should not be taken uncritically as definitive proof for or against a hypothesis. A holistic perspective on the matter would suggest that, because the scattered points do not lie on a simple straight line, the relationship between international trade and per capita GDP depends on other influences. That is, the relationship is part of a bigger system in which other variables influence per capita GDP. Perhaps by adding more observations, that is, more countries, the slope of the regression line will change again. And, using observations for each of the countries for multiple years will no doubt cause the statistical program to calculate yet another slope for the line and, thus, a different economic relationship.

If the three observations shown in Figure 1.3 were for three countries that export mostly primary products like coffee, cocoa beans, oil, diamonds, palm oil, and copper, while the additional countries shown in Figure 1.4 exported mostly manufactured goods, a development economist would not be very surprised by the very different pictures presented by the two figures. Widespread evidence suggests that most people in countries that export mostly primary products, like oil, gold, or diamonds, do not often see their incomes rise when their country's exports rise. Of course, if you were a heterodox economist who respected the interrelationships between the economic, social, and natural spheres, you would never have estimated such simple two-dimensional regressions. You would already have delved more thoroughly into how exporting affects other variables associated with economic development, such as investment, innovation, and the distribution of income. You would probably also have classified imports more precisely and differentiated between primary exports, industrial exports, and services exports, suspecting that the income effects from different types of exports were unlikely to be the same. Also, when there are many other variables that influence international trade and GDP per capita, as there most definitely are, then we should indeed expect to observe different relationships between GDP and exports in different countries or at different points in time. A broader perspective thus suggests that exports will not have the same effect on per capita GDP in a country where a few foreign-owned mining companies produce raw materials such as oil,

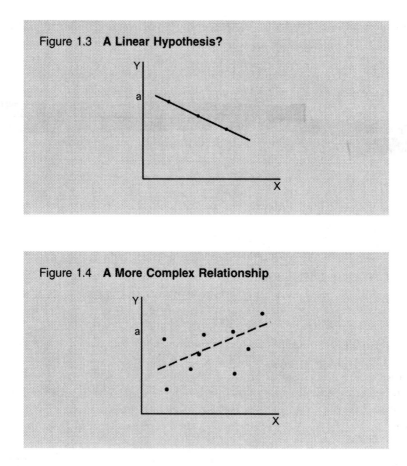

Figure 1.3 **A Linear Hypothesis?**

Figure 1.4 **A More Complex Relationship**

gold, or diamonds as they do in a country where highly trained and well-paid workers produce manufactured products.

More sophisticated statistical regression models, which simultaneously account for the influence of many variables and, effectively, look at more "dimensions" than the simple relationships shown in Figures 1.3 and 1.4, can be used to uncover other variables that affect how exports translate into GDP per capita. Heterodox economists are, therefore, quite skeptical of most statistical results. They understand that there are no simple relationships where only one variable, X, entirely determines the value of another variable, Y. In short, observations on two isolated social phenomena seldom line up neatly along a straight line as shown in Figure 1.3.

Modeling is difficult in economics because economists never have enough math, data, or statistical methods to accurately represent the true level of complexity of our economic, social, and natural environments. Since we cannot just throw our hands up and give up probing for the truth about international economic integration, we must be practical and state hypotheses that are, inevitably, simplified models of what we think is reality. And if we do not lose sight of the potential complexities of the issues we investigate, we can at least avoid jumping to conclusions, such as that the relationship between international trade and GDP is the precise one suggested in Figure 1.3.

The Tyranny of Models and Paradigms

The particular set of models that economists use determines the perspective they take on the subjects they seek to understand and analyze. It is common to call such a set of verbal, graphic, or mathematical models a **paradigm**, which is a conceptual framework for organizing thought. Students are misled by most textbooks to believe that there is just one paradigm in the field of international economics, namely the **neoclassical paradigm**, and that models that fit the neoclassical paradigm—neoclassical models, in other words—can be used to analyze all economic issues. The fact is that there are many paradigms in economics. Conclusions about international trade, investment, finance, and migration differ substantially depending on which paradigm is used and, therefore, which simplifying assumptions underlie the models used to carry out economic analysis.

International economists most often embrace the neoclassical paradigm. They generally ignore other paradigms that have been developed since the late nineteenth century, such as the various institutionalist paradigms, the dynamic Schumpeterian paradigm, the aggregate analysis of the Keynesian paradigm, the multidisciplinary paradigm of Karl Marx, and the innovative paradigms of the structuralist, dependency, and Austrian schools of economic thought. The shift to mathematics as the preferred medium for modeling economic phenomena has limited the realism of the neoclassical paradigm.

The Pro-Globalization Culture of International Economics

The neoclassical paradigm has generated a strong pro-globalization culture in the field of international economics. The standard neoclassical assumptions are familiar to most students: individual consumers are welfare maximizing, consumers shop in perfectly competitive markets for goods and services and earn their income in competitive factor markets, profit-maximizing producers acquire factors of production in competitive factor markets and sell their goods and services in competitive product markets, money is a neutral medium of exchange, assets are used to store wealth, risk can be diversified away, and government is a benevolent regulator and arbiter. Models based on these assumptions inevitably predict that free trade, unrestricted international investment, unregulated international finance, and unrestricted immigration are welfare maximizing.

As later chapters will show, orthodox neoclassical economic models have a lot to say about how trade, investment, finance, and immigration affect the distribution of income across countries and people within economies, how they shift production between countries and industries, and how they influence economic growth. That is, the neoclassical models are useful for dealing with many issues that concern social scientists. And, with some adjustments, the neoclassical models can be used to qualify and elaborate on many of their conclusions. But international economists seem to have become reluctant to extend the models to bring in phenomena from beyond the economic sphere, to drop some of the neoclassical assumptions in favor of more realistic assumptions of imperfect competition, exploitation in labor markets, or undiversifiable risks, and to focus on broader issues. Perhaps mainstream economists fear undermining the pro–international economic integration culture of the field. This culture takes the neoclassical models' conclusions as truth, to the point that mainstream international economics textbooks spend relatively little time on cases that contradict the main neoclassical conclusions.

Mainstream international economists often justify their exclusive reliance on the neoclassical paradigm by appealing to its "rigor" and its exact numerical predictions. Indeed, by very precisely defining "human wants" in terms of sets of goods and services with market prices, it becomes relatively straightforward to judge and evaluate economic policies and outcomes. Whether human well-being actually depends exclusively on the amount of stuff consumed is seldom questioned.

Neoclassical economists also make economic analysis more rigorous by limiting the scope of their analysis. For example, note the following definition of international economics from a typical textbook that we once used in an introductory international economics class:

> International economics studies how a number of distinct economies interact with one another in the process of allocating scarce resources to satisfy human wants.[21]

This definition places the study of international economics clearly in the mainstream of economic thinking, which is that the "economic problem" consists of maximizing human well-being subject to limited resources. Another leading international economics textbook offers this definition of the field:

> The study of international economics, like all branches of economics, concerns decision making with respect to the use of scarce resources to meet desired economic objectives.[22]

Note the use of the term *economic objectives* in the second definition above. By limiting the field of economics to a small subset of human activities, and effectively avoiding those determinants of human well-being that are more difficult to observe and quantify, the (reduced) economic problem becomes easier to solve.

But that is enough discussion of neoclassical economic analysis for now. There will be ample opportunities for more detailed critiques throughout the textbook as we evaluate a range of models of international economic activity.

This textbook takes a heterodox approach to international economics. It covers most of the same topics and issues covered in mainstream international economics courses, but it differs from mainstream international economics textbooks in that it uses a variety of models from many different paradigms.

Heterodoxy, by definition, implies a willingness to analyze a situation from multiple perspectives. Heterodoxy also recognizes the broader spheres within which economic activity takes place, which will often mandate the use of models from different fields and specializations.

The advantages of heterodoxy over orthodox neoclassical analysis in international economics merit a much more thorough discussion. That is the purpose of the next chapter. It will also explain why the heterodox approach provides a more accurate and useful framework for understanding, analyzing, and designing policy for managing international trade, investment, financial transactions, and migration, as well as the interdependence among humans and countries implied by international economic integration.

CONCLUSIONS

The purpose of this textbook is to teach international economics. International economics studies the evolutionary process of international economic integration that has accompanied the much broader process of economic and human development. Specifically, international economic integration refers to the process whereby people increasingly transact and engage with people in distant countries and regions. Today, people are linked throughout the world by trade, investment, finance, and migration. Overall, international economic integration has had many advantages for human well-being, but this chapter also explained some of the general reasons why the growing interdependence among greater numbers of people can be problematic and is often resisted by individuals, firms, governments, and interest groups.

The field of international economics seeks to clarify what this interdependence means for human well-being and to prescribe policies to shape this interdependence in ways that improve people's lives. This textbook often uses the term *international economic integration* instead of the traditional term *international economics* in order to underscore the interdependencies between international trade, international investment, international finance, and immigration. Furthermore, the term *integration* suggests that the growth of international economic activities is part of an evolving process of economic and social development that is increasing the interdependence of human beings on earth.

Of special importance is Figure 1.1, which placed international economic activity within the economic, social, and natural spheres of human existence. Economic activity is intimately related to human social behavior. Also, humanity's relationship with its natural environment must be explicitly recognized, especially today when the earth's seven billion human inhabitants and their rapid growth of production are threatening the ecosystem's ability to support and sustain human life and many other forms of life. Orthodox international economics has not done a very good job of analyzing international economic activity's social and environmental effects; heterodox economics has the potential to do much better.

This chapter provides the basic ideas that led us to adopt a heterodox approach to international economics. The next chapter explains why the heterodox approach is much more likely than the traditional one to get us closer to the fundamental understanding that we need to advance human well-being in the complex, internationally integrated world that we inhabit.

CHAPTER SUMMARY

1. The purpose of this textbook is to explain what international economists know about the process of international economic integration, which is defined as the growth of international economic activity relative to overall economic activity.

2. International economic integration has four main components: (1) international trade, (2) international investment, (3) international finance, and (4) international migration.

3. All components of international integration have been expanding rapidly since the close of World War II.

4. Forms of international economic integration have been occurring, off and on, for at least ten thousand years, when the discovery of agriculture led humans to build more complex societies with expanded interaction with strangers.

5. As Seabright suggests, there are three main reasons why interactions among strangers have grown: interdependence enables greater specialization, risk reduction, and spread of knowledge.

6. Interdependence is inherently problematic, however. Greater interaction with foreigners has also led to violence, exploitation, and theft.

7. International economic integration is far from complete, however. There is scope for further growth of international trade, international investment, international finance, and immigration.

8. This textbook will present both mainstream and heterodox perspectives on international economic integration. The orthodox neoclassical models are inherently limited in their capacity for studying complex issues that transcend narrow economic perspectives. Many concerns about international economic integration are related to social and environmental issues, which neoclassical models are not designed to analyze.

9. Heterodox perspectives are necessary because international economic integration is not exclusively an economic process, nor is economic behavior exclusively determined by economic variables. International economic integration occurs within the broader social and natural spheres, which surround the economic sphere observed by traditional economic analysis.

10. The complexity of international economic integration is reflected in the fact that globalization has been stopped or reversed many times throughout history. There is no guarantee that governments will continue to create the institutions necessary for international trade, international investment, international migration, and international finance to occur.

KEY TERMS AND CONCEPTS

abstract reasoning
Central American Free Trade Agreement (CAFTA)
cross-section data
culture
ecological footprint
economies of scale
economic growth
economic integration
ecosystem
empirical evidence
Green Revolution
greenhouse gas (GHG) emissions
heterodoxy
heterodox economics
institutions

international economic integration
learning by doing
model
monoculture
neoclassical paradigm
North American Free Trade Agreement (NAFTA)
orthodox economics
outsourcing
paradigm
risk
specialization
technological change
time-series data
uncertainty

QUESTIONS AND PROBLEMS

1. The portion of human economic activity that involves foreigners has grown over the past century. Do you find this expansion of international trade, international investment, international migration, and international financial flows troubling or encouraging? Explain the pros and cons of international economic integration.

2. Describe how international trade has grown over the past two centuries, using the information provided in the chapter as well as any outside sources you can find. Has the growth been steady? Have all countries integrated into the international economy to the same extent?

3. In the opening sentences of Chapters 1 and 2 of Volume 1 of his *An Inquiry into the Nature and Causes of the Wealth of Nations* (1776) Adam Smith wrote:

   > The greatest improvements in the productive powers of labour, and the greatest part of the skill, dexterity, and judgment with which it is any where directed, or applied, seem to have been the effects of the division of labour. . . . As it is the power of exchanging that gives occasion to the division of labour, so the extent of this division must always be limited by the extent of that power, or, in other words, by the extent of the market.

   Interpret the meaning of his words for international trade.

4. Is the world truly internationally integrated? If not, how much further does international economic integration still have to go before we live in a truly integrated world economy?

5. Why has international economic integration not progressed further than it has? What could have prevented international trade, international investment, and immigration from growing more than they did over the past fifty years?

6. Economists and all scientists use models of varying degrees of realism and simplicity, depending on the circumstances and purposes at hand. Can you think of a decision that you faced recently that required you to reach a conclusion about the likely outcome of a complex process? How did you reach your decision? What was your reasoning? Describe the "model" of the situation that you used in your thought process. How accurate was your model?

7. How many examples of international economic integration can you find in your community? List them and classify them as falling under international trade, international investment, or immigration.

8. The textbook writes: "Human survival has always depended on a careful balance between closer interaction and keeping one's distance." Evaluate this statement and offer real world observations of both advantages and disadvantages of international trade, investment, finance, and migration.

9. The textbook provides an example that links immigration from Mexico to the United States to international trade. Can you think of other examples of how two or more of the components of international economic integration are related? Describe and explain. (Hint: Financial flows between countries can be used to finance other activities such as investment or trade.)

10. This chapter decribes the difficulties that the Native Americans and the Dutch immigrants had in dealing with each other in what is today New York. Can you think of other examples from history where contacts between strangers did not turn out to be beneficial to all participants? Can you think of examples of international trade, international investment, international finance, or immigration that are not beneficial to one or more of the countries involved? Describe and explain.

NOTES

1. The case of Jinfeng is taken from Joseph Kahn and Mark Landler (2007), "China Grabs West's Smoke-Spewing Factories," *New York Times,* December 21, and James Kynge (2006).

2. Keith Bradsher and David Barboza (2006), "Pollution from Chinese Coal Casts a Long Shadow," *New York Times,* June 11.

3. Quoted in John Authers and Alison Maitland (2004), "The Human Cost of the Computer Age," *Financial Times,* January 26.

4. Paul Seabright (2010), pp. 3–4.

5. Adam Smith (1776 [1976]), p. 7.

6. William Petty (1682).

7. Adam Smith (1776 [1976]), p. 13.

8. Paul Seabright (2010), p. 257.

9. Douglass C. North (2005), p. 15.

10. Ibid., pp. 15–16. Deepak Lal (1998) makes a very similar argument but calls the nonrational portion of our overall belief system "cosmological beliefs."

11. Legend has it that the Dutch paid $24 for Manhattan Island, but this sum was arrived at by a nineteenth-century U.S. ambassador to the Netherlands, who calculated that 60 Dutch guilders in 1626 were about equal to 24 U.S. dollars in 1839.

12. Quoted in Stuart Ferguson (1999), "Going Dutch: Manhattan for Sale," *Wall Street Journal,* November 19, p. W10.

13. Lance Davis and Robert Gallman (1999).

14. Joe Duggan (2001), "Changing Faces in Rural Places," *Lincoln Journal Star,* March 18.

15. Jeffrey Frankel (1999), p. 52.

16. John Maynard Keynes (1920).

17. Dani Rodrik (1998), p. 4.

18. Robert J. Blendon et al. (1997).

19. Herman E. Daly (1999).

20. World Wildlife Fund (2008), p. 2.

21. Miltiades Chacholiades (1990), p. 2.

22. Dennis Appleyard, Alfred Field, and Steven Cobb (2010), p. 2.

CHAPTER 2

The Heterodox Approach

> The composition of this book has been for the author a long struggle of escape, and so must the reading of it be for most readers if the author's assault upon them is to be successful—a struggle of escape from habitual modes of thought and expression. The ideas which are here expressed so laboriously are extremely simple and should be obvious. The difficulty lies, not in the new ideas, but in escaping from the old ones, which ramify, for those of us brought up as most of us have been, into every corner of our minds.
>
> —John Maynard Keynes, 1936, p. viii

The term *heterodox economics* refers to an approach to economic analysis that is being embraced by an increasing number of economists. To grasp what this term means, note first that the prefix *hetero* has its origins in ancient Greek, where it meant "other" or "different." The word *doxy* refers to a doctrine, a framework of analysis, or what many social scientists would call a **paradigm. Heterodoxy** thus suggests a set of ideas, perspectives, and models that are different from the orthodox perspective or approach to economic analysis.

The relationship between *heterodoxy* and *orthodoxy* is not a comfortable one. To understand the conflict, note that the word element *ortho,* which also comes from Greek, means "straight," "right," or "correct." Thus, we might conclude that according to these meanings of the terms *heterodox* and *orthodox,* the latter refers to mainstream thinking, which its adherents view as the right way to think, while heterodox effectively refers to viewpoints that fall outside the accepted mainstream culture of economics. That is, the linguistic origin of the term *orthodoxy* reinforces the viewpoint in mainstream economics that those who embrace heterodoxy are little more than outside agitators, not worthy of attention by the mainstream group. In the United States today, the orthodox paradigm in economics is the **neoclassical paradigm**. All other paradigms, such as those advanced by institutionalists, Marxists, Keynesians, behaviorists, libertarians, Austrians, structuralists, and dependency theorists, are thus assigned to heterodox economics.

This textbook follows many heterodox economists by interpreting heterodoxy generally as a **multi-paradigmatic approach**. Heterodoxy is a form of economics multiculturalism. Heterodox economists do not entirely reject neoclassical models, but they do diminish them to the status of one of the many alternative approaches that must be considered in addressing the complexity of human economic, social, and natural existence. Under this definition of heterodoxy, heterodox economists are not simply anti-neoclassical. They do firmly reject the idea that economic phenomena can be accurately understood and analyzed using only the neoclassical paradigm, or any single paradigm.

If you think of a paradigm as a language, heterodoxy enables economists to speak many languages, which enables them to discover many viewpoints, discuss issues with many different interests, and uncover more information and evidence to support or refute many more hypotheses. In short, one must understand other paradigms (languages) in order communicate with other people and comprehend what they say.

This chapter brings together some of the ideas presented in the previous chapter as well as several new concepts to explain more precisely what we mean by heterodox economics and why this textbook embraces heterodoxy. There is a compelling logic to heterodoxy that goes well beyond merely rejecting the generality of the neoclassical paradigm. Heterodox economics embraces alternative paradigms because it recognizes the limits of models and the need to apply different models under different circumstances and to compare the results of different models for any given set of circumstances. As will be discussed in the first section of this chapter, heterodox economics recognizes the need to think holistically about economic phenomena. In fact, the concept of **holism** is central to heterodox economics. Heterodox economics also embraces the scientific method, as every social science should, although it is careful to distinguish its **holistic scientific** approach from the **scientific reductionism** of orthodox neoclassical economics. Heterodox economics seeks to identify and actively compensate for the biases inherent in any one paradigm, a goal that it sees as critical for a social science that studies the complexity and uncertainty of human existence. This chapter concludes with a "sociology of economics" that clarifies how heterodoxy reduces bias and inaccuracies inherent to analysis limited to one dominant paradigm.

HOLISM AND ECONOMICS

Recall from the previous chapter how economists are challenged to understand the complexity of the overall economic system and its multiple interactions with the social and natural spheres of human existence. The example of how the North American Free Trade Agreement (NAFTA), which purported to liberalize trade between Canada, Mexico, and the United States, led to an expansion of illegal immigration from Mexico to the United States showed that economic and social behavior combine to generate overall social outcomes. Interestingly, it was heterodox economists who first predicted NAFTA's consequences on immigration and the U.S. labor market. The neoclassical paradigm, static in its view of time and with its focus on purely economic phenomena, was not designed to analyze the broad relationships between trade, immigration, and social change. But, if we are to get closer to those optimal outcomes, we need to at least formally recognize the interdependence of economic, social, and natural phenomena. And, we need to adopt an efficient method for increasing our knowledge about this complex reality. The advantage the heterodox economists enjoy over orthodox economists is that they are willing to embrace a perspective that we call holism.

The term *holism* is derived from the Greek word *holos,* meaning "entire, total, whole." The term was initially used in the early twentieth century to describe new dynamic theories in the physical sciences, such as Charles Darwin's theory of evolution, Henri Becquerel's theory of radioactivity, and Albert Einstein's theory of relativity. These new theories described the world as evolving dynamic systems, in which each part is related to all other parts in complex ways that effectively condition how each individual part functions. Holism is the explicit recognition that the component *parts* of the *whole* cannot be understood in isolation and their functions cannot be predicted without knowing the whole environment in which they exist. In the case of international economic activity, the overall economic, social, and natural outcomes are a function of both the international economic system's parts *and their interactions.* In the case of NAFTA, the opening of the border between the United States and Mexico to the flow of goods resulted in imports of cheap U.S. corn, driving over a million Mexican farmers off their small farms and into other economic activities, just as trade theory predicts. But, orthodox economics assumed that the displaced farmers would seek work in other sectors of the Mexican economy, and they ignored the possibility that the farmers would cross the border to seek better paying jobs in the United States. Economists looked at international trade

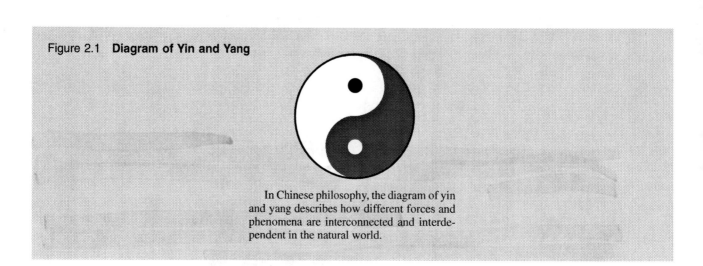

Figure 2.1 **Diagram of Yin and Yang**

In Chinese philosophy, the diagram of yin and yang describes how different forces and phenomena are interconnected and interdependent in the natural world.

in isolation, and they ignored another part of international economics: immigration theory. It took heterodox economists, who are accustomed to looking at the relationships between the parts of the overall system, the international economic system in this case, to put all the parts together and make a more accurate prediction of NAFTA's overall economic effects.

The System versus the Parts

On March 28, 1979, the second reactor of the Three Mile Island nuclear power plant in Pennsylvania released radioactive water. Soon thereafter, radioactive gas was detected near the plant. Something was clearly going dreadfully wrong, but no one seemed to know what the problem was. "I think it's safe to say chaos was the best way to describe it," wrote Samuel Walker, the U.S. Nuclear Regulatory Commission's historian.[1] Because the governor of Pennsylvania was not given any information for three days, he did not immediately order a limited evacuation. "I needed facts, and we simply weren't getting them," the governor said later in an interview.[2] Only later was it apparent that the plant had come very close to a critical meltdown that would have devastated the entire region, including perhaps even Washington, DC. One scientist in the U.S. Nuclear Regulatory Commission, which oversees all U.S. nuclear power plants, later commented that among the many experts the commission had consulted to try to understand what had gone wrong, not one fully understood the whole Three Mile Island plant. No one was able to grasp why the separate parts of the plant, each performing well within its established performance parameters, could interact in a way that would have destroyed the whole system had it been permitted to operate a bit longer.

The example of Three Mile Island reminds us of how difficult it is to monitor and manage complex systems. Clearly, complex systems cannot work unless each of their components works well. But it is also true that even when each of the complex system's components is managed very well, the whole system may still fail if the parts are not well integrated or the linkages between them are misunderstood. "This is true for atomic power plants, large enterprises operating in many countries and sectors, and the international financial system," writes the international economist Vito Tanzi.[3] Indeed, the failures of the international financial system during the Great Depression or the 2008 financial crisis, triggered by dangerous combinations of predatory behavior and faulty systems designs, caused much more economic damage than did the Three Mile Island nuclear accident."[4]

The holistic approach to understanding, which is the simultaneous focus on the parts and the systemic interactions of those parts, has been pursued in many fields. In sociology, Émile Durkheim argued against the notion that society was nothing more than a collection of individuals.

He showed that a **community** can take on many different forms depending on how the individuals who make up the group organize themselves and behave within their particular organization. In medicine, the holistic approach to healing analyzes how the emotional, mental, and physical elements of each person work together. Modern psychological research widely confirms that a person's relationship to society shapes his or her behavior. The International Electrical Engineering Association has published guidelines suggesting engineers should take a holistic approach to their work in order to avoid incompatibilities between specific projects and the societies in which the projects are carried out. And, of course, holism is fundamental to the field of ecology. For example, the biologist E.O. Wilson (2002) documents the evidence on the hundredfold increase in the rate of extinction of living species in the twentieth century. Wilson reminds us that human economic activity seems to have inadvertently triggered an ecological collapse of major proportions, the consequences of which we cannot yet fully comprehend. These holistic perspectives in a wide variety of intellectual fields suggest that economists would be in good company if they too embraced holism. The economist Kenneth Boulding (1956, p. 197) appropriately described holism over half a century ago as the approach that links "the specific that has no meaning and the general that has no content."

Do Systems Move toward Stable Equilibria?

The holistic view of human existence not only crosses disciplinary boundaries with many other fields in the natural and social sciences, but it also straddles distinct time periods. Holism views events as part of an evolving dynamic system that links past, current, and future events. That is, there is an important time dimension to everything we experience and observe. Such a dynamic perspective is quite useful for analyzing international economic integration because international trade, investment, finance, and migration cannot be understood from single-point-in-time observation. Today's international economic integration is the cumulative result of past trade flows, investments, financial arrangements, and migrations. And today's integration shapes future integration. Furthermore, the results of these international economic activities have had other, broader dynamic consequences. Over the past hundred thousand years, humans have increased their exploitation of their natural environment, they have employed more tools (capital), and they have improved their technology. Most important for social scientists like economists, humans have developed very sophisticated social and economic communities.

By looking at economic systems, social organization, and natural ecosystems as dynamic systems that are continually evolving in relation to each other, it becomes possible to analyze whether these systems are stable or subject to sudden instability. Since the 2008 financial crisis hit most of the world's economies, there has certainly been much discussion about whether economic systems are prone to recurring booms and busts. There are many hypotheses suggesting that economic systems are unstable. Karl Marx, of course, predicted the imminent collapse of capitalism in the nineteenth century. More recently, Hyman P. Minsky (1982) presented his financial instability hypothesis, which predicts that in a capitalist system every economic boom is inevitably followed by a financial crash. Sociologists, anthropologists, and historians have examined why human societies tend to "disintegrate" after extended periods of economic and social integration.

There is currently also an active debate about whether our ecosystem, the natural sphere, is stable. Some scientists argue that the ecosystem is characterized by **homeostasis**. Claude Bernard used this term in 1865 to describe a living organism that automatically or instinctively regulates its internal environment in order to survive within a variable external environment. The maintenance of constant body temperature by endothermic animals, such as mammals and birds, in response to changes in external temperatures is one form of homeostasis. Exothermic animals like reptiles and some sea creatures survive in changing environments by letting their body temperatures change with the external temperature and then mitigating body temperature changes by adjusting their behavior. Snakes, for example, actively seek out sunshine to raise their body temperatures. Each of these homeostatic mechanisms, internal regulation or conformism, has advantages and disadvantages. One disadvantage of internal regulation is that it takes more energy. Snakes eat once a week or less; mammals and birds spend the greater part of their lives seeking food.

James Lovelock's (1972) famous **Gaia hypothesis** states that the planet Earth functions as a large homeostatic organism that actively adjusts its "internal" natural conditions. For example, plants absorb carbon dioxide from the air, effectively reducing the amount of carbon dioxide in the atmosphere. And, when some event increases the carbon in the atmosphere and raises temperatures, plants grow faster and absorb more carbon, thus reducing the greenhouse gases in the air. The hypothesis is named for the Greek goddess Gaia, who personified Mother Earth. It seems to suggest that somehow the system will adjust so that the overall ecological environment remains stable. Note, however, that while the whole system may be homeostatic, the ongoing adjustment process of evolution causes a continual string of extinctions of species.

Peter Ward (2009) offers his **Medea hypothesis**, which he named in honor of the mythological Greek sorceress who killed her own children in a fit of rage against her husband. Ward points out that the paleontological record suggests that Mother Earth occasionally drives a very large proportion of species into extinction at the same time. Like economic and social systems, the ecosystem is subject to booms and busts. Ward contends that because humanity evolved in the relatively stable natural environment over the past few million years, the recent unprecedented growth of the human population and its economic activity will cause the earth's system to adjust in ways that could overwhelm humans' own homeostatic adjustment mechanisms. For example, if global warming exceeds 15° C or species depletion increases another order of magnitude, then humanity may not survive. In short, neither humanity's spheres of existence nor the entire system is stable in the sense that all the parts will survive the adjustment process that humanity's expansion has set in motion.

In this unstable environment, it would not be appropriate to frame economic analysis under the assumption that economic outcomes are stable equilibria within unchanging social and natural environments. That is exactly what mainstream economic analysis does, which explains why nearly all mainstream economists failed to foresee the 2008 financial collapse and global recession.

Holism and Science

Holism accepts that complex systems can only be fully understood by analyzing how the components of the system operate together. For this reason, holism has been described as the diametric opposite of scientific reductionism. The latter approach assumes that we can understand the whole by learning about its parts, one part at a time. In effect, scientific reductionism accepts that the whole is the straightforward sum of its parts. Holistic scientists, on the other hand, argue that to understand a complex process or system, one must understand not just each part, but also how the parts interact. Scientific reductionism is, in fact, not scientific if there are good reasons to suspect that the interactions between the components of the system determine the outcomes of the overall system. A brief review of the scientific method makes it clear why holism is more scientific than scientific reductionism.

The development of **science** is often cited as humanity's most important intellectual achievement, but we seldom give much thought to what we mean by science. Since we strive to apply the scientific method throughout this book, we had better understand precisely what science is.

Strictly speaking, science is defined as the body of knowledge about a set of natural or social phenomena that is gathered in accordance with the **scientific method**. The scientific method consists of the following steps:

Step 1. Carefully and accurately observe some phenomenon or fact; this constitutes a **scientific observation**.

Step 2. Use reason to invent a **hypothesis**, which is a carefully stated or presented relationship or idea that accurately and logically explains the facts you observe.

Step 3. Confront the hypothesis with real world outcomes or perform experiments to generate outcomes that can be compared to the hypothesis' predicted outcomes.

Step 4. Perform many experiments or observe large amounts of real world outcomes under a variety of circumstances in order to avoid conclusions driven by unseen forces not taken into consideration in your hypothesis, observations, and experiments.

Step 5. Record everything you do and observe, so that others can see exactly how your hypothesis was tested.

Step 6. Carefully examine whether all the observed outcomes consistently conform with your hypothesis.

Step 7. If these tests of your hypothesis reveal that the real world outcomes or experimental outcomes are not consistent with your hypothesis, modify your hypothesis and return to step 2.

Step 8. If your experiments, observations, or other objective tests consistently confirm your hypothesis, your hypothesis becomes a **theory** (a confirmed hypothesis). The scientist must publish all results, accompanied by all the details of the tests that confirm the hypothesis so that others can replicate the experiments and confirm the methods and results.

If you follow these steps in your quest for knowledge, you are a scientist. When you apply the scientific method to gain understanding about social phenomena, you are a **social scientist**.

With regard to the steps of the scientific method, a few important points are in order. First, note that the popular definition of the word *theory* does not match the scientific definition. Most people think of a theory as some vague or abstract idea. In science, however, a theory is a precise conceptual framework that consistently explains known facts and accurately predicts facts that may be known in the future. The scientific method classifies an idea as a hypothesis until it is proven by an objectively obtained set of data, direct observations of real phenomena, or carefully designed tests. A hypothesis is no more than a carefully thought-out probe into the space between what we know and what we don't know.

Because a theory is a hypothesis that withstood the challenges of tests and accurate observations of reality, a **scientific hypothesis** must be falsifiable. For example, the hypothesis that immigration between two countries depends on the difference in wages between the two countries is truly a scientific hypothesis because we can observe wages and the flows of immigrants and, potentially, confirm or falsify it. Repeated and careful examination of the evidence suggests that this is more than a hypothesis; the evidence seems to have repeatedly confirmed this hypothesis across different pairs of countries, under different circumstances, and at different periods of history. On the other hand, it is not scientific to propose a hypothesis that is not falsifiable with the evidence we currently have available and then claim that it is true because there is no evidence refuting it. For example, there is no way to refute the hypothesis that the universe was created by a flying spaghetti monster. As crazy as this idea sounds, given our current understanding of physics and culture, we really do not have enough scientific evidence to definitively determine that a flying spaghetti monster did *not* create the universe. Since we really have no evidence (at this point in time) about what may have caused our universe to come into being or what it emerged from, the scientific approach in this case is to simply say: "We don't know."

Sometimes we optimistically think we have uncovered a theory, but then our ongoing scientific investigations uncover new evidence that refutes it. An example of such a false theory is Isaac Newton's theory of gravity. Newton's theory that gravitational force between two objects is directly proportional to the bodies' mass and inversely proportional to the square of the distance between them was confirmed repeatedly by a great amount of evidence. Then, in the nineteenth century, more accurate instruments found that there were some discrepancies, such as the observed fact that the planet Mercury did not orbit quite the way Newton's theory predicted. Einstein's theory of relativity seemed to more accurately explain what was observed in the universe, but recent experiments using a set of satellites orbiting the earth uncovered some slight variations in the orbits predicted by Newton's theory of gravity and Einstein's theory of relativity. Truth is hard to find.

The scientific method is designed to overcome the human tendency to hold on to old ideas that are inconsistent with observed evidence. Perhaps the best-known example of the persistence of bad ideas was the ancient Greek hypothesis, argued most elegantly by Aristotle and Ptolemy, that the earth is the center of the universe. Despite growing evidence that it was incorrect, this hypothesis was so entrenched in human thinking that it became a central tenet of Christianity, the religion that came to dominate Western culture over the past two millennia. Thus, when Galileo convincingly questioned this hypothesis in the seventeenth century, he was convicted of heresy and placed under house arrest for the rest of his life.

Interestingly, Galileo also ruffled feathers when he used logic and reason to dispute Aristotle's widely accepted claim that heavy objects fall faster than lighter ones. Galileo was so confident of his reasoning, however, that he did not see the necessity for testing the hypothesis. It was the defenders of Aristotle who conducted tests to try to prove Galileo wrong.[5] They dropped a set of different weights from the leaning tower of Pisa to see which ones would hit the ground first, and to their disappointment, the weights all hit the ground simultaneously, proving Galileo's reasoning to have been correct. The critics of Galileo followed the scientific method by confronting opposing hypotheses with evidence. Galileo's reliance on his reasoning rather than carefully testing his conclusions reflects the tendency for people to skip steps of the scientific method.

The scientific method is a systematic, gradual, step-by-step process that builds knowledge and, by definitively rejecting failed hypotheses and publishing how confirmed hypotheses gained theory status, prevents losses of previous knowledge. The expanded interaction with strangers brought by international economic integration can enhance the power of the scientific method by providing more ideas to test and more evidence with which to test hypotheses.

The scientific method naturally demands that we take a holistic approach when we analyze complex systems such as the global economy and the social and natural systems within which humans carry out economic activities. Science and holism are fully compatible, and their joint application can be termed holistic science. In general, holistic science is the scientific study of *complex systems*. Since complex systems generally extend across many sectors of our social and natural environments, and because complex systems tend to be evolutionary rather than one-time occurrences, holistic science generally looks for dynamic paths rather than events observed at one point in time. International economic integration is just such a complex and evolving phenomenon whose study demands a holistic scientific approach.

Can the Scientific Method Ever Uncover Absolute Truth?

To some people it is discouraging that the scientific method has not yet led us to the absolute truth about everything in the universe. Indeed, our ignorance about our natural and social environments is still very large. The failure of science to answer all our questions has often caused people to reject science altogether and to fall back on what behavioral economists call **heuristics**, or those rules of thumb and traditional solutions that societies come to see as useful in dealing with problems even though they lack a scientific verification. Humans seem to have evolved not only the ability to think scientifically, but also a desire for shortcuts and a willingness to proceed with only partial knowledge when confronted by an urgent problem.

The sheer complexity of humanity's current existence complicates the application of the scientific method. Holism requires more complex hypotheses, which are more difficult to test than simple hypotheses. Secondly, holism tends to lead to hypotheses that hold under more restrictive circumstances. For example, there are plausible reasons why free international trade is likely to stimulate economic growth. However, our holistic approach reveals that economic growth requires many favorable conditions, so that international trade, by itself, may not always cause economies to grow. This finding means we need a more complex hypothesis that permits us to test whether trade *together* with those other conditions promotes economic growth. If we do not take such a holistic approach and we test the simple hypothesis that more international trade leads to faster economic growth, our results will still depend critically on those other unspecified conditions but we will not know to what extent our observations are influenced by those other conditions. For example, if we test the hypothesis for a group of developed economies during the latter half of the twentieth century, when the other conditions happened to be largely favorable to economic growth, we would be led to accept the hypothesis, but if we tested it for a group of developing economies that exported mostly raw materials during the late nineteenth and early twentieth centuries, we would reject the hypothesis. Simple hypotheses often lead to conclusions that are subsequently refuted.

Despite not (yet) having found absolute truth, the more frequent application of the scientific method has clearly enabled us to accelerate the accumulation of knowledge in recent centuries. Realistically, we will have to be content with improving our knowledge, in confirming new hypotheses, and in gaining insights that inspire ever more ambitious hypotheses. On the bright side, we have a lot of exciting work ahead of us!

ECONOMISTS AND COMPLEX SYSTEMS

As social scientists, many economists have looked beyond the immediate variables of interest to explain why economic phenomena occur. Most economists would agree that, where practical, general equilibrium analysis that relates a specific economic activity of interest to some representation of the "rest of the economy" is clearly preferable to partial equilibrium analysis, which looks at only a narrow relationship under the ceteris paribus, or "all other things equal," assumption. For example, in 1799, Thomas Malthus linked economic growth closely to population growth. In the nineteenth century, Marx linked the evolution of the social system to the dynamics of a capitalist economic system. There is no denying, however, that economists and other social scientists have often limited their perspectives to phenomena within their own narrow fields.

Of special concern is the neoclassical paradigm's embrace of the scientific reductionist approach, in which the economic system is hypothesized to be the simple sum of its parts. Models based on the assumption that the system is a static set of relationships that make the whole a sum of its parts are unlikely to include the real outcomes of the complex, dynamic process of international economic integration.

Economists' Embrace of Scientific Reductionism

Despite the holism of Adam Smith, the classical economists, and Marx, economists in the late nineteenth and early twentieth centuries embraced the unsound strategy of scientific reductionism by concentrating on individual markets, banking and finance, and, above all, resource allocation. They implicitly assumed that a good understanding of the economic system's component parts would be sufficient for designing the policies and institutions necessary to support the economic system. Textbooks often used the *ceteris paribus* assumption in order to focus on specific markets and sectors of the economy, freed from the need to deal with more complex systemic relationships and feedback. The best-selling economics textbook beginning in 1890 was Alfred Marshall's *Principles of Economics*, the eighth edition of which was published in 1920. It reflected the belief, not a proven hypothesis, that a market economy would always move toward a stable equilibrium.

Of special interest for our discussion of holism is the mathematical model of a complete economic system developed by the French-born, Swiss-based economist Léon Walras in the late nineteenth century. Walras modeled the economy as a huge system of equations, each representing one of the economic system's many markets in which transactions simultaneously occur. For example, his mathematical model had equations for each of the markets where consumers purchase the great variety of goods and services from producers, where the government purchases goods and services from producers, and where producers acquire capital goods from other producers, labor from individuals, land from landowners, and other resources from resource and factor owners.

Specifically, in Walras' model there are m products, n factor services, m product prices, n factor prices, and mn technical coefficients. The latter specify how many of each of the n productive services are used to produce each of the m products. There were thus $2m + 2n + mn - 1$ unknowns, since according to Walras' law, one of the products serves as "numéraire," the measure in which all other variables are valued. In general, a system of equations can be solved if the number of unknowns is equal to the number of equations. And, indeed, there are $m-1$ demand equations for products, m cost equations for products, n quantity equations and n supply equations for productive services, and mn technical relationships.

In a sense, Walras' model is holistic because it shows every part of the economy related to every other part. Ironically, Walras' elaborate simultaneous equations model probably discouraged economists from adopting a true holistic approach to analyzing economic issues and economic development. For practical reasons, Walras' mathematical model specified the system as a set of equations with fixed parameters that did not permit the relationships among the component parts to vary. In other words, it was a static system. He was never able to find a mathematical solution to his system, but he, and most other economists of his time, assumed that if all markets automatically tend to move toward their respective equilibria, then the entire system would also automatically move toward an overall stable equilibrium.

The impossibility of solving the system of equations encouraged economists to focus on the system's individual markets and refrain from trying to analyze how the overall economic system performed. Walras' intuition that some solution must exist was accepted as obvious. Thus the complexity and impossibility of solving the Walrasian model, combined with the faith that the system did have a solution, seem to have justified scientific reductionism and the focus on individual markets rather than on interconnections and the overall system. Interestingly, it was only in the latter half of the twentieth century that topology was used to prove that a solution to Walras' static system of fixed equations even existed!

These reductionist tendencies in economics were reversed only when the world economy plunged into the Great Depression during the 1930s. At that point, mainstream economists recognized that a system of individual product markets, factor markets, asset markets, and money markets does not always result in a stable equilibrium at which human welfare is maximized. Also, the Great Depression showed that an economy's equilibrium could change drastically even when the component parts, such as the number of workers, the capital stock, and natural resources, remained the same. The Great Depression of the 1930s shifted economists' focus from the component parts to how the overall system performed.

In 1936, British economist John Maynard Keynes published his *General Theory of Employment, Interest, and Money,* the work that effectively created the field that is today known as macroeconomics. He developed a model that explicitly showed how the major components of the economy interacted to determine the total levels of output and employment, and how that system could generate bad outcomes such as the high unemployment and negative growth that characterized the 1930s. Keynes's macroeconomic model helped policy makers design policies to address the obvious failure of the world's major economies to reach the full employment general equilibrium economists had assumed would automatically occur in a market system. Keynes, therefore, restored interest in looking at an entire economic system rather than just its individual components.

The model of international trade that still dominates textbooks of international economics was developed during the period between Marx's and Keynes's major publications. More recently, the 2008 global financial crisis made it clear that the field of finance had, once again, abandoned holism and, specifically, the systemic approach of Keynes. Modern financial economics had adopted a new neoclassical paradigm that assumed financial markets would remain stable under all circumstances and that there would be no systemic failures that could disrupt the macroeconomy. A holistic heterodox approach quickly uncovers what were the disruptive consequences of international trade and finance that sank the world economy in 2008.

A Historical Note on Neoclassical Economics

The school of economic thought associated with Marshall and other late nineteenth-century economists, who we described as having implicitly accepted the unsound strategy of scientific reductionism in order to focus their analytical attention on individual producers, consumers, and markets, is now commonly referred to as the neoclassical school.[6] Since neoclassical thought has dominated mainstream economic thought for the past several decades, it is important at this stage to clarify where it differs from the other schools of thought described above. The principal feature of neoclassical thinking is that it views the economy as a static, fixed set of resources, which implies that the economy's principal problem is to seek the allocation of that finite set of resources that maximizes consumers' welfare. The neoclassicals have developed an elaborate modeling structure that supports Smith's idea that the "invisible hand" operates through free markets to channel self-interest into an optimal level of human welfare. Neoclassical models largely ignore Smith's writing about the failures of markets and the potential breakdown of market competition.

Neoclassical analysis is not exclusively microeconomic in nature. In fact, neoclassical analysis followed in the footsteps of Walras by seeking a consistent model that systematically links the economy's individual consumers, workers, producers, bankers, and investors to the economy's aggregate performance. Neoclassical economists spearheaded the search in macroeconomics for **microfoundations**, which are the logically consistent models of individual consumers and producers that explain how their actions brought about the observed macroeconomic outcomes. Just like Walras found more than one hundred years ago, strong simplifying assumptions are necessary in order to build practical macroeconomic models that are logically compatible with simple models of individual and firm behavior. The quest for microfoundations resulted in unrealistic microeconomic models of individual behavior to match unrealistic macroeconomic models.

Labor markets were modeled as competitive markets where workers were paid their full marginal product. Ignored was the power of large employers in setting wages, the presence of unions, the need for employers to motivate workers, the costs of hiring and firing workers, or the common presence of unemployed and underemployed workers in all Western economies. Even more inaccurate was the common neoclassical assumption that suppliers of products always face rising costs, necessary for economists' assumption of perfect competition and the absence of any tendency for production to become concentrated in oligopolies or monopolies. Given today's industrial concentration, this assumption could be described as delusional, surpassing any reasonable standard of simplification that is appropriate for economic modeling. Also notable is the widespread acceptance of the **Coase theorem** after Ronald Coase (1960). This theorem states that **externalities** will not, in general, cause markets to fail because people, firms, and governments are motivated to find ways to negotiate the sharing of the external costs imposed on others outside a particular market or benefits gained from others outside a particular market and, thus, to enable the mutually beneficial transactions to be carried out. In reality, market participants are seldom aware of the externalities they generate, the extent of those externalities they are aware of, or the externalities that others' actions impose on them. They are even less aware of how to negotiate ways to accurately account for externalities.

The field of finance has come to accept as practical approximations of reality several other highly questionable models, such as Eugene F. Fama's (1970) model of efficient markets that assumed all available information was always built into asset prices, Milton Friedman's (1953) hypothesis that **speculation** always stabilizes financial markets, and Michael C. Jensen and William H. Meckling's (1976) management model that assumes managers of private firms act as faithful servants to the firm's stockholders. Financial markets were described as highly efficient in motivating people to save and financial firms to allocate those savings to the economy's most profitable investments and innovative projects. The microfoundations for this faith in the efficiency of financial markets was informally based on the work of Kenneth Arrow and Gerard Debreu (1954) and Debreu (1959), who constructed elaborate general equilibrium models reminiscent of Walras' model. In reality, borrowing, lending, and long-term projects with high up-front costs and delayed future payoffs must deal with uncertainty, which makes such activities inherently risky. Long-term financial transactions may not be carried out because information about the future is simply not available, nor are even the probabilities of alternative outcomes known. In reality, financial markets often fail. But Arrow and Debreu ignored uncertainty by assuming financial markets only face risk defined by known probability distributions, and they then eliminated risk by assuming competitive markets in **contingent commodities**. These commodities are transactions and payments that occur only when certain prespecified conditions are met. Wrote Debreu: "This new definition of a commodity allows one to obtain a theory of uncertainty free from any probability concept and formally identical with the theory of certainty."[7]

While a modern financial industry does indeed provide insurance against contingencies such as fire, theft, automobile accidents, and other reasonably predictable events, the 2008 financial crisis and the massive government bailouts of financial firms suggest that the financial sector has been unable to create viable insurance instruments that cover the many complex and unpredictable contingencies that can arise. Arrow and Debreu's contingent markets are nothing more than a theoretical fantasy that serves to hide the complexity of risk and uncertainty. Keynes (1936) provides a more realistic assessment of long-term risk:

> Most, probably, of our decisions to do something positive, the full consequences of which will be drawn out over many days to come, can only be taken as a result of animal spirits—of a spontaneous urge to action rather than inaction, and not as the outcome of a weighted average of quantitative benefits multiplied by quantitative probabilities.[8]

If we broaden financial transactions to include innovation, invention, research, and development activities, Keynes's description of investment as being driven by "animal spirits," that is, emotion, rather than precise mathematical calculations of probable economic outcomes is even more accurate. Arrow and Debreu's narrative and models led many economists to believe that the touted financial innovation that preceded the 2008 economic collapse must have created contingent markets that made the international financial system more stable and efficient. The near complete deregulation of financial markets and the abandonment of government oversight, in combination with neoclassical models served to provide a very false intellectual justification for financial innovation that did little more than increase profits in the financial industry. The innovations did not provide greater insurance against risk and uncertainty.

Finally, according to neoclassical analysis, the basic objective of the economy is to produce final consumption goods. The neoclassical welfare function simply relates goods and services consumed to individual welfare. Many other activities in the economy, such as the accumulation of capital and wealth, are effectively modeled as an incidental by-product of individuals' consumption decisions and producers' resource allocation decisions. Neoclassical models and their hypothesized competitive markets have trouble explaining capitalist profit and the growing inequality of wealth, something that the classical economists and Marx were able to do in their models of competing economic sectors and economic classes, respectively. Nor could neoclassical analysis provide useful insight into economic instability, as Keynes's macroeconomic model from the Great Depression could.

International economic integration, whose growth was detailed in the previous chapter, has effectively created a global economic system that links the nearly seven billion humans, governments at many levels, millions of small firms, and an increasingly concentrated declining number of transnational corporations. It is unlikely that this integrated world economic system is more stable than individual national economies were earlier. In the remainder of this chapter we will illustrate why heterodox analysis is likely to accurately analyze international economic activity.

THE COMMON THEMES OF HETERODOXY

The concept of holism underlies all of heterodox economics. Recall that holism calls for models that are *systemic, dynamic,* and *multidisciplinary.* Holism clashes directly with neoclassical economics and its scientific reductionism, its limited focus on only "economic" issues, and its widespread use of the "all other things equal" assumption to justify its static equilibrium models. Heterodox economists reject the exclusive reliance on neoclassical theory precisely because it is not holistic. But there are many more fundamental ideas that motivate heterodox economists.

Heterodox economists generally agree that economic models need not be stated in mathematical form or graphic form, as has become common practice in neoclassical economics. Relationships can also be represented verbally. In fact, many of the models of international economic integration detailed in this textbook were originally presented without equations or diagrams. It was not until the late 1800s that graphic illustrations became popular in economics, and mathematical models did not become popular until the middle of the twentieth century. Given the complexity of human existence, a verbal model can often more accurately and consistently describe observations of real phenomena than mathematical or graphic models that are constrained by practical mathematical forms or the number of dimensions that can be depicted on a flat screen. Note that the scientific method can be followed using words as well as mathematics.

Fundamental Ideas of the Heterodoxy Paradigm

Heterodox economists do not make up a homogeneous group. In fact, the very nature of heterodoxy, which demands a choice of alternative paradigms to study economic issues, leads to individual economists taking many alternative directions in their research and analysis. A reading of the heterodox economics literature reveals at least twenty fundamental ideas that appear to persistently guide the thinking of most heterodox economists. These ideas are often interrelated, which is perfectly understandable given the complexity of social phenomena.

1. *Humans simultaneously live in economic, social, and natural spheres.* Heterodox economists recognize that human economic activity occurs within the broader social and natural systems in which humans exist. Humans engage in a variety of activities that inevitably transcend the economic sphere, which means that human activity cannot be understood using narrow models of economic behavior that take "noneconomic" events and feedbacks as exogenous to the analysis. It is inaccurate to restrict the analysis of economic activity to the economic sphere and to ignore the influence of the social and natural spheres on human economic activity.

2. *Objectivity requires that the scientific method be respected.* Social scientists can never escape the influence, and bias, of culture. If we recognize the likelihood of violating the ideal scientific method

but find ways to compensate for and mitigate our cultural biases, we can maintain the spirit of the scientific method. The neoclassical approach of pretending to be objective by using models that completely ignore cultural influences and the social and natural spheres of existence constitutes a serious violation of the scientific method.

3. *Culture influences economic thought.* The history of economic thought is intimately related to the evolution of human culture. The economic paradigm economists use in their research, analysis, and writing can be as much a result of the economic and social forces it tries to explain as an objective explanation of the economic outcomes. Heterodox economists recognize that culture is a collective phenomenon, which consists of the widely held and reinforced views and perspectives that are directed at, or imposed on, individuals by their peers and the broader collective of people that we call society. Culture does not fit into the methodological individualism adopted by neoclassical economics, which generally assumes that everyone is on the same page—that everyone on both sides of an international transaction plays by the same rules, has the same basic motivations, and sees the entire transaction from the same perspective.

4. *The analysis of economic activity requires an interdisciplinary approach.* Since economic activity occurs within complex social and natural systems, economists must take advantage of the knowledge base in other fields of study. Not only should economists purposely examine economic phenomena and policy prescriptions from a variety of economic paradigms, but they should also incorporate specific knowledge from other fields into their models. For example, findings from psychology should shape economists' models of human behavior and their welfare function. Findings from political science should guide studies of economic policy, and the field of ecology can contribute greatly to the accurate estimation of externalities, true opportunity costs, and cost functions.

5. *Economists must know the history of economic thought.* Human memory is short, and successive generations of economists have often forgotten the worlds of earlier generations. Knowledge grows according to a combinatoric process in which new ideas emerge from combinations of earlier ideas. Today's focus on only the neoclassical paradigm has caused economists and their students not only to lose valuable contributions to our economic understanding, but to ignore alternative paradigms that provide the necessary alternative perspectives for understanding our complex modern economic environment.

6. *Complexity must be respected, not assumed away.* From the time of Walras, economists have conveniently assumed that the economic system is linear and that the parts add up to the aggregate total. In truth, economic analysis and economic policy must recognize that the economic system and the combined economic, social, and natural systems are almost certainly not linear. Multiple equilibria are possible. Complexity requires policy approaches that include the **precautionary principle**, build flexibility into policies so that they can be adjusted as unpredictable results become apparent, and accept the need for continual experimentation and new initiatives to deal with unanticipated problems and opportunities.

7. *Human well-being does not depend on material goods and services alone.* Psychology, neuroscience, happiness studies, and behavioral economics have all demonstrated beyond any doubt that human welfare is not accurately represented by the neoclassical aggregate welfare function, which is specified as the sum of individual welfare functions. People value their social status, the company of others, their overall social environment, as well as their relationship with the natural environment. Individuals in most circumstances value their relative income and social status much more than gains in absolute material wealth. People also care about the well-being of their offspring.

8. *The bottom line in economic analysis is not output or per capita GDP.* This idea stems directly from the previous idea, but it is worth emphasizing because it largely invalidates most mainstream economic analysis based on the aggregate welfare function. This is not to say that measures of per capita income are useless, but it is clear that if increases in per capita real GDP are the result of large shifts in economic activity and resource allocations, as is inevitably the case when international trade, international investment, international finance, and immigration are part of the growth process, then increases in average income will not accurately reflect the changes in income distribution and true human well-being.

9. *Human society continually evolves; it is not static.* Heterodox economics rejects static models of economies, in which all other things remain equal in the face of some policy shift or noneconomic shock. Not only do all economic policies and changes in specific outcomes generate feedback and reactions throughout the economy, society, and the natural environment, but the outcomes and feedbacks operate dynamically over time to generate a string of subsequent economic events. An accurate assessment of economic policies must estimate the long-run dynamic path that such policies put the economy on.

10. *Social and economic institutions are fundamental to economic outcomes.* A society's formal and informal institutions shape individual and firm behavior. This is why heterodox economists often favor interdisciplinary analysis in order to fully understand society's institutions, especially the informal institution that we refer to as **culture**. Heterodox economists are commonly concerned with the dynamics of social institutions that determine economic outcomes, such as racial and gender discrimination, cultural oppression, and political power structures.

11. *Feminist perspectives contribute greatly to economic understanding.* Economics does not always pay attention to how economic activity and policies specifically affect people with distinct positions in human society. In fact, the consequences of economic change are often very different depending on whether you work in the labor market or in the home, or on how society defines your social position. Gender, race, class, ethnic identity, and other personal characteristics are important for determining who bears the costs and benefits of international economic integration. Mainstream economics usually assumes all individuals are identical and that they occupy identical economic power and social status as suppliers of labor, as consumers, and as long-term planners and investors. Feminist economists have shown that this clearly is not the case.

12. *Environmental consequences of economic activity must be internalized.* Environmental economics and ecological economics are important fields in economics. Mainstream economics, with its focus on market activity, has largely failed to recognize, analyze, or prescribe policies to deal with the environmental consequences of economic activity. Mainstream economics has also paid relatively little attention to the effect of the natural environment on economic outcomes or economic activity's effect on the natural sphere. Heterodox economists are more likely to build the natural environment into their analysis.

13. *People are both individuals and social beings.* Margaret Thatcher's comment that "there are no societies, only individuals" reflects the assumptions of neoclassical economics, not actual, observed human behavior. To the contrary, heterodox economists recognize the overwhelming evidence that people are social beings, and social institutions and culture are dominant factors in human economic behavior. Heterodox economics also accepts the need for government to carry out collective actions in a complex society; efficient individual behavior, by itself, cannot deal with complex economic and social issues.

14. *Mathematics is useful, but not required in economic analysis.* Heterodox economists dispute the frequent claim that mathematics permits economists to formulate more complex models than they can with words or diagrams. To the contrary, mathematics introduces more biases into economic thinking because it is not nearly as powerful as mainstream economists suggest. For example, neoclassical economists have had to limit their dynamic analyses to a small set of very simplistic models for the simple reason that they are the only models that can be solved mathematically. Fortunately, humans have developed a variety of ways to communicate and store information, with mathematics but one medium. Complex ideas are often better communicated in words rather than with mathematics.

15. *Make selective use of multiple models rather than relying on one paradigm.* Since all models are simplifications of reality, and since we only very partially understand reality, modeling introduces inaccuracies into economic analysis. Heterodoxy recommends the use of models whose assumptions most closely parallel the phenomenon and situation being analyzed. Also, it is advisable to use multiple models with diverse assumptions in order to examine the robustness, or generality, of specific conclusions and predictions. For example, the short-term models used by the financial industry just before the 2008 financial collapse illustrate how dangerous it is to rely on simplifications that have proved valid only across very short periods of time or very small samples of outcomes.

16. *The fallacy of composition distorts human thinking.* The choices that improve an individual's well-being, all other things equal, may not improve anyone's welfare if everyone makes the same decision. In macroeconomics, personal saving is often given as an example of the fallacy of composition: Personal saving is good for every individual, but if everyone saves more, the economy may end up with higher unemployment and lower real savings in the long run. In international economics, it is not necessarily true that cheap imports improve national well-being. If cheap imports force down wages in domestic manufacturing industries, then the lower domestic purchasing power will reduce aggregate demand for output and potentially increase unemployment and income throughout the economy.

17. *Smaller government is not generally better than larger government.* Heterodox economists recognize the need for collective decisions and actions in a complex modern economy. Many problems humanity faces cannot be solved by means of individual choices and actions. Individuals seem to have little or no power to deal with major problems like national defense, global warming, the massive extinction of living species, a global financial crisis, et cetera, by altering their personal behavior. Heterodox economists are, therefore, not as likely as orthodox neoclassical economists to favor relying on individual actions over collective government action to deal with economic problems.

18. *Economic transactions do not take place only in markets.* Of all the interactions between humans over the course of a day, very few occur in organized markets. Most interactions occur informally under a variety of social norms, family customs, acquired routines, mandated rules and regulations, legal parameters, corporate structures, business procedures, and other cultural habits that guide human behavior. Even among market transactions, very few exchanges are made in the competitive marketplace that economists assume in their models. Imperfect competition is the norm in markets; the model of a perfectly competitive market is a myth—there are no such markets. For this reason, heterodox economics takes an interdisciplinary approach to analyzing economic activity; social, political, historical, technical, and cultural parameters dominate economic activity. Heterodox economics seeks to understand transactions between parties with different levels of market power, as well as the exploitation, oppression, and unequal outcomes that tend to accompany unequal market power. Heterodox economics also analyzes the many other ways in which humans interact in the economy.

19. *Economic policy must address the distribution of income.* Heterodox economics recognizes the importance of the distribution of income for human well-being because people's satisfaction with life depends on social and economic status. Relative income and employment are main determinants of human well-being. It is therefore impossible to judge economic outcomes and policies without explicitly taking into consideration the distribution of the gains and losses associated with economic change and evolution.

20. *No man is an island.* The first chapter emphasized human interdependence as the critical concept for understanding international economics. The expansion of international trade, international investment, international finance, and immigration offers many benefits. However, the sudden expansion of human interdependence from small groups to the entire world over a period of just ten thousand years represents a huge increase in the complexity of human economic and social organization. The heterodox approach and its interdisciplinary perspectives offer a much more realistic framework of analysis for understanding the welfare implications of the rise in the complexity of human existence.

These twenty themes by no means present a complete listing of what heterodox economists think about and do. This textbook will present many more ideas related specifically to international economics. But these ideas, we hope, help to show where heterodox economics diverges from mainstream economic analysis.

Heterodoxy and Economic Policy

Economics consists of both the **positive** task of figuring out how the economy works and the **normative** task of judging whether the economy's performance is good or bad. And, after judgments are made, economists inevitably end up discussing economic policy. It is in the area of economic policy that the different perspectives of orthodox and heterodox economics are most apparent.

Policies that appear appropriate under one paradigm may be inadvisable according to models from another paradigm. Because heterodox analysis uses alternative models and dynamic analytical frameworks that more accurately reflect the complexity of systems, heterodox economists' policy prescriptions are usually much less specific than the policy prescriptions suggested by orthodox economists. "It depends" is a common heterodox response, and flexibility is seen as a positive attribute for policy and institutions. Mainstream economics has sought to minimize indeterminacy in its analysis and to limit flexibility in its prescribed policies.

Heterodox economics may put itself at a disadvantage in the policy realm because people prefer firm answers to an "it depends" or "we'll find out" answer. Yet, the complexity of our human existence and the global economic, social, and environmental problems we face cannot be accurately addressed given our current state of knowledge. For example, orthodox economists are programmed by their paradigm to estimate the costs and benefits of global warming under a set of assumptions and assumed probability distributions in order to arrive at a specific forecast. The uncertainty of the future state of humanity makes a mockery of such calculations, and heterodox economists are usually satisfied to conclude that there is a range of possible outcomes. They do not normally insist on one specific predicted estimate or outcome. In recognition of the uncertainty of what will actually come to pass, they are likely to invoke the precautionary principle in cases where some of the possible outcomes are truly catastrophic. For example, the precautionary principle suggests that the world's governments should take strong action to limit the greenhouse gas emissions that cause global warming precisely because we do not know exactly how much damage a rise in temperatures of several degrees will do to human well-being.

Heterodox economists' freedom in choosing paradigms, models, and methods according to their interpretation of the issues and circumstances leaves them open to the criticism that they are intentionally biasing their analysis. Of course, the neoclassical paradigm is almost certainly biased, but heterodox economists nevertheless face a strong challenge to maintain objectivity and impartiality when they conduct analysis and make policy prescriptions. The advantage that heterodox economists have over orthodox neoclassical economists is that they openly recognize the economic and cultural pressures that can bias their analysis. By explicitly recognizing our cultural and methodological biases, as heterodoxy does, the scientific method can be maintained, and, hopefully, the biases can be mitigated.

A SOCIOLOGICAL JUSTIFICATION FOR HETERODOXY

In this section, we explain why mainstream economics, and thus orthodox international economics, largely ignores the biases of its economic analysis. Specifically, we explain why international economics continues to teach students about international economic integration using a very restrictive set of models that ignore many of the causes and consequences of international economic activity.

Institutions and Culture

In the previous chapter, we discussed the role of institutions in enabling large groups of humans to live productively in complex societies (see "The Crucial Role of Institutions" and "Institutions Evolve Slowly and Unevenly"). Recall that institutions include cultural norms, social customs, formal laws, and explicit government regulations; that is, there are both informal and formal institutions. Institutions are needed because hardwired human behavioral instincts evolved when social and natural environments were different, and these instincts are not appropriate for dealing with the complexity of modern societies. The section titled "Institutions Evolve Slowly and Unevenly" also pointed out that informal institutions, like culture, change very slowly and thus are often inappropriate for dealing with the immediate circumstances that continually evolving modern human societies face.

But while mainstream economics has appropriately recognized the importance of institutions, and thus human culture, in explaining the performance of an economy, mainstream economists have not recognized the cultural struggle within their own profession. The behavior of economists is as much influenced by culture as is the economic behavior of all human beings. In fact, it is precisely *culture,* itself a set of informal institutions such as half-baked ideas, beliefs, conventions, habits, and customs, that tends to obscure the intellectual biases of economists. For example, orthodox mainstream economics has developed a particular subculture in which the neoclassical paradigm is viewed as the correct way to analyze all economic phenomena. When mainstream economists challenge students to learn to "think like an economist," they really mean for the student to frame economic questions within the neoclassical paradigm. In effect, the neoclassical paradigm has become the culture of mainstream economics in the United States and most other countries, which follow the example of the United States in their universities.

Culture has been thoroughly studied by sociologists. This section of the chapter, therefore, borrows heavily from sociology in order to examine the culture of the field of international economics. What follows is a *sociology of economics.* The conclusions of this exercise provide a clear justification for heterodoxy.

Pierre Bourdieu's Analysis of Cultures

The early twentieth-century sociologist Max Weber (1978) wrote that society cannot be analyzed in terms of specific and clearly defined classes or cultures because individual status in society often cuts across traditional concepts of class or subcultures. No doubt the coexistence of cultures and subcultures within societies has become more pervasive with the advances of international economic integration in the latter half of the twentieth century. Among these subcultures is that of a person's professional field. The simultaneous existence of cultures and subcultures is perhaps best analyzed using the framework provided by the French sociologist Pierre Bourdieu. Bourdieu (1988, 2005) famously called for a "sociology of sociology," by which he meant that sociologists should use their own methods to clarify how their professional culture biases their analysis.

Bourdieu's (1977, 2000) lifetime of work also provided a detailed conceptual framework that enables social scientists to break down the components of the cultures and subcultures that influence the behavior of an individual. Bourdieu's work is especially relevant for analyzing how the subculture of international economics evolved within the broader cultures of economics, social science, the workplace, and society as a whole, and, more important, why a particular subculture is so persistent even in the face of scientific evidence that refutes its relevance.

Bourdieu begins by defining a **field** as the social or intellectual arena within which people spend much of their day and within which they focus their efforts to advance their primary social interests. Even though people identify with a broad national or ethnic culture, in going about their daily activities they tend to pay attention almost exclusively to their immediate professional or social environment. Often, a field is one's work, which means that people identify themselves with the culture of a particular job, industry, or profession. For academics, the term *field* is especially appropriate, because so much of one's life is spent within a well-defined "intellectual field." Bourdieu's concept of a field is more general than an academic field, however. He describes how young people tend to embrace the culture of their school environment, members of the military adopt a distinctive military culture, and regular patrons of coffee shops embrace certain rules of behavior that are not found in either fast-food restaurants or high-end restaurants. These fields are often referred to as subcultures by other sociologists, but Bourdieu's connection between subcultures and people's daily lives gives a clearer reason for subcultures' existence.

Bourdieu develops two additional concepts that help to more precisely define a subculture. First of all, when people embrace the subculture that permeates the field they identify with, they adopt certain attitudes and dispositions, or what Bourdieu defines as **habitus**. Bourdieu borrows this concept from earlier social thinkers such as Aristotle and Weber. Specifically, habitus is a set of *subjective* but persistent perceptions, customs, conventions, norms, and forms of outward behavior and expression. The habitus determines both a person's personal disposition and how others judge her within the field. A person develops the subjective dispositions and takes on the attitudes of the habitus in order to be successful in the well-defined objective field he participates in. A soldier whose field is the military is likely to adopt a habitus characterized by a willingness to engage in aggressive behavior, an unquestioning acceptance of rank and authority, and a strong affirmation of nationalism. A small-businessperson's habitus is most likely characterized by open admiration for enterprising people, disdain for government regulators, and a strong positive attitude toward monetary rewards.

It is inherently difficult for a thinking person to psychologically deal with the combination of an objective field and a subjective habitus. The individual, therefore, develops a complex set of beliefs that effectively explain the reality of one's field, which Bourdieu calls **doxa**. Doxa are the fundamental, but mostly unproved, set of beliefs that a person comes to rely on for survival within a particular field. These are the "'half-baked' theories" referred to in the quote from Douglass North in the previous chapter, which people latch on to in order to deal with the inevitable lack of full understanding of their complex existence. Psychologists and neurologists have found that people come to accept certain patterns as normal if they are repeated long enough, so we should think of doxa as the justification for the patterns of human thinking and action that people come to accept as normal and appropriate. Bourdieu specifically states that one's doxa serve to rationalize, justify, and, therefore, legitimize the subjective habitus necessary to successfully participate in the particular objective arrangement of one's field.

Defining a subculture as the combination of a habitus supported by doxa makes it clear why cultures do not change very quickly. Habitus and doxa, or simply culture, change slowly even when people face substantial changes in economic outcomes, social shifts, or the natural environment. Incompatibilities between reality and people's perceptions and beliefs are common in rapidly changing economic, social, and natural environments.

Symbolic Violence

Bourdieu argues that culture can be oppressive because it effectively enforces and perpetuates hierarchical social structures. In the case of an intellectual field, a subculture can similarly become oppressive by perpetuating a particular paradigm. Using Bourdieu's terminology, doxa and habitus combine to justify, and thus strengthen, the dominance of a particular paradigm.

To explain the oppressive nature of culture, Bourdieu introduced the concept of **cultural capital**. Specifically, cultural capital consists of acquired behavioral characteristics, material goods, and formal institutional certifications that give a person status in a specific field or in society in general. **Inherited cultural capital** includes specific traditions and culture that can take considerable time to transfer and absorb, such as habits developed during years of training and education, specific terminology and models, social behavior and professional procedures, and, of course, personal relationships. Cultural capital also includes objects, such as a musical instrument, an office, or an intellectual's library of books. Bourdieu calls this **objectified cultural capital**, and it is important for solidifying a person's status in a field or broader society. For example, an economist most likely owns a sports jacket with patches on the elbows! Finally, there is **institutionalized cultural capital**, which consists of institutional recognitions of cultural capital held by individuals, such as diplomas, awards, certifications, and other official credentials. Cultural capital is intimately wrapped up in a field's habitus and thus is a source of power, quite apart from a person's real economic, physical, or intellectual capabilities.

When a holder of cultural capital uses this power against someone who holds less cultural capital, and seeks to alter that person's actions or social position, Bourdieu calls this **symbolic violence**. Exploitation, oppression, and harassment are overt forms of symbolic violence. Symbolic violence is often more implicit than explicit, especially within intellectual fields such as economics. For example, a frown or angry look by a conference participant can make a speaker retreat from arguing a new idea. In general, symbolic violence among economists is fundamental to the perpetuation of bad ideas and paradigms that produce biased and inaccurate ideas. Bourdieu (2001) shows that symbolic violence leads people to act against their own interest because the prevailing doxa effectively make cultural capital a legitimate determinant of the social hierarchy. People who are the object of symbolic violence are often complicit in their own subordination because they adjust their habitus and doxa to justify the reality of the social or professional field they inhabit.

Therefore, economics graduates of lower-rated universities (say, the University of Nebraska) see the professional success of the graduates of higher-ranked universities (Harvard or MIT) as a legitimate reflection of the latters' greater ability or harder work, even though in reality the institutionalized cultural capital (the diplomas) are seldom more than the result of class-based inherited cultural and economic capital. Similarly, orthodox economists have come to dominate the field of economics because individuals have been pushed into adopting the neoclassical paradigm. Promotion, salaries, and prestige within the field depend on adhering to the habitus of the field.

A Sociology of International Economics

In the spirit of Bourdieu, a sociological examination of the culture of the field of international economics reveals many reasons for the failure of international economics to provide relevant and convincing analyses of our internationally integrated economy. An example of bias in subject matter is the tendency for economists to focus exclusively on market activities, use data generated by markets, and interpret the observed results as if all economic activity occurred in well-defined competitive markets. Hence, most economic research analyzes activities included in measured GDP, uses market prices and quantities to quantify human economic activity, and judges outcomes in terms of market-generated incomes and quantities. There are relatively few economic studies of household activity, largely the work of feminist economists. In international economics, there are few studies that look at the social and ecological consequences of international economic activity. An example of this limited vision is the unexpected impact of the North American Free Trade Agreement (NAFTA) described in the previous chapter: liberalized trade resulted in the devastation of rural society in Mexico and sharply increased immigration to the United States. Economists had only calculated immediate gains from increased imports and exports according to the comparative advantage as determined by a simple neoclassical model of international trade. The broader societal effects of the decline of rural communities and the immigration it induced had been detailed in sociological studies but were ignored in the economics literature, where such issues were generally deemed to be outside the scope of economics. Interdisciplinary study in U.S. academia is still shunned. Despite claims to the contrary by university administrators, the professional journals where interdisciplinary research is published are still considered to be second or third tier journals, not as worthy for raises and promotions.

The most egregious logical error committed by mainstream international economists, and perpetuated in the field's most popular textbooks, is the defense of the limited perspective of their field with the claim that noneconomic issues such as human psychological happiness, environmental problems, and nonmarket household activities are beyond the scope of economics. Heterodox economists, on the other hand, argue that nothing is beyond the scope of economics because when economic issues are addressed holistically it becomes obvious that all economic activity occurs within the broader social system and the natural environment.

Jerry Ravetz (1995, p. 165) uses the term "elite folk science" to describe how the neoclassical framework "can have functions other than those of the increase of positive knowledge." He accuses neoclassical economics of providing "reassurance for a general worldview." The well-known economic historian Robert Heilbroner is more to the point: "The best kept secret in economics is that economics is about the study of capitalism."[9]

Fortunately, there has been more dissent. For example, the field of behavioral economics, which has brought together psychologists and economists, has grown substantially, and several of its members have been awarded Nobel prizes for their heterodox contributions. Behavioral economics, and its closely related field of experimental economics, has addressed economic issues using much more realistic models of human behavior and broader measures of human welfare. We will detail some of these advances after we introduce the orthodox model of international trade in the next part of the book. Ecologists, natural scientists, and environmental economists are filling the huge gaps left by mainstream economics' failure to incorporate the natural environment into economic models. And political scientists have provided valuable insights and models that enable economists to better understand the making of, and the failures of, economic policies.

International economics, however, has yet to *endogenize,* that is, include in its models, the many influences from the broad social and natural spheres. Nor has it seriously analyzed the many stresses that international economic activity puts on society and the ecosystem. For example, it should be no surprise that international economists and environmental economists are often on opposite sides of debates about globalization, free trade, and international investment. The very restrictive market-based focus of neoclassical international economic models leads to conclusions that often differ sharply with the conclusions of the more holistic models that environmental economists use to estimate the ecological and social consequences of international economic activity. When environmental externalities are accounted for, the costs and benefits of economic activity change drastically, as do the gains from international trade and investment. Specifically, when environmental externalities are accounted for, free trade is no longer guaranteed to benefit all countries, as neoclassical trade theory so unambiguously asserts.

The likelihood of bias within an intellectual field, as described by the above sociological analysis of international economics, provides a clear justification for heterodoxy over the orthodox mainstream neoclassical framework that currently dominates the field. Heterodoxy calls for a multidisciplinary approach to analyzing economic phenomena. By looking at issues from the perspective of more than one field, social scientists are less likely to be blinded by their own field's imposed habitus and its supporting doxa. Whether heterodoxy indeed does permit us to overcome the biases in the neoclassical models used in mainstream international economics will be for you to judge. We do argue that heterodox economics is less likely to give you a biased perspective of international economic integration.

CONCLUSIONS AND FURTHER THOUGHTS

The first two chapters of this book have presented the foundations of heterodox economics. The discussion of the three spheres of human existence and economic modeling in the previous chapter, plus this chapter's discussions of holism and Bourdieu's sociological analysis of culture complete the justification for our heterodox approach to international economics. The list of twenty prominent heterodox ideas gives you details on the types of issues the heterodox approach tries to address and where it seeks to take the understanding and analysis of economic activity and policy. The remaining chapters will further clarify heterodoxy as we address a great variety of international economic issues.

Before we set off on our journey through international economics and the many alternative perspectives that our voyage will provide you with, let us once again note how knowledge is accumulated. In the words of Einstein:

> Creating a new theory is not like destroying an old bar and erecting a skyscraper in its place. It is rather like climbing a mountain, gaining new and wider views, discovering unexpected connections between our starting point and its rich environment. But the point from which we started out still exists and can be seen, although it appears smaller and forms a tiny part of our broad view gained by the mastery of the obstacles on our adventurous way up.[10]

In other words, new ideas and knowledge do not appear as a sudden bolt of lightning out of the blue. Knowledge grows because humans actively seek answers to life's questions, they exert considerable effort to find those answers, and they take care to preserve their new knowledge so that others can build on it. The creation of knowledge is a costly, dynamic, and cumulative process in which new ideas are derived by building on combinations of existing ideas.

International economists should understand this better than most other economists. Recall from the previous chapter that one of the main reasons it is advantageous to engage in international economic activities and "deal with strangers" is to share knowledge. Heterodox economics and its preference for dynamic analysis, as opposed to static analysis, gives us an advantage in understanding complex processes such as the accumulation of knowledge and technological change.

Steven Mark Cohn (2007) argues that neoclassical economists are a bit like native English speakers; because their language is so prominent and so many others speak it, they are not pushed to learn other languages. Because learning a new paradigm is always a major investment, most neoclassical economists do not learn about other paradigms. But Cohn observes: "In contrast, because of the dominance of the neoclassical paradigm in contemporary economics, all heterodox economists must take the time to become fluent in its language. This gives heterodox thinkers a bilingual perspective that can leave them more open to new ideas than neoclassical economists."[11] As economists we must admit that the culture of the field of economics has seriously hampered economists' search for new ideas. Ominously, economists' reluctance to venture beyond orthodox paradigms of mainstream economics has given an entire generation of students an inaccurate and incomplete view of human economic activity.

This textbook takes its inspiration from Keynes, who in effect rebelled against the prevailing economic culture when he wrote *The General Theory of Employment, Interest, and Money* as a response to the Great Depression in the 1930s. The quote from his preface to *The General Theory* given at the opening of this chapter is relevant. Keynes's "escape from old ideas" and holistic approach influenced macroeconomic policy in most Western countries for about forty years. During that time there were no major economic crises in any of the developed economies of the world, and both developed and less-developed economies enjoyed the fastest rates of growth ever experienced before or since. Today the culture of mainstream economics has shifted back to the neoclassical paradigm that justifies policies that increase income and wealth inequalities, lower labor income, increase business concentration, and reduce the role of collective government activity in the economy. Just as these policies brought on the Great Depression that Keynes addressed, the last three decades' return to unfettered financial markets and the elimination of restrictions on international investment and financial transactions caused in 2008 the largest decline in economic activity since the Great Depression.

This textbook frees international economics from the confines of the neoclassical paradigm by both revealing the weaknesses of that paradigm on the one hand and, positively, presenting the broader perspectives from heterodox economics. Hopefully, you will be inspired by the freedom of thought that heterodoxy encourages. The holism of this textbook's heterodox approach will give you insights into the fascinating process of international economic integration well beyond what orthodox international economics textbooks can offer.

CHAPTER SUMMARY

1. In the United States today, the *orthodox* paradigm in the social science discipline of economics is the neoclassical paradigm.
2. All other paradigms, such as those advanced by institutionalists, Marxists, Keynesians, behavioral economics, libertarians, Austrians, structuralists, dependency theorists, and other social scientists are assigned to heterodox economics.
3. Heterodox economics embraces alternative paradigms, plus the neoclassical paradigm, because it recognizes the limits of any particular model; it applies different models under different circumstances and compares the results of different models for any given set of circumstances.
4. Heterodox economics accepts that economics is a social science; thus, social phenomena must be studied in accordance with the *scientific method.*
5. The concept of holism underlies all of heterodox economics because, like holism, it embraces models that are *systemic, dynamic,* and *multidisciplinary.*
6. Holism clashes directly with neoclassical economics and its scientific reductionism, its limited focus on only "economic" issues, and its widespread use of the "all other things equal" assumption to justify its static equilibrium models.
7. A reading of the heterodox economics literature reveals at least twenty fundamental ideas that appear to persistently guide the thinking of most heterodox economists, and this chapter details these ideas.
8. Because heterodox analysis uses alternative models and dynamic analytical frameworks, and recognizes the complexity of systems, heterodox economists' policy prescriptions are usually much less specific than the policy prescriptions suggested by orthodox economists.
9. In recognition of uncertainty within a complex system, such as our economic, social, or natural systems, heterodox economists are likely to invoke the *precautionary principle* in complex cases such as financial deregulation, environmental policies to deal with climate change or bioversity, and international economic integration.

10. The neoclassical paradigm has become the dominant culture of mainstream economics in the United States and most other countries, which follow the example of the United States in their universities.
11. In the spirit of Pierre Bourdieu, a sociological examination of the culture of the field of international economics reveals why the intellectual bias of international economics often causes it to fail to provide relevant and convincing analyses of our internationally integrated economy.
12. Habitus and doxa, which constitute culture, change slowly even in the face of substantial changes in economic outcomes, social shifts, or clear trends in the natural environment. Incompatibilities between reality and people's perceptions and beliefs are common in rapidly changing economic, social, and natural environments.
13. Bourdieu argues that culture can be oppressive because it effectively enforces and perpetuates hierarchical social structures. The subculture of an intellectual field like economics can similarly become oppressive by perpetuating a particular paradigm, such as the neoclassical paradigm in international economics.
14. The discussion of the three spheres of human existence and economic modeling in the previous chapter, plus this chapter's discussions of holism and Bourdieu's sociological analysis of culture, complete the justification for our heterodox approach to international economics.

KEY TERMS AND CONCEPTS

Coase theorem
community
contingent commodities
cultural capital
culture
doxa
externalities
fallacy of composition
field
Gaia hypothesis
habitus
heterodox economics
heterodoxy
heuristics
holism
holistic science
homeostasis
hypothesis

inherited cultural capital
institutionalized cultural capital
Medea hypothesis
microfoundations
multi-paradigmatic approach
neoclassical paradigm
normative economics
objectified cultural capital
paradigm
precautionary principle
science
scientific method
scientific observation
scientific reductionism
social scientist
symbolic violence
theory

PROBLEMS AND QUESTIONS

1. The maintenance of constant body temperature by endothermic animals, such as mammals and birds, in response to changes in external temperatures is one form of homeostasis. Exothermic animals like reptiles and some sea creatures survive in changing environments by letting their body temperatures change with the external temperature and then mitigating body temperature changes by adjusting their behavior. One disadvantage of internal regulation is that it takes more energy. Snakes eat once a week or less; mammals and birds spend the greater part of their lives seeking food. Is human society endothermic or exothermic? Write a brief essay to answer this question.

2. Why is holism more scientific than scientific reductionism?
3. Describe scientific reductionism. Have you ever engaged in scientific reductionism? Which of your college courses engage in scientific reductionism? What would such courses look like if they embraced holism?
4. Describe the scientific method. Do economists follow the scientific method? Can you find examples of the scientific method in economics? Can you find violations of the scientific method?
5. The popular definition of the word *theory* does not match the scientific definition of a theory. Explain the difference.
6. Why does step 4 of the scientific method prescribe that a scientist perform many experiments or observe large amounts of real world outcomes under a variety of circumstances in order to avoid conclusions driven by unseen forces not taken into consideration in your hypothesis, observations, and experiments? Explain why a single experiment or observation is not sufficient to "prove" a relationship.
7. Explain the potential implications of failing to observe each step of the scientific method.
8. The nineteenth-century French economist Frédéric Bastiat wrote: "Between a good and a bad economist this constitutes the whole difference—the one takes account of the visible effect; the other takes account both of the effects which are seen, and also those which it is necessary to foresee." Explain what Bastiat meant with reference to the concept of holism described in the chapter.
9. Explain precisely how the "sociology of economics" leads to the conclusion that heterodox economics is less likely to generate biased conclusions than orthodox neoclassical economics. (Hint: review Bourdieu's arguments and concepts, and fit both descriptions of heterodox economics and neoclassical economics into Bourdieu's framework for analyzing culture.)
10. Review the twenty fundamental ideas of heterodox economics. Are there additional ideas that do not fit neatly into the neoclassical paradigm and should, therefore, be added to the field of heterodox economics? Explain.

NOTES

1. Quoted in "Three Mile Nuclear Fears Revealed," BBC News, June 17, 2006.
2. Ibid.
3. Vito Tanzi (2006).
4. We do not yet know the ultimate cost of the 2011 Japanese nuclear tragedy, where the interaction of two complex systems, nature and human technology, combined in unexpected ways. We will discuss how heterodox economics analyzes the interactions between international economic activity and nature in later chapters.
5. This incident is described in John Gribbin (2002).
6. Usually included among the neoclassical thinkers of the late nineteenth century are, in addition to Walras and Marshall, Stanley Jevons, Kurt Wicksell, J.B. Clark, and Stanley Fisher. The Walrasian neoclassical model was extended by Gerard Debreu (1959) in the twentieth century.
7. Gerard Debreu (1959), p. 98.
8. John Maynard Keynes (1936), pp. 161–162.
9. Quoted in Thomas Palley (1998), p. 15.
10. Quoted in Gary Zukav (1979), *The Dancing Wu Li Masters: An Overview of the New Physics*, New York: William Morrow.
11. Steven Mark Cohn (2007), p. 14.

PART TWO

INTERNATIONAL TRADE THEORY

Most people equate globalization with international trade. In fact, the broad process of what we prefer to call international economic integration consists of international investment, international finance, and immigration as well as international trade. And these distinct processes do not occur separately; they interact in complex ways within the broader and continuously evolving economic, social, and natural spheres of human existence. Nevertheless, international trade is different from other types of international economic activity, and its special features and behaviors need to be examined and understood in order to place it within the broader economic, social, and natural systems. That is the purpose of Part Two of the textbook.

Chapter 3 details the orthodox neoclassical model, or, in honor of its originators, the Heckscher-Ohlin (HO) model of international trade. This model is featured in all international economics textbooks, and it provides the guiding framework for most economic analysis of international trade. The chapter presents both the model's useful results and insights as well as its many weaknesses and biases. Chapter 4 examines how mainstream economists have extended and adjusted the orthodox model to explain real world phenomena that are not in conformity with the predictions of the pure model. This chapter concludes by showing why alternative perspectives and models, not just ad hoc extensions to the orthodox model, are necessary to understand the full causes and consequences of international trade.

Chapter 5 presents an alternative model of international trade that drops the orthodox model's convenient, but inaccurate, assumptions of perfect competition and efficient markets. Nearly all manufacturing in the real world is, in fact, carried out by rather small numbers of very large firms, not by large numbers of independent and competitive firms. Even agricultural production is today dominated by a few large transnational firms. Once the assumption of perfect competition is dropped, very different conclusions about international trade are reached. Chapter 5 also describes transnational corporations, which dominate international trade. To understand modern international trade, it is important to recognize that transnational corporations do not operate in accordance with the orthodox models of trade.

Chapters 6 and 7 look at international trade as a dynamic, evolutionary, long-run process of change, rather than a comparatively static shift, as the orthodox model of international trade assumes. The dynamic perspective leads to some very different conclusions about international trade. Chapter 7 specifically brings the issue of inequality into the discussion of international trade, drawing on interdisciplinary evidence from psychology, experimental economics, neuroscience, and sociology. While the orthodox Heckscher-Ohlin model described in Chapter 4 does analyze how the gains from trade are distributed within each country under the "all other things equal" assumption, its static approach does not capture the large long-run distributional consequences of economic change that accompany the continuing and evolving process of international economic integration. More importantly, the HO model does not capture how inequality evolves across countries.

In order to better understand the long-run evolution of how international economic activity affects the income distribution, Chapter 7 also describes the process of agglomeration. Agglomeration is the observed tendency for much of the world's economic activity to concentrate in specific geographic locations. In a highly integrated world economy, agglomeration is likely to favor some nations over others, and international trade and the related forms of international economic integration may end up increasing rather than decreasing income inequality across countries. This is a very different conclusion from the one reached by orthodox neoclassical models, which effectively assume that well-functioning markets arbitrage differences and, therefore, equalize economic outcomes across countries.

CHAPTER 3

Orthodox International Trade Theory: Why Mainstream Economists Like Free Trade

> The proposition that freedom of trade is on the whole economically more beneficial than protection is one of the most fundamental propositions economic theory has to offer for the guidance of economic policy.
>
> —Harry G. Johnson (1960)

The most popular model of international trade, which is taught in nearly all courses of international economics, is the Heckscher-Ohlin (HO) model, named after the two Swedish economists, Eli Heckscher and Bertil Ohlin, who developed it early in the twentieth century. The HO model reflects mainstream neoclassical thinking and methodology. Like all neoclassical models, the HO model of international trade is based on an extensive set of unrealistic assumptions. For example, the HO model assumes that all product and factor markets are perfectly competitive, factor supplies are fixed in quantity, aggregate consumer preferences are the sum of individual preferences, preferences are stable and consistent over time, and market prices accurately reflect all the costs and benefits associated with the production of a good or service.

The HO model's popularity is, in large part, based on its logical derivation of the intuitive principle of **comparative advantage**. The model also concludes that international trade changes a country's production mix, reallocates its resources, changes individuals' incomes, and alters the country's demand. Technically, the HO model does not conclude that free trade maximizes every individual's real income in every economy; it only shows that the total value of output, and thus total income, rises in all countries that engage in free trade. But, under the convenient assumption, implicitly accepted in most orthodox economic analysis, that national welfare can be estimated by adding up individual welfare levels, the HO model shows that all economies increase aggregate national welfare by opening their borders to free trade.

The HO model is clearly not holistic. Its assumption of fixed preferences and supplies of productive factors means it is not dynamic. The assumed absence of externalities that could cause market prices to diverge from the true underlying costs and benefits of production implies the model ignores many influences from the social and natural spheres of human existence. And, the neoclassical approach largely rules out interdisciplinary analysis. Yet, it is this model, more than any other, that has shaped economists' thinking on international trade to the point that Harry Johnson's quote above seems entirely reasonable to most mainstream economists today. In order to understand mainstream economists' arguments for free trade, we must understand the model on which they base those arguments. This chapter presents the basic HO model. Subsequent chapters discuss how heterodox economists and some mainstream economists have moved beyond the confines of the HO model.

MAINSTREAM ECONOMIC ANALYSIS OF INTERNATIONAL TRADE

The Heckscher-Ohlin model's conclusions are the result of carrying out a simple maximization problem that determines the economy's mix of production under the alternative states of restricted trade and free trade, explains the international trade flows that result under free trade, and compares national welfare in each case. In order to carry out its maximization exercise, the model closely follows *neoclassical general equilibrium* analysis and assumes rather simple models to represent the demand and supply sides of the economy. We begin with the supply, or production, side of the economy.

The Production Possibilities Frontier

Suppose the economy of the tiny country of Smalland has the resources and know-how to produce, at most, those combinations of two goods, food and clothing, represented by the **production possibilities frontier (PPF)** in Figure 3.1. For example, combinations such as 200 pounds of food and 350 pieces of clothing or 300 pounds of food and 300 pieces of clothing can realistically be produced. Of course, a point below the PPF, such as the combination of 200 units of clothing and 200 units of food, could also be produced, but such a combination implies the economy is not using all of its resources or its best technology. On the other hand, a combination of food and clothing outside the PPF, such as point A at 350 pounds of food and 350 pieces of clothing, is not feasible given Smalland's resources and know-how. The PPF illustrates the **economic problem** of **scarcity**: When the economy has no unemployed resources and it produces a combination on the PPF curve, an increase in output of one product necessarily requires a decrease in output of the other.

The PPF curve is typically drawn so that it has a bowed-out shape, as in Figure 3.1. Such a PPF curve that is concave to the origin means that the production of food and clothing is characterized by **increasing costs**; the higher the level of production of food, the greater the **opportunity cost** in terms of the value of the clothing, the other product, that can no longer be produced. The PPF can shift. For example, an increase in productive resources from investment in more physical capital or a technological breakthrough would shift the PPF out. A decline in productive capacity because of a destructive war or overexploitation of the ecosystem shifts the PPF inward.

Consumer Demand and Indifference Curves

The PPF, the **supply side** of the economy, gives the combinations of food and clothing that the economy could produce. But which of the feasible combinations of food and clothing will Smalland actually choose to produce? To answer this question, we need the **demand side** of Smalland's economy.

Orthodox neoclassical economic analysis assumes that every person maximizes his or her welfare by allocating personal income among the available alternative products so that each additional, or *marginal,* dollar spent adds the most to personal welfare. A person's demand for products is assumed to be determined by his or her **welfare function**, which is the relationship between personal welfare and all possible combinations and quantities of products available in the economy. This welfare function is usually translated graphically into a set of **indifference curves**, which illustrate how people value one good relative to another. That is, indifference curves are sets of combinations of goods that are valued equally by a consumer, the combinations to which a consumer is "indifferent." Figure 3.2 illustrates a typical set of indifference curves for a simplified world of two goods. The combinations of food and clothing represented by the points k, m, n, and q all leave consumers equally well off, or indifferent, so they lie on the same indifference curve I_1.

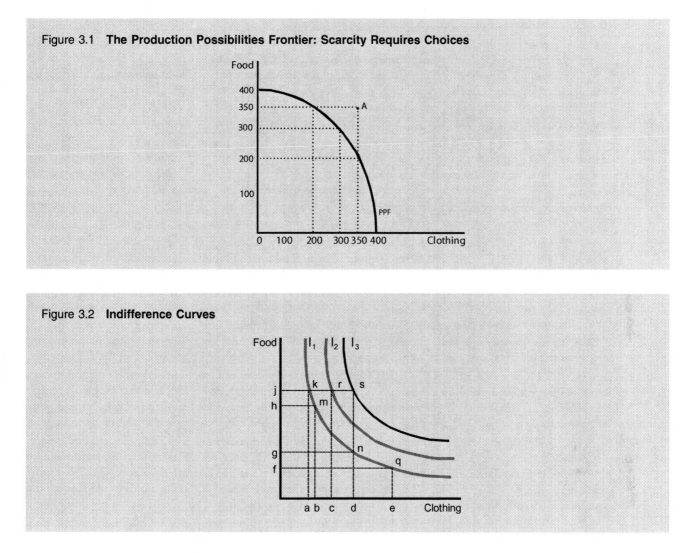

Figure 3.1 **The Production Possibilities Frontier: Scarcity Requires Choices**

Figure 3.2 **Indifference Curves**

The combinations r and s in Figure 3.2 represent higher levels of welfare than the combination k because they combine the identical amount of food at k with higher amounts of clothing. If we assume, as the neoclassical model normally does, that all goods are indeed "goods" that improve human well-being, then the combination r must lie on a higher indifference curve than k, and s must lie on an even higher indifference curve than r. The two points r and n are more difficult to compare because r combines a higher amount of food than at the combination n with a *lower* amount of clothing than at n. Logical reasoning makes it clear that r is preferable to n because (a) consumers are indifferent between n and k, and (b) r is clearly preferable to k. In short, the higher the indifference curve, the higher the level of welfare associated with the combinations of goods on the curve.

The indifference curves in Figure 3.2 are drawn convex to the origin, which means their slope gradually declines as clothing is substituted for food. The curves' convexity reflects the assumption that consumers value one good more highly the less of it they have relative to the other good. For example, if a consumer selects the combination k on the indifference curve I_1, which combines the quantity a of clothing and j of food, a decline in food consumption from, say, j to h requires that he be compensated with an increase in clothing from a to b. At the combination n, however, the consumer requires a larger increase in clothing consumption to fully compensate for a reduction of food consumption. For example, a decline in food consumption from g to f, which is identical to the decline in the quantity of clothing from j to h, requires a larger offsetting increase in clothing from g to e. The convexity of the indifference curves implies that the more consumers have of one good, the less valuable an addition is in terms of the other good. Implicitly, this assumes that consumers prefer some of both to a lot of just one, or as they say, "Variety is the spice of life."

Individual Indifference Curves and Society's Indifference Curve

There are many objections to using indifference curves to model a person's welfare function, not the least of which is that welfare is a notoriously difficult concept to define, much less measure. As we will discuss in later chapters, the field of behavioral economics, which brings in evidence from the fields of psychology, neuroscience, sociology, and experimental economics, concludes that individual welfare functions are often logically inconsistent, easily manipulated, and continually changing in response to a person's social and economic surroundings. For this reason alone, the use of a stable set of indifference curves to judge the welfare effects of some change in consumption is not accurate.

Despite these objections, international economics and the HO model not only assume that individual welfare functions are stable over the period of analysis for which the model is used; they also assume that these individual welfare functions can somehow be combined into a social welfare function that can be represented by a stable set of **aggregate** or **social indifference curves** that represent the preferences of the entire society. Unless we make incredibly unrealistic assumptions about an individual's welfare function, however, there is no logical way to derive a unique set of social indifference curves from all the sets of individual indifference curves. For example, even under the inaccurate assumption that the sets of individual indifference curves are stable and unchanging, it is only possible to combine the individual indifference curves into a set of social indifference curves if we also assume that (1) individual welfare is completely isolated from the perceived welfare of others (that we are not capable of empathy or jealousy, for example); (2) individual welfare is somehow measurable and comparable; and (3) people do not in any way relate their personal welfare to the overall economic and social outcomes of the whole society (people are not nationalistic or group oriented). These assumptions clash with all evidence that shows humans are group animals who, for example, care about close relatives, instinctively root for the home team, and are very conscious of their social status. Yet, the HO model is entirely based on the existence of stable social indifference curves.

Combining the Supply and Demand Sides

The HO model finds that the welfare-maximizing production combination of food and clothing occurs at the point where the PPF and the aggregate indifference curve have exactly the same slope and are just tangent to each other, illustrated by the point A in Figure 3.3. At point A, the slope of the PPF curve shows how much production of one good must be reduced in order to make available the resources needed to produce one more unit of the other good. The slope of the aggregate indifference curve shows how much of one good people are willing to give up in exchange for one more unit of the other good. Since the slopes of the PPF and indifference curve are identical at A, the relative opportunity costs of food and clothing, respectively, are proportional to the relative marginal benefits from consuming food and clothing.

The tangency point A represents society's best possible outcome because it is impossible to increase consumption or production of one good without decreasing consumption or production of the other. At every other point on the PPF it is possible to improve national welfare by reallocating productive resources and/or switching consumption expenditures. For example, at the point B in Figure 3.3, where the slope of the PPF is –½, the economy can produce two more units of clothing

Figure 3.3 **Equilibrium in the Closed Economy**

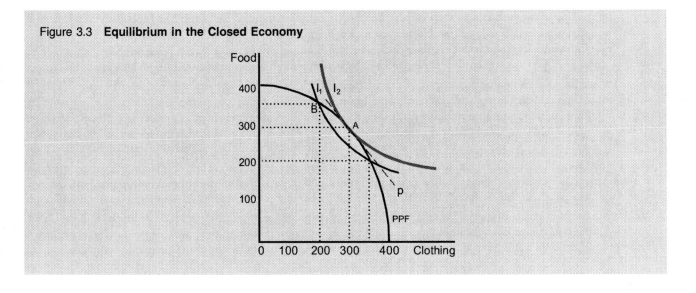

if it reduces food production by one pound. But, the slope of the indifference curve at point B is –2, so consumers are willing to give up two pounds of food in exchange for one unit of clothing. Thus in the aggregate consumers improve their welfare when the economy provides an additional unit of clothing at the opportunity cost of only half a pound of food.

The concave PPF and the convex indifference curves imply that the trade-offs change as production shifts along the PPF toward A. Specifically, the marginal cost of clothing rises, and the marginal value of clothing falls as more clothing is substituted for food. Only when the economy provides consumers with the combination of food and clothing represented by the tangency point A is the trade-off permitted by the PPF exactly equal to the trade-off people would be willing to accept. This trade-off is represented by the price line p, whose slope represents the relative prices of food and clothing.

The Gain from International Trade

In general, the relative prices of goods in the rest of the world are not the same as in the isolated Smalland economy illustrated in Figure 3.3. Relative prices differ because, first of all, the quantities of productive factors and the levels of technology are unlikely to be identical in every country. In general, the PPF of the combined world economy will tend to be shaped differently than Smalland's PPF. Secondly, on the demand side consumer preferences are also unlikely to be the same everywhere. Hence, the rest of the world's indifference curve schedule will be shaped differently from Smalland's preference schedule. According to the HO model, it is this difference between relative prices at home and relative prices abroad that makes international trade welfare improving for Smalland.

To illustrate how differences in relative prices of food and clothing create potential gains from trade, suppose that in Smalland the slope of the price line at the tangency point A in Figure 3.3 is exactly –1. A slope of –1 implies that consumers value a pound of food and a piece of clothing equally and that the economy can increase its output of clothing by one piece if the resources made available by a one-pound reduction in food production are applied to clothing production instead. Suppose also that in the rest of the world the relative prices are reflected in a price line whose slope is –1/3, or –0.33. That is, in the rest of the world, a pound of food costs three times as much as a piece of clothing, perhaps because the rest of the world has much better clothing manufacturing know-how (technology) than does Smalland or because the rest of the world has relatively more of the relevant resources, such as workers and sewing machines, than Smalland does.

Suppose, finally, that Smalland, as its name suggests, is a very small economy and that world prices will not be affected by its participation in the world markets for food and clothing. In effect, Smalland is "a perfect competitor" in the huge world market. This assumption lets us conveniently treat the world price ratio of 0.33 as a constant that Smalland consumers and producers can take advantage of but cannot influence. Thus, a Smalland consumer who values a pound of food the same as a piece of clothing can go overseas and exchange a pound of food for three pieces of clothing.

Figure 3.4 illustrates the gain from international trade for Smalland. If Smalland continues to produce 300 pounds of food and 300 pieces of clothing at point A, then international trade permits Smalland consumers to acquire any combination of food and clothing along the **consumption possibilities line** CPL_1 that passes through A with a slope of –0.33. Given indifference curves such as I_2 and I_3, Smallanders would find it advantageous to exchange food for clothing. But as more and more food is exchanged for clothing, the relative values to Smallanders of food and clothing change. The substitution of clothing for food continues until the point B is reached, where the relative preferences are the same as the international relative prices. The combination of clothing and food at B is clearly a preferred outcome to the consumption point A, and the model is interpreted as showing that international trade raises national welfare.

The amount of international trade that takes Smalland to its higher level of welfare is determined by the **trade triangle** linking the points ABD in Figure 3.4, which shows how much domestically produced food, measured along its vertical height, is exported in exchange for imports of foreign clothing, measured along the horizontal width. The slope of the hypotenuse measures the **terms of trade**—how much needs to be exported in exchange for imports. In Figure 3.4, 67 units of food are exchanged for 200 units of clothing. The gain from international trade is represented by the gain in welfare associated with the jump from I_2 to I_3.

The Gain from International Specialization

There is a way for Smalland to achieve even greater welfare gains from trade than it does in Figure 3.4. The world price ratio defines not only the trade-offs that consumers face, but on the production side it also defines the relative gains to producers from producing food or clothing. International trade gives producers the option to sell overseas as well as at home, so it is no longer optimal for Smalland producers to produce the combination A of food and clothing. At A, the relative marginal opportunity cost of producing an additional unit of food is less than the world price of food, and the opportunity cost of producing an additional unit of clothing is greater than the world price of clothing. Profit-maximizing producers will therefore seek to employ more productive factors to produce food, which is relatively more expensive in the rest of the world, and fewer factors to produce the relatively cheaper clothing. In Figure 3.5, perfectly competitive producers thus collectively end up shifting production to point P, where the relative opportunity costs of producing food and clothing are the same as in the rest of the world. In the open economy, the value of production at point P defines higher real income and a higher consumption possibilities line, CPL_2. Welfare-maximizing consumers will thus consume the combination of food and clothing given by the point C, where marginal gains now equal relative prices. The gain in welfare represented by the shift from consuming a combination of goods lying on I_3 to a combination lying on I_4 is the gain from specialization.

This simple "small country" version of the HO model thus shows that the gains from trade are greater when a country takes advantage of both the *gain from trade* and the *gain from specialization*, as evidenced by the larger trade triangle PCD in Figure 3.5, compared to the trade triangle ABD in Figure 3.4. Note, also, that the HO model shows that when the full gains from specialization are achieved, one industry is smaller than it was before the opening of international trade.

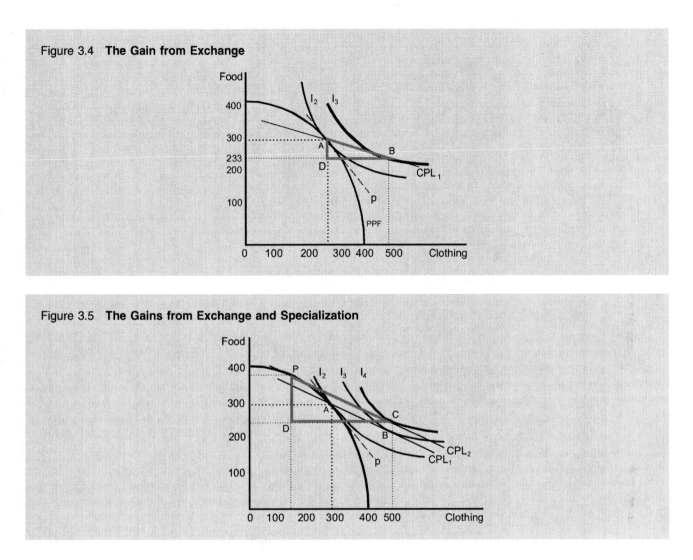

Figure 3.4 **The Gain from Exchange**

Figure 3.5 **The Gains from Exchange and Specialization**

DO ALL NATIONS GAIN FROM TRADE?

The *small country assumption* is not realistic for a model used to analyze international trade among large economies like the United States, Germany, Japan, China, India, or France. When a large country increases its imports and exports, this has a noticeable effect on overall world demand and supply. Therefore, prices of goods and services in other countries cannot be assumed to remain constant when a large economy opens its borders to international trade. To analyze this possibility, this section develops a more general two-country HO model.

Why Production Possibilities Frontiers Differ

In this section's two-country HO model of international trade, we depict the distinct production possibilities frontiers of two countries. In general, the PPFs of the two countries have different shapes. Recall from the previous discussion that the shape of a country's PPF is determined by (1) the country's set of factors of production and resources and (2) the level of technology with which those factors and resources can be transformed into final output. Because Heckscher and Ohlin were interested in examining how international trade was linked to countries' resources, they assumed that technology

Table 3.1

Factor Endowments Relative to the World Mean (= 100) for Selected Countries

	Capital per worker	% of labor poorly educated	% of labor highly educated	Farmland per worker
Argentina	55	130	63	278
Australia	139	55	155	1,240
Japan	99	84	120	1
Mexico	63	159	29	80
Netherlands	130	79	126	6
United Kingdom	74	97	103	12
United States	124	13	205	67

Source: James Harrigan and Egon Zakrajšek (2000), "Factor Supplies and Specialization in the World Economy," working paper, August, Federal Reserve Bank of New York, Table 3.

was identical in both countries. This is a normal modeling strategy: isolate the effects of a specific change in one variable by assuming other variables remain unchanged. Under these assumptions, the HO model describes how different amounts of resources, or factors of production, determine the shapes of countries' PPFs. Then, the model traces how differing PPFs affect international trade.

Differences in the quantities of factors, like labor and capital, are important because different industries use factors in different proportions. The technology for producing computer chips is different from the technology for producing shirts. Different again are the technologies used in the oil industry, retailing, university education, or banking. For any given set of factor prices, each productive activity will select a different combination of productive factors. The shirt industry employs more labor relative to physical capital than the oil industry. Retailing employs less educated labor, or human capital, than universities do. Therefore, depending on the relative amounts of each of the factors available in an economy, the ability to produce different goods will vary, and the economies' PPFs will vary as well.

Table 3.1 presents data on factor endowments. Note that high-income countries such as Australia, the Netherlands, and the United States have relatively higher amounts of physical capital per worker, and they also have the largest percentages of highly educated workers. Argentina and Australia have the greatest amount of farmland per worker, a proxy measure that the economists who compiled the data used to represent a country's total stock of natural resources.

A Two-Country Model of Trade

Suppose that there are two countries in the world, Here and There, each producing two goods, food and clothing. Assume also that Here and There have different productive capacities and, therefore, different production possibilities frontiers. The differences in productive capacity may be due to different factor endowments or different technologies, as discussed above. The result is that the two countries' PPFs have different shapes. In order to isolate the effects of different productive capacities, assume also, for the time being, that consumer tastes are the same in both countries. In other words, assume that the indifference curve schedules are the same but the PPFs differ in the two countries.

Figure 3.6 illustrates the equilibria in Here and There when the two economies do not engage in exchange and are completely self-sufficient. Here's self-sufficiency equilibrium is at the point A; There's is at the point A*. Notice that Here's PPF suggests that it has some advantage in producing food. There has an advantage in producing clothing. Given the identical sets of indifference curves

Figure 3.6 Two-Country Model: Equilibria with No Trade

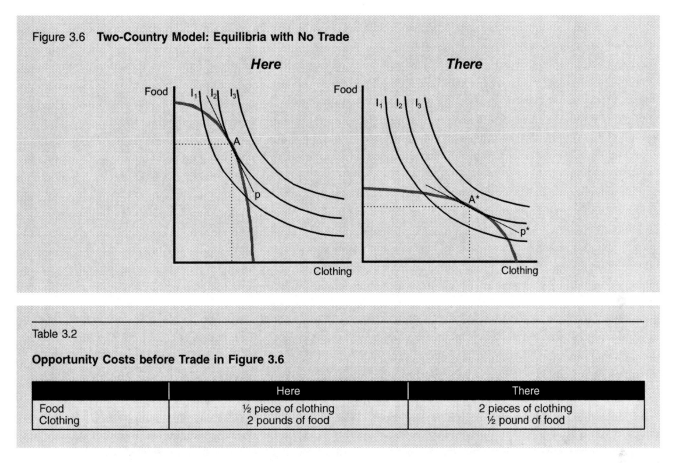

Table 3.2

Opportunity Costs before Trade in Figure 3.6

	Here	There
Food	½ piece of clothing	2 pieces of clothing
Clothing	2 pounds of food	½ pound of food

and sharply different PPFs, the equilibrium price ratios in self-sufficiency are obviously different. In Here, the slope of the price line p is −2. In There, the price line p* has a slope of −0.5. In Here, where the stock of resources or technology favors food production, the price of food is one-half that of clothing. In There the price of food is twice that of clothing. These relative price differences create potential gains from exchange and specialization for both countries.

Here's producers and consumers will view There's price ratios as an opportunity to export their relatively cheap food and import There's relatively cheap clothing. There's producers will find it advantageous to export their relatively cheap clothing to Here's market, where it sells for twice the price of food. And, There's consumers look at the relatively low price of food in Here as an opportunity to increase their purchasing power by substituting relatively cheap foreign food for relatively expensive domestic food. Hence, food will be exported from Here to There, and There will export clothing to Here. The price of food will rise in Here and fall in There, and the price of clothing will fall in Here and rise in There.

In the graphic model, Here's price line p will turn counterclockwise and become less steep. Production will shift along the PPF upward and to the left from A. Consumption will move out beyond the PPF. In There, the initiation of foreign trade will cause the economy to specialize in the production of clothing, so production will shift toward some combination on the PPF downward and to the right from the self-sufficient production combination at A*. Unlike the small country model of the previous section, in which foreign relative prices were assumed to be unaffected by the opening of trade, in this world of two similarly sized countries, the initiation of trade changes relative prices in both. The world price ratio settles somewhere between the relative price ratios that prevailed in each country before trade. With free trade, each country shifts more productive resources toward producing the good that was relatively cheaper in self-sufficiency.

Figure 3.7   **Two-Country Model: Equilibria with Free Trade**

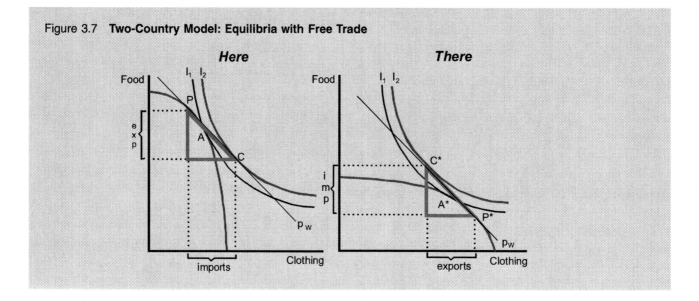

International trade expands until the situation depicted in Figure 3.7 is reached. In a two-country world, and assuming nothing falls overboard during the voyage from one country to another, Here's imports of clothing must equal There's exports of clothing. And, of course, Here's exports of food equal There's imports of food. Since trade equalizes relative prices in the two countries, equilibrium in each country will be determined by a common terms of trade or world price line p_W. The terms of trade are said to improve if the relative price of exports to imports rises and lets a country obtain more imports for a given volume of exports. In a two-country world, what one country exports, the other imports, and the trade triangles have identical shapes for the two countries.

The Principle of Comparative Advantage

The two-country HO model shows that a country's trade reflects the relative opportunity costs of production of food and clothing in each economy as given by the PPFs at the self-sufficiency equilibria A and A^*. Table 3.2 summarizes the **opportunity costs** of each product, which in a two-product world can be stated in terms of how much of the other product must be foregone. Before trade commences, the opportunity cost of a pound of food in Here is one-half of a piece of clothing, which is the flip side of the opportunity cost of a piece of clothing, which is two pounds of food. In There, the opportunity cost of a pound of food is two pieces of clothing and the opportunity cost of a piece of clothing is half a pound of food.

Each country reaches a higher level of welfare by specializing in, and exporting, the good that has the lower opportunity cost. That is the good for which the country is said to have a comparative advantage. In the case of food, Here clearly has the lower opportunity cost. Thus, Here has a comparative advantage in producing food. In this two-country, two-product world, There must then necessarily have the comparative advantage in clothing production. In sum:

- Each country exports the product for which it enjoys a comparative advantage, and this trade is welfare enhancing for both countries.

The two-country HO model thus suggests that international trade is a **positive-sum game** in which both countries come out ahead.

Table 3.3

Opportunity Costs in Ricardo's Original Example

	Portugal	England
Wine	8/9 unit of cloth	6/5 unit of cloth
Cloth	9/8 unit of wine	5/6 unit of wine

David Ricardo's Example of Comparative Advantage

The HO model's conclusion that all countries gain from free trade is not limited to cases where two economies are of roughly similar size or technical efficiency. David Ricardo is the economist who is credited with first presenting the concept of comparative advantage. In his 1817 economics textbook *On the Principles of Political Economy and Taxation*, Ricardo used an example in which two countries, England and Portugal, each produced two products, wine and cloth, but Portugal was more productive in producing both products.

Ricardo assumed that Portugal could produce a bolt of cloth using 90 workers for a day and a barrel of wine using 80 workers. In England, on the other hand, it took 100 workers to produce cloth and 120 workers to produce wine. Ricardo's numbers on how much labor is needed to produce wine and cloth in Portugal and England are given in Table 3.3 in the form of opportunity costs. Even though Portugal had the lower absolute costs in producing both wine and cloth (in terms of labor resources used), it only had the lower opportunity cost, and hence comparative advantage, in wine. England had the lower opportunity cost for producing cloth.

Ricardo's example described a different situation than the one described in 1776 by Adam Smith, who had suggested that countries should specialize in those things that they can do better than others can do them. Smith essentially implied that countries gained from trade by exporting goods for which they enjoyed an **absolute advantage**. Ricardo showed that trade was beneficial whenever countries had different opportunity costs and, therefore, a *comparative advantage,* regardless of whether they had an absolute advantage in producing anything. The principle of comparative advantage means that trade between two countries at different levels of technological development is still quite beneficial to both, provided they concentrate on what they can do *relatively* more efficiently.

Ricardo's assumption that England and Portugal had different productive technologies reminds us that there are many reasons why relative prices differ across countries. Differences in countries' stocks of resources are just one of the potential sources of differing price ratios and relative opportunity costs across countries. Differences in technology also matter, as do differences in macroeconomic conditions that affect overall employment of labor and other resources. On the demand side, differences in consumer preferences also cause relative prices to differ across countries and, thus, to influence international trade.

INTERNATIONAL TRADE AND THE DISTRIBUTION OF INCOME

The simple two-product HO model shows that the opening up of international trade increases the demand for output in the export industry and decreases the demand for the output in the import-competing industry. Since each industry has a distinct set of technologies that call for different combinations of factors of production, the expanding industries are unlikely to demand additional factors of production in the same proportions as the contracting industries used those same factors.

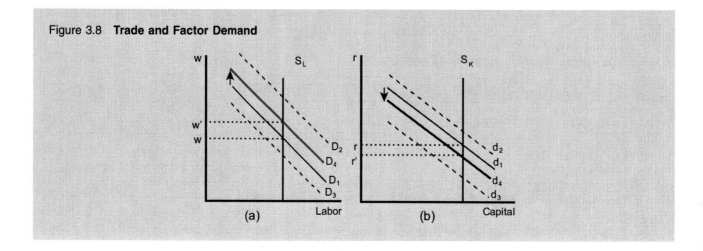

Figure 3.8 Trade and Factor Demand

Hence, the expansion of international trade will cause the overall demand for the economy's factors of production to change, and thus the prices, or returns, of these factors will change.

International Trade and Factor Returns

Suppose that output in each of the economy's two industries, clothing and food, requires just two factors of production, capital and labor. Suppose, also, that all resources are fully employed so that the economy is always on the production possibilities frontier. Figure 3.8 illustrates the markets for the two factors in the form of supply and demand curves. In the country that has the comparative advantage in producing clothing, the clothing industry will expand output because the price of clothing rises relative to the price of food. In order to produce more clothing, additional resources must be attracted to the clothing industry. In the case of full employment, the expanding clothing industry has to attract labor and capital from the food industry. It attracts labor and capital by outbidding the food industry in the labor and capital markets, which it can do because the price of its final output has risen while the price of food has fallen. That is, just when the clothing industry seeks to expand output, the falling-price food industry finds that it can no longer afford to continue employing the number of workers and the amount of capital it did before free trade.

The clothing industry's expansion does not exactly offset the food industry's contraction in each of the two factor markets, however. Unless the clothing and food industries have exactly the same production technologies, the demand for each type of factor changes.

Suppose that the clothing industry uses more labor relative to capital than does the food industry for any given set of factor prices. In this case, the clothing industry is said to be relatively labor intensive, which, in a two-industry world, necessarily means that the food industry is relatively capital intensive. Thus, at pre-trade factor prices, a shrinking food industry releases more capital than the clothing industry wishes to acquire and less labor than the clothing industry seeks to hire. Diagrams (a) and (b) in Figure 3.8 illustrate the changes in demand for labor and capital, respectively, that result from the shift in production from A to P in Figures 3.5 or 3.7. Note that these diagrams simplify by following the standard practice of the HO model and assuming constant supplies of labor and capital, as illustrated by the vertical supply curves S_L and S_K.

Suppose that the demand for labor and capital are initially D_1 and d_1, respectively. The expansion of international trade and the growth of the clothing industry cause demand for both labor and capital to increase, from D_1 to D_2 for labor and from d_1 to d_2 for capital. But, the labor-intensive clothing industry's demand for labor increases considerably more than its demand for capital. The contraction of the capital-intensive food industry, on the other hand, causes its demand for labor and capital to fall, as illustrated by downward shifts in the demand from D_1 to D_3 for labor in (a) and from d_1 to d_3 for capital in (b). The contraction of the capital-intensive food industry causes the demand for capital to decline a lot, but the demand for labor falls relatively little. The demand curves D_4 and d_4 represent the *net* effects of the shifts in demand for the two factors. As a result of free trade and specialization in the production of Y, the economy's net demand for labor rises and net demand for capital falls. Thus, the wage rate rises and the price of capital falls.

The Heckscher-Ohlin Theorem

Under a restrictive set of assumptions, the HO model provides a very specific prediction about international trade. Among the assumptions are, for example, that in a two-country, two-factor world the differences in the shapes of production possibilities frontiers (PPFs) across the two countries are due exclusively to differences in factor endowments. Technology is assumed to be equally available and consumer preferences are identical everywhere. This means each country's comparative advantage is determined exclusively by its stock of factors. In the case where everything is the same except that one country has more labor relative to capital, this country is defined to be relatively *labor abundant*. In a two-country, two-factor world, this means that the second country must then necessarily be relatively *capital abundant*. Finally, the model assumes that there are no transport costs, trade barriers of any kind, or costs associated with shifting resources between one industry and the other.

This specific version of the **Heckscher-Ohlin model** then predicts that:

- In the case of two countries, two products, and two factors, free trade will result in each country exporting the product whose industry *intensively* uses the country's relatively *abundant* factor.

This result is known specifically as the **Heckscher-Ohlin theorem**.

This theorem was derived under assumptions that effectively eliminate all other influences on trade. Therefore, the Heckscher-Ohlin theorem is logically correct only in the case where factor endowments are absolutely the only determinant of trade that differs across countries. Recall that the "all other things equal," assumption is an analytical procedure that mainstream economists use in neoclassical analysis to logically isolate specific causes of economic outcomes under hypothetical circumstances. But we must recognize that it is nothing more than that, an analytical procedure. The Heckscher-Ohlin theorem is, therefore, not a general rule that can be expected to be satisfied in a different set of circumstances in the real world. It is not necessarily true, as later chapters will show, that a poor country with a lot of people relative to its stocks of capital and natural resources must operate labor-intensive assembly plants (often referred to as sweatshops) in order to expand international trade and maximize its national welfare. Yet, the acceptance of the HO model as a general model by most international economists often forces them to argue that low-wage factories are a positive development in poor countries.

The Stolper-Samuelson Theorem

The reasoning laid out in the section "International Trade and Factor Returns," and the specific version of the model assumed to generate the Heckscher-Ohlin theorem in the previous subsection have been combined to generate one of the best-known theorems in international economics, commonly known as the **Stolper-Samuelson theorem**. Wolfgang Stolper and Paul A. Samuelson (1941) logically derived the following theorem:

- When an economy shifts from self-sufficiency to free trade, the real income accruing to the factor used relatively intensively in the expanding export industry rises and the real income accruing to the factor used relatively intensively in the shrinking import-competing industry falls.

The only difference between the Stolper-Samuelson theorem and the intuitive analysis of shifting demand curves in Figure 3.8 is that the theorem states not only that the price of the abundant factor rises with free trade, but that the total real income earned by the abundant factor rises. This is an important result because Figure 3.8 could be interpreted as suggesting the change in the real income of each factor is indeterminate; it might seem that it is possible for the owner of the falling-price factor to increase her real income if trade also causes the prices of imports to fall more than the factor returns fall. Or, the owner of the factor rising in price could experience a fall in income if the price of imports rises a lot. Under the assumptions that led to the Stolper-Samuelson theorem, that will not happen.

Under the HO model's assumptions, Stolper and Samuelson explain that the price of the relatively scarce factor falls by more than the import price falls, and the price of the abundant factor rises by more than import prices rise. In our example of the clothing and food industries, the release of capital by the capital-intensive food industry increases the amount of capital that each unit of labor has to work with in the labor-intensive industry, thus increasing labor's marginal product and, therefore, its real income.

The Stolper-Samuelson theorem suggests that capital-abundant countries will see their returns to capital rising and their labor force's real wages falling all other things equal. Labor-abundant countries, on the other hand, will find that free trade causes real wages to rise and the return to capital to fall. This theorem has important implications for a capital-abundant country like the United States. Economists often quote the Stolper-Samuelson theorem to "explain" why organized labor in the United States lobbies against free trade agreements. The theorem is also used to criticize protectionist trade policies in poor countries, which are assumed to be labor abundant. Economists have often been heard questioning why a poor country with many poorly paid workers would want to restrict trade and, therefore, miss out on raising its workers' incomes as the Stolper-Samuelson theorem predicts.

The Factor Price Equalization Theorem

If we combine the Heckscher-Ohlin theorem and the Stolper-Samuelson theorem in a two-country, two-good, and two-factor model under the assumptions of identical preferences and technologies, free trade, no transport costs, and perfect competition, the HO model of international trade leads to another prediction:

- Under completely free trade, not only will the price of each of the final products be equalized across countries, but the price of each factor of production will also be the same in every country.

As with the other theorems derived from the HO model, the assumptions of completely free trade, zero transport costs, and perfect competition are critical to this result. In this case, free trade effectively unifies separate national markets into fully integrated single-product markets. In terms of the model presented above, free trade will make the price of clothing the same in both Here and There. Similarly, the price of food will end up the same in each country. Then, we also assume that markets are perfectly competitive, so that the price of final goods is exactly equal to the costs of the resources used to produce them. We further assume that technology and production methods are the same in both countries, so that the production functions of the clothing industries in Here and There are the same, as are the production functions of the food industries in both Here and There. In this case, identical product prices translate into identical factor prices. Therefore, with completely free trade, perfect competition, no transport costs, and the other assumptions of the HO model, workers earn the same wage regardless of which country they work in. Similarly, the return to capital is the same everywhere. This result is formally known as the **factor price equalization theorem**.

The factor price equalization theorem seems to verify rich-country workers' worst fear, which is that free trade will drive wages down to the levels of sweatshops in Bangladesh and India. That interpretation is not quite correct, of course. The theorem also suggests that free trade will raise the wages of poor Indian workers closer to current American workers' wages. The model suggests that all workers' wages will end up somewhere between the world's highest and the world's lowest wages. Even this prospect is not comforting for workers in high-wage countries.

Interestingly, those who use the HO model to justify free trade often reject the factor price equalization theorem as unrealistic, especially when they face criticism of free trade by worker groups in high-income countries. Of course, it is not consistent to accept one theorem but not another derived from the same model and assumptions.

Estimating the Precise Distributional Effects of Trade

There have been many studies to estimate the effects of international trade on the distribution of income. Casual observers have noted that in a number of countries, such as the United States, Great Britain, and China, the growth of international trade over the past several decades has coincided with a sharply rising income inequality and stagnant real wages.[1] More detailed studies have shown, however, that international trade is just one of several reasons why income inequality has increased in many high-income countries. At the same time, some high-income countries have not experienced a large rise in income inequality despite growing international trade.

One reason trade may not alter relative incomes very much is that people may own more than one type of factor of production. For example, increased levels of education and increasingly sophisticated jobs give people **human capital**, which is the acquired and embodied productive resource that enhances a worker's income. Work experience increases people's human capital, as evidenced by the fact that experienced workers are usually paid more than new entrants to the labor force. The wage a person earns is the return to basic labor plus human capital. In a modern economy, where people spend years in school, learn a lot on the job, and accumulate assets that entitle them to the returns to physical capital and new innovations, the return to any one type of factor becomes less important for the welfare of an individual.

A simple exercise makes it clear that in most high-income countries today human capital is more important than basic labor as a source of income. The average number of years of education accumulated by people living in the developed economies of North America, Europe, and the Asia-Pacific region is about twelve. According to available research, such as that of George Psacharopoulos (1994) and Psacharopoulos and Harry Patrinos (2004), in the developed economies education augments basic labor by 7.7 to 12 percent for each year of schooling. Setting the income for basic labor equal to 100, then in developed economies the return to the combination of labor *and* human capital will be at least $100(1.077)^{12} = 244$, which shows that the return to the human capital component of total compensation exceeds the return to basic labor. If returns are 12 percent per year, then the total returns to labor and human capital will be $100(1.12)^{12} = 390$, and the return to human capital is nearly three times as large as the return to basic labor. It should be clear, therefore, that education and other forms of human capital provide people with income from a source that, in general, is affected differently by international trade than basic labor. If a country's comparative advantage is in industries that use human capital intensively, such as biotechnology, higher education, electronics, or financial services, and its workers have high levels of human capital, then international trade will not reduce wages.

It is interesting to note that high-income countries where income inequality has not increased as a result of expanded international trade, such as the Scandinavian countries, provide the most equitable access to educational opportunities and offer the greatest social mobility. By providing people with a variety of productive factors, the Stolper-Samuelson and factor price equalization theorems are less onerous for individuals. In sum, these theorems must be applied carefully when people are diversified.

EVALUATING THE HECKSCHER-OHLIN MODEL

The HO model lies firmly behind mainstream economists' pro-trade stance. The justification for economists' advice on trade policy thus depends, in large part, on the validity of the HO model. In this section, we first review the main conclusions reached by the model. Then we follow with a review of the restrictive assumptions that underlie the model. Finally, we critique the model's conclusions.

Evaluating the HO Model and the Gains from Trade

The simple version of the Heckscher-Ohlin model presented above generates several important conclusions about the effects of international trade:

- International trade increases the total value of goods and services consumed.
- To capture the gains from trade and specialization, resources must be shifted from import-competing industries to export industries.
- Consumption patterns change because exported products become more expensive and import-competing goods become less expensive.
- Estimates of the welfare gained from the shift to international trade illustrated by the movement to a higher indifference curve are very small.

To reach these conclusions, the HO model makes some very strong assumptions, where by "strong" we mean very specific and restricted. That is, the model does not apply to conditions that are generally satisfied in real world situations.

It is therefore important to examine those assumptions:

(a) Perfect competition makes product prices exactly equal to the sum of costs of the factors employed in their production.
(b) There are no externalities that cause product prices to diverge from the true underlying opportunity costs of production.
(c) Consumer welfare functions and preferences are stable, and indifference curves do not shift when trade causes production and consumption to shift.
(d) Overall human welfare in an economy is a stable aggregation of the individual welfare functions of the people living in the economy.
(e) Society's resources are fully employed and society's technology is fully applied so that the economy is always on the edge of the production possibilities frontier.
(f) There are no costs associated with shifting resources from one industry to another as an economy adjusts to free trade.

(g) There are no transportation, distribution, or other transactions costs that drive a wedge between the price paid by importers and the price received by exporters.

(h) Production technologies are immediately available and fully applied in all countries.

(i) Total supplies of productive inputs like labor and capital are constant even as factor prices change.

(j) International trade is always balanced so that the value of exports is always equal to the value of imports.

These assumptions are necessary to reach the conclusions derived from the HO model presented in this section. Economists have examined many cases where one or more of the above assumptions do not hold, but most of these examinations were theoretical in nature. For example, international economists have worked out the Heckscher-Ohlin theorem for cases of multiple goods and factors (comparative advantage becomes somewhat indeterminate for most products and countries), the Stolper-Samuelson theorem for multiple goods and countries (a similar indeterminacy sets in), and the effect of transportation costs on trade (trade will diminish, factor prices will not equalize, and human welfare is reduced).

Some Especially Dangerous Assumptions of the HO Model

One particularly objectionable assumption of the neoclassical HO model is that the indifference curves represent the aggregate preferences of the group of all individual consumers. Even if it is reasonable to assume that each individual consumer has well-defined preferences that could be represented by indifference curves, and it is not, it is quite a stretch to assume that national preferences and welfare levels can be represented by a given set of indifference curves. As explained in the previous chapter, a huge body of evidence from psychology, neuroscience, experimental economics, and behavioral economics suggests that preferences are variable and often rather unstable and inconsistent under the rules of logic. In case you doubt this, note that great efforts go into advertising and public relations in order to change our preferences and our conceptions of well-being; this money would not be spent if we had well-defined and fixed preferences. Also, individual preferences and welfare depend on the welfare of others because humans are group animals who are both envious of and empathetic toward others. Welfare functions are not truly individual, or separable in neoclassical terminology, and thus cannot be added up into some measure of aggregate welfare.

The neoclassical HO model assumes a stable aggregate preference function because it is convenient. This is an especially inappropriate assumption for a model of international trade, which describes how an economy shifts resources from one industry to another and from one set of tasks to another. The increase in specialization that accompanies the expansion of international trade thus involves shifts in income from some industries and people to other industries and people. If individuals all have different preferences, then such shifts in income change the *aggregate indifference curves* representing the whole social group. And if trade is correlated with economic growth, which further redistributes income, this model's predictions of the gains from trade become even more questionable. But because economists lack an easy way to represent aggregate preferences in the face of structural economic changes, they routinely ignore these potential complications, wave their hands, and just assume that aggregate welfare can be represented by a fixed set of indifference curves while the production and consumption points change.

Another serious shortcoming of the HO model is that it is *static;* that is, it describes how, *all other things equal,* a nation is always better off trading with others as opposed to remaining self-sufficient. Economic and social development are closely intertwined dynamic processes, however, and all other things *do not* remain equal. Many things change when countries expand trade and economies develop. Admittedly, it becomes very difficult to analyze the causes and consequences of international trade when everything in the human economic and social spheres is changing. But the HO model's restricted static framework of analysis most surely cannot accurately capture the full causes and consequences of international trade in an economy, much less the broader human society.

From a holistic perspective, a potentially much more damaging weakness of the HO model is that it does not very directly address the concerns about international trade that people often voice, such as the loss of particular jobs, the struggles of industries facing import competition, the loss of government sovereignty as transnational firms spread their distribution systems across political jurisdictions, the macroeconomic effects of the investment flows that accompany trade flows, the financial effects of the accumulation of national debt when trade does not balance, and the dependence of firms on foreign markets, foreign inputs, and foreign natural resources. The HO model is also completely silent on an issue that excites people's emotions everywhere: the growth of international trade seems to be accompanied by the spread of foreign cultures. When a country imports Coca-Cola, it not only imports a sweet drink; it imports an image, an attitude, and a behavior that reflect American culture. This phenomenon was famously projected by Coca-Cola's "one world" global advertising campaign, which pictured young people from many different countries sharing their enjoyment of drinking the product. And when a country imports U.S. films and television programs, it puts U.S. culture on prominent display before its citizens. The spread of transnational firms, a process that, as Chapter 5 will detail, is intimately related to the growth of international trade, has introduced new consumption patterns, new labor practices, and new management practices that all combine to alter national cultures. In sum, the HO model paints a very restricted picture of international trade.

How Important Is the Welfare Gain from Trade?

The limited scope of the HO model also becomes more explicit when economists use it to estimate the gains from international trade. There have been numerous studies in which economists use the HO model's general framework, assuming specific functional forms for the welfare functions that underlie preferences and the production functions that underlie the economy's supply side, in order to estimate how the predicted price changes from shifting to free trade affect overall national welfare. The conclusion of virtually all of these studies is that the welfare gains from abolishing restrictions on international trade are very small.

One of the earliest studies, by Giorgio Basevi (1966), estimated that trade restrictions cost the United States one-tenth of one percent of the value of its GDP. This is not a very large loss. Robert Feenstra (1992) surveyed a set of pre-1990 studies on the costs of protection to the U.S. economy and found that estimates of the total loss to the United States from its protectionist tariffs and quotas across all industries was $30 billion at 1986 prices, or about three-quarters of one percent of U.S. GDP. U.S. protectionism also caused losses in other countries, of course, and Feenstra concluded that these foreign losses were about equal to the United States's losses, which implied that the total cost of U.S. trade restrictions to the world was about $60 billion. By itself, this is by no means a small number, but it is a very small percentage of total world income. More recent studies based on the conceptual framework of the HO model presented above provided estimates of the gains from international trade that ranged from 0.5 to 1 percent of a country's GDP.

Such small percentages add up to hundreds of billions of dollars per year throughout the world, but relative to GDP such results do not translate into an overwhelming case for free trade. After all, economic growth routinely adds more than 1 percent to income in most economies every year. It is difficult to reconcile these small estimated gains from trade with mainstream economists' enthusiasm for free trade. Perhaps the model, and thus estimates based on the model, misses much of the action surrounding international trade. Or is international trade really not so beneficial for human well-being?

A common method for calculating the gains from trade is to estimate the gains and losses from expanding imports or exports in a sample of individual markets. The next section explains this method in detail, including how supply and demand models for individual markets are theoretically related to the Heckscher-Ohlin model.

SUPPLY AND DEMAND ANALYSIS

International economists have used simple supply and demand models of markets, built on the same assumptions that lie behind the HO model, to detail various distortions and complications that the HO model ignores. Supply and demand diagrams are partial equilibrium models that determine the equilibrium in one market while all variables outside that particular market are assumed to remain unchanged. The "all other things equal" assumption is often made in microeconomics when analyzing the effects of some specific change in a particular market. Partial equilibrium models are thus even more restrictive than the HO model. Nevertheless, these models are often used because it is easier to put specific parameters on the functions. And they form the basis for estimating the total gains from international trade.

Producer and Consumer Surplus

Figure 3.9 illustrates the market for shirts. The supply and demand curves S and D intersect at the price of $12 and the quantity of 50. A shift in demand or supply causes the equilibrium price to change: for example, if demand falls to D′, then, all other things equal, the price of shirts falls to $10, and the quantity exchanged falls to 40. In addition, under neoclassical assumptions such as competitive markets, the absence of externalities, and stable individual preferences, microeconomic analysis has used supply and demand curves to quantify producers' and consumers' gains from exchange and to calculate how changes in prices alter those gains from exchange.

According to standard microeconomics, the supply curve indicates how many units suppliers are willing to supply at every market price. Suppliers supply additional units of a product so long as the marginal revenue received is greater than the marginal costs incurred in supplying the additional units. In market equilibrium, marginal revenue equals the marginal costs of production. The supply curve is also known as the marginal cost (MC) curve.[2] The sum of the marginal costs of each additional good is the total variable cost of the entire quantity of products supplied. The area below the MC curve represents total variable costs. Yet, because the producer earns the same price for all goods supplied to the market, total revenue exceeds total costs if the supply curve is upward sloping as in Figure 3.9.

For example, Figure 3.10 again presents the market for shirts in which the equilibrium price is $12 at a quantity supplied of 50 units. Total revenue accruing to the producer is, therefore, the dark-bordered box whose size is 50 x $12 = $600. Total variable costs are less than $600 because the first shirt's marginal cost is only about $2, the second a little more than $2, and so forth. The shaded area in Figure 3.10 is the difference between total revenue and total variable costs, and it is commonly called the **producer surplus**.

Similarly, the demand curve reflects the values that consumers attach to each additional shirt. The marginal value to some consumers is very high for the first shirt. Other consumers value their first shirt less, and those consumers who value their first shirt highly probably value a second shirt somewhat less. Hence, the demand curve is downward sloping. The area underneath the demand curve, bordered by the thick black lines in Figure 3.11, represents the sum of the benefits to consumers of

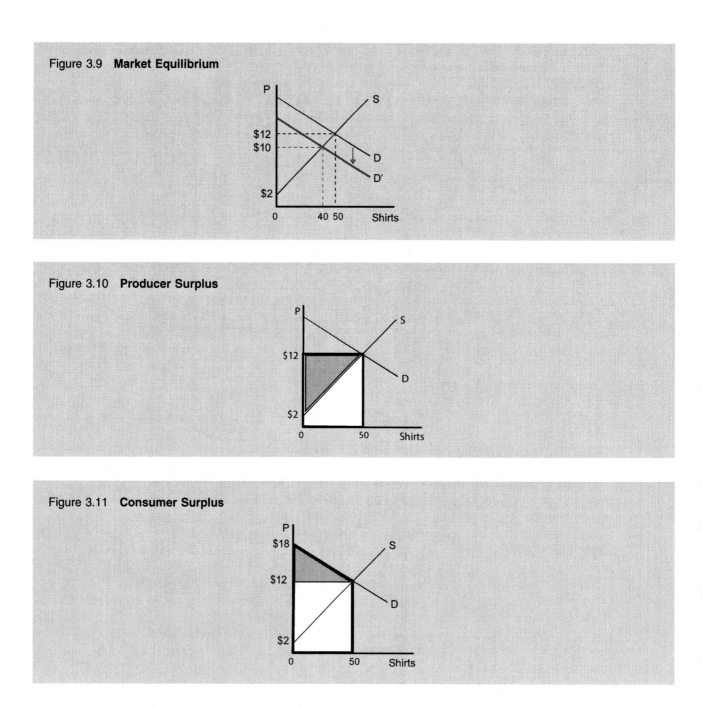

Figure 3.9 **Market Equilibrium**

Figure 3.10 **Producer Surplus**

Figure 3.11 **Consumer Surplus**

each additional shirt, or the total gain from acquiring shirts. Therefore, the net benefits to consumers from being able to buy fifty shirts at the market price of $12 is the difference between the total gains and the total amount paid, which is equal to the shaded area underneath the demand curve in Figure 3.11 and above the market-clearing price of $12. This is called **consumer surplus**. Producer surplus and consumer surplus represent the net gains to producers and consumers, respectively, from participating in the market for shirts.

The concepts of producer surplus and consumer surplus let us put actual dollar figures on the gains to consumers and producers. For example, consumer surplus is the area of the triangle with a height of $6 (the difference between $18 and $12) and a base of 50 units, or $6(50)/2, which equals

$150. Producer surplus is the area of a triangle with a height of $10 (the difference between $12 and $2) and a base of 50 units, or $10(50)/2, which equals $250. Thus, the existence of a market for T-shirts provides society with net welfare gains of $400.

From the HO Model to the Partial Equilibrium Model

Partial equilibrium models that look at single markets are convenient for illustrating the details of how economies are affected by international trade. However, individual markets are related to all other markets in the economy, and we should not forget that partial equilibrium models present a close-up picture of just one detail of the overall economy. A supply and demand model for a single market can be derived from the HO model that is used to represent the whole economy.

Suppose that there are two economies in the world, Home and Away. Suppose, also, that Home and Away both produce two products, guns and butter. The economies of Home and Away are represented by the production possibilities frontiers (PPFs) and indifference curves in Figure 3.12. The PPFs and preferences in the two countries are such that in the absence of international trade, the relative price of guns is half the price of a ton of butter in Home and twice the price of a ton of butter in Away. With free trade, the relative prices, represented by the price line p_w, are equal to 1. The actual quantities produced and consumed at the self-sufficiency relative prices and the free trade relative prices provide points on the supply and demand curves for guns and butter.

Let's focus on the market for guns in each country. In a self-sufficient Home, the tangency between the indifference curve and the PPF is at point A, which is where the production of guns is equal to the consumption of guns, and guns cost half as much as a ton of butter. With free trade, however, the relative price of guns rises to where it is equal to the price of a ton of butter. At the opportunity cost (price) of 1, supply exceeds demand by 30 guns. Similarly, at the opportunity cost (price) of 1, the demand for guns in Away exceeds supply by 30 guns, and the supply and demand curves in Away intersect at opportunity cost 2. This latter case is illustrated in the right-most supply and demand diagram in Figure 3.13.

The partial equilibrium model of trade assumes that the differences between supply and demand define either exports or imports when the international price deviates from the equilibrium domestic price. When we know the supply and demand curves for the gun markets in the two countries, it becomes possible to derive the supply and demand curves for guns in the international market. Specifically, the international supply of guns is the difference between domestic supply and demand. Therefore, when the opportunity cost (price) of guns in the international market exceeds the equilibrium domestic opportunity cost of 0.5, Home suppliers increase the quantity of guns supplied. Note that the actual amount of guns supplied to the international market increases more rapidly than Home suppliers increase their quantity supplied because, as the opportunity cost (price) rises above 0.5, Home consumers demand fewer guns, which leaves more guns available for export. In sum, at every price, the international supply curve of guns in the center diagram is exactly equal to the horizontal difference between the low-cost country's upward-sloping supply curve and its downward-sloping demand curve.

The international demand curve for guns in the international market is the difference between the demand and supply of Away (the high-cost producer). Below the opportunity cost of 2, Away consumers demand more guns than Away's guns suppliers can profitably supply, and this difference between demand and supply spills over into the international market as international demand. In Figure 3.13, equilibrium in the international market occurs when the relative price of guns is equal to 1. At that opportunity cost (relative price), the excess supply of guns by Home is exactly equal to Away's excess demand for guns.

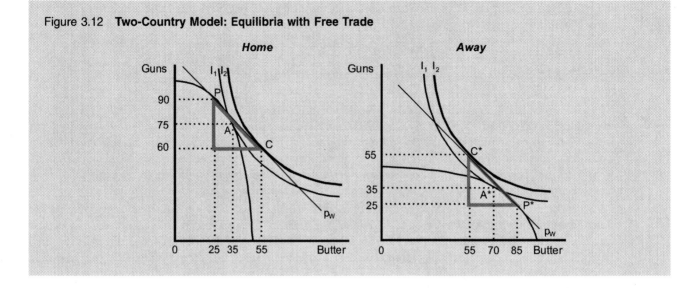

Figure 3.12   Two-Country Model: Equilibria with Free Trade

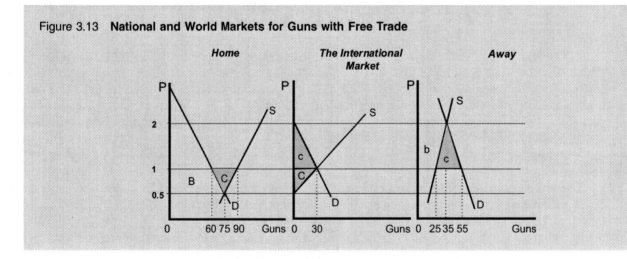

Figure 3.13   National and World Markets for Guns with Free Trade

From the Supply and Demand Diagram to the Gains from Trade

The welfare gain from international trade can be estimated using the concepts of consumer and producer surplus. When shifting from self-sufficiency to free trade in guns, Home and Away experience changes in the price of guns. When the price changes, so do consumer and producer surplus in each country's market for guns. Because the price of guns rises in their economy, Home consumers lose part of their surplus. But, because the price of guns falls in Away, consumers there gain surplus. Producers in each country experience opposite fates. The net welfare effects in each country are positive, however. Note that Home's consumers lose the area B, but its producers gain areas B + C. In Away, consumers expand their consumer surplus areas by b + c, but producers lose surplus equal to the area b. The net gains are, therefore, the areas C and c in Home and Away, respectively.

In Figure 3.13, the exact gains and losses in Home and Away from adopting free trade in guns can be found by calculating the areas of the triangles:

	Home		Away	
Change in Consumer Surplus:	–B	= –$33.75	(b + c)	= $45.00
Change in Producer Surplus:	(B + C)	= $41.25	–b	= –$30.00
Net Change in Welfare:	+C	= $7.50	+c	= $15.00

In each country, there are gains as well as losses, but the gains are greater than the losses. Shifting to free trade brings net welfare gains to both countries.

We can now answer the question of how economists estimate the gains from international trade. As in the above example, economists use information on what the demand and supply curves look like in a number of product markets, and then they estimate how much the expansion of international trade changes the prices in these markets. After calculating the changes in consumer and producer surplus caused by the price changes, they use the total changes in the surpluses from the sample of markets to generate a total estimate for the whole economy. For example, if the surpluses estimated cover about ten percent of all product markets in the economy, they multiply the estimated surpluses by a factor of ten. Note that estimates such as these are closely related to the HO model's perspective of international trade because the supply and demand curves in individual markets are assumed to be derived, theoretically, from a general equilibrium model that represents the entire economy.

Comparing the Partial and General Equilibrium Models

The partial equilibrium model is compatible with the HO model in that it shows that trade benefits both countries. However, it only shows the gains from trading one product, not both products as in the HO model. Strictly speaking, the partial equilibrium model shows that trade in guns raises total welfare in both countries, all other things equal.

The *partial equilibrium model* pits consumers against producers in individual product markets. The Heckscher-Ohlin *general equilibrium model* pits the owners of the different productive factors against each other in a global market. Recall the Stolper-Samuelson theorem derived from the HO model, which is stated entirely in terms of incomes accruing to specific factors of production. Arguably, the general equilibrium model gives a better picture of how people are affected by international trade because it takes into consideration all the changes throughout the economy rather than just the isolated effect in one market of the economy. But, many people and firms have difficulty tracing all the direct and indirect effects that an increase in international trade has on their lives or their bottom lines. Hence, the immediate effect of trade as seen in one market, and explained by the partial equilibrium model, may better reflect how people think international trade affects them and why they pressure their governments for protection.

There have been many studies on whether these models accurately reflect how people view international trade, and whether observed trade flows are accurately explained by the HO model and the partial equilibrium model. The evidence is somewhat inconclusive, although the models do capture some of the relationships. For example, two economists who are not noted as strong advocates of unfettered free trade, Anna Maria Mayda and Dani Rodrik (2005), analyzed the links between attitudes about international trade and people's economic and social assets. Interestingly, they found that, all other things equal, U.S. workers with a high level of human capital tend to be pro-trade. This is compatible with what the Stolper-Samuelson theorem of the HO model suggests. And as the partial equilibrium model suggests, Mayda and Rodrik found that people's views on trade also depend on the exposure to trade of the industry in which they are employed. They found that people who work in the non-traded goods and services sectors of the economy tend to be most pro-trade, and individuals in industries with the greatest comparative *dis*advantage tend to be most anti-trade.

It may be that neither model provides an accurate picture of the gains and losses from trade, however. Obviously, the presence of externalities makes prices inaccurate. For example, if the sale of guns increases violence, which obviously lowers human welfare, then consumer surplus based only on product prices overestimates the gain from trade in the partial equilibrium model above. On the other hand, if international trade in food reduces the need for individual countries to stock food to deal with emergencies, then the gains from trade based purely on product prices may fail to capture the positive externality of reduced warehousing and spoilage costs. This is the risk reduction mentioned by Seabright (2010) and discussed in Chapter 1.

Both models also assume perfect competition, an assumption that is especially dangerous for the partial equilibrium model in which a supply curve cannot even be defined, much less estimated, when markets are not competitive. Estimates of consumer and producer surplus, which have been used to supplement the more elaborate estimates of the gains from trade using the HO model, are thus suspect as well. At best, such estimates are rough measures of the short-term gains from trade.

CONCLUSIONS

The models examined in this chapter suggest that international trade influences human welfare in a number of ways. The small country general equilibrium model of international trade shows that, under a long list of assumptions about human preferences, production functions, competitive markets, and the like, international trade changes production and consumption patterns in both the domestic and the foreign economies, it permits an economy to exchange goods and services that its citizens value relatively less for more highly valued goods and services produced by people in other countries, and it permits producers to specialize and thus use society's scarce resources more efficiently by producing the products for which the economy has a comparative opportunity cost advantage. The small country HO model also shows that when an economy opens its borders to international trade, all other things equal, one industry expands and the other contracts and consumers reallocate their income. This suggests that people in the economy do not share the gains and losses from increased trade equally. The model concludes that whenever the relative prices of goods are not the same at home and abroad, countries can enhance national welfare by engaging in international trade.

The two-country general equilibrium model shows that, under an even longer list of assumptions about the economies in the two countries, international trade changes production and consumption patterns in both the domestic and the foreign economies. The two-country general equilibrium model also clearly illustrates the principle of comparative advantage, which says that countries will export the goods that have the relatively low opportunity costs at home and import those that have relatively high opportunity costs. The traditional HO model assumes that it is differences in factor endowments that drive international trade because, under the assumption of perfect competition and product prices that perfectly reflect underlying factor prices, different factor supplies cause final product prices to differ and accurately reflect opportunity costs. It is differences in relative prices that generate international trade's positive welfare effects.

The partial equilibrium, or supply and demand, model of international trade focuses on one market of the economy and effectively ignores what happens elsewhere in the economy, not to mention the social and natural spheres. Such partial equilibrium models have proved useful for studying certain details about international trade, and we will use them in later chapters, but the underlying assumptions are often just as unrealistic as the assumptions underlying the HO model.

In sum, mainstream international economics derives its near unanimous conclusion that free trade maximizes human welfare from the HO model and the partial equilibrium (supply and demand) model. Mainstream international economists usually ignore that both of the models are built on a large set of assumptions that do not reflect the real circumstances under which international trade is carried out. For example, among many other assumptions, the Heckscher-Ohlin model of trade assumes that social welfare is the sum of individual welfare levels, that all the products that contribute to human welfare are transacted in markets at prices that accurately reflect all opportunity costs, and all transactions are voluntary. Holistically, international trade causes structural changes in the economy that affect individuals' employment and income in potentially adverse ways. The structural changes that international trade introduces into the economy have many broader social implications. International trade also has adverse environmental effects.

The next chapter will discuss these broader perspectives of international trade. First, the chapter will examine how the models' predictions change if some of the strongest assumptions are relaxed. Then, the analysis is extended to include issues that the HO model ignores entirely.

CHAPTER SUMMARY

1. This chapter began with a simple "small country" version of the Heckscher-Ohlin (HO) general equilibrium model of international trade that, under a large set of strong assumptions about consumer and producer behavior, shows how international trade increases welfare.

2. The small country HO model also shows how trade permits an economy to exchange less-valued goods and services for more highly valued goods and services, and how trade leads producers to specialize by producing the products for which their economy enjoys a comparative advantage.

3. The small country general equilibrium model shows that when an economy opens its borders to international trade, all other things equal, one industry expands and the other contracts and consumers reallocate their income.

4. In general, whenever the relative prices of goods are not the same at home and abroad, countries can enhance national welfare by engaging in international trade.

5. The gains from exchange are the result of domestic consumers substituting the relatively cheaper foreign products for the relatively more expensive domestic products.

6. The gains from specialization are the gains from shifting domestic resources away from producing products that are relatively cheaper overseas to those products that are relatively more expensive in the rest of the world.

7. An economy can enjoy the gains from exchange without specializing, but it cannot enjoy the gains from specialization without trading with foreigners.

8. The two-country general equilibrium, or HO, model illustrates that all nations gain from international trade.

9. The two-country general equilibrium model also shows that international trade changes production and consumption patterns in both the domestic and the foreign economies.

10. The two-country general equilibrium model illustrates the principle of comparative advantage, which says that countries will export the goods that have relatively low opportunity costs at home and import those that have relatively high opportunity costs.

11. The economist who is usually credited with first exposing the concept of comparative advantage is David Ricardo, who described it in his 1817 book *On the Principles of Political Economy and Taxation.*

12. Economists also often use the partial equilibrium model of international trade, which is based on the same set of neoclassical assumptions as the HO model, and which focuses on how individual markets, producers, and consumers are affected by trade.

13. The aggregate gains in welfare as described by the general equilibrium models of this chapter are the net outcome of economic activities undertaken by individual people who pursue their own interests and are, in all likelihood, not aware of exactly how their activity affects the overall welfare of society. The partial equilibrium models may better reflect the incentives that drive individual behavior than do the broader general equilibrium models.

14. The partial equilibrium model of trade exploits

the concepts of producer surplus and consumer surplus, which are used to derive measures of the net gains to producers and consumers from being able to participate in a particular market.

15. A partial equilibrium supply and demand model for a single market can be derived from the general equilibrium model that we used to represent the whole economy under the "all other things equal" assumption.

16. The partial equilibrium model of trade shows that in each country there are gains as well as losses, but in each case the gains are greater than the losses so that free trade brings net gains to both countries.

17. In the case of imports, import-using consumers gain and import-competing domestic producers lose welfare, but the consumers gain more than the import-competing firms lose.

18. In the case of exports, consumers lose welfare when the competition from foreign consumers forces them to pay more for products, but the exporting producers gain more welfare than the consumers lose.

19. The partial equilibrium model, based on the broader HO model, makes many of the same assumptions, which undermines the generality of its conclusions.

KEY TERMS AND CONCEPTS

absolute advantage
aggregate indifference curves
capital intensive
comparative advantage
consumer surplus
consumption possibilities line
demand side
economic problem
factor price equalization theorem
general equilibrium model
Heckscher-Ohlin (HO) model
Heckscher-Ohlin theorem
human capital

indifference curves
labor intensive
opportunity cost
partial equilibrium model
producer surplus
production possibilities frontier (PPF)
social indifference curves
Stolper-Samuelson theorem
supply side
terms of trade (ToT)
trade triangle
welfare function

PROBLEMS AND QUESTIONS

1. Carefully set up the simple two-good general equilibrium model for a "small country," then show how a shift from isolation to free trade improves national welfare. Highlight international trade's gains both from exchange and from specialization.

2. Show how two economies that have identical production possibilities frontiers can still gain from trade if their populations have different tastes.

3. Suppose two countries enjoy gains from trade with each other because they have different factor endowments (their PPFs are different). Then suppose that one economy's PPF shifts out because of economic growth. Show how both economies are affected by one country's growth. Is the non-growing country better off because of the other economy's growth? Why or why not?

4. A poll in 1999 asked American consumers if they would be willing to pay more for American goods than they would be willing to pay for identical foreign products. Only 31 percent of the respondents said they were not willing to pay more for American products, and 39 percent said they were willing to pay more (30 percent were undecided). In fact, the 39 percent offered to pay, on average, about $41 dollars per month more for the opportunity to buy only American-made products. Why would

people be willing to pay extra in order to help domestic workers who they do not personally know? Why would others not be willing to pay extra?

5. News stories on international trade often praise exports and depict imports as a problem. Use the models presented in this chapter to critique the negative image of imports. Do the HO and partial equilibrium models provide any reasons why imports are harmful to an economy?

6. Assume two economies that have identical production possibilities frontiers. Then show how they can still gain from trade if their populations have different tastes. (Hint: Define two different sets of indifference curves to represent the differing tastes, and then determine the relative price ratios in each country in the absence of trade.)

7. The chapter summary includes this item: An economy can enjoy the gains from exchange without specializing, but it cannot enjoy the gains from specialization without trading with foreigners. Explain precisely using the small-country HO model.

8. Prove the Heckscher-Ohlin theorem. (Hint: Set up the two-country HO model under the usual assumptions, assume two different sets of factor abundancies for the two countries, and derive the resulting free trade triangle. Does each country export the good that uses the country's abundant factor intensively?)

9. Review the partial equilibrium model shown in Figure 3.13. Then explain what happens to the Home country's gains from trade if, in the case of an export good the foreign country demand curve shifts up because, say, foreign incomes are rising. Show exactly what happens to the price and quantity of exports. (Hint: Shift the foreign demand curve and derive the new international demand curve.)

10. The estimates of the gains from trade reported in this chapter were mostly derived using estimated supply and demand models for a sample of exports and imports. Can you think of how you might select such a sample of goods and translate your estimates of consumer and producer surplus changes into an overall estimate of your country's gains of trade? Explain your procedure.

11. Why do you think the estimated gains from international trade are so small? Do these small estimates, often less than one percent of gross domestic product, justify economists' enthusiasm for free trade? Discuss.

Notes

1. See, for example, Gary Burtless (1995) and Paul R. Krugman (2008).
2. This is true only in the short run and under perfect competition.

CHAPTER 4

International Trade: Beyond the Neoclassical Perspective

When the facts change, I change my mind. What do you do, sir?

—John Maynard Keynes

The previous chapter described the Heckscher-Ohlin (HO) model, which combines simple neo-classical production and welfare functions that represent the supply and demand sides of the economy into a framework within which the causes and consequences of international trade can be analyzed. The HO model is, as the previous chapter showed, built on many simplifying assumptions that undermine the model's accuracy. The simplifying assumptions permit the model to generate the clear conclusion that free trade is the optimal policy for maximizing human welfare. Technically, the HO model only proves that trade is welfare maximizing under a very special set of assumed circumstances. Economists who base their advocacy of free trade on the HO model, therefore, are open to questions about whether the welfare superiority of free trade holds in the real world.

There are many examples from history in which long-distance trade and the human interactions that accompany the exchange of goods were not beneficial to everyone involved. For example, the arrival of Spanish explorers in the Western Hemisphere, allegedly to find new products to trade for, ended up introducing diseases that killed over three-fourths of the population of the Western Hemisphere. The opening of trade clearly had high adjustment costs, a problem the HO model ignores entirely. Over the past five hundred years, European countries imposed colonial regimes on Africa, Asia, and Latin America that effectively resulted in the theft of products and resources rather than the voluntary exchange of goods depicted by the HO model. The dominance of trans-national corporations (TNCs) in international trade today completely invalidates the HO model's assumption that trade occurs under conditions of perfect competition. History also makes clear that the growth of international trade has been an integral part of the more general process of economic development, much as Adam Smith suggested over two centuries ago. But, the HO model assumes unchanging factor supplies, technology, and consumer preferences, not very realistic assumptions for a phenomenon closely related to a rapidly changing economy. And, counter to all evidence on human behavior, the HO model assumes that the aggregate consumer preference function is the sum of fixed and "separable" individual preferences.

This chapter examines how some of the HO model's predictions change if we drop some of its strong assumptions. Before we begin our discussion, it would be useful to review the ten main assumptions of the HO model of trade, which are listed in the section titled "Evaluating the Heckscher-

Ohlin Model" in Chapter 3. Dropping or changing these assumptions leads us naturally away from the orthodox neoclassical perspective on international trade and toward heterodox perspectives.

Many mainstream international economists have examined the cases where one or more of the above assumptions are dropped, without abandoning the HO framework. Heterodox economists, on the other hand, have gone much further than mainstream economists and have stopped relying exclusively on the neoclassical framework of economic analysis. They point to fundamental weaknesses of the HO model that cannot be remedied by changing a few assumptions. For one thing, the HO model is a **static model** that seeks to describe the inherently dynamic process of international economic integration. Also, the neoclassical HO model ignores the consequences of international trade in the broader social and natural spheres that humans inhabit and does not recognize the potential feedback on trade from those spheres. Heterodox economists contend that orthodox international economics and the HO model needlessly restrict economic analysis to the narrow economic sphere, when interdisciplinary analysis is essential for understanding trade's effects on society and the natural environment. This chapter begins examining how we can escape from the narrow vision of the HO model.

TRANSPORT AND TRANSACTIONS COSTS

This first section extends the basic HO model by dropping the assumption that there are no transport, distribution, or other transactions costs related to the export and import of goods and services [assumption (g)]. In fact, it is costly to move goods and services between countries. Evidence shows that it was the decline in transport costs that enabled the rapid growth of trade in the nineteenth century. Even so, today we do not trade houses or haircuts with distant countries, because the costs of shipping such goods, or transporting people to acquire the foreign services, are still prohibitive.

Transport Costs

A standard supply and demand diagram of an international market, such as that in Figure 4.1, can be used to demonstrate how transport costs drive a wedge between the price received by suppliers in the exporting country and the price paid by consumers in the importing country. For example, suppose that Figure 4.1 illustrates the international market for bananas. In the absence of any transport costs, which is the assumption we implicitly made in the previous chapter when we used this model, the equilibrium price in the world market would be $50 and a quantity of 40 million boxes of bananas would be traded. Recall the discussion of consumer and producer surplus from the previous chapter. The importing country's net gain in welfare is represented by the consumer surplus area A, and the exporting country's net welfare gain from trade is equal to producer surplus area B.

Suppose now that transport costs are not negligible. Specifically, suppose that it costs $40 to transport a box of bananas from the exporting country, which is located somewhere in the tropics, to the importing country, located far to the north where bananas cannot be grown. For trade to occur, consumers in the importing country must pay $40 more for a box of bananas than suppliers charge for them in the exporting country. This case is illustrated in Figure 4.2. From the consumers' point of view, transport costs raise the supply curve from the solid supply curve S to the dashed curve S_T lying $40 above the solid supply curve. This raises the price to $70, and consumers accordingly demand fewer bananas, 20 million instead of 40 million boxes. The supply curve in the exporting country shows that suppliers will supply 20 million boxes at the price of $30, which is exactly $40 less than the sale price in the importing country. The difference between the consumers' price and the producers' price is the transport cost of $40. The volume of trade is reduced from the "no transport costs" case in Figure 4.1 by 20 million boxes of bananas, and the gains from trade are reduced from the areas A and B in Figure 4.1 to the smaller areas a and b in Figure 4.2.

Figure 4.1 **The Market without Transport Costs**

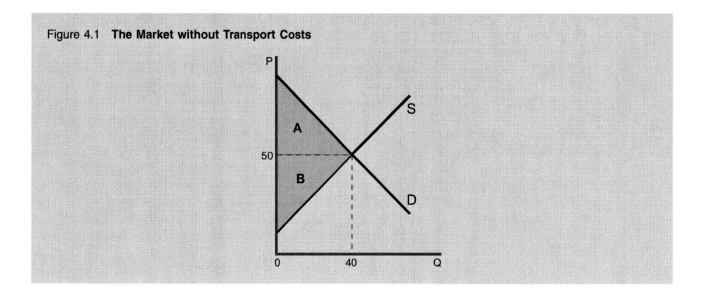

Figure 4.2 **Decreasing Transport Costs Permit Increased Trade**

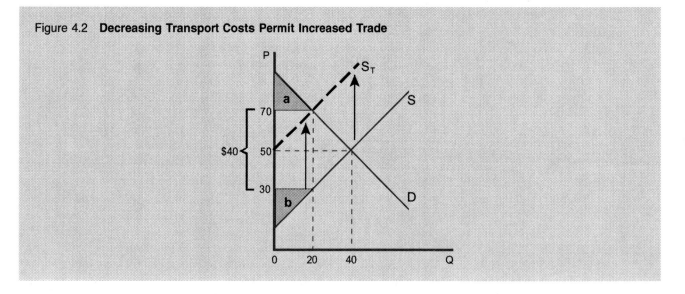

Now suppose that more efficient ships are developed and a less expensive way of refrigerating the bananas during their journey is discovered, so that the transport cost falls from $40 to $20 per box of bananas. Figure 4.3 illustrates this case: The lower transport cost lowers the supply curve to S_{T2}, from S_{T1} (the case of $40 transport costs), and the equilibrium prices settle at $60 and $40 in the importing and exporting countries, respectively. Trade increases from 20 million boxes to 30 million boxes per year. Note also that consumer welfare in the importing country rises by the shaded area c, and producer surplus rises by the area d in the exporting country.

In general, the supply and demand model shows that international trade is inversely related to transport costs. Transport costs thus reduce the gains from trade. It seems that transport costs can be analyzed in the neoclassical supply and demand model of trade. We will, in fact, use the partial equilibrium supply and demand model again when we discuss trade policy in later chapters. Import tariffs, for example, have some of the same effects as transport costs do; all other things equal, they both increase the cost of getting the goods from one country to another.

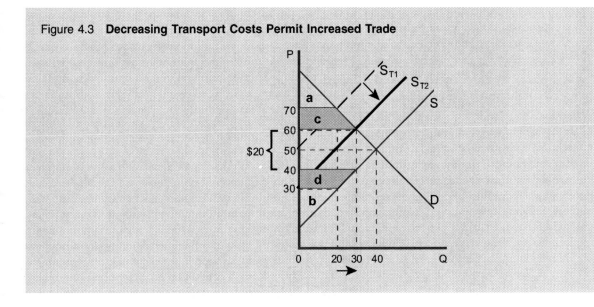

Figure 4.3 **Decreasing Transport Costs Permit Increased Trade**

Transport Costs and Trade Throughout History

In 1800, about 1 percent of the world's output was exported beyond countries' borders. This is a surprisingly small percentage, given that during the previous three hundred years exploratory journeys and colonization had opened trade between Europe and the Western Hemisphere, Africa, and Asia. But in 1800, we still used small sailing ships, horse-drawn wagons, and people's backs to transport goods over long distances. Also, as discussed in the next chapter, colonial trading arrangements often limited trade. During the 1800s many advances in transportation technology caused international trade to grow to nearly 5 percent of GDP by 1870 and nearly 8 percent at the start of the twentieth century.

During the course of the nineteenth century, ocean transport was revolutionized by the iron steamship, which was much safer, faster, and easier to operate than the sailing ship, not dependent on the winds, and able to sail on fixed schedules. The invention of the screw propeller and steel hulls further shortened shipping times and increased the size of ships. Also, without the need for masts to hold sails, steamships could be more flexibly designed to meet specific needs, such as the transport of passengers, iron ore, grain, and lumber. The cost of shipping coal between continents fell by 70 percent between 1840 and 1910, for example.[1] The use of steam engines rather than sails permitted the development of refrigerated ships to carry chilled and frozen foods. By the 1870s frozen beef was transported across oceans from the United States, Argentina, and Australia to Europe. Projects like the Suez and Panama canals lowered transport costs further.

Beginning in the middle of the nineteenth century, railroads greatly improved land transportation. As in the case of ocean shipping, the development of refrigeration permitted railroads to carry fresh and frozen foods across large distances. Railroads effectively eliminated water transport's great comparative advantage and virtual monopoly on long-distance bulk transport.

We can estimate the decline in transport costs by tracing the trends in price differences between different parts of the world for specific products. For example, in 1870 wheat prices in Liverpool in Great Britain were 58 percent higher than in Chicago, where wheat shipments from the fertile midwestern U.S. farmlands originated. The price gap had narrowed to 18 percent by 1895, and to 16 percent by 1912.[2] The price gap for bacon between Chicago and Liverpool narrowed from 92 percent in the late 1800s to just 18 percent in 1913. Also, between 1870 and 1913 the U.S.-British price gap for cotton textiles fell from 14 percent to near zero, the iron bar price gap from 75 to 21 percent, and the gap for cowhides from 28 to 9 percent. The opening of the Suez Canal and the introduction of steamships to the India trade reduced the price gap for cotton between Bombay and Liverpool from 57 percent to 20 percent, and the jute price gap between London and Calcutta narrowed from 35 to 4 percent.[3] Michael Mussa (2000) compared export and import prices for trade partners from balance of payments statistics in the 1800s; he estimates that transport costs as a percentage of the value of goods exported fell from 30 percent in 1800 to about 3 percent around 1900, a 90 percent decline over the entire century. Other studies conclude that transport costs declined by nearly 50 percent just from 1870 to 1910.[4]

Transportation efficiency continued to improve in the twentieth century. Further improvements in ocean shipping brought the 1990 per-ton cost of ocean freight to less than 30 percent of 1920 per-ton costs. In the mid-1950s, containerization greatly reduced **cabotage** costs, which are the costs of transferring shipments from one mode of transportation to another. Pilferage and theft, known as **shrinkage**, were reduced.

Air freight has made the transportation of fresh flowers, fruit, vegetables, fish, and other perishables possible. Large jet aircraft like the Boeing 747 permitted the outsourcing of critical components throughout the world even as manufacturers demanded **just-in-time supply systems** for quicker delivery of parts. Data for the United States show that in 1965 just 6.2 percent of all imports and 8.3 percent of exports, in terms of dollar value, traveled by air, but by 1998 those percentages were approaching 30 percent.[5] David Hummels (1999) estimated that for trips of 5,000 kilometers, air-freight rates fell by one-third over the twenty-five years between 1973 and 1998, and for trips of 9,000 kilometers, rates fell by nearly one-half.

Afghan Warlords and Transport Costs

When the Portuguese and Spanish monarchs hired sea captains such as Vasco da Gama and Christopher Columbus to search for alternative routes to the Far East, it was largely to circumvent the troublesome southern Asian region through which the **Silk Road** had passed centuries earlier. Warlords had dominated what are today the countries of Afghanistan, Uzbekistan, and Tajikistan, among others, and had routinely robbed merchants or demanded hefty tolls for their safe passage. The warlords, of course, had destroyed the goose that laid the golden eggs by extorting excessively high payments, and trade between Europe and the Far East moved to the sea. The Silk Road lost its role in world trade.

Shortly after the fall of the fundamentalist Islamic Taliban government in Afghanistan in 2001, various warlords and local criminals reportedly began demanding tolls from truckers passing through their territories. According to one tank truck driver, under the centralized Taliban control of Afghanistan he used to pay a duty equal to about US$7 for a cargo of diesel fuel at the border between Iran and Afghanistan, and he could drive the cargo all the way to Kabul without further payments. Now, he pays as much as US$300 at numerous points along the way between Iran and Kabul. On the bright side, "Things are not as bad as they were before the Taliban came to power," says another Afghan trucker. "Sometimes they would take your whole truck (Charles Clover 2002)."

The loss of safe travel and trade in the early 1990s had led Afghan businessmen and even some foreign businesses to fund the Taliban in the hope that they would restore order. Once in power, the Taliban government did establish order, but with a heavy loss of personal freedom for many people. The chaos that followed the U.S. invasion in 2001 eventually permitted the Taliban, which still enjoy considerable support in the religiously conservative regions of Afghanistan, to reestablish power in many areas of the country. The forces of the North Atlantic Treaty Organization (NATO), highly distrusted and unwanted, have been unable to restore safe travel. Truckers, their customers, and trade in general are paying the price, just as the model of transport costs suggests.

Network Effects and Trade

International trade data suggest that national borders matter much more for international trade than can be explained by tariffs, transportation costs, and other costs of moving and marketing products to other countries. Daniel Trefler (1995) refers to the unexplainable low level of trade as "the missing trade." James E. Anderson and Douglas Marcouiller (2002) contend that much of this missing trade may be due to the anticipated costs of losses from (1) theft and (2) imperfect contract enforcement. Anderson and Marcouiller use data on corruption and the ability of countries' legal institutions to enforce contracts, and they are able to explain much of the world's missing trade. Based on their statistical results on the importance of legal systems and law enforcement, Anderson and Marcouiller calculate, for example, that Latin America would trade 34 percent more if its legal institutions were as "good" as those of the European Union. Trade among the developed economies of Europe, which on average have better legal systems and law enforcement, is just less problematic and, therefore, less costly than trade with developing economies such as those in Latin America.

The problems of theft and contract enforcement have always plagued international traders. This is why centuries ago traders often traveled with their goods rather than relying on others to transport and sell their goods overseas. Also, trade was often limited to certain familiar foreign locations where institutions were trusted. During the time of the Roman Empire, a uniform legal system and consistent contract enforcement throughout the Mediterranean region facilitated long-distance transactions. After the fall of Rome and the dismantling of the common institutions, trade continued because alternative arrangements were made. Specifically, traders in informal networks devised ways to enforce agreements despite the lack of a uniform legal structure. Trade remained largely free of explicit restrictions and tariffs throughout the Muslim-controlled Mediterranean region, which included North Africa, Sicily, Egypt, and Palestine.

Avner Greif (1989) investigated a network of eleventh-century Mediterranean traders known as the **Maghribi traders**. Greif used old documents that had recently been uncovered in Cairo to reconstruct how the merchants operated. He found that they organized into peer organizations or coalitions, within which each member found it in his own interest to operate according to established rules that ensured the best outcome for the group. These coalitions of merchants were necessary because: (1) the legal systems across the large region were not useful for enforcing agreements and contracts, (2) it was inefficient for merchants to travel with their cargoes to distant locations, and (3) the variability of market conditions around the Mediterranean required on-the-spot decisions about when to buy and sell at prices that could not be predicted. Therefore, it was advantageous to create a coalition of merchants located throughout the region, each of whom could act as agent on behalf of all other merchants who formed part of the coalition. Goods could then be shipped with the assurance that they would be sold at the best possible price and that the proceeds would be sent to the seller in due course.

"Agency relations in the period under study were characterized by asymmetric information, since the revenues the agent received depended upon circumstances that were not directly observed by the merchant,"[6] Greif wrote. Hence, in a perfectly competitive market, where "faceless" buyers, sellers, and firms interact in anonymity, an overseas agent would, in the absence of some other force compelling him to be honest, be tempted to misreport the price of the transaction in order to gain more of the revenue.

Greif found that the Maghribi traders minimized the risk of cheating by establishing a clear and well-understood set of rules of behavior: (1) each coalition merchant will employ only coalition merchants to serve as their agents abroad, (2) all members agree to immediately stop dealing with any member who is caught cheating another member, and (3) all members will be encouraged to cheat or otherwise punish any member who is caught cheating one of the members. This implicit contract "enables merchants to employ agents for assignments which both parties know ahead of time will be of short duration. Since an agent who considers cheating a specific merchant threatens his business with *all* the coalition members, the agent's lifetime expected utility is rather robust with respect to the length of his associations with a specific merchant."[7] Thus, the Maghribi traders bought and sold their goods throughout the Middle East and Mediterranean region despite the lack of legal institutions to prevent theft and support of formal contractual arrangements.

Of course, Maghribi trade was limited to the major trade areas within which coalition members were certain of substantial repeat business. The interesting field of game theory has shown that one-time games are much more volatile than repeated games because players have no incentive to maintain reputations in one-time encounters. It certainly would have been easier for everyone if they could have trusted local legal institutions and dealt with a wider number of foreign merchants in a greater number of foreign locations. But, nevertheless, the Maghribi network enabled trade where otherwise there would have been none.

Transactions Costs and the Gravity Model of Trade

Transportation costs and contract enforcement costs are but two examples of what we generally call **transactions costs**, which are all the explicit costs, the time, and the preparation necessary in order to carry out the exchange of goods and services. Transactions costs include business activities such as marketing. Without advertising, distribution arrangements, warehousing, market research, sales staff, pricing strategies, and many other common and costly marketing activities, few goods and services would be exported or imported. The HO model assumes that transactions between countries are costless in order to avoid introducing complicating factors that obscure what it hypothesizes is the fundamental determinant of trade, namely comparative advantage based on resource endowments. But, as the discussion on transport costs and contract enforcement costs makes clear, transactions costs are also fundamental determinants of international trade. The history of trade is mostly a history of transactions costs.

Mainstream international economics research confirms the importance of transactions costs for international trade. International economists have for many years statistically tested the importance of various hypothesized determinants of trade flows between countries using the **gravity model of trade**. As its name suggests, this model is based on the equation for gravity from physics, and it thus hypothesizes that the volume of trade between a pair of countries is a negative function of the distance between the countries and a positive function of the "mass," or size, of the two economies. The size of economies is usually quantified by gross domestic product (GDP). In this case, the gravity model becomes

(4.1)
$$\text{TRADE}_{ij} = f[(\text{GDP}_i \cdot \text{GDP}_j) / \text{DIST}_{ij}]$$

where TRADE_{ij} is the total value of bilateral trade between countries i and j, GDP_i is the gross domestic product of country i, and DIST_{ij} is the physical distance between the economic centers of the two countries. Taking the natural logs of both sides yields a convenient linear equation (in which logs are written in lowercase) whose coefficients can be estimated using standard statistical regression analysis:

(4.2)
$$\text{trade}_{ij} = a_0 + a_1(\text{gdp}_i \cdot \text{gdp}_j) + a_2(\text{dist}_{ij}) + u_{ij.}$$

In this model, the coefficient a_2 measures the influence of distance, which can be taken as a proxy for transport costs.

Other variables can be added to the model to represent additional transactions costs. For example, demographic, geographic, ethnic/linguistic, and economic conditions can be added to proxy various transactions costs. A gravity model commonly found in the international trade literature is

$$(4.3) \qquad trade_{ij} = a_0 + a_1(gdp_i \cdot gdp_j) + a_2(pop_i \cdot pop_j) + a_3(dist_{ij}) + $$
$$a_4 FTA_{ij} + a_5 LANG + a_6 CONT_{ij} + a_7 LINK_{ij} + u_{ij},$$

in which $pop_i \cdot pop_j$ is the log of the product of the populations in countries i and j, and FTA, LANG, CONT, and LINK are variables that indicate whether a pair of countries has a common free trade area agreement, common language, contiguous border, and colonial links, respectively. These variables are included under the assumption that transactions costs are lower if there is a trade agreement, language and other cultural similarities, a long history of trade due to a common border, and colonial links.

Since Jan Tinbergen's (1962) first use of the gravity model to explain international trade patterns, economists have consistently found that a model such as equation (4.3) statistically "explains" almost all of the variation in international trade flows between countries. In short, distance is an important determinant of international trade, and the assumption (g) of the HO model is clearly unrealistic.

Tentative Conclusions

This section has begun our search for the determinants of trade beyond those that are incorporated in the HO model. International trade depends on (1) transport costs, (2) institutional failures that raise transaction costs for international traders, and (3) other types of transactions costs and risks that cut into the gains from trade. The volume of trade and, thus, the gains from trade are reduced by these factors. Accordingly, by focusing only on countries' productive resources, technologies, and consumer preferences and ignoring these additional costs of trade, the HO model appears to overstate the volume and gains of trade.

THE COSTS OF ADJUSTING TO FREE TRADE

The HO model illustrated in Figure 3.5 of the previous chapter showed how the opening of a closed economy to trade shifts production along the production possibilities frontier (PPF) from the closed-economy equilibrium at point A to point P. The HO model assumes that the shifts in productive inputs from one industry to another occur instantaneously and without any frictions or costs. In reality, these shifts normally cause at least temporary, and often permanent, unemployment, costly rebuilding of physical capital, and suboptimal consumption decisions while consumers evaluate their new options relative to their past habits. There are also likely to be real costs when equipment and buildings (capital) are abandoned in one industry and new investment must be undertaken in another industry, or when workers find their old skills are not needed and they must invest in learning new skills.

Costly Economic Adjustments to Free Trade

We can still use the graphic HO model to illustrate a costly adjustment process. For example, Figure 4.4 illustrates a hypothetical dynamic path of adjustment of an economy that shifts from isolation to free trade under the alternative assumption that producers, workers, investors, and consumers do not adjust instantaneously. A sudden shift in international trade is likely to cause unemployment and the closing of factories. In this case, the trade-induced change in relative prices of X and Y causes production to move inside the PPF as the economy shifts from point A to point P, perhaps along the path through point P' in Figure 4.4, rather than along the edge of the PPF. The adjustment path

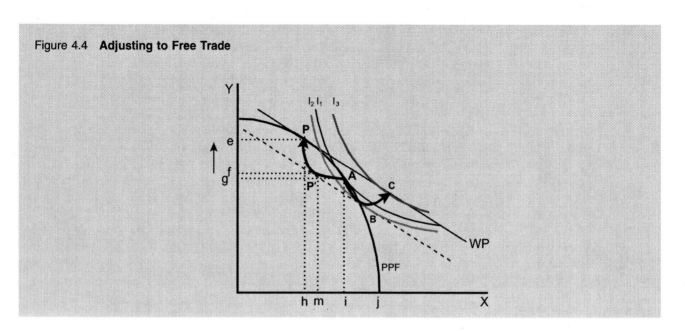

Figure 4.4 **Adjusting to Free Trade**

between A and P′ reflects a rapid fall in the production of X, from i to m, that is matched by little growth in the production of Y from g to f. Even if consumers immediately allocate their incomes in the most efficient way possible, production at point P′ caused by temporarily unemployed resources generates only enough real income to permit consumers to consume at point B in the lower indifference curve I_2. And, if consumers also adjust slowly to the new prices and allocate their diminished income according to past habits, they may not even reach I_2.

The adjustment costs depend, in part, on how quickly people can change jobs. Thus, adjustment costs depend on whether workers have sufficient human capital to perform other tasks, and whether they have the financial wherewithal to cover the costs of moving to other parts of the country where the new jobs in growing industries are located. Also, adjustment costs depend on how quickly banks and financial markets can shift the flow of savings from financing investment in shrinking industries to financing investment in the expanding export industries. Of course, the owners of specialized physical and human capital that can be applied only in the industry X, the declining industry in Figure 4.4, will suffer substantial losses. In the real world, there will always be a time lag in shifting physical capital from one sector to another. It simply takes time to build new factories, infrastructure, and the specialized equipment necessary in the industries that enjoy the comparative advantage, and for people to find new employment operating the new capital.

It is interesting to note that Adam Smith, who in a sense laid the foundations for the Heckscher-Ohlin model of trade with his praise of international trade and the "invisible hand" of free markets, recognized the costs of adjustment to foreign trade and the losses in declining industries:

> The undertaker of a great manufacture, who, by the home markets being suddenly laid open to the competition of foreigners, should be obliged to abandon his trade, would no doubt suffer very considerably. That part of his capital which had usually been employed in purchasing materials and in paying his workmen, might, without much difficulty, perhaps, find another employment. But that part of it which was fixed in workhouses, and in the instruments of trade, could scarce be disposed of without considerable loss. The equitable regard, therefore, to his interest requires that changes of this kind should never be introduced suddenly, but slowly, gradually, and with a very long warning.[8]

More recently, Alan Blinder, President Clinton's advisor on trade who helped sell the North American Free Trade Agreement (NAFTA) to skeptical legislators and an unconvinced public in

1993, has qualified his support for free trade by recognizing the adjustment costs of opening borders. Blinder describes today's trade-driven shifting of jobs between countries as a phenomenon of similar severity to the Industrial Revolution, which caused huge changes in "how and where people lived, how they educated their children, the organization of businesses, the form and practices of governments."[9] The case of Mexico after NAFTA, described in Chapter 1, makes it clear that the effect of cheap grain imports on rural communities in Mexico has been no less costly than the **enclosure** of communal land in Britain that forced millions to flood into the industrial cities in search of work and survival two centuries ago.

The Fixed-Factors Model

An economy that suddenly faces a new set of relative prices after opening its borders to international trade may not only find it very costly to shift resources; it may not be able to shift resources at all. For example, machines and factories for making clothing are not at all useful for growing and harvesting corn. Also, human capital, the skills and knowledge that people accumulate from learning and experience, is often specialized and appropriate only for certain jobs. If agriculture is the declining industry and clothing the expanding industry, for example, farm equipment and a vast knowledge about working the land cannot be employed in producing clothing. Hence, international trade results in the abandonment of productive factors. The impossibility of shifting all resources between industries has led to a version of the HO model called the **fixed-factors model**.

Figure 4.5 begins with the production possibilities frontier from Figure 3.5, labeled "PPF," as well as the pre-trade and post-trade equilibria from that case. Figure 4.5 then draws an alternative PPF for the case in which only some factors can be shifted because some factors are industry specific and simply cannot be employed in other industries. In this case, the rate at which one product can be transformed into another is reduced, and the opportunity costs of increasing the output of a product rise. This alternative is reflected in the more sharply curved production possibilities frontier labeled PPF_{FF}. With some factors fixed in each industry, the Y industry grows from f to k, which is less than from f to e in the case of full-factor mobility. The X industry contracts less as well, from i to m rather than to h. Compared to the HO model in Figure 3.5, output does not rise as much, and the gain from trade and specialization is lower. In Figure 4.5, free trade only takes the economy with industry-specific factors to the indifference curve I_2 at point B, not I_3, under the assumption that all factors are mobile across industries.

Trade and Jobs

Most discussions of international trade in the press or the political arena focus on jobs, not overall estimates of welfare as the HO model does. Typical is a recent Economic Policy Institute report:

> The growth of U.S. trade with China . . . has had a devastating effect on U.S. workers and the domestic economy. Between 2001 and 2007 2.3 million jobs were lost or displaced, including 366,000 in 2007 alone. New demographic research shows that, even when re-employed in non-traded industries, the 2.3 million workers displaced by the increase in China trade deficits in this period have lost an average $8,146 per worker/year.[10]

Because the HO model assumes that all factors are always fully employed in the economy so that the opening of international trade shifts the economy along the edge of the production possibilities frontier, the shift to free trade results in "no jobs lost." Jobs are merely shifted from one industry to another. That is not to say the HO model has nothing to say about the shift in productive inputs. Recall that the

Figure 4.5   **The Short-Run PPF**

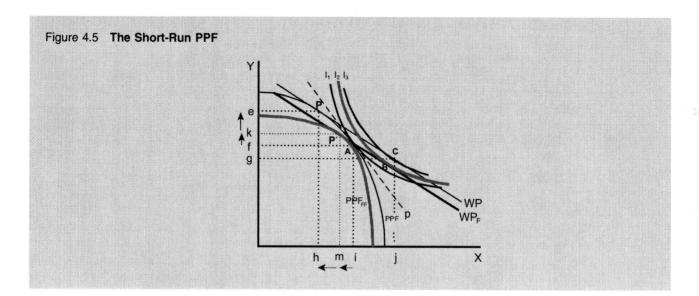

Stolper-Samuelson theorem of the HO model seems to address the decline in wages of displaced, or shifted, workers. The theorem indeed predicts clearly that returns to factors change when an economy opens to trade. But most discussions of international trade's effect on jobs go beyond the capacity of the HO model. For example, this section discussed the likelihood that there would be temporary, and quite possibly permanent, job losses during and after the economy's adjustment to the opening to free trade. These very real costs must be added to the calculations of the gains and losses from trade.

The discussion of how trade decreases or increases the number of jobs also often turns into an argument about who should share the burden of the costs of opening an economy to international trade. Not all factors have to move when industries contract or grow, so inevitably some people seem to bear the cost of the economy's adjustment to free trade while others capture most of the gains. There is clearly a fairness issue. The neoclassical paradigm in general, and the HO model in particular, is not well positioned to discuss the distribution of income, much less the fairness of the distribution. The HO model's assumption of an aggregate welfare function that is, effectively, some aggregation of independent individual welfare functions makes it difficult to track the distribution of individual welfare, either absolutely or relative to others. The HO model's argument that a shift to free trade is worthwhile because across the population income increases exceed income losses is not convincing. There is vast literature from psychology, behavioral economics, and happiness studies that shows people are very concerned about the distribution of welfare, their status in society, and above all their jobs.

INTERNATIONAL TRADE, INCOME INEQUALITY, AND WELFARE

A simple application of consumer surplus and producer surplus can clarify some of the microeconomic ramifications of trade liberalization. This example specifically shows why not everyone gains from the expansion of trade among more people. Suppose that there are two people, Joe, a consumer of widgets, and Mary, a supplier of widgets. Joe's demand curve, D_J, and Mary's supply curve, S_M, are given in Figure 4.6. These are standard demand and supply curves, as we would encounter in perfectly competitive markets where production is subject to increasing costs. At the equilibrium price of $7, Joe gains consumer surplus equal to area J and Mary gains area M in Figure 4.6.

Suppose now that two other people, José, who consumes widgets, and María, who supplies widgets, are represented by the demand and supply curves in Figure 4.7. The equilibrium price in José

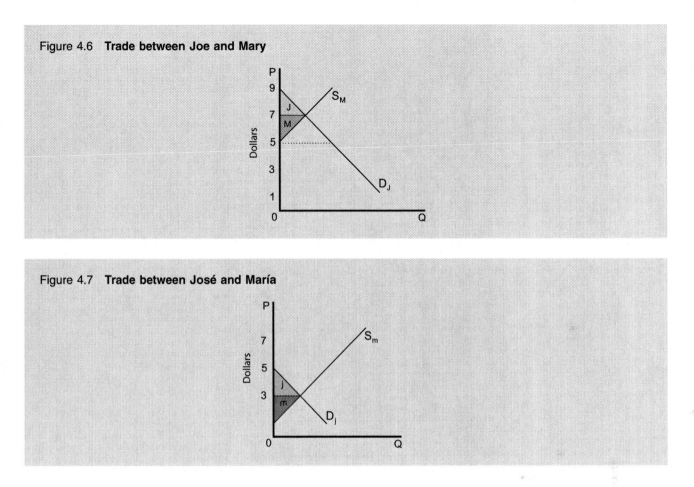

Figure 4.6   Trade between Joe and Mary

Figure 4.7   Trade between José and María

and María's market is $3, and they gain consumer and producer surpluses of j and m, respectively. Notice that the equilibrium price in the two markets differs quite a bit. María seems to be able to begin supplying widgets at a much lower price than Mary, perhaps due to her superior manufacturing skills or just her willingness to work for a lower income because she does not have the same high-paying options to use her labor elsewhere as Mary does. Joe's demand for widgets is much higher than that of José, perhaps because Joe has a higher income than José or just because Joe likes widgets a lot more. The exchanges as shown in Figures 4.6 and 4.7 definitely make Joe, Mary, José, and María better off. However, in looking across the two sets of exchanges, some of traders notice that they could gain much more from trade.

María eyes the price of $7 in Joe and Mary's market, and she decides that she could gain by selling to Joe. After all, Joe should be quite willing to buy widgets from María at any price below the $7 he now pays Mary. So, Joe and María agree to form a new market, which is depicted in Figure 4.8. Note that Joe's demand curve and María's supply curve would result in an equilibrium price of $5, and the gains from exchange to Joe and María are J and m, respectively. Clearly, Joe and María are better off than they were before: area J in Figure 4.8 is larger than consumer surplus area J in Figure 4.6. And, area m in Figure 4.8 is larger than area m in Figure 4.7. Does this mean that overall welfare improved, however?

With Joe and María now exchanging widgets and dollars, José and Mary suddenly face a less attractive situation. In fact, José and Mary find they cannot gain from trading with each other. Figure 4.9 illustrates why: their supply and demand curves do not intersect at a positive quantity of widgets. That is, Mary's supply curve reflects opportunity costs of supplying widgets that exceed José's

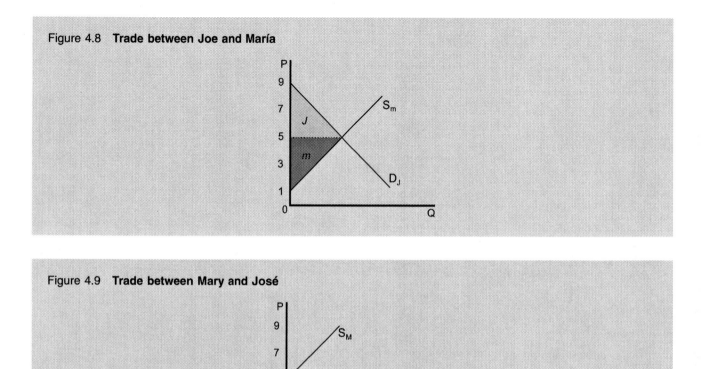

Figure 4.8 **Trade between Joe and María**

Figure 4.9 **Trade between Mary and José**

opportunity costs of acquiring widgets. Thus, they have lost the ability to gain from the exchange of widgets because Joe and María are no longer willing to exchange with either of them. José and Mary are worse off than they were before.

The question of which set of exchanges makes society better off seems difficult to answer. Two people are better off, compared to the initial situation, and two people are worse off. What is the net effect? The most common approach to this question has been to simply sum the individual welfare gains and losses. Figure 4.10 shows the gains and losses clearly. The original gains from exchange, as shown in Figures 4.6 and 4.7, are given by the areas J, M, j, and m. After switching trade partners, Joe ends up with consumer surplus of J + M + A, which is equal to the area J in Figure 4.8. María gains a producer surplus of m + j + a, equal to area m in Figure 4.8, after switching. Clearly, Joe gains more than Mary loses when he stops buying widgets from her. Similarly, María gains more than José loses when she stops exchanging widgets for dollars with him. Therefore, when the gains and losses are added up, there is a net gain. National welfare seems to have increased, but the switch in exchange partners leaves some people worse off.

This simple example illustrates why there might be some opposition to international exchange. If there were a border separating Joe and Mary from José and María, it should not be difficult to imagine Mary lobbying her government to protect her market with Joe from the "unfair" competition from cheap imports from suppliers like María. José might decide to lobby his government to prohibit María from selling widgets to foreign consumers like Joe. We will return to these policy questions in Part 3 of this book. This example also clarifies the point already made with the Stolper-

Figure 4.10 **Summary: The Gains from Trade**

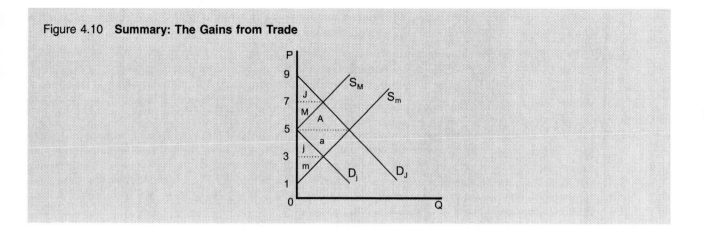

Samuelson theorem and the analysis of consumer and producer surplus in the previous chapter: the gains from extending trade to more people do not benefit everyone. The HO model of international trade, therefore, suffers from an internal inconsistency: the model cannot simultaneously assume that an economy's social welfare function remains unchanged while, at the same time, explicitly showing that individual welfare is redistributed as a result of opening the economy to free trade.

Defining Happiness

We use the aggregate welfare function to help us judge the performance of the economy and the efficiency of economic policies. When neoclassical analysis judges a policy for putting society on a higher indifference curve, it is effectively assuming that people are somehow happier, or more satisfied with life, after the policy is instituted. Mainstream economists seem to be content to leave it at that.

Even though neoclassical economists seem to accept that people are happier when they have more income to acquire more products, few philosophers would agree. For example, Aristotle wrote:

> We may define happiness as prosperity combined with excellence; or as independence of life, or as the secure enjoyment of the maximum of pleasure; or as a good condition for property and body, together with the power of guarding one's property and body and making use of them. That happiness is one or more of these things, pretty well everyone agrees. From this definition of happiness it follows that its constituent parts are: good birth, plenty of friends, good friends, wealth, good children, plenty of children, a happy old age, and also such bodily excellences as health, beauty, strength, large stature, athletic power, together with fame, honour, good luck and excellence.[11]

There is little doubt that the things Aristotle mentions are important for human happiness. Note, however, that not all of his determinants of human happiness can be achieved by simply increasing the economy's material output or average income. Some, such as health, education, and longevity, are indeed closely related to average income; a wealthier economy makes it easier to provide people with better health, more education, and longevity. However, it is not obvious that the growth of GDP increases fame or friendship. And how do we improve our luck? Clearly, it is difficult to measure individual happiness, and given the importance of things like friendship, it is even more difficult to measure aggregate happiness in society when individual levels of happiness depend on what other people do.

An interesting way to judge what has made people happy at different points in history is to analyze their fantasies and dreams. For example, Herman Pleij, professor of literature at the University of Amsterdam, surveyed the arts, literature, and popular culture to reconstruct **Cocagne**, a mythical, ideal place that existed in the minds of medieval European writers and artists (Pleij 2001). Life in medieval times was not nearly as comfortable as life today. People were more directly impacted by the changing seasons. Starvation was always around the corner, and without advanced technologies of food storage and preservation, people were forced to greatly vary their diets over the seasons. There were also disease, war, and the arbitrary demands for labor and donations by kings and priests. So people dealt with the harshness of life by fantasizing about paradise. Pleij summarizes popular descriptions of Cocagne:

> It was a country, tucked away in some remote corner of the globe, where ideal living conditions prevailed: ideal, that is, according to late-medieval notions. . . . Work was forbidden, for one thing, and food and drink appeared spontaneously in the form of grilled fish, roast geese, and rivers of wine. One only had to open one's mouth, and all that delicious food practically jumped inside. . . . The weather was stable and mild—it was always spring—and there was the added bonus of a whole range of amenities: communal possessions, lots of holidays, no arguing or animosity, free sex with willing partners, a fountain of youth, beautiful clothes for everyone, and the possibility of earning money while one slept.[12]

Both Cocagne's and Aristotle's sources of happiness suggest people do not find happiness by themselves. Aristotle's fame and friendship require the cooperation of other people. Cocagne's availability of sex, communal possessions, and social harmony clearly link happiness to one's social environment.

Psychology and Life Satisfaction

Some psychologists have defined happiness more generally as people's comparison of their actual life to their expectations of what life should be like. A.C. Michalos (1985), for example, proposes a "multiple discrepancy theory" of happiness based on the differences between people's desires, hopes, and expectations in five main categories relative to what they actually have. Specifically, Michalos hypothesizes that individual happiness depends on the satisfaction of:

1. Basic needs and wants
2. What one was accustomed to having earlier in life
3. What one expects to have later in life
4. What others in society have
5. What one deserves

Michalos points out that his multiple discrepancy theory implies that happiness is a very complex state of human consciousness that depends on how we evaluate the past, how we predict the future, how we compare ourselves to others, who are those others that we compare ourselves to, and how we determine what we deserve. These hypotheses present happiness as a relative concept that changes over time, across cultures, and during lifetimes. Also, because expectations are not related to absolute levels of income, happiness also is not systematically related to the measures of income that social scientists like to use to measure economic growth. Note, finally, that Michalos' multiple discrepancy theory is holistic because the term "wants" is general enough to include much more than material wants. Michalos' wants can include Aristotle's "fame, friends, or good luck."

Happiness Surveys

Some social scientists have approached the challenge of measuring human happiness by simply asking people how happy they are. The results of these **happiness surveys** have been converted to numerical measures and used in statistical tests of various hypothesized determinants of happiness. These surveys have been carried out for many years in many countries, so it is now possible to compare happiness across countries and over time. Research studies using these data are referred to as **happiness studies** and are often reported and discussed in the *Journal of Happiness Studies.*

Many happiness studies have used the results from surveys by the University of Michigan's Survey Research Center (SRC), which asked people the question:

> Taken all together, how would you say things are these days—would you say that you are (1) very happy, (2) pretty happy, or (3) not too happy?

Another popular source of happiness data is the *World Value Surveys,* conducted every few years across a large sample of countries. And, in Europe, the level of happiness is routinely revealed in the annual Eurobarometer survey, which asks:

> On the whole are you (1) very satisfied, (2) fairly satisfied, (3) not very satisfied, or (4) not at all satisfied with the life you lead?

The average values of these surveys take the form of a number between 1 and 3 for the three-option question by the University of Michigan, and between 1 and 4 for the latter two surveys. These numbers represent a ranking, not an absolute measurement of happiness, because there is no way of knowing precisely how, for example, *very happy* compares to *pretty happy.* These survey results are useful for social scientists because they allow us to relate changes in the happiness index and hypothesized determinants of happiness such as income, health, age, marriage status, gender, educational achievement, and myriad other human conditions.[13]

Results of Recent Surveys of Happiness

Table 4.1 presents data from surveys on happiness in Europe and the United States. Notice that the proportions of people in each of the categories barely changed at all between 1972 and 1998. If anything, Table 4.1 suggests that the proportion of people who classify themselves as *very happy* or *very satisfied* declined slightly from 1972 to 1998. During this period real per capita GDP increased substantially and continually. There certainly is no indication that people became happier as their incomes rose over these two-and-a-half decades.

Also interesting are the findings from happiness studies of post–World War II Japan. According to survey responses, Japanese citizens did not experience any increase in personal happiness over the four decades between 1950 and 1990, when the Japanese economy increased per capita real GDP sixfold. This period is still referred to as the Japanese "economic miracle." The results are illustrated in Figure 4.11: As Japanese per capita real GDP consistently increased, the average life satisfaction index remained about the same. These findings for Japan are similar to what Table 4.2 reveals for the United States and Europe.

Studies that have looked at a large sample of different countries at a given point in time do seem to suggest that life satisfaction or happiness is positively related to income. However, the relationship is not linear. Figure 4.12 suggests a clear, direct relationship between income and happiness for countries with average annual incomes under US$5,000. Yet, once average income exceeds US$5,000, the surveys do not show much systematic variation in how satisfied people are with their lives. People's life satisfaction in the average country with an average per capita income of US$7,500 is not much different from the average reported life satisfaction in a country with an average per capita income of US$30,000. A broad study of a large number of countries for an extended period (1960 through 2005) by Rafael Di Tella and Robert MacCoulloch (2008) confirms the lack

Table 4.1

Life Satisfaction in the United States and Europe: 1972–1998

United States	1972–76	1977–82	1983–87	1988–93	1994–98
Not too happy	14%	12%	12%	10%	12%
Pretty happy	52	54	56	58	58
Very happy	34	34	32	33	30

12 European Countries[1]	1973	1983	1997
Not at all satisfied	4%	6%	5%
Not very satisfied	16	16	17
Fairly satisfied	58	59	59
Very satisfied	22	19	19

[1] Belgium, Denmark, France, Greece, Ireland, Italy, Luxembourg, the Netherlands, Portugal, Spain, the United Kingdom, and West Germany.
Source: Eurobarometer; taken from David G. Blanchflower and Andrew J. Oswald (2000), "Well-Being Over Time in Britain and the USA," NBER Working Paper w7487, January.

Figure 4.11 **Happiness and Real Per Capita GDP in Japan: 1958–1991**

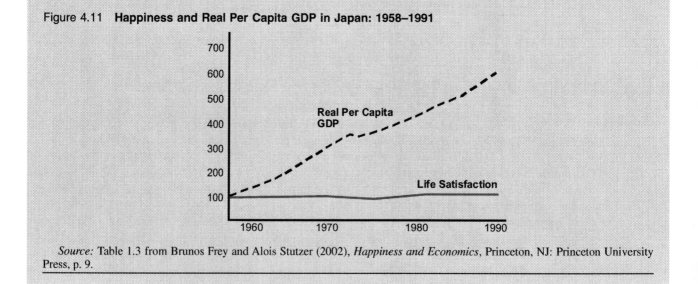

Source: Table 1.3 from Brunos Frey and Alois Stutzer (2002), *Happiness and Economics*, Princeton, NJ: Princeton University Press, p. 9.

of effect of income on happiness after "basic needs" are met, which it estimates occurred at 1960 GDP per capita in Europe.

The time-series data on happiness do not give the complete story, however. Cross-section studies comparing people across different income groups in each country in any given year suggest that rich people are, on average, happier than poor people. Table 4.2 shows that average levels of happiness differ across income groups within individual countries. The lowest income *quartile* (the 25 percent of the population at the bottom of the income distribution) contains the highest proportion of people reporting they were *not too happy* in the United States and not very happy or *not at all happy* in a group of European countries. Nearly 20 percent of the poorest Americans were not happy, but only 5 percent of wealthy Americans were *not happy*. Less than 25 percent of poor Americans, but over

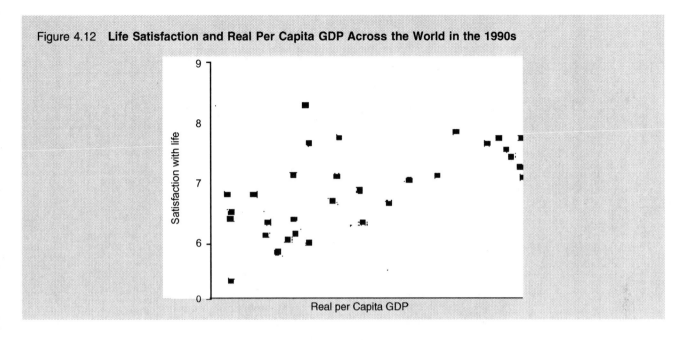

Figure 4.12 **Life Satisfaction and Real Per Capita GDP Across the World in the 1990s**

40 percent of wealthy Americans, were *very happy*. Within a single country, or society, rich people are much more likely to be happy than poor people.

Statistical Studies of Happiness

Many studies have used happiness survey data in statistical regression equations in order to test which hypothesized determinants of human happiness significantly "explain" the variation in happiness survey results. Typical of such happiness studies is the paper by David Blanchflower and Andrew Oswald (2004), who use data from the Michigan survey for the United States and from the Eurobarometer survey for the United Kingdom over the period 1972–1998 to explain the variations in happiness across different groups of people. Their statistical regressions estimate whether (1) age, (2) gender, (3) race, (4) marital status, (5) employment status, (6) student status, and (7) the presence of a spouse have an effect on individual happiness. Table 4.3 presents the regression results for both countries. A survey of the many similar happiness studies for other countries, time periods, and data sets by Paul Dolan, Tessa Peasgood, and Matthew White (2008) confirm Blanchflower and Oswald's findings. Specifically, their survey finds that happiness is positively and significantly correlated with being female, having many friends, being young, being married or cohabiting, being educated, being healthy, having a relatively high income, being self-employed, having low blood pressure, having sex at least once per week with the same partner, being a right-wing voter, being religious, being a member of an organization, doing volunteer work, and exercising regularly.

In both the United Kingdom and the United States, people are less happy when, all other things equal, they are unemployed, not married, older, male rather than female, or retired, or they have lost their spouse. Blanchflower and Oswald's statistical results thus seem to suggest that, in order to achieve greater happiness, people should get married, stay married, stay employed, become educated, and never retire. Males should contemplate a sex change. More generally, the similarity of the results from happiness studies across many different countries suggests that humans across different cultures react similarly to their economic and social circumstances. The many happiness studies clearly confirm a positive relationship between happiness and people's sense of belonging and being valued.

Table 4.2

Life Satisfaction in Europe and the United States: 1975–1994

	Income Quartiles:			
United States	Lowest	2nd	3rd	Highest
Not too happy	18.28	13.20	8.56	5.81
Pretty happy	57.43	58.07	57.53	52.48
Very happy	24.28	28.73	33.91	41.71
12 European Countries[1]				
Not very/not at all satisfied	28.58	21.10	16.48	12.47
Fairly satisfied	49.52	54.54	56.71	54.96
Very satisfied	21.90	24.36	26.81	32.58

[1] Belgium, Denmark, France, Greece, Ireland, Italy, Luxembourg, the Netherlands, Portugal, Spain, the United Kingdom, and West Germany.

Source: Eurobarometer; taken from David G. Blanchflower and Andrew J. Oswald (2000), "Well-Being Over Time in Britain and the USA," NBER, Working Paper w7487, January.

Table 4.3

Marginal Influences on Happiness: 1972–1998

	United States	United Kingdom
Age	−0.0220	−0.0424
Male	−0.1595	−0.1555
Black	−0.4494	
Unemployed	−0.8321	−1.1337
Retired	−0.0410	−0.0371
Student	0.1245	0.0141
2nd marriage	−0.1063	
Widowed	−1.1109	−0.2894
Divorced	−0.9874	−0.6061
Separated	−1.2523	−0.6531
Never Married	−0.7384	−0.7830
Married		0.3972
Education	0.0482	

[1] Belgium, Denmark, France, Greece, Ireland, Italy, Luxembourg, the Netherlands, Portugal, Spain, the United Kingdom, and West Germany.

Source: Eurobarometer; taken from David G. Blanchflower and Andrew J. Oswald (2000), "Well-Being Over Time in Britain and the USA," NBER Working Paper w7487, January.

Having reviewed some examples of the results from happiness surveys as well as from the statistical analysis of these survey responses, we can take stock of what the research suggests. Happiness research reveals that:

- Average human happiness does not change as real average per capita income grows over time.
- At one point in time within the same country, people with high incomes are happier, on average, than people with low incomes; this suggests that people are conscious of their relative income and status.

- Overall happiness rises with average per capita income levels only up to US$10,000, and further rises in average real per capita GDP have little effect on average happiness.
- The strong reaction to loss of a spouse or a job confirms that humans are social animals who value friendship and respect from others.

In short, relative income matters more than absolute income, probably because it defines social status. Sudden losses also matter a lot. This puts international trade in a different light. Is it really worth causing a lot of people to lose their jobs in order to increase the income of others in society?

Evidence from Neuroscientific Research

Evidence on the sources of human happiness has also been provided by neuroscientists, who have devised techniques to directly monitor how the human brain reacts to specific changes in those circumstances. Neuroscientific analysis has determined that the actions and choices that define human behavior are controlled from distinct parts of the brain. The brain's **automatic processes** occur with little or no awareness or feeling of effort. Reactions to pain, danger, and physical trauma, for example, are mostly automatic. These evolved automatic brain processes, and the behavior they trigger, do not follow normative axioms of inference and choice. They are more like *constants* than behavioral *variables.* The *emotional* processes occur in a part of the human brain that has evolved more recently. Hence, many of the **emotional processes** are unique to humans and humans' more recent mammal ancestors. The word *instinct* is often used to describe emotional behaviors, although automatic processes are also instinctive in the sense that no active thought process triggers them. Finally, there are the *deliberate processes* which developed the most recent human ancestors. These processes are closest to the rational behavior economists often assume.

The distinct sectors of the brain work together in many different combinations that depend on the type of decision to be made and the circumstances under which the decision is made. In contrast to what economists normally assume, most of the brain's activity is *automatic* and *emotional* rather than *deliberative* (and thus potentially rational). And, even when the deliberative brain functions are called into action, the emotional processes often still dominate the outcome.

According to Joseph E. LeDoux (1996), "the wiring of the brain at this point in our evolutionary history is such that connections from the emotional systems to the cognitive systems are stronger than connections from the cognitive systems to the emotional systems." The faster automatic and affective processes direct cognitive or deliberate processes to deal with the most urgent issues first. Another neuroscientific discovery is that specialization within the brain is, at least in part, a learning process. That is, people can learn to change their instinctive behavior in given circumstances by altering the sequence in which different parts of the brain are activated in response to external events. For example, one study that tracked the brain activity of foreign exchange floor traders showed that seasoned traders reacted calmly to the same events that agitated novice traders. It is, of course, well known in sports that a team with some older, experienced players often performs better than a younger, physically superior but less experienced team.

As confirmed by Robyn Aimee LeBeouf (2002), Douglas Medin and Max H. Bazerman (1999), and many other experiments, the automatic and emotional processes in the brain depend largely on the recognition of patterns. The brain becomes agitated when unfamiliar patterns emerge or familiar patterns cannot be found; its ability to handle information when unfamiliar, confusing patterns must be interpreted is limited, and it ends up making mistakes. An interesting experiment by Shane Frederick (2005) finds that people often misinterpret a problem or an observation because their emotional processes get ahead of their deliberative process and place the problem in a familiar pattern that does not exactly match the true pattern. In other words, they jump to conclusions.

When the senses tell the brain that something is not familiar, reactions are triggered that attempt to restore equilibrium. This reaction of the human brain to deviations from familiar patterns is referred to by neuroscientists as **homeostasis.** Most of the brain processes triggered are automatic and emotional, which is why immediate reactions to change are so often irrational. Homeostasis in the brain's processes thus explains why humans react much more intensely to *changes* in their circumstances than they do to a continuation of familiar circumstances, but it also explains why humans are very adaptable in the long run. Despite short-term overreactions, people eventually adjust to changed circumstances. For example, a well-known study of lottery winners found that one year after the elation of becoming rich, they fall back to their normal level of brain activity and, apparently, life satisfaction. A.J. Oswald and N. Powdthavee (2008) found that people who become permanently disabled recover much of their pre-injury level of happiness over time. "It's better to win the lottery than to break your neck, but not by as much as you'd think," concludes Jonathan Haidt (2006) after comparing people's happiness immediately after unexpected major events, such as financial windfalls and permanently debilitating injuries, to their happiness one year later. If these conclusions surprise you, think about what would have happened to our ancestors over the course of millions of years of economic hardships, personal setbacks, natural disasters, and other changes in their social and natural environments had they not been able to adjust and get on with their lives.

Neuroscience has also confirmed the social nature of human beings, as suspected by Aristotle and other philosophers over the centuries. We cannot do justice to the many neuroscientific studies that have confirmed human empathy, which is the ability to understand what others feel. Jean Decenty and Claus Lamm (2006) of the University of Chicago confirm that these feelings of empathy stem from all three neural processes, so they are a natural behavioral characteristic, not only a socially acquired behavior. Maël Lebreton et al. (2009) specifically trace humans' dependence on social rewards to the brain's orbitofrontal cortex, basal ganglia, and temporal lobes, regions that have previously been shown to be involved in processing primary rewards. They interpret these results as "evidence for a brain's structural disposition to social interaction."

Evidence from Behavioral Economics and Psychology

Happiness studies have been supplemented by other types of research in recent years. For example, David Lykken (1999), a psychologist of the University of Minnesota, studied a sample of identical twins who, for one reason or another, grew up apart from each other. He found that the twins' stated levels of happiness were very closely correlated, regardless of the differences in lifestyles they experienced. He concluded that happiness is 90 percent genetic, and only minimally influenced by environmental factors in the long run. In the short run, however, environmental factors could alter happiness substantially. Lykken suggests that each person has a happiness set point around which his or her happiness fluctuates.[14] People experience changing levels of happiness over their lifetimes, but in the long run their average happiness diverges little from their genetically determined set point of happiness.

The field of behavioral economics, which combines the disciplines of economics and psychology plus other interdisciplinary ideas and evidence, has carried out human experiments to test some of the neuroscientific findings reported above. For example, in their now-classic study, Daniel Kahneman and Amos Tversky (2000) conducted a series of experiments that confirmed that people disproportionately value their current situation over other options. In one experiment, Kahneman and Tversky found that people value the object A that they have over the object B that they do not possess, but when they find themselves in possession of object B while object A belongs to someone else, a surprisingly large number of people then claim to prefer the object B to object A! Kahneman and Tversky refer to this phenomenon as the "endowment effect." This result implies that people are loss averse, and that they will fight harder to hold on to what they have than to acquire something new. Many animals exhibit this kind of behavior, and we often refer to it as **territoriality.**

People are not comfortable with change, and to justify their aversion to change, they adapt to their "territory" and convince themselves they like it more than some other territory, even though there is no apparent rational reason for this preference.

Lykken's set point hypothesis, along with the vast evidence from happiness studies and neuroscience showing that people dislike major changes but eventually adjust to changes in life and income begs an interesting question: Why do economists advocate policies that substantially change people's economic and social circumstances if it is unlikely to make them much happier in the long run? This question is relevant to the growth of international trade, the rise in economic growth, and the shifts in social status that people have experienced over the past two hundred years.

International Trade: Happiness, Inequality, and Change

The main findings from happiness studies, neuroscience, and psychology for our search for a welfare function are: (1) human happiness depends on much more than money income and material wealth, (2) people actively seek social interaction, (3) they are very conscious of their position in society, (4) they quickly detect changes in their patterns of life, and (5) they resist change and attempt to preserve the status quo, although (6) people do like improvements in their well-being and (7) they are adaptable and eventually come to accept changed circumstances. The economic implications of these conclusions are several. First, short-term and long-run human happiness probably do not depend on the exact same set of variables, and, therefore, economic policies designed to satisfy people today do not necessarily maximize humans' lifetime happiness. In terms that economists are familiar with, welfare functions are not constant, or stable, over time. Secondly, the social welfare function is not a simple aggregation of individual welfare functions. The fact that people have empathy and the conscious awareness of social status means that the aggregate social welfare function, provided one even logically exists, depends on the distribution of income. Every change in the distribution of income must result in a new social welfare function and, therefore, a different set of social indifference curves. Finally, the demonstrated human aversion to change and, especially, loss means economists must change their estimates of the costs and benefits of opening an economy to free trade. More generally, the neoclassical social welfare function, in which human welfare is a direct function of goods and services or just GDP, is clearly not an accurate guide for judging economic activity.

The economic historian Richard Easterlin (2003b) emphasizes the findings from happiness studies that suggest life events such as marriage, divorce, widowhood, and physical disability can have a lasting effect on well-being even if increases in income and material consumption have no lasting influence on life satisfaction once basic needs are taken care of. Easterlin therefore argues that we need a better set of policies to maximize happiness:

> A better theory of well-being builds on the evidence that adaptation and social comparison affect utility more in the pecuniary than nonpecuniary domains. The failure of individuals to anticipate that these influences disproportionately undermine utility in the pecuniary domain leads to an excessive allocation of time to pecuniary goals at the expense of nonpecuniary goals, such as family life and health, and reduces well-being. There is need to devise policies that will yield better-informed individual preferences, and thereby increase individual and societal subjective well-being.[15]

Easterlin effectively urges people to stop and smell the roses. Or better yet, make sure you have lots of friends who will join you in the rose garden.

What this all means for the study of international trade is that economists should not measure the gains and losses from trade purely in terms of material output or per capita GDP. The costs of adapting to new jobs, losing investment incomes, or changing social status may be substantial, but orthodox models, such as the HO model, assume a stable set of indifference curves that remains unchanged even as the gains and losses from trade are spread unevenly across the populations. And, the importance of relative income over absolute income in today's high-income countries means that the role of international trade in accelerating economic growth may not be as important as the fear that free trade will alter relative incomes and social status. We are still faced with the question we asked after looking at the happiness studies' conclusions: Is it really worth causing a lot of people to lose their jobs in order to increase the income of others in society?

EXTERNALITIES AND INTERNATIONAL TRADE

Not all the costs and benefits are reflected in a product's price. Producers do not always pay the full costs of the resources used in production, nor do buyers pay a price that exactly represents benefits provided by a product. The Chinese steel mill described in Chapter 1 is an example; the plant emits carbon into the air, which causes pollution locally and climate change globally, but the firm does not take such externalities into consideration because it is not charged for them. Consumers do not pay for the external carbon emissions related to the international transport of products using the Chinese steel. When steel producers avoid certain costs, the industry supply curve is too low.

Modeling Externalities

Suppose the only externalities associated with steel production are the carbon emissions during the production. These emissions produce both local pollution as well as climate change. Economic efficiency demands that these external costs be internalized and included in the supply curve so that the market can set an accurate price that takes the full costs into consideration. Internalizing these emissions costs raises the supply curve from S_1 to S_2 in Figure 4.13. Note that this diagram is the same two-country supply and demand diagram as in Figure 3.13, which we derived from the HO model in the previous chapter. An upward shift in China's supply curve to capture the true costs of producing steel raises the world price of steel because the shift in the Chinese supply curve also shifts up the international supply curve in the center diagram. Recall from Figure 3.13 that this international curve was the difference between the exporting country's domestic supply and demand curves; hence, an upward shift in one curve reduces the "excess" supply over domestic demand that China has available for export. The net gains from trade for Germany, the importing country, are also reduced because the price rises. And, because the gains from trade are less, the volume of trade is reduced.

In short, the internalization of the external cost of carbon emissions seems to reduce the gains from international trade. It should be apparent, however, that the external costs were always present, and the internalization of those costs to where they are captured by the product price actually results in a more efficient allocation of resources. Steel production is really too large in China because neither the producers nor the consumers took the costs of carbon emissions into consideration in deciding how much steel to produce and how much to consume. At the level of production Q in China, the amount of steel produced when carbon emissions are ignored, the true marginal cost of production is at j, well above the market price. Too much steel is produced, and its true cost exceeds its marginal benefits reflected in what consumers of the steel are willing to pay.

Shifting GHG Emissions to Developing Countries

This discussion of carbon emissions is especially interesting because it involves both local pollution as well as the global problem of climate change. When the steel plant was moved from Dortmund to China, air pollution was reduced in Germany, but it increased in China where the plant was reassembled. In the former case, international specialization and trade have shifted pollution from one country to another.

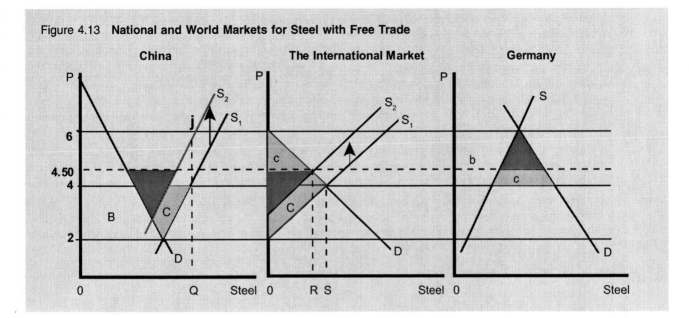

Figure 4.13 **National and World Markets for Steel with Free Trade**

But the sale of the German steel plant to a Chinese firm has no apparent effect on the plant's **greenhouse gas (GHG) emissions**. In this case, international trade does not seem to change anything.

Further analysis suggests otherwise, however. Since the Chinese plant produces steel that is incorporated into other Chinese products, many of which are exported, new carbon emissions are generated when the steel and the products made with the steel are shipped around the world. Furthermore, the Chinese coal-fired power plants that provide most of the electric power to the transplanted steel plant emit more GHGs than do current German power generators, which increasingly consist of natural gas plants and wind farms. Therefore, the shipment of dirty steel plants from Germany to China, and the subsequent international trade that this relocation of production caused, increased global GHG emissions.

The HO model of international trade suggests that the shift of industries like steel and manufacturing to labor-abundant economies like China, India, and Brazil is a simple matter of comparative advantage. But externalities mean that comparative advantage must be based on more than just factor endowments: differences in environmental policies across countries also determine relative production costs across countries. If costs are not accurately accounted for in all countries, then trade will not reflect true comparative advantage.

Transnational corporations often shift production to countries where environmental regulations are weakest or most easily ignored. The large variations in national environmental regulations have caused a "race to the bottom" in environmental regulation because governments fear they will lose industries, and jobs, to countries with more lax rules. For example, Arik Levinson and Scott Taylor (2008) examine data for a set of twenty industries impacted by new environmental regulation in the United States, and find that about half the increase in U.S. imports is statistically "explained" by the increases in regulation. In other words, U.S. producers shifted a substantial amount of production to plants overseas in response to U.S. efforts to internalize environmental costs.

Externalities Associated with Transport

At the start of this chapter, we noted how steady declines in transportation costs have expanded international trade. With lower transport costs, transnational food retailers Walmart, Tesco, Carrefour, and others that are also food distributors have created global networks that keep consumers supplied with the full range of fresh foods year-round, from producers spread throughout the world. These distributors and retailers have grown by increasingly shifting food production to countries where labor costs are lowest. For example, labor costs for processing codfish in Norway are US$1.36 per pound, but they are only US$0.36 in China. As a result, cod caught off Norway's shores is shipped to China for processing before being shipped back to Norway to be sold. But according to Elisabeth Rosenthal (2008), "the movable feast comes at a cost: pollution—especially carbon dioxide, the main GHG, from transporting the food." The environmental costs are not being paid in full by the shippers who shift food around the world. In fact, international shippers pay fewer taxes than do domestic shippers in most countries. The 1944 **Convention on International Civil Aviation** established that fuel for international air travel and transport of goods, including food, is exempt from national taxes. There is a similar international agreement for ocean shipping. These rules were put into effect in order to prevent taxes being used to restrict trade, in violation of other trade agreements. But such rules also prevent countries from imposing welfare-improving taxes to compensate for market failures such as externalities from GHG emissions.

GHGs Embedded in Trade

Standard accounts of GHG emissions only look at where products are produced. A few studies have included transportation as a source of GHG emissions. Those studies arbitrarily allocated emissions across countries according to either the ownership of the steamship companies, airlines, and trucking companies involved or the country where the transport originated or terminated. The logic of international trade theory suggests that the physical location of the sources of GHG emissions is not what matters in assigning either national obligations or congratulations for reducing GHG emissions. Since the ultimate gains from trade are measured in terms of consumption, not production, it is appropriate to calculate an individual country's GHG emissions in terms of final consumption rather than production. If Germans still consume steel from the transplanted ThyssenKrupp plant, Germany's GHG emissions have not really been reduced.

A study by T. Wiedman et al. (2008) for the U.K. Department for Environment, Food and Rural Affairs (DEFRA) recalculated Britain's emissions according to its consumption rather than its production. Figure 4.14 describes how the study first classified data on the production of GHGs. The location of production, represented by boxes 1 through 6, may be in foreign countries or in the domestic country (the United Kingdom). Consumption occurs where the arrowheads are located, again either in the foreign economy or in the domestic economy. If GHG emissions are attributed to production, the domestic economy's GHG emissions are equal to the sum of emissions produced in the boxes 1, 2, 5, and 6. On the other hand, if GHG emissions are attributed to final consumption, then the domestic economy's total GHG emissions are the sum of emissions produced in the boxes 1a, 1, 3, 5, and 6. The difference between these two sets, 1a + 3 − 2, is the excess of consumption GHGs over production GHGs. Table 4.4 presents Wiedman et al.'s actual estimates. From a consumption perspective, the U.K.'s GHG emissions have not stopped growing at all, even though direct production emits the same GHGs it did a decade ago.

Another Example of Embedded GHGs

The "race to the bottom" effect of international trade is also illustrated by the surge in U.S. exports of used automobiles to Mexico after 1994 when the North American Free Trade Agreement (NAFTA) eliminated trade restrictions between the two countries. Before NAFTA went into effect, Mexico had banned the import of used vehicles in order to protect its domestic automobile industry. After NAFTA, Mexico imported between half a million and a million automobiles aged ten years or older from the United States, where such cars have little value and are often scrapped or used very

Table 4.4

CO₂ Emissions Embedded in the U.K.'s International Trade

Year	U.K. Producer Emissions (1+2+5+6)	U.K. Consumer Emissions (1+1a+3+5+6)	Balance of Emissions Embedded in Trade (1a+3–2)
1992	620.0	647.2	26.8
1993	607.7	638.8	31.1
1994	601.0	634.0	33.0
1995	593.5	652.3	58.9
1996	620.8	651.0	30.2
1997	600.8	660.6	60.0
1998	606.3	680.3	73.9
1999	597.7	664.9	67.2
2000	609.0	680.7	71.7
2001	624.4	732.1	107.5
2002	609.7	730.1	120.4
2003	624.8	763.6	138.8
2004	630.6	762.4	131.8

Source: Table 2 in Wiedman, T., R. Wood, M. Lenzen, J. Minx, D. Guan, and J. Barrett (2008), *Development of an Embedded Carbon Emissions Indicator*, report to the U.K. Department for Environment, Food and Rural Affairs (DEFRA) by the Stockholm Environment Institute at the University of York and Centre for Integrated Sustainability Analysis at the University of Sydney, June, London: DEFRA.

Figure 4.14   GHG Emissions from National Production and Consumption

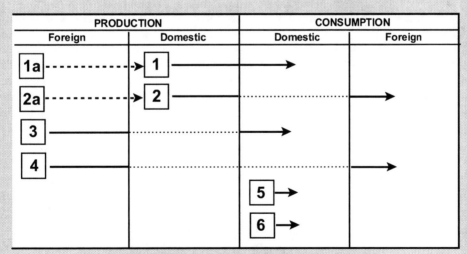

1 - U.K. emissions from production for domestic consumption
2 - U.K. emissions from production for export
1a - Imported emissions through intermediate inputs to U.K. production for domestic consumption
2a - Imported emissions through intermediate inputs to U.K. production for export
3 - Imported emissions for U.K. domestic consumption
4 - Imported emissions for U.K. export
5 - U.K. emissions generated by households (excluding use of private automobiles)
6 - U.K. emissions generated by households from private use of automobiles

little. Because they are old, these vehicles, on average, emit more carbon and other GHGs than the average automobile on the road in the United States, but they emit less than the average vehicle on the road in Mexico. As a result, this used-vehicle trade has led to a decrease in average emissions per vehicle in both the United States and Mexico. This result has led some to interpret this trade as beneficial for the environment.

Lucas W. Davis and Matthew E. Kahn (2010) estimate, however, that total global GHG emissions have increased because this trade gives new life to old vehicles that otherwise would have been scrapped. They report that this trade has caused no discernible decline in the number of vehicles on the road in the United States, but it has caused a large increase in the number of vehicles operating in Mexico because their low price makes them affordable to Mexican consumers who would otherwise not acquire a motor vehicle. Also important to their calculations is the Massachusetts Institute of Technology Energy Laboratory's (2000) finding that for a lifetime driving distance of 300,000 kilometers, 93 percent of carbon emissions associated with an automobile come from fuel usage, and only 7 percent come from the vehicle's production.

In a conclusion that is relevant for used steel mills as well as used cars, Davis and Kahn (p. 60) write:

> With durable goods, how and where goods are consumed is potentially more important than how and where they are produced. . . . With global pollutants the location of consumption is irrelevant, but the magnitude of lifetime consumption is not. As a result, policies aimed at reducing greenhouse gas emissions may not achieve aggregate gains when fuel inefficient durable goods can be traded.

Thus, international trade can cause GHG emissions to increase. This is not a necessary outcome, but it certainly is a possible outcome given the world's lack of international institutions or agreements to deal with environmental externalities.

Policies for Adjusting Trade for Embedded GHGs

The European Union has proposed taxing airlines for their GHG emissions, a measure that is scheduled to go into effect in 2012. It is hoped that, if transport services fully account for the cost of GHG emissions, international trade in food will more accurately reflect true comparative advantage that takes the cost of carrying the goods into consideration. A **carbon tax** on transport appears to be a more accurate way of dealing with the externalities associated with international trade than, say, a simple ban on certain food imports. But a carbon tax on transport will not capture the fact, for example, that grass-fed beef from New Zealand produces much fewer GHG emissions than feedlot-fed U.S. beef. If the transport tax stops U.S. imports from New Zealand in favor of feedlot-fed domestic beef, GHG emissions could actually rise. To avoid such a perverse result, the U.S. government must simultaneously tax U.S. feedlot operators for their GHG emissions. Blocking imports in order to internalize foreign environmental costs while ignoring the environmental destruction by domestic producers would be an especially egregious form of trade protectionism.

Pricing international trade appropriately so that it accurately reflects all direct and indirect costs and benefits is a huge challenge. Getting the prices of the world's goods and services to accurately reflect their true contributions to global warming is the most urgent issue facing international trade negotiators. Part 3 of this textbook deals with international trade policy in more detail.

CONCLUSIONS

This chapter began with a discussion of adjustment costs associated with shifts in international trade. The HO model assumes these away, but they could be quite significant, at least for some people who lose jobs or end up with unusable capital. The fixed-factor model formalizes the situation where capital cannot be transferred to other uses. Also discussed were a variety of transport costs, networking costs, and other transactions costs that the HO model assumes away. Evidence suggests that transport and transactions costs may be the single most important determinant of international trade.

This chapter introduced the issue of how international trade affects the number of jobs. The HO model and its Stolper-Samuelson theorem seem to address this issue. The Stolper-Samuelson theorem also explicitly addresses the issue of how international trade affects the distribution of income. However, heterodox economists extend the analysis of how trade affects the distribution of income far beyond what the HO model covers. For one thing, the vast evidence from behavioral economics, psychology, and neuroscience shows that the orthodox neoclassical welfare function does not accurately reflect how people really judge their personal welfare. Furthermore, the interdisciplinary evidence contradicts the neoclassical assumption of a stable social welfare function that is an aggregation of separable individual welfare functions. Once we recognize that one person's welfare is influenced by others' welfare, there is no longer a unique social welfare function. Variations in how people react to each other imply a near-infinite number of possible national aggregate welfare functions, each dependent on a particular distribution of income, jobs, and other variables that influence our well-being. Many of these variables are themselves influenced by the same international trade that we want to judge using the social welfare function!

The discussion of human happiness hopefully convinces you that orthodox welfare analysis is not valid. Instead, international trade must be judged not only according to whether average per capita GDP rises or falls, but by how total GDP is distributed, how variables not included in GDP but shown to be important for human happiness, like friendship, social status, job stability, and risks of death are affected. The conclusions of the HO model must be adjusted to reflect changes in social status, disruptions to people's valued lifestyles, the distribution of the costs and benefits of trade, and the fact that continued increases in material consumption do not provide a useful measure of human progress. The benefits of international trade as predicted by models from the orthodox neoclassical paradigm have to be reassessed.

Finally, this chapter introduced externalities, which are costs and benefits not included in the prices at which products are traded. The HO model assumes those problems are not present, but heterodox economists familiar with the broader social and natural spheres of human existence and the holistic interactions between those spheres know that market prices never capture all costs and benefits associated with economic activities. Adjustments are possible and, in the case of pressing social and environmental problems, urgently needed.

CHAPTER SUMMARY

1. This chapter examines how some of the HO model's predictions change if we drop some of the model's strong assumptions.

2. The first section of this chapter extends the basic HO model by dropping the assumption that there are no transport or other transactions costs related to the export and import of goods and services.

3. The supply and demand model of trade shows that, when transport costs are explicitly accounted for, the volume of and the gains from trade are reduced, all other things equal.

4. Transportation costs and contract enforcement costs are but two examples of what we generally call transactions costs, which are all the explicit costs, the time, and the preparation necessary in order to carry out the exchange of goods and services. Transactions costs include business activities such as marketing.

5. Since Jan Tinbergen's (1962) first use of the gravity model to explain international trade patterns, economists have consistently found that a model such as equation (4.3) statistically "explains" almost all of the variation in

international trade flows between countries. In short, distance is an important determinant of international trade.

6. A sudden shift in international trade is likely to close factories and cause unemployment.

7. An economy that suddenly faces a new set of relative prices after opening its borders to international trade may not only find it very costly to shift resources; it may not be able to shift resources at all.

8. Studies that have looked at a large sample of different countries at a given point in time do seem to suggest that life satisfaction or happiness is positively related to income. However, the relationship is not linear.

9. Happiness research reveals that average human happiness does not change very much as real average per capita income grows over time, and people are much more conscious of their relative income and status.

10. Producers do not always pay the full costs of the resources used in production, nor do buyers pay a price that exactly represents benefits provided by a product, which means there are important externalities to international trade that are not accounted for.

11. The internalization of the external cost of carbon emissions seems to reduce the gains from international trade, but the external costs were always present, of course, and a model that ignores them is inaccurate.

12. Economists should measure the gains and losses from trade after duly taking into account the costs of adapting to new jobs, losing investment incomes, or changing relative incomes and social status.

13. The conclusions of the HO model must be adjusted to reflect the fact that continued increases in material consumption do not provide a useful measure of human progress.

KEY TERMS AND CONCEPTS

automatic processes
cabotage
carbon tax
Cocagne
Convention on International Civil Aviation
deliberative (cognitive) processes
emotional processes
enclosure
fixed-factors model
gravity model of trade
greenhouse gas (GHG)
greenhouse gas emissions

happiness studies
happiness surveys
homeostasis
just-in-time supply systems
Maghribi traders
neuroscience
shrinkage
Silk Road
static model
territoriality
transactions costs

PROBLEMS AND QUESTIONS

1. Our fantasies about what constitutes "paradise" have changed somewhat, but not entirely, since medieval times. How are our visions of an ideal world still similar to what Pleij found through his survey of literature and art from medieval times?

2. Describe the main conclusions from evidence on transport costs over the past several centuries. Will the trends continue in the future? Explain.

3. Use the supply and demand model of transport costs to explain how falling transport costs affect international trade. Supplement your graphic model with a verbal explanation of the model and how it illustrates your main points.

4. Happiness surveys tend to use either the term *happy* or the term *life satisfaction.* Is there a difference? Which do you prefer?

5. Describe and explain the main conclusions derived from surveys of human happiness and the happiness research that uses these survey results to explain human behavior.

6. Given the results of happiness research, answer the question at the end of the section titled "International Trade, Income Inequality, and Welfare" in this chapter: Is it really worth causing a lot of people to lose their jobs in order to increase the income of others in society?

7. Arik Levinson and Scott Taylor (2008) examine data for a set of twenty industries impacted by new environmental regulation in the United States, and they find that about half the increase in U.S. imports can be statistically explained by the increases in regulation. What policies could address this "race to the bottom?"

8. What are the consequences of ignoring externalities? Can you think of specific examples in which externalities are ignored? What are the losses from ignoring the externalities in your examples?

9. Explain how the DEFRA-sponsored study on Britain's carbon footprint differs from common production-based estimates of countries' carbon footprints.

10. Write a brief essay to address the question: Is increased international specialization and trade good for the environment?

11. Contrast the HO model presented in Chapter 3 with Figure 4.4 in this chapter. Specifically, how does each model explain the adjustment of the economy in response to the opening of international trade? Which do you think is more realistic?

12. Many people equate international trade with either the loss or gain in the number of jobs in their economy. How does the HO model address the "jobs issue"? Does trade create or destroy jobs? Discuss.

Notes

1. C.K. Harley (1988); Douglass C. North (1958).

2. Philippe Aghion and Jeffrey G. Williamson (1998), p. 136.

3. Ibid.

4. Kevin H. O'Rourke and Jeffrey G. Williamson (1999), p. 36.

5. U.S. Bureau of the Census (1998), *Statistical Abstract of the United States,* Washington, DC: GPO.

6. Avner Greif (1989), p. 865.

7. Ibid., p. 868.

8. Adam Smith (1776 [1976]), p. 494.

9. Alan Blinder (2006). See also David Wessel and Bob Davis (2007).

10. Robert Scott (2008).

11. Aristotle, *Rhetoric.*

12. Herman Pleij (2001), p. 3.

13. The results of these surveys are in the World Database of Happiness, directed by Ruut Veenhoven of Erasmus University, Rotterdam, the Netherlands, http://worlddatabaseofhappiness.eur.nl/.

14. The results of the study Lyken led are reported in detail in: T.J. Bouchard Jr., D.T. Lykken, M. McGue, N.L. Segal, and A. Tellegen (1990). "Sources of human psychological differences: the Minnesota Study of Twins Reared Apart." *Science* 250 (4978): 223–228. The results and the set point concept are discussed in Lykken (1999).

15. Richard A. Easterlin (2003b).

CHAPTER 5

International Trade: Imperfect Competition and Transnational Corporations

> How does the market, whose principle is one-dollar/one-vote, properly coexist with a political democracy whose basic rule is "one person/one vote"?
>
> —Robert Kuttner (1999)

The assumption of perfect competition is very convenient for justifying laissez-faire economic policies. In neoclassical economic models, the assumption of perfect competition in combination with other assumptions such as the absence of externalities, no transactions costs, perfect information, and rising marginal costs means that prices can be assumed to perfectly reflect underlying opportunity costs. It then becomes possible to conclude that profit maximization by producers and welfare-maximizing behavior by budget-constrained consumers indeed brings about efficient outcomes that maximize overall human well-being. The problem with the assumption of perfectly competitive markets is that there are no perfectly competitive markets in a real economy. Those perfectly competitive markets assumed in neoclassical economic models are a myth, not a reasonable approximation of real world market behavior.

Recognizing the bias that the assumption of perfect competition introduced into neoclassical models of international economics, in the early 1980s several international economists began looking at models of international trade that assumed that most product markets are imperfectly competitive. Models were developed in which production was characterized by **increasing returns to scale** and, therefore, international trade occurred in markets in which just a few large and differentiated producers supplied products at prices that exceeded marginal costs. This chapter examines a simple model of trade in which production is subject to increasing returns to scale and producers are, therefore, not perfectly competitive.

This chapter also examines another outcome of increasing returns to scale and the resulting concentration of production in the hands of a few large, imperfectly competitive producers, namely the growth of **transnational corporations (TNCs)**. TNCs dominate international trade as well as international investment and international finance. An important question thus arises: Are the neoclassical models of international trade, which are based on the assumption of perfect competition, accurate in a world in which nearly all international trade is carried out by TNCs? In this world, does free trade maximize welfare in all countries?

INCREASING RETURNS TO SCALE AND INTERNATIONAL TRADE

The Heckscher-Ohlin (HO) model concludes that the gains from trade are greatest when countries with very different relative price ratios exchange goods and services. The more the slope of the world price line differs from the slope of the domestic price line, the greater is trade and the higher is the new indifference curve reached. But, is it that most of the world's international trade takes place between fairly similarly developed economies where price ratios are very similar. This section examines this puzzle and provides an alternative model of trade based on the concept of increasing returns to scale.

Intra-industry Trade

The exchange of products produced by the same industry is referred to as **intra-industry trade**. Economists have measured such trade by carefully classifying actual trade data, and these data reveal several interesting patterns. Nigel Grimwade (1989) calculated an index to measure the proportion of intra-industry trade in a country's overall international trade and found that this index is several times larger for developed economies than for developing ones. Bela Balassa (1986) compared a group of eighteen developed economies and twenty developing economies and found that intra-industry trade increases systematically as a country's per capita income rises. If developed countries indeed engage in more intra-industry trade than developing economies, and if world incomes keep rising, then intra-industry trade as a share of total trade will keep rising as well. The HO model of trade is therefore caught in the position of not being able to explain a large portion of world trade.

The HO model suggests that the greatest gains from trade result from trade between those countries that are most different in terms of their productive capacity or their tastes. Yet, as Figure 5.1 shows, as recently as 1998, nearly 60 percent of the world's trade was occurring between high-income economies that have relatively similar production possibilities frontiers (PPFs) and consumer preferences. Only about one-third of world trade was between developed and developing countries, trade partners that are much more diverse in terms of their factor endowments, their technologies, and their consumer preferences. Ten years later, however, trade among high-income countries was close to 50 percent of the total. World Trade Organization (WTO) 2010 data show that trade between developed and developing countries was boosted by the rapidly growing industrial exports by China, India, Brazil, and other developing economies. The WTO data show that in 2008 about 20 percent of U.S. imports were from China alone, up from under 8 percent as recently as 2000. Still, the majority of trade was disproportionately between relatively similar economies.

The conflict between the HO model of international trade and the observations that (1) a large proportion of trade is intra-industry trade and (2) most trade takes place among similar countries suggests the HO model of trade is not a general model that can explain all, or even most, international trade. In the 1980s, trade economists found that by assuming increasing returns to scale and imperfect competition, they could explain a pattern of specialization and exchange that enhances intra-industry trade among similarly endowed countries.

Modeling Increasing Returns to Scale

The increasing returns to scale model of trade drops the assumption of perfect competition and assumes that producers become more efficient the larger they grow and the more they produce. This assumption is compatible with the observation that just about all international trade in manufactured goods is carried out by large, multinational firms rather than large numbers of small, competitive firms.

The shapes of the production possibilities frontiers that were used to model the two-product economy in the previous chapter were drawn concave to the origin. Such PPFs imply increasing costs; ever-greater sacrifices of one good are necessary in order to gain additional units of the other good. Many production processes are not subject to increasing costs, however. In many industries the cost of producing additional units of output actually decreases, at least over some range of output. Such industries are said to operate under increasing returns to scale. For example, increasing

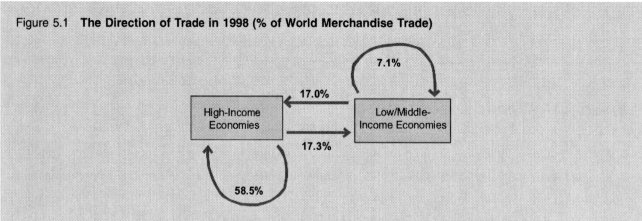

Figure 5.1 **The Direction of Trade in 1998 (% of World Merchandise Trade)**

Source: The World Bank (2000), *World Development Indicators 2000*, Washington, DC, Table 6.2.

returns to scale define the situation where an increase in inputs of 10 percent raises output by more than 10 percent.

A common example of an industry that exhibits increasing returns to scale is the automobile industry. It would take quite an effort to produce an automobile in your garage, even if you could acquire an extensive set of machines, tools, and raw materials. You would go through a lot of trial and error as you learned to make the parts and assemble them, and you would probably forget some of what you learned before you would be called on to perform the same task again. The final cost of the automobile in terms of your labor, machinery, and raw materials would be very high. Henry Ford proved nearly a century ago that an assembly-line process in which each worker performs identical tasks can turn out a large number of identical automobiles at a much lower per unit cost and with superior quality. Today, nearly all manufacturing is subject to increasing returns to scale, at least over a substantial range of output, as evidenced by the fact that there are usually only a few large firms in markets for manufactured goods. Mining and transportation industries also have small numbers of large firms. Even in agriculture and the food industry, larger operations are dominant.

What does the PPF look like if one or both of the industries exhibit increasing returns to scale? A possible PPF is given in Figure 5.2, where it is assumed that two industries, automobiles and frozen pizzas, both exhibit increasing returns to scale. The PPF is convex to the origin, with the diminishing slope reflecting the increasingly *smaller* amounts of one product that must be sacrificed in order to achieve ever *greater* amounts of the other.

In general, if large firms can produce at lower cost than small firms, the market will tend to have one or a small number of large firms rather than a large number of small competitors characteristic of perfectly competitive markets. Large firms do not behave as price takers; rather, they explicitly take into consideration the effects of their actions on prices. Figure 5.3 depicts a typical large firm with declining average and marginal cost curves facing a downward-sloping demand curve. The profit-maximizing imperfect competitor equates marginal cost and marginal revenue. Monopoly profits are possible, as in the case of the shaded area in Figure 5.3. Note that when sellers have some degree of monopoly power, the assumption that prices of goods exactly reflect the costs of the resources used to produce the goods no longer holds.

Large manufacturers often differentiate their products and promote their brands in order to raise demand for their products and make it less elastic. A Ford Focus is not the same as a Nissan Altima. Coca-Cola is not the same as a Pepsi-Cola. The question here is: Does international trade still increase welfare when production is characterized by increasing returns to scale and there is imperfect competition? This is an important question because mainstream perfect competition models in Chapter 4 concluded that free trade

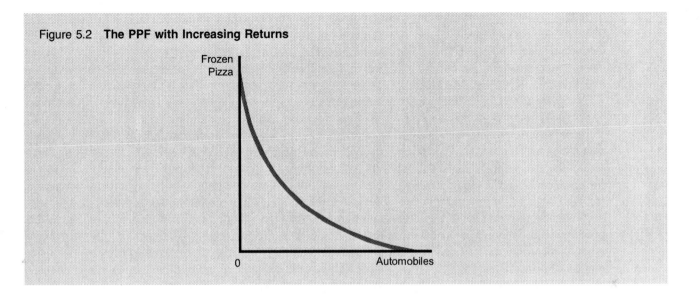

Figure 5.2 **The PPF with Increasing Returns**

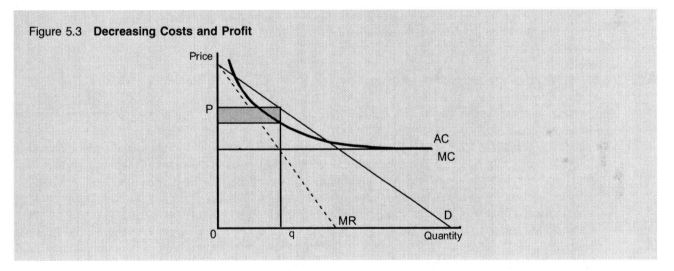

Figure 5.3 **Decreasing Costs and Profit**

improves a country's overall level of welfare. But with increasing returns to scale and declining costs, there will be no perfect competition. We will find that trade may still increase national welfare under increasing returns and imperfect competition, but the reasons why trade increases welfare are different.

An Example of Two Identical Countries

Suppose there are two economies in the world, each producing only books and pizza. (What more could you need?) Suppose also that they have identical PPFs, and that both the book industry and the frozen pizza industry operate under increasing returns to scale. Both countries' PPFs are therefore convex to the origin and look like the PPF in Figure 5.3 above. Suppose also that consumers have typical tastes represented by the standard indifference curves that exhibit varying preferences that depend on the relative quantities of books and pizzas. These assumptions eliminate differences in tastes, differences in the availability of productive resources, or differences in technology as possible influences on trade.

In the absence of trade, each economy produces and consumes where its PPF is tangent to the indifference curve I_1, as in Figure 5.4, and the relative prices of books and pizza will be the same in both countries. The equilibria in the two identical economies are at A and A*, respectively. Neither country appears to have a comparative advantage: the opportunity costs are the same in each country at 1 book equals 1 pizza. Welfare in each country is represented by the indifference curves I_1 and I_1*, respectively. But, if both tastes and the PPFs are the same in both countries, how can there be gains from trade?

Increasing returns to scale create an interesting conflict: consumers prefer more variety to less variety, but the cost of each product is lower if consumers opt for less variety by consuming only one of the two goods. This conflict becomes more benign if countries A and B agree to trade freely. Suppose each country specializes in producing just one of the two goods, fully exploiting increasing returns to scale, and then exchanges books for pizzas or pizzas for books so that their consumers continue to enjoy the variety of both books and pizza. For example, if Country A specializes in the production of books and produces at d, and Country B produces only pizzas at b*, then they can set relative prices as given by the dashed lines and exchange books and pizzas as illustrated by the identical shaded trade triangles in Figure 5.5. This lets the two countries consume the combinations of books and pizza B and B*, respectively, and reach the higher indifference curves I_2 and I_2*. So, trade raises human welfare in each nation even though Country A and Country B are identical. With increasing returns and identical resources, each country effectively gains a comparative advantage when an increasing-returns-to-scale industry lowers its costs below those of the same, but smaller, industry in the other country.

Krugman's Model of Variety, Increasing Returns, and Trade

Paul Krugman extended the basic logic of the simple example of two countries and two goods above and developed a more general model of international trade when production is characterized by increasing returns to scale. In his classic article "Increasing Returns, Monopolistic Competition, and International Trade (1979)," he assumed that the world consisted of several identical economies, each with the potential for producing a wide range of products whose production functions are all subject to increasing returns to scale. He also assumed that consumers preferred more variety to less variety. As in the case of the simple model above, with increasing returns to scale making large-scale production cheaper but consumers preferring more variety to less variety, a choice would need to be made. The economy thus has to decide whether to concentrate production in a small number of large industries that produce very large amounts of just a few products very inexpensively or in a large number of different small-scale, high-cost industries.

Krugman showed that international trade makes possible a one-time gain in welfare from both *lower unit costs* and *increased variety*. By specializing, each country produces a larger quantity of fewer goods, thereby taking advantage of increasing returns to scale. And, by exchanging some portion of each of the goods for different foreign goods, each country increases the variety of goods available to its consumers. For example, suppose that in the absence of international trade each identical country balances variety and unit-cost results by producing 1,000 differentiated products. In the case of free trade, however, new options become available. For example, each country could continue producing their 1,000 products and send half of the total of each product overseas in exchange for half of each of the 1,000 products produced by the other country. In this case, consumers in each country would enjoy a doubling of the variety of products without any increase in unit costs. On the other hand, each country could cut the number of different products it produces in half, thus more than doubling the production of each of the remaining products, and then export half of each of those products. In this case, consumers in each country would enjoy lower prices while still enjoying 1,000 different products. Most likely, since consumers value *both* variety and low costs, trade will

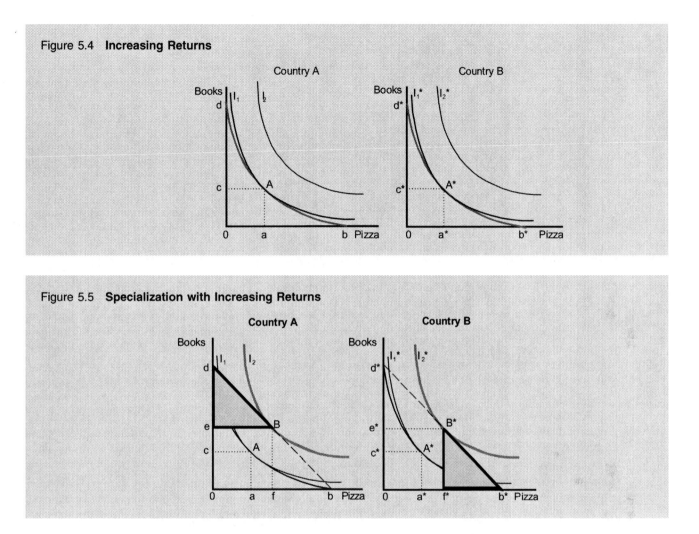

Figure 5.4 **Increasing Returns**

Country A

Country B

Figure 5.5 **Specialization with Increasing Returns**

Country A

Country B

result in some intermediate solution—for example, each country produces larger quantities of 750 different products and consumers thus have access to 1,500 different products. Under this idealized scenario, international trade permits more favorable compromises between costs and variety.

Some Further Implications of the Model

An interesting implication of the simple economies of scale trade model above is that the direction of specialization by each of the two initially identical economies is arbitrary. What made one country specialize in pizza and the other in books? Nor is the model clear on why the two countries would settle for the terms of trade necessary to bring countries A and B to points B and B*, respectively. In practice, these decisions are made by large firms that think and act strategically. Therefore, depending on the size of the firms, their market positions, and consumer demand, a great variety of outcomes are possible. There is also a timing issue: the first firm to expand and exploit increasing returns gains the comparative advantage.

There may be competition among imperfectly competitive corporations to gain a competitive advantage in those businesses that will in the future generate the greatest profits. For example, the **income elasticity of demand** may be such that, as economies grow and income increases, demand increases more for pizza than for books. To illustrate this possibility, suppose that, unlike

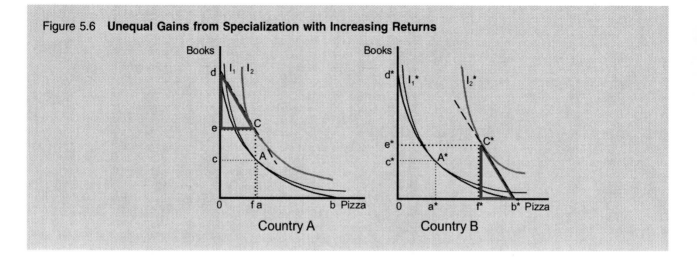

Figure 5.6 **Unequal Gains from Specialization with Increasing Returns**

the nice equal outcomes in Figure 5.5, the relative prices at which trade occurs brings the two identical countries very different gains from trading books and pizza. Figure 5.6 shows Country A gaining relatively less than Country B. People value pizza more than books, which means that the higher demand for pizza moves the **terms of trade** in favor of Country B, the country that arbitrarily ended up specializing in pizza production and gaining the comparative advantage in that industry.

Research on trade under increasing returns to scale and imperfect competition suggests that (1) international trade can still be welfare enhancing, but (2) completely free trade is not necessarily the optimal trade policy. Or, as Krugman points out, "showing that free trade is better than no trade is not the same thing as showing that free trade is better than sophisticated government intervention."[1] Perhaps government policy can push the direction of international trade toward a more favorable outcome, such as the point C* in Figure 5.6. In a world where some governments actively support their exporters, a country whose government remains inactive would effectively default to inferior outcomes such as point C.

Policies to protect and promote industries with the greatest growth potential are called **strategic trade policies**. In the example above, policies by the government of country B to protect, subsidize, or otherwise encourage the pizza industry would constitute such a strategic trade policy. In Chapter 10, we will return to this issue of whether, under imperfect competition, policies that intentionally attempt to influence international trade flows can be welfare improving for a country.

Another Implication of Imperfect Competition: Transnational Corporations

Increasing returns to scale are common in manufacturing, mining, agriculture, and many other productive activities. The model of two identical countries above suggests that national welfare can still increase from international trade when production is subject to increasing returns to scale. This is reassuring because so many of the products traded are produced in factories and firms whose activities are subject to economies of scale.

Economists have also found that once they drop the Heckscher-Ohlin model's assumptions of perfect competition and increasing costs, some new conclusions become apparent. As already noted, it becomes clear why most trade occurs between very similar economies. Second, strategic trade restrictions protecting a specific industry or set of industries can be welfare increasing for a country.

Third, perfect competition breaks down when there are increasing returns to scale, which means that international trade is conducted by monopolistic producers that charge prices that exceed their production costs.

The standard HO model of trade is no longer accurate when international trade is the concentration of business activity dominated by transnational corporations (TNCs) with economies of scale in production, marketing, research, and distribution. The growth of TNCs links international trade to international investment, market structures, and institutional factors that are not covered in the HO model of trade. TNCs with market power can increase profit margins and gain income at the expense of consumers and workers, thus altering the distribution of the gains from trade. When a large portion of the gains from trade is in the form of corporate profits, the country with the most stockholders of TNCs gains the most from international trade, while workers and many other groups across all countries may experience declining real incomes.

These conclusions about the role of TNCs in the international economy will be viewed as radical by many mainstream economists. But, ironically, it is the analysis developed by mainstream economists, as well as the data collected by these same economists, that brings us logically to these conclusions. The fact is that TNCs, not small national firms, dominate international trade, and the foreign direct investment that constructs these TNCs dominates long-run international investment flows. There is also vast evidence from economists who study trade policy that the concentration of wealth in the hands of TNCs has enabled them to influence and, in many cases, permanently shape international institutions in ways that favor the further growth of TNCs. Part 3 of this textbook discusses international trade policy and the role of special interest groups in setting policy. The remainder of this chapter examines the TNC in detail.

FOREIGN DIRECT INVESTMENT

Foreign direct investment (FDI) is investment in overseas facilities in which the investor has a controlling interest. It is fundamentally different from the purchase of many other types of financial assets, such as buying 100 shares in a foreign firm, buying a bond, or making a bank loan. FDI involves active participation in the management and financial monitoring of the foreign investment.[2] FDI is closely related to TNCs because it is FDI that creates TNCs. There are, apparently, advantages to direct ownership and control of foreign businesses. FDI has grown very large in the second half of the twentieth century.

We examine FDI here because it is closely related to international trade. For example, in the early 2000s close to 90 percent of U.S. imports and exports involved a transnational corporation on at least one side of the transaction. Over one-third of global merchandise exports are to foreign branches of the same TNC! Evidence suggests that international trade now often occurs because TNCs intentionally invest in factories and **marketing** organizations to exploit the comparative advantages of different economies.

Given the growing role of TNCs in both international trade and international investment, it is obvious that the simple economic models cannot, by themselves, accurately describe either phenomenon. In fact, TNCs complicate the analysis of international economic integration in many ways.

The Growth of Foreign Direct Investment and Transnational Corporations

FDI has grown rapidly in recent decades. During the 1960s, FDI accounted for about 6 percent of all international investment, in 1990 for about 20 percent, and by the 2000s it occasionally surpassed 30 percent. During the 1990s, FDI grew at a rate about three times as fast as overall investment worldwide.[3] The accumulated stock of FDI has grown from about $3.2 trillion in 1990 to well over

$10 trillion in 2005. In real terms, this amounts to a doubling of total FDI in fifteen years. Over $1.25 trillion was added in 2000 alone, the year when FDI reached its all-time one-year high. In 2006, there were about 160,000 foreign affiliates belonging to almost 60,000 TNCs throughout the world.[4] Table 5.1 provides some details. Notice that FDI to developing countries has grown much faster, from $21 billion to over $1 trillion, than overall FDI. Most FDI still flows from developed to other developed economies, however. Also, note that "finance" accounts for about half of services FDI. We will discuss international banking in later chapters.

By extending a business organization across borders, FDI effectively creates *transnational corporations* (TNCs), which are firms that manage and own production and distribution facilities in more than one country. Hence, by definition, multinational firms carry out all of the world's FDI in foreign firms or foreign real assets. The presence of TNCs also implies that international trade is carried out not only between different firms located in different countries, but now often between different branches of the same firm located in different countries. Such trade is called **intra-firm trade**, and it means that the same management now often controls both the exporter in one country and the importer in another country.

Vertical and Horizontal Foreign Direct Investment

Vertical FDI occurs when a TNC builds or acquires foreign facilities that comprise one stage of its complete production process. An example of a vertical foreign direct investment is the Ford Motor Company's engine plant in Brazil, which supplies engine blocks to Ford assembly plants in Brazil, Europe, and the United States. Similarly, Toyota Motor Corporation's wholesale organizations, located in nearly every country of the world, are vertically related to its manufacturing plants, located in just a few countries.

Horizontal FDI, on the other hand, duplicates facilities and operations that the TNC already owns and operates in other countries. The huge French retailer Carrefour, for example, operates distribution centers and chains of retail stores in a number of countries, and its investment in distribution, warehousing, and retail facilities is similar in every country. Ford and Toyota operate assembly plants producing the same cars in several different countries.

TNC investments across developed economies are more often horizontal investments, and TNC activity in developing countries more often serves to vertically integrate the supply chain. Howard Shatz and Anthony Venables (2000) estimated that less than 4 percent of production by European affiliates of U.S. TNCs was sent back to the U.S. market, but 18 percent of U.S. affiliate production in developing economies was exported to the United States. U.S. affiliates in Mexico sent 40 percent of their output to their parent firms in the United States. Shatz and Venables also confirmed S. Lael Brainard's (1997) finding that a TNC's geographic distribution of production was more likely to be horizontal when transport costs and trade barriers are large relative to the gains from economies of scale at the factory level. Vertical FDI is, therefore, driven by factor cost differences, a principal determinant of comparative advantage. This seems to be a restatement of a pattern of international trade noted half a century ago: factor endowments drive trade between developed and developing countries and increasing returns to scale more often determine trade between developed countries.

Richard E. Caves (1996) warns that FDI is a complex phenomenon driven by a combination of many factors. For example, horizontal foreign subsidiaries of the TNCs engaging in manufacturing in different countries often still exchange products in order to fill out their lines with imports from corporate affiliates in other countries. In effect, differences in comparative advantages, transactions costs, transportation costs, tariffs and quotas, and market size across countries and industries lead TNCs to engage in a variety of investment projects throughout the world, some horizontal, some vertical.

Table 5.1

Estimated World FDI Stock, by Sector and Industry: 1990 and 2005 (billions of US$)

	1990			2005		
	MDCs*	LDCs**	World	MDCs*	LDCs**	World
Primary	161.5	2.2	163.8	584.1	35.4	618.6
Agriculture, forestry, and fishing	5.2	0.3	5.6	4.3	1.6	5.9
Mining, quarrying, petroleum	156.3	1.9	158.2	577.4	33.8	610.2
Manufacturing	793.6	6.4	800.0	2,655.3	117.4	2,774.3
Food, beverages, tobacco	75.6	0.4	76.0	298.8	2.5	301.4
Textiles, clothing, leather	19.6	0.2	19.7	132.2	3.2	135.5
Wood and wood products	21.5	0.0	21.6	81.7	2.1	83.8
Publishing, printing, recorded media	2.3	—	2.3	15.6	0.0	15.7
Coke, oil refining, nuclear products	39.3	—	19.3	35.7	0.0	35.7
Chemicals	150.9	0.8	151.7	560.0	3.6	564.5
Rubber and plastic products	14.5	0.1	14.6	33.7	2.2	35.9
Nonmetallic mineral products	13.1	0.2	13.3	35.3	0.8	36.2
Metal products	66.4	0.9	66.4	266.3	1.5	268.1
Machinery and equipment	42.0	0.0	42.1	108.9	0.5	109.5
Electrical and electronic equipment	97.5	1.0	98.5	240.6	9.0	149.6
Precision instruments	13.5	—	13.5	50.8	0.3	51.0
Motor vehicles, transport equipment	60.3	0.0	60.3	427.4	1.3	428.7
Other manufacturing and unspecified	177.1	3.5	181.6	368.3	90.3	458.7
Services	834.9	11.6	846.6	6,264.0	830.7	7,095.6
Electricity, gas, water	9.6	—	9.6	96.5	6.8	103.7
Construction	18.2	0.2	18.4	73.1	8.7	81.1
Trade	139.9	1.9	141.8	631.1	107.2	738.4
Hotels and restaurants	7.1	—	7.1	96.2	8.6	104.8
Transport, storage, communications	39.8	0.5	40.3	557.4	53.6	611.2
Finance	400.0	7.2	407.2	2,208.9	176.7	2,385.8
Real estate sales	—	—	—	1.7	—	1.7
Business activities	55.1	1.3	56.4	2,127.2	454.3	2,582.1
Public administration and defense	—	—	—	4.0	—	4.0
Education	0.4	—	0.4	0.4	—	0.4
Health and social services	0.9	—	0.9	1.2	—	1.2
Community, social services	3.4	—	3.4	19.5	1.7	21.2
Other services and unspecified	160.5	0.5	161.0	448.5	13.1	461.6
Total	1,794.2	20.9	1,815.2	9,570.4	1,005.1	10,577.1

* More developed countries; ** Less developed countries

Source: UNCTAD (2007), *World Investment Report 2007*, New York: United Nations Conference on Trade and Development, Annex Table A.1.11.

A Brief History of Transnational Corporations

Business firms have spread their operations across borders for centuries. In fact, some 2,500 years ago Sumerian merchants stationed employees abroad to sell goods or receive foreign products to be sent back home, thus technically satisfying the definition of FDI. By 1600, private companies began setting up permanent operations in colonial regions protected by their governments' armies and navies. Mira Wilkins (1970) describes the 1606 settlement at Jamestown, Virginia (the first European settlement in what is today the United States), as FDI by the British-based Virginia Company.

Some historians point to the **Verenigde Oost-Indische Compagnie (VOC)**, or the **Dutch East India Company**, as the first transnational corporation. In 1602, the company was granted a charter to conduct colonial activities in Asia, and it financed itself by selling stock on the Amsterdam Stock Exchange. The VOC issued two types of stock, one type for *participanten,* or general stockholders, and another for *bewindhebbers,* or managing partners. Dutch joint-stock companies were unique in that both types of stockholders had limited liability. Also, both types of stock were permanent during the lifetime of the firm, and liquidation of stock ownership could be done only by selling the stock on the stock exchange. Interestingly, the VOC was encouraged by the Dutch monarchy in order to create a private monopoly that could counter the colonial enterprises of Spain and Portugal. The Netherlands had just gained independence from Spain, whose royal family had ruled the Low Countries until the latter part of the sixteenth century, and by 1600 Dutch traders were clashing with Portuguese and Spanish traders in the Far East spice trade. The VOC was organized into six divisions (chambers) located in six Dutch ports, and stock was issued for each division. But the enterprise operated as a whole, and overall policy was set by a board of seventeen directors, with less than a majority from any one of the six cities.

The VOC became very profitable. It operated ports throughout India, Ceylon, the Philippines, China, and Indonesia. The overseas headquarters of the firm moved among several ports until, in 1619 with a fleet of nineteen ships and a small private army, the VOC conquered the port of Jaya-karta (today's Jakarta) in Indonesia. It renamed the city and port Batavia, which was retained until Indonesia gained independence in 1949. The VOC used a combination of force, money, and business sense to build the largest overseas trading network of its time. The VOC was even permitted to maintain its trading post in Nagasaki, Japan, after that country otherwise closed itself completely to foreign trade in the seventeenth century. The VOC thus served as the outside world's only trade channel with Japan until the United States Navy and its black ships forced Japan to reopen trade with the outside world two hundred years later.

The VOC remained profitable and solvent until the very late 1700s, when changing global trade patterns made its trading network obsolete and internal corruption weakened its financial state. The Dutch government took over the colony of Indonesia that the VOC had cobbled together from a large number of islands, and Indonesia became a true Dutch colony after two hundred years of being a private colonial enterprise.

The examples of Jamestown and the Dutch East India Company suggest that there was a direct connection between transnational companies and **colonialism**. That is indeed a correct interpretation of the period before the start of the nineteenth century. Most private overseas business ventures operated either in colonies of their European home countries, or, as in the case of the VOC, in what would later become official colonies controlled by European governments but which were initiated by the private transnational companies. It was not until the nineteenth century that the modern transnational enterprise, not directly linked to colonial governments, emerged.

The Singer Company's opening of a sewing machine factory in Scotland in the late 1860s is often given as the earliest example of modern FDI. I.M. Singer and Company was formed in New York in 1851 after Isaac Singer perfected the bobbin, the technological breakthrough that made mechanical sewing possible. Singer's early business plan was to set up manufacturing in Elizabeth, New Jersey, and to offer exclusive territories within the United States to local independent distributors. It soon found it more advantageous to organize its own marketing organization, as the performance of independent distributors was mixed, at best. The Singer Company took a different approach to foreign markets, however; in 1855 it authorized a French company to manufacture its sewing machines in France for a royalty of 15 percent. This arrangement did not prove to be profitable either. The French firm was found to be underreporting how many machines it manufactured in France in order to reduce its royalty payments. Singer therefore switched to expanding its own sales organizations overseas as well. By 1861, Singer had sales offices with its own employees in Glasgow and London.

After the Civil War, U.S. sales grew very rapidly, and Singer had trouble supplying the British and other European markets from its New Jersey factory. Rather than expand its New Jersey manufacturing capacity even faster, Singer decided in 1867 to open a factory in Glasgow, Scotland, thus becoming a truly transnational manufacturer. By the end of the nineteenth century, Singer operated a network of sales organizations, retail stores, distribution centers, and factories in over 100 countries.[5]

In 1914, nearly three-fourths of U.S.-owned assets abroad were direct investments. This was not the case for other countries; most British investment overseas consisted of bonds and bank lending. Early in the twentieth century, when the United States was still a net debtor to the rest of the world overall, its FDI greatly exceeded foreigners' FDI in the United States. As recently as 1960, half of the world's accumulated stock of FDI was owned by U.S.-based TNCs.

Foreign TNCs began to invest much more heavily in the United States in the 1980s and quickly made up for lost time. In 2000, foreigners' new FDI in the United States was nearly twice as great as U.S. FDI abroad.[6] Worldwide, in 2000 U.S. TNCs owned less than one-fourth of the world's accumulated stock of FDI, compared to about half some forty years earlier. The growth of TNCs in other countries is evidenced by the fact that in the early 2000s about 10 percent of the accumulated stock of FDI was owned by TNCs based in developing countries.[7] Among such developing-country FDI are the recent purchases of the personal computer business of International Business Machines Corporation (IBM) by the Chinese firm Lenovo and of Ford's Jaguar division by the Indian firm Tata Motors.

Transnational Corporations and International Trade

In 1982, a U.S. government study on the TNCs' share in U.S. foreign trade revealed that of the total U.S. exports of $212.2 billion in 1982, $203.4 billion (95.9 percent of the total) were made by U.S. TNCs (72.2 percent of total exports) and affiliates of foreign TNCs (23.7 percent). At the same time, U.S. and foreign TNCs in the United States imported 77 percent of all goods imported into the United States. The data also highlighted the fact that a substantial portion of exports and imports were intra-firm trade. Specifically, the data showed that of total exports of $212.2 billion, $46.6 billion were by U.S. TNCs to their foreign affiliates and $20.2 billion were by U.S. affiliates of foreign TNCs to their own firms' home-country operations. That is, 31.5 percent of all U.S. goods exports were intra-firm transfers. For imports the situation was similar: 36.6 percent of all U.S. imports were intra-firm transfers.

More recent studies suggest that TNCs' role in international trade has certainly not diminished since the detailed study of the 1980s.[8] According to William J. Zeile (2005) and Raymond J. Mataloni, Jr. (2005), the percentages of intra-TNC imports and exports in the United States in 2003 were 32 percent and 38 percent, respectively—slightly larger shares than in the 1980s.

EXPLAINING THE GROWTH OF TRANSNATIONAL CORPORATIONS

There are many reasons for the growth of transnational corporations, but most of the explanation centers around the advantages of **internalizing transactions** within a single business organization. In general, if a business firm finds it is less costly to *internalize* transactions than to engage in "arm's-length" transactions with other firms, managers will elect to allocate resources *administratively* rather than using market transactions. According to Richard Caves (1996, pp. 1–2):

> The Darwinian tradition holds that the most profitable pattern of enterprise organization should ultimately prevail: Where more profit results from placing plants under a common administrative control, multiplant enterprises will predominate, and single-plant firms will merge or go out of business. In order to explain the existence and prevalence of [TNCs], we require models that predict where the multiplant firm enjoys advantages from displacing the arm's-length market and where it does not. In fact, the prevalence of multiplant (multinational) enterprises varies greatly from sector to sector and from country to country.

In short, if a firm believes that it can best manage its unique assets, talents, technology, and reputations in other national markets by extending its own organization to those locations, then it will opt to become a TNC. The next section details the many advantages of internalization.

Why Transnational Corporations Dominate the Economic Sphere

There are many advantages in spreading a business organization across political borders. The brief list below summarizes the explanations commonly found in the management and finance literature.

1. *Economies of scale*—Firms may become more efficient at a certain tasks the larger their operations become, and therefore a single firm spread throughout the world may be able to produce more efficiently than independent firms located in each of the countries of the world. Certain tasks such as research, product development, central administration, marketing design, and product design are the same no matter how many products are sold. A firm already in possession of a product design or a large research facility would be at a **competitive advantage** vis-à-is a smaller local firm that must start from scratch to develop a product.

2. *Knowledge and technology are difficult to sell*—As the Singer Company discovered in 1856, knowledge and technology are very difficult to trade in markets. Some types of know-how are not easily transferable. Know-how is often unique to the firms that built up the experience that gradually produced the know-how. Thus, these firms must establish overseas units to reap the economic rewards of their accumulated know-how.

3. *The hold-up problem*—Outside suppliers of specialized inputs into a firm's production process are often reluctant to make large investments in capacity and technology to supply specialized products to a specific firm. In fact, a purchasing firm has a real incentive to induce a supplier to make substantial investment in building capacity and know-how for supplying specialized products, and then to "renegotiate" the terms of the contract once the supplier is locked in to this new supplier capacity. Suppliers are leery of opening themselves to such pressure, and they can strengthen their hand by **holding up** their investments until the outsourcing firm agrees to contractual terms more favorable to the supplier. Or, the supplier may insist that the outsourcing firm provide technology, machinery, or other assets up front in order to even out their bargaining positions. The growth of TNCs suggests that it is often easier for a firm to squeeze its own foreign subsidiaries than it is to pressure outside suppliers.

4. *Exploiting core competencies*—**Core competencies** are those activities that provide the firm with its highest markup and profit margins. Modern management theory advocates that firms outsource all activities except for their core competencies, which will guarantee the highest profits. FDI is a logical extension of a core competencies strategy. Rather than let other firms in other countries gain part of the profits from the firm's core competencies, FDI enables the firm to extend its organization globally in order to keep all the core activities in house.

5. *Exploiting reputations*—Many firms build up considerable reputations over the years, and often the only way to exploit a reputation in other markets is to set up operations in those markets. Licensing a foreign firm to produce a product may not transfer the reputation effectively if local consumers know that the product is not produced by its true originator. Successful TNCs are often those firms that have established strong reputations and brands. The importance of reputation and brand recognition tends to favor large firms, which can devote more resources to establishing their brands in the market.

6. *Jumping trade barriers*—If a firm has a reputation, know-how, or fixed product development costs that can be profitably exploited in foreign markets, but trade barriers prevent the export of its products to other markets, then it may be profitable to invest in factories behind the tariff and quota walls that block trade. Protection stimulated FDI activity in the European Union, as non-European TNCs sought to do business in the region after it established common tariffs vis-à-vis the rest of the world but permitted the free flow of goods within its borders.

7. *Avoiding taxes and regulations*—TNCs are often accused of evading environmental and labor regulation by moving production overseas. Since firms seek to minimize costs, there should be little doubt that they would prefer environmental and labor regulations to impose as few costs as possible, all other things equal. Differences in regulation and taxation may make certain business activities more profitable in some countries than others.

8. *Diversification*—By spreading its production and marketing operations more evenly across countries, and thereby better balancing expenses and revenue in each currency, TNCs reduce their exposure to foreign exchange fluctuations. Also, TNCs can reduce their financing costs because, with operations in many countries, they effectively represent a diversified portfolio of assets. Lower costs of financing should lead to (1) the expansion of TNCs at the expense of national firms and (2) more national firms expanding overseas and becoming TNCs. Fang Cai and Francis E. Warnock (2004) find that stock in TNCs throughout the world is valued more highly relative to non–TNCs, because purchasers of stock prefer TNCs' inherent reduction in business risk.

9. *Access to financing*—Recent flows of capital to the so-called **emerging markets**, or developing economies, suggest that TNCs are better able to deal with the difficulties of financing investment in economies where financial systems and institutions to enforce contracts are not as well developed. For example, net portfolio flows to emerging markets showed no growth trend during the 1990s and early 2000s, and the net inflows went almost entirely to Asia. FDI, on the other hand, expanded rapidly during the 1990s and early 2000s.

10. *Reducing competition*—The spread of TNCs is usually described as an increase in global competition, as a greater number of firms from a variety of countries compete in the many individual national markets formerly dominated by a few domestic firms. That is often indeed the case in the early stages of FDI and the growth of TNCs. However, we are now observing FDI fueling a worldwide consolidation of industries into a sharply reduced number of global TNCs. The automobile, financial, pharmaceutical, and food processing industries are examples of rapid consolidation across borders.

11. *Enhancing innovative success*—Joseph Schumpeter (1934) famously argued that firms organize themselves, at least in part, to maximize their performance as innovators. Hélène Blanc and Cristophe Sierra (1999) hypothesize that innovation is driven by a process that is (1) subject to large economies of scale yet (2) very dependent on outside ideas. We normally see R&D activities concentrated at research centers, which are commonly concentrated in specific geographic regions such as Silicon Valley. On the other hand, new knowledge and technology follow a combinatorial process in which old knowledge and technologies are combined to form new ideas. The regional concentration of R&D activity, as suggested by increasing returns to scale, may result in an increasing isolation from critical information and knowledge available elsewhere in the world. A firm in Schumpeterian competition, therefore, seeks an optimal combination of centralization (internal proximity) and dispersion (external proximity) of research activity. A TNC has more options than a purely domestic firm in reaching the most efficient compromise between external and internal proximity in organizing its R&D activity.

12. *Weaken the power of labor unions*—The ability of TNCs to shift production from one country to another gives these firms great power over their workers. The weakening of labor unions has been proportionate to the ability of TNCs to shift production overseas. The stagnation of wages in the United States, for example, has been closely correlated with the growth of international trade in general. The fall in real wages of industrial workers has been, in part, the result of labor negotiations carried out under the threat of shifting production overseas.

The explanations for the growth of TNCs listed here are by no means exhaustive. They are not mutually exclusive either; several explanations may apply to each actual case of FDI. For example, the large inflow of FDI to Ireland over the past two decades has been driven by the desire to jump over the European Union's trade barriers, to take advantage of Ireland's low corporate taxes, and to exploit Ireland's particular comparative advantages for production within the European Union. Whatever the particular reasons for the rise of individual TNCs in specific countries and regions, overall many factors have combined to make TNCs the dominant form of business organization in the global economy.

Transnational Corporations Are Controversial

Because TNCs directly affect international trade and investment, they are also intimately involved in the reallocation of employment across borders. The traditional "jobs argument," namely, that international trade eliminates jobs in one country and adds jobs in another, is too simplistic and, in most cases, inaccurate. With proper macroeconomic policies, all countries can maintain full employment even when trade alters the mix of jobs performed in individual countries. However, increased international trade and investment most definitely alter the *types* of jobs in an economy. More important, shifts in trade and investment change the wages workers and other factors of production earn from the production carried out in their country. Since TNCs carry out most international trade and physical investment, they are the ones who effectively make the decisions that bring about this shift in jobs within countries and across borders.

TNCs are often viewed as dangerous and detrimental to human well-being. Labor organizations are quite aware of how shifting production abroad weakens their bargaining power. Some labor organizations have begun to seek international alliances, effectively creating transnational labor unions that can better deal with transnational corporations. Another controversial result of TNCs has been the gradual shift in taxation from capital to labor and consumption. The international mobility of capital reduces governments' power to tax capital because the failure to remain "competitive" in terms of corporate taxation can cause outflows of FDI and, therefore, losses of tax revenue. TNCs have effectively threatened governments, and corporate taxation has declined substantially in most countries over the past three decades. Today we even see the spectacle of major political parties in most high-income economies accepting the call to cut corporate taxes further, and dealing with the expected tax shortfalls by cutting job creation programs and assistance to unemployed workers, and even reducing pension payments, medical assistance, and other parts of the social safety net. The TNCs' active pursuit of profit by political means has sharply tilted the distribution of income in favor of the owners of capital.

COMPARATIVE ADVANTAGE AND INTERNATIONAL MARKETING

The dominance of transnational corporations in the integrated international economy has channeled most of the world's wealth to international business organizations that have considerable power to manipulate the demand for their products and, therefore, the profits that increase the amounts of money they can spend lobbying governments to shape economic policy and business regulation in their favor. This section focuses on the active marketing activities of TNCs. The success of marketing in shaping international product demand and consumer preferences further undermines neoclassical trade models and their assumptions of perfect competition and stable preferences. TNCs often work very hard to reduce competition and manipulate consumer demand.

This section also shows that international trade is not a simple reflection of comparative advantage. All other things equal, lower opportunity costs are obviously very helpful for exporting, but as the old business saying goes, "nothing happens until someone sells something." International trade usually requires **international marketing** activities to translate comparative advantage into actual exports and imports. Products must be designed, positioned, promoted, advertised, distributed, priced, and supported. Marketing in other countries is usually also more difficult than marketing in one's own economy and national culture.

Comparative Advantage and Competitive Advantage

In marketing, the term *comparative advantage* is seldom used. Instead, marketing is usually concerned about competitive advantage, which refers to a firm's advantage in providing its customers or potential customers with a greater **value** of goods or services than its competitors. Value only partially depends on price; it also depends on quality, convenience, prestige, ease of use, and any number of other product traits and cultural perceptions.

A product's *value,* V, is often defined by the **value equation**

$$(5.1) \qquad\qquad V = B/P,$$

where B and P are the product's benefits and price, respectively. Product benefits are the perceived characteristics of a product, which are influenced by tastes, culture, traditions, habits, and active marketing activities such as advertising, public relations, pricing strategies, market positioning, distribution strategies, and sales organizations. The value of a good increases if (1) its price falls or (2) its perceived benefits increase. The comparative advantage that economists talk about is related mostly to the variable P; marketing tends to focus on the B term in the value equation. The concept of value is important; potential customers must be convinced that the benefits relative to the price of the good or service are greater than from other suppliers and for other goods and services that compete for customer demand. Producers must "sell" their products. TNCs sell in many different markets, political jurisdictions, and cultures.

Marketing and the Perceived Value of a Product

Marketing is sometimes narrowly defined as consisting of sales promotion, advertising, and market research.[9] But the field of marketing itself views marketing much more broadly as the entire range of activities beginning with the conceptualization of goods and services, continuing through the research and development stage, the design of the manufacturing process, the distribution network, and culminating with promotion and sales activities. Essentially, we adopt the definition of marketing as consisting of all activities that enhance the perceived *value* of a product to customers.

Marketing activities, shown in bold italics in Figure 5.7, include *promotion and advertising,* which are the sales-related activities that try to raise the perceived value of a product. *Pricing* strategies, *sales* organizations, and *distribution* systems are marketing activities that affect the price of products and the costs of acquiring them. Finally, *market research* affects production directly by investigating what firms should produce and the specific characteristics that the products should have. Market research may precede product development, engineering, and production. Marketing activities are intertwined with product development and production because the business success of a product is in large part determined by its perceived value.

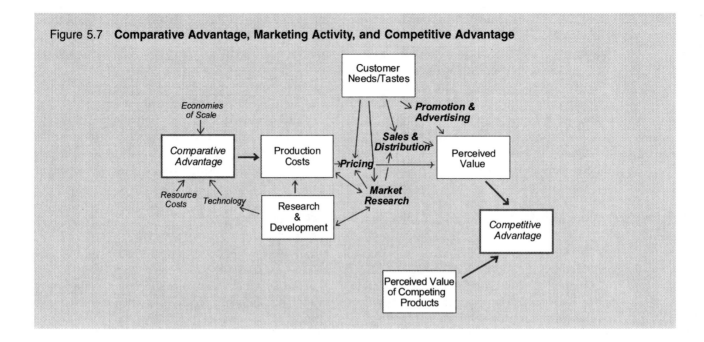

Figure 5.7 **Comparative Advantage, Marketing Activity, and Competitive Advantage**

Providing value to overseas customers is often much more difficult than marketing in a producer's home economy. The perceived benefits of goods and services in export markets are often different from the perceived benefits of those same goods and services in producers' home markets. Not only do customers' specific tastes, needs, and incomes differ across countries, but the marketing activities needed to enhance products' perceived benefits are also likely to be different. The sales techniques and advertisements that work well at home may not work well overseas.

Customers Are Not All the Same

U.S. automakers are still ridiculed for trying to sell cars with steering wheels on the left in Japan, a country that drives on the left-hand side of the road, more than twenty years ago. German car makers sold cars with steering wheels on the right and gained significant market shares in Japan. However, some other U.S. firms have taken a more enlightened approach to selling in other countries than the unmotivated U.S. automakers. For example, Domino's Pizza operates in forty-six countries and has developed pizza flavors to meet local tastes. It sells mayonnaise and potato (*mayo jaga*) pizza in Japan and pickled ginger pizza in India. It also developed a non-beef pepperoni topping for its India stores. Pizza Hut sells a *tom yam*–flavored pizza in Thailand and salmon pizza in Japan. McDonald's offers wine in its French fast-food restaurants and sells beer in its German outlets. PepsiCo's Frito-Lay division sells seafood-flavored chips in China. Ben and Jerry's, the ice cream company, tried selling its chocolate chip cookie dough flavor in Great Britain, but according to cofounder Jerry Greenfield, "People didn't grow up in this country [Britain] sneaking raw cookie-dough batter from mom."[10] Ben and Jerry's opted to hold a contest for new flavors that British consumers would like. One successful flavor has been "Cool Britannia," which is a combination of vanilla ice cream, strawberries, and chocolate-covered Scottish shortbread.

Foreign markets sometimes call for distribution systems that are very different from those in a TNC's home country. For example, developed economies in Western Europe and North America sell most food and household products through supermarkets, department stores, and large discount stores. But in most low-income developing economies, household goods are sold through many very small retailers. In Tanzania, 33 million people purchase food and household products in some hundred thousand small retail shops, often market stalls or small shacks. With half the Tanzanian population earning less than US$1 per day, most customers buy in very small quantities each day. Unilever, the Dutch/British TNC, therefore distributes its soaps and detergents in Tanzania through a "bicycle brigade" of wholesalers, who visit every retail stall and store throughout the country daily. These distributors pedal bicycles loaded with small, 50-gram packages of detergent and soap; the bicycles can negotiate the narrow paths and alleyways where stores are located. They often sell just a few items each day to stallkeepers, who in turn sell just a few bars of soap each day to their poor clientele. According to one account, a typical bicycle brigade wholesaler sells between 50,000 and 100,000 Tanzanian shillings (US$62.50 and US$125) worth of Omo detergent, Key soap, and Blue Band margarine per day. The bicycle driver earns between US$2.50 and US$5 per day.[11]

Maintaining different marketing policies across different countries can also cause problems, as Toshiba recently learned. The company had agreed to pay US$1.05 billion to U.S. customers to settle a lawsuit over potential floppy disk malfunctions on its laptop computers. But it refused to compensate Chinese users of its products because, Toshiba claimed, it offered a different warrantee in China. A wave of protests spread quickly throughout China.[12] The official newspaper *China Daily* even carried a cartoon of a Toshiba executive bowing before an American customer who was sitting comfortably next to a pile of dollar bills. Modern communications make it more difficult for companies to discriminate between markets.

Should the Product Look Local or Foreign?

Some foreign firms deal with nationalistic consumers by emphasizing how "local" they really are. For example, the Japanese automaker Toyota has for years run advertisements in the United States emphasizing its U.S. operations. One typical ad mentions Toyota's investment in its Indiana manufacturing plants and the three hundred thousand "Hoosier-built" vehicles that are produced annually. Another ad about its Indiana truck factory shows a group of young basketball players and the headline: "Indiana team spirit, it's building more than just great athletes."[13] The U.S. software giant Microsoft at one time employed a thousand people at its Dublin, Ireland, office to *localize* its software products. And, Microsoft's *localization* experts decided to credit Guglielmo Marconi, the Italian physicist, as the inventor of the telephone in the Italian version of their encyclopedia, *Encarta,* not Alexander Graham Bell, who is credited in the U.S. version and most other versions.[14]

On the other hand, some foreign firms exploit their foreign image. French perfume manufacturers use French-looking models to promote their fragrances. German beer brewers tout their German heritage and brewing prowess. Colombian coffee producers for years used the image of Juan Valdez and his mule, Conchita, to promote Colombian coffee. The advertising campaign is estimated to have added as much as $2 billion to the annual value of Colombian coffee exports. Other countries have now copied Colombia and promoted their national brands. Today, coffee is increasingly marketed like wine, with the country of origin an important contributor to the product's value.

Market Segmentation

International trade is often depicted as an arbitrage process that tends to equalize prices across different national markets. Neoclassical analysis suggests that such price arbitrage is "efficient" in that it equalizes price incentives across countries. Because they internalize the international markets for the products they produce, TNCs are often able to avoid the arbitrage process and, instead, discriminate across national markets. The TNCs increase their profits by such discrimination, or what marketers call **market segmentation**.

Figure 5.8 uses orthodox microeconomic theory to illustrate how a supplier can raise profits by setting different prices in markets with different demand characteristics. For example, the figure

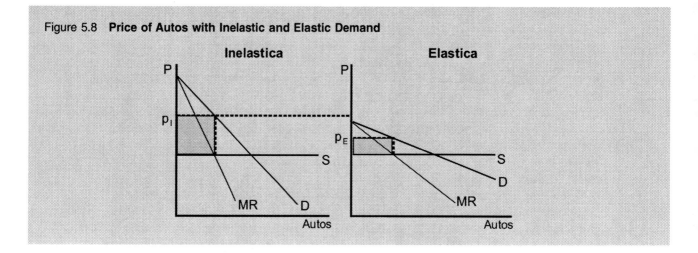

Figure 5.8 **Price of Autos with Inelastic and Elastic Demand**

illustrates the case of an automobile producer based in the country of Inelastica, which is assumed to produce under constant marginal costs and market autos in its home market as well as the neighboring country of Elastica. The markets in the two countries are both imperfectly competitive, and the auto producer faces downward-sloping demand curves. But, the market in the country of Inelastica is characterized by demand that is relatively inelastic, while in Elastica, perhaps because of more domestic competition, demand is relatively elastic. Orthodox models suggest that the profit-maximizing firm will set its price so that marginal costs are equal to marginal revenue. Figure 5.8 shows that the supplier will set a lower price in the market with the more elastic demand, as evidenced by the prices p_I and p_E in Inelastica and Elastica, respectively. Notice that if the producer set the price p_I in both markets, there would be no sales in Elastica at all, and no profits. But if the price p_E is set in both markets, the producer undermines profits in Inelastica.

Market segmentation is a common practice that permits firms to enhance profits by charging prices in accordance with the characteristics of different markets. But it does take some degree of control over markets. Market segmentation is often accomplished by differentiating products slightly, perhaps by varying the size of a package, the payment terms, or the advertising image of the product. Or, a producer may appoint different distributors in different markets. Most often, the marketing is carried out by large TNCs with market power; **price discrimination** then becomes an internal marketing decision.

Marketing and Transnational Corporations

In sum, international trade is not simply the international extension of perfectly competitive markets across borders, as the HO and other orthodox trade models would have us believe. Nor is it even the exploitation of economies of scale by imperfectly competitive firms. Rather, the growth of international trade is part of a massive construction of international business organizations built up with massive amounts of capital, persistent marketing efforts, and, as the next section will describe, the active shaping of favorable government institutions. The marketing power of TNCs is increasingly used not only to sell products, but to sell a way of life, a culture, that favors the TNCs' economic interests.

WHAT DOES THE GROWTH OF TRANSNATIONAL CORPORATIONS REALLY MEAN?

Peter Drucker (1987), the popular management guru, noted more than twenty years ago that FDI was replacing international trade as the driving force of international economic integration. FDI built the

TNCs that today dominate world trade. TNCs also increasingly directly and indirectly drive international migration, either by moving personnel between parts of companies or altering labor market conditions as they shift production between countries. These close relationships between FDI, finance, the movement of people, and international trade complicate the analysis of international trade.

Managed Trade

Increasingly, what a nation imports depends on TNC management structures, marketing strategies, investments in factories, and their complex business relationships with suppliers, customers, and competitors. A 2005 newspaper article on U.S. trade in aircraft and aircraft components provides an interesting example:

> Aircraft engines and engine parts, a category that has experienced a 24 percent increase in imports in the latest 12 months, are . . . affected by global sourcing, but in a more complex way. General Electric in the United States and Snecma of France, for example, jointly manufacture the jet engine for Boeing's 737 and Airbus's 320. G.E. makes the "hot section" at its plant in Cincinnati, while Snecma manufactures the giant fans in France. They ship these components to each other and each partner does the final assembly of the engines for its customers. In addition, G.E. makes smaller jet engines for the commuter planes that Bombardier makes in Canada and Embraer in Brazil. These are exported to those countries, but 24 percent of the value of the engines is composed of components imported from Japan. The upshot is that exports of engines and engine parts are rising, but so are imports.[15]

Are these trade flows explained by comparative advantage as it is illustrated in orthodox trade theory? The growth of FDI, and the huge TNCs FDI clearly represent a challenge to international economists. Again, according to Drucker (1987):

> We . . . have no theory for an international economy that is fueled by world investment rather than by world trade. As a result, we do not understand the world economy and cannot predict its behavior or anticipate its trends.

The state of international trade theory has not changed much since Drucker wrote these words. The continued use of the HO model, or any model that explains international trade in isolation, prevents orthodox economists from accurately explaining the trade flows we observe in the world today.

Transnational Corporations and Economic Policy

FDI is intimately mixed up with the disruptive processes of economic growth, such as the shifting of jobs across borders, the stagnation of workers' wages in many developed economies, and the volatile prices of commodities. After presenting evidence that FDI significantly boosts the international trade and economic growth of a host country, Robert Lipsey (2002, p. 60) nevertheless notes:

> The association of FDI with more trade and faster growth would not necessarily please critics of multinationals. Trade links reduce the freedom of action of a country's government domestically, if not that of its people. Fast growth involves disruptions and the destruction of the value of old techniques of production and old skills. Those who value stability over economic progress will not be convinced of the worth of the gifts brought by foreign involvement. That is especially true if the gains are captured by small elements of the population or if no effort is made to soften the impact of the inevitable losses.

Heterodox economists and many other critics of TNCs have also questioned whether the economic growth TNCs bring to a country is worth the economic and social disruption. Also of concern are the environmental damage and political corruption often observed in developing countries, especially when TNCs invest in extractive industries. After two decades of active pursuit of FDI and its alleged growth benefits, largely endorsed by mainstream economists and international development institutions such as the World Bank, some national political leaders have begun to question the benefits of inviting foreign TNCs into their countries. For example, President Evo Morales of Bolivia and his economic advisors have opposed several recent proposals by TNCs to mine Bolivia's large deposits of lithium, a raw material used in the manufacture of batteries for electric and hybrid automobiles. Politicians like Morales and heterodox economists also question whether the economic growth that sometimes accompanies FDI really brings true improvements in human welfare. Orthodox economic analysis, and the neoclassical models it is based on ignore many long-term economic, social, and environmental consequences of the spread of multinational business organizations. Morales insists that Bolivia's lithium deposits "cannot be another Cerro Rico," Bolivia's rich silver mine that was exploited by the Spanish colonists and left the former mining city Potosí one of the poorest cities on earth.[16] Not all FDI improves human welfare.

Transnational Corporations and National Sovereignty

There is also the fear that the extension of business organizations across borders threatens not only national sovereignty, but the concept of nationhood itself. Which country does a TNC have allegiance to? Can a sovereign nation really exist when all economic power is in the hands of transnational business organizations whose ownership is not defined by nationality? Today's large TNCs are often owned by stockholders in many different countries. They operate in many countries, their managers are nationals from many different countries, they have employees from many different countries, and their customers are spread across the globe. There have been many cross-border mergers and acquisitions that effectively give TNCs dual or multiple corporate citizenship. And, increasingly, the shares of corporations are held by retirement funds and mutual funds for individuals dispersed across many countries: This indirect ownership further cuts the channel of control between the "owners" and management. TNCs are largely "ownerless," according to John Plender (2010), which leaves control in the hands of managements whose rewards are determined by the corporations' bottom line.

Does a TNC owe its allegiance only to the stockholders? To employees as well? To customers? The growing concentration of economic activity within fewer and fewer increasingly large multinational business and financial firms does not seem to be consistent with the notion that private business naturally maximizes the welfare of all people. There are obvious dangers associated with the concentration of immense economic power in the hands of mostly unaccountable business organizations staffed by compliant employees indoctrinated to believe in their employer's benevolence but managed by people facing incentives that appeal directly to personal greed. An examination of the root causes of the 2008 financial crisis makes it clear that many domestic corporations do not hesitate to take profitable actions that diminish the welfare of their fellow citizens. Therefore, why should we expect foreign TNCs to behave in a manner that optimizes the well-being of people in their host countries?

CONCLUSIONS

Increasing returns to scale are common in manufacturing, mining, agriculture, and many other productive activities. Over the past thirty years, international economics has investigated what dropping the assumption of increasing costs in favor of the assumption of increasing returns to scale does to models of international trade. The model of two identical countries above suggests that national welfare can still increase with international trade when production is subject to increasing returns to scale. This is reassuring because so many of the products traded are produced in factories and firms whose activities are subject to increasing returns to scale, not the increasing opportunity costs that are assumed in the HO model.

On the other hand, economists have also learned that once they drop the Heckscher-Ohlin model's assumptions of perfect competition and increasing costs, many other conclusions are possible. For one thing, economies of scale in many industries explain why so much trade occurs between very similar economies that seem to have nearly identical resource-based and technological comparative advantages. Secondly, perfect competition breaks down when there are increasing returns to scale, and this means that international trade is conducted by monopolistic producers that charge prices that exceed their production costs. This divergence of costs and prices will tend to alter international trade patterns as envisioned by the Heckscher-Ohlin model.

Economies of scale contribute fundamentally to the concentration of business activity into transnational corporations (TNCs). Economies of scale in production, marketing, research, and distribution give firms that expand across borders distinct advantages. From a dynamic holistic perspective, TNCs are able to increase profit margins and gain income at the expense of consumers and workers. The growth of TNCs thus alters the distribution of gains from international trade. When a large portion of the gains from international trade appears in the form of corporate profits, the country with the most stockholders of TNCs appears to gain the most from trade, while workers and many other groups across all countries can simultaneously experience declining real incomes.

These conclusions about the role of TNCs in the international economy will be viewed as radical by many mainstream economists. They really should not be surprising, given that it is the analysis developed by mainstream economists, as well as the data collected by these same economists, that brings us logically to these conclusions. Recall Krugman's analysis that used standard microeconomic models to illustrate trade under imperfect competition. The fact is that evidence clearly shows TNCs, not small national firms, dominate international trade. Also, the foreign direct investment (FDI) that constructs these TNCs dominates long-run international investment flows. National and international institutions seem to have been shaped in ways that favor the growth of TNCs.

There is no consensus on what the full economic, political, and social consequences of the concentration of economic power in the hands of TNCs will mean for international trade specifically, or the welfare of humanity in general. It is clear, however, that in international economics we need much more understanding of the role of TNCs in our increasingly integrated world economy. It is surprising, therefore, how few mainstream international economists have recognized the broad processes of economic, social, and environmental change, such as the growing political and economic power of large transnational businesses, that have accompanied the growth of international economic activity. Fortunately, heterodox economists, aided by their holistic approach to economics, have not been reluctant to examine these tough but urgent issues. We will return to these issues in later chapters.

CHAPTER SUMMARY

1. The assumption of perfect competition is not a reasonable approximation of real world market behavior.

2. Economies of scale in many industries explain why so much trade occurs between very similar economies that seem to have nearly identical resource-based and technological comparative advantages.

3. Perfect competition breaks down when there are increasing returns to scale, and this means that international trade is conducted by monopolistic producers that charge prices that exceed their production costs.

4. In the early 1980s, several international economists developed models in which production was characterized by increasing returns to scale by assuming that producers become more efficient the larger they become and the more they produce. These models are compatible with the observation that just about all international trade in manufactured goods is

carried out by large multinational firms rather than large numbers of small, competitive firms.

5. Increasing returns to scale create an interesting conflict in that consumers prefer more variety to less variety, but the cost of each product is lower if consumers opt for less variety by consuming only one of the two goods.

6. Krugman showed that international trade makes possible a one-time gain in welfare from both *lower unit costs* and *increased variety,* effectively mitigating the conflict between cost and variety.

7. An interesting implication of the simple economies of scale trade model above is that the direction of specialization by each of the two initially identical economies is arbitrary, which may justify strategic trade policies that seek to influence which industries develop in a country.

8. Imperfect competition enables the growth of TNCs, which links international trade to international investment, market structures, and institutional factors that are not covered in the HO model of trade.

9. *Foreign Direct Investment* (FDI) is investment in overseas facilities in which the investor has a controlling interest. FDI effectively creates *transnational corporations* (TNCs), which are firms that manage and own production and distribution facilities in more than one country.

10. *Vertical* FDI occurs when a TNC builds or acquires foreign facilities that comprise one stage of its complete production process. *Horizontal* FDI duplicates facilities and operations that the TNC already owns and operates in other countries.

11. This chapter outlines many reasons for the growth of transnational corporations. Most of the explanations center around various advantages of *internalizing* transactions within a single business organization rather than conducting arm's-length exchanges with other independent persons or groups of persons.

12. Because increased international trade and investment alter the *types* of jobs available for workers in an economy, and because they carry out most of the trade and investment in real productive facilities, TNCs are controversial.

13. In marketing, the term *comparative advantage* is seldom used; instead, marketing is usually concerned about *competitive advantage,* which is a firm's advantage in providing its customers or potential customers with goods or services that are valued more highly than those of its competitors.

14. *Market segmentation* is a common practice that permits firms to enhance profits by charging prices in accordance to the characteristics of different markets; TNCs commonly seek to segment international markets.

KEY TERMS AND CONCEPTS

colonialism
competitive advantage
core competencies
Dutch East India Company
emerging markets
foreign direct investment (FDI)
hold up problem
horizontal FDI
internalizing transactions

intra-industry trade
market segmentation
marketing
strategic trade policy
terms of trade (ToT)
transnational corporations (TNCs)
Verenigde Oost-Indische Compagnie (VOC)
vertical FDI

PROBLEMS AND QUESTIONS

1. List and explain the reasons for the growth of transnational corporations (TNCs). Which of the many reasons do you think were most responsible for the dominance of TNCs in the international economy?

2. One of the reasons given for the growth of transnational companies is the popularity of the management concept of *core competencies.* Explain how the focus of a firm on its core competencies

stimulates its international expansion. Is the concept of core competencies related to the concept of comparative advantage? Explain.

3. Another reason often given for the growth of transnational corporations is their advantages in circumventing national regulations and taxes. Explain how they do this. Is this good for human welfare? Why or why not?

4. Explain market segmentation. What are the advantages for a firm? What are the costs to society? Are transnational corporations better able to engage in market segmentation than national firms importing and exporting?

5. Explain how increasing returns to scale undermine the Heckscher-Ohlin model of international trade. Is international trade still possible if firms' production is subject to increasing returns to scale? (Hint: Use the model developed in the first section of this chapter.)

6. What role do increasing returns play in the growth of transnational firms?

7. Explain Krugman's model of trade under imperfect competition. How does his model differ from the two-diagram model presented in the first section of this chapter?

8. Discuss the potential implications of the growing dominance of transnational firms in the integrated international economy. Should we be concerned about the growth of transnational business firms? What harm could they cause?

9. Explain how trade based on comparative advantage derived from the expansion of increasing returns to scale industries points to potentially beneficial strategic trade policies. (Hint: Use the example presented in Figure 5.6.)

10. Write an essay on how the predominance of transnational corporations (TNCs) in the global economy affects the accuracy of the Heckscher-Ohlin (HO) model as a descriptive framework of international trade. Specifically, you should focus on how the presence of TNCs invalidates the HO model's assumptions. Also, compare a TNC's behavior with the firm behavior implied by the HO model's assumption that trade is carried out by large numbers of competitive importers and exporters.

NOTES

1. Paul R. Krugman (1991).

2. See Robert E. Lipsey (2001), "Foreign Direct Investment and the Operations of Multinational Firms: Concepts, History, and Data," National Bureau of Economic Research working paper 8665, December, for a thorough discussion of the various definitions of FDI and TNCs. The 10 percent rule is fairly standard across the criteria used in the literature.

3. *The Economist* (1997), "A Worldbeater, Inc.," November 22.

4. UNCTAD (2007), Annex Table A.1.5.

5. Isaac Singer may have had another motivation for setting up a factory in Scotland: he was being prosecuted for bigamy in the United States, and found it convenient to move to Scotland with one of his wives.

6. Harlan W. King (2001) and Maria Borga and Raymond J. Mataloni, Jr. (2001).

7. Lipsey (see note 2).

8. William J. Zeile (1997), p. 23.

9. See, for example, David W. Pierce (1989), *The MIT Dictionary of Modern Economics*, Cambridge, MA: MIT Press, p. 264.

10. Quoted in Tara Parker-Pope (1996), "Custom-Made," *Wall Street Journal*, September 26, p. R22.

11. Mark Turner (2000), "Bicycle Brigade Takes Unilever to the People," *Financial Times*, August 17.

12. James Kynge (2000), "Toshiba Runs into a Storm of Protest in China," *Financial Times*, May 27–28.

13. This was a full-page ad in the *Wall Street Journal*, August 22, 2000.

14. John Murray Brown (2000), "Ireland Fine-Tunes Software with Ear to Cultural Nuance," *Financial Times*, November 29.

15. Louis Uchitelle (2005), "Made in the U.S.A. (Except for the Parts)," *New York Times*, April 8.

16. The history of Potosí is described in Eduardo Galeano (1997), *Open Veins of Latin America: Five Centuries of the Pillage of a Continent*, New York: Monthly Review Press. The quote by Morales is taken from Lawrence Wright (2010), "Lithium Dreams," *The New Yorker*, March 22.

CHAPTER 6

International Trade and Economic Development

Orthodox mainstream economic models suggest that there is an inherent similarity between trade and growth: both processes imply an increase in the value of economic output. In the mainstream economic paradigm, economic growth is often described as an increase in the economy's productive capacity. In terms of the Heckscher-Ohlin (HO) model, economic growth can be illustrated as an outward shift in the production possibilities frontier (PPF), shown in Figure 6.1 as the shift from PPF_1 to PPF_2. Since such economic growth enables the economy to reach production points on a higher social indifference curve, orthodox neoclassical analysis concludes that economic growth directly raises human welfare.

Figure 6.1 also shows how international trade enables the economy to reach the same higher indifference curve that the outward shift in the PPF made accessible. The only difference between international trade and economic growth is that consumers select a slightly different combination of clothing and food under free trade compared to what they opt for under economic growth in a closed economy, the points C and B, respectively. These different consumption points are due to the fact that trade changes relative prices differently than economic growth does. But, otherwise, trade and growth seem to be quite similar.

There is one important difference between growth and trade, however. In the static framework of the HO model, which assumes no changes in factor endowments or **technology**, once the economy has shifted to complete free trade no further gains in welfare are possible. But, in the dynamic framework of economic growth, further shifts in the PPF are not ruled out. If the economy can continue to grow and shift the PPF out, then welfare can continue to rise as well.

This difference between trade and growth has important welfare implications. Recall from Chapter 4 that when economists used the neoclassical static HO model of trade to estimate the gains from trade, their calculations turned up very small welfare gains. Recently, mainstream economists have taken a more dynamic approach and linked international trade to the long-run process of economic growth. They reason that continual economic growth brings the power of compounding into play. If free trade causes the economy's annual rate of growth to rise even just slightly, in the long run this will lead to large improvements in human well-being.

Compare, for example, two economies with identical populations depicted by the PPFs labeled A and B in Figure 6.2. For the economy B at the bottom left corner of Figure 6.2, a one-time static improvement in welfare brought about by opening up to international trade does not do much to close the 1,000 percent difference in per capita income between it and the more developed economy A. For most people living in the less developed economies of Africa, Latin America, and Asia, economic development is not about moving from I_1 to I_2 in Figure 6.2. Rather, what is needed are welfare gains on the order of moving from I_1 to I_{20}. According to the neoclassical paradigm, such

Figure 6.1   The Similarity between Trade and Growth

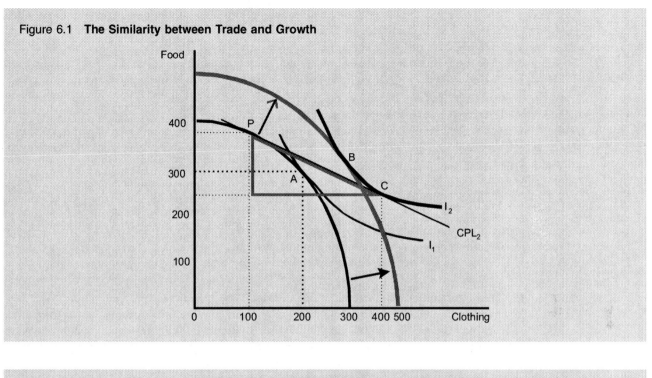

Figure 6.2   The Welfare Gain from Trade versus Economic Growth

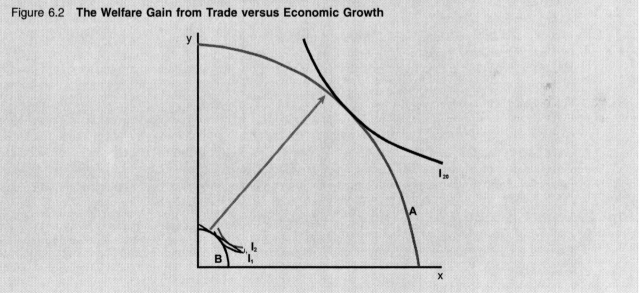

a gain requires a persistent outward shift of the PPF that only steady growth of welfare-enhancing economic output can bring about.

But is there such a positive link between expanding international trade and an economy's long-run rate of economic growth and development? This chapter and the next examine the relationship between international trade and an economy's long-run economic development. We first introduce two models from the field of economic growth and discuss the insights they provide. We then link these models to the various effects of international trade discussed in the previous two chapters.

Orthodox growth theory defines economic growth as an increase in per capita output. Economic growth thus requires that the **production function** shift out faster than the growth in population, which can be accomplished either (1) because the economy's factors of production are increased or (2) because technology improvements permit the economy to produce more output for a given set of resources. The former is sometimes referred to as growth through **factor accumulation**. This type of growth is examined by means of a model developed by Robert Solow around the middle of the twentieth century. **Technological change**, on the other hand, is examined using a **dynamic model** first proposed by Joseph Schumpeter nearly a century ago and generalized by the contemporary growth economist Paul Romer in 1990. This chapter also includes a detailed discussion of technological change and how international trade can advance knowledge.

THE GROWTH OF INTERNATIONAL TRADE

One of the characteristics of the past two hundred years of rapid economic growth is the increase in international trade. The main reason trade grew so rapidly after 1820 was the sharp reduction in transport costs, as discussed in the previous chapter. Politics also played a role; many of the major economies of the world reduced or abolished tariffs and other trade barriers during the nineteenth century, although those policies were reversed during the first half of the twentieth century.

Figure 6.3, which is based on Table 1.1 from Chapter 1, graphs the evolution of world trade and economic growth over the past two hundred years. Only 1 percent of the total value of world output was exported beyond individual countries' borders in 1820. By 1870, the advent of railroads and steamships, as well as the reduction of tariffs and other trade restrictions, had increased trade to where about 5 percent of the world's output was destined for foreign markets. By 1929, the year before the Great Depression set in, exports had reached 9 percent of world gross domestic product (GDP). After the sharp increase in protectionist trade policies during the Great Depression of the 1930s and a second devastating World War in the first half of the 1940s, exports fell to just 5.5 percent of world GDP by 1950. Since 1950, however, world trade has again grown rapidly both in absolute terms and as a proportion of world output. About 30 percent of world industrial output was being exported by 2010.

As shown in Figure 6.3, the growth of trade and the growth of per capita real GDP seem to be related. When international trade grew rapidly in the nineteenth century, standards of living grew faster than the world had ever experienced. During the 1930s, protectionist trade policies caused trade to shrink, and economic growth slowed dramatically. After World War II, record economic growth coincided with very rapid growth of trade. Of course, correlation does not imply causation.

Why Growth Matters: The Power of Compounding

To fully appreciate the implications of economic growth you must understand the concept of **compounding**. Romer, a noted growth economist, provides an interesting example to illustrate the power of compounding. Suppose that a recently graduated economics major has just begun working at her exciting and high-paying new job, and she wants to buy a house. She goes to her local bank to seek a loan for US$200,000, fully knowing that such a sum of money is going to take a long time to pay off. To her surprise, the loan officer at the bank makes her a strange, but tempting, offer: The bank will issue her a check for US$200,000 today if she signs a contract that requires her to come back in ten years with a chessboard and enough pennies to place one on the first white square of the board, two on the second white square, four on the third white square, eight on the fourth, and so on until all of the white squares are covered. Should she take the bank up on this offer?

Romer claims that "we systematically underestimate how fast things grow," and many people would thoughtlessly jump at the opportunity of filling a chessboard with "just pennies." But a

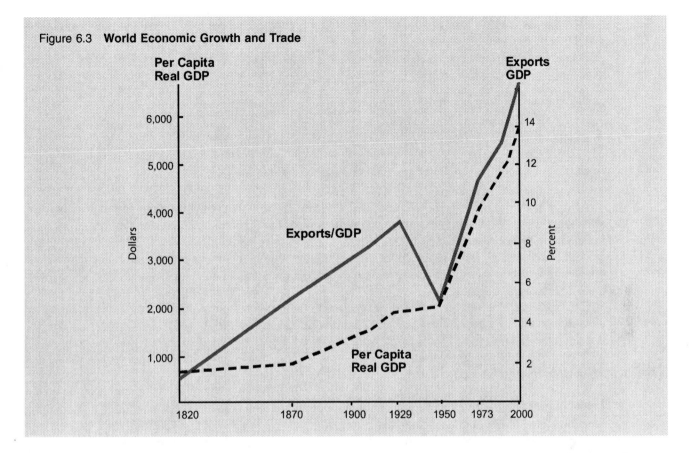

Figure 6.3   **World Economic Growth and Trade**

serious economics major would, no doubt, carefully calculate that, with thirty-two white squares on a chessboard, the repayment scheme is equal to 1 cent plus thirty-one consecutive amounts that are each 100 percent larger than the previous amount. The total payment is therefore 1 cent plus 2 cents to the thirty-first power, which adds up to about US$21.5 million! The bank's offer is a bad deal.[1]

The lesson of Romer's example is that the **power of compounding** is great. Small differences in economic growth rates soon add up to very large differences in standards of living. Specifically, the general formula for a **compound growth process** shows that if per capita real GDP grows at an annual rate of R, then after T years the level of per capita real GDP will be:

$$(6.1) \qquad PCGDP_T = PCGDP_{t+0}(1 + R)^T.$$

For example, if a country with a per capita real GDP of US$2,000, about equal to that of Honduras, India, Indonesia, or Uzbekistan, grows for ten years at an annual rate 2.5 percent, the average growth rate for low-income countries, per capita real GDP will rise from US$2,000 to

$$(6.2) \qquad PCGDP_{T+10} = \$2,000(1 + .025)^{10} = \$2,560.$$

Suppose that another country grows a little faster, say at 3.5 percent per year. After ten years, this economy's per capita real GDP will be:

$$(6.3) \qquad PCGDP_{T+10} = \$2,000(1 + .035)^{10} = \$2,821.$$

Notice that its slightly faster economic growth gives the second country about a 10 percent higher standard of living after a decade.

If the two countries grow at 2.5 percent and 3.5 percent, respectively, for 100 years, then standards of living diverge much more:

$$(6.4) \qquad PCGDP_{T+100} = \$2,000(1 + .025)^{100} = \$23,627$$

and

$$(6.5) \qquad PCGDP_{T+100} = \$2,000(1 + .035)^{100} = \$62,383.$$

After just one century, which is not a long period of time over the course of human history, an annual growth rate of 2.5 percent brings a very poor country up to the standard of living of today's most developed economies in Western Europe and North America. But, a growth rate of just 1 percentage point higher takes a very poor country to a standard of living more than twice as high as the wealthiest countries enjoy today and nearly three times higher than the first country. The power of compounding is great.

Could such a 1 percentage point difference in growth rates depend on whether a country is open or closed to international trade? There is some evidence that international trade, in fact, has a positive effect on economic growth.

Statistical Evidence on Trade and Growth

There is considerable **uncertainty** about how international trade affects a country's economic development. This uncertainty has led many economists to seek data about and apply statistical methods to measure the relationship between international trade and human well-being. Such statistical analyses have been done for many countries over many different time periods. Many have used **time-series data** consisting of observations spread over long periods of time for individual countries. Others carried out **cross-section studies** using sets of observations for many countries at a given point in time. More recently, **panel studies** that simultaneously apply time-series data for a cross-section of countries have become popular. The results of the statistical studies often find that expanding trade is correlated with growing output. But, doubts remain because it is difficult to separate the many causes of economic growth. There is also great variation in the statistical results.

The results of statistical studies examining the relationship between international trade and economic growth often suggest that trade liberalization is positively related to economic growth.[2] And, the estimated effect of trade on growth often appears to be **economically significant** as well as **statistically significant**. The latter term refers to the estimated probability that a statistical analyst will accept as a confirmation of a hypothesized statistical relationship; the former refers to whether the estimated parameters of a statistical relationship generate outcomes that have a meaningful effect on human well-being or some other important economic outcome. On average, the cross-section and time-series studies suggest that the rate of growth of real GDP rises by about 0.20 percentage points for every 1 percentage point increase in the growth rate of international trade. That is, an economy whose exports and imports grow 5 percentage points faster than those of its more protectionist neighbor will grow about 1 percentage point faster than that neighbor, all other things equal. The power of compounding expands such an increase of 1 percentage point in annual growth into a per capita GDP that is 2.7 times as large as its neighbor's after one century.

Empirical studies of the relationship between foreign trade and economic growth most often specify linear econometric models of the form

(6.6) $$G_{GDP} = a_0 + a_1 G_K + a_2 G_L + a_3 TRADE + a_4 Z + u$$

where G_{GDP}, G_K, and G_L are the growth rates of real gross domestic product, capital stock, and labor force, respectively. TRADE represents the growth of trade, Z is a set of other variables thought to explain economic growth, and u is the standard error term that statisticians use to represent a random variation not accounted for by the explanatory variables. If the regression program estimates the coefficient a_3 is greater than zero with a 95 percent confidence level, we can conclude that trade has a positive influence on the growth of output. Data to proxy the model's variables are readily available from national accounts and large databases such as Angus Maddison's (1995, 2001, 2006) historical time series.

There are many reasons why linear regressions fail to provide accurate estimates of how the independent variables influence the dependent variable, however. Often, data are inaccurate or incomplete, so that the sample is a biased representation of the population. Also, the dependent variable is influenced by many variables not included in the regression model. When the regression equation does not include all the variables or explicitly model all the true interrelationships between all the relevant variables, statistical methods attribute causality to the included variables that really belongs to variables omitted from the analysis. These are, respectively, the **measurement error** and **omitted variable bias** problems that students of statistics learn to deal with.

Cross-Section Studies

Joshua Lewer and your author (Van den Berg and Lewer 2007) conducted a detailed survey of the many statistical tests of the relationship between international trade and growth in order to verify the robustness of the reported results. We found thirty-four studies in major economic journals that included a total of 196 separate regressions using a model like equation (6.6) above and cross-section data for different samples of countries. The average value of the coefficient of the growth of real exports variable was 0.22. However, there was a substantial variation across the 196 regressions; only 111 of the 196 estimated coefficients fell between 0.15 and 0.45. With the variables all in terms of growth rates, a coefficient value of 0.22 implies that for each 1 percentage point increase in the growth rate of trade, the economy's rate of growth increased by one fifth (0.22/1.00) of 1 percentage point. Figure 6.4 illustrates the variability of the statistical estimates. The left-hand diagram shows the estimated regression coefficients for the growth of exports from each of the 196 cross-section regressions, listed from left to right in order of publication date. The right-hand diagram shows the 95 percent confidence intervals of the 196 coefficient estimates. Over 90 percent of the coefficient values covered by the confidence intervals are positive, but a large number of these are very close to zero. The studies differ in terms of data sets, sample size, other variables included in the equations, et cetera.

One interesting feature of showing the results in order of the date of their publication in Figure 6.4 is that we can observe whether the coefficient estimates or the confidence intervals show a distinct trend over time. The fact that there is no obvious time trend suggests there were no systematic biases in the early studies compared to the later studies. Note, however, this set of cross-section studies does not address the main criticism of regression studies of trade and growth, namely that trade is probably closely correlated with institutions and economic efficiency. It is difficult to quantify institutions across countries, so such variables were usually left out of cross-section studies. The predominantly positive but wide-ranging coefficient estimates are, therefore, likely biased by omitted variable bias. Time-series data may be better able to avoid omitted variable bias.

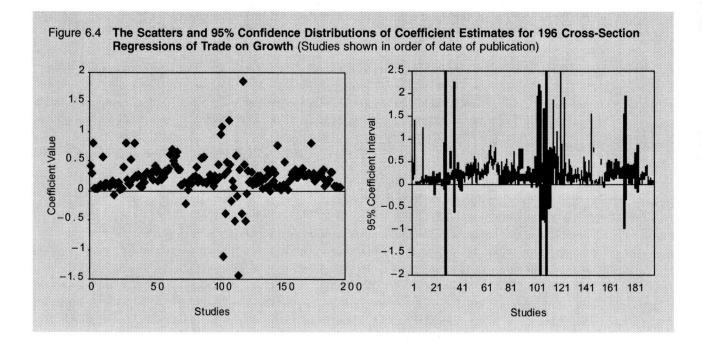

Figure 6.4 **The Scatters and 95% Confidence Distributions of Coefficient Estimates for 196 Cross-Section Regressions of Trade on Growth** (Studies shown in order of date of publication)

Time-Series Studies

Where cross-section analysis uses observations at one point in time for a group of different countries, time-series analysis uses many observations, usually done annually, for a single country. Time-series regressions offer some advantages over cross-section analysis. Because institutions and other social and economic characteristics often vary less over time than they do across a broad sample of different countries, time-series analysis may, therefore, be less vulnerable to Francisco Rodriguez and Dani Rodrik's (2001) critique that the trade variable mistakenly captures the effects of other institutional and structural factors that vary across countries. Time-series analysis for individual countries has the added benefit of permitting researchers to generate and compare country-by-country results and, therefore, to explicitly analyze the potential causes of the country-by-country differences.

Time-series regressions are not free of problems, however. Among other things, they are likely to generate *spurious regression results* in cases where all the time-series variables increase over time, which is normal when economies grow. Even when there is no direct causal relationship between them, the statistical programs will, therefore, tend to find positive and significant coefficients for the explanatory variables in the regression equation even if there is no direct causality.

In Van den Berg and Lewer (2007), we tabulate the results for 402 time-series regressions that specified regression equations similar to the regression equation (6.6). The average value of the 402 coefficients for the growth of real exports variable is 0.22, surprisingly similar to the average cross-section results.

The top two diagrams of Figure 6.5 show the scatter of point estimates and the accompanying 5 percent confidence intervals for the 299 regressions that used the traditional *ordinary least squares (OLS) method* to estimate the coefficient values and confidence levels. As pointed out earlier, OLS estimates may be biased by spurious correlations among time-series variables. Most time-series studies now apply tests and, when necessary, adjustments to the data in order to mitigate the effects of spurious correlations of variables moving over time. The bottom two diagrams plot the point estimates and 5 percent confidence intervals for the 103 regressions that applied those recommended

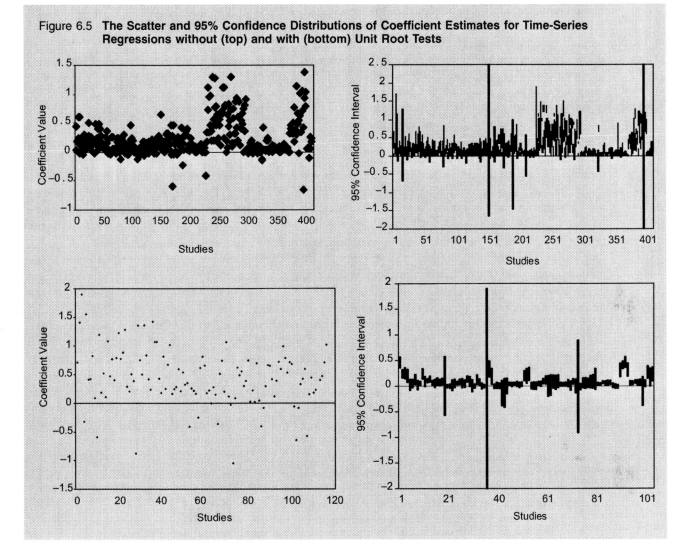

Figure 6.5 **The Scatter and 95% Confidence Distributions of Coefficient Estimates for Time-Series Regressions without (top) and with (bottom) Unit Root Tests**

adjustments. There is a very large difference between the results of the regressions that did not apply the best time-series methods and those that did. The average value of the 299 coefficients from time-series regressions was 0.26, which is over three times as large as the average 0.08 value for the trade coefficients from 103 time-series regressions for which time-series estimation procedures were adjusted. It appears that spurious correlations may have biased the average coefficient estimate of 0.22 reported for the whole set of time-series regressions. The long-run gains from international trade may not be as great as the average regression results seem to suggest.

Some researchers have split the sample of countries according to the World Bank's (2002) classification of high-, upper-middle-, lower-middle-, or low-income countries. A survey of these studies shows that the average coefficient on export growth for high-income countries is 0.43 and is 0.15 for upper-middle-income countries, 0.22 for lower-middle-income countries, and 0.21 for low-income countries. The different growth rates may be due to developing countries' lower capacity to apply the foreign technology that potentially flows along with traded goods and services. Also, the transnational corporations that dominate international trade may be able to exploit exporters in developing countries to a greater degree, thus leaving fewer gains from trade in developing countries. Finally, recall from the previous chapter that lower-income countries more often export raw materials and primary products, and such exports do not seem to generate the same technology spillovers and incentives for **innovation** that industrial products generate. The low coefficient values for upper-middle-income countries are of special concern. Are these countries at the stage where the shift to more industrial production requires protection from imports?

The Relationship between International Trade and Institutions

Rodriguez and Rodrik (1999, 2001) show that international trade policy is too closely correlated with factors such as legal structures, quality of government programs, protection of human rights, cultural factors, and many other social institutions for statistical programs to differentiate between the trade's effect on growth and the growth effects of the various institutions. That is, it may not be the case that an **open economy** grows faster because it trades more, but that institutional and policy variables really are the cause of faster economic growth and also happen to facilitate international trade. Thus, liberalizing trade will not expand growth if institutions remain unchanged.

Rodrik, Arvind Subramanian, and Francesco Trebbi (2004) show that the coefficient for trade actually becomes statistically insignificant when variables representing institutions are also included in a growth regression such as equation (6.6). The rule of law, property rights, human rights, **patents** and **copyrights**, a consistent legal system, and many other institutions seem to be more important for growth than opening the borders to trade. When Roberto Rigobon and Dani Rodrik (2005) controlled for the simultaneous effects of many other variables, including many institutional variables, the estimated regression coefficient for overall international trade, not just raw materials trade, was *negative*. All other things equal, trade reduced economic growth.

It is clear that international trade's effect on economic growth is intertwined with many other influences on growth. In the conclusion to his survey of case studies and statistical studies on the relationship between international trade and growth, Robert E. Baldwin (2003) sums up as follows:

> It is true developing countries are often given the advice that decreasing trade barriers is a more effective way of achieving higher sustainable rates of growth than tightening trade restrictions. But . . . those giving such advice also emphasize the need, as a minimum, for a stable and non-discriminatory exchange-rate system and usually also the need for prudent monetary and fiscal policies and corruption-free administration of economic policies for trade liberalization to be effective in the long-run. It seems to me that the various country studies do support this type of policy advice and the cross-country statistical studies do not overturn this conclusion. But the recent critiques of the latter studies demonstrate that we must be careful in attributing any single economic policy, such as the lowering of trade barriers, as being a sufficient government action for accelerating the rate of economic growth.

The intellectual debate over whether trade is "the engine of growth" or merely a "handmaiden of growth" has, therefore, not yet been settled. The empirical evidence does not clearly establish whether international trade itself drives economic growth or whether it merely *accompanies* economic growth. As we showed in Chapter 4, even the HO model that economists most often use to frame their pro-trade policy prescriptions does not rule out that there may be substantial adjustment costs associated with the expansion of international trade; resources must be reallocated and entire sectors of an economy may shrink, making specialized capital obsolete. There are also likely to be significant changes in how income is distributed in society.

The Stolper-Samuelson Theorem and Long-Run Economic Change

In the long run, trade's effect on the welfare of individuals and groups of individuals can be quite different from the changes suggested by the HO model or the Stolper-Samuelson theorem. Recall from Chapter 4 how the Stolper-Samuelson theorem predicted incomes accruing to the owners of the fixed stock of factors of production would change when an economy opens itself to international trade. But, in the long run, the stocks of factors of production are not fixed. In a dynamic setting, economic development changes both the amount of factors of production and the technology with which those factors are transformed into output. Technological progress is seldom **neutral** in the sense that all factors have their marginal productivities expanded by the same proportion. Many studies suggest that recent shifts in technology have favored those factors that are most abundant in wealthy economies. That is, to the extent that international trade stimulates technological change, it seems also to have shifted comparative advantage in a way that favors capital and human-capital abundant countries. These were precisely the countries that already enjoyed higher incomes, of course. Therefore, trade's positive effect on technological progress and economic growth will dynamically alter the static effects on relative factor incomes described by the Stolper-Samuelson theorem.

The relative earnings of factors of production have also been affected by the reduction in competition among producers, as described in the previous chapter. Large transnational corporations that can exercise market power across borders have been able to extract growing shares of the gains from international trade. The growing inequality of income and wealth throughout the world is in part the result of the growing share of corporate profit in the national incomes. Since the ownership of transnational corporations is concentrated in high-income countries, the gains from international trade also tend to be concentrated in a small number of countries. In short, some countries gain much more from trade than others, contrary to what the HO model, and its assumption of perfect competition, seems to suggest.

In reference to the above statistical studies, the growth effect of international trade is almost never found to be positive in the case of countries whose comparative advantage is in exporting raw materials. As first confirmed by Jeffrey Sachs and Andrew Warner (1995) and reconfirmed by Jeffrey Frankel's (2010) survey of the literature, in the case of raw material exporters, statistical results consistently show that expanding trade *reduces* economic growth. This finding is referred to as the **natural resource curse**, and many explanations have been given: (1) the transnational firms who dominate trade have the power to suppress prices of natural resources, (2) the elasticity of demand for natural resources is low, and (3) the concentration of ownership of resources keeps export earnings in the hands of local elite business and resource groups that use their earnings to control political institutions that restrict economic and social change.

THE SOLOW GROWTH MODEL

The model most often used to describe the process of economic growth is the model developed by Robert Solow (1956, 1957). This model is featured in nearly all textbooks that cover the topic of economic growth and has come to be known as simply the **Solow model**. Solow's model incorporates the "marginalist" thinking of neoclassical economics, and the model is also referred to as the **neoclassical growth model**.

Technological Progress and Factor Accumulation

Recall that an economy can grow because (1) investment increases the stock of productive factors or (2) technological change improves the efficiency with which factors combine to produce welfare-enhancing output. There are fundamental differences between economic growth generated by **technological progress** and economic growth generated by *factor accumulation*. The differences can be illustrated using a simple aggregate economy-wide production function.

The simplest example of an aggregate production function is where total national output is specified as a function of just two factors of production, labor and capital. In this case, the economy's aggregate production function is

(6.7) $$Y = f(K, L)$$

where Y is total output, K is the economy's stock of capital, and L is the number of workers. Suppose also that each of the inputs has a positive effect on output. Or, for example, if $K_2 > K_1$, then:

(6.8) $$f(K_2, L_1) > f(K_1, L_1).$$

Thus, investing in more capital causes output to grow, all other things equal.

The function f(K, L), which specifies how inputs like capital and labor are transformed into output, effectively represents the economy's state of technology. Technological change implies a shift to a new production function that translates the same inputs into a different amount of output. Technological change that increases total output is often referred to as *technological progress* in the economic development literature, and can be described symbolically as an increase in output achieved by the same set of productive factors. That is, for a given amount of capital, K_1, and labor, L_1, technological progress takes the economy to the new production function g(K, L) that increases output from Y_1 to Y_2:

(6.9) $$Y_2 = g(K_1, L_1) > Y_1 = f(K_1, L_1).$$

The Solow model furthermore incorporates the neoclassical assumption that when only one input is increased, holding the others constant, the expansion of the variable input is subject to **diminishing returns**. The logic of diminishing returns is straightforward: each additional unit of capital provides the fixed labor force with more identical tools and machines, but it becomes increasingly difficult for labor to use those additional tools and machines to increase output. For example, give a ditch digger a shovel, and she can certainly dig a much bigger hole than if she had to use her bare hands. A wheelbarrow would also help to move the dirt. But how much bigger a hole could she dig with two shovels and two wheelbarrows? Over a year's time it could prove useful to have more than one shovel or wheelbarrow in case one breaks, leaving the digger temporarily without her tools. How much would a third shovel do for the worker's digging capacity?

Diminishing returns is illustrated in Figure 6.6, which shows the technical relationship between Y and K, assuming L and all other factors of production remain fixed. The curved production function in Figure 6.6 depicts diminishing returns because each subsequent equal addition to the amount of capital increases output by smaller and smaller amounts. Notice that with labor constant, output is effectively a function of the capital stock, and we can conveniently write the production function as Y = f(K).

Diminishing returns appears to suggest that growth slows down with ever-increasing investment, but Solow (1956) concluded that output growth comes to a complete stop even if investment continues to occur. The reason for this stunning conclusion is that Solow also recognized that capital wears out, that is, it *depreciates*. Some portion of the capital stock must be replaced, repaired, or serviced every year to keep the total stock of capital from decreasing. And, the larger the capital stock, the greater the amount of capital that needs to be replaced or repaired. Solow assumed that **depreciation** is a constant fraction, δ, of the stock of capital, K. In this case, the change in the stock of capital over the course of the year, denoted as ΔK, is equal to the difference between total new investment, I, and the amount of existing capital that depreciates:

(6.10) $$\Delta K = I - \delta K.$$

If the capital stock K or the depreciations rate δ are large, then δK may be greater than I, and the capital stock may shrink even when I is positive.[3]

Figure 6.6 **A Production Function Subject to Diminishing Returns to Capital**

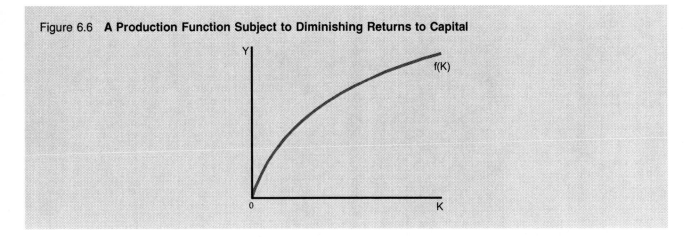

Investment depends on people's willingness to save instead of consume. If people save a constant fraction, σ, of income Y, then total saving, S, and investment, I, are

(6.11) $I = S = \sigma Y.$

In this case, $I = \sigma f(K)$ and equation (6.10) can be rewritten as:

(6.12) $\Delta K = I - \delta K = \sigma Y - \delta K = \sigma f(K) - \delta K.$

This dynamic equation of the change in the economy's stock of capital shows that when total investment is greater than what is needed to replace that portion of the capital stock that wears out, or $\sigma f(K)$ is greater than ΔK, the total stock of capital increases and so does total output $Y = f(K)$. If, on the other hand, when $\sigma f(K) < \delta K$, total investment in new capital is not large enough to replace the capital that depreciates, and the total stock of K and output $Y = f(K)$ decreases.

It is easy to represent the Solow model graphically because depreciation, investment, and output are all functions of the capital stock K. Therefore, the three functions can all be included in a single diagram in which capital is shown on the horizontal axis and the quantities Y, I, and depreciation are measured along the vertical axis. With output assumed to be subject to diminishing returns to capital, the production function slopes upward at a decreasing rate in Figure 6.7. With a constant savings rate, savings is a constant proportion, σ, of income, or $\sigma f(K)$. The investment function $I = \sigma f(K)$ is therefore a diminished version of the production function $f(K)$, and its slope also decreases as the capital stock K increases. The constant rate of depreciation implies that depreciation is represented by a straight-line function of capital, δK. Figure 6.7 combines all three functions.

An important conclusion of Solow's model is that, given the economy's production function, savings rate, and depreciation rate, the size of the economy's capital stock automatically adjusts toward the stable equilibrium level K^* where investment just equals depreciation. To the left of K^*, the investment curve $I = \sigma f(K)$ lies above the depreciation line δK, and thus the capital stock grows at these levels of capital. But, because of diminishing returns, the slope of $\sigma f(K)$ declines and, eventually, investment only adds just enough to income and saving to cover the increased depreciation of the constantly increasing stock of capital. At that point, there is no further growth of K. To the right of K^*, the situation is reversed; investment is less than depreciation, and K declines back toward K^*.

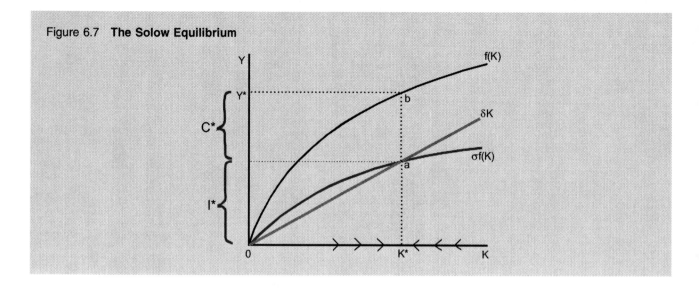

Figure 6.7 **The Solow Equilibrium**

Since output is a function of K, it also moves toward a stable equilibrium level of $Y^* = f(K^*)$. At Y^* consumption and investment are C^* and $I^* = \sigma Y^*$, respectively. Solow called these stable equilibrium levels of the capital stock and output the economy's **steady state equilibrium**. In this equilibrium, investment is positive but, because of depreciating, output growth is zero.

Increased Investment Brings Only Medium-Run Growth

Solow's model contradicts the common belief that investment, that is, *factor accumulation,* is the source of long-run economic growth. To grasp why that belief is inaccurate, suppose that there is a sudden change in the economy-wide rate of saving from σ_1 to σ_2, and, as illustrated in Figure 6.8, the saving function shifts up from $\sigma_1 f(K)$ to $\sigma_2 f(K)$. Now, at the initial steady state levels of capital and output, K_1^* and Y_1^*, saving exceeds depreciation. Thus, the capital stock grows. But as the capital stock grows, the amount of saving required to cover the cost of replacing depreciating capital increases, and because of diminishing returns to capital, total saving and investment do not grow in proportion to the capital stock. The economy, therefore, moves to a new steady state equilibrium, where the capital stock and output settle at K_2^* and Y_2^*, respectively.

The shift from Y_1^* to Y_2^* is, therefore, best described as **medium-run** or **transitional economic growth**, not *permanent* economic growth. Output growth gradually slows and eventually again stops when the new steady state is reached. Of course, a further increase in the rate of saving can spur another round of transitional growth. However, the rate of saving cannot be raised forever. The savings rate cannot increase to 100 percent of output because people would starve. Saving in the most frugal countries today does not exceed 30–40 percent of income.

Does International Trade Create Only Medium-Run Growth Too?

The Solow model also suggests that international trade does not increase an economy's rate of growth in the long run. Recall from Figure 6.1 that the gain from trade described by the Heckscher-Ohlin model can be illustrated as a one-time shift of the economy's production-possibilities curve. Within the framework of the Solow growth model, such a one-time improvement in welfare constitutes an upward shift in the production function because international trade effectively permits the economy to generate a higher value of output for a given set of inputs. Richard Baldwin (1992) shows that this

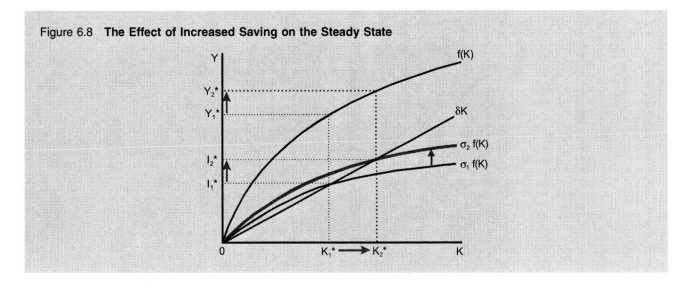

Figure 6.8   **The Effect of Increased Saving on the Steady State**

upward shift in the production function causes a secondary increase in real output as the economy transitions to a new steady state.

Figure 6.9 depicts such a trade-induced shift in the production function. For example, the shift from f(k) to g(k) changes the economy's steady state capital-output ratio and per capita income from K_1^* and Y_1^* to K_2^* and Y_3^*, respectively. These changes are the result of an immediate increase in per worker output from Y_1^* to Y_2^* before the capital stock, K, begins to change. This is the traditional static gain from trade. Assuming a constant rate of saving, the increase in real income raises the economy's saving function as well. Therefore, the steady state equilibrium shifts up and generates a secondary spurt of medium-run growth that gradually moves to the new steady state equilibrium at K_2^* and Y_3^*.

Note, however, that the traditional gain from trade does not cause permanent economic growth in the Solow model. The economy eventually settles at the new steady state equilibrium. Therefore, if international trade does generate permanent economic growth, this effect must operate through some other channel. The Solow model actually provides an important insight into how trade might stimulate more permanent economic growth.

Technological Change and Permanent Growth

The continuous and rapid growth of material output over the past two centuries suggests that at least some countries have experienced more than a transition from one steady state to another. Average real GDP in the world as a whole increased about tenfold between 1820 and 2000, and in today's most developed economies, real income per capita increased about twentyfold to thirtyfold.[4] But, if this growth could not have been the result of only saving and investment, what else went on that the simple Solow model illustrated above did not reveal?

Solow (1956) used his model to show that the growth in material output over the previous two centuries was the result of technological progress. He argued that there is a difference between giving a bookkeeper more pens and ink, the bookkeeper's tools in 1800, and giving him a calculator. Recall that we defined technological change as a shift in the economy's aggregate production function. As shown in Figure 6.10, in the absence of technological progress, the first unit of capital added to a given amount of other productive resources results in 100 units of output being produced. Diminishing returns results in the second unit of capital adding only 40 units of output, however.

Figure 6.9   Trade and the Solow Growth Model

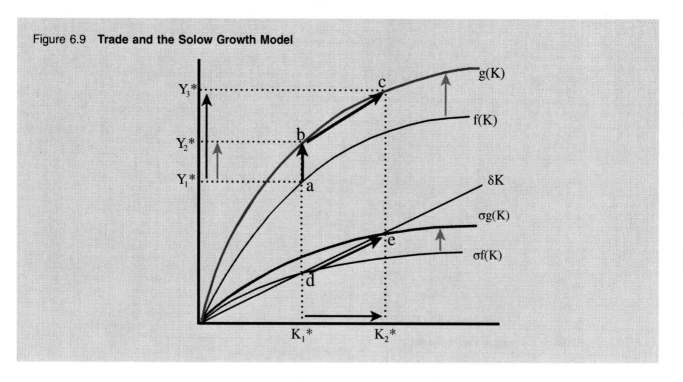

Alternatively, when the doubling of capital is combined with a shift in technology and, therefore, an upward shift in the production function from $f_1(K)$ to $f_2(K)$ in Figure 6.10, output also doubles, to 200 units. This example suggests that technological progress enables the economy to avoid diminishing returns.

Permanent economic growth thus requires continued shifts in the production function, or continual technological progress. Figure 6.11 illustrates how repeated upward shifts of the production function in the Solow model shift the economy's steady states from points a to b and then to c, which represent the steady state combinations of K^* and Y^*, K^{**} and Y^{**}, and K^{***} and Y^{***}, respectively, rather than along a single production function with diminishing returns.

By shifting the production function, technological progress induces additional investment in capital that raises the capital stock from K^* to K^{**} and K^{***}. But note that it is technological progress that induces investment, not investment that causes the continued growth. In terms of our earlier example, for the bookkeeper to make use of computer technology, he must invest in a computer. But it takes the invention of the computer to enable the investment. In general, the Solow model suggests that the rising standards of living that people in most countries have experienced over most of the past two hundred years have been the result of both *more* tools and machines and *better* tools and machines as well as better knowledge and production methods. According to Solow's neoclassical model with diminishing returns, without technological progress the economy cannot avoid diminishing returns to investment.

If you doubt that technological progress is really necessary for economic growth, try imagining what our standard of living would be like today if after 1800 we had only increased the number of horses rather than inventing motorized tractors, we had used only larger doses of cod liver oil rather than developing antibiotics to fight infections, and we had only raised more carrier pigeons rather than inventing the Internet. Or, can the earth support twice as much electricity generation using coal and today's technology, twice as many cars putting twice as much exhaust into the air, and twice as many acres for growing food for the 12 billion or so humans that will likely inhabit the earth in a hundred years? Obviously, for continued growth of output to be possible, we need to figure out

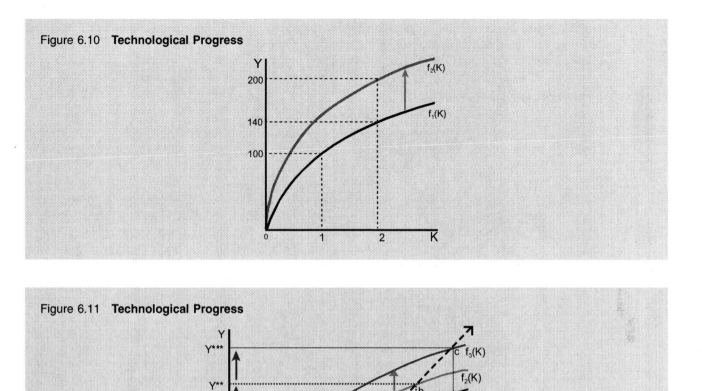

Figure 6.10 **Technological Progress**

Figure 6.11 **Technological Progress**

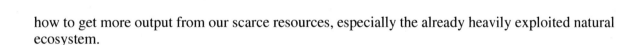

how to get more output from our scarce resources, especially the already heavily exploited natural ecosystem.

TECHNOLOGY AND TECHNOLOGICAL PROGRESS

The Solow model does not tell us anything about how to generate technological progress, only that there is no long-run growth without it. In order to discern whether international trade might generate permanent economic growth by stimulating technological change, we need to examine technology and the process of technological change in greater detail. This section first discusses what we mean by technology, and we emphasize that technology is an accumulation of knowledge and ideas that follows a **combinatorial process**. Second, this section presents a popular dynamic model of economic change built on the idea that technological change is a costly human activity that requires scarce resources to be applied to generate new ideas, inventions, improvements in quality, more attractive designs, reductions in cost, better management practices, more efficient plant layouts, and all other forms of innovations.

Human Technology

Earlier in this chapter, we presented the neoclassical definition of technological progress as an upward shift in the economy's aggregate production function. Technological progress was effectively defined as an improvement in method, practice, procedure, or organization that increases the amount of output produced from a given set of inputs. From a social perspective, the concept of technology is much more than the economy's production function. Among many other complications, technological change can affect (1) the production process, (2) the quantities of productive inputs that humans can make use of, and (3) how humans perceive that production to affect their well-being. But, even if we take the neoclassical growth definition at face value, economists need to know more about the process in order to design policies to raise the rate of economic growth.

Romer (1993, p. 543) broadens the definition:

> The word technology invokes images of manufacturing, but most economic activity takes place outside of factories. Ideas include the innumerable insights about packaging, marketing, distribution, inventory control, payments systems, information systems, transactions processing, quality control, and worker motivation that are all used in the creation of economic value in a modern economy. If one looks carefully at the details of the operations of a corporation like Frito-Lay, one sees that there are as many subtle ideas involved in supplying potato chips to a consumer as there are in making computer chips. In addition, the ideas involved in supplying potato chips are probably more important for successful development in the poorest countries.

Indeed, since the Solow model seeks to represent the entire economy, and not just one factory or industry, we are interested in more than the cutting-edge technology of a few industries like electronics, biotechnology, or information technology. But, even Romer's description of technology is not broad enough.

What most distinguishes humans from other animal species is not just the extraordinary amount of knowledge and techniques that they apply to their daily routine of going about life, but that so much of their knowledge and techniques were developed separately from the evolution of the physical human being. That is, we humans draw on a huge body of ideas, knowledge, techniques, methods, procedures, and other forms of behavior that is passed on from generation to generation through culture, language, and various codified means. On the other hand, much more of the knowledge or technology that nonhuman animals apply is hardwired in the instinctive and automatic processes of their brains. Most of the observed behavior of nonhuman living creatures is passed on through genes, so that changes in the way they live, how they interact with each other, and how they deal with their natural environment occur through the slow process of evolution. The biologist Edward O. Wilson (1975) describes the life-enhancing techniques and practices of nonhuman animals as "bound by a tight **biological leash**."

All animals, of course, pass on at least some knowledge and technology through communications between generations in addition to the selective biological passing on of genes. Scientists have observed and documented intergenerational communicative learning by primates, elephants, and many other animal species. However, scientists have also observed that for nonhumans the "biological leash" does not seem to get longer, at least not for as long as humans have been observing fellow animal species. Recent human history is different, however. According to Katherine Nelson and Richard R. Nelson (2002, p. 720):

Humans today cannot run much faster or shout much louder than humans of a century—or fifty centuries—ago, nor are our eyes any better. But we can get where we are going far faster by bike, by car, or by airplane. We can communicate over long distances by flags, telegraph, wireless, and now e-mail. We can see the galaxies an incredible distance away, and also the smallest molecules, through the technologies we have progressively developed over time. The biological leash has become longer and longer, so that today our species knowledge capabilities in many arenas appear very loosely attached to our biological makeup.

Human technology has gotten a life of its own, so to speak, able to survive separately from humans. This is not to say that the evolution of the human brain is not an important determinant of human technology. Indeed, the human brain's past evolution to where it can now store and process very large amounts of knowledge certainly is a major factor in the growth of human technology. But, as Nelson and Nelson note, the storage of knowledge outside the human brain has come to characterize much of human technology:

> [T]he minds of individual human actors are extended through the collective memories of the community as well as through the artifacts and symbols—especially spoken and written language—of their social worlds. (p. 721)

Humans have developed a social structure and methods of communication that permit the accumulation of knowledge well beyond what can be carried in the mind. Humans hold much of their technologies in the form of social culture that is passed from generation to generation by communicating through various languages, including spoken language and cultural body language. Increasingly, humans hold knowledge in the form of written instructions that can be communicated to, or accessed and read by, anyone at any time.

We define *technology* as this entire set of techniques, knowledge, methods, procedures, and culture that exist outside the physical human body and brain. Unlike the instinctive knowledge that is passed biologically from generation to generation, and which enters the production function as a factor of production, technology is very diverse. It includes the techniques and processes that humans use to produce specific products, but it also includes the social culture that defines how humans interact within their societies, and it includes the techniques and systems that permit the external storage and accumulation of technologies. Technology therefore includes everything from social norms learned from parents to the information stored on Internet servers.

Technological Progress Is a Combinatorial Process

New knowledge generally builds on previous knowledge by *combining* existing ideas and knowledge in order to create new ideas and knowledge. According to Martin L. Weitzman (1996, p. 211): "An abstract case could be made that *all* innovations, being expressions of human imagination, are in a sense combinatoric."[5] The combinatorial nature of the accumulation of human knowledge is very important for explaining international trade's positive effect on economic growth. The more knowledge we have, the easier it is to come up with new ideas and increase our knowledge. In fact, a combinatorial process can grow explosively.

Table 6.1 provides a simple example of a combinatorial process of technological progress. Suppose that in each successive period of time, the number of new ideas created is equal to the number of all possible pairs of ideas created in the previous period. As the table shows, if the stock of knowledge in a hypothetical economy consists of four ideas numbered 1 through 4, then all the possible combinations of the initial four ideas results in six new ideas A through F. Thus, after one period of innovation, this specific combinatorial process has expanded four ideas into six new ideas, which

Table 6.1

A Combinatorial Growth Process (new idea = the unique combination of two old ideas)

Begin with 4 ideas:		New Ideas	Accumulated Ideas	Percentage Growth
Period 1	Begin with	4	4	
Period 2	4!/(2!·2!) =	6	10	150
Period 3	6!/(4!·2!) =	15	25	150
Period 4	15!/(13!·2!) =	105	130	420
Period 5	105!/(103!·2!) =	5,460	5,590	4,200

Period 1:	Period 2:	Period 3:		
1	1,2 = A	A,B	B,C	C,E
2	1,3 = B	A,C	B,D	C,F
3	1,4 = C	A,D	B,E	D,E
4	2,3 = D	A,E	B,F	D,F
	2,4 = E	A,F	C,D	E,F
	3,4 = F			

In general, a combinatorial process consists of n elements taken r at a time, which equals $n!/[(n-r)!\cdot r!]$. The symbol "!" represents a product of descending integers beginning with the number preceding the !, for example, $5! = 5\cdot4\cdot3\cdot2\cdot1 = 120$. In this example, we take n as the number of ideas generated in the previous period and combine them 2 at a time, so r = 2.

implies a total stock of knowledge equal to ten ideas, an increase of 150 percent over the previous stock of four ideas. By the fifth round, there are 5,460 combinations of the previous period's 105 new ideas. This potentially explosive expansion of knowledge under the combinatorial process led Weitzman (1998) to conclude that technological progress is likely to accelerate over time.

The example in Table 6.1 is obviously unrealistic. The state of knowledge consists of more than four ideas. If knowledge consists of millions or even billions of ideas, then the simple example above suggests that the combinatorial process of technological progress must indeed be very explosive. Furthermore, older ideas can also be combined with later ideas, in which case the examples above understate the rate of technological progress. On the other hand, knowledge can also be forgotten or lost, in which case the combinatorial process will be diminished. Resources must be employed to teach each successive generation of people the knowledge that was already accumulated by previous generations. And, perhaps most importantly, it is unlikely that all combinations of previous ideas produce useful new ideas. Many of the new ideas that were useful in one period do not lead to further useful ideas when they are combined with other existing ideas. All in all, the process of technological progress is very complex and the combinatorial process described above probably does not capture all the nuances and variations. However, the idea that the greater the stock of knowledge, the more combinations are possible remains a very important insight.

Technological Change Is Path Dependent

The combinatorial nature of knowledge explains why technological change tends to be a **path-dependent process**, in which the ability to create new technologies depends on the technologies already accumulated. The path-dependent nature of the step-by-step process of technological change also means that even momentous technological advances, such as the development of agriculture, the wheel, the factory system, or electricity, took place through a fairly well-defined sequence of steps that built on previously acquired knowledge, experiments, and technological change.

The gradual, step-by-step combinatorial nature of technological change is evidenced by the fact that there is some dispute over who exactly is responsible for many of humanity's greatest discoveries and inventions. For example, the myth is that Alexander Graham Bell suddenly thought up his design for the telephone while sitting on a log over the Grand River near his parents' house in Brantford, Ontario, mulling over what he had up to that point discovered about sound. Yet, the same day that Alexander Graham Bell filed a patent application for the telephone, another inventor, Elisha Gray, filed a similar application. Malcolm Gladwell (2008) describes the common phenomenon of simultaneous discovery as follows:

> In order to get one of the greatest inventions of the modern age, . . . we thought we needed the solitary genius. But if Alexander Graham Bell had fallen into the Grand River and drowned that day back in Brantford, the world would still have had the telephone, the only difference being that the telephone company would have been nicknamed Ma Gray, not Ma Bell.[6]

Similarly, it is not entirely clear whether the Wright brothers were really the first ones to fly. Brazilians argue that their compatriot, Alberto Santos-Dumont, was the first to fly a heavier-than-air craft. Charles Darwin and Alfred Russel Wallace are both credited with discovering evolution. And there were four independent discoveries of sunspots in 1611, by Galileo in Italy, Christoph Scheiner in Germany, Johannes and David Fabricius in Holland, and Thomas Harriott in England. Isaac Newton and Gottfried Wilhelm Leibniz both discovered calculus. It is difficult to attribute even one of the steps in many innovations to any particular person because many people walk along the same path.

Path dependency provides another reason why new ideas are often rejected or ignored. An interesting example of how hard it is to change technology is the popular layout of the keys on your computer keyboard. The current layout is known as "QWERTY," in reference to the six letter keys at the upper left-hand side of the keyboard. Early typewriters were unpowered mechanical machines, and each key activated levers that pushed a reverse mold of a letter or symbol toward a roller that contained a sheet of paper. These levers obviously had to be activated in succession; if the typist hit two at once, they would get tangled and stuck near the point where they hit the paper. The layout of the keyboard was designed to minimize the likelihood of levers hitting each other when experienced typists typed at high speed. The characters that were often typed in succession were thus placed some distance away from each other so mechanical collisions were less likely. Today we have electronic keyboards, and there is no longer any problem of levers getting tangled up. But no one has begun producing keyboards with another layout. Why not? People are used to it, and the gain in efficiency from an alternative layout would at best be very small. If we could start from scratch today, we might choose a different path. But technology never starts from scratch.

On a broader scale, the United States has been reluctant to adopt the metric system, and China and Japan have no plans to change their cumbersome systems of writing. The world today seems to be locked into technologies that require the use of fossil fuels that add to the greenhouse gases in the atmosphere. There are obvious alternative technologies available, but there are apparently few incentives for anyone to apply them. Most cars sold today still use an internal combustion engine fueled by gasoline. Most electric power plants use coal, the "dirtiest" fossil fuel in terms of greenhouse gas emissions, and in 2010 there were several hundred more coal-fired power plants under construction throughout the world.

Not All New Technology Constitutes Progress

Changes in technology have a variety of effects on the way humans work and live. Some production may increase, but life may become less pleasant. For example, we all enjoy many benefits from technologies that take advantage of electric power. But, does an electric power plant represent technological progress?

Coal, oil, natural gas, and hydropower are the most often used sources of power for electricity generation. Of these four sources, three emit carbon into the atmosphere. The fourth, hydroelectric power, requires the construction of dams and other systems to divert water from natural rivers and lakes. In short, electricity generation alters the natural environment. The damage such power plants do to the environment must be seen as part of the broad range of technological changes brought about by the development of electricity and the application of electric power in factories, homes, and throughout human society.

There is little doubt that the development of electric power has enhanced both labor and physical capital. Better lighting and communications, air-conditioning, individually controlled machinery—all of these things have made labor more productive. The assembly line, office equipment, teaching aids, and transportation are all more efficient because of electric power. But, the carbon emissions of electric power plants contribute to global warming, which threatens to cause climate changes that will diminish the services of the ecosystem that humans have come to depend on. If greenhouse gas emissions are permitted to continue increasing at their current rate, humanity may find its standard of living seriously diminished. The worst-case scenario is that human exploitation of nature destroys the natural services that support human life.

JOSEPH SCHUMPETER'S MODEL OF CREATIVE DESTRUCTION

Other fundamental characteristics of technical progress were brought out by Joseph Schumpeter, who criticized neoclassical economists who were his early twentieth-century contemporaries for being too concerned with resource allocation in static circumstances and, therefore, not paying attention to the fact that the economies around them were undergoing continual and huge changes. Schumpeter (1934, p. 84) wrote that the important issue is not "how capitalism administers existing structures, . . . the relevant problem is how it creates and destroys them." Recent models of technological progress have built on **Schumpeter's model** of **creative destruction**, which is also described as an **evolutionary model of economic change**.

Fundamental Ideas behind Schumpeter's Model

First of all, Schumpeter recognized that it takes resources to create new ideas, work out new technologies, install new methods, and teach new knowledge. Therefore, someone must bear the costs of innovation. Schumpeter noted that by the twentieth century, private firms were more often willing to bear the costs of innovation because they were able to capture the profits generated by it. Schumpeter saw profit very differently than traditional neoclassical economists did. Schumpeter did not view *profit* as a problem or as a form of inefficiency. In fact, he saw profit as necessary to induce innovative activity, and believed that efforts to reduce firms' profits by breaking up large firms and promoting traditional price competition could slow down innovation and economic growth.

Your microeconomics or business economics course no doubt explained that under perfect competition, the market price exactly covers the cost of the resources used in *production*. This outcome of the mythical state of perfect competition is desirable in that it means prices exactly reflect underlying costs, and price signals thus lead individual producers and consumers to allocate society's resources most efficiently. However, perfect competition, if it existed, would leave no income to cover the upfront cost of innovation. So, it is easy to see why Schumpeter clashed with mainstream economists, whose orthodox microeconomic theory suggests that monopoly profit is a form of "market failure" that is costly to society. Schumpeter viewed profits as necessary for the economic growth that was so rapidly raising living standards at the start of the twentieth century.

Schumpeter was not blind to the dangers of letting large firms gain market power. He pointed out, however, that market power gained through innovation would be only temporary as long as vested interests were prevented from stifling innovation by others. New innovations would, sooner or later, destroy monopoly positions created by earlier innovation. Every time an innovator, or **entrepreneur**, *creates* a new business opportunity, it *destroys* the market power and profits that its competitors had gained as a result of their earlier innovations. Schumpeter thus described the capitalist economy as a "perennial gale of *creative destruction*." This continual creation and destruction prevents monopolies from permanently reaping profits, and, in the process, society enjoys constant technological progress.

Schumpeter's concept of *creative destruction* captures another important characteristic of economic growth, which is that the creation of something new requires that resources be reallocated, and often some existing economic activity must be eliminated. New activities require resources, which, in the absence of unemployment or excess capacity, must be transferred from existing activities. Growing economies are therefore characterized by **structural change** as old economic activities are replaced by new economic activities. This point is very relevant today, given that we have reached limits to the earth's capacity to provide resources.

Recent "Schumpeterian" Models of Technological Progress

A number of economists have developed models of technological progress based on the Schumpeterian assumption that technological progress is the result of entrepreneurs intentionally applying resources to develop better products, improve the organization of firms, or use resources more efficiently. These models are often referred to as **Schumpeterian growth models** because they incorporate the idea that entrepreneurs compete for monopoly profits by engaging in costly research and development (R&D) activities in order to *creatively destroy* their competition and capture the profits of their innovations.

All Schumpeterian innovation models are dynamic optimization models that hypothesize that innovators increase their R&D activity whenever expected marginal profits exceed the marginal costs of innovation. More specifically, the dynamic Schumpeterian optimization problem depends on:

- The expected likelihood that intentional costly R&D activity will generate new ideas and knowledge (innovations)
- The opportunity costs of acquiring resources to carry out R&D
- The benefits that entrepreneurs expect (hope) to reap from an innovation

The first two items above, research productivity and resource costs, determine the *cost* of innovation. The latter item reflects the *gains* from innovation. The above distinctions between productivity of R&D, opportunity costs of employing resources to engage in innovative activities, and future benefits are important for distinguishing more specific contributors and barriers to innovation.

Growth theorists identified several key variables that impacted the costs and gains of technological innovation. Obviously, the innovator's expected profit or the economy's overall welfare gains are key to estimating the future gains from innovation. Therefore, economic conditions and policies that enable innovators to reap greater profits or policies to distribute new ideas and better products to more people enhance the gains from innovation. The efficiency with which innovators can produce new technologies or new products, or society can generate new ideas and knowledge, is an important variable.

Growth theorists hypothesize that the efficiency of innovation depends on the quality and quantity of productive factors, as well as the economic and social institutions in which those factors are employed. Innovation requires an educated labor force, for example. In the case of institutions, Schumpeter argued that a society's tolerance of change, of "deviant" behavior by entrepreneurs, and of resistance by vested interests to creatively destructive innovation ultimately determine an economy's rate of technological progress. Finally, how a society views the future versus the present determines how willing people, firms, and government policy makers are to allocate current resources toward activities that bring uncertain gains in the future. Hence, most Schumpeterian models of technological change have as principal variables the rate of profit, the stock of factors of production, various proxies for institutions like economic freedom, social mobility, protection of property rights, and others, and the social discount rate.

This model is useful only as a general guide to technological change. Each of the variables in the model is difficult to determine precisely. Not least is the problem of how expectations are determined. Innovation is a most uncertain process, and future gains from innovative activity are equally nebulous at the time innovators are undertaking research, experiments, tests, and so on. When it comes to innovative activity, we must deal with uncertainty, not calculable risk.

Recall from the previous chapter and the discussion of financial transactions and investment activity that risk implies there is at least a known set of probabilities for alternative outcomes, but uncertainty admits some degree of ignorance of the probabilities of specific outcomes and even of the existence of all possible outcomes. Entrepreneurs' estimates of future costs and benefits are volatile because they depend on future economic conditions, human sentiments, and very partial information sets. Decisions to undertake costly innovative activities are, inevitably, influenced by emotion, past experience, poorly supported judgments of the future, and, in John Maynard Keynes's (1936) terminology, "animal spirits." Innovative activity, therefore, will tend to be volatile unless, somehow, economic conditions can be stabilized, emotions can be controlled, and more complete and transparent information can be made available.

The Cost of Innovation

Innovation requires engineers, scientists, laboratory assistants, test pilots, agronomists, computer programmers, marketing consultants, cost experts, and a great number of other people to create new ideas and carry out innovative projects. These people need time, equipment, laboratories, offices, raw materials, libraries, and many other things to help them innovate. Resources for innovation have opportunity costs, namely the value of the things that can no longer be produced when the economy's scarce resources are allocated to R&D activity. The quantity of resources used in innovative activities are, therefore, limited by the economy's total stock of factors of production, and the cost of those resources depends on total demand for those resources by producers, investors, and innovators.

An expansion of R&D activity, all other thing equal, increases the total demand for factors and resources and thus increases the price of productive resources. Hence, Schumpeterian models of innovation assume that, given the total supply of factors of production, the cost of innovation is an increasing function of the amount of resources applied to R&D activity. The price of resources is lower, all other things equal, the greater the total amount of factors and resources available to both producers and innovators.

To estimate the actual cost of generating an innovation, one also needs to know how *many* resources it is likely to take to generate new knowledge, ideas, and innovations. That is, Schumpeterian models assume some form of *production function* for knowledge and technology. As Keynes explained (1936), innovators never know exactly when, or even if, their research and development activities will bear fruit and deliver a breakthrough. Such an innovation function is a very uncertain conceptual relationship; it can be further qualified by linking the relationship between resources and new discoveries to influences ranging from economic conditions to society's cultural norms.

The Gains from Innovation Depend on the Speed of Innovation

In the case of private innovation, say to develop a new and better product, the eventual gains to the entrepreneurs depend on how much of a premium price the new product commands in the market.

Second, the eventual gains depend on *how long* that new product can command a premium price. The length of time that an innovator enjoys monopoly profits from her innovation depends on how soon another innovator *creatively destroys* that profit by introducing an even better product or a more efficient production method. Thus, the gains from innovation depend on the rate at which new innovations are generated. Specifically, the length of time that an innovation generates profit is thus an inverse function of the number of innovations per year. Therefore, innovation can be too rapid, with no single improvement ever recouping the costs of innovation.

An illustration of the conflict between the cost of innovation and the gains from innovation is the suggestion by the chief technology officer of Taiwan Semiconductor Manufacturing, Calvin Chenming Hu, that computer chip makers should slow their pace of technological development. "The industry would be better off if we paid more attention to the bottom line and less attention to the beauty contest of technology introduction," said Mr. Hu.[7] He blamed the losses of chip makers during the early 2000s on the rapid rate of change in the industry. Of course, Mr. Hu was equally quick to point out that his firm would not fall behind others in the industry, and the speech in which he called for a slowdown in introducing new products also described the new generation of chips that his firm would soon introduce. In short, he was not about to abandon the innovative competition his firm was in, but he sure would enjoy having less innovative competition and a longer product life for his innovations.

Finally, because there is a time delay between when costly R&D activity is undertaken and when the gains from the innovation are earned, the value of an innovation depends on the rate at which we discount the future. Therefore, as mentioned earlier, the present value of an innovation is a negative function of the rate at which future profit is discounted, that is, how society values the welfare in the future over welfare today.

The Equilibrium Rate of Technological Progress

In sum, the Schumpeterian model of technological progress concludes that, all other things equal, innovation will be greater, and thus technological progress will be faster, in a society in which:

- Potential gains from a successful innovation are larger.
- Future gains are valued more highly relative to current costs.
- The supply of resources is greater and, hence, the opportunity cost of innovation in terms of lost current output is lower.
- Resources are employed more efficiently to generate new innovations.

Even though Schumpeter modeled the behavior of profit-maximizing entrepreneurs, his model can be generalized to illustrate all types of innovative activity in an economy. This generality of the model explains its popularity in mainstream economics. Interestingly, the model is dynamic in nature, which places it in the realm of heterodox economics, but it became popular in mainstream economics because it could still be stated as a standard maximization problem that orthodox economists were familiar with. Of course, it also seemed to promote entrepreneurship, which fit the neoliberal paradigm that underlies neoclassical economics.

In line with the Schumpeterian model, economic policies to promote economic growth might include linking society's expected gains from innovation more closely to entrepreneurs' profits from innovation, building institutions that prevent vested interests from blocking the creative destruction process in order to stretch out the gains from past innovations, promoting society's tolerance for change and entrepreneurship, creating the productive resources that are critical to innovation, advancing education, maintaining a communications infrastructure through which knowledge can spread, and creating public institutions such as universities and national institutes to undertake the most *uncertain* types of innovation, such as basic scientific research. Other policies may include encouraging the arrival of immigrants who can bring new ideas from abroad, instituting taxes and subsidies to account for externalities and market failures, and establishing clear rules for patents and copyrights that accurately balance the need to provide incentives for creating new ideas as well as incentives for current innovators to build on ideas. In short, the Schumpeterian model shows that permanent economic growth requires complex policies that go well beyond the traditional policies for increasing saving and investment.

INTERNATIONAL TRADE AND ECONOMIC DEVELOPMENT

The Schumpeterian dynamic framework provides a convenient way to examine how international trade is likely to influence technological progress and, therefore, economic growth in the long run. In this section we discuss, specifically, how international trade might affect the cost of resources, the efficiency with which resources are employed in innovative activities, and the eventual gains from innovation.

The Combinatorial Process and International Trade

International trade can forge ties between people in different countries and, therefore, increase international **technology transfers**. International trade and the accompanying activities of international marketing, market research, product planning, and international travel all serve to spread knowledge and technology. Thus, by effectively integrating individual economies into a single global economy, international trade expands the knowledge and ideas that innovators can draw on.

This latter point, that international trade expands the stock of knowledge available to innovators, is important because technological progress is a combinatorial process whose rate depends directly on the amount of already accumulated knowledge. The more we already know, the easier it is to increase knowledge. Table 6.2 provides an example. Suppose the economy begins with three ideas rather than the four ideas in the example presented earlier in this chapter. In this case, the rate of technological progress actually *decreases* over time. A problem at the end of the chapter asks how technology changes if the initial stock of knowledge consists of two useful ideas.

This last example of the combinatorial process is obviously unrealistic. The state of knowledge certainly consists of more than three ideas, which suggests that technological progress is not just inevitable, but likely to accelerate in the future. However, it is unlikely that all combinations of previous ideas produce useful new ideas. As mentioned earlier, knowledge can also be forgotten, and there may be institutional barriers against certain combinations, such as legal restrictions on stem cell research in some states of the United States or patents that give private ownership to intellectual developments. All other things equal, therefore, the greater the stock of knowledge, the less likely that restrictions on certain combinations or the inevitable dead ends of some of the available combinations will cause the process of innovation to stagnate. By making more ideas available, international trade can prevent such stagnation.

The real worth of any new idea depends on how many more ideas are generated along the path of new combinations that follow. The term **meta-ideas** was coined by Romer (1993) to define those ideas that set society on a path to an exceptionally large number of subsequent high-impact innovations. There is an important role for international trade to play: not only can it create more combinations by helping to move ideas and knowledge across borders, but it may enable exceptionally fruitful combinations. Different countries are likely to have followed slightly different combinatorial paths if they were not previously fully integrated. In the words of the French mathematician and intellectual Jules Henri Poincaré (1908): "To create consists precisely in not making useless combinations and in making those which are useful. . . . Among chosen combinations the most fertile will often be those formed of elements drawn from domains which are far apart" (Weitzman 1998). Economists have begun to examine in more detail trade's role in moving knowledge.

Table 6.2

A Slowing Combinatorial Growth Process (new idea = the unique combination of two old ideas)

		New Ideas	Accumulated Ideas	Percentage Growth
Period 1	Begin with	3	3	
Period 2	$3!/(1! \cdot 2!) =$	3	6	100
Period 3	$3!/(1! \cdot 2!) =$	3	9	50
Period 4	$3!/(1! \cdot 2!) =$	3	12	33
Period 5	$3!/(1! \cdot 2!) =$	3	15	25

The number of combinations for n ideas taken r at a time is $n!/[(n-r)! \cdot r!]$; we take n as the number of ideas generated in the previous period and combine them 2 at a time, so r = 2. The symbol "!" represents a product of descending integers beginning with the number preceding the !, e.g., $5! = 5 \cdot 4 \cdot 3 \cdot 2 \cdot 1 = 120$.

The Geographic Diffusion of Technology

The combinatorial nature of ideas and the Schumpeterian model of innovation combine to suggest that, all other things equal, technological progress is positively related to the size of an economy. As the seventeenth-century English intellectual William Petty (1682) noted three centuries ago: "It is more likely that one ingenious curious man may rather be found among 4 million than among 400 persons." More recently, Michael Kremer (1993) modeled change in technology as a direct function of population size. He reasoned that large countries grow faster than small ones. Evidence does not support this hypothesis, however; there are many small countries with high incomes and the countries with the largest populations, China and India, are among the poorest countries.

Several economists have suggested that international trade enhances the economic growth of small countries by facilitating the movement of technology and ideas across borders.[8] Indeed, international trade has over the centuries served as a major motivation for contacts among people of different countries and regions, the dissemination of new ideas, and the transfer of new technologies. An early example of how contacts between regions of the world spread technological progress is the development of agriculture some ten thousand years ago. Evidence suggests that about 10000 B.C.E., humans began farming in the region now known as the Fertile Crescent in the Middle East. Their new farming technologies spread throughout Asia, Europe, and Africa over the next two thousand years, first to the regions closest to the Middle East, then to the regions farthest away. Those regions not connected to the Middle East by existing trade routes did not benefit from the new technology. Evidence suggests that people in the Western Hemisphere invented agriculture and animal husbandry independently, and those practices did not appear until several thousand years later.

Today, scholars can read books from other countries, and the Internet makes the latest research in science and the latest achievements in the arts instantaneously available throughout the world. People can watch television and see how those in other countries live, think, and behave in a great variety of real and fictional situations. Entrepreneurs travel to observe and copy ideas from other countries. Buying foreign books, watching foreign television programs, and traveling overseas to observe foreign production methods are all forms of international trade, of course.

CONCLUSIONS AND IMPLICATIONS

In the field of international economics, there is a growing appreciation for international trade as an important variable in the process of economic development. The very modest estimates of the gains from trade based on the Heckscher-Ohlin model versus some of the statistical estimates of the long-run growth effect of international trade have shifted the justification for free trade policies toward trade's role as the "engine of growth."

This chapter discussed the ideas behind the Schumpeterian model of technological change. Recent growth economists have generalized Schumpeter's original model to where it provides a plausible explanation of why international trade, by facilitating the flow of ideas and technology across borders, causes economic growth to increase. At the same time, economists have used a variety of statistical methods and models to examine data from many countries and different time periods. In the mainstream economics literature, these studies are interpreted as confirming a positive relationship between international trade and economic development. Between the appeal to the Schumpeterian model and some of the statistical studies, the former U.S. Federal Reserve Chair Alan Greenspan (2001) probably reflected the culture of mainstream economics quite accurately when he testified before Congress that:

> The international trading system . . . has enhanced competition and nurtured what Joseph Schumpeter a number of decades ago called "creative destruction," the continuous scrapping of old technologies to make way for the new.

The statistical evidence on the relationship between international trade and economic development is not as strong as international economists often suggest, however. Statistical results vary significantly depending on what other variables are introduced into the analysis. Institutions seem to play a much more important role than international trade in determining a country's economic development. Unfortunately, more detailed studies of how international trade influences the flow of technology across borders are difficult because it is nearly impossible to measure technology flows. Isolating trade's effect on such a poorly measured phenomenon using available statistical methods is equally difficult. As a result, economists do not have a very good idea of the strength of the causal relationship between trade and technology.

This is not intended to suggest that international trade has no potential positive benefits for economic development and human standards of living. To the contrary, the analysis in this chapter was intended to show that there are many potential channels through which international trade could be very beneficial for increasing human welfare in the long run. In general, it is difficult to see how economic isolation could increase the rate at which a country accumulates new knowledge and generates new ideas. Historical evidence suggests that isolated countries, such as China and Japan in the 1700s and 1800s, and Albania and North Korea today, fall behind in technology. On the other hand, there are many countries that engage in international trade but still lag far behind in technology.

A complicating factor in assessing the role of international trade in the process of economic development is the tendency for innovative activity to **agglomerate**, that is, to concentrate in a few regions rather than spread uniformly. Internationally, the concentration of innovative activity in certain regions and countries may explain the divergence of incomes across countries over the past two hundred years. This is also the period in which international trade grew very rapidly. Trade both enables and mitigates the problem of agglomeration driven by the concentration of innovative activity, economic growth, and its profits and high incomes. Trade and specialization could enable innovative activity to be centered where it is most likely to bring welfare-enhancing new technologies and knowledge, and that same trade could then also help to disperse that new knowledge around the world. Or, trade could fail to spread the gains from new technology because technology may not be easy to transfer between countries, or international trade is dominated by transnational firms that organize production and international trade to maximize profits for their managers and owners concentrated in high-income countries. The following chapter examines the long-run distribution of the gains from international trade in greater detail.

CHAPTER SUMMARY

1. Economic growth and international trade are similar in that they increase real national income.
2. Both per capita output and international trade have grown rapidly over the past two hundred years, suggesting a cause and effect relationship.
3. Statistical evidence is not definitive in confirming cause and effect from international trade to economic growth, however.
4. The power of compounding implies that any continuous growth process will always outgrow any one-time gain in welfare, no matter how large the one-time gain may be. This means that if international trade can raise a country's growth rate even modestly, the effects on human welfare will eventually be large.
5. The Solow growth model shows that a constant rate of investment, no matter how high, cannot generate permanent economic growth without being accompanied by technological change.
6. The Solow model thus also concludes that, in the absence of technological progress, international trade cannot bring permanently faster economic growth.
7. International trade can cause economic growth if it, in some way, motivates or enables the creation or adoption of new technologies.
8. The Schumpeterian model relates innovation to (1) the eventual rewards, (2) the availability of the resources needed to create new knowledge, (3) the efficiency of research and development activity, and (4) the willingness of people to incur short-run costs to generate long-run technological progress.
9. Joseph Schumpeter's concept of creative destruction, which is that continued technological change introduces new technologies at the expense of old ones, illustrates the potential for resistance against new technology, and if international trade facilitates the introduction of new technology, there is likely to be resistance to trade.
10. Schumpeter also emphasized that innovation requires the application of scarce resources, which implies that innovation has opportunity costs.
11. International trade can accelerate technological change by (1) expanding the market for, and thus increasing the eventual gains from, innovation; (2) facilitating the flow of knowledge across borders and thus making it easier to create new knowledge; and (3) improving the allocation of resources and thus making more resources available to innovation.
12. New knowledge generally builds on previous knowledge by *combining* existing ideas and knowledge in order to create new ideas and knowledge.
13. The combinatorial nature of knowledge explains why technological change tends to be a *path-dependent* process, in which the ability to create new technologies depends on the technologies already accumulated.
14. The combinatorial and path dependent nature of technological change implies that international trade, by stimulating the international flow of knowledge and ideas, can accelerate a country's technological change. Also, by introducing more diverse ideas, the combinatorial process is less likely to bog down or get stuck on a less efficient path.
15. Not all technological changes benefit humanity. This chapter gives the example of increased greenhouse gas emissions that accompany energy use.
16. The very modest estimates of the gains from trade based on the Heckscher-Ohlin model versus some of the statistical estimates of the long-run growth effect of international trade have shifted the justification for free trade policies toward trade's role as the "engine of growth."

KEY TERMS AND CONCEPTS

agglomeration
biological leash
combinatorial process
compound growth process
compounding

creative destruction
cross-section data
depreciation
diminishing returns
economically significant

entreprenuer

evolutionary model of economic change

factor accumulation

human technology

innovation

measurement error

medium-run economic growth

meta-ideas

natural resource curse

neoclassical growth model

neutral technological change

omitted variable bias

open economy

ordinary least squares (OLS) method

panel studies

path-dependent process

power of compounding

production function

Schumpeter model

Solow model

spurious regression results

statistically significant

steady state equilibrium

structural change

technological change

technology

time-series data

transitional economic growth

PROBLEMS AND QUESTIONS

1. What do you think Paul Romer has in mind in saying, "[T]he ideas involved in supplying potato chips are probably more important for successful development in the poorest countries"?

2. According to the Schumpeterian model, the rate of innovation depends on:

   - The size of the potential gains from a successful innovation
   - The value society places on future gains relative to current costs
   - A greater supply of resources and, hence, a lower opportunity cost of innovation in terms of lost current output
   - More efficient employment of resources to generate new innovations

   Explain how each of these variables might be influenced so as to speed up technological progress.

3. Suppose for the moment that the general framework of the Schumpeterian model is accurate. Then go to the next step and contemplate whether the profit motive can lead the private sector of the economy to generate all the new knowledge that could possibly be necessary for human progress and survival.

4. Table 6.2 illustrates a case where the combinatorial process starts with three ideas and generates a constant amount of new innovations each subsequent period. Table 6.1 shows a more explosive process under the assumption that there are initially four ideas. What about the case in which we start with two ideas? Show and explain what happens in this case.

5. Explain the link between the combinatorial nature of knowledge accumulation and the observed path-dependency of technological change.

6. Why are there so many cases of simultaneous discovery? Explain.

7. Explain how human technology and knowledge differs from the procedures, techniques, and methods used by other living species. Do you agree with the discussion on human technology in the textbook?

8. Theodore Roosevelt once said that "The only thing worse than a regulated monopoly is an unregulated monopoly." Based on what you know about his model of technological change, do you think Joseph Schumpeter would agree with Roosevelt's statement? Explain why or why not.

9. Explain Schumpeter's model of technological change. Then discuss how international trade affects technology. Conclude with an answer to the question: Does expanding international trade increase economic growth?

10. The Solow growth model takes the rate of technology growth as a given, determined somewhere outside the model. Do you believe that technology "just happens," or is technological change a function of specific causes? What might cause the rate of technological change to increase or decrease? Are there government policies that can affect the rate of technology growth?

11. Paul Krugman claims that the East Asian Tigers grew because, among other things, they greatly increased the levels of education of their labor forces. Use the Solow model to explain why economic growth cannot continue forever if only human capital is expanded.

12. After reading about the declining rate of economic growth in the Soviet Union, what do you think the Soviet central planners could have done to avoid the growth slowdown? Use the Solow model to frame your answer.

13. Write a brief essay explaining how international trade can raise an economy's permanent rate of growth. Hint: Use the Solow and Schumpeter models to frame your discussion, and link international trade to the specific variables that drive each of the two models.

14. Explain precisely how the Solow model reaches the conclusion that a high rate of investment does not, in the long run, make an economy grow faster. (Hint: State the model's assumptions and focus on the logic behind each of the curves in the graphic model.)

NOTES

1. From Paul M. Romer (1998); this is a short piece consisting of material later published as "Economic Growth," *The Fortune Encyclopedia of Economics,* David R. Henderson (ed.), Warner Books (Boston, MA: 2003).

2. Useful surveys of the empirical literature include Joshua J. Lewer and Hendrik Van den Berg (2003), Sebastian Edwards (1998), Robert E. Baldwin (2003), and Chapter 2 of Van den Berg and Lewer (2007).

3. The assumption of a constant rate of depreciation is often justified by the fact that we really do not have any convincing information to suggest any other particular shape for the function. Clearly, depreciation rises when the capital grows, so a linear function in this conceptual model is as reasonable as any other rising function.

4. Angus Maddison (2003), *The World Economy, Historical Statistics,* Paris: OECD.

5. See also Martin L. Weitzman (1998).

6. Malcolm Gladwell (2008), p. 56. See also Matt Richtel (2008) for a report on the many disputes about who invented what.

7. Don Clark (2002), "One Executive Suggests It's Time for Chip Makers to Slow Down," *Wall Street Journal,* April 9.

8. See, for example, Alberto Alesina, Enrico Spolaore, and Romain Wacziarg (2000) and Alberto F. Ades and Edward L. Glaeser (1999).

CHAPTER 7

International Trade, Human Happiness, and Unequal Economic Development

> [A] society is well-ordered when it is not only designed to advance the good of its members but when it is also effectively regulated by a public conception of justice.
>
> —John Rawls (1971)

Static models of international trade suggest that there are immediate gains to expanding opportunities for people to exchange goods and services. Our analysis shows, however, that there may be substantial costs in shifting an economy's production and consumption patterns, thus making the shift to free trade less attractive. Furthermore, the static framework of analysis has not given economists very large estimates of the improvement in human well-being associated with the expansion of trade.

A more dynamic focus on the relationship between international trade and economic growth suggests that there may indeed be very substantial improvements in human well-being associated with the expansion of international trade. Simple correlations are often misleading, of course, and the wide variations in estimates imply that there are other forces at work behind the scenes. Standard statistical methods have a limited capacity to uncover complex systemic relationships, and economic data are notoriously incomplete, imprecise, and just plain inaccurate. The previous chapter, began a broader examination of how international trade and economic growth interact as our human society evolves over time.

There are many reasons why people would engage in more exchanges of goods and services as human society develops and becomes more complex. There is no doubt that humans would live under substantially riskier and much less comfortable circumstances if there was no trade among people, communities, and nations. But that conclusion does not automatically imply that all increases in trade, and thus interdependence, bring improved living conditions. This chapter examines one of the fundamental problems of the growth of specialization, exchange, and interdependence, namely the growth of economic and social inequality. The tenfold increase in per capita economic production that has accompanied the equally stunning growth of international trade over the past two hundred years has itself been accompanied by a sharp rise in inequality within countries and across countries. Some of these changes in the distribution of human wealth can be explained by the orthodox models of trade and growth that we have already examined. A more holistic approach provides further insight into the twin processes of international trade and economic growth.

INCOME INEQUALITY

The international economy is characterized by huge differences in income. There are large differences in household income within individual countries, and because average income levels differ so much across countries, differences in per capita incomes across countries are much greater than within any single country. Worldwide income inequality has not been reduced during the post–World War II period despite the hypothesized leveling effects of increased international economic integration. In this section of the chapter, the international distribution of income is examined. Subsequently, we will discuss more specifically what role international trade may have had in determining worldwide income inequality.

Measuring Inequality

The degree of income inequality is often measured by comparing the proportion of total national income captured by different income groups. The most popular measure of income distribution divides the population into even-sized groups according to their incomes and then ranks the groups beginning with the one with the lowest incomes. We can then observe what portion of total income is captured by each of those income groups.

Table 7.1 divides the population of each country into *quintiles* of households, each consisting of 20 percent of the total population and ranked from the lowest to the highest household incomes. In Bolivia in 2002, the lowest quintile of households earned 1.5 percent of total GDP. The second quintile earned 5.9 percent of national income; thus the poorest 40 percent of Bolivian households earned just 7.4 percent of total national income. The third quintile of households earned 10.9 percent of national income, which gave them an average income of half the national average. Even the fourth quintile earned less than the national average. The top 20 percent earned 63.0 percent of Bolivia's GDP.

In contrast, in South Korea in 1998 the lowest 20 percent of households earned 7.9 percent of national income and the second 20 percent earned 13.6 percent of national income. The second quintile in South Korea enjoyed a substantially higher percentage of national income than did the third quintile in Bolivia. And, in South Korea the fourth quintile enjoyed above-average income with its 23.1 percent share. Korea's highest income quintile earned less than twice the national average, compared to over three times the national average for Bolivia's top 20 percent. Clearly, income inequality was much lower in South Korea than in Bolivia.

The Lorenz Curve

The distribution of income in an economy is sometimes represented graphically using the distribution data above. Figures 7.1 and 7.2 show the population quintiles, ranked by income levels from the lowest to the highest, beginning at the southwest corner on the horizontal axis. The percentage of income earned is depicted along the vertical axis. In the case of Bolivia, the fact that the first quintile earned 1.5 percent of national income is shown by the point a, which represents 20 percent along the horizontal axis and 1.5 percent up the vertical axis. The points b, c, and d represent the 2nd, 3rd, and 4th quintiles, respectively. The curve connecting the points is known as the **Lorenz curve**.

It should be readily apparent that the more curved the Lorenz curve, the less equal the distribution of income. The dashed straight line 0T represents a hypothetical perfectly equal income distribution where each quintile earns exactly 20 percent of total national income. In general, the closer the Lorenz curve lies to 0T, the more equal the income distribution. Figure 7.2 shows both Bolivia's and South Korea's Lorenz curves. South Korea's Lorenz curve lies above Bolivia's curve.

A convenient numerical measure of income inequality called the **Gini coefficient** is derived from the Lorenz curve. The Gini coefficient is calculated using the areas A and B in Figure 7.1; specifically, it is equal to B/(A + B). The Gini coefficient thus must fall between zero and one (zero and 100 in Table 7.1), and the smaller the Gini coefficient, the more equal the income distribution. In

Table 7.1

Income Distribution for All Countries with Available Data

Country	Survey Year	Gini*	Lowest 10%	Lowest 20%	Second 20%	Third 20%	Fourth 20%	Highest 20%	Highest 10%
Albania	2004a	31.1	3.4	8.2	12.6	17.0	22.6	39.5	24.4
Algeria	1995a	35.3	2.8	7.0	11.6	16.1	22.7	42.6	26.8
Argentinab	2004c	51.3	0.9	3.1	7.6	12.8	21.1	55.4	38.2
Armenia	2003a	33.8	3.6	8.5	12.3	15.7	20.6	42.8	29.0
Australia	1994c	35.2	2.0	5.9	12.0	17.2	23.6	41.3	25.4
Austria	2000c	29.1	3.3	8.6	13.3	17.4	22.9	37.8	23.0
Azerbaijan	2001a	36.5	3.1	7.4	11.5	15.3	21.2	44.5	29.5
Bangladesh	2000a	33.4	3.7	8.6	12.1	15.6	21.0	42.7	27.9
Belarus	2002a	29.7	3.4	8.5	13.2	17.3	22.7	38.3	23.5
Belgium	2000c	33.0	3.4	8.5	13.0	16.3	20.8	41.4	28.1
Benin	2003a	36.5	3.1	7.4	11.3	15.4	21.5	44.5	29.0
Bolivia	2002c	60.1	0.3	1.5	5.9	10.9	18.7	63.0	47.2
Bosnia and Herzegovina	2001a	26.2	3.9	9.5	14.2	17.9	22.6	35.8	21.4
Botswana	1993a	60.5	1.2	3.2	6.0	9.7	16.0	65.1	51.0
Brazil	2004c	57.0	0.9	2.8	6.4	11.0	18.7	61.1	44.8
Bulgaria	2003a	29.2	3.4	8.7	13.7	17.2	22.1	38.3	23.9
Burkina Faso	2003a	39.5	2.8	6.9	10.9	14.5	20.5	47.2	32.2
Burundi	1998a	42.4	1.7	5.1	10.3	15.1	21.5	48.0	32.8
Cambodia	2004a	41.7	2.9	6.8	10.2	13.7	19.6	49.6	34.8
Canada	2000c	32.6	2.6	7.2	12.7	17.2	23.0	39.9	24.8
Central African Republic	1993a	61.3	0.7	2.0	4.9	9.6	18.5	65.0	47.7
Chile	2003c	54.9	1.4	3.8	7.3	11.1	17.8	60.0	45.0
China	2004c	46.9	1.6	4.3	8.5	13.7	21.7	51.9	34.9
Hong Kong, China	1996c	43.4	2.0	5.3	9.4	13.9	20.7	50.7	34.9
Costa Rica	2003c	49.8	1.0	3.5	8.2	13.1	21.2	54.1	37.4
Côte d'Ivoire	2002a	44.6	2.0	5.2	9.1	13.7	21.3	50.7	34.0
Croatia	2001a	29.0	3.4	8.3	12.8	16.8	22.6	39.6	24.5
Czech Republic	1996c	25.4	4.3	10.3	14.5	17.7	21.7	35.9	22.4
Denmark	1997c	24.7	2.6	8.3	14.7	18.2	22.9	35.8	21.3
Dominican Republic	2004c	51.6	1.4	4.0	7.8	12.1	19.3	56.7	41.1
Ecuador	1998c	53.6	0.9	3.3	7.5	11.7	19.4	58.0	41.6
Egypt, Arab Rep.	2000a	34.4	3.7	8.6	12.1	15.4	20.4	43.6	29.5
El Salvador	2002c	52.4	0.7	2.7	7.5	12.8	21.2	55.9	38.8
Estonia	2003a	35.8	2.5	6.7	11.8	16.3	22.4	42.8	27.6
Ethiopia	2000a	30.0	3.9	9.1	13.2	16.8	21.5	39.4	25.5
Finland	2000c	26.9	4.0	9.6	14.1	17.5	22.1	36.7	22.6
France	1995c	32.7	2.8	7.2	12.6	17.2	22.8	40.2	25.1
Gambia, The	1998a	50.2	1.8	4.8	8.7	12.8	20.3	53.4	37.0
Georgia	2003a	40.4	2.0	5.6	10.5	15.3	22.3	46.4	30.3
Germany	2000c	28.3	3.2	8.5	13.7	17.8	23.1	36.9	22.1
Ghana	1998–99a	40.8	2.1	5.6	10.1	14.9	22.9	46.6	30.0
Greece	2000c	34.3	2.5	6.7	11.9	16.8	23.0	41.5	26.0
Guatemala	2002c	55.1	0.9	2.9	7.0	11.6	19.0	59.5	43.4
Guinea	2003a	38.6	2.9	7.0	10.8	14.7	21.4	46.1	30.7

(continued)

Table 7.1 *(continued)*

Country	Survey Year	Gini*	Lowest 10%	Lowest 20%	Second 20%	Third 20%	Fourth 20%	Highest 20%	Highest 10%
Guinea-Bissau	1993a	47.0	2.1	5.2	8.8	13.1	19.4	53.4	39.3
Haiti	2001c	59.2	0.7	2.4	6.2	10.4	17.7	63.4	47.7
Honduras	2003c	53.8	1.2	3.4	7.1	11.6	19.6	58.3	42.2
Hungary	2002a	26.9	4.0	9.5	13.9	17.6	22.4	36.5	22.2
India	2004–05a	36.8	3.6	8.1	11.3	14.9	20.4	45.3	31.1
Indonesia	2002a	34.3	3.6	8.4	11.9	15.4	21.0	43.3	28.5
Iran, Islamic Rep.	1998a	43.0	2.0	5.1	9.4	14.1	21.5	49.9	33.7
Ireland	2000c	34.3	2.9	7.4	12.3	16.3	21.9	42.0	27.2
Israel	2001c	39.2	2.1	5.7	10.5	15.9	23.0	44.9	28.8
Italy	2000c	36.0	2.3	6.5	12.0	16.8	22.8	42.0	26.8
Jamaica	2004a	45.5	2.1	5.3	9.2	13.2	20.6	51.6	35.8
Japan	1993c	24.9	4.8	10.6	14.2	17.6	22.0	35.7	21.7
Jordan	2002–03a	2.7	6.7	10.8	14.9	21.3	46.3	30.6	38.8
Kazakhstan	2003a	33.9	3.0	7.4	11.9	16.4	22.8	41.5	25.9
Kenya	1997a	42.5	2.5	6.0	9.8	14.3	20.8	49.1	33.9
Korea, Rep.	1998c	31.6	2.9	7.9	13.6	18.0	23.1	37.5	22.5
Kyrgyz Republic	2003a	30.3	3.8	8.9	12.8	16.4	22.5	39.4	24.3
Lao PDR	2002a	34.6	3.4	8.1	11.9	15.6	21.1	43.3	28.5
Latvia	2003a	37.7	2.5	6.6	11.2	15.5	22.0	44.7	29.1
Lesotho	1995a	63.2	0.5	1.5	4.3	8.9	18.8	66.5	48.3
Lithuania	2003a	36.0	2.7	6.8	11.6	16.0	22.3	43.2	27.7
Macedonia, FYR	2003a	39.0	2.4	6.1	10.8	15.5	22.2	45.5	29.6
Madagascar	2001a	47.5	1.9	4.9	8.5	12.7	20.4	53.5	36.6
Malawi	2004–05a	39.0	2.9	7.0	10.8	14.8	20.7	46.6	31.8
Malaysia	1997c	49.2	1.7	4.4	8.1	12.9	20.3	54.3	38.4
Mali	2001a	40.1	2.4	6.1	10.2	14.7	22.2	46.6	30.2
Mauritania	2000a	39.0	2.5	6.2	10.6	15.2	22.3	45.7	29.5
Mexico	2004a	46.1	1.6	4.3	8.3	12.6	19.7	55.1	39.4
Moldova	2003a	33.2	3.2	7.8	12.2	16.5	22.1	41.4	26.4
Mongolia	2002a	32.8	3.0	7.5	12.2	16.8	23.1	40.5	24.6
Morocco	1998–99a	39.5	2.6	6.5	10.6	14.8	21.3	46.6	30.9
Mozambique	2002–03a	47.3	2.1	5.4	9.3	13.0	18.7	53.6	39.4
Namibia	1993c	74.3	0.5	1.4	3.0	5.4	11.5	78.7	64.5
Nepal	2003–04a	47.2	2.6	6.0	9.0	12.4	18.0	54.6	40.6
Netherlands	1999c	30.9	2.5	7.6	13.2	17.2	23.3	38.7	22.9
New Zealand	1997c	36.2	2.2	6.4	11.4	15.8	22.6	43.8	27.8
Nicaragua	2001a	43.1	2.2	5.6	9.8	14.2	21.1	49.3	33.8
Niger	1995a	50.5	0.8	2.6	7.1	13.9	23.1	53.3	35.4
Nigeria	2003a	43.7	1.9	5.0	9.6	14.5	21.7	49.2	33.2
Norway	2000c	25.8	3.9	9.6	14.0	17.2	22.0	37.2	23.4
Pakistan	2002a	30.6	4.0	9.3	13.0	16.3	21.1	40.3	26.3
Panama	2003c	56.1	0.7	2.5	6.6	11.4	19.6	59.9	43.0
Papua New Guinea	1996a	50.9	1.7	4.5	7.9	11.9	19.2	56.5	40.5
Paraguay	2003c	58.4	0.7	2.4	6.3	10.8	18.6	61.9	46.1
Peru	2003c	52.0	1.3	3.7	7.7	12.2	19.7	56.7	40.9
Philippines	2003a	44.5	2.2	5.4	9.1	13.6	21.3	50.6	34.2

Table 7.1 (continued)

Country	Survey Year	Gini	Lowest 10%	Lowest 20%	Second 20%	Third 20%	Fourth 20%	Highest 20%	Highest 10%
Poland	2002a	34.5	3.1	7.5	11.9	16.1	22.2	42.2	27.0
Portugal	1997c	38.5	2.0	5.8	11.0	15.5	21.9	45.9	29.8
Romania	2003a	31.0	3.3	8.1	12.9	17.1	22.7	39.2	24.4
Russian Federation	2002a	39.9	2.4	6.1	10.5	14.9	21.8	46.6	30.6
Rwanda	2000a	46.8	2.1	5.3	9.1	13.2	19.4	53.0	38.2
Senegal	2001a	41.3	2.7	6.6	10.3	14.2	20.6	48.4	33.4
Serbia and Montenegro	2003a	30.0	3.4	8.3	13.0	17.3	23.0	38.4	23.4
Sierra Leone	1989a	62.9	0.5	1.1	2.0	9.8	23.7	63.4	43.6
Singapore	1998c	42.5	1.9	5.0	9.4	14.6	22.0	49.0	32.8
Slovak Republic	1996c	25.8	3.1	8.8	14.9	18.7	22.8	34.8	20.9
Slovenia	1998a	28.4	3.6	9.1	14.2	18.1	22.9	35.7	21.4
South Africa	2000a	57.8	1.4	3.5	6.3	10.0	18.0	62.2	44.7
Spain	2000c	34.7	2.6	7.0	12.1	16.4	22.5	42.0	26.6
Sri Lanka	2002a	40.2	3.0	7.0	10.5	14.2	20.4	48.0	32.7
Swaziland	2000–01c	1.6	4.3	8.2	12.3	18.9	56.3	40.7	50.4
Sweden	2000c	25.0	3.6	9.1	14.0	17.6	22.7	36.6	22.2
Switzerland	2000c	33.7	2.9	7.6	12.2	16.3	22.6	41.3	25.9
Tajikistan	2003a	32.6	3.3	7.9	12.3	16.5	22.4	40.8	25.6
Tanzania	2000–01a	2.9	7.3	12.0	16.1	22.3	42.4	26.9	34.6
Thailand	2002a	42.0	2.7	6.3	9.9	14.0	20.8	49.0	33.4
Trinidad and Tobago	1992c	38.9	2.2	5.9	10.8	15.3	23.1	44.9	28.8
Tunisia	2000a	39.8	2.3	6.0	10.3	14.8	21.7	47.3	31.5
Turkey	2003a	43.6	2.0	5.3	9.7	14.2	21.0	49.7	34.1
Turkmenistan	1998a	40.8	2.6	6.1	10.2	14.7	21.5	47.5	31.7
Uganda	2002a	45.7	2.3	5.7	9.4	13.2	19.1	52.5	37.7
Ukraine	2003a	28.1	3.9	9.2	13.6	17.3	22.4	37.5	23.0
United Kingdom	1999c	36.0	2.1	6.1	11.4	16.0	22.5	44.0	28.5
United States	2000c	40.8	1.9	5.4	10.7	15.7	22.4	45.8	29.9
Uruguayb	2003c	44.9	1.9	5.0	9.1	14.0	21.5	50.5	34.0
Uzbekistan	2003a	36.8	2.8	7.2	11.7	15.4	21.0	44.7	29.6
Venezuela, RB	2003c	48.2	0.7	3.3	8.7	13.9	22.0	52.1	35.2
Vietnam	2004a	34.4	4.2	9.0	11.4	14.7	20.5	44.3	28.8
Yemen, Rep.	1998a	33.4	3.0	7.4	12.2	16.7	22.5	41.2	25.9
Zambia	2004a	50.8	1.2	3.6	7.9	12.6	20.8	55.1	38.8
Zimbabwe	1995–96a	1.8	4.6	8.1	12.2	19.3	55.7	40.3	50.1

* The World Bank Gini's vary from 0 to 100, which is [A/(A+B)] x 100.
a: Refers to expenditure shares by percentiles of population, ranked by per capita expenditure.
b: Urban data.
c: Refers to income shares by percentiles of population, ranked by per capita income.
Source: 2007 World Development Indicators, Washington, DC: World Bank.

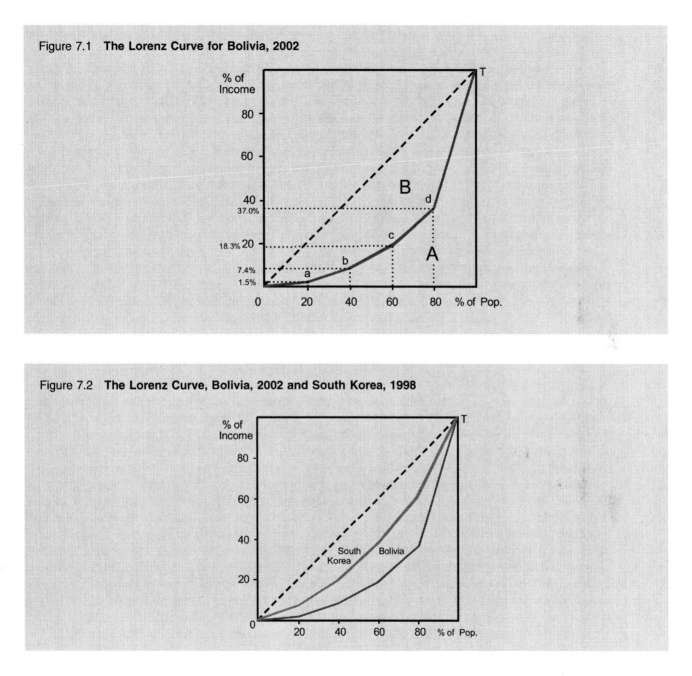

Figure 7.1 **The Lorenz Curve for Bolivia, 2002**

Figure 7.2 **The Lorenz Curve, Bolivia, 2002 and South Korea, 1998**

Figure 7.2 we see that the Lorenz curve for South Korea lies much closer to the line 0T than does Bolivia's. Thus, South Korea's Gini coefficient is lower than Bolivia's: 31.6 compared to 60.1. Table 7.1 presents Gini coefficients for most of the world's countries.

The Distribution of Income in Distant History

At the height of the Roman Empire, about half of all people were slaves or indentured servants whose lives were controlled by somebody else. Obviously, slaves did not earn income, and slave owners had little incentive to provide much more than the bare minimum consumption to keep their investment alive and working. Slavery and other forms of extreme oppression were also common in many other parts of the world two thousand years ago, including Africa, Asia, and the Americas. And, even though the very slow positive rate of population growth throughout human history suggests that average per capita income must have been slightly above bare subsistence, high mortality rates suggest that many individual people ended up with incomes below subsistence. There is also plenty of evidence that small privileged groups had incomes and wealth that exceeded the average by huge multiples. Kings, emperors, pharaohs, popes, tribal chiefs, army generals, and other political and religious rulers enjoyed lifestyles quite different from those of ordinary people.

For example, in comparing current economic inequalities with those of medieval England, D.G. Champernowne and F.A. Cowell (1998, p. 52) suggest that "in some respects the underlying inequality of social and economic power was much greater then: the pre-industrial medieval lord had much wider powers in his right to tie workers to the land, his control over appointments and through other forms of patronage." Champernowne and Cowell compile a simple index of inequality that suggests the distribution of income in England was less equal in the fifteenth century than in the twentieth. They also present evidence that income in medieval Augsburg was more equal than income in that same German region in the sixteenth century, but it was less equal than the distribution of income in twentieth-century Germany.

Europe was not unique in its economic inequality. When the Spanish arrived in the Western Hemisphere five hundred years ago, they found that the Aztec and Inca empires in present-day Mexico and Peru, respectively, had rigid hierarchies not very different from what they themselves had. For example, the Aztec emperor was both the political and religious leader of his nation, much like the king of Spain, who represented the church as well as the political organization of that country. The Aztec emperor lived in rather ostentatious surroundings compared to the subsistence level experienced by most Aztecs, who in turn enjoyed better standards of living than the many neighboring peoples who had been subjected by the conquering Aztecs. Eleventh-century Ghana was ruled by Caliph Tenkaminen. According to one historical account, reported by Rachel Emma Silverman (1999, p. R6), "If gold nuggets are discovered in the country's mines, Tenkaminen reserves them for himself and leaves the gold dust for his subjects." Historians estimate that Tenkaminen took about half the caliphate's income for his household. He imported glass windows from northern Africa for his palace, he wore silk from the Far East, and his horses were decorated with gold rings. Genghis Khan, who conquered most of China, Iran, Iraq, Korea, and nearly all of Russia in the twelfth century, is alleged to have said that "[t]he greatest joy is to conquer one's enemies, to pursue them, to seize their property, to see their families in tears, to ride their horses and to possess their daughters and wives" (Silverman ibid.). Suryavarman II, the ruler of Cambodia in the twelfth century, built one of the largest religious monuments of all time, Angkor Wat. When he traveled, he rode in a throne on top of an elephant, accompanied by hundreds of young women carrying his gold and silver on open platters for everyone to see. These examples all suggest extreme inequality.

Using historical accounts, we could depict the Lorenz curves for the ancient empires, as we do for Tenkaminen's caliphate in Figure 7.3. With the caliph and a privileged few taking half of the nation's income and the remaining 99 percent of the population having an equal, subsistence level of income, as historical accounts suggest, the Gini coefficient is clearly greater than that of South Korea or most developed economies today. Branko Milanovic (2006) brings together a wide variety of historical information about Byzantium, which covered roughly the eastern half of the Roman Empire, during the rule of Basil II from 976 to 1025 C.E. He finds evidence showing that large landowners comprised just 1 percent of the rural population but enjoyed income seven times that of the remaining small farmers, landless tenants, and slaves, who all lived at or just above bare subsistence. Incomes in the Byzantine cities were higher, on average; artisans and craftsmen earned five times the subsistence level of income. However, this class of workers comprised just half of the urban population and thus 5 percent of the total population of Byzantium. Other urban workers, beggars, soldiers, and marginals lived at less than double the subsistence level. Byzantine nobles,

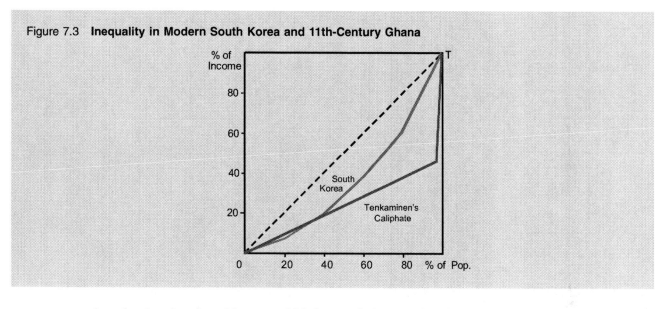

Figure 7.3 **Inequality in Modern South Korea and 11th-Century Ghana**

on the other hand, enjoyed incomes 100 times subsistence, but they comprised less than one-half of 1 percent of the population. Putting all this information together, Milanovic calculates a Gini coefficient for Byzantium in the year 1000 of a little less than 0.45. This is lower than Ginis for today's developing countries like Brazil and South Africa, but substantially larger than the Ginis of nearly all of the more developed countries today, except, perhaps, the United States and Russia.

Milanovic, Peter H. Lindert, and Jeffrey G. Williamson (2007) estimate the Gini coefficients for fourteen historical societies, including the Roman Empire in the year 14 C.E. Table 7.2 presents the their estimates of the principal economic measures in addition to their Gini estimates. Note that Milanovic, Lindert, and Williamson also use their evidence on social classes and income levels to estimate the maximum feasible Gini coefficients. All in all, Table 7.2 suggests that income inequality within individual countries is in some cases less today than it was some centuries ago. But in other cases, inequality seems to have risen over the past several centuries. It is not clear, therefore, whether the growth of international trade has reduced or increased income inequality.

Global Measures of Income Inequality

A number of economists have gathered and combined national income data into a world distribution of income and estimated **global Gini coefficients**. In his appropriately entitled book, *Imagine There's No Country*, Surjit S. Bhalla (2002) adjusts the income levels of people in all countries according to the purchasing power of the national currencies, combines the national data into a world population by income groups, and estimates global Gini coefficients for 1950, 1960, 1970, 1980, 1990, and 2000. His global Gini coefficient varies between 0.63 and 0.69.

Bhalla's results plus those of several other studies on global income distribution are reported in Table 7.3. Each of the authors reported in the table uses slightly different methods to aggregate national income distribution data into a global measure. Each also uses different original data sets for differently sized groups within countries. Yet, the final estimates are quite similar. The authors of the survey that compiled the results in Table 7.3, Sudhir Anand and Paul Segal (2008), conclude that "there is insufficient evidence to determine the direction of change in global interpersonal inequality in recent decades." Overall, the estimated global Gini coefficients are much higher than the Ginis for individual countries. For individual countries, Gini coefficients are seldom greater than .50; most high-income countries have Ginis between .25 and .40.

Table 7.2

Gini Coefficients for 14 Historical Countries

Country-Date	Population (Millions)	GDI/capita	Gini	Today's Gini
Roman Empire-14	55.0	844	39.4	Italy (2000): 35.9
Byzantium-1000	15.0	710	41.0	
Holland-1561	1.0	1,129	56.0	Netherlands (1991): 31.5
England & Wales-1688	5.7	1,418	45.0	U.K. (1999): 37.4
Holland-1752	2.0	2,035	63.0	Netherlands (1991): 31.5
Moghul India-1750	182.0	530	48.9	India (1994): 27.9
Old Castille-752	2.0	745	52.5	Spain (1990): 32.5
Nueva España-1790	4.5	755	63.5	Mexico (2000): 53.8
England & Wales-1801	30.0	2,006	51.5	U.K. (1999): 37.4
Bihar (India)-1807	3.3	533	32.8	India (1994): 27.9
Kingdom of Naples-1811	5.0	752	28.4	Italy (2000): 35.9
Brazil-1872	10.2	721	43.3	Brazil (2002): 58.8
China-1880	377.5	540	24.5	China (2001): 41.6
British India-1947	346.0	617	49.7	India (1994): 27.9

GDI = gross domestic income

Source: Branko Milanovic, Peter H. Lindert, and Jeffrey G. Williamson (2007), "Measuring Ancient Inequality," National Bureau of Economic Research working paper 13550, October, Tables 1 and 2, pp. 76, 77.

Table 7.3

Global Income Gini Coefficients: 1960–2000

Author(s)	1960	1970	1980	1990	2000
Bhalla 1	0.66	0.69	0.68	0.67	0.65
Bhalla 2	0.63	0.66	0.67	0.66	0.63
Bourguignon and Morrison	0.635	0.650	0.657	0.657[1]	
Chotikapanich, Valenzuela, and Rao			0.658	0.648	
Dikhanov and Ward		0.668	0.682	0.686	0.683[2]
Dowrick and Akmal 1		0.659	0.636[3]		
Dowrick and Akmal 2		0.698	0.711[3]		
Milanovic 2005			0.622[4]	0.641[4]	
Sala-i-Martin		0.653	0.660	0.652	0.637

[1] 1992; [2] 1999; [3] 1993; [4] 1988 and 1998.

Source: Table 1 in Sudhir Anand and Paul Segal (2008), "What Do We Know about Global Income Inequality?" *Journal of Economic Perspectives* 46, no. 1, pp. 57–94.

The global Gini coefficient estimates from Tables 7.2 and 7.3 suggest that the very substantial growth of international trade over the past two hundred years has not reduced or increased global income inequality. This contradicts the Heckscher-Ohlin model and its factor price equalization theorem, which, as discussed in Chapter 4, predicts that international trade effectively makes returns to the factors of production more equal across countries. The Solow and Schumpeterian growth models are more compatible with the Gini estimates. Differences in endowments of productive factors, combined with differences in national institutions and cultures, can affect technological change and economic growth and, therefore, cause incomes to become less equal across countries. Given that several large poor countries, such as China and India, have grown exceptionally fast recently, other poor countries must have grown more slowly if the global inequality index has remained about the same.

The Distribution of Wealth versus Income

The Gini coefficient has been used to measure the world distribution of *wealth* as well as the distribution of *income*. Income distribution is more often studied because annual income data are more readily available than estimates of accumulated wealth, but from the perspective of economic inequality, it may be more useful to look at the distribution of accumulated wealth. Wealth is defined as the accumulated value of assets and capital in people's possession. Income is the *flow* of new purchasing power acquired, and when these flows are adjusted for expenditures and depreciation of accumulated assets, they indicate how the *stock* of accumulated wealth changes. It is the accumulated set of assets, not annual income, that has most often been equated with economic power.

Many societies have suffered internal conflicts over the distribution of ownership of land. The Mexican Revolution (1910–1920) was fought, in large part, over the very concentrated ownership of land by a small number of families and the church. Recently, political parties representing indigenous populations in Bolivia and Ecuador won elections because they favored redistribution of land and wealth. In Brazil, the "sem-terras" (landless) movement has often engaged in occupations of land in order to demand its redistribution. Violent clashes have left many injured and dead over the past ten years.

On a more abstract level, Marxist economists argue that the capitalist system results in *incomes* becoming increasingly unequal over time. Because the growing ranks of the workers, the **proletariat**, live at bare subsistence, they cannot save, and, therefore, the distribution of *wealth* grows even more unequal over time. Karl Marx reasoned that the owners of the means of production, the **bourgeoisie**, gain an increasingly larger share of the economy's income as they invest in ever-greater amounts of capital in an effort to maintain profits by reducing labor costs. As a result, labor income is reduced as growing unemployment creates a "reserve army of the unemployed" that pushes wages to subsistence.

Marx predicted a social revolution in which the proletariat would collectively take ownership of all wealth. Marxist revolutions occurred, among other places, in Russia in the early twentieth century, in China in the middle of the twentieth century, and in Cuba during the 1950s. These revolutions did not bring "workers' paradises" as Marxists predicted, and some communist societies came to be ruled by oppressive Communist Party organizations. Still, income and wealth distributions in communist states were much more equal than in market economies. Gini coefficients for income in the formerly communist states of the Soviet Union and Eastern Europe still have relatively equal income distributions (see Table 7.1). As predicted by the Marxist model, the income Gini coefficients of Russia, China, and other former communist states have increased in recent years as those countries have shifted from collective ownership of industry and land to more private ownership.

Table 7.4 shows the Gini coefficients for wealth for a small number of countries for which we have reliable data. This data does not entirely support Marx's hypothesis. While the wealth Ginis are substantially higher than the income Ginis for the same countries, as Marx predicted would happen in capitalist economies, Table 7.4 does not show a uniform relationship between income inequality and wealth inequality. Note that China has the second lowest wealth Gini among the countries listed, but it has the highest income Gini! Switzerland, on the other hand, has the highest wealth Gini, but one of the lower income Ginis. Private wealth accumulation is a very recent

Table 7.4

Global Wealth Shares: 2000 (*Adjusted for PPP*)

| | Lowest | | | | | Ratio of Ginis for |
	50%	90%	Top 10%	Wealth Gini	Income Gini	Wealth and Income
Australia	9.0	56.0	45.0	0.622	0.352	1.77
Canada	47.0	53.0	—	0.663	0.326	2.03
China	14.4	58.6	41.4	0.550	0.469	1.17
France	—	39.0	61.0	0.730	0.327	2.23
Germany	3.9	55.7	44.4	0.671	0.283	2.37
India	8.1	47.1	52.9	0.667	0.368	1.81
Indonesia	5.1	34.6	65.4	0.763	0.343	2.22
Italy	7.0	51.5	48.5	0.609	0.360	1.69
Japan	13.9	60.7	39.3	0.547	0.249	2.20
Korea, South	12.3	56.9	43.1	0.579	0.316	1.83
Spain	13.2	58.1	51.7	0.565	0.347	1.63
Switzerland	—	28.7	71.3	0.803	0.337	2.38
U.K.	5.0	44.0	56.0	0.697	0.360	1.94
U.S.A.	2.8	30.2	69.8	0.801	0.408	1.96
World	1.6	29.9	71.1	0.802	0.660	1.22

PPP = purchasing power parity
Source: James B. Davies, Susanna Sandstrrom, Anthony Shorrocks, and Edward N. Wolff (2006), "The World Distribution of Household Wealth," WIDER Report, December 5, Tables 9, 10.

phenomenon in China; private property is a centuries-old institution in Switzerland. The histories of most northern European countries suggest that the growing inequality of wealth predicted by Marx is not an inevitable outcome.

The simplicity of the Gini coefficients used here to make inferences about inequality should serve as a warning that they may not be very accurate representations of how a society shares its overall economic and social assets. Indeed, the Gini coefficient can be criticized for many of the same shortcomings as GDP and other quantitative measures of complex economic phenomena like economic development and international economic integration. Nevertheless, the differences in the distribution of even the incomplete set of material goods included in GDP and measured by a simple statistic like the Gini coefficient are so large that it is safe to say that human welfare is distributed unequally. The remainder of this chapter examines further models and ideas related to how international trade and economic growth rates interact to influence the global distribution of income.

IS THERE AN OPTIMAL LEVEL OF EQUALITY?

You might ask yourself: If I had magical powers and could impose any distribution of wealth and income on the economy where I live, what kind of a distribution would I choose? You might be tempted to take a lot for yourself, leaving little for the rest of the population. If you do, you had better also give something to a substantial number of people with guns, tanks, and prisons to protect you from all the hungry people with little left to lose. On the other hand, you might opt to do exactly the opposite and give everybody an equal share of the total economic pie. But, if it is true that humans have some choice over their own destiny, then a perfectly equal distribution of income and wealth would eliminate what economic theory assumes is the key incentive for people to work, save, and innovate. We need to examine the options more thoroughly.

Elements of a Just Society

Most people will agree that, in the abstract, fairness, or justice, requires that all people have an equal opportunity to pursue their interests and an equal chance to improve on their own and their families' well-being. Most people also will agree that racial, gender, or ethnic discrimination is not fair or just. Similarly, oppression, theft, coercion, and threats of violence are not just. Discrimination and oppression are generally the result of unequal levels of power in society, the result of one person's power over those with less power. In practice there are sharp disagreements about what equal opportunity means or what exactly constitutes an oppressive position of power. What, exactly, does **equal opportunity** look like or how can we tell whether people really interact under their own volition, completely free from personal or cultural oppression? All we can observe are the outcomes of human activity, and unequal outcomes do not necessarily imply an unjust process. Reverse-engineering economic and social outcomes in search of justice is difficult.

Some argue that differences in economic and social outcomes must be entirely due to individual effort and choices for them to be fair or just. But even if economic outcomes accurately reflect people's individual effort and preferences, are they just? Are preferences and capabilities randomly distributed, or are they, at least in part, determined by heredity or society itself? Sociology and behavioral economics find evidence that in a complex, interdependent society, human capital and personal capabilities are determined by culture, upbringing, and personal lifestyles. These three influences on personal behavior, in turn, are determined by the decisions, efforts, and actions of many people other than the individuals themselves.

It can also be argued that even pure luck is not just. Are events and economic outcomes that are beyond the control of humanity also beyond the responsibility of humanity toward those individuals impacted by those events? The popularity of insurance and social safety nets suggest that societies in fact often assume responsibility for helping those members who are adversely affected by events beyond their control. Often, families and entire societies help those whose "bad luck" is obviously partly their own fault. Most developed countries tax the general population in order to provide health care to everyone, regardless of whether they exercise regularly, drink heavily, or eat unhealthy foods their entire lives. Most cultures have some provision for compassionate responses to others' suffering no matter what the cause of that suffering.

Most cultures also embrace some concept of equal effort, that just outcomes should reflect effort and work, not luck. Of course, it is difficult to determine effort, capability, or preferences. A social system, in the form of culture, tends to set rules of behavior, and people then use that culture to shape their judgments of other people's behavior and the associated outcomes. There are great differences across cultures, which no doubt explain the large differences in how societies deal with income and wealth inequality. For example, the very different rates of incarceration in the United States and Europe—the United States has about seven times as many people imprisoned per capita as Europe—reflect very different attitudes toward whether crime is the fault of the individual or a failure of society.

Rawls's Veil of Ignorance

The **social-contractionist** philosophy of John A. Rawls (1971) provides a reasonable definition of a just society and what its distribution of income might look like. In seeking to define what makes a society just, Rawls reasoned that a truly unbiased definition of social justice can only be arrived at from behind a "veil of ignorance" that hides one's own personal characteristics, background, culture, and circumstances. That is, a just society is the one people would design if, hypothetically, they did not know their actual social class, race, gender, sexual orientation, level of wealth, education, talent, and other personal and social characteristics. Rawls reasoned that, from behind their veil of ignorance, people would be especially concerned about the conditions of the least well-off people in a society because they would realize that they could be among those unfortunates.

The prevalence of hierarchical structures in all cultures suggests that people have collectively built informal institutions that favor some over others, and it is difficult to dismantle unjust formal institutions if they are supported by unjust, but well-established, informal institutions or culture. To be just, according to Rawls, society must provide not only personal freedom and equal opportunity to acquire education, wealth, and social status, but also assistance for the unfortunate who, for reasons not entirely of their own doing, are prevented from taking advantage of all their opportunities. Modern societies are likely to use their governments to achieve such justice.

From behind Rawls's "veil of ignorance," many people are likely to decide that a just society would probably seek "equal outcomes for equal effort," thus leaving individuals the freedom to choose how much effort they want to expend. Equal outcomes for equal effort requires not only equal opportunity in its fullest sense (including equal preparation and endowment), but in a complex social and natural environment, it implies some form of social insurance like progressive taxation, collective government services, and even direct government transfers to compensate for uncontrollable adverse individual outcomes. In short, a *just society* strives not only for equal opportunity, but to the extent that outcomes are determined in part by forces beyond the control of individuals, for mechanisms by which the lucky compensate the unlucky.

The Psychological Basis for Economic Equality

Rawls's perspective on social justice represents what people might choose if they indeed chose their future from behind a veil of ignorance. But people live in a real world, and their views are strongly influenced by the formal and informal institutions of their society. Humans are also hardwired by evolution to behave in ways that contradict Rawls's criteria for social justice.

Recall the research on human behavior discussed in Chapter 4, which showed that people's preferences depend on their status quo. Recall that Daniel Kahneman and Amos Tversky (2000) found that people disproportionately value their current status quo over other possibilities. In one of their many experiments, they found that people value the object A that they have over the object B that they do not possess, but when they find themselves in possession of object B while object A belongs to someone else, a surprising number of people then claim to prefer the object B to object A. Kahneman and Tversky refer to this phenomenon as the "endowment effect," which makes people **loss averse**. Like so many living creatures that exhibit **territoriality**, people will fight harder to hold on to what they have than to acquire something new. Numerous studies show that people need an extra inducement to get them to abandon their status quo and embrace change. For example, Richard Thaler and Henrik Conqvist (2004) summarize research on pension plan choices and conclude that default settings unduly determine people's choices. This research is nicely summarized in the popular book by Richard Thaler and Cass Sunstein entitled *Nudge*. It should not be surprising, therefore, that people seldom willingly surrender positions of power. The human capacity for abstract thought, so well described by Paul Seabright (2010), means that people quickly find mental justifications for the status quo; even when it is clear that they enjoy an advantage over others, people find ways to justify that privilege. Societies are likely to develop informal institutions, or culture, that justify social hierarchies. In practice, it is very difficult for any society to view justice from behind a Rawlsian veil of ignorance.

Further reinforcing the tendency for societies to distribute their income and wealth unequally is the fact that people are hardwired to be very conscious of their status in society. Recall from the discussion of happiness studies in Chapter 4 that data for high-income developed countries shows that people's average level of happiness does not change as real per capita income grows, but at any point in time, people with high incomes are happier, on average, than people with relatively lower incomes living in the same country. That is, people are much more conscious of their relative income status than they are of their absolute income, provided their basic needs for living without hunger and physical suffering are satisfied. Figure 7.4 illustrates the finding of

Figure 7.4   Life Satisfaction: Relative vs. Average Happiness

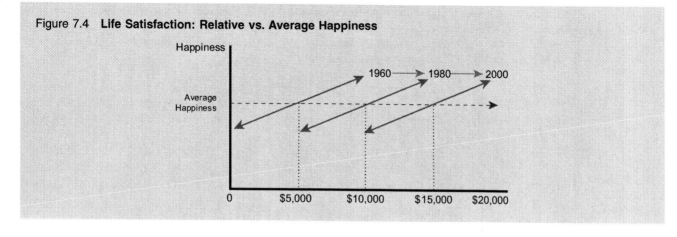

happiness studies: individuals' relative levels of happiness rise and fall with income in each year, but the entire relationship between income and happiness shifts as average per capita income in society rises over time. Hence, average happiness does not rise with personal income, but any individual who experiences a sudden rise or fall in relative income experiences a rise or fall in life satisfaction or happiness.

The importance of relative income for human happiness no doubt reflects income's role in signaling a person's status in a modern capitalist economy. Happiness studies clearly confirm the positive relationship between happiness and people's sense of belonging and being valued. An egalitarian society, where more people feel valued, therefore is likely to come closer to maximizing human welfare than an unequal society, in which many people interpret their relatively low income as a rejection by their fellow humans.

The Relationship between Social and Economic Justice

When Rawls concludes that people would choose an egalitarian economic structure from behind a hypothetical veil of ignorance, he effectively argues that the basic human rights that underlie social justice are inseparable from basic economic rights. Rawls's idea that economic rights are necessary to enable fundamental human rights goes back at least to the Enlightenment of the seventeenth and eighteenth centuries. And, at the midpoint of the last century, nearly all governments of the world explicitly accepted the idea when they signed the United Nations' *Universal Declaration of Human Rights*. This declaration supplements basic human rights, such as political rights, freedom of speech, freedom of assembly, freedom from torture and degrading punishment, a ban on servitude and slavery, and equal rights before the law, with a set of specific economic rights. Among the explicit economic rights declared are:

> **Article 22**: Everyone, as a member of society, has the right to social security and is entitled to realization . . . of the economic, social and cultural rights indispensable for his dignity and the free development of his personality.

> **Article 23**: (1) Everyone has the right to work, to free choice of employment, to just and favourable conditions of work and to protection against unemployment; (2) Everyone, without any discrimination, has the right to equal pay for equal work; (3) Everyone who works has the right to just and favourable remuneration ensuring for himself and his family an existence worthy of human dignity, and supplemented, if necessary, by other means of social protection; (4) Everyone has the right to form and to join trade unions for the protection of his interests.

Article 25: (1) Everyone has the right to a standard of living adequate for the health and well-being of himself and of his family, including food, clothing, housing and medical care and necessary social services, and the right to security in the event of unemployment, sickness, disability, widowhood, old age or other lack of livelihood in circumstances beyond his control.

Article 26: Everyone has the right to education. Education shall be free, at least in the elementary and fundamental stages. Elementary education shall be compulsory. Technical and professional education shall be made generally available and higher education shall be equally accessible to all on the basis of merit.

The *Universal Declaration* was adopted by the United Nations General Assembly on December 10, 1948 by a vote of 48 in favor and 0 against, with 8 abstentions. By including such a broad range of political, social, and economic rights, the world's political leaders effectively adopted Rawls's definition of a just society.

Some years earlier, in his 1944 State of the Union address to Congress, U.S. President Franklin D. Roosevelt provided a political justification of economic rights:

As our nation has grown in size and stature, however—as our industrial economy expanded—these political rights proved inadequate to assure us equality in the pursuit of happiness. We have come to a clear realization of the fact that true individual freedom cannot exist without economic security and independence. "Necessitous men are not free men." People who are hungry and out of a job are the stuff of which dictatorships are made. In our day these economic truths have become accepted as self-evident. We have accepted, so to speak, a second Bill of Rights under which a new basis of security and prosperity can be established for all—regardless of station, race, or creed.

Roosevelt detailed a set of economic rights he felt were necessary to create the conditions in which people could enjoy human rights such as free speech, freedom of thought, political freedom, or freedom of religion, such as:

- The right to a useful and remunerative job
- The right to earn enough to provide adequate food and clothing and recreation
- The right of every businessman to trade in an atmosphere of freedom from unfair competition and domination by monopolies
- The right to adequate medical care and the opportunity to enjoy good health
- The right to protection from the economic costs of old age, sickness, accident, and unemployment
- The right to a good education

Most, but not all, developed economies today provide their citizens with the majority of these economic rights. Interestingly, among the high-income countries, President Roosevelt's United States provides the fewest of the economic rights listed above.

Political debate continues in all countries about whether countries can afford all of these economic rights. International trade often enters these debates because many people are willing to accept the suggestion that foreign imports are the main reason they are losing the economic benefits they thought they had achieved. In fact, foreign competition is often held up by employers as the reason they have to cut health benefits or pension contributions. Transnational firms continually threaten to shift production overseas if governments do not reduce taxes, eliminate regulations, or revise labor laws. Employers use the same threats when they deal with labor unions, threatening to pull up stakes or to outsource parts of their domestic production to foreign plants if unions do not agree to wage and benefits cuts. Governments take these threats seriously, and indeed corporate tax rates have been substantially reduced in many countries. Subsequently, the decline in tax revenues has strained governments' ability to provide their citizens with the economic rights prescribed in the *Universal Declaration.*

INTERNATIONAL TRADE'S EFFECT ON THE DISTRIBUTION OF INCOME

The Heckscher-Ohlin (HO) model addresses the distributional effects of international trade with its Stolper-Samuelson theorem and its factor price equalization theorem. These theorems were explained in Chapter 4. But the assumptions of the HO model, such as increasing costs, perfect competition, fixed-factor inputs, and no international mobility of factors, as well as the static nature of the neoclassical model, limit its ability to explain all the distributional concerns brought up above. For one thing, the real world is dynamic, not static. Stocks of productive factors and technology do not remain constant, and thus neither does comparative advantage in the long run. Also, international trade itself influences the accumulation of factors of production and technological change. Thus, the distribution of income described by the Stolper-Samuelson and price equalization theorems is continually changing in ways that are likely to be very different from the HO model's static predictions.

Second, in the real world, trade is in the hands of imperfectly competitive transnational corporations (TNCs), not perfectly competitive small firms that trade at arm's length. Trade thus becomes intimately embedded with the international investment and long-run business strategies of large corporations that extend across many countries. Where these transnational corporations decide to produce, innovate, invest, and market their wares ultimately has a great effect on people's incomes, both within countries and across countries. With the increasing returns to scale that characterize both industrial production and innovation, international trade and the concentration of economic activity in large corporations may cause incomes to become less equal rather than more equal. While the neoclassical HO model and the factor price equalization theorem suggest trade is an arbitrage process that equalizes incomes, economies of scale cause trade to increase inequality.

Vernon's Model

There is an interesting set of models that combine dynamic technology flows with the concept of comparative advantage in order to explain the divergent paths of economic development observed across the global economy. These models are sometimes referred to as **leader-follower models**, in which developed economies are hypothesized to lead in innovation and economic growth, and less developed economies are hypothesized to also grow but continue to lag behind under some process of gradual technological transfers. Raymond Vernon (1966) presented one of the earliest such models, which describes how trade patterns change as a product goes through its life cycle. It is called the **product cycle model** of trade.

During a product's early life, production and consumption are concentrated in the most developed countries, where resources for innovation are relatively abundant and where high income levels provide a market for expensive new products. We have earlier pointed out that innovation is highly concentrated in a few regions of the most developed economies. But once a new product has been developed, and as it becomes known throughout the world, an increasing proportion of production is exported from the country where the product originated. Later, as the product matures, consumption growth slows and production levels off in the originating country. With manufacturing experience, production costs decline because production methods are perfected and standardized production equipment is developed. Key components and parts are increasingly outsourced to lower-cost suppliers. This development of standardized production methods and equipment also makes overseas production easier, and the originator of the new product may be more willing to license production by others as profit growth slows in the more mature market.

Every new product eventually becomes a **standardized product**, meaning that its production technology is widely understood and its production equipment can be easily acquired. And as less skilled labor can do more of the production work, the comparative advantage shifts to low-wage countries. Production may cease altogether in the country where the product originated, and international trade flows completely reverse themselves so that low-wage countries export the product back to the country that originated the product. Of course, by this time producers in the originating country are producing and exporting newer products, and they are already performing the R&D for even newer products that will replace the products they are currently producing and exporting.

Figure 7.5 illustrates how production and trade evolve according to Vernon's product cycle model. The most advanced economies with the best-educated labor force specialize in developing new products. They export new products to the rest of the world during the early phases of the product cycle and then develop new products as the production of older, standardized products moves to developing economies. Low-wage countries adopt products that have already been developed, produced, and exported by the advanced economies. All countries gain from this continually changing pattern of trade. The shifting patterns of international trade described by Vernon's product cycle model are often the result of multinational firms moving production from high-cost countries to low-cost countries as soon as the technology becomes easier to transfer.

Although it is often presented as an alternative to standard models of trade, Vernon's dynamic model is actually compatible with the static HO model of trade. It hypothesizes a pattern of trade that constantly changes in accordance with shifts in technology over a product's life cycle. Advanced economies with highly educated labor forces and sophisticated financial and scientific infrastructures have a comparative advantage during the early stages of a product cycle. Labor abundant countries have the comparative advantage in production later, in the standardized-product phase of the product cycle.

Vernon's model also describes a pattern of technology diffusion. First, the technology for producing the new product remains at home, and if it does spread to other countries, it is only to other developed economies that have the resources most appropriate for adopting the new technology. Eventually, the new technology becomes *standardized* and easy-to-use machinery becomes available. This means that the technology to produce the product can be applied in economies with few specialized resources, located far from the large markets for the product, and with little experience in producing similar products. While Vernon did not explicitly hypothesize this, it is obvious that transnational corporations often manage these shifts in production from developed to developing countries over the product life cycle. It remains an interesting question whether the growth of TNCs has accelerated Vernon's hypothesized international product cycle.

Examples of Vernon's international product cycle are clothing and shoes in the nineteenth and early twentieth centuries, radios and televisions after World War II, and computers and computer chips at the end of the twentieth century. In each case, the leading industrial economy developed the products, techniques, and machinery to manufacture the products. These same countries were once great exporters of the products, production of which first moved to other developed economies but eventually moved to developing economies. Computer chip production moved from the United States to Japan, then to Taiwan and Singapore, and then to Malaysia and China.

More Leader-Follower Models

The well-known Stolper-Samuelson theorem derived from the Heckscher-Ohlin model states that, if high-income countries are capital or skill abundant, then international trade will increase wage inequality in rich countries and decrease wage inequality in poor economies. However, wage

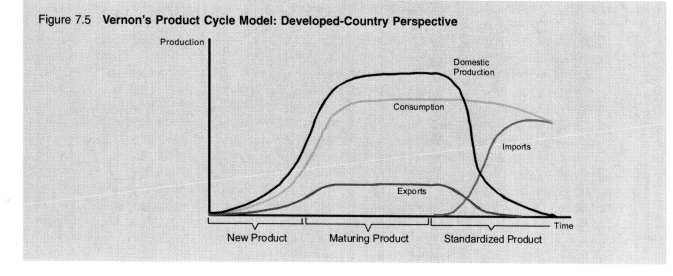

Figure 7.5 **Vernon's Product Cycle Model: Developed-Country Perspective**

inequality has increased in both poor and rich countries. Susan Chun Zhu (2005) shows that in the case where technological innovation continually increases the productivity in the advanced countries while older, less skill-intensive production is continually shifted to poor countries, the skill-intensity of production rises in both poor and rich countries and wage inequality increases everywhere. The leader-follower process benefits elite skilled workers in both the leader and follower countries. If the followers do not catch up to the leaders, world inequality rises despite growing international trade.

Leader-follower models bring out two important points about technology diffusion and economic growth. First, the worldwide pace of economic growth depends on the incentives for innovation in the leader countries and for technology adoption in the follower countries. These models make assumptions about the costs of innovation versus the costs of copying and adopting existing technologies. Second, Vernon's model suggests that comparative advantage drives the shifting trade pattern over the life of a product. Taiwan, South Korea, and Singapore are examples of how countries can assume different positions in the product cycle as their factor endowments, and thus their comparative advantages, change. For example, the average level of education in Taiwan in the early 1950s was three years; today it is approaching twelve years, about the same as in most developed countries. Hence, Taiwan is now a leader because it has developed a comparative advantage in R&D activity and new product introductions. Taiwanese computer chip manufacturers are now opening factories in China. Singapore similarly increased its human and physical capital stocks to where it is now promoting itself as a center for biotechnology research.

Some leader-follower models suggest that as long as there is technology diffusion, countries will tend to grow at similar rates in the long run. The absolute levels of technology will be quite different across countries, however, if the diffusion of technology is slow. Vernon's model is an example of such a model. On the other hand, if an acceleration of technology diffusion suddenly occurs, say by the liberalization of international trade or the improved absorptive capabilities in follower countries, then the opportunity to copy rather than invent technologies may permit follower countries to achieve higher rates of economic growth and catch up to the technology leaders. Models by Elise Brezis, Paul Krugman, and Daniel Tsiddon (1993) and Dan Ben-David and Michael Loewy (1998) even predict "leapfrogging" if the countries that catch up gain enough "momentum" to pass the leaders and reverse roles with them. In general, whether less developed economies can catch up depends on how easily knowledge and technology are transferred.

International Trade and Technology Diffusion

Technology is often modeled as a blueprint or design that can be used by people and firms to produce a new product, reduce costs, improve quality, and so forth. If such a blueprint or design is obtained at less than the original cost to the inventor, then there is said to be a **technology spillover**. When ideas and knowledge are transferred in the form of designs, directions, instructions, blueprints, or diagrams that can be used directly by people to learn, understand, and apply the ideas and knowledge, the international transfers of technology are usually referred to as **direct transfers of technology**. International trade may enable direct transfers by creating contacts between people, creating competition that requires producers to acquire new technology, or simply stimulating curiosity through the introduction of new products.

International trade may also bring about **indirect transfers of technology**, which occurs when a country can import capital goods and intermediate inputs that *embody* the technology. As long as the cost of technology embodied in the capital and intermediate goods is less than the cost of developing the technology from scratch, there is a gain to the importing economy. A great deal of technology is transferred between countries in this form.

In the case of direct transfers of technology, the process depends on others' ability to understand and apply the blueprints that are available. It also depends on the willingness of people and firms to pay for and apply the blueprints. The influence of international trade in increasing direct international technology transfers depends on trade's competitive effects, its demonstration effects, and the network effects that facilitate international transactions. In the case of indirect transfers, international trade plays a necessary and direct role. Without trade in capital goods and intermediate goods there are no indirect technology transfers: the transfer of technology is directly proportional to the amount of international trade in capital equipment.

Geographic Concentration of Innovative Activity

Regional economists have amassed evidence over the decades that shows new technologies spread very slowly geographically. The concentration of information technology firms in California's Silicon Valley, financial firms in London, and the auto industry in Detroit are common examples of how applications of new technologies tend to agglomerate close to where they were initially developed. Edward Glaeser et al. (1992, p. 1126) used some simple intuition to explain agglomeration in observing that "intellectual breakthroughs must cross hallways and streets more easily than oceans and continents."

Nearly a century ago, the microeconomist Alfred Marshall devoted an entire chapter of his popular economics textbook to the "Concentration of Specialized Industries in Particular Localities." Marshall (1959 [1920]) attributed concentration to three factors: (1) the availability of specialized labor, (2) the development of specialized suppliers of intermediate goods and services, and (3) the flows of technology between the industries. Economists from the field of **regional economics** have hypothesized models that explain the development of cities, urban concentration, and the differences in the economic development across regions of a country.

Fundamentally, most explanations of agglomeration rely on economies of scale and economic growth. That is, the process of economic growth often exploits economies of scale, a process that is inherently concentrated. Evidence suggests that such concentration of economic activity tends to be geographic as well as organizationally within ever-larger business firms. Industrial production is more often characterized by economies of scale than, say, agriculture and personal services.

Agriculture is, by nature, linked to the land. It therefore tends to disperse across a country's territory. In the global economy, agricultural production tends to disperse throughout the world in accordance with the natural conditions of the land and the availability of other factors that complement the land in producing agricultural products. Agriculture requires other services, especially as technology improves and incomes rise, and that is why, historically, towns and cities have developed and spread out wherever agricultural activity has flourished. But it was the Industrial Revolution that gave towns and cities a much stronger reason to exist: cities and towns were the best location for factories that needed large numbers of workers and outside suppliers of other inputs and support services.

Paul Krugman (1991) attributes the agglomeration of industrial activity to **increasing returns to scale**, which seem to characterize industrial production. In manufacturing, it tends to be more efficient to produce a large amount of output in one large factory than to produce the same amount of output in a large number of small factories scattered throughout the economy. Krugman hypothesizes that the rate at which industrial activity agglomerates depends on the cost of transportation and the scope of increasing returns to scale. When transport costs are high, economies of scale cannot be exploited and industry remains scattered around the country to service the dispersed population still engaged in agricultural activities and the service activities related to agriculture. However, technological change and economic development gradually lower transport costs, as detailed in Chapters 1 and 4, thus permitting increasing returns to scale to be further exploited and causing industry and its supporting economic activities to agglomerate in a few geographic locations. That such economies of scale are important was shown by David Davis and David E. Weinstein (2001), who estimated that Japan's real GDP would be 20 percent lower if production were evenly distributed throughout the country rather than concentrated in a smaller number of towns and cities.

Not only industrial activity agglomerates. Because industrial firms require more and more outside support services as their output grows, and the workers at the factories spend a large portion of their income where they live and work, the services sector agglomerates in the same locations where industrial activity agglomerates.

This agglomeration of much of our modern economic activity requires workers to move out of the dispersed agricultural sector and to the industrial and services activities concentrated in urban areas. The process whereby people leave agriculture and move to towns and cities to find work in industry and services is a well-known characteristic of economic growth over the past ten thousand years almost everywhere in the world, but the process greatly accelerated over the past two hundred years. Note that this process of agglomeration shows up in the form of increased specialization of tasks, more concentrated investment, and human migration from rural to urban areas. And, because the forces that bring about agglomeration cross borders, the process leads to international specialization and trade, international investment, and immigration.

The Agglomeration of Innovative Activity

Krugman's story of agglomeration is incomplete, however. Economic activity should be broken down into agriculture, industry, services, *and* innovative activity. As highlighted in the Schumpeterian model of technological change, the latter is the centerpiece of the economic growth that drives agglomeration, and is itself a process that thrives on agglomeration.

There is widespread evidence that innovative activity is especially prone to concentrate geographically. The regional economist Richard Florida (2005, p. 50) explains this phenomenon:

> Ideas flow more freely, are honed more sharply, and can be put into practice more quickly when large numbers of innovators, implementers, and financial backers are in constant contact with one another, both in and out of the office. Creative people cluster not simply because they like to be around one another or they prefer cosmopolitan centers with lots of amenities, though both those things count. They and their companies also cluster because of the powerful productivity advantages, economies of scale, and knowledge spillovers such density brings.

Florida uses data on copyrights, patents, and scientific citations to show that creative and innovative activity are much more concentrated than human production of goods and services.[1] In fact, data on the residences of the most often cited scientists and scholars suggest that innovation and creativity occur not just in a very small number of countries, but in a small number of cities within those countries. Florida (ibid.) concludes: "As far as global innovation is concerned, perhaps a few dozen places worldwide really compete at the cutting edge." China and India, countries that are often described as "catching up" in terms of technology, barely register on Florida's map of innovation. This is not to say that Chinese and Indians are not creative. To the contrary, AnnaLee Saxenian (2002) finds that Chinese and Indian entrepreneurs started over one-third of new firms in Silicon Valley. But that is precisely Florida's point: creative and innovative people tend to agglomerate in specific locations because it is quicker to go where the knowledge is than to wait for knowledge to spread.

The geographic concentration of innovative activity is partially driven by the geographic concentration of the resources most important for innovative activities. Countries with large numbers of highly educated people tend to have a comparative advantage in generating new ideas and technologies. Since innovation consists of building new knowledge on top of existing knowledge, those people most likely to combine existing ideas into new ideas are those who have access to, and a good understanding of, existing knowledge. There is, therefore, a "virtuous cycle" at work here: the regions that have the resources critical for innovative activity accumulate more knowledge, which in turn makes further technological progress more likely.

The explanation of the geographic concentration of innovation still requires another condition to be satisfied, however. Technology is, at least in part, a **nonrival good**; once an idea is conceived, it can be used by many people. This nonrival nature of knowledge suggests that knowledge should be nearly free and, therefore, will be passed from one economy to another so that, in the end, it will not matter for subsequent technological change where any one innovation takes place. However, when Adam Jaffe, Manuel Trajtenberg, and Rebecca Henderson (1993) compared the locations of the owners of patents with citations in later patent applications, they found that "[l]ocalization fades over time, but only very slowly."

Why does innovative activity not move more readily across regions, countries, and continents? One reason for the agglomeration of innovative activity is that the adoption and application of existing technologies are not free. Technology transfers are costly, even when knowledge and technology are openly available. Applying existing technology normally involves a learning process, an adaptation of the technology to one's specific circumstances, or both. David Teece (1977) estimated the costs of technology transfers across countries in the chemicals, petroleum refining, and machinery industries, and found that, on average, the cost of adopting foreign technologies was equal to 19 percent of total project costs. Edwin Mansfield, Mark Schwartz, and Samuel Wagner (1981) also found the costs of adopting existing technologies to be substantial; for forty-eight product introductions in the chemical, drug, electronics, and machinery industries in the United States, the estimated cost of imitation was about 65 percent of the total cost of innovation.

Relevant here is Michael Polanyi's (1958) description of most knowledge as tacit, by which he means that it is passed on "by example from master to apprentice" (p. 53). The tacit nature of most **knowledge** and technology means adoption requires costly and time-consuming person-to-person interactions. Technology is not normally transferred in the form of precise blueprints that are easily copied. Hence, the transfer of technology is likely to follow foreign direct investment (FDI). The lack of easy instructions for applying foreign technologies also means that countries must have the resources necessary to learn, adopt, and apply technologies from other countries. Recent research has, therefore, increasingly focused on human capital and institutions as the critical elements for technology adoption. A TNC may enjoy a cost advantage in transferring technology because its organization already has people that understand the technology and have experience applying it.

Because it takes time and effort to learn about, adapt, and put into use new technologies, knowledge and technology are not pure nonrival goods that are entirely free for the taking. And, the developers of new ideas have many ways to keep trade secrets from reaching their competitors. Formal, government-enforced intellectual property rights in the form of patents and copyrights have further made knowledge and technology increasingly excludable.

This is not to say that knowledge flows more slowly today than it did in the past. To the contrary. Moses Abramovitz (1986, p. 405) concluded that "differences among countries in the productivity levels create a strong potentiality for subsequent convergence of levels, provided that countries have a 'social capability' adequate to absorb more advanced technologies. . . . [T]he institutional and human capital components of social capability develop only slowly as education and organization respond to the requirements of technological opportunity and to experience in exploiting it." All other things equal, technological change will be faster in those locations where there are more resources and wealth to pay for the absorption of new technologies. As wealth rises, more knowledge and technology can be acquired. Also, technology may flow more easily to where business practices most closely fit the capitalist traditions. Hence. TNCs are best positioned to carry out technology transfers.

Changing Patterns of Economic Activity

We are now ready to add innovative activity, which seems to be the most agglomerative economic activity of them all, to Krugman's explanation of agglomeration. Since innovation is closely correlated with economic development, economies will increasingly agglomerate as they grow and develop.

The economies of scale in industrial production and innovative activities, and the greater economies of scale in the latter compared to the former, are fundamental to the process of international economic integration. Agglomeration increases regional and national specialization, which means agglomeration leads to more regional and international trade. Agglomeration, of course, also tends to bring about a concentration of physical investment. And, because investment is increasingly in the form of private foreign direct investment, the integrated global economy is increasingly dominated by transnational business organizations.

The growing flows of immigrants, as evidenced by the over 3 percent of the world's population that now live outside their countries of birth, are in large part driven by this international agglomeration of economic activity. The so-called brain drain, in which relatively talented and educated people leave countries where their skills are scarce and move to locations where there are many other talented people, is a direct consequence of the agglomeration of innovative activity, which raises the wages of people best able to contribute to innovation in the regions and countries where innovation is most efficient.

Specialized Agglomeration

Agglomeration is limited by the availability of productive resources in any given geographic location, however. If nothing else, the amount of land available is naturally limited. Also, increased innovation takes labor away from other economic activities, such as production and investment. With both industrial production and innovation tending to concentrate, the cost of production in an innovative region will rise relative to the costs of production elsewhere. As workers' wages rise, new migrants will be attracted, and the population will grow to meet the increased demand for labor. But space is a fixed resource, and implicit and explicit land prices will rise, making land-intensive activities more costly. Increased congestion will require people to spend more scarce time getting around the region. More people will strain the existing capital infrastructure, and the local ecosystem may not be able to support more concentrated economic activity. The rising costs of agglomeration will then tend to drive away and disperse those activities least subject to increasing returns to scale and those least affected by transport costs. Agglomeration will, therefore, increasingly become specialized agglomeration based on either production or innovation.

Some regions have become known as high-tech centers, such as San Francisco, Boston, Austin, and San Diego in the United States, while others have become industrial centers, such as the state of São Paulo in Brazil and the coastal region of China. Communications and computer technologies developed in California's Silicon Valley have enabled customer services to concentrate in Bangalore, India. Centuries of banking experience, plus special tax incentives offered by the British government, give London an advantage in financial services. The above examples show to what degree the process of agglomeration crosses national boundaries.

TRANSNATIONAL CORPORATIONS, AGGLOMERATION, AND THE SPREAD OF TECHNOLOGY

Transnational corporations (TNCs) carry out most of the world's private research and development. Most patents are issued to corporations and inventors working in corporations. Therefore, TNCs control much of the world's industrial knowledge and technology, and they thus have the potential to play a major role in the dissemination of technology throughout the world. Furthermore, as our discussion of agglomeration made clear, most innovative activity occurs in a relatively small number of countries. According to Magnus Blomström and Ari Kokko (1998, p. 249), "over four fifths of the global stock of FDI originates from the half dozen home countries that dominate the world's research and technology: the U.S., the U.K., Japan, Germany, Switzerland, and the Netherlands."

Foreign Direct Investment, Trade, and Technology Flows

Many economists have thus focused on FDI as a channel for transferring technology. Theodore H. Moran (1998, p. 158) surveys this literature and concludes:

> Local subsidiaries exhibit an integration effect when they become part of the parents' strategy to maintain a competitive position in world markets that provides more rapid upgrading of management, technology, and quality control than any other form of transfer. Thus, they create a dynamic link to the global frontier of best practices, most advanced technologies, and most sophisticated operational techniques in an industry. Simultaneously, they generate direct and indirect spillovers and externalities for domestic suppliers. FDI that creates a proprietary network of suppliers introduces a powerful interaction between parents and subsidiaries and between subsidiaries and host countries.

These conclusions are not entirely confirmed by irrefutable evidence yet, however. It has been difficult to study the geographic spread of technology because, as Krugman (1991, pp. 53–54) noted, technology flows "leave no paper trail by which they may be measured and tracked, and there is nothing to prevent the theorist from assuming anything about them that she likes."

Krugman may have been a bit too pessimistic. Innovative researchers *have* found some useful evidence. One strategy for uncovering the flow of technology and ideas has been to examine patent data. Patent applications require an explicit listing of prior ideas and discoveries on which the new idea is based, and in many countries patent applications require that the country of origin of the prior patents and ideas be listed as well. Hence, patent applications provide a paper trail of where knowledge came from. However, patent data capture only a small portion of all innovative activity that occurs in an economy. Most new knowledge is not patented. Nor do patents accurately reflect the importance of each innovation. Finally, patent data are of little help in tracing technology transfers within TNCs, since a patent held by a TNC tells us nothing about where the firm applies a technology.

Despite the difficulties, there have been numerous studies of technology transfers between countries. According to the survey of these studies by Hendrik Van den Berg and Joshua Lewer (2007), the main conclusions of the many studies of technology diffusion can be summarized as follows:

- Foreign countries are the principal source of new technologies for all but the very largest economies.
- Small developed economies and all developing economies depend on foreign sources for nearly all of their technological change.
- In general it takes longer for technology to move across borders than within countries.
- Developed economies absorb more foreign technology than developing economies, which is compatible with many authors' suggestion that technology diffusion depends critically on a country's absorptive capacity and institutional compatibility.
- The volume of bilateral trade explains a significant share of the variation in bilateral technology flows.
- Developing countries gain more technology from trade with developed economies than they do from trade links with other developing economies.

In sum, there is some evidence that international trade helps to spread technology across borders.

Reassessing the Gains from Trade When It Diffuses Technology

Paul Samuelson (2004) looks at the static welfare effects in a rich country when its poorer trading partner improves its technology. He suggests that, all other things equal, as the economy with less technology acquires more technology and "catches up" to the high-tech economy, the two economies become more similar. Hence, the gains from trade are reduced. Samuelson goes one step further, however, by linking international trade directly to the transfer of technology from the technology leader to the technology follower. Because international trade transfers technology, Samuelson argues that trade directly causes a loss of welfare in the leader economy.

Supporting Samuelson's hypothesis is Lewer and Van den Berg's (2001, 2003a) finding that the most developed countries are net exporters of capital goods and developing countries are net importers of capital goods. Since capital goods have technology embedded in them, international trade itself directly transfers technology from capital-producing countries to capital-importing countries. By shifting production abroad, often by means of foreign direct investment in developing economies, to take advantage of low wages, transnational corporations supply the capital and the technology that effectively make the poorer economies more similar to high-income economies.

Samuelson (2004, p. 137) describes how foreign direct investment and transfer of technology by U.S. firms to China "gives to China some of the comparative advantage that had belonged to the United States." Furthermore, he warns that this loss of comparative advantage can result in "permanent lost per capita real income" in the United States:

> Historically, U.S. workers used to have kind of a *de facto* monopoly access to the superlative capitals and know-hows (scientific, engineering and managerial) of the United States. All of us Yankees, so to speak, were born with silver spoons in our mouths—and that importantly explained the historically high U.S. market-clearing real wage rates for (among others) janitors, house helpers, small business owners and so forth. (2004, p. 144)

In short, as international trade and the accompanying technology transfers cause the terms of trade to deteriorate for the leader economy, all factors' incomes can fall.

An Example of Samuelson's Argument

Saul H. Hymans and Frank P. Stafford (1995) illustrate how the growth of a poor country can cause a deterioration of a rich country's welfare. Suppose that there are two economies in the world,

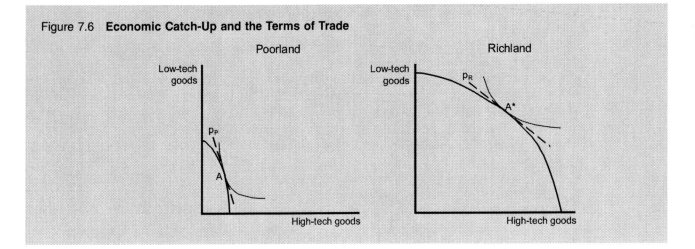

Figure 7.6 **Economic Catch-Up and the Terms of Trade**

Richland, which is a developed economy that provides its residents with high standards of living, and Poorland, a developing economy where average per capita output is much lower. Suppose also that both Richland and Poorland have about the same number of residents; Poorland's relative poverty is thus due to (1) its much lower stock of physical and human capital and (2) its lower level of technology. In Figure 7.6, Richland's production possibilities frontier (PPF) is much larger than Poorland's, and Richland's PPF is more skewed toward high-tech goods.

The different levels of per capita output also influence demand. At high levels of per capita income, Richland's consumers show a much greater preference for high-tech goods, and Poorland's relatively poor consumers show a greater relative preference for low-tech necessities like food and clothing. The differences in preferences thus reinforce the underlying productive capacities of the two economies. It is clear that capital-abundant and technologically advanced Richland has a comparative advantage in producing high-tech goods, and Poorland therefore has the comparative advantage in producing low-tech goods. Notice in Figure 7.6 that the price line in a self-sufficient Poorland is much steeper than in a self-sufficient Richland.

Free trade between Richland and Poorland is depicted in Figure 7.7 as a typical HO model. The terms of trade will be reflected in the international price line p_1, at which the value of Poorland's exports of low-tech goods to Richland is exactly equal to the value of Richland's exports of high-tech goods to Poorland. Each country attains a higher level of welfare with free trade than they would under self-sufficiency, but Richland reaches a much higher indifference curve than does Poorland. Remember, the assumption that the countries' populations are the same size implies that the much higher indifference curve reached by Richland's economy provides much higher per capita levels of welfare.

Now, suppose that Poorland uses a large portion of its low per capita output to expand physical and human capital, but Richland saves only enough to cover depreciation and maintain its physical and human capital stock. Assume, also, that international trade enables Poorland to gain new knowledge and raise its level of technology. But, the low savings in Richland hinder research and development activity, and there is no accumulation of new knowledge. Richland's PPF remains exactly the same, therefore. On the other hand, in Poorland there is economic growth and its PPF shifts outward. The accumulation of physical and human capital, plus the transfer of knowledge from Richland, improves Poorland's ability to produce high-tech goods, and Poorland's PPF thus becomes more similar in shape to Richland's PPF. The change in Poorland's PPF will cause its comparative advantage to change, and therefore the pattern of international trade will change.

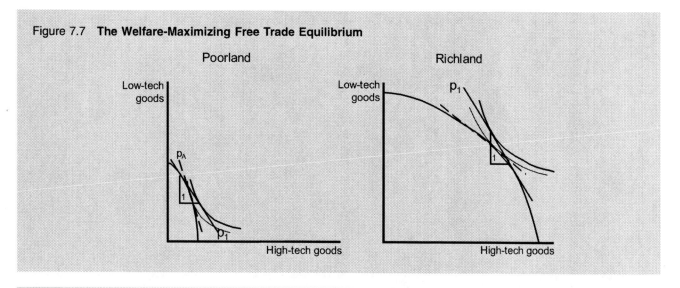

Figure 7.7 **The Welfare-Maximizing Free Trade Equilibrium**

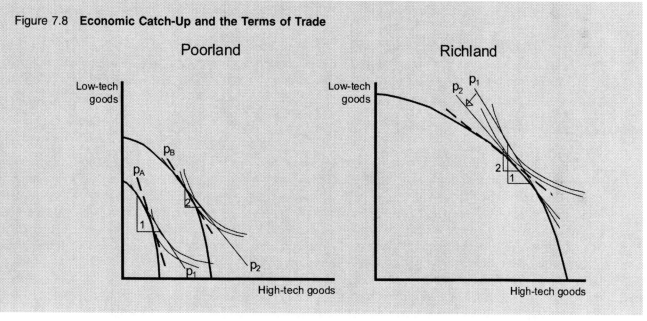

Figure 7.8 **Economic Catch-Up and the Terms of Trade**

Figure 7.8 illustrates the outcome of the hypothesized catch-up growth in Poorland: even though absolutely nothing has changed in Richland, the changing pattern of trade caused by Poorland's growth reduces Richland's welfare! Notice, first of all, that the self-sufficiency equilibrium in Poorland shifts to a point on the new PPF at which the price ratio between high-tech and low-tech goods is less steep, which implies the relative price of high-tech goods falls as Poorland improves its capacity to produce them. With free trade, Poorland's expanded capacity to produce high-tech goods increases the world supply, which reduces the relative price of those goods in the world market. That is, the terms of trade deteriorate for Richland and improve for Poorland. This deterioration in its terms of trade, as illustrated by the change in the international price line from p_1 to p_2, reduces Richland's per capita welfare.

Would Richland have been better off not trading with Poorland? The answer seems to be no. Poorland's economic growth has not eliminated all of Richland's gains from trade; it has only

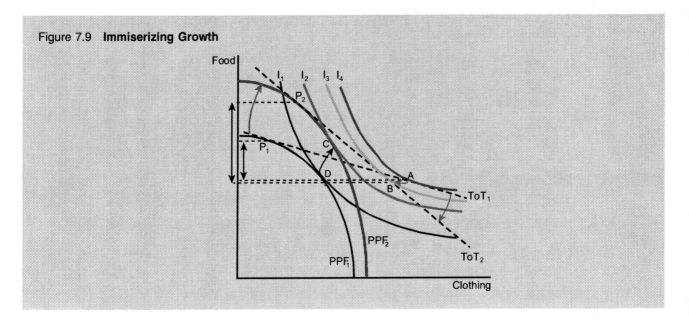

Figure 7.9 **Immiserizing Growth**

reduced them. Richland still consumes a bundle of goods that lies outside of its PPF. If Richland closes its economy to international trade, it will be worse off than with free trade and deteriorating terms of trade. But, it is not as well-off as it was before trade enabled the flow of its technology to Poorland.

Immiserizing Growth

The example above shows how changing terms of trade, the rate at which a country exchanges its real exports into real imports, affect the welfare of a country's citizens. Interestingly, the traditional HO model can be used to show how, in the case of a country large enough to influence international prices, the gains from increased international trade may be undermined by adverse price movements. One such case, which international economist Jagdish Bhagwati (1958) called **immiserizing growth**, effectively refutes the generally accepted hypothesis that economic growth and international trade are always welfare enhancing and never cause any misery.

Figure 7.9 illustrates how economic growth that is biased toward expanding a country's capacity to export can cause national welfare to decline. Suppose the economy's productive capacity is initially represented by the production possibilities frontier PPF_1. If the world's terms of trade are given by the line ToT_1, then the country open to trade can specialize by producing at the point P_1 and trading to consume at the consumption point A, thus reaching the indifference curve I_4. The country exports food in exchange for clothing at the terms of trade given by the slope of the line ToT_1. Then, suppose the economy grows and the production possibilities frontier shifts out to PPF_2. The diagram suggests that the economy's growth seems to have been concentrated in the economy's export sector, the food industry. This will often be the case in developing economies where the export sector is the only part of the economy that has ready access to financing. If, furthermore, the country is a major supplier of food to the world economy, the price of food will decline. In Figure 7.9, the country's terms of trade are assumed to decline from ToT_1 to ToT_2 as exports of food increase. The diagram shows that this terms of trade decline can more than offset the positive welfare effect of an increase in productive capacity. Hence, after the growth in capacity and the increase in exports, the country consumes at the point B, which lies on a lower indifference curve! Had the country not been open to trade, the growth of production would have provided a gain in welfare.

Note that Figure 7.9 does not suggest that closing the economy to international trade will reverse the welfare loss from immiserizing growth. Comparing the consumption points A and B with C and D shows that a closed economy does not suffer immiserizing growth, but it never attains the levels of welfare achieved by an open economy before or after the immiserizing growth.

Even though under specific circumstances economic growth and increased trade can be immiserizing, how likely is such an outcome? Miltiades Chacholiades (1990) lists the conditions that make immiserizing growth possible: (1) the exporting country's growth in productive capacity is concentrated in the sectors of the economy that export, (2) the price elasticity of demand for the export product is inelastic, (3) exports account for a large share of the country's GDP, (4) technological change is minimal, (5) the export country supplies a large portion of total world output, and (6) the export country does not restrict trade. Not all six of these conditions have to be satisfied for growth to be immiserizing; even when demand is elastic, satisfaction of the other five conditions may still be enough to cause immiserizing growth.

Some documented cases of immiserizing growth include developing countries that dominated commodity markets in which demand was price inelastic. For example, in the early twentieth century, Brazil supplied over half the world's coffee, coffee accounted for a very large percentage of Brazilian GDP, the coffee industry's growth was based mostly on factor accumulation rather than technological change, and the demand for coffee was highly price inelastic. Brazil was especially vulnerable to immiserizing growth because it takes six to eight years before a newly planted coffee tree produces its first harvest of coffee beans. Hence, the feedback from coffee prices to investment is delayed, and farmers do not know for many years whether they invested too much or too little.

Development economists argue that developing economies are especially prone to suffering immiserizing growth because they are often predominantly suppliers of raw materials and agricultural products. Mining projects are long-term investments that are made for uncertain long-run returns. Agricultural production is often closely integrated in a country's culture, which only responds to economic changes with a long lag. Hence, developing countries' economies are relatively inflexible and unable to alter their structures in response to price movements. Therefore, developing economies that currently enjoy a comparative advantage in raw materials may want to restrict trade and push production toward other types of output for which demand is more elastic.

The Long-Run Dynamics of International Investment and Knowledge Transfers

The Hymans and Stafford model, in which a poor country catches up through rapid investment, and the Samuelson model, in which the poor country catches up by acquiring technology, both assume that things stay the same in the rich economy. In his critique of Samuelson, Bhagwati points out that "we can change the terms of trade by moving up the technology ladder."[2] That is, if the high-technology economy continues to develop new technology when old technology is transferred to the poor economy, then it can maintain enough of a difference between the two countries to keep the terms of trade gains from systematically changing. This is like the dynamic process that Vernon (1966) described in his product cycle model of trade.

Samuelson suggests that Vernon's model, and thus Bhagwati's critique, may not be correct. For one thing, in an increasingly global, integrated world economy, technology will tend to flow more quickly and, therefore, reduce the period during which the technology leaders can exploit their technologies. The quickening of the pace at which technology spreads may reduce the benefits from innovation, and this may reduce the rate of innovation, and hence income, in the wealthy country. And, of course, the leader in the technology race may falter for other reasons. For example, the United States has become hopelessly bogged down in two foreign wars, and the resulting budget deficits have forced the government to reduce spending on education, scientific research, infrastructure, and employment. Another ominous development for the traditional technology leaders has been the severe financial collapse caused by the irresponsible deregulation of their financial sectors, which has pushed the U.S. and European economies into recession, which, in turn, has greatly reduced investment and innovation there. In the meantime, foreign direct investment has been flowing into the so-called "**emerging economies**" of Brazil, China, and India.

The discussion above also did not consider the effects of the dynamic relationship between international trade and economic growth. It is quite possible that the economic growth in Poorland will increase its ability to generate knowledge, and the gains from Poorland's rate of technological progress will spill over to Richland and enhance growth there. Before you reject such a scenario as unlikely, you need only look at Japan, Taiwan, and Finland, all countries that at one time lagged substantially in terms of technology but have today become important developers of new knowledge and technology.

Also not considered in the Hymann-Stafford and Samuelson models is the likelihood that, as Poorland becomes more similar to Richland, it will tend to produce more of the increasing-returns-to-scale products that the most developed economies excel in. In this case, variety and increasing returns provide the gains from trade, not the traditional comparative advantage based on factor endowments and technology differences. Thus, as one type of gain diminishes, another gain from trade becomes more likely.

Finally, we did not consider whether the increased competition between Poorland and Richland will push Richland to take measures to spur investment and innovation. Political systems are seldom very good at dealing with complex issues. Blaming trade with Poorland for the country's troubles often gains politicians more votes than, say, raising taxes to pay for better education and infrastructure. Sometimes, outside competition can push a society to make difficult choices. As the model above shows, international trade is not the true cause of Richland's loss of income; the fundamental cause is Richland's lack of economic growth. Of course, an even more daunting issue is how to increase output growth in both Richland and Poorland without destroying the natural environment. Leadership is never easy.

TRADE AND THE WORLD DISTRIBUTION OF INCOME: A CONCLUSION

This chapter continued the previous chapter's discussion of international trade's role in the dynamic processes of economic development and technological change. It is clear that from a dynamic perspective, international trade does not necessarily operate as an arbitrage process that equalizes prices, incomes, and welfare levels across countries. When embedded in the broader processes of economic development and technological change, trade can contribute to the agglomeration of economic activity and the concentration of income.

The eighteenth-century Dutch philosopher Bernard de Mandeville in his "Fable of the Bees" (1714), tells the story of two different beehives. In one, the bees have developed a cooperative society in which they jointly agree to work fewer hours, have more time to enjoy life, and spend more time developing the personal relationships that, as you will recall, Aristotle described as keys to personal happiness. They reached their decision after discovering that with everyone working more hours and increasing their material consumption, they were each still at the same point in the social hierarchy and, therefore, felt no better off for all their effort. In fact, there was a net loss of welfare because the competition and long hours of drudgery at work destroyed the personal friendships they all valued.

Meanwhile, in the second beehive, no collective agreement was discussed, and individual bees just worked long hours under the false impression that each individual would become happier if only they worked harder and earned more income to buy more stuff. They did not yet notice, as the bees in the first hive had, that they were failing to achieve any gain in social stature or happiness as they and their fellow bees all raised their consumption of stuff. Still, the bees believed in their leaders' exhortations to work even harder and propaganda touting material rewards and the potential for moving up in the ranks.

The result was that the first beehive was much happier, but it did not grow very rapidly. The second hive was less happy, but its leaders used the bees' long hours of labor to build a much bigger, and more powerful, hive. Eventually, the second beehive conquered the first beehive, at which point the latter's happiness came to a sudden end. The bees in the first hive, deprived of their own collective culture and governance, saw no other option than to maximize individual welfare by working longer hours and thereby at least avoid any further deterioration in their relative material welfare. Psychologically, many of the first hive's bees found it convenient to believe the propaganda of their new leaders, which told them they would be fully welcomed into their new society if only they worked harder.

Mandeville's fable suggests that a society in which people futilely toil for individual advancement but achieve no permanent rise in status is less well off than a society in which people arrange for a social system with more leisure and freedom from the hedonic treadmill. However, he also provocatively points out that if the two societies inhabit the same world, the happy society will eventually be overtaken, and effectively conquered, by a society of unhappy individuals focused on their work for fear of losing status to even harder-working compatriots.

Interestingly, this colonization of the happy society by the unhappy society ends up boosting the happiness of the latter because after the conquest, the people in the colonizing society now see that they are relatively richer than the poor people of the conquered colony. And, after the conquest, the formerly happy people in the colonized society now find themselves relatively poor and, therefore, less happy than before. This is a redistribution of happiness, not a rise in global welfare.

Mandeville wrote in 1700s Holland, a country that was in the process of "conquering" overseas colonies. His fable was a critique of Dutch colonialism, which led to the deaths of many Dutchmen during their overseas ventures and also greatly reduced the well-being of people in Holland's conquered lands. On the other hand, some readers might interpret Mandeville's fable as justifying the seemingly senseless toil in the second beehive because it ultimately led to a larger bee colony.

A more farsighted observer might wonder if there is not some way to arrive at a cooperative, global solution, say an economic disarmament treaty under which all countries agree to abandon their futile attempts to raise their welfare above that of others and to reduce work hours. Such a worldwide agreement would cause conventionally measured economic growth to slow, but happiness would rise. Workers of the world, unite! The practical problem, of course, is that if only one country failed to join the scheme, say, secretly keeping its population chained to their hedonic treadmills while other countries enjoyed their greater leisure, the country that cheated would eventually take over the world and perhaps raise its happiness somewhat while decimating others' happiness.

Perhaps this difficulty of keeping individuals from narrow-mindedly seeking greater status by working harder and thus undermining welfare-improving collective action explains why the world has not yet adopted a twenty-four-hour workweek. France currently has a thirty-five-hour workweek, but its center-right government is trying to raise work hours again. Modern technology would certainly permit us to live quite well materially on twenty-four hours of work, and the natural environment would be more likely to accommodate human society. But we live in a world where international trade has brought all 7 billion of the world's people together in an integrated economic system, and those countries unilaterally adopting a twenty-four-hour workweek would lose out on capturing the agglomeration of the most profitable economic activities. They would become less developed and, some time in the future, might be conquered by profitable transnational corporations from the high-income countries seeking low-wage economies for outsourcing their labor-intensive production.

Mandeville's fable brings up questions that the orthodox neoclassical paradigm is not designed to answer. We need such alternative perspectives because the very real stresses that people face in today's integrated international economy cannot be dealt with using the orthodox international trade models that are currently in vogue among political leaders and the transnational corporations that increasingly dictate economic and social policies in the countries that have joined the global trading system. Do you think the world could agree on international institutions and policies that would put all societies on a less stressful and more equitable path to economic development? How likely is it that trade negotiations will set rules so that international trade is not used to compel the world's entire labor force into a useless competition for ever-greater material wealth? Will the productivity gains from international trade be used to reduce hours worked to say, twenty hours per week?

CHAPTER SUMMARY

1. This chapter examines whether, and how, the growth of international trade affects economic and social inequality.
2. There are large differences in household income within individual countries, and, because average income levels differ so much across countries, differences in per capita incomes across countries are much greater than within any single country.
3. A convenient numerical measure of income inequality called the *Gini coefficient* is derived from the Lorenz curve; the global Gini coefficient has not changed during the post–World War II period.
4. In practice there are sharp disagreements about what equal opportunity means or what exactly constitutes an oppressive position of power.
5. The popularity of insurance and social safety nets suggests that societies often assume responsibility for helping those members who are adversely affected by events beyond their control.
6. The *social-contractionist* philosophy of John Rawls (1971) provides a reasonable definition of a just society. Rawls reasoned that a just society is the one people would define from behind a "veil of ignorance" that hides their own personal characteristics, background, culture, and circumstances.
7. Rawls effectively shows that the basic human rights that underlie social justice are inseparable from basic economic rights.
8. The increasing returns to scale that characterize both industrial production and innovation imply that international trade, as part of the more complex processes of international economic integration and the concentration of economic activity in large corporations, may cause global incomes to become less equal rather than more equal.
9. The concentration of innovative activity in a few countries is modeled in Vernon's model as continuous shifts in comparative advantage, which continuously change the pattern of trade in accordance with products' life cycles.
10. Since Alfred Marshall, many economists have suggested hypotheses for why some economic activities agglomerate in specific geographic locations. Fundamentally, most explanations rely on economies of scale and economic growth.
11. There is widespread evidence that innovative activity tends to agglomerate, a finding that, combined with the finding that knowledge moves slowly geographically, seems to explain why income is unequal across countries.
12. Evidence showing that innovative activity is the most agglomerative economic activity means that economies will increasingly agglomerate as they grow and develop.
13. There is some evidence that international trade helps to spread technology across borders. Because capital goods have technology embedded in them, so trade directly transfers technology from capital-producing countries to capital-importing countries.
14. Paul Samuelson hypothesizes that trade, by transferring technology overseas, can reduce welfare in the most technologically advanced countries.
15. The traditional HO model can be used to show how, in the case of a country large enough to influence international prices, the gains from increased international trade may be undermined by *immiserizing growth*, which is investment-driven growth that increases a country's exports fast enough to deteriorate its terms of trade.
16. In sum, when embedded in the broader processes of economic development and technological change, trade can contribute to the agglomeration of economic activity and a concentration of income that worsen some countries' overall welfare.

KEY TERMS AND CONCEPTS

agglomeration
bourgeoisie
direct transfers of technology
equal opportunity
Gini coefficient
global Gini coefficient
immiserizing growth
increasing returns to scale
indirect transfers of technology

leader-follower models
Lorenz curve
loss averse
nonrival good
product cycle model of trade
proletariat
standardized product
tacit knowledge
territoriality

PROBLEMS AND QUESTIONS

1. Evaluate the *Universal Declaration of Human Rights.* Explain why you agree or disagree that the items from it listed in the chapter are necessary to guarantee human rights. Does trade affect these rights?

2. Using the discussions on happiness, neuroscience, and psychology in the section entitled "International Trade, Income Inequality, and Welfare" in Chapter 4, explain why the distributional effects of international trade are important.

3. Describe the trend in income inequality over the past several centuries. Has the rapid international economic integration of the past two centuries made the world more equal in terms of income and wealth? Provide specific evidence to support your answer.

4. Explain how international trade affects the distribution of income:
   (a) using the neoclassical HO model
   (b) adopting a more dynamic perspective that takes investment, innovation, and economic growth agglomeration into consideration

5. Explain why conclusions about how international trade affects the worldwide distribution of welfare differ depending on whether you use the static HO model of trade or a more dynamic model that incorporates technological progress and economic growth.

6. Why does some economic activity tend to agglomerate geographically?

7. Jagdish Bhagwati's model of immiserizing growth has been described as the only exception to the conclusion that free trade is welfare superior to restricted trade. Explain how protection can make a country better off according to the graphic model of immiserizing growth. Is it the only "exception?"

8. Does faster growth in poor countries make rich countries worse off? Use the two-country model in Figures 7.6 and 7.7 to answer this question. (Hint: Present both the case of technological change and the case of investment in capital.)

9. Explain Paul Samuelson's (2004) argument on how international trade can reduce a developed economy's income. (Hint: Be sure to explain all the steps of his argument.)

10. Discuss Mandeville's "Fable of the Bees." What does this fable have to do with international trade?

11. Write an essay answering the questions at the end of this chapter: Do you think the world could agree on international institutions and policies that would put all societies on a less stressful and more equitable path to economic development, one where international trade is not used to compel the world's entire labor force into a useless competition for ever-greater material wealth. How likely

is it that international negotiations will set rules so that productivity gains from international trade are used to reduce hours worked to say, twenty hours per week?

NOTES

1. See also the data on R&D expenditures as a percentage of GDP given in UNESCO (2002), *Statistical Yearbook,* Geneva: UNESCO, or in World Bank (2002), *World Development Indicators,* Washington, DC: World Bank, Table 5.11, pp. 320–322.

2. Quoted in Steve Lohr (2004), "An Elder Challenges Outsourcing's Orthodoxy," *New York Times,* September 9.

PART THREE

INTERNATIONAL TRADE POLICY

This part of the textbook introduces and analyzes international trade policy, the formal institutions that govern a country's exchange of products with foreigners. Both mainstream international economics and heterodox interpretations of international trade provide useful explanations for how national governments deal with international trade. In practice, we observe a wide range of policies, from nearly complete free trade to elaborate systems to control inflows of imports and outflows of exports. There are no countries that do not in some way interfere with international trade.

Chapter 8 presents the ways in which governments interfere with trade. Import tariffs and quotas are explained. The orthodox supply and demand model of international trade is used to analyze the short-run costs and benefits, and their distribution, of tariffs and quotas. This model is static, and it therefore cannot address the long-run consequences of international trade, such as those processes that were discussed in Chapters 6 and 7. Nevertheless, the model provides useful insight into how the short-term interests drive the political process. There is also a discussion of export subsidies and taxes, as well as the many variations on tariffs and quotas that governments use to restrict trade.

Chapter 9 presents the history of international trade policy, with special emphasis on the past two hundred years. Preceding the historical discussion, there is a brief presentation of some of the political economy models of why governments interfere with international trade. These models can be applied to explain the historical trends in trade policy as described in the remainder of the chapter. The chapter ends with a discussion of recent trade negotiations, including regional free trade arrangements such as the European Union and the failure of the World Trade Organization's Doha Round of trade negotiations.

Chapter 10 continues the discussion of trade policy, focusing on specific policy regimes that address some of the dynamic effects of international trade that were discussed in Chapter 7. This discussion is especially important for analyzing how trade policy influences a country's long-run economic development. This chapter presents several alternative approaches to trade policy. The chapter begins with a discussion of mercantilism and attempts by special interests to shape international trade in their favor during the fifteenth through the eighteenth centuries. There is a full description and analysis of dependency theory, structuralism, and the import substitution policies that were popular in developing countries in the second half of the twentieth century after World War II. Finally, there is a discussion of strategic trade policy, which seeks to maximize national welfare by influencing long-run trade patterns within a framework that assumes imperfect competition and the strategic behavior of transnational corporations.

CHAPTER 8

Tariffs, Quotas, and Other Trade Restrictions

> On the one hand, democracy makes leaders more accountable to their citizens,
> promoting trade liberalization to the extent that this is good for society as a whole.
> On the other hand, democracy also empowers distributional coalitions with
> intense interests, making higher levels of protection more likely.
>
> —Geoffrey Garrett (2000)

The discussion of *trade policy* is usually framed by the standard neoclassical Heckscher-Ohlin (HO) model of international trade. Just as the HO model permits economists to determine the comparative static gains from free trade, that same model is also used by mainstream economists to estimate the costs and benefits of trade barriers. This first chapter on trade policy presents the orthodox neoclassical analysis of the standard measures that government policy makers use to interfere in international trade, such as tariffs, import quotas, and export subsidies. As already discussed in earlier chapters, the neoclassical HO model of trade misses many important causes and consequences of international trade, and in this chapter we point out the most obvious cases where the orthodox analysis of trade may miss the full effects of trade policies. Orthodox comparative static analysis does provide good insight into why governments restrict trade, even if it is not fully holistic.

After we review the history of trade policies in the next chapter, Chapter 10 reexamines the trade policies detailed in this chapter from more heterodox and holistic perspectives. Throughout these three chapters on trade policy, we seek to answer the question: If there are circumstances under which free trade is not the optimal long-run welfare-maximizing policy, then what active trade policy does maximize human welfare?

TARIFFS

One of the most often used types of trade restrictions is the **tariff**, which is simply a tax on imports. Since ancient times, governments have imposed tariffs to raise revenue and to protect domestic economic interests from import competition. Tariffs are either *ad valorem* or *specific*. An **ad valorem tariff** is a tax on imports that is specified as a percentage of the value of the product on which the tariff is levied. For example, an ad valorem tariff of 20 percent on, say, coffee requires that the importer of a pound of run-of-the-mill robusta coffee worth $5 pay a tariff of $1. An importer of organic fair trade gourmet coffee worth $10 would pay a tariff of $2. A **specific tariff** levies a designated amount of money per unit of imports. For example, if the imported coffee is taxed at the

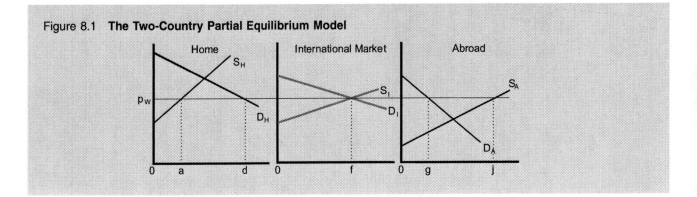

Figure 8.1 The Two-Country Partial Equilibrium Model

specific rate of $2 per pound, then the importer must pay the government $2 for every pound of coffee imported, regardless of what the price of coffee is.

Ad valorem tariffs are often used because it is easier to set a single ad valorem tariff for a whole category of products of different values than to set specific tariffs for each product within that category. Also, ad valorem tariffs, because they are a constant percentage of the actual prices of the imports, maintain their real value over the long run as inflation causes prices to rise. Specific tariffs denoted in terms of actual dollar amounts would gradually decrease in real terms as inflation raises the prices of imports.

Other important differences include the fact that ad valorem tariffs reward low-cost foreign suppliers by in effect charging a lower absolute tax on their products than is charged on more expensive products in the same category. Specific tariffs, on the other hand, lead to less tampering with shipping documents in order to mislead customs agents about the true value of imported goods. Ad valorem tariffs are used more often, but there are plenty of specific tariffs.

The Welfare Gains and Losses of a Tariff

The effects of a tariff can be illustrated using the partial equilibrium supply and demand model of international trade that you have already encountered in Chapter 3. For easy reference, Figure 3.12 is repeated here as Figure 8.1. Suppose that Figure 8.1 represents the markets for bicycles in a world consisting of two countries, Home and Abroad. The equilibrium price is lower in Abroad than in Home, so it is clear that Abroad enjoys the comparative advantage in producing bicycles.

Figure 8.2 illustrates the case where one of the two countries in the world, Home, levies a 50 percent ad valorem tariff on bicycles. The figure includes the Home market and the international market as seen by the residents of Home, the left and center diagrams from Figure 8.1.

A tariff forces importers to pay not only the foreign supplier of the product, but also their own country's government. From Home's perspective, the tariff appears to raise the international supply curve of the import good, represented by the shift of the supply curve S_W, to S_T in the international market (Figure 8.2). The distance between S_W and S_T represents the tariff revenue to the government. With an ad valorem tariff the specific amount of the tariff increases as the price rises; hence the distance between the foreign supply curve S_W and the tariff-inclusive foreign supply curve S_T is greater for higher supply prices. The upward shift in the international supply curve means that the intersection with Home's import demand curve occurs at a higher price and a lower quantity. Home's price of bicycles rises from p_W to p_T, and international trade of bicycles is reduced from 0f to 0e.

The decline in Home's quantity demanded of imports also affects the market in Abroad. Figure 8.3 shows the bicycle market from Abroad's perspective. Exporters in Abroad effectively

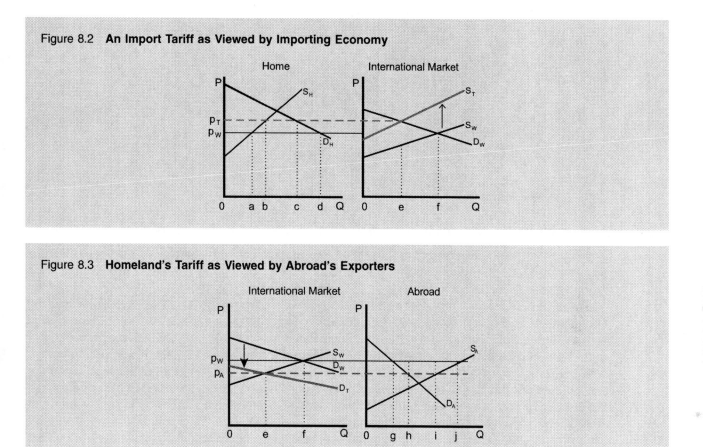

Figure 8.2 **An Import Tariff as Viewed by Importing Economy**

Figure 8.3 **Homeland's Tariff as Viewed by Abroad's Exporters**

interpret the 50 percent ad valorem tariff as a decline in foreign demand, from D_W to D_T. The price of bicycles in Abroad therefore falls from p_W to p_A. The quantity of bicycles exported by Abroad after the tariff is hi = 0e = bc; the latter quantity is what Home wants to import at the tariff-inclusive price.

Figure 8.4 combines Figures 8.2 and 8.3 and gives us a full picture of the world market for bicycles. Figure 8.4 permits the application of the concepts of consumer and producer surplus explained in Chapter 3. The imposition of Home's tariff on bicycles reduces consumer surplus and raises producer surplus in Home. Home's tariff raises consumer surplus and lowers producer surplus in Abroad. Specifically, Home consumers lose areas A+b+C+d, and Home producers gain area A. In Abroad, producers lose areas W+x+Y+z, and consumers gain W. The tariff also generates revenue for Home's government, of course. The Home government's tariff revenue is equal to the shaded areas C and Y. The parts of the former consumer and producer surpluses that are lost when the tariff is imposed are usually referred to as the **deadweight losses**.

Who Pays the Tariff?

In Figure 8.4 the source of the tariff revenue to the home government is clearly illustrated. The tariff box in the center diagram is made up of two areas, one from the surplus lost by consumers in Home, the other from the surplus lost by producers in Abroad. The incidence of the tax thus falls on groups in both countries. Even though importers technically pay the tariff, part of the tariff is effectively paid by the producers from Abroad who supply the lower quantity of bicycles

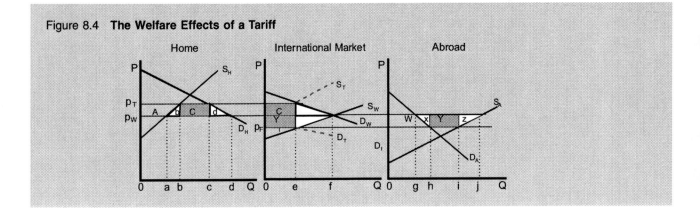

Figure 8.4 The Welfare Effects of a Tariff

at a lower unit cost. Just as in the case of transportation costs in Chapter 4, the tariff drives a wedge between foreign and domestic prices, raising the price at home and pushing down the price abroad, preventing arbitrage from equalizing prices.

The tariff changes a country's **terms of trade** by lowering the price that Home pays for its imports, and this constitutes a gain for Home. Of course, the tariff also reduces the level of trade, which is welfare diminishing. Home's net losses from a tariff depend on the degree to which the improvement in its terms of trade offsets the deadweight losses from restricting trade. In fact, Home could gain net welfare from its tariff if it sets the tariff at a level so that $Y > (b+d)$. Abroad definitely suffers a net loss because it suffers the deadweight losses x and z in addition to having to pay part of Home's tariff, the area Y. The world as a whole loses welfare because even though Home's gain of Y is equal to Abroad's loss of Y, there are still the four deadweight losses, b, d, x, and z. It should be intuitive why the tariff must reduce world welfare: International trade is artificially reduced below the level where arbitrage fully equalizes prices across countries. The world has lost some of the gains from trade.

A Numerical Example of a Specific Tariff

Suppose that the Home and Abroad markets for calculators are given in Figure 8.5, in which prices are in dollars and quantities are given in millions of calculators. In the absence of trade, the equilibrium prices and quantities would be $10 and 10 million, respectively, in Home and $6 and 10 million in Abroad. Under free trade, the world price would settle at $8. According to the center diagram of the international market, when there is free trade Home imports 8 million calculators from Abroad. Home also still produces 6 million calculators itself. Abroad produces 14 million calculators, of which it exports 8 million to Home.

Suppose that domestic producers of calculators in Home complain to their government about the "unfair" competition from low-priced producers in Abroad, and Home's government responds by levying a $3 per calculator specific tariff on imports. The tariff shifts the foreign supply curve in the center diagram up by $3 at each quantity, which results in a new equilibrium price of $9.50 in the Home market. The price in Abroad falls to $6.50 as Home reduces its imports from 8 million to 2 million units. The incidence of the tariff, which is equal to areas C + Y, falls in part on Home's consumers and in part on Abroad's producers. For Home, the welfare effects of a tariff on calculators to a $3 specific tariff are as follows:

Home Consumer Surplus	$= -(A + b + C + d)$	$= -\$18.75$ million
Home Producer Surplus	$= +(A)$	$= +\$11.25$ million
Home Gov't Tariff Revenue	$= +(C + Y)$	$= +\$\ 6.00$ million
Net Change	$= Y - b - d$	$= -\$\ 1.50$ million.

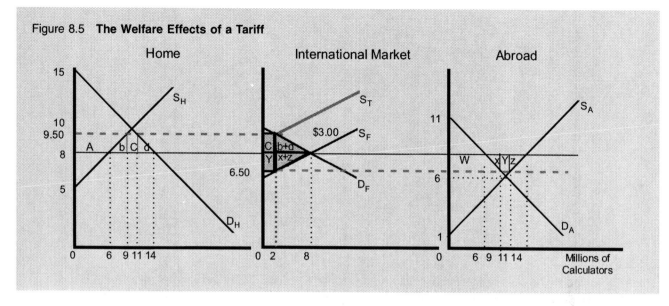

Figure 8.5   The Welfare Effects of a Tariff

Home thus suffers a net welfare loss. Its consumers of calculators pay for some of the gains by its calculator producers. Ultimately the gains from the tariff revenue depend on how Home's government spends or distributes its tax revenue. Abroad's loss is greater than Home's because it actually pays part of Home's tariff revenue:

$$\text{Abroad's Consumer Surplus} = +(W) \qquad\qquad = +\$11.25 \text{ million}$$
$$\text{Abroad's Producer Surplus} = -(W + x + Y + z) = -\$18.75 \text{ million}$$
$$\text{Net Change} \qquad\qquad = -Y - x - z \qquad = -\$\ 7.50 \text{ million}.$$

The net loss for the world is now:

$$\text{World deadweight losses} = -(b + d + x + z) = -\$9.0 \text{ million}.$$

These results show that both Home and Abroad lose net welfare from the $3 tariff, although Home loses less than Abroad loses. By effectively reducing its demand, Home improves its terms of trade effect and thus shifts part of the tariff payment to producers in Abroad.

A Tariff in the Heckscher-Ohlin Model

We justified showing the effects of a tariff in the supply and demand model of trade by claiming that this model can be derived from the more general HO model of trade. We can actually show the effect of a tariff directly in the HO model. Although we lose the convenient consumer and producer surplus areas with which to judge the effects of a tariff, the HO model is useful for understanding the effects of a tariff beyond the particular market where the tariffs are levied.

To keep things as simple as possible, let's begin by looking at a **small country** that has no influence on world prices and, hence, takes the world price ratio of the two products, say X and Y, as a given. The immediate effect of a tariff is to raise the price of the taxed import good relative to the prices of other goods produced in the economy. An ad valorem tariff of t percent on the import good X will raise the domestic price of X from the world price of P_X to $(1+t)P_X$. For example, if the ad valorem tariff t = 50 percent and the world price P_X = $100, then $(1+t)P_X = (1.50)\$100 = \$150$. As illustrated in Figure 8.6, the ad valorem tariff on imports of X causes the slope of the price line

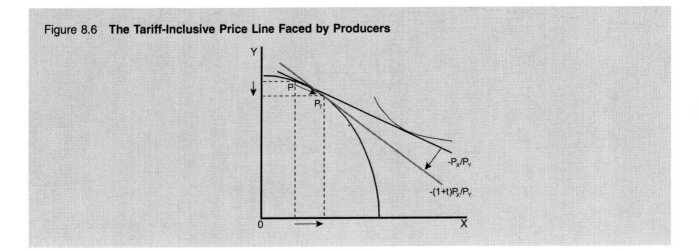

Figure 8.6 **The Tariff-Inclusive Price Line Faced by Producers**

$-P_X/P_Y$

$-(1+t)P_X/P_Y$

faced by domestic producers to become steeper. Specifically, if the world price line has a slope of $-(P_X/P_Y)$, then the tariff-distorted domestic price line will have a slope of $-[(1+t)P_X/P_Y]$. As a result of this change in domestic relative prices, domestic production shifts to P_T. The shift in production from the free trade equilibrium P to the tariff-induced production point P_T implies an increase in X production and a decrease in Y production.

We will not illustrate the full effects of a tariff on the economy; that is given in the Appendix to this chapter for those of you who are interested in a more detailed analysis of a tariff using the Heckscher-Ohlin model. What is important to note here is that the tariff reverses the effects of liberalizing international trade.

The Lerner Symmetry Theorem

The two-industry HO model further shows that a tariff on imports of good X not only reduces imports and lets the X industry expand its output, but it also ends up contracting the Y industry and reducing exports. The intuition behind this result is that the tariff protection of the X industry, which raises the price of X, permits that industry to attract more of the economy's resources. The X industry's increased demand for resources necessarily raises the cost of resources for the Y industry, which reduces that industry's ability to produce and export. If you have trouble grasping this idea, just think of what happens if a country applies a **prohibitive tariff**, which is a tariff that raises the price of imports so far above the price of domestic goods that domestic producers earn enough to acquire enough of the economy's resources to satisfy all domestic demand for the import-competing products and no one imports anything. Such a tariff would take the economy back to self-sufficiency, where there are no imports and no exports at all. Thus, the prohibitive tariff eliminates both imports and exports.

There is a second mechanism through which import tariffs work to reduce exports: exchange rates. When a tariff raises the price of imports and causes domestic consumers to buy fewer imports, the demand for foreign exchange falls and the exchange rate appreciates. An appreciation makes domestically produced exports more expensive for foreigners, and foreigners will therefore tend to reduce their purchases. We will discuss exchange rates later in the textbook. There is, in fact, a well-known theorem, the **Lerner symmetry theorem**, named in honor of Abba P. Lerner (1934), who first rigorously proved it, that says that an import tariff, by raising opportunity costs to exporters, is a tax on exports as well as imports. Protectionist trade policies might be more strenuously resisted if everyone understood that a tariff on imports effectively acts as a tax on exports. Given that the effects of tariffs extend beyond a single industry or country, you should always be suspicious of suggestions that a tariff will help some firm or industry without having any effects on anyone else.

Summarizing the Welfare Effects of a Tariff

The two-country supply and demand model of a tariff, which assumes both countries are large enough to influence each other's prices, shows that the imposition of a tariff by one country on the other's exports causes:

- A transfer of welfare from domestic consumers to domestic producers in the importing country
- A transfer of welfare from producers to consumers in the exporting country
- A transfer of consumer surplus in the importing country to the government in the form of tariff revenue, which ultimately benefits the recipients of the government transfers or services paid for with the tariff revenue
- A transfer of producer surplus in the exporting country to the government of the importing country and, ultimately, the recipients of the government transfers and services paid for by the tariff revenue in the importing country
- Deadweight losses in both importing and exporting countries

The net welfare loss to the world as a whole is equal to the deadweight losses, although the importing country may lose less than its deadweight losses because the tariff may improve its terms of trade. Of course, the terms of trade gains come at the expense of the exporting country, which consequently suffers a welfare loss in excess of its deadweight losses.

The HO model shows that restrictions on imports end up restricting exports as well because the tariff causes a shift of resources from the export to the import industries. This is the important Lerner symmetry theorem. It is possible to extend the general equilibrium analysis to include a second country, in which case a tariff imposed on one product by one country causes exports and imports in the rest of the world to also decline, thus causing welfare losses and industry shifts overseas as well as at home.

How Much Protection Does a Tariff Really Provide?

The amount of protection provided to a domestic industry by a tariff is often quantified by how much the tariff raises the domestic price of the industry's products. That is, if the tariff raises the domestic price by, say, 10 percent, then the tariff can be described as providing a protective margin of 10 percent. This is often not an accurate measure of the true degree of protection provided to a specific industry, however, because the final price of a product usually includes a substantial amount of inputs from other industries.

A tariff on imported pickup trucks, currently 25 percent in the United States, offers a good example. The automobile industry purchases steel from the steel industry, hoses and belts from the rubber industry, computer chips from the chip industry, radios from the consumer electronics industry, and so forth. Suppose that half of the total cost of producing a US$10,000 pickup truck consists of actual production costs incurred by the automobile industry for metal stamping, parts manufacture, and product assembly, and the other 50 percent of the cost of producing a truck consists of purchases of parts and services from other firms and industries. The automobile industry's value added is therefore US$5,000. Suppose also that there are no tariffs or other trade restrictions placed on the importation of any of the things the auto industry buys from others, so that arbitrage keeps the prices of those goods at or near world prices. In this case, suppose that the 25 percent ad valorem tariff causes the domestic price of pickup trucks to rise by, say, 20 percent, from US$10,000 to US$12,000, because part of the tariff is absorbed by foreign suppliers. This will actually increase the value of the production of the automobile industry, its **value added**, from US$5,000 to US$7,000, or by 40 percent! That is, by increasing the price of the pickup truck by US$2,000 while the prices of the goods and services responsible for half of total costs remain the same, the 25 percent tariff increases the truck industry's value added by 40 percent. This 40 percent is the **effective tariff** on value added of the truck industry. Figure 8.7 illustrates the above example.

An effective tariff can also have a negative effect on an industry. Suppose that instead of a tariff on complete trucks, the government imposes a 25 percent tariff on auto parts, raw materials, and other inputs used by the auto industry. If there is no tariff on finished autos, then the automakers will see their value added squeezed: Suppose again that the 25 percent tariff actually raises the price of inputs, both imported inputs and protected domestic inputs, by 20 percent because foreign suppliers absorb part of the tariff. Thus, the total cost of inputs rises from US$5,000 to US$6,000. If truck makers face sharp competition from foreign truck suppliers, they will be unable to raise their prices above the market equilibrium US$10,000 per truck. Therefore, value added falls from US$5,000 to US$4,000, a 20 percent decline in value added. The tariff on truck components, parts, and other inputs serves as an *effective tariff* of –20 percent on trucks. Figure 8.8 illustrates this example.

The effective protection that a country's tariffs provide is difficult to estimate without a detailed analysis of how tariffs affect prices for finished products as opposed to intermediate inputs. In general, a tariff on final output provides a higher level of effective protection than the tariff rate suggests if intermediate goods and services are subject to lower tariffs. The effective level of protection of an industry is lower than the explicit tariff on that industry's final output if inputs and intermediate services purchased from other firms and industries are protected by tariffs that are higher than the tariff on the final good. The discrepancy between actual tariffs and effective tariffs would not occur in the case of completely free trade in all goods and services or in the case where all goods and services imports are subject to exactly the same ad valorem tariff. There are few countries that have ever applied such a uniform tariff rate. Chile stands out as an exception; in 2000 it began applying the same 9 percent tariff to all imports, no matter whether they were final goods, intermediate goods, or raw materials.

Average Tariff Rates

Tariff rates vary greatly across product categories, so it is difficult to compare the overall trade policies of different countries. Countries may have very low tariffs for certain categories of products, but levy very high tariffs on other products. The World Bank calculates a weighted mean tariff rate for most countries of the world. This measure "weighs" each tariff category by its share of the country's overall value of trade, and the countries for which recent estimates are available (after 1997) are listed in Table 8.1. Notice that the developed economies tend to have the lowest tariff rates and developing countries impose the highest tariffs, although there are many exceptions. And because these are averages, it may be the case that developed countries levy some high tariffs, or that developing countries do not block all imports with equally high tariffs.

QUOTAS

As other seemingly straightforward way to restrict trade is to simply prohibit goods from crossing the border and to back up that prohibition with force and the threat of punishment. Often, rather than banning all imports, a government sets limits on how many goods enter the country from abroad. Such **quantitative trade restrictions** are commonly called **quotas**. In general, a quota can be set at any quantity. A quota may be set in terms of value, weight, volume, or the number of items. The

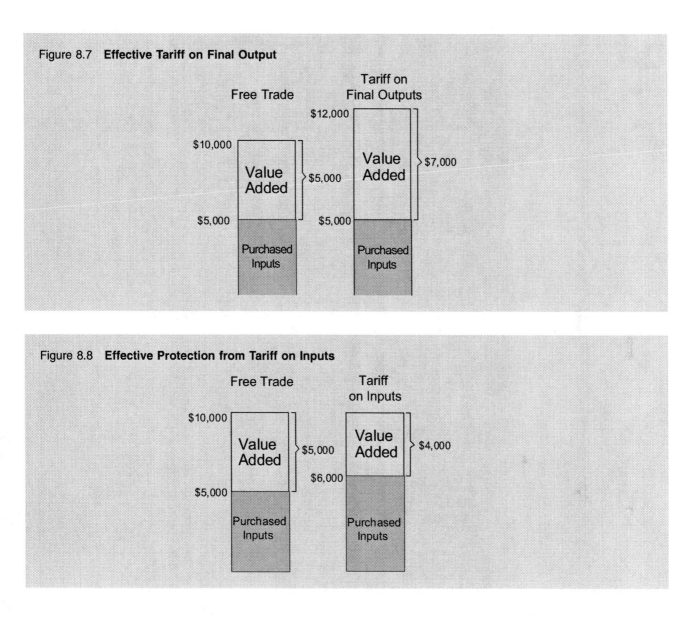

Figure 8.7 **Effective Tariff on Final Output**

Free Trade

Tariff on
Final Outputs

Figure 8.8 **Effective Protection from Tariff on Inputs**

Free Trade

Tariff
on Inputs

smaller the quota, the more restrictive of trade it is. A quota of zero is effectively a complete ban on imports. The analysis that follows will focus on the intermediate case of a nonzero quota.

A Quota in the Supply and Demand Model of Trade

Just like the tariff, the effects of a quota can be illustrated using the partial equilibrium model of imports and exports from Chapter 4. Suppose that we are interested in the market for cheese in a world consisting of the same two countries whose bicycle market we analyzed earlier, Home and Abroad. Suppose also that Abroad has a comparative advantage in producing cheese.

A quota on imports of cheese set by Home's government is illustrated in Figure 8.9. In this case, the quota is set at one-half the level of imports that would normally enter Home under free trade. Foreigners supply products as given by their supply curve until the quota becomes binding at quantity 0e. After that, foreign supply effectively becomes completely inelastic; the quantity supplied from Abroad no longer responds to price increases once the quota is filled. The foreign

Table 8.1

A Sample of Average Tariff Rates

Developing Economies:				Developed Economies:	
Algeria	17.3%	Laos	14.7%	Australia	9.1%
Argentina	10.5	Lebanon	19.1	Canada	6.0
Bangladesh	21.0	Libya	21.3	European Union	1.8
Bolivia	9.4	Malawi	11.5	Hong Kong	0.0
Brazil	12.7	Mali	10.3	Iceland	3.6
Burkina Faso	21.7	Mauritius	11.9	Japan	2.0
Cameroon	13.9	Mexico	15.4	Korea	5.9
Cen. African Rep.	14.1	Morocco	25.8	New Zealand	2.3
Chad	14.6	Mozambique	17.4	Norway	1.1
Chile	9.0	Nepal	17.7	Singapore	0.0
China	14.7	Nicaragua	2.9	Switzerland	0.0
Colombia	11.0	Nigeria	20.0	Taiwan	3.9
Congo Republic	16.7	Pakistan	41.7	United States	1.8
Costa Rica	3.7	Panama	7.8		
Cote d'Ivoire	14.1	Paraguay	10.5	*Transition Economies:*	
Dominican Rep.	15.8	Peru	12.6	Belarus	9.5
Ecuador	11.1	Saudi Arabia	10.3	Czech Republic	5.7
Egypt	13.7	South Africa	4.4	Estonia	0.4
El Salvador	6.5	Sri Lanka	7.4	Georgia	10.1
Equatorial Guinea	15.3	Tanzania	14.2	Hungary	4.5
Ethiopia	18.1	Trinidad	17.0	Latvia	3.2
Gabon	16.0	Tunisia	28.8	Lithuania	2.3
Guatemala	5.8	Turkey	5.7	Poland	7.4
Honduras	8.3	Uganda	6.1	Romania	12.4
India	28.5	Uruguay	6.2	Russia	12.4
Israel	4.0	Venezuela	13.4	Slovenia	11.4
Jamaica	9.6	Vietnam	18.7	Ukraine	5.2
Jordan	18.9	Zambia	13.1		
Kenya	12.4	Zimbabwe	16.4	*Newly-Industrialized Economies:*	
				Indonesia	5.2
				Malaysia	6.0
				Philippines	3.8
				Thailand	10.1

Source: World Bank (2002), *World Development Indicators 2002*, Washington, DC: World Bank, Table 6.6, pp. 348–350.

supply curve therefore looks like the "kinked" curve in the international market diagram. The price in the international market thus rises to p_Q, which is higher than the free trade price of p_W. The total supply curve, which is the sum of the domestic supply curve S_H and the restricted foreign supply curve S_Q, becomes S_{H+Q} in the Home cheese market. Home therefore consumes the quantity 0c of cheese at price P_Q.

Figure 8.10 shows the quota from Abroad's perspective. The limit on Home's imports of cheese is seen in Abroad as a decline in demand, from the dashed D_W curve under free trade to the heavy, dark "kinked" curve D_Q after the quota is enforced. The sum of foreign and domestic demand in Abroad becomes the heavy, dark total demand curve D_T, which intersects domestic demand at p_F. Thus, Home's import quota causes the price of cheese to fall in Abroad, which benefits Abroad's consumers but hurts its cheese makers.

Figure 8.11 combines the results from Figures 8.9 and 8.10 into the standard two-country partial equilibrium diagram. The import quota by Home causes the domestic price in Home to diverge from

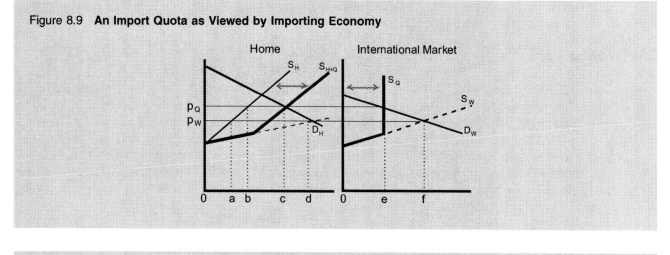

Figure 8.9   **An Import Quota as Viewed by Importing Economy**

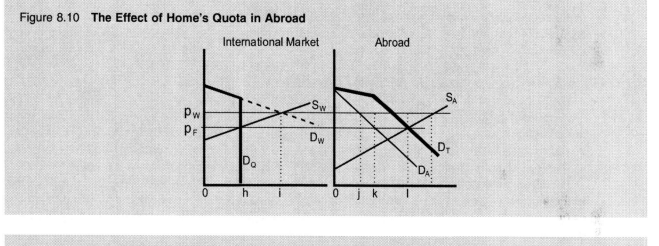

Figure 8.10   **The Effect of Home's Quota in Abroad**

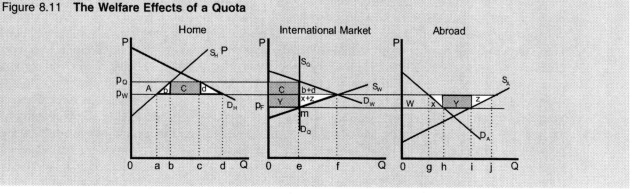

Figure 8.11   **The Welfare Effects of a Quota**

the price for the same good in Abroad. This price difference comes about because the quota prevents arbitrage from being carried out in sufficient volume for it to equalize prices in both markets. This means that those who are able to buy in one market and sell in the other stand to gain substantial arbitrage profits. Indeed, an import quota provides exceptional profits to the restricted number of people who are able to trade. These exceptional profits created by the quota's restriction on trade are called **quota rent**; the economic term *rent* applies to earnings that are over and above those necessary to lead producers to supply the market. The existence of different prices in the two markets and the presence of quota rents for a privileged few traders complicates the analysis of the welfare effects of a quota.

The Welfare Effects of a Quota

Recall that producer surplus is equal to the area between the supply curve and the market price. The quantity supplied by Home's domestic producers after the imposition of the quota is equal to the quantity 0b in Figure 8.11. Under free trade, the quantity supplied is ab and the price is p_W. The quota thus increases producer surplus in Home by the area A. The quota's effect of raising the price from p_W to p_Q causes Home's consumers to lose surplus equal to areas A, b, C, and d. Home's consumers therefore lose more than Home's producers gain. In Abroad the consumers gain welfare and the cheese makers lose welfare. Abroad's cheese makers lose the surplus area consisting of W, x, Y, and z, but its consumers gain W.

The key to understanding the partial equilibrium effects of a quota is to recognize that a quota provides some people with rent. When the prices of a good or service in different countries diverge and only some importers or exporters are able to arbitrage the price differences between the domestic economy and the rest of the world, the price differences do not disappear, and the selected arbitragers continually earn high rents. Such rent is represented by the shaded areas in the center diagram of Figure 8.11. Either importers or exporters, or both, get the rent.

Who Gets to Import and Collect the Quota Rent?

An important question for determining the welfare costs and benefits of a quota is who gets to earn the quota rent, and, equally important, who doesn't? Because a quota limits imports below the level that would exist under free trade, the imposition of an import quota by the government requires that some rationing scheme be established to decide who will be allowed to import and earn the quota rent.

A common method for rationing quota privileges is to issue a number of import permits equal to the number of items permitted to enter the country under the quota. Anyone with an import permit is allowed to import the foreign good, and everyone else is limited to domestic sources of the restricted good. Such import permits can be issued according to a variety of criteria. For example, it might be deemed fair to issue import permits in proportion to past imports. That is, suppose that last year imports amounted to 200 units and this year the quota is set at 100. Under this scheme, if someone imported ten units last year, they would be issued five import permits this year. Alternatively, governments may set criteria that would-be importers must satisfy. For example, they could require lengthy documentation detailing the exact use of the product, the availability of domestic substitutes, the employment effects of the imports, and so forth for would-be importers to "justify" their need for import permits. Sometimes a lottery system is used. In the absence of any specific criteria for awarding import permits, a first-come, first-served system becomes the de facto rationing scheme. Of course, because the quota rents are often quite large, bribery and other forms of legal and illegal influence peddling often become part of the rationing process. Given the many possible ways in which quota rents can be rationed, the theoretical model cannot tell us precisely which suppliers and demanders actually get to satisfy their wishes and trade.

It is not even clear whether quota rent is earned by exporters or by importers. Most manufactured goods exported throughout the world are branded products marketed by the multinational firms who produce them. Import permits for branded products will often result in quota rent that accrues to foreign exporters. For example, in the case of Toyota automobiles produced in Japan and sold in the United States, it is Toyota's U.S. subsidiary, Toyota of America, which essentially collects the difference between the cost of making the car in Japan and the price at which that the car is sold to dealers in the United States. If a quota increases the difference between Japanese costs and U.S.

prices, Toyota's U.S. sales subsidiary earns higher profits. These profits are then remitted back to Japanese stockholders, and the quota rent effectively accrues to the exporting country.

On the other hand, in the case of foreign-made blue jeans sold by Walmart in the United States, it is Walmart that buys the clothes overseas and imports them. If a quota on jeans lowers the price of jeans in Bangladesh, China, and Costa Rica, but raises their price in the United States, it is the importer and marketer in the quota-restricted U.S. market, Walmart, that earns the quota rent.

In general, quota rent tends to accrue to domestic firms for products that are relatively homogeneous and sold in competitive worldwide markets. Agricultural commodities, for example, are sold at world prices through world commodity exchanges. In this case, import permits are awarded to domestic import firms, who can then capture the difference between the world and domestic prices. But, in the case of most branded consumer goods and specialized industrial inputs that are marketed by the foreign producers themselves, the quota rent is effectively an improved profit margin captured by the foreign producers.

A Numerical Example of a Quota

In the previous section on tariffs, a numerical example showed how you can quantify the effects of a $3 specific tariff on calculators. Suppose that, instead of the tariff, the government of Home imposes an import quota on calculators that reduces imports by the same amount and causes the exact same price distortions as the $3 specific tariff. As illustrated in Figure 8.12, imports can be reduced by 6 million units, from 8 million to 2 million, and the domestic price raised to $9.50 by imposing a quota of 2 million calculators. The welfare effects of a quota turn out to be very similar to those of a tariff previously illustrated. If the quota rent is captured by Home importers, then the welfare effects of shifting from free trade in calculators to an import quota of 2 million calculators are as follows:

$$
\begin{aligned}
\text{Home Consumer Surplus} &= -(A + b + C + d) &&= -\$18.75 \text{ million} \\
\text{Home Producer Surplus} &= +(A) &&= +\$11.25 \text{ million} \\
\text{Home Quota Rent} &= +(C + Y) &&= +\$\ 6.0 \text{ million} \\
\hline
\text{Net Change} &= Y - b - d &&= -\$\ 1.5 \text{ million.}
\end{aligned}
$$

Home thus suffers a net loss from the quota. Home's consumers suffer huge losses, but calculator producers and calculator importers actually gain from the quota. Abroad suffers a net loss that exceeds Home's net loss by the quota rent:

$$
\begin{aligned}
\text{Abroad's Consumer Surplus} &= +(W) &&= +\$11.25 \text{ million} \\
\text{Abroad's Producer Surplus} &= -(W + x + Y + z) &&= -\$18.75 \text{ million} \\
\text{Abroad's Quota Rent} &= 0 &&= +\$\ 0.0 \text{ million} \\
\hline
\text{Net Change} &= Y - x - z &&= -\$\ 7.5 \text{ million.}
\end{aligned}
$$

The net loss for the world is equal to the deadweight losses in both countries:

$$
\text{World deadweight losses} = -(b + d + x + z) = -\$9.0 \text{ million.}
$$

The above results depend critically on the assumption that Home's importers earn the quota rent. To see why, suppose that the rent from Home's quota accrues to foreign exporters, perhaps because they market their products directly to consumers in Home. In this case, Abroad's exporters capture the difference between foreign production costs and the domestic sales price. The welfare effects in Home will then be as follows:

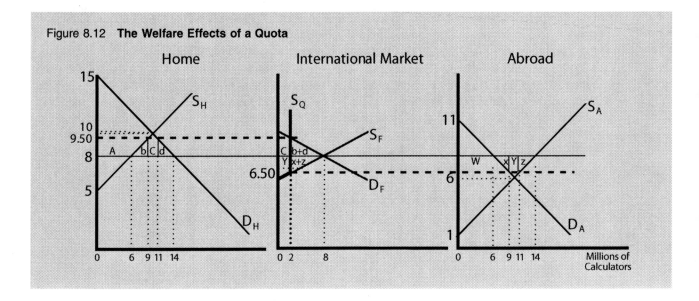

Figure 8.12 **The Welfare Effects of a Quota**

$$\text{Home Consumer Surplus} = -(A + b + C + d) = -\$18.75 \text{ million}$$
$$\text{Home Producer Surplus} = +(A) \qquad\qquad = +\$11.25 \text{ million}$$
$$\text{Home Quota Rent} \qquad = 0 \qquad\qquad\quad = +\$\ 0.0 \text{ million}$$
$$\text{Net Change} \qquad\qquad = Y - b - d \qquad = -\$\ 7.5 \text{ million.}$$

In Abroad, the welfare gains and losses are allocated as follows:

$$\text{Abroad's Consumer Surplus} = +(W) \qquad\qquad\quad = +\$11.25 \text{ million}$$
$$\text{Abroad's Producer Surplus} = -(W + x + Y + z) = -\$18.75 \text{ million}$$
$$\text{Abroad's Quota Rent} \qquad = +(C + Y) \qquad\quad = +\$\ 6.0 \text{ million}$$
$$\text{Net Change} \qquad\qquad\qquad = -(Y + x + z) \qquad = -\$\ 1.5 \text{ million.}$$

Now Home suffers the larger net loss from the quota. Just like before, the net loss for the world as a whole is:

$$\text{World deadweight losses} = -(b + d + x + z) = -\$9.0 \text{ million.}$$

In summary, while there is no doubt over which country gains the revenue from a tariff, the welfare effects of a quota are less certain because quota rent can accrue to exporters or importers.

Voluntary Export Restraints (VERs)

An interesting variant of the quota is the **voluntary export restraint (VER)**. A VER, as the name suggests, is a limitation of exports voluntarily agreed to by an exporting country at the insistence of an importing country. How voluntary VERs really are is debatable. The VER was introduced as a way of limiting imports without violating the General Agreement on Tariffs and Trade (GATT) that most nations of the world have signed. The GATT rules prohibited the unilateral imposition or expansion of tariffs and quotas, but they did not explicitly prohibit a country's agreeing to export less at the request of an importing country.

In the early 1980s, for example, when Japanese automobiles were rapidly expanding their share of the U.S. automobile market just as an economic recession was causing earnings losses for the major U.S. automakers, the U.S. Congress and President Ronald Reagan's administration were anxious to come up with some way of helping the large, and politically powerful, automobile industry without openly breaching the GATT. So the U.S. government pressured the Japanese government to bring together its automobile makers and get them to agree to "voluntarily" limit the number of cars they would ship to the U.S. market. While technically such a VER is not a quota imposed by the importing country, the final effect is exactly like a quota. In terms of welfare costs, the automobile VER negotiated with Japan was a very costly quota.

U.S. consumers lost consumer surplus to the tune of about US$1,500 per car purchased in the 1980s, according to several studies. The domestic automobile producers, Chrysler, General Motors, and Ford, were able to increase profits and finance the development of new products. Chrysler was very close to bankruptcy in the early 1980s. Ironically, the Japanese automakers were able to increase their profits even further and used some of these increases to finance new plants in the United States that further eroded the market share of domestic U.S. automobile producers. The gains by the Japanese automakers should have been expected. By asking the Japanese manufacturers of automobiles to limit shipments to the United States, the U.S. government was effectively asking them to collude, split up the market, restrict supply, and have their U.S. marketing subsidiaries raise prices to consumers. That is, the Japanese manufacturers were effectively invited to capture the full quota rent. No wonder they did not object very loudly to the U.S. insistence on a VER.

Auction Quotas

One way to avoid the loss of quota rent to foreigners is for the quota-imposing government to hold a competitive auction for import permits. Since an import permit allows the holder to import a good whose price is higher in the domestic market than it is in the international market, each import permit has a value equal to the difference between the foreign and the domestic price. If bidding for the permits is truly competitive, the winning bid will be very close to the full value of the permit. In this way the government would receive virtually all of the quota rent, which is equal to the number of imports times the difference between the domestic and world prices, or the areas C and Y in Figure 8.11. A competitive quota auction would therefore make the welfare effects of a quota virtually the same as those of an "equivalent" tariff that limits imports to the same degree because the quota rent becomes government revenue, just as in the case of a tariff.

Auction quotas have seldom been used, however. Perhaps it is the likelihood of foreign **retaliation**; recall that VERs often let the foreign exporting country capture the quota rent, which means they essentially pay off the foreign country for going along with the scheme.

Are Tariffs and Quotas Equivalent?

Within the modeling framework we have used here, there is, hypothetically, always an equivalent tariff for any given quota, and, vice versa, there is always an equivalent quota for any given tariff. The numerical examples of a tariff and a quota above make that clear. Quickly review Figures 8.4 and 8.11 (or Figures 8.5 and 8.12). The areas representing transfers from one group to another and deadweight losses seem to be the same in both diagrams. The only exception is the area C, which represents tariff revenue in the case of the tariff and quota rent in the case of the quota. Otherwise, the welfare effects appear to be virtually identical. The decision on how to protect domestic importers therefore seems to hinge on political issues such as whether the government wants to earn tariff revenue, whether importers have political clout and can get the government to let them collect the quota rent, and whether the nation's trading partners will need to be "bribed" into accepting the trade restriction by awarding their exporters the quota rent.

International economists have pointed out some important differences between tariffs and quotas that are not immediately obvious in the static partial equilibrium diagrams. First of all, if demand and supply shift, as they are bound to do as time passes and economies change and grow, a tariff and quota that were initially "equivalent" will come to have very different price and welfare effects.

For example, suppose that supply and demand for steel in the international market are the curves S and D_1 in Figure 8.13. The tariff that pushes the supply curve up to S_T and the quota that sets the kinked supply curve at S_Q are *equivalent* in the sense that they cause the domestic price to settle at the same level p_1. But, if there is a shift in the demand curve from D_1 to D_2, assuming the supply curve remains the same, the new equilibrium price and quantity differ for the formerly equivalent tariff and quota. The shift in demand causes the price to rise to p_t under the tariff and the higher level of p_q under the quota. The tariff does not keep the quantity imported from rising but the quota does. Therefore, as demand shifts out over time, a fixed quota will become increasingly more restrictive than a fixed tariff rate; that is, the quota will give domestic producers increasingly more "protection" in the form of higher import prices.

Second, a quota may not ration rent opportunities efficiently, in which case it will cause losses beyond those represented by the deadweight loss areas in Figure 8.11. In that diagram, it was implicitly assumed that, as a result of the quota, only those consumers along the highest portion of the demand curve and producers along the lowest section of the supply curve—the thick sections of the supply and demand curves in Figure 8.14—engaged in trade. What if the political process rations import permits to people who are only marginally interested in importing, as for example the people on the demand curve at point A in Figure 8.14, effectively denying import permits to some consumers at the upper end of the demand curve? A quota could even result in people on the demand curve below the free trade price p_e getting import permits, such as those at point B in Figure 8.14. Or, what if those handing out import permits deny some of the lowest-cost foreign suppliers import permits and instead let relatively high-cost producers at point C on the foreign supply curve engage in trade? Clearly, this will result in fewer gains from trade, and the deadweight loss areas will understate the actual losses from the quota. Even producers with marginal costs greater than the free trade price could end up exporting when the quota pushes up the world price, for example those at point D, while lower-cost producers are denied import permits. In short, a quota does not necessarily reward the lowest-cost producers or the consumers that benefit the most from the products, and trade could even be diverted to consumers and suppliers who would otherwise not find it worthwhile to participate in trade at all. A tariff, on the other hand, causes the price to rise equally for everyone in the importing country and fall for everyone in the exporting country, thus guaranteeing that supply and demand are efficiently allocated to the lowest-cost producers and highest-demand consumers and deadweight losses are kept to their minimum.

These efficiency losses as well as the potentially more restrictive nature of quotas in the long run are two of the reasons that economists favor tariffs over quotas, *if protection is necessary*. The level of protection will not increase as much as under quotas in the case of growing demand, and trade will be carried out by those who value it the most. International trade agreements have sometimes included provisions to convert quotas to tariffs in order to make later reductions in quotas easier to achieve.

In sum, tariffs and quotas are, in many ways, similar in their immediate effects in a competitive import market. In fact, in the static neoclassical supply and demand model of international trade, in which supply and demand curves remain fixed, if the rationing of import permits efficiently maximizes the gains from trade under the quota, then:

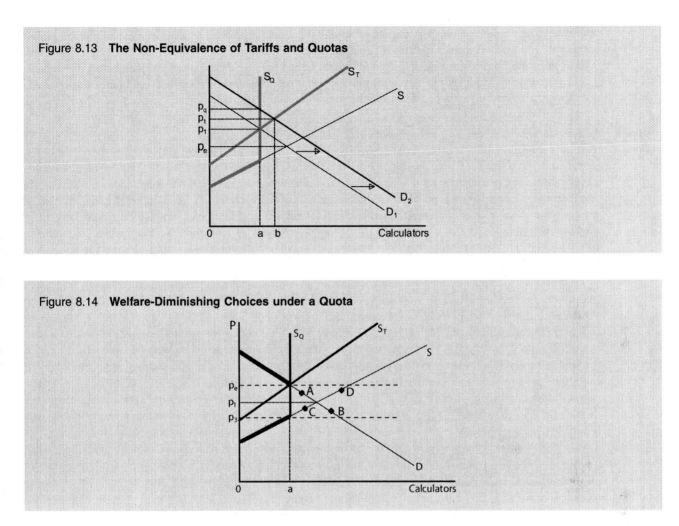

Figure 8.13 **The Non-Equivalence of Tariffs and Quotas**

Figure 8.14 **Welfare-Diminishing Choices under a Quota**

- There is always an *equivalent* tariff for any given quota, and, vice versa, there is always an *equivalent* quota for any given tariff, where *equivalent* means the tariff and quota generate the equivalent level of imports, domestic and foreign prices, and producer and consumer surpluses.

Of course, the quota always involves some quota rent while the tariff generates revenue for the government. In the long run, however, tariffs and quotas will tend to have diverging effects because supply and demand curves shift and the rationing scheme for the quotas becomes less appropriate. Lobbying activity suggests that it matters to special interests whether trade is restricted by tariffs or quotas.

OTHER TRADE BARRIERS

Over the past half century, quotas have been loosened and tariffs have been reduced in most countries. Overall, however, trade has not been liberalized as much as those changes in tariffs and quotas suggest. The special interests that had successfully pressured their governments to raise tariffs and tighten quotas in the past did not suddenly disappear when governments signed international agreements to reduce the most obvious trade barriers. As some trade barriers fell, governments have come up with other ways to protect domestic groups from international competition. Governments use a variety of methods to make it difficult to import goods and services, and domestic producers and consumers often take matters into their own hands to make importing or exporting more difficult. The costs of such trade barriers are similar to the costs of the more formal tariffs and quotas, but they are often not perceived as the trade barriers that they effectively are.

Export Bans to Insure Against Domestic Shortages

Countries have often restricted exports, motivated by the desire to guarantee the domestic availability of products deemed critical to the survival of society. For example, Solon, the magistrate who came to rule Athens in ancient Greece in 594 B.C.E., prohibited the export of wheat and other food products with the explicit intent of keeping food plentiful and its prices low for Athenian consumers. The frequent occurrence of crop failures and famines no doubt made restrictions on exports of food, even in times of surplus, seem more like a rational insurance against future starvation than a trade restriction intended to benefit one group at the expense of others.

Proponents of free trade argue that international trade by all countries provides the lowest-cost insurance against famine. But how does a famine-struck country guarantee that others will export food to them? Note that in 2010 Russia immediately banned the export of wheat when its crop was reduced by drought. Wheat prices increased by over 50 percent worldwide as other countries followed Russia's lead and also banned exports. The World Trade Organization (the governing body for international trade matters) was no match for the human fear of not having enough to eat.

In the early twenty-first century agricultural prices surged, first in 2008 and again in 2011. Fears of shortages again surfaced, especially as it became apparent that worldwide stocks of grains and many other foods were very low by recent historical standards. These low stocks were partially the result of an exceptional number of droughts and other adverse weather conditions, but they were also caused by the convergence of several long-term trends: the shift to just-in-time inventory management by the dominant industrial agricultural transnational corporations, the growth in income in countries such as China and Brazil, the increasing use of grains for manufacturing biofuels, and the slowdown in technological improvement in agriculture. With food shortages looming, full or partial bans of food exports may become a more common phenomenon in the global economy.

Using Bureaucratic Procedures to Impede International Trade

Bureaucratic procedures can add substantial costs to international trade, which makes them very effective at stopping trade. Proponents often disguise them by relating them to issues such as health, safety, national security, or the protection of national culture. Because they are superficially linked to politically popular goals, such trade restrictions are often difficult for free trade advocates to confront directly.

Health regulations are often used to keep foreign food and medicines out of the domestic market. For example, the European Union has banned the import of beef from cows that were fed growth hormones or antibiotics. The World Trade Organization has ruled that there is no scientific evidence to support such a ban, but European governments operate or the precautionary principle and continue to impose it anyway. Another example is Japan, which has always required all foreign drugs to be tested in Japan before they can be sold domestically, even if they have been fully tested in other countries. This makes it costly and time consuming for foreign pharmaceutical firms to enter the Japanese market.

Another example is the U.S. ban on imports of potatoes from Prince Edward Island, the province where 30 percent of Canada's potatoes are produced, in 2001. Canadian agricultural inspectors found a few potatoes blighted with potato wart on one plot of land. The U.S. Department of Agriculture

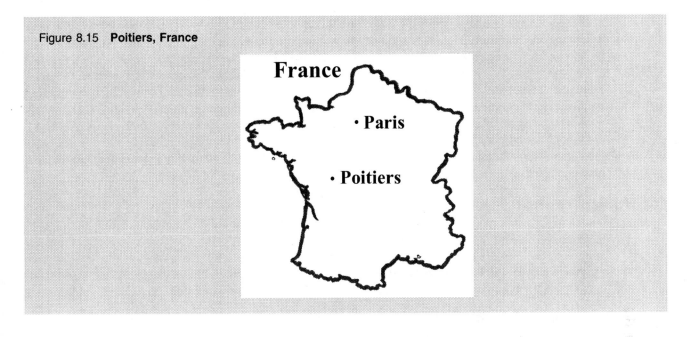

Figure 8.15 **Poitiers, France**

France

· Paris

· Poitiers

responded by banning all imports of potatoes from Prince Edward Island after being urged to do so by senators from Idaho and Wisconsin, two large potato-producing states.[1]

An interesting case of bureaucratic procedure serving as a hidden trade restriction is France's method of keeping imports of Japanese and Korean video players and recorders out of its market. In the 1980s foreign imports began taking market share away from French manufacturers of video players, and French politicians sought ways to assist them without violating France's international agreements. Foreign manufacturers, anxious to make inroads into Europe's electronics market, balked at agreeing to VERs. Creative French bureaucrats then issued a procedural order instructing importers of video players to deal only with its customs agency in the small city of Poitiers, which was to "specialize" in handling such equipment. Not coincidentally, Poitiers was far from any of the large ports where the video players normally entered the country. The video players would therefore have to be shipped in sealed containers from the ports to Poitiers. Shipments often had to be held at the ports because of the limited availability of bonded warehousing in Poitiers. When the video players were finally cleared by customs, in strict accordance with regulations, they could then enter their normal distribution channels. In the meantime, the strange procedure of shipping the video players to the interior of France and holding them in various warehouses awaiting inspection by the small Poitiers customs office significantly increased the cost of the imports, and thus increased the surplus of French producers.

"Buy Domestic" Regulations

Government **buy domestic regulations**, which restrict purchases to domestically produced goods and services, are quite common. For example, most countries limit their military to using arms produced at home. This policy supposedly maintains a viable domestic arms industry for national security reasons. Yet, government agencies are also frequently limited to buying nonstrategic products from domestic sources simply because it might appear unpatriotic for the government to spend taxpayers' money on foreign goods. The U.S. government, for example, requires that its officials fly on U.S. flag airlines when traveling overseas; foreign airlines may be used only if waiting for a flight on a U.S. airline would cause a delay of more than one full day.

Most recently, the United States was widely criticized for the "buy American" provision in the federal economic stimulus law passed in 2009 (the American Recovery and Reinvestment Act) to reduce unemployment and lift the economy out of its deep recession. Because the bill was intended to boost domestic demand for U.S. firms, lawmakers argued that the increased government expenditures it called for would have the greatest effect if they were directed at domestic firms and their employees. Of course, the provision ran afoul of international trade agreements. If foreign countries retaliated, as some threatened to do, then U.S. aggregate demand would suffer from the loss of export demand. Economists brought up the Lerner symmetry theorem to argue against the "buy American" provision. Negotiations between the White House and the Senate resulted in a watering down of the provision, but a weak form of it did remain in the bill that was passed in early 2009.

Local Restrictions on Foreign Trade

Restrictions on international trade are not applied only at a country's national border; they are often applied at the borders of local jurisdictions. For example, Massachusetts passed a law in 1996 that sanctions companies doing business in Myanmar (Burma), a country that is widely seen as violating the civil rights of its citizens. Specifically, the Massachusetts law adds a 10 percent price penalty to contract bids for state work submitted by companies who do business in Myanmar, effectively making their bids uncompetitive. Dade County of Florida imposed sanctions on certain trade with Cuba.[2] Nebraska has a law that prohibits foreign nationals from engaging in private-detective activity there. These state and local laws end up affecting international trade if, for example, a British detective agency needs to perform part of its work in Nebraska or a German company that imports raw materials from Myanmar wants to do business with a Massachusetts state agency. Local governments are often accused of interfering with international trade in China, a country where local governments have become very active in promoting the growth of local industries. According to a 2000 newspaper report by Karby Leggett (2000), "City, county and provincial governments in China use licensing fees, taxes, subsidies and even outright sales bans to prevent foreign companies from entering their local markets." For example, General Motors' Chinese **joint venture** that assembles Buicks had achieved reasonable sales in many parts of China, but it had problems selling anything in the northern province of Jilin. It seems that the provincial government had a financial stake in another automobile factory there that manufactured cars under license to the German automobile manufacturer Audi. According to the Buick dealer in Jilin, "Local government agencies at all levels are forbidden from buying Buicks" (Leggett 2000).[3]

EXPORT TAXES AND SUBSIDIES

Export bans discussed previously are not the only tools governments use to interfere with exports. Often, they tax or subsidize exports. Governments of some countries routinely tax exports in order to raise government revenue. Also, negative taxes, or **subsidies**, are often used to promote exports of certain goods or services. All trade taxes can be analyzed using the same graphic models that were used to explain the costs and benefits of tariffs and quotas.

Export Taxes

An export tax tends to reduce the amount of exports. It drives a wedge between the prices of the export good in the home market and the foreign market. And, it causes a variety of gains and losses at home and abroad. An export tax is illustrated in Figure 8.16, which presents a two-country partial equilibrium supply and demand model in which Home is the exporter and Abroad the importer of orange juice.

To Home's producers, the export tax appears as a decline in foreign demand for orange juice, as in the case of a shift from D_W to D_T in the center diagram of Figure 8.16. As a result, the domestic

Figure 8.16 The Effect of an Export Tax by Home

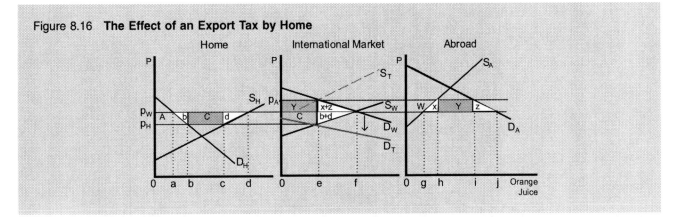

price of orange juice falls from p_W to p_H in the Home market. Compared to free trade, the export tax causes producer surplus to fall by the areas $A+b+C+d$. Home's consumers clearly gain area A. Exports fall from $ad = 0f = gj$ to $bc = 0e = hi$. Export tax receipts for Home's government are equal to the areas $C+Y$. The area C represents that part of the export tax effectively paid by domestic exporters. To Abroad's consumers and producers, Home's export tax looks like a decrease in supply of orange juice from S_W to S_T, which raises the price of orange juice in Abroad. The area Y is the part of the export tax effectively paid by Abroad's consumers of orange juice, who end up paying the higher price of p_A after the imposition of Home's export tax. There are the usual deadweight losses because the export tax distorts prices in both countries, which pushes producers and consumers away from the equilibria that accurately reflect marginal costs and benefits.

Note that, compared to a tariff, an export tax reverses the gains and losses at home and abroad. In fact, the partial equilibrium model looks very similar to that of the tariff. Just as in the case of a tariff, the exporting country can end up gaining from its tax if foreign consumers pay a large portion of the tax. As the volume of trade is reduced, the importing country's consumers in effect pay part of the tax because the restricted supply causes the foreign price of the export product to rise.

Summarizing the effects on Home of an export tax:

$$
\begin{aligned}
\text{Home Consumer Surplus} &= +A \\
\text{Home Producer Surplus} &= -(A + b + C + d) \\
\text{Home Govt. Tax Revenue} &= +(C + Y) \\
\text{Net Change} &= Y - b - d.
\end{aligned}
$$

Home thus enjoys a net gain from the export tax if $Y > b+d$, although its producers in effect pay for the gains by Home's consumers of orange juice and by the beneficiaries of the Home government's expenditures paid for out of the tariff revenue. And, of course, Abroad suffers a net loss of $Y+x+z$. World welfare declines by the total deadweight losses in both countries:

$$
\begin{aligned}
\text{Abroad's Consumer Surplus} &= -(W + x + Y + z) \\
\text{Abroad's Producer Surplus} &= +W \\
\text{Net Change} &= -(Y + x + z).
\end{aligned}
$$

The net loss for the world is:

$$
\text{World deadweight losses} = -(b + d + x + z).
$$

In summary, an export tax is just like a tariff, except that the revenue is collected by the exporting government instead of the importing government.

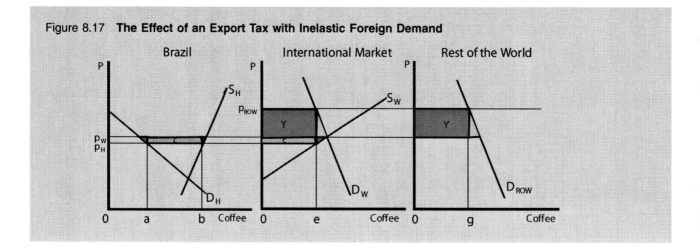

Figure 8.17 **The Effect of an Export Tax with Inelastic Foreign Demand**

Price Elasticity and Export Taxes

Export taxes are most often used by countries that are exporters of agricultural products or natural resources that, in the short run, are inelastically supplied and demanded. For example, the government of Brazil, a major exporter of coffee, used export taxes to raise revenue while keeping the price of the national drink low at home. The Brazilian government, no doubt, also hoped to exploit the low price elasticity of demand and effectively let foreign coffee drinkers pay most of the export tax. The importance of the price elasticity of foreign demand is illustrated in Figure 8.17, in which the foreign demand curve for the export product is steep (inelastic).

Figure 8.17 also assumes there is no production of coffee in the export market, a realistic assumption in the case of coffee, so that the foreign demand curve in the center diagram is equally inelastic compared to the domestic demand curve in the importing country. Figure 8.16 shows that even a large export tax causes the domestic price in the exporting country to fall relatively little, but the price in the rest of the world rises a lot. Thus, foreigners pay most of the tax; politically powerful producers in the exporting country suffer little loss of welfare.

Governments of oil-producing countries used export taxes to extract greater earnings from oil exports. But, as OPEC (the Organization of Petroleum Exporting Countries) learned to its dismay after it sharply increased administered oil export prices in the 1970s, in the longer run, supply and demand for oil were not as inelastic as it had hoped. In the short run, oil-importing countries were unable to reduce their oil consumption very much when prices rose sharply, and alternative sources of oil could not be brought into production very quickly. But, by the late 1980s, the higher price of oil had indeed encouraged consumers to find alternative sources of oil or to economize on the use of oil. New oil fields were developed in the North Sea, Mexico, Alaska, and Africa, and automobiles were redesigned to operate more efficiently, for example. So, while the price of oil rose to over US$30 per barrel in 1979, by the late 1990s the price had fallen back below US$15 per barrel. Of course, the lower price eventually caused demand for oil to grow again, and by 2008 the price of oil again reached the same high real price it had reached in 1979.

Why Doesn't the United States Tax Exports?

The United States does not use export taxes at all. The U.S. Constitution explicitly states, "No Tax or Duty shall be laid on Articles exported from any State" (Article I, Section 9). When the thirteen colonies united to form the United States, the southern states were major exporters of agricultural goods, such as tobacco and cotton. The northern states did not export nearly as much, their economies being much more oriented toward the domestic market. The southern states were afraid the federal government would tax exports; it certainly would have been a convenient source of revenue for the cash-strapped new government. Therefore, delegates to the Constitutional Convention from the southern states insisted on including a prohibition on export taxes in order to prevent a simple majority in Congress from imposing a tax that would fall disproportionately on exporters from southern states. Import restrictions were not banned, however, because northern industries wanted protection from British industrial imports. The *Lerner symmetry theorem* suggests the southern states did not really win on this issue.

Export Subsidies

Export subsidies are simply negative export taxes that, in effect, offer a payment to exporters rather than extracting a payment from exporters. Subsidies are just as costly as tariffs or any other trade restrictions that distort the prices that serve as the incentives for consumer and producer behavior. Subsidies effectively take an economy beyond its comparative advantage to where the marginal opportunity costs of producing exports exceed the price that those exports command on the world market. The subsidies raise the domestic price of export products above the free trade world price, and they lower their price abroad. In the short-run framework of the HO model, an export subsidy appears to benefit foreign consumers by providing them with cheaper products. The Lerner symmetry theorem suggests that a subsidy on exports effectively subsidizes imports as well because an inefficiently large amount of resources is pulled toward the export industry and away from the import-competing industry. Foreign retaliation is also likely, of course, and such retaliation may even be sanctioned by the World Trade Organization (WTO). For example, in 2001 the WTO ruled that the $4 billion tax break that the United States provided its exporters violated international law and that the European Union, which had brought the case to its attention, could retaliate by banning $4 billion worth of U.S. exports to Europe (Alden 2001). The dispute continued for most of the decade that followed, as the United States tried to change its tax laws as little as possible and Europe challenged its lack of seriousness in the WTO. The United States finally agreed to eliminate the implicit export subsidy, but it nevertheless allowed its exporters to repatriate their profits tax-free for one year in 2006 under the pretext of promoting investment in the United States. This measure sharply reduced U.S. tax receipts, spurred little domestic investment, and was still challenged by the European Union at the WTO.[4]

More recently, developed economies have come under fire for their agricultural subsidies. They effectively promote overseas sales and suppress the price farmers in developing economies receive for their crops.

ANTIDUMPING PROCEDURES, SURGE PROTECTION, AND SANCTIONS

Often, the same imports or exports are viewed favorably by some and unfavorably by others. These different perspectives, and the search for politically viable justifications, have resulted in many different procedures for restricting imports and exports. In this section, we examine several different justifications for trade restrictions, each based on a specific interpretation of how international trade affects a country's welfare.

Defining Dumping

Allegations of foreign **dumping** have often served as a justification for tariffs or quotas. Few people ask what dumping really is, but public opinion usually sides with "innocent" domestic producers who claim to be "dumped" on. Whatever the definition, the number of tariffs levied to offset alleged cases of foreign dumping has grown rapidly even as other trade restrictions have been reduced in recent decades.[5]

Dumping is usually defined as selling below cost. In foreign trade, dumping is also defined simply as selling in a foreign market at a lower price than the identical good sells for in the producer's home market. These two either/or criteria were adopted by negotiators of the General Agreement on Tariffs and Trade (GATT) back in 1947 at the insistence of the United States; the definition carried over to the WTO's rules when it superseded the GATT in 1994. Article VI (Part 1) of the GATT says dumping occurs when:

> (1) the price of the foreign product is less than the comparable price, in the ordinary course of trade, for the like product when destined for consumption in the exporting country, or

> (2) in the absence of such domestic price, the price of the foreign product is less than either the highest comparable price for the like product for export to any third country in the ordinary course of trade, or the cost of production of the product in the country of origin plus a reasonable addition for selling costs and profit.

The *margin of dumping* is defined as (1) the difference between the selling price in the foreign market and the average production cost plus transport, selling costs, and "reasonable" profit, or (2) the difference between the foreign price and a home price or third-country market price.[6] If either definition of dumping is satisfied, countries are permitted to levy a tariff to exactly offset the alleged dumping.

For example, if the foreign cost of producing wicker laundry baskets is $3, but the foreign supplier is selling them in your market for $2, then the dumping margin is 50 percent. An importing country is permitted to levy a 50 percent ad valorem tariff to bring the price of the foreign good up to the "true" cost of $3. Many countries add transport costs, selling costs, and a "reasonable" profit to the production costs, thus making the dumping margin greater than 50 percent. Such a tariff is referred to as an **antidumping duty**, and it is supposed to exactly offset the allegedly unfair advantage that the foreign producer gains by selling below cost. The alternative definition of dumping can be used to determine whether the price of $2 constitutes dumping if it can be shown that the foreign producer charges $3 in its home market or in some other foreign market. The WTO requires countries to formally prove dumping, and most countries have set up procedures that give the appearance of objectivity in determining the degree of dumping. However, the procedures are easily, and often, corrupted.

Economists generally accept that dumping is detrimental to a country's economic welfare if it is predatory and reduces competition, as in the case where a seller dumps products in order to drive competitors out of business and then raises prices to reap monopoly profits after its competitors' demise. **Predatory dumping** is illegal in many countries; it is prohibited in U.S. antitrust law. For example, to successfully accuse a firm of predatory dumping in the United States under the Sherman Antitrust Act requires proof that (1) the alleged predator had the *intent* to drive out the competition in order to monopolize the market, (2) the predator had a reasonable chance of succeeding in its attempt to drive out the competition, *and* (3) that the loss of competition would cause damage to the economy. These are much tougher criteria than those of the GATT/WTO cited above. U.S. antitrust laws and their antidumping provisions are intended to prevent monopolization of markets, not to protect individual firms from their competitors.

How the U.S. Government "Proves" Dumping

The first U.S. law dealing with dumping by foreigners, the 1916 *Anti-Dumping Duty Act,* extended existing provisions of antitrust legislation to foreign firms selling in the United States. In 1921, when the electorate was in a more protectionist and isolationist mood, a second law dealing with foreign dumping, called the *Anti-Dumping Act,* was passed. This act accepted selling overseas at prices below those in the firm's home market as proof of dumping. It was enacted because foreign dumping was difficult to prove under the 1916 act, which, like the Sherman Antitrust Act, required proof of *intent* to monopolize. The 1921 act was also different from the 1916 act in that it was not a criminal statute on which individuals could pursue damages and punishment in the courts. Rather, the 1921 act mandated government action directly against the foreign firms found to be dumping. In effect, alleged foreign dumpers were denied the due process of law and foreign competitors were to be treated differently from domestic competitors. The purpose of the 1921 act was clearly to protect U.S. companies from foreign competition, not to prevent monopolization of markets. It was this broad view of dumping that was incorporated into the GATT in 1947 at the insistence of the United States.

Most countries have established seemingly fair procedures to deal with charges of foreign dumping. Following is an outline of the United States' procedure, which has been copied by many other countries:

1. A producer in the United States seeking protection from alleged dumping must first petition the United States Department of Commerce for a ruling on whether or not there is dumping. The petitioner presents evidence to support its case, but the Department of Commerce may also gather evidence.
2. If the Department of Commerce finds dumping is taking place, the case is referred to the International Trade Commission (ITC), a separate office of the U.S. government, which must then rule on whether or not the dumping has a "material" effect on the well-being of the U.S. industry. The ITC is composed of four members, two representing each of the two major political parties of the United States, the Democrats and the Republicans. The petitioning U.S. producer could be required to present more evidence.
3. If both the Department of Commerce and the ITC rule in favor of the petitioner's request for protection, the matter is referred to the President of the United States, who then decides whether or not to implement a tariff equal to the estimated margin of dumping.

This three-step procedure seems to provide ample protection against phony claims of dumping. But, in recent years, application of antidumping tariffs has increased, despite the seemingly difficult process.

Richard Clarida (1997) describes how the U.S. Department of Commerce often compares the *average* annual selling price in the exporter's country with each individual sale made in the United States in order to determine whether there is dumping. Under this method, when sales in the United States are below the average foreign price, the sales are recorded as dumped and used to calculate the dumping margin. When U.S. sales are above the average foreign selling price there is no dumping and the prices are ignored. As a result, the seasonally or exceptionally high prices are not used to offset the instances of dumped sales.

This procedure is clearly inappropriate for agricultural products, which often vary substantially over the course of the year. Yet, in the late 1990s, the United States used this procedure to threaten antidumping tariffs on tomatoes imported from Mexico. Mexico exported tomatoes during the winter months, and actually imported tomatoes from the United States during summer months. Mexican prices were low in winter, when its production peaked, and were high in summer. The U.S. Department of Commerce used only those several months' prices that were below the average price to estimate dumping for the full year. Not surprisingly, the Commerce Department determined that antidumping duties were called for. Mexican producers agreed to raise their prices in unison, U.S. consumers paid more, and Mexico's seasonal comparative advantage could not be fully exploited.

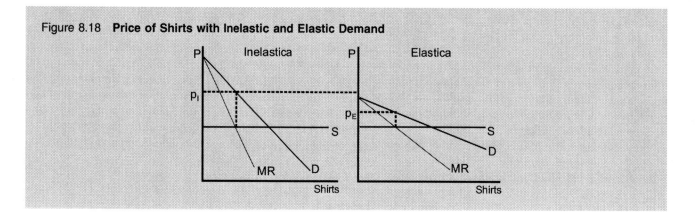

Figure 8.18 **Price of Shirts with Inelastic and Elastic Demand**

Robert McGee (1993, p. 496) puts U.S. antidumping procedures into perspective:

> Imagine a system of civil litigation in which a party serves a massive discovery request, consisting of interrogatories and requests for production of documents. Imagine further that the serving party has the sole authority to prescribe the time within which responses must be made and the format. . . . Imagine still further that the serving party is the sole judge of the adequacy of the response and of the merits of all objections as to relevancy or burdensomeness of the request; that the serving party also is the imposer of sanctions for failure to comply, and the ultimate decision maker in the underlying matter for which the information is sought.
>
> Such a system would be intolerable in the state or federal courts of the United States. It would raise serious questions of due process in a system of administrative law that separates the investigative from the judicial functions within a single agency. But this is the inquisitorial system that was ordained by Congress for the administration of antidumping [laws]. Torquemada, no doubt, would be right at home with it. But this is hardly a recommendation for the system.

The real reason for the proliferation of antidumping actions by the United States and many other countries is political pressure from domestic producers facing import competition. Thomas Prusa and Susan Skeath (2001) find that the recent increases in antidumping actions cannot be fully explained by an increase in unfair trading practices under even the broadest definition of dumping.

Price Discrimination Does Not Necessarily Imply Dumping

Price differences across different markets are common. In fact, if demand differs from one market to another, price differences are almost certain to occur. Figure 8.18 illustrates the case of a shirt manufacturer based in the country of Inelastica, who produces under constant marginal costs and markets shirts in its home market as well as the neighboring country of Elastica. Notice that the markets in the two countries are both imperfectly competitive because the shirt maker faces downward-sloping demand curves in both markets. The market in the country of Inelastica is characterized by demand that is relatively inelastic, while in Elastica, perhaps because of more domestic competition, demand is relatively elastic. In each market, the profit-maximizing firm will set its price so that marginal costs are equal to marginal revenue. Obviously, the supplier will set a lower price in the market with the more elastic demand, as evidenced by the prices p_I and p_E in Inelastica and Elastica, respectively.

According to the official definitions of dumping, the Inelastican shirt manufacturer that exports to Elastica is dumping in the latter market because it sells there at a price lower than it does in its home market. Local producers in Elastica can appeal to either of the GATT/WTO's two definitions of dumping to "prove" dumping and insist that their government apply an antidumping tariff. A tariff equal to the margin of dumping would raise the price of imported shirts to p_I. Of course, at that price, the Inelastican producer cannot sell any shirts in Elastica, and the politically astute shirt producers in Elastica can exploit the rules to keep a competitor out of their market.

Countervailing Duties

Under international trade rules, countries are also permitted to levy **countervailing duties** to offset government subsidies that protect domestic industries and firms against foreign competition or that help uncompetitive industries or firms compete in world markets. In general, countervailing duties work about the same as antidumping duties, and they have often been abused as well. Arguments about what is a subsidy and the effects of subsidies on international trade are invariably complex and imprecise. As in the case of antidumping duties, it is the accusing country that controls the evidence, the procedures, and the final decisions.

The WTO's Uruguay Round of international trade talks, which were begun in the late 1980s and completed in 1994, set a specific timetable for developing countries to phase out subsidies that distort international trade. In fact, all countries except for the very poorest eliminated export subsidies and protectionist subsidies for uncompetitive domestic producers by 2002. The developing countries agreed to the phasing out of subsidies reluctantly because they felt that it was they, not the developed countries, who faced the most blatant examples of trade-distorting subsidies. Agricultural products are largely exempt from the countervailing duties rules, however, a condition that developed countries wrote into the GATT/WTO rules decades ago.

Surge Protection

There is yet another provision in the GATT/WTO rules that allows a country to selectively impose tariffs on imports: the **escape clause** in Article XIX. This clause permits countries to apply trade restrictions in the case of increasing imports that seriously harm a domestic industry. Needless to say, the criteria for applying tariffs, quotas, or VERs under this provision are rather open ended. The general consensus among the framers of the GATT was that the escape clause should be used only temporarily, to give the harmed industry time to adjust but not to provide permanent protection.

The United States has used the escape clause to provide protection to its steel industry since at least the 1950s. In each case, it was claimed that the protection was temporary, intended to help the industry modernize and compete on its own. Yet, invariably, when the protectionist tariffs, quotas, or VERs were about to elapse, new measures were passed by Congress or initiated by the president. The ritual continued in the early 2000s, nearly fifty years after the steel industry first sought protection under the escape clause. For example, in 2001 the chairman and CEO of USX-U.S. Steel Group said, after a favorable ruling on his firm's petition for antidumping duties on foreign steel, "The objective of this remedy is to give the industry breathing time." The president of the United Steelworkers of America, the labor union that organizes many U.S. steel plants, was more direct: "We want strong quotas and substantial tariffs for as long as we can get them." That may be a long time. As an international economist at a Washington think tank, the Institute for International Economics, accurately noted, "We haven't seen any administration be tough on steel—they all cave in."[7] In 2002, President George W. Bush ordered "emergency" tariffs of up to 30 percent on imported steel. President Barack Obama in 2010 approved special tariffs on certain steel imports from China.

Trade Sanctions

Governments often apply **trade sanctions** on countries for a variety of misdeeds unrelated to international trade per se. Trade sanctions are intended to inflict economic damage on countries in order to punish them or, more positively, to convince them to change their ways. What is often conveniently forgotten is that trade sanctions, protection, and export restrictions cause welfare losses in the country imposing them. They also seldom achieve their stated objectives.

Writing in the *Wall Street Journal,* Gerald F. Seib (1998) described sanctions as follows: "Congress right now has fallen prey to a bad habit with global implications: the impulse to slap economic sanctions on other countries whenever lawmakers can't figure out what else to do." In fact, economic sanctions have been applied well over a hundred times by the United States since World War II. In 2000, for example, more than seventy-five countries containing about two-thirds of the world's population were subject to some U.S. trade sanctions. The United States has imposed strict trade sanctions on countries such as Cuba, North Korea, Iraq, Iran, and Burma. U.S. trade sanctions on Cuba go back more than fifty years to 1960, when Cuba's communist government expropriated all U.S.–owned property. The United Nations authorized a trade ban by all its members on Iraq at the close of the Gulf War in 1991 in order to pressure that country to dismantle its capacity to build "weapons of mass destruction" and to reveal the whereabouts of the dangerous weapons it was believed to posess.

Like all trade restrictions, sanctions cause losses in many industries and countries. The greatest costs are not necessarily felt in those countries that are targeted by the sanctions. The costs of the trade sanctions on Iraq fell not only on Iraq, as expected, but also on Greece, Jordan, and Turkey, the three countries that traditionally traded most with Iraq. Ironically, the countries that gained the most from the sanctions on imports of oil from Iraq were Libya and Iran, two other oil exporters whose political behavior made them targets of a number of different trade sanctions by the United States and other countries. General equilibrium analysis shows that the gains and losses from the trade sanctions are spread around the world in complex ways seldom foreseen, much less accurately estimated, by politicians eager to use the sanctions as a public show of their concern for some international issue.

Sanctions seldom achieve their goals. In fact, they can make things even worse. Trade sanctions have been blamed for killing half a million Iraqis during the 1990s, while Iraq's dictator, Saddam Hussein, profited from the clandestine trade that circumvented the sanctions. According to the United Nations, as a result of the trade sanctions, "hundreds of thousands of Iraqis, particularly children under five, have died from dehydration, malnutrition, cholera, tuberculosis and other easily preventable diseases."[8] As subsequent United Nations investigations revealed, including one commission headed by Paul Volcker, the former U.S. Federal Reserve chair, billions of dollars worth of petroleum was exported illegally to pay for imports of consumer goods for Iraq's middle- and upper-class consumers.[9]

One case where trade sanctions seem to have been successful in bringing about political change is in South Africa. Economic sanctions were applied by most countries of the world when South Africa maintained apartheid policies that severely limited the rights of black South Africans. The effectiveness of worldwide trade sanctions on South Africa has been disputed, however. According to Philip I. Levy (1999), there were other forces for change within South Africa that were much stronger than the sanctions, which were not, in any case, applied so as to inflict maximum damage on the South African economy. Contrary to what most people believed to be the case, Anton Lowenberg and William Kaempfer (1998) contend that the trade sanctions on South Africa inflicted relatively little hardship on South Africa. Rather, they found that the sanctions seemed to have been designed to limit the costs to domestic interests in the sanctioning countries. Foreign governments continued to buy strategic metals and other raw materials from South Africa. European governments even continued to permit imports of South African fruits and vegetables during the European winter season because European consumers would have objected to their cutoff. Hence, it may not have been the trade sanctions that brought down the despicable apartheid regime.

The example of U.S. trade sanctions on Cuba, among the most thorough of any trade sanctions, is most condemning. The United States has maintained its sanctions for over fifty years, but the communist government remains firmly in power. The sanctions have also bolstered the exiled Cuban community in Florida to maintain hope of recovering their former property in Cuba that was confiscated during the communist revolution in 1958, thus making any withdrawal of the sanctions politically difficult in the United States.

Today, many countries maintain sanctions on trade with Iran and North Korea. Whether these will be successful in inducing the governments of these countries to do what the sanctioning countries want remains to be seen at the time of this writing.

National Security

Many industries claim they deserve protection because their industry is crucial for national security. Recently, the U.S. steel industry has used this approach. While this argument may make sense to the general public, it is difficult to argue that any specific product is any more crucial to national security than any other. The U.S. economy would obviously collapse if, for some reason, trade were cut off. The United States imports much of its oil, much of its clothing, most of its toys, a considerable portion of its food products, many of its electronics, most of computer components, and so forth. Is steel more important than computer chips?

The argument for banning the export of certain strategic products may seem more compelling. After all, why simply give away technologies that could be used to strengthen the armed forces of potential enemies? The reply is twofold. First, foreigners pay for exports, and those with the most advanced technologies are especially expensive. Second, not exporting a country's best and most advanced products can retard the development of even more advanced products. Recall that one of the reasons an open economy is likely to have a faster rate of technological progress is that innovators can earn higher returns from selling their innovations in a large world market. Continued innovation is probably a better assurance of strategic advantage than hiding behind an export barrier. In addition, the openness of most countries makes it difficult to hide anything, with or without export bans.

CONCLUSIONS

The most important thing to remember from this chapter is that the effects of protection are widely dispersed throughout the domestic and foreign economies. Earlier chapters showed how opening an economy to international trade had many effects throughout the home economy and the rest of the world. Protective measures such as tariffs and quotas similarly have widespread effects. Trade policy is, therefore, never strictly a sectoral policy, nor is it even just a national policy. Trade policy is always an international policy with international repercussions.

Because protectionism is not exclusively a gain to one group in one country, but a complex set of gains and losses distributed throughout all economies of the world, protectionism cannot so easily be defended as a clear issue of fairness or compassion. A new tariff or the elimination of a quota may benefit one group, but it is likely to hurt some others. And the trade policy that benefits some group today may hurt that group in the long run. In other words, protectionism seldom has a clear moral cause. Arguments for protection must take a very broad, holistic approach in order to explain how blocking or taxing imports and exports benefits humanity.

Despite the costs of protectionist policies, many quotas, VERs, tariffs, and assorted other barriers to trade are still in place throughout the world. There must, therefore, be incentives for policy makers to place barriers in the way of international trade and, once the barriers are in place, to resist taking them down. This chapter has, in fact, already hinted at some of the reasons why trade barriers exist, namely that some groups and individuals gain welfare, at least in the short run, when trade is restricted. The next chapter takes a more systematic and historical look at *why* governments so often interfere with international trade. Chapter 10 then extends the analysis of trade policy by taking a more dynamic and holistic perspective. As the next chapter will show, trade policy is an integral component of the long-run evolution of an economic and social system.

Trade policy must be analyzed holistically as a complex phenomenon with many causes and consequences. It is part of a dynamic process of economic and social change, and it can only be understood from an interdisciplinary perspective. In the meantime, governments continue to impose trade restrictions even though mainstream economists have, for the most part, failed to analyze them holistically.

CHAPTER SUMMARY

1. The two-country supply and demand model of trade shows that one country's tariff on the other's exports changes the prices of all products in both economies, which causes a transfer of welfare from domestic consumers to domestic producers in the importing country and a transfer of welfare from producers to consumers in the exporting country.

2. A tariff also causes a transfer of consumer surplus in the importing country to the government in the form of tariff revenue as well as a transfer of some producer surplus from the exporting country to the government of the importing country.

3. A tariff causes deadweight losses in both importing and exporting countries.

4. The net welfare loss of a tariff to the world as a whole is equal to the deadweight losses, but the importing country most likely loses less than its deadweight losses because a tariff tends to change the terms of trade in favor of the importing country.

5. The Lerner symmetry theorem states that restrictions on imports end up restricting exports as well because the tariff causes a shift of resources from the export to the import industries.

6. The *effective protection* that a tariff provides to a certain industry is measured as the size of the ratio of the tariff over the industry's value added.

7. An import quota, or quantitative import restriction, is a limit on the quantity of a certain product that is permitted to enter the country. An import quota usually involves the issuance of import permits in the quantity of the quota.

8. A quota is very similar to a tariff; for example, in the case of fixed supply and demand curves and efficient rationing of import permits there is always an *equivalent* tariff for any given quota, which results in the same quantity of imports and domestic and foreign prices.

9. An important difference between a quota and a tariff is that a tariff generates revenue for the government and a quota creates rent for the importers who have the limited quantity of import permits.

10. A voluntary export restraint (VER) is identical to an import quota, except that the quota rent is effectively ceded to the foreign exporters.

11. Economists do not necessarily view tariffs and quotas as equivalent, however, because the assumption of fixed supply and demand curves is unrealistic in an ever-changing world and lucrative import permits are seldom rationed efficiently.

12. There are many other ways in which government can interfere with trade, including export tariffs or quotas, export and import subsidies, "buy domestic" mandates, national security concerns, health relations, and simple bureaucratic obstructionism.

13. Antidumping duties have become especially common because they effectively permit countries to restrict imports from specific countries and even specific foreign exporters. The procedures for applying antidumping duties are very imprecise and thus permit countries to apply the duties under a great variety of circumstances.

14. International trade regulations permit governments to impose temporary trade barriers in the case of sudden surges in imports, foreign export subsidies, or national security. Also common are trade sanctions, imposed for various political, social, and military reasons.

KEY TERMS AND CONCEPTS

ad valorem tariff
auction quota
buy domestic regulations
countervailing duties
deadweight losses
effective tariff
export subsidy
Lerner symmetry theorem
prohibitive tariff
quantitative trade restrictions
quota rent

quotas
rent
small country assumption
specific tariff
tariff
terms of trade (ToT)
trade policy
trade sanctions
value added
voluntary export restraint (VER)

PROBLEMS AND QUESTIONS

1. Explain the difference between an *ad valorem tariff* and a *specific tariff.* Explain the advantages and disadvantages of each.
2. Under what assumptions are tariffs and quotas similar? Under what assumptions does the "equivalence" of tariffs and quotas not hold?
3. In each of the following cases, calculate the effective rate of protection of the final product, assuming that markets are competitive and all other things remain the same:

   (a) A tariff on intermediate inputs raises the price of intermediate inputs by 10 percent in a market where, prior to the tariff, intermediate inputs accounted for 50 percent of the total cost of the final product.

   (b) A quota on intermediate inputs raises the price of intermediate inputs by 50 percent in a market where, prior to the quota, intermediate inputs accounted for 20 percent of the total cost of the final product.

   (c) A quota on imports of the final product raises the price of the final product by 22 percent in a market where, prior to the quota, intermediate inputs accounted for 65 percent of the total cost of the final product.

   (d) A tariff on imports of the final product raises the price of the final product by 40 percent in a market where, prior to the quota, intermediate inputs accounted for 10 percent of the total cost of the final product.

4. Figure 8.17 illustrates the case of inelastic foreign demand and the incidence of an export tax falling largely on the importing country. Illustrate the case of an export tax when foreign demand is highly elastic. What conditions will cause foreign demand to be elastic?
5. Antidumping procedures were on the agenda of the World Trade Organization's Doha Round of negotiations begun in 2001 but still not completed. First, discuss how antidumping procedures should, or should not, be reformed. Second, why do you think the Doha Round negotiations have stalled on this issue (and several others)? Who gains and who pays for antidumping duties?
6. Explain why economists often prefer tariffs to quotas if protection is called for.
7. What is the best way to allocate import permits under a quota? Explain precisely how each of several alternative allocation procedures would affect welfare. What other objectives should be taken into consideration when choosing a rationing scheme for import permits?
8. In the two-country partial equilibrium model of a tariff presented in the section of this chapter titled

"A Tariff in the Heckscher-Ohlin Model," why does the importing country that imposes the tariff suffer a smaller welfare decline than the exporting country?

9. Use a two-country supply and demand diagram to illustrate how, starting from completely free trade, a tariff on wool blankets affects both the domestic and foreign markets for blankets.

   (a) Label the important geometric areas in your diagram, and explain how the tariff changes the consumer and producer surpluses in both countries, as well as the well-being of other relevant groups.

   (b) Compared to free trade, how does the quantity of imports and the price of wool blankets change in each economy?

   (c) Then compare trade with a tariff to a complete ban on trade in wool blankets.

10. Explain the frequent use of VERs by developed economies. Are VERs less harmful than tariffs or quotas? Illustrate the effect of a VER using a two-country supply and demand model of international trade.

11. The chapter mentions a number of ways in which countries restrict trade beyond the usual tariffs and quotas. Can you think of any additional ways in which laws, regulations, coercion, or bureaucratic procedures discriminate against foreign products?

12. Use a partial equilibrium model to explain the costs and benefits of an auction quota. Also, suggest some reasons why they are seldom, if ever, used when countries impose import restrictions.

13. Explain quota rent. Where does it come from? How can an importer gain the quota rent? How can the exporter reap the quota rent?

14. Explain what happens to the effects of a fixed quota if the demand for imports declines. How would the effect of a decline in import demand differ if imports were restricted by a specific tariff?

15. Cotton farmers in West Africa have complained that U.S. cotton subsidies make their farms uneconomical to operate. Use the two-country model of export subsidies to explain the effect of U.S. cotton subsidies on the world market for cotton. (Hint: Assume that without export subsidies, U.S. cotton costs more than West African cotton, and then show how the U.S. subsidy can reverse trade.)

16. Write a brief essay explaining why trade sanctions seldom achieve their stated goals. (Hint: Be sure to discuss the effects on third countries of a ban on trade between two countries.)

APPENDIX

THE COMPLETE ANALYSIS OF A TARIFF IN A GENERAL EQUILIBRIUM MODEL

This appendix picks up the discussion on general equilibrium effects where we left off on page 206. The new production point P_T and the domestic price ratio of $(1+t)P_X/P_Y$ seem to point to a new consumption equilibrium at C_1 in Figure 8.19, where the indifference curve is tangent to the consumption possibilities line that passes through the production point. But, from a general equilibrium point of view the full effect of a tariff is more complex. Even though consumers face a steeper price line, the economy does not pay as much for X as consumers do because the tariff is paid by the consumers' government, which presumably returns it to the citizens of the country in some form. Where, then, does consumption end up after government tax revenue is reflected in consumers' real income?

Figure 8.20 illustrates how the income generated by production at P_T leads to a consumption equilibrium that is different from the point C_1 shown in Figure 8.19. Consumers face the price ratio $(1+t)P_X/P_Y$, so they take their income from producing P_T and move toward the combination of X and Y given at point C_1. But, as they proceed toward C_1, as shown by the arrow extending from P_T, they find their income declining less than their expenditures on X would imply because they receive goods or income payments from their government, funded by the tariffs that they are paying as they acquire imported X. Suppose that the goods or transfers that the government provides are equal in

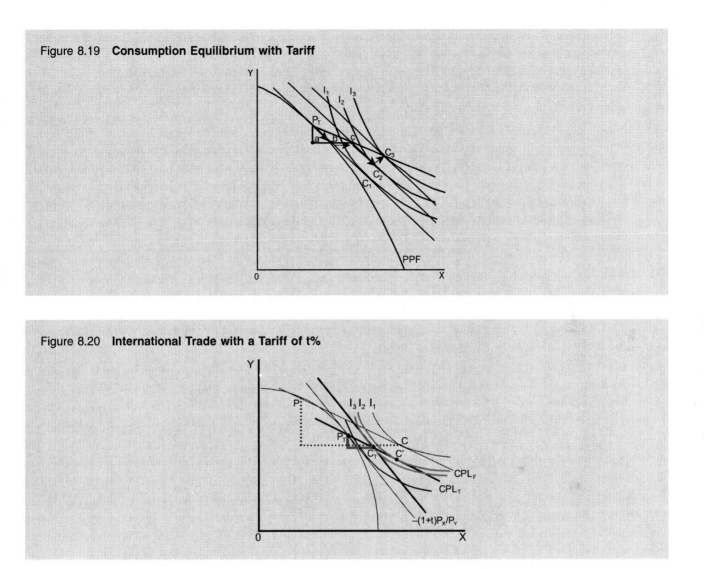

Figure 8.19 **Consumption Equilibrium with Tariff**

Figure 8.20 **International Trade with a Tariff of t%**

value to X. Then, after consumers use their income earned by producing the combination of goods given by P_T to buy an additional amount of X goods equal to ab, the government earns enough tariff revenue to transfer income that could provide an additional bc worth of X for its citizens. Thus, consumers end up at point c, instead of b. Once at point c, consumers prefer the combination of X and Y given by C_2, and they seek to add more X to their consumption basket, which increases imports and again increases tariff revenue, which in turn again moves consumers to a higher consumption possibilities frontier. The whole process stops when consumers reach a consumption point where, at the tariff-distorted prices that they observe, they have no further desire to increase purchases of the import good. This occurs when the point C_3 in Figure 8.19 is reached, which is where consumer preferences reflect the tariff-distorted price ratio $(1+t)P_X/P_Y$ but lies on the consumption possibilities frontier that passed through the tariff-distorted production point P_T with a slope equal to the world price ratio. This is shown as the C_T in Figure 8.20.

In summary, consumption does not occur along the tariff-distorted price line $-(1+t)P_X/P_Y$ because that line ignores the fact that the tariff is paid by importers to their country's own government, which presumably returns it to its citizens in the form of transfers, reductions in other taxes, or government goods and services. The tariff-distorted production point P_T therefore provides consumers with sufficient income to acquire goods along CPL_T, whose slope reflects the small country's unchanged terms of trade. Thus, the tariff's distorting effect on production implies that the economy can at best reach the indifference curve I_2, not I_1. However, consumers do not increase their consumption of X enough to move to C in Figure 8.20 because they make their decisions according to the tariff-distorted price of X that they observe in the market. Hence, consumption ends up at C_3, and welfare is represented by the indifference curve I_3.

Trade with the tariff of t percent on imports of X still generates some gains from trade. The indifference curve I_3 reached in Figure 8.20 represents a greater level of welfare than can be reached if there were no trade at all and consumption points were limited to the economy's own production possibilities frontier. But the tariff-distorted trade triangle is smaller than the dotted free trade triangle whose corners consist of points P and C, and the welfare gains from trade are smaller.

NOTES

1. Christopher J. Chipello (2001), "Canadian Island's Potato Shipments Shrivel on U.S. Ban," *Wall Street Journal,* March 5.

2. Robert S. Greenberger (1998), "States, Cities Increase Use of Trade Sanctions, Troubling Business Groups and U.S. Partners," *Wall Street Journal,* April 1; Patti Waldmeir (2000), "Supreme Court to Rule on Burma Boycott," *Financial Times,* March 22.

3. Karby Leggett (2000).

4. See, for example, Sam Laird and Alexander Yeats (1990) and World Trade Organization (2010).

5. Floyd Norris (2009), "Tax Break for Profits Went Awry," *New York Times,* June 4.

6. For additional details on the GATT's definition of dumping, see John H. Jackson (1997).

7. Frances Williams (2001), "New Blow for U.S. Steel Industry," *Financial Times,* August 25; see also Robert Guy Matthews (2001), "Trade Panel Rules for U.S. Steelmakers," *Wall Street Journal,* October 23.

8. As described in Ali Abunimah and Anthony Arnove (2000), "An Embargo on Common Sense," *Financial Times,* August 10.

9. See, for example, Stephen J. Glain (2000), "Oil, Smuggling Grease Iraq's Economy," *Wall Street Journal,* May 1, and Robert Corzine (2000), "The Merchants of Baghdad Find Their Way Round Sanctions," *Financial Times,* February 27.

CHAPTER 9

The History of Trade Policy

[T]he lowering of tariffs has, in effect, been like draining a swamp. The lower water level has revealed all the snags and stumps of non-tariff barriers that still have to be cleared away.

—Robert Baldwin (1970)

The intervening thirty years have witnessed completion of the swamp draining, but the stumps have started to grow.

—Richard Baldwin (2001)

Worldwide, average tariffs on imports of manufactured goods are today one-tenth what they were right after World War II. In the United States, average tariff levels on imports of manufactures have fallen to just 2.5 percent from their peak of over 50 percent in 1930. Most foreign goods now enter the countries with the highest incomes without paying any tariff. The lowering of trade barriers over the past sixty years does not represent an irreversible trend, however. Just eighty years ago, the world sharply increased tariffs and other trade barriers.

In fact, when we compare today's tariffs to those of the mid-nineteenth century, we conclude that trade barriers have not been reduced much at all over the past 150 years, and current tariffs seem low only compared to the post–World War I period's sharp shift to protectionism. Also, as suggested by the quotes above, a more detailed examination of the current barriers to trade reveals that while tariffs have indeed been reduced, importers and exporters still encounter numerous other barriers that were explicitly introduced to take the place of the tariffs. For example, over the past several decades, the United States has pressured trade partners to set voluntary export restraints (VERs) on automobiles, steel, chemicals, cheese, and consumer electronics, among many other products. European, North American, and Asia-Pacific countries have all stealthily introduced new trade restrictions to offset official reductions in tariffs. Also, the latest round of international negotiations to reduce tariffs and other trade barriers is hopelessly bogged down and unlikely to result in a new free trade agreement. In short, trade policy, which is the sum of government laws, regulations, and taxes directed at international trade, is better depicted by an up-and-down wave pattern than a continually declining curve.

This chapter begins with some models of the political processes that drive trade policy to help explain the dynamic shifts in such policy. Then, we combine these political models with the economic models of international trade from earlier chapters to examine the history of trade policy.

THE POLITICAL ECONOMY OF INTERNATIONAL TRADE

Most government-imposed barriers to trade are the result of political pressure by special interests who expect to gain from the protection. The models of international trade described in Chapter 4 and the models of tariffs and quotas in Chapter 7 showed how trade barriers help various groups of people at home and abroad. Therefore, in order to understand why governments impose trade barriers, economists have sought to explain why national policy makers institute policies that effectively redistribute welfare among citizens by combining models of trade and political science. This section discusses several popular models from the field of **political economy** that are useful in explaining trade policy.

The Median Voter Model

One popular political model that has been used to explain trade policy is the **median voter model**. This model was developed by political economists from the public choice school, which sought to explain political outcomes as the result of individual actions motivated by self-interest.[1] Here, we combine the median voter model with the Heckscher-Ohlin model's **Stolper-Samuelson theorem**, discussed in Chapter 3, in order to generate some specific predictions of trade policy.

To make our conclusions more precise, suppose that there are just two factors of production, labor and capital, and that the country's comparative advantage is in labor-intensive production. Therefore, people are assumed to view their own gains or losses from trade as depending on whether they are owners of labor or owners of capital. Free trade will, in this case, benefit the owners of labor and reduce the incomes of the owners of capital, according to the Stolper-Samuelson theorem. Suppose that every person in the economy has one vote to cast for the economic policy makers who will decide to either restrict imports or permit free entry of foreign goods. Then, if we also assume that policy makers are democratically elected officials, or bureaucrats whose jobs and pay depend on elected officials, they can be expected to enact the trade policy that gains the greatest number of votes. These are strong assumptions that, no doubt, oversimplify the political process; we will suggest more realistic assumptions below.

The median voter model predicts that under a one person, one vote political system, trade policy depends on how many owners of labor there are relative to the number of owners of capital. If there are more owners of labor, then the policy maker who commits to maintaining free trade will win the election.[2]

Figure 9.1 graphs the absolute welfare gains from free trade on the vertical axis and the proportions of total voters along the horizontal axis. Figure 9.1 assumes that 20 percent of the voters are capital owners and the remaining 80 percent are owners of labor. The Stolper-Samuelson theorem thus suggests that capital owners will lose from lower tariffs, and laborers will gain. Note that the diagram is drawn to show that the welfare losses from free trade for each of the capital owners, listed first from left to right, are much greater than the welfare gains for each of the labor owners. But, because there are more labor owners and there is no way of reflecting the intensity of the gains or losses in the voting, the policy makers who promise free trade will be elected. Hence the name *median voter model;* the policy favored by the median voter, who is the one exactly in the middle, is the one enacted regardless of the intensity of each voter's preferences. The result is that trade policy can both increase and decrease welfare under the median voter model.

The Uninformed Voter Model

According to some Public Choice school economists, such as James Buchanan and Gordon Tullock (1962), the *median voter model* is unrealistic because it assumes people vote for political candidates on the basis of their preferences concerning a single issue. Policy makers hold office for extended periods of time, and over the course of their political careers they make decisions on a great variety of issues. People therefore seldom vote for or against a candidate solely on the basis of the candidate's decisions with regard to trade policy.[3] In fact, most people have no idea how a candidate will act when it comes to the many issues that will come up in the future. Nor do people understand, or even care about, all the issues. Voters are largely *uninformed*.

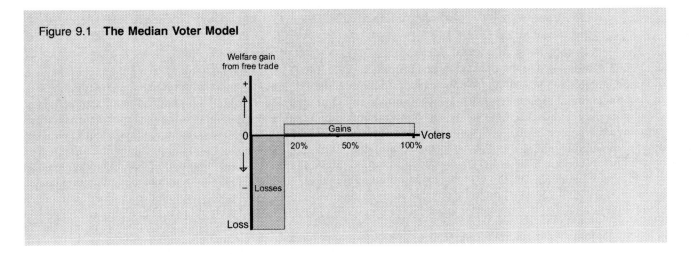

Figure 9.1 **The Median Voter Model**

But the situation is even more difficult. Even when certain issues are very important to them, voters have difficulty letting candidates know what their specific preferences are. Because votes do not clearly signal people's specific policy preferences to policy makers on specific issues like tariffs, those voters who are greatly concerned about specific policies must influence policy makers by engaging in activities such as lobbying, advertising, campaign contributions, or just plain old bribery. These activities are costly, however, and only those groups who stand to gain or lose a lot from certain government policies have an incentive to spend money. Therefore, lobbying is no more likely to accurately reflect the true costs and benefits of actual and potential trade policies than individual votes in the median voter model. Specifically, the **uninformed voter model** suggests that small groups with large gains or losses will exercise a disproportionately large influence on trade policies.

In terms of Figure 9.1, suppose the losses to the 20 percent of the population who are capital owners from, say, a ban on imports of bananas, substantially exceed the gains from free trade for the remaining 80 percent who are laborers. Domestic owners of capital may find it worth their while to lobby against the free trade policy because they are small in number and each of them suffers a large loss under free trade.

Mancur Olson (1965) argued that an organization is more likely to effectively promote its interests if it has a small number of members that each have a large stake in the issue. Olson based his reasoning on the well-known **free rider problem**. In the case of trade policies, it is especially tempting to free ride on the efforts of others because trade policies are not aimed at individual firms; rather, trade policy deals with protection of entire industries, sometimes even entire sectors of the economy, and all firms in an industry or sector experience the effects of a policy shift, whether they contributed to the lobbying effort or not. According to Olson, concentrated industries in which just a few firms dominate the domestic industry will be much better able to organize and coordinate their efforts than a widely dispersed industry consisting of many firms where the temptation to free ride will be greater because each individual firm matters less to the lobbying effort. Olson's observations are especially useful in explaining why a small number of producers are often better able to lobby *for* protection than a large group of consumers are able to lobby *against* protection.

Case Study: The U.S. Sugar Quota

U.S. import quotas on sugar are an example of how a special interest group with a small number of members is able to influence trade policy. Traditionally, U.S. sugar is made from sugarcane and sugar beets. Sugarcane is grown in the warmer states of Florida, Hawaii, and Louisiana, and sugar beets are grown mostly in Minnesota, North Dakota, Idaho, and other midwestern farm states. Most farms are relatively large and are organized into one of several cooperatives to handle marketing and promotion. Sugar producers, therefore, are already organized, and they have a large stake in protection from imports. Sugar consumers, on the other hand, consist of 300 million individual citizens, each of whom spends just a few dollars per year on sugar. Consumers have little interest in organizing a sophisticated lobbying effort to counter the producers' push for protection; in fact, very few U.S. consumers even know that they are paying prices far above the international price for sugar. Of course, there is also a smaller number of large food processors who purchase sugar as inputs, and these firms may lobby actively.

U.S. barriers to imports of foreign sugar are part of a long-running policy; out of the past two hundred years, there were only four in which the U.S. government did not in some way interfere in the domestic market for sugar.[4] Since 1982 the U.S. sugar support program has consisted of: (1) a loan program by the U.S. government that lets sugar processors borrow money to buy sugar from farmers at a predetermined (usually high) price and permits them to default on the loans if the price falls below that support price, and (2) import quotas that limit imports and keep domestic prices above the support price. By keeping the quotas tight enough, domestic prices remain high enough to avoid defaults, and the government never incurs any costs that appear in the budget. Consumers effectively pay for the sugar support program in the form of high prices for sugar and sugar-laden food.

In some recent years, the world sugar price has been nearly as high as U.S. support prices, but in most years the support price is well above the world price. For example, in 2000 the support price was eighteen cents for raw cane sugar, while the world price for sugar was just over seven cents (U.S.) per pound. The partial equilibrium model of a quota is useful for understanding the protection of sugar producers. Figure 9.2 illustrates the U.S. sugar market using the approximate prices and quantities from the past twenty-five years: domestic production of sugar of about 15 million tons per year and consumption of about 16 million tons, which implies imports of about 1 million tons at the support price of twenty cents per pound, five cents above the world price. According to David Tarr and Morris Morkre (1984), U.S. demand for sugar is very inelastic, as might be expected for a basic food product whose cost accounts for a negligible share of total consumer expenditures; supply is more elastic because producers do face substantial opportunity costs.

In Figure 9.2, consumers lose areas a+b+c+d, and domestic producers gain area a at the expense of U.S. consumers. Foreign suppliers gain the quota rent c, and the price distortion causes deadweight losses equal to the areas b+d. According to Tarr and Morkre's elasticity estimates, a = $1.2 billion, b = $300 million, c = $100 million, and d = $50 million. Consumers suffer a consumer surplus loss of $1.65 billion, and domestic producers gain $1.2 billion. These estimates are similar to what others have found. Tarr and Morkre found that, in 1983, consumers suffered a loss of $1.266 billion and producers gained $616 million. Gary Clyde Hufbauer and Kimberly Ann Elliott (1994) estimated consumer surplus losses in the U.S. sugar market to be $1.357 billion, producer surplus gains to be $776 million, and quota rent for foreign exporters to be $396 million. A 1988 study by the U.S. Department of Commerce estimated that sugar price supports cost consumers as much as $3 billion. Keith E. Maskus (1987) surveyed available studies and found estimates of consumer surplus losses to range from $1 billion to $2.7 billion.

U.S. protection of sugar is a classic example of a small, well-organized group of producers, each of whom stands to gain a lot from protection, imposing its interests at the expense of a much larger but very diverse group of consumers, each of whom stands to lose very little from the protection. Producer surplus gains averaged about $500,000 per farmer, which is worth a few contributions to the political campaigns of key politicians. A consumer surplus loss of even $1.5 billion, the average estimate from the various studies of the welfare effects of sugar quotas, implies a loss of only a little more than $5 per person, hardly an amount to get excited about. These losses have continued year

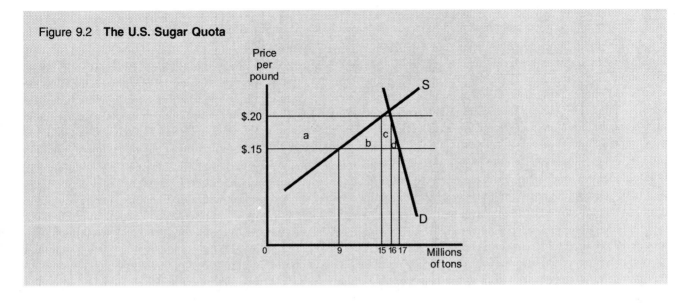

Figure 9.2 **The U.S. Sugar Quota**

after year and have come to add up to quite a sum, but, still, they are small compared to people's overall food expenditures and incomes.

The Endogenous Tariff Model

Stephen P. Magee, William A. Brock, and Leslie Young (1989) developed a model of voters who are uninformed about how government laws, regulations, taxes, subsidies, and other programs affect them. Politicians running for office must use advertising, public relations, and other marketing activities to influence these voters. Such activities require money, of course, which effectively leads office-seeking politicians to "sell" their policy-making power in exchange for the contributions necessary to fund political campaigning and advertising. Magee, Brock, and Young show how this situation results in some positive level of protectionism even if trade restrictions always cause more harm than good. Their model, known as the **endogenous tariff model**, is presented in Figure 9.3. This political economy model is different from the tariff model in the previous chapter, in which the tariff level is taken as a given. In the real world, tariffs clearly are not *givens;* policy makers set tariffs in accordance with the economic and political forces that they see as critical to their political survival.

Magee, Brock, and Young assume that there are diminishing marginal returns to campaign expenditures. Therefore, in the top diagram of Figure 9.3, the total number of votes gained by promising increased tariffs to the special interests and gaining more campaign funds for campaign advertising and activities to influence voters are represented by a curve with a declining slope. At the same time, voters normally do not find it worth their time and effort to be informed about trade policies, but if tariffs get too high and cover too many products, they begin to take notice. Thus, as tariffs rise, more voters decide to become informed, and there are more losses of votes, as illustrated by the increasing-slope curve in the top diagram of Figure 9.3.

The curve in the bottom diagram of Figure 9.3 represents the difference between the gains from more campaign contributions from those who are favored by protectionist legislation and the losses from those who are hurt by the protectionism. The curve peaks at the tariff level where the marginal votes gained from campaign expenditures are equal to the marginal votes lost from those adversely affected by the tariffs in the upper diagram.

According to this model, the more informed voters are, the less campaign expenditures are likely to secure votes, and the lower will be the "votes gained" curve in the top diagram of Figure 9.3.

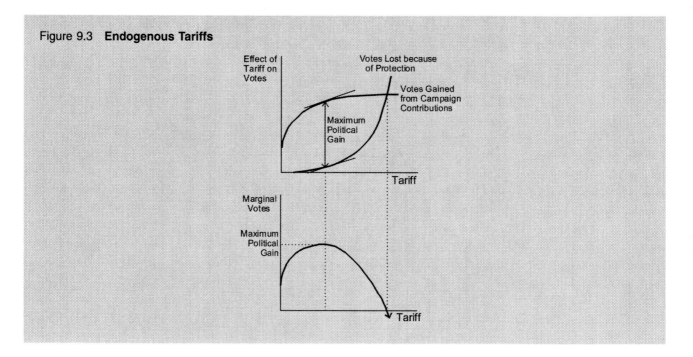

Figure 9.3 **Endogenous Tariffs**

However, astute political observers would, no doubt, note that campaign contributions are often used in advertising and other campaign messages that intentionally obscure the real issues and make voters *less* informed. Thus, a higher level of protection for special interests may be self-perpetuating. In any case, trade policy seldom attracts much attention even from politically aware citizens. Hence, Magee, Brock, and Young's model suggests that lobbyists will have relatively free rein to push for at least modest amounts of tariff protection.

The Adding Machine Model

Richard E. Caves (1976) and Robert Baldwin (1985) suggested that because politicians cannot satisfy the special interests of every voter, policy makers are most likely to use trade policy to protect import-competing industries with large numbers of workers. This simple model is referred to as the **adding machine model** because policy makers add up the number of jobs in an industry in order to gauge the need to favor that industry's well-being. Statistical evidence using data on protection and industry size suggests that indeed the adding machine model helps to explain protectionism in the United States. The clothing and textile industry, the steel industry, and, of course, the auto industry have traditionally received the greatest amount of protection from U.S. policy makers, and the adding machine model would say that this is because these industries employ the greatest number of people who can, potentially, vote.

Rent-Seeking Behavior

Firms, organizations, and groups that share certain interests often exert considerable effort and incur substantial costs in order to influence their governments' trade policies. These costly and intentional efforts are often referred to as **rent-seeking activities**. This term was first used by Anne O. Krueger (1974) in an influential paper in which she analyzed the welfare effects of import restrictions in Turkey. The concept had been presented earlier by Gordon Tullock (1967). Krueger observed that many very talented individuals spent most of their working hours lobbying the government officials

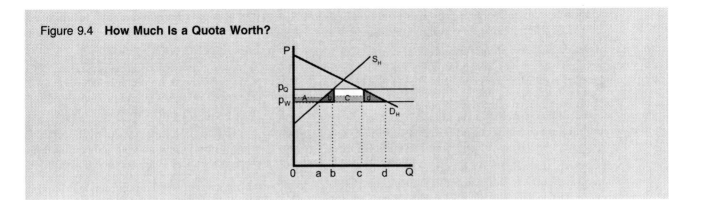

Figure 9.4 **How Much Is a Quota Worth?**

who had the authority to issue import permits. The goal of these costly efforts was to gain the rent created by the Turkish government's widespread quotas on imports. Import permits were scarce commodities, and it was worth devoting some effort to obtain them. Krueger calculated that the cost of rent seeking in Turkey in the early 1970s was as much as 14 percent of the national product.

Like the political economy models above, the rent-seeking literature views government as an organization made up of self-interested officials who maximize their personal welfare within the constraints they face. Because government officials have the power to create and enforce laws and regulations, they can, potentially, be persuaded or pressured into favoring the interests of some people over those of others. If lobbying costs consume half of the area A in Figure 9.4, then some portion of area A must also be added to the costs of protection. How much will special interests spend to lobby their government?

According to the partial equilibrium model of trade, the value of the import permits to importers is equal to the quota rent, area C in Figure 9.4. Potential importers would be willing to spend some of this potential quota rent on lobbying activities in order to gain the rent. Note, however, that rent seeking reduces the ultimate gain from international trade. If, for example, lobbying activities consume resources equal in value to half of the area C, then the total costs to the economy of the quota of bc would be equal to the deadweight loss areas b+d plus half of C. Krueger assumed competitive rent seekers in Turkey ended up consuming most of the area C.

Importers may not be the only ones who engage in rent seeking. There may be lobbying by domestic producers seeking to increase their surplus, area A in Figure 9.4. Consumers may also organize to protect themselves against rent-seeking producers. If they could indeed organize and get all their members to contribute to the lobbying effort, consumers would be willing to spend up to the sum of the areas A, b, C, and d to avoid the quota altogether. Conceivably, total lobbying expenses in the economy by producers seeking protection, consumers trying to avoid protectionist policies, and potential importers seeking scarce import permits, could exceed the total area A+b+C+d being disputed.[5] The difficulties of organizing and the free rider problem may prevent this from happening, but it should be obvious that the real costs of tariffs and quotas are often found not as much in the deadweight loss triangles as they are in the opportunity costs of rent seeking.

Consumers of imports that are taxed or otherwise restricted from entering the country occasionally engage in **smuggling** to avoid paying the cost of protecting domestic producers. Smuggling is effectively a form of **rent-evading activity** intended to avoid the costs imposed as a result of rent-seeking behavior by producers. Smuggling is one of the oldest ways in which consumers of imports have dealt with government-imposed trade barriers.

In sum, each of the models discussed in this section suggests unique explanations for how trade policy is shaped in the real world of politics. There is some support for each model, but none by itself explains all policy outcomes. Politics is complex, and it is difficult to precisely explain the economic policies that emerge from the political process. A heterodox approach that applies models on a selective basis and compares explanations across different models is most likely to add to our understanding of how trade policy evolves in a dynamic political and economic environment.

TRADE POLICY BEFORE THE TWENTIETH CENTURY

Governments have restricted foreign trade to varying degrees throughout history. For example, as far back as 516 B.C.E. the Athenian ruler Solon prohibited the export of wheat by farmers around Athens because citizens complained that booming foreign demand for wheat was raising bread prices at home. It is probably safe to say that, historically, most trade restrictions were driven either by special interests who sought to gain at the expense of others or by government's need for revenue, either in the direct form of tariff revenue or, indirectly, from rent seeking.

Tariffs and export taxes also served as important sources of government revenue, especially before modern monetized economies made it easier to tax other economic activities. International trade was always a convenient target for the tax collector, in part because international commerce was usually more likely to involve the exchange of money than the barter of goods. Also, international trade was often easier to monitor and tax than other economic activities because it tended to pass through a small number of ports or along a small number of roads and rivers. Taxes on international trade were often seen as less objectionable than other taxes because they could be presented as charges on foreigners and merchants, two groups that were often viewed unfavorably.

The Ups and Downs of Trade Policy

Human history has passed through periods of increasing global economic integration, each followed by a period of increasing isolation. For example, two thousand years ago, during the time of the Roman Empire, trade was unrestricted throughout the Mediterranean region. The flows of goods, people, and ideas through the region linked the people of Africa, Asia, and Europe. However, the fall of the Roman Empire led to Europe's fragmentation into separate nations and the emergence of a feudal socioeconomic system in which local economic and political structures dominated. The Middle East and Asia remained open to outside influences and trade for the next few centuries after Europe withdrew into itself. During the Sung dynasty (960–1279 C.E.), China was the technological and economic leader of the world. The Muslim states of the Middle East also stood out for their technological developments. The Silk Road through central Asia is still romanticized because it carried exotic goods and ideas between China and the Middle East.

In the first few centuries of the second millennium of the Christian era, trade policies again shifted. The Muslim Middle East gradually closed itself to trade and outside influence, reversing the openness that had distinguished the region during the previous millennium. The murderous Christian Crusades spurred on by corrupt popes and other European leaders helped to raise fears of foreigners and foreign ideas among Muslim nations in the Middle East. The fear of outside ideas grew; the printing press was even banned in many Muslim states to stem the spread of foreign knowledge. High taxation of trade by various rulers plus increased piracy and extortion by various warlords in Asia destroyed the Silk Road, which linked China to the Middle East. China and Japan eventually closed themselves completely to foreign trade and all other contacts with foreigners. In China's case, the cause was repeated invasions by the Mongols; in Japan's case, it was the inroads made by European Christian missionaries. Interestingly, the Far East's closing in coincided with Europe's gradual abandonment of its economic isolation. The revival of international trade in Europe was led by independent city-states, such as Venice in the Mediterranean region and the network of Baltic city states that formed the trade area known as the **Hanseatic League** in northern Europe.

Mercantilism

Beginning in the Renaissance, international trade was increasingly seen as an important contributor to a nation's welfare in Europe, provided it was carefully controlled and guided to benefit certain privileged groups. The policies evolved by European monarchs to promote and shape international trade after 1500 are now often referred to as **mercantilism**. The definition of mercantilism as no more than a set of protectionist trade policies intended to generate a positive trade balance dates from seventeenth- and eighteenth-century writings that attempted to justify protectionism. In the original words of one mercantilist writer, Thomas Mun (1664):

> Although a Kingdom may be enriched by gifts received, or by purchase taken from some other Nations, yet these are things uncertain and of small consideration when they happen. The ordinary means therefore to increase our wealth and treasure is by Forraign Trade, wherein wee must ever observe this rule; to sell more to strangers yearly than wee consume of theirs in value.

During the early stages of the industrial revolution, in the eighteenth century, the promoters of mercantilism justified the protection of manufacturing industries as a tool for generating trade surpluses. Mercantilist writings also often claimed that a country's level of employment grew with exports and declined with rising levels of imports. Adam Smith's trashing of the mercantilists in order to contrast their approach with his call for free trade (1776 [1976]) helped to perpetuate this image of mercantilism as merely an argument for promoting protection against imports. In fact, mercantilism was a complex economic and political arrangement that reflected circumstances in Europe between 1500 and 1800.

As the political economy models recognize, trade policies are shaped by many social, political, and economic factors. Mercantilism was a system of government regulations and controls over economic activity that was intended to favor certain economic groups, usually merchants, artisans, and early European industrialists, who found it in their interest to support national monarchs. The economic historians Robert B. Eckelund and Robert Tollison (1981) describe mercantilism as the "supply and demand for monopoly rights through the machinery of the state." Trade of monopoly rights was nurtured by Europe's monarchs to solidify their political power.

At the start of the Renaissance, Europe was still largely a feudal society consisting of small economic and political units. The consolidation of national power by a few kings, queens, and emperors required central governments to develop sources of revenue free from the complex feudal arrangements between local and regional aristocracies. In order to enhance their political and military power so they could overcome the influence of the local aristocracies, the monarchs who headed the central governments of England, France, Spain, and other parts of Europe saw an advantage in forging relationships with artisans, merchants, and bankers located in towns and cities who were not linked to the local aristocracies. At the same time, the artisans, merchants, and bankers gained prestige and freedom from the restrictive taxes and other obligations of the feudal system. In seventeenth-century England and the Netherlands, merchants came to occupy the highest positions in society.

The reason mercantilism came to be identified with trade barriers was that the monarchs of England, Holland, France, Spain, and Portugal also saw that they could tax foreign trade and colonial enterprises, gaining revenue and an advantage over the traditional feudal lords, who could not collect the taxes on foreign ventures and trade. It was not intellectual curiosity that led Queen Isabela of Spain to finance Columbus's attempts to find a shorter and safer route to the spices of the Far East, nor was it the pure quest for national glory that led the House of Orange in the Netherlands to invest in the Dutch East India Company. These first transnational enterprises were commercial ventures that used politics and the power of government to further their ends, and government leaders willingly cooperated because they found special interest politics to be quite useful for maintaining their power.

Mercantilist trade policies discouraged or prohibited the importation of finished products and the export of raw materials because the new industrialists in, for example, England and France sought protection. On the other hand, in Spain and Portugal, where manufacturing was not as well developed, mercantilist trade policies were designed to benefit artisans, merchants, and shippers. Portugal, for example, required that all goods exported from its colony in Brazil be carried on Portuguese ships and pass through Portugal, even if they were ultimately destined for some other country. Most European governments required their colonies to purchase all imports from the mother country, to the benefit of domestic manufacturers, artisans, and merchants.

The Intellectual Attack on Mercantilism

During the Enlightenment, social thinkers criticized mercantilist trade policies. Most notably, in his classic *An Inquiry into the Nature and Causes of the Wealth of Nations,* Adam Smith (1776 [1976]) argued that an economy should be judged by how much welfare it provides for the country's citizens, not whether a positive trade balance permits the nation's treasury to accumulate gold and silver. Smith reasoned that specialization and exchange were the true source of economic growth, which meant that the protection sought by the mercantilists must reduce the long-term growth of human welfare. Other classical economists, most notably David Ricardo, helped to spread the idea of comparative advantage and free trade on into the 1800s.

To suggest that classical economists such as Smith and Ricardo caused mercantilism's downfall would be an exaggeration. Some would argue that mercantilism is still alive and well. On the one hand, the movement toward removing trade barriers was already well under way when Smith was working out his logical arguments for free trade. In 1784, Britain lowered many import tariffs, and two years later, in a treaty with France, cut tariffs even further. Specific trade restrictions were abandoned because they imposed high costs on the new industrialists who rose to political prominence during the Industrial Revolution, which began in the late eighteenth century.[6] It is premature to talk about mercantilism's demise; it is found today in the form of transnational corporations and the extensive lobbying networks they employ to bend government policy in their favor.

Rather, the apparent end of mercantilism in the nineteenth century was really a shift in policy that reflected changing economic interests as the Industrial Revolution transformed European economies. The British **Corn Laws** offer a good example of how shifting interests translated into policy changes. At the end of the eighteenth century, Britain's very limited democracy gave voting rights only to large landowners, the landed gentry. Landowners supported the Corn Laws, which mandated high protective tariffs on grain imports in order to keep grain prices and the returns to land high. The new industrialists who gained prominence during the Industrial Revolution argued that the Corn Laws kept food prices artificially high in Britain, and high food prices raised the costs of labor in the new textile, clothing, and metalworking industries.

The growing economic importance of merchants, industrialists, and the urban population changed Britain's political landscape in the early nineteenth century. The Reform Act of 1832 extended voting rights to all middle-class men and shifted the balance of political power in Parliament away from the landed gentry.[7] Political pressure to repeal the Corn Laws intensified. The Irish potato famine in 1845 and 1846 also helped to swing sentiment toward freeing the importation of food. In addition, the Industrial Revolution led forward-looking British landowners to diversify their wealth by investing in industrial and commercial ventures, which, according to Cheryl Schonhardt-Bailey (1991), reduced their opposition to the repeal of the Corn Laws. In 1846 the Corn Laws were finally repealed. By 1860 the British government had eliminated nearly all import tariffs.

At the beginning of the Industrial Revolution, Britain's textiles, iron, and machinery industries enjoyed strong market positions because of their technological superiority, and they needed raw materials from other parts of the world. But, for Britain to gain the full benefits from trade, other countries would have to reduce their trade restrictions as well. Britain therefore used diplomacy to open borders to trade in Europe. For example, in 1860, the Cobden-Chevalier Treaty, admittedly rammed through an unwilling French political system by the dictatorial Napoleon III, reduced many tariffs on trade between Britain and France.

International trade was further liberalized when France negotiated tariff reductions with other European countries. Most of the trade agreements contained a **most favored nation** (MFN) clause, which obligated the signatories to grant every concession given to any other country in later treaties. Thus, when France negotiated a reduction in tariffs with the *Zollverein,* the free trade area formed by most of the German states, the inclusion of an MFN clause in the agreement obliged France to immediately extend to the Zollverein all the reductions in trade barriers that France had granted Britain earlier and to extend any new tariff reductions negotiated with the Zollverein to Britain as well. The MFN clause effectively made bilateral trade negotiations **multilateral**. According to A.G. Kenwood and A.L. Lougheed (1992, p. 61), during the decade 1860–1870, Europe "came close to attaining the ideal trading conditions postulated by classical economic theory."

Because British trade policy can be fully explained by changing economic and political conditions, it is difficult to argue that trade was expanded because policy makers were convinced by classical economic theory. In fact, mercantilism did not end; it only led to different trade policies because the new economic conditions had created new interest groups and the accompanying social and political changes opened channels through which these new interest groups could gain government support. In the 1800s, these interest groups favored free trade.

U.S. Trade Policy before World War I

Unlike Europe, the United States maintained very high tariffs throughout the nineteenth century. U.S. protectionism had its roots in its revolution, when the former British colonies were isolated from Britain and forced to produce a variety of industrial products previously imported from Britain. After the hostilities with Britain ended, the U.S. industries lobbied for tariff protection from British industrial products.

Actually, it was the new industries in the northern states that favored high tariffs. The predominantly agricultural South favored free trade because it enjoyed a comparative advantage in tobacco, cotton, and other agricultural products, and it preferred to import manufactures from low-cost British and other European producers rather than purchase high-priced products from the less efficient industries in the North. This situation was a classic case of gainers and losers from tariff protection, with consumers and mostly southern exporters losing while mostly northern import-competing industries gained. The northern states seemed to gain the upper hand in 1828 with the infamous Tariff of Abominations, which raised average tariffs to about 60 percent, an extremely high level. The public reaction to these high tariffs soon altered the composition of Congress, and the Compromise Tariff of 1833 lowered rates to an average of about 40 percent. Further reductions in tariffs followed, although the demographic superiority of the northern industrial states kept tariffs averaging well above 20 percent until just before the Civil War. Some historians claim the Civil War was fought over tariffs, not slavery. That conclusion is not correct, given the overwhelming importance of the slavery issue, but there is little doubt that the general animosity between northern and southern states that prevented a peaceful resolution to the slavery issue was partially the result of the repeated arguments over the protectionist trade policies that the northern majority imposed on the South.

After the Civil War began, the U.S. government, now minus the southern states, further raised tariffs above the level of the 1860 Morrill Tariff. Political leaders argued that higher tariffs were necessary to protect industries penalized by very high excise taxes necessary to fund the Civil War. But, when the Civil War was concluded, the tariffs somehow remained in place. In fact, U.S. tariffs remained between 40 and 50 percent for the rest of the nineteenth century, with increases coinciding with presidents affiliated with the Republican Party, which more closely represented industry, and modest declines coming during Democratic administrations, which were more attuned with the interests of labor and farmers. When Woodrow Wilson, a Democrat, became president in 1913, he pushed through sharp reductions in tariffs and other forms of protection. This trend toward trade liberalization was short lived, however. World War I broke out in 1914, disrupting all trade flows.

Historians still argue over whether the United States was a closed economy to trade in the nineteenth century. The answer is not as easy as it seems because in terms of the three other components of globalization, the United States was very open. Immigration was not restricted, and new arrivals grew steadily, reaching 1 million persons per year at the start of the twentieth century. Also, foreign capital flowed into, and out of, the country with ease. Many of the U.S. railroads, steel mills, and other projects critical to U.S. economic development were financed by foreign investors. Therefore, while it is true that the U.S. economy was closed in terms of trade policy, in terms of immigration, finance, and investment, it was very open. This combination of trade barriers and free entry of foreign financing and immigrants was fully compatible with the interests of U.S. industry, which sought cheap labor, low-interest financing, and protection from foreign competition for its products.

Forced Trade Liberalization in the Far East

A country's trade policy is not always a choice by that country's government; sometimes, trade policy is imposed by another country. Such was the case for nineteenth-century China and Japan. Recall that both China and Japan had closed their economies to foreign trade centuries earlier in response to what they felt were unwelcome impositions of foreign cultures. The general expansion of international trade by European countries clashed with the closed Chinese and Japanese economies.

British merchants were eager to acquire Chinese goods, and they sought ways to pay for them. The Chinese permitted some foreign trade through the port of Guangzhou, but the Chinese government demanded payment in silver for all goods. British merchants sought a product that the Chinese would buy in order to balance trade and economize on silver, and they found it in opium. The British could acquire opium in their colony of India. Chinese authorities soon banned the import of opium, however, as they realized that large numbers of their citizens were quickly becoming addicted to the drug. After repeated disputes between British merchants and the Chinese government, and specifically the seizure and burning of one large shipment by the mayor of Canton, Britain sent an army and naval forces into China in 1842. The British quickly defeated the Chinese forces in what would be called the first Opium War, and China agreed to the Treaty of Nanjing, which gave the British access to Chinese ports, ceded the territory of Hong Kong to Britain, and permitted opium imports. A second Opium War was fought in the 1850s, and the 1860 Treaty of Tianjin further opened the Chinese market to Europeans, expanded the opium trade, and even gave foreign missionaries free rein in China. The Boxer Rebellion in 1900 represented a nationalistic resistance to foreign imperialists, but the "rebellion" was put down by an eight-nation military force of some twenty thousand soldiers. Not only was the Chinese market kept open, but the Qing Dynasty was undermined in favor of the Chinese Republic, which Western powers expected to be more likely to keep China open to foreign trade.

The Japanese market was opened to foreign trade when Commander Matthew Perry of the United States sailed his warships into Tokyo Bay in 1853 and again in 1854. Perry's naval superiority resulted in a group of anti-isolation forces within Japan gaining power. These new leaders were convinced that Japan had fallen far behind the rest of the world in terms of technology. The following year, a treaty was signed that gave U.S. traders limited access to Japan's market. Treaties between Japan and Russia, England, Holland, and France followed. The treaties that the Western powers signed with Japan and China contained most favored nation clauses. Thus, as each foreign country gained market entry on better terms, the most favorable terms were immediately extended to all foreign countries. Trade between Europe, the United States, and the Far East grew rapidly in the second half of the nineteenth century.

Europe Reverses Course in the Late 1800s

Cheap wheat from the United States, Argentina, and Russia, among other places, began to flood European markets in the late nineteenth century as transport improved and Western Hemisphere countries settled by European immigrants rapidly expanded their agricultural production. Food prices fell, and farmers in Germany and France suffered declines in income. At the same time, growing industries in Germany and France competed with the well-established British industrialists. This created a natural coalition in France and Germany between new industries and farmers that sought to impose trade barriers. Then, an extended slowdown of economic growth from 1873 to 1879 made foreign imports a convenient target for politicians. Germany increased tariffs in 1879, and France followed in 1892 with the Méline Tariff. The governments of Britain, Holland, and Denmark resisted, at least for a while, the growing domestic political pressures for increased protection.[8]

Despite the unmistakable shift toward protectionism at its end, the nineteenth century can nevertheless be characterized as one of international economic integration. Raw materials exports from Latin America, Africa, and Asia were exchanged for capital goods and consumption goods from the new industries in Europe and the United States. New methods of communication and transport facilitated the growth in trade. However, it was not clear to everyone that the growth of international trade was such a good thing. The increase in international economic integration and the rapid economic and technological changes left many people uncomfortable and insecure. Under the colonial structure and the overall pattern of primary product exports by poor nations in exchange for industrial products from the rich nations, not everyone benefited from international commerce. Politics would shift trade policy back toward protectionism in the twentieth century.

DESTROYING TRADE DURING THE INTERWAR PERIOD

World War I (1914–1918) changed the world in a great many ways. There were many more national borders after the war than there had been before 1914. Austria-Hungary was split up into Czechoslovakia, Hungary, Austria, Romania, Yugoslavia, and Poland. Russia lost substantial territory to new countries, including Finland, Estonia, Latvia, Lithuania, and Poland. Secondly, after the war, the United States and most of Western Europe would erect barriers to trade. Also, the post–World War I period was complicated by the terms of the peace treaty that closed the war.

The Treaty of Versailles

The **Treaty of Versailles**, which formally ended the war in 1919, determined that Germany would compensate the Allies for their war losses. Losses were assessed at US$30 billion at 1920 prices, which was more than double Germany's annual GDP at that time.[9] The British economist John Maynard Keynes (1920), a member of the British delegation to the Paris meetings where the treaty was drafted, accurately predicted its consequences:

> If the European Civil War is to end with France and Italy abusing their momentary victorious power to destroy Germany and Austria-Hungary now prostrate, they invite their own destruction also.

Allied countries such as France and Britain saw the reparations payments that Germany would owe them as the source of repaying their own debts to the United States. The European Allies had borrowed heavily during the war to purchase arms, food, and other imports.

For this scheme to work, somehow tax payments by German citizens to their government in German marks had to be converted to dollar payments by British and French governments to their U.S. lenders. Specifically:

- Germany would have to increase taxes or borrow from its citizens, and it would have to run a large trade surplus with the Allied countries in order to earn the British pounds, French francs, and Italian lira needed to pay war reparations.
- The Allied countries would then have to run trade surpluses with the United States in order to earn the dollars with which to pay their debts to U.S. lenders.

Unfortunately, political conditions in Germany, the Allied countries, and the United States would not let these things happen.

The German government ran huge budget deficits, in part to pay for its reparations payment obligations. These budget deficits were at first financed by domestic borrowing, but when doubts arose over the German government's ability to repay their domestic debt, Germans became reluctant to purchase their government's bonds. The German government was forced to simply print money to cover the budget deficit, and rapid inflation was the predictable result. The faster prices rose, the more money the government had to print to cover its expenditures. By 1922, prices were rising by thousands of percentage points per month. A huge aid package from the United States and Britain, combined with increased taxes and reduced government expenditures, helped to restore stability to the German economy in 1924. Nevertheless, Germany struggled under the fiscal burden, and unemployment remained high throughout the 1920s. Also, Germany was never able to run consistent trade surpluses to earn the foreign currency needed to pay the reparations payments because the Allied countries restricted imports in an effort to boost their own employment after World War I.

The second part of the trade pattern that would be necessary for the world economy to handle the post–World War I reparations and debt repayments also failed: the United States sharply raised tariffs. U.S. industry, which had expanded rapidly during World War I, felt vulnerable to foreign competition after the war. It clamored for protection, and the new Republican administration that took office in 1921 immediately set out to enact protectionist legislation. The Fordney-McCumber Tariff of 1922 doubled average tariff rates.

The Smoot-Hawley Tariff

The political pressures for protectionist trade policies increased when the U.S. economy fell into deep recession after 1929. Industry after industry demanded protection, and the U.S. Congress was eager to comply. Representatives pushing for protection of the industries concentrated in each of their congressional districts soon put together a trade bill that raised average U.S. tariffs to about 50 percent. This tariff bill, which had begun in 1929 as a simple bill to provide protection to a few select industries, became the **Smoot-Hawley Tariff Act** of 1930, named after the senator and representative who headed the committees that put the bill together. The Smoot-Hawley Tariff caused a **trade war** that quickly engulfed much of the world. Faced with unemployment due to the spread of the U.S. recession to most other parts of the world, politicians faced calls for protection at home, which meant that few countries accepted the increased U.S. tariffs without retaliation.

The trade war caused trade volume to fall by more than 50 percent from its 1929 level within two years, and by 1933, world trade had fallen by about 70 percent.[10] Rather than create new jobs, the global trade war caused all countries' exports to decline. There were also political consequences to the trade war. According to the international economist Richard N. Cooper (1992, p. 2123):

What is less well known is the influence of the Smoot-Hawley Tariff and the sharp down-turn in world economic activity in undermining the position of internationally minded officials and politicians in Japan, in favor of an imperialistic nationalism which led to the Japanese invasion of Manchuria in late 1931, the real beginning of the Second World War.

Trade policies obviously do not excuse the atrocities of the military regimes in Japan and Germany that set off World War II. However, the circumstances leading up to World War II remind us that shifts in trade policies alter economic conditions in other countries, and these changes can have dire political consequences.

Another Policy Reversal

Four years after the Smoot-Hawley Tariff Act was passed, the United States took the lead in proposing negotiations to reduce tariffs among the major economies of the world. At the urging of President Franklin D. Roosevelt, the **Reciprocal Trade Agreements Act (RTAA)** was passed by Congress in 1934. This act marked the first time that the Congress of the United States, which has the constitutional power to determine trade policy, gave the executive branch of government the authority to negotiate tariffs without direct congressional participation. Congress did impose some severe limitations on U.S. trade negotiators, however. President Roosevelt had to promise that he would not agree to trade policies that "injured" U.S. industry, a promise that severely limited what U.S. negotiators could offer during trade negotiations.

As a further recognition of their inability to resist protectionist measures favored by special interest groups, Congress also agreed to give the president **fast-track authority**, which specified that any trade agreement that the executive branch negotiated would be given a straight up or down vote by Congress without the possibility of adding amendments or making changes to parts of the agreement. This would not only prevent specific exceptions and new trade restrictions from working their way back into law, but it would also make negotiations easier. Clearly, if everyone around the negotiating table knew that Congress would chop up the agreement afterward, foreign negotiators would offer fewer concessions and instead save some offers for later when Congress took up the measure. Executive-branch responsibility for carrying out negotiations and fast-track authority have been features of U.S. trade negotiations ever since.

It remains an open question whether giving the executive branch more responsibility for negotiating trade policy results in more or less protectionism. The immediate effect of the RTAA was small, but that should not be surprising given that by the mid-1930s the world was rapidly splitting into opposing political camps that would soon declare war on each other. Nevertheless, between 1934 and 1945 the United States negotiated thirty-two bilateral agreements to reduce tariffs.[11]

TRADE POLICY AFTER WORLD WAR II: THE GENERAL AGREEMENT ON TARIFFS AND TRADE

The real effects of the RTAA appeared shortly before the end of World War II. In recognition of the role that economic recession and unemployment played in permitting fascist politicians to come to power in Germany, Japan, Italy, and elsewhere, the United States and its allies set out to design a postwar economic system that would, they hoped, generate a rapid economic recovery. In July of 1944, one year before the end of World War II, delegates from all the Allied countries met at a U.S. resort hotel in Bretton Woods, New Hampshire, for three weeks to hammer out an economic blueprint for the post–World War II world. That blueprint included the formation of the **International Trade Organization (ITO)**, an organization that would encourage negotiations to reduce trade barriers and enforce international rules for trade. It was believed by most of the delegates that an expansion of international trade among all countries would reduce the likelihood of further war. However, when it came time to implement the agreement after the war, the United States had second thoughts about creating an international agency with the power to regulate countries' trade policies. The ITO was seen as a threat to national sovereignty. Instead, in 1947, a group of the largest Western economies negotiated the **General Agreement on Tariffs and Trade (GATT)**. This was not a formal organization but a treaty with rules to guide countries' international trade policies and international trade negotiations. The GATT was signed by twenty-three countries in 1947, and thirteen more had signed on by 1951; the thirty-six signatories included nearly all the major market economies.

The Key Provisions of the General Agreement on Tariffs and Trade

The GATT rules proved to be quite durable, and today they still serve as the basis of the international trade regime, formally adhered to by over 150 countries worldwide. The GATT specified, among other things, that:

- Countries commit to never raising their tariffs above initial 1947 levels.
- Countries can offer reductions in their limits on tariffs as concessions in order to induce other countries to reduce their tariffs.
- Signatories give all other signatories most favored nation (MFN) status.
- Countries do not discriminate between foreign and domestic goods and services once they have entered their country.
- Countries should use tariffs rather than quotas or other, less visible, **nontariff barriers** whenever possible.

The principle of establishing formal limits to protection recognized that a critical first step was to get countries to agree to never again raise tariffs and other trade barriers. Countries were thus required to submit a list of their current tariffs, quotas, and other trade barriers when they signed the GATT, and the tariff-equivalent levels of protection then became *limits* that could not be surpassed and would serve as the starting points in future negotiations to reduce tariffs. The MFN and the so-called **national treatment** clauses in the GATT reflect economists' dislike for discrimination. Different treatment of products from different trade partners or between foreign and domestic products is economically inefficient because, by diverting trade away from the lowest-cost producers, the world's allocation of resources would remain inefficient and the potential gains from trade would be reduced or eliminated altogether. Finally, tariffs were deemed preferable to other forms of protection because they were seen to be more visible and thus easier to monitor and negotiate. In fact, multilateral trade negotiations under the GATT have generally sought proportional reductions in tariffs for specific categories of products by all countries so that all countries would appear to be making the same sacrifice, proportionally, in lowering protection. As shown in Chapter 8, tariffs are likely to be less costly than quotas.

As noted in the previous chapter, the GATT has an escape clause that permits countries to temporarily increase protection if (1) imports are increasing very rapidly and (2) domestic industry is suffering severe hardship. This clause was included in the GATT at the insistence of the United States. Trade restrictions applied under this clause have, over the years, caused a lot of animosity between trade partners since interpretation of the clause is arbitrary. What constitutes a "severe hardship"?

The GATT Rounds

The GATT provided a framework within which countries were encouraged to participate in multilateral trade negotiations to reduce the high barriers to trade that had been erected during the first half of the twentieth century. The early GATT negotiating "*rounds*" produced only modest reductions in tariffs and other trade barriers. One can imagine how difficult it was for some fifty countries, each with a very different tariff structure and occupied with rebuilding its economy after World War II, to agree on some common form of trade liberalization that would inevitably affect the future structure of their economies.

In practice, the negotiating approach that worked best was to have all countries negotiate a common percentage reduction in tariff rates. For example, if Britain's ad valorem tariff on automobiles was 30 percent and the United States's rate was 10 percent, then the countries could agree to reduce automobile tariffs by, say, 50 percent; Britain's tariff would fall to 15 percent and the U.S. tariff would fall to 5 percent. This approach was successful because, first of all, all countries were perceived to be making comparable concessions. Second, no countries were able to increase the tariffs on particular goods.

Table 9.1 summarizes the tariff reductions of successive negotiating rounds under the GATT. Negotiations between small groups of countries after the RTAA and before the formal ratification of the GATT in 1947 had actually already lowered average tariffs by about one-third from the 1930 trade-war levels. The First Round, held in Geneva, Switzerland, reduced tariffs by another 21 percent on average, leaving average tariffs at about half of their post–Smoot-Hawley levels. Further negotiating rounds in the 1950s produced few additional tariff reductions, however.

The U.S. Reluctance to Open Its Market

Despite its claim that it favored free trade, the United States more often reverted to its traditional protectionist tendencies after the First Round of GATT negotiations, in 1947. The slow progress through the Dillon Round (1961–1962) was in large part due to severe restrictions that Congress and the president placed on U.S. trade negotiators. Not only did Presidents Harry S. Truman and Dwight D. Eisenhower, like President Franklin Roosevelt, promise "no injury" to any U.S. industry, but Congress grabbed back some of its power by insisting on formal procedures to determine injury. The U.S. Tariff Commission, a six-person committee appointed by the president, was created to formally determine whether imports were causing injury to U.S. industries. Congress passed a national security amendment to the Trade Agreements Act of 1955, which gave the U.S. administration nearly open-ended freedom to protect its industries from foreign competition. A provision to the 1955 act required the president to present a list of all products on which he planned to offer tariff reductions in upcoming GATT negotiations so that the Tariff Commission could determine beforehand how large the tariff cuts could be before they reached the so-called *peril point* at which U.S. industry would be injured. This provision severely tied the hands of U.S. negotiators. For example, when in 1960 the six countries that made up the European Economic Community offered to uniformly reduce all tariffs by 20 percent, the United States was unable to respond because the peril points had been estimated at far less than 20 percent for many industries.[12] Europe withdrew its offer, and the 1961–1962 Dillon Round accomplished only a very small decrease in overall tariffs.

Trade without Injury: Further Analysis

In terms of the Heckscher-Ohlin model, the no-injury rule effectively limits the gains from trade to the gains from exchange without specialization, as distinguished in Chapter 3. As illustrated here in Figure 9.5, the neoclassical model shows that the trade gains from exchange *without* specialization are positive but limited by the requirement that domestic production remain at the self-sufficiency production point A. Welfare gains are represented by the movement of the economy's consumption point from A in the indifference curve I_2 to the consumption point B on the indifference curve

Table 9.1

Tariff Reductions during the GATT Rounds

	% Cut in All Tariffs	Average Tariff Level as % of 1931 Level
Negotiations between 1934 and 1947		66.8
1st Round (Geneva, 1947)	21.1	52.7
2nd Round (Annecy, 1949)	1.9	51.7
3rd Round (Torquay, 1950–51)	3.0	50.1
4th Round (Geneva, 1955–56)	3.5	48.9
Dillon Round (Geneva, 1961–62)	2.4	47.7
Kennedy Round (Geneva, 1964–67)	36.0	30.5
Tokyo Round (Geneva, 1974–79)	29.6	21.2
Uruguay Round (Geneva, 1987–94)	38.0	13.1

Sources: Real Phillipe Lavergne (1983), *The Political Economy of U.S. Tariffs: An Empirical Analysis*, Ottawa, Canada: North-South Institute, pp. 32–33. Updated for Uruguay Round.

Figure 9.5   The Gain from Exchange without Specialization

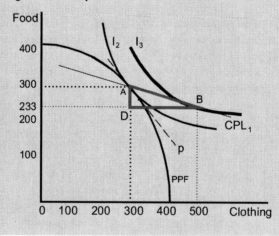

I_3. But, the gains from exchange without specialization are not as great as the welfare gains when exchange is also permitted to push the economy toward international specialization.

Figure 9.6 illustrates the gains from exchange that accompany an increase in specialization in accordance with comparative advantage. Production shifts from A to P, and real income rises to the consumption possibilities frontier CPL_2, which permits the economy to reach the consumption point C on the higher indifference curve, I_4.

The no-injury clause thus meant that the negotiators would have to seek only gains from exchange without specialization. Since that implied relative prices could not change much, U.S. negotiators could not offer very large reductions in tariffs and other trade restrictions. Consequently, other countries made few substantial counteroffers to reduce their trade barriers. Table 9.1 reveals the modest tariff reductions achieved in the 1950s.

This is not to say that the U.S. Congress was entirely wrong in imposing a no-injury clause on the executive branch's trade negotiators. More rapid trade liberalization after 1960, described next,

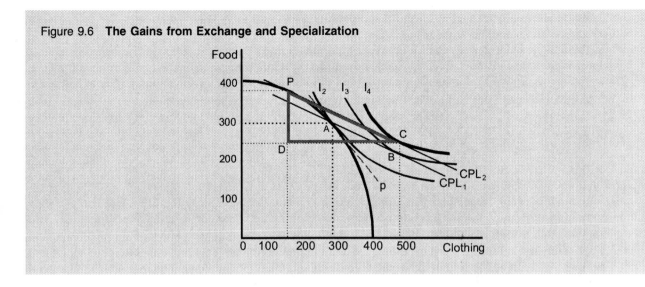
Figure 9.6 **The Gains from Exchange and Specialization**

would greatly accelerate the deindustrialization of the U.S. economy. The opening of U.S. borders to unrestricted imports of manufactures had, by 2000, resulted in the loss of tens of millions of manufacturing jobs, not to mention a sharp decline in real industrial wages.

The Emergence of the Stumps: Nontariff Barriers

In the mid-1950s, the U.S. textile and clothing industry faced strong competition from Japanese textile producers, and textile interests lobbied the U.S. government for protection. The Eisenhower administration responded in 1957 by formally urging Japan to "voluntarily" limit its exports of cotton textiles and apparel to the United States. This practice of pressuring foreign governments to "voluntarily" reduce exports by their countries' producers became a popular way for countries to *increase* protection for specific industries, and against specific foreign countries, without technically violating the GATT.

The political economy models discussed in the previous chapter shed light on why the Eisenhower administration, despite its stated goal of liberalizing world trade, would insist that Japan set a voluntary export restraint (VER) on textiles and clothing products. First of all, the adding machine model suggests that industries with large numbers of employees and votes are better able to lobby for protection. Also, the textile and clothing industries employed very large numbers of people in a small number of states and congressional districts. Thus, a few senators and representatives would fight very hard to protect them. The clothing and textile industries were mostly unionized, which meant that workers were already organized and able to avoid the free rider problem. On the other hand, consumers of clothing included the entire U.S. population, a very large group that was difficult to organize. Furthermore, because clothing generally did not account for a terribly large share of most people's expenditures, it was unlikely that consumers would mount opposition to the protection.

After Japanese VERs limited U.S. imports of Japanese cotton textiles and clothing, U.S. importers began bringing in textiles and clothing from other low-wage countries. The U.S. industry therefore resumed its lobbying activities, and in 1961 President John F. Kennedy pressured all the major exporting countries to sign the **Long-Term Arrangement (LTA) on Cotton Textiles**. This agreement set specific "voluntary" limits on exports to the United States on a country-by-country and product-by-product basis. The LTA tended to lock in market shares and prevent any competitive shifts among suppliers because its quotas were not transferable; if one country did not fill its entire quota for some specific item of clothing, it could not substitute other products or let other countries fill its unused allotment.

The LTA restricted only cotton goods, and it was not long before foreign producers started exporting wool and synthetic textiles and clothing to the United States. Further lobbying by the U.S. textile and clothing industries pushed the U.S. government to pressure labor-abundant developing countries into a new agreement covering all three categories of fibers: cotton, wool, and synthetics. In 1973, the **Multi-Fiber Arrangement (MFA)** agreement between the United States and nearly fifty developing countries went into effect. Like the LTA, the MFA specified exactly how much of each category of textiles and clothing each country could export to the United States. When the MFA came up for renewal in 1977, the European Economic Community joined the scheme, which meant that nearly all the world's trade in textiles and clothing had fallen under the elaborate country-by-country quota scheme of the MFA. Annual growth rates of developing-country exports of textiles and clothing to the United States and Europe were limited to between 2 and 4 percent, roughly in line with the growth of market demand. Arguably, comparative advantage would have resulted in labor-abundant countries gaining market share for products such as clothing. The LTA and MFA were in violation of the principles of the GATT, but because the quotas had technically been agreed to by exporting countries, albeit under the threat of even more restrictive trade barriers under the escape clause of the GATT, the MFA survived into the early twenty-first century.

The Kennedy and Tokyo Rounds

Interestingly, at the same time that President Kennedy was pressuring Japan to limit its clothing exports to the United States, he initiated a new round of multilateral trade negotiations. The creation of the European Common Market in 1958 presented the United States with a serious threat to its exports to Europe. With its common external tariffs and free trade among its six members, the Common Market was likely to increase imports from fellow members at the expense of outsiders like the United States. The Kennedy administration therefore sought to negotiate a reduction in the Common Market's external tariffs.

Kennedy understood that he would have to scrap the no-injury clause in order to offer Europe serious tariff reductions. The administration therefore came up with a program of **trade adjustment assistance (TAA)** to deal with the loss of production and jobs to foreign competition. The new program extended unemployment compensation to workers laid off by foreign competition, provided tax benefits to induce industries to modernize and switch production, and subsidized worker retraining. Kennedy was able to convince enough members of Congress, and their union supporters, to go along with substituting trade adjustment assistance for the no-injury clause in the fast-track authority. This marked an important shift in U.S. trade policy. The United States and its trade partners could now negotiate to exploit the gains from specialization. After President Kennedy's assassination, the round was named in his honor. As Table 9.1 shows, the **Kennedy Round** lowered average tariff levels to one-third their 1930s level.

In the early 1970s, the administration of President Richard M. Nixon organized another round of trade negotiations. Congress passed enabling legislation, the Trade Act of 1974, that again included a Trade Adjustment Assistance Program. The round ended up being named for the location of the opening meeting, Tokyo, even though most meetings were held in Geneva. Table 9.1 shows that at the end of the 1970s, average tariffs on manufactures were just 20 percent of their 1930 levels.

The Effectiveness of Trade Adjustment Assistance

An interesting question is why organized labor in the United States accepted trade adjustment assistance as a substitute for the no-injury clause it had hitherto insisted on. These programs actually provided little real assistance to workers who lost their jobs to import competition.

According to the Trade Act of 1974, workers who lost their jobs because of increased imports became eligible for job retraining, job search subsidies, relocation allowances, and even temporary income support. In practice, establishing eligibility was difficult. To gain certification, a group of three or more workers, their union, or a company official had to petition the U.S. Department of Labor, which was instructed to approve the petition only if it was determined that (1) workers had indeed been laid off, (2) sales and production had actually declined, and (3) imports contributed substantially to the layoffs. The assistance was to be administered by state agencies, and benefits varied quite a bit from state to state. In the most generous states, workers could apply for up to 104 weeks of retraining, up to one year of income support, and the full cost of searching for a job and moving outside their commuting area. In other states, however, procedures were difficult and benefits were substantially smaller.

A study by Leah E. Marcal (2001) found that, once the sample was adjusted for the self-selection bias that led workers with the worst job prospects to participate in the TAA program more often, training under the TAA program significantly increased workers' likelihood of getting new jobs, although wages were generally lower than in their old jobs. Most displaced workers did not use the benefits because they were unable to meet certification requirements or they found new employment. Whatever the merits of the TAA program, similar schemes are likely to be used in the future in order to induce potentially hostile groups to support, or at least not vigorously resist, trade liberalization. In 2001, President George W. Bush proposed wage insurance in order to blunt organized labor's opposition to his request for fast-track authority. The fast-track bill that became law in 2002 included a provision to pay workers a portion of their former income if they are laid off because of import competition.

Evaluating the GATT Rounds through Tokyo

The Kennedy and **Tokyo Rounds** dealt mainly with tariff rates on manufactured goods. While the negotiations reduced tariffs on manufactures to nearly zero in most countries by the end of the 1970s, the GATT rounds had ignored trade restrictions in several important economic sectors. The MFA and restrictions on clothing and textiles have already been discussed. Previous GATT rounds had also ignored the widespread protection of agricultural products by most developed countries. Since the early twentieth century, agriculture had been protected from imports in most developed, and many developing, economies. Also, international trade in services remained restricted by a whole range of regulations and protectionist measures. For example, air and sea transport were strictly regulated, the financial industries of most countries were usually closed to foreign competition, communications were nearly always required to be in the hands of national companies or government agencies, and public utilities were often regulated by government or were government-owned monopolies. Also, the early GATT rounds had ignored nontariff barriers to trade.

Nontariff barriers to trade, those "stumps" the Baldwins mentioned in the quotes at the start of the chapter, were being used more often to take the place of the permanent tariffs that the negotiators had agreed to lower. It is likely that the availability of alternative means to restrict imports permitted government officials to sign, and legislatures to ratify, major trade agreements to lower tariffs, knowing quite well that they could impose new targeted quotas, administrative procedures, anti-dumping duties, VERs, and other innovative forms of protection to keep important special interests and political donors happy. From a political perspective, the "stumps" were often more attractive because they could be tailored to the interests of specific industries and even specific firms. They were, therefore, often the target of intensive lobbying efforts and substantial campaign contributions for members of Congress.

THE URUGUAY ROUND

The last GATT negotiating round to be completed was the **Uruguay Round**, so named because the opening session was held in the Uruguayan seaside resort of Punta del Este in 1985. The Uruguay

Round was not completed as scheduled in December 1990; the negotiations stalled over trade restrictions on agricultural products, textiles, and services such as transportation and banking. After several extensions of the negotiations, a formal agreement was signed in April 1994, even though some parts of the negotiations were left to be completed later. The reason for the delay was that the Uruguay Round tried to do much more than had ever been attempted in a single round of trade negotiations.

More Players Put Everything on the Table

Many more countries participated actively in the negotiations. By the end of the round, there were 125 countries involved in at least some of the negotiating sessions. Most of these countries were developing economies whose immediate interests differed quite a bit from those of the more developed countries that had dominated the earlier rounds of GATT negotiations. The first two GATT rounds, in 1947, had included only twenty-three active participants. Even the very successful Kennedy Round in the 1960s had included just sixty-two of the world's nations. Finding common ground among 125 very different countries would clearly be more difficult. Dealing with the many new trade issues, such as agricultural protection, trade in services, and nontariff barriers, proved even more difficult.

The interests of the high-income industrialized economies and the many low-income developing economies were very different. Orthodox international economists never tire of pointing out that all countries gain from trade, no matter what their level of development, as their favored Heckscher-Ohlin model predicts. But developing countries, and some developed economies, were nevertheless leery of opening their borders to trade with countries at very different levels of economic development and technology. Some high-income countries feared that free trade with countries where labor costs were an order of magnitude lower would put many of their workers out of a job. Many developing countries entered the negotiations with some reluctance after having largely shunned free trade during the 1950s, 1960s, and 1970s and, in fact, having enjoyed record-high rates of economic growth. Some were afraid that current comparative advantage would condemn them to exporting mostly raw materials and agricultural products; they had all seen the statistical evidence showing that countries that export commodities grow more slowly.

Some developing countries were no doubt pressured to participate by the International Monetary Fund (IMF) after they sought assistance after defaulting on their foreign debt during the **1982 debt crisis**. Among the policy reforms the IMF insisted on was the opening to international trade and investment as a way to improve developing countries' ability to increase exports and repay foreign debts. The advisability of these policy shifts is still under debate, and it is a fact that very few of the Asian, African, and Latin American developing economies that agreed to drop their protectionist trade policies in favor of free trade grew as fast after 1982 as they did earlier. Many African countries ceased to increase their per capita output at all. In any case, the commitment of developing countries to free trade was tepid, at best, and this made expanded Uruguay Rounds much more difficult than the earlier rounds among more developed economies whose governments were more enthusiastic about eliminating trade restrictions.

The Uruguay Round did not accomplish everything that was on its agenda.[13] On the one hand, Table 9.1 shows that tariffs on industrial goods were indeed further reduced. It was also agreed to phase out the Multi-Fiber Arrangement by 2005. The "voluntary" quotas to tariffs were converted to equivalent tariffs over the ten-year phase-out period, after which the lowering of tariffs began.

On the other hand, little progress was made to eliminate barriers to trade in services. Most countries continue to regulate (or deregulate) their own financial industries. Trade in films and television programs remains restricted in many countries because, at the insistence of some major countries, trade in so-called *cultural* products, which included films, television programs, and recorded music, was simply not negotiated at all. Transportation services also remained protected in most countries. Recall from Chapter 4 that a recent World Bank study suggested that ending the protection of national shipping lines and the collusion among shipping lines could reduce ocean shipping costs by as much as one-third. This may explain why labor unions and key industries in a number of countries urged their governments to walk out on negotiations to eliminate the protection of international air and ocean shipping services.

The Uruguay Round made only a small dent in agricultural trade restrictions. Europe reduced some protections very modestly, and Japan agreed to allow foreign producers to supply 4 percent of its domestic rice requirements immediately and as much as 8 percent by 2005. Europe continued to protect its farmers as part of its programs to maintain rural communities and green areas in densely populated European countries. In the early 2000s, the United States sharply increased agricultural subsidies even as it insisted other countries cut their support for farmers and food production. Meanwhile, the European Union has responded to the wishes of the citizens of most member countries by continuing the ban on genetically engineered crops and seeds or meat from animals raised on growth hormones or antibiotics.

Intellectual Property Rights

Intellectual property rights, such as patents and copyrights, were a contentious issue during the Uruguay Round. The final agreement signed by all countries at the end of the round requires all countries to honor others' patents, copyrights, and trademarks. Ideas, information, processes, and artistic creations have become very valuable in modern economies. Recall how the Schumpeterian R&D model showed that costly innovation and R&D activity requires mechanisms through which innovators can recover the up-front costs. Private corporations carry out much of the applied research and technology development in the world, and they do so in part to take advantage of the property rights for ideas and technologies made possible by the enforcement of patents and copyrights. Transnational corporations lobbied hard to extend patent and copyright rules to all countries. The lack of enforcement of patents and copyrights in some countries essentially permits people and firms in those countries to avoid payment for the use of privately created ideas and technologies. It was argued that such "theft" effectively reduces the amount of innovation in the world and, hence, the rate of technological progress.

Most countries agreed to establish compatible patent and copyright laws by the year 2000 if they did not already have them in place. The lowest-income developing countries negotiated to delay the effective date of compliance until 2006. In fact, many developing countries argued that their acceptance of intellectual property rights was a "concession" that had to be balanced by developed countries' opening their markets to developing-country exports. They claimed that because most patents and copyrights are owned by firms and citizens in high-income developed countries, where higher levels of R&D spending and more formal innovative systems create most of the world's patented inventions and copyrighted artistic creations, uniform enforcement of intellectual property rights would result in large payments by developing countries to developed countries.

Replacing the GATT with the World Trade Organization

The other huge task before the Uruguay Round negotiators was the proposed establishment of the **World Trade Organization (WTO)**, a permanent organization to replace the informal organization and staff that oversaw the GATT. Recall that the GATT system as it existed in the 1980s offered no place where countries could effectively seek retribution for others' increasingly frequent violations of the GATT rules. A hearing process had been set up in Geneva, but parties to a trade dispute had to volunteer to participate, rulings were nonbinding, and they could be appealed indefinitely. The GATT, of course, was an agreement, not an organization that could serve as arbiter or judge in case of disputes. As mentioned earlier, the initial provision for an International Trade Organization with some power to rule on disputes, agreed to at Bretton Woods in 1944, was not put into effect, largely due to the objections of the United States and its fear of losing national sovereignty. Without an official enforcement mechanism, however, individual countries could retaliate against violators only by imposing restrictions of their own, but misunderstandings could easily cause such retaliation to escalate into a trade war. Worse yet, unfounded allegations of violations of the GATT were sometimes used as an excuse to reimpose trade restrictions negotiated away earlier.

By the 1990s, the lack of a permanent arbiter for the rising number of trade disputes was becoming a problem. The Uruguay Round did succeed in establishing a dispute settlement procedure within the WTO that can be petitioned by any country. It was set up to rule on cases within fairly tight time frames. This new dispute settlement procedure has been used more frequently than most proponents expected. Not all of the WTO's decisions have been accepted by the countries involved. For example, in 2001 the United States was ruled to be guilty of subsidizing exports by as much as $4 billion dollars per year. The United States ignored the ruling, and the European Union, which had lodged the complaint, was eventually authorized by the WTO to levy **retaliatory tariffs** against a set of U.S. products. In 2010, Brazil won a case on cotton subsidies against the United States. It remains to be seen whether the United States will eliminate the illegal subsidies. And the European Union is holding out against the insistence by the United States that it change its policy of restricting imports of hormone-fed U.S. beef. In this case, the WTO sided with the United States on technical grounds, but many scientists support the European Union's refusal to permit imports of genetically engineered foods, hormone-fed beef, antibiotics-fed pork, and other industrialized U.S. food products of dubious quality. Some have questioned whether the WTO can survive with the largest economies increasingly ignoring its decisions. Others argue for giving individual countries more leeway to restrict objectionable imports.

THE DOHA ROUND

In November 2001, delegates of the WTO's 142 member states agreed to launch another round of negotiations to address trade issues left undecided after the ratification of the Uruguay Round seven years earlier. Also on the agenda were some problems created by the Uruguay Round, such as developing countries' dissatisfaction over intellectual property rights and the lack of attention given to workers' rights and the environmental consequences of international trade. The 2001 meeting was held in Doha, the capital of the Persian Gulf country Qatar, a location chosen because it was difficult for protestors to travel to. A meeting of WTO delegates in Seattle, Washington, in 1999 had been disrupted by massive street protests that prevented delegates from getting to the conference hall. The negotiations were scheduled to be completed by January 1, 2005, but after several extensions the **Doha Round** came to a complete stop in 2010. It appears to have become the first post–World War II trade round to fail to reach an agreement.

The Agenda of the Doha Round

First on the agenda were further reductions in tariffs on industrial goods. Industrial goods tariffs had already been reduced from an average of about 40 percent in 1947 to less than 4 percent in 2001. An exception to the lowering of industrial tariffs were the new higher tariffs on textiles and clothing following the conversion of MFA quotas to their tariff equivalents. Developed-country textile industries continued to fight hard for protection, and the United States insisted at Doha that strong language about opening markets for textiles be toned down.

Agriculture was a contentious issue at the Doha meeting. France nearly prevented a final agreement by refusing to accept any mention of the elimination of farm subsidies. It finally agreed to language that called for negotiations "without prejudging the outcome" to open agricultural markets, reduce export subsidies, and substantially reduce trade distorting domestic subsidies. But while it took the brunt of the criticism from developing countries eager to gain access to the closed developed-country markets for food products, France was far from the only resister to opening its market. In fact, no other developed countries made significant concessions, and the United States blatantly increased its agricultural subsidies shortly after the Doha meeting, making it even more difficult for developing-country farmers to compete in the global food market.

Equally contentious was the issue of patents and copyrights. During the Uruguay Round, developing countries had agreed to a uniform system of patents and copyrights to be enforced worldwide. In Doha, developing countries, led by the delegation from India, fought hard to lighten the cost of **intellectual property rights** on developing countries. India and others claimed that the developed countries had not delivered on their promise to open markets to developing-country exports, which had been the quid pro quo for developing countries' acceptance of uniform patent and copyright enforcement. At the start of the Doha Round, developed countries agreed to let poor countries avoid the costs of patents on a wide range of medicines, but many developing countries refused to accept this partial concession as a substitute for developed countries' opening their markets to all developing-country products.

The United States made a major concession by agreeing to negotiate its controversial antidumping laws that essentially give the U.S. government great leeway to charge foreign suppliers with dumping and levy **countervailing duties**. The U.S. Congress had in fact prohibited U.S. negotiators from even putting this issue on the table, but because the wording of the Congressional resolution was fuzzy, the U.S. delegation made the concession anyway. Some commentators on the Doha meeting credited the U.S. delegation's willingness to negotiate antidumping rules as the critical factor in getting an overall agreement at Doha. The domestic U.S. politics surrounding this issue soon undermined later negotiations, however, and the credibility of the U.S. delegation was diminished.[14]

It was also agreed to bring WTO rules in line with those of multilateral environmental agreements. Trade barriers to environmental goods and services were to be eliminated, worldwide rules on eco-labeling of products were to be negotiated, and countries' rules on limiting trade in what they deem to be environmentally harmful products were to be harmonized. Services trade liberalization was also to be attempted again. In addition, competition rules and investment policies were to be harmonized, which left countries with the prospect of having to change their domestic antitrust laws, merger and acquisition laws, national ownership laws, and many other laws and regulations that have traditionally been seen as the domain of individual national governments. Finally, rules covering Internet commerce were to be negotiated. This latter issue is no doubt very important given the trends in online sales, but given the uncertainty of the technologies involved and the difficulty for any group to determine what its interests were, negotiations on Internet commerce were difficult to carry out. All in all, the issues that made it onto the agenda of the Doha Round were too much for the diverse WTO members—whose numbers had grown to 150—to deal with. With the United States not able to impose its will on the rest of the world, conflicting interests within the United States made preserving the status quo the default U.S. negotiating strategy.

The Role of the Developing Countries

The Doha Round was different from previous trade rounds in that developing countries had increased their international political clout, especially after the entry of China into the WTO and the strengthening of cooperation among the major developing economies. For example, countries like Brazil, Russia, India, China, and South Africa, known as the BRICS, increasingly present a unified front in international political and economic negotiations. At the same time, policy makers in developed countries face strong domestic political pressures for protection after years of job losses in traditional industries.

Developed-country protectionism is related to a fundamental characteristic of economic growth, namely that it, along with technological change, alters the structure of an economy. Some sectors grow faster than others, and some may even decline in size. Agriculture and the labor-intensive clothing and textile industries are among the sectors of the economy that shrink relative to others as an economy grows and standards of living rise. Income elasticity of demand is low for the products produced by these sectors, and the labor-intensive nature of some of these industries gives the comparative advantage to low-wage labor-abundant countries. Workers and owners of these declining sectors and industries naturally seek to avoid the inevitable adjustment costs, and they lobby very hard for protection. In short, the protected industries in developed economies are precisely the industries where developing countries enjoy their comparative advantages.

Developed-country protectionism shows up as **tariff escalation**, which is the practice of levying higher ad valorem tariffs for manufactured products than for raw materials. Table 9.2 shows that, at the start of the Doha Round, industrialized countries in Europe, North America, and the Pacific region levied tariffs on fully processed agricultural products that were, on average, almost three times as high as their tariffs on unprocessed agricultural products. But, interestingly, developing economies also engaged in tariff escalation; their tariffs on fully processed agricultural products were about 50 percent higher than their tariffs on unprocessed products. And, at all levels of processing, developing countries' tariffs were much higher than industrialized-country tariffs. Developing economies appeared to be preventing each other from specializing in higher-value products as well.

As of 2010, the now 150-plus members of the WTO had been unable to reach an agreement. The Doha Round is technically still underway, but negotiations are largely on hold. An agreement is, at the time of this writing, not in sight. The world thus continues under trade rules based on previous rounds.

THE SHIFT TO TRADE BLOCS

While the Doha Round has stalled in its tracks, individual countries have continued to negotiate regional trade agreements. These are various forms of preferential treatment among small groups of countries, in apparent violation of the GATT/WTO rules and the most favored nation principle. Liberalizing trade among only a small group of countries is not the same thing as liberalizing trade among *all* countries of the world. The formation of a regional free trade area may actually *reduce* welfare in one or more of the region's countries, something that according to orthodox models, cannot happen if free trade is established among all countries of the world. Furthermore, regional free trade areas will almost certainly reduce the welfare of those countries that remain outside the regional group. Nevertheless, regional free trade groups abound, and numerous regional trade agreements are being proposed by political leaders in all parts of the world.

Defining Regional Economic Integration

Technically, a group of national economies that eliminates barriers to the flow of goods and services between them but maintains restrictions on trade with other countries is called a **regional trade bloc**- or just a **trade bloc**. The act of forming a regional trade area is often referred to as "*regional economic integration.*" There are many degrees of regional economic integration, as summarized in Figure 9.7.

The lowest degree of economic integration is the formation of a **preferential trade area (PTA)**, which is an arrangement where the member countries agree to lower trade barriers within the group

Table 9.2

Tariff Escalation: 1994–2000

	Agricultural Products			Industrial Products		
	1st Stage	Semi-processed	Fully processed	1st Stage	Semi-processed	Fully processed
Less Developed Countries' Average Tariff	17.9	23.2	27.7	10.7	11.9	15.5
Industrialized Countries' Average Tariff	4.8	8.6	12.0	3.2	3.6	5.1

Source: World Bank website, www.worldbank.org, August 2, 2001.

Figure 9.7 **Levels of Regional Economic Integration**

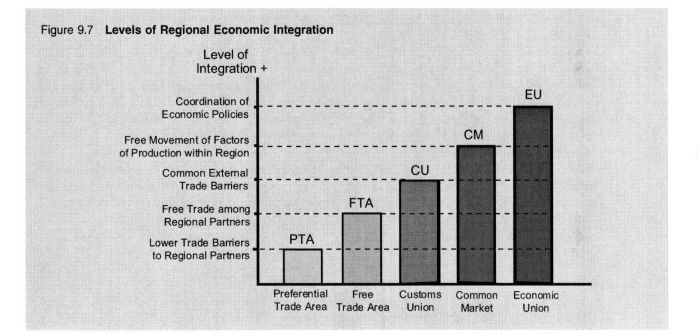

to levels below those erected against outside economies. A PTA does not imply the complete elimination of trade barriers. An example of a PTA is an agreement by which member countries halve the tariffs on products traded between themselves while maintaining existing tariffs on products from all other countries. The GATT/WTO specifically prohibits developed economies from forming a PTA, although it gives developing economies some leeway in forming regional groups that lower, but not completely eliminate, tariffs among themselves.

The GATT/WTO rules generally require that, if countries want to pursue some form of regional economic integration, they must at least form a **free trade area (FTA)**. An FTA completely eliminates all restrictions on the flow of goods between members of the trade bloc, while each country maintains its own restrictions on trade with outside countries. FTAs do not eliminate the need for maintaining customs operations for monitoring the borders between the member countries. In fact, the continuation of individual trade barriers against outside countries by each of the members creates an incentive for importers to import goods into the member country that levies the lowest tariff on the particular good in question and then transshipping it on to the other member countries. Each country's customs officials are faced with the difficult task of determining the origin of all goods crossing their borders so that they can levy tariffs or enforce quotas for the goods that originate outside the region. In today's global economy, many goods contain parts and components from other countries, and what does or does not constitute a national good is a very arbitrary determination. The **North American Free Trade Area (NAFTA)**, for example, sets specific percentages of the value of products that must be of regional origin for them to be considered as being regional rather than foreign and subject to tariffs.

A **customs union (CU)** is a regional arrangement in which the member countries agree not only to allow the free trade of goods between their economies, but also to negotiate a set of common tariffs and other trade restrictions against nonmember countries. The negotiations for a customs union are more difficult than for an FTA because tariff rates must be equalized among all countries. A CU may force some countries to make very substantial changes in their trade policies vis à vis outside countries. If a traditionally high-tariff country joins a low-tariff country to form a customs union, the negotiations will be especially difficult. The low-tariff country may have to raise its pre-CU tariffs against nonmember countries in order to match the common tariffs in effect for all CU members.

The next-highest form of economic integration is the **common market (CM)**, which allows for the free trade of goods among member countries, sets common tariffs and other trade restrictions against outside countries, *and* permits the free movement of factors of production. This last characteristic sets a CM apart from an FTA and a CU. A common market implies that labor, capital, and factor payments can move freely between member countries. The free movement of labor across borders often clashes with opposition to immigration by people who, justifiably or not, fear the social effects of foreigners taking up residence in their countries.

The highest level of economic integration is the **economic union (EU)**. An EU has all the characteristics of a CU *plus* members agree to a uniform set of macroeconomic and microeconomic policies. The fifty states of the United States are, in a way, an economic union, because goods and factors can move freely and economic policies are set by the national government and Federal Reserve Bank in Washington. Before its demise, the Soviet Union was an economic union. The European Union is the latest example of an economic union.

Trade Creation versus Trade Diversion

The two-country partial equilibrium model can be used to show how a trade bloc distorts international trade. Suppose that the international and domestic Homeland markets for hammers are as illustrated in Figure 9.8. Under free trade, Homeland would face the world price for hammers of p_w, but with a tariff levied equally on all trade partners the price rises to p_t. The various gains and losses are given by the deadweight loss triangles and the gray tariff box, and are in part effectively paid by foreign producers just as was shown in Chapter 8. Suppose now that Homeland forms a free trade area with the country of Neighbor, and both countries continue to levy tariffs on products from the rest of the world. Suppose also that Neighbor is not the world's lowest-cost producer of hammers; suppose, rather, that Neighbor's international supply curve for hammers is S_N, which lies above the world supply curve S_W. This translates into a free trade area price of p_f, which is higher than P_w but lower than the tariff-inclusive price of p_t. Homeland consumers will buy their hammers from Neighbor at the higher price p_f. And, the Homeland government earns no tariff revenue, part of which was effectively paid by foreign suppliers.

The free trade area results in more trade than would have occurred with a uniform tariff levied on all countries. The number of hammers imported is equal to $0f = ad$ rather than $0e = bc$, the quantity that would be imported in the case of the tariff levied on imports from all countries. Thus, the free

Figure 9.8 **Trade Diversion versus Trade Creation**

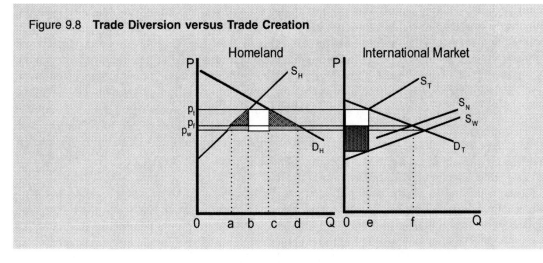

trade area *creates* additional trade. But the free trade area also *diverts* trade by inducing importers to buy hammers in Neighbor rather than from the world's lowest-cost suppliers. Whether a country gains from establishing a free trade area depends on whether the positive welfare effects of **trade creation** exceed the negative welfare **effects of trade diversion**. The expanded trade reduces the deadweight losses of the tariff by the checkered gray triangles. But, the **trade diversion** eliminates the government's tariff revenue, part of which was effectively paid by foreign suppliers. Also, Neighbor's hammers cost more. In Figure 9.8, the net welfare effect of a trade bloc depends on whether the gray checkered triangles, which represent the gains from **trade creation**, are greater than the hatched area in the right-hand diagram, which is loss from trade diversion. The latter area is the sum of the tariff absorbed by foreign suppliers and the price premium of Neighbor's hammers.

Regional Free Trade Is Not Necessarily Welfare Increasing

Compared to no trade at all, a trade bloc increases national welfare. If the tariff applied to all countries was prohibitive and prevented all trade, then freeing trade among a regional group of countries must increase welfare because there was no trade to be diverted and there can only be trade creation. On the other hand, if there is completely free trade in the world, and a group of countries forms a trade bloc that places tariffs on nonmembers' products, then there must be a loss of welfare. In this latter case, trade is already at a maximum and no further trade creation is possible; the trade bloc can only divert trade.

In the general case of a world with some trade restrictions, the formation of a trade bloc has ambiguous welfare effects. Whether a country gains from forming a free trade area depends on how close the costs of the regional free trade area partner are to the world's true low-cost producers. Conversely, the higher is the regional partner's international supply curve S_N compared to the world's international supply curve S_W, the less trade creation there is and the smaller are reductions in deadweight losses (gray checkered triangles) relative to the price premium of the Neighbor's products plus the portion of the tariff revenue that would have been absorbed by foreign suppliers (checkered rectangle). In summary, the common belief that regional economic integration represents a movement toward free trade that must be welfare improving for every participating country is simply incorrect. Only multilateral free trade guarantees positive net welfare gains in all countries.

CONCLUSIONS AND COMMENTS

As you will recall from the quotes at the start of this chapter, in 1970 the noted trade economist Robert Baldwin described emerging nontariff barriers as "stumps" in a drained swamp; his son,

Richard Baldwin, an equally accomplished international economist, observed in 2001 that the stumps were alive and growing! This remains true today. Among the stumps that are not only more visible with the declining overall level of tariffs but actually growing to replace lowered tariffs are the antidumping duties discussed in the previous chapter. Antidumping duties are usually country specific, sometimes even firm specific, and given their poorly defined procedures, they effectively give individual governments arbitrary power to restrict many imports. The fact that the Doha Round intended to negotiate uniform antidumping procedures promised to put some limits on this loophole in the WTO rules, but the failure of the round has meant that countries are free to expand use of antidumping procedures. The revived and growing stumps also include the trend toward regional trade agreements, such as common markets and free trade areas. The expansion of the European Union and the Free Trade Area of the Americas (FTAA) proposed in 2001 by U.S. president George W. Bush are examples of such regional agreements. The fact is that world trade is not necessarily well served by the formation of regional groups; such groups can distort trade flows because they liberalize trade among some countries but maintain trade barriers against others. A successful completion of the Doha Round would help diminish the emphasis on regional trade agreements and return the focus to worldwide trade liberalization and the negotiation of international agreements to deal with global issues. By the time you read this textbook, the prospects for expanding international cooperation and collective action to deal with international trade issues will, hopefully, look brighter than they do at the time of this writing.

CHAPTER SUMMARY

1. Political science provides a number of models that apply to trade policy, and these models suggest various reasons why tariffs, quotas, and other trade restrictions vary across time and countries. Especially relevant to modern democracies is the uninformed voter model, which shows that there is likely to always be some trade protection.

2. History shows that international trade policy has changed directions often as economic, social, political, and technological conditions have changed.

3. From 1500 through the early 1800s, many countries followed mercantilist policies that protected domestic industry and pushed governments to colonize foreign societies.

4. In the nineteenth century, Britain and much of the rest of Europe greatly reduced trade barriers by negotiating bilateral trade agreements that contained most favored nation clauses.

5. The United States, on the other hand, more often protected its new industries throughout the nineteenth century.

6. Around the middle of the nineteenth century, China and Japan were forced by European and U.S. military pressure to open their economies to trade.

7. After World War I, the world took a more protectionist turn that culminated with the U.S.'s infamous Smoot-Hawley Tariff in 1930, which triggered a trade war that caused international trade to decline drastically.

8. Four years later, the new Roosevelt administration and Democratic Congress reversed course with the Reciprocal Trade Agreements Act (RTAA).

9. Since World War II, the world has steadily reduced trade restrictions under the institutional rules of the General Agreement on Tariffs and Trade (GATT) and, in 1994, the World Trade Organization (WTO).

10. The details of the United States's post–World War II trade policy suggest that the country's commitment to free trade was not always strong; even as major GATT agreements to reduce trade barriers were being successfully negotiated, the United States increasingly used nontariff barriers to protect politically sensitive industries and interest groups.

11. The nine rounds of trade negotiations under the auspices of the GATT and WTO have been successful in reducing tariffs on most manufactured goods, but barriers remain on services and agricultural products, as well as the various innovative barriers such as sanctions, antidumping duties, and countervailing duties.

12. The Uruguay Round, which was concluded in 1994, addressed trade in agricultural products, trade in services, and intellectual property rights, but few changes were made. The Uruguay Round established the WTO as a permanent international institution to oversee trade rules and establish dispute settlement procedures.

13. In 2001 in Doha, Qatar, the 142 members of the WTO agreed to launch a new round of trade negotiations, whose agenda includes further tariff reductions on industrial goods, the liberalization of agricultural trade, the setting of rules for antidumping tariffs, and liberalization of services trade. As of 2010, the round was dormant, and there was little interest in completing the negotiations.

KEY TERMS AND CONCEPTS

adding machine model
common market (CM)
Corn Laws
countervailing duties
customs union (CU)
Doha Round
economic union (EU)
endogenous tariff model
fast-track authority
free rider problem
free trade area (FTA)
General Agreement on Tariffs and Trade (GATT)
Hanseatic League
intellectual property rights
International Trade Organization (ITO)
Kennedy Round
Long-Term Arrangement (LTA) on Cotton Textiles
median voter model
mercantilism
most favored nation (MFN)

multi-fiber arrangement (MFA)
multilateral trade negotiations
North American Free Trade Agreement (NAFTA)
political economy
preferential trade area
Reciprocal Trade Agreements Act (RTAA)
rent-evading activities
rent-seeking activities
retaliatory tariffs
Smoot-Hawley Tariff Act
Stolper-Samuelson theorem
tariff escalation
Tokyo Round
trade adjustment assistance (TAA)
trade blocs
trade creation
trade diversion
uninformed voter model
Uruguay Round
World Trade Organization (WTO)

PROBLEMS AND QUESTIONS

1. Using the political economy models, explain U.S. trade policy in the 1800s.
2. Explain why in the United States the debates about NAFTA and the WTO in the early 1990s attracted different levels of attention from the general public and special interests.
3. Can you think of any case of discrimination in international trade that results in an economic outcome that is less than the optimum that would result in the absence of discrimination?
4. When the U.S. delegation at the first meeting of the Doha Round agreed to include antidumping procedures on the agenda for further negotiation, many members of the U.S. Congress criticized the U.S. negotiators, claiming that the United States should never limit its ability to impose antidumping duties as it deems appropriate. Why would U.S. politicians want to maintain the arbitrary and discriminatory antidumping procedures that increasingly have been used to restrict U.S. imports?
5. As discussed in this chapter, the fundamental principles of the GATT specify that, among other things: (1) countries commit to keeping their tariffs below explicit limits; (2) countries can offer

reductions in their limits on tariffs as concessions in order to induce other countries to reduce their tariffs; (3) countries who sign the agreement agree to give all other signatories most favored nation (MFN) treatment; (4) countries do not discriminate between foreign and domestic goods and services, once they have entered the country and tariffs have been paid; and (5) countries should use tariffs rather than quotas or other, less visible, nontariff barriers if trade must be restricted. Explain why each of these provisions was inserted into the GATT.

6. Explain how the U.S. Congress's insertion of the no-injury clause into fast-track authority effectively prevented much progress in liberalizing trade in the 1950s.

7. Explain clearly, using a general equilibrium model of a small economy, why a country cannot gain the full welfare benefits from trade liberalization if it maintains a policy of no-injury to any of its industries.

8. Explain clearly how the political economy models discussed in the previous chapter help to explain why the Eisenhower administration, despite its stated goal of liberalizing world trade, insisted that Japan set a VER on textiles and clothing products.

9. Explain the rationale for the trade adjustment assistance (TAA) program, established in 1962 to replace the no-injury clause that had been part of all previous U.S. legislation on international trade.

10. Briefly describe the trends in tariff reductions during the latter half of the twentieth century, using Table 9.1 as your guide. Then, explain the major changes in the trends. For example, what led to the slow progress in the 1950s and the speed-up in tariff reductions after 1960? What led to the increase in the use of nontariff barriers in the 1980s and 1990s?

11. Why has international trade been taxed so often by governments throughout history?

12. Use the general equilibrium model of trade to illustrate both the long-run loss in welfare and the transitional costs of shifting resources as a result of the Smoot-Hawley Tariff of 1930, which very sharply reduced international trade. (Hint: Assume that trade shifts from the free trade equilibrium to the self-sufficiency equilibrium, and show first the transition path and then the long-run move from P to A, similar to the description of the transition to free trade in the small country model of trade in Chapter 3.)

13. Explain why a shift to free trade necessarily implies injury to some industries. (Hint: Use the general equilibrium model of trade and the section "Trade without Injury: Further Analysis.")

14. Explain why the threat of potential antidumping duties probably has much higher costs than does levying antidumping duties.

15. Write in the five types of regional economic integration in order of their degree of integration, from the least integrated to the most integrated. In the space to the right describe the principal features of each category of regional economic integration:

Type of integration: Key Features:

1. _____
2. _____
3. _____
4. _____
5. _____

16. Explain why the welfare effects of a regional trade bloc, such as a regional free trade area, are ambiguous. (Hint: Use a partial equilibrium model such as Figure 9.8.)

17. Explain fast-track authority. Why is it important for negotiators to be given fast-track authority by legislatures?

18. Explain why the most favored nation principle is an important element of any trade agreement.

19. Describe how the no-injury clause limits the potential gains from trade. Also, describe how the clause prevented the United States from taking a leadership role in the GATT multilateral trade negotiations during the 1950s. How did the Kennedy Round circumvent this obstacle?
20. Carefully illustrate how a regional free trade area both creates trade and diverts trade. Use the diagrams developed in this chapter.

NOTES

1. See Kenneth J. Arrow (1963).

2. This model may help to explain why politicians often avoid committing to specific policies that benefit some people at the expense of others.

3. Ross Perot's opposition to NAFTA as his main political plank in the 1992 U.S. presidential election campaign was a notable exception to the rule.

4. See Rigoberto A. Lopez (1989).

5. This possibility is discussed by John T. Wenders (1987).

6. See, for example, Barry Baysinger, Robert B. Eckelund, Jr., and Robert D. Tollison (1980).

7. Described in detail by William D. Grampp (1987).

8. A.G. Kenwood and A.L. Lougheed (1992), p. 71.

9. Based on data from Angus Maddison (1991).

10. Charles P. Kindleberger (1973).

11. John H. Jackson (1992), p. 31.

12. Peter B. Kenen (1967), p. 43.

13. Thorough descriptions of the results of the Uruguay Round are provided by John Whalley and Colleen Hamilton (1996) and by the General Agreement on Tariffs and Trade (1994).

14. Helene Cooper and Geoff Winestock (2001), "Poor Nations Win Gains in Global Trade Deal as U.S. Compromises," *Wall Street Journal,* November 15; Guy de Jonquières (2001), "All-Night Haggling in Doha Ends in Agreement," *Financial Times,* November 15.

CHAPTER 10

International Trade Policy: A Holistic Perspective

> The idea that some form of protection is in order to enable a country to establish its place in the world economy, in order to establish an economy that is flexible and resilient, is a fundamental idea.
>
> —Henry Bruton (1989)

Our discussion of international trade in Part Two and the history of trade policy in the previous chapter make it clear that international trade policy needs to be analyzed from a holistic and heterodox perspective. The static neoclassical analysis detailed in Chapter 8 is useful for analyzing some of the short-run costs and benefits of trade policies, but in the long run, trade policy has much broader and often very different consequences than those that are predicted by the static and narrow neoclassical models.

Recall from Chapters 5, 6, and 7 that once the Heckscher-Ohlin (HO) model's assumptions of perfect competition and increasing costs are dropped, many different logical conclusions about international trade are possible. For one thing, increasing returns to scale explain why most trade occurs between similar high-income economies rather than the most different economies. Also, because perfect competition breaks down when there are increasing returns to scale, it is obvious why international trade is mostly conducted by monopolistic producers that charge prices that exceed their production costs. Consequently, the divergence of costs and prices generates international trade patterns that differ from those predicted by the Heckscher-Ohlin model. The distribution of the gains and losses from opening an economy to foreign trade also differs from the patterns predicted by the neoclassical HO model and its factor price equalization theorem and Stolper-Samuelson theorem. These deficiencies of the neoclassical paradigm make it inappropriate not only for analyzing international trade, but also for analyzing international trade policy.

Perhaps most damaging to the orthodox neoclassical paradigm and the HO framework is the rapid concentration of business activity into transnational corporations (TNCs) during the twentieth century. Economies of scale in production, aggressive marketing, research, and distribution, and TNCs' influence on international trade policy have created a real world that does not match the assumptions of the neoclassical paradigm. The growth of TNCs links international trade to international investment, market structures, and institutional factors that are not covered in the HO model of trade. TNCs have been able to increase profit margins and gain income at the expense of consumers and workers, thus altering the distribution of gains from international trade. Many heterodox economists argue that trade policy and the international institutions that help shape national trade policies have been seriously biased toward assisting the growth of TNCs.

The dominance of TNCs in international trade has an important implication for the study of trade policy: TNCs increasingly directly influence policy makers and the trade policies they institute. Wealth and political power have always been closely correlated, of course. The liberal perspective on social policy that emerged from the Enlightenment, and which so strongly influenced the field of international economics, was fundamentally the rejection of wealth-based politics as usual. The concentration of economic power in the hands of TNCs, and their political influence, suggest that the link between wealth and economic policy is still as tight as ever, however. In international economics, this link between wealth and political power has been disguised by the neoclassical paradigm's conclusion that international trade is always beneficial for human welfare. That is, according to this paradigm, because international trade enhances human welfare, and TNCs seem to expand international specialization and trade, they too must have a positive effect on human welfare. What is surprising, however, is how few mainstream international economists have followed the liberal tradition and examined the broader economic and social changes, such as the concentration of economic power in TNCs, that have accompanied the growth of international economic activity.

This chapter seeks to bring our understanding of international trade *policy* in line with heterodox perspectives of international trade in general. We begin by examining colonialism, an important economic system in which commercial interests captured government power in order to use military force to support international trade and investment. Only heterodox perspectives on international trade, which suggest that there are many circumstances under which unrestricted international trade harms human welfare, can adequately analyze colonialism and twentieth-century trade policy in developing countries impacted by the colonial experience.

MERCANTILISM AND THE COLONIAL SYSTEM

The Heckscher-Ohlin model suggests that the gains from international trade are greatest between countries that are very dissimilar in terms of their resources endowments, their technology, or their consumer preferences. In terms of the HO model presented in Chapter 3, the improvement in human welfare from trade is greatest the more different are countries' production possibilities frontiers and indifference curve schedules. This means that trade between highly developed and poorly developed countries provides the greatest gains. However, Chapter 4 pointed out that most international trade takes place between countries with relatively similar, high levels of income, technology, and consumer preferences. Alternative models that explicitly recognize economies of scale and imperfect competition, therefore, do a better job of explaining the world's trade patterns. Heterodox economists, especially those who favor a historical perspective, explain why the *unequal exchange* between dissimilar trade partners—for example, rich and poor countries, or militarily powerful and weak countries—brought about very unequal shares of the gains and losses from international trade.

Colonialism Is a Form of Mercantilism

When Adam Smith (1776 [1976]) was writing about why free trade is beneficial for human well-being, most international trade was being carried out within colonial empires among very unequal trading partners, and trade was subject to many restrictions imposed by the colonial governments. The government-sponsored capture and occupation of foreign countries by Europe's monarchies that started some five hundred years ago is what is usually referred to as **colonialism**, but colonialism is really a more general arrangement in which one party to the exchanges uses the coercive power of government to extract disproportionate gains at the expense of other trade partners. Rome was a colonial power, as was the Soviet Union in Eastern Europe.

Charles Wilson (1963, p. 26) describes **mercantilism** as "all the devices, legislative, administrative, and regulatory, by which societies still predominantly agrarian sought to transform themselves into trading and industrial societies." Recall also from the previous chapter Robert B. Eckelund and Robert Tollison's (1981) description of mercantilism as the "supply and demand for monopoly rights through the machinery of the state." That is, a mercantilist society is an active rent-seeking one in which commercial interests bid for, and gain control of, government mechanisms that provide them with special privileges and monopoly powers over sectors of the economy. In 1500s Europe, mercantilism solidified the control of national monarchs over the local power bases that remained from earlier feudal societies. When these alliances between central governments and commercial interests were extended overseas, mercantilism became colonialism, which was essentially the joint government-private conquest of foreign territory and resources.

Smith [1776 (1976)] famously railed against "the mercantilists" for their protectionist trade policies designed to spur exports and deter imports. His description of mercantilism in such simple terms let him show his logical argument for free trade in a more favorable light. In fact, European countries were content to run trade deficits, and European countries regularly used gold and silver to cover their trade deficits with the Far East, as documented by Timothy Brook (2008). Smith also failed to directly equate mercantilism and colonialism, but he did devote many pages to describing colonialism and comparing the colonial trade relationships to his ideal of free trade.

The Case of Brazil

It is always risky to generalize from different historical events, but there were many common characteristics across the colonialization episodes carried out by the European powers after 1500. In each case, European powers sent their navies and armies overseas to pursue the commercial interests of their elites. For illustration, we focus below on the very interesting case of Brazil. After its "discovery" by the Portuguese explorer Pedro Cabral in 1500, Brazil's economic growth and social development were shaped by international trade carried out under a colonial regime.

Cabral claimed Brazil as a Portuguese territory in 1500 after having been blown off course while on a government-sanctioned voyage to sail around the Horn of Africa and trade for spices in India. Government funding for such trips was usually granted by the Portuguese monarch on the condition that the Crown be paid a substantial tax on the eventual profits of the venture. The Crown awarded merchants monopoly privileges in overseas territories and provided the navies and armies to protect the merchants in those territories. In the fifteenth century, King Henry the Navigator of Portugal had taken an especially active role in promoting overseas commercial ventures. The monarchs of other European countries, such as Spain, England, France, and Holland, similarly awarded privileges to their merchants to conduct overseas ventures in exchange for a share of the earnings.

Portugal was a small country, and it initially sought trading posts in Africa and the East Indies rather than control of overseas territories. This strategy did not work well in Brazil, however, because there were few products to trade for in the vast jungle territory. Brazil's most valuable early resource export was brazilwood, which was processed to produce a red dye, but it ultimately proved to be of little value beyond giving the new territory its name. The Portuguese, therefore, adopted what was quickly becoming a common colonization strategy: it awarded large tracts of land (*capitanias*) to Portuguese adventurers (*donatários*) willing to go to Brazil, invest in their properties, and attract colonists. In exchange for the land titles and nearly free rein in the allotted lands, the Crown demanded a share of the revenues generated by the private investments. According to William P. Glade (1969, p. 156), this system made early Brazilian colonization "a business venture, combined with aspects of private subgovernment." A small local elite came to dominate Brazil's society and economy.

The donatarios introduced new crops from elsewhere in the Portuguese empire, such as Middle Eastern sugarcane, which had already been cultivated profitably in the Portuguese Azores and Cape Verde islands in the Atlantic. Sugar grew well in Brazil, but it was a labor-intensive crop most efficiently produced on large plantations. Labor was in short supply in the capitanias because there were few Portuguese settlers, the introduction of European diseases had killed the greater portion of the natives, and those remaining had fled into the interior of the huge country to escape the disease and hard labor. Brazilian landowners began importing slave labor from Portuguese outposts in Africa, thus initiating the Atlantic slave trade. By 1600, Brazil was the world's leading sugar producer and the largest importer of African slaves. Slaves greatly outnumbered the Portuguese in Brazil.

Brazilian sugar production was centered in what is today northeast Brazil, the region where Cabral first touched land and where the early capitanias were established. Brazilian plantation society was characterized by huge income inequalities and little lasting economic development, although substantial wealth was accumulated by the plantation owners. Brazilian sugar production stagnated in the late seventeenth century when other European colonial powers introduced sugar to their own colonies in the Caribbean, the Americas, and Africa. Most colonial powers limited foreign trade to their own colonies whenever possible. Unfortunately for Brazil, its mother country, Portugal, offered a very small market for sugar. Its sugar production center stagnated economically and Brazil's northeast remains the poorest region of the country today.

Around 1700, gold and diamonds were discovered in the interior of Brazil, in a region that is today the state of Minas Gerais. A gold rush quickly developed, and nearly half of the world's output of gold during the eighteenth century came from Minas Gerais. Some sugar planters from the northeast moved their slaves to Minas Gerais to work in the gold mines, but the region was mostly settled by eager new arrivals from Portugal and elsewhere. The gold rush generated more diverse economic development than the sugar plantations did because gold mining was carried out more often on individual operations. Miners' demand for food and transportation stimulated farming and the raising of mules to carry supplies in and products out of the interior region to the coastal city of Rio de Janeiro.

The gold boom led to a more direct Portuguese government presence in Brazil. To facilitate tax collection and reduce evasion, Portuguese bureaucrats and soldiers intentionally limited transport to a single mule trail between Rio and Minas Gerais. Also, all ships leaving Brazil had to sail together in convoys accompanied by government escorts back to Portugal, allegedly for protection against pirates but mostly to prevent tax evasion. All trade from Brazil was also required to pass through Portuguese merchants authorized by the Portuguese royal government. Of course, smuggling occurred, but the economically oppressive measures mostly fueled resentment of the Portuguese Crown among the miners, farmers, and local Brazilian business elite. The first open uprising against the Portuguese colonial government occurred in Minas Gerais in the late 1700s. It was not easy for a small country like Portugal to colonize and control a large territory like Brazil.

It was these types of mercantilist policies that Smith criticized in *The Wealth of Nations* (1776 [1976]). His calls for free trade were largely intended to break up the trade monopolies established during colonial times. In the case of Brazil, the spread of slavery, the awards of huge territories to the privileged, the regulation of trade, and the inefficient procedures to ensure tax collections did not maximize the benefits from trade or spread the diminished benefits equitably among all concerned.

Mercantilism after Brazil's Independence

Brazil gained a sudden increase in stature when, in 1807, the Portuguese royal court fled Napoleon's Iberian invasion and moved to Brazil, making its small capital city, Rio de Janeiro, the de facto capital of the entire Portuguese empire. When the Napoleonic wars ended and the Crown returned to Lisbon and tried to restore Brazil's status as nothing more than a distant colony, the elite families that held an estimated two-thirds of Brazil's wealth at the start of the nineteenth century declared independence. The Brazilian elite, which was an integral part of the Portuguese mercantilist-colonial system, opted to establish a monarchy rather than a republican form of government; in contrast, nearly all of the newly independent former Spanish colonies in Latin America had chosen republican governments. The Brazilian elite that headed the new government convinced the son of the Portuguese king to remain as emperor of Brazil. In a clear show of who held power in the new country, the elite quickly replaced that first emperor, Dom Pedro I, with his five-year-old son in 1831 when the former remained too loyal to Portugal. An appointed regent ruled in the young emperor's place until 1840, when Dom Pedro II assumed the Brazilian throne. Brazil remained a monarchy and did not abolish slavery until 1889. Throughout this period the country was effectively ruled by a somewhat shaky coalition of elite commercial and agricultural families, a type of plutocracy. A republican form of government was formally adopted in 1889 after years of debate within the elite about slavery and monarchy. The shift in government also came about because of the growing economic influence of the new commercial elite, the coffee barons.

This first century of Brazilian independence brought little change from colonial times. As has so often happened in countries that formally shed their colonial masters, the elite that had gained economic wealth during the colonial era ended up effectively governing the country after independence. The distribution of income and wealth remained essentially the same. Commerce, shipping, and banking had been monopolized by chartered enterprises, and these enterprises usually remained in the hands of the privileged elite after independence. Hence, the highly unequal societies, created during the colonial era remained in place in the nineteenth century in Latin America.

The Coffee Economy

Coffee had been introduced to Brazil from the Middle East early in the eighteenth century. Coffee trees require a temperate climate but cannot withstand frost. Such a delicate combination of cool but never cold weather is often met in the higher altitudes of tropical countries, and the vast coastal highlands of Brazil fit that description perfectly. Coffee production and exports grew rapidly with worldwide demand from the increasingly numerous and wealthy middle-class consumers in Europe and the United States. No longer colonists, Brazilian coffee producers could trade with everyone. Also, the iron steamship transformed ocean transportation, cutting costs by over 70 percent between 1840 and the early twentieth century.[1] Coffee cultivation in Brazil spread south from the Paraíba River valley near Rio toward the state of São Paulo and westward into the former mining region of Minas Gerais. The port of Santos, just below the extensive São Paulo plateau, became the world's largest coffee port.

The coffee boom put huge amounts of capital into the hands of the coffee farmers, most in the interior region of São Paulo. Coffee farming required large amounts of labor, and because the importation of slaves was no longer permitted by Brazil's largest trade partner, Great Britain, Brazil instead attracted large numbers of immigrants from Portugal, Italy, Spain, Germany, and most other parts of Europe. The southern part of Brazil, from São Paulo to the Uruguayan border, became a melting pot of European immigrants, augmented by later immigrations from Japan and the Middle East as well as continual internal migration of Brazilians from the relatively poor northeast region. British investment in railroads followed, and rail lines soon fanned out from Santos to the city of São Paulo and the interior of the state. By 1900, Brazil produced half the world's coffee, and coffee exports accounted for 80 percent of the country's export earnings.

The substantial wealth accumulation by São Paulo coffee producers funded Brazilian industrialization. Already in the first decade of the twentieth century, a growing immigrant population created a market for locally produced textiles, clothing, footwear, woodworking, and processed foods. Most new industries were established in the city of São Paulo. However, coffee's role as an engine of growth in Brazil was diminished by the volatility and decline of coffee prices as other countries, such as Colombia and Mexico, expanded production. The politically powerful coffee barons pushed the Brazilian government to guarantee prices and purchase excess stocks. Coffee prices rose in the 1920s as the world economy recovered from World War I, but collapsed by two-thirds at the start of the Great Depression. Brazil's predictable political response to the 1930 coffee bust would radically change the process of economic development in Brazil.

In summary, during the nineteenth century Brazil's international trade and its integration into the world economy accelerated through the expansion of coffee production in the southern part of the country. A new class of merchants arose that gained domestic political power from the huge profits derived from coffee exports. The coffee farmers used their political clout to push the government, and the taxpayers, to protect them from adverse climate and market conditions. This mercantilistic commerce-government collaboration enabled the country to fund much of its early industrialization from export earnings rather than from foreign borrowing.

From Accidental to Planned Industrialization

Brazilian economic historian Celso Furtado (1963) estimated that Brazil's terms of trade fell by about 50 percent at the start of the Great Depression, which meant that 1930 exports of coffee and other primary products purchased only half as many real imports as in 1929. Brazil was able to balance its balance of payments (see Chapter 11) only by severely devaluing its currency and making imports much more expensive relative to domestic products. Exactly as exchange rate theory predicts, this shift in relative prices of imports to domestic products led domestic consumers to substitute domestic goods for foreign goods. Brazilian trade thus remained in balance despite the collapse of export earnings because it suddenly became economical to produce many products in Brazil that, before 1929, were imported from abroad.

The boom in Brazilian industrial production was only partially caused by the devaluation's effect on import prices, however. Domestic demand was also stimulated by the Brazilian government's very expansionary fiscal and monetary policies. These policies were actually an unintentional by-product of traditional domestic mercantilist rent seeking. When coffee prices fell sharply, the Brazilian government responded to coffee barons' demands for help by providing huge subsidies that essentially maintained domestic coffee farmers' incomes despite the fall in international prices. To pay for these subsidies, the Brazilian government printed money and substantially increased the domestic money supply. Therefore, in 1930 Brazil unintentionally carried out precisely the expansionary monetary and fiscal policies later advocated by John Maynard Keynes (1936) to reduce the Depression's high unemployment in Britain, the United States, and elsewhere. In the words of Furtado (1963, p. 212):

> It is therefore quite clear that the recovery of the Brazilian economy which took place from 1933 onward was not caused by any external factor but by the pump-priming policy unconsciously adopted in Brazil as a by-product of the protection of coffee interests.

The year 1933 marked the deepest point of the Great Depression in most developed countries of the world, but that year industrial production in Brazil had recovered its 1929 level. By 1937, Brazil's industrial production was 50 percent greater than it was in 1929, and overall real domestic product was 20 percent greater in 1937 compared to 1929, quite a feat in the 1930s. The new industries were located mostly in the urban area around the city of São Paulo, where the coffee wealth was concentrated.

The good economic performance during the 1930s influenced Brazilian policy makers in the 1940s. World War II increased demand for raw materials, and Brazil's exports to the United States expanded rapidly. Even after the war, demand for Brazil's traditional exports was strong, fueled by the world economy's recovery from the war. The value of the Brazilian currency had to rise, relative to other currencies, for its balance of payments to remain in balance. This rise in the value of the currency would change the relative prices of domestic goods versus foreign goods, this time in the opposite direction from what had occurred in the 1930s. The government and the many new industrialists feared that the process of import substitution would be reversed. There was concern that the many new industries would be unable to survive a cheapening of imports from the traditional industrial countries.

Lobbied by the new industrialists and the labor unions whose members worked in the new industries, the Brazilian government decided to institute trade restrictions to offset the improved terms of trade. These explicit trade barriers after World War II were very different from the effective trade barrier provided by the general depreciation of Brazil's currency in the 1930s. In 1948 Brazil passed a **law of similars**, which authorized a complete ban on all imports of "similar" products as soon as any domestic firm could show it was capable of supplying a particular product to the domestic market.

Under this law, any product, whether it cost twice as much or five times as much to produce in Brazil as it did in the rest of the world, would be protected. The law of similars also provided permanent protection, unlike an exchange rate that is subject to future change. Thus, the law of similars and the broad protection it offered any and all domestic producers went well beyond the traditional **infant industry argument for protection**, which justified only temporary protection of a specific industry that could reasonably be expected to gain a comparative advantage in free markets after a period of protection. The law of similars effectively severed all links between comparative advantage and domestic production. It awarded domestic producers near-permanent subsidies by Brazilian consumers, who were forced to pay the high prices charged by producers protected from foreign competition. Economists are still questioning whether this was a good policy choice.

The Law of Similars and the Infant Industry Argument

Brazil was certainly not the first to embrace the idea of protecting new industries from foreign competition. The United States and Germany, two of the world's leading industrial economies, had built their industries behind protectionist trade barriers in the nineteenth century. The United States and Germany had openly appealed to the *infant industry* argument for protection. That argument had been elegantly presented as early as 1791 by Alexander Hamilton, the first U.S. Secretary of the Treasury, in his *Report on Manufactures*. The argument was further legitimized in the mid-1800s when John Stuart Mill included it in his popular economics textbook:

> The only case in which, on mere principles of political economy, protective duties can be defensible, is when they are imposed temporarily (especially in a young and rising nation) in hopes of naturalizing a foreign industry, in itself perfectly suitable to the circumstance of the country. The superiority of one country over another in a branch of production often arises only from having begun it sooner. There may be no inherent advantage on one part, or disadvantage on the other, but only a present superiority of acquired skill and experience. A country which has this skill and experience yet to acquire, may in other respects be better adapted to the production than those which were earlier in the field. . . . A protecting duty, continued for a reasonable time, will sometimes be the least inconvenient mode in which the nation can tax itself for the support of such an experiment. (1848, p. 922)

Mill qualified his endorsement of infant industry protection in the same chapter of his textbook, however:

> But the protection should be confined to cases in which there is good ground of assurance that the industry it fosters will after a time be able to dispense with it; nor should the domestic producers ever be allowed to expect that it will be continued to them beyond the time necessary for a fair trial of what they are capable of accomplishing.

The argument that there must be a reasonable probability that an industry will become profitable in the future for it to be awarded protection has come to be known as the Mill criterion. Note that Brazil's law of similars does not meet the Mill criterion, even though the *infant industry argument* for protection was often brought up to justify the new import law.

Later economists distinguished additional assumptions that implicitly lie behind the infant industry argument, namely that (1) there is some kind of **learning-by-doing** process that relates production costs to accumulated output, (2) only domestic production experience can help the learning process because technology and know-how cannot be acquired from abroad (technology is country specific), and (3) know-how and technology are industry specific, so that they cannot be acquired from other sectors of the economy. Despite these qualifications, it is nevertheless quite possible that firms or whole sectors of developing economies qualify as *infant industries*. Technology does not move freely from one country to another, and there are costs to applying and adapting foreign technologies. The use of trade restrictions to protect and nurture new industries is further justified in developing countries, where the financial sector is often not well developed or able to provide funds to new industries over long periods. There may be external benefits that cannot be captured by the individual owners or the financial sector. Finally, governments may not have well-run tax systems that can cover the costs of direct subsidies to infant industries. Hence, the indirect method of having consumers of imports effectively pay for the temporary cost of protection may be the most efficient way to bring a potentially profitable infant industry into existence.

A group of developing economies is currently pushing for amending World Trade Organization (WTO) rules to permit low-income economies to protect their infant industries, as they were indeed permitted to do before the WTO rules came into effect after 1994. Under the General Agreement on Tariffs and Trade (GATT), the set of international trade rules that preceded the more formal current regulatory framework of the WTO (see Chapter 9), developing countries were given great leeway to protect their economies from import competition. Developing-country governments often point out that today's leading industrial economies, the United States, Germany, and Japan, all protected their industrial sectors during the formative years with a wide array of tariffs, quotas, regulatory restrictions on imports, and strong appeals to nationalism.

Interpreting Brazil's Colonial and Postcolonial Experiences

Brazil's choice of explicit trade restrictions after World War II was not arrived at casually or accidentally. Of course, domestic politics played a role, but the country's colonial and postcolonial experiences weighed heavily in the political process that led to the policy shifts. A feature of colonialism that did not escape many Brazilian intellectuals was that trade relationships did not become more fair or equitable when formal colonial links were severed. Brazil, and virtually all other colonies and former colonies, remained exporters of raw materials and importers of industrialized products even after political independence. There is evidence suggesting that trade and investment between European countries and their colonies had not been beneficial for the colonies.[2] When per capita incomes rose persistently in Europe and the United States during the 1800s and early 1900s, the developing countries and colonies remained poor. This is the period when incomes across countries diverged sharply. In the case of Brazil, only when it effectively cut itself off from international trade by means of its 1930 devaluation did it experience rapid industrialization. It moved away from its colonial role of supplier of raw materials to one of the world's more industrialized countries.

The colonial and postcolonial experiences provided evidence to support a school of economists who called for developing countries to sever all economic ties with their former colonial masters. This interpretation of colonialism came to be known as **dependency theory**. This perspective was developed by the German-born and American-educated economist Andre Gunder Frank (1967) who built on the works of Karl Marx, the socialist economist Paul Baran (1957), and numerous Marxist Latin American economists.

Frank challenged the common perception that developing countries were in a stage of development that the more developed countries had passed through earlier. He claimed that poor countries were in a unique, unprecedented state, which he called "**underdevelopment**," that no country had experienced before. Developed countries had never passed through a stage during which they had had to coexist with much wealthier and more highly industrialized countries and to play the role of subservient provider of those countries' economic needs. According to Frank (1967, p. 100):

> [E]ven a modest acquaintance with history shows that underdevelopment is not original or traditional and that neither the past nor the present of the underdeveloped countries resembles in any important respect the past of now developed countries. The now developed countries were never *under*developed, though they may have been *un*developed. It is also widely believed that the contemporary underdevelopment of a country can be understood as the product or reflection solely of its own economic, political, social, and cultural characteristics or structure. Yet historical research demonstrates that contemporary underdevelopment is in large part the historical product of past and continuing economic and other relations between satellite underdeveloped countries and the now developed metropolitan countries. Furthermore, these relations are an essential part of the structure and development of the capitalist system on a world scale as a whole.

Note that Frank's explicit recognition that countries are all part of a greater global economic system is not what distinguishes his thesis from those of mainstream economists. Mainstream trade theory likewise recognizes that individual countries are part of an integrated world economy. Rather, Frank and the other dependency theorists distinguished themselves by claiming that economic interdependence with wealthy countries *prevents* less developed economies from ever developing:

> When we examine this metropolis-satellite structure, we find that each of the satellites, including now-underdeveloped Spain and Portugal, serves as an instrument to suck capital or economic surplus out of its own satellites and to channel part of this surplus to the world metropolis of which all are satellites. Moreover, each national and local metropolis serves to impose and maintain the monopolistic structure and exploitative relationship of this system . . . as long as it serves the interest of the metropoles which take advantage of this global, national, and local structure to promote their own development and the enrichment of their ruling classes. (p. 101)

Dependency theorists hypothesized that rather than serving as an engine of growth, trade is the channel through which rich *center* countries exploit poor *peripheral* countries and effectively perpetuate the unequal distribution of world income.

Dependency theory was closely related to the **structuralist school of economics**, which was another popular philosophical trend in Latin America after World War II. Structuralist economists explicitly rejected mainstream economics' fundamental assumption that economic outcomes were the result of free choices made by individuals who sought, rationally, to maximize their individual welfare. Structuralists argued that human behavior is holistically influenced by, among other things, culture, institutions, and psychological factors that lead people to favor the status quo. The structuralists further emphasized that international trade perpetuated unequal economic and social structures, such as, for example, the way the export of sugar by Brazil in the sixteenth and seventeenth centuries created a plantation society whose slavery and unequal wealth still distorted Brazilian society. Thus, where modern economic analysis assumes smooth functions and continuous marginal adjustments to price signals, structuralists argued that developing economies were plagued by structural rigidities, such as culture and institutions, that prevented smooth adjustments. The structuralists were convinced that if developing countries followed their current comparative advantages, they would forever be locked in to exporting primary products and to deteriorating terms of trade.

The structuralist school was related to the French philosophical movement led by, among others, the anthropologist Claude Lévi-Strauss. This philosophical movement, called **structuralism**, replaced existentialism as the dominant philosophical mood in the late 1940s and 1950s. Like the structuralist school of economics, philosophical structuralists rejected the idea that humans make choices according to their free will. Rather, structuralists hypothesized that human behavior is determined by various structures, or in terms of our holistic language, systems. They therefore concluded that human economic behavior could be explained and predicted only if the basic social, political, natural, and economic structures were understood. Like these structuralists in philosophy, anthropology, sociology, and other fields, structuralist economists accepted that human economic behavior was tightly bound by broader economic systems and, for developing countries, the international economic system, within which they lived.

In line with these philosophical trends and economic ideas, many developing-country governments took the same route that Brazil did after World War II and began intentionally changing the system by restricting international trade and international investment. These protectionist policies were often justified by the Brazilian experience of the 1930s. Protectionist policies were, no doubt, fundamentally an emotional reaction to colonialism. After World War II, many of the developing countries in Africa and Asia finally gained independence from their former exploiters. There was clearly little sentiment in favor of continuing traditional trade channels through which colonialists had exploited their colonies.

IMPORT SUBSTITUTION INDUSTRIALIZATION

The protectionist economic policies Brazil adopted in the 1940s and 1950s came to be known as **import substitution industrialization (ISI)**. In the many developing economies that adopted them, ISI policies usually consisted of a broad assortment of trade bans, quotas, and high tariffs on imports, all intended to *protect* domestic industries so that they could effectively defy comparative advantage and *substitute* domestic industrial production of goods for formerly imported goods.

ISI Gets a Life of Its Own

Policy makers seldom based their support of ISI policies on rigorous economic models and paradigms. Their thinking more often reflected the belief that expansion of manufacturing would lead to a more rapid growth of technology and technology spillovers. Henry Bruton (1998) points out that many **development economists** and developing-country policy makers saw their economies as a dualistic coexistence of large "traditional" agricultural sectors and smaller "modern" sectors that looked more like those sectors in developed countries. Bruton argues that development plans were thus designed around a process of shrinking the traditional sector, and the institutions that guided it, and expanding the growth of the modern industrial sector. Add to this pro-industrial view the fact that policy makers in developing countries had little respect for international trade because, even with political independence, their trade still looked like the colonial trade arrangements that these countries were forced to conform to before their independence. ISI seemed to be a way to end once and for all what were seen as abusive trade relationships.

In addition to the dependency theorists and the structuralists mentioned above, other important intellectual supporters of ISI policies were the development economists Arthur Lewis (1954), Gunnar Myrdal (1956), and John Fei and Gustav Ranis (1964). The active advocacy of ISI policies by the United Nations Economic Commission for Latin America (ECLA) was also very important. The director of ECLA, Argentinean economist Raúl Prebisch (1950, 1959), presented a detailed rationale for ISI policies in Latin America and other developing regions of the world.

Prebisch's Development Plan

Prebisch began with the fact that in a world with free trade, developing economies' comparative advantage in trade lay with primary products. He then drew on evidence showing that the income elasticity of demand for primary products was inelastic and demand for such products would not grow in proportion to world income. On the other hand, he saw that the demand for the industrial products that the wealthier, developed countries produced had an income elasticity greater than one. Prebisch therefore predicted that the terms of trade of countries that exported primary products would, in the long run, continually deteriorate. If export prices fall while import prices rise, the country's **terms of trade** are said to decline, and the country effectively has to export more of its production to pay for the products it imports. Prebisch concluded that with deteriorating terms of trade, international trade would serve as a greater engine of growth for the industrialized countries than it would for the primary product exporters in the third world, and developing countries would thus fall further behind industrialized countries if they continued to produce according to current comparative advantage.

For most of the twentieth century, commodity prices indeed trended downward, the occasional oil price spike notwithstanding. More recently, the decline in primary product prices has been accompanied by the growth of the margin between the prices paid to primary product producers and the prices earned in final product markets by the users of primary products. Jacques Morisset (1998) examined the price differences between raw primary products in exporting countries and processed primary products in import markets (beef cows/beef, coffee beans/coffee, crude oil/fuel oil, crude oil/gasoline, rice/rice, sugar/sugar, and wheat/bread) over the period 1975–1994. He finds that "the spread between world commodity prices and domestic consumer prices has increased over time, by about 100 percent on average for the seven commodities analyzed here for 1975–94" (p. 520). These findings are troubling because they suggest that even the low measured income elasticity of demand for primary products overstates the expected growth of primary product demand. As the differential between export prices and the prices consumers pay in developed-country markets grows, it takes ever larger export price declines in developing economies to raise exports because the export price declines are only partially, or not at all, passed on to the final users.

Morisset examined many possible explanations for this rapid expansion of the differential between export prices of raw materials and prices in the final export markets, including changes in trade policies, transport and insurance costs, and marketing and processing costs. He finds that these explanations are not supported by the evidence. A more likely cause is the increased demand for processed food products in high-income countries and the growing concentration of the food processing industry in the hands of a small, and shrinking, number of large transnational corporations that capture most of the final price paid by consumers.

As we noted above for coffee prices, price volatility is problematic for all exporters of primary commodities. Not only have primary commodity prices declined over time, but as we pointed out in Chapter 6, primary product prices have fluctuated rather wildly around the long-term downward trend. Christopher Blattman, Jason Hwang, and Jeffrey Williamson (2004) use statistical analysis to show that it is the volatility of export prices, not persistent price declines, that most significantly depresses economic growth in developing countries. Their explanation for this finding is that economies can deal with gradual changes much more easily than sudden, unpredictable changes. Therefore, an economy should diversify its export earnings across more and different products in order to stabilize the engine of growth.

The second main strand of Prebisch's argument for ISI policies was derived from the structuralist and dependency theory schools of thought discussed above. Prebisch saw how the international economic system had shaped the structure of Latin American economies and other developing economies. He therefore called for explicit government policies to free economies from the structures imposed by comparative advantage and foreign investments owned and operated by foreigners. His suggested ISI policies were intended to expand the manufacturing sector by drawing resources away from traditional primary economic activities like agriculture and mining. ISI policies that closed a country's borders and intentionally defied its current comparative advantage were seen as a "necessary short-run cost" to force a long-run structural change in the economy. The structuralists and Prebisch claimed that the forced structural change would more than pay for itself in the form of higher rates of economic growth in the long run.

An important factor that enabled the rapid spread of ISI policies throughout the developing world, especially Latin America, was their viability within the dominant political realities in many developing countries. For example, in most Latin American developing countries, the national government was supported by an implicit coalition of traditional economically dominant families in rural areas, urban small businesses, and urban workers. Under ISI policies, it was the latter two groups that would gain from the trade protection at the expense of consumers and farmers, in general. Coincidentally, ISI was also acceptable to the intellectual elite of Latin America, whose Marxist and dependency theory views made them suspicious of international trade with capitalist economies. Interestingly, the growing sense of nationalism, actively promoted by fascist-leaning leaders such as Juan Perón in Argentina and Getúlio Vargas in Brazil, also increased support for policies that cut traditional ties to the rest of the world.

An Assessment of ISI Policies

Table 10.1 shows that while international trade grew as a percentage of overall economic activity in most of the world between 1950 and 1973, in Latin America and South Asia, where countries most actively embraced import substitution, trade declined as a percentage of gross domestic product (GDP). On the other hand, in East Asian economies such as Taiwan and South Korea, which abandoned protectionism in the 1950s and early 1960s, respectively, trade grew relative to these countries' rapidly growing GDPs.

The question, therefore, is whether the decline in trade led to a more rapid rise in standards of living. The experience with ISI is complex and very difficult to assess. ISI was not the dismal failure that many neoclassical economists and free trade proponents have suggested. The industrial sectors in countries like Brazil, South Africa, Mexico, and India were first developed under ISI, and it is very doubtful that they would be as large today without ISI's protectionist policies. But neither were ISI policies a clear success; they brought rapid economic development to the third world, but it was not sustainable. The financial crises in most developing countries in the 1980s and 1990s were, in large part, the result of foreign debt incurred under ISI. In the 1980s most countries that had adopted ISI policies stopped growing.

In contrast, a small group of East Asian economies *were* able to sustain very high rates of economic growth in the late twentieth century. The growth of per capita GDP in Hong Kong, Indonesia, Malaysia, Singapore, South Korea, Taiwan, and Thailand slowed only briefly in 1982, when a worldwide debt crisis hit, and these countries quickly resumed their rapid growth of GDP thereafter.

In a widely distributed report, the World Bank (1993) attributed the East Asian success to their **export orientation**, which stood out in sharp contrast to the ISI policies adopted by other developing economies. Table 10.1 shows how, indeed, international trade grew as a share of GDP in countries such as Taiwan, South Korea, and the other *Asian Tigers*. East Asian economic growth was not simply the result of openness to trade, however. In fact, East Asian governments actively protected their new industries even as they also encouraged these protected firms to export.

The Taiwanese bicycle industry provides an interesting example of East Asian industrial development. The assembly of bicycles began right after World War II in Taiwan, but this business was threatened by imports from Japan when Taiwan opened trade with its former colonial master

Table 10.1

Merchandise Exports as Percentage of GDP

	1929	1950	1973	1992
Western Europe	13.3	9.4	20.9	29.7
Canada	15.8	13.0	19.9	27.2
United States	3.6	3.0	5.0	8.2
Argentina	6.1	2.4	2.1	4.3
Brazil	7.1	4.0	2.6	4.7
Mexico	14.8	3.5	2.2	6.4
Total Latin America	9.7	6.2	4.6	6.2
China	1.7	1.9	1.1	2.3
India	3.7	2.6	2.0	1.7
Indonesia	3.6	3.3	5.0	7.4
Japan	3.5	2.3	7.9	12.4
Korea	4.5	1.0	8.2	17.8
Taiwan	5.2	2.5	10.2	34.4
Thailand	6.6	7.0	4.5	11.4

Source: Angus Maddison (1995), *Monitoring the World Economy 1820–1992,* Paris: OECD, Table 2–4, p. 38.

(after Taiwan became the home of the Nationalist Chinese government that had been forced out of mainland China by Mao Tse Tung's Communist government). In response, Taiwanese authorities simply banned imports of bicycles and soon restricted even imports of bicycle parts. Bicycle parts manufacturers set up shop, and several large bicycle manufacturers took shape during the 1950s. The bicycle market stopped growing when the local market was saturated by the end of the 1950s and rising incomes led Taiwanese consumers to buy motorcycles instead of bicycles. Annual production of the four main bicycle manufacturers did not exceed thirty thousand units during the 1960s.

The bicycle industry turned around when, with government encouragement and financial incentives, Taiwanese producers began exporting to the United States. In 1972, bicycle exports reached 1 million units. Taiwanese bicycle exports to the United States resumed their growth, reaching 10 million units ten years later, in 1986.

Wan-wen Chu (1997) describes how the Taiwanese bicycle industry could never have reached its efficient levels of production had it produced only for its domestic market. He also describes how the small manufacturers arose during the period of import substitution and protection from foreign competition.

> The history of the industry indicates that the causes of growth were several. The progress made under import-substitution, and the favourable factors on both the overall and industry level in Taiwan, made it the choice of production site when international capital wanted to move sourcing offshore. All three—import-substitution, a favourable environment, and globalisation of production—were necessary conditions for the growth of the bicycle sector. . . . Accumulated learning during the import-substitution period enabled the bicycle industry to expand its capacity quickly, and it enjoyed a high rate of parts self-sufficiency in the early 1970s. Thus, import-substitution is not really a waste, as the neoclassical school has asserted. (p. 68)

ISI policies could therefore substantially change the structure of a developing economy, as its proponents claimed. They could even spur the growth of specific industries and turn them into global competitors. But protectionism is a double-edged sword in that it not only provides an industry time to develop; it can also suppress the foreign competition that induces continued technological upgrading and development. The next case shows that not all trade protection results in efficient industries.

An Example of ISI Failure

In the early 1960s, the government of Chile had committed to ISI policies, and it was decided to establish an automobile industry. Chilean policy makers envisioned an industry that would initially consist of assembly plants using imported components and parts, but, by gradually banning the import of foreign parts, domestic auto producers would be pressured to buy more parts from local suppliers. It was hoped that the new domestic automobile assembly industry would generate "spillovers" to the local economy by providing incentives for the establishment of parts suppliers and new manufacturers of glass, tires, upholstery, et cetera.

The government let other political priorities interfere, however, and it required the automobile assembly plants to set up in the northern city of Arica, approximately one thousand kilometers north of the central region where nearly all of Chile's 10 million inhabitants lived. This measure was intended to provide a boost to an isolated region of the country where the opposition political party had recently exploited the poor economic situation to gain a majority in local elections. Thus, ISI policies were mixed with politically motivated regional development objectives, and the cost of producing automobiles in Chile was increased.

Further complicating the new auto industry was the Chilean government's regulation of foreign exchange dealings. All requests to exchange Chilean escudos for foreign currency had to be directed to the central bank, and it often took months before an exchange was approved because Chile's poor export performance kept foreign exchange in short supply. The uncertainty about whether foreign exchange would be available for imports of auto parts and components turned what should have been a year-round industry into a seasonal one. Each of the automobile factories in Arica would, at the beginning of the year, request foreign exchange in order to import parts. In the meantime, the factories had to wait with their orders for domestically produced parts such as batteries, tires, and windshields. Only toward the end of the year would they have all of the needed foreign and domestic parts to begin manufacturing, so most cars were produced over a brief period at the end of the year. When the inventory was used up, production stopped until, at the end of the next year, there would be another flurry of automobile manufacturing. Workers were thus hired only temporarily, and the protected industry did not have the employment effect that was the aim of sending the auto industry to Arica.

The most surprising feature of the Chilean automobile industry in the 1960s was the small size of each of the assembly plants. No fewer than twenty different assembly plants were set up, and together they produced just 8,180 cars in 1963 and 7,558 cars in 1964! The assembly plants in Arica were little more than large warehouses, the assembly process was very slow and labor intensive, and the final price of an automobile was about eight times the cost of the imported components. Leland Johnson (1967) estimated that, at international prices, 70 percent of all components going into each car were imported, but seven-eighths of the domestic price of each car covered the remaining 30 percent of local components and assembly cost. A car that cost about $2,500 in the United States cost over $8,000 in Chile.

None of the goals of Chile's ISI policies were met. There was little learning by doing because few workers were permanently employed in Arica and the production methods were almost artisan in nature. The uncertainty about the future of what was clearly an uneconomical arrangement slowed investment in modern equipment. There were few externalities that benefitted other industries or firms. Ironically, the opposition socialist party whose election win in Arica had led the national government to force automobile production to move there went on to win the national elections in 1970. In 1973, a military dictatorship was established after a brutal coup and the new military regime abandoned Chile's attempt to create an automobile industry.

How Protection Can Slow Innovation

Thomas J. Holmes and James A. Schmitz, Jr. (1995, 1998) set up an interesting variation on the Schumpeterian model of creative destruction. They assume that a country has two imperfectly competitive manufacturers who engage in Schumpeterian competition, each trying to establish technological superiority, but they also assume that the two firms have the option of using resources to obstruct the other's innovative activity. In Schumpeterian fashion, technological innovation makes one of the two firms the **technological leader**, and it earns a monopoly profit. The **technological follower**, no longer able to profitably produce its obsolete product, then devotes all available resources to research and development in order to recapture technological leadership. The leading firm must decide how many resources to allocate to production of its profitable innovation and how many to allocate to research to generate new innovations and establish technological leadership in the future. Holmes and Schmitz permit the technological leader to allocate resources to a third activity: *obstructing* the efforts of the follower to regain leadership.

According to the Holmes and Schmitz model, the decision to produce, research, or obstruct depends on the potential payoff from each form of activity. Resources should be allocated to R&D so long as the expected payoff is positive, or, in terms of the Schumpeterian R&D model described in Chapter 6, so long as the present value of profit from innovation exceeds the current cost of innovation. Obviously, the more resources are devoted to R&D activity, the faster is the rate of technological progress. Therefore, if resources are allocated to obstructing the follower, and the obstructive activity is successful, then technological progress may slow down. The welfare costs of obstructive activity consist of:

- The resources that are spent on obstructive activity rather than production or innovation.
- The lost future economic growth if the obstructive activity is successful.

The economic cost of obstructing innovative activity can be very large. Recall how the power of compounding magnifies even small changes in growth rates into large welfare changes.

Holmes and Schmitz's model concludes that there will be more obstruction under protection when domestic producers face foreign competition. The logic behind this conclusion is that in a protected domestic economy, the technological leader only has to obstruct domestic competitors while, in an open economy, the domestic firm has to compete with foreign innovators as well as domestic innovations. Therefore, all other things equal, obstructive activities become more difficult, and thus more costly, when there is foreign as well as domestic innovative competition.

Lessons from ISI

An important lesson from the ISI policies of the past is that ISI must be applied with care. A blunt tool like a law of similars may work reasonably well in a large country like Brazil, where indeed many industries can grow to operate at efficient levels, but it makes little sense for a small economy like Chile. Chile was unlikely to develop an automobile industry. More recent promotion, and protection, of the food processing industry has been very successful in Chile, however.

Another lesson from the experience with ISI is that the period of protection must be used to build flexibility into the structure of the domestic economy because a modern industrial economy must be able to deal with continuous change. No example makes this more clear than the Taiwanese bicycle industry. Today, bicycle manufacturing is centered in China, not Taiwan. Taiwanese management and marketing skills are still involved, since most of the Chinese plants are Taiwanese owned. But in Taiwan, industrial production is now centered in industries such as computers, computer chips, and, most recently, biotechnology. These new industries have also received protection and government assistance, and so ISI policies are still applied. Alice Amsden and Wan-wen Chu (2003) detail the extensive measures that were used to nurture new high-tech industries in Taiwan. Among them was the 1992 Development of Critical Components and Products Act, which formalized government assistance for the electronics industry.

The effectiveness of ISI policies thus comes down to how the policies are applied. Bruton (1989; p. 1641) concluded:

> The idea that some form of protection is in order to enable a country to establish its place in the world economy, in order to establish an economy that is flexible and resilient, is a fundamental idea. To get the form of this protection right and to get the changes that take place behind this protection to produce this kind of economy, is what import substitution is all about.

Not everyone will agree even with Bruton's nuanced conclusion. Opponents of globalization want permanent barriers to trade, and free market proponents prefer to throw open the borders and let private initiative fend for itself. But the successes of ISI policies in transforming formerly resource-based economies into industrial societies makes it clear that policy makers managing the complex and dynamic process of economic development would be well advised to retain the temporary protection of specific industries as a policy option.

MERCANTILISM, AGGLOMERATION, AND THE INTERNATIONAL ECONOMY

There is more to ISI policies than the desire to anticipate and manipulate shifts in comparative advantage. As pointed out in Chapter 7, economic development is usually a process of **agglomeration** that causes economic activities to become increasingly concentrated in certain regions or countries. International economic integration means agglomeration becomes a global process that tends to concentrate economic activities in certain countries. We now have an international economic system that is increasingly specialized and agglomerated. Key creative human activities such as innovation, art, scientific research, corporate research and development, upper-level education, the management of transnational corporations, and the high-end business services, such as advertising, design, and public relations, that transnational corporations (TNCs) need all agglomerate in certain countries and regions of the world. Since these activities generate the greatest incomes and profits, this agglomeration has also concentrated the greatest sources of wealth in certain countries and regions of the world.

The agglomeration of economic activity, especially the highest-income jobs and the most profitable business activities, means that the gains from international economic integration, which enables this process of agglomeration, are not equally shared among countries. The Heckscher-Ohlin model's conclusion that all countries gain from international trade must, therefore, be qualified. Trade policy must take into consideration the role of trade in advancing the agglomeration of economic activity. You can easily imagine cases where active government interference in the evolution of this agglomeration process could reap large long-run rewards for a country. Alternatively, remaining inactive while leaving other governments to interfere could place the country on a development path where it ends up with the least profitable industries.

Agglomeration and TNCs

The key to understanding the agglomeration of wealth creation is the recognition that international economic integration is being carried out by TNCs. TNCs are responsible for most of the world's international trade and international investment. By means of the brain drain, they employ the most educated and most talented people to perform the management, research, and marketing jobs that enable TNCs to grow and prosper. Also important are the transnational financial corporations (TFCs) who carry out most of the world's international financial transactions and operate the world's financial markets.

The fact that national governments are increasingly eclipsed in size and wealth by transnational business and financial organizations greatly changes the way we have to look at international trade policy. This is not to say that national political leaders no longer have power. Technically, as the overall stakes from international economic integration rise, policy makers' power to close borders gives them great power over TNCs and TFCs. On the other hand, TNCs seem to be getting the upper hand in the mercantilist relationship with governments because international economic integration lets TNCs play one government against another. That is, commercial interests no longer only bargain with a single national government about how much they will pay for protection and favoritism, but now they also threaten to take their taxes, political contributions, investment projects, and jobs elsewhere if a government's terms are not to their liking.

The Reappearance of Mercantilism

One of the criticisms of TNCs is that they, through their concentrated wealth, acquire political as well as economic power. Wealth and the political power it brings enable TNCs to shape national and international institutions in their favor. They engage in lobbying, public relations, advertising, and marketing that reduce competition and solidify their political and economic power. It is important to note that even when Smith (1776 [1976]) was writing about why free trade is beneficial for human well-being, most international trade was being carried out within colonial empires, and among very unequal trading partners. When Smith criticized mercantilism, he chose to focus on the allocative inefficiency of trade barriers; he ignored the possibility that trade generates unequal benefits.

Mercantilism is much more than the simplistic attempt by countries to accumulate gold by boosting exports and restricting imports that Smith emphasized in order to explain the benefits of free trade. A more holistic definition is Wilson's, quoted earlier (that mercantilism is "all the devices, legislative, administrative, and regulatory, by which societies still predominantly agrarian sought to transform themselves into trading and industrial societies," (1963, p. 26). Mercantilism was, in fact, an integral part of the shift in Europe away from fragmented, small administrative units to centralized nation-states. Mercantilism was effectively a system of government regulations and controls over economic activity designed to protect and favor the government's commercial allies and financial supporters, usually merchants, artisans, early industrialists, and bankers. That is, mercantilism is an active process in which commercial interests continually bid for, and gain control of, government institutions and agencies that then provide them with special privileges and monopoly powers in certain sectors of the economy.

The political leaders are complicit in this corruption of government because they find the income, taxes, and bribes that the business and banking interests provide to them useful for their own goals and interests. For example, as discussed in Chapter 9, in 1500s Europe mercantilism solidified the political base of national monarchs at the expense of the local power bases that remained from earlier feudal societies. When the same alliances between central governments and commercial interests were extended overseas, mercantilism became colonialism, the joint government-private conquests of overseas territory and resources.

Some heterodox economists see the growth of modern TNCs, which increasingly shape government policy by using a combination of direct monetary influence and indirect threats to shift investment and employment overseas, as a new phase of mercantilism. As a result of the political clout of wealthy and footloose TNCs, the internationally integrated economic system is increasingly characterized by institutions that raise TNC profits and reduce political and economic opposition to corporate power and profit. Taxes on capital are lowered, labor laws and union power are scaled back, and "the market" has become the symbol of justice and economic efficiency. Markets are no longer recognized as human creations that must be supported by sophisticated government institutions. Markets cannot function without a legal system that enforces property rights and contractual arrangements, a justice system that arbitrates business disputes, regulations that require information on products and firms' financial conditions, and, as we will detail in Part 4 of this textbook, regulations that prevent the financial sector from stealing the savings entrusted to its care. It is this need for collective institutions in a market system that has led many intellectuals since the time of the Enlightenment to argue that government should be democratic. The self-interested behavior of individuals and wealthy firms will not maximize overall human well-being unless the institutions that shape the individual behavior are designed with the public interest in mind.

Today, markets are often misrepresented as independent and unbiased mechanisms that are the polar opposites of government involvement in the economy. But in reality, the collective social and economic institutions needed for markets to function efficiently require government involvement as intense as the direct government provision of goods and services. Without collective institutions to regulate and guide the behavior of business organizations, economies quickly deteriorate into a chaotic competition among mafia-like organizations and local warlords. Effectively, without collective government institutions, humanity goes back to operating in small groups. In today's crowded world, even small groups inevitably clash, and the result is conflict or oppression. TNCs are using their huge financial wealth to corrupt democratic political systems and to shape institutions that give them greater freedom of operation. TNCs even control the main news media around the world, and they increasingly use their money to influence universities and other educational institutions to manipulate people's beliefs and society's cultures. TNC-funded advocacy groups have even influenced appointments to the U.S. Supreme Court, which in 2010 returned the favor by ruling that corporations are effectively individuals with unlimited freedom to directly fund political campaigns. Both the economic and the political systems of the United States now operate on the principle of one dollar, one vote. Similar growth of political influence by TNCs in most countries of the world means that mercantilism is alive and well in the modern economy.

TNCs and the Power to Set Policy

Critical to this conflict between national governments and TNCs is the degree to which TNCs increasingly control the power of national governments and use that power to shape the world to their commercial ends. In short, modern mercantilism is international, not national in nature. As TNCs and TFCs gain control of national government institutions, other national constituencies, such as farmers, labor organizations, bureaucrats, professionals, regional ethnic groups, small businesses, intellectuals, and national political parties, among others, are losing the influence they had gained under the spread of democracy and the creation of democratic institutions during the nineteenth and twentieth centuries.

Modern mercantilism is potentially very destructive of democracy and social justice. TNCs and TFCs are enriched by the profits from international economic integration, agglomeration, and the monopolization of global product and labor markets, and this wealth permits them to capture national government institutions. Instead of the democratic principle of one person, one vote, modern mercantilism puts economic policy in the hands of inherently autocratic organizations that tolerate little dissent from their single-minded pursuit of profits. Corporations are certainly not democratic organizations, which means that their control of national governments is an inherently antidemocratic shift in political power. As the wealth of TNCs and TFCs lets them gain greater control of mercantilistic commerce-government alliances, it becomes even less likely that international trade, investment, finance, and migration will maximize human welfare or spread the gains from international economic integration equitably.

Under these ominous circumstances, it also becomes less likely, even impossible, that trade policy will be used to improve human welfare. Calls for free trade will fall on deaf ears or be applied selectively to favor the most powerful corporate interests. And, policies that seek to maximize long-run national incomes will be undermined by TNC and TNC-sponsored political shifts that give corporations greater political power. It is difficult to see how serious ISI policies that favor broad structural economic changes will ever become possible again under modern mercantilism.

A Dramatic Example of Mercantilism

Joseph Conrad's short novel *Heart of Darkness* (1899 [2003]) is a tale about an English captain hired by a colonial enterprise to navigate a riverboat to an ivory-trading post deep in the Belgian Congo in the late nineteenth century. The local manager of this outpost for the Belgian government, Kurtz, is described by Conrad as not only "an emissary of pity, and science, and progress," but also an egotistical tyrant: "'my ivory, my station, my river, my—' everything belonged to him." Conrad also noted that "Kurtz had been educated partly in England. . . . His mother was half-English, his father was half-French. All Europe contributed to making Kurtz" (p. 92).

Especially interesting is the English captain's description of a company report that Kurtz wrote. The following passage, which consists of the captain repeating and describing the lofty language of the report, is relevant:

> 'By the simple exercise of our will we can exert a power for the good practically unbounded,' etc. etc. From that point he soared and took me with him. The peroration was magnificent, though difficult to remember, you know. It gave me the notion of an exotic Immensity ruled by an august Benevolence. It made me tingle with enthusiasm. This was the unbounded power of eloquence—of words—of burning noble words. There were no practical hints to interrupt the magic current of phrases, unless a kind of note at the foot of the last page, scrawled evidently much later, in an unsteady hand, may be regarded as the exposition of a method. It was very simple, and at the end of that moving appeal to every altruistic sentiment it blazed at you, luminous and terrifying, like a flash of lightning in a serene sky: 'Exterminate all the brutes!' (p. 92)

In short, stated good intentions do not prevent bad behavior by overseas personnel facing the day-to-day struggle to manage a large, profit-oriented business in a foreign business environment. At the same time, bad behavior is encouraged by the profit-based incentive systems that easily overwhelm noble mission statements.

Granted, Conrad described the colonial system and the colonial businesses that exploited foreign workers and resources in the nineteenth century. This mercantilist colonial system was characterized by private business ventures closely allied with their respective governments. Today, the world faces the extraordinary economic power and political influence of TNCs that do not always identify themselves with single home governments, and those governments do not always provide the explicit military and administrative support for their overseas ventures as colonialist governments did. Yet, there are many similarities. TNCs shape the lives of people throughout the world and act according to their own interests wherever they do business. It is important, therefore, to ask whether today's TNCs are managed all that differently from the colonial enterprises of the past. More specifically: How much different are today's self-righteous corporate mission statements, the TNCs' profit-linked employee incentives, their autocratic top-down management structures, and their behavior in foreign lands?

In June 2009, the Royal Dutch Shell Oil Company agreed to a $15.5 million settlement in U.S. court over alleged killings of opponents of its oil operations in Nigeria. Among the dead were the environmentalist and writer Ken Saro-Wiwa, who had organized a worldwide campaign to stop Shell's projects on the Ogoni tribe's lands in Nigeria. According to company documents obtained by lawyers representing the families of those killed and reported on in 2009 by the London newspaper *The Independent,* Shell had written to the local governor requesting "the usual assistance" after Ogoni activists blocked the laying of a pipeline in 1993.[3] One death resulted when government soldiers disrupted the protests. A few days later, Shell went to the country's military leadership to "request support from the army and police." Eventually, the military's clampdown on the Ogoni resulted in about two thousand deaths, thirty thousand people made homeless, and numerous reported cases of rape, plunder, and theft by the brutal forces of Nigeria's military government. Modern TNCs like Shell apparently are not hesitant to demand the extermination of local resistance to their commercial activities.

STRATEGIC TRADE POLICY

Intellectual arguments for ISI such as those based in dependency theory, structuralism, and Marxism suggest that less developed economies need "protection" from economic forces that prevent them from raising the welfare of their citizens. These arguments suggest that high-income industrial economies gain disproportionately from international trade, and that they will, logically, favor free trade. That has not been the case, as the history of trade policy in Chapter 9 makes clear. Today, developed-country policy makers often use dynamic arguments for protection not unlike those made by the proponents of ISI in developing countries. In this section, we discuss an example of **strategic trade policy**, the general term given to intentional government interference with international trade in order to support large national firms over foreign firms.

Recall from Chapter 6 that in the case of economies of scale and imperfect competition, it is possible for government policy to direct the economy toward alternative future growth paths, some of which will prove to generate more income than others. One way dynamic strategic trade policy has been carried out in recent decades is for governments to assist specific firms or entire industries. Most governments have protected their agricultural sectors, and in many cases government subsidies have enabled farmers and commodity traders to sell agricultural products overseas. Governments have also selected specific industries for assistance. This section presents a strategic trade model of the commercial aircraft industry. This model shows how, hypothetically, policy makers can increase national welfare by means of carefully constructed policies of tariffs or subsidies to influence multinational firms' strategic behavior in a duopolistic market.

Strategic Competition: Boeing versus Airbus

A popular example of strategic behavior is the commercial aircraft industry, which is dominated by two large multinational firms, the Boeing Company of Seattle, Washington, in the United States and Airbus Industrie based in the French city of Toulouse. Airbus has received huge amounts of financial aid from various European governments whose suppliers are part of Airbus Industrie, and Boeing has accused Airbus of "unfair" competition. Boeing has also received substantial government subsidies, mostly in the form of military projects. For example, the first commercial jet produced by Boeing, the Boeing 707, was derived from a military tanker that the U.S. government paid Boeing to develop in the 1950s. The reason why development subsidies are so important is that so much of the total cost of producing an aircraft consists of fixed, or *sunk,* costs, often totaling billions of dollars, that must be recovered over the period of actual production. If few planes are sold, the fixed costs will not be recovered, in which case the firm cannot service its debt incurred to develop the aircraft.

In the example developed here, suppose that there is a new market segment in the airline industry that requires an aircraft of a certain size, range, weight, and performance. Both Boeing and Airbus must decide whether to incur the cost of several billion dollars to develop the aircraft. Obviously, if only one of the two firms develops the aircraft, that producer is very likely to earn considerable profits, as all planes for the specific market segment will have to be purchased from that single producer. However, if both firms decide to produce competing models aimed at the same market segment, the expected number of sales will have to be split among the two, and price competition between the two firms may further erode profits.

Both firms calculate how many airplanes they will sell, what production costs will be, and how much profit they will earn in case their rival enters, or does not enter, the market with a competing model. Table 10.2 presents this known information. Boeing estimates that if both companies incur the development costs and enter the market, it will lose US$1 billion on the project because it will not be able to recoup its development costs. Airbus calculates it will end up with a loss of US$2 million if Boeing also develops a competing airplane and enters the market. This is shown in the upper left-hand combination in Table 10.2. However, if Boeing decides not to enter, it would earn no profit but, of course, also incur no development costs; hence, in the lower two quadrants, which represent the cases where Boeing does not enter the market, Boeing is shown to earn zero profit. If Airbus then enters the market, it will capture all sales and be able to recoup its development costs and also earn a US$2 billion profit, which would be distributed to its European shareholders and lenders. If Boeing enters but Airbus does not, then Boeing makes a profit of US$3 billion and Airbus neither earns a profit nor suffers a loss. Of course, if neither firm incurs the development costs, both earn zero profit, as in the lower right-hand side of Table 10.2.

The decision each firm must make is called a strategic decision because it must take into consideration the likely actions of the other firm. For example, if Boeing knows that Airbus is definitely *not* going to develop an airplane for the new market segment, its choices are among the two right-hand boxes. Obviously, Boeing's *best* strategy would be to go ahead and produce the plane for a profit of US$3 billion versus zero. However, if Boeing knows that Airbus is definitely going ahead with development and production of the plane, then Boeing's choices are confined to the left-hand column: lose US$1 billion or break even. Under these circumstances, Boeing's best strategy is to not enter this segment of the market. For Airbus the numbers are slightly different, but it too will decide to enter (not enter) the market if it knows that Boeing will not enter (enter).

Note that the outcome of this strategic game is indeterminate. The winner of the strategic game between Boeing and Airbus will be the firm that can somehow convince the other firm that it is definitely proceeding with the project, thus leading the other to examine its options with the its rival's entry as a given fact. In that case, the second firm will not enter the market, thus guaranteeing the first firm a healthy profit. But how do you convince your rival that you are definitely proceeding? In the real world, we often see aircraft companies stage product presentations, make formal announcements, and stage other public relations events to convince the market that they are definitely proceeding with the development of a new aircraft. All market participants know, however, that these are public relations events, not solid commitments. Aircraft producers have often abandoned projects even after major celebrations to launch new projects. But what *is* a credible event? This is where government intervention can be helpful.

Suppose that several European governments pass legislation that earmarks the equivalent of US$2.5 billion for development costs of the new Airbus aircraft. In this case, the numbers from Table 10.2 change to those in Table 10.3. Now, Airbus will earn a profit from developing and producing the aircraft no matter what Boeing does. The uncertainty about future profits has been eliminated by the promised subsidy payment equaling $2.5 billion. Since Airbus will now defi-

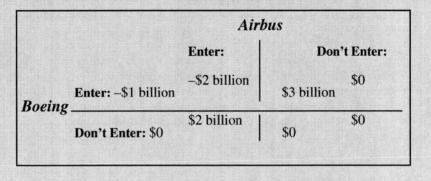

Table 10.2

Hypothetical Profits or Losses for Boeing and Airbus

		Airbus	
		Enter:	**Don't Enter:**
Boeing	**Enter: –$1 billion**	–$2 billion	$0
			$3 billion
	Don't Enter: $0	$2 billion	$0
		$0	$0

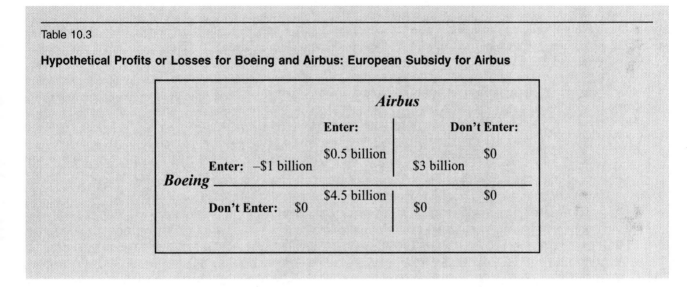

Table 10.3

Hypothetical Profits or Losses for Boeing and Airbus: European Subsidy for Airbus

		Airbus	
		Enter:	**Don't Enter:**
Boeing	**Enter: –$1 billion**	$0.5 billion	$0
			$3 billion
	Don't Enter: $0	$4.5 billion	$0
		$0	$0

nitely enter the market, Boeing's best choice between a US$1 billion loss and $0 is to concede the market to Airbus.

The subsidy enables Airbus to earn a profit of US$4.5 billion. Thus, Europe appears to have a net gain in welfare of US$2 billion, the profit minus the government subsidy. Some of this profit will come at the expense of higher aircraft costs for European airlines and higher airline ticket prices for European travelers because the monopoly price charged by Airbus raises the cost of the airplanes. But if a sufficiently large portion of the aircraft are sold and flown outside of Europe, the net gain to Europe is likely to still be positive and the subsidy can be considered to have been successful in increasing European income, albeit at the expense of U.S. income.

Strategic Trade Policy Can Reduce National Welfare

Note that the above example could have been used to show how a U.S. subsidy of Boeing would have pushed Airbus out of the market. In fact, it is quite conceivable that after European policy

Table 10.4

Hypothetical Profits or Losses for Boeing and Airbus: Subsidies for both Airbus and Boeing

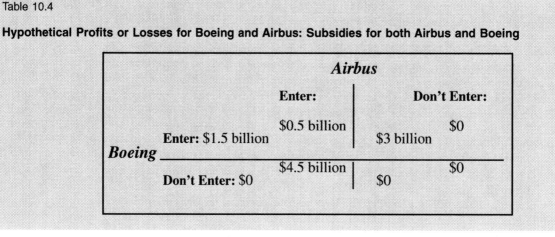

	Airbus	
	Enter:	**Don't Enter:**
Boeing **Enter: $1.5 billion**	$0.5 billion $1.5 billion	$0 $3 billion
Don't Enter: $0	$4.5 billion $0	$0 $0

makers decide to subsidize Airbus, the United States's government will counter Europe's subsidy with some form of subsidy of its own. After all, two can play the game! Suppose that the U.S. government offers Boeing $1.5 billion to design and develop an aircraft for the new market segment. Table 10.4 reflects both the subsidy to Airbus and the subsidy to Boeing. Both Airbus and Boeing will proceed with the development of their new aircraft. They will enjoy positive profits only if they produce their new aircraft, no matter what their rival does. This situation is not welfare enhancing for Europe or the United States, however. Note that in Table 10.4 in the upper left-hand box, both Boeing and Airbus earn positive profits, but the two firms are receiving government subsidies of US$1.5 billion and $2.5 billion, respectively. Thus, the two firms gain, but the taxpayers lose and overall national welfare declines. The two firms still lose money, except it is no longer their own money that they lose. Company profits are positive because of the subsidies.

This example of strategic trade policy brings out a serious weakness of strategic trade arguments, which is that governments end upsetting policies that favor the welfare of the producers lobbying for assistance, not the general public. Also, the model unrealistically assumes that the government has information that is not normally available to government policy makers. In the above example, the government needs the information given in Table 10.2, but in the real world such information about future profits is little more than speculation. In fact, the government is likely to be at least partly dependent on the domestic firm for even this information, and the firm has an incentive to cook the data in its favor by overstating its expected losses from its competitor's entry into the market, in order to receive a higher subsidy.

In sum, strategic trade policy may improve a country's overall level of human welfare, or it can leave everyone worse off. Thomas Palley (2006), a research associate of the Levy Economics Institute of Bard College, summarizes the case for strategic trade policies as follows:

> Although there are always gains from trade, countries can suffer from further globalization—their future gains from trade may fall, making them worse off than before. This sobering conclusion derives from pure trade theory [neoclassical theory], which assumes away macroeconomic problems such as unemployment, trade deficits, and financial instability. When these problems are factored in, the case for strategic trade policy becomes even stronger. (p. 22)

But the ultimate success of such policies depends on how they are carried out within a realistic political environment. Once again, economists have to reply: "It depends."

CONCLUSIONS

The discussion on import substitution industrialization (ISI), agglomeration, and strategic trade policy leads to an important conclusion: government interference with international trade can have a beneficial long-run effect on human welfare. It also leads to another equally important conclusion: government interference with international trade can have a detrimental long-run effect on human welfare. Whether active trade policies by national governments have positive or negative welfare effects depends on the circumstances and the specific policies that governments put in place. This part of the book's discussion of trade policy suggests that governments have been far from efficient in using trade policy to promote human well-being. Governments often make bad choices, and special interests often influence the government and use its power to promote their particular interests at the expense of the overall welfare of the country's citizens.

The strong political influence of special interests complicates trade policy in most countries. Trade policy is seldom carried out objectively by honest and independent policy makers who have only the interests of the country's citizens in mind. Trade policy has been likened to sausage: it may taste good, but you do not want to know how it was made.

Clearly, having governments refrain from interfering with international trade is not the solution, because then world trade is substantially determined by large, private transnational corporations. No government interference with international trade is also a trade policy; it is a trade policy that explicitly leaves the decisions to large, autocratic business organizations with well-focused interests that almost certainly do not closely match the interests of the world's 7 billion people. TNCs have the wealth and power to determine where production occurs, how production is marketed, and which countries will gain how much in the global economy.

TNCs dominate business in most countries. By spreading technology, shaping consumer demand, and integrating economic activity across borders, TNCs are reshaping human societies. They have gained disproportionate power within government to shape policy, and they use that power to shape trade policy. And since TNCs also provide many of the most-sought-after jobs as well as the products people both need and crave, coping with the autocratically run TNCs will be difficult.

Note that we are not suggesting that there is a well-orchestrated conspiracy by TNCs to take over the world. To the contrary, the discussion of agglomeration in this chapter suggests that there are natural economic and technological reasons for the concentration of economic activity within large transnational corporations. And even though TNCs shape the world economy, their actions are not well coordinated, because each firm and industry has its particular interests and imperfectly competitive constraints. The mercantilist alliances between commercial interests and governments are an evolving and gradual process driven by self-interest based on imperfect knowledge and understanding of the overall economic, social, and natural systems within which firms and people operate.

Unfortunately, the fact that we face a changing, complex system beyond the full control of any firm or government rather than an organized conspiracy is not reassuring. We need to understand much more about how this system works and how it interacts with the broader economic, social, and natural systems before we can design policies that effectively deal with international trade or any other issues related to international economic integration.

This chapter completes our discussion of international trade. The next part of the textbook moves on to international investment and finance. This does not mean we will not discuss international trade further, however. The upcoming discussion of additional dimensions of international economic integration will help you better understand the holistic, dynamic processes of economic change that we suggest affect international trade.

CHAPTER SUMMARY

1. This chapter seeks to bring our understanding of international trade *policy* in line with heterodox perspectives of international trade in general. For example, the growth of transnational corporations (TNCs) links international trade to international investment, market structures, and institutional factors that are not covered in the HO model of trade.

2. TNCs have been able to increase profit margins and gain income at the expense of consumers and workers, thus altering the distribution of gains from international trade. Many heterodox economists argue that trade policy and the international institutions that help shape national trade policies have been seriously biased toward assisting the growth of TNCs.

3. The liberal perspective on social policy that emerged from the Enlightenment and that so strongly influenced thinking in the field of international economics, was fundamentally the rejection of wealth-based politics as usual. The concentration of economic power in the hands of TNCs, and their political influence, suggest that the link between wealth and economic policy is still as tight as ever, however.

4. The HO model of trade concludes that the welfare gains from trade are greatest when countries are very different. Heterodox economists, especially those who favor a historical perspective, find many cases of *unequal exchange* between dissimilar trade partners—for example, rich and poor countries, or militarily powerful and weak countries—that brought about very unequal shares of the gains and losses from international trade.

5. A mercantilist society is an active *rent-seeking* one in which commercial interests bid for, and gain control of, government mechanisms that provide them with special privileges and monopoly powers over sectors of the economy. When these alliances between central governments and commercial interests are extended overseas, mercantilism becomes *colonialism*, which is the joint government-private conquest of foreign territory and resources.

6. This chapter presents a detailed case study of the colonial and postcolonial trade and economic development of Brazil. Each trade cycle brought different economic effects to different regions of Brazil, which resulted in different gains and losses from international trade.

7. The infant industry argument for trade barriers and Prebisch's case for import substitution industrialization (ISI) are detailed in this chapter, as are the concepts of dependency theory and structuralism that supported the ISI policies.

8. Protection is a double-edged sword: it can increase the gains from innovation but it can also reduce the competition that drives Schumpeter's creative destruction process. ISI policies in the many developing economies that applied them illustrate both the gains and losses from dynamic protectionism.

9. This chapter returns to the issue of agglomeration and the concentration of economic activity in transnational corporations, first discussed in Chapter 7. TNCs represent a modern form of mercantilism, as their concentrated wealth permits them to acquire political power that enables them to shape national and international institutions in their favor.

10. A holistic definition of *mercantilism* is: all the devices, legislative, administrative, and regulatory, by which societies still predominantly agrarian sought to transform themselves into trading and industrial societies. Mercantilism is also characterized by a close alliance between business and government.

11. This chapter presents an interesting example of *strategic trade policy*, which is the intentional government interference with international trade in order to support locally based TNCs over foreign-based firms operating in a highly concentrated global market.

12. This chapter shows that trade restrictions can both improve human welfare and decrease it, depending on the circumstances and the interactions of the many dynamic influences of trade. The strong political influence of special interests further complicates trade policy in most countries, as trade policy is seldom carried out objectively by honest and independent policy makers who have only the interests of the country's citizens in mind.

KEY TERMS AND CONCEPTS

agglomeration
colonialism
dependency theory
export orientation
Heart of Darkness
import substitution industrialization (ISI)
infant industry argument for protection
law of similars
learning-by-doing

mercantilism
strategic trade policy
structuralism
structuralist school of economics
technological follower
technological leader
terms of trade
underdevelopment

PROBLEMS AND QUESTIONS

1. Describe exactly why Prebisch logically concluded that developing countries needed to use protectionist trade policies to stimulate domestic industrialization. (Hint: include the philosophical background, trade trends, and his assessment of the structure of developing economies.)
2. Define an infant industry. Under what circumstances is the infant industry argument for protection correct?
3. Which economic activities are most prone to agglomeration? Explain.
4. Can you think of examples of agglomeration? Describe them and determine whether these examples match the discussion on agglomeration in this chapter.
5. Why do a country's terms of trade change over time? List and explain as many reasons as you can think of.
6. Do you think Prebisch was correct in his assessment of the future terms of trade for developing economies? Explain.
7. Are heterodox economists correct in their concern about transnational corporations in the world economy? How does the presence of TNCs alter the world economy?
8. What could Brazil have done differently in 1930 when its export prices fell and its balance of payments turned sharply negative?
9. Should Brazil have kept its borders open after World War II? How do you think the economy would have performed if Brazil had not opted for import substitution industrialization?
10. Assess Frank's view of economic development. Has he been vindicated by the past fifty years' history, or have his ideas been refuted?
11. Define mercantilism. Does mercantilism still exist today? Provide examples to match your definition.
12. How does structuralism clash with neoclassical economy theory? (Hint: Remember, neoclassical economic models assume smooth curves and adjustment processes.)
13. Was import substitution industrialization (ISI) justified by the infant industry argument? (Hint: Explain how the infant industry argument for protection differed from the application of ISI policies.)
14. Explain Brazil's various development cycles (sugar, gold, coffee) and how they differed in their effects on Brazil's economic development.
15. The "Conclusions" section of this chapter states: "No government interference with international trade is also a trade policy." Explain the meaning of this statement within the context of the alternative policy approaches to international trade discussed in this chapter.

NOTES

1. C.K. Harley (1988); Douglass C. North (1958).
2. Paul Bairoch (1993). Adam Smith (1776 [1976]) described colonialism as disadvantageous to the colonies.
3. Andy Rowell (2009), "Secret Papers 'Show How Shell Targeted Nigeria Oil Protests,'" *The Independent,* June 14.

PART FOUR

INTERNATIONAL INVESTMENT AND FINANCE

This part of the textbook examines the second and third components of international economics: international investment and international finance. It is important to explain the difference between international investment and international finance. These are two types of international economic activity that introductory international economics textbooks often confuse. In fact, international investment is the process of moving physical and human capital from one country to another; international finance involves the purchase and sale of financial assets. International financial flows may be linked to international investment, as when a transnational corporation transfers funds to another country to purchase a foreign firm or when a foreign government borrows overseas to finance an infrastructure project. But often international lending and international investment are separate processes, with different costs, benefits, and potential destabilizing effects.

Many economists feel that, by combining the static models of international investment with models of economic growth, a strong case can be made for policies that encourage international investment. From a heterodox perspective, however, there are many issues to discuss that go well beyond the orthodox models of international investment and economic growth. International investment shifts the factor endowments across countries, which affects international trade. And, international finance creates creditors and debtors with different interests. Also, the accumulation of international debt can cause financial instability and massive economic damage, as the recent 2007–2008 Great Recession has made all too clear. It does not make sense to keep expanding the complexity of our economic environment in pursuit of gains hypothesized in some orthodox economic models when the real world continually experiences massive losses in human welfare because international financial flows trigger financial crises and economic recessions. The international financial system does not function the way orthodox economic models suggest. This part, and the next, present a fascinating picture of the international monetary system and how international investment and finance operate.

Chapter 11 introduces the balance of payments, which are the standard accounts where international transactions are recorded. The world currently faces unprecedented imbalances in countries' balance of payments, the result of the liberalization of international financial flows over the past four decades.

Chapter 12 details the foreign exchange markets. Both the spot and forward markets are discussed, and the various processes of geographic and intertemporal arbitrage are explained. Foreign exchange rates are shown to be, in part, expectational variables whose values depend on market expectations of the future values of those currencies. This chapter emphasizes that, because the future is uncertain, and foreign exchange markets depend on governments' macroeconomic policies, foreign exchange markets are not the efficient and smooth markets most textbooks suggest. Foreign exchange markets are often volatile and disruptive, and they are subject to manipulation by both private financial interests and government policy makers. The question of whether foreign exchange markets should be controlled by governments or permitted to fluctuate freely is explained.

Chapter 13 presents a straightforward introduction to international banking and financial markets. It describes the growth of the Eurocurrency markets beginning in the 1960s and continuing up to the present. Today, international finance is dominated by a concentrated group of private transnational financial corporations. The development of the international financial industry is also described. Both the advantages and disadvantages of international lending and borrowing are analyzed. The usefulness of financial innovation is also discussed, and recent evidence is examined.

Chapter 14 describes how the international financial system has been characterized by foreign exchange crises that, in turn, have caused severe financial crises and economic crises. The cases detailed illustrate some points made about foreign exchange markets in the previous chapter as well as the foreign payments imbalances discussed in Chapter 12. Many countries, especially developing economies, have been hurt by the volatility of foreign exchange markets and the financial crises that have accompanied the sudden shifts in international financial flows and exchange rates.

These four chapters provide the details necessary for understanding the history of the international financial system that will be presented in Part Five.

CHAPTER 11

International Investment and International Finance

[T]he claims of enormous benefits from free capital mobility are not persuasive.

—Jagdish Bhagwati (1998)

This chapter introduces two additional forces of international economic integration: **international investment** and **international finance**. Strictly speaking, the former consists of international sales and purchases of physical capital, such as houses, factories, machines, tools, roads, and power plants. Finance deals with *intertemporal transactions*, which are exchanges *over time,* that is, transactions that involve a payment or payments in one period or periods of time in exchange for an expected, or hoped for, receipt or set of receipts in some later period or periods of time. Explicitly or implicitly, finance consists of borrowing and lending, which implies the creation of real or financial assets. Of course, some international financial transactions may be related to purchases of physical capital, but the world's international financial flows also include massive international flows of money purely for purchasing financial assets.

The previous chapters showed how international trade has grown consistently over the past sixty years, at least until the worldwide recession in 2007 and 2008 caused trade to decline for the first time since the close of World War II. International investment and financial flows have grown even more rapidly than trade, but their growth has been inconsistent, not only fluctuating widely from year to year within all countries, but also varying greatly among countries. Many countries, especially developing countries, often have suffered sudden reversals of financial flows that caused equally sudden reversals in economic growth and human welfare. The disruptions caused by the volatility of international financial flows led one of the most ardent advocates of free trade, Jagdish Bhagwati, to suggest restricting international capital flows. In the same article from which the quote above is taken, he also notes that "[e]ach time a crisis related to capital inflows hits a country, it typically goes through the wringer."

It is important to distinguish between *investment* in economic terms, which is the acquisition of physical capital, and the more popular meaning of *investment,* which is the purchase of both real and financial assets. In general, all real investment explicitly or implicitly involves finance because there is an exchange of a current payment (opportunity cost) for an asset with some hoped-for future returns. That is, there is a process of lending and borrowing. However, it is useful to distinguish between the investment in physical or human capital and the explicit financial flows that comprise borrowing and lending.

International financial flows must be added to the international payments made for international trade of goods and services. In order to help us understand how the international payments are related to international financial transactions, this chapter begins with an explanation of the **balance of payments (BoP)**. The BoP is the accounting scheme for recording all payments between countries. Just as business accounting is designed to help managers understand and run their businesses, BoP accounting is designed to help economic policy makers carry out macroeconomic policy.

The volatility of both international investment and international financial flows is a major contributor to economic instability in an integrated international economy. Intertemporal exchanges of assets are inherently difficult, of course, and they are even more difficult in an international setting. For example, the problems with informational asymmetries, enforcement of contracts, and monitoring of borrowers' performance are even more difficult to deal with when assets are exchanged across national boundaries, between different autonomous political systems, and between different cultures. Despite the difficulties, however, politicians, policy makers, and business leaders in nearly all countries continue to seek loans from foreign banks, push for tax incentives to attract foreign firms to build factories in their countries, and negotiate agreements to facilitate the flow of international borrowing and lending. Presumably, international investment provides benefits that overcome the potential dangers of sudden reversals of investment flows and the difficulties in servicing foreign debt.

This chapter thus also explains the inherent difficulties of carrying out international intertemporal transactions, which prepares the reader for later chapters on financial crises. To help explain why countries continue to liberalize international financial flows, this chapter presents a simple orthodox model that illustrates the logic used by mainstream economics to describe the gains from international financial investment. Supplementing this model is one that distinguishes how international investment can help to reduce risk. The traditional analysis is then extended to account for the growth effects of international financial flows.

Most important, this chapter makes it very clear that international economic integration consists of much more than the growth of international trade. International investment and especially international financial investment in an increasing variety of financial assets have created a complex web of interdependencies across people, industries, countries, and time.

THE BALANCE OF PAYMENTS

The balance of payments is a balance sheet that states the international transactions carried out by a country's citizens, businesses, organizations, and government agencies. Among other things, the BoP shows a country's exports and imports of goods and services, its private and public transfer payments to foreign individuals and governments, foreign direct investment inflows and outflows, domestic investors' stock and bond purchases overseas and foreigners' purchases of stocks and bonds in the domestic economy, and the interest, dividends, profits, and other earnings on foreign assets. By international agreement, all countries follow the same standard double-entry accounting procedures when they compile the BoP.

The Circular Flow of Economic Activity

John Maynard Keynes effectively created the field of macroeconomics when he developed his macroeconomic model during the Great Depression of the 1930s. His model proved to be useful not only for explaining the Great Depression, but for conducting overall economic policies in general. In his 1936 work, ***The General Theory of Employment, Interest, and Money***, Keynes showed policy makers how to design economic policies aimed at specific groups and sectors of the economy in order to most effectively push the economy back toward full employment. He also explained how individuals, firms, and government agencies can end up functioning in ways that result in total output in the world's major economies falling well below levels at which all resources and workers are fully employed.

Keynes's macroeconomic model focused on an economy as a system within which the parts interact. To keep the number of parts to a practical level, Keynes aggregated the millions of individual consumers, producers, banks, and other units into groups that can be reasonably hypothesized to behave in similar ways and react to similar sets of incentives. For example, macroeconomics treats "consumers" as behaving according to a uniform consumption function. Similarly, "producers" are treated as a single group of firms that behave according to a production function that links output to a set of inputs and the level of technology. By modeling the complex economy as a smaller, more manageable number of relationships among aggregate groups rather than the complex system of relationships linking the millions of consumers, firms, agencies, and organizations that it really is, Keynes not only made sense out of the complexity, but he made it possible for policy makers to design economic policies that could be practically applied across broad groups of individuals, firms, and markets. The aggregation also permitted Keynes to discuss systematic connections between the groups.

To illustrate the basic logic of Keynesian macroeconomic aggregation, the economy is often represented by a **circular flow diagram**. A circular flow model traces the main flows of payments among aggregate groups of people and organizations within an economy and, thus, reveals how the various groups interact in an economy. The balance of payment accounts are a natural extension of the circular flow diagram. Once you understand the logic of the circular flow of payments, the BoP is easy to grasp.

Figure 11.1 shows a circular flow diagram of an economy consisting of (1) individual consumers and (2) firms that produce the economy's goods and services. The most fundamental components of the circular flow in any economy are the combination of wage payments, dividend payments, interest payments, and other **factor payments**, from producers to individuals, labeled as FP, and the flow of payments by individuals to producers to acquire consumption goods, which is labeled as C. Because individuals spend their income to acquire products, producers can afford to pay them for their labor and the other factors they own. And, because they sell their labor and other factors of production to producers, individuals have income with which to acquire producers' goods and services. Note that the direction of the flows in the circular flow diagram follows the direction of the payments, not the direction of the goods or services provided. The payment flows C and FP measure the money value of the consumption goods and factors' incomes, respectively.

Production does not consist entirely of consumption goods, of course. An economy also produces *capital goods* and **intermediate goods**. Investment involves an up-front payment for equipment, buildings, and machines that are then used to produce goods and services over some extended period into the future. In Figure 11.1, the flow of capital goods is labeled I, for investment. These payments flow between producers of capital goods and producers who purchase the capital goods for use in production.

Firms also acquire goods and services from other producers that are incorporated into the goods that they, in turn, sell to consumers or other producers for further processing. These *intermediate goods* are labeled IG in Figure 11.1. The trend for businesses to increasingly focus on their core competencies and to outsource more stages of production to other producers means that the exchanges among producers are growing in proportion to final production. For the group of producers as a whole, intermediate inputs tend to cancel out. In fact, in the simple model of Figure 11.1, we show the IG payments leaving and returning to the producers box. National income accounting arrives at the total value of production, such as gross domestic product (GDP), by summing the **value added** by all producers. Value added is the difference between the final price of the product and the cost of the raw materials, parts, components, and other inputs acquired from other producers. In an

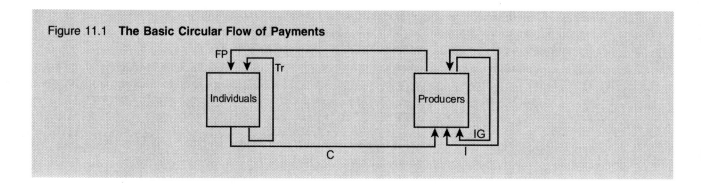

Figure 11.1 **The Basic Circular Flow of Payments**

open economy, some of the intermediate transactions by producers spill across the border and thus generate international payments that are recorded in the balance of payments.

There are transactions among individuals. For example, children do not earn income but they still consume clothing, pizza, video games, and other products. Children consume more than they earn because they receive transfers from their parents. Transfers, denoted as Tr in Figure 11.1, are really more like gifts, as opposed to factor payments for productive activity, which pay for specific services. Depending on an individual's personal situation and the society he or she lives in, social norms call for a variety of interpersonal transfers, such as the care of children, elders, and the unfortunate, compensation for social activities, the maintenance of social institutions, and the maintenance of common assets. Theft and extortion are also transfers, although most societies try hard to prevent such types of involuntary transfers. People also transfer income to relatives, friends, and unrelated people as pure acts of personal kindness.

Adding the Financial Sector and Government to the Circular Flow

The **financial sector** serves to allocate resources in the economy by channeling funds from savers to borrowers. When it performs this function well, the financial sector channels savings to the most productive investments and innovative projects. The financial sector lets savers earn high returns from projects they are not able to carry out themselves, and it enables individuals and firms with high-return projects to carry them out even though they do not have the wealth to pay for the projects' up-front costs. A well-functioning financial sector also lets people sustain long-run consumption levels when their income temporarily falls below long-run trends, and it helps firms to maintain production despite temporary fluctuations in cash flows. The financial sector is, therefore, important for long-run economic growth and reducing risk. If people cannot borrow money or acquire assets for storing purchasing power (saving) for future use, each individual in the economy must exactly balance income and expenditures at all times.

The financial sector consists of banks, pension funds, venture capitalists, stock markets, bond markets, and other organizations that provide intermediary financial services and maintain the markets where financial assets are bought and sold. In a modern economy, the financial sector consists of a great variety of public and private firms that provide a great many different services that are, fundamentally, related to saving and borrowing.

In Figure 11.2, the savings flows between individuals and producers on the one hand, and the firms that make up the financial sector, S_I and S_P, respectively, are net flows. While some individuals save part of their income, others borrow in order to consume more than they earn. Producers save or borrow, depending on whether their earnings exceed or fall short of their expenditures. The payments labeled S_I and S_P in Figure 11.2 are thus *net* flows that can be positive or negative.

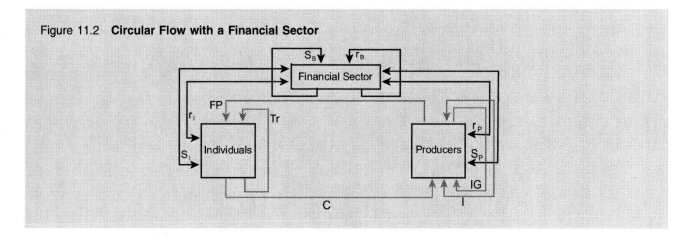

Figure 11.2 **Circular Flow with a Financial Sector**

Assets such as loans, property, and stocks generally produce *net* flows of *returns,* which are labeled r_I and r_P. The letter *r* is used to represent these returns on assets, which include such things as interest, rents, profits, and dividends.

Note that Figure 11.2 also shows savings S_B and returns r_B flowing within the banking and financial sector. Some of the institutions in the financial sector, such as banks, pension funds, and insurance companies, themselves may acquire or sell assets and thus earn or pay returns on assets. That is, the financial sector is not just a conduit through which individual, producer, and government savings flow. A modern financial sector itself engages in a large volume of lending and borrowing by means of exchanging various financial assets.

The fourth aggregate component of an economy consists of the various levels of government and the economy's various public agencies. No modern economy can function without a government to carry out collective actions; transfer income between individuals, groups, and households; operate institutions to moderate individual and firm behavior; and provide public goods and services. To provide public goods, the government acquires goods and services from producers, which we label G in Figure 11.3. The government may pay producers out of revenue from taxing individuals and producers; we label these taxes TX_I and TX_P, respectively. Transfer payments to individuals and producers, labeled TR_I and TR_P, respectively, may also be paid for out of tax revenue. Governments often do not exactly balance tax revenue TX_I and TX_P and expenditures on goods and services G and transfer payments TR_I and TR_P. If, for example, the government is a net borrower, the *net* flow of government saving, S_G in Figure 11.3, is negative. Also, if there has been net borrowing in the past, then the government must make interest payments on its debt. In this latter case, *net* interest payments to the government, r_G, are negative.

In the self-contained, or *closed,* economy represented by the circular flow diagram in Figure 11.3, total payments by consumers, producers, and government to the banks and other intermediaries in the financial sector (**financial intermediaries**) must equal total receipts from the financial sector. Net saving throughout the economy, plus the net returns paid to the holders of assets in which savings are stored, must sum to zero. What one person borrows, another must lend, and one person's receipt of a return on an asset is another person's payment. Therefore, the following condition must hold:

(11.1) $$S_I + S_P + S_G + r_I + r_P + r_G = 0.$$

Total net savings and returns flowing to the financial sector must sum to zero in a closed economy. The total demand for goods and services is equal to:

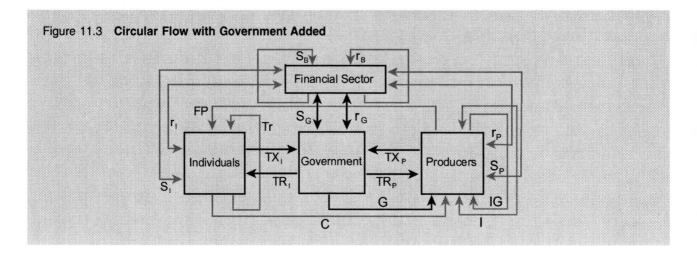

Figure 11.3 Circular Flow with Government Added

(11.2) $Y = C + I + G.$

Total demand for those goods and services is enabled by income flows, such as factor payments, as well as government transfers and borrowing from others.

The circular flow of payments reveals how interdependent we all are in a modern economy. Any change in activity by one individual, firm, bank, or government agency has effects on others throughout the economy. The circular flow must balance. The circular flow diagram suggests that consumers cannot consume more than producers produce. Producers are limited by how much labor people are willing to supply. Government tax revenue depends on others' incomes, sales, and accumulation of wealth. Borrowers depend on others to save. Individual choices thus depend on the choices others make. And, the overall performance of an economy is the result of the many individual actions and decisions of consumers, managers, bankers, government officials, and all the other people who influence the many flows in the circular flow of the economy.

It is important to point out that the circular flow diagram is based on standard macroeconomic accounting, which ignores many human activities as well as the services provided outside the market by our natural environment. For example, tomatoes produced in your home garden are not counted, nor are parental child care or home-cooked meals counted either as production or consumption. The life-sustaining services of nature, such as the reverse osmosis that produces oxygen, pollenation of fruit trees by bees, or the vitamin D we get from sunshine, are not counted as production or consumption either unless they are incorporated in other products that are paid for in the marketplace. This omission of many types of economic activity and benefits in standard economic data was dealt with in Chapter 4 when we discussed **externalities**.

Opening Up the Circular Flow

The world consists of about two hundred national economies, each of which can be represented by a circular flow diagram. These economies are integrated into the world economy through trade, investment, and finance. A realistic circular flow diagram must, therefore, incorporate the foreign payments for trade, investment, borrowing, and lending that flow into and out of open and interdependent economies.

Figure 11.4 shows a circular flow diagram for an open economy, in which each of the economy's four main aggregate sectors are linked to the rest of the world. First of all, consumers, investors, and governments in an open economy can import goods and services from foreign producers. Total

Figure 11.4 **Circular Flow of an Open Economy**

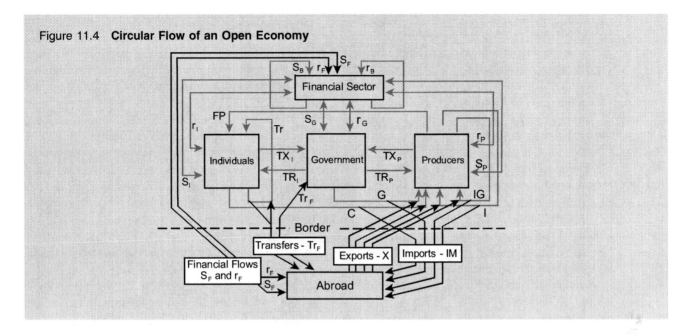

imports, denoted as IM, are the sum of the payments for foreign consumption goods, foreign capital goods, foreign intermediate goods, and foreign goods and services purchased by government. On the other hand, the sum of goods and services sold by domestic producers to foreign consumers, producers, and governments, are called exports and denoted as X.

Unlike the closed economy circular flow model in Figure 11.3, in an open economy some of the sales and purchases of intermediate products leave the domestic producer box and cross the border. A country can be either a net exporter of intermediate goods or a net importer. In the balance of payments account, sales of intermediate goods and services to foreign producers are tallied as exports; purchases by domestic producers of intermediate goods and services from abroad are recorded as imports. Outsourcing, which is the contracting to other firms for the production of some portion of a firm's output, explains a large part of the international trade in intermediate goods and services. This rapid growth of international trade in intermediate products is also referred to as the growth of **vertical specialization**.[1] Typical of vertical specialization are the **maquiladora** firms located in northern Mexico along the border with the United States. These firms import raw materials, semi-finished products, and parts and components; use low-wage Mexican labor to further transform the imports; and then export the finished products to the United States and other countries.

Statistics on trade in intermediate goods overstate the amount of actual value added that a country trades internationally. The price of exports reflects the cost of the imported intermediate inputs plus the value added by the domestic producers. The growth of international outsourcing means that, in most countries, the total value of exports exceeds the actual value added, the country's true export.

While international trade gets most of the attention in international economics, people make payments across borders for many reasons other than to pay for imports and exports. Some payments across borders are not directly for any particular product, service, factor input, or asset. As discussed above, just as there are transfers between domestic individuals and between the government and domestic producers, there are also international transfers. For one thing, governments make transfers to other governments and foreign organizations. Government transfers to foreigners are often referred to as **foreign aid**. Private individuals and organizations also make cross-border transfers. Private transfers have grown rapidly in recent decades while government-to-government foreign aid has stagnated.

The growth of private transfers is largely the result of the rapidly increasing number of immigrants. Today, with over 3 percent of all people in the world living outside their native countries, there are many immigrants who have moved to other countries specifically to earn higher incomes and transfer part of those incomes back to family in their native countries. These transfers, usually called **immigrant remittances**, are estimated to have exceeded $200 billion in 2008. Transfers are shown in Figure 11.4 as *net* payment inflows. They are labeled Tr_F.

As we did for domestic assets, we sum together purchases and sales of foreign assets into *net* flow. The net purchases of domestic assets by foreigners are denoted by S_F (net foreign saving) in Figure 11.4. Be careful to note the direction of the payments related to the purchase and sale of assets. For example, foreigners' purchases of domestic assets, such as bonds, checking accounts, or houses, involve payment inflows, which constitute a positive addition to S_F. The purchase of foreign assets by domestic investors results in a payment *outflow*. Hence, if a country's balance of payments shows a positive value for S_F, the value of domestic assets that foreigners purchased exceeded the value of foreign assets that domestic savers purchased abroad. A negative S_F means that domestic citizens, firms, and government agencies bought more assets overseas than foreigners acquired in the domestic economy.

Finally, the stock of foreign assets held by domestic individuals, producers, and government generates inflows of interest, profits, rents, and dividends from abroad. Foreign holdings of domestic financial assets will result in outflows of interest, profits, and dividends. The net *inflow* of returns to assets is denoted as r_F. When inflows exceed outflows, r_F is positive.

In sum, the open-economy circular flow diagram in Figure 11.4 highlights the following categories of international payments:

- Exports of goods and services, X, to foreign consumers, producers, and governments
- Imports, IM, of goods and services from abroad by domestic consumers, producers, and governments
- Net inflows of international transfers, Tr_F, between governments, individuals, and organizations, abroad and at home
- Savings outflows and inflows of foreign saving, S_F
- Payments of returns on assets to foreigners and receipt of returns from abroad in the form of interest, dividends, rents, profits, et cetera, r_F

For the circular flow of payments to be maintained, all payments leaving the domestic economy must be balanced by payments entering the country. That is, total payments *to* the rest of the world must be equal to the total receipts *from* the rest of the world. This balance occurs quite automatically because any receipt from abroad not used to explicitly purchase something becomes a de facto acquisition of an asset (currency or a bank balance). Therefore, the *net* inflows of payments for goods and services, or exports minus imports, plus net asset purchases, net returns on accumulated foreign assets, and net transfer payments must sum to zero. That is:

$$(11.3) \qquad (X - IM) + S_F + r_F + Tr_F = 0.$$

Each of the four different subcategories of foreign payments may have a net positive or negative value, however. When the circular flow is extended beyond the border, it becomes clear that in an open economy everyone's choices are affected not only by what others do in the domestic economy, but also by what others do throughout the rest of the world. The linkages between the rest of the world, or what we label as "Abroad" in the diagram, and the domestic entities in the model imply that everyone's choices are potentially altered by foreign events and decisions made overseas. On the other hand, international transactions offer domestic consumers, producers, governments, savers, and borrowers choices that are not available in a closed economy.

THE DESIGN OF THE BALANCE OF PAYMENTS ACCOUNT

Countries throughout the world compile balance of payments accounts according to a uniform set of guidelines. In 1996, the International Monetary Fund (IMF) issued the fifth edition of its *Balance of Payments Manual,* which introduced some minor changes to the accounting rules. The discussion below follows these latest changes.[2] The IMF publishes all countries' BoP accounts in its quarterly *Balance of Payments Statistics.* In this section, we focus on the U.S. BoP. We could, however, detail any other country's BoP in a similar manner.

The Basics

The balance of payments sums the inflows and outflows of payments over a period of time, either a year, a quarter, or a month. In the case of annual flows of international payments, the BoP of the United States for the year 2010 measures the payments *by* people, firms, organizations, and government agencies living in Spain to people, firms, organizations, and government agencies in all other countries and all the payments *from* people, firms, organizations, and government agencies in the rest of the world to people, firms, organizations, and government agencies located in Spain during 2010.

We use the term **credits** for those transactions that involve payment *inflows* and the term **debits** for those international transactions that lead to payment *outflows.* For example, the export of a product from Japan to the United States would show up as a credit in the Japanese BoP equal to the yuan value of the export. It would show up as a debit in the U.S. BoP as the U.S. dollar value of the transaction. The purchase of 100 shares of stock on the New York Stock Exchange by a Japanese investor would show up as a credit in the U.S. BoP, since the payment is from Japan to the United States. This same purchase of 100 shares of U.S. stock by a Japanese citizen shows up as a debit in the Japanese BoP. It is common practice to use a "+" for a credit and a "−" for a debit in the BoP. The circular flow diagram made it clear that all flows are related; an individual flow is just one component of the overall economic system. Hence, "+" items are not better than "−" items. Each economy generates an equal amount of debits *and* credits: the balance of payments must balance.

The Current Account and the Financial Account

A country's BoP account is divided into two main parts. The first is called the **current account** and the second the **financial account**. The current account contains all transactions related to the trade of goods and services. Thus, in the current account of the BoP are items such as merchandise exports and service expenditures (X–IM). The current account also contains payments related to the returns to factors of production and assets (r_F). Finally, the current account contains all private and government transfers (Tr_F). In terms of the notation used in the circular flow earlier:

$$(11.4) \qquad \text{Current account balance} = (X - IM) + Tr_F + r_F$$

The current account thus includes all cross-border payments except those made for purchasing and selling assets.

The BoP rules allocate to the financial account all international payments associated with the sale and purchase of assets. Again, in terms of the notation used for the circular flow above:

(11.5) $$\text{Financial account balance} = S_F.$$

Detailed accounts distinguish between short-term and long-term assets, as well as private asset transactions versus transactions undertaken by the government and its various agencies. The financial account registers transactions such as net purchases of government bonds by foreigners (credit) and the net increase in overseas bank accounts held by domestic residents (debit).

Equation (11.3) made it clear that the current account and the financial account must sum to zero. Therefore:

(11.6) $$(X - IM) + Tr_F + r_F = -S_F.$$

A deficit (surplus) on a country's current account must be balanced by a surplus (deficit) of the same absolute value on the financial account. Also, a change in one item of the current account must be offset by changes in one or more other items elsewhere in the BoP. For example, an increase in the trade balance, $(X-IM)$, must be offset by reductions in one or more components of S_F, r_F, or Tr_F. Any number of combinations of changes in the items of the BoP can end up offsetting a change in any one item. However, in the end total outflows must always equal total inflows.

The split of the BoP into *current* and *financial* accounts dates from the early post–World War II period, when most activity on the BoP of most countries was related to trade in goods and services. At that time, the acquisition of foreign assets was restricted by most countries. For example, citizens of most European countries, Japan, New Zealand, and nearly all developing countries were not permitted to open foreign bank accounts or acquire stock in foreign companies. As will be explained in Chapter 16 on the history of the international financial system, much of the activity recorded in countries' financial accounts at that time consisted of **official transactions**, which were intentional purchases or sales of foreign money by central banks for the exclusive purpose of compensating for deficits or surpluses in the current account or influencing exchange rates. Today, few countries ban their citizens or firms, banks, or other organizations from acquiring foreign assets, and their financial accounts now record large flows of private purchases and sales of assets.

A case can still be made for the separation of current account and financial account transactions based on their temporal nature, however. Current account transactions are mostly one-time transactions for which equal values are exchanged at one moment in time, but financial account transactions involve assets for which one side of the transaction pays today and the other expects payment at some time or times in the future. Of course, this reasoning suggests payments of interest, rent, and other asset returns should also be in the financial account. The size of these financial transactions is an important variable; the exchange of assets played a critical role in the financial crises experienced in many countries in recent decades. Hence, the separation of international transactions into separate current and financial accounts is still useful.

The Current Account

Exports and imports of physical goods, like toys, automobiles, wine, and corn, are referred to as goods or merchandise exports and imports. In the years from 2000 to 2010, these two large items in the U.S. current account (called "Exports of goods" and "Imports of goods" in Table 11.1) summed to a large net minus balance called the **merchandise trade balance**, given at the bottom of the table. In 2010, U.S. consumers, governments, and producers imported $646 billion more merchandise than they exported.

The deficit between total U.S. *exports* of goods and services and total U.S. *imports* of goods and services is not as large as the merchandise trade balance, because the U.S. services trade balance showed a surplus of $146 billion. When both services and goods are included in exports and imports, the 2010 total trade balance is –$500 billion versus –$646 billion for the merchandise trade balance.

Table 11.1

The U.S. Balance of Payments: 2000–2010 (billions U.S. $)

	2000	2002	2004	2006	2008	2009	2010
Current Account:							
Exports of goods	$771.9	682.4	807.5	1,023.1	1,307.5	1,069.5	1,288.7
Exports of services	299.5	294.9	343.9	422.6	535.2	505.5	548.9
Asset returns from abroad	350.9	281.2	401.9	650.5	813.9	599.5	663.2
Imports of goods	−1,224.4	−1,167.4	−1,477.1	−1,861.4	−2,137.6	−1,575.4	−1,934.6
Imports of services	−225.3	−250.4	−292.2	342.8	−403.4	−380.9	−403.0
Asset returns to foreigners	−329.9	−253.5	−345.6	−613.8	−666.8	−471.5	−498.0
Unilateral transfers (net)	−58.8	−63.6	−84.4	−89.6	−125.9	−123.3	−136.1
Financial Account:							
Change in U.S. assets abroad	−$560.5	−294.0	−1,055.2	332.1	−139.3	−1,005.2	−905.0
Official assets	−0.3	−3.7	2.8	2.3	−4.8	−52.3	1.8
Direct investment	−159.2	−154.5	−279.1	−235.4	−329.1	−303.6	−351.9
Foreign stocks & bonds	−127.9	−48.6	−146.5	−289.4	197.3	−226.8	−151.9
Bank loans to foreigners	−133.4	−38.3	−359.8	−454.6	542.1	−242.9	−515.0
Other claims on foreigners	−138.8	−50.0	−124.1	−83.5	456.2	144.9	7.4
Change in foreign assets in U.S.	1,046.9	797.8	1,461.8	1,859.6	431.4	335.8	1,245.7
Official assets	42.8	115.9	397.8	440.3	554.6	480.2	349.8
Direct investment	321.3	84.4	145.8	180.6	310.1	158.6	236.2
U.S. treasury bonds	−70.0	100.4	93.6	−35.9	162.9	−14.9	256.4
Private stocks & bonds	459.9	283.3	381.5	592.0	−162.9	4.0	120.5
Foreign bank borrowing	117.0	96.4	334.7	434.4	−428.3	−317.1	177.1
Other claims by foreigners	170.7	95.9	93.5	235.8	−31.5	12.4	77.5
Statistical Discrepancy	−69.4	−42.1	85.8	−17.8	−59.4	130.8	216.8
Capital Account:	0.8	−1.5	−2.4	−3.9	−6.0	−0.1	−0.2
Merchandise Trade Balance:	−452.4	−485.0	−669.6	−838.3	−830.1	−505.9	−645.9
Balance on Services:	74.1	61.2	57.5	79.7	131.8	124.6	145.8
Balance on Goods and Services:	−378.3	−423.7	−612.1	−758.5	−698.3	−381.3	−500.0
Current Account Balance:	−416.0	−459.6	−640.2	−811.5	−677.1	−376.6	−470.9

Source: U.S. Department of Commerce, Bureau of Economic Analysis; downloaded August 5, 2011 from www.bea.doc.gov.

Until recently, few services were traded across borders, and, since goods are easier to track, most countries focused on compiling the merchandise trade balance. In a modern economy, services claim an increasingly large share of total production, and more and more services are traded internationally. The balance of both goods and services is thus a more accurate estimate of the country's true trade balance.

The current account balance also includes factor payments, returns on assets, and net unilateral transfers. In 2010, U.S. owners of foreign assets received $663 billion in interest, rent, profits, royalties, dividends, wages, and salaries from their overseas investments and labor services, while foreign-owned assets and labor used toward production in the United States were paid $498 billion. Thus, the United States had a surplus of $165 billion on factor payments and returns to foreign assets. Net U.S. unilateral transfers were −$136 billion in 2010. These payments included military and other forms of foreign aid by the U.S. government to foreign governments, humanitarian aid by nonprofit organizations, and gifts sent by immigrants to their families in their home countries. That last item has almost always been negative for the United States, not just because the United States is a relatively wealthy country, but also because its relative wealth has in recent years attracted a large number of immigrants who still have close ties to overseas family.

Summing the $646 billion merchandise trade deficit, the $146 billion surplus on services trade, the $165 billion surplus on asset returns and factor income, and the $136 billion net unilateral transfers to foreigners leaves an overall current account balance of –$471 billion for 2010. In dollar terms, this is not the largest current account deficit that the United States has ever registered for a calendar year, but it is still much larger than any deficits before 2000. This deficit is also a sharp increase over 2009. As a percentage of GDP, other countries have had larger deficits than the United States has had in recent years. Nevertheless, there is concern that the U.S. current account deficit is not sustainable. Most other countries whose deficits as a proportion of GDP were as large as that of the United States recently ultimately were forced to make major macroeconomic adjustments. U.S. consumers, producers, and governments can continue buying more goods and services from foreigners than they sell to foreigners only if foreigners remain willing to buy large amounts of U.S. assets. That is, the United States can sustain huge current account deficits only if there are equally large surpluses on its financial account.

Notice that in 2010 foreign firms and investors acquired a controlling interest in U.S. firms and enterprises at about the amount that American firms and investors acquired foreign business facilities and businesses. In 2010, new foreign direct investment overseas by U.S. firms, investors, and financial firms was $352 billion, a high amount by historical standards. Foreigners invested $236 billion to acquire direct ownership in U.S. firms and enterprises. Table 11.1 also makes it clear that net U.S. foreign direct investment abroad has fluctuated quite a bit from year to year. Foreigners acquired almost $256 billion more U.S. Treasury bonds than they sold in 2010, and they also purchased an additional $121 billion in U.S. bonds and stocks. And, after sharply reducing their loans to U.S. borrowers in 2008 and 2009, foreign banks increased lending in the United States by $177 billion in 2010.

The central bank of the United States, the Federal Reserve Bank, engaged in very little foreign exchange market intervention during the period 2000–2010. The official assets item was just a net –$4.8 billion in 2008, although the Fed purchased an exceptionally high $52 billion in foreign currencies in 2009 as it made dollars available to foreign central banks to support their private banks' foreign losses as a result of the 2008 financial meltdown. In 2010, however, the Federal Reserve Bank of the United States sold only a small quantity of reserves on the foreign exchange market, just $1.8 billion. Note that with $350 billion in purchases of dollars and dollar assets, well over half of the U.S. current account deficit was financed by foreign central banks. This suggests that the value of the dollar would have been substantially lower if there had not been so much foreign central bank **intervention** in the foreign exchange markets. Intervention will be explained in the next chapter.

FINANCIAL INVESTMENT

Financial investment is defined as the acquisition of real and financial assets. Real assets include buildings, land, works of art, gold, and other physical objects. Financial assets include cash, checking account balances, corporate stock, government and private bonds, foreign exchange, other bank deposits, and a great variety of explicit and implicit loans to financial firms, businesses, organizations, and individuals. Financial assets such as these are often referred to as **cash instruments** because their values are determined in markets where these instruments can be bought and sold for cash. Also included among financial investments are **derivative instruments**, or just **derivatives**, such as options, futures, swaps, and other instruments whose values are "derived" from other assets, such as cash instruments and assorted real assets such as real estate. Derivative instruments are acquired in order to reduce risk, to provide insurance against certain losses and negative events, or just to gamble or speculate.

Uncertainty and Expectations

The prices of financial instruments usually depend on expectations of uncertain future outcomes. For example, stock prices depend on the expected future performance of corporations, and in the case of foreign stocks, they depend on the expected health of the foreign economies. Information about the future is incomplete, and prices of financial instruments and their derivatives, therefore, may be driven by emotions and heuristics (simple rules of thumb). Prices can diverge from fundamental long-run factors over extended periods of time, and price movements can be volatile when there is uncertainty about the future.

Financial investment is distinct from what economists define as economic investment, which is the direct creation of physical capital such as a factory, a machine, or a bridge. The purchase of newly issued stock or bonds may, of course, end up funding the building of the factory or bridge or the purchase of the machine, but such financial investment and economic investment are two separate things. Financial investment is not always directly related to economic investment, however, as when someone buys stock issued years ago or opens a savings account at a bank that uses the money to provide credit card debt to consumers.

The Financial Sector of the Economy

In most countries, the financial sector consists of **intermediaries**, formal **financial exchanges**, and **over-the-counter markets** for assets. Intermediaries are institutions that offer one set of financial arrangements to those contributing funds and another set to those borrowing the funds. For example, commercial banks offer depositors a variety of checking and savings accounts and certificates of deposit with different interest rates and maturities, and they offer borrowers a variety of loans of different lengths, methods of payment, and charges. Intermediaries channel funds from one set of financial assets to another set of financial assets, usually deposits to business and consumer loans, and in the process they assume risks and incur costs.

Financial exchanges are centralized markets where large numbers of buyers and sellers—that is, those who demand and those who supply—interact directly and set asset prices. Examples of exchanges are stock markets, livestock auctions, and foreign exchange futures markets.

Over-the-counter markets consist of dealers who maintain stocks of merchandise or assets and stand ready to sell or buy upon demand. Most bonds, foreign exchange, and financial derivatives are traded in over-the-counter markets. These markets are less transparent than exchanges because they reveal little information about prices and trading volumes; buyers and sellers only see the price of one particular transaction since dealers are rarely required to reveal price and volume data.

The Economic Purpose of Financial Investment

The fundamental economic purpose of the financial sector, and thus financial investment, is to channel savings to economic investment. The financial sector's role in channeling funds to new projects and research activities is critical to the economy's long-run rate of growth. For example, without financial intermediaries to connect savers and investors, there would be less investment and innovation, all other things equal, because investors and innovators would have to also be savers.

Financial investment also channels funds to cash-constrained consumers, a process that is economically beneficial if it permits consumers to better allocate their purchases over time. For example, without mortgage loans people would have to build their homes gradually as their income flows permit the purchase of building materials and construction services. Also, financial investment reduces life's risks because it permits people to save for contingencies and borrow during emergencies.

The Costs of Financial Investment

Financial intermediaries, exchanges, and markets are costly to operate, however, and they may introduce new risks and uncertainties. The financial sectors in today's high-income countries cost several percent of GDP to operate. Banks earn a spread between deposit rates and borrowing rates, and brokers, dealers, and financial firms charge high fees for their services.

Modern financial sectors are also prone to systemic instability. For one thing, all intertemporal transactions are subject to default. Also, the complexity of today's financial instruments and derivatives makes it impossible for any one investor, financial firm, or government regulatory agency to fully grasp all the risks of every financial investment. Because there are many levels of derivative instruments available in modern financial sectors, any one default or market failure can trigger many more defaults and failures throughout the system. From an economic perspective, when the financial sector falters in its role of channeling savings to investment, innovations, and consumption, there are very real economic consequences.

Instability in financial intermediaries, exchanges, and markets also results from the divergence in purpose of sellers and purchasers of financial assets. In explaining the financial collapse during the Great Depression, Keynes (1936) observed that before the development of modern financial systems "enterprises were mainly owned by those who undertook them or by their friends and associates, [and] investment depended on a sufficient supply of individuals of sanguine temperament and constructive impulses who embarked on business as a way of life" (p. 150). But "as a result of the gradual increase in the proportion of the equity in the community's aggregate capital investment which is owned by persons who do not manage and have no special knowledge of the circumstances, either actual or prospective, of the business in question, the element of real knowledge in the valuation of investments by those who own them or contemplate purchasing them has seriously declined" (p. 153). Keynes feared that "when the capital development of a country becomes a by-product of the activities of a casino, the job is likely to be ill-done." (p. 159). Keynes focused on the stock market as a source of instability, but the same problem exists in all **financial markets**. For example, government bond prices are determined by savers, **speculators**, financial firms, gamblers, and business firms that have no interest in the underlying government agency that issued the bond.

Financial investment has thus become a major contributor to the booms and busts observed in modern economies. It has proved difficult to find the optimal balance between the need for larger financial sectors to facilitate the flow of funds from savers to investors, innovators, and consumers on the one hand, and the increasing complexity that seems to generate occasional economic crises on the other. The over-the-counter markets that dominate trade in most assets have added to the volatility because they do not reveal much information and, according to substantial evidence, they enable substantial amounts of fraud.

Why Financial Transactions Are Not Always Completed

There are several fundamental problems in carrying out financial transactions:

Default—Intertemporal trades involve a payment today in exchange for a promise of future payments or opportunities for future payments. Between the time the financial asset is acquired and the time the promised payments or opportunities are to become available, circumstances may unexpectedly change, and the payments or opportunities may not materialize. Also, there are incentives (listed in the three definitions that follow) for the party with the obligation to make the future payments to renege, or default, on its obligation. There is also ample room for fraud by intentionally misrepresenting the likelihood of meeting future obligations. It takes a sophisticated set of legal, judicial, and other institutional arrangements to enforce contracts in today's impersonal and often opaque financial markets in order to minimize the likelihood that the seller of an asset will default on future obligations.

Adverse selection—This refers to the likelihood that borrowers or issuers of bonds will be more of a risk than the average population. That is, borrowers form a group that is, on average, more likely to default than people in the entire population because those with the least likelihood of defaulting will be more likely to use their own money to invest in the asset.

Moral hazard—This refers to the likelihood that once borrowers have acquired borrowed money, they behave less responsibly than promised.

Asymmetric information—Default, adverse selection, and moral hazard occur because one side of a financial transaction, the borrower, often has more information about future returns and the likelihood of repayment than the supplier of the savings.

Information asymmetries point to a role for government policy. In the developed economy of the United States, the **Securities and Exchange Commission (SEC)** was created to oversee financial markets. Among other things, it requires firms that issue stock or bonds to provide financial information to prospective buyers. In most countries, the government agencies that supervise banks require periodic public financial information so depositors and other holders of bank liabilities can judge the bank's ability to meet its obligations. Government-mandated information permits financial transactions to be completed where the fear of default, adverse selection, or moral hazard would otherwise cause prospective buyers or sellers to shy away.

Financial intermediaries introduce a **principal-agent problem**. Banks, money managers, and hedge funds (the agents), among other intermediaries, effectively play with money belonging to other people (the principals), and they may have incentives that lead them to treat funds differently than how financial investors would prefer. For example, a profit-maximizing bank may be tempted to invest in excessively risky assets because if things work out, then the bank owners enjoy high profits, but if things do not work out, it is the depositors who suffer most of the losses. The fear of bank failures has led many countries to provide depositors with **deposit insurance**. But unless banks and other intermediaries are closely regulated, such insurance can worsen the principal-agent problem because principals have less motivation to monitor agent activity.

The debacle known as the "savings and loan crisis" that occurred after a weakening of U.S. banking regulations in the late 1970s and early 1980s illustrates several problems that plague financial intermediaries. Savings banks were suddenly permitted to freely determine interest rates on deposits and to make commercial loans after decades in which interest rates were regulated and lending was restricted to home mortgages. The newly deregulated savings banks offered higher interest rates on government-insured accounts in order to attract funds for making risky commercial loans they had little experience with. In some cases, thieves acquired savings banks in order to channel the savings of unaware depositors to their own phony projects or those of closely allied business friends. U.S. taxpayers paid nearly $200 billion in 2010 dollars to cover the bank losses and the stolen deposits.[3]

Explaining the Variety of Financial Markets and Institutions

The problems of moral hazard, adverse selection, asymmetric information, fraud, and contract enforcement, explain why intermediaries, exchanges, and over-the-counter markets coexist: each has its advantages and disadvantages in dealing with these problems. For example, relatively inexpensive financial markets such as bond and stock markets can exchange the stocks and bonds of well-known corporations whose value can be easily judged by most savers. But less well-known borrowers rely on banks, which have the resources to investigate and monitor small business firms and their proposed projects. Financial intermediaries such as banks, pension funds, mutual funds, and insurance companies are also able to pool risk by taking deposits and contributions by many people and spreading them across many different loans and other financial instruments.

The creation of new financial institutions and instruments is called **financial innovation**. An economy that has experienced a large amount of financial innovation and thus has a variety of intermediaries and markets is said to have a "deep" financial sector. **Financial depth** is often touted as the financial industry's greatest success. However, financial depth can be problematic.

A recent example of how financial innovation can damage rather than improve the financial system is the growth of **collateralized debt obligations (CDOs)**, which are derivatives consisting of claims to shares of large bundles of financial instruments. For example, a CDO is created when a bank originates mortgages, puts them together into one large bundle, and then sells shares in the earnings from the mortgages or auto loans to investors, pension funds, hedge funds, and other banks. CDOs are not simple shares, however. To make the CDOs as profitable as possible for the loan originators, they are split into separate **tranches**, each with a different rate of return and a different priority for receiving the returns on the underlying mortgages. Purchasers of a share in the top tranche are the first to get paid from the returns on the whole bundle of mortgages, and the purchasers of the other tranches are paid only after the higher tranches are paid. The bottom tranche, sometimes referred to as "toxic waste," is paid a relatively high stated interest rate but, again, only after all the other tranches are paid. The tranches are carefully structured to gain the highest possible ratings for each one. The top tranche is normally awarded a AAA rating, a rating given only to financial instruments with no risk. Its share of the total bundle must be small enough to make it highly unlikely that the total returns on the whole bundle will not be large enough to fully service that upper tranche.

The AAA tranche may be quite large even when the underlying instruments are risky. For example, the top tranche of U.S. CDOs of subprime mortgages, home loans to relatively risky borrowers issued from 2005 through 2007, included about 80 percent of all the mortgages in the total CDO (Greenlaw et al., 2008). Only if more than 20 percent of the subprime borrowers stopped servicing their debt would the AAA-rated top tranche no longer earn full returns, which was considered highly unlikely during the optimistic 2000s.

CDOs of subprime mortgages played a central role in causing global financial markets to collapse in 2007 and 2008. It turned out that many banks that originated subprime mortgages had enticed U.S. borrowers with easy introductory interest charges for the first two or three years, while housing prices were clearly in a bubble in many parts of the country. **Securitization** also led banks to encourage loan officers to issue mortgages with little concern for borrowers' ability to service the debt, since the banks would not have any risk once the loans were sold as part of CDOs. Regulators and the banks themselves should have become suspicious when loan officers openly began to refer to the subprime mortgage market as "the liar's market" (Kane 2008). When the housing price bubble burst, defaults became much more likely than the ratings suggested they would (Lowenstein, 2008).

A second financial innovation meant to enhance the safety of CDOs also failed: **credit default swaps (CDSs)**. CDSs covering CDOs were options that paid out the full value of the CDO in the case of default. CDSs are a form of insurance. Interestingly, these derivative instruments were purchased not only by investors in CDOs, but also by hedge funds, speculators, and plain old gamblers who did not own any CDOs but just wanted to place a bet that the CDOs would default in the future. Such gambles are comparable to your purchase of a fire insurance policy on your neighbor's house; if your neighbor's house burns down, you receive a windfall equal to the value of the house without actually owning and losing the house. Of course, your neighbor could also have purchased insurance, in which case the insurance company has to pay out twice the value of the house. CDSs many times the value of the underlying CDOs were sold, exposing the sellers of the CDSs to huge potential payments in the case of the default of specific CDOs.

The over-the-counter CDS market is another example of Keynes's (1936) point about the divergence of interest between the financial instruments and the economic activities that underlie the financial instruments. It is estimated that, by 2007, over US$50 trillion in credit default swaps had been contracted by investors, hedge funds, banks, and other assorted gamblers throughout the global financial industry.

One of the largest sellers of CDSs for tranches of the sub-prime mortgage CDOs was the U.S. insurance firm AIG, which sold the CDSs through its London-based Financial Products Division. By 2008, the AAA-rated top tranches of the subprime mortgage CDOs proved to be rather risky after all, and AIG was called on to pay out the losses. It turns out that AIG had set aside too few reserves to cover the losses in the unregulated London banking environment, and the U.S. government had to channel over $180 billion to AIG to keep the large insurance firm solvent. With its widespread life insurance, fire insurance, auto insurance, and other insurance businesses, AIG was deemed to be too important to the U.S. economy to fail and leave millions of people and businesses uninsured.

The Value of Financial Investment

An earlier comment on the frequent lack of a direct relationship between true economic investment in capital and most financial investment is quite relevant to today's debate about the real value of the financial industry. Ultimately, the value added of the financial sector is measured in terms of the increase in human welfare that financial transactions create. The mere shuffling around of money and assets does not, in and of itself, benefit anyone. Only if the financial transactions and the increased variety of financial instruments result in an increase in real investment and true welfare-enhancing innovation or a more efficient allocation of consumption over time can we say that the financial sector produces something of value.

The description of the recent failure of the market for CDOs in the United States again reminds us that the financial sector of the economy does not always provide benefits to the rest of the economy. Rather than spreading risk, lowering finance costs, and permanently increasing home ownership, the recent new financial tools seem only to have enabled bankers and financial executives to increase their incomes at the long-run expense of misinformed investors, deceived pensioners, unrepresented future taxpayers, and foreclosed homeowners. This massive financial fraud was not foreseen in the orthodox economic models, which predicted instead that growing financial markets and the increased variety of financial instruments would bring greater stability, an increase in real investment, and a more efficient allocation of scarce savings toward the economy's more productive investments. The next section reviews some of the most basic of these models. What did these models miss?

ORTHODOX MODELS OF INTERNATIONAL INVESTMENT

Orthodox economics defines *international investment* as the sum total of purchases and sales of foreign assets. An asset is anything that holds value over time. A distinction is often made between **real assets**, like buildings, land, and factories, and **financial assets**, which are claims on future payments. Thus, an asset can take the form of tangible property, or it can be a verbal promise to pay "next month when I get my paycheck." In general, an asset is something that has value today because it is expected to have value in the future, either because it generates future returns or it can be redeemed or resold in the future. An asset is sometimes referred to as a **store of wealth**.

Among the financial assets that are commonly traded internationally are stocks, bonds, bank deposits, and bank loans. Internationally traded real assets include real estate, factories, office buildings, inventories, and entire business firms. As shown in Table 11.1, a major share of international investment consists of **foreign direct investment (FDI)**, which is overseas investment by transnational firms (TNCs). Examples of FDI are building factories overseas, establishing foreign marketing organizations, and acquiring controlling interests in existing foreign firms. This latter form of FDI is referred to as **mergers and acquisitions (M&A)**; the first two are examples of **greenfield investments**, which are the establishment of new overseas businesses and production facilities by a

TNC. Other major categories of international investment include bank lending, portfolio investment in stocks and bonds, and international lending by governments and international agencies.

A Traditional Model of International Investment

Figure 11.5 presents a supply and demand model of a country's financial market where loanable savings are exchanged. The demand curve for savings, or loanable funds, can be represented as a downward-sloping curve that represents, in descending order according to rates of return, the various real and financial investment opportunities for employing the loanable funds. The downward-sloping demand for loanable funds curve reflects a country's investment and innovative projects listed in descending order of expected returns. The supply curve of savings or loanable funds is shown as an upward-sloping curve, which suggests higher interest rates are necessary to induce savers to lend their purchasing power to investors and innovators. Savers require higher and higher returns to induce them to forego more current consumption.

In Figure 11.5, the equilibrium interest rate is 10 percent. The area under the demand curve D represents the total returns to the descending order of financial and real investments. The area under the supply of funds curve represents the opportunity cost of foregone consumption by savers. Both savers (suppliers) and borrowers (demanders) in the financial market enjoy net gains, or surpluses, from being able to lend and borrow, respectively. In Figure 11.5, borrowers receive returns equal to the distance below the demand for funds curve, while they must pay the equilibrium interest rate of 10 percent for borrowed funds. Borrowers therefore earn a surplus equal to the area a. Savers earn a surplus over and above their perceived value of foregone consumption equal to the area b. The total area beneath the demand for investment in new projects, the sum of areas a, b, and c in Figure 11.5, is the total return to all the projects carried out with the loanable funds.

Figure 11.6 shows a two-country version of the single-economy partial equilibrium loanable funds market model in Figure 11.5. Suppose, for example, that the world consists of two countries, Greece and Turkey. Suppose, also, that supply and demand conditions set equilibrium rates of return in the two countries at 6 percent and 4 percent, respectively. This difference in rates of return creates arbitrage opportunities for savers and borrowers in Greece and Turkey.

Savers will, in the absence of restrictions on the movement of money, place their wealth where the returns are greatest. Therefore, savings will move from Turkey to Greece. Figure 11.7 illustrates the result of this international financial investment. The supply curve of funds to purchase assets in Greece shifts out from S_I to S_{I+F}, where the F in the subscript stands for the amount of foreign savings that move from Turkey to Greece. The supply of savings in Turkey shifts to the left by an equal amount, as given by the shift of S_I to S_{I-F}. In effect, there is an international market for savings, which is illustrated in the center diagram of Figure 11.7 as international investment. The center diagram represents the net supply and demand that spill over from the domestic markets for loanable funds whenever interest rates in the international market differ from domestic interest rates. The model shows that the amount of savings that move from the low-interest market to the high-interest market, or the amount of international financial investment, is equal to $I_I = 0k = eg = hj$.

Figure 11.7 shows that savers in Turkey gain because the rate of interest rises. Turkish savers gain the areas c and d in the right-hand diagram of Figure 11.7. The shaded area c represents that part of the total returns that used to be captured by borrowers in Turkey but now accrue to savers. The net gain to Turkish citizens is the area d, which is the difference between (1) the additional returns earned by Turkish savers from being able to lend their savings in both Turkey and Greece and (2) the higher returns that must be paid to savers by Turkish borrowers. In summary, Turkish savers enjoy the opportunity to lend in next-door Greece where the returns are higher. Turkish borrowers have to compete with the higher returns on loans in Greece. Borrowers in Turkey prefer that Turkish savers not be permitted to acquire Greek assets, of course. In Greece, savers in Greece lose the

Figure 11.5 **The Market for Loanable Funds**

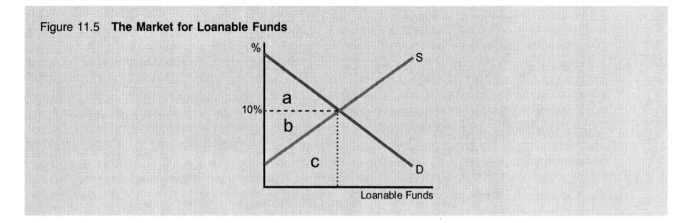

Figure 11.6 **Two-Country Partial Equilibrium Investment Model**

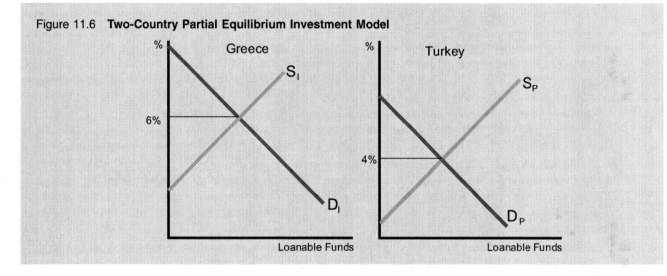

Figure 11.7 **Two-Country Partial Equilibrium Investment Model with International Investment**

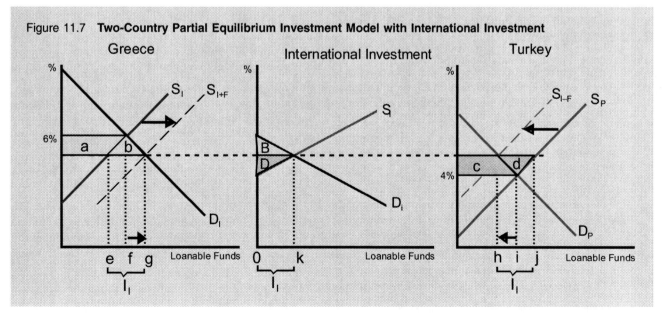

area a, but Greek borrowers find that the lower interest rate provides gains equal to the areas a and b. Thus, in each country the gainers gain more than the losers lose, although the roles of savers and borrowers are reversed.

Note that by opening the border to financial inflows and outflows, the total amount of financial investment falls in Turkey, and it rises in Greece. By sending savings to Greece and increasing Greece's financial assets, Turkey's savers enjoy higher returns in Greece and total Turkish income rises despite the fall in total returns on assets located in Turkey. In Greece, the gains to borrowers are greater than the losses to Greek savers following the interest rate decline. Like in the case of international trade, there are gainers and losers in each economy. International financial investment changes the distribution of economic welfare in each economy.

The partial equilibrium model of investment presented here is very simplistic, of course. First of all, it ignores the flows of savings and returns to assets in later periods. Eventually, loans have to be paid back, and international financial flows will tend to be redirected among the many different countries of the world. However, the simple two-country model of the market for loanable funds also helps to explain why some groups lobby against international investment. Savers in Greece are likely to press for curbs on savings inflows that lower the rates of return on real and financial assets. On the other hand, in countries with low rates of return on investment, borrowers are likely to object to investment outflows.

This traditional model of international investment thus concludes that savings flow from a country with lower interest rates to another with higher interest rates. As a result of this arbitrage process, returns on financial and real assets become equal across countries, and while the process favors some groups over others, the net welfare effects in both countries are positive. The model does not detail why there are differences in returns to financial assets across countries. Such differences may be the result of differing intertemporal preferences that are due to the variety of people's tastes, ages, family responsibilities, and present and expected wealth and income, and lenders' willingness to bear risk. They may also be the result of differences in the availability of factors of production and in the levels of technology. Intertemporal preferences may also differ because of differences in institutions or macroeconomic policies. Of course, because international investment may alter the preferences or productive capacities of countries by, say, adding to physical capital stocks or letting consumers borrow at lower interest rates, a static model of international investment cannot give us a very accurate long-run picture.

Risk and Diversification

The simple model above predicts investment flows between countries in one direction only, from the low-return economy to the high-return economy. Yet, the balance of payments data for individual countries generally show both sales of real and financial assets to foreigners and purchases of foreign real and financial assets. Therefore, there must be other motivations for international investment beyond the mere arbitrage of interest rate differentials. One of these other motivations for international asset exchanges is **diversification**. Virtually all assets have some risk in the sense that no one is ever perfectly certain that the assets will hold their value and pay out the promised or expected returns, although the risk generally varies greatly across different types of assets.

Purchasers of assets are wealth holders who want to maximize their income over time, all other things equal. But risk implies all other things are not equal. Wealth holders also tend to be **risk averse** in the sense that, all other things equal, they prefer less risk to more risk. Thus, the attractiveness of an asset to wealth holders depends on both risk and return, where risk reduces the attractiveness of an asset and higher returns increase its attractiveness. There is clearly a trade-off between risk and return.

Diversification improves the trade-off between risk and return. When wealth is spread across a diverse set of assets whose values vary differently in response to economic conditions, the value of a large set of assets fluctuates much less than the value of each of the assets in the portfolio. For example, when the value of one asset falls, other assets may not fall as much or may rise in value, thus keeping the average value of the portfolio from changing as much as the price of one asset.

International investment increases a wealth holder's opportunities for diversifying asset holdings because assets in different countries are less likely to be closely correlated than assets within a single economy. Thus, pooling assets from different countries should permit a greater amount of diversification than if diversification is limited to domestic assets. The diversification motive has been one of the reasons why international investment in stocks and bonds, or what is normally referred to as **portfolio investment**, has grown so much in the past twenty-five years.[4] Mutual funds of foreign stocks and bonds have proliferated, making it even easier for individuals to diversify their wealth holdings internationally. The gain from reducing risk is that wealth holders can store their wealth in riskier but, on average, more profitable investments. The ability to cross borders, therefore, seems to enable the financial system to more efficiently carry out its task of channeling savings to the most productive investment projects.

Normally, models of **portfolio diversification** assume that the risk of an asset can be defined in terms of a set of outcomes distributed around an expected mean. Risky assets are those whose distribution of possible returns is spread widely across many possible outcomes. The asset with the tightest distribution is defined as the least risky asset. In reality, however, financial assets are often characterized by a high degree of **uncertainty** rather than well-defined risk. Uncertainty describes the situation where the distribution of possible outcomes is not known, and the full range of possible outcomes is not known with certainty. In such a case, people's expectations can be subject to sudden changes as new information becomes available. Worse yet, because uncertainty implies a high degree of ignorance about the true future prospects of an asset, people resort to rules of thumb or pure instinct; this means that simple shifts in group sentiment or completely unrelated events can move market prices. Sudden shifts in expectations, well founded or completely unfounded, can cause large shifts in international financial flows.

THE DYNAMIC GAINS FROM INTERNATIONAL INVESTMENT

The gains from international investment shown in the orthodox standard model in the previous section do not accurately represent the complex gains and losses that countries experience when they open their borders to international investment and international financial flows. Most obvious is the inherent contradiction between static models and the long-run nature of investment. Investment, and the financing to pay for it, are part of the long-run dynamic process of economic development. In this section, therefore, we analyze international investment by linking it to both the Solow growth model and the Schumpeterian R&D model of technological progress.

The Solow Model and the Returns to Capital

The basic graphic representation of the Solow model from Chapter 6 is repeated here as Figure 11.8. Recall that the Solow model's steady state equilibrium occurs where the saving function, $\sigma f(K)$, is equal to the rate of depreciation line, δK, which defines the steady state levels of capital K^* and output $Y^* = f(K^*)$. Chapter 6 showed how variations in the rate of saving σ changes the steady state levels of capital and output in the economy; the higher the rate of saving, the higher the steady state level of output. This point is important because international financial flows consist of inflows and outflows of savings that, respectively, raise or lower the rate of saving in an economy. According to the Solow model, a change in saving directly changes investment in new capital.

The Solow model explains the returns to capital in an economy. Specifically, the return to investment is given by the slope of the production function $Y = f(K)$. A steep slope implies a high return

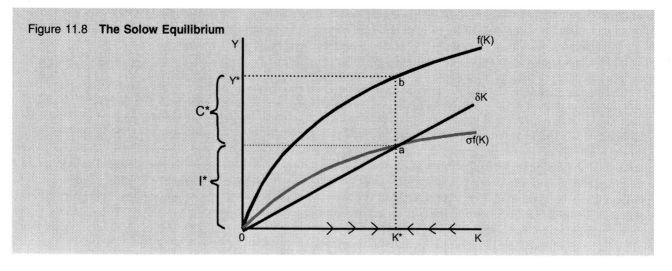

Figure 11.8 **The Solow Equilibrium**

because an increase in K causes a large increase in output; a flat slope implies a low return. The slope of the production function depends on:

- The stock of capital
- The stock of other substitute factors of production
- The level of technology

These three determinants of the return to investment are illustrated in Figure 11.9. Suppose the production function is given by $f_1(K,L_1)$, where K is variable and the labor supply L is fixed at quantity L_1. If the production function is subject to diminishing returns, as in Figure 11.9, then at the lower stock of capital K^*, the slope of the production function r_1 is greater than the slope r_2 at the larger stock of capital K^{**} (point a versus point b). Diminishing returns means that the greater the stock of capital, all other things equal, the lower the return to an additional unit of capital.

The return to capital is also affected by how many other factors of production are available. For example, an increase in the amount of labor, say from L_1 to L_2, will raise the entire production function from $f_1(K,L_1)$ to $f_1(K,L_2)$ in Figure 11.9. If the capital stock is given by K^{**}, in Figure 11.9 this increase in labor from L_1 to L_2 causes the marginal rate of return to investment (capital) to rise from r_2 to r_3 (point c versus point b).

The higher production function in Figure 11.9 may reflect a higher level of technology rather than a greater quantity of complementary inputs. Figure 11.9 assumes that improvements in technology increase the slope of the new production function $f_2(K,L_1)$ at K^{**} so that it is steeper than the slope of $f_1(K,L_1)$ at that same level of capital K^{**}, as evidenced by the steeper slope of the tangent r_3 compared to r_2. This is an example of labor-saving technological change. Labor-saving technological change increases the effective stock of labor and, therefore, raises the return to capital. This type of technological change will, all other things equal, increase the inflow of foreign capital to fund increased investment. Accordingly, the economy will tend to grow.

Why Savings Do Not Flow to Poor Countries

Robert E. Lucas, Jr. (1990) asked an interesting question some years ago: Why doesn't most capital flow from rich to poor countries? After all, poor countries have much less capital than rich countries, which means that, all other things equal, the marginal return to capital should be much higher in

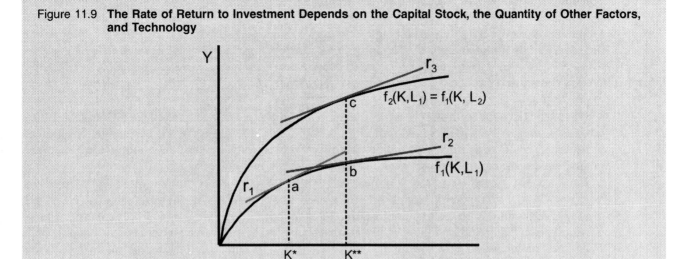

poor countries than in rich countries. In practice, international investment flows mostly from high-income countries to other high-income countries, not to poor countries.

Lucas examined several possible explanations for the lack of foreign investment in countries with little capital: (1) technology is not as advanced in low-income economies; (2) people have more human capital as well as physical capital in the rich countries, and human capital is complementary to physical capital; (3) there are large risks associated with intertemporal transactions between countries because long-term contracts cannot be effectively enforced in low-income countries; and (4) there are explicit restrictions on international investment. The first two explanations suggest that the slope of the production function is not steeper in developing countries; the latter two explanations suggest that even if the return to capital *is* higher in developing countries, international investment does not occur because it is in some way prevented or discouraged from responding to the incentive of higher returns. Lucas suggested that policies to promote a greater flow of savings to capital-scarce poor countries should focus on education, eliminating barriers to capital flows, and improving institutions that encourage people to enter into long-term contracts and otherwise enable intertemporal transactions to be carried out successfully.

The discussion above on labor-saving and capital-saving innovation provides another possibility: low labor costs in developing countries lead firms to employ labor-using and capital-saving technologies, which suppress returns to capital. As a result, there is less demand for foreign borrowing.

The Welfare Effect of International Investment in the Solow Model

The traditional two-country loanable funds model in the section "Orthodox Models of International Investment," showed that both countries gain from international investment even though investment falls in one of the countries. But the simple model does not take into consideration the adjustments in each economy that tend to occur subsequent to the investment flow. The Solow growth model takes at least some of these adjustments into consideration, and it appears to suggest that international savings flows raise investment and output in the destination country and reduce investment and the steady state level of output in the **source country**. Both countries may still gain from international borrowing and lending, however. The reason income can grow in both countries is the same reason savers in Turkey gained from being able to acquire assets in Greece in the partial equilibrium loanable funds model earlier: The citizens and firms who acquire higher-return foreign assets earn higher income than they would if they could acquire only lower-return domestic assets. Some of the gains from the higher returns on capital in the country receiving foreign savings are returned to the savers in the finance-exporting country in the form of interest, profit, or dividends.

Long-Run Growth Effect of International Investment

The Solow model shows that increased saving and investment can bring the economy only medium-term economic growth; permanent, continuous economic growth requires continual technological progress. Therefore, in order to examine the role of international investment on long-run economic growth we must examine how foreign investment affects technological change.

Recall from Chapter 6 that the Schumpeterian model hypothesizes innovation to be the result of *intentional* and *costly* innovative activities undertaken by profit-seeking entrepreneurs. We extended the logic of the model to include welfare-maximizing policy makers, nonprofit organizations supporting various interests, and educational institutions. The Schumpeterian process of innovation is essentially a dynamic maximization problem. The gains from innovation depend on (1) how much each new innovation improves human welfare, (2) how great is the opportunity cost of the resources employed to generate innovations, (3) how efficiently those resources in fact generate new ideas and technologies, and (4) how much society values future welfare relative to the current welfare lost because resources are redirected from production toward innovation.

International financial investment is likely to affect technological progress in several ways. Because it contributes to the integration of national and regional economies into a single world economy, international investment raises the potential profits from innovation. The gains for human welfare are greater when innovations are quickly applied throughout the world rather than just within one firm or one country. International financial investment can reduce the cost of innovation by facilitating the flow of ideas. As discussed in Chapter 10, there is evidence that foreign direct investment (FDI) leads to the transfer of technology to the recipient countries, and other forms of investment may also facilitate information flows between economies.

Statistical studies have found a positive correlation between economic investment in capital equipment and countries' rates of economic growth.[5] Studies have also found that the effect of equipment investment on economic growth is stronger in developing economies in the early stages of industrialization than it is in more developed economies.[6] Since FDI includes such things as the building of foreign factories, the acquisition of existing foreign firms and facilities, and the erecting of a marketing and distribution organization in a foreign market, FDI can lead to a substantial transfer of know-how abroad. Transnational firms also often transfer people, designs, business philosophies, and management techniques across borders.

International technology flows through FDI are not automatic. E. Borensztein, J. De Gregorio, and J-W. Lee (1998) trace international flows of technology and find that technology moves only when institutions in the destination country provide a stable economic environment so that investors are confident about the long-run performance of their investment. These authors also find that technology flows depend on education levels and the availability of educated local employees who can learn and apply new technologies. Institutions thus again come into play.

INTERNATIONAL FINANCIAL FLOWS: SOME CONCLUSIONS

The models that are most often used to analyze international investment all seem to suggest that national economies benefit from inflows of foreign savings. International financial flows, or what we might more accurately refer to as international trade in assets, mostly parallel the effects of international trade. From a static perspective, international investment causes short-run gains from an improved allocation of savings to investment projects. The Solow and Schumpeter models suggest that there may be further medium-run welfare gains from a transition to a higher steady state or a steeper growth path. Finally, there may be long-run gains from increased innovation due to greater flows of ideas and knowledge.

Many economists feel that, by combining the static models of international investment with our models of economic growth, a strong case can be made for policies that encourage international investment. Overall returns to investment improve as financial flows are more efficiently directed to the highest-return projects, risk is reduced through international diversification, innovation may increase, and FDI is likely to carry technology across borders.

Before concluding that development policies should include measures to expand international investment and international financial flows, however, we must examine Bhagwati's point that financial flows are potentially destabilizing and, thus, detrimental to long-run economic development. Looking at international investment and international financial flows more holistically, many other concerns become apparent. For one thing, when savings shift from one country to another, the macroeconomies of both countries are affected. The international sale or purchase of assets can change the aggregate demand for the economy's output. Also, savings affect the long-run path of national debt, national wealth, and the cost of loanable funds.

Also important are the practical problems of finance, such as default, fraud, adverse selection, information asymmetries, and other market failures. These failures are often much greater when intertemporal transactions occur across borders. Upcoming chapters show that international financial investment can be very destructive of human well-being. Sudden reversals of capital flows between countries have occurred with regularity over the past two hundred years, and they have often reduced people's income substantially and for long periods of time. This does not mean that international financial flows should be completely abolished, but a good case can be made for better regulation and monitoring of the financial flows on the financial account of the balance of payments. It does not make sense to keep expanding the complexity of our economic environment in pursuit of some gains in efficiency hypothesized in some orthodox economic models when the world continually suffers very real losses in human welfare because we are unable or unwilling to manage the complex international financial system.

Before we can fully address all these difficult issues, there is much more to learn about the international financial system. The next six chapters provide the necessary details as well as the world's historical successes and failures in dealing with financial complexity.

CHAPTER SUMMARY

1. This chapter introduces two additional forces of international economic integration: international investment, which consists of international sales and purchases of physical capital, such as houses, factories, machines, tools, roads, and power plants, and international finance, which includes all international asset sales and purchases that represent intertemporal exchanges.

2. International investment and financial flows have grown even more rapidly than trade, but their growth has fluctuated widely from year to year in all countries and has varied greatly among countries.

3. The balance of payments shows a country's exports and imports of goods and services, its private and public transfer payments to foreign individuals and governments, foreign direct investment inflows and outflows, domestic investors' stock and bond purchases overseas, foreigners' purchases of stocks and bonds in the domestic economy, and the interest, dividends, profits, and other earnings on foreign assets.

4. The balance of payments is the international extension of the circular flow of economic activity; each international payment flow connects to an individual economy's internal flows.

5. The circular flow diagram is based on standard macroeconomic accounting, which ignores many human activities as well as the services provided outside the market by our natural environment, which means the balance of payments also ignores many international transactions between the economic, social, and natural spheres of human existence.

6. The open-economy circular flow diagram in Figure 11.4 highlights the main flows of payments between countries.

7. The balance of payments account is divided into two main parts. The first is called the current account, and the second is the financial account. All the payment flows in the international circular flow diagram appear in either the current or financial accounts of the balance of payments.

8. Financial investment is broadly defined as the explicit or implicit acquisition of real and financial assets. This chapter gives many examples of the great variety of such assets.

9. An asset is anything that holds value over time. A distinction is often made between real assets, like buildings, land, and factories, and financial assets, which are claims on future payments.

10. Since assets are part of all intertemporal transactions, which involve payments at one point in time for payments later in time, the prices of financial instruments in large part depend on expectations of uncertain future outcomes that determine the later payments.

11. The limited information on the future, and the resulting uncertainty, mean that the prices of financial instruments and their derivatives are often driven by emotions and heuristics. Asset prices can diverge from fundamental long-run factors over extended periods of time, and asset price movements can be volatile.

12. The fundamental economic purpose of the financial sector is to channel savings to economic investment.

13. Financial investment also channels funds to cash-constrained consumers, a process that is economically beneficial if it permits consumers to better allocate their purchases over time.

14. The financial intermediaries, exchanges, and markets are costly to operate, however, and they may introduce new risks and uncertainties that cause default, moral hazard, adverse selection, and numerous other information problems.

15. The complexity of today's financial instruments and derivatives makes it impossible for any one investor, financial firm, or government regulatory agency to fully grasp all the risks of financial transactions. The complexity also implies that any one default or market failure can trigger many more defaults and failures throughout the system.

16. Instability in financial intermediaries, exchanges, and markets also results from the divergence in purpose of sellers and purchasers of financial assets.

17. International finance increases opportunities for diversifying asset holdings because assets in different countries are less likely to be closely correlated than assets within a single economy.

18. The diversification motive has been one of the reasons why international investment in stocks and bonds, or what is normally referred to as portfolio investment, has grown so much in the past twenty-five years.

19. The Solow model suggests that increased saving and investment can bring the economy only medium-term economic growth; international investment can increase long-run growth if it facilitates innovation.

20. International finance may affect innovation and technological change in several ways, each illustrated by how intertemporal transactions across borders affect the variables in the Schumpeterian model.

KEY TERMS AND CONCEPTS

adverse selection
asymmetric information
balance of payments (BoP)
cash instruments
circular flow diagram
collateralized debt obligations (CDOs)
credits

credit default swaps (CDSs)
current account
debits
default
deposit insurance
derivative instruments
derivatives

diversification
externalities
factor payments
financial account
financial asset
financial depth
financial exchanges
financial innovation
financial intermediaries
financial investment
financial market
financial sector
foreign aid
foreign direct investment (FDI)
General Theory of Employment, Interest,
    and Money, The
Greenfield investment
immigrant remittances
intermediate goods
international finance

international investment
intervention
maquiladora
merchandise trade balance
mergers and acquisitions (M&A)
moral hazard
official transactions
over-the-counter market
portfolio diversification
portfolio investment
principal-agent problem
real asset
risk aversion
Securities and Exchange Commission (SEC)
securitization
store of value
store of weath
uncertainty
value added
vertical specialization

PROBLEMS AND QUESTIONS

1. Explain why the acquisition of foreign assets can reduce the overall risk of an individual's portfolio of assets.
2. Why is a contemporaneous exchange of apples for oranges different from an intertemporal exchange of today's apples for the promise of similar apples next year?
3. Why have capital flows to developing countries increased so rapidly over the past decade, compared to earlier periods? Discuss.
4. Do you agree with Lucas's policy suggestions for stimulating more flows of savings from high-income to low-income economies? Explain using the simple production function model presented in Figure 11.9.
5. Why could intertemporal exchanges across national borders be more welfare enhancing than intertemporal exchanges within borders? Why might such international investment be more difficult to carry out than asset exchanges within borders?
6. Explain why the growth of international investment, in part driven by the diversification motive, has reduced the gains from international asset diversification.
7. Is gross national product a better measure of individual welfare than gross domestic product if a country engages in a large amount of international investment? Explain your answer.
8. Figure 11.10 shows the equilibrium in the markets for loanable funds (savings) in two isolated countries, Portugal and Spain. Describe the international investment that would result if the governments of the two countries permitted their citizens and firms to borrow and lend with people and firms in the other country. (Hint: Follow the discussion on the two-country partial equilibrium model of international investment as given in Figure 11.7, with a center diagram describing international investment and specific areas that represent the gains and losses to savers and borrowers in each country.)
9. Explain how international investment influences a country's rate of economic growth using (1) the Solow growth model and (2) the Schumpeterian R&D model of technological progress. Contrast the conclusions of the two models.

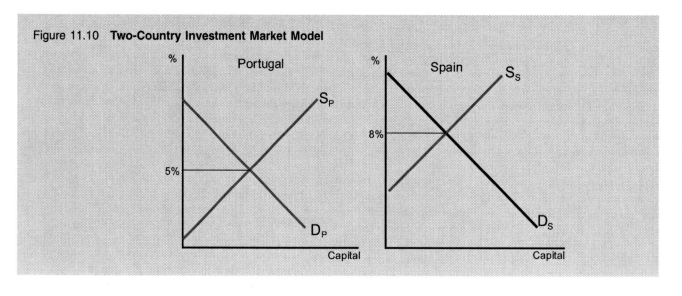

Figure 11.10 **Two-Country Investment Market Model**

10. Explain why moral hazard is likely to be a greater problem for international investment than for domestic investment.

11. What government institutions can mitigate the problems of fraud, moral hazard, and adverse selection? Provide some examples.

12. Review the example of AIG and the credit default swaps, and explain the roles played by fraud, adverse selection, and moral hazard.

13. Review the open-economy circular flow diagram presented in this chapter (Figure 11.4) and explain how the past accumulation of foreign assets by a country's citizens and businesses permits the country to run trade deficits without adding to its foreign debt.

14. Go to the website of the Bureau of Economic Analysis of the U.S. Department of Commerce (http://www.bea.gov/international/index.htm) and look at the spreadsheet of the U.S. balance of payments from 1960 to the present. Describe the trends that you observe in the numbers. (Hint: You should notice that the individual categories of the U.S. balance of payments have not all grown proportionately; describe why some international transactions have grown more rapidly than others.)

15. Table 11.1 shows that the United States has in recent years run very large trade deficits. Can the United States continue to import much more than it exports? Explain how trade deficits are offset by other payments flows and why these other flows could prove difficult to sustain in the long run.

NOTES

1. Vertical specialization is analyzed by David Hummels, Jun Ishii, and Kei-Mu Yi (2000), for example.

2. International Monetary Fund (1996), *Balance of Payments Manual,* 5th ed., Washington, DC: IMF. Some of the terminology in this book may clash with that of older books based on earlier balance of payments accounting conventions.

3. "Financial Audit: Resolution Trust Corporation's 1995 and 1994 Financial Statements," www.gao.gov, quoted in Mary Bottari (2010), "Of Bubbles and Bailouts: New Wall Street Bailout Accounting Puts Numbers in Perspective," *Dollars & Sense,* July–August, p. 22.

4. See *The Economist* (1997), "All Fall Down," November 8.

5. The classic articles are J. Bradford De Long and Lawrence H. Summers (1991) and De Long and Summers (1992).

6. See, for example, Jonathan Temple (1998) and A.J. Aurbach, K.A. Hassett, and S.D. Oliner (1994).

CHAPTER 12

The Foreign Exchange Market

> The puzzling thing is that despite the obvious gain from the use of one money, it appears to be quite difficult to introduce one money in the international economy which will be acceptable to everyone.
>
> —Paul De Grauwe (1989)

If you have traveled overseas, you are already familiar with *exchange rates,* the prices at which one country's money is exchanged for another country's money. In your travels, you probably viewed changing money as part of the "international experience." Importers, exporters, and international investors are more likely to see the many different moneys as a complication that adds to the cost of international transactions. Evidence suggests that there would be more international trade and international investment if importers, exporters, and investors did not face the cost of having to exchange currencies every time they exchanged products or assets across borders.

The existence of different national currencies effectively gives all the products traded between countries many prices rather than just one. For every traded product, there is the price in the currency of the country where the product is produced, and then there are the prices in terms of other countries' currencies. There are many reasons why prices differ from one country to another, but the main long-run determinant of the price differences are the exchange rates between the world's many different currencies. Exchange rates are very important for international trade because the attractiveness of buying foreign goods or selling domestic goods overseas depends on how exchange rates translate foreign currency prices into prices denominated in the domestic currency.

Exchange rates also impact international investment. Potential buyers of foreign assets must take into consideration both the current and future prices as well as the expected future returns on foreign assets compared to the current prices, future prices, and future returns on domestic assets. Prices of and returns on foreign assets must be translated into domestic currencies before they can be compared to domestic assets and returns. In the case of assets, decisions to buy or sell are based on both current known exchange rates and expected future exchange rates. Foreign investment decisions, therefore, face not only the usual risks and uncertainty of long-run investment, but, because the exchange rates at which the future selling prices and returns are translated back into the investor's home currency cannot be predicted with certainty, foreign investment is also subject to **foreign exchange risk**.

Foreign exchange markets are not mere inconveniences. The exchange rates set in foreign exchange markets have a direct bearing on economic activities in the global economy. As will be detailed later in this chapter, by determining the relative prices of products and assets across different economies, the exchange rate plays a critical role in balancing the flow of payments between countries. In short, the exchange rate is a major determinant of the international payments flows that are recorded in the balance of payments.

This chapter will begin to make it clear that there are distinct advantages, and disadvantages, to maintaining a national currency as opposed to using another country's money or adopting an international money jointly with a group of other countries. Among other things, a national money gives a national government the power to conduct a national **monetary policy**, which can be quite useful for macroeconomic management of the economy. On the other hand, as already noted, separate currencies create transactions costs for exporters, importers, travelers, and international investors. Also, sudden changes in foreign exchange rates have very real, and potentially devastating, consequences for national economies.

Major newspapers report foreign exchange rates every day. Exchange rates between the major currencies are also continuously available on the websites of major newspapers. Table 12.1 reports the values of each of the world's currencies in terms of the two major currencies, the U.S. dollar and the euro, reported by the *Financial Times* on May 27, 2009. The *Financial Times* reported the values of 216 national currencies. Many of the exchange rates listed are determined on active markets where the forces of supply and demand determine the price of a currency in terms of other currencies. These markets are referred to as *foreign exchange markets,* or collectively as the **foreign exchange market**.

In markets where the forces of supply and demand are free to drive the prices of currencies, the exchange rates are said to *float*. The foreign exchange market is not a true free market, however. The uncertainty associated with **floating exchange rates** and concern about their potential negative effects on international trade and investment often lead governments to interfere in the foreign exchange market. Governments often influence the price of their currencies by selling or buying currencies to offset shifts in supply and demand that would otherwise cause the exchange rate to change. When governments intervene in the foreign exchange market in order to keep a currency's value perfectly constant, the exchange rate is said to be *fixed*. We will show in later chapters that it is very difficult to maintain **fixed exchange rates** when the fundamental forces of supply and demand shift in today's global economy. Governments nevertheless often interfere in foreign exchange markets, and some even attempt to rigidly *fix* the values of their currencies by constantly intervening in the market or directly restricting supply and demand. As we will see, there are advantages to preventing exchange rates from changing import and export prices and the relative prices of domestic and foreign assets.

THE EVOLUTION OF THE FOREIGN EXCHANGE MARKET

Markets for exchanging foreign money have operated for over two thousand years, ever since there have been distinct national moneys. In ancient times, gold and silver coins from different parts of the world were used by the merchants who carried goods from one region to another. Even though all coins were made of the same precious metals, they varied greatly in weight and purity. The early foreign exchange markets were money changers who had expertise in measuring the relative worth of coins minted by the many different regions, empires, and city-states.

The Foreign Exchange Market in Ancient Times

The origin of money is not known with certainty, but historians agree that the region of Lydia (located in modern-day Turkey) issued coins as early as 650 B.C.E. The practice of minting coins spread from the cities of ancient Greece to other regions in the Middle East, Asia, and the Mediterranean.[1] Most ancient coins were made of bronze (for small transactions) and silver (for larger and foreign

Table 12.1

A Sample of Exchange Rates: May 26, 2009

Currency per:

Country:	Dollar	Euro	Country:	Dollar	Euro
Argentina (peso)	3.7413	5.2327	Philippines (peso)	47.355	66.2331
Australia (dollar)	1.2802	1.7905	Poland (zloty)	3.1567	4.4150
Bahrain (dinar)	0.3770	0.5273	Romania (new leu)	2.9876	4.1786
Bolivia (boliviano)	7.0200	9.8185	Russia (ruble)	31.3265	43.8148
Brazil (real)	2.0353	2.8467	Saudi Arabia (riyal)	3.7502	5.2453
Canada (dollar)	1.1216	1.5687	Singapore (dollar)	1.4484	2.0257
Chile (peso)	562.95	787.37	South Africa (rand)	8.2900	11.5947
China (yuan)	6.8306	9.5536	South Korea (won)	1262.90	1766.36
Colombia (peso)	2210.6	3091.9	Sweden (krona)	7.5687	10.586
Costa Rica (colon)	576.395	806.176	Switzerland (franc)	1.0837	1.5156
Czech R. (koruna)	19.0877	26.697	Taiwan (dollar)	32.655	45.6729
Denmark (kroner)	5.3227	7.4446	Thailand (baht)	34.475	48.2185
Egypt (pound)	5.6235	7.8653	Tunisia (dinar)	1.3502	1.8885
Estonia (kroon)	11.1869	15.6465	Turkey (lira)	1.5545	2.1742
Hong Kong (dollar)	7.7520	10.8423	U.A.E. (dirham)	3.6727	5.1368
Hungary (forint)	201.301	281.550	U.K. (pound)*	1.5943	0.8773
India (rupee)	47.930	67.037	1 mo. forward	1.5941	0.8771
Indonesia (rupiah)	10335.0	14455.1	3 mo. forward	1.5937	0.8769
Israel (shekel)	3.9666	5.5479	1 yr. forward	1.5924	0.8766
Japan (yen)	94.7750	132.557	Ukraine (hryvnia)	7.6575	10.7102
1 mo. forward	94.7417	132.467	Uruguay (peso)	23.5500	32.9382
3 mo. forward	94.6824	132.316	U.S.A. (dollar)	—	1.3987
1 yr. forward	94.1988	131.490	1 mo. forward	—	1.3982
Kenya (shilling)	78.150	109.305	3 mo. forward	—	1.3975
Kuwait (dinar)	0.2879	0.4027	1 yr. forward	—	1.3959
Malaysia (ringgit)	3.5125	4.9128	Venezuela (bolivar)	2.1473	3.0033
Mexico (peso)	13.1380	18.3755	Vietnam (dong)	17781	24869
New Zealand (dollar)	1.6138	2.2572	Euro*	1.3987	—
Nigeria (naira)	148.00	207.00	1 mo. forward	1.3982	—
Norway (krone)	6.4008	8.9525	3 mo. forward	1.3975	—
Pakistan (rupee)	80.615	112.752	1 yr. forward	1.3959	—
Peru (new sol)	2.9993	4.1950	SDR	0.6479	0.9062

* Exchange rates for the British pound and the euro are from the dollar perspective; all other rates are local currency per dollar.
Source: Closing rates, 16:00 Greenwich Mean Time, published in the *Financial Times*, May 27, Marketing and Investing Section, p. 20. Also, see www.ft.com/markets/data.

transactions). Because of their scarcity and high value relative to the prices of most goods, gold and gold coins served mostly as a store of value rather than a medium of exchange.

The ancient money changers plus the various suppliers of coins comprised the ancient international financial system. By the fifth century B.C.E., money changers were active in Greece and Persia and throughout the Middle East. Their job was

> to know the value of foreign coins and the proper exchange rates and to make the exchanges. There were, after all, a great many different coinages in circulation in Greece and they were on several different standards. . . . While the coins of some cities were sound, those of others were more or less debased. On the simplest level exchanges would be freely made and, allowing for the money changer's commission, such exchanges should have reflected the metallic contents, weights, and relative purity of the gold, silver, and bronze in the coins. (William L. Davisson and James E. Harper 1972, p. 157)

The ancient money changer's job was complicated by the variety and unreliability of the coinage in circulation. Rulers who minted coins sometimes tried to pass them off as containing more gold and silver than they really did. Money changers therefore carefully weighed and analyzed coins in order to determine their true content of gold, silver, or other precious metals. The risks involved in exchanging coins were high, and ancient money changers demanded high margins between buying and selling prices in order to cover their risk.

Even honest governments found the minting of coins a profitable business, and as time passed, emperors, kings, queens, pharaohs, and other heads of state increasingly monopolized coinage within their territories. With the supply restricted, coins normally gained value over and above the implicit value of the gold or silver they contained because they provided some reassurance to their holders that they indeed were of the stated value. Merchants were usually willing to accept standard coins for payment over unminted gold or silver of unknown purity and weight. The difference between the value of the gold or silver in a coin and the value at which the coin circulated came to be called **seignorage**, which was the gain that the seigneur, or the monarch, derived from the monopoly right to mint coins. The ancient gold and silver coins were often **debased** by intentional scraping of some of a coin's gold or silver from its edges.

The Development of Banking

Foreign exchange markets became more complicated after the development of banking and the introduction of new types of payments to supplement the traditional use of coins made from precious metals. In the Middle Ages, merchants in the major European trading centers increasingly made payments using **bills of exchange** that were linked to deposits of gold or silver coins or bullion in banks, a procedure very similar to the current practice of writing checks on money deposited in a checking account. Bills of exchange were a financial innovation that freed merchants from having to carry gold or silver over long distances under the risk of loss or theft. The paper claims on gold or silver deposited in distant but known banks were exchanged among merchants multiple times before being redeemed. A merchant from one country might buy goods in another country and pay for them with a bill of exchange drawn on a bank in his home country. The merchant who sold the goods could sell the bill to a money changer for local money, and the money changer could then sell the bill to someone going to the country where the bank was located. Or, the merchant could use the bill to pay for goods purchased from another merchant, who could then sell the bill to a money changer or use it to yet again buy goods.

The banks that provided the bills of exchange were usually the same ones that financed merchants and their trade costs. These banks enjoyed good reputations among merchants, and they naturally came to dominate the exchange of bills of exchange from banks in other kingdoms and cities. In effect, the most reputable commercial banks became not only suppliers of foreign exchange and bills of exchange, but also, effectively, wholesale money changers, exchanging the new negotiable financial claims denominated in different currencies. In other words, the financing of foreign trade and the exchange of currencies went hand in hand. Today, foreign exchange markets are still operated by the world's largest commercial banks.

Fiat Money and Exchange Rates

Paper money was allegedly invented in China, and the practice later spread to Europe. Gold and silver were known commodities that had value all over the world, but paper money's value depended only on the expectation that it could be used to purchase some quantity of goods or assets some time in the future. Paper money is a **fiat money**, which has value only if people trust they will be able to exchange it for something of value in the future. With paper or *fiat* money, the job of the money changer became much more difficult. Now the price of one fiat money in terms of other fiat moneys reflected not the value of some well-known precious metal, but only an expectation of the fiat money's future **purchasing power**. That is, the relative value of each paper money depended on what it, and all other currencies, could buy currently and, most importantly, what it was expected to be able to buy in terms of real goods and services in the future.

This fundamental difference between using gold or silver coins and bullion to back financial instruments, such as the bills of exchange mentioned above, and using fiat money should be obvious. In the former case, the relative values of instruments denominated in different currencies can never deviate very much from the relative values of the gold and silver that back the instruments. But, if paper money and bills of exchange backed by fiat paper money are exchanged in the foreign exchange markets, then it is the perceived relative values of the paper money that determine exchange rates. Bills of exchange drawn on accounts containing deposits of fiat money will be accepted in payment for goods so long as people expect the fiat money can be used to acquire goods or assets of the stated value. If people suspect, for example, that the government may abuse its privilege to print money by printing much more than is needed for the exchange of goods, services, and assets, then people will expect inflation to rise and the purchasing power of the fiat money to diminish over time. Sellers of goods will then demand to be paid in other currencies, thus reducing the value of the diminished money even further. And those who hold the currency or bills drawn on accounts denominated in that currency may begin to exchange those bills for other currencies or assets denominated in other currencies. In the end, demand for a currency that is expected to lose purchasing power will decline, and there will be growing demand for currencies whose value is expected to rise in the future. The exchange rate at which the currencies are traded reflects these shifts in supply and demand.

Specifically, expectations of fiat money exchange rates depend on a variety of information about current economic conditions and policies, as well as people's understanding of how economic and political conditions are likely to evolve in the future. Demand for fiat currencies issued by governments less likely to engage in inflationary money creation will tend to rise. Exchange rates among fiat moneys tend to continually change as news about political and economic events becomes known and people's understanding of the world changes. Given that today's moneys are nearly all fiat moneys, backed only by the monetary policies of the issuing government agency or designated central bank, it should not be surprising that exchange rates are often volatile.

This brief discussion of the history of money and foreign exchange markets has, hopefully, served to distinguish several important relationships that help explain how foreign exchange markets work today. The role of expectations about future purchasing power is key to understanding exchange rates among modern fiat moneys. Now let's add some more details about today's money changers, or what we call the foreign exchange market.

CONTEMPORARY FOREIGN EXCHANGE MARKETS

When you travel overseas and exchange dollars for foreign money at an airport foreign exchange counter, you are dealing in what is called the retail foreign exchange market. The retail market accounts for a very small part of the world's foreign exchange transactions, however. Nearly all of the US$3 to $4 trillion worth of currencies that are exchanged every working day are traded through a worldwide network of dealers that are collectively referred to as the **over-the-counter market**.

The Over-the-Counter Market

The term *over-the-counter* implies that the dealers maintain stocks of currencies and they are open to buying from and selling to whoever "steps up to the counter." The details of each query, offer, and actual exchange are known only to the customer and dealer, although most market participants have some knowledge of recent prices at other counters. The foreign exchange dealers are more like wholesalers, dealing only with large sales and purchases. A US$1 million deal is referred to as "thin" in the foreign exchange market. Dealers are often located mostly in the offices of large banking organizations, linked by the most sophisticated electronic communications network available. The dealers make a market for international businesses, financial firms, pension funds, insurance companies, hedge funds, and other large investors. The dealers both sell to and buy from the same group of customers, and the dealers also trade for themselves in order to balance their inventories of currencies, to exploit arbitrage opportunities, and occasionally to take speculative positions. The dealers buy and sell foreign exchange to customers on demand.

Foreign exchange dealers are exposed to exchange rate risk for the simple reason that they are what we call **market makers**, who are dealers who hold stocks of currencies and stand ready to quote both bids and offers for one or more currencies. The market makers provide the price information that guides the market and permits trades upon demand. These foreign exchange dealers, trading on behalf of their customers and for their own accounts, make up the single largest financial market in the world.

Today's foreign exchange market evolved from the banks that provided trade credit and dealt in foreign bills of exchange centuries ago. The modern over-the-counter dealer market is located wherever commercial banks and other financial organizations have gone into the business of dealing in foreign exchange. According to the Bank for International Settlements (BIS), traders located in the United States accounted for 17.9 percent of the world's foreign exchange transactions in 2010. London accounted for 36.7 percent, or well over one-third, of the world's foreign exchange transactions. London's current prominence in foreign exchange dealings is the result of centuries of banking experience. The British authorities' deregulation of international financial transactions has also helped to solidify London's current position in the world financial markets. Worldwide, over 1,300 active dealers reported to the BIS in 2010 (BIS 2010).

About 85 percent of foreign exchange transactions involve the U.S. dollar as one of the currencies exchanged. This percentage seems rather high, given that the United States accounts for less than 20 percent of world trade in goods and services. But, many international transactions are denominated in dollars even when they are by people, firms, agencies, banks, or other organizations from countries that do not use the dollar as their currency. Commodities such as oil, coffee, copper, and most others are usually priced in dollars, regardless of who is supplying or buying the oil. Also, most international loans by large commercial banks to firms and governments of developing economies are denominated in U.S. dollars, and many foreign firms and governments issue bonds in dollars.

The dollar's prominence in the foreign exchange market also reflects the fact that it serves as a **vehicle currency** for many trades of less common currencies. For example, if you want to exchange Uruguayan pesos for Malaysian dollars, you will have to first trade pesos for dollars and then dollars for ringgit. Such roundabout trades may appear to be cumbersome, but they are actually more efficient than trading pesos directly. A peso-ringgit market would be very "thin," and it would not clear very frequently. Also, exchange rates could fluctuate excessively because small random shocks would easily overwhelm a very small market. The peso-dollar and ringgit-dollar markets are much larger than the missing peso-ringgit market would be; the peso-dollar and ringgit-dollar markets therefore provide more accurate information and greater *liquidity* to market participants. Greater **market liquidity** means market participants can more often close trades in precisely the quantities of currencies desired. Costs are also often lower with two trades through larger markets than with one trade through a small, illiquid market. Economies of scale are substantial and come into play because with a smaller number of markets, dealers and other market participants need to hold fewer working balances in different currencies.

A Worldwide Market

Modern communications have created an integrated world market for foreign exchange that essentially functions twenty-four hours per day. There are major financial centers where large dealers are located in nearly every time zone of the world. When it is late afternoon in San Francisco and financial markets close there, markets in Auckland, New Zealand, in Sydney, Australia, and in Tokyo, Japan, are just opening. And, before those markets close, other markets in Singapore in Southeast Asia and Bahrain in the Middle East will have opened, followed by the foreign exchange dealers in the financial centers of Europe. Then, as the London, Paris, and Frankfurt markets are in their afternoon trading, dealers in New York open, followed by dealers in Chicago and San Francisco, at which point the whole cycle starts over again.

The foreign exchange market is, by far, the largest financial market in the world. Table 12.2 provides some estimates of the size of the foreign exchange market compiled by the Bank for International Settlements (BIS 2010). According to the latest BIS data, the overall volume of the spot, forward, and swap markets is about US\$4 trillion per day. Notice from Table 12.2 that the overall 2001 volume declined relative to 1998. This contraction in trading volume was caused by the introduction of the euro, the new currency that replaced twelve separate European currencies. The single currency eliminated the large volume of currency trades that had occurred between German marks, French francs, Dutch guilders, Spanish pesetas, Italian lira, Belgian francs, and the other national currencies that the euro replaced. But, after that adjustment, worldwide currency trading resumed its growth, and by 2004 the total of the three markets reached a new daily turnover of about US\$1.8 trillion.

Table 12.2 splits trading on the foreign exchange market into several categories. There are **spot transactions** that consist of exchanges of currencies immediately at current exchange rates. There are also **forward transactions**, which consist of contractual arrangements agreed to today for an exchange of currencies to be carried out at some future date. In practice, spot and forward market transactions are settled two days after the exchange in order to give banks ample time to confirm the agreement and arrange for the necessary crediting and debiting of accounts in different business locations, but the prices and volumes are determined at the moment they are agreed to. As will be explained later in this chapter, forward transactions are an important method by which international traders and investors reduce uncertainty about the future value of currencies.

A growing proportion of foreign market transactions are *swaps,* which are contractual arrangements where a party buys (sells) foreign exchange for delivery on one date and agrees to sell (buy) it back at some later date. Some swaps combine a spot and a forward transaction that reverses the spot transaction. Many swaps involve two offsetting forward transactions for distinct future dates. Table 12.2 shows the growth of swaps as a proportion of total foreign exchange transactions. Swaps permit investors to temporarily acquire foreign assets without incurring the risk of future exchange rate changes, an important attribute for short-term investors, speculators, and the financial managers of international businesses.

Online Trading

In 2000, a small multi-bank website called Currenex.com began to accept currency trades online. Shortly thereafter, another small firm launched FXTrade.com, which took trades directly from retail customers such as small exporters and importers. Its computer system could handle 100 trades per second, and all trades were taken regardless of size.[2] This entrance of "outsiders" into the foreign exchange trading business prompted seven of the largest foreign exchange banks, Bank of America, Goldman Sachs, J.P. Morgan, Morgan Stanley Dean Witter, HSBC, Credit Suisse First Boston, and UBS Warburg, to offer an online foreign exchange trading service named Fxall.com in June 2000.

Table 12.2

Global Foreign Exchange Market Turnover: 2010 (Daily Averages on April 1, US$ billions)

	1989	1992	1995	1998	2001	2004	2007	2010
Spot transactions	317	394	494	568	386	621	1,005	3,981
Forward transactions	27	58	97	128	130	208	362	1,490
Foreign exchange swaps	190	324	546	734	656	944	1,714	475
Currency swaps	—	—	—	10	7	21	31	43
Options and other products	—	—	—	87	60	119	212	207
Total turnover	590	820	1,190	1,705	1,505	2,040	3,370	3,981

Source: BIS (2010), "Trennial Central Bank Survey of Foreign Exchange and Derivatives Market Activity in April 2010," Basel: Bank for International Settlements, September (downloaded from www.bis.org).

These seven firms together already accounted for slightly over 30 percent of all foreign exchange transactions on the conventional over-the-counter dealer market. In August 2000, the three largest foreign exchange banks, who controlled about 28 percent of all foreign exchange business—Citibank, Chase Manhattan, and Deutsche Bank—linked up with Reuters to create a competing foreign exchange trading service on the Internet. Reuters was already operating a worldwide interbank system used by major dealers in competition with Electronic Broking Services (EBS) run by a consortium of major banks. These two dealer networks should not be confused with the direct access online networks. The online dealer networks effectively replaced the telephone networks used by the dealers since the early twentieth century, while the direct access networks opened direct trading to nontraditional dealers and major bank customers. EBS is today owned and operated by ICAP, the London-based financial services provider that operates a number of interdealer financial trading networks.

In 2005 another new online trading platform, Hotspot FX, gained market share because its procedures maintained the anonymity of clients, a feature that hedge funds in particular liked. Hedge funds suspected that their trades through dealers generated market gossip that revealed their trading strategies and, therefore, reduced their earnings. At the same time, the largest of the interbank communications networks used by dealers, EBS, began a pilot program to let some pension funds, large multinational firms, hedge funds, and other large customers act directly on dealer quotes without the active involvement of the traditional dealers. The BIS (2010) estimates that today about half of all foreign exchange trades still pass through the traditional dealers or their online platforms, but the potential competition from online platforms has caused the margins of dealers to fall.

Centralization of the Market

The foreign exchange market has, for the past century, been characterized by its decentralized structure. Foreign exchange trades were carried out by dealers located throughout the world who communicated by telephone. Deals closed over the phone were followed up by paperwork delivered by mail. Research on market structure in general suggests that the degree of centralization of a market influences its performance. Centralized markets more quickly eliminate arbitrage opportunities, and they do a better job of executing trades in accordance with traders' specific requirements. Information is disseminated much more slowly in decentralized markets than in **centralized exchange markets**, or simply *centralized exchanges*, where everyone can observe price movements immediately. For example, Robert Flood (1994) found significant inefficiencies in the foreign exchange markets related to inventory imbalances inherent in a decentralized market. Dealers must engage in frequent and large transactions to keep inventories in balance, and such transactions are costly. Bid-ask price margins tend to be larger in decentralized markets because of the higher costs, but, of course, dealers can demand higher margins because they have greater market power due to the fact that customers have less information about competing prices. Overall, decentralized over-the-counter markets are more costly than centralized exchanges.

In decentralized markets not all dealer quotes are observable to market participants. Different deals may be closed with different prices at the same time. A centralized foreign exchange market is more transparent because one price applies to all deals and every participant can observe the bids and offers of other participants. The foreign exchange markets in most countries have no disclosure requirements, and trades are observed only by the buyer and seller. Outside customers can observe only those bid and ask prices they are offered directly and at which they actually trade currencies.

The electronic brokering systems have changed the process of price discovery and the way price information is disseminated among dealers and to the public. These electronic systems have been referred to as "virtual centralization" because they communicate with all market participants at once. When the foreign exchange market consisted exclusively of decentralized two-way telephone conversations, market participants were aware of prices in just a very small segment of the market at any one time. In order to gain more information about market prices and the underlying demand and supply, dealers would regularly execute small trades throughout the day.

Table 12.3 shows the ten largest dealers in the market for foreign exchange for 2004 and 2009. The top ten dealer institutions are all large, private, international banking firms. Note that in 2009, three banks handled almost one-half of the total value of foreign exchange transactions in the over-the-counter market. In 2009, the top dealer institution, Deutsche Bank, handled 21 percent of the total market's volume. Five years earlier, the largest dealer, Union Bank Switzerland, handled just over 12 percent of a much smaller total volume. Less than twenty years ago today, the largest dealer, Citibank, handled little more than 4 percent of the total market volume.

Since the foreign exchange market is largely unregulated and open for any firm to enter, the increased concentration and the decline in the overall number of dealers over the past decade suggests that there are natural reasons for the industry concentration. Most likely, there are economies of scale to dealing in foreign exchange. A firm interested in dealing in foreign exchange needs only to connect to one or both of the interbank communications platforms, Reuters and EBS, hire a competent staff, and attract customers who want to buy and sell foreign exchange. To make a profit, however, a foreign exchange dealer must gain a large enough volume of business to be able to offer clients the liquidity they demand and to make money at the small margins between buy and sell prices.

Retail Currency Exchange

There is also a separate retail market, which you can see in the form of booths at airports, border crossings, and tourist destinations. Currency exchange offices can also be found in retail businesses; for example, Marks & Spencer department stores in Britain exchange currencies on a cash basis. These retail exchanges often charge a 10 percent premium above the over-the-counter exchange rates plus additional fees. Your author is, at the time of this writing, still carrying around a £20 note from a trip to Britain a year earlier because he obstinately refused to pay the $5 fee plus a 12 percent premium charged in the retail market at the airport.

The retail market has now gone online. In 2009, newspapers like the *Financial Times* and the *Wall Street Journal* contained many advertisements for online foreign exchange trading. These retail online systems move the retail market well beyond the traditional business of changing

Table 12.3

Top Ten Dealer Banks' Market Shares

2009		2004	
Company	Share	Company	Share
Deutsche Bank	21.0%	UBS	12.4%
UBS	14.6	Deutsche Bank	12.2
Barclays Capital	10.5	Citigroup	9.4
RBS	8.2	J.P. Morgan	5.8
Citigroup	7.3	HSBC	4.9
J.P. Morgan	5.4	Goldman Sachs	4.5
HSBC	4.1	Barclays	4.1
Goldman Sachs	3.4	CSFB/Credit Suisse	3.8
Credit Suisse	3.1	RBS	3.5

Source: Euromoney, as published in the *Financial Times*, May 27, 2004; Euromoney (2009), "FX Poll 2009: Embattled Banks Boosted by Performance in Booming FX Markets," www.euromoneyfix.com.

money for travelers, other individual consumers, and small businesses. These online traders are set up mainly to attract individual speculators, or better said, gamblers. The online systems therefore offer leverage as high as 100:1, in some cases even 200:1.[3] For example, a gambler who deposits $10,000 can bet that the dollar will appreciate the next day relative to the one-day forward exchange rate by committing to buy $1 million in dollars forward one day. If the dollar becomes 1 percent more expensive the next day, the speculator simultaneously buys the $1 million as contracted and sells them on the **spot market** for 1 percent more to earn $10,000 (1 percent of $1 million), or 100 percent of the $10,000 deposited with the trading system. Hence, the 100:1 leverage converts a 1 percent change in the exchange rate into a 100 percent profit on the $10,000 deposited.

Such leverage also means that if the currency appreciates and moves 1 percent in the "wrong" direction, then the gambler must sell the dollars she has committed to buy the currency at 99 percent of the purchase price, which brings a $10,000 loss that completely wipes out the initial deposit. The inherent dangers of high leverage ratios are why currency traders for banks and hedge funds are seldom permitted to leverage more than 10:1.

The National Futures Association, the self-regulatory organization for the U.S. futures markets, offers this legalistic cautionary message:

> Like many other investments, off-exchange foreign currency trading carries a high level of risk and may not be suitable for all investors. In fact, you could lose all of your initial investment and may be liable for additional losses. Therefore, you need to understand the risks associated with this product so you may make an informed investment decision. This . . . does not suggest that you should or should not participate in the retail off-exchange foreign currency market. You should make that decision after consulting with your own financial advisor and considering your own financial situation and objectives. (National Futures Association 2004, p. 1)

This weak warning in a booklet promoting online foreign exchange speculation suggests that self-regulation by financial firms does not work. With regard to these retail speculative foreign exchange markets, much stronger warnings are in order, such as: "On average, participants will lose money." Just as in Las Vegas or Macao, China, these online casinos (online trading platforms) take a small fraction of every transaction. And, leveraging adds further borrowing costs and fees. Therefore, what may seem like a zero-sum game, given that foreign exchange rates seem to fluctuate randomly in the short run, is really a negative-sum game.

There is also the problem of "gambler's ruin." In a repeated fair (zero-sum) game in which gains and losses occur randomly in each stage of the game, the participant with the least capital will tend to go bankrupt first. In the foreign exchange market, participants effectively play against the entire market, which collectively has nearly infinite amounts of capital. Hence, an individual with a limited amount of capital will eventually lose everything. It is only a matter time.

The large dealers (banks) in the over-the-counter market have welcomed the growth of online retail trading because retail trades are cleared through the over-the-counter wholesale market. There is no evidence that the added volume from speculative trading in the online retail market increases liquidity or lowers transactions costs. In fact, online speculation may make foreign exchange markets, and exchange rates, more volatile, and thus more costly for those who use the foreign exchange market for international trade and investment.

THE SUPPLY AND DEMAND MODEL OF FOREIGN EXCHANGE

The market for foreign exchange is commonly represented by supply and demand curves. As we will show below, arbitrage among related foreign exchange markets for the world's approximately two hundred currencies, across geographic regions and over time, makes a single foreign exchange market between two currencies, such as the one depicted in Figure 12.1, highly dependent on other markets and events. Nevertheless, the supply and demand diagram is useful for understanding some of the critical aspects of foreign exchange markets. Be sure to pay attention to the qualifications brought out in the remainder of this chapter, however.

A Simple Example of a Foreign Exchange Market

Figure 12.1 depicts the market for Argentinean pesos. The horizontal axis shows the quantity of pesos, and the vertical axis shows the dollar price of pesos. In Figure 12.1, the demand curve intersects the supply curve at the price $.50. That is, the dollar price of the foreign currency, the Argentinean peso in this case, is fifty U.S. cents. The letter e is often used to represent this price, which you know as the foreign *exchange rate.* Therefore, the equilibrium in Figure 12.1 is written as e = $.50.

Our depiction of the equilibrium exchange rate between dollars and pesos as e = $.50 is somewhat arbitrary. The equilibrium could equally well have been represented as e = 2.00 pesos. Such a price would result if we depict the market where dollars and pesos are traded as the market for dollars in terms of pesos. Figure 12.2 illustrates this alternative view of the market: the quantity of dollars traded is shown along the horizontal axis and the peso price of dollars along the vertical axis.

The *supply* curve for dollars in Figure 12.2 is nothing other than the *demand* curve for pesos from Figure 12.1 multiplied by 1/e, and the *demand* curve for dollars is the peso *supply* curve multiplied by 1/e. Thus the intersection, or the equilibrium exchange rate, in Figure 12.2 is 1/e = 1/0.5 = 2. For example, Figure 12.1 shows that at the dollar price of $.75 per peso, demand for pesos is 100 million pesos. That translates into a supply of 75 million dollars, that is, $100 multiplied by 1/e = 1/.75 = 1.33, at the peso price of 1/e = 1/.75 = 1.33 pesos per dollar. The equilibrium exchange rate of e = .50 where the peso demand and supply curves intersect in Figure 12.1 is equivalent to the equilibrium peso price of dollars 1/e = 2 at which 250/2 = 125 million dollars are exchanged. The two alternative, but equally appropriate, views of the same dollar/peso foreign exchange market reflect the fact that when a holder of dollars demands pesos, in order to acquire some good or asset priced in pesos, he or she simultaneously supplies dollars to the foreign exchange market. Similarly, pesos are supplied when dollars are demanded.

Figure 12.1 **The Foreign Exchange Market**

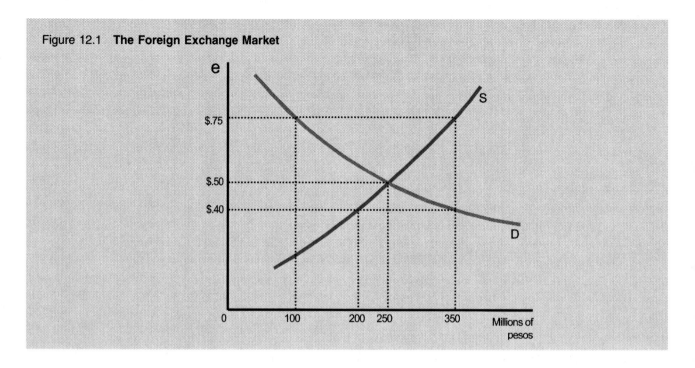

Figure 12.2 **The Foreign Exchange Market**

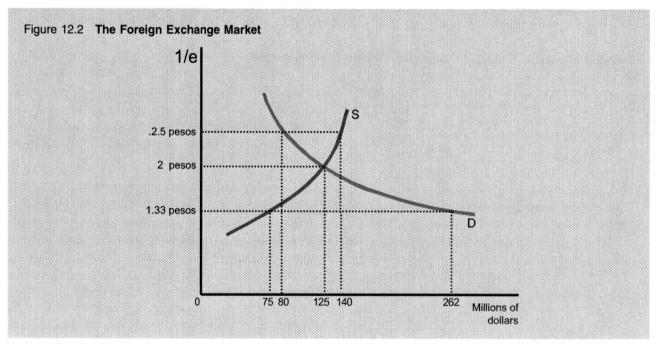

Since either e or 1/e represents the same foreign exchange rate, you need to be clear about how you define e. Economists commonly adopt the rule that e represents the home country currency price of the "foreign" exchange. If you are in the United States, you would, therefore, reply with the answer "two" if you were asked what the equilibrium exchange rate between dollars and pesos is. But, since this does not help us much in deciding how to depict the yen/euro exchange rate in London, tradition now determines how exchange rates are commonly shown in the major foreign exchange markets. Nevertheless, there is always potential for confusion; be careful and explicitly define in which currency you are setting your exchange rates.

Arbitrage

Foreign exchange markets are characterized by several forms of **arbitrage**. Arbitrage is any process that causes distinct markets to effectively merge into a single integrated market. Such a process occurs when profit-seeking *arbitrageurs* buy goods or assets in those segments of a general market where prices are low and sell where prices are high; these arbitrageurs cause the price differences to diminish between the market segments. A simple example of arbitrage follows.

Suppose that there are two separate markets for cucumbers, one in Toronto, Canada, and the other in Chicago, in the United States. Suppose also that there is a large number of cucumber producers in the regions around each city and millions of consumers interested in buying cucumbers. The producers around Toronto and Chicago are not identical. Labor costs differ in the two locations, land rents may be different, and perhaps technology or management may be different as well. Consumers of cucumbers are not the same in the two cities, either. Differences in tastes, culture, income, and the total number of people make the demand curves different in Chicago and Toronto. Suppose the two isolated markets for cucumbers are as shown by the supply and demand curves in Figure 12.3. The price of cucumbers is higher in Toronto.

The large price difference between the two cities is likely to come to the attention of buyers in Toronto and producers in Chicago, who see opportunities for gains. Some smart merchants from Toronto might decide to go to Chicago and buy cheaper cucumbers to haul back to Toronto with them. Some equally observant merchants in Chicago might also decide to load a truck with cucumbers and drive to Toronto to sell them there. This shift of demand from high-priced markets to low-priced markets and supply from low-priced to high-priced markets is precisely what economists call *arbitrage.*

Arbitrage in cucumbers reduces demand in Toronto and increases demand in Chicago. When the Chicago merchants load their trucks with cucumbers and drive to Toronto, they reduce supply in Chicago and increase it in Toronto. Figure 12.4 illustrates the shifts of supply and demand as a result of the arbitrage in cucumbers. The final effect of the arbitrage is to make prices more similar. In fact, if there are no costs to moving cucumbers from Chicago to Toronto, then prices will equalize at the international price of p_{INT}. At that point, there are no further arbitrage opportunities, and the demand and supply curves define the level of trade in cucumbers between Chicago and Toronto.

This simple example of cucumbers and the assumption of zero transportation costs is not very realistic. It is costly to ship a perishable product like cucumbers from Chicago to Toronto. However, the example of complete arbitrage is quite realistic for the foreign exchange markets located around the world. Transport costs for money are virtually nil, and communications about prices in all the foreign exchange markets around the world are instantaneously available in all other locations. There should be no differences in exchange rates across geographic locations. Indeed, the low transaction costs of the foreign exchange market imply that even differences in exchange rate of one ten-thousandth of one cent provide a profitable arbitrage opportunity. The electronic communications also imply that these small arbitrage opportunities cause large amounts of money to move almost instantaneously. The result of this foreign exchange arbitrage implies that at any moment in time exchange rates are virtually identical worldwide for every pair of currencies in the world.

The world's many far-flung foreign exchange dealers are in practice very tightly linked by a state-of-the-art electronic network. Furthermore, the several hundred major commercial banks who house foreign exchange dealers nearly all have branches in each of the world's major financial centers, so many of the global communications are, in a sense, in-house. Dealers from the different banks are in continuous contact to manage their foreign exchange exposures, always seeking to balance

Figure 12.3 **Two Isolated Markets for Cucumbers**

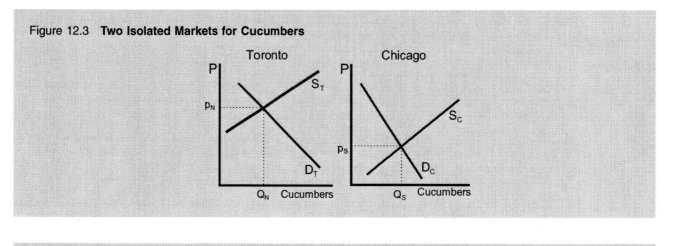

Figure 12.4 **Arbitrage and Price Equalization**

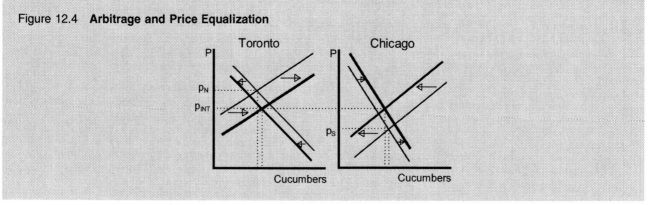

assets and liabilities in each currency so that they do not suddenly find themselves carrying excessive foreign exchange risk. Dealers also continuously trade foreign currencies in order to take advantage of differences in prices across the different geographic locations of foreign exchange dealers. This continuous arbitrage by profit-seeking foreign exchange dealers effectively keeps exchange rates the same in all locations. This activity is referred to as **geographic arbitrage**.

As an example of how *geographic arbitrage* in the foreign exchange markets works, suppose that dealers in the New York trading room of Citicorp are trading U.S. dollars at 90 yen per dollar. Suppose also that, at that same moment, dealers at Barclays Bank in London are exchanging yen and dollars at 91 yen per dollar. In such a case, there is an obvious arbitrage profit to be made. The New York dealers would immediately begin selling the dollars they purchased at 90 yen to Barclays in London, receiving 91 yen for a net gain of 1 yen for every dollar sold. Barclays traders in London would take their yen gained from selling dollars and offer to buy back the dollars in New York for 90 yen each, pocketing 1 yen for every dollar. A huge amount of yen would be purchased for dollars from Citicorp traders in New York and sold for dollars to Barclays traders in London. This trading activity would very quickly raise the price of yen in New York and lower the price of yen in London. Or, seen from the alternative perspective, the huge volume of transactions would lower the price of the dollar in New York and raise its price in London. The process ends when the exchange rate becomes the same, say somewhere around 90.5 yen per dollar, in both locations. Of course, the large differential as in the example here would never occur in today's world of electronic transactions; differences of even one-thousandth of one percent are quickly erased by arbitrage.

Table 12.4

Example: Four Countries and Four Currencies

Currencies:	α	β	γ	δ
Country A	1	α/β	α/γ	α/δ
Country B	β/α	1	β/γ	β/δ
Country C	γ/α	γ/β	1	γ/δ
Country D	δ/α	δ/β	δ/γ	1

Geographic arbitrage in the foreign exchange market did not always work so quickly, however. Before modern communications permitted continuous contacts between different parts of the world, sailing ships and horses took a long time to carry price information from one part of the world to another. Foreign exchange dealers required much larger spreads between bid and offer prices to cover potential risks of unknowingly buying or selling currencies at prices that differed from those in the rest of the world. The profits from being the first to discover discrepancies and exploit arbitrage opportunities were greater, of course, because prices diverged more than they do in today's electronic system. The potential gains from being the first to know motivated foreign exchange dealers to quickly adopt new channels of communication as they became available. For example, among the very first commercial messages on the trans-Atlantic telegraph cable in the mid-nineteenth century were foreign exchange trades. Similarly, the first commercial messages on the trans-Atlantic telephone cable involved currency trades.

Triangular Arbitrage

There are close to two hundred countries in the world, and most issue their own money. With nearly 200 different currencies, there are a very large number of exchange rates. Not only are there exchange rates between U.S. dollars and Japanese yen, dollars and British pounds, dollars and Mexican pesos, and U.S. dollars and Canadian dollars, but there are also exchange rates linking yen and pounds, yen and pesos, yen and Canadian dollars, pounds and pesos, and pesos and Canadian dollars.

Assuming 200 currencies that all trade for each other, you could set up a 200 x 200 grid containing 40,000 currency combinations. This counts each exchange rate twice because, for example, the amount of dollars per Swiss franc and the amount of francs per dollar are two sides of the same rate. Are there 20,000 exchange rates then? Well, nearly that many.

Table 12.4 illustrates the case of four countries, A through D, each with its own currency, say α, β, γ, and δ, respectively. There are markets for exchanging α for β, α for γ, and α for δ. Furthermore, there must be markets to trade β for γ, β for δ, and γ for δ. The exchange rate between currencies α and β can be expressed as either the amount of β per unit of α, that is β/α, or as the amount of α per unit of β, α/β. The grid in Table 12.4 has a diagonal set of 1s; these trivial cases of α/α, β/β, et cetera are not foreign exchange rates, because one currency is priced in terms of itself.

In the case of four currencies, there are only six different foreign exchange markets and exchange rates. The total size of the grid is $4 \times 4 = 16$, but after subtracting the four diagonal values of 1 and half of the remaining exchange rates, there are 6 actual exchange rates. In general, for n different currencies, there are $[n(n-1)]/2$ different foreign exchange markets. In the real world of 200 countries and moneys, there are thus $[200(199)]/2 = 19,900$ foreign exchange rates. This is still a very large number of exchange rates.

Table 12.5

Arbitrage with Incompatible Exchange Rates

Price of:	a	b	c
in:			
Country A	1a	.5a	.25a
Country B	2b	1b	1b
Country C	4c	1c	1c

Arbitrage links all of these exchange rates. In fact, when people, firms, and banks are free to move money across borders and shift their wealth from one currency to another, the world's foreign exchange markets are effectively reduced to a set of 199 out of the 19,900 exchange rates. The process is called **triangular arbitrage** because it involves transaction across at least three currencies.

An Example of Triangular Arbitrage

To grasp the concept of triangular arbitrage, suppose that there are three countries, A, B, and C, with three currencies a, b, and c. In Table 12.5 we hypothesize a set of exchange rates so that a is worth two units of b (or, b equals one half unit of a, which is the same thing), a is worth four units of c, and b trades for one unit of c.

A foreign exchange trader, seeing these exchange rates on her terminal, would immediately detect some arbitrage opportunities. For example, she could sell 1 million a's and acquire 4 million c's (since a = 4c), then exchange the c's for an equal amount of b's (since 1b = 1c), and, finally, exchange the 4 million b's for 2 million a's (since a = 2b). She would end up with 1 million more a's than she started out with by just making three quick trades! Many attentive traders would do the same thing. There would be a massive increase in supply of a in order to demand c, an increase in supply of c to demand b, and then an increase in supply of b in order to demand a. This would cause the price of c to rise relative to a, the price of b to rise relative to c, and the price of a to rise relative to b.

Triangular arbitrage will result in a price of c > .25a, a price of b > 1c, and the price of a > 2b. Arbitrage will of course continue until the exchange rates have moved to where there is no longer any way of making a few trades and ending up with more money than you start out with. One possible final outcome of the arbitrage and the exchange rate changes that it causes is given in Table 12.6.

In this scenario there are no longer any arbitrage profits to be had. If the foreign exchange trader now carries out the trades that made her a lot of money at the original exchange rates, she will have to pay .29a per unit of c, exchange 1 million a's for 3.5 million c's, use the c's to buy 3.5(.71) = 2.5 million b's, and then use the b's to get exactly 1 million a's again. You can now try any series of trades at these new exchange rates, and you will find that you neither gain or lose money in the process. Thus, the forces of supply and demand, fueled by triangular arbitrage profits, moved exchange rates so that they became consistent across all currencies.

Notice from Table 12.6 that you only need to know the exchange rates between a and b and a and c to find the exchange rate between b and c. That is, $(b/a)/(c/a) = b/c = 2.5/3.5 = .71$. Therefore, if there are n currencies and the foreign exchange traders are not restricted from carrying out profitable triangular arbitrage trades, then, in the general case of n currencies, you only need to know the rates of exchange between one of the n currencies and the other $(n-1)$ currencies to calculate the remainder of the $[n(n-1)]/2$ exchange rates.

Table 12.6

Compatible Exchange Rates After Arbitrage

Price of:	a	b	c
in:			
Country A	1a	.4a	.29a
Country B	2.5b	1b	.71b
Country C	3.5c	1.4c	1c

You can easily confirm that triangular arbitrage works in the real world. Every day, the *Financial Times* presents the exchange cross rates for nine currencies. The *Wall Street Journal* and all other business and financial newspapers present similar tables daily, as do most business sections of major general newspapers. In the published tables you can see that (1) rates in the southwest half of the table are reciprocals of corresponding rates in the northeast half of the table and (2) all rates can be derived from the n–1 rates in one column or row. In Table 12.7, you can see that (1) rates in one half of the table are reciprocals of corresponding rates in the opposite half of the table and (2) all rates can be derived from the n–1 rates in one column or row. March 1, 2002, the date of the table, was the first day that the euro fully replaced the individual currencies of the twelve European countries that form the European Monetary Union; hence, unlike all earlier *Financial Times* cross-currency tables, the euro appears in the place of the German mark, the French franc, the Italian lira, and the nine other currencies that the euro replaced.

Triangular arbitrage has an important implication, which is that if any one exchange rate changes, then arbitrage will cause all other exchange rates to change. This implication makes it difficult to fix the value of an exchange rate. Because it is very difficult to keep *each and every* one of the $[n(n–1)]/2$ exchange rates constant, it is difficult to keep *any* one of the n-1 exchange rates constant.

EFFECTIVE EXCHANGE RATES

With about two hundred currencies in the world, it is very difficult to determine whether a specific currency appreciates or depreciates. On any particular day, an individual currency may depreciate against some foreign currencies and appreciate against others. To provide better information about a currency's appreciation or depreciation, government agencies, private banks, and international organizations compile broader exchange rate measures called **effective exchange rates**, which are weighted averages of sets of foreign exchange rates.

The Effective Value of a Currency

In the United States, the Federal Reserve Bank compiles the *Broad Dollar Index,* which is a weighted average of twenty-six exchange rates between the U.S. dollar and other currencies, weighted for each country's share of U.S. exports plus imports. The *Major Currencies Index* weights just the exchange rates of Australia, Canada, Japan, Sweden, Switzerland, the United Kingdom, and the euro area, and the *Other Important Trading Partner Index* is a weighted average of the nineteen exchange rates that are in the Broad Index but not the Major Currencies Index. The weights are summarized in Table 12.8. Because Canada is the United States's largest trade partner, the Canadian dollar exchange rate has the highest weight in both the Broad Index and the Major Currencies Index. The weights are continually changed to match the United States's

Table 12.7

Cross-Currency Rates Reported in the *Financial Times*, March 1, 2002

February 28		C$	Dkr	€	¥	NKr	SKr	SFr	£	$
Canada	(C$)	1	5.354	0.721	83.41	5.554	6.522	1.062	0.441	0.623
Denmark	(Dkr)	1.868	10	1.346	155.8	10.37	12.18	1.984	0.823	1.164
Euro	(€)	1.388	7.431	1	115.8	7.708	9.051	1.474	0.612	0.865
Japan	(¥)	1.199	6.420	0.864	100	6.658	7.819	1.274	0.528	0.747
Norway	(NKr)	1.801	9.641	1.297	150.2	10	11.74	1.913	0.793	1.122
Sweden	(SKr)	1.533	8.210	1.105	127.9	8.516	10	1.629	0.676	0.956
Switzerland	(SFr)	0.941	5.040	0.678	78.52	5.228	6.139	1	0.415	0.587
UK	(£)	2.269	12.15	1.635	189.3	12.60	14.80	2.411	1	1.414
USA	($)	1.605	8.591	1.156	133.8	8.911	10.46	1.704	0.707	1

Note: Danish Kroner, Norwegian Kroner, and Swedish Kroner per 10; Yen per 100

Table 12.8

Broad Dollar Index: Trade Weights

	1997	2003		1997	2003
Canada	17.49	18.80	Thailand	1.59	1.43
Euro Area	16.92	16.43	**Australia**	1.31	1.25
China	6.58	11.35	**Sweden**	1.22	1.16
Japan	14.27	10.58	India	0.88	1.14
Mexico	8.50	10.04	Philippines	1.18	1.06
U.K.	5.73	5.17	Israel	0.84	1.00
Korea	3.68	3.86	Indonesia	1.25	0.95
Taiwan	3.77	2.87	Russia	0.78	0.74
Hong Kong	2.65	2.33	Saudi Arabia	0.80	0.61
Malaysia	2.25	2.24	Chile	0.53	0.49
Singapore	2.87	2.12	Argentina	0.61	0.44
Brazil	1.82	1.79	Colombia	0.49	0.41
Switzerland	1.43	1.44	Venezuela	0.58	0.30
			Total	***100.0***	***100.0***

Note: Boldface indicates the countries that make up the Federal Reserve's Major Currencies Index.
Source: Mico Loretan (2005), "Indexes of the Foreign Exchange Value of the Dollar," *Federal Reserve Bulletin,* Winter, Table 3, p. 5.

changing trade patterns. Table 12.8 gives the weights for the Broad Index in 1997 and 2003 published in the *Federal Reserve Bulletin.*

Recent Behavior of Effective Exchange Rates

Figures 12.5 and 12.6 graph the Broad Dollar Index for 1995 through 2009 and the Major Currencies Index for 1974 through 2009, the time periods for which the Federal Reserve Bank published these indexes. Note that two indexes trace similar but not identical paths. It makes a big difference which exchange rates are included in an effective exchange rate index. As you can see from comparing the ups and downs with the index on the vertical axis, the U.S. dollar fluctuated much more against the

Figure 12.5 **The Broad Index, 1995–2009**

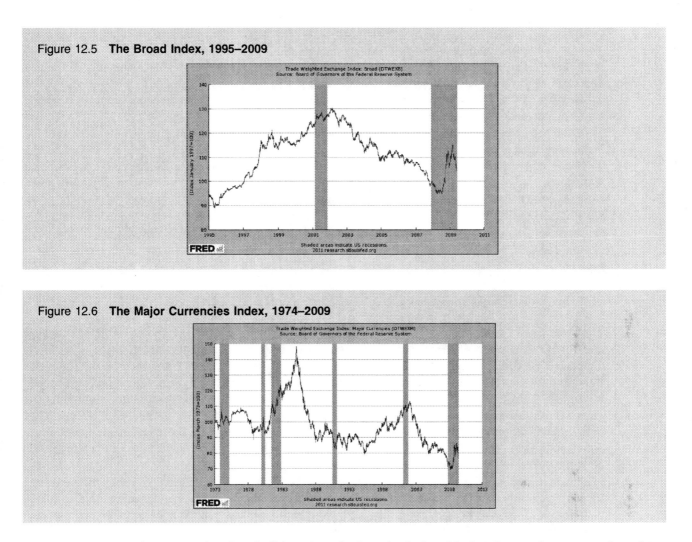

Figure 12.6 **The Major Currencies Index, 1974–2009**

seven major currencies than it did against the broader index. Market forces also seem to have kept these latter currencies more closely aligned to the dollar. This means that when the dollar depreciated rapidly against the major currencies after 2001, many of the currencies in the broader index, such as those of Asian economies like Taiwan, Hong Kong, and China, as well as other developing economies, generally depreciated against those same major currencies in tandem with the dollar. As a result, the U.S. dollar depreciated much less against the Asian currencies. This may help to explain the further rise in the U.S. trade deficit vis à vis the Asian economies.

Figure 12.5 also shows how volatile exchange rates have been over the past twenty-five years. As an average of individual exchange rates, an effective exchange rate should be less volatile than they are. But notice that even the effective exchange rates of the U.S. dollar have fluctuated widely, changing by more than 10 percent in many years. The decline of the Major Currencies Index from nearly 150 to under 100 between early 1985 and the middle of 1986 stands out. Only a bit less surprising is the equally sharp increase in the effective value of the dollar during the first half of the 1980s.

INTERTEMPORAL ARBITRAGE AND THE INTEREST PARITY CONDITION

Table 12.2 showed that the majority of transactions on the world's foreign exchange markets are **forward transactions**. These are contracts to exchange currencies at some future date. Forward contracts set a firm price *today* for the delivery of currencies at some future date. The forward markets for foreign exchange are similar to the *futures* markets for commodities, where corn, sugar, pork bellies, petroleum, et cetera are bought and sold for delivery and payment at a specific future date. And, the same way that futures markets for corn enable farmers to *hedge* the uncertainty of future prices by setting a firm price they will receive for their crops before they plant their seeds, the forward market for foreign exchange permits exporters, importers, and international investors to *hedge* their *foreign exchange risk* by contractually fixing the future exchange rate for expected foreign currency receipts or payments.[4]

The forward markets for foreign currencies are operated by the same dealers who operate the spot markets. This market grew quickly after 1973, when the **Bretton Woods system** of pegged exchange rates was abandoned in favor of letting exchange rates *float* in response to the continually shifting forces of supply and demand. The floating exchange rates were quite volatile after 1973, so exporters, importers, and foreign investors immediately sought ways to hedge their foreign exchange risk in the new floating rate regime. This chapter explains in detail what forward markets mean for exchange rates.

Intertemporal Arbitrage

The **spot** and **forward exchange** rates are determined by supply and demand for currencies today and for purchase/sale in the future, respectively. Between now and the future, price levels will change, economies will grow at different rates, and many other things that influence international trade and international investment will change. The forward exchange rate will, therefore, reflect how people, firms, and international investors expect all of these things to change over time. In general, their supply and demand for currencies at some future date will tend to be different from their current supply and demand for currencies. Of course, knowledge about the future is not complete; in fact, we know very little about what future supply and demand for foreign exchange will be some years into the future.

The first important point about the forward markets for foreign exchange is that the spot and forward exchange rates are not determined independently of each other. Wealth and obligations can be held over from one period to another, and when exchange rates in the spot and forward markets differ a lot, foreign exchange purchases and sales will be shifted forward or backward. In fact, the spot and forward rates will tend to be related by a type of arbitrage we refer to as **intertemporal arbitrage**. The term "intertemporal" means "over time." This intertemporal arbitrage process does not, in general, cause the spot and forward exchange rates to be equal. However, the spot and forward exchange rates will be related in a way that also reflects the differences in returns to holding assets denominated in the different currencies and the perceived risk of not hedging.

A Simple Example of Intertemporal Arbitrage

Suppose that you have the option to store your wealth in assets denominated in your domestic currency or in a foreign currency. Specifically, suppose that you can deposit your savings in a bank in your hometown, buy a bond from your government, or buy stock in a company in your country, all denominated in your country's currency. Or, you can shift your savings overseas to buy foreign currency and then open a deposit in a foreign bank, buy a foreign government's bond, or buy stock in a foreign corporation. Your choice between foreign and domestic assets normally depends on the expected risk and return on the domestic and foreign assets. For the time being, let's assume that you are not concerned about the risk of holding foreign versus domestic assets and that you care only about the relative rates of return on potential investments at home and abroad. In making your decision as to where to store your wealth, you therefore compare only the expected returns on domestic and foreign assets. Suppose, finally, that the domestic country is the United States and the foreign country where you are looking to purchase assets is the United Kingdom.

Say your wealth consists of $10,000, and you seek to buy the highest-return asset you can find for that $10,000. We denote this $10,000 of wealth as $w(\$)_t$, where the subscript stands for the current year, and the dollar sign denotes that the wealth is denoted in U.S. dollars. Suppose that a dollar-denominated asset in the United States will earn an annual return of r, which means that over the period of one year your wealth would grow to

$$(12.1) \qquad w(\$)_{t+1} = w(\$)_t(1 + r) = \$10,000(1 + r).$$

Alternatively, you could invest in a British asset denominated in British pounds (designated by the symbol "£"). To purchase British assets, you would first need to exchange the $10,000 for pounds. The amount you actually invest in Britain is the pound equivalent of $10,000, or

$$(12.2) \qquad w(£)_t = w(\$)_t / e_t = \$10,000/e_t.$$

That is, your current wealth in pounds, $w(£)_t$, is equal to the $10,000 divided by the spot exchange rate, e_t, which is defined here as the dollar price of a British pound. For example, if the spot rate $e_t = \$2$, then your wealth in pounds will be equal to $\$10,000/\$2 = £5,000$. If r^* is the rate of return on foreign (British) assets, then after one year your wealth in British pounds will be

$$(12.3) \qquad w(£)_{t+1} = w(£)_t(1 + r^*) = (\$10,000/e_t)(1 + r^*).$$

Before you can make your final decision about which assets to buy, you must convert the future pound value of your investment back to dollars at next year's exchange rate, e_{t+1}. You do not know e_{t+1} with certainty, but if you have reason to believe that the exchange rate will change between now and next year, you can eliminate this uncertainty by contracting today for the sale of your pounds one year from now on the forward market at the forward exchange rate f_t^{t+1}. In writing the forward exchange rate, we let the subscript stand for the point in time when the forward exchange is contractually agreed to, and we let the superscript stand for the time when the exchange of currencies actually occurs.

To get next year's dollar value of your British investment, multiply next year's pound value of your British asset by the forward exchange rate:

$$(12.4) \qquad w(\$)_{t+1} = w(£)_{t+1}(f_t^{t+1}) = (\$10,000/e_t)(1 + r^*)(f_t^{t+1}).$$

Now you can compare this dollar value of the British investment to the dollar value of the U.S. investment:

$$(12.5) \qquad \$10,000(1 + r) \leftarrow ? \rightarrow (\$10,000/e_t)(1 + r^*)(f_t^{t+1}).$$

Note that the forward foreign exchange market eliminates exchange rate risk, and if it is possible to assume that the returns r and r^* are also riskless in that they can be contractually established today, your choices on each side of relationship (12.5) are both said to be *covered* against risk. Your best investment strategy is thus the side of the relationship (12.5) that has the greater value.

The Covered Interest Parity Condition

To understand the process of *intertemporal arbitrage,* suppose that the relationship between the right-hand and the left-hand terms in (12.5) is:

(12.6) $$\$10{,}000(1 + r) < (\$10{,}000/e_t)(1 + r^*)(f_t^{t+1}).$$

In this case, U.S. wealth holders will elect to shift their wealth to British assets, and if British investors had their wealth invested in dollar assets, they will shift funds back toward pound assets. Thus, holders of dollars and dollar-denominated assets will purchase pounds and pound assets. If a lot of people do this, e_t will rise (provided we continue to define the exchange rate from the U.S. perspective as the dollar price of pounds). The dollar therefore falls in value relative to the pound. American purchasers of pound assets will simultaneously want to buy dollars with their pounds next year after they gain their asset values and returns, which will increase the demand for dollars and the supply of pounds on the forward market and, therefore, cause the forward exchange rate to fall. Notice that the rise in e_t and the fall in f_t^{t+1} cause the right-hand side of inequality (12.6) to diminish. Of course, if the shift in wealth from the United States to Britain is very large, it will also affect the rates of return on assets in the two countries, r and r^*. With more being invested in British pound assets, their returns r^* would fall, thus decreasing the right side of (12.6), and with savings leaving the United States, rates of return would rise there, thus increasing the left-hand side of (12.6).

In a perfect world devoid of transfer costs and other frictions, the process of international investment arbitrage will cause international transfers of wealth to expand until the inequality (12.6) becomes an equality:

(12.7) $$\$10{,}000(1 + r) = (\$10{,}000/e_t)(1 + r^*)(f_t^{t+1}).$$

This equation is the *intertemporal arbitrage* condition that links the present spot rate to the future. It is more commonly known as the **covered interest parity** condition, where *covered* refers to the use of the forward market to eliminate all exchange risk from storing wealth in foreign assets.

A little mathematical manipulation of equation (12.7) will reveal a convenient equation that in turn reveals the logic of the relationship between the spot and forward exchange rates. First, divide each side by \$10,000, which leaves

(12.8) $$(1 + r) = (1/e_t)(1 + r^*)(f_t^{t+1}).$$

Then divide each side of (12.8) by $(1 + r)$ and multiply each side by e_t:

(12.9) $$e_t = [(1 + r^*)/(1 + r)](f_t^{t+1}).$$

This equation says that the spot exchange rate is related to the forward exchange rate by the factor $[(1 + r^*)/(1 + r)]$, which reflects the relative rates of return for pound and dollar assets. Note that the spot rate e_t is equal to the forward rate f_t^{t+1} only if $r = r^*$. If, for example, $r > r^*$, then $[(1 + r^*)/(1 + r)] < 1$ and $e_t < f_t^{t+1}$.

A More General Form of the Interest Parity Condition

Forward foreign exchange markets exist only for the currencies of the world's larger economies, and then only for up to one or two years into the future. Unless a market processes some minimum amount of transactions, the banks who run the foreign exchange markets cannot afford to maintain inventories of currencies, employ the dealers, and operate the sophisticated communications systems to make a market. If you are contemplating purchasing assets in Egypt or Chile or debating whether to build a factory in a foreign country that will generate returns for the next fifty years, you will not be able to eliminate your exchange rate risk by using the forward market; the markets for Chilean pesos or for delivery of even the major currencies fifty years from now are said to be "too thin."

The next chapter will describe some other methods for hedging exchange rate risk when there are no forward markets. These methods require hedgers to base their decisions on their expectations of the future. For example, in the absence of a forward market to quote you a price for future foreign exchange transactions, you will have to compare returns on domestic and foreign assets based on your *expectations* about exchange rates in the future. That is, you must effectively alter equation (12.5) by entering your expectation of the spot rate one year from now in place of the forward rate f_t^{t+1}.

The expectation at time t of the exchange rate at time t+1 is denoted as $E_t(e_{t+1})$. To evaluate the expected earnings from, say, a Chilean asset, you must use the expected future exchange rate, $E_t(e_{t+1})$, to convert the future value of your Chilean assets from Chilean pesos to dollars. This dollar value of the Chilean investment can then be compared to the dollar value of the alternative U.S. investment:

$$(12.10) \qquad \$10,000(1 + r) \leftarrow ? \rightarrow (\$10,000/e_t)(1 + r^*)(E_t e_{t+1}).$$

Intertemporal arbitrage will still tend to occur so long as the difference between the right-hand and left-hand sides of (12.10) is large enough to overcome the perceived risk associated with the exchange rate uncertainty. There will be a tendency for the following relationship to hold approximately:

$$(12.11) \qquad \$10,000(1 + r) \approx (\$10,000/e_t)(1 + r^*)(E_t e_{t+1}).$$

The sign $\approx$ stands for "approximately equals." Manipulating the terms just as we did above for the covered interest parity condition then shows that the spot exchange rate is directly related to the expected future exchange rate:

$$(12.12) \qquad e_t \approx [(1 + r^*)/(1 + r)](E_t e_{t+1}).$$

Equation (12.12) is known as the *uncovered interest parity* condition or simply as the **interest parity condition**. This is one of the most important relationships in international economics. The covered interest parity condition is thus a special case of the more general interest parity condition, one in which there is a formal market where expectations are effectively revealed in the form of a forward exchange rate through market participants' willingness to buy and sell currencies in the future.

Equation (12.12) effectively tells us that, if people are free to move their wealth to other countries and to store their wealth however they want, so that intertemporal arbitrage can freely occur, then the spot exchange rate is a function of expectations about the future exchange rate and the relative rates of return on assets at home and abroad. Hence, if the assumptions behind the interest parity condition are accurate, the spot exchange rate effectively depends on expected future exchange rates, which depend on the expected future supply and demand for currencies and, therefore, expected future economic conditions.

The conclusion that the current exchange rate is determined by the "market's" expectations about the future depends on a number of assumptions, of course. For one thing, the interest parity condition assumes that there is perfect arbitrage, that there is no risk or uncertainty associated with the acquisition of foreign assets, that people have unbiased knowledge about the future, and that people behave objectively and rationally in assessing the likelihood of future events.

The logical application of the rational expectations hypothesis to the foreign exchange markets leads to another interesting conclusion: future changes in exchange rates are unpredictable. The reasoning is straightforward. If the interest parity hypothesis is accurate and people rationally use their full information sets to quantify their expectations about the future in accordance with Eugene Fama's (1970) efficient market hypothesis, then the spot exchange rate and the expected time path that links the future to the present must already reflect everything that we now know about future exchange rates. Therefore, the only thing that can change the spot exchange rate is new knowledge that changes the information set, that is, *news,* which by definition is information and knowledge that were not previously known or predictable. Hence, when expectations are rationally set and the interest parity condition holds (international investment is not restricted), future *changes* in the exchange rates are effectively unpredictable.

Alan Greenspan implied this when he said: "My experience is that exchange markets have become so efficient that virtually all relevant information is embedded almost instantaneously in exchange rates to the point that anticipating movements in major currencies is rarely possible."[5] Was Greenspan right?

An Exercise in Interest Parity

The predictive value of the interest parity condition comes down to whether it offers a reasonable approximation of what really happens in the foreign exchange market. Economists have carried out many empirical tests of the interest parity condition using data on forward and spot exchange rates and interest rates from many countries.

You can perform a simple test of the interest parity condition using readily available information published every day in the *Financial Times.* For example, Table 12.9 presents interest rates in the *Eurocurrency* market as well as the spot and 1-year-forward exchange rates for an arbitrarily selected day, namely January 12, 2005, as reported by the *Financial Times* on the following morning, January 13, 2005. These data were given to students in an international finance class in that year by your author. The Eurocurrency market will be discussed in the next chapter, in which we detail international banking. For now, it is enough to know that Eurocurrency markets are worldwide financial markets where the world's major commercial banks lend and accept deposits in most of the major currencies. The Eurocurrency interest rates are often stated in terms of the **London interbank offered rates**, or **LIBOR**. These are the interest rates at which the large London banks lend currencies to each other. Outside bank customers would pay slightly above LIBOR to borrow, and they would receive slightly below LIBOR on deposits in each of the currencies shown. Table 12.9 also includes the foreign exchange rates that you need to test the interest parity condition.

Looking at the dollar and pound first, Table 12.9 tells us that on January 12, 2005, the rate of return on a 1-year dollar deposit in the Eurocurrency market was 3.22 percent, and a similar pound deposit in the Eurocurrency market returned 4.895 percent. At the end of the normal trading day in London on January 12, the spot exchange rate was 1.8932 dollars per pound, and the 1-year forward exchange rate was quoted by dealers at 1.8642 dollars per British pound. Using equation (12.9):

$$(12.13) \quad e_t = [(1 + r^*)/(1 + r)](f_t^{t+1}) = [(1.04895/1.0322)]1.8642 = 1.01623(1.8642) = 1.8945.$$

The calculated spot rate is almost exactly the actual spot rate of 1.8932 reported by the *Financial Times* for the same day. Thus, the interest parity condition seems to hold almost exactly. The small difference could easily be explained by the fact that the reported exchange rates are from 4:00 P.M. the previous day and the reported interest rates are those that were observed at 11:00 A.M.

Similarly, the reported forward rate and the interest rates for dollars and euros can be used to "predict" the spot rate at 4:00 P.M. on January 12, 2005:

$$(12.14) \quad e_t = [(1 + r^*)/(1 + r)](f_t^{t+1}) = [(1.023245/1.0322)]1.3346 = 0.99132(1.3366) = 1.3250.$$

The calculated spot rate of 1.3250 is very close to the the reported spot exchange rate of 1.3286.

Table 12.9

Interest Rate Parity on January 12, 2005

	1-year LIBOR	Spot	1-year forward
U.S. dollar	3.22000	—	—
British pound	4.89500	1.89320	1.86420
Euro	2.32450	1.32860	1.33460
Swiss franc	0.97167	0.85950	0.87900
Japanese yen	0.09313	0.00977	0.01010

As reported in the January 13, 2005, *Financial Times.*

Note how well the covered interest parity condition holds for dollars-pounds and dollars-euros. As an exercise, calculate the spot dollar-franc and dollar-yen rates from the given information on interest rates and forward exchange rates in Table 12.9. How well does the covered interest parity condition hold for those currency combinations? By the way, be sure that all your exchange rates are given from the same perspective; in the examples above the rates were all from the U.S. perspective, that is, dollars per unit of foreign currency. Also, be sure to match 1-year forward exchange rates with the differences in the 1-year interest rates; newspapers typically report forward rates for 90 days, 180 days, and 1 year forward.

Further Evidence on Interest Parity

The fact that the spot and forward interest rates accurately reflect the interest parity condition does not tell us whether the interest parity condition is an unbiased predictor of future exchange rates, however. For this, it is necessary to compare the forward rate with actual future spot exchange rates. Jeffrey Frankel (2008) recently examined evidence on the forward exchange rate, and he found that forward rates usually differ greatly from future spot rates. He also notes that:

> The forward rate is not just a poor predictor of the future exchange rate, but a biased predictor. Only in developing countries with high inflation rates do currencies with high inflation rates or high forward discounts tend to point in the right direction (toward depreciation)—and even then, the bias does not fully disappear. (p. 41)

The reasons for interest parity's inaccurate predictions of future exchange rates are not clear. Many studies also find persistent bias in forward exchange rates.

Others have found other potential causes of interest parity's failure by examining historical data on spot and forward exchange rates. For example, Martin Evans and Richard Lyons (2005) found that news events explained only a very small part, less than 3 percent, of the immediate and subsequent variation in exchange rates, which calls into question the efficiency of foreign exchange markets. Other studies have documented great variations in the **risk premium** over time and across different pairs of currencies, which suggests that the foreign exchange market is influenced by variations in confidence. Finally, Walter Isard (2006) suggests that the foreign exchange market may simply not be fully rational, at least not as rationality is defined in macroeconomics.

Isard draws on the work of John Maynard Keynes in arguing in favor of the use of backward-looking rather than popular "rational," forward-looking exchange rate models such as the interest parity condition. Isard (2006, p. 5) writes: "Keynes was well aware that investor choices between foreign and domestic assets do not depend on interest rates and exchange rates alone." For example, when he wrote his *Tract on Monetary Reform* shortly after World War I, Keynes emphasized how foreign exchange risks and credit risks made exchange rates volatile and unpredictable. Later, during the Great Depression, Keynes (1936) argued that people's expectations depend on *confidence* and **convention**. The latter term refers to people's rough understanding of how things normally work. For example, investors remain confident, and willing to invest in inherently uncertain assets, as long as the outcomes from the investments seem to pan out in ways that they have come to view as normal or "conventional." While Keynes focused on domestic asset markets, the same reliance on convention pervades the foreign exchange market. According to Keynes's thinking, supply and demand in the foreign exchange market remain stable as long as expectations are roughly validated. In general, people keep doing the same things they were doing as long as the consequences of their decisions turn out as expected. Keynes argued that people's short memories reinforce such conventional thinking; people base their expectations on outcomes in the recent past, which is most vivid in their memories.

De Grauwe (1989) described exchange rates as "near-rational," a term he borrowed from George Akerlof and Janet Yellen (1987). Akerlof and Yellen's experiments and observations of human behavior had confirmed that people are strongly influenced by current prices in deciding on a price to charge or pay. Thus De Grauwe argues that, in the absence of overwhelming evidence that some very different exchange rate clearly reflects future values more accurately, exchange rates tend to remain relatively stable around some initial **anchor** price that people are familiar with.

The problem with using an *anchor*, or what Keynes called *convention*, to guide decisions is that, inevitably, the anchor comes loose when something upsets the "conventional" world as we know it. When confidence is eroded because conventional beliefs turn out to have been wrong, unexpected shifts in the supply or demand for foreign exchange can occur; this can cause exchange rates to suddenly change. An exchange rate may collapse or surge, and for lack of any accepted conventions, a period of extreme exchange rate volatility may follow. The volatility may last for a long time before a new anchor value takes hold and confidence in new conventions grows.

A Modern Case Study of Expectations: The Carry Trade

The interest parity condition suggests that, if the rate of return is the only thing that matters, it should not matter whether financial investors buy foreign or domestic assets. Any difference in returns should, on average, be exactly compensated by **currency appreciation** or depreciation. Yet, people routinely exploit interest rate differences by borrowing money in low-interest countries in order to invest in high-interest countries. This practice is known as the **carry trade**, in which people "carry" assets denominated in currencies with high interest rates and pay for them by borrowing currencies with low interest rates. Effectively, carry traders bet that the interest parity hypothesis will not hold in the short run and, if it does hold in the long run, they can unwind their foreign investments before the prescribed depreciation of the high-interest currency occurs. The carry trade has been described as a "free lunch in front of a steamroller."[6] If you eat fast, you may do very well.

One example of the carry trade was when Japanese savers sought alternatives to near-zero interest rate yen accounts during the 1990s. These savers began seeking higher returns, and they found them overseas. Japanese investors borrowed at near-zero interest rates in Japan, exchanged yen for foreign currencies to open accounts or purchase other assets in the United States, Brazil, Australia, New Zealand, and other countries where interest rates were high. For quite a few years, these Japanese carry traders enjoyed what was, literally, a free lunch as the Bank of Japan kept interest rates in Japan low during the recessionary 1990s. During this time, the Bank of Japan also intervened in the foreign exchange market to keep the value of the yen low in order to stimulate exports, which it saw as another tool for fighting recession in Japan. Thus, for many years, the yen did not appreciate against the other currencies as the interest parity condition predicts.

More recently, home buyers in high-interest countries in Eastern Europe, such as Poland and Hungary, took out low-interest loans in Switzerland, confident that the Polish zloty and the Hungarian forint would not depreciate, because their countries, which had just become members of the European Union, were stabilizing their currencies in order to prepare to adopt the euro. The 2008 financial crisis changed conditions, and the zloty and forint depreciated sharply. Those Poles and Hungarians who were unable to quickly sell their local assets and repay their Swiss bank loans are now stuck having to pay much more local currency to service their loans.

Frankel, who was quoted earlier disputing the validity of the interest parity condition, does not find the carry trade to be irrational:

> When one currency pays a high interest rate, it does not later, on average, depreciate correspondingly. If anything, the markets seem to behave perversely, with currencies that can be borrowed at low interest rates more often than not depreciating with respect to high-interest rate currencies! (2008, p. 5)

Frankel is, of course, referring to the same violations of the interest parity hypothesis that others have found and we previously reported. The past twenty-five years suggest, however, that the interest parity hypothesis does not hold well enough in the short run to prevent renewed interest in carry trades. As Keynes noted, people do not look back very far and they often underestimate the chances that things will go wrong. It does not take long for conventions supporting exchange rates that violate the interest parity condition to take hold and thus make the carry trade profitable for some extended period of time.

Still, the carry trade is risky. The fortunate free lunch of high returns will eventually come to an end. When confidence in the foreign currency begins to erode and investors begin unwinding their carry trades, the sale of the high-interest currencies will cause the borrowed currency to begin depreciating. The depreciation can turn into a crash if the depreciation triggers further desperate attempts to unwind the carry trades, and thus an even faster depreciation of the foreign currency. Some investors will not be able to get out of the way of the steamroller in time and will be crushed by the loss of the value of their overseas investments.

Exchange Rate Futures

When you read the *Financial Times* or the financial pages of most major newspapers, you may see a table reporting *foreign exchange futures*. These are contracts traded on several exchanges located in the United States and elsewhere. These *futures markets* for foreign exchange are similar to, but completely distinct from, the forward markets discussed in this chapter.

In the United States, there are organized exchanges in Chicago, Philadelphia, and New York that trade foreign exchange futures contracts to buy or sell fixed amounts of foreign exchange, usually in multiples of $10,000, at standard times in the future. Because they deal in uniform contracts, these futures markets can provide foreign exchange hedges to small foreign traders, investors, and speculators at a reasonable cost. However, restricting the market to contracts of uniform length and value means that they do not offer hedgers contracts that meet their precise needs. Also, these futures contracts are available only for certain major currencies. But, because they are relatively inexpensive, futures markets permit smaller players to at least partially hedge their foreign exchange risk or to speculate on future foreign exchange rates. The futures exchanges make up a very small segment of the foreign exchange market; they account for less than 1 percent of the turnover on all the foreign exchange markets.

EXPLAINING THE $4 TRILLION PER DAY VOLUME

The huge volume of trade on the foreign exchange market cannot be explained by the underlying international trade, international investment, immigrant remittances, and other international payments categorized in the balance of payments of the world's 200-plus economies. International trade of goods and services plus total international investment in real and financial assets by private citizens and businesses account for just a couple of percentage points, certainly less than 5 percent, of the daily volume of the foreign exchange markets around the world. Why are the other 95 percent or more of the more than $4 trillion daily currency trades carried out?

Arbitrage Trades

A very substantial portion of currency trades are motivated by arbitrage opportunities. Recall the three types of arbitrage that keep exchange rates unified across the distinct geographic locations of the market, across the many cross-currency rates, and between the current spot and expected future spot rates. Arbitrage opportunities develop every time an exchange rate changes in one location, between one pair of currencies, or at one point in time.

For example, suppose an Indian call center signs a contract for $5 million to provide customer service calls for a U.S. firm. Payment for the services will be made in one month. The Indian firm calls its bank in India to purchase $5 million worth of rupees forward one month, an act that increases the supply of dollars and the demand for rupees in the forward market. Thus, the forward price of rupees will rise, which results in arbitrage opportunities between various forward markets and the spot market. The shifts in the spot and forward rates will generate opportunities for geographic arbitrage, resulting in more trades to reunify exchange rates throughout the world. There may also be a variety of triangular arbitrage opportunities when the rupee-dollar exchange rates change, thus spreading the change in one exchange rate to exchange rates between other currency pairs. In short, a currency trade directly related to one of the fundamental international transactions recorded on the balance of payments triggers a series of subsequent dealer-to-dealer currency trades to exploit the arbitrage opportunities created by the initial currency trade.

Hot Potato Process

Arbitrage is not the only reason why the volume of foreign exchange trades swamps the volume of fundamental trade and investment-driven trades. Also important is the continual management of currency inventories by dealers. Any trade carried out by a market-making dealer in one institution with a dealer in another institution immediately alters the inventories of currencies in the possession of each market-making institution. Dealers have a strong incentive to carefully manage their currency inventories because the impact of exchange rate changes on total value of a dealer institution's inventory depends on the mix of currencies in the inventory. Richard Lyons (1996, 1998) and Christopher J. Neely and Paul A. Weller (2001) had access to privileged, detailed data on intraday trading and found that most dealers try to end the day holding a predetermined balance of currencies. That is, the dealers conduct currency trades to eliminate what they see as excessive holdings of any single currency. For this reason, customer-initiated trades usually trigger further interdealer trades to correct the inventory imbalance.

A simple example illustrates how inventory adjustments by dealers can trigger a series of follow-up currency trades. Suppose that foreign exchange dealers are risk averse, and each dealer currently has the mix of currencies deemed optimal. If a customer then purchases US$10 million worth of Canadian dollars from one of the market-making dealers, that dealer's inventory probably deviates from its optimal mix of currencies. Not wanting to carry 10 million extra U.S. dollars and so many fewer Canadian dollars, the dealer thus begins to adjust its inventory. Suppose, specifically, that the firm the dealer works for wants to hold on to no more than 10 percent of the newly acquired U.S. dollars. We assume here that the dealer's bank is willing to increase its holdings of U.S. dollars a little because the previous sale may have pushed the price of the dollars slightly below its long-run value, suggesting dollars may appreciate soon. The mid-office therefore instructs one of its traders to call another dealer and unload US$9 million in exchange for Canadian dollars. Suppose that this other dealer similarly seeks to adjust its inventory after making a market for the first dealer. This second dealer thus calls yet another dealer to sell 8.1 million in U.S. dollars. In the limit, the total interdealer volume generated from the US$10 million customer trade is ($9 million)/(1–0.9) = $90 million. Thus, the example produces a tenfold increase in foreign exchange transactions. Notice also that international trade accounted for just 10 percent of the total increase in foreign exchange transactions. Lyons (1996) calls this inventory adjustment process among dealers the **hot potato process**.

Explaining the $4 Trillion Daily Volume

We have now essentially answered the question about why the foreign exchange market volume is so much larger than the fundamental transactions of the global economy, such as exporting, importing, lending, borrowing, and sending remittances to overseas relatives. These latter sources of demand and supply account for only a couple of percentage points of the $4 trillion daily volume. Some shifts in supply and demand are initiated by changes in expectations, which can induce both outside customers and dealers to *speculate* and take **open positions** in the market. But most activity in the foreign exchange market consists of arbitrage and inventory adjustments. Lyons (1998) estimates that less than 10 percent of dealer-to-dealer trades can be considered speculative. According to Neely and Weller (2001), "there is little doubt that a much greater volume of transaction is accounted for by traders who close their positions at the end of the day than by those who take open positions with horizons of weeks or months" (p. 22).

CONCLUSIONS

This chapter introduces the foreign exchange rate, which is set in the foreign exchange market. This variable is one of the most important prices in our global economy, as it has a substantial long-run influence on the flows of payments between countries. It should be clear from the discussion in this chapter that exchange rates can be volatile and difficult to predict. That is, exchange rates contribute to the uncertainty and instability of international economic activity. Exchange rates have, in fact, often destabilized the international financial system and diminished human welfare.

The instability of exchange rates stems from the fact that they are determined by expectations of future economic international economic transactions, which depend on future economic conditions. But we cannot predict the future very well. We do not have any data on the future. Nor do we have a time machine so that we can go and take a look at the future. In this case of uncertainty, we therefore fall back on emotion, habit, half-baked ideas, rules of thumb, or other shortcuts to set our expectations. Keynes suggested that people use recent experience to establish conventions as to what seems appropriate. They then continue doing what they have been doing as long as their decisions bring results that are roughly in line with what they see as conventional. Of course, eventually things change and outcomes do not fit the conventions. This will certainly happen if people's actions are fundamentally inconsistent or unsustainable. Then, in the case of exchange rates, a period of large price changes and, often, an extended period of exchange rate volatility will ensue.

We are now ready to return to the main subjects of this part of the book, international investment and international finance. Investment and finance are also intertemporal decisions whose current value depends on future outcomes. They are, therefore, also guided by convention and, potentially, unstable and subject to excessive volatility. The next two chapters detail how the exchange rates combine with international investment and international finance to destabilize the international financial system and, subsequently, the entire integrated international economy.

CHAPTER SUMMARY

1. For every traded product, there is the price in the currency of the country where the product is produced, and then there are the prices in terms of other countries' currencies. There are many reasons why prices differ from one country to another, but the main long-run determinant of the price differences are the exchange rates between the world's many different currencies.

2. Because the exchange rates at which the future selling prices and returns are translated back into the investor's home currency cannot be predicted with certainty, foreign investment and finance are subject to *foreign exchange risk* or *uncertainty.*

3. In markets where the forces of supply and demand are free to drive the prices of currencies, the exchange rates are said to *float.*

4. Governments sometimes rigidly *fix* the values of their currencies by constantly intervening in the market or directly restricting supply and demand.

5. Markets for exchanging foreign money have operated for nearly three thousand years, ever since there have been distinct national moneys.

6. Foreign exchange markets became more complicated after the development of banking and the introduction of new types of payments to supplement the traditional use of coins made from precious metals.

7. With the invention of paper or *fiat* money, the price of one fiat money in terms of other fiat moneys came to reflect not the value of some well-known precious metal, but only an expectation of the fiat money's future *purchasing power.*

8. Today, nearly all of the US$4 trillion worth of currencies that is exchanged every working day is traded through a worldwide network of dealers that is referred to as the *over-the-counter foreign exchange market.*

9. Decentralized over-the-counter markets are more costly and less efficient than centralized exchanges. Dealers engage in frequent transactions to keep inventories in balance, they take advantage of arbitrage opportunities between segments of the markets, and customers have less information about competing prices.

10. There are economies of scale in dealing in foreign exchange because, to make a profit, a foreign exchange dealer must gain a large enough volume of business to be able to offer clients the liquidity they demand and to make money at the small margins between buy and sell prices.

11. The market for foreign exchange is commonly represented by supply and demand curves, although arbitrage among related foreign exchange markets for the world's nearly two hundred currencies, across geographic regions and over time, makes a single foreign exchange market between two currencies such as the one depicted in Figure 12.1 highly dependent on other markets and events.

12. Foreign exchange markets are characterized by three forms of *arbitrage:* geographic arbitrage, cross-currency (triangular) arbitrage, and intertemporal arbitrage.

13. Triangular arbitrage implies that if any one exchange rate changes, then arbitrage will cause all other exchange rates to change; this interdependence among all exchange rates makes it difficult to fix the value of an exchange rate because a change in any one will tend to change all exchange rates.

14. To provide better information about a currency's appreciation or depreciation, government agencies, private banks, and international organizations compile broader exchange rate measures called *effective exchange rates,* which are weighted averages of sets of foreign exchange rates.

15. The forward market for foreign exchange permits exporters, importers, and international investors to *hedge* their *foreign exchange risk* by contractually fixing the future exchange rate for expected future foreign currency receipts or payments.

16. The interest parity condition is often used to represent the intertemporal arbitrage condition, and it shows that the spot exchange rate is determined by the expected future exchange rate, tempered only by the interest rates for the pair of currencies.

17. The *covered interest parity condition* is a special case of the more general interest parity condition, one in which there is a formal market where expectations

are effectively revealed in the form of a forward exchange rate through market participants' willingness to buy and sell currencies in the future.

18. Isard (2006) suggests that the foreign exchange market may simply not be fully rational, at least not as rationality is defined in macroeconomics. Isard draws on the work of Keynes in arguing in favor of the use of backward-looking, rather than popular "rational," forward-looking exchange rate models such as the interest parity condition.

19. De Grauwe argues that, in the absence of overwhelming evidence that some very different exchange rate clearly reflects future values more accurately, exchange rates tend to remain relatively stable around some initial *anchor* price that people are familiar with.

20. The problem with using an *anchor,* or what Keynes called *convention,* to guide decisions is that, inevitably, the anchor comes loose when something upsets the "conventional" world as we know it. Therefore, foreign exchange markets are volatile and, sometimes, unstable.

21. The huge daily volume of trade on the foreign exchange market cannot be explained by the underlying international trade, international investment, immigrant remittances, and other international payments categorized in the balance of payments of the world's 200-plus economies, but it can be explained by the over-the-counter market's need to continually engage in arbitrage and inventory-adjustment transactions.

KEY TERMS AND CONCEPTS

anchor
arbitrage
bills of exchange
Bretton Woods system
carry trade
centralized exchange
convention
covered interest parity condition
debased (currency)
effective exchange rates
fiat money
fixed exchange rate
floating exchange rate
foreign exchange futures market
foreign exchange market
foreign exchange risk

forward exchange rate
forward transactions
geographic arbitrage
hot potato process
interest parity condition
intertemporal arbitrage
market liquidity
market makers
over-the-counter market
purchasing power
seignorage
spot exchange rate
swaps
triangular arbitrage
uncovered interest parity condition
vehicle currency

PROBLEMS AND QUESTIONS

1. What are the implications of triangular arbitrage for any one currency's exchange rate? Explain.
2. Explain precisely what the uncovered interest parity condition tells us about the spot exchange rate. (Hint: Use the interest parity condition to state the spot rate in terms of interest rates and forward rates.)
3. Describe and explain in detail the three forms of arbitrage that seem to characterize today's foreign exchange markets.

4. Suppose that there are two separate markets where bananas are sold. Suppose that the price for bananas is $1.00 per pound in the first and $0.25 per pound in the other.
   a. Draw two hypothetical supply and demand diagrams depicting these two markets and the equilibrium prices of $1.00 and $.25, respectively.
   b. Then, assume that arbitrage between the two markets occurs. Explain precisely how arbitrage would shift the supply and demand curves in the two markets. (Assume that perfect arbitrage occurs and prices are eventually equalized.)
5. Suppose that the spot exchange rate between Canadian dollars and U.S. dollars is equal to e = US$0.50. The current return on high-quality Canadian financial assets is 13 percent per year while the interest rate in the United States for comparable assets is 9 percent per year. Suppose that there is perfectly free asset trade between Canada and the United States. Use the interest parity condition to calculate what the 360-day forward exchange rate must be.
6. Explain precisely, using the relationships detailed in this chapter, what the difference is between the covered interest parity condition and the uncovered interest condition.
7. Explain the intuition behind the interest parity condition. Given this intuition, explain why the interest parity condition may fail to hold.
8. Summarize the evidence on the interest parity condition. Given this evidence, is the interest parity condition a useful concept for understanding foreign exchange markets?
9. Describe the carry trade. What does the presence of the carry trade imply about the interest parity condition?
10. Explain what economists mean by an effective exchange rate. Give an example of an effective exchange rate. For what purpose is an effective exchange rate more useful than an individual exchange rate that links two specific currencies?
11. You are given the following exchange rates between U.S. dollars, Canadian dollars, European euros, Swiss francs, and British pounds below:

	US$	CAN$	€	SFr	£
US$ per	1	.60	___	2.50	___
Can$ per	___	___	___	___	___
€ per	2.50	___	___	___	___
SFr per	___	___	___	___	___
£s per	___	___	___	0.20	___

Complete the grid by filling in all the blanks.

12. Use Table 12.9 to calculate the spot dollar-franc and dollar-yen rates from the given information on interest rates and forward exchange rates. How well does the covered interest parity condition hold for those currency combinations? (Hint: Be sure that all your exchange rates are given from the same perspective; in Table 12.9 the rates are all from the U.S. perspective, that is, U.S. dollars per unit of foreign currency. Also, be sure to match 1-year forward exchange rates with the differences in the 1-year interest rates; newspapers typically report forward rates for 90 days, 180 days, and 1 year forward.)
13. Explain why the daily volume of the foreign exchange markets is a huge multiple of the daily volume of international trade and finance.
14. Explain what De Grauwe (1989) meant when he described exchange rates as "near-rational." How does De Grauwe's thinking relate to that of John Maynard Keynes, who described the role of "convention" in determining market prices under uncertainty?

15. Online foreign exchange trading is now readily available for anyone willing to put up a few thousand dollars. Explain the risks of foreign exchange speculation for individuals. How likely is it that a small trader will reap profits from such speculation in the long run?

NOTES

1. See, for example, William L. Davisson and James E. Harper (1972), Glyn Davies (1996), and Rondo Cameron (1993).

2. *The Economist,* "Enter the Little Guy," April 12, 2001.

3. Jack Egan (2005), "Check the Currency Risk. Then Multiply by 100," *New York Times,* June 19.

4. The term *hedge* suggests the "hedging in," or strict delineation, of the area within which the effects of future exchange rate shifts will be confined.

5. From Alan Greenspan's remarks at the twenty-first Annual Monetary Conference, cosponsored by the Cato Institute and *The Economist,* Washington, DC, November 20, 2003 (downloaded from www.federalreserve. gov).

6. From an editorial in the *Financial Times* (2007), "Carry on Trading: Free Lunches—Queue in Front of the Steamroller," February 24.

CHAPTER 13

International Financial Markets

> We should have a safer, cleaner banking system.
>
> —Joseph Stiglitz (2009)

> The only useful banking innovation was the invention of the ATM.
>
> —Paul Volcker (2010)[1]

The ownership of foreign assets has grown to unprecedented levels over the past three decades. Never before have so many individuals, firms, governments, banks, and pension funds owned so many foreign assets. Of course, this also means that never before have so many people, firms, and governments *owed* so much to banks, stockholders, lenders, and owners in other countries.

Another characteristic of today's international investment and finance is that cross-border flows of lending and borrowing have become much more diverse. International financial flows consist, in part, of traditional bank lending. However, with banking increasingly extending beyond its traditional role of making loans directly to borrowers and, instead, creating new instruments sold on financial markets, banks in most countries have become active participants in the global financial markets where many different types of financial assets are traded. At the same time, stock markets and bond markets in more than seventy countries now permit foreigners to buy and sell corporate equity and a great variety of bonds issued by governments, government agencies, and private firms. Finally, the financial flows recorded in the financial accounts of countries' balance of payments show large private and government transfer payments and, in the case of a growing list of developing economies, large official transactions. These latter purchases and sales of foreign currencies and liquid foreign assets have become one of the more controversial issues in international finance.

The first goal of this chapter is to detail the many different international financial flows that have built the huge stock of foreign-owned assets. Second, this chapter begins to examine the economic implications of the growth of international finance. Among these is the potential for greater financial and economic instability, as alluded to at the end of the previous chapter. Third, this chapter discusses how financial deregulation in individual countries has enabled a number of national banks to grow into large transnational financial services conglomerates that do business in many countries and spread their ownership across many countries.

By 2009, the worldwide economic recession had revealed the downside of the globalization of finance and the concentration of the control of private financial flows in the hands of a small group of growing private financial enterprises. Not long ago held up by many economists and policy makers as the major achievement of the modern global economy, the private international financial industry is now seen as the party responsible for plunging the global economy into the first annual decline in measured overall worldwide output since the end of World War II. Financial instability is not a new phenomenon, however. Economists still debate the causes of the Great Depression of the 1930s and many other financial panics that caused severe economic recessions and depressions over the past two hundred years of capitalist economic development. This chapter's discussion of financial instability is fundamental to understanding these momentous shifts in economic conditions.

STOCKS AND FLOWS IN INTERNATIONAL FINANCE

The **balance of payments (BoP)** outlined in Chapter 11 records annual flows of payments between countries. The payments noted in the financial account of the BoP effectively represent the net increase or decrease in the amount of foreign assets owned by a country's citizens, firms, organizations, governments, and public agencies. That is, the *flow* of payments that reflect purchases and sales of foreign assets changes the *stock* of foreign assets owned.

There is another frequently reported international account that records the state of a nation's net stock of foreign assets. This account is the **net international investment position**, which we will also refer to as the net investment position, for short.

The Net International Investment Position

There is a fundamental difference between a country's *balance of payments* and its *international investment position*. Whereas the BoP is a compilation of flows of payments over some period of time (usually one calendar year), the international investment position is a measure of a country's net stock of foreign assets at one given moment in time (usually midnight, December 31). Specifically, the international investment position of a country measures how many foreign assets are owned by private citizens, firms, and government agencies of a country versus how many of its private and public assets are owned by foreign citizens, foreign firms, and foreign governments. Since the BoP records the flows of financial payments to buy and sell assets across the border, and the net international investment position measures the value of the accumulated stocks of those assets, the total accumulated assets in the net international investment position reflect past activity on the financial account of the BoP.

Table 13.1 presents the United States's international investment position through the end of 2010. The table shows the clear trend over the past thirty years: the United States went from being a net creditor to a net debtor to the rest of the world. In fact, the United States is today the largest net debtor in the world.

The trend from a surplus to large deficits, shown in Table 13.1, clearly is related to the United States's large current account deficits beginning in the early 1980s. For example, in the early 1980s the rising value of the U.S. dollar combined with the rapid growth of the U.S. economy caused U.S. imports to surge ahead of exports. Large current account *deficits* during the 1980s were matched by equally large financial account *surpluses,* which imply that U.S. citizens, corporations, and governments sold many more assets to foreigners than they purchased from foreigners. Large financial account surpluses, in turn, significantly changed the net investment position of the United States, and as shown in Table 13.1, the United States went from being a net creditor to a net debtor sometime during 1986. Even larger current account deficits during the 1990s and 2000s pushed the U.S. net investment position further into deficit. By the end of 2010, foreign citizens, firms, organizations, and governments owned nearly $3 trillion more assets in the United States than American citizens, firms, organizations, and governments owned in foreign countries. The net debt of the United States was about 20 percent of GDP in recent years.

Table 13.1

The International Investment Position of the United States (US$ billions, current cost basis)

	U.S.-owned assets abroad	Foreign-owned assets in U.S.	U.S. net international investment position	NIIP as % of GDP
1979	$786.7	$471.0	$315.7	12.3%
1980	929.8	569.5	360.3	12.9
1981	1,001.7	661.3	340.4	10.9
1982	1,108.4	$777.0	331.4	10.2
1983	1,211.0	908.6	302.4	8.5
1984	1,204.9	1,038.2	166.7	4.2
1985	1,287.4	1,225.7	61.7	1.5
1986	1,469.4	1,497.2	−27.8	−0.6
1987	1,646.5	1,717.4	−70.9	−1.5
1988	1,829.7	1,997.2	−167.5	−3.3
1989	2,070.9	2,317.1	−246.2	−4.5
1990	2,179.0	2,409.4	−230.4	−4.0
1991	2,286.5	2,578.2	−291.8	−4.8
1992	2,331.7	2,742.7	−442.0	−7.0
1993	2,753.6	3,038.1	−284.5	−4.3
1994	2,987.1	3,286.6	−298.5	−4.2
1995	3,486.3	3,916.5	−430.2	−5.8
1996	4,032.3	4,495.6	−463.3	−5.9
1997	4,567.9	5,345.1	−786.2	−9.4
1998	5,095.5	5,953.9	−858.4	−9.8
1999	5,974.4	6,705.5	−731.1	−7.3
2000	6,238.8	7,575.8	−1,337.0	−13.4
2001	6,308.7	8,183.7	−1,875.0	−18.2
2002	6,649.1	8,693.7	−2,044.6	−19.2
2003	7,638.1	9,731.9	−2,093.8	−18.8
2004	9,340.6	11,593.7	−2,253.0	−19.0
2005	11,961.6	13,893.7	−1,932.1	−15.3
2006	14,428.1	16,619.8	−2,191.7	−16.4
2007	18,339.9	20,255.6	−1,915.7	−13.6
2008	19,244.9	22,738.8	−3,493.7	−24.3
2009	18,379.1	21,116.9	−2,737.8	−19.4

Source: Table 2 in Elena L. Nguyen (2010), "The International Investment Position of the United States at Year-end 2009," *Survey of Current Business*, July 2010, pp. 18–19, 2007–2010 updated from www.bea.gov/international/.

From the Balance of Payments to the Net Investment Position

The financial account in the BoP and the year-on-year change in the net international investment position are not perfectly correlated. The stocks of foreign-owned domestic assets and domestically owned foreign assets must also be adjusted each year for asset price changes, depreciation, and exchange rate changes. Specifically:

> Net Investment Position of the United States at the end of 2009
> + Net Purchases of Foreign Assets by Americans from BoP
> − Depreciation of Foreign Assets Owned by Americans
> + Net Change in the Value of Foreign Assets Owned by Americans
> + Adjustment in Foreign Asset Value from Exchange Rate Changes
> − Net Purchases of U.S. Assets by Foreigners from BoP
> + Depreciation of U.S. Assets Owned by Foreigners
> − Net Change in the Value of U.S. Assets Owned by Foreigners
>
> = Net Investment Position of the United States at the end of 2010

There are always changes in the values of assets over the course of the year. For example, the sharp declines in stock prices in most countries between 2000 and 2001 caused major revaluations of stock holdings. Also, the large depreciation of the U.S. dollar during the early 2000s caused the value of U.S.-owned foreign assets to rise in value relative to foreign-owned assets in the United States; note that there were years when the net investment position of the United States rose in value even though the United States ran huge financial account surpluses that financed its $500 billion-plus trade deficits. We should, therefore, not expect the net international investment position to change exactly in line with the international investment flows from the BoP.

In the long run, however, there is clearly a relationship between the annual flows in the BoP and the measured stocks of assets in the net investment position. The net investment position will, therefore, continue to grow more negative as the continued U.S. current account is financed by even more foreign purchases of U.S. assets.

Asset Stocks and Asset Returns

The rapid increase in foreign ownership of U.S. assets implies that there will be a shift in net interest, rent, profit, and dividend payments recorded in the current account, a category where the United States has always recorded net positive payment inflows. Interestingly, despite the large and growing deficit in the United States's net international investment position, the nation continued to record positive net asset returns. According to the U.S. BoP figures presented earlier, in 2010 earnings by American individuals, firms, banks, et cetera on their foreign assets amounted to $663.2 billion while payments to foreigners for returns on their U.S. assets were $498.0 billion. Thus, U.S. financial and real investments abroad earned $165.2 billion more than foreign investors earned in the United States. Given that foreigners owned nearly $3 trillion more assets in the United States than U.S. individuals, firms, governments, and organizations owned overseas, we might have expected the net earnings flows to be negative too.

It appears that U.S. investors earn much higher returns on their foreign investments than foreigners earn on their U.S. investments. One reason may be that foreign-owned U.S. companies are more concentrated in low-profit industries. Also, much foreign investment in the United States consists of government bonds, which are a less risky investment, but also a lower-return investment. Foreign investors in the United States may also not be sending all of their earnings back home, and thus foreign earnings of U.S. assets are not fully reflected in the BoP. It is also possible that, because foreign direct investment in the United States is newer on average than U.S. direct investment abroad, foreign investment in the United States is not as profitable; new investments often take time to mature and generate large profits.

Finally, there have been suggestions that the rush by foreigners to acquire U.S. assets after foreign governments removed restrictions on overseas investment during the 1980s led to careless investment decisions. An article in the *Financial Times* in 2004 quotes Alan Gregory, a British professor of corporate finance, concluding that the data "shows that on average . . . UK companies make disastrous acquisitions in the US."[2] The same research does not explain why British overseas direct investments have such poor returns. The U.S. BoP in Table 11.1 revealed that, compared to U.S. holdings of foreign assets, the total holdings of foreign-owned assets in the United States are divided very differently among official assets, stocks and bonds, government bonds, foreign direct investment, and bank loans. Do you think these differences can explain the differences in asset returns?

Some economists have interpreted the net positive inflow of earnings on overseas investments as indicating the net international investment position is incorrectly measured. Ricardo Hausman and Frederico Sturzenegger (2006) perform an interesting exercise in reverse engineering. They begin with the data on international income flows, specifically the net flows of returns to assets, that show the United States earns more on its overseas investments than foreigners earn on their U.S. investments. They interpret that result as evidence that the United States owns more foreign assets than the net international investment position reports. Specifically, they capitalize the recorded flows of returns to assets, assuming a 5 percent average annual return. This calculation generates an estimate of U.S. net wealth of $724 billion in 2004. Hausman and Sturzenegger refer to the unrecorded wealth as "dark matter," borrowing a scientific term for the unknown forces in the universe that physicists have hypothesized must exist, given the movements of planets, stars, comets, and other observable objects in the universe. The authors speculate that financial "dark matter" could consist of accumulated know-how that gives U.S. firms operating abroad higher returns to their productive and innovative activities. Or perhaps it reflects the better marketing abilities of U.S. firms.

Hausman and Sturzenegger's article was well received by many analysts because it not only eliminated the need to worry about the growing U.S. net foreign debt, but also reflected the popular myth of the superiority of the U.S. economy. Other researchers point out, however, that the dark matter calculated by Hausman and Sturzenegger was not large enough to keep net wealth positive given the rate at which the United States continues to accumulate new debt. Even if the growth of true dark matter continues equal to Hausman and Sturzenegger's estimated $125 billion per year since the 1970s, current trade deficits still show the United States holding a large, and unsustainable, level of net foreign debt. Also, reported flows of returns are not necessarily accurate either. Many foreigners keep returns in the U.S. financial markets, which means their holdings become accumulated debt that may come due if foreigners eventually decide to invest the earnings elsewhere. There are also some worrisome indications that the actual net investment position of the United States is worse than the numbers suggest because foreign companies report abnormally low profits in the United States to avoid high U.S. corporate profits taxes. Finally, foreign ownership of U.S. portfolio investment is also likely to be underreported.

Is the Growth of the Net Investment Deficit Sustainable?

As in the case of the U.S. current account deficits, many people have asked whether the U.S. international investment position is sustainable. Will foreign investors eventually earn larger returns and "repatriate" more of the earnings that they now use to add to their U.S. asset holdings? These questions are important because they have implications for future financial stability. Since the BoP must balance, sudden changes in the inherently volatile financial flows can cause large changes in exchange rates that, in turn, cause large changes in trade flows, interest rates, or both. Changes in exports, imports, and investment activity have real effects on national output and human welfare. It is difficult to predict when unsustainable trends in specific items of the BoP will undergo the inevitable adjustment, but experience suggests the adjustments can come very suddenly and unexpectedly. Recall Jagdish Bhagwati's quote at the head of Chapter 11, in which he signals the very real dangers of unregulated international financial flows.

THE GROWTH OF INTERNATIONAL BANKING

Bank lending still accounts for a large share of international flows of capital. However, during the early 2000s there was a notable shift toward **financial markets** and away from **financial intermediaries** like traditional banks. This shift occurred not only in the more developed economies of the world, but also in many developing economies with the opening and expansion of stock markets, bond markets, and overnight money markets. Traditional banks have responded by consolidating and expanding into investment banking, brokerage, and other financial services. They also increasingly *intermediate* between traditional banking and the financial markers.

Shifts in the Ranks of the Financial Transnational Firms

Table 13.2 shows the twenty-five most globalized financial transnational firms in 2006. This ranking is based on the Geographical **Spread Index** of the United Nations Conference on Trade and

Development (UNCTAD), which consists of the square root of the ratio of foreign affiliates to all affiliates, multiplied by the number of host countries. Many of the banks that are part of these transnational financial firms have been internationally active for decades or even centuries. Some of these corporate conglomerates started out as insurance companies. Almost all became larger and more global through mergers and acquisitions, a trend that continued in 2007. For example, the Royal Bank of Scotland (RBS) briefly became the largest transnational financial firm in 2007 after acquiring ABN Amro, a Dutch bank already in the top twenty-five by size. In 2009, RBS was taken over by the British government, and its acquisition, ABN Amro, was handed over to the Dutch government. Others on the top twenty-five list, including Citigroup, BNP Paribas, UBS, ING, AIG, Credit Suisse, Fortis, Dexia, JP Morgan Chase, and Merrill Lynch were also in various states of insolvency, government takeover, or forced consolidation in early 2009. Future rankings will be very different from what you see in Table 13.2.

The ranking of financial firms for 2006 in Table 13.2 reflects the global economy just before the financial crisis that began in 2007 and became a global recession in 2008 and 2009. At the time of this writing, some of these financial giants have been taken over by governments, have large ownership stakes by governments, or have been merged into other financial firms. The shift toward ever-larger global firms making up the critical financial sector in the circular flow of the global economy thus continues, despite their failure to provide sustainable financial intermediation and markets to stabilize international economic integration.

The Eurocurrency Markets

International banks and international financial markets differ from purely domestic banks and markets because they operate across a variety of institutional environments with different rules, regulations, traditions, and levels of local competition. Transnational banking firms have learned to take advantage of the many institutional differences; international banking effectively operates outside the jurisdiction of any single country's banking authorities in what effectively has become an unregulated business environment. The growth of international banking is closely related to the emergence and growth of the so-called **Eurocurrency markets**.

Eurocurrency is money deposited in banks located in countries other than those where the currency was issued. For example, U.S. dollar deposits in a bank in France, a country where euros normally circulate, would be considered Eurocurrency deposits. The sum total of private transnational banks that take deposits and make loans in foreign currencies make up the **Eurocurrency market**. Because they deal in foreign currencies, the Eurocurrency markets are not closely regulated by the national banking authorities of the countries where they operate. Overall, Eurocurrency markets are largely unregulated. The majority of banking centers around the world permit banks to provide financial services denominated in non-national currencies. For example, a firm can borrow Japanese yen in New York and open a yen account in Singapore. You can also deposit dollars in the Bahamas and borrow British pounds in the Grand Cayman Islands.

Eurocurrency first arose in the 1950s in London, which had lost its dominant position in international banking because Britain no longer had a large empire and the British pound was no longer the dominant world currency. After World War II, the rise of the U.S. dollar as the international currency gave U.S. banks a great advantage in providing trade finance to the global banking market. But London banks were able to grasp a unique opportunity in 1956. In that year, the British government feared that foreign governments opposed to its involvement in the Israeli-French-British attack on Egypt, known as the Suez crisis, would sell pounds and put downward pressure on the exchange rate, so British banking authorities prohibited British banks from lending pounds overseas. Their rationale was simple: if foreigners had no pounds, they could not sell them on the foreign exchange markets and drive the value of the pound down. This regulation seemed to be the

Table 13.2

The 25 Most Globalized Financial Transnational Firms, Ranked by UNCTAD's Spread Index[1]
(2006, millions of US$, and number of employees)

Financial TNF	Home	Assets (billions US$)	Employees	Affiliates Total	Affiliates Foreign	Affiliates Ratio	Affiliates Countries
1 Citigroup Inc.	U.S.	1,884.3	337,000	773	506	65	75
2 GE Capital Corp.	U.S.	543.7	81,000	1,117	785	70	51
3 Alianz	Germany	1,357.7	166,505	824	613	74	48
4 BNP Paribas	France	1,898.2	132,507	746	517	69	49
5 Axa	France	939.8	76,339	603	504	84	38
6 Generali Group	Italy	486.4	63,770	359	305	85	37
7 ABN Amro	Netherlands	1,297.6	107,535	887	624	70	43
8 Societe Generale	France	1,261.5	115,134	495	298	60	50
9 UBS AG	Switzerland	1,961.3	78,140	328	293	89	33
10 Deutsche Bank	Germany	1,481.0	68,849	974	745	76	38
11 ING Groep NV	Netherlands	1,606.7	119,801	939	539	63	46
12 Unicredit Group	Italy	1,077.2	139,061	794	738	93	31
13 Zurich Financial	Switzerland	351.2	52,286	338	327	97	29
14 HSBC	U.K.	1,857.5	300,920	985	574	58	47
15 AIG	U.S.	979.4	106,000	574	342	60	43
16 Credit Suisse	Switzerland	1,025.1	44,871	251	221	88	28
17 Credit Agricole SA	France	1,662.6	77,063	387	195	50	40
18 Fortis NV	Belgium/ Netherlands	1,020.1	59,747	431	306	71	27
19 Natexis B. Populaire	France	604.4	21,138	268	119	44	41
20 Dexia	Belgium	747.0	21,490	234	192	82	22
21 JP Morgan Chase	U.S.	1,351.5	174,360	491	278	57	31
22 Banco Santander	Spain	1,088.0	129,749	316	231	73	22
23 Merrill Lynch	U.S.	841.3	58,200	196	124	63	24
24 KBC Groupe SA	Belgium	428.5	50,189	308	245	80	19
25 Bank of Nova Scotia	Canada	336.3	53,251	86	60	70	20

[1] UNCTAD's Geographical Spread Index consists of the square root of the ratio of foreign affiliates to all affiliates, multiplied by the number of host countries.

Source: UNCTAD (2007), *World Investment Report 2007,* New York: United Nations Conference on Trade and Development, Table A.1.15.

final death knell for London banks because it forced them out of international banking altogether. Unwilling to give up so easily, however, several London banks reacted to the British government's ban on foreign lending in pounds by offering very attractive interest rates on deposits in U.S. dollars and using those deposits to make foreign dollar loans instead of traditional pound loans. This was a radical financial innovation; never before had banks anywhere accepted deposits and made loans in anything other than their national currency. The British regulatory authorities signaled that they had no objections to this business strategy, and to many bankers' surprise, their dollar business grew very quickly.

Some borrowers and depositors of dollars rather liked the opportunity to do their dollar banking in London rather than in the United States. One early customer was the Soviet Union, which engaged in a limited amount of foreign trade and was forced to receive and make payments in dollars, the currency of its Cold War adversary, the United States. The Soviet Union was not very comfortable depositing money in the United States, even for a short while, because their deposits could easily be confiscated by a hostile U.S. government. Hence, when London banks began accepting dollar deposits, the Soviet Union was an eager customer. The U.S.S.R. even opened its own London branch of the Moscow Narodny Bank to handle its dollar accounts.

The British government realized that the dollar business was an opportunity to revive London as the world's leading banking center even though the U.S. dollar had become the world's dominant currency. Soon British authorities provided explicit incentives for banks to do **Eurodollar** business. For example, the government exempted banks' business in foreign currencies from bank taxes, minimum reserve requirements, and most other forms of regulation and control. Eurodollar banks could therefore pay above-market rates on deposits and charge below-market rates on loans to reputable and trusted customers. As hoped, many foreign banks set up branches in London to take advantage of the deregulated environment and the vast pool of banking talent working in London. Now it was possible to borrow and deposit dollars in a unique unregulated environment outside the United States.

The U.S. government inadvertently helped to expand the Eurodollar market in the 1960s when it restricted international lending from the United States in an effort to contain dollar outflows and maintain the value of the dollar in the regulated foreign exchange market. U.S. firms that wanted to invest overseas could no longer borrow in the United States and export the money, so they borrowed on the Eurodollar market instead. The higher deposit rates meant that U.S. exporters found it more advantageous to deposit their overseas earnings in London than to bring the money back to the United States where it would earn lower interest rates. More deposits meant the London banks had more dollars to lend, and thus the Eurodollar market grew. London banks later began to accept other currencies for deposit. Soon other countries began to permit their banks to lend and accept deposits in foreign currencies too. What developed was essentially a large **offshore banking** market that came to be known as the *Eurodollar market*. Later, as banking centers in Asia and the Western Hemisphere also began to permit unregulated banking in foreign currencies, the market became the Eurocurrency markets; for some reason the *euro* portion of the term *Eurodollar* stuck even though the market became global. Even the U.S. government eventually caved in to competitive forces, and rather than seeing international banking activity going offshore, it permitted banks in the United States to deal in foreign banking under more favorable conditions. As a result, New York has been able to remain a major international banking center. Among other Eurocurrency banking centers are Paris, Frankfurt, Zurich, Tokyo, Hong Kong, Sydney, and Singapore. Eurocurrency centers have also arisen in Dubai, the Grand Cayman Islands, Aruba, Bermuda, Panama, and other **tax havens** as international banks and their customers have sought to escape even the reduced regulations in the major banking centers.

Most of the offshore bank centers offer bank secrecy for their customers. Switzerland is the best known for enforcing strict **bank secrecy laws**, which prohibit banks from revealing any information about their customers' banking activities to anyone, including governments. Bank secrecy protects bank customers, but, of course, it ends up hiding tax evasion, business fraud, and other illegal activities. Banks in offshore banking centers are often accused of **money laundering**, which refers to the process of exchanging tainted money for new, clean money.

After the World Trade Center attack in New York by political-religious terrorists in 2001, efforts to control the funding of international criminal activities further singled out the offshore banking centers as likely conduits for such funding. The European Union and the United States have pressured Switzerland, Luxembourg, and the smaller offshore banking centers to reveal the identities of their depositors so that they can be monitored for tax evasion. A major shift in Swiss banking policy was attempted in early 2009 when the Swiss bank UBS settled a criminal case with the U.S. Department of Justice by agreeing to disclose the names of nearly three hundred U.S. clients suspected of tax evasion in the United States. The Swiss courts have declared this agreement illegal since then. The United States and Swiss governments were still negotiating on this issue and in 2011, the Swiss Federal Assembly voted against weakening bank secrecy laws in defiance of U.S. pressure.

PORTFOLIO INVESTMENT

In most developed countries, and in an increasing number of developing economies, we see a growing variety of financial markets and intermediaries functioning simultaneously. The complexity of financial intermediation, especially the problems of moral hazard, adverse selection, asymmetric information, fraud, and contract enforcement that we discussed in the introduction to international finance in Chapter 11, explains this variety. For example, relatively inexpensive financial markets such as bond and stock markets can exchange the stocks and bonds of well-known corporations whose value can be easily judged by most savers. But small, unknown firms must rely more on commercial banks, which have traditionally been equipped to investigate and monitor small business firms and their projects. Financial intermediaries such as banks, pension funds, mutual funds, and insurance companies are good at pooling risk, something that individual savers cannot easily do by themselves. Therefore, stock and bond markets coexist with banks, pension funds, and insurance companies in what we broadly term the financial sector of the economy or the **financial industry**.

In the following section we briefly examine stock and bond markets, where savers can engage in what we normally call **portfolio investment**. Portfolio investment, as the term suggests, lets savers diversify their portfolios of assets and, therefore, reduce risk. The establishment of stock and bond markets in most countries has greatly facilitated international portfolio investment.

Defining Portfolio Investment

Portfolio investment consists of purchases and sales of securities, such as bonds and stocks, in amounts that do not imply any direct management control or influence on the businesses issuing the securities. For example, international portfolio investment includes a foreign investor buying 1,000 shares in General Electric or an American buying a €10,000 bond issued by the government of France. It would also include a U.S. mutual fund buying several thousand shares in the Danish windmill manufacturer Vestas or a German pension fund buying a wide variety of foreign stocks across many different countries and industries in order to reduce its portfolio's overall risk. During the early 2000s, before the 2007–2008 Great Recession, portfolio investment was either the largest or second largest category of international investment. The prominence of international portfolio investment is a very recent phenomenon, however. International portfolio investment was negligible before 1980.

International Equity Markets

You can appreciate the globalization of stock, or "equity," trading by looking in the *Financial Times* or any of the world's leading business newspapers. In 2010, for example, the *Financial Times* showed the indexes covering stock exchanges in sixty-two countries in its Global Equity Markets section. Of course, stock market activity is still highly concentrated, and the New York Stock Exchange still trades nearly half of the world's stocks in terms of their value. The New York Stock Exchange's dominance reflects the historical leadership of the United States in developing **equity markets** as well as the current trend toward consolidation of stock markets. The stock of over four hundred non-U.S. corporations are traded in New York, so the capitalized value of the companies whose stocks are traded on the New York Stock Exchange includes the values of many foreign transnational financial firms. It is simply more efficient to trade more stocks on fewer markets.

The advantages of size have favored existing stock markets in developed countries and hampered the development of small stock exchanges in developing economies. With small volumes and trading stocks in companies that are not well known outside their home markets, volume at many developing-country stock exchanges has remained small despite the increased purchases of stock in emerging-market corporations. In order to attract buyers, larger corporations from developing economies have increasingly listed their stocks on exchanges in developed countries. Many foreign stocks are traded on the New York Stock Exchange and the over-the-counter Nasdaq in the United States.

American Depository Receipts Make Foreign Stock Look Like a Domestic Asset

The development of the **American Depository Receipt (ADR)** has made international investment in corporate stock easier. For example, when British Petroleum (BP) completed its $55 billion acquisition of Amoco in 1998, Amoco's U.S. stockholders were not given stock in BP; rather, they were given ADRs, which are receipts for BP stock deposited in a U.S. bank. The BP ADRs are traded on the New York Stock Exchange, unlike the BP stock, which was issued in the United Kingdom and is traded on the London Stock Exchange. The advantage of ADRs for the American stockholders is that they are valued in U.S. dollars, and they pay out dividends in U.S. dollars even though the underlying BP stock is valued and pays dividends in British pounds. According to the detailed data in the U.S. net investment position in 2010, Americans owned nearly $3 trillion in foreign equities. It is estimated that close to half of these equities were in the form of ADRs issued on the stock of foreign corporations. Foreign corporations find the arrangement attractive because American investors' greater willingness to acquire ADRs than foreign stock effectively lowers their financing costs. American investors apparently like the convenience of transacting exclusively in dollars and avoiding the often higher transactions costs of acquiring foreign equities on foreign exchanges.

Unintended Consequences of the Globalization of Financial Markets

Stock and bond markets are not the only national financial markets that have been internationally integrated by the participation of increasing numbers of foreign investors. The countries whose banks have engaged in financial innovation have also led the way in opening their markets to foreign investors. Therefore, when U.S. banks began creating **collateralized debt obligations (CDOs)**, which are securities backed by bundles of mortgages and other types of debt, they immediately marketed them to buyers throughout the world. Similarly, the **credit default swaps (CDSs)** that were used to insure the CDOs were also marketed throughout the world. New types of financial instruments like CDOs and CDSs are generally marketed through over-the-counter markets. Recall our discussion of over-the-counter markets in Chapter 11: These are markets run by dealers who maintain inventories and sell and buy their wares upon demand. In the case of financial instruments like CDOs and CDSs, the dealers are large, international, private financial firms that operate in many countries, and the trade thus was global from the outset.

Until 2008, most international financial economists openly praised the global financial system that had developed and the innovations, such as CDOs, that were produced by the multinational commercial banks, investment banks, stock markets, bond markets, insurance firms, and other financial firms. The globalization and innovations were believed to facilitate the flow of savings to the world's most profitable investment projects. The apparent liquidity of the global financial markets and the pooling of assets and liabilities by specialized intermediaries and by means of new financial instruments like the credit default swaps that were marketed globally were believed to reduce overall risk.

In 2008, it became very clear that something had gone dreadfully wrong in the international financial system. Because over-the-counter markets, such as the market for CDOs, lacked **transparency**, no one knew who owed what to whom. In 2008, the financial markets froze after declines in the prices of CDOs created a panic; it was impossible to determine who owned how many of those assets. Many of the CDOs were held off the balance sheets of the banks and other financial firms in what are known as **conduits**, or in other dependent entities created explicitly to hold such assets. Yet, there were commitments and guarantees issued by the banks and other financial firms, implicit and explicit, backing the various derivative assets. This lack of transparency contributed to a sharp slowdown in interbank lending because no one could judge the financial health of borrowers.

Now, the reality of the global financial meltdown has changed economists' views of the international financial system. By 2009, bank lending had diminished, government bailouts of banks and other financial institutions throughout the world summed to several trillion dollars, and institutions such as the International Monetary Fund and regional development banks were being called on to resume lending to developing countries in place of the sharply diminished private flows. For the first time since World War II, the total world economy contracted in 2009. With short-term interest rates in the United States, Japan, and the United Kingdom approaching zero, the average saver was happy to just maintain her nominal wealth, quietly hoping that the growing debts of her government would not undermine its obligation to insure her savings account nor trigger future inflation that could destroy the real purchasing power of her savings. What, exactly, triggered this financial collapse?

FINANCIAL INNOVATION

The two sections above on international banking and portfolio investment describe recent innovation and expansion of new business in the financial industry. The Eurocurrency markets and offshore banking centers are clearly forms of **financial innovation**, as are the securitization of traditional mortgages and credit card debt. The term *financial innovation* generally refers to new financial institutions and new financial instruments. But the consolidation of financial services into ever-larger conglomerates and the spread of these transnational banking and financial firms across borders also constitute a form of financial innovation, one that may be more significant than any other recent change (except for the ATM, as Paul Volcker states at the start of this chapter). The international financial industry has changed drastically over the past twenty-five years.

It is still an open question whether financial innovation has improved the performance of the world's economies. Innovation certainly improved the earnings of the transnational banking firms, at least until the financial crisis hit. For example, in 2007 financial firms' profits accounted for over one-fourth of total corporate earnings in the United States. The global financial collapse following the Lehman Brothers default in 2008 suggests that financial innovation has failed, rather spectacularly some say, to carry out its fundamental roles in the economy, which were described in Chapter 11 as improving the allocation of the world's savings to the most productive investments and reducing risk. The quotes at the start of this chapter by a noted former chairman of the U.S. Federal Reserve Bank and a Nobel Prize–winning economist suggest that there is no convincing evidence that banks have notably improved their service to humanity. The following section of this chapter details how the financial innovation of securitization destabilized the global financial system and caused world economic output to fall for the first time since World War II.

Collateralized Debt Obligations

Recall from Chapter 11 that collateralized debt obligations (CDOs) are securitized bundles of loans. These were one of the highly-touted financial innovations of the past ten years. CDOs permitted banks to originate loans and, rather than holding the loans as assets over their full term, they bundled the loans into CDOs and sold them on the international over-the-counter market for securities. Specifically, savings banks and commercial banks issued mortgage loans, auto loans, credit card debt, and consumer loans as they have always done, but then, rather than hold the loans as assets over their full term, they bundled this debt together into CDOs and issued new securities that promised returns based on the expected returns to the underlying loans and debt. Recall also that CDOs were seldom simple average samples of the full bundle of loans and debt. To make these securities more profitable for the sellers, the bundles of mortgages, auto loans, credit card debt, and so on were split into separate **tranches**, each of which represented the order in which returns derived from the whole bundle of underlying loans and debt would be paid out. For example, the top tranche of the CDO offered purchasers a relatively low interest rate but placed them at the front of the line in getting paid that rate of return from the payments made on the original loans and credit card debt. The purchasers of each subsequent tranche would receive their returns only after the higher tranches were paid. The tranches were carefully *structured* to include the largest possible number of mortgages, loans, and credit card accounts that still met the minimum requirements for high ratings from one of the major ratings agencies, such as Standard and Poor's, Fitch, or Moody's.

In order to maximize the overall profits from bundling loans and debt into CDOs, the financial firms that created the CDOs made the top tranche of each CDO as large as possible because AAA tranches of the CDOs sold at the highest price (paid the lowest return). Despite the obvious risk of **subprime mortgages**, the AAA-rated top tranche of subprime mortgage CDOs issued during 2005–2007 included about 80 percent of all such mortgages, as D. Greenlaw et al. (2008) find in their examination of confidential data from the bond rating firm Moody's. Therefore, if more than 20 percent of the subprime borrowers stopped servicing their debt, the AAA rated top tranche would no longer earn its full returns.

Many of the underlying subprime mortgages were also configured to entice borrowers with low introductory interest charges for the first two or three years, which would then rise to a much higher rate for the remainder of mortgage. And, many of these mortgages were issued for 100 percent of the purchase price of homes that were being sold in a market that by 2004 was clearly experiencing a massive price bubble. It was thus highly likely that housing prices would eventually fall and the value of the homes purchased would fall below the value of the mortgage loans. In short, defaults on the subprime mortgages were likely, and the AAA rating on tranches consisting of over 80 percent of the overall CDOs should have been seen as too optimistic. But we have to understand that these private, profit-motivated ratings firms issued their overly optimistic ratings on CDOs bundled by financial firms who were paying them directly for the ratings! This arrangement between private ratings agencies and other private financial firms may have been viewed by some as a profitable financial innovation, but more sober observers see this clever innovation as a clear conflict of interest.

Credit Default Swaps Insured the CDOs

A second highly-touted financial innovation was the *credit default swap* (CDS). Recall also from Chapter 11 that CDSs are *options* that, for an initial fee or *premium,* promise to pay out the full value of remaining CDO obligations if the underlying CDO defaults. CDSs were acquired not only by purchasers of CDOs, however. Incredibly, the financial industry also sold CDSs to hedge funds, speculators, and plain old gamblers who did not actually own any of the CDOs on which CDSs would pay out in the case of default. These investors in **naked CDSs**, as they are called, just wanted to place a bet that a specific tranche of a specific CDO would default in the future. In a sense, the purchasers of naked credit default swaps are like bettors on a football match who observe the game but have no direct participation in its outcome. And, just as with bets on a football game, there are multiple bets on the future performance of a single CDO.

Some perceptive economists noted, however, that the purchase of a CDS by a hedge fund that did not actually own the underlying CDO is equivalent to your purchasing a fire insurance policy on your neighbor's house or a life insurance policy on a friend's life. There may be an incentive for you to take action to ensure a favorable outcome! Financial conglomerates intentionally created exceptionally risky CDOs for which they then purchased CDSs from other financial firms to cover the expected losses.[3] This is equivalent to purchasing a house cheaply because it has bad electrical wiring and a broken fire alarm, and then buying fire insurance priced on the assumption that the house is in compliance with the fire codes. Seventy-five years ago, Keynes, the noted British economist, questioned the usefulness of letting gamblers with no interest in the underlying corporations dominate daily transactions in the stock market. Keynes (1936) advocated making it more difficult for gamblers to dominate the day-to-day movements in the stock market, which, after all, was there to promote investment, not gambling.

It is, therefore, debatable whether these innovations constituted improvements in the financial industry. Nevertheless, by 2007 over US$50 trillion in credit default swaps had been contracted by investors, hedge funds, banks, and assorted gamblers throughout the global financial industry.

The purchasers of the highly rated top tranches of mortgage CDOs duly insured with CDSs no doubt felt their financial investments were secure. When the housing bubble in the United States burst in 2007, mortgage defaults increased and these tranches proved to be much riskier than their initial AAA ratings had suggested. Belatedly, the ratings firms downgraded the ratings. This created another problem, however. Many of the purchasers of CDOs were banks, insurance companies, pension funds, and other intermediaries that were required by regulators to hold specific percentages of their assets in the form of safe AAA assets. So when the CDOs were downgraded, they had to sell them and acquire other assets that were still rated as AAA assets. The panic selling caused the prices of the CDOs to plummet, which further lowered their ratings. The holders of subprime mortgage CDOs lost billions of dollars from their balance sheets, and banks and financial firms around the world were suddenly in deep financial trouble. Banks stopped lending, and in order to prevent a financial meltdown and a downturn in economic activity, governments in most countries "bailed out" their banking systems in 2008 and 2009 by paying cash at face value for the banks' downgraded CDOs.

DEREGULATION AND FINANCIAL FRAUD

Because the 2008 financial crisis originated in the United States, many analysts blamed the crisis specifically on the dismantling of U.S. banking and financial regulations. Indeed, the story of how financial innovation caused a global economic recession is much more complicated than the story above lets on. To the shortsighted, profit-motivated behavior must be added bad policy decisions, a disregard for history, and very large doses of good old fraud and deception. Among other regulations, the U.S. government had erected **firewalls** to separate the different banking and financial businesses. These regulatory limits were instituted during the Great Depression in response to the risky financial behavior that was seen as having contributed to the sharp decline in lending and investment after the stock market crash of 1929.

The Glass-Steagall Act

The 1933 **Glass-Steagall Act** set strict rules for what each type of financial firm could, and could not, do. Savings banks were limited to taking deposits and making mortgages, commercial banks were limited to making business and consumer loans, and investment banks, which took greater risks, were not permitted to solicit deposits from the general public. These rules were intended to prevent a financial institution from directing the savings deposited by people who wanted safe retirement accounts toward risky speculative investments. If risky investments fail, then savers' deposits are underfunded.

Glass-Steagall was overturned in 1999, however, after years of strong lobbying by the financial industry. Senator Phil Gramm, the top recipient of campaign contributions from commercial banks between 1989 and 2002, sponsored the legislation. Gramm's law received strong support from President Bill Clinton and his treasury secretary, Lawrence Summers (who was later chosen to be chief economic advisor in the Obama administration in 2004 and 2010).[4] Said Summers in 1999:

Today Congress voted to update the rules that have governed financial services since the Great Depression and replace them with a system for the 21st century.[5]

After 1999, financial conglomerates were permitted to lend the savings of depositors buying low-risk certificates of deposit to high-risk hedge funds. Reserves set aside by insurance companies to cover risks for fire and life insurance were effectively mixed with the reserves backing the credit default swaps that insured financial derivatives like CDOs and the bets of those who gambled on the CDOs' failure.

Not everyone thought it was a good idea to abolish Glass-Steagall. Senator Byron Dorgan of North Dakota said on the day the Great Depression–era law was overturned: "I think we will look back in 10 years' time and say we should not have done this but we did because we forgot the lessons of the past, and that that which is true in the 1930s is true in 2010."[6] Dorgan's estimate of how long it would take before the deregulated financial system would succumb to excessive risk taking and fraud was too optimistic. The fraud came within a few years, the financial cash in just eight years.

Globalization and Financial Deregulation

Some viewed the 1999 repeal of the Glass-Steagall Act as nothing more than a long-overdue recognition of the fact that the firewalls had already been breached by the globalization of banking and financial enterprises. Because the world's major banks and financial firms operated in many countries, they routinely "shopped around" for the regulatory structure that let them do what they wanted. If, for example, a U.S. bank was not permitted to underwrite bond issues, then perhaps its London or Frankfurt branch could do it under the regulations of the United Kingdom or Germany. In this global environment, it helped little if one country maintained strict firewalls while other countries did not. The globalization of banking was, in fact, used as an argument for eliminating all remaining limits on financial firms. "If we don't pass this bill, we could find London or Frankfurt or years down the road Shanghai becoming the financial capital of the world," said Senator Charles Schumer before the decisive final Senate vote on abolishing Glass-Steagall in 1999.[7]

An example of how globalization effectively disabled existing national financial regulation is the case of AIG, the American International Group that was described in Chapter 11 as a major issuer of credit default swaps (CDSs), the derivatives that served as insurance for risky financial assets. AIG decided it would be more convenient, and profitable, to open a London office to sell CDSs covering the upper tranches of mortgage CDOs issued in the United States. In London, as long as its models showed reserves were not necessary, AIG was not required to hold reserves to back the insurance commitments issued. AIG's London office used a financial model that showed there was absolutely no chance that the upper tranches of the mortgage-backed CDOs would default, and its American management apparently agreed that reserves were not necessary to cover the risk of default on the hundreds of billions of dollars of CDOs that the London office covered with the CDSs it issued.[8]

AIG's customers thought there was risk; why else would they have paid billions of dollars in premiums to AIG for the CDSs? But, AIG's London office booked the premiums as pure profit, which nicely augmented AIG's profit by hundreds of millions of dollars per year. So impressed was AIG's management with the 400 employees in its London office that it paid each one of them more than $1 million per year in bonuses, or about one-third of the premiums collected on the CDSs. The CEO of AIG, of course, also increased his own bonuses as the company's profits and stock value rose. The manager of AIG's Financial Products Division in London, Joseph Cassano, earned £280 ($400) million over the 2000–2008 period. It was Cassano who stated in 2007:

It is hard for us, without being flippant, to even see a scenario within any kind of realm of reason that would see us losing one dollar in any of those transactions.[9]

As described in Chapter 11, when the CDOs proved to be risky after all, and AIG was called on to pay out on the losses, there were no reserves to cover them. By early 2009, the U.S. government had channeled over $180 billion to AIG to enable the large insurance firm to meet its insurance obligations. AIG was deemed to be too important for the U.S. economy to let it fail and suddenly leave people and businesses uninsured, although it turns out that some of biggest recipients of the payouts AIG had to make, and effectively funded by U.S. taxpayers, were to other large financial firms, most notably Goldman Sachs.

The Great Monetary Expansion

The financial innovations and expansion of the financial industry discussed above took place in an extremely accommodative monetary policy environment. Since the 1980s, the U.S. Federal Reserve Bank had kept monetary policy exceptionally loose. Despite concerns that the Fed was printing too much money and that it would cause inflation to rise, official price indexes remained stable throughout the 1990s. The chairman of the Federal Reserve, Alan Greenspan, explained that inflation was not a problem because there was rapid growth in technology that expanded the supply of products. Surely, the rapid rise in imports from low-cost countries like China and rising immigration, both legal and illegal, also moderated prices in the United States. The monetary expansion did fuel a stock market bubble in the late 1990s, however, and it burst spectacularly in 2000.

The stock market bubble was followed by the September 11, 2001, terrorist attacks, and the Federal Reserve Bank responded by again increasing the money supply. Over a two-year period, the Fed lowered the discount rate from 5 percent to just 1 percent, but this monetary expansion again did not generate inflation in the United States or any other developed economies. Again, rapid growth of imports from China and other low-wage economies, plus even more legal and illegal immigration, kept wages low or even declining during the economic recovery in the United States, Britain, Ireland, and elsewhere.

The lack of general inflation was even more surprising because the expansionary Federal Reserve monetary policy was magnified by the **securitization** of debt, as for example, the CDOs that securitized mortgages. The expanded money supply flowed into sectors where securitization was most common, such as housing, auto loans, and credit card debt. While imports kept most consumer product prices stable, the rapid growth of the global market for securitized and **structured financial products** like the tranched CDOs did cause a massive housing price bubble in the United States. Securitization permitted the banks to issue many more mortgages than they could have supported with only the money they captured through deposits at their bank, because they could now issue mortgages, sell them on to others in CDOs, use that money to issue yet more mortgages, create more CDOs, and so forth. Securitization also encouraged banks to permit their loan officers to issue mortgages with little concern for borrowers' ability to service the debt. Some reasoned that as long as housing prices kept rising, borrowers could always sell their houses at a profit if they ran into trouble servicing their debt. But the housing bubble had already lifted prices to unsustainable levels.

One news report accurately observed that "the nation's mortgage system was set up to promote and encourage outright fraud in order to close a loan—and everyone, from brokers to loan officers to Wall Street, looked the other way."[10] Everyone seemed to profit: the bank officers who received bonuses for originating the mortgages, the real estate brokers who earned commissions on the ever-higher house prices, the Wall Street financial executives who earned bonuses for creating CDOs and the CDSs to insure the CDOs, and the growing number of employees working in the booming financial centers of the world. Regulators and the banks themselves should have become suspicious when loan officers openly began to refer to the subprime mortgage market as "the liar's market."[11] Neither lenders nor borrowers told the truth about the terms of the loans or the ability to pay. But as long as the global markets absorbed the securities, the mortgage lenders continued to make loans, bundle them up into new securities that could be sold on to other investors and banks throughout the world, and earn more fees and bonuses. In short, rather than spreading risk and permanently increasing home ownership, the system mostly boosted the bonuses of bankers and financial executives at the long-run expense of taxpayers, duped investors, pensioners, stockholders, and foreclosed homeowners.

Financial Crisis to Recession

The financial expansion came to an end when the housing price bubble began to pop in 2006 and the securitized mortgages, often bundled together with other securities, had to be downgraded to reflect their diminished value. Many banks and other financial institutions, required by regulators to carry mostly AAA-rated assets, scrambled to shore up their balance sheets and avoid violating regulatory guidelines. The market for securitized bundles of mortgages and other debt quickly dried up, sharply reducing financing for housing and other loans. Borrowing costs rose, and building and investment activity slowed sharply.

As construction activity fell and bank lending slowed, the United States fell into recession in late 2007. More important, this collapse of lending in the United States was repeated in many other countries around the globe. For example, when the U.S. online banking subsidiary of the Dutch financial group ING became insolvent in the United States, it required help from its holding company, and therefore ING in Europe also stopped lending. Other countries, most notably Ireland, Spain, and the United Kingdom, had experienced housing booms and housing price bubbles not unlike those in the United States, even though the European Central Bank had not expanded the money supply as rapidly as the U.S. Federal Reserve had. This suggests that the financial innovations of securitization and their insurance through credit default swaps were the real culprit in causing the global financial collapse.

The financial innovations were to blame for the global recession for another reason: the fact that the CDOs and CDSs were sold in over-the-counter markets, where there is no public disclosure of who is buying what from whom, made it impossible to calculate risk throughout the financial system. Lenders could not trust borrowers' balance sheets because they did not know what assets backed CDOs or who held and backed the CDSs that insured or gambled on the unknown CDOs. Instead of lending, financial sectors in economies exposed to U.S. CDOs "fled to safety" by holding cash or government bonds. Lending stopped, investment collapsed, and unemployment rose.

The recession spread throughout the world very quickly. Even countries that were not directly affected by the financial crisis were eventually affected by declining international trade. For example, U.S. consumers bought fewer foreign products when their economy slowed, so foreign employment fell. Immigrants in the United States and Europe became unemployed and stopped sending remittances back home. Hence, the Mexican, Chinese, Indian, and many other emerging economies also slowed as well. In sum, deregulation and questionable banking practices in the United States triggered a global financial crisis and economic recession.

From Financial Crisis to Economic Crisis

The above example of the 2008 financial crisis and the discussion in the previous chapter on exchange rate volatility have one thing in common: in each case a financial market failed. This failure caused most other financial intermediation to cease, which, in turn, caused real economic activity and employment to fall.

There are many similarities between the cases of economic disruption discussed in the previous chapter and above in this chapter. Most obvious is the propensity for financial markets, whether it be the ages-old market for foreign exchange or the more recent markets for complex financial derivatives, to remain relatively stable for extended periods and then suddenly undergo very large changes in price and volume. In the next section we generalize the brief discussion in the previous chapter on the volatility of foreign exchange markets. All financial markets are potentially volatile because they are driven by expected future prices rather than present market conditions. Financial markets operate in a state of uncertainty.

FINANCIAL INSTABILITY

The 2007–2008 economic recession seemed to take economists, bankers, policy makers, pundits, and business leaders by surprise. Up through 2007, economic growth rates were positive almost everywhere. The U.S. economy was seen as an example of good macroeconomic management; since the 1980 recession, the U.S. economy had been characterized as the Great Moderation because its macroeconomic performance seemed to have become much less volatile compared to earlier periods of the twentieth century. And, of course, the extraordinarily high reported economic growth rates for China and India were interpreted as a validation of globalization and the Western free market model, since the spurt in Chinese and Indian economic growth had come after those countries "opened up" to the rest of the world.

This is not to suggest that the U.S. economy, the largest economy in the world, was in fact healthy. Economists had pointed out a number of unsustainable trends. For example, we noted above that the U.S. economy generated growing trade deficits and an ever-larger negative net investment position. China's growing official accumulation of foreign assets was taking on astounding proportions, approaching $2 trillion by 2007. U.S. households had stopped saving any income, on average. Government deficits grew very large after President Bush cut taxes and escalated spending to initiate what would become the two longest foreign wars of the many the United States had waged. Much of the government deficit was financed by foreign borrowing. Table 11.1 shows that foreigners bought very large numbers of U.S. Treasury bonds, as did foreign central banks through official transactions to prevent their currencies from appreciating.

But until the sharp decline in financial asset prices in 2008, financial markets seemed to believe that the United States would be able to somehow deal with these unsustainable imbalances. Recall from the previous chapter how receptive pundits were to the suggestion that the "dark matter" of U.S. business superiority explained why the net investment position was not the true net investment position. And, above all, financial experts and pundits interviewed on television's financial channels and writing in the financial pages of the world's newspapers regularly confirmed their belief that the U.S. financial industry and its efficient markets would be capable of handling the imbalances and any future risks that might arise. The increases in asset values and corporate profits during the 1990s and early 2000s, save for the brief setback after the 2000 stock market bubble and the terrorist attacks in 2001, were constantly touted by financial pundits as signs of the strength and resiliency of the U.S. economy. The fundamental imbalances were largely ignored by the press and, to their detriment, by investors.

What was most surprising about the 2007–2008 recession was that economists largely failed to anticipate it. Clearly, the mainstream neoclassical paradigm was not useful for detecting the inherent unsustainability of trends or the precarious state of the financial sector. Interestingly, there has been a revival of interest in Keynes's ideas in the mainstream of economics because his macroeconomic analysis seems to provide insight into why the financial system suddenly caused a worldwide economic recession, something the neoclassical paradigm could not do.

Neoclassical Analysis Cannot Explain Crises

In general, neoclassical economic analysis uses models that are static in nature and that assume smooth continuous functions and fundamental forces, such as producers' profit maximization and consumers' utility maximization, that drive the economy toward stable equilibria. The debate within the mainstream of macroeconomic thought, therefore, has focused on how fast the economy moves back to full employment when the system is disrupted by some exogenous shock. The so-called post-Keynesian school of economic thought has tried to fit into this neoclassical mindset by distinguishing mechanisms that prevent the rapid return to full employment after, for example, a financial crisis. According to this analysis, the slow reaction time of the economy justifies active fiscal and monetary policies.

On the other hand, Milton Friedman and Anna Jacobson Schwartz (1963) concluded in their popular *Monetary History of the United States 1867–1960* that the macroeconomic performance of the U.S. economy closely tracked movements in the money supply. Friedman further argued that fiscal policy was not only ineffective but often perverse because of the long lag time between policy decisions and economic effects. He suggested that the U.S. Federal Reserve Bank should, therefore, steadily expand the monetary base at exactly the long-run rate of real growth of the U.S. economy, which in the 1960s was about 3 percent per year. Friedman (1968) and the labor economist Edmund Phelps (1968) provided a further justification for more passive macroeconomic policies by contesting the conventional wisdom that there was a trade-off between unemployment and inflation. The evidence of an inverse relationship between unemployment and inflation had become known as the *Phillips curve,* in honor of A.W. Phillips (1958), who first uncovered an inverse relationship between unemployment and prices in studying Britain over the extended period 1861–1957. If true, such a trade-off between inflation and employment could be exploited by policy makers to raise employment by means of faster money growth. Friedman (1968, p. 1) claimed, however, that even though "there is always a temporary trade-off between inflation and unemployment; there is no permanent trade-off." By the start of the 1980s, policy makers in the United States, Britain, and many other countries increasingly accepted the monetarist assumption that free labor markets would take care of unemployment.

Another important development in the history of neoclassical macroeconomic thought is the work of Robert E. Lucas, Jr. (1972, 1973), who drew on John F. Muth's (1961) concept of **rational expectations**. Muth hypothesized that people are fully rational in the sense that they use all available information to reach objective conclusions about the future. Lucas used Muth's hypothesis to provide a precise justification not only for Friedman's argument that there was no trade-off between employment and inflation, but for the more general argument that financial markets are rational and unbiased predictors of the future. Rational expectations lie behind the interest parity condition described in the previous chapter.

There are many other potential problems that prevent markets from clearing efficiently, but neoclassical economists came up with various microeconomic models that offered the **microfoundations** to justify the frequent conclusions that laissez-faire policies are welfare-superior to active government macroeconomic policy. First, neoclassical models generally assumed that product markets are supplied exclusively by rising-cost producers, so there is no tendency for market power to become concentrated in oligopolies or monopolies. In reality, of course, labor and product markets are far from fully competitive, and prices normally do not accurately reflect true opportunity costs. Also notable is the widespread acceptance of the **Coase theorem**, attributed to Ronald Coase (1960), which states that **externalities** will not, in general, cause markets to fail because people and firms are motivated to find ways to negotiate the mutually beneficial sharing of the external costs or benefits. The Coase theorem leads, arguably, to the greatest leap of faith to be found in mainstream economics; it is safe to say that in most cases few market participants are even aware of the existence of externalities, much less able to negotiate a market solution to incorporate them in prices. To assume that firms and consumers can seriously negotiate some way to share the externalities is completely unrealistic.

In the area of finance, mainstream neoclassical macroeconomic analysis accepts as practical approximations of reality several other highly questionable models, such as Eugene F. Fama's (1970) model of efficient markets that built all available information into asset prices, Friedman's (1953) hypothesis that speculation always stabilizes financial markets, and Michael C. Jensen and William H. Meckling's (1976) model of managers of private firms as faithful servants of the stockholders. Most interesting given our discussion here of the recent failures of the financial industry, the seemingly blind faith in the efficiency of financial markets was justified by the work of Kenneth Arrow and Gerard Debreu (1954) and Debreu (1959), who constructed elaborate general equilibrium models that introduced a technical gimmick that seemed to eliminate risk: they assumed competitive markets in **contingent commodities**, which are commodities that come into being only when certain pre-specified conditions are met. Think of contingent commodities as insurance, which kicks in only when some disastrous event occurs. Wrote Debreu: "This new definition of a commodity allows one to obtain a theory of uncertainty free from any probability concept and formally identical with the theory of certainty" (p. 98). Effectively, the inclusion of contingent commodities to cover every possible contingency eliminated all risk. Noeclassical economists view financial innovation positively because it is a potential source of Arrow and Debreu's contingent markets. In short, the widely accepted assumptions outlined here permitted neoclassical economics to create a convenient but completely unrealistic modeling framework for analyzing real world macroeconomic issues.

Back to Keynes

The 2008 financial crisis shows that the financial sector has been unable to create viable insurance instruments that cover the more complex contingencies Arrow and Debreu incorporated into their neoclassical general equilibrium model. Arrow and Debreu's contingent markets are a theoretical fantasy that obscures the uncertainty, not risk, that an economy faces. The financial industries in most modern economies indeed do provide insurance against well-understood risks such as fire, theft, automobile accidents, and other predictable events. But only a small proportion of future events are so predictable. Most future events are uncertain.

We discussed some of Keynes's (1936) ideas about financial instability in Chapter 11. His ideas are very important for understanding instability, so here we pick up on the earlier discussion and detail Keynes's analysis. Most important, Keynes highlighted the difference between risk and uncertainty fully. Long-run decisions like investment, innovation, and financial transactions involve uncertainty, not well-defined risk as neoclassical analysis assumes. Keynes's words on uncertainty are worth repeating:

> The actual results of an investment over a long term of years very seldom agree with the initial expectations. Nor can we rationalise our behaviour by arguing that to a man in a state of ignorance errors in either direction are equally probable, so that there remains a mean actuarial expectation based on equi-probabilities. For it can easily be shown that the assumption of arithmetically equal probabilities based on a state of ignorance leads to absurdities. . . . [O]ur existing knowledge does not provide a sufficient basis for a calculated mathematical expectation. (p. 152)

Keynes thus would explicitly reject Muth's assumption that expectations are "a weighted mathematical average" of possible outcomes. Keynes understood that for events in the distant future, no one has enough facts with which to specify the probabilities associated with the many possible known and unknown outcomes. Experiments and research in psychology, neuroscience, and behavioral economics have also thoroughly refuted human rationality as Muth hypothesized it. People are not entirely rational; human evolution apparently has not designed the brain to function precisely according to the rules of mathematical logic. This latter point should not be taken as a criticism of the human brain; rather, it is a criticism of the rational expectations model of human economic behavior.

But if there are no contingent markets where investors and innovators can insure against risk, and they cannot or will not use such information rationally even if they miraculously discover a crystal ball that provides the full information on the future, how do they decide whether to incur current debt, implicitly or explicitly, in order to pursue future gains? Keynes had a realistic perspective on expectations:

> Most, probably, of our decisions to do something positive, the full consequences of which will be drawn out over many days to come, can only be taken as a result of animal spirits—of a spontaneous urge to action rather than inaction, and not as the outcome of a weighted average of quantitative benefits multiplied by quantitative probabilities. (pp. 161–162)

When we broaden investment to include innovation, invention, research, and development activities, Keynes's description of investment as being driven by animal spirits rather than precise mathematical calculations of probable economic outcomes is further validated.

The difficulty in predicting events, possibilities, and the value of long-term assets in the distant future, into which investment and innovative projects must be projected, makes it unlikely that a stable economy will persist. Sooner or later, expectations will not be met, and either lenders or borrowers will pull back. Then economic growth will slow, disappointing more investors and their lenders, and a downward economic spiral develops. In the little-read but most important chapter of his *General Theory of Employment, Interest, and Money* (1936), Keynes hypothesized that the volatility of the market depends on confidence and the continuation of what people perceive as normal or conventional, in accordance with some popular model. People remain confident and willing to engage in uncertain investment and innovative activities as long as outcomes from our investments and innovations are in accordance with conventional and familiar models.

But if Keynes is correct in that expectations are anchored in recent experience and a very limited understanding of the true process that generated the recent results, then the economy will be vulnerable to occasional shocks and, subsequently, revisions of expectations that can severely change people's behavior. Keynes (1936) thus argued for active fiscal policies during the Great Depression, not explicitly because aggregate demand was less than aggregate supply at the full employment level of output, but because, with their conventions invalidated, bankers, investors, innovators, and consumers all became defensive in the face of uncertainty. Only the government could simply increase spending and raise aggregate demand. Keynes furthermore showed that at times like the Great Depression or a severe recession, monetary policy would have little effect on macroeconomic outcomes, either as a stabilizing force or a corrective measure, because the lowering of interest rates has little impact when bankers do not want to lend and potential borrowers do not want to invest, innovate, or buy. This condition is known as the **liquidity trap**, and monetary expansion in this situation has been referred to as "pushing on a string."

The Separation of Finance and Investment

Keynes's emphasis on the role of uncertainty in the macroeconomy is based on his thorough understanding of the financial sector of a modern economy, both from his active personal investing and his perceptive study of the sector. He stated that uncertainty is an especially powerful force for instability in a modern capitalist economy with a modern financial sector that uses complex financial instruments. To explain this point, Keynes first described the environment in which investment and innovative activities occurred before the development of modern financial systems:

> In former times, when enterprises were mainly owned by those who undertook them or by their friends and associates, investment depended on a sufficient supply of individuals of sanguine temperament and constructive impulses who embarked on business as a way of life, not relying on a precise calculation of prospective profit. . . . Decisions to invest in private business of the old fashioned type were, however, decisions largely irrevocable, not only for the community as a whole, but also for the individual. (1936, p. 150)

With the development of securities markets, however, investment decisions have become revocable, at least for the individual. Keynes writes:

> The daily revaluations of the Stock Exchange, though they are primarily made to facilitate transfers of old investments between one individual and another, inevitably exert a decisive influence on the rate of current investment. For there is no sense in building up a new enterprise at a cost greater than that at which similar existing enterprise can be purchased; whilst there is an inducement to spend on a new project what may seem an extravagant sum, if it can be floated off on the Stock Exchange at an immediate profit. (1936, p. 150)

For the community, however, investment cannot be undone so easily. Once built, factories, bridges, and machines continue to exist even if their ownership or market value changes. Keynes saw the fact that financial markets make investments "liquid" for the individual, but keep them "fixed" for the community, as the major source of instability in the economy. Short-term prices and returns in financial markets end up influencing what for the community are long-term decisions on where and how much to invest and innovate.

Keynes observed that in the short run asset prices on financial markets bear little connection to the long-term views of investors:

> As a result of the gradual increase in the proportion of the equity in the community's aggregate capital investment which is owned by persons who do not manage and have no special knowledge of the circumstances, either actual or prospective, of the business in question, the element of real knowledge in the valuation of investments by those who own them or contemplate purchasing them has seriously declined. (1936, p. 153)

Surely this observation is even more relevant today, when many more people buy and sell stock, bonds, foreign exchange, and many other financial assets and derivatives. Also, the use of preprogrammed computerized trading, the high-speed trading that now accounts for at least half of all stock market trades, raises further concerns about the separation of short-term trading from long-term views. In Keynes's famous words:

> When the capital development of a country becomes a by-product of the activities of a casino, the job is likely to be ill-done. (1936, p. 159)

Keynes thus argued that financial markets would function better if financial transactions were heavily taxed, so that short-term transactions to exploit short-run fluctuations in prices would not so easily interfere with long-run purchases and sales of assets.

In sum, Keynes provided ample explanations as to why a modern capitalist economy with a sophisticated financial system can fall into recession and depression. The next section presents Hyman P. Minsky's financial instability hypothesis, which is derived from a model that both strengthens Keynes's arguments and extends them to show that financial crashes are not only likely, they are inevitable and predictable.

Three Categories of Finance

The stability of the financial system depends on the characteristics of the debt that the financial sector issues. Every intertemporal transaction that involves some payment today in exchange for a future payment or set of payments is financed. The finance may be implicit, as when a person or firm uses its own funds to make an up-front payment for some asset or project in the hope of receiving future income. When the financial sector gets involved, such as when a bank provides a loan to an individual entrepreneur or a government agency sells a bond to raise money for building a railroad, the finance is explicit.

Minsky (1982) identified three broad categories of financial arrangements: **hedge finance**, **speculative finance**, and **Ponzi finance**. A project's financing is characterized as hedge if its cash flow is sufficient to meet all debt payment obligations. That is, the cash flow from the project not only covers all the required interest or dividend payments, but also suffices to pay off the debt by the scheduled due dates.

Speculative finance characterizes investment projects whose cash flow covers all of the interest and dividend payments and some, but not all, of the scheduled principal repayments. Speculative projects are financially sound in the sense that they meet their interest, dividend, or expected profit payments, but the financing arrangement will have to be "rolled over" or renewed, at least partially, when the final settlement comes due. Many new projects, newly formed businesses, and innovative activities are speculative in nature, and while such projects individually are not a concern for the health of the financial system, if a large proportion of an economy's investment projects are financed this way, credit could suddenly become less plentiful or financial markets could freeze up, making the financial system unstable. Such a change in circumstances occurred after the real estate bubble burst in 2007, for example.

Projects whose cash flows from operations are not sufficient to meet even the contractual interest or expected dividend payments, much less cut into the outstanding debt, were termed by Minsky to be Ponzi ventures because, in the tradition of *Ponzi schemes*, to stay alive they must borrow just to meet day-to-day payments.

According to Minsky, the precise mix of hedge, speculative, and Ponzi financing determines whether an economy has a stable or unstable financial system. If most financing arrangements in the economy are hedge financing, and there are few cases of Ponzi financing, then the financial system will be relatively stable and unlikely to generate panics and widespread economic distress. It takes a very substantial shift in economic circumstances to convert hedge financing into Ponzi financing. On the other hand, if speculative and Ponzi financing are prominent throughout the economy, then even a modest change in actual or perceived economic conditions can trigger a sudden rise in defaults that the financial industry cannot cover from its reserves and accumulated capital. In the latter case, the financial sector will become defensive and stop lending, in which case investment and consumption of durables will fall sharply, and the economy will fall into recession.

In sum, Minsky provides a thorough justification for Keynes's assertion that capitalism's inherent instability is caused by the precarious nature of capitalist finance. Financial decisions must be made in a state of uncertainty. As unpredictable events cause the nature of existing financial arrangements to shift from hedge to speculative and Ponzi, default becomes more frequent, and financial contraction, recession, and unemployment follow.

Minsky's Financial Instability Hypothesis

Minsky took a second step in his reasoning that generated a provocative conclusion: every prolonged period of economic growth, if left to run its course without government policy to change its course, will *always* end with a financial collapse! Good economic times generate the very forces that inevitably cause the good times to come to an end. In Minsky's words: "Stability—or tranquility—in a world with . . . capitalist financial institutions is destabilizing" (1982, p. 101).

Minsky's second theorem comes directly from Keynes's view of investment under uncertainty. Like Keynes, Minsky points out that a capitalist economy requires that real activities such as investment and research remain consistently successful over extended periods of time if aggregate demand is to remain compatible with the growing aggregate supply in the economy. According to Minsky, "if the short run equilibrium implicit in the state of long run expectations is attained and then sustained, a 'stable' or a 'tranquil' behavior of the economy will result" (1982, p. 100). This is exactly what Keynes meant when he wrote that investors, lenders, and borrowers follow the convention that they continue to do what they were doing as long as things work out roughly as expected, and this behavior will be "compatible with a considerable measure of continuity and stability in our affairs, *so long as we can rely on the maintenance of the convention*" (Keynes's italics; 1936, p. 152). Recall that we used Keynes's rationale to explain exchange rate behavior in Chapter 11.

Minsky also draws on Keynes's explanation of why investors and lenders rely on recent experiences rather than long-run trends to predict the future. Keynes wrote: "It is reasonable . . . to be guided to a considerable degree by the facts about which we feel somewhat confident, even though they may be less decisively relevant to the issue than other facts about which our knowledge is vague and scanty" (1936, p. 148). Keynes has been fully validated by recent psychological research that finds that people discount the past as well as the future relative to today. Such shortsighted backward vision was actually institutionalized by many financial firms recently; they used only a few years of historical data to estimate the parameters of the financial models they were using to project the future.

Minsky then uses Keynes's points that we use past experience to set our expectations and that our expectations are more influenced by recent experience than distant experience, to "prove" his second theorem:

> Such a stable or tranquil state of the economy, if sustained for a while, will feed back and affect long term expectations about the performance of the economy. This will affect views of the uncertainties involved which, in turn, will affect asset values and permissible liability structures. (1982, p. 100)

Thus, an acceleration in economic growth is initially seen as a pleasant surprise, and investors react cautiously by not increasing investment immediately. But the longer growth is sustained, the more investors and lenders begin to view the growth as normal. Soon they forget the recessions in the more distant past, or they convince themselves that the world is now in some way different, and they ratchet up their expectations. Investment then increases, which increases aggregate demand and economic growth and effectively makes the higher expectations self-fulfilling. This process of rising expectations may continue for some time, but as expectations rise, the likelihood of not meeting those expectations also rises.

Keynes and Minsky effectively explain why the world was surprised by the 2008 financial crisis and the depth of the Great Recession. Since we are all influenced most by recent experiences, the relatively tranquil years of the Great Moderation (1982–2007) were more than enough to establish a pattern or model in the minds of investors, bankers, and economists.[12] Gradually, over the twenty-five-year period, economics textbook dropped what had become a rather distorted Keynesian model for rational expectations, the Coase theorem, the efficient markets hypothesis, and, in international finance, the interest parity condition. Economists trained in leading U.S. graduate schools in the 1970s learned about rational expectations before they entered the world that would, superficially at least, seem to validate laissez-faire economics. Never mind the repeated developing-country financial crises, the growing income inequality, the stagnant wages, and the growing international imbalances fueled by grossly inaccurate exchange rates. When the 2008 financial crisis needed an explanation, the work of Keynes and Minsky was revisited by the mainstream. However, once there were slight signs of economic recovery in 2010, mainstream economists began warning against excessive re-regulation of finance.

The 2008 Financial Collapse Again

One of the more common features of the many subprime mortgages issued in the United States during the early 2000s was that many low-income home buyers were lured into signing mortgage agreements that offered special, low interest rates for the first two or three years of the mortgage, after which rates would rise to much higher levels normally associated with relatively risky mortgages. Therefore, holders of such mortgages often found they were automatically switched from hedge financing to speculative financing, or worse, from speculative financing to Ponzi financing, when the higher interest rates kicked in. In 2007, when the market for securitized mortgage debt and other collateralized debt obligations (CDOs) dried up because of the rising default rates, the housing bubble burst and housing prices began to decline steeply. Suddenly, borrowers with "liar loans" that were in the state of speculative financing or Ponzi financing saw no reason to continue to service even part of their debt because the housing price declines ruled out any possible long-term gain from reselling their house in the future. Then, when the recession hit and unemployment rose sharply to 10 percent in the United States, the default rate rose further. As already explained, the CDOs into which the mortgages had been bundled were downgraded, and the world ended up with a financial crisis and a deep recession.

Looking back now, it should have been obvious that in the early 2000s U.S. housing prices were rising to well above sustainable levels in a bubble sustained, no doubt, by the same (limited) persistence of unsustainable trends that Keynes discussed, and housing prices were likely to fall eventually. It should have been clear that the programmed rises in mortgage interest rates would trigger defaults if housing prices declined. And it should have been anticipated that the CDOs built on subprime mortgages would not accurately price in these eventualities. Clearly, Muth (1961) and Lucas (1972), who argued that people use all available knowledge and information to, on average, accurately anticipate future events, could not explain the housing bubble, the CDOs, the CDSs, and the silence by economists. The rational prediction would have been that the housing bubble would pop, and rational bank managers would have refrained from making subprime loans, home seekers would not have taken on loans they could not pay back, financial groups would not have bought the derivative securities based in these loans, and construction firms would have refrained from building the houses that would not be paid for. The financial crisis clearly validates Keynes's suggestion that the recent past disproportionately determines our expectations. In fact, many of the risk models used in the financial industry, such as those that led Joseph Cassano of AIG's London Financial Products Division to claim that he did not "see a scenario within any kind of realm of reason that would see us losing one dollar," were estimated using data going back only five years. The financial models would have predicted more accurately if their parameters had been estimated taking into consideration the Great Depression from seventy years prior. But that is not how people, even those really smart people who were paid very high salaries, actually set their expectations of an unknown future or, apparently, how they estimated their sophisticated financial models.

Note that the rational expectations hypothesis gives the bankers, home buyers, inattentive government regulators, and neoclassical economists cover for their poor predictions. Had heterodox economics been more often invited into economic discussions, it would now be much easier to prove fraud against the bank employees who issued the "liar loans" and the bank CEOs who took bonuses paid out of what should have been reserves set aside for very predictable defaults. Neoclassical economics failed, and as long as it continues to be used to explain the financial collapse of 2008, it will continue to fail. Since neoclassical macroeconomics cannot explain the collapse, it continues to give the impression that what happened was beyond the ability of anyone to anticipate or understand. It thus is of no help in dealing with those who are responsible for the fraud and carelessness that caused the recent recession, nor can it be of much help in shaping new policies to prevent the next capitalist boom-and-bust cycle.

CONCLUSIONS

Clearly, the financial sectors of the world's economies have not performed their task of efficiently channeling savings to society's most profitable and welfare-enhancing investments. The international financial system permitted financial failures in one major economy to disrupt the entire world economy to such an extent that in 2009 per capita real GDP declined from the previous year's level for the first time since the end of World War II. Since the financial sector in each country operates within the rules and norms of the international financial order, many political leaders and the economists who advise them have called for reform of the international financial system. Of course, it was the irresponsible deregulation and lax oversight of the banking sector in the United States that triggered the economic downturn, but even countries that had sound banking systems with active regulatory structures felt the effects of the U.S. financial failure. Many national leaders have made specific proposals for new markets and exchanges where financial assets can be traded openly according to basic standards and rules. And there have been proposals for reform of the international financial and monetary rules.

Internationally, financial crises have occurred with some regularity over the past thirty years. But because they did most of their damage in developing economies, most people living in the world's high-income countries did not pay much attention or notice any spillover effects. The next chapter discusses some of these breakdowns in the international financial and monetary system. It also provides yet more evidence that the 2008 financial crisis should have been foreseen; financial instability is nothing new, and even a short memory should have alerted us to the very real possibility of financial collapse, if only policy makers and economists in wealthy countries had paid more attention to what was going on overseas in developing economies.

CHAPTER SUMMARY

1. The international investment position of a country measures how many foreign assets are owned by private citizens, firms, and government agencies of a country versus how many of its private and public assets are owned by foreign citizens, foreign firms, and foreign governments.

2. The total accumulated assets in the net international investment position reflect past activity on the financial account of the balance of payments, adjusted for depreciation, asset price changes, and ownership transfers.

3. Despite the large and growing deficit in the United States's net international investment position, it continues to record positive net asset returns.

4. As in the case of the U.S. current account deficits, it is difficult to predict when unsustainable trends will undergo their inevitable adjustment, but experience suggests the adjustments could come very suddenly and unexpectedly.

5. The international financial system has changed with the opening and expansion of stock markets, bond markets, overnight money markets, and over-the-counter markets for derivatives such as collateralized debt obligations (CDOs) and credit default swaps (CDSs).

6. Traditional banks have responded by consolidating

and expanding into investment banking, brokerage, and other financial services.

7. The growth of international banking has included the growth of Eurocurrency markets, which consist of a growing network of transnational banking firms that accept deposits of many currencies in banks they operate in countries other than those where each currency was issued.

8. The term *financial innovation* generally refers to new financial institutions and instruments, but the consolidation of financial services into ever-larger conglomerates and the spread of these transnational banking and financial firms across borders also constitute a form of financial innovation, one that may be more significant than any other recent innovation.

9. It is still an open question whether financial innovation has improved the performance of the world's economies; there is no convincing evidence that banks have in recent years improved their service to humanity, especially since the innovation of securitization destabilized the global financial system and in 2009 caused world economic output to fall for the first time since World War II.

10. The 2008 financial crisis that originated in the United States is blamed on the dismantling of

U.S. banking and financial regulations, such as the reversal of the Glass-Steagall Act in 1999.

11. The 2008 financial crisis shows how the failure of a financial market caused most other financial intermediation to cease, which, in turn, caused real economic activity and employment to fall. This is not the first time such a sequence of events has occurred.

12. The reason so few economists predicted the 2007–2008 recession is that they relied on their neoclassical economic models, which were based on assumptions that effectively ruled out financial market failures and biased asset prices.

13. As Keynes argued seventy-five years ago, finance operates under uncertainty, not predictable risk. Keynes further argued that under uncertainty people base their expectations on conventions built up during recent experience, not long-run historical evidence.

14. Like exchange rates, all asset prices are subject to sudden, sharp changes as new information comes to light.

15. Keynes also showed that during recessionary times, monetary policy has little effect on macroeconomic outcomes, either as a stabilizing force or a corrective measure, because the lowering of interest rates has little impact when bankers do not

want to lend and potential borrowers do not want to invest, innovate, or buy.

16. When the economy is caught in such a liquidity trap, only fiscal policy will change aggregate demand.

17. Hyman Minsky built on Keynes's thinking to develop his financial instability hypothesis, which says that in the absence of strong regulation to keep expectations based on short-term experience from pushing asset prices away from their long-term trends, every extended period of exceptional growth will ultimately cause a financial collapse and a long economic recession.

18. Minsky argued that when unpredictable events differ from conventions developed during tranquil times or an above-average growth period, as they eventually do, finance shifts from hedge finance to speculative and Ponzi finance, and defaults and failures drive the economy into financial instability.

19. Had economists not been influenced by neoclassical models that fit recent stable economic times, they would have seen that in the early 2000s U.S. housing prices were rising to well above sustainable levels in a bubble sustained by upwardly revised expectations and were likely to fall eventually.

KEY TERMS AND CONCEPTS

American Depository Receipt (ADR)
balance of payments (BoP)
bank secrecy law
Coase theorem
collateralized debt obligation (CDO)
conduit
contingent commodities
credit default swap (CDS)
Eurocurrency
Eurocurrency market
Eurodollar
externalities
financial industry
financial innovation
financial intermediary
financial market
firewall

Glass-Steagall Act
hedge financing
liquidity trap
microfoundations
money laundering
naked CDSs
net international investment position
offshore banking
Ponzi finance
portfolio investment
rational expectations
securitization
speculative finance
structured financial product
subprime mortgage
tranche (of a CDO)

PROBLEMS AND QUESTIONS

1. This chapter pointed out that the very negative net investment position of the United States points to net payments overseas of returns on assets. But, the balance of payments in Table 11.1 shows receipt of asset returns by Americans exceeds such payments to foreigners. Does this make sense? Explain. (Hint: The U.S. balance of payments in Table 11.1 reveals that, compared to U.S. holdings of foreign assets, the total holdings of foreign-owned assets in the United States are divided very differently among official assets, stocks and bonds, government bonds, foreign direct investment, and bank loans.)

2. Describe how a country's international investment position is related to its balance of payments over time. Make use of the information on the U.S. balance of payments and the U.S. net investment position to support your verbal description. Why is there not a perfect relationship between the flows in the balance of payments and the subsequent changes in the net investment position?

3. Describe American Depository Receipts (ADRs). What advantages do they hold over the direct purchase of foreign stocks?

4. Over the past decade, securitization has exceeded traditional banking as the source of financing in many developed economies. How does securitization differ from traditional bank finance? Is securitization more stable than traditional bank lending? Explain.

5. Are the U.S. trade deficits, and accumulation of foreign debt, sustainable? When will the U.S. economy have to undergo a fundamental shift toward trade surpluses?

6. Carefully trace the reasoning of Hyman Minsky, which leads him to conclude that not only is the financial sector of a modern capitalist economy the main source of instability, but that instability is inevitable and predictable.

7. The assumptions behind the neoclassical macroeconomic model, discussed above in the section titled "Neoclassical Analysis Cannot Explain Crises," have been accepted as a reasonable approach to modeling macroeconomies. Why do you think these assumptions have been so rarely questioned by mainstream economists?

8. Explain the difference between risk and uncertainty. Provide some examples of risk. Then provide some examples of uncertainty. How do these examples illustrate your explanation of risk and uncertainty?

9. Trace the development of the subprime loan bubble and the subsequent financial collapse. How well were these events explained by the Keynes/Minsky model of financial instability? Provide exact details of where the facts fit the model and where they do not.

10. Do you agree with former Federal Reserve Bank Chair Paul Volcker that, other than the ATM, there have been no useful innovations in the financial industry? Discuss.

11. Is there any validity to Hausman and Sturzenegger's concept of "dark matter"? Is dark matter really mitigating the reported U.S. current account deficit? Discuss.

12. Kenneth Arrow and Gerard Debreu (1954) and Debreu (1959) constructed elaborate general equilibrium models that introduced a technical gimmick that seemed to eliminate risk: they assumed competitive markets in contingent commodities. Has financial innovation been able to create such contingent commodities? Explain why or why not.

13. Recount the history of the Eurocurrency markets. How has their development changed national banking sectors?

14. Investigate the Glass-Steagall Act. Explain its importance. Why do some economists argue that the elimination of the Glass-Steagall rules in 1999 caused the Great Recession of 2007–2008?

15. What is the relationship between Joseph Casano's suggestion that there was no chance that the

securitized assets his company (AIG) insured would ever fail and Keynes's suggestion that human memory focuses on the recent past? Discuss. How might humans be prodded into taking more distant human history into consideration?

NOTES

1. Joseph Stiglitz quoted in Louis Uchitelle (2009), "Volcker Fails to Sell a Bank Strategy," *New York Times,* October 21; Paul Volcker quoted in *The Week,* 10, no. 449, February 5, 2010.

2. Quoted in Kate Burgess (2004), "Acquisitions in US 'Disastrous' for British Companies," *Financial Times,* October 11.

3. Wolfgang Münchau (2010), "Time to Outlaw Naked Credit Default Swaps," *Financial Times,* March 1.

4. *The Guardian* (2009), "Twenty-Five People at the Heart of the Meltdown," January 26.

5. Quoted in Stephen Labaton (1999), "Congress Passes Wide-Ranging Bill Easing Bank Laws," *New York Times,* November 5.

6. Ibid.

7. Ibid.

8. This information on AIG is from Gretchen Morgenson (2008); Bloomberg News (2009), "Britain Investigates AIG Unit in London," reported in the *New York Times,* February 13; and Cyrus Sanati (2009).

9. Quoted in Morgenson (2008).

10. Mary Kane (2008).

11. Ibid.

12. The Great Moderation was not as much of a moderation as often suggested because the period included the build-up of many unsustainable trends, including stock market and real estate bubbles, growing balance of payments imbalances, growing government budget deficits, and falling savings rates. But yes, economic growth and unemployment were fairly stable by historical standards, at least in the United States.

CHAPTER 14

Exchange Rate Crises

Each time a crisis related to capital inflows hits a country, it typically goes through the wringer.

—Jagdish Bhagwati (1998)

In 1982, the world economy was rocked by financial crises in most developing countries. Capital flows from private banks to developing countries ended suddenly, causing exchange rates to collapse and economies to fall into deep recession throughout Africa, Asia, and Latin America. Chile's per capita gross domestic product (GDP) fell by 18 percent after the Chilean peso lost about half its value and many heavily indebted domestic firms and banks went bankrupt. Ironically, Chile had recently been praised for its government's budget surplus. But the collapsing exchange rate's effect on Chile's private foreign debt proved to be as devastating as similar currency collapses were on foreign government debt elsewhere in Latin America. The cause of each of these economic crises was a large change in exchange rates caused by sudden shifts in international financial flows. These shifts were the result of monetary policy decisions in the United States, the United Kingdom, and elsewhere, but the losses in income and employment were felt in the world's developing economies.

Since 1982, there have been many similar exchange rate crises followed by financial crises and deep economic recessions in other developing countries. These crises have not only diminished policy makers' enthusiasm for further opening their countries' borders to international financial flows, but caused even the most ardent supporters of free trade, such as economist Jagdish Bhagwati, to conclude, as he put it, that the "the claims of enormous benefits from free capital mobility are not persuasive" (Bhagwati 1998).

International financial flows are subject to sudden reversals, as discussed in the previous chapter. When they change direction, the supply and demand curves for currencies shift sharply, causing sharp changes in exchange rates. In developing economies with large amounts of foreign debt, either private or public, exchange rate depreciations proportionately increase the burden of such debt because it is almost always denominated in foreign currencies like the dollar or euro. Therefore, exchange rate changes can trigger a financial crisis, which, as discussed in the previous chapter, can drive an economy into a deep and lengthy recession.

Each economic crisis triggered by a shift in international financial flows inevitably leads to the question of whether the countries involved would have been better off if their citizens, firms, banks, and governments had not borrowed as much from overseas banks, sold as much equity to foreigners, or floated as many bonds in foreign financial markets. Are the gains from international investment described in Chapter 11 really worth the risk of an exchange rate collapse followed by economic recession, unemployment, and widespread bankruptcies?

This chapter complements the previous chapter's discussion of financial crises by detailing the mechanism, namely **reversals of international financial flows**, by which foreign economic events and policy shifts are transformed into economic crises in indebted countries through the foreign exchange market. This chapter also clarifies the **trilemma** faced by governments that have opted to participate in the global economy by opening their economies to international trade and investment.

THE ECONOMICS OF EXCHANGE RATE CRISES

Chapter 12 showed that, in the case of unrestricted international investment, it is very difficult to keep exchange rates from changing when new information continually causes people to adjust their expectations. This represents a problem for policy makers, because there are some advantages to keeping exchange rates *fixed.* For one thing, the volatility and uncertainty of *floating* exchange rates makes international trade and investment more risky and, therefore, less attractive. Also, changing exchange rates can have very large wealth effects when people own assets or owe debt denominated on currencies other than their own, and these wealth effects can have recessionary or inflationary macroeconomic effects.

Fixing the Exchange Rate under Rational Expectations

The general interest parity condition from Chapter 12 provides some insight into *why* it is difficult to keep exchange rates fixed in an open economy with free international trade and investment. The equation for the interest parity condition is repeated here as

$$(14.1) \qquad e_s = E_t e_{t+n} [(1 + r^*)/(1 + r)]^n,$$

in which r and r^* are the domestic and foreign rates of return on assets, respectively, e_s is the spot exchange rate, and $E_t e_{t+n}$ is the expected exchange rate n periods into the future. That is, the spot exchange rate depends on the future spot rates and the relative rates of returns of foreign and domestic assets. According to equation (14.1), the spot exchange rate remains unchanged if all variables on the right-hand side of the equation remain the same; that is, if:

1. Expectations about future exchange rates, $E_t e_{t+n}$, do not change.
2. Rates of return on assets are the same at home and abroad, that is, $r = r^*$, so that $[(1 + r^*)/(1 + r)]^n = [(1 + r^*)/(1 + r)]^{n-1} = [(1 + r^*)/(1 + r)]^{n-2} = \ldots = [(1 + r^*)/(1 + r)]$.

Technically, equation (14.1) suggests that the spot exchange rate can also remain unchanged even when one of the right-hand variables changes, provided that:

3. Policy makers immediately adjust domestic policies when expectations change or interest rates change in order to shift exchange rate expectations back to where they were, to change domestic returns so that they again are equal to foreign returns, or to change some variables to offset changes in others.

This latter condition requires a country's policy makers to stay attuned to exchange rates and adjust their economic policies to satisfy the interest parity condition, regardless of any other policy objectives they might have. These conditions are very difficult to satisfy. Of course, if expectations are not rational as equation 14.1 assumes, it becomes even more difficult to fix exchange rates.

Using Intervention to Stabilize the Exchange Rate

Despite the difficulties, governments nevertheless have frequently tried to fix exchange rates. Several exchange rate arrangements after World War II sought to maintain fixed exchange rates by means of central bank intervention in the foreign exchange markets. The Bretton Woods exchange rate system kept exchange rates constant among all major world currencies for twenty-five years between 1946 and 1971, and the European Monetary System attempted to fix exchange rates among a group of European economies during the period 1979–1993. Both systems required the central banks of the participating nations to buy and sell foreign exchange in the foreign exchange markets to keep supply and demand for their currencies intersecting at previously agreed-to target exchange rates.

Foreign exchange market intervention is easy to understand. Figure 14.1 illustrates the foreign exchange market for Chilean pesos as seen from the U.S. perspective, with the supply and demand curves for pesos intersecting at $.10. Suppose that instead of the equilibrium exchange rate of $.10 shown as the intersection of the supply and demand curves for pesos in Figure 14.1, policy makers in the United States or Chile wanted to keep the exchange rate fixed at $.08 per peso. This can be accomplished by, for example, having Chile's central bank create pesos and sell them on the foreign exchange markets. Alternatively, the central bank of the United States, the Federal Reserve Bank, could use reserves of pesos and sell them on the foreign exchange market. In either case, the supply of pesos would increase and the exchange rate would fall to $.08.

From the Chilean perspective, the equilibrium exchange rate prior to intervention would have been 10 pesos per dollar in the market for dollars. The sale of pesos by the Chilean or U.S. central banks appears as an increase in demand for dollars in Figure 14.2. The central bank intervention thus shifts the demand curve just enough to raise the peso price of dollars to 12.50 pesos, which of course is simply the flip side of the dollar rate of $.08 per peso.

Intervention Is Not a Long-Run Tool

Despite its apparent simplicity, intervention is not always an effective tool for preventing long-run movements in exchange rates. One weakness of intervention is that, in the case of a fundamental disequilibrium in the foreign exchange market, central banks have to supply the necessary amounts of foreign exchange for long periods of time. In the example of the dollar-peso market above, the Federal Reserve Bank of the United States will eventually run out of pesos from its reserves of foreign currencies. Only the Chilean central bank can print pesos, and if it is not willing to intervene itself or to lend pesos to the U.S. Federal Reserve, eventually the Federal Reserve will have to stop intervening and let the exchange rate float.

The Federal Reserve does have another option for keeping the exchange rate from changing: it can tighten its monetary policy. A tighter monetary policy raises U.S. interest rates and lowers the rate of U.S. inflation, which then, according to equation (14.1), appreciates the spot exchange rate. For example, a higher domestic interest rate means that the ratio $[(1 + r^*)/(1 + r)]$ in equation (14.1) becomes smaller, and thus, all other things equal, $E_t e_{t+n}$ translates into a lower spot rate e. Furthermore, the Federal Reserve's tighter monetary policy may convince people that there will be less inflation, relative to Chile, in the United States in the future, which could change expectations about the future competitiveness of U.S. producers in the world market and, hence, lower $E_t e_{t+n}$. In either case, a shift to tighter monetary policy can offset people's increased supply of dollars and demand for pesos and keep the exchange rate at $.08.

It may have occurred to you that the monetary policy and foreign exchange market intervention described above are essentially the same thing. Recall from your principles of economics course that a central bank like the Federal Reserve in the United States usually manages the money supply by carrying out **open market operations** in which it buys or sells government

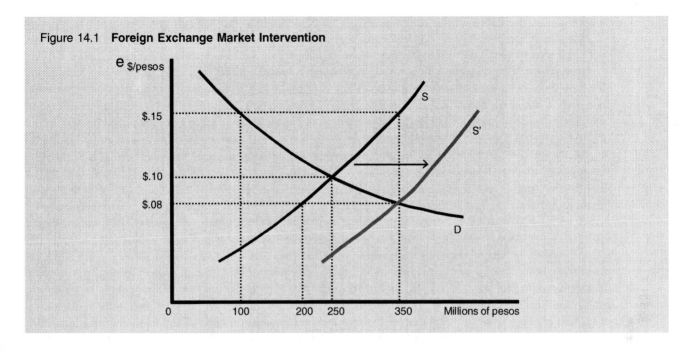

Figure 14.1 Foreign Exchange Market Intervention

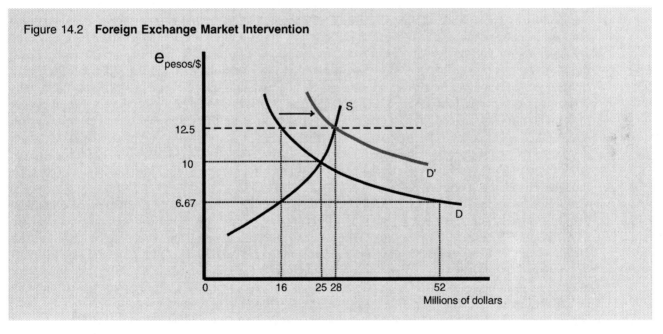

Figure 14.2 Foreign Exchange Market Intervention

bonds. In the example above, the Federal Reserve can tighten the money supply by selling bonds to the public, which reduces the sellers' balances in their checking accounts and thus reduces the money supply. But there is nothing unique about government bonds when it comes to changing the amount of money in circulation. Government bonds are convenient because the bond market is so large (liquid), which lets the central bank make purchases and sales quickly. The Federal Reserve Bank could just as well decrease the amount of money in circulation by selling its office building in Washington, DC; the buyer would write a check on his or her account just as would the buyers of bonds. Or, the central bank could sell foreign exchange. Foreign exchange market intervention, therefore, *is* monetary policy. The Federal Reserve's buying of dollars using pesos also tends to cause the U.S. interest rate to rise and expected inflation to fall, therefore causing the spot rate to decline from $.10 to $.08.

Conventional monetary policy might seem like a more viable long-run policy than using the limited peso reserves to purchase dollars. However, monetary policy is not an unlimited tool either because it has effects on the economy that can be very costly. Tight monetary policy and higher interest rates slow economic activity, reduce tax revenues, and increase the costs of servicing debt. For example, Brazil in 1998 and Turkey in 2001 had high levels of government debt that were suddenly judged to be likely to force governments to default on their loans in the near future. In each case, an increase in interest rates to "defend the currency" caused the currencies' values to fall further, rather than to rise as hoped. Government budgets were pushed further into deficit as governments had to borrow to pay interest payments on their large debts, which caused potential lenders to expect an even smaller likelihood that foreign debt would be serviced on schedule. A tight monetary policy and high interest rates also tend to reduce investment and economic growth, which was expected to reduce the future competitiveness of the economy. Thus, even as a rise in domestic interest rates increases the ratio $(1 + r^*)/(1 + r)$, which would, all other things equal, lower the spot exchange rate, the expected future exchange rate $E_t e_{t+n}$ could rise, leaving the net effect on the spot rate ambiguous. In sum, there may be a conflict between short-run measures to influence the exchange rate and the expectations of the long-run consequences of those short-run measures. Expectations translate future economic events into present economic effects, thus making it harder for policy makers to use short-run intervention to influence the exchange rate.

A study from the Federal Reserve Bank of Cleveland concluded that "most economists now regard foreign-exchange-market intervention as generally ineffectual."[1] On the other hand, Kathryn Dominguez and Jeffrey Frankel (1993) examined a very large set of episodes of central bank intervention through 1990, and they concluded that intervention *can* have an effect on exchange rates provided it is interpreted as a credible signal of a true underlying policy shift by policy makers. Lucio Sarno and Mark Taylor (2001) reexamine the cases surveyed by Dominguez and Frankel plus many more studies of exchange rate intervention through the end of the twentieth century and state that "the evidence . . . seems to us to be sufficiently strong and econometrically sound to allow us to conclude cautiously that official intervention can be effective, especially if the intervention is publicly announced and concerted and provided that it is consistent with the underlying stance in monetary and fiscal policy."

It could be argued that Sarno and Taylor's work actually shows that it is fundamental economic policies that determine exchange rates, not intervention per se. Intervention can serve as a *signal* of government policy in a foreign exchange market where information about the future is seldom clear, and when the intervention is *concerted,* meaning it is carried out simultaneously by the central banks of several countries, the signal is even clearer. But to be successful in the long run, there have to be accompanying shifts in policies, such as monetary policies, trade policies, and policies on government expenditures and taxes, to validate the change in expectations.

FIXED EXCHANGE RATES AND ECONOMIC CRISES

There is evidence that exchange rate volatility discourages international trade and international investment. As has been shown earlier in this textbook, exchange rate changes alter competitive advantage and thus disrupt trade flows. Also, exchange rate uncertainty increases the risk of foreign finance and investment. This suggests that fixed exchange rates are indeed a worthy goal. The problem is that, in order to keep exchange rates constant, policy makers may have to give up other policy goals because those are incompatible with the monetary and fiscal policies needed to maintain interest rates and expectations of long-run price levels that satisfy the interest parity condition. In the language of international finance, policy makers may lose "policy independence" in a financially integrated international economy if they insist on keeping exchange rates stable around some target rate.

Policy Choices

One obvious way that a country can set its monetary and fiscal policies independently of what the interest parity condition mandates *and* keep the exchange rate fixed is to stop people from moving their wealth between assets denominated in different currencies. If individuals, firms, pension funds, and other financial intermediaries cannot buy or sell assets across the border, then central bank intervention in the foreign exchange markets only has to deal with trade imbalances.

Prohibiting asset exchanges has an opportunity cost, however. This cost is equal to the lost welfare gains that would have come from allocating savings to the most productive investments, smoothing consumption, reducing risk, and expanding technology transfers for economic growth. Also, by effectively preventing exporters from giving foreign customers credit and prohibiting importers from borrowing overseas in order to finance their foreign purchases, international trade will be reduced. Hence, placing barriers on international borrowing and lending in essence places barriers on many other forms of international economic integration. Policy makers concerned about exchange rate volatility therefore face a dilemma: Should they restrict financial account transactions and, possibly, international trade that depends on **trade credits** and foreign direct investments in overseas plants and distribution networks? Or, should they keep the economy open and conduct their domestic monetary and fiscal policies with an eye on exchange rates rather than domestic policy objectives?

The Options When Policy Independence Is the Priority

The dilemma described above makes it seem as though the choice for policy makers is between policy independence and international economic integration. That is technically correct only if a fixed exchange rate is the supreme objective. If, on the other hand, it is policy independence that really matters, then foreign finance and trade can still be pursued, provided policy makers are willing to give up their quest for a fixed exchange rate. They could just let the exchange rate float. Floating exchange rates have their own costs, however.

Floating exchange rates add to the uncertainty that traders and investors must factor in to their decisions to engage in transactions with foreigners. The uncertainty of exchange rates may "divert" exchanges of products and assets to the domestic market and reduce the overall welfare gains from international trade and investment. The welfare losses from reduced trade and investment could be large, especially if the long-run growth effects of international trade and investment are taken into consideration. Policy makers seeking the freedom to pursue a variety of policy objectives unrelated to the exchange rate therefore face another dilemma: Should they fix exchange rates and limit their economy's contacts with the rest of the world? Or, should they let the exchange rate float so that they do not have to restrict financial account transactions?

Two Dilemmas Equal One Trilemma

The two dilemmas discussed above imply that policy makers face a *trilemma*.[2] In the words of international economist Maurice Obstfeld:

> A country cannot simultaneously maintain fixed exchange rates and an open capital market while pursuing a monetary policy oriented toward domestic goals. Governments may choose only two of the above. If monetary policy is geared toward domestic considerations, either capital mobility or the exchange rate target must go. If fixed exchange rates and integration into the global capital market are the primary considerata, monetary policy must be subjugated to those ends. (1998, pp. 14–15)

The global economy forces a nation's policy makers to make choices. No country can simultaneously fix its exchange rate, set economic policies with only domestic goals in mind, and permit the free flow of goods and assets across national borders. For example, if policy makers opt for unrestricted investment flows between countries and a fixed exchange rate, then they must align their economic policies with the rest of the world. On the other hand, if policy makers opt for fixed exchange rates and economic policies focused on domestic objectives, such as low inflation, high productivity growth, or increased government spending, regardless of the effects on asset returns or long-run expectations, then they cannot let people freely move their wealth across the border. In effect, the trilemma implies that policy makers must select one of the three sides of the triangle in Figure 14.3, which means they can reach only two of the three corners.

The trilemma makes clear how difficult it is to keep exchange rates fixed when policy makers are faced with domestic political pressures to deal with a variety of macroeconomic issues as well as pressure from business to keep the border open to international trade, investment, and financial flows. Jay C. Shambaugh (2004) used time-series analysis to examine whether, during the period 1973–2000, countries that pegged exchange rates had less policy independence than countries that let their exchange rates float. He confirms that indeed pegged exchange rates give countries less policy leeway, and concludes that "the open-economy trilemma is alive and well." Maurice Obstfeld, Jay C. Shambaugh, and Alan M. Taylor (2004) examined numerous historical episodes starting with the use of the gold standard in the nineteenth century. They conclude that economic policy has effectively been constrained by the trilemma in every period.

THE 1982 DEBT CRISIS

The international monetary system suffered a huge shock in 1982, when some forty developing economies were forced to rescheduled debt payments, renegotiate terms, or simply default on their foreign debt. This debt crisis followed a period of increasing international financial flows that seemed to have successfully offset the growing trade imbalances after the oil price hikes during the 1970s. But something changed in 1982, and the sudden shift in international financial flows triggered crises that effectively marked the end of an unprecedented period of economic growth in most developing countries in Africa, Asia, and Latin America that stretched over the 1950s, 1960s, and 1970s. Nearly all of the debtor countries who ran into trouble meeting their debt obligations stopped growing in the 1980s.

Thirty years later, most of the countries still have not returned to the economic growth rates they achieved before the **1982 debt crisis**. This section details the events leading up to and following the 1982 debt crisis.

Recycling Petrodollars

When the Organization of Petroleum Exporting Countries (OPEC) cartel sharply raised the price of oil in 1973, the trade balances of many countries were upset. The rise from US$4.00 per barrel to $10.00 per barrel suddenly left oil-producing countries with large current account in surpluses. The oil-importing countries, of course, suddenly saw their trade balances turn sharply negative, and their real incomes also fell with the adverse shift in the terms of trade.

Specifically, the OPEC countries' aggregate trade surplus rose from zero in 1972, the year before the price hikes, to a positive $60 billion in 1974, the year after the price of oil was raised. The sharp changes in current accounts caused great concern. Would oil-importing countries have to limit imports, or would they have to slow down their pace of economic growth in order to reduce or even reverse the growth of oil consumption? Somewhat surprisingly given the alarmist warnings in 1973, most oil-importing countries were able to continue growing because they were able to borrow enough in the world capital markets to offset the deteriorating current accounts. The

Figure 14.3   The Trilemma: Select Any Two of Three

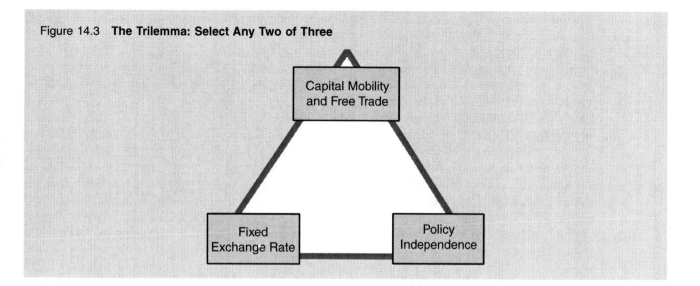

international financial system proved able to **recycle petrodollars**. Most oil-exporting countries deposited the petrodollars in the **Eurocurrency** market, that is, in dollar accounts in the branches of the world's large commercial banks in London and other major banking centers. This money was, in turn, lent to oil-importing countries, who thus gained access to the dollars needed to pay for the more expensive oil without reducing economic growth. The International Monetary Fund (IMF) assisted the *recycling* of petrodollars by creating a special financing facility to provide loans for the poorest developing countries. This facility was funded by money lent to the IMF by the principal oil-exporting countries. Overall, there was little immediate pressure for oil-importing countries to adjust their economies for the deteriorated terms of trade. Oil-importing countries began to accumulate debt that had to be serviced, that is, on which interest and principal had to be paid, in dollars.

The OPEC trade surplus began to diminish after 1974 as the OPEC countries gradually increased their imports. In OPEC countries with large populations, such as Iran, Nigeria, and Venezuela, there were many pressures for governments to spend the windfall revenues of their state-owned oil companies. By the late 1970s the OPEC surplus was gone. But again to the surprise of many observers, the international credit markets nevertheless remained flush with money. This time it was the central banks of most developed economies who were expanding money supplies in response to economic recessions triggered by the oil price supply shock.

The expansion of money supplies made many domestic developed-country banks, not just the largest banks with overseas branches in the Eurocurrency centers, eager to lend overseas. Many private bank loans to developing countries were syndicated loan packages in which as many as 100 different banks participated, usually with one of the major international banks serving as the manager. A substantial amount of the expanded money supply thus moved overseas.

A second way in which the monetary expansions in the United States, Japan, and Europe stimulated overseas lending was that they caused inflation to rise domestically and in the international commodity markets. By the late 1970s, the prices for all commodities, not just oil, rose sharply. For example, Brazil saw its oil import bill triple, but its export earnings from coffee, iron ore, sugar, cotton, tobacco, and soybeans rose nearly as much. The oil price hikes, therefore, did not hurt current account balances very much, and lenders concluded that developing-country borrowers would have little trouble servicing their rising debt burdens.

Inflation sometimes exceeded nominal interest rates, which meant *real* interest rates were often negative for borrowers in the late 1970s! Thus, despite the heavy international borrowing, most developing countries found that the ratio of debt service to export earnings was not growing very much, and they were able to continue borrowing to roll over existing loans while adding substantial new loans. Some governments of oil producers, such as Ecuador's, Mexico's, Nigeria's, and Venezuela's, took advantage of the liquid financial markets to contract foreign bank loans in anticipation of future oil revenues. The low real interest rates and expected further rises in commodity prices made foreign borrowing seem prudent.

When OPEC raised oil prices again in 1979, from about US\$12 per barrel to over \$30 per barrel, there was a new need for recycling petrodollars. Initially the price hike was easily maintained, and like the 1973 price increase, it seemed to reflect underlying market conditions. The OPEC countries' aggregate current account surplus rose from the near-zero level it had returned to in 1978 to over \$100 billion in 1980. This surge in deposits in the Eurocurrency banking system again stimulated a massive recycling of petrodollars. Borrowing by developing countries expanded rapidly in 1979. During the period 1979–1981 Brazil added US\$16 billion, Argentina \$11 billion, and Mexico \$21 billion to their foreign debts. Would everything continue as before, with oil importers able to keep growing through borrowing, fed by OPEC's surpluses and developed countries' expansionary, and inflationary, monetary policies?

The Macroeconomics of International Financial Flows

Before we answer the question above, let's digress a moment and examine in more detail what happens when a country borrows overseas. Effectively, when a country's government, citizens, or firms borrow money from foreigners, they acquire purchasing power with which to buy foreign goods and services, and the country is able to consume and invest more than its economy produces in the current period. The term for the sum of domestic expenditures, namely consumption plus investment plus government purchases, used in this context is **absorption**. Thus, all other things equal, foreign borrowing (the sale of assets to foreigners) allows a country to *absorb* more goods and services than its economy produces.

If the citizens, firms, and government of a country sell assets (borrow) abroad equal in value to 2 percent of their national product, they can absorb 102 percent of their national product, a net gain of 2 percent in welfare-enhancing consumption, investment, or both. Such a net gain in current absorption implies, of course, a trade deficit equal to 2 percent of national product. Many developing economies in the 1970s absorbed more than they produced, and funded this by selling assets to foreigners that consisted mostly of loans by foreign private banks to governments, government agencies, and government-owned firms and agencies.

When further foreign borrowing is no longer possible and countries must repay outstanding loans, absorption must fall below national production. For example, if foreign **debt service**, the required payment of interest and principal over and above any new foreign borrowing, is equal to 2 percent of GDP, then in effect 2 percent of national product must be transferred abroad and domestic absorption can then be no more than 98 percent of national production. Thus, if foreign lending is disrupted and a country faces the sudden need to repay more than it borrows, the necessary reduction in absorption will have a substantial welfare effect. Such a sudden decline in domestic consumption is not easily achieved. It can be forced by a drastic reduction in government expenditures, which is effectively a contractionist fiscal policy that can push the economy toward a recession and rising unemployment. Also, the reversal of financial inflows into a net outflow can cause a sharp decline in the exchange rate, which can lead to an **exchange rate crisis**.

What Changed in 1982?

The second oil price rise, in 1979, turned out to be unsustainable. By 1980, some developed-country central banks had already stopped reacting to rising unemployment by increasing money supplies because inflation was exceeding 10 percent per year. The new chairman of the U.S. Federal Reserve Bank began tightening money supplies. By 1980, money supplies were tight throughout the world, and the U.S. economy and others were falling into recession. The international financial markets' main source of new funds was the OPEC surplus, but that source dried up very quickly as the oil price soon fell back under US$20 per barrel after reaching $36 in 1979. Many OPEC countries found themselves in balance of payments difficulties, and the huge OPEC surplus of US$100 billion in 1980 had become a deficit of $10 billion by 1982.

Ironically, in early 1982, it was an oil producer, Mexico, that first defaulted on its loan obligations. Mexico had borrowed heavily for a wide range of government projects in infrastructure, industry, and oil exploration, using its future oil revenues as implicit collateral. Private banks were quite willing to lend as long as money flowed to the Eurocurrency market. But when money tightened and the OPEC surplus disappeared, banks were not able to make as many new loans and interest rates shot up sharply to over 15 percent. Mexico technically defaulted when it was unable to engage in what Hyman Minsky would classify as Ponzi finance by obtaining new loans to pay for its sharply higher interest payments. Soon Brazil, Argentina, and some forty other developing countries in Asia, Africa, and Latin America similarly were seeking Ponzi financing to cover interest and principal payments on what they and their lenders thought were hedge or, at worst, speculative loans. The private banks that operated in the Eurocurrency markets no longer had enough deposits to offer the new financing and **rollovers** of old loans sought by the public and private borrowers in developing countries. In fact, they sought only repayment of old loans.

This constituted a large *reversal* of international financial flows, and the consequences were devastating. The transfer of purchasing power from lenders to borrowers that had taken place throughout the 1970s not only stopped in 1982, but the servicing of the debt suddenly required a reverse transfer of purchasing power from developing countries to developed-country banks. Developing countries suddenly were instructed to export more than they imported in order to pay for the interest flows due on accumulated debt and adjust to a world where little new lending could be expected.

Table 14.1 details the state of indebtedness of less developed countries in 1982. Brazil had the largest foreign debt, followed by Mexico, Argentina, Korea, Venezuela, and Egypt. As a percentage of gross national product (**GNP**), Costa Rica, Côte d'Ivoire, Egypt, the Sudan, Zambia, and Jamaica had the highest **debt burdens**. Another useful indicator of a country's debt burden is annual interest payments as a percentage of GNP. This measure shows that Costa Rican absorption was at most 85.2 percent because Costa Rican debtors had to transfer 14.8 percent of GNP to foreigners for interest payments. Actual debt repayments would lower absorption further.

Table 14.1 also shows foreign debt and interest payments as a percentage of exports. These are frequently used measures that can provide a good indication of a country's ability to sustain the servicing of its foreign debt. Interest payments and eventual repayments of principal require foreign currency that must be earned by exporting goods and services. Foreign debt exceeded 400 percent of 1982 exports in Argentina, Brazil, Egypt, Morocco, and the Sudan. The rising real interest rates in the early 1980s increased interest payments to 47.1 percent of 1982 export earnings in Brazil, 43.5 percent in the Sudan, and 40.5 percent in Chile. It is difficult to see how those countries could have met their debt obligations without further borrowing to cover the high interest payments. How much can a country reduce absorption without causing extreme misery for its citizens? Of course, borrowing to pay interest on outstanding loans is a classic indicator of bankruptcy.

To grasp the meaning of these various measures of a country's debt burden, contrast Brazil and Korea (South Korea) in Table 14.1. As a percentage of its national product, Korea's foreign debt was larger than Brazil's, 48.4 percent of GNP for the former as compared to 34.6 percent for the latter. Yet, interest payments as a percentage of exports were much more burdensome for Brazil: 1982 interest payments for Korea were just 12.8 percent of exports but Brazil used nearly half of its 1982 export earnings to cover its foreign interest payments. Among the reasons for these differences

Table 14.1

Foreign Debt of 30 Selected Developing Economies in 1982

	(1)	(2)	(3)	(4)	(5)	(6)	(7)
	Gross External Debt US$millions	Debt as a % of 1982		Interest Payments as % of		Long-Term Claims of Commercial Banks	
Country		GNP	Exports	GNP	Exports		(6)/(1)
Algeria	$17,641	34.7%	108.4%	2.9%	9.2%	$4,439	.25
Argentina	43,634	79.0	447.8	5.9	33.3	18,104	.42
Bolivia	3,328	101.4	348.6	3.1	10.5	901	.27
Brazil	92,961	34.6	405.3	4.0	47.1	57,605	.62
Chile	17,315	68.7	333.9	8.3	40.5	12,100	.70
Colombia	10,306	16.8	145.7	1.4	12.5	3,758	.36
Costa Rica	3,646	157.1	306.3	14.8	28.9	1,190	.33
Côte d'Ivoire	8,945	126.7	319.6	9.8	24.7	3,487	.39
Ecuador	7,705	64.2	273.3	8.2	34.9	3,600	.47
Egypt	29,526	121.1	422.8	4.3	15.1	923	.03
India	27,438	12.6	190.2	0.0	0.3	1,800	.07
Indonesia	25,133	24.4	108.6	1.6	7.0	6,848	.27
Jamaica	2,846	97.6	219.9	6.5	14.6	467	.16
Korea	37,330	48.4	125.3	4.9	12.8	11,346	.30
Malaysia	13,354	37.5	70.2	1.2	2.2	7,589	.57
Mexico	86,081	52.0	328.0	6.0	37.8	46,666	.54
Morocco	12,536	83.4	422.0	5.1	25.9	2,744	.22
Nigeria	12,954	12.4	89.6	1.1	8.3	5,531	.43
Pakistan	11,638	35.1	339.6	1.0	9.2	624	.05
Peru	10,712	37.8	229.1	3.7	22.2	3,061	.29
Philippines	24,412	59.9	344.7	5.7	32.7	6,786	.28
Sudan	7,218	101.1	823.5	5.3	43.5	1,276	.18
Syria	6,187	43.6	241.0	0.9	4.9	0	.00
Thailand	12,238	30.5	125.1	2.5	10.2	4,216	.34
Turkey	19,716	36.2	238.7	3.0	19.7	4,873	.25
Uruguay	2,647	27.9	79.7	1.7	4.8	1,276	.48
Venezuela	32,158	32.9	145.7	1.2	5.5	14,800	.46
Yugoslavia	19,900	30.3	126.9	2.6	11.0	12,004	.60
Zaire	5,079	36.1	292.7	2.6	21.0	531	.10
Zambia	3,689	99.9	332.0	5.1	17.0	132	.04

Sources: From William R. Cline (1995), *International Debt Reexamined,* Washington, DC: Institute for International Economics, which were compiled from the World Bank's *World Debt Tables* and the International Monetary Fund's *International Financial Statistics* and *Balance of Payments Statistics Yearbooks.*

in debt burden was that Korea exported over four times as much of its total national production as did Brazil. But Korea also paid a lower rate of interest on its outstanding debt than Brazil, which was seen as a riskier borrower precisely because its debt burden was higher. Korea was able to fully service its private and public foreign debt after the rise in interest rates in 1982, and it avoided any kind of financial crisis or economic recession.

The case of Egypt was different again. Even though Egypt had one of the highest levels of foreign debt, 121.1 percent of GNP, its interest payments in 1982 were only 4.3 percent of GNP. This was because Egypt's foreign borrowing consisted largely of low-interest loans from foreign governments and multilateral aid agencies. The last column of Table 14.1 shows that virtually none of Egypt's loans were from commercial banks. When market interest rates were low in the 1970s, private bank loans seemed like a great bargain. But when tight monetary policies pushed Eurocurrency interest rates into double digits, Egypt was very lucky to be carrying mostly subsidized, low-interest debt.

Dealing with the 1982 Debt Crisis

In many countries, the fall in real per capita welfare after 1982 was severe. The reversal in financial flows caused the value of national currencies to fall sharply on the foreign exchange markets. Some policy makers and economists welcomed this exchange rate collapse because they saw it as necessary for generating the trade surplus, the excess of export earnings over import payments, that could offset the negative financial account balance caused by the reversal of financial flows. But the exchange rate collapses also precipitated severe financial crises in most of the debtor economies. When currencies depreciated, the value of the foreign debt of developing-country firms, banks, and governments rose in terms of their domestic currency and their domestic income. Domestic firms and banks that had borrowed overseas faced bankruptcy as their liabilities suddenly exceeded the value of their domestic assets. As bankruptcies spread, especially in the banking sectors, financial intermediation, and thus investment, came to a sharp halt. Economic growth turned negative.

Most of the foreign borrowing had been carried out by governments and various government agencies. The higher debt service in 1982 meant that government budgets were suddenly highly negative, which obligated policy makers to cut expenditures, raise taxes, or borrow. But no foreign borrowing was available and the domestic financial crisis and economic recession meant there was little money available to borrow. Budget cuts thus ended up making the economic recessions worse in many countries. In sum, the 1982 debt crisis turned into a long economic crisis in many developing economies.

Solving this global debt crisis turned out to be very difficult. The difficulties were related not only to the size of the debt, but also to the conflicting interests of the parties involved and the incentives each of these interests faced under the institutional arrangements within the financial system.

An obvious problem with debt incurred by a sovereign government is that creditors have virtually no access to any type of collateral. Bond holders or banks in foreign countries normally find it difficult to go to court to demand payment from a foreign government. There have been times when loans to sovereign governments have been enforced with battleships and invading armies. For example, in 1902, when the government of Venezuela defaulted on its foreign debt, British, German, and Italian naval ships blockaded the country's ports until the government again began servicing its debt. Back in 1881, when the Ottoman Empire defaulted on its foreign loans, several European countries sent in commandos to seize the empire's customshouses and then helped themselves to customs revenues until the debt was paid up.[3] Such occurrences are rare, however, because they are very costly for creditor nations. They are constitutionally impossible in many countries. However, creditors do have some leverage over debtors.

Most important, creditors can threaten to never lend again. Settlements of debt disputes are often quite favorable to creditors because debtors have some strong incentives to maintain a reputation for reasonable behavior even under the most trying economic conditions. There are potential gains from being able to borrow and lend across borders, as explained in Chapter 11, which means countries, or at least some people in them, have an incentive to maintain their access to international capital markets. Running up debt and then defaulting for a short-run gain will imply long-run costs from losing the capacity to use international borrowing for intertemporal consumption smoothing, a more efficient allocation of savings, and more diversification.

Debtors also know that a large proportion of international trade is financed using trade credits, which are short-term loans. They provide exporters with cash to cover their production costs while they wait for payment from their overseas customers; they may also finance importers who are required to pay up front for goods that will arrive and be resold locally much later. Trade credits are usually for terms of less than one year. The international economists Kenneth Rogoff (1999, p. 31) writes: "The strongest weapon of disgruntled creditors, perhaps, is the ability to interfere with short-term credits that are the lifeblood of international trade." Andrew Rose (2005) examines historical data on trade and defaults and finds that less access to trade credit can keep trade between creditor and debtor countries below long-run trends for up to fifteen years after a default.

The Three Sides of the Negotiations

A typical dispute over debt pits a debtor against a creditor. The 1982 debt crisis turned into a three-party dispute when the governments of the world's major developed economies realized that total loans to foreign governments exceeded the capital of most of their major commercial banks. A total default by a large number of debtor governments and firms in the indebted developing economies would have meant the failure of most of the world's largest commercial banks and a serious financial crisis in their countries. This concern for the health of the global private banking industry pushed developed-country governments and central banks to join in the search for a solution to the "debt problem."

The debt crisis in effect became a **three-person game**, with each side—foreign borrowers, the private lending banks, and developed-country governments—bargaining with the two other interested parties. Developed-country governments often used the IMF and World Bank, institutions that they controlled, to do their bidding. The debtor country governments attempted to negotiate a reduction in their obligations to the foreign creditor banks at the same time that they attempted to get foreign governments and international institutions like the International Monetary Fund to foot part of the bill. Creditor private banks also negotiated with one eye on their own governments (taxpayers) and the IMF as a source of funds to supplement the limited ability of the debtor countries to repay their foreign obligations. The IMF, of course, gets its funds from its member countries; every member is required to contribute capital to the IMF in proportion to the size of its economy.

The governments of the high-income countries whose banks had done most of the lending sought to unwind the debt without causing the banks to curtail their domestic lending at a time when many high-income countries were just emerging from recessions triggered by the tight anti-inflationary monetary policies instituted at the end of the 1970s and early 1980s. The difficulty of negotiating agreements among three different interest groups in many different countries dragged out the negotiations. A list of questions that a viable proposal would have to address to the satisfaction of all three parties illustrates the complexity of the negotiations:

- How much debt should be forgiven—all, some, or none?
- Who bears the costs of writing off debt?
- Should *all* debtor countries enjoy some debt relief?
- If just some, which ones?
- How much debt should be rescheduled as opposed to forgiven?
- How much new lending should creditors provide to debtors?
- Should debtors reform their economic policies, and if so, how?
- How costly will reform be in terms of current welfare of the citizens of debtor countries?

The first question must be answered through negotiation. Obviously debtors preferred to repay less rather than more, with creditors taking the opposite view. But all sides recognized that some debt relief was necessary because debtors simply could not meet current debt obligations. Exactly how much relief was necessary was not clear, however. In fact, depending on the economic policies adopted, debtor countries could effectively service various levels of debt.

Perhaps more problematic was the issue of deciding which countries merited what degree of debt reduction. Should the poorest countries enjoy the greatest reductions in debt? Or should those countries that had adopted the most serious economic reforms enjoy the greatest forgiveness of debt? And what about those countries that continued to service their foreign debt despite great sacrifices in terms of short-run economic welfare? Economists urged governments not only to look at past problems, but also to establish incentives for more efficient international lending and borrowing in the future.

It took the entire decade of the 1980s for debtor countries, banks, and developed-country governments to agree on the answers to the difficult questions listed above. Toward the end of the decade, the United States introduced a framework for solving the debt crisis known as the **Brady Plan** (named for U.S. Secretary of the Treasury Nicholas Brady). The essential elements of the plan were:

- Debtor countries would adopt economic reforms designed to improve their ability to repay foreign loans.
- The International Monetary Fund would send its economists to judge and certify debtor countries' reform programs.
- Creditors would write down outstanding debt to reflect the market value of the debt on the secondary market for sovereign debt.
- Developed-country governments would directly, or indirectly through the International Monetary Fund, offer guarantees on the remaining debt so that creditors would be assured of future debt service.

The Brady Plan thus consisted of a combination of debt write-offs by the creditors, substantial policy changes to improve debt repayment by debtor governments, and subsidies by developed-country governments in the form of loan guarantees.

Critics of the Brady Plan pointed to the unfair allocation of costs in the agreements that were negotiated based on the plan. Problem debtors, whose debt was nearly worthless on the secondary market, in effect had most of their debt forgiven, while those countries that had sacrificed to service their debt, and whose debt therefore sold for a high percentage of face value on the secondary market, had relatively less debt forgiven. While this seems to be a clearly inequitable outcome, remember that all loan defaults inevitably result in similar outcomes. Bankruptcy proceedings often appear to reward those who behaved irresponsibly.

In 1989, Mexico became the first country to negotiate a debt relief plan along the lines of the Brady Plan. Mexico's creditors accepted some reductions in future debt service payments, Mexico issued new **Brady bonds** whose principal was backed by U.S. Treasury notes, and it committed to very substantial economic reforms designed to restore economic growth and the ability to meet interest and principal payments on its reduced foreign obligations. Among the reforms was the formation of the **North American Free Trade Area (NAFTA)**, consisting of Mexico, the United States, and Canada, which for Mexico was a radical departure from the *import-substituting industrialization* policy it had developed in its high-growth years of the 1950s and 1960s. Many other developing countries followed Mexico in negotiating final resolutions to their debt problems along the lines of the Brady Plan.

The Role of the International Monetary Fund

The IMF played a central role in implementing the Brady Plan. In its traditional role as the "central banker for central banks," it was an important source of short-term credit to debtor governments. But as the source of financing, the IMF enjoyed great leverage to push the debtor countries to undertake the economic reforms that its donor high-income governments deemed necessary for the debtor countries to service their foreign debt. Under the Brady Plan, the IMF and its staff economists served as judges of debtor countries' economic reforms.

The IMF's role makes perfect sense from the perspectives of the creditor banks and the high-income countries' governments. They faced a moral hazard problem: debtor governments could promise to institute certain economic policies that the creditors thought would be in the best interest of servicing debt, but, because the interests of the political leaders of the debtor countries were not compatible with the economic reforms that would maximize the likelihood that outstanding debt would be serviced on schedule, the debtors were likely to succumb to domestic political pressures and renege on the agreed to reforms. The IMF's role as monitor of borrower economic policies could reduce the likelihood that debtors would not carry out the agreed-to economic reforms.

The IMF's mandated economic reforms came to be known as the **Washington consensus**. These reforms included free trade, reduced government involvement in the economy, a realistic foreign exchange rate, conservative monetary policies to reduce inflation, balanced government budgets, privatization of government assets, reduced labor market regulation, and diminished financial regulation. These types of economic reforms were often strenuously opposed by many groups, especially labor groups and small farmers, in the debtor countries. The IMF was regularly depicted as a bully that sought to repay the transnational banks with the sweat of the poor. On the other hand, because debtor governments were often slow in implementing the economic reforms pushed by creditors and the IMF, the IMF came under frequent criticism from developed-country banks and politicians for not "enforcing" the agreements reached under a Brady plan.

Economists still debate the role of the IMF in the world economy. The designers at the 1944 Bretton Woods Monetary Conference who established the IMF could not have foreseen the role that the institution performed in the 1980s and 1990s, but they did build an institution that was perfectly poised to play the role of judge. At Bretton Woods, the IMF was seen as maintaining the stability of the international monetary system. Member countries contributed reserves that could be lent to governments to protect the value of their currencies, and they were authorized to hire a large staff of economists to judge countries' economic policies. The voting rights in the IMF were awarded roughly in proportion to the size of members' economies, so the rich countries dominated the institution. The next part of this textbook will look at the historical origins of the IMF in more detail. Meanwhile, below we provide some insight into what happened after 1990, after the Brady Plan and the Washington consensus reforms were put into effect.

FOREIGN EXCHANGE CRISES OF THE 1990S

The Brady Plan did not stop further foreign exchange crises from slowing growth in developing economies. In this section we detail three of the many exchange rate crises that would occur with nagging regularity during the 1990s and early 2000s. It seems as though the Washington consensus reforms did little to stabilize the international monetary system. Like the 1982 exchange rate and financial crises, these subsequent crises began as reversals in financial flows that triggered exchange rate collapses, which then produced financial crises and, finally, deep recessions.

The Mexican Peso Crisis in 1994

Mexico's economy had gone through a major transformation during the 1980s as policy makers shifted from import substitution industrialization to free trade, privatization of government assets, less regulated labor markets, financial liberalization, and less government involvement in the economy. After the "lost decade" of the 1980s, during which per capita income did not increase at all, the Mexican economy began to grow again in the early 1990s. Many economists interpreted this resumption of economic growth as a validation of the Washington consensus policies. Note, however, that the growth in the early 1990s was still substantially below the growth rates achieved in the 1950s, 1960s, and 1970s. The Mexican government also made headway in reducing inflation by cutting monetary expansion and stabilizing the peso-dollar exchange rate after fifteen years of continual depreciation. The government's apparent commitment to reducing inflation was often credited for strengthening the value of the Mexican peso. The reduced inflationary expectations lessened the perceived exchange rate risk associated with investing in Mexico. The good economic news encouraged foreign investors to buy Mexican stocks and bonds, and it encouraged Mexican firms, banks, and government agencies to again begin borrowing overseas. Then, in 1994, the confidence suddenly dissipated.

It was an election year. In order to gain favor with voters, the Mexican government sharply increased spending and loosened monetary policy. The ruling party, the Institutional Revolutionary Party (PRI), had been in power since the 1920s, but its hold on power was no longer solid after the 1980s' economic stagnation. Rumor has it that the PRI had resorted to massive election fraud to win the previous presidential election, in 1988, and 1994's election was expected to be close again despite the resumption of economic growth. The PRI resorted to increased government expenditures to benefit voters, and the political spending caused the economy to grow rapidly during 1994. The PRI won the election, but it had become obvious to many Mexicans and foreigners that the government was attempting to defy the trilemma by simultaneously keeping the peso fixed to the dollar, greatly increasing spending and the money supply, and opening the borders to trade and investment as prescribed by the implementation of the new North American Free Trade Area (NAFTA). A political uprising in the very poor southern region of the country, the assassination of the relatively popular PRI presidential candidate, and his replacement by a less charismatic economist over the course of the year did not help confidence either. Individuals, banks, and firms who had previously acquired Mexican assets began exchanging peso-denominated assets for dollar-denominated assets.[4] To counter this **capital flight**, the Mexican central bank spent over $20 billion of its U.S. dollar reserves purchasing the many pesos being supplied to the foreign exchange market. Capital flight reached panic proportions toward the end of the year, and Mexico's reported reserves of US$24 billion were nearly exhausted. In December, the government had to stop intervening in the foreign exchange market, and the peso promptly lost half its value.

According to script, this collapse of the peso caused a severe slowdown in economic activity in Mexico. The peso depreciation instantaneously bankrupted much of the Mexican banking sector. Mexican banks and manufacturers had borrowed heavily in the United States and the worldwide Eurocurrency markets in order to lend to customers in Mexico anxious to invest and expand businesses in the growing Mexican economy. As part of its preparations for joining NAFTA and its overall economic reforms to restore growth in the Mexican economy, the government had deregulated the banking industry. The liberalization of banking stimulated aggressive competition among banks to build market share by capturing funds and attracting new customers. The banks borrowed overseas to capture funds, apparently believing that the government would continue to stabilize the value of the peso. Furthermore, many poor loans were made by inexperienced bank personnel spurred by their managers to capture market share in the newly deregulated industry. When the peso depreciated by 50 percent at the end of 1994, the liability side of bank balance sheets grew precipitously. The banks' foreign debt suddenly doubled in size in terms of pesos. Many of the banks' largest customers had also borrowed overseas, and thus defaulted on their Mexican loans, further weakening banks' balance sheets. The bankrupt banks stopped lending, investment collapsed, and the economy contracted sharply. Mexico's real per capita GDP fell by nearly 10 percent in 1995.

A bank bailout was organized at great expense to the Mexican taxpayer. Although the downward spiral was stopped within a year, it took until the very end of the 1990s before per capita income regained its 1994 level. President Clinton of the United States, one of Mexico's NAFTA partners (the other is Canada), found a way to provide a $50 billion loan to help stabilize the peso despite the opposition of the U.S. Congress.

Economists blamed the 1994 Mexican crisis on the government's public commitment to stabilizing the exchange rate. By stating that it would support the value of the peso, the government had implicitly provided domestic borrowers of dollars with a guarantee, so borrowers acted as if there was little exchange rate risk. The government's bailout of the banks confirmed borrowers' expectations, which means that any future commitment by the Mexican government to fixed exchange rates may trigger even greater disregard for exchange rate risk. This may explain why the Mexican government has let the peso float freely since 1995. The 1994 exchange rate collapse and economic crisis had another interesting effect: In 2000, Mexican voters handed the PRI its first defeat in a presidential election in nearly eighty years. The winner was a conservative candidate who continued the Washington consensus policies that the 1994 PRI candidate, U.S.-educated economist Ernesto Zedillo, had already put firmly in place between 1994 and 2000.

The Asian Crisis of 1997

The world economy was surprised in 1997 by a sudden massive outflow of money from several fast-growing East Asian economies. Hong Kong, Singapore, South Korea, and Taiwan had been among the fastest-growing economies of the world since the 1950s. They were commonly referred to as the *Asian Tigers*. Southeast Asian countries such as Indonesia, Malaysia, the Philippines, and Thailand, referred to as the new tigers, had also grown spectacularly since the 1970s and 1980s. These economies were often held up as examples of successful developing economies. After the financial crisis in 1997, in fact, many people wondered how it was possible that economies that had apparently done so many things right could suffer crises commonly associated with less successful economies.

The governments of most Southeast Asian countries had avoided the accumulation of large amounts of government debt, and government budgets were in balance. Inflation was not high compared to that in most developing economies in the 1980s. The Southeast Asian economies were also export oriented, and the Asian Tigers were widely used as an example of how free trade policies promoted economic development. As mentioned in Chapter 10, East Asian policy makers' commitment to free trade was weak at best. What is definite, however, is that the tiger governments ignored the trilemma.

The governments of most of the fast-growing Asian countries had fixed their exchange rates to the U.S. dollar, using reserves of foreign exchange to intervene when necessary to keep the market from raising or lowering the rates. By 1997, these government-controlled nominal exchange rates had become overvalued. Inflation rates that were higher than those of the countries' principal trade partners were one cause. Another was the appreciation of the U.S. dollar relative to most other currencies after 1995; as the dollar rose in value, so did the East Asian currencies that were fixed to the dollar by their governments. Most important, the 1994 depreciation of the yuan by China further overvalued the Tigers' currencies. China's devaluation hurt most because China produced and exported many of the same types of labor-intensive manufactures that the Asian Tigers were exporting.

Since the East Asian governments had committed to fixing their currencies to the U.S. dollar, they continued to intervene to keep the exchange rate from changing. Gradually, expectations of an eventual change in the fixed exchange rates grew stronger, and the owners of assets increasingly decided to store their wealth in assets denominated in other currencies, especially U.S. dollars. Demand for foreign currencies thus expanded, and the supply fell. As much as US$80 billion is reported to have left Indonesia, Korea, Malaysia, the Philippines, and Thailand in 1997 and 1998.[5] The central banks of Thailand, Malaysia, Indonesia, South Korea, Taiwan, and other Asian economies used large amounts of their accumulated reserves of foreign exchange, which were initially quite substantial because of their countries' success in exporting, to make up the difference between market demand and supply in order to keep the exchange rate from changing. But when reserves dwindled, the fixed exchange rates had to be abandoned. The national currencies fell sharply in value relative to the major currencies of the world. Just as in Mexico, the sudden rise in foreign liabilities caused the balance sheets of banks and firms that borrowed overseas to deteriorate, a financial crisis set in, bank lending ceased, investment stopped, and economic activity fell sharply. In 1998, real GDP fell by 13 percent in Indonesia, 11 percent in Thailand, and nearly 8 percent in Malaysia.

Weak banking systems in many of the East Asian economies were also blamed for the crash. It appears that many state and private banks had already been weakened with large amounts of non-performing loans even before the collapse of the national currencies. Housing bubbles in several countries made matters worse. Some studies even suggest that it was not the exchange rate crisis that caused the financial the crisis, but a domestic problem of **crony capitalism**.[6] Crony capitalism is the common phenomenon where the financial industry favors certain borrowers over others, most notably the politically well connected and those firms that currently dominate the economy. The fact of the matter is that all banking sectors tend to favor existing borrowers over new, unknown borrowers because the informational problems cause adverse selection and moral hazard. Most likely, the fundamental cause of the crisis was the trilemma. When the Chinese devaluation began to push current accounts into deficit, governments maintained their commitments to fix the exchange rate, they did not adjust domestic macroeconomic policies to changing foreign circumstances, and they increased their countries' dependence on foreign trade and finance.

The Russian Crisis

Not all currency crises occurred in developing economies. One of the more disruptive loan defaults and currency depreciations occurred in Russia in 1997. Russia is the largest of the sovereign countries that emerged from the political collapse of the Soviet Union. The fall of U.S.S.R.'s communist regime in 1990 was followed by a variety of schemes to transition the economy from a central-planning system. By 1997, having gone through seven years of transition, Russia defaulted on its foreign debt, and the collapse of the ruble resulted in a widespread economic collapse characteristic of the foreign exchange crises in developing economies.

Russia was a very different economy from the developing economies discussed above, however. The pre-transition Soviet economic model was based on state ownership of all means of production and central planning of all major economic decisions. What was to be produced, how it was to be produced, and who was to receive the output were all determined by government bureaucrats according to a national plan.

The centrally planned economy was relatively successful in terms of material output for many decades. For example, when most of the world's capitalist economies were experiencing the Great Depression, total output in the Soviet Union grew rapidly, driven by very high rates of saving and investment. Of course, the saving was not entirely voluntary; central planners determined that consumer goods would be produced in limited amounts, leaving consumers no alternative but to save. The weakness of the Soviet system was that it was not able to generate lasting economic growth. As estimated by Gur Ofer (1987), economic growth declined steadily from the 1950s to the 1980s. First, factor productivity declined and eventually turned negative. By the late 1970s, output was growing more slowly than inputs, which means that it was taking increasing amounts of labor, capital, and other resources to produce the same amount of output. Second, the return to capital fell over time. Because the growth of capital exceeded the growth of other inputs, the marginal return to capital fell. Thus, when technology stopped improving, as evidenced by the negative rates of factor productivity, diminishing returns to capital set in.

The collapse of the Soviet system in 1990 did not improve the growth performance of Russia. Instead, per capita real output declined sharply. Between 1991 and 1997, output in Russia fell by 40 percent. The shifting of an entire economy's resources from the centrally planned and state-owned economy to a fundamentally different private market economy proved difficult. Capital from the state sector was not immediately useful in the private sector. In fact, according to Irina Dolinskaya (2002, p. 156), "part of the capital stock inherited from the socialist era is so outmoded it will never be used again and thus has to be replaced, which requires time and resources." Another reason for the slow transition from state firms to new private firms was the breakdown of production networks caused by the transition from central planning to a market economy. This is what Olivier J. Blanchard and Michael Kremer (1997) called *disorganization.*

By 1997, however, it began to look as though Russia's sharp economic decline had come to an end, and there were solid signs of a reversal in economic fortunes. Negotiations were completed to deal with Russia's outstanding foreign debt, most of which had been contracted by the former Soviet regime. Over US$80 billion in payments on old debt was rescheduled, greatly easing Russia's lingering debt burden. International trade moved toward balance, inflation was brought under control, the price of oil, Russia's largest export, rose, and the rate of economic growth was positive for the first time since the collapse of the Soviet government. There were predictions that Russia's credit rating would soon be raised, and Russian banks were increasingly able to expand their foreign borrowing to fund domestic lending. The Russian central bank was successfully keeping the exchange rate within a narrow band of 5 to 6 rubles per dollar. On the negative side, only 40 percent of Russian workers had paying full-time jobs, the government budget deficit was still very high, and falling real wages suppressed consumer demand.[7]

Then, in late 1997, the Asian currency crisis spooked the international capital markets, and Russia's central bank spent US$6 billion to defend the ruble against speculators betting on its depreciation. Russia's President Yeltsin added to the deteriorating economic uncertainty by firing his entire cabinet in early 1998. The speculative attacks on the ruble increased in early 1998, and as it was running out of foreign reserves to intervene in the foreign exchange market, the Russian central bank raised interest rates from an already high 30 percent to 50 percent. Emergency aid from the IMF of nearly US$5 billion in the summer of 1998 did little to stem the speculation, and in August 1998 the government first devalued the ruble and, when speculation continued, let it float. The ruble depreciated from about 6 rubles per dollar to nearly 30 per dollar by the end of the year. As feared by the Russian government, the massive fall in the value of the ruble resulted in widespread defaults by banks and firms with foreign debt, a financial crisis, and a decline in real output of over 5 percent. The recovery of the Russian economy from its costly transition would have to wait a few more years.

Common Threads to 1990s Exchange Rate Crises

At this point, it is useful to stop and examine the similarities between the 1994 Mexican crisis, the 1997 Asian crisis, and the 1998 Russian crisis. All of the countries concerned had made substantial economic policy changes, such as balancing government budgets, opening the economy to foreign competition, privatizing much of the economy, and suppressing inflation through conservative monetary policy. Also, financial account transactions were liberalized and foreign loans and investment had grown rapidly. Finally, all the governments were openly committed to maintaining fixed exchange rates. That is, they had picked globalization and fixed exchange rates from the trilemma's menu.

In each case, when it became apparent that underlying economic conditions and policies were not compatible with the exchange rates at which the currencies were being fixed, investors began to shift their wealth out of assets denominated in these countries' national currencies and into assets denominated in U.S. dollars, Japanese yen, and other currencies expected to appreciate relative to the domestic currencies. The shifts in wealth eventually turned into panics when it became apparent that the government was running out of reserves or politically unable to continue intervening to prevent the exchange rate from changing. In all cases, both domestic and foreign wealth holders reacted in similar fashion as they tried to protect the value of their wealth or use their wealth to make speculative gains from an expected devaluation.

The cases are also interesting in that detailed information shows that when confidence in the exchange rate erodes, everyone becomes a speculator. In Mexico and East Asia, importers began making advance purchases of foreign goods, sometimes even making advance payments to foreign suppliers for later deliveries of goods, because they feared a currency devaluation would raise the domestic price of foreign goods in the future. Exporters often kept their overseas receipts parked in foreign bank accounts, awaiting the possible devaluation that would increase the amount of domestic currency earned from the earlier exports. All of these actions further increased demand for foreign exchange and reduced the supply, and central banks found themselves spending reserves of foreign exchange more and more rapidly in order to bridge the growing gap between demand and supply. After losing substantial amounts of foreign reserves, the central banks gave up and let their currencies float freely according to supply and demand, as the millions of large and small speculators had expected.

Why the Exchange Rate Crises Were So Damaging

The economic slowdowns in Mexico, Southeast Asia, Russia, and elsewhere during the 1990s and 2000s were damaging because the *exchange rate crises* triggered *financial crises,* which then killed investment and pushed the economy into recession. In each case, governments, banks, and firms had borrowed overseas in dollars and lent to domestic firms in domestic currency. Therefore, exchange rate depreciation caused liabilities to suddenly rise in terms of the domestic currency. There was, therefore, a sudden deterioration of balance sheets; an increase in liabilities was not matched by a concurrent increase in assets. Bankrupt banks cannot lend, and for this reason the financial crisis turned into a sharp slowdown in investment and any other economic activities that needed credit and financial intermediation. In some cases, most notably in Asia, the availability of credit from overseas also helped to create speculative bubbles in real estate markets, stock markets, and investment in general, which then made the eventual reversal of financial flows even more devastating. In Hyman Minsky's terminology, when many loans are already mostly speculative or Ponzi before an adverse change in economic circumstances, the financial crisis will be much more severe than when most financing before the change in economic circumstances is hedge financing.

An important detail to remember about the above cases is that the financial crises were caused, fundamentally, by a mismatch of liabilities and assets across currencies. Borrowers owed dollars but their assets and expected earnings were in local currency, and they had not hedged their foreign exposure. Banks, governments, and firms in Korea, Malaysia, Mexico, Thailand, and Russia earned their income (or taxed) in domestic currency, but they had to pay foreign loan principal, interest, and dividends in U.S. dollars and other major foreign currencies.

Most developing and small developed countries have little choice but to borrow overseas in terms of dollars or other major currencies. That is, they have to bear all of the exchange rate risk. Foreigners' unwillingness to carry the exchange rate risk may reflect their belief that the currencies in question are more likely to depreciate than to appreciate. Indicative of the difficulty for developing economies to borrow abroad in their own currencies is Colombia's attempt in 2005. It offered a 12.5 percent interest rate on the equivalent of US$250 million in bonds denominated in Colombian pesos. Just two months earlier, Colombia had sold $500 million in bonds denominated in U.S. dollars yielding 8.5 percent.[8] Colombia therefore had to pay a 4.0 percent premium to sell peso bonds instead of U.S. dollar bonds.

It is not only the governments of poorly managed economies that cannot borrow abroad in their own currencies. Many well-governed countries are also forced by the markets to borrow internationally in terms of one of the major world currencies. This phenomenon is often referred to as *original sin* because there is often no evidence that countries have done anything to bring this disadvantage upon themselves.[9] Contrast this situation with the United States, which, as you saw in Chapter 11, also has huge net foreign obligations. The United States's foreign obligations are almost entirely in terms of U.S. dollars, however, and a depreciation of the dollar would not change U.S. borrowers' dollar obligations to foreigners. There would be no financial crisis in the United Sates; rather, it would be the foreign lenders who would suffer, and the dollar depreciation could trigger a financial crisis abroad.

Finally, the reversals of international investment flows that triggered the exchange rate crises in Mexico, Southeast Asia, Russia, and elsewhere were very costly for human welfare. For example, when Mexico's citizens, firms, and government borrowed money from foreigners, they were able to absorb more than their country produced. But when Mexico was forced to reduce its outstanding debt, its absorption fell below national production. When a financial crisis caused production to plummet, that loss was added to the loss of absorption.

BRAZIL'S 2004 TIGHTROPE WALK

In 1998 Brazil adopted an IMF-sponsored fiscal stabilization program after suffering a modest exchange rate crisis and recession. As part of this program, Brazil committed to reducing its government budget deficit, decreasing its debt-to-GDP ratio, and maintaining conservative monetary policies to keep prices steady. Six years later and after a brief crisis that led the government to let the currency float and depreciate by 50 percent in 1999, the fiscal picture looked much better, but, according to most financial market analysts, not good enough. By 2004, the possibility of yet another currency crisis loomed.

Sustainability of Public Sector Debt

At the beginning of 2004, Brazil's government debt burden was very large. Gross public sector debt was estimated at about 80 percent of GDP, a very high ratio by IMF standards. *Net* public sector debt was considerably less, at 58 percent of GDP, but about half of the government's assets, which were used to calculate the net debt, were loans to public enterprises and credits committed to the Labor Assistance Fund, a contributor-designated unemployment insurance fund whose assets could not be touched by the government.

The foreign exchange market was seeing the Brazilian real fall in value. One reason for this was the discovery and public revelation of many *esceletos* (skeletons, as in "skeletons in the closet") by the newly elected administration of President Luiz Inácio Lula da Silva. These skeletons were government obligations that had been hidden from public and were correctly being brought into the visible government budgeting process.[10] Also causing a loss in confidence in the future value of the real were the growth of government debt and the high interest rates the government had to pay on it. Slow economic growth did not help confidence either. And, of course, the currency depreciations in 2004 further increased the debt burden because Brazil's foreign debt is denominated entirely in foreign currencies. One estimate suggests that Brazil's net debt-to-GDP ratio would have been only 42 percent, rather than 58 percent, had no Brazilian debt been dollar-denominated.[11]

A country's public sector debt can be viewed as *sustainable* if the country can service its debt without policy changes. This is because a country's capacity to generate revenue to service its debt depends on its tax system and the economy's rate of economic growth, which are both influenced by government policy. A key indicator of sustainability is the path of the debt-to-GDP ratio. Clearly, the debt-to-GDP ratio cannot rise indefinitely.

Tracing the Path of Public Sector Debt: An Example

The change in a country's real total government debt at time t, ΔD_t, that is, the difference between real total government debt at time t, D_t, and at time $t-1$, D_{t-1}, depends on the real interest rate at time t, r_t, and the real government **primary budget surplus** (government receipts minus non-interest expenditures) at time t, S_t, as follows:

(14.2) $$\Delta D_t, = D_t - D_{t-1} = r_t \cdot D_{t-1} - S_t.$$

Dividing equation (14.2) by GDP_t gives us

(14.3) $$D_t / GDP_t = D_{t-1}/GDP_t + (r_t \cdot D_{t-1})/GDP_t - S_t/GDP_t.$$

Since $GDP_t = (1+g_t)GDP_{t-1}$, where g_t is the annual growth rate of real GDP in period t, we can rewrite equation (14.3) as

(14.4) $$D_t / GDP_t = D_{t-1}/(1+g_t)GDP_{t-1} + (r_t \cdot D_{t-1})/(1+g_t)GDP_{t-1} - S_t/GDP_t.$$

By shuffling terms, this equation can be more clearly written as:

(14.5) $$D_t / GDP_t = [(1 + r_t) / (1 + g_t)] (D_{t-1} / GDP_{t-1}) - S_t/GDP_t.$$

Then, if we write the ratios of each of the variables to GDP as their lowercase equivalents, we end up with

(14.6) $$d_t = [(1 + r_t) / (1 + g_t)] d_{t-1} - s_t.$$

This relationship makes it clear that, for a primary budget surplus equal to zero and initial debt burden d_{t-1}, the debt-to-GDP ratio d_t will continue to rise if the real interest rate on debt r_t exceeds the growth in real GDP, g_t.

A simple example using equation (14.6) shows why a high debt burden is problematic. Suppose a country has a debt burden of 100 percent ($d_{t-1} = 1$), the primary budget is in balance ($s_t = 0$), the real interest rate $r_t = 10\%$, and GDP growth $g_t = 2\%$, then its public sector debt grows by

(14.7) $$d_t = [(1.10)/(1.02)]1 - 0 = 1.078.$$

That is, $d_t > d_{t-1}$ means that the budget deficit grows over time and the public debt ratio is not sustainable. On the other hand, if a country has a debt burden of 50 percent ($d_{t-1} = .5$), the primary budget is a positive 4 percent ($s_t = .04$), the real interest rate is 10 percent, and GDP growth is 2 percent, then the public sector debt *is* sustainable. Specifically

(14.8) $$d_t = [(1.10)/(1.02)].5 - .04 = .5392 - .04 = .4992.$$

Now $d_t < d_{t-1}$, and the deficit-to-GDP ratio does not grow. We can conclude that the deficit is sustainable. Thus, the lower the debt burden and the greater the primary budget surplus, the more likely the government debt is sustainable.

Tracing Brazil's Public Sector Debt

This example is very relevant to Brazil's situation in 2004. In Brazil, the real interest rate on government debt had exceeded the growth of real GDP in almost every year since 1995. Brazil's average growth rate of real GDP has been a little more than 2 percent since the mid-1980s, yet real interest rates have exceeded 10 percent per year. In an interesting paper from early 2004, Patrick Higgins and Owen Humpage (2004) assumed a variety of interest rates, economic growth rates, and primary budget surpluses for Brazil over the subsequent ten years in order to see under what circumstances Brazil's debt would be sustainable and, therefore, unlikely to trigger an exchange rate crisis. Given

Table 14.2

Changes in Brazil's Debt-to-GDP Ratio under Alternative Assumptions

Real Interest Rate	Real GDP Growth Rate				
	2.0%	3.0%	3.5%	4.0%	4.5%
8.0%	−11.2	−18.1	−21.2	−24.2	−27.0
9.0%	−4.0	−11.6	−15.1	−18.4	−21.5
10.0%	4.0	−4.5	−8.4	−12.0	−15.4
11.0%	12.7	3.3	−1.0	−5.0	−8.8
12.0%	22.2	11.9	7.2	2.7	−1.5
13.0%	32.6	21.2	16.0	11.1	6.5

Source: Table 3 from Patrick C. Higgins and Owen F. Humpage (2004), "Walking on a Fence: Brazil's Public-Sector Debt," Federal Reserve Bank of Cleveland Policy Discussion Paper no. 6, February.

Brazil's 57.8 percent debt-to-GDP ratio and primary budget surplus of 4.25 percent at the end of 2003, they found the percentage point changes in the debt-to-GDP ratio given in Table 14.2 under various assumed combinations of annual real GDP growth rates and annual real interest rates. It is clear from the table that Brazil's financial situation was tenuous. Slight variations from recent trends in real interest rates and real GDP growth rates would critically shift Brazil's debt burden from sustainable to unsustainable. The calculations in Table 14.2 assume that the exchange rate does not change. A depreciation of the real lowers all of the numbers in the table; if the Brazilian real depreciates further, the debt burden will rise and become more difficult to sustain, all other things equal.

Brazil seemed to be walking on a ridge between sustainable and unsustainable public debt dynamics at the start of 2004. With high real interest rates in the 10–13 percent range, the debt is sustainable only if economic growth is high. But how can the economy grow rapidly with such high real interest rates? A lowering of real interest rates would benefit growth, but it would also cause capital outflows to increase and capital inflows to diminish, thus causing a possible depreciation and a rise in the debt burden. The hope was that the economy would grow faster and that the decline in real interest rates would be tolerated by the financial markets because the growth-driven increases in tax revenues would improve the primary budget surplus. Another hope was that Brazilian growth would be export driven, in which case the real would not depreciate. With luck, the real might even appreciate and reduce the debt burden faster than the primary budget surplus would by itself.

The balancing act between a rising debt burden and a falling debt burden was further complicated by the tenuous state of expectations in a situation of uncertainty. Recall Keynes's emphasis on confidence and conventions rather than expectations when people face uncertainty. If the international capital markets suspected that the debt burden was likely to spiral upward in the near future, there would most certainly be a sharp outflow of money from Brazil, causing a sharp depreciation in the real. The expectation of a rising debt burden and a default on government debt would in effect be self-fulfilling. On the other hand, if everyone expected Brazil's debt burden to be fully sustainable, then capital would continue to flow into Brazil, interest rates would fall, growth would pick up, tax revenues would grow, and the expectation of sustainability would be equally self-fulfilling.

Fortunately, the second scenario is what played out. In 2004, the Brazilian economy grew by 5.2 percent in real terms, interest rates declined somewhat, and the primary budget surplus increased to 4.6 percent of GDP—and it reached a stunning 5.5 percent of GDP at the start of 2005.[12] The net debt-to-GDP had fallen below 50 percent at the start of 2005. Interest rates were still 12.75 percent at the end of 2004, however. But since everything else worked out—the real did not collapse and the government debt proved to be sustainable—the interest rate finally began to fall after 2004. Overall, economic growth was fairly good later in the decade. Interestingly, Brazil would be one of the few countries to get through the 2007–2008 worldwide recession without a decline in real per capita GDP.

Brazil's 2004 tightrope walk is interesting in that it shows that countries can overcome looming exchange rate crises by taking decisive macroeconomic measures. The fact that Brazil still came so close to a true crisis, with all its economic disruption and human suffering, also shows that countries may wish to examine their situation relative to the effective international system they have selected. Perhaps Brazil should have long ago undertaken more fundamental reforms in the way its economy was linked to the international monetary system, so that its government's budget deficit could not have come so close to triggering a major exchange rate crisis and economic recession.

CONCLUSIONS

The discussion of the trilemma and exchange rate crises in this chapter suggests that the many financial crises in developing economies during the 1980s, 1990s, and 2000s are the result of failed attempts by policy makers to maintain the policies necessary to keep exchange rates fixed in the face of changing economic conditions and expectations. The crises are generated by shifts in circumstances and expectations, or confidence, which, in turn, causes sharp reversals in financial flows, which then have very real effects that we observe as rising unemployment and declines in real income.

The examples in this chapter also show that exchange rate collapses are not necessarily the result of bad economic decisions by the country's policy makers. Often, it was a change in international financial conditions, as in the case of tight monetary policy to combat inflation in rich countries in 1982, or the depreciation of a major trading partner's currency, such as China's depreciation before the 1997 Asian crisis, that caused a foreign exchange crisis. At the same time, there were several policy choices that countries who suffered exchange rate crises intentionally made:

- Economies were permitted, or encouraged, to become integrated into the world economy.
- The country was permitted, or encouraged, to accumulate net private and public foreign debt.
- The exchange rate was fixed or manipulated, and the countries' investors, exporters, importers, and savers were explicitly or implicitly assured the fixed rates would be maintained.

This means that the very costly economic recessions triggered by exchange rate crises were avoidable. However, as the trilemma suggests, the above measures in effect imply giving up certain types of international economic integration. To avoid foreign debt, international trade in goods and services must remain in balance. On the other hand, letting exchange rates float, and thus fluctuate, makes international trade, finance, and investment less attractive and may, therefore, reduce either or all of these activities.

It is interesting to note that in the early 2000s, Argentina and Ecuador have taken different approaches to exchange rate crises. After Argentina's currency lost 75 percent of its value following a ten-year period of fixed exchange rates, its GDP fell by almost 20 percent. Unemployment soared. After arguing with the IMF throughout 2002, Argentina quit its negotiations with creditors and the IMF and imposed a settlement on its creditors. Argentina offered each creditor less than one-third the face value of the debt, take it or leave it. At the start of 2004, the holders of nearly 75 percent of Argentina's defaulted US$103 billion in government foreign debt agreed to accept the government's offer of about thirty cents on the dollar and lengthened terms of repayment. Creditors appear to have taken such a bad offer simply because they expected no better offers would be forthcoming. At the beginning of 2004, the Argentinean economy had recovered most of the ground it had lost after the currency collapse in 2002, and it has grown consistently ever since. Argentina has faced some difficulties in obtaining further borrowing, but it has not been entirely frozen out of the international financial markets. It has been able to obtain trade credits and short-term foreign financing.

The newly elected government of Ecuador made the stunning decision in 2006 to not repay its government's foreign debt. It simply repudiated the debt, claiming, with good justification, that the debt had been incurred by irresponsible previous government leaders, often at the urging of private international banks, who did not legitimately represent the interests of Ecuadorians. Ecuador has faced strong retaliation, both financially by private international banks and the IMF and politically by the United States, for this **debt repudiation**. Ecuador has struggled to balance its trade, now that it is cut off from long-run foreign borrowing. On the other hand, it is under no obligation to institute Washington consensus policies.

In sum, there are many options for government policy makers to shape how their countries, and economies, participate in the global economy. Large developing countries can, in fact, participate in the process that shapes the international monetary system, such as the BRICS (Brazil, Russia, India, China, and South Africa) have effectively done. Smaller countries have to face the reality that they must either form broad coalitions with many others or remain content to simply adjust to the system that is imposed on them. But they do still have some choice on how they integrate their economies into the global system. They can do what Argentina did and refute some of their debt.

The next part of the textbook traces the history of the international monetary system and how individual countries fared in those systems. You will see that the trilemma helps to explain the failures of past international monetary systems as well as the problems individual countries face within each system, as exemplified by the cases detailed in this chapter. In fact, you will have to draw on many of the things you have learned about foreign exchange markets, international trade and trade policy, the balance of payments, and international finance to understand the fascinating history of the international monetary system. You will also see that we have not yet found a monetary system that satisfies all countries and functions well for more than a few decades. The world, therefore, faces not only the instability of investment, financial flows, and exchange rates, but also the instability of the entire international economic system within which individual economies must function.

CHAPTER SUMMARY

1. Since 1982, there have been many exchange rate crises in a great variety of countries.
2. International financial flows are subject to sudden reversals that sharply shift the supply and demand curves for currencies and thus change exchange rates. Exchange rate depreciations proportionately increase the burden of debt denominated in foreign currencies like the dollar or euro, and such exchange rate crises can trigger financial crises, which, in turn, tend to drive economies into deep and lengthy recession.
3. Foreign exchange market intervention is not always an effective tool for preventing long-run movements in exchange rates. One weakness of intervention is that, in the case of a fundamental disequilibrium in the foreign exchange market, central banks are unable to supply the necessary amounts of foreign exchange for long periods of time.
4. Conventional monetary policy may seem like a more viable long-run policy than using the limited reserves to support a currency, but monetary policy is not an unlimited tool either because it has effects on the economy that often run counter to other economic priorities.
5. Intervention can serve as a *signal* of government policy in a foreign exchange market where information about the future is seldom clear and when the intervention is *concerted*. But to be successful in the long run, there have to be accompanying shifts in policies, such as monetary policies, government expenditures, taxes, and trade policies, to validate the change in expectations.

6. The trilemma implies that policy makers cannot simultaneously maintain fixed exchange rates and an open capital market while pursuing a monetary policy oriented toward domestic goals; governments may choose only two of the above.

7. If monetary policy is aimed toward domestic goals, either capital mobility or the exchange rate target must be abandoned. If fixed exchange rates and integration into the global capital market are the main policy goals, then monetary policy must be adjusted to those ends, regardless of other macroeconomic goals.

8. The trilemma makes it clear how difficult it is to keep exchange rates fixed when policy makers are faced with domestic political pressures to deal with a variety of macroeconomic issues as well as pressure from business to keep the border open to international trade, investment, and financial flows.

9. The international monetary system suffered a huge shock in 1982, when some forty developing economies were forced to rescheduled debt payments, renegotiate terms, or simply default on their foreign debt.

10. This debt crisis followed a period of increasing international financial flows that seemed to have successfully offset the growing trade imbalances after the oil price hikes during the 1970s.

11. Most oil exporting countries deposited their *petrodollars,* earned after the oil price increases in the 1970s, in the *Eurocurrency* market, and this money was, in turn, lent to oil-importing countries, who thus gained access to the dollars needed to pay for the more expensive oil without reducing economic growth.

12. In 1982, some forty other developing countries in Asia, Africa, and Latin America, facing financial flow reversals triggered by monetary policy shifts in developed countries, effectively sought Ponzi financing to cover interest and principal payments on what they and their lenders had thought were hedge or, at worst, speculative loans.

13. Solving the 1982 debt crisis proved to be very difficult because not only was the size of the debt very large, but the conflicting interests and incentives led to an extended period of posturing and negotiation to settle the long list of questions involved.

14. The 1982 debt crisis effectively caused a three-party dispute when the governments of the world's major developed economies realized that total loans to foreign governments exceeded the capital of most of their major commercial banks.

15. The 1982 debt crisis was eventually solved under the *Brady Plan,* which consisted of a combination of debt write-offs by the creditors, substantial policy changes to improve the likelihood of debt repayment by debtor governments, lending and oversight of policy changes by the IMF, and subsidies by developed-country governments in the form of loan guarantees.

16. Under the Brady Plan, the IMF and its staff economists served as judges of debtor countries' promised economic policy reforms, known as the Washington consensus, a broad range of policies that included free trade, reduced government involvement in the economy, a realistic foreign exchange rate, conservative monetary policies to reduce inflation, balanced government budgets, privatization of government assets, reduced labor market regulation, and diminished financial regulation.

17. After the Brady Plan, there were many more exchange rate crises during the 1990s and early 2000s, suggesting that the Washington consensus reforms did little to stabilize the international monetary system.

18. Each of these subsequent crises began as reversals in financial flows triggered by a variety of changes in economic circumstances, each of which caused exchange rate collapses that then produced financial crises and, finally, deep recessions.

19. Brazil's 2004 tightrope walk is interesting in that it illustrates how debt dynamics can drive a country into default, with all its economic disruption and human suffering.

20. The examples in this chapter show that debt crises are, fundamentally, caused by international financial integration, the accumulation of private and public foreign debt, and sudden collapses of exchange rates that were intentionally held fixed or were managed to remain at unsustainable levels. Policies to avoid debt crises, therefore, include setting more realistic exchange rates, avoiding foreign debt, and limiting financial flows between countries.

KEY TERMS AND CONCEPTS

1982 debt crisis
absorption
Asian Tigers
Brady bonds
Brady Plan
capital flight
crony capitalism
debt burden
debt repudiation
debt service
Eurocurrency
exchange rate crisis

foreign exchange market intervention
intervention
North American Free Trade Area (NAFTA)
open market operations
primary budget surplus
recycle petrodollars
reversals of international financial flows
rollovers
three-person game
trade credits
trilemma
Washington consensus

PROBLEMS AND QUESTIONS

1. Use a diagram of the foreign exchange market to describe how central bank intervention can keep the exchange rate from changing. Explain precisely what the central bank must do if the equilibrium exchange rate is not the same as the target exchange rate and how the central bank's actions return the curves to an intersection at the target exchange rate.
2. Why is exchange rate intervention seldom successful in the long run? (Hint: Examine the conditions presented in the textbook necessary to keep the exchange rate at a specific value.)
3. Explain the difference or similarity between exchange rate intervention and open market operations. Then discuss the effects of each on the foreign exchange rate.
4. Use the equation that relates the spot exchange rate to the future expected exchange rate to show what it takes to keep the exchange rate fixed over time.
5. Explain precisely the *trilemma* that policy makers face in a global economy. What are policy makers' options with regard to the trilemma?
6. How does the trilemma explain exchange rate crises? What conditions must be present for an abrupt and large change in the exchange rate to cause a major economic slowdown?
7. In the 1982 debt crisis, why did the sharp decline in the value of the national currency not trigger a boom in exports that stimulated the overall economy, as some exchange rate models suggest, but instead caused a sharp downturn in investment and economic activity? (Hint: Explain exactly what happens when an exchange rate collapse triggers a financial crisis.)
8. Provide some examples of government economic policies that can conflict with a particular exchange rate. (Hint: Use the simple supply and demand model of the foreign exchange market and show how specific policy shifts affect either the supply or demand curve for a currency and shift equilibrium away from the target exchange rate.)
9. How much can a country reduce absorption without causing extreme misery for its citizens? What choices do policy makers have?
10. It is well known that the United States in 2010 had a government primary budget surplus of −8 percent, an economic growth rate of 1 percent, and a real interest rate of zero percent. Is the U.S. budget deficit sustainable? (Hint: Use the analysis from the section titled "Tracing the Path of Public Sector Debt: An Example.")

11. Explain the causes of the 1982 debt crisis, including the historical events that affected debt and borrowing up to 1982. What could the debtor countries and the creditor banks have done differently?
12. Review the conditions of the Brady Plan. Was it a fair plan for all parties concerned? Discuss.
13. Investigate the Washington consensus economic policies that were imposed on debtor countries under the Brady Plan. What do you think was the real purpose of the Washington consensus policies?
14. John Maynard Keynes once proposed a plan to make it impossible for countries to accumulate international debt. He claimed that international debt inevitably causes financial crises. Examine what would have been the benefits and costs of Keynes's arrangement for the countries that experienced one or more financial crises after 1980.

NOTES

1. Owen F. Humpage and William P. Osterberg (2000).

2. The term was coined by Alan Taylor and used in Maurice Obstfeld and Alan M. Taylor (1998).

3. These examples of "enforcement" of loan obligations are from "A Victory By Default?" *The Economist,* March 3, 2005.

4. Despite criticism of foreign investors, it was mostly domestic wealth that moved out of the country first, as documented by Jeffrey A. Frankel and Sergio L. Schmukler (1996).

5. Eric van Wincoop and Kei-Mu Yi (2000).

6. See, for example, Anne O. Krueger and Junho Yoo (2001), Robert J. Barro (2001), Yung Chul Park and Jong-Wha Lee (2001).

7. Abbigail J. Chiodo and Michael T. Owyang (2002).

8. Mike Esterl (2004), "Colombia Plans Peso Offering," *Wall Street Journal,* November 9.

9. See, for example, Barry Eichengreen and Ricardo Hausman (2002), "How to Eliminate Original Financial Sin," *Financial Times,* November 22. The widespread use of this Roman Catholic religious term reflects the Western cultural bias in international finance.

10. Ilan Goldfajn and Eduardo Refinetti Guardia (2003).

11. Ibid.

12. For a brief account of Brazil's recent economic performance, see "The Dangers of Tax and Spend," *The Economist,* March 3, 2005.

PART FIVE

THE HISTORY OF THE INTERNATIONAL MONETARY SYSTEM

Experience is the name we give to past mistakes, reform that which we give to future ones.

—Henry Wallich (1972)

Since the early 1970s, exchange rates between the major currencies of the world have been determined in the foreign exchange markets. These are not entirely free markets, of course, since many of the world's governments still actively interfere in them by supplying their own currencies or using their holdings of foreign reserves to demand foreign currencies. Nevertheless, exchange rates fluctuate daily in response to the shifts in market demand and supply driven by the traders, investors, arbitrageurs, speculators, and financial firms that operate in the integrated international economy. We have become accustomed to the current order, and we view the daily reports on exchange rates in the financial section of the newspaper on par with the daily stock and mutual fund reports. We do not have to go very far back in history, however, to see that the international monetary system did not always operate this way.

For example, during the latter part of the nineteenth century and the beginning of the twentieth century, nearly all governments followed the rules of a system called the *gold standard,* and exchange rates never changed or fluctuated. World War I forced most governments to suspend the rules of the gold standard, and for some years after the war exchange rates were left free to fluctuate. By the middle of the 1920s, however, most countries had gone back to following the rules of the gold standard. But just a few years later the Great Depression led most governments to abandon it, and the international monetary system disintegrated into a chaotic mix of trade restrictions, managed exchange rates, and tight controls on the trade and financial activities that are the source of supply and demand for foreign currencies.

After World War II, the Bretton Woods agreement among the major Western economies established a system of *pegged exchange rates* that kept exchange rates among the major convertible currencies constant for twenty-five years. This financial arrangement coincided with twenty-five years of the fastest economic growth the world has ever experienced. Nevertheless, in the early 1970s the pegged rates were abandoned by most of the major market economies in favor of the system of floating exchange rates that is still in place today. Not everyone was happy with this regime, however, and in 2002 twelve members of the European Union abandoned their national currencies, and the exchange rates between those currencies, in favor of a single currency called the euro.

Chapters 15 and 16 outline the history of the international monetary system. The focus is on the changes in foreign exchange arrangements and exchange rate policies over the past two hundred years. This historical account will show that some arrangements worked better than others, but in the end, all except the current system ultimately failed and were replaced. And, now, the growing imbalances in trade and financial flows call into question the sustainability of the current global monetary order. Chapter 17 examines our options and the likelihood that the world's governments will agree on reforming the international monetary system. Henry Wallach's quote is still relevant.

Describing the International Monetary System

Historians can be both descriptive and normative with regard to the events and outcomes they recall from the past. The three chapters of this part of the textbook are intended to present both the details of past international monetary systems and an assessment of how those systems affected human welfare.

To describe an international monetary system, economic historians often distinguish the incentives that drive the human behavior that generates the observed outcomes. In the case of a monetary system, the set of informal and formal incentives are normally referred to as the **international monetary order**. According to Nobel laureate Robert Mundell:

> An *order* . . . is a framework of laws, conventions, regulations, and mores that establish the setting of the system and the understanding of the environment by the participants in it. A monetary order is to a monetary system somewhat like a *constitution* is to a political system.[1]

John Maynard Keynes referred to the international monetary order as *the rules of the game* when he described the unwritten rules that policy makers followed during the time of the gold standard. This term is still often used by financial economists.[2] In the next three chapters, we will clearly distinguish each of the orders that characterized the distinct phases of the international monetary system over the last two centuries.

Judging the International Monetary System

In order to compare and judge the many exchange rate arrangements and other government rules, laws, and regulations that have defined the international monetary system over the centuries, we must first establish a set of criteria for determining how well a particular monetary order worked. Economists normally judge economic policies by how they affect human welfare. Therefore, we should judge an international monetary system by:

1. How well the economies participating in the system were able to maintain full employment in the short run;
2. How fast they grew and raised people's standards of living in the long run;
3. How well individual economies were able to integrate into the international economy and engage in welfare-enhancing international trade and investment;
4. Whether the system enhances or diminishes a government's ability to address what it sees as its country's economic, social, political, and institutional problems;
5. Whether the system tends to maintain price stability; and
6. How well the system distributes the gains and losses from international economic activity among countries and within individual economies.

As we describe the evolution of the international monetary system, we will base our judgments on these six criteria.

NOTES

1. Robert A. Mundell (1972), "The Future of the International Financial System," in A.L.K. Acheson, L.K. Chant, and M.F.J. Prachowny, *Bretton Woods Revisited,* Toronto: University of Toronto Press, p. 92.

2. See Ronald I. McKinnon (1993), p. 1.

CHAPTER 15

Early Monetary History: Ancient Times Through the End of the Gold Standard

> A closer look reveals that the economic repercussions of a stock market crash depend less on the severity of the crash than on the response of economic policy makers, particularly central bankers. After the 1929 crash, the Federal Reserve mistakenly focused its policies on preserving the gold value of the dollar rather than stabilizing the domestic economy.
>
> —Ben Bernanke (2000)

For much of human history, plunder and pillage of neighboring communities has been a common method for raising one group's economic welfare. Such one-way transfers do not require the use of money, just an army sufficiently large to subdue another society. However, there is ample evidence suggesting that for thousands of years separate groups and nations have also often found it convenient to engage in voluntary and mutually beneficial transactions. When one group's army is not large and the outcome of an invasion is in some doubt, most groups of people come to the conclusion that it is preferable to engage in voluntary exchanges. Voluntary exchanges between individuals and groups in different nations and regions are not easy to carry out, however.

Voluntary exchanges can be carried out using barter, which is the direct exchange of one product for another. Barter is a very costly method for exchanging products, however, because every seller has to find someone who has precisely the things the seller wants to acquire and is willing to exchange them for precisely the things the seller wants to sell, all at precisely the moment the seller wants to make the exchange. The coordination problems and costs of barter become especially onerous as economies develop and produce greater varieties of products, as wealth increases and people seek to store their wealth in assets of varying types, and as exchanges are carried out over greater distances.

Nearly three thousand years ago, people began to use scarce commodities that could serve as an intermediate **medium of exchange** and also as a **store of value**. Such commodities enabled people to exchange a much greater variety of products among a greater variety of people with wants and needs that extended over longer time horizons. When they became widely used, such commodities also served as *units of account* in which the values of the products bought and sold were measured. Commodities that simultaneously serve as medium of exchange, store of value, and unit of account are commonly referred to as **money**, of course. When people began to use money to conduct trade over long distances and to exchange the different moneys from different parts of the world, the international monetary system effectively came into existence.

BIRTH OF THE INTERNATIONAL MONETARY SYSTEM

Precious metals often served as money because they were scarce and, therefore, high in value relative to their weight, and pretty much indestructible. The benefits of using money over simple barter are so great that people resorted to using many other things as money when precious metals were not available. Some small island communities used rare seashells. In World War II prisoner of war camps, cigarettes were used as money. In war-ravaged Germany after World War II, when strict price controls were in effect and the new German monetary system had not yet been created, cigarettes, nylon stockings, and Parker fountain pens circulated as money. Today, beautifully printed pieces of paper do. We also exchange money over the Internet by changing the entries in digital accounts.

Throughout history, regions and political states tended to develop their own moneys. The development of different moneys complicated international trade because exporting and importing products across borders came to involve not only the movement of products, but also the exchange of moneys. When money came into general use and traders crossed borders to carry out exchanges of products, foreign exchange markets naturally came into being. The procedures and rules under which foreign exchange markets operate define the order of an **international monetary system**. In this section, we take a brief look at how the earlier international monetary systems operated.

Ancient Monetary Arrangements

Silver ingots whose weight and purity were guaranteed by the state were used as money in Babylon as early as 2000 B.C.E. Rare cowrie shells from islands in the Indian Ocean were used as money three thousand years ago throughout the world from China to Africa. The oldest known minted coins date back to 687 B.C.E. in the city-state Lydia in Asia Minor (modern-day Turkey).

In ancient times, the international monetary system consisted of a variety of minted coins plus an informal network of money changers located in the main cities where merchants from other cities and states frequently traded goods. In some cities and states, money changers were allowed to operate freely, in others they were restricted, and in some places they were banned altogether. In the cities where foreign trade flourished, money changers must have been tolerated; payments between merchants from different places could not have been made without them.

The rise of the Roman Empire brought the entire Mediterranean region under the jurisdiction of one political power. The political capital of the empire, the city of Rome, ran a considerable trade deficit with the rest of the empire, which was covered by the inflow of tax revenues from the provinces throughout the region.[1] Roman taxation, which had to be paid in the form of coinage, expanded the use of money throughout the economy since taxpayers had to earn coins in order to pay taxes. The control of the Mediterranean region by the Romans also created a large free trade area with a single currency, not unlike today's euro area. However, the Roman Empire traded with many other regions of the world, such as present-day India, China, and Africa, which issued their own coins. Roman coins have been found in foreign regions, which suggests that these coins must have been exchanged for goods or moneys from these regions. It also shows that during the Roman Empire, distant nations engaged in international trade that was facilitated by the use of money and the exchange of moneys.

The Growing Complexity of International Finance

By the late Middle Ages, certain coins dominated international trade. Especially popular for international trade were gold *florins* issued by the city of Florence in Italy. Venetian *ducats* were also greatly valued throughout Europe and Asia. The florin was minted in large denominations, and

Florentine minters were trusted to maintain their coins' gold content. Florins were, therefore, trusted and highly valued.

In order to better accommodate long-distance trade, in the twelfth and thirteenth centuries the medieval fairs in the French region of Champagne established the use of "letters of fair," which were paper assets that let merchants accumulate debts and credits from one year to the next.[2] Storage depositories for precious metals and coins began offering checking services on those deposits, and then they evolved into full-fledged lending institutions that even provided overdraft privileges to reputable customers. The earliest surviving check was drawn on the Castellani bank of Florence in 1368 and made out to a draper in payment for black cloth for a funeral. The use of bank drafts, or checks, proved to be more convenient and safer than carrying coins from place to place. Money changers gradually evolved into bankers, and some banks began to exchange checks denominated in different moneys, creating commercial banking institutions that provided both loans and foreign exchange. As described in Chapter 12, foreign exchange over-the-counter markets are still operated by large international banks today.

Bank drafts also provided a practical way to get around the Roman Catholic Church's ban on charging interest. Since bank drafts in foreign currencies involved some degree of exchange risk, the church permitted some discounting of the drafts. Raymond De Roover (1948) suggests that the development of bank drafts was an early example of how international transactions between offshore banks were used to overcome "domestic" banking regulations.

In fourteenth-century Europe, exchange rates changed frequently. Official records of exchange rates were meticulously maintained, and the daily closing exchange rates in Venice and Florence in Italy, and Bruges in what is today Belgium, are still available to researchers. News of exchange rates was carried across Europe by the same couriers who carried business letters, bills of exchange, and other business and bank documents. Not until the nineteenth century would railroads, steamships, the telegraph, and finally the telephone accelerate the speed of communications beyond what it was in the fourteenth century.[3]

Fiat Money

The arrival of paper money not convertible into any commodity complicated the job of money changers, and it brought the potential for greater instability in the international monetary system. With paper money, the value of a currency came to depend on the value of goods that people *expected* to be able to purchase with the money, called its **purchasing power**. A currency's value was no longer measured by the generally accepted worth of precious metals incorporated in coins or into which paper was convertible. Paper money was usually officially sanctioned by a government, which is why paper money not officially backed by some other commodity of value is often referred to as **fiat money**, money authorized by government fiat. Because fiat money was inexpensive to create—it took only a printing press—revenue-hungry governments were often tempted to print too much, which creates inflation. Inflation undermines the purchasing power of money, and expectations of divergent rates of inflation across countries will then cause exchange rates to change. Exchange rates between fiat moneys are therefore inherently more volatile than the exchange rates between moneys fully backed by or actually consisting of scarce commodities like gold or silver, whose supply cannot be easily increased.

THE ORIGINS OF THE GOLD STANDARD

Most people are surprised to learn that the monetary order known as the **gold standard** existed for only a brief period before World War I. Even though money had often been closely related to gold, or made out of gold, for several millennia, there are important differences between gold-backed moneys and the worldwide gold standard that prevailed between 1870 and 1914.

The gold standard had its origins in Britain's high inflation during the Napoleonic wars in the early nineteenth century, which had been caused by the Bank of England's printing of large amounts of pound notes to finance the war effort. The government had stopped offering to back the notes with gold when, in 1797, the amount of pound notes in circulation began to exceed the amount of gold in its possession. The pound thus became a fiat currency, and the government printed enough currency to cause price inflation. After the war, the landowners and merchants who dominated Parliament sought to prevent future losses of purchasing power by passing the Coinage Act of 1816, which instructed the government to mint gold coins in accordance with strict purity standards.[4] Then, in 1819, Parliament passed another law that required the Bank of England to redeem its pound notes for gold at the fixed parity rate established in the 1816 Coinage Act. With this regulation, the Bank of England would no longer be able to print pounds without limitation. As hoped, inflation came to an abrupt end. At this point, Britain was on a national gold standard, but the rest of the world still had different rules and different currency standards.

Why Britain Had a Gold Standard and Not a Silver Standard

According to economic historian Barry Eichengreen (1996, p. 7), the gold standard "was one of the great monetary accidents of modern times." One reason for the "accident" was that in 1717, when Sir Isaac Newton briefly served as master of the British mint, he for some reason offered to buy and sell silver at a lower price relative to gold than did other European countries. This discrepancy in relative prices created a profitable arbitrage opportunity for anyone buying silver in Britain, hauling it overseas, trading it for relatively less expensive gold, hauling the gold back to Britain, and then converting the gold back to a larger amount of silver than they started out with. Of course, the British mint soon ran out of silver and ended up with only gold in its vaults. Therefore, when the British Parliament passed the Coinage Act in 1816, they linked the pound to gold because that is what the British treasury had available. Had Newton set the prices of silver and gold differently, Britain, and eventually the whole world, might have gone to a silver standard. History over the past two centuries might have been completely different as well.

The International Gold Standard

When Britain adopted a gold standard in the early nineteenth century, other countries had different monetary arrangements. For example, following its independence from Britain, the United States maintained a policy of **bimetallism**, which was the simultaneous circulation of both gold and silver coins. France, Belgium, Switzerland, and Italy formed the **Latin Monetary Union**, in which each of the four countries was authorized to issue identical silver and gold coins that were legal means of payment throughout the region. (The euro, introduced in Europe in 2002, is thus not the first attempt at creating a single currency for European countries.) China and most other Far Eastern countries had long favored silver as a store of wealth, as had most other European countries engaged in trade with Asia, such as Holland, Spain, and Portugal.

But then the tide turned in favor of gold. In 1870, newly unified Germany opted for the gold standard after the Franco-Prussian War. Germany's sales of its stock of silver and purchases of gold altered the relative prices of gold and silver in Europe, and discoveries of huge silver deposits in the United States and elsewhere further depressed the price of silver. Silver soon began flowing to countries that had bimetallic or exclusive silver standards that guaranteed a fixed price for silver. The inflows of silver, which was converted to currency, increased the money supply and raised prices. The fear of inflation led the Latin Monetary Union to switch from backing its currency with silver to gold in 1878. With large countries like Germany and France joining Britain on the gold standard, most other European countries soon followed suit.

Christopher Meissner (2005) characteristics such momentum toward a single worldwide system as a type of network effect. The more trade and investment partners are on the gold standard, the more advantageous it becomes for every other country to also be on the gold standard. J. Ernesto Lopez-Cordova and Meissner (2003) in fact found strong evidence that countries on the gold standard traded much more with each other than they did with non–gold standard countries. Adherence to the gold standard also gave countries better access to international capital markets; it was taken as evidence of their commitment to stable fiscal and monetary policies.

The Order of the International Gold Standard

By 1879, most of the world's currencies were freely convertible into gold at specific gold parities. Under the rules of the gold standard, the order that governments adhered to was the following:

1. Fix an official gold price, or **gold parity**, for the national currency.
2. Permit the conversion of gold into domestic money and domestic money into gold at the parity price.
3. Eliminate all restrictions on foreign exchange transactions and allow the import and export of gold.

The weak point of this order was the temptation that revenue-hungry governments had to issue more paper currency than they could back with the gold stored in their vaults. If holders of paper money suspected that the government was printing too much money, they would "run" on gold, and when the government ran out of gold, it would have to suspend *convertibility* of money into gold and effectively leave the gold standard. Ronald McKinnon (1993) described how, in order to maintain faith in the system, governments effectively followed at least two other implicit rules of the game:

4. Keep the domestic money closely linked to the stock of gold reserves.
5. If the central bank must serve as a lender of last resort in the case of short-term credit crises in the domestic banking sector, always charge interest rates well above those charged in the credit markets in order to keep such lending to a minimum.

The latter was known as **Bagehot's rule**, in honor of a former director of the Bank of England who rigorously applied it to ensure that private banks would borrow from the central bank only when they truly faced an emergency. Bagehot's rule gave the central bank some room to act as a lender of last resort in emergencies without immediately raising fears that it was abusing its power to print money.

The Gold Standard's Fixed Exchange Rates

As long as governments followed the rules of the game, exchange rates remained fixed. For example, because with the **Coinage Act of 1816** the British government established free convertibility of pounds for gold at the parity rate of 4.24 pounds per 1 ounce of gold, and the U.S. government offered to exchange dollars at the rate of $20.67 per ounce after 1872, the parities in effect defined the exchange rate as 4.24 pounds per 20.67 dollars, or £1.00 = $4.87 over the gold standard period. As long as the governments of Britain and the United States maintained the full convertibility of currency to gold and gold to currency at the stated parities, the exchange rate could not differ very much from £1.00 = $4.87.

Suppose that the supply curve of British pounds shifts so that it intersects the demand curve at £1.00 = $4.00, perhaps because there is a sudden surge in demand for U.S. products in England or

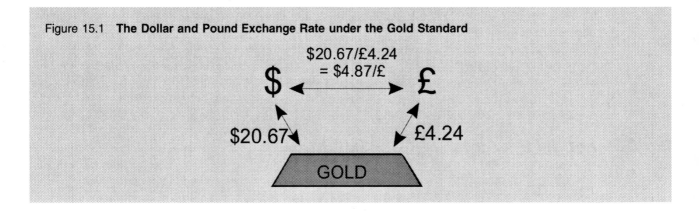

Figure 15.1   **The Dollar and Pound Exchange Rate under the Gold Standard**

$20.67/£4.24
= $4.87/£

$ ←————→ £

$20.67   £4.24

GOLD

increased lending to U.S. borrowers by British savers. Clearly, it would not be advantageous for English importers or U.S. borrowers to convert pounds to dollars at the £1.00 = $4.00 exchange rate, thus getting only 4 dollars for every pound spent. English importers or U.S. borrowers should, instead, use their pounds to buy gold from the Bank of England at the official price of £4.24 per ounce, ship the gold to the United States, and exchange it at the dollar price of gold, $20.67 per ounce, at the U.S. Treasury in Washington. This effectively gives them $4.87 for every pound. Thus, if the exchange rate fell much below £1.00 = $4.87, gold would move from Britain to the United States. Remember, another gold standard rule was the free import and export of gold.

How the Gold Standard Really Worked

It practice, it was not necessary for importers of goods or international borrowers to demand gold in Britain and ship it to the United States. If short-run shifts in the supply and demand for foreign exchange moved equilibrium away from the gold parity exchange rate, expectations were that the problem would correct itself; after all, respectable governments adhered to the rules of the game! Thus, speculators would "bet" that the gold parity rate would prevail by buying the currency that was slightly depreciated with the temporarily appreciated currency, fully expecting to capture the gains from selling high and buying low. Such speculation would, of course, cause the exchange rate to move back toward its gold parity level. So long as there was faith in governments' commitment to the gold standard, speculation was a stabilizing force, and short-run variations in trade and financial flows did not greatly upset the system of fixed exchange rates.

Nor did governments always match the money supply to their gold stock. Changes in the gold stocks statistically "explain" little more than half of the changes in money growth rates during the period 1880–1913. A likely explanation for the stable exchange rates was the large volume of capital movements between countries in the late 1800s and early 1900s. Especially important were the large flows of capital from Great Britain to the newly settled economies of the world, such as the United States, Australia, Canada, and Argentina. Railroads, electric power plants, harbor facilities, mines, and a great variety of other capital projects in these countries were financed with British money. Capital flows from the United States and the major European economies also played a role, and they were often channeled through London. These capital flows, which were large relative to overall economic activity even compared to capital flows in today's global economy, offset trade deficits and kept supply and demand for currencies in equilibrium at the gold parities.

Also important for the stability of exchange rates was the Bank of England's manipulation of interest rates to influence international capital flows. Whenever gold stocks fell in Britain, perhaps because trade deficits were causing gold to flow out of the country, the Bank of England would raise interest rates in order to attract financial flows back to Britain. Such fluctuations in British interest rates and, therefore, financial flows into and out of Britain often hurt foreign countries that relied on borrowing through the London financial market, but that did not deter the dominant colonial power of the world, Great Britain, from protecting its own interests and reputation under the gold standard system.

The governments of the major European countries also cooperated in dealing with pressures against one another's currencies. For example, after the collapse of Barings, a large London bank, as a result of defaults on its risky loans to the government of Argentina, investors questioned whether, after a period of exceptionally large outflows of saving to foreign borrowers, the Bank of England had enough gold reserves to both serve as a lender of last resort to Barings and defend pound convertibility as well. Gold began flooding out of England, forcing Bank of England officials to quickly arrange loans of gold from the Bank of France and the Russian state bank. An overnight emergency shipment from Paris permitted the Bank of England to continue selling gold until the panic subsided. According to Eichengreen (1996, p. 8):

> The dilemma for central banks and governments became whether to provide only as much credit as was consistent with the gold-standard statutes or to supply the additional liquidity expected of a lender of last resort. That this dilemma did not bring the gold-standard edifice tumbling down was attributable to luck and to political conditions that allowed for international solidarity in times of crisis.

Despite these close calls, there was confidence in the permanence of the gold standard. Banks, savers, and governments seldom worried about exchange rate risk, and they routinely shifted large amounts of their wealth across borders, secure in their expectations that exchange rates would not change and undermine their foreign assets. This confidence was, allegedly, dependent on governments and their central banks following the order of the gold standard. This period is further evidence of how lenders, investors, banks, policy makers, and everyone else interpret recent history as if it represents the normal long-run situation. By the late 1800s, the gold standard's parity exchange rates had become Keynes's *conventional model* or DeGrauwe's *anchor* discussed in Chapter 12.

In the long run, governments did behave in ways that appeared to adhere to the rules of the game. This was evidenced by the data on money supplies and prices during the late 1800s and early 1900s, the heyday of the gold standard. Long-run prices roughly responded to the supply of gold because national money supplies did not deviate much from actual supplies of gold. Until 1890, prices around the world gradually declined as economic activity expanded more rapidly than the gold-based world money supply. By the mid-1890s, however, the development of the potassium cyanide process for extracting gold from ore and a series of major gold discoveries in Alaska, South Africa, Russia, and elsewhere expanded the money supply more rapidly than overall economic activity. Thus, with money supplies tied to gold, prices trended consistently upward between 1895 and 1914.

Figure 15.2 illustrates that the overall price levels in the United States and Canada just before the end of the gold standard period were about the same as at the start of the gold standard. This price stability is held up by advocates of a "return to gold" as a justification to abandon today's exchange rate regime for a new gold standard order. Figure 15.2 shows, however, that there was a long period during which the trend in prices was downward, followed after 1895 by a nearly continuous upward trend in price levels throughout the world. There were also year-to-year fluctuations in prices. But there were no high rates of inflation similar to those we experienced under floating exchange rates in the latter three decades of the twentieth century.

International Investment in the Late Nineteenth Century

International borrowing and lending grew very rapidly under the gold standard in the late 1800s. International financial flows actually exceeded the huge international flows we observe today when

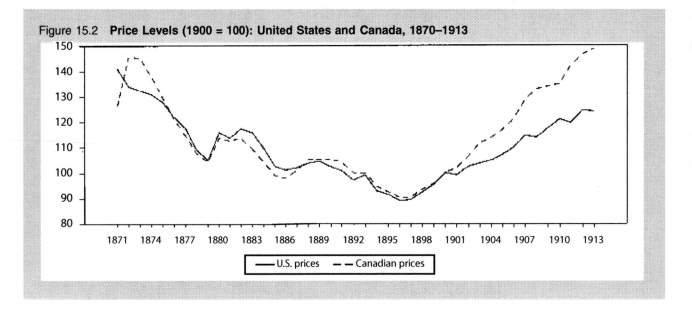

Figure 15.2 **Price Levels (1900 = 100): United States and Canada, 1870–1913**

they are measured as a proportion of gross domestic product (GDP). For example, over the period 1880–1914, annual capital outflows averaged about 5 percent of GDP in the United Kingdom, nearly half of its savings, and reached a phenomenal 9 percent in 1913. Outflows of savings frequently reached 5 and 6 percent of GDP in France. Germany averaged capital outflows equal to 2 percent of its GDP over the same 1880–1914 period.

Outflows of savings from one country of course imply inflows elsewhere in the world. The major importers of savings in the late nineteenth century were the newly populated countries, such as Australia, Canada, Argentina, the United States, and New Zealand. Sweden and Norway were also major importers of capital during the late 1800s. These were all rapidly growing economies, and returns to investment there were high. During the 1880s, inflows of foreign savings averaged nearly 10 percent of GDP in Australia, before falling to a more modest 2.5 percent during the 1890s. Of course, 2.5 percent is still very high even by the standards of the 1990s. Savings inflows into Canada exceeded 6 percent of GDP in the 1880s, averaged about 4.5 percent in the 1890s, rose to 7 percent in the first decade of the twentieth century, and reached an astounding 14 percent of GDP between 1910 and 1913. As a percentage of total investment, foreign saving accounted for nearly 35 percent of total saving in New Zealand and Canada over the entire 1880–1914 period, and nearly 25 percent in Australia and Sweden. In contrast, foreign savings financed less than 4 percent of all investment in developing countries of the world during the 1980s, and even in the 1990s foreign saving financed only 10 percent of investment in developing economies. The remainder of international investment occurred among the developed economies in North America, Europe, and the Pacific.

A large portion of international lending in the 1800s was in the form of bonds that were intermediated by British investment banks, or **investment houses** as they were commonly referred to, in London. The London investment houses earned hefty fees of between 1.5 and 4.0 percentage points.[5] The role of the investment houses included negotiating the bonds' terms and promoting their sale, and the advance of funds to the issuers of the bonds in anticipation of the sale. The investment houses also played an important role when defaults occurred because large groups of diverse bondholders cannot negotiate as easily with defaulters as can a single bank or small group of private banks. The investment houses acted as principal negotiators on behalf of the bondholders, and records show that default settlements were usually relatively favorable to the bondholders.

In many ways, the international financial system became tightly integrated during the gold standard period. With London at the center, international banking and financial trading spread to all corners of the world. Maurice Obstfeld and Alan M. Taylor (2004, pp. 23–24) describe the period as follows:

> Finance also advanced through the development of a broader array of private debt and equity instruments, through the expansion of insurance activities, and through international trade in government bonds. By 1900, the key currencies and instruments were known everywhere and formed the basis for an expanding world commercial network, whose rise was equally meteoric. Bills of exchange, bond finance, equity issues, foreign direct investments, and many other types of transaction were by then quite common among the core countries, and among a growing number of nations at the periphery.

This is not to say that financial markets were as "deep" in terms of variety of instruments as they are today, but their worldwide development was without a doubt unprecedented. With the intermediation of London, and given the relatively high per capita income in the British economy, it was British investors who financed many of the world's railroads, electric utilities, and other infrastructure projects.

THE UNITED STATES AND THE GOLD STANDARD

The previous discussion is somewhat misleading in its optimistic interpretation of the historical facts. Confidence in the system was not shared by everyone. There was strong opposition to the gold standard in the United States, even though the leadership did not in fact end up reducing the government's commitment to the system. But a difference of just a few percentage points in the vote totals in the 1896 presidential election would probably have led the United States to reject the gold standard and its rules of the game.

Social Conflict and the Gold Standard

In the late 1800s, several fundamental political battles were raging in the United States. There was conflict between industrial interests in the eastern and Great Lakes regions of the country and the farming sector in many midwestern states. There was also conflict between labor and capital in general, which began to show up in the form of labor strikes and the violent repression of strikers by private security forces, police, and National Guard troops. In addition there were clashes between pro-immigrant and anti-immigrant groups, especially in the early 1890s, when the U.S. economy sank into a deep and lengthy recession and experienced high unemployment. These diverging economic interests often showed up in the ongoing political debate between the Republican Party and the Populist Party, which was closely allied with the national Democratic Party.

The Populists were against the gold standard, which they saw, correctly, as the cause of the gradual deflation that often made life difficult for debtors, which is what most farmers were most of the time. Farmers routinely borrowed to finance the purchase of land, equipment, and the seeding of their crops. Under the rules of the international gold standard, the U.S. money supply could expand only as rapidly as the amount of gold in the government vaults increased. With the U.S. economy growing quickly in the late 1800s because of rapid immigration, large investments in industry and railroads, and rapid technological progress, the supply of gold did not keep up with the expansion of real GDP. Recall the gradual decline in prices through the mid-1890s shown in Figure 15.2; that meant that *real* interest rates were even higher than the already high nominal rate.

The United States also did not yet have a central bank, so the amount of money in circulation was effectively a function of how much paper currency the U.S. Treasury printed in response to gold purchases and sales, and how much the banking system multiplied that monetary base. In the latter half of the nineteenth century, the money supply was very volatile as cyclical variations in economic activity in the young capitalist economy were aggravated by the banking system's role in expanding the money supply. **Bank runs** were frequent occurrences, and financial panics generated frequent recessions.

Bimetallism and William Jennings Bryan

Most opponents of the gold standard promoted the alternative of *bimetallism,* the pre–gold standard U.S. system that backed the money supply with the combined stocks of gold and silver. The perception was that with more commodities backing money, there would be more money in circulation and, therefore, prices would be higher and interest rates lower. There were some gaps of logic in the thinking of the *bimetallists,* but in principal their linkage of money supplies and prices was correct, as Milton Friedman and Anna Jacobson Schwartz (1963) and Friedman (1990a) would later point out. No politician used the issue of gold better than William Jennings Bryan. A Populist from the agricultural state of Nebraska, Bryan enthralled the Democratic Party convention and gained the party's nomination to oppose William McKinley, the pro–gold standard Republican candidate, in the 1896 presidential election.

Bryan had been given little chance of winning the nomination at the Democratic convention in Chicago in the summer of 1896. Several other bimetallists were ahead of him in the party pecking order, and a number of party leaders from industrial states openly supported maintaining the gold standard. When the support for the leading candidates faltered, however, Bryan made his famous "Cross of Gold" speech, which still stands as one of the most emotional and stirring political speeches in American history. It was part populist rhetoric:

> There are two ideas of government. There are those who believe that, if you will only legislate to make the well-to-do prosperous, their prosperity will leak through on those below. The Democratic idea, however, has been that if you legislate to make the masses prosperous, their prosperity will find its way up through every class which rests upon them.

Bryan also directly appealed to midwestern farmers:

> You come to us and tell us that the great cities are in favor of the gold standard; we reply that the great cities rest upon our broad and fertile prairies. Burn down your cities and leave our farms, and your cities will spring up again as if by magic; but destroy our farms and the grass will grow in the streets of every city in the country.

And Bryan fully exploited nationalism by depicting the gold standard being imposed on the United States by foreigners:

> It is the issue of 1776 over again. Our ancestors, when but three millions in number had the courage to declare their political independence of every other nation; shall we, their descendants, when we have grown to seventy millions, declare that we are less independent than our forefathers?
> . . . Having behind us the producing masses of this nation and the world, supported by the commercial interests, the laboring interests and the toilers everywhere, we will answer their demand for a gold standard by saying to them: You shall not press down upon the brow of labor this crown of thorns, you shall not crucify mankind upon a cross of gold.

Bryan concluded the speech with his arms spread as if he were being crucified, and the convention burst into long, enthusiastic applause. The little-known politician from Nebraska was voted in as the Populist/Democratic candidate the next day.[6]

Bryan nearly became president of the United States in 1896 despite being outspent by 30 to 1 by the Republican candidate, William McKinley. A number of prominent fellow Democrats openly opposed Bryan's anti-gold campaign, and most of the country's major newspapers actively supported McKinley. Bryan nevertheless received 47 percent of the popular vote to McKinley's 51 percent. Bryan's voter support, based largely on his stance on the gold standard, surprised many pundits. Feelings had clearly been inflamed by the various conflicts between urban and rural communities, workers and employers, and natives and immigrants.

The United States Remains on the Gold Standard

After 1896 the gold issue lost its urgency, largely because gradual inflation replaced the gradual deflation that had characterized the economy up to the early 1890s. As Figure 15.2 showed, by 1913 overall prices had risen back to their 1870 level. Bryan again ran for president in 1900, but without the emotional issue of the gold standard and a recovered economy, he lost by a much greater margin. It nevertheless remains an important fact that in 1896 the United States came very close to electing a populist candidate who almost certainly would have taken the United States off the gold standard.

Bryan's challenge to the established regime in 1896 had created a mini-panic that briefly sent interest rates soaring and disrupted financial transactions. What the consequences of the United States abandoning the gold standard would have been makes for interesting speculation.

Several economists have seriously examined what would have happened if the United States had never adopted the gold standard and had stayed with bimetallism. For example, Friedman (1990a) used a monetarist model to estimate what the world would have looked like under the assumption that the United States had continued to freely mint silver dollars after 1873 at the pre–Civil War silver content. He concluded that the world price level would have been more stable than the actual alternation of deflation followed by inflation under the actual gold standard. François Velde (2002) uses a different model and concludes that:

> The U.S. would have remained a bimetallic country for twenty years, and its price level (indeed, price levels around the world) would have been more stable. However, abandonment of silver by other countries would have ultimately forced the U.S. off bimetallism and onto the silver standard, where it would have been alone with China. The sharp depreciation of silver in the early 20th century would have induced considerable inflation. In short, the stability of the price level in the 1870s and 1880s would have been paid with higher inflation in the 1890s.

There is considerable debate about whether the persistent deflation between 1870 and 1895 was harmful to human welfare. Michael Bordo, John Landon Lane, and Angela Redish (2004) show that the deflation during the gold standard was the result of rapid growth of aggregate supply that exceeded the somewhat slower, but still rapid, growth of aggregate demand. Bordo et al. argue that deflation is bad only if it is the result of declining aggregate demand that exceeds the decline in aggregate supply, as during the Great Depression, for example. But the period from 1880 to 1914 was one of rapid economic growth fueled by scientific discoveries and technological advances. Real wages consistently rose, and even in years of declining prices, nominal wages did not decline as rapidly as prices. According to Thomas F. Dernberg (1989, p. 377):

> Adjustment in such an environment of growth is far easier and less painful than in a stationary or stagnant one. For example, with productivity and real wages growing rapidly, adjustment to a payments deficit could be achieved by a barely noticeable slowdown in the rate of wage increase rather than by the need to lower the absolute wage level, which would be required in the absence of growth in labor productivity.

Indeed, world GDP had never grown as rapidly as it did during the gold standard period, and technological progress was also unprecedented. Electricity, the telephone, the horseless carriage, the airplane, the record player, central heating, the refrigerator, and mass vaccinations against disease were just a few of the many revolutionary new technologies and products introduced to the world. But people also had to withstand the effects of frequent economic booms and busts, high unemployment, and high indebtedness made worse by price deflation. Economic growth was certainly volatile, and given that there was no social safety net and extended families were rare in a country of recent immigrants, economic volatility weighed heavily on people's perceptions of well-being.

Evaluating the International Gold Standard

The gold standard was a qualified success. Table 15.1 presents a "report card" on the gold standard based on the criteria laid out in the introduction to Part Five of this textbook. As mentioned above, economic growth was unprecedented, though it came along with substantial instability and frequent surges in unemployment. Furthermore, the world became much more economically integrated as world merchandise exports tripled between 1880 and 1914 in real terms. It is impossible to say with complete certainty that it was the gold standard that caused the unprecedented economic growth, however. Perhaps it was the good economic conditions that allowed the gold standard to operate successfully. It is safe to conclude that, at the very least, the gold standard was not a serious impediment to international economic integration, economic growth, and rising living standards in Europe and North America. Overall, prices were fairly stable; there were none of the episodes of rapid inflation that had characterized periods of war before the gold standard and that would become even more common throughout periods of both peace and war in the twentieth century.

The gold standard did not satisfy the first, fourth, fifth, and sixth criteria of success for monetary orders nearly as well, however. The rules of the gold standard, notably the prohibition against engaging in active monetary policy, often caused financial panics and severe ups and downs in economic activity in many countries. The order of the gold standard mandated that central banks keep the money supply in line with gold stocks to maintain convertibility.

Furthermore, not all countries gained similar increases in standards of living. Some countries raised the standard of living of their citizens by multiples of 2, 3, or even more, but many parts of the world saw only modest gains. Countries with one third of the world's population, including China and India, experienced no gains in real per capita income at all during the gold standard. The manipulation of interest rates by the Bank of England to balance Britain's payments caused international capital flows to vary from year to year, and the fluctuations in investment flows occasionally caused liquidity problems and defaults on foreign loans in Latin America and Asia. The gold standard did not prove to be automatic and self-correcting. Frequent adjustments by the Bank of England and other central banks were necessary to maintain credibility and prevent runs on currencies, and, therefore, suspensions of convertibility.

In terms of the trilemma, illustrated in Figure 15.3, under the gold standard policy makers effectively chose **capital mobility** and a fixed exchange rate over policy independence. The exchange rates of all the major currencies remained unchanged for over thirty-five years. But individual governments had no power to carry out long-run monetary and fiscal policies in response to domestic economic conditions. Of course, not all governments were interested in using macroeconomic policies at that time in history. The United States did not have a central bank until 1913, and Bryan's political campaign notwithstanding, governments largely ignored unemployment and social suffering.

THE AGONIZING END OF THE GOLD STANDARD

The world changed during the nineteenth century. Economic growth and technological progress were unprecedented, and few people in the world's major economies failed to see their lives change drastically during their lifetimes. The century also saw unprecedented international economic inte-

Table 15.1

Report Card for the International Gold Standard (1870–1914)

1. Stability/employment	Fail
2. Economic growth	Pass
3. Globalization	Pass
4. Policy independence	Fail
6. Mutually beneficial	Fail
5. Price stability	Pass

Figure 15.3 **The Trilemma during the Gold Standard (1926–1931)**

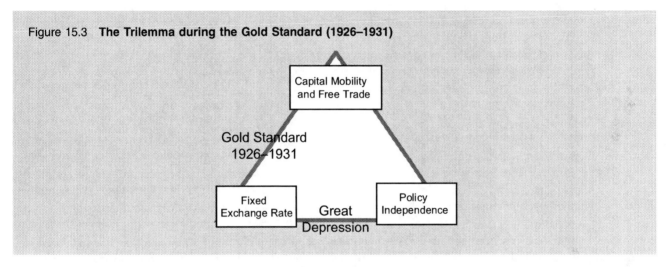

gration. Jules Verne's popular novel, *Around the World in 80 Days,* with its steamships, railroads, telegraph messages, hot air balloons, global banking services, and widespread use of the British pound, epitomized the times. Recall John Maynard Keynes's (1920, pp. 11–12) description of life in London just before the outbreak of World War I:

> The inhabitant of London could order by telephone, sipping his morning tea in bed, the various products of the whole earth, in such quantity as he might see fit, and reasonably expect their early delivery upon his doorstep; he could at the same moment and by the same means adventure his wealth in the natural resources and new enterprises of any quarter of the world, and share, without exertion or even trouble, in their prospective fruits and advantages; or he could decide to couple the security of his fortunes with the good faith of the townspeople of any substantial municipality in any continent that fancy or information might recommend.

This integrated world economy came to a sudden end in 1914. World War I broke out, and many countries promptly suspended convertibility. In fact, nearly all countries effectively abandoned convertibility within the first year of the war.

Back to "Normal" after World War I?

World War I was fought almost exclusively in Europe, but millions of soldiers from non-European countries and colonies participated and died in the conflict. The historian Margaret MacMillan (2001, pp. xxv–xxvi) argues that the war's toll was largely human: "Away from the battlefields,

Europe still looked much the same. The great cities remained, the railway lines were more or less intact, ports still functioned." But the psychological effects of the huge loss of human life during the "Great War" came at a time when the human psyche already had to deal with unprecedented changes in the economic, social, and political structures of the world.

After the war, world leaders declared their intention to establish a lasting peace. In practice, however, the leaders of most countries sought to return to the prewar economic environment described by Keynes. The leaders of most countries (those of the new communist regime in Russia and in Europe's overseas colonies were the dissenters) also accepted that a return to the gold standard was necessary. The "normal, certain, and permanent" state as described by Keynes could not be so easily brought back, however. New political forces emerged after the war. Russia threw out its feudal society in favor of communism. In Europe and in its cultural offshoots in Latin America, political systems slid toward fascism when the pre–World War I order could not be revived. And where democracy was strong enough to resist totalitarianism, that same democracy forced governments to pay more attention to the interests of broader segments of their populations. As already seen in the United States in 1896, the gold standard and its implicit rules constrained government policy in ways that disadvantaged many segments of society.

The Costs of the War

The cost of the First World War was large when compared with the costs of earlier wars. The number of dead was in the millions. Nearly all governments had been forced to stop redeeming their currencies for gold because they had had to print money to finance the war. All countries involved in the war suffered severe economic upheaval that would not be easy to set right. Entire industrial sectors had been converted to wartime production, and the well-established international trade patterns had been completely disrupted. The cost of recovery was underestimated by most policy makers.

Yet policy makers' biggest postwar failure was their inability to see that the world had changed in fundamental ways, and that these changes had been brewing well before World War I broke out. That is, there was no "normal" to go back to. The rapid economic growth and the extraordinary technological progress achieved during the decades before the war had changed not only the way the global economy worked, but also the political and social environments within which policy makers had to operate. The most obvious evidence of the changing economic, political, and social conditions staring the policy makers in the face was the war itself. World War I was the result of fundamental economic, political, and social forces that, obviously, policy makers and their constituencies did not grasp.

Again, Keynes (1920, p. 12) provided insight into prewar attitudes:

> The projects and politics of militarism and imperialism, of racial and cultural rivalries, of monopolies, restrictions, and exclusion, which were to play the serpent to this paradise, were little more than the amusements of his daily newspaper, and appeared to exercise almost no influence at all on the ordinary course of social and economic life.

Imperial rivalries had been growing for years, especially between the early colonial powers like Britain, France, and the Netherlands, and the latecomers to imperialism like Germany and Italy. These rivalries pushed leaders to negotiate political and military alliances, and as is well known, it was those alliances that caused the rather insignificant murder of an archduke to quickly escalate into a world war. But the alliances were popular in the uncertain world of the early twentieth century. Individual countries feared being isolated, so they rushed to join either the Central Powers, which included Germany, Austria-Hungary, Romania, and the Ottoman Empire, or the Triple Entente of Britain, France, and Russia. On top of this international political mosaic, there were ethnic tensions within many of the larger countries. Governments fomented growing nationalism and militarism with the help of an aggressive press willing to stimulate people's basest instincts to sell newspapers. Rapid technological advances in weaponry also inflated assessments of likely military victories, which meant that the world was poised for war. Yet very few people saw the changes, even after the war.

The unexpectedly long four-year war did not sort things out. The same conflicts that sparked the war severely hampered efforts by the world's leaders to restore order. The failure of the post–World War I order was not the result of a lack of effort to deal with the pressing issues. Rather, it seemed as though the complexity of human society had outpaced human comprehension, rising technological progress and literacy notwithstanding.

Reviving the Gold Standard under Changed Circumstances

When World War I ended in 1918, foreign exchange markets expected the gold standard to be resumed. According to Leland Yeager (1976, p. 311):

> Towards the end of the war speculation centered on belief that exchange rates would soon return to "normal." At the time of the armistice, the rates of the Netherlands, Spain, the United States, Great Britain and the Empire, Japan, France, Sweden, Argentina, Brazil, and Italy diverged remarkably little from the prewar pattern, considering the circumstances.

An immediate return to the old rules was simply not possible. For one thing, the United States had stayed on the gold standard; because it had supplied large amounts of arms, food, raw materials, and many other goods to the belligerents, it had run very large trade surpluses and accumulated large amounts of gold.

The war years were inflationary. For example, the U.S. Federal Reserve Bank converted the inflows of gold to money as the rules of the game mandated. Inflation ensued, and U.S. prices doubled during the war. Most other countries, no longer bound by the gold standard, had printed money to finance their war efforts and, therefore, also suffered high rates of inflation. Because inflation had increased all countries' price levels, in 1919 there was not enough gold in the world to back all of the currency in circulation if the old gold parities were applied. Furthermore, since everyone's rates of inflation had been different, the prewar exchange rates did not reflect postwar relative purchasing power parities of the currencies.

Unable to restore convertibility, most countries let exchange rates float freely during the years immediately after World War I. At the same time, most policy makers prepared for the world's return to the gold standard at the old gold parities. For example, the U.S. Federal Reserve Bank tightened monetary policy, and prices fell by nearly 20 percent between 1920 and 1922. Deflation raised the real interest rate, and unemployment surged. After 1921 the Federal Reserve opted to just maintain price stability rather than try to push prices down any further.

Other countries, most notably Britain, also instituted deflationary monetary policy in order to return to the gold standard under the old gold parities. These deflationary policies were harshly criticized by Keynes (1923). He argued that the tight monetary policies required to restore the real value of gold relative to the world's money supplies under the old gold parities would cause a continual recession. The cost in terms of unemployment, falling investment, and lost output would be too great, he claimed. He instead suggested that countries wanting to return to the gold standard should set new parities in line with existing gold reserves, which meant they only had to maintain price stability at the higher price levels instead of first having to deflate prices. If the price of gold had been raised as Keynes suggested, there again would have been enough gold to back the money in circulation, and lengthy recessions to drive down prices would not have been necessary.

But British policy makers pushed ahead with their deflationary policies in order to bring Britain back on the gold standard, which they understood to mean the same gold parity for the pound that had existed before the war. Had the rules of the gold standard become an unalterable element of a culture that people equated with modern civilization rather than just an international financial arrangement?

The Treaty of Versailles

The post–World War I period cannot be understood without taking note of the Paris Peace Conference in 1919. President Woodrow Wilson of the United States, the prime ministers of France and Britain, Georges Clemenceau and David Lloyd George, and nearly all other world leaders led large delegations of diplomats, economists, bankers, and lawyers to Paris to negotiate a new world order that would establish permanent peace. For six months, these leaders lived in Paris and participated in the daily negotiations. Effectively, the world's governments operated from Paris for half a year! Agreement was reached on the creation of the League of Nations, an international body that would serve to deal with international issues and conflicts. The conference also created the International Labour Organization (ILO), which today falls under the auspices of the United Nations. The conference redrew the world political map. The Austro-Hungarian Empire was split into Austria, Hungary, Czechoslovakia, Romania, and Yugoslavia. Poland, Lithuania, Latvia, and Estonia were created out of former Russian territory. The Middle East was completely reorganized, with Turkey, Syria, Iraq, Palestine, and other countries created out of the former Ottoman Empire. Some of these countries reflected older ethnic and political realities, but the new borders often separated ethnic groups and threw together bitter enemies. Also, the conference negotiated a set of treaties that defined the terms of surrender of Germany, Austria, Hungary, Bulgaria, and Ottoman Turkey.

The treaty between the Allied countries and Germany was signed in June 1919 in the Paris suburb of Versailles. This treaty and those signed with the other countries that fought on the side of Germany determined that Germany and its allies should compensate Britain, France, and its allies for their war losses. Losses caused by Germany alone were assessed at US\$30 billion at 1920 prices, which was slightly more than double Germany's annual GDP at that time.[7] A rigorous time line for **reparations payments** was laid down. Later to become even better known for his role in shaping the Bretton Woods agreement after World War II, John Maynard Keynes, as chief treasury advisor, was also a member of the British delegation to the Paris conference. He became disillusioned by the negotiations, and after returning to his academic position at the University of Cambridge, he wrote a book critical of the Paris conference entitled *The Economic Consequences of the Peace* (1920). In that insightful work, Keynes warned:

> If the European Civil War is to end with France and Italy abusing their momentary victorious power to destroy Germany and Austria-Hungary now prostrate, they invite their own destruction also. (p. 5)

It is debatable whether France, Britain, and Italy really wanted to *destroy* Germany, although some leaders, and their electorates, clearly had revenge on their minds. Rather, countries such as France and Britain simply saw the reparations payments as a convenient way to finance their own debt repayments to the United States. The Allies had borrowed heavily from the United States during the war to purchase arms, food, and other imports. The United States also made known to its allies that they viewed the loans as commercial transactions that could not be canceled or even renegotiated. It was not a coincidence that the reparations payments from Germany and its allies called for in the Treaty of Versailles were about equal to the wartime foreign borrowing by Britain, France, Italy, and other Allied countries. The United States's allies in World War I hoped to use the reparations to repay their debts from the war that Germany was now being blamed for.

The German reparations payments posed a serious problem. In order for tax payments by German citizens in German marks to be converted to dollar payments by British and French governments to their U.S. lenders, a number of things had to happen:

- Germany would have to increase taxes or borrow from its citizens.
- Germany would also have to run a large current account surplus with the allied countries in order to earn the British pounds, French francs, and Italian lira needed to pay war reparations.
- The Allied countries would, in turn, have to run current account surpluses with the United States in order to retire their debts with U.S. lenders.

Political conditions in Germany, the Allied countries, and the United States prevented things from unfolding in this required manner.

Reparations payments are effectively transfers, which you may recall appear in the current account of the balance of payments. Therefore, barring large private investment inflows, Germany would have to offset these transfers to Britain, France, and others with a trade surplus. The German government also ended up running large budget deficits in order to pay the reparations. These budget deficits were at first financed by domestic borrowing, but when the weak government was reluctant to raise taxes, doubts arose over its ability to pay back its growing debt. German citizens and banks became reluctant to acquire government bonds. At that point, the German government was forced to print money to cover its budget deficit, and accelerating inflation was the predictable result. The faster prices rose, the more money the government had to print to cover its expenditures. By 1922, prices were rising by thousands of percent per month. Many of Germany's allies, such as Austria, Hungary, Poland, and Bulgaria, similarly ended up with what came to be called **hyperinflation** as they struggled to make reparations payments. People's savings were reduced to near zero in real terms.

An aid package by the United States and Britain, known as the **Dawes Plan**, provided Germany with loans with which it could meet its reparations payments. Germany's 1924 budget reform increased taxes and reduced expenditures, and inflationary monetary expansion was ended. Private lending also resumed, and Germany was in fact able to borrow enough to more or less cover its balance of payments deficit for much of the remainder of the 1920s. But it was never able to run consistent trade surpluses, because high unemployment and difficulties in recovering from the war led the Allied countries in Europe to increasingly restrict imports. The same countries that demanded the reparations payments effectively prevented Germany from running a current account surplus with which to finance its reparations payments. In the end, the "victors" collected only a small fraction of the reparations specified in the Treaty of Versailles. The United States eventually canceled the remaining debts of its allies, but only years after the economic damage had been done.

Glorious Isolationism in the United States

The second link in the intricate trade pattern that would be necessary for the world economy to handle the post–World War I reparations and debt repayments also failed: the United States refused to permit imports from its former allies to increase and refused to tolerate the trade deficit that would permit its allies to repay their debts. The United States instead raised tariffs. U.S. industry, which had expanded rapidly during the war, felt vulnerable to foreign competition after the war and clamored for protection. The Republican administration that took office in 1921 obliged its business constituency by pushing for trade protection. The **Fordney-McCumber Tariff** of 1922 doubled average U.S. tariff rates.

The sharp isolationist turn by the United States after World War I also led the U.S. Congress to refuse to ratify U.S. participation in the League of Nations. Creating this new international body was one of the "Fourteen Points" President Wilson presented to the Paris conference. After the conference,

Wilson traveled by train across the United States promoting ratification of the Treaty of Versailles and participation in the League of Nations, but he could not muster enough support. The Congress insisted that a number of "reservations" be added to the treaty. When Wilson's health deteriorated and he returned to Washington late in 1919, no one else took up the fight for ratification. Congress simply did not act. In 1920, American voters, apparently tired of war and world politics, effectively rejected Wilson's plan by voting for the Republican candidate, Warren Harding, who had actively campaigned against participation in the League of Nations or any other international organization.

Another sign of its isolationist national mood was the U.S. reversal of its long-standing policy of open immigration. After extensive debate, which became more acrimonious as it proceeded, Congress set strict limits on all immigration for the first time in U.S. history. The *Immigration Act of 1924* limited immigration from any particular country to 2 percent of the number of descendants of immigrants of that nationality residing in the United States in 1890. The racist quotas appealed to the many Americans who feared that the recent immigration from southern and Eastern Europe was upsetting the country's culture. Legislators apparently thought that by going back to the 1890 census, the "traditional" ethnic makeup of the United States could be preserved. The world's largest economy thus gained a political culture focused on domestic issues, not world leadership.

Return to the Gold Standard

Most countries struggled to restore convertibility to gold during the 1920s, but by 1926 most of the major economies of the world claimed to again be "on the gold standard." As described earlier, the return to the gold standard did not come easily. Most European countries remained in recession with high levels of unemployment as monetary and fiscal policies were designed to deflate price levels and effectively expand the monetary value of national gold stocks. As a result, the revival of the pre–World War I international financial order resulted in a system that was not quite like the gold standard.

Most countries did not rigorously adhere to the unwritten rules of the game that had been largely adhered to before the war. Domestic political pressures did not permit them to do so. The constant pressure of unemployment and slow growth often led governments to reverse their policies and expand money supplies. The incompatibility between monetary expansion, government borrowing, and full convertibility led countries to limit free convertibility. Also, many countries held foreign currencies instead of gold, allegedly under the justification that the foreign reserves were backed by gold. This practice effectively created a **gold-exchange standard** rather than a gold standard. This was a type of fractional reserve monetary system that increased the world money supply relative to the gold base, a convenient result given the difficulties of deflating prices fully to the point where money supplies could be fully backed by gold. However, it also meant that changes in the availability of reserve currencies would affect the world's money supply. And, any loss of confidence in the gold-exchange standard that might trigger attempts to seek currencies backed exclusively by gold would cause the world's money supply to shrink sharply.

Obstfeld and Taylor (2002) compared interest rates on government foreign debt during the classic gold standard period, 1870–1914, and during the interwar return to the gold standard between 1925 and 1931. During the former period, interest rates on loans to countries that adhered to the gold standard were 40 to 60 basis points lower, all other things equal, than on loans to countries whose currencies were not convertible to gold. During the latter period, however, for many countries the announced adherence to the gold standard did not result in lower interest rates. In other words, countries' commitments to gold convertibility were not as credible as their pre–World War I commitments to full convertibility to gold.

U.S. loans helped to finance German reparations payments for a time, and they enabled Germany to restore limited convertibility to gold in 1926. But toward the end of the 1920s U.S. capital flows overseas fell sharply as the booming U.S. stock market pulled money back home. Then interest rates rose in 1928 because the Federal Reserve Bank tightened monetary policy in response to what it saw as a developing stock price bubble. Under the rules of the gold standard, the struggling democratic Weimar government in Germany had to contract the money supply as money flowed back to the United States and the balance of payments went into deficit once again. Eichengreen (1996) explains that as the outflow caused prices to deflate, debtors' real liabilities increased, and bankruptcies and loan defaults rose sharply. The financial crisis caused German unemployment to rise even higher than it already was, and social unrest became commonplace in many German cities. Once the U.S. economy slowed after the 1929 stock market crash, German exports declined, further driving the German economy into a deep recession. One German politician who exploited the deteriorating economic condition was the leader of the small National Socialist Party, Adolph Hitler. When economic times are difficult, fear drives some people toward leaders who activate the worst human instincts.

Germany's export decline was made worse by the increased protectionism of its trade partners. Recall from Chapter 9 that in the United States the isolationist tendencies that had already increased tariffs in the 1920s. In 1930, the enactment of the Smoot-Hawley Tariff Act and immediately caused a trade war that engulfed much of the world. Faced with unemployment and calls for protection at home, few countries accepted the increased U.S. tariffs without retaliation. Most major trading countries imposed equal or more severe tariff increases. The consequences of the Smoot-Hawley tariffs and other countries' retaliation were that by 1931 world trade volume had fallen by more than 50 percent from its 1929 levels. Charles P. Kindleberger (1973) estimated that by 1933 world trade had fallen by about 70 percent. Alternative data is provided in Table 15.2. Either way, trade fell sharply. In the United States and elsewhere, the new protectionism did not create any new jobs because, even though import-competing industries may have benefited from the protection, foreign retaliation caused exports to decline. All other things equal, real income fell because, effectively, foreign protectionism reduced the size of each country's most competitive and efficient industries and expanded its least competitive industries slowly, at best, in the recessionary environment.

DID THE GOLD STANDARD CAUSE THE GREAT DEPRESSION?

The Great Depression began in October 1929 with the sudden collapse of the U.S. stock market, which caused economic activity to spiral downward in nearly all countries of the world. In the United States, for example, real economic output had fallen by about one-third by 1933. Unemployment in the United States rose from about 4 percent in 1929 to 9 percent in 1930, 16 percent in 1931, and near 25 percent in 1932 and 1933 as demand for output fell each time employment fell. The United States, and most other countries throughout the world, did not have built-in stabilizers in place, such as government assistance that automatically kicks in when unemployment or income losses increase.

Explaining the Great Depression

The discussion on financial crises in Chapter 13, especially Hyman P. Minsky's financial instability hypothesis, provides a good framework for explaining why the stock market crashed and the U.S. financial sector froze after 1929. The Great Depression was, fundamentally, a failure of the U.S. financial system that subsequently caused a real fall in demand and, therefore, a sharp rise in unemployment. Recall that Minsky (1982) hypothesized that every extended period of rapid economic expansion will inevitably shift expectations to where financial arrangements are increasingly speculative or Ponzi-like. Within Minsky's framework, it is obvious that the stock market collapse would convert hedge and speculative financing into Ponzi financing, which would in turn force the financial system to scramble for safety and reduce lending.

Economists from across the political spectrum agree that the decline in economic activity that began in 1929 was made much worse by the Federal Reserve Bank's contraction of the money supply. That is, when a contraction in the financial sector was already under way in late 1929, the Fed

Table 15.2

World Merchandise Exports: 1919–1934

Years	Export Value (US$ billions)	Value Index (1929 = 100)	Export Volume (1929 = 100)
1929	32.7	100	100
1930	26.2	80	93
1931	18.6	57	86
1932	12.6	38	73
1933	14.8	45	75
1934	18.6	58	78

Source: Angus Maddison (1995), *Monitoring the World Economy 1820–1992*, Paris: OECD.

tightened the money supply further and thus accelerated the downward spiral. The Fed's monetary contraction also came on top of a decline in prices that had started in 1929, with the result that its tight monetary policy raised real interest rates to where they killed off almost all remaining demand for borrowing. Why did the Fed behave this way?

The Fed's contraction in 1930 has been widely studied, and except for simple incompetence, the only justification for monetary contraction in the face of deflation and rising unemployment was that the Fed sought to maintain convertibility of the dollar to gold as mandated by the gold standard's rules of the game. This suggests that the fundamental cause of the Great Depression was the partial return to the gold standard.

Spreading the Recession

The gold standard's rules of the game have also been singled out as the primary reason why the U.S. recession spread so quickly to the rest of the world. It is true that the U.S. recession reduced its demand for foreign imports and the United States could have spread its recession abroad by triggering declines in aggregate demand in other economies. But the severity of the economic contractions everywhere suggests additional channels.

According to Robert A. Mundell (2000, p. 331), "Had the price of gold been raised in the late 1920's, or, alternatively, had the major central banks pursued policies of price stability instead of adhering to the gold standard, there would have been no Great Depression." Eichengreen (1992) explicitly attributes the perverse behavior of central banks around the world in the face of economic recession to the need to follow the rules of the gold standard. He claims that fixed exchange rates caused the U.S. recession that followed the 1929 stock market crash to be quickly transmitted to other economies. The rules of the gold standard mandated that central banks facing declining exports to the United States contract their money supplies in order to maintain convertibility and fixed exchange rates. The depression that began in 1930 in the United States was primarily due to the Federal Reserve Bank's contractionary monetary policies after the stock market crash.

The Culture of the Gold Standard

Eichengreen and Peter Temin, also an economic historian, contend that the fundamental cause of the Great Depression was the "ideology" of the gold standard. This ideology led policy makers to continue following the rules of the game well after it should have become obvious that the consequences of rigid monetary policies were causing economic devastation:

> The constraints of the gold standard system hamstrung countries as they struggled to adapt during the 1920s to changes in the world economy. And the ideology, mentalité, and rhetoric of the gold standard led policy makers to take action that only accentuated economic distress in the 1930s. Central bankers continued to kick the world economy while it was down until it lost consciousness. (2000, p. 183)

By "mentalité" Eichengreen and Temin mean "the mind set of policy makers, which shaped their notions of the possible." They go on to explain:

> Historians have pondered why policy makers failed to counteract the Depression and why the actions they took in fact aggravated its severity. The recent literature shows that they saw no other option, given the international system they confronted and the ideological lens [model] through which they viewed it. (Ibid.)

Their model mandated that they respond to balance of payments deficits and gold losses by restricting credit and deflating the economy with the goal of reducing domestic prices and costs until international balance was restored.

In the 1930s, Keynes (1936) argued for a completely new macroeconomic policy approach that included active government fiscal and monetary policies to increase aggregate demand. But such policies would have to wait as long as the politicians in power had the gold standard mentalité. The rationale for the monetary contraction and the reluctance to engage in expansionary fiscal policy was the belief that maintaining the gold standard was the best solution to solving the unemployment problem. So convinced were many central bankers, economists, and others of this approach, that many would later suggest that it was the abandonment of the gold standard that caused the Great Depression.

When the U.S. commitment to the gold standard came into question in 1931 after Britain abandoned it, the U.S. Federal Reserve Bank raised interest rates in order to confirm its commitment. This contractionary policy in the midst of rapid economic decline was "inept" according to Friedman and Schwartz. They wrote, "The Federal Reserve System reacted vigorously and promptly to the external drain. On October 9, the Federal Reserve Bank of New York raised its discount rate to 1.5 percent and on October 16, to 3.5 percent—the sharpest rise within so brief a period in the whole history of the System, before or since" (1963, p. 317). And so the culture, or what Eichengreen and Temin call mentalité, drove the U.S. economy into the Great Depression.

Some Further Consequences of the Economic Decline

The spread of economic recessions and rising unemployment were exploited by opportunistic political leaders. To finish the comment from Mundell (2000) quoted above: "Had the price of gold been raised . . . there would have been no Great Depression, no Nazi revolution, and no World War II." Adolf Hitler exploited a dismal economy to gain control in Germany. Fascist military leaders came to power during the Great Depression. According to the international economist Richard N. Cooper (1992, p. 2123):

> What is less well known is the influence of the Smoot-Hawley Tariff and the sharp down-turn in world economic activity in undermining the position of internationally minded officials and politicians in Japan, in favor of an imperialistic nationalism which led to the Japanese invasion of Manchuria in late 1931, the real beginning of the Second World War.

It may seem somewhat of a stretch to argue that the international financial order was the cause of the Depression, the Nazi atrocities, and World War II, as Mundell does. Nevertheless, the fact that the leaders of the Allied nations convened the Bretton Woods conference in 1944 suggests that they had effectively concluded that the financial order was indeed a very important determinant of world peace and economic well-being.

The End of Gold

In 1931, Britain was among the first countries to abandon its commitment to convert its currency to gold. Tom Johnson, former parliamentary secretary for Scotland, famously exclaimed, "Nobody told us we could do that!" The United States did not abandon gold convertibility until 1933, after elections brought Franklin D. Roosevelt into the White House and Democrats gained majorities in both houses of Congress. On the other hand, Switzerland, France, and the Netherlands continued to defend gold convertibility well into the 1930s by trying to increase their holdings of gold and reducing the share of foreign exchange in their reserves.

The 1920s gold-exchange standard, under which reserves of one or more of the major currencies were often substituted for actual gold in many countries, was effectively abandoned in favor of a pure gold-based system, which central bankers felt would better enable them to maintain credibility. This "flight to the safety" of real gold further reduced money supplies when tighter monetary policy and the freezing of the financial sector, and thus the money multiplier, were already restricting the money supply.

Some economists have tried to estimate how much better off countries would have been if they had abandoned the gold standard sooner. For example, Michael Bordo, Thomas Helbing, and Harold James (2007) use a macroeconomic model to calculate how the Swiss economy would have performed under a depreciated exchange rate instead of maintaining gold convertibility at the traditional parity rate. They estimate that if Switzerland had devalued with Britain in 1931, Swiss real GDP would have been 18 percent higher in 1935. Even if Switzerland had waited to devalue its franc with the U.S. dollar in 1933, its 1935 real GDP would still have been 15 percent higher.

A CHANGE OF ORDER

Cultures and ideologies are not easily changed. Sometimes it takes a change in leadership to change a mind-set or an ideology. Eventually a failing ideology will be replaced, but there is, of course, little guarantee that the new leadership will improve matters. The rise to power of totalitarian governments like those headed by Joseph Stalin and Adolph Hitler was made possible by failing economic systems, but the new orders were not good for humanity. In the United States, President Herbert Hoover was defeated at the polls by Franklin D. Roosevelt. One of the first things Roosevelt said was that "[t]he sound internal economic situation of a nation is a greater factor in its well-being than the price of its currency."[8]

Reversing the Financial Chaos

As the Great Depression spread over the world, politicians grasped for possible solutions. In 1933, at the depths of the Depression, a World Monetary Conference was organized in London in the hope that a cooperative effort to restore prosperity might succeed where the strict adherence to conservative monetary policy was clearly failing. Discussions centered around restoring the gold standard, reducing tariffs and other barriers to trade, and setting rules for improving the international coordination of economic policies. In particular, there was concern over the competitive exchange rate devaluations being carried out by some governments that had abandoned the gold standard. These governments were accused of trying to raise their economy at the expense of the rest of the world, and, of course, their actions were seen as undermining the efforts of those governments that were desperately trying to stay on the gold standard. The conference failed. Policy makers had become leery of restoring the gold standard, yet there was no consensus on what international financial order should replace it.

Competitive Devaluations

As mentioned above, many countries that had abandoned convertibility to gold began to actively intervene in the foreign exchange markets. Ragnar Nurkse (1944, pp. 8–9) described the situation as follows:

> [F]reely fluctuating exchange rates were far from common in those years. Exchange rates changed indeed; but the changes were usually controlled. For considerable periods at a time, rates were "pegged" or kept within certain limits of variation.

Some economists have referred to this period as one of **managed exchange rates** because governments interfered with exchange rates in so many ways, from exchange market intervention to direct restrictions on international trade and financial flows. Many countries established **exchange rate stabilization funds**, which were really governmental agencies located in the finance ministry or central bank and authorized to use accumulated foreign exchange reserves to intervene in the foreign exchange market. These funds were officially designated to smooth out seasonal and speculative fluctuations in exchange rates, as most governments were reluctant to just let currencies float freely in the volatile economic environment of the Great Depression. But as described in the previous subsection, many governments used the stabilization funds to actively undervalue their currencies in order to give their exporters an advantage in international markets.

In the deflationary environment of the Great Depression, flooding the foreign exchange market with domestic currency to drive down its value was quite compatible with domestic economic goals; the expanded money supply was a desirable policy on its own to combat economic deflation. The problem with such competitive devaluations was that they tended to cause retaliatory devaluations by other countries. There were repeated calls for more coordination among countries to stabilize exchange rates at their "realistic" levels.

New approaches to exchange rates were just part of the paradigm shift that occurred during the Great Depression. In addition to abandoning the permanently fixed exchange of the gold standard, new political leaders also abandoned the hands-off approach to the economy. Keynesian macroeconomic policies became more pronounced as the economic difficulties of the Great Depression gradually brought about the replacement of old political leaders with new ones who were not handicapped by the gold standard mentalité. For example, when Franklin D. Roosevelt assumed the presidency in the United States in 1933, he pushed a stimulative government budget through the Congress controlled by his political party, began negotiations to undo the Smoot-Hawley tariff, instituted new financial regulations to prevent future financial bubbles and collapses, created various programs to increase employment, established social security and minimum wages, and began discussions with close allies on a new international financial order.

The Tripartite Agreement

Governments had to decide whether to definitively abandon the gold standard or just adopt temporary policies to stimulate economic activity before they could, eventually, return to the gold standard. Many economists and the political leaders they advised were leery of returning to the system that they had come to see as the source of the recent economic troubles. But central bankers and the heads of the major private banks lobbied hard to restore the old rules of the game, pointing to the exchange rate instability caused by competitive devaluations and other managed interventions in the foreign exchange market. This instability was interpreted by some prominent economists as evidence not for a return to the rigidities of a commodity standard, but rather as a reason for central banks to stop their intervention and let exchange rates float freely. The noted international economist Gottfried Haberler (1937) argued that flexible exchange rates would have prevented the transmission of booms and busts from one country to another as occurred at the start of the Great Depression. James W. Angell (1933) and Seymour Harris (1936) analyzed contemporary policies and economic outcomes, and they concluded that trade by the countries with floating or frequently changed exchange rates did not contract as rapidly as trade by countries who maintained fixed gold parities.

The governments of the major economies were, mostly, reluctant to accept the idea of completely freely floating exchange rates, especially since there was no way to stop governments from again using exchange rates to boost exports and aggregate demand at the expense of other countries. Hence, something of a consensus developed around a system of pegged exchange rates with enough flexibility to permit governments to use stimulative fiscal and monetary policies in the case of a serious recession. That was the thinking behind the **Tripartite Monetary Agreement**, negotiated by the United States, Great Britain, and France in 1936.

This agreement fixed exchange rates between the currencies of the three signatory countries. But the exchange rates were not fixed by means of unlimited convertibility to gold; rather, central bank intervention in the foreign exchange markets would be used to keep exchange rates at their agreed-to levels. In light of the experience since 1929, the designers of the Tripartite Agreement added the provision that the target rates could be changed under certain circumstances. In the case of rising unemployment and economic deflation, they felt, domestic macroeconomic policy should not be held captive to the exchange rate.

By the time the Tripartite Monetary Agreement went into effect, the world was sharply divided into conflicting political camps. There was little hope of extending the agreement to more countries. It would take another world war before further cooperation among countries would be sought. But when the time was ripe, the Tripartite Monetary Agreement would serve as a model for the world-wide financial order.

ASSESSING THE GOLD STANDARD DURING THE INTERWAR PERIOD

There really are not many good things to say about the international monetary system between the two world wars. High levels of unemployment plagued all of the major economies, and the unemployment worsened as the Great Depression wore on. The Great Depression was caused, in large part, by the contractionary monetary policies demanded by the rules of the game, specifically the requirement that convertibility of money for gold be protected under all circumstances. It took the massive spending on another world war to finally eliminate the unemployment that plagued the United States, Britain, and much of the rest of the world. In short, the report card for the return to the gold standard is not good.

A Bad Report Card

Our rationale for the failing grades shown in Table 15.3 is easy to understand. Economic growth was slow or nonexistent in most of the major economies. Only the United States grew rapidly during the 1920s, but even that was reversed in the 1930s when the nation suffered a deeper depression than most other industrial countries. The protectionist policies of the United States and retaliatory measures by most other countries, compounded by the complete cessation of international lending and borrowing, effectively destroyed globalization. The world separated into isolated economic spheres defined by ideologies rather than comparative advantage or common economic interests. Prices were fairly stable during the 1920s but then they mostly fell during the 1930s. It is not clear that price stability is a positive outcome when it comes at the cost of unemployment, stagnation,

Table 15. 3

Report Card for the Gold Standard in the Interwar Period

1. Stability/employment	Fail
2. Economic growth	Fail
3. Globalization	Fail
4. Policy independence	Fail
5. Price stability	n/a
6. Mutually beneficial	Fail

Figure 15.4   **The Trilemma during the Interwar Period**

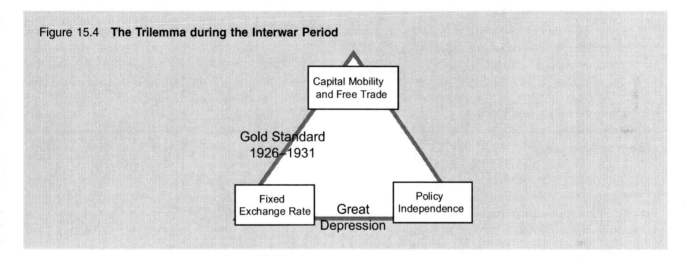

and declining world trade. In the report card, we rule that this criterion is not applicable in the Great Depression. Finally, the gold standard failed criterion 6 because its fixed exchange rates caused the U.S. recession to be quickly transmitted to all other economies, and the one-at-a-time abandonment of the gold standard made any constructive international cooperation difficult.

The Trilemma between the Wars

The interwar period saw economic policy come to the forefront of political debate. This had already occurred in the United States before World War I, when William Jennings Bryan almost won the 1896 presidential election by linking people's perceived economic difficulties to the gold standard. During the interwar period, the power of the trilemma undermined the mentalité of the gold standard and, eventually, gave way to the more popular macroeconomic focus on unemployment and inflation. More fundamentally, it was the rise of democracy, organized labor, and the popularity of socialism that shifted political pressures and made policy makers more uncomfortable with the lack of policy independence under the rules of the game of the gold standard.

Economic policies varied greatly during the interwar period, and it is impossible to generalize across all countries. But Figure 15.4 presents a general picture of how the trilemma was dealt with by most countries between 1920 and the end of the 1930s. Immediately after the close of World War I, most countries had few gold reserves, and they had experienced widely differing inflation rates that had driven the traditional gold parities far away from their **purchasing power parity** equilibria. A quick return to the gold standard was thus impossible, and, instead, the world operated with what was effectively a system of floating exchange rates. In the meantime, policy makers tried to conduct economic policies that would put their economies once again in a position to go back on the gold standard.

Indeed, by 1926, the major economies of the world again claimed convertibility to gold, and exchange rates remained fixed until the early 1930s. When the Great Depression spread across the globe, however, countries gradually abandoned the gold standard in favor of greater policy independence in response to political events that pushed the unemployment rate ahead of the fixed exchange rate in the ranking of policy priorities. After they abandoned gold convertibility, policy makers seldom opted for floating exchange rates. Rather, they generally selected the combination of managed exchange rates and domestic policy independence, effectively recognizing the collapse of international trade and investment as the inevitable results of the Smoot-Hawley trade war, the Depression's low aggregate demand, and the global political divisions. It is impossible to locate the 1930s on the trilemna diagram.

The bad report card omits one important event: the Tripartite Monetary Agreement. Because political divisions made it impossible to extend the agreement to more than the three signatory countries, we cannot use it to improve the report card for the interwar period. But eight years later, when the end to the Second World War was beginning to come into sight, the Tripartite Monetary Agreement from 1936 became the model for the world's next monetary system. We take up that story in the next chapter.

CHAPTER SUMMARY

1. An international monetary order is a set of written and unwritten rules, laws, agreements, conventions, regulations, and traditions as well as institutions such as central banks, legislatures, and regulatory agencies, that influence the individual, firm, and bank behaviors that generate the aggregate outcomes that characterize the international monetary system.

2. In ancient times, the international monetary system consisted of the minting of coins by various governments and an informal network of money changers.

3. The Roman Empire, which was a large free trade area with a single currency that was used throughout a large region, was an early example of an economic union.

4. The gold standard's origin was the British Parliament's 1819 law that limited the Bank of England's power to print money by requiring that each pound note be freely convertible into a fixed amount of gold set by the 1816 Coinage Act.

5. By the end of the 1870s, most governments had adopted similar laws that made their currencies freely convertible into gold at specific gold parities, and the world in effect had the monetary system that came to be called the international gold standard.

6. The gold standard was an order built on the faith that money could always be converted to pure gold at any time without restrictions.

7. The gold standard's rules of the game included the requirement that (1) each national currency be fixed to gold according to an official gold parity, (2) there be no restrictions on converting gold into domestic money and domestic money into gold at the parity price, (3) there be no restrictions on foreign exchange transactions, and (4) gold imports and exports remain completely unrestricted.

8. In the long run, governments did behave in ways that appeared to adhere to the implicit rules of the game, as evidenced by the fact that over the long run prices did roughly reflect the world supply of gold.

9. The gold standard was a qualified success in that it permitted economic growth and technological progress to accelerate, but the rigid rules of the game often caused financial panics and severe ups and downs in economic activity in many countries.

10. The 1896 election in the United States, in which William Jennings Bryan openly campaigned on abandoning the gold standard, shows that there was popular discontent with the rigid monetary system that seemed to favor creditors over debtors.

11. World War I led most governments to suspend convertibility of their currencies to gold, as more urgent needs to finance the war took precedence.
12. The rapid money creation to fund the war caused inflation to rise, and the variation in inflation rates made a return to the gold standard after the war at the old gold parities impossible.
13. Only in 1926, eight years after the war ended, did countries officially announce their return to a gold standard order. Some countries, like France, changed their gold parities, but Britain insisted on returning to the gold standard under its old gold parity, which required price deflation and an economy on the brink of recession throughout the 1920s.
14. The 1926 gold standard was really a gold-exchange standard because many countries held currencies rather than gold as reserves, which implied the global money supply was a large multiple of the actual gold supply.
15. The onset of the Great Depression led most central banks to shrink their money supplies in misplaced efforts to maintain gold convertibility even though unemployment soared and economic growth turned sharply negative.
16. The economic historians Barry Eichengreen and Peter Temin (1997) contend that the fundamental cause of the Great Depression was the "ideology" of the gold standard, which led policy makers to continue following the rules of the game well after it should have become obvious that the consequences of rigid monetary policies were causing economic devastation.
17. Governments did eventually change course as voters elected new parties to power, including, tragically, Hitler's National Socialists in Germany, and most governments abandoned the gold standard in the early 1930s.
18. Once the link to gold was cut, some governments resorted to excessive devaluations in order to boost their exports as a stimulative macroeconomic measure, and "competitive devaluations" became a major international issue.
19. In 1936, the United States, Great Britain, and France negotiated the Tripartite Monetary Agreement in an attempt to restore stability to the world monetary system; under this accord, the three countries agreed to maintain pegged exchange rates between their currencies by having their central banks intervene in the foreign exchange market.

KEY TERMS AND CONCEPTS

Bagehot's rule
bimetallism
Coinage Act of 1816
Dawes Plan
exchange rate stabilization funds
fiat money
Fordney-Mccumber Tariff
gold parity
gold standard
gold-exchange standard
hyperinflation
international monetary order

international monetary system
investment houses
Latin Monetary Union
managed exchange rates
medium of exchange
monetary order
money
purchasing power
reparations payments
store of value
Tripartite Monetary Agreement

PROBLEMS AND QUESTIONS

1. Explain the difference between a financial system and a financial order. Give examples of each.
2. Noted economist Milton Friedman explained that a floating exchange rate was simpler than a fixed exchange rate because under a floating rate only the exchange rate has to change to restore balance to the foreign exchange market; under a fixed rate, all other prices in the economy have to change. Apply this insight to the gold standard before and after World War I.

3. Do you think that the gold standard could work as the financial order in the world today? Why or why not?

4. Explain precisely how the gold standard dealt with the trilemma.

5. One of the rules under the order of the gold standard was that governments would return to convertibility under the old gold parity as soon as possible in the case of an emergency that required the temporary suspension of convertibility. Why was this rule important to the continued maintenance of fixed exchange rates during the gold standard?

6. Using the criteria for judging a monetary system developed in the introduction to Part Five of the textbook, discuss the performance of each of the major financial orders, and the resulting systems that functioned from the beginning to the end of the twentieth century. Was any one particularly good?

7. Write an alternative history that begins with a narrow electoral victory by William Jennings Bryan in the 1896 U.S. presidential election. How would world events have differed if the United States had abandoned the gold standard?

8. Would a bimetallic standard, such as William Jennings Bryan advocated during his 1896 presidential campaign, have created more stable economic conditions in the United States? Recall that two of the criticisms of the gold standard were the volatility of money supplies and the frequent financial panics.

9. Why did world leaders feel it was necessary to reinstate the rules of the game for the gold standard after World War I?

10. Precisely explain the "rules of the game" of the gold standard. Could the system have worked if anyone of the rules were not followed?

11. Why was it so hard to return to the gold standard after the war? (Hint: Begin by listing all the things that changed between 1913 and 1919.)

12. Was the gold standard responsible for the Great Depression? Discuss.

13. Describe the "rules of the game" of the Tripartite Agreement. How did it differ from the gold standard?

14. Describe why Germany had such difficulty in making its reparations payments. What had to happen for it to be able to meet the obligations imposed on it at the Versailles Conference?

15. Do you agree with the report cards given in this chapter? Why or why not?

NOTES

1. William L. Davisson and James E. Harper (1972), p. 196.

2. Rondo Cameron (1993).

3. Peter Spufford (2002), "An Encore for the Merchant of Venice," *Financial Times,* October 19–20.

4. Leland B. Yeager (1976), *International Monetary Relations: Theory, History, and Policy,* 2d ed., New York: Harper & Row, p. 295.

5. Michael Edelstein (1982).

6. For those who like politics, the appendix provides Bryan's complete "Cross of Gold" speech.

7. Based on data from Angus Maddison (1991).

8. Quoted in Edgar B. Nixon (1969), p. 269.

CHAPTER 16

The International Monetary System: Bretton Woods to the End of the Twenty-first Century

> [C]ontrol of capital movements, both inward and outward,
> should be a permanent feature of the postwar system.
>
> —John Maynard Keynes (1943)

The night of June 30, 1944, a special train from New York raced along the Connecticut River between Vermont and New Hampshire. The engineer's orders read: "Run passenger extra Springfield to White River Junction. Has right over all trains." The order meant that all other trains, even scheduled express trains, had to let them pass. The train rushed past Greenfield, Massachusetts, and Bellows Falls, Vermont, and at Whitefield, New Hampshire, it turned onto a connecting line to Bretton Woods, New Hampshire, a small resort located at the base of Mount Washington, the highest mountain in the eastern half of the United States. At the Bretton Woods station, a line of taxis was waiting to carry the six hundred passengers the last mile of their journey to the luxurious Mount Washington Hotel.

The fireman on the steam locomotive had read that President Franklin D. Roosevelt and the Soviet Union's Joseph Stalin were having confidential meetings, so he assumed that it was they who were on his special train. He later revealed his disappointment at learning that the train's passengers were economists and finance ministers from forty-four countries. Among the passengers were the British economist John Maynard Keynes, U.S. Treasury Secretary, Henry Morgenthau, and the chief international economist at the Treasury Department, Harry Dexter White. These passengers were on their way to one of the most important international meetings of the twentieth century. When another train carried the delegates back to New York three weeks later, the delegates to the *Bretton Woods Monetary Conference* had completed the blueprint, or order, for the international monetary system that would follow World War II.

To grasp the unique nature of the Bretton Woods conference you need to place yourself back in history. Think, for a moment, about those first three weeks of July 1944. World War II was still raging, and the final outcome was not yet certain. The Allied invasion of Normandy was just a few weeks old. The German concentration camps were in full operation, millions were dying on the Russian front, and naval battles were raging in the Pacific Ocean. And as if the war was not dismal enough, there was not much consolation from bringing up memories of life before the war. In the 1930s, the Great Depression had spread unemployment, hunger, misery, and a huge loss of prosperity throughout the world. There was also the rise of fascism in Germany and millions of deaths under Stalin's brutal regime in the Soviet Union. And just one generation earlier, World War I had devastated economies and populations in many countries. In short, the delegates to the Bretton Woods conference were clearly challenged to try to put the world on a new path. But could a new order for the international monetary system put world history on a more enlightened track? More importantly, what exactly should that path be? This chapter examines the post–World War II period and the role of the Bretton Woods order in shaping the world economy.

THE BRETTON WOODS CONFERENCE

The previous chapter, on the gold standard, leaves little doubt that the international monetary system plays a central role in setting the course of history. Recall how the attempts to return to the gold standard's rules of the game complicated economic recovery after World War I, and then how the gold standard mind-set drove the world economy into a depression and empowered political factions that ultimately drove most nations into yet another world war. The future order of the international monetary system was an important matter because the rules that govern international payments largely determine how much countries trade with each other, lend to each other, borrow from each other, and invest in each other. The rules of the system also determine how much foreign debt governments, businesses, and financial groups can accumulate and, therefore, how stable the global economy is. The rules of the international monetary system thus determine the degree of international economic integration.

A Holistic Perspective of Bretton Woods

Most delegates selected to attend the conference believed that World War II had been, in part, caused by countries isolating themselves from each other, politically and economically, after World War I. Some delegates to the conference, such as Keynes, also feared that international economic integration under the wrong rules could create more conflicts. Humanity has, of course, always been challenged by this choice: Should we deal with foreigners, or should we keep our distance?

The delegates in Bretton Woods sought a system that would expand international trade and reverse the economic isolationism that characterized the period just before World War II. They discussed the merits of different exchange rate systems and whether international payments should be restricted or deregulated. Should exchange rates be allowed to float freely, managed through intervention, or fixed permanently by means of a commodity standard like the gold standard? Stable exchange rates facilitate international trade because exporters and importers can more easily compare domestic and foreign prices. Floating exchange rates make international investment more risky, and they make it difficult to judge the future returns on international investments. As discussed in the previous chapter, it is not easy to keep exchange rates from changing as economic conditions, world events, and the full complexity of human society evolve over time. The trilemma reminds us that the goal of keeping international payments stable conflicts with other policy goals, such as maintaining full employment and price stability.

White and Keynes

Harry Dexter White, the chief economist at the U.S. Department of the Treasury, oversaw the negotiations. According to the monetary historian James Boughton (1994), "The core of White's thinking . . . was a belief that cooperation among governments was necessary for global prosperity." White had already decided that the system should strive for exchange rate stability. He, therefore, advocated pegging exchange rates by means of continual central bank purchases and sales of currencies in the foreign exchange markets. White also aggressively sought to give the U.S. dollar a central role in this new international monetary system. Over the three weeks in Bretton Woods, White gently but persistently steered consensus toward pegged exchange rates and dollar dominance.

The British delegation was headed by Keynes, who enjoyed universal respect as an economist and as a statesman. Keynes had been a member of the British delegation to the **Paris Peace Conference** at the close of World War I, and was noted for resigning because he disagreed with the punishing reparations payments that the leaders of Britain, France, and Italy were demanding from Germany and Austria-Hungary. After the Paris conference, Keynes wrote *The Economic Consequences of the Peace,* in which he predicted that the harsh terms imposed on Germany would fuel resentment that would lead to renewed warfare. His prediction, sadly, came true.

Keynes was even better known for his *General Theory of Employment, Interest, and Money* (1936), which had become the prescription for economic policy in most Western economies. In that work, Keynes prescribed active monetary and budgetary policies to keep an economy at or near full employment. In Bretton Woods, therefore, Keynes consistently argued that the international monetary system should give national governments and their policy makers some flexibility to pursue economic policies aimed at maintaining full employment even if it made exchange rate stability more difficult to achieve. Keynes had become convinced, as many economists of his time had, that Britain's economic troubles during the Great Depression stemmed from attempts to tie the British pound to gold under the rules of the pre–World War I gold standard. By forcing monetary authorities to link each country's money supply to its stock of gold, the rules of the game of the gold standard had made it impossible for a central bank to act as a lender of last resort for failing banks or to expand the money supply to stimulate investment and economic activity in times of high unemployment. Keynes thus argued that exchange rates be pegged, not permanently fixed. He defined **adjustable exchange rate pegs** as targets that could be adjusted if the foreign exchange market was characterized by a **fundamental disequilibrium**, which he defined as an exchange rate that was not compatible with the monetary and fiscal policies necessary for maintaining full employment in each national economy.

White and Keynes agreed on the adjustable pegs, but they disagreed on other matters. Keynes, as a representative of the United Kingdom, sought a financial system in which Britain and the United States would enjoy equal stature. White represented U.S. financial interests, and he pushed for a system that appeared multilateral but was designed to make the U.S. dollar the dominant currency in which international trade and financial assets were priced so it would become the world's reserve currency. The conference attendees would agree to establish the **International Monetary Fund (IMF)**, a type of "central bank for central banks" that would serve as lender of last resort to national central banks and as monitor of the international economy. Keynes was in agreement on creating the IMF, but he envisioned the new institution as the manager of a new international reserve currency, not as the superintendent of an international monetary system based on dollar reserves.

Another area where White and Keynes disagreed was on how to treat financial account transactions. Keynes recognized that pegging exchange rates and maintaining some degree of policy independence would put the system in conflict with the trilemma if financial account transactions were not restricted. He had argued in advance of the conference "that control of capital movements, both inward and outward, should be a permanent feature of the postwar system" (1943, p. 31). Specifically, Keynes had proposed an **International Clearing Union** that would penalize countries that ran persistent deficits or surpluses on their international accounts in order to force both surplus and deficit nations to balance trade. This proposal was never considered at Bretton Woods. White's U.S. delegation, under pressure from U.S. politicians lobbied by the financial industry, insisted that countries should have the option of keeping their financial markets open to foreigners. The U.S. position prevailed, and no explicit controls on financial account transactions were mentioned. Still, in a sign of respect for Keynes and their European allies, the United States went along with keeping any explicit mention of liberalizing financial flows out of the final agreement. The following clause was included in the Bretton Woods agreement:

> No member shall, without the approval of the Fund, impose restrictions on the making of payments and transfers for current international transactions. (International Monetary Fund [1944], Article VIII)

It was most delegates' understanding that current transactions included normal trade credit, but not other capital movements. Hence, international trade and the direct financing of trade was not to be restricted, but every country was free to regulate, or not, capital inflows and outflows.

A large part of the three weeks at Bretton Woods was spent arguing over voting rights in the IMF. In the end, it was agreed that voting rights would be in proportion to countries' contributions of capital to the IMF and that those contributions were to be in rough proportion to countries' gross domestic products (GDPs). It was also agreed that the IMF should operate on the basis of consensus, not majority voting. Specifically, major actions and rules would require an 85 percent supermajority. This rule gave the United States a unique position of power in the IMF: the U.S. economy accounted for over 20 percent of world GDP, and with the corresponding proportion of votes the United States effectively gained veto power over IMF decisions.

Finally, the Bretton Woods conference agreed to create two additional institutions: the **World Bank** and the International Trade Organization. The World Bank, more formally called the **International Bank for Reconstruction and Development**, was to provide financing to help countries rebuild after World War II. Like the IMF, the World Bank was set up with funds provided by the signatories to the Bretton Woods agreement, each paying in proportion to its share of world GDP. Later, after reconstruction had been completed, the World Bank's role shifted to providing development financing to low-income developing economies, a role it continues to fulfill today.[1] The purpose of the International Trade Organization (ITO) was to oversee negotiations to reduce trade barriers and resolve trade disputes between countries. The ITO never materialized after the war, however. The United States had second thoughts about giving up national sovereignty over trade policy to an international agency that it might have trouble controlling, and the world had to settle in 1947 for the **General Agreement on Tariffs and Trade (GATT)**, which was a set of rules on how countries could conduct trade policy. This was an agreement, not a permanent organization with oversight or regulatory powers.

The U.S. Dollar Assumes a Special Role

On paper, the Bretton Woods agreement depicted a system in which all currencies have equal standing. All countries were to contribute their national currencies to the IMF to serve as reserves that could be borrowed by member states. In practice, however, the Bretton Woods system would function as a **fixed-rate dollar standard**. The United States and the dollar assumed special roles in the system. While the Bretton Woods agreement mandated every central bank to intervene to peg its currency's value in the foreign exchange market, only n–1 central banks actually needed to intervene to keep all exchange rates constant. Recall from Chapter 12 that if there is enough triangular arbitrage across all n currencies, there are only n–1 fundamental exchange rates. Therefore, in a world with n countries and currencies, all exchange rates can be kept fixed if n–1 of the central banks actively intervene to keep their currency pegged to the nth currency. In practice, all central banks intervened to keep their currencies pegged to the dollar, and the U.S. central bank remained passive. The United States was the nth country.

As the nth country, the United States implicitly accepted a different and unique responsibility: by controlling the world's reserve currency, it effectively set the world's monetary policy. With all other countries pegging their currencies to the dollar, it effectively occupied the same place in the system as did gold under the gold standard. Recall how under the gold standard, the supply of gold relative to worldwide economic growth determined world price levels. Now, with all currencies pegged to the dollar, it was the supply of dollars that effectively determined the world's money supply.

Keynes had argued against making the U.S. dollar the world's reserve currency. In lectures before the conference, he had proposed a separate international reserve currency, which he named the **bancor**, to assume the role of gold. The IMF would create and manage the new international money. However, the U.S. delegation avoided discussion of the bancor at Bretton Woods. Clearly, the United States wanted the U.S. dollar to become the reserve currency.

Interestingly, gold was not entirely eliminated from the monetary system. Although nearly all countries cut the link between their currencies and gold, there was still a high regard for gold as an anchor for the monetary system. It was therefore decided to link at least the U.S. dollar, the currency to which all other currencies were to be linked, to gold. But the dollar would not be freely convertible to gold; only other central banks could turn in their dollars for gold. The parity price was set at $35 per ounce of gold.

The Bretton Woods Order

The Bretton Woods order was different from the gold standard order in that it was based on a set of rules that were explicitly written down in Bretton Woods. The gold standard was an order whose rules were essentially a culture, a mind-set that world leaders and central bank presidents implicitly accepted and followed.

The Bretton Woods order thus went into practice after the war with the following rules:

1. Countries other than the United States intervene in the foreign exchange market to keep their exchange rate within 1 percent of their currencies' dollar peg.
2. The United States does not intervene in the foreign exchange markets, but stands ready to convert dollars to gold at $35/oz. only for foreign central banks.
3. The International Monetary Fund (IMF) acts as the central bankers' central bank, lending reserves (usually U.S. dollars) to intervene in the foreign exchange markets and providing economic and financial advice.
4. Exchange rate pegs should be adjusted only in the case of a fundamental disequilibrium; otherwise, countries must intervene in the foreign exchange market or adjust domestic monetary policies to keep the exchange rate fixed.
5. The United States effectively anchors the world price level with its monetary policy because its currency serves as the world's reserve currency.
6. Currencies are freely convertible for current account transactions, but governments have the option to restrict financial account transactions.
7. The International Bank for Reconstruction and Development (the World Bank) will provide funding for rebuilding after the war and, in the longer run, fostering economic growth and development where funding would otherwise not be available.

Harry Dexter White managed to keep all delegations in Bretton Woods on board to sign the final agreement, including the Soviet Union's. There was some doubt about the Soviet delegation's intentions throughout the three weeks, but in the end Stalin gave his consent for the delegation to sign the agreement. Of course, when the Cold War began, after 1945, the Soviet Union had second thoughts and declined to participate in the IMF and the Bretton Woods system, despite White's controversial continued communications with the Soviets. The Bretton Woods system was essentially designed for a capitalist world economy, and the Soviets saw little to gain from integrating their centrally planned communist economy into this system. After the Cold War erupted, the Bretton Woods system was operated by, and for, the Western market-oriented economies with the United States's economy at the center.

The Marshall Plan and European Economic Integration

The pegged exchange rates and the World Bank did not bring instant economic recovery to Europe. In 1947, two years after the war, Europe barely survived one of the worst winters on record. There was little the devastated European economies could produce for sale abroad in order to earn dollars to pay for imports such as food and the capital equipment to restore destroyed railways, water systems, power plants, and other infrastructure. U.S. Secretary of State George C. Marshall, the retired U.S. Army chief of staff, understood the situation in Europe was desperate, and he feared that the humanitarian crisis would play into the hands of the Soviet Union, which was actively trying to convince Europeans to embrace communism and side with it in the Cold War. Marshall proposed a huge aid package of $200 billion (in today's dollars) that would permit Europe to import equipment, food, and other scarce products without being constrained by its limited export capacity. This program came to be known simply as the **Marshall Plan**. Freed from their balance of payments constraints, European governments could begin to stimulate their economies and eliminate price controls and trade restrictions. The U.S. aid worked, and by the mid-1950s, Western Europe's economies were growing. As hoped, by then international trade between Western economies grew rapidly.

The United States offered aid to the Soviet Union under the Marshall Plan, although U.S. officials could not realistically have expected the U.S.S.R. to accept the offer. Marshall Plan aid came with strong requirements attached. The U.S.S.R. would have had to participate in the European bureaucracy that would administer and monitor the aid, for example. Also, some of the aid was intended to fund capitalist institutions, such as central banks, tax systems, and democratic government agencies. When, not surprisingly, Stalin decided that the Soviet Union would not participate in the Marshall Plan, Europe was effectively split into West and East.

The Performance of the Early Bretton Woods System

The Bretton Woods system worked well during the 1950s. There were two small devaluations of the French franc in 1957 and 1958, but otherwise the pegged exchange rates came under little pressure. World trade started to grow rapidly, and the countries that had been destroyed by the war recovered impressively. West Germany and Japan were the big economic success stories of the decade; their rapid recoveries were often referred to as **economic miracles**. Even though their rapid growth can be fully explained, it was impressive nonetheless. It appears as though the designers of the Bretton Woods system had been right: A pegged exchange rate, adjustable under extreme circumstances, would help create an economic climate appropriate for rapid economic growth. But it turned out that the system was not really tested in the 1950s.

The trilemma, which is the conflict between policy independence, increased international trade and finance, and fixed exchange rates, was not applicable before 1960. Until then, the United States conducted a moderately expansionist monetary policy that was acceptable to other countries in the system. Current accounts were small as world trade was just beginning to recover from the protectionism of the 1930s, and financial account transactions were tightly controlled by most governments. With foreign exchange transactions related mostly to international trade, not international investment, required intervention to maintain the exchange rate peg was not very large even when desired monetary and fiscal policies differed somewhat from those necessary to match U.S. policies.

The 1960s Reveal the System's Inconsistencies

In the 1960s, the U.S. Federal Reserve Bank greatly expanded the money supply in an attempt to hold down interest costs of the growing U.S. government budget deficits. These deficits stemmed from tax cuts to spur the economy after a nagging recession early in the 1960s, the expensive Vietnam War, and expanded social spending during the administration of President Lyndon Johnson. The Federal Reserve targeted interest rates, and inflation rose steadily during the 1960s. With pegged exchange rates, the dollar therefore lost purchasing power in the world economy, and the resulting decline in the demand for dollars and increased supply of dollars were causing the dollar to depreciate in value. In order to keep their currencies "pegged" to the dollar, the Bretton Woods rules required foreign central banks to supply their own currencies in order to buy the excess U.S. dollars in the foreign exchange market and thus keep the exchange rate pegged. The increased supply of U.S. dollars effectively forced other countries to increase their money supplies, which threatened to cause inflation in other countries. Recall that, just as the supply of gold determined world price levels under the gold standard, under Bretton Woods rules the supply of dollars determined global price levels. Foreign central bankers complained that the United States was "exporting inflation."

Toward the end of the 1960s, after expansionary monetary policy in the United States raised U.S. inflation above inflation in most of its trade partners, speculative pressure against the dollar strengthened. This speculative pressure consisted of growing amounts of U.S. dollars being sold on the foreign exchange market in exchange for other currencies to purchase nondollar assets that would instantaneously gain in value if the dollar were devalued. The term **devaluation** refers to an intentional one-time lowering of the value of a currency under a fixed exchange rate arrangement. That is, many wealth holders believed that the current pegged exchange rate was no longer an accurate reflection of the long-run supply and demand for the dollar and that the United States would have to change the dollar's peg sometime soon. It would, therefore, be safer to place one's wealth in assets denominated in another currency, like the German mark, Dutch guilder, or Swiss franc, whose value would rise.

Robert Triffin (1960) had warned, in a widely read book, that there was a fundamental inconsistency in the Bretton Woods order: because the U.S. dollar was the world's reserve currency, the United States was obligated to run trade deficits so that the rest of the world could "earn" dollars for their reserves, but the more dollars were held by foreigners, the more likely that the dollar could come under speculative attack and the less foreigners would want to hold dollars. This came to be known as the *Triffin paradox*. By the late 1960s, growing U.S. trade deficits meant foreign governments were accumulating more dollars than they wanted to hold. Then the central bank of France began using its accumulated dollars to purchase U.S. gold, as the Bretton Woods rules allowed. But as Triffin had predicted, when it appeared that there were more U.S. dollars held as reserves by foreign governments than there was gold in the United States at the $35 parity rate, expectations of a devaluation of the dollar grew stronger and fewer financial investors wanted to hold dollars or dollar-denominated assets. If the central banks of all countries sought to exchange their dollars for U.S. gold, wouldn't the United States have to devalue the dollar?

In the late 1960s more and more people, firms, banks, and other wealth holders began to move their wealth out of dollar-denominated assets and into nondollar assets. Even more intervention by Germany and others was required. In 1970, the German mark and Dutch guilder were, in fact, **revaluated**, that is, repegged at a higher value relative to the dollar. But pressure on the dollar continued when there was no evidence of any change in U.S. macroeconomic policy.

The Final Collapse of the Bretton Woods System

In 1971, President Nixon devalued the U.S. dollar against all other currencies by raising the gold parity from $35 to $38. This was a devaluation of about 8.5 percent. Nixon acted in accordance with the spirit of Bretton Woods Articles of Agreement that permitted exchange-rate flexibility; the U.S. government duly informed the International Monetary Fund of its decision. But the dollar devaluation violated the unwritten rules of the game of the fixed-rate dollar standard. The United States was not supposed to interfere in the foreign exchange markets, because its currency served as the "commodity" in which all other currencies were valued. Nixon also suspended foreign central banks' conversion of dollars to gold, which broke another of the Bretton Woods rules of the game. The U.S. actions were designed to stem the speculation against the dollar, but they seemed only to increase uncertainty and increase the supply of dollars in the foreign exchange market. Further devaluations were expected.

Germany, the Netherlands, Switzerland, and several other European governments reacted to the speculation against the dollar by suspending their central bank intervention in the foreign exchange markets and effectively letting their currencies float. Without the central bank intervention, the U.S. dollar quickly lost value, as did the British pound. As expected, the German mark, the Swiss franc, the Dutch guilder, and numerous other currencies all rose in value relative to the dollar. World leaders were not yet willing to embrace floating exchange rates, however. Throughout 1971 there were active negotiations among the governments of the United States, Japan, and the European countries, with the intent of modifying the Bretton Woods agreement so that the basic system could continue to function.

At a meeting at the Smithsonian Institution in Washington, DC, in late 1971, the signatories of the Bretton Woods agreement agreed to try to return to a fixed exchange rate system. This time, however, the dollar would not be linked to gold. New pegs were set to reflect market exchange rates during the brief period of floating exchange rates. And currencies would be permitted to fluctuate within a band of plus or minus 2.25 percent of the "pegged" exchange rate. The foreign exchange market settled down for a few months, but by early 1973 the U.S. dollar came under attack again.

The U.S. government, much too concerned with the Vietnam War, student protests, a slowing economy, and presidential elections in 1972, did not fundamentally alter its monetary and fiscal policies after the Smithsonian meeting. In early 1973, Switzerland saw so many dollars converted to Swiss francs that it took the desperate measure of requiring negative interest rates on bank deposits by foreigners, in what proved to be an unsuccessful effort to stem the tide of dollars flowing into Swiss banks. Apparently, a 1 percent negative interest rate on a Swiss franc bank account was preferable to a dollar asset expected to suffer a capital loss from a sharp devaluation. The continued inflow of foreign money had serious inflationary consequences in Switzerland, so in early 1973, Swiss authorities decided to stop intervening in the foreign exchange market and let the franc float upward. Then people, firms, and financial institutions immediately began to switch their wealth to the still-pegged German mark, Dutch guilder, and Japanese yen, and other currencies that were still viewed as undervalued relative to the dollar.

In February 1973, the United States announced that the dollar would be devalued by 10 percent against other major currencies. There was no clear evidence that the dollar was overvalued by 10 percent, but it seemed like a convenient number. At first, the foreign exchange markets reacted by pushing the value of the dollar back up, probably the result of demand for dollars by profit-taking speculators who had earlier moved out of dollars. But by March, the dollar was again sinking below its new peg. On March 11, Germany, France, Belgium, the Netherlands, and Denmark floated their currencies, and soon most other central banks also stopped intervening to keep their currencies fixed. The dollar has been floating ever since. In terms of the trilemma, policy makers effectively opted for capital mobility and policy independence in 1973. They abandoned their attempts to simultaneously maintain capital mobility, peg exchange rates, and conduct independent macroeconomic policies.

Evaluating the Bretton Woods System

Many writers have judged the Bretton Woods system harshly. Admittedly, it did eventually fail. However, in a broader sense the system was a tremendous success. In fact, its collapse was caused

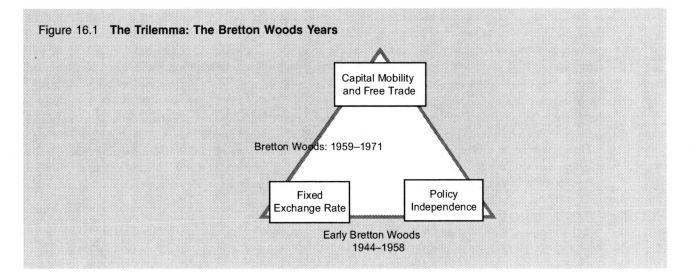

Figure 16.1 **The Trilemma: The Bretton Woods Years**

Capital Mobility and Free Trade

Bretton Woods: 1959–1971

Fixed Exchange Rate

Policy Independence

Early Bretton Woods 1944–1958

by that very success in achieving the idealistic goals of the Bretton Woods delegates. Recall that the purpose of the Bretton Woods conference was to establish an international financial order that would help to reverse economic isolation and promote economic growth of all countries, thereby hopefully avoiding the unemployment and economic stagnation that could cause another wave of dictators and wars. The Bretton Woods order had enabled the world to accomplish those goals beyond most people's expectations. World GDP grew at unprecedented rates during the 1950s and 1960s. Never had material output risen as fast as it did during these two decades. Also, unemployment rates were generally low as growing economies created many new employment opportunities.

As suggested in Figure 16.1, there really were two distinct phases of the Bretton Woods system. The system appeared quite stable from the end of World War II until the shift to full currency convertibility for current account transactions in Europe in 1958. This stability was due to widespread trade restrictions and strict control of financial account transactions by most countries. Without financial flows to upset the foreign exchange markets, the trilemma was not violated. But after 1960, the system became less stable. The liberalization of international trade and financial flows, which was a goal of the delegates at Bretton Woods, made it more difficult to maintain the pegged exchange rates. The Triffin paradox undermined confidence in the dollar, and the expansionary U.S. fiscal and monetary policies meant the trilemma became more likely to upset the pegged exchange rates. Figure 16.1 summarizes the trilemma over the Bretton Woods period. In the first period, 1944 through 1958, the market economies that adhered to the Bretton Woods order effectively opted for fixed exchange rates and policy independence as they recovered from World War II. After 1958, the year when the European economies lifted restrictions on the foreign exchange markets, countries lost their ability to focus their macroeconomic policies exclusively on domestic needs, and they effectively opted for the combination of international economic integration and fixed exchange rates.

The loss of policy independence meant that the Bretton Woods system limited countries' ability to maintain domestic economic stability. Despite the rapid long-run growth of world GDP, it is not possible to conclude that all economies performed smoothly all the time. The business cycle and its very noticeable ups and downs in employment and business activity were an expected and accepted macroeconomic phenomenon in nearly all major market economies, especially in the United States and the United Kingdom.

The Bretton Woods order clearly failed in some respects. Prices and output were not stable. In fact, as discussed above, U.S. inflation became a problem that ultimately undermined the pegged exchange rates. Furthermore, the Bretton Woods system was not equally beneficial for all countries. The United States seemed to assume it had special privileges where other countries thought it had special responsibilities for managing the world's reserve currency. When the benefits from participation are not equally shared, dissent arises and the system becomes less stable. It was, in fact, when the United States began exporting inflation, in part because it wanted to reduce the costs of its unpopular Vietnam War, that many countries lost their enthusiasm for intervening in the foreign exchange markets to keep exchange rates pegged. First in 1971, and then definitively in 1973, the Bretton Woods order was abandoned, one dissenting country at a time. Regaining international cooperation to piece together a new system would be difficult.

AFTER BRETTON WOODS

When the Bretton Woods system was unable to solve the trilemma, floating exchange rates effectively became the order of the day. Floating exchange rates are the default order when other specific measures are not taken. But governments did continue to seek an alternative to fully free floating exchange rates. Finding an alternative order and system proved to be very difficult, however.

Many Meetings, No Agreement

John Williamson, in his appropriately entitled book, *The Failure of World Monetary Reform, 1971–1974* (1977), describes the many meetings that were held after the 1973 failure of the Bretton Woods order. The mind-set, or perhaps we should use Barry Eichengreen and Peter Temin's (1997) term *mentalité,* was not ready for the new realities of the 1970s, and countries were unable to agree on a new order that could create a stable exchange rate system in the increasingly integrated world economy. In 1973 and 1974, there were many meetings of officials from the finance ministries and central banks of the major economies. The meetings attempted to establish a system with more flexibility for individual countries to pursue their national policies while maintaining exchange rate stability.

Some countries wanted to maintain a system of pegged exchange rates, albeit a reformed one. They proposed strict fiscal and monetary rules that countries would have to adhere to. The French also sought to limit the United States's privilege of being able to finance its external liabilities in dollars, which France argued relieved the United States from the international market discipline that all other countries faced. The United States naturally objected to that plan. Instead, it offered to accept the responsibility of stabilizing exchange rates within wide bands, provided that other countries agreed to help maintain the bands by promising to revalue undervalued currencies.

There were many meetings during the 1970s and 1980s, some including national leaders, others central bank chiefs, and some just officials from lower-level government agencies. Several of these meetings stand out in importance. At the **Rambouillet Summit** in 1975, countries agreed to work toward a "stable system" of exchange rates, but not a "system of stable exchange rates," as the French had wanted. Finally, in 1978, countries agreed on the **Second Amendment** to the original Bretton Woods *Articles of Agreement,* which legalized the floating exchange rates that had been a fact since 1973. The *Second Amendment* also required that countries maintain stable economic policies in order to minimize exchange rate volatility. Finally, the IMF was authorized to monitor and critique countries' economic policies on a continual basis.

There was little consensus among economists on how the system should be reformed. Central bankers longed for policy independence, and economists such as Milton Friedman advocated flexible exchange rates as central to a stable monetary system. Others were apprehensive about floating

Figure 16.2   **Real Exchange Rates 1975–1989**

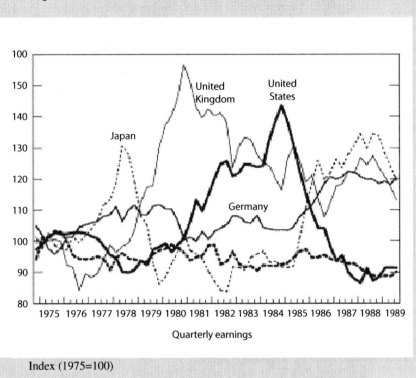

Index (1975=100)

exchange rates, but because of the diverging national interests, there appeared to be no possibility of maintaining a system of pegged exchange rates. When in 1978 the new world order of flexible exchange rates gained official status, many economists were surprised by the results. The world didn't sink after the fall of Bretton Woods, as some had feared. Rather, it floated. On the other hand, the proponents of floating exchange rates were surprised that those rates were not stable. The waters turned out to be rather choppy, and the voyage was not to most passengers' liking.

Exchange Rate Volatility

Proponents of flexible exchange rates had reasoned that, so long as long-run expectations were stable, arbitragers and speculators would smooth out short-term fluctuations. In fact, exchange rates fluctuated wildly after 1973, much more than even some of the critics of floating exchange rates believed possible. Figure 16.2 illustrates the volatility of exchange rates after the fall of the Bretton Woods order. For example, the dollar fell from 3.65 German marks per dollar in 1970 to 2.28 marks in 1979, a 38 percent decline. Such a change means it took 50 percent more dollars to buy the same amount of marks in 1979 as it did in 1970! Then, from 1979 to 1985, the dollar recovered all of its value lost relative to the mark after 1973, but by 1989 it again fell to less than it was worth in 1979.

The U.S. dollar's gradual fall in value relative to most other major currencies came to an end in 1979. With inflation reaching 15 percent per year, the new chairman of the Federal Reserve Bank, Paul Volcker, applied the brakes to monetary policy. Volcker announced that he would tighten the money supply as much as was necessary to reduce inflation to single digits, regardless of the consequences on the **real exchange rates**. The dollar appreciated by 28 percent in real terms between 1980 and 1982. The expansionary fiscal policy of President Ronald Reagan, who cut income taxes and raised defense expenditures in 1981, combined with the tight monetary policy to raise real interest rates in the United States to nearly 15 percent. This monetary tightening, you may recall from Chapter 14, was one of the decisive triggers of the 1982 debt crisis in many developing economies. The high real interest rates strengthened the U.S. dollar as wealth holders abandoned foreign assets for high returns on U.S. dollar assets.

The gap between foreign interest rates and U.S. interest rates reached a peak in early 1984, but the dollar nevertheless continued to rise in value relative to other major currencies throughout the year. The dollar's appreciation finally stopped in February 1985, after which it began to depreciate. As you read in Chapter 11, the U.S. current account fell deeply into deficit. These growing trade deficits were viewed with concern by most economists, politicians, and commentators, who worried that large exchange rate adjustments could cause financial crises even in the large, developed economies.

The Plaza Accord

The popular story about the turnaround of the dollar in 1985 involves the secret meeting of finance ministers and central bankers of France, West Germany, Japan, the United Kingdom, and the United States in the Plaza Hotel in New York City in September 1985. Only at the close of that meeting was a public announcement made and a formal agreement presented to the press. As part of that agreement, the United States would cut its government deficit, Japan promised to expand its monetary policy and to push forward stalled reform of its financial sector, and West Germany agreed to cut taxes. There was also agreement on the need for concerted intervention in the foreign exchange markets to bring currencies into alignment with economic fundamentals. According to paragraph 18 of the agreement:

> The Ministers and Governors agreed that exchange rates should play a role in adjusting external imbalances. In order to do this, exchange rates should better reflect fundamental economic conditions than has been the case. They believe that agreed policy actions must be implemented and reinforced to improve the fundamentals further, and that in view of the present and prospective changes in fundamentals, some further orderly appreciation of the main non-dollar currencies against the dollar is desirable. They stand ready to cooperate more closely to encourage this when to do so would be helpful.[2]

At the end of 1987, the dollar had fallen by 54 percent against the German mark and the Japanese yen from its peak in February 1985.

It is not clear that the **Plaza Accord**, as the agreement became known, was the cause of the currency realignment. The dollar had already begun falling in value in early 1985, and it had declined sharply by the time of the Plaza Hotel meeting in September 1985. The Plaza Accord is important because it illustrated that the leading economies were willing to cooperate and even alter their policies in the interest of stability in the international monetary system. Not all of the suggested policy changes were implemented; domestic politics often intervened. But enough of the countries adhered to enough of their commitments so that, when the accord was combined with the clear coordination of exchange rate intervention by the five central banks, market expectations were reinforced and the foreign exchange markets continued to drive down the value of the dollar as hoped.

The dollar fell so far in value that some countries expressed fears that world trade would be disrupted and international financial flows would even be reversed. Another meeting was held in 1987, and another agreement, similar to the Plaza Accord, was hammered out. Called the **Louvre Accord** because the meeting was held at the Louvre Museum in Paris, this agreement committed the United States to tighten its fiscal policy and for Japan to loosen its monetary policy, among other things. Concerted exchange rate intervention by all central banks was also called for. The post-Louvre appreciation of the dollar was small, however. And although the United States followed through on some of its promises made in the Plaza and Louvre Accords, by the early 1990s U.S. authorities had reverted back to their customary policy of benign neglect of the dollar, preferring to let the markets (and other governments) determine the value of the dollar. Indicative of the U.S. dollar policy in the early 1990s was President George H.W. Bush's comment to a reporter asking about the dollar: "Once in a while, I think about those things, but not much."[3]

The Bretton Woods Institutions

The IMF and the World Bank were given specific tasks in the Bretton Woods agreement, namely to manage the pegged exchange rate system and provide financing for postwar reconstruction, respectively. But once the pegged rates were abandoned, the IMF switched to helping countries deal with the volatility of international investment flows and exchange rates. Recall from Chapter 14 how the IMF became involved in the 1982 debt crisis by lending temporary funds and overseeing developing countries' economic reform programs. The World Bank, on the other hand, came to focus exclusively on raising economic growth rates in the developing countries. The World Bank finances long-term projects to promote economic growth, such as education, transportation facilities, communications, and electricity generators.

The IMF's emergency lending is usually closely linked to a set of policy changes that it deems necessary for countries to solve the fundamental imbalances that caused the shifts in international investment flows. The IMF and World Bank often insist on policies that reduce government budget deficits, tightly restrict monetary expansion, reduce government interference in the economy, privatize government assets, and rationalize tax systems, a set of goals that is often referred to as the Washington consensus. For this reason, the IMF and World Bank are often depicted as U.S.-dominated institutions that dictate economic policies to borrowers for the benefit of lenders in general and the United States in particular. The truth of the matter is much more complex, but there is no doubt that the two Bretton Woods institutions operate within the neoclassical paradigm and adhere to a free market ideology. There has been much talk of reforming the two institutions and giving developing-country governments a greater voice in their operation and decision making, but so far little has changed.

Evaluating the Post–Bretton Woods Period

Despite the fears of the delegates at the Bretton Woods conference, there is no evidence that floating exchange rates have depressed world trade and investment. Many studies covering the period since 1973 when trade volumes have been expanding and exchange rates floating conclude that the volume of international trade would not have grown any faster if exchange rates had still been pegged, although, admittedly, counterfactuals are difficult to estimate.[4] International investment has also grown especially rapidly since the 1970s.

Other goals of the international financial order, such as low unemployment and economic growth, have not been as clearly met, however. Exchange rate volatility seems to have played a role in the many currency crises that have occurred during the post-1973 period. The many currency crises and accompanying financial crises in developing countries, discussed in the previous chapter, show that the post–Bretton Woods system has not been an improvement on the Bretton Woods system. Even many developed economies have experienced rising unemployment, especially in Europe. On the other hand, the U.S. economy enjoyed relatively stable economic growth from the 1980s into the early 2000s, although the enthusiasm about U.S. technological progress has been overstated. Michael Kouparitsas (2005) of the Federal Reserve Bank of Chicago shows that early 2000s U.S. technological progress was on its post-1960 trend, not above trend as some new economy enthusiasts have suggested. It was below trend between 1985 and 1995.

In the first decade of the 2000s, the international monetary system permitted increasingly large trade imbalances among countries and the accumulation of large foreign debts. Economic growth rates began diverging, with a few large developing economies, especially China, growing nearly 10 percent per year while others in Africa, South Asia, and Latin America continuing to stagnate. The United States's trade deficits continued to grow, reaching an unprecedented 6 percent of GDP in 2007. Western Europe had difficulties dealing with growing unemployment. The long and consistent growth episodes in Germany and Japan came to an end in the 1990s. In terms of GDP per capita, the Japanese economy has stagnated for the last two decades, although it can also be argued that it has successfully maintained its very high standard of living while other countries have gone through sharp ups and downs in income and social welfare. Eastern European countries have struggled to recover from their sharp economic declines after the fall of the U.S.S.R. and the transition to new economic paradigms.

Not only were there continuing financial crises in developing countries, but the United States suffered a major stock market collapse in 2000. This collapse was the outcome of the Federal Reserve Bank's excessively expansionary monetary policy in the late 1990s. The monetary expansion was justified by the fact that the measured inflation rate remained stable. U.S. product prices did not rise, because of the rapid expansion of international trade and the seemingly unlimited supply of low-priced Chinese manufactures. The increased money supply fueled a stock bubble instead. When this bubble popped in 2000, the decline in perceived wealth quickly slowed U.S. economic growth. And when the September 11, 2001, terrorist attacks in the United States further weakened the U.S. economy, the Federal Reserve launched yet another aggressive expansion of the money supply. This time a housing bubble resulted.

More serious than the stock market bubble, the housing bubble was also driven by financial innovation and lax financial oversight by the Federal Reserve Bank. As discussed in Chapter 13, in 2007 and 2008 this housing bubble created a worldwide financial crisis that caused the first worldwide economic recession since World War II. The official U.S. unemployment rate reached 10 percent in 2009; alternative measures suggest true unemployment and under employment rose to nearly 20 percent. Youth unemployment surpassed 25 percent in the United States and in many other high-income economies, which meant that this deep recession would have lasting effects. In sum, by 2010 the post–Bretton Woods international monetary system appeared to be neither stable nor equitable.

The post-1973 period has a mixed record with respect to inflation. Inflation exploded in both developed and developing economies during the 1970s as many countries loosened monetary policies. Developed countries revised their policies, and they brought inflation under control. However, developing countries experienced even worse inflationary episodes after the 1982 debt crisis, especially Latin America. In the 1990s and early 2000s, however, inflation has been subdued in nearly all of the world's economies. This experience makes it clear that floating exchange rates accommodate inflation, in large part because floating rates give governments the freedom to establish whatever macroeconomic policies they want. But floating exchange rates do not necessarily result in higher inflation. That is, they effectively eliminate a source of price discipline for central banks, but there is nothing about floating exchange rates that prevents central banks from controlling money supplies.

When it comes to the issue of policy independence, floating rates do seem to permit the major economies to carry out macroeconomic policies more independently, although complete policy independence has been an illusive dream for all but the largest countries in the increasingly global economy. By 2005, some economists began to suggest that even the United States will find that it has become so dependent on foreign capital flows that it would have to rein in its fiscal deficits if it was to avoid a long-term currency crisis.

As the report cards in Tables 16.1 and 16.2 show, the post–Bretton Woods international monetary system has not performed as well as the Bretton Woods system before it. Granted, the Bretton Woods system ultimately became unsustainable. But the current system does not appear to be sustainable

Table 16.1			Table 16.2		
Report Card: The Bretton Woods System			**Report Card for the Post–1973 Period**		
1. Stability/employment	Marginal Pass		1. Stability/employment	Needs work	
2. Economic growth	Pass		2. Economic growth	Inconsistent	
3. Globalization	Pass		3. Globalization	Pass	
4. Policy independence	Fail		4. Policy independence	Fail	
5. Mutually beneficial	Marginal Pass		5. Mutually beneficial	Fail	
6. Price stability	Fail		6. Price stability	Fail	

either, and in the meantime the economic outcomes are not improving nearly as much they did under the Bretton Woods system.

THE EURO

The volatile floating exchange rates after 1973 were very costly to Europe. The volume of trade between the European countries was very large. Small European economies like Belgium, the Netherlands, and Luxembourg exported over half of their output and imported over half of the products they consumed. Even larger European countries exported at least one quarter of their production, about twice as high a percentage of GDP as the average country in the world. Hence, for Europe floating exchange rates added a disproportionate amount of expense and risk to their international transactions.

European policy makers realized it would be impossible to keep their exchange rates fixed in terms of the U.S. dollar, the Japanese yen, or other major world currencies. But they thought it would be possible to peg exchange rates among the European currencies, which would at least isolate intra-European trade and financial transactions from exchange rate uncertainty. The enthusiasm in Western Europe for continuing some kind of pegged exchange rate system among their currencies was enhanced by their experience in forming a common market in which goods were freely traded among themselves. As discussed in the Chapter 9, the European Union had already achieved many forms of economic cooperation. This section discusses the monetary union in Europe that culminated in the creation of a single European currency, the euro, in 2002.

The Early Steps toward Economic Union

The idea of a politically united Europe did not arise only in the late twentieth century. For example, emperors and kings had on many occasions attempted to unite Europe through conquest. This propensity for Europe's nations to go to war led the nineteenth-century French novelist Victor Hugo to advocate a peaceful "United States of Europe" guided by the humanistic ideals of the Enlightenment. European countries ignored Hugo's idea and continued to wage war on each other, however, and the hostilities culminated in World War II. At the end of World War II, more enlightened leaders acknowledged their electorates' fatigue with war and began a serious process to fundamentally change the economic and political environment of Western Europe.

A renewed interest in a peacefully united Europe coincided with the Marshall Plan, which, as discussed earlier, established a European organization to administer the distribution of U.S. financial assistance. One of the conditions for receiving Marshall Plan aid was that countries participate in this new European organization. There was considerable reluctance to participate, however, because wartime animosities had not entirely subsided. There was concern among the

Allied countries after the war that an economic recovery of German industry would enable that nation to rearm for yet another war. Even many U.S. officials, including Secretary of the Treasury Henry Morgenthau, Harry Dexter White's boss, opposed letting Germany rebuild its industry after the war.

Accepting the reality of Germany's industrial development, French Foreign Affairs Minister Robert Schuman and his fellow French statesman Jean Monet came up with a holistic, and as it turned out, fully realistic, proposal: the **European Coal and Steel Community (ECSC)**. This was to be a multinational authority for governing the production and distribution of coal and steel in France, West Germany, Italy, and the Benelux countries (Belgium, the Netherlands, and Luxembourg). Under the treaty signed in Paris in 1950, these six countries agreed to eliminate all tariffs and quotas on the trade in coal and steel among themselves. They also agreed to establish a regional authority with executive powers, an assembly consisting of delegates from the individual countries, a council of ministers to safeguard the countries' national interests, and a court of justice to settle disputes. The goal of Schuman and Monet was to create a regional organization to monitor German industry and to put a crucial part of that country's industry under the control of a supranational body. Such an arrangement would overcome fears that Germany would use its Marshall Plan aid to rearm its military.

In practice, the ECSC turned out to be the first of many steps toward European cooperation and economic integration that led to today's European Union and the introduction of the euro. The six members of the European Coal and Steel Community signed two more agreements in 1957, the first establishing the **European Atomic Energy Community (Euratom)** and the second, the *Treaty of Rome,* establishing the **European Economic Community (EEC)**. The Treaty of Rome mandated the elimination of all restrictions on trade between the member states. It also mandated that the members of the EEC set common external tariffs; that is, the members would have to agree to a common trade policy. Technically, the EEC was soon to become a **customs union** (recall Figure 9.7 in Chapter 9).

There was more to the Treaty of Rome than the creation of a common market, however. Article 2 of the Treaty of Rome set much broader aims for the EEC. It was to

> promote throughout the Community a harmonious development of economic activities, a continuous and balanced expansion, an increase in stability, an accelerated raising of the standard of living and closer relations between the States belonging to it.[5]

These were lofty goals. To achieve them would require not just the opening up of borders to goods, services, people, and capital, but also genuine cooperation among governments and their willingness to surrender some degree of national sovereignty. To the surprise of many observers, European countries not only proceeded to meet the goals set out in the Treaty of Rome, but over the remainder of the twentieth century they set, and achieved, even loftier goals for economic cooperation and unification.

Enlarging the EEC

In 1960, seven other Western European countries negotiated a more modest free trade area. The Stockholm Convention established the **European Free Trade Area (EFTA)** among Austria, Denmark, Norway, Portugal, Sweden, Switzerland, and the United Kingdom. Finland joined in 1961. EFTA eliminated trade restrictions among its member countries, but the agreement did not address the more ambitious goals of the EEC. EFTA was seen by some of its members as a temporary step toward eventual membership in the EEC and its higher level of economic integration. Others preferred to limit the level of integration to free trade because they were not willing to give up their autonomy in setting trade policies toward countries outside EFTA or they were not willing to pursue higher levels of cooperation with other countries because of the loss of policy autonomy and national sovereignty that such cooperation would imply.

Meanwhile, the six members of the EEC achieved the customs union foreseen in the Treaty of Rome on July 1, 1968, when the last remaining tariffs between the six countries were removed. Common external trade policies were also negotiated and implemented during the 1960s. The long-term goal of a **Common Agricultural Policy (CAP)** was also achieved during the 1960s, and the CAP remains a major feature of European cooperation. The CAP's protectionist subsidies have made it a major stumbling block in multilateral trade negotiations at the start of the twenty-first century, but it was a major step toward political cooperation and unification in Europe. The EEC was enlarged in 1973, when Denmark, Ireland, and the United Kingdom joined. This enlargement had been blocked by the French government throughout the 1960s because the French president, Charles de Gaulle, was afraid that the United Kingdom would tilt the EEC away from the French-German axis and reduce French cultural and economic influence. With De Gaulle's resignation from the French presidency at the end of the 1960s, however, France became open to British membership in the EEC.

The EEC after the Collapse of Bretton Woods

The shift to floating exchange rates was not welcomed by European governments, because it made the large volume of trade among European countries more costly to carry out. There was strong support by business groups for renewed efforts to restore some kind of pegged exchange rate system. In fact, when in 1971 the Smithsonian Agreement permitted exchange rates to fluctuate within a band of 2.25 percent to each side of the pegged rate compared to the Bretton Woods rule plus or minus 1 percent, EEC and EFTA countries agreed to keep their exchange rates within 1.125 percent of their pegs. These tighter fluctuations among European currencies while the whole group of currencies varied by plus or minus 2.25 percent against the rest of the world's currencies were referred to as the **snake in the tunnel**. With the complete abandonment of the Bretton Woods order in 1973, five European economies—Belgium, Denmark, Germany, the Netherlands, and Luxembourg—agreed to continue to respect the snake's tighter margins. This arrangement proved successful because each of the four smaller countries in the group of five maintained monetary policies in strict concert with the German central bank's monetary policy.

In 1979, the five snake countries plus France and Italy, all members of the EEC, established a more formal system of pegged exchange rates called the **European Monetary System (EMS)**. They agreed to use central bank intervention to peg the exchange rates between their currencies within narrow bands using central bank intervention and float as a group against all other currencies. For example, the central banks of Germany and the Netherlands intervened in the foreign exchange markets to maintain the guilder-mark exchange rate within 2.5 percent of an agreed value, but they let the mark and guilder float freely against the U.S. dollar or the Japanese yen. Each country's central bank would maintain supplies of other European currencies in order to intervene in the foreign exchange markets if necessary. The EMS grew in size when Great Britain, Spain, Portugal, Denmark, and Austria joined later in the 1980s.

The EMS functioned just like the Bretton Woods system. Each country agreed to intervene in the foreign exchange markets to keep their currencies within 2.5 percent of each currency's pegged exchange rate. In recognition of the trilemma, and the failure of the Bretton Woods system to successfully deal with it, the European countries participating in the EMS also agreed to coordinate economic policies and keep the underlying supply and demand curves for foreign exchange intersecting at or near the targeted exchange rates.

The EMS did not work as hoped, however. Table 16.3 shows how frequently the pegs were changed for each of the participating currencies. With some of the countries changing pegs almost yearly in the early 1980s, the EMS was not a fixed exchange rate system. Since forward markets

Table 16.3

Realignments of EMS Exchange Rates (percent changes in currency pegs)

Date	BLF	DK	DM	ESC	FFR	IL	IP	DG	PTA	UKP
9–24–79	—	-2.86	+2.0	*	—	—	—	—	*	*
11–30–79	—	-4.76	—	*	—	—	—	—	*	*
3–23–81	—	—	—	*	—	-6.0	—	—	*	*
10–5–81	—	—	+5.5	*	-3.0	-3.0	—	+5.5	*	*
2–22–82	-8.5	-3.0	—	*	—	—	—	—	*	*
6–14–82	—	—	+4.25	*	-5.75	-2.75	—	+4.25	*	*
3–21–83	+1.5	+2.5	+5.5	*	-2.5	-2.5	-3.5	+3.5	*	*
7–22–85	+2.0	+2.0	+2.0	*	+2.0	-6.0	+2.0	+2.0	*	*
4–7–86	+1.0	+1.0	+3.0	*	-3.0	—	—	+3.0	*	*
8–4–86	—	—	—	*	—	—	-8.0	—	*	*
1–12–87	+2.0	—	+3.0	*	—	—	—	+3.0	*	*

↑
five years of stability
↓

Date	BLF	DK	DM	ESC	FFR	IL	IP	DG	PTA	UKP
9–13–92	—	—	—	—	—	-7.0	—	—	—	—
9–17–92	—	—	—	—	—	*	—	—	-5.0	*
11–23–92	—	—	—	-6.0	—	*	—	—	-6.0	*
2–1–93	—	—	—	—	—	*	-10.0	—	—	*
5–14–93	—	—	—	-6.5	—	*	—	—	-8.0	*

* Not part of the EMS at the time
— No change
BLF: Belgian franc; DK: Danish Kroner; DM: German mark; ESC: Portuguese escudo; FFR; French franc; IL: Italian lira; IP: Irish pound; DG: Dutch guilder; PTA: Spanish peseta; UKP: British pound.
Source: From Table 2 in Bryon Higgins (1993), "Was the ERM Crisis Inevitable?," Federal Reserve Bank of Kansas City, *Economic Review,* 4th Quarter, p. 31.

permitted buyers and sellers of foreign currencies to hedge their short-run exchange rate risks, the benefit of a fixed exchange rate system depending on its ability to stabilize long-run exchange rates that are not easily hedged by exporters, importers, and international borrowers and lenders. But beginning in 1987, the participating countries increased efforts to synchronize policies, and the pegged exchange rates remained unchanged for the next five years. Then, suddenly, in 1992 speculative attacks on the British pound and Italian lira forced those countries to leave the EMS. The following year, there was further speculation against other European currencies, and the EMS was suspended.

The Trilemma Again!

The EMS could not permanently fix exchange rates because the macroeconomic policies of the member countries diverged in the early 1990s. This was triggered by the fall of the Berlin Wall in 1989. When West Germany absorbed East Germany, it had to unify the monetary systems by exchanging West German marks for the East German marks held by the former citizens of East Germany. Officially, East Germany had always maintained that one East German mark was equal to one West German mark, but the real purchasing power of the East German mark was much lower than that of the West German mark, a fact long recognized in the black market where the West German mark had traded for three, four, or even five East German marks. Therefore, had the West German authorities wanted to keep the real money supply unchanged, in respect of the EMS and the looming trilemma, they should have exchanged West German marks for East German marks at somewhere near the purchasing power parity exchange rate between the two currencies. Instead, the West German government decided to exchange a large portion of East German marks at the official but inaccurate one-to-one exchange rate, which constituted a large subsidy for East Germans. Perhaps West Germany's politicians thought this would help the political unification of the two countries. Or perhaps it was deemed necessary to extend aid to the poorer regions that made up East Germany. In any case, the one-to-one conversion also greatly increased the total real money supply of the unified Germany.

The surge in the German money supply threatened a rise in inflation, and the German central bank tightened monetary policy. Interest rates rose sharply, which in turn caused an equally sharp increase in demand for German assets and the marks to acquire the assets. The West German central bank at first intervened to keep the German mark from appreciating; the bank reportedly spent about 100 billion German marks to buy francs, kroner, pounds, pesetas, and other currencies. The French central bank spent US$55 billion of its foreign reserves to keep the franc from depreciating relative to the mark. The foreign exchange market intervention necessary to keep the mark from appreciating would, of course, undo the German central bank's tight money supply to fight inflation by injecting marks back into the banking system, so the central banks eventually gave up and let the currencies float.

The EMS experience once again reminded policy makers that they face a trilemma: it is impossible to fix exchange rates, liberalize international capital flows, and pursue independent domestic economic policies. The experience made it clear to most policy makers that they would have to do one of the following things: accept floating exchange rates, restrict international transactions, or find a way to permanently resist political pressures for independent macroeconomic policies. By 1992, the trilemma had become more restrictive with the 1991 signing of the **Maastricht Treaty**, in which the then-twelve member countries of the European Union agreed to completely liberalize all services trade, all investment and financial flows, and immigration among themselves. In recognition of the trilemma, the twelve also agreed to work toward the introduction of a single currency for all of Europe managed by a single central bank. Such a single currency in place of separate national currencies effectively creates permanently fixed exchange rates between the currencies. The European Economic Community changed its name to **European Union (EU)** to signify its intent to establish a complete economic union in which goods and services were freely traded, people and capital could cross borders without restrictions, and a single monetary policy would apply to all member countries.

In fact, the EEC had taken a big step toward becoming a complete economic union some years earlier. In 1985, a widely publicized white paper by a group of EU leaders headed by European Commission President Jacques Delors had proposed creating a true single market serving more than 300 million consumers by eliminating remaining obstacles to trade, such as inspections at border crossings, assorted technical barriers, and closed markets for public contracts. The European Commission is an EU's policy-making board consisting of national officials from member countries.[6] The cost of this inefficiency—the annual "cost of non-Europe" as the white paper called it—was put at around 200 billion euros. The twelve EEC member states transformed the white paper into the **Single European Act** in 1986. This act set out a precise timetable for completing 275 steps necessary for achieving the single market by the start of 1993. The act effectively moved Europe toward a full common market by 1993. In 1995, Austria, Finland, and Sweden joined the economic community. And in 1997 the Amsterdam Treaty formalized European rules on citizenship, standardized employment laws and regulations across the member countries, harmonized some social policies across countries, and further improved the organization of a common European trade policy vis-à-vis the rest of the world. The Amsterdam Treaty gave the European Union many new powers and responsibilities over individual European nations. The European Union was definitely moving toward political as well as economic union.

Establishing the Monetary Union

In December 1995, the European Union's fifteen members finalized the procedures for creating a single currency and the European Central Bank to manage it. The new currency would be called the **euro** and be denoted by the symbol €. They also agreed to a three-step procedure for admitting EU countries to the single currency area beginning in 1999. Each prospective member was required to meet these five macroeconomic criteria:

1. The currency's exchange rate must have remained fixed for two years.
2. Inflation must be less than 1.5 percent above the average inflation rate of the three European Union countries with the lowest inflation rates.
3. Interest rates on openly traded government bonds must be less than 2 percentage points above the average rates for the three European countries with the lowest rates.
4. The government budget deficit must be less than 3 percent of GDP.
5. Total government debt must be less than 60 percent of GDP.

At a meeting in May 1998, the European Union officially ruled that of the fifteen member countries, only Greece had failed to make "satisfactory progress" toward meeting the criteria for joining the euro system. Not all the fifteen countries wanted to join the scheme, however; Denmark, Sweden, and Britain opted to keep their own currencies for the time being. European Union rules permitted countries to opt out of the single currency agreement.

On January 1, 1999, the eleven approved and willing countries permanently fixed their exchange rates relative to each other and ceded all monetary policy to the new **European Central Bank (ECB)**. Greece was later deemed to have come into compliance with the stated guidelines and joined in 2000, although there is now evidence that Greece manipulated its numbers. During this initial phase of monetary unification, each national currency continued to circulate but its supply was managed by the ECB. This transitional phase came to an end between January 1 and March 1, 2002, when the national currencies were all exchanged for euros at the exchange rates set in 1999.

Further Expansion of the European Union

The political and economic environment of Europe changed dramatically with the fall of the Berlin Wall in 1989. Germany was reunified, and the other formerly communist countries of central and eastern Europe broke away from Soviet control and sought to reintegrate with Western Europe. Soon after Austria, Finland, and Sweden joined the ambitious EU, another twelve states applied for membership: the former Soviet-controlled eastern European countries (Bulgaria, the Czech Republic, Hungary, Poland, Romania, and Slovakia), three Baltic states that had once been part of the Soviet Union (Estonia, Latvia, and Lithuania), one of the republics of the former Yugoslavia (Slovenia), and two small Mediterranean island countries (Cyprus and Malta). The early supporters of the European Coal and Steel Community in 1950 would no doubt have been surprised by how far European economic and political integration had proceeded when negotiations were completed in December 2002 for ten of the applicants to officially join the European Union at the start of 2004. More recently, Romania and Bulgaria were also admitted, bringing membership to twenty-seven states in all.

In recent years, many politicians in Europe have openly spoken out against extending membership to more countries. Discussions with Turkey have proven to be an especially contentious issue.

Eastern European countries such as Ukraine, Belarus, and Moldova and former Yugoslavian states such as Serbia, Bosnia, and Croatia are seen as likely future members of the EU. By 2010, Cyprus, Malta, Slovenia, and Slovakia had also qualified for the euro area of the European Union, bringing the number of euro countries to sixteen.

Trade Effects of the European Monetary Union (EMU)

Many studies have looked at the effects of the **European Monetary Union (EMU)** on trade between the EU members. Perhaps most often cited is the statistical analysis by Andrew Rose and Eric van Wincoop (2001, p. 390), who find that international trade greatly expands among countries adopting a common currency. They conclude:

> Currency union reduces trade barriers associated with national borders, leading to substantial increases in both trade and welfare. That is, a national currency seems to be a significant barrier to trade. Reducing these barriers through currency unions like EMU or dollarization in the Americas will thus result in increased international trade. Our empirical work indicates that this effect may be large, in excess of 50 percent for EMU.

Jeffrey Frankel and Andrew Rose (2002) look at all countries in the world, and they estimate that belonging to a currency union triples trade with currency union partners, all other things equal. Silvana Tenreyro and Robert J. Barro (2007) use a different statistical procedure but reach the same conclusion as Frankel and Rose.

There have now been dozens of studies investigating the effect of a currency union on trade. Andrew K. Rose (2005) looks at all of these studies to pick out their consistent conclusions in what he calls a "meta-analysis" that combines the statistical results of each study. He concludes that (1) a currency union increases trade among the countries that share a currency over and above what trade would be in the absence of the common currency, and (2) the increase in trade is probably somewhere between 30 and 90 percent. However, given the broad range of results that cannot be linked to specific sample sizes or statistical methods, we should not accept these conclusions without reservations. And because some of the studies that Rose compiles examined common currency areas other than the euro area, the conclusions above may not accurately represent the precise positive effect of a currency union on EU trade.

Fiscal Policy in the European Union Countries: Some Potential Problems

As the euro area was just coming into existence, Olivier Blanchard and Francesco Giavazzi (2002) examined financial flows between the member countries of the European Union and found a clear rise in capital mobility. They found that correlations between domestic saving and investment had declined sharply, and individual countries were running larger financial account deficits and surpluses than in the past. Clearly, money was moving across borders more readily. This financial mobility represents one of the vulnerabilities of a monetary union, often referred to as the **fiscal free rider** problem. Even though individual countries in the EU still have a great deal of freedom to set their own taxation and expenditure policies, during the first few years of the euro, financial markets did not distinguish much between governments. That is, countries with large government deficits could borrow at about the same rate as countries with balanced or positive fiscal balances. Governments thus faced less market discipline that would discourage excessive borrowing. According to two *Financial Times* writers:

> Indeed, bond investors' complacency may be fuelling the fiscal problem, since it is reducing pressure on countries with bigger deficits to cut their debt. So is the behaviour of the European Central Bank, which

treats all eurozone debt equally in its daily monetary operations. This means that an investor can post Greek bonds as collateral, for example, and get German bonds in return. This reinforces the convergence of yields and further reduces the market pressure on governments to reform.[7]

How serious was this danger that the single currency is, in fact, subsidizing the countries with the largest fiscal deficits?

The European Union addressed the free rider problem when it imposed its set of criteria for joining the euro area, as detailed earlier. Also, the EU countries negotiated a **Stability and Growth Pact** in 1992, which extended the accession criteria into a set of ongoing rules of behavior. But in recent years, some of the largest members of the EU, such as France and Germany, missed many of the targets. And they offered no apologies for doing so. In March 2005, the European Council, which is effectively the executive cabinet of the EU, agreed that circumstances justified the flouting of the rules. This apparent willingness to weaken the Stability and Growth Pact may have encouraged countries to free ride and suggests that local political pressures can still trump EU rules and guidelines. The trilemma thus remained a threat. In fact, it emerged with a vengeance when the 2007–2008 Great Recession suddenly increased the government budget deficits and accumulated debt burdens of many EU member governments. The recent troubles of the euro will be discussed in the next chapter, in which the post-2000 performance of the entire international monetary system is examined.

SOME TENTATIVE CONCLUSIONS

The second half of the twentieth century was, overall, probably much better for humanity than the first half. There were no more world wars, and no new economic depression that bred worldwide economic suffering and political isolation. Instead, the last fifty years of the twentieth century brought unprecedented material wealth for most people, rapid international economic integration, and a hesitant acceptance of the international monetary order by nearly every country of the world. The weakness of the latter half of the twentieth century, however, is that by 2000 the international monetary system had permitted unsustainable trade and financial deficits to accumulate. Also, environmental problems were ignored and the distribution of incomes became less equal in many countries.

The next chapter will examine these imbalances in more detail. For now, it is useful to think about how the system evolved as it did. First, recall Paul Seabright's (2004) point about the benefits and dangers of dealing with strangers from Chapter 1. Holistically, there are many benefits, but also many dangers, in dealing with other countries. International economic integration creates interdependence, and this both limits and expands individual choices. Interdependence also limits a government's policy options, as illustrated by the trilemma and the arguments about fixed and floating exchange rates.

The Bretton Woods conference seemed to exhibit an enthusiastic acceptance of greater economic interdependence. The delegates accepted the need for cooperation. The two world wars and the Great Depression had made it clear that a purely national focus was a disastrous strategy for achieving economic progress and improving human well-being. This willingness to cooperate in order to improve economic and social outcomes was also exhibited by European governments throughout the latter half of the twentieth century as they worked toward creating a single political and economic entity called the European Union. These same countries had in the past shown little hesitation to march into each others' territories. Do these experiences indicate a shift in human attitudes toward strangers?

John McClintock (2009) takes a more practical approach and suggests that the European experience indicates that, even though people's instinctive feelings toward strangers have probably not changed, national governments have at least found a practical formula for cooperating to deal with complex systemic global issues. McClintock argues that the resistance to surrendering national sovereignty can be overcome more easily when integration begins with regional groups of countries such as the European Union. He adds a sense of urgency to Europe's example when he argues that the surrender of national sovereignty is not just an option that will prove beneficial, but it is an absolute necessity because the modern world's greatest challenges are global. Humanity faces global warming, nuclear proliferation, global economic inequality, the growing influence of global corporations, and global financial instability, among other things. International cooperation and the creation of global institutions are essential for dealing with such complex global problems.

McClintock's optimism notwithstanding, by 2010 there was a growing resistance in many European countries to further expansion of the EU. The loss of enthusiasm for continued European integration was further fueled by the possibility that several EU member governments would default on their foreign loans to banks in other EU countries, thus making it likely that taxpayers in the latter countries would have to pay for what they often saw as irresponsible behavior by debtor country government officials.

In general, it becomes more difficult to continue the process toward economic and political integration when the integrating countries are more diverse. Many people apparently still view sovereignty from a national perspective. Furthermore, the broad acceptance of, or resignation toward, the United States's war on terror shows that people are still quite willing to distrust, fear, and mistreat strangers. To understand this current rise in fear of and aggression toward foreigners, it is instructive to go back to the period right after World War II, just a year or two after the delegates signed on to the noble words about international cooperation in the **Bretton Woods agreement**. Recall that Harry Dexter White led the U.S. delegation at Bretton Woods and achieved the U.S. goals of establishing the U.S. dollar as the world's major currency and placing the United States solidly at the center of the international monetary system. White firmly pushed aside the proposal by John Maynard Keynes for a more multilateral system based on the bancor and in which international financial flows would be permanently restricted. The Bretton Woods order that White pushed through the conference became the basis for the economic recovery of the Western capitalist economies after the war. Yet, in the United States, Harry Dexter White was accused of treason.

In August 1948, White was called before the U.S. House of Representatives' Un-American Activities Committee, accused of meeting with Soviet officials. White had indeed met with Soviet officials after the war, when the United States and the Soviet Union were in the beginning stages of what was to become the Cold War. White's contacts were interpreted by some Congressmen as proof that he had engaged in espionage. Also, the fact that White had held the Nationalist government in China closely accountable for hundreds of millions of dollars of U.S. aid during World War II was taken as evidence that he had intentionally undermined the Nationalists in order to help Mao Tse-tung's communist forces in China's civil war. White also supported a $10 billion loan by the United States to aid postwar reconstruction in the Soviet Union. He argued that such a loan was necessary for the economic recovery of Europe, but the Cold War mind-set kept many Americans from seeing aid to the Soviet Union as anything other than active support of communism.

Three days after his appearance before the Congress, White died from a heart attack. Incredibly, White's death was immediately interpreted by some pundits of the day as proof of his guilt. In fact, White had been suffering from a serious heart condition for some time. His emotional defense of his reputation most likely did lead to his final heart attack. Among the most memorable moments of the hearing was his response to a question about his loyalty to the United States:

> I believe in freedom of religion, freedom of speech, freedom of thought, freedom of the press, freedom of criticism, and freedom of movement. I believe in the goal of equality of opportunity, and the right of each individual to follow the calling of his or her own choice, and the right of every individual to have an opportunity to develop his or her capacity to the fullest. . . . I consider these principles sacred. I regard them as the basic fabric of our American way of life, and I believe in them as living realities, and not mere words on paper. This is my creed.[8]

When he finished these words, White was applauded by most officials and spectators present. His critics were undeterred, however.

Several years after White's death, the director of the Federal Bureau of Investigation (FBI), J. Edgar Hoover, continued investigations into his alleged treason. In 1953, Wisconsin's Senator Joseph McCarthy named White as one of the many foreign agents that he claimed had infiltrated the U.S. government. At that same time, President Dwight Eisenhower's attorney general, Herbert Brownell, even accused former President Harry Truman of appointing a known Soviet spy (White) to the executive board of the new International Monetary Fund in 1947. President Truman successfully fought a subpoena to testify before Senator McCarthy's committee, but in the process White's reputation was further damaged.

The attacks on White's national loyalty were never substantiated, and Senator McCarthy, J. Edgar Hoover, and Attorney General Brownell never presented the evidence they claimed they had. This episode of personal destruction leaves open the question of why prominent politicians and members of the U.S. government would so viciously attack Harry Dexter White years after his death when his biggest accomplishment, the Bretton Woods system, was beginning to successfully achieve precisely the goals that business and financial interests in the United States had demanded of the U.S. delegation.

Perhaps White's biggest mistake was to openly lament the Soviet decision to withdraw behind its iron curtain. He also refused to engage in the anticommunist rhetoric that signaled the beginning of the Cold War. Given the political climate at the time, White naively invited criticism when he maintained contacts with Soviet operatives in the United States.[9] Perhaps he did provide the Soviets with some information. However, it is more likely that White was singled out as a convenient target of anti-internationalist anger by the American public, and of course there were politicians ready to exploit Americans' distrust of strangers.

Incredibly, sixty-five years after Bretton Woods, the unsubstantiated allegations lodged against him often still seem to outweigh the fact that Harry Dexter White played the dominant role in shaping an international monetary system that would prevail throughout the latter half of what has come to be known as the American Century. Textbooks and historical accounts still minimize his accomplishments and treat him very carefully. And White does not feature prominently in the various displays of photos and records in the fully refurbished Mount Washington Hotel in Bretton Woods that your author visited a couple of years ago. Why are people so inclined to distrust the efforts of those who seek cooperation with strangers over isolation and conflict?

The next chapter looks at the current state of the international monetary system. The world is still struggling to find an international financial order that can maximize the gains from international cooperation while minimizing the losses from the increased interdependence imposed by international economic integration.

CHAPTER SUMMARY

1. The delegates to the 1944 Bretton Woods Monetary Conference sought a system that would expand international trade and reverse the economic isolationism that characterized the period just before World War II. They discussed the merits of different exchange rate systems and whether international payments should be restricted or deregulated.

2. Harry Dexter White, the chief economist at the U.S. Department of the Treasury, oversaw the negotiations, and the British delegation was headed

by John Maynard Keynes, who enjoyed universal respect as an economist and as a statesman.

3. Keynes consistently argued that the international monetary system should give national governments and their policy makers some flexibility to pursue economic policies aimed at maintaining full employment even if it makes exchange rate stability more difficult to achieve.

4. White and Keynes agreed on *adjustable pegs,* but they disagreed on other matters.

5. Keynes, as a representative of the United King-

dom, sought a financial system in which Britain and the United States would enjoy equal stature; White represented U.S. financial interests, and he pushed for a system that appeared multilateral but was designed to make the U.S. dollar the dominant currency in which international trade and financial assets were priced so it would become the world's reserve currency.

6. Major International Monetary Fund actions would require the approval of an 85 percent supermajority; since the U.S. economy accounted for over 20 percent of world GDP and the United States thus had 20 percent of the votes, the United States effectively gained veto power over IMF decisions.

7. Keynes had argued in advance of the Bretton Woods conference "that control of capital movements, both inward and outward, should be a permanent feature of the postwar system," but he was overruled by White, who represented the U.S. financial industry that wanted open financial markets.

8. In practice, the Bretton Woods system functioned as a *fixed-rate dollar standard,* with the United States assuming a passive stance in the foreign exchange markets while the n-1 other countries actively pegged their currencies to the dollar.

9. Keynes's preference for creating a neutral reserve currency, which he called bancor, and the International Clearing Union to force both surplus and deficit nationals to balance trade, was never considered at Bretton Woods.

10. The Marshall Plan played an important role in restoring the international monetary system by giving countries the foreign reserves they needed to open their countries to trade and international payments.

11. Toward the end of the 1960s, after expansionary monetary policy in the United States raised U.S. inflation above the world average, speculative pressure against the dollar grew to where constant intervention in the foreign exchange markets was necessary to prevent dollar depreciation. France also began demanding gold in exchange for its growing holdings of U.S. dollars.

12. Robert Triffin (1960) warned that there was a fundamental inconsistency in the Bretton Woods order: As the owner of the world's reserve currency, the United States was obligated to run trade deficits so that the rest of the world could "earn" dollars for their reserves, but the more dollars were held by foreigners, the more likely that the dollar could come under speculative attack and the less foreigners would want to hold dollars as reserves.

13. Pegged exchange rates were first altered in 1971, and then they were abandoned altogether in 1973 in favor of a mixed system, including floating, dirty floating, and otherwise manipulated exchange rates, in which each country determines their own exchange rate policy.

14. The mind-set of policy makers was not ready for the new realities that began in the 1970s, however, and countries have been unable to agree on a new order that could stabilize exchange rates in an increasingly integrated world economy.

15. There have been regular meetings between central bankers, including formal meetings at the Plaza Hotel in 1985 and the Louvre Museum in 1987, but no cohesive system like Bretton Woods, under which all countries played by the same rules of the game, has emerged to date.

16. European countries resisted the shift to floating exchange rates because they were so closely linked through trade, and they sought to maintain exchange rate stability among European currencies.

17. The European Monetary System (EMS) was established in 1979 to keep exchange rates pegged within narrow bands, and after some success, this system failed in similar fashion to the Bretton Woods system when the monetary and fiscal policies of Germany, its largest member (accounting for over 25 percent of EU GDP), became incompatible with those of the rest of the EMS countries.

18. At a meeting in Madrid in December 1995, the European Union reiterated its intent to create a single currency, to be called the euro and denoted by the symbol €.

19. In 2010, the euro was the currency of sixteen countries, but serious questions had arisen about the group's viability, especially after the 2008 global financial crisis and global recession had increased government debt to unsustainable levels in Greece, Ireland, Portugal, and several other countries.

20. The trilemma thus continues to haunt pegged exchange rate systems, from Bretton Woods to the EMS and now to the euro area of sixteen European countries; it is impossible to maintain stable exchange rates (or a single currency) if money is free to move across borders and domestic macroeconomic policies need to address a pressing domestic problem such as high unemployment.

KEY TERMS AND CONCEPTS

adjustable exchange rate peg
bancor
Bretton Woods agreement
Common Agricultural Policy (CAP)
customs union
devaluation
economic miracles
euro
European Atomic Energy Community (Euratom)
European Coal and Steel Community (ECSC)
European Economic Community (EEC)
European Free Trade Area (EFTA)
European Monetary System (EMS)
European Monetary Union (EMU)
European Union (EU)
fiscal free rider
fixed-rate dollar standard
fundamental disequilibrium
General Agreement on Trade and Tariffs (GATT)
General Theory of Employment, Interest, and Money

International Bank for Reconstruction and
   Development (World Bank)
International Clearing Union
International Monetary Fund (IMF)
International Trade Organization (ITO)
Louvre Accord
Marshall Plan
Maastricht Treaty
monetary order
monetary system
Paris Peace Conference
Plaza Accord
Rambouillet Summit
revaluated
Second Amendment (to the Bretton Woods
   agreement)
Single European Act
snake in the tunnel
Stability and Growth Pact
World Bank

PROBLEMS AND QUESTIONS

1. Write a brief essay explaining why the Bretton Woods order eventually was abandoned in the early 1970s in favor of a new set of rules after nearly twenty-five years of apparent stability.
2. Discuss how the trilemma was dealt with under each of the following international financial orders:
   a. The gold standard
   b. The Bretton Woods system
   c. The EMS
   d. The European Monetary Union
3. How do you foresee the international financial system evolving in the future? Explain and justify your prediction.
4. Describe how well the Bretton Woods system met the goals of its designers. What could have been done better? Explain.
5. The world has gone through several different international financial orders over the past hundred years. Explain how each one came into being, why that particular order seemed to be a good set of rules at the time, and why the order eventually ran into difficulties and was superseded by another order.
6. Explain the Bretton Woods system: Why did it work reasonably well for a time but eventually collapse?
7. Explain precisely how (1) the gold standard, (2) the Bretton Woods system, and (3) the single currency in Europe dealt with the trilemma.
8. Present a concise history of the international monetary system since World War II, pointing out exactly why certain institutions were established and why changes took place.
9. Explain precisely why the trilemma became a problem in the 1960s after causing little concern during the 1950s.

10. Given the difficulties encountered by the Bretton Woods order and the EMS, should the difficulties of the European Monetary Union and the euro after the 2007–2008 recession been foreseen? Discuss.

11. In light of the various foreign exchange crises studied in earlier chapters and the recent troubles in the euro area of the EU, reevaluate Keynes's proposal for an International Clearing Union that included penalties for running deficits and surpluses that forced countries to accumulate international debt.

12. Explain the Triffin paradox. Is Triffin's warning still relevant today? Explain.

13. Should the European Union continue to expand its membership? Evaluate the potential gains and losses from further expansion. Specifically, evaluate the potential gains and losses from expansion of the euro area.

14. Investigate the alleged treason of Harry Dexter White (many historians have written about him). Was he guilty of treason? Evaluate the evidence.

Notes

1. Today The World Bank Group consists of the original International Bank for Reconstruction and Development and several other entities created after 1960.

2. Taken from the agreement text reproduced in Funabashi, Yoichi (1988), *Managing the Dollar: From the Plaza to the Louvre,* Washington, DC: Institute for International Economics.

3. Quoted in Randall Henning (1994).

4. See, for example, Phillippe Bacchetta and Eric van Wincoop (2000), M.D. McKenzie (1999), and S. Wei (1996).

5. From the official European Union website, "publications and documents." The words for the quote were downloaded on August 10, 2011 from http://europa.eu/documentation/index_en.htm.

6. Readers interested in more details on the governance structure of the EU can go to the EU website at http://europa.eu/about-eu/institutions-bodies/index_en.htm, where the institutions are described in great detail.

7. George Parker and John Thornhill (2005), "An Unhappy Union: Why Europe Is in Danger of Becoming Hollow at the Core," *Financial Times,* April 27.

8. Quoted in J. Bruce Craig (2004).

9. In his very interesting book *Treasonable Doubt: The Harry Dexter White Spy Case* (2004), J. Bruce Craig describes the meager evidence against White. White apparently did have contact with Soviet operatives in the United States, but it is not clear that he passed them any confidential or secret information.

CHAPTER **17**

Another Bretton Woods Conference?

> The outstanding faults of the economic society in which we live are its failure to provide for full employment and its arbitrary and inequitable distribution of wealth and incomes.
>
> —John Maynard Keynes (1936)

Over the past century and into this new one, exchange rate policies varied from completely fixing exchange rates to letting them float freely. National governments often pursued many variations and combinations of those two extremes. Today, the international monetary system is a complex and variable mixture of fixed exchange rates, clean floats, dirty floats, currency boards, regional currency unions, crawling pegs, systematic undervaluations, and other managed exchange rate strategies. This mixture is difficult to analyze because it is continually evolving as national governments respond to domestic interests, foreign governments' actions, increasing international economic integration, and changing economic outcomes.

Today's eclectic mixture of exchange rate regimes carried out with varying degrees of consistency may be the most practical response by national policy makers to the changing economic environment they face. Given the complexity of human society today, it is difficult to imagine that a universally accepted gold standard or a Bretton Woods–like system of pegged exchange rates could be sustained for very long. On the other hand, there are still many economic, social, and environmental problems facing humanity, and it would be comforting to know that we had the best possible international monetary system in place to address those problems. Keynes's quote addresses two of the most pressing economic issues. Developing countries in Africa, Asia, and Latin America have not grown enough to narrow the huge income gaps across countries. The extreme poverty of nearly one-third of the world's population that lives on US$2 per day is a human-made tragedy, given human technology and knowledge. High unemployment, especially among youth, has not been seriously addressed even in high-income countries. In addition to such economic issues, the repeated financial crises and the global 2007–2008 Great Recession have made it clear that we do not yet have what we could call a fully successful international financial order. Is it time for another Bretton Woods conference?

Before the world's economics ministers and financial experts pack their bags for New Hampshire, however, we need some consensus on what, exactly, the world's economic and social problems are. Despite the continuing recessions and financial turmoil in many countries, a consensus on reforming the international monetary system has been difficult to achieve. Perhaps by the time you read this, world leaders will have made good choices from among their many options. But at the time of this writing, they were not ready to agree on an exchange rate regime, the precise level of international economic integration, or a common set of macroeconomic policies.

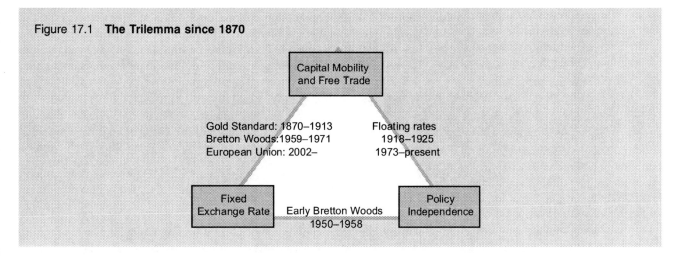

Figure 17.1 **The Trilemma since 1870**

Capital Mobility and Free Trade

Gold Standard: 1870–1913
Bretton Woods:1959–1971
European Union: 2002–

Floating rates
1918–1925
1973–present

Fixed Exchange Rate

Early Bretton Woods
1950–1958

Policy Independence

International economists often interpret financial history from the perspective of how governments choose to deal with the trilemma. Figure 17.1, for example, uses the trilemma to summarize the history of the international monetary system. Policy makers have made radically different choices throughout this history. Since the early 1970s, there has been a pronounced shift from fixed to floating exchange rates. The trilemma suggests that this shift permits increased integration into the international economy without sacrificing policy makers' ability to address domestic political interests. However, even as a growing number of countries let their exchange rates float, the European Union (EU) has opted for a single currency. The EU has effectively sacrificed national policy independence in an attempt to gain exchange rate stability in its integrated economic region.

There have been other creative attempts to deal with the trilemma. In 2000, Ecuador and El Salvador abolished their own currencies and adopted the U.S. dollar in their place, essentially closing their central banks and letting the U.S. Federal Reserve Bank and international financial transactions determine their monetary supplies. They follow Panama, which, since its U.S.-manipulated secession from Colombia to allow the United States to build the Panama Canal through its territory, has always used U.S. dollars as its national currency.

The somewhat forgotten third solution to the trilemma, which is to maintain policy independence and fixed exchange rates by restricting a country's international economic integration, has not gained much traction in recent years. Perhaps there is a rational fear that this choice would cause a country to lose the many gains from international trade and international investment. Or, perhaps the economic and political dominance of transnational corporations has pushed this option off the table in most countries. It is also possible that the predominant culture of globalization has blinded policy makers to the perfectly viable option of partially restricting cross-border transactions.

This chapter completes the history of the international monetary system by presenting a mosaic of current financial issues. It also describes how multilateral negotiations to reform the system were progressing as of late 2010. It concludes by seeking to answer the question: Is it time for another Bretton Woods conference?

ECONOMIC INSTABILITY

A quick review of the report cards for past international monetary systems reveals many deficiencies. Economic instability ranks as one of the areas where the international monetary system consistently failed. The gold standard not only permitted continual financial crises in individual countries or regions, but its rules of the game ultimately pushed the entire world into the Great Depression. The Bretton Woods system worked well for a while, but it eventually failed too, leaving the world once again without a clear set of rules. The mixed system that followed the Bretton Woods order has resulted in numerous financial and economic crises, including the 2007–2008 financial crisis and, in 2009, the first year-on-year decline in real GDP since the Great Depression.

Chapters 13 and 14 discussed financial instability and exchange rate crises in detail. In this section we highlight some other failures of the post–Bretton Woods system that effectively still provides the rules of the game for today's policy makers. As this section details, these failures include inflation, growing international debt by the United States, huge trade imbalances, and instability in the newly created euro single currency area.

Inflation

Most of the post–World War II period, which includes the Bretton Woods order and the post–Bretton Woods mixture of orders, is characterized by inflation. Figure 17.2 provides a very vivid illustration of the exceptional behavior of prices in the latter half of the twentieth century. It is taken from a Federal Reserve Bank report and shows real prices in England, France, Spain, and the United States from 1600 until 2000. Notice how prices fluctuated but did not exhibit any discernable trend for over three hundred years. Then, after World War I, prices began to show a definite inflationary trend. After World War II and beginning with the Bretton Woods system, prices rose very rapidly by historical standards.

At first glance, the eruption of inflation seems to be explained by the increased active use of monetary policy to reduce unemployment or increase economic growth, combined with the severance of links between money and gold or other commodities. The rises in prices shown in Figure 17.2 seem to coincide with the suspension of the gold standard during World War I, the abandonment of the gold standard after 1930, and the Bretton Woods period when the United States effectively determined the world money supply. Interestingly, even though no countries abandoned fiat money or linked their currencies to other commodity-backed moneys, inflation began to subside in the 1990s. Inflation effectively stopped during the first decade of the twenty-first century, and after the 2007–2008 recession, economists actually began to worry about deflation. Does this mean that policy makers have finally learned to take advantage of the flexibility of floating exchange rates and fiat money without succumbing to the temptation to print too much money?

Interestingly, the huge budget deficits and the large amounts of foreign debt accumulated as a result of persistent trade deficits raise the possibility of future inflation. Governments' ability to print money becomes a tempting way to reduce debt. This issue lies behind many of the current debates about macroeconomic policy and reform of the international monetary system.

Financial Instability in Europe

The 2008 financial crisis and, in 2009, the first global decline in GDP since World War II put a strain on the euro area. The euro countries did not all decline in tandem. Ireland, for example, experienced a decline in GDP of close to 10 percent in 2009, while French GDP fell by little more than 1 percent. The **European Central Bank** took a fairly conservative approach to the economic collapse, and it was largely left to individual governments to deal with the financial crisis and the subsequent economic recession. With the very different economic performances across countries, different macroeconomic responses were called for in each country. Yet, there was only one area-wide monetary policy available. And with so many European governments carrying high levels of debt, it was not clear whether deficit spending, the standard fiscal remedy for reversing an economic recession, was an available policy option in all countries.

Figure 17.2 **Inflation since 1600**

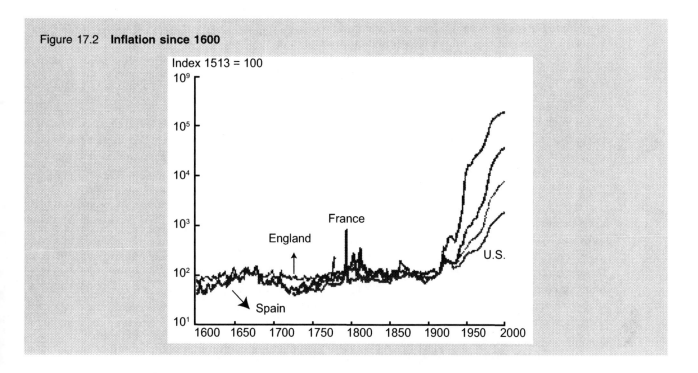

Greece gained attention in 2010. By that year, its government had accumulated an extremely high level of debt equal to 113 percent of its GDP. To understand the difficulties that Greece faced, recall the analysis used in Chapter 14 to analyze Brazil's precarious debt situation in 2003. Greece's total accumulated government debt as a percentage of GDP in 2010 (d_{2010}) depends on Greece's total government debt as a percentage of GDP in 2009 (d_{2009}), the real interest rate that the government must pay on its accumulated debt in 2010 (r_{2010}), the growth of GDP between 2009 and 2010 (g_{2010}), and the real government **primary budget surplus** (government receipts minus non-interest expenditures) as a percentage of GDP in 2010 (s_{2010}) as in:

$$(17.1) \qquad d_{2010} = [(1 + r_{2010} / (1 + g_{2010})] \, d_{2009} - s_{2010}.$$

This formula shows how much new debt is necessary to cover the difference between the government's current expenditures and its tax receipts, and how much new debt must be acquired to pay interest on the accumulated debt from earlier years. The ratio of the Greek government's debt to GDP will rise, all other things equal, when the real interest rate exceeds the growth in real GDP and when the primary budget surplus is negative.

In 2010, the Greek economy was in recession and contracting by 2 percent per year, and the interest rate it had to pay on borrowing was high; the 6.5 percent interest rate on Greek debt was about three percentage points above what the German and Dutch governments paid on their euro borrowing. The previous chapter described the incentives for countries like Greece to accumulate debt because the single currency would tend to offer lower interest rates than Greece could obtain if it continued with its own currency. Euro interest rates were expected to reflect average budget deficits in the euro area, not the deficits of any one particular euro member. But once actual default or the collapse of the euro area became a real possibility, Greece suddenly faced much higher interest rates as lenders began to doubt its ability to avoid default or currency depreciation if it abandoned the euro. Finally, the Greek government's annual budget deficit had risen to 12.5 percent of GDP as the recession lowered tax receipts drastically and rising unemployment increased government payments for social benefits. In terms of equation (17.1), r_{2010} = 6.5%, g_{2010} = –2%, d_{2009} =113%, and s_{2010} = –12.5%, and the ratio of Greece's government debt to GDP in early 2010 was about:

$$(17.2) \qquad d_{2010} = [(1.065) / (.98)]1.13 - (-0.125) = 1.35.$$

That is, Greece's debt-to-GDP ratio rose from 113 percent of GDP in 2009 to about 135 percent of GDP in 2010, an increase of about 20 percent. The same interest rate, growth rate, and primary budget deficit through the following year, 2011, caused the debt ratio to grow to well over 150 percent of GDP. Clearly, this path was not sustainable, and economists and the financial press began discussing the possibility that Greece would withdraw from the euro area and return to managing its own depreciated currency.

To prevent such an unraveling of their new single currency, leaders in other EU countries urged Greek authorities to take strong measures to reduce, and ultimately eliminate, the primary budget deficit. This would require both tax increases and expenditure reductions. There were massive street protests by labor groups, government employees, retirees, and others who feared they would bear large consequences from government fiscal adjustments. Greece and other EU governments agreed to a goal of reducing the primary budget deficit from 12.5 percent to 7.5 percent in 2011. But note that even such a large reduction in expenditures, equal to 5 percent of national income, would not stop the debt ratio from rising further:

$$(17.3) \qquad d_{2010} = [(1.065) / (.98)]1.13 - (-0.075) = 1.30.$$

This is still a 15 percent rise in the ratio of debt to GDP compared to 2009. Obviously, the Greek government would have to commit to not just cutting the budget deficit but turning the primary budget surplus positive. Also, for this strategy to work, lenders would have to be willing to continue lending at favorable interest rates until the Greek debt ratio began falling. Guarantees of Greek loans were, therefore, promised by the other EU governments. Direct loans from the International Monetary Fund (IMF) were also negotiated to placate the market. As much €750 billion was pledged by the IMF and the European Union countries in May 2010. The financial market had raised its likelihood of a Greek default.

In late 2010, however, Greece was paying interest rates of over 11 percent. This changes equation (17.3) to:

$$(17.4) \qquad d_{2010} = [(1.11) / (.98)]1.13 - (-0.075) = 1.35.$$

That is, despite the projected reduction in the budget deficit, the fear of Greek default offset that promise and kept Greek debt as a percentage of GDP on track to rise to 135 percent. By mid-2011, the situation had not improved, and Greek GDP continued to decline, by 8.1 percent in the first quarter of the year and 6.9 percent in the second quarter according to the national statistical agency.[1] You should be able to plug these negative numbers into equation 17.4 to calculate the rise in the ratio of indebtedness to GDP that such negative growth rates imply.

If Greece abandoned the euro and reissues its national currency at a sharply depreciated exchange rate to the euro, there would be devastating short-run consequences in Greece and throughout the EU. If Greek debt were converted to debt denominated in a new national currency that would likely depreciate rapidly, foreign lenders would suffer huge losses. Since the lenders to the Greek government consist mostly of European banks, other European governments would then have to provide loans or direct capital infusions to its banks to avoid further disruption of banking systems still reeling from the 2007–2008 financial collapse.

The future of the euro thus remains in doubt in 2011. This makes it difficult to reach a definitive conclusion on whether the euro has been a positive development for the European Union members.

Table 17.1

Report Card for the Euro, 2001–2007

1. Employment	Needs Improvement
2. Economic growth	Marginal Pass
3. Globalization	Pass
4. Policy independence	Fail
5. Mutually beneficial	Fail
6. Price stability	Pass

Even over the 2000–2007 period, before the 2007–2008 recession had much impact, some of the euro countries experienced relatively high levels of unemployment. Most countries were able to reduce unemployment rates, however, until the recession raised unemployment in nearly every EU country. Still, compared to the 1980s and 1990s, economic growth actually improved in the early 2000s, and the euro economies grew substantially faster than Japan and compared favorably to the United States. As reported above, statistical evidence suggests that a common currency increases the volume of trade among countries that share the currency, and trade among euro countries grew rapidly during the 2001–2007 period. However, the common currency may have diverted trade from countries outside the currency union. The European Union has often been referred to as "fortress Europe" because of Europe's protectionist trade policies in agriculture and services.

The 2007–2008 recession made it clear that the euro severely limits national governments' ability to conduct independent macroeconomic policies. The national central banks of the euro area members had all been replaced by the European Central Bank (ECB). The ECB was designed with the former German Central Bank in mind; that bank was noted for its singular focus on price stability. The ECB indeed has kept price levels near constant over the first decade of the twenty-first century. To prevent conflicting macroeconomic policies and economic outcomes from reviving the trilemma, the euro countries had negotiated a **Stability and Growth Pact** that limited countries' freedom to engage in fiscal expansion. The euro has a mixed record on spreading the costs and benefits of a common currency. Table 17.1 presents the report card for the euro from 2001 through 2007, just like the report cards for earlier systems covered in Chapters 15 and 16.

Developing Countries' Accumulation of Dollar Reserves

Following the Asian financial crises, many developing or emerging countries in the Far East and elsewhere began to build up large stocks of foreign reserves by using central bank intervention to keep their currencies undervalued in order to run large trade surpluses year after year and to accumulate foreign reserve currencies. These developing economies accumulated mostly U.S. dollars and liquid dollar assets like U.S. Treasury bonds. Many politicians and commentators in the United States and Europe have described this exchange rate manipulation as a **beggar-thy-neighbor policy** to boost aggregate demand at home through import substitution and export growth. Others have accused the governments of East Asian economies of simply supplying political favors to export industries. However, the accumulation of reserves may not have been undertaken only to benefit export industries or to boost overall GDP.

Given the huge costs of the recent foreign exchange crises in terms of lost GDP and employment, it is likely that the developing countries wanted to accumulate dollar, euro, and yen reserves in order to protect themselves from future exchange rate crises. The reserves effectively enable countries to credibly fix exchange rates. Because accumulated reserves permit central banks to intervene in the foreign exchange market for long periods of time, the hope is that speculators would recognize that their chances of gaining from their speculation are substantially diminished and refrain from attacking the currency of a country whose central bank holds large reserves.

The accumulation of large foreign exchange reserves thus serves as an insurance policy to protect an open economy from sudden exchange rate changes triggered by changing economic circumstances over which the country has little control. Recall from Chapter 14 that exchange rate crises are not always caused by faulty policies in the countries that suffer speculative attacks on their currencies. Jeffrey Frankel and Nouriel Roubini (2002) document that shifts in developed-economy macroeconomic policies have often been the cause of developing-country financial crises. They mention, among other events, the tightening of U.S. monetary policy as the cause of the 1982 financial crises throughout the developing world. Interestingly, they also point to the easing of monetary policy in the United States and the decline in U.S. interest rates as helping to finally solve the 1997 Asian crisis. To the extent that domestic policies and institutions cannot prevent foreign events and circumstances, developing countries interested in controlling their currencies' value thus concluded that they have to accumulate large reserves to prevent exchange rate instability.

It is still too early to tell if large stocks of reserves permit pegged exchange rates to coexist with domestically oriented macroeconomic policies and the ever-deeper participation of the East Asian and other developing economies in the global economy. Also worrisome is the fact that the developing countries' trade surpluses are the flip side of the large U.S. current account deficits. The United States must run large trade deficits in order for foreign economies to accumulate dollar reserves, and these current account deficits may ultimately undermine the faith in the dollar. Recall the **Triffin paradox** discussed in the previous chapter; growing trade deficits in the United States led to speculation against the dollar, and the speculators eventually won when the U.S. dollar was devalued in 1971. The entire Bretton Woods order was soon abandoned as well because it appeared to be impossible to maintain pegged exchange rates between all currencies. In 2010, there was again fear that a sudden shift of reserves from dollar assets to assets in other currencies could cause massive exchange rate shifts. The instability would, no doubt, have very real effects by reducing international investment and financial transactions.

To Fix or to Float?

Discussion of the current international monetary order's weaknesses invariably returns to the question of whether a government should seek to peg or float its currency. Chapter 14 suggests that certain foreign exchange rate crises were the result of failed attempts by policy makers to maintain the policies necessary to keep exchange rates fixed in the face of changing economic conditions and expectations. Milton Friedman, who had argued for floating exchange rates since early in the Bretton Woods order, responded to the collapse of the European Monetary System (EMS) in 1992 as follows:

> How many more fiascos will it take before responsible people are finally convinced that a system of pegged exchange rates is not a satisfactory financial arrangement?

The fiasco that Friedman was referring to was the attempt by the members of the European Union to fix exchange rates between their currencies after the fall of the Bretton Woods pegged exchange rate system. Friedman believed that countries with independent political systems would inevitably enact economic policies that reflected domestic political pressures but conflicted with the goal of maintaining a fixed exchange rate, and the trilemma would trigger an exchange rate crisis.

Toward the end of the twentieth century, Paul A. Volcker, the former chairman of the Federal Reserve Bank of the United States, had come to quite another conclusion about exchange rates, however:

> I think the idea of a small country freely floating its exchange rate is unworkable. (1999, p. 268)

Volcker's quote was part of an explanation of why developing-country governments continued to peg the values of the currencies even though such pegs were prone to fail in the long run. Who is correct? Does the world need another Bretton Woods–like system of pegged exchange rates or a system of freely floating exchange rates?

The Case for Pegged Exchange Rates

It is worth reading more of the context of Volcker's quote above. He also argued that:

> The exchange rate is a multilateral phenomenon. There are a lot of sides to it. You cannot float and have other people fixed. We cannot fix and have other people float. There has to be some coherence in the system. I do not think there is any coherence in the system now, and these people in the Asian countries are not going to be able to pick a sensible exchange rate. Conceptually, it is easy to think of Mexico with a fixed dollar rate because so much of its trade is with the United States. But what do you do if you are Thailand or Indonesia? A third of your trade is with Japan and 30 percent is with the United States and 25 percent is with Europe and 10 percent is with each other. You have nothing obvious to fix to. (Ibid.)

Volcker's words remind us of Keynes's (1936) point, described in Chapter 12, that people base their expectations on confidence and convention. Similar was De Grauwe's (1989) hypothesis that, in the absence of overwhelming evidence suggesting that some other exchange rate clearly reflects future values more accurately, exchange rates tend to remain relatively stable around some initial anchor price that people are familiar with. The problem with using an anchor, or what Keynes called a *convention,* to guide decisions is that, inevitably, the anchor comes loose when something upsets the conventional world as we know it. Volcker effectively argued that not only would the anchor inevitably come loose, but in a world where many countries let their currencies float, there is no anchor. That is, it is nearly impossible for any country to peg its exchange rate when most other currencies are continually changing their values. Then, as he says, "You have nothing obvious to fix to." Therefore, Volcker argued for an international monetary system that took explicit measures to maintain exchange rate stability, throughout the world.

There are many positive consequences of fixed exchange rates. For example, at the end of the nineteenth century, when the exchange rates of most countries remained fixed for over thirty years under the gold standard, investment flows to the world's poorest economies were much higher than they were at the end of the twentieth century.[2] Fixed exchange rates also serve to discipline policy makers and prevent inflationary monetary policies. A study by the International Monetary Fund examined the economic performances of all its member countries (which were most of the noncommunist countries) over the thirty-year period 1960–1990 and found that countries with floating exchange rates tended to have higher rates of inflation than countries with fixed exchange rates.[3] Specifically, countries with floating exchange rates averaged 16 percent annual inflation while countries that fixed their exchange rates averaged 8 percent inflation.

The Case for Floating Exchange Rates

On the other hand, the IMF study mentioned just above also found that countries with floating exchange rates grew faster than countries with fixed exchange rates. Countries with floating exchange rates had higher productivity growth, which was partially due to the fact that the floating exchange rate countries traded more; exports grew 3 percentage points faster, on average, in countries with floating exchange rates. Studies relating trade and growth suggest that, on average, economic growth is about 0.15 percent faster for every 1 percentage point increase in the growth of international trade. This conclusion is interesting because it is often claimed that exchange rate risk, which should be higher under floating exchange rates, discourages trade. Perhaps policies to open an economy to trade are accompanied by floating exchange rates in order to avoid the wrath of the trilemma. Or, floating exchange rates may be less disruptive of international trade and international investment, on average, than the occasional devastating exchange rate crisis.

So, which exchange rate regime is better? When inflation is the overriding concern, a fixed exchange rate system may be the best choice. However, if unemployment or slow economic growth is the overriding issue, then floating exchange rates may be the appropriate exchange rate regime choice. The world has frequently shifted between fixed and floating exchange rates, and recent central bank actions and government decisions show that there is still no general consensus on the superiority of fixed or floating exchange rates.

Have Transnational Financial Firms Changed the Monetary System?

Investors and lenders generally favor fixed exchange rate systems. Recall the presidential campaign of 1896, in which the Populist anti-bank candidate William Jennings Bryan opposed the gold standard and his opponent, who was heavily funded by financial interests, favored the gold standard. This suggests that politics may have something to do with the choice of exchange rate regimes.

Profit-driven financial innovation and the persistent dismantling of financial regulatory structures have radically changed the private financial systems in nearly every country. As a result of the ease with which money flows across borders today, the growth of private finance has also changed the international monetary system.

The deregulation of finance became near-universal because individual governments did not act to stop it. Even when individual countries attempted to maintain their regulations and oversight, the fact that some countries disabled substantial parts of their financial regulatory structures made it more difficult for any country to maintain control of its financial sector. Modern communications and the financial industry's innovations driven by its relentless quest for short-term profits made a mockery of the fragmented and often-weak political institutions that were intended to protect a country's broader economic and social interests. Furthermore, the financial deregulation itself reinforced the pressure for further deregulation by increasing the concentration of finance into fewer and larger international financial conglomerates that increasingly used their wealth to pressure for, or simply buy, more favorable national regulatory structures.

Today's international financial order is very different from the one created at Bretton Woods in 1944. The international financial system during the Bretton Woods era (1947–1971) was characterized by controls on cross-border financial transactions and pervasive regulation and oversight of the financial sector in each national economy. Even the United States, which at Bretton Woods argued for liberalizing both financial and current account transactions, tightly regulated its banks and financial markets. After fifty years of active lobbying by the financial industry and the fading of the Great Depression from humanity's collective memory, the regulations were gradually eliminated or easily avoided. In 2007, on the eve of the 2007–2008 economic recession, financial regulation in many countries could be described as regulatory neglect.

The Path to Reform after the 2007–2008 Great Recession

The 2007–2008 Great Recession was of concern to policy makers, in part, for its sheer size. In 2009, world GDP per capita fell for the first time since World War II. And by 2010, per capita income was still below that of 2007. But more troublesome was the fact that the recession was a direct result of the failure of the international monetary system and, more specifically, the failure of the private financial industry that had been allowed to grow within the international monetary system.

The response by the leaders of all the major economies was quick, at least compared to the governments' response after the 1929 U.S. financial crisis. It seemed as though policy makers had learned from the Great Depression. But the international monetary system was fragmented, with every country setting its own policies, and the response was inconsistent and inefficient. In general, the policy response to the financial crash and economic recession consisted of some combination of (a) fiscal expansion in the form of increased government spending and cuts in taxes, (b) monetary expansion, (c) direct infusions of cash into the private banking system in order to reverse its sudden seizure in 2008, and (d) beginning discussions on how to change the regulations and government agencies responsible for overseeing the financial sector. There were even calls for another Bretton Woods conference. John Maynard Keynes and Hyman Minsky were suddenly popular again. M.E. Sharpe quickly reprinted Minsky's *Can "It" Happen Again? Essays in Instability and Finance* (1982).

Avoiding a Repeat of the Great Depression

Standard macroeconomic analysis suggests that monetary or fiscal policy, or both, can be applied to deal with the sudden increases in unemployment in most of the world's economies. However, in the case of a severe financial crisis, the money mechanism may not work. An increase in the money supply may not induce banks to lend more or cause financial markets to grow.

At the depth of a recession, when unemployment is high and the economy's productive capacity is not being fully used, there are few investors interested in borrowing to expand productive capacity. Monetary policy, therefore, will not have much immediate effect on increasing investment and, thereby, expanding aggregate demand and employment. Keynes (1936) explained that during a deep recession, the economy is stuck in a **liquidity trap**. Keynes reasoned that the interest rate will stop falling before it reaches zero percent because no one will acquire long-term assets with a very low positive interest rate for fear of suffering capital losses when the interest rate goes back up in the future. Hence, a liquidity trap develops once interest rates are very low, and no amount of monetary expansion will lower interest rates further to stimulate additional investment.

A liquidity trap was not the only problem an economy faced after a financial crisis, however. Keynes (1936, p. 158) also pointed out that merely creating the conditions under which prospective investors are willing to borrow and invest again is, by itself, not enough to end a financial crisis because

> we must also take account of the other facet of the state of confidence, namely, the confidence of the lending institutions toward those who seek to borrow from them, sometimes described as the state of credit. But whereas the weakening of either is enough to cause a collapse, recovery requires the revival of both.

As documented by Carmen Reinhart and Kenneth Rogoff (2009) in their study of eight hundred years of economic crises, financial crises trigger especially long economic recessions compared to those caused by direct shifts in aggregate demand (say, a sudden shift in government budgets or a decline in foreign demand for exports). It takes time to restore the confidence of both borrowers and lenders.

In 2008, many governments, and their central banks, began to assist banks and some of their customers in cleaning up their balance sheets. Governments lent banks cash and government bonds in exchange for "toxic" securities such as the subprime mortgage CDOs described in Chapter 13. Central banks also engaged in much routine monetary expansion, injecting great amounts of money into the banking system through open market operations. These policies had little immediate effect, however. Unemployment continued to grow throughout 2008 and 2009, and the negative effects of the financial crisis and the deep recession had not yet been dealt with in 2010. The large outstanding euro debt of Greece, Spain, Ireland, and Italy made it difficult for these governments to borrow more and use fiscal expansion to stimulate economic activity.

Why the Reluctant Fiscal Response?

The experience of Greece and other European Union countries points to the role of the international monetary system in the Great Recession. In their review of Reinhart and Rogoff's conclusion that financial crises provoke exceptionally long recessions, Yeva Nersisyan and Randall Wray (2010a, 2010b) found no cases of such recessions in countries that let their currencies float and issued debt only in their own currency. Policy makers in these countries, they conclude, were able to quickly borrow and increase government expenditures, thus solving the liquidity trap and aggregate demand problems. Nersisyan and Wray point out that a country with debt issued in its own currency is thus unconstrained by the obligation to keep its exchange rates stable and can always issue more money to pay for increased government expenditures; Greece's need to reduce government expenditures and raise taxes is entirely the result of its being a member of the euro area. Yet, at the time of this writing, the European Union governments were finalizing tighter fiscal rules for euro area governments in order to "save" the single-currency system.

Recall how the order of the gold standard tied the hands of policy makers after the 1929 U.S. stock market bubble popped and forced them to "protect" the gold value of their currencies by keeping monetary policy tight and avoiding an expansion of government debt. Now, the monetary order of the euro area is transforming the financial crisis, triggered by the fraudulent securitization of carelessly issued subprime mortgages in the United States, into a long period of high unemployment not only in Greece, but in all EU countries. The EU even issued stricter rules that further limit fiscal policy. The problem is that Greece and all other euro-country governments cannot print more money to pay for government expenditures; they must borrow in the "foreign" euro. The Greek government, headed by the Socialist Party, did not even contemplate new borrowing for an expansionary fiscal policy. It could only complain that it was being pushed by other EU countries, whose banks hold most of Greece's government debt, to engage in fiscal austerity by reducing expenditures and increasing tax revenues.

One of the more interesting policy responses to the 2007–2008 Great Recession was that of the United States. The U.S. Congress passed a modest fiscal stimulus in the form of a tax rebate plan under the Bush government in 2008. Under the Obama administration in 2009, Congress authorized a large expenditure and tax-cut package. In an attempt to clean up the banks' questionable balance sheets, Congress in late 2008 had also approved the Bush administration's program to acquire questionable assets from the banks in exchange for government bonds. This came to be known simply as the *bank bailout*. In the meantime, the Federal Reserve Bank expanded the money supply and drove short-term interest rates to near zero. Most longer-term interest rates also fell to historic lows. Official U.S. unemployment nevertheless rose to 10 percent, and it remained close to 10 percent through 2011. Despite the lack of a clear recovery from the recession, the U.S. Congress refused to pass a further fiscal stimulus, with many politicians arguing that the economy would improve only if the U.S. government reduced its budget deficit rather than increasing it. It was not clear what economic model they were using. The U.S. government's near-zero interest rates meant that it could easily borrow in dollars. In fact, it could create as many dollars as necessary to buy its own debt if no one else would buy it, provided it allowed its exchange rate to float. Keynesian analysis mandated further deficit spending, given that the economy was still stuck in a liquidity trap.

In sum, after the 2007–2008 recession became obvious, U.S. and European governments engaged in some, but seldom enough, fiscal expansion to restore aggregate demand to near full employment levels. Monetary expansion was carried out, and interest rates were low in nominal terms, but the liquidity trap prevented the monetary expansion from having much effect. By 2010, bank bailouts in many countries had restored bank solvency, at least on paper. Questions remained about the true value of assets listed on financial firms' balance sheets, however. How did the governments fare in their remaining response to the financial crisis, which was to reform the regulations and government agencies responsible for overseeing the financial sector in order to reduce the chances of another crisis in the future?

Restoring Financial Regulation and Oversight

Since the 2008 financial crisis, discussions on systemic reform have focused on the failure of national regulatory agencies to notice, much less prevent, the risky activities in the private financial industry that caused the financial crisis. The activities of AIG's London office, detailed in Chapter 13, are but one example of the aggressive pursuit of profit by any means possible by private global financial firms.

After considerable debate within its ranks, the European Union agreed to present five specific proposals at a November 15, 2008, summit on reforming the international financial system:

1. Supervisory panels for all large private international financial firms
2. Stronger risk control mechanisms, such as reserve requirements and diversification requirements, for all private international financial firms
3. Strict codes of conduct on risk-taking behavior in the financial industry
4. Tighter rules for credit ratings firms
5. Harmonization of accounting definitions to improve international coordination of regulatory requirements

Even Jean-Claude Juncker, the prime minister of Luxembourg, a country that has exploited global financial deregulation and innovation to build a large financial industry, openly blamed the global financial crisis on a "deregulatory frenzy" and agreed to the reforms.[4]

In late 2008, however, the global financial industry was already lobbying most governments to limit regulatory changes. In the United States, it was only a month after JPMorgan, Chase, Goldman Sachs, Citigroup, and Bank of America accepted billions in government assistance that they created a lobbying group, the CDS Dealers Consortium, to fight any increased regulation of derivatives trading. The financial reform legislation that passed the Congress in 2010 was deemed by most impartial economists to be useful but by no means sufficient to prevent future financial crises. The new measures required more reserves, better reporting, and more information for consumers, and gave more power to the Federal Reserve to regulate the banks, but there were no measures to reduce the size of banks, limit their activities, or clamp down on profit-motivated innovation. Financial reform met similar resistance in the United Kingdom and the rest of the European Union. Britain has taken a somewhat different position from Germany and France when it comes to regulation and institutional changes. Britain's government is anxious to protect London's prominence in the global financial markets, of course, and new regulations that limit financial industry growth would severely impact London employment and British tax revenues.

In addition to the obvious lobbying by the financial industry, the reluctance by policy makers to enact strong new restrictions on the banking industry may also have been influenced by culture. John Lanchester (2009) suggests that embarrassment explains the reluctance of the United States and British governments to expand regulation:

> The Anglo-Saxon economies [Britain and the United States] have had decades of boom mixed with what now seem, in retrospect, smallish periods of downturn. During that they/we have shamelessly lectured the rest of the world on how they should be running their economies. We've gloated at the French fear of debt, laughed at the Germans' 19th-century emphasis on manufacturing, told the Japanese that they can't expect to get over their "lost decade" until they kill their zombie banks, and so on. It's embarrassing to be in worse condition than all of them.

Lanchester also suggests that instituting new regulations on British and American banks or breaking up "too-big-to-fail" conglomerates "would mean that the Anglo-Saxon model of capitalism had failed."

Differences in national regulatory policies are problematic; in fact, they constitute a problem that, by itself, merits an international conference of its own. The global nature of the financial industry means that internationally coordinated reform is urgently needed, not a diverse set of national regulatory agencies with incompatible mandates. The ability of financial firms to move between political jurisdictions tends to make the most lax national regulatory structure effectively the world's regulatory structure.

DO WE NEED A NEW BRETTON WOODS CONFERENCE?

Many political leaders and a number of economists claim that a coordinated reform of the international monetary system is not needed. After all, there have been no more world wars, and many international institutions have already been created. The IMF and the World Bank are still in place to deal with international financial crises and lagging economic development, the World Trade Organization is well structured to deal with trade disputes and to coordinate trade policies, and numerous other international organizations and institutions are already working to harmonize regulation and government oversight throughout the world.

Those who call for more international cooperation can point to areas where individual economies are not performing as well as they might. Poverty remains a problem in today's global economy, with about 1 billion people still existing on income of just US$1 per day. The World Bank has not been effective in promoting economic growth throughout the world. The Bretton Woods goal of increasing international trade has been substantially met, but the benefits of trade and other global economic activity have not spread across all countries. The world economy is dependent on sources of energy supplied by a few countries, some of which teeter precariously on the verge of political and social collapse. Currently, numerous civil wars, foreign interventions, violent border disputes, and guerilla uprisings are under way. And there are huge, looming environmental problems that are being ignored by national policy makers.

More specific to the international monetary system, the current international monetary order, including the IMF, has not been able to prevent repeated financial crises in Mexico, Brazil, Argentina, Southeast Asia, Russia, Turkey, and many other developing countries. Each of these financial crises began with overvalued pegged exchange rates, followed by speculative attacks on the currencies, reversals of capital flows, declines in investment, bankruptcies, and deep recessions. Each of these financial crises had very lasting effects. Economic growth in sub-Saharan Africa stopped almost entirely after the 1980 debt crisis, and growth slowed drastically during the 1980s and 1990s in most Latin American countries. Clearly, the international monetary order did not lead to economic stability or consistent economic development.

Then, in 2008, the belief that financial crises happen only to poor countries was shattered. The deregulation of private banking and financial markets throughout the world since the 1970s caused the housing bubble and financial crisis in the United States to spread throughout the financially integrated world. Specifically, the sudden fall in housing prices undermined a widely distributed class of assets based on the mortgages that financed purchases of housing during the run-up in prices. When housing prices fell, bank lending and financial markets froze up because no one understood the true value of the mortgage-based assets held by banks and as collateral by prospective borrowers.

In short, the whole integrated economic system failed when one of its parts failed. This possibility was anticipated by Keynes, which is why at Bretton Woods he argued for limiting the financial flows across borders. Keynes was overruled by the American delegation and Harry White, who sought to make the dollar the center of both the international monetary system and the private international financial industry. Only recently has the idea of limiting financial flows between countries, and thus the debt that these flows create, been brought up in policy circles again.

Keynes's Bancor

Recall that at the Bretton Woods conference, Keynes had wanted to create an institution called the **International Clearing Union (ICU)** to regulate the exchange of currencies and act as a lender of last resort to national central banks. The latter function was instead given to the **International Monetary Fund (IMF)**, and the clearing union was never created. The exchange of currencies was thus left unregulated at the international level, and the foreign exchange markets were free to develop into what they are today, private and secretive over-the-counter markets.

Keynes saw the ICU as the financial intermediary for all trade and currency transactions. He also proposed a new international reserve currency, which he named the **bancor**. The bancor would take the role that, at the insistence of the United States, the Bretton Woods agreement instead gave to the U.S. dollar. Keynes also proposed that the ICU regulate the exchange of currencies. He did not merely suggest that foreign exchange markets be regulated to ensure their efficient operation; rather, he wanted to limit international financial flows with the express purpose of preventing countries from accumulating either large foreign debts or large stocks of foreign reserves.[5] Keynes correctly saw foreign debt as the fundamental reason why large exchange rate adjustments cause financial crises and economic recessions. He wanted the Bretton Woods order to include measures to prevent such financial crises.

The ICU would work as follows. Say someone in France exports a product to Italy. The Italian importer would pay lira to the ICU, the ICU would debit Italy's bancor account at the ICU according to the pegged lira-bancor rate, the ICU would then transfer those bancors over to France's bancor account at the ICU, and French francs would be issued to the French exporter according to the pegged franc-bancor rate. The exporter and importer would deal through their own private or public commercial bank, much as international traders now go through their bank to buy and sell foreign exchange. But rather than deal with private foreign exchange dealers, the banks would deal with the ICU.

To prevent the accumulation of large foreign debts or reserves, Keynes proposed rules that would limit both trade deficits and trade surpluses. Limiting trade deficits was not difficult: when continued trade deficits eventually depleted a country's bancor account, importers would no longer be able to acquire bancors to pay foreign exporters. The ICU would provide overdraft privileges up to one half the value of a country's average annual exports, but when that ran out, there would be no more bancors available for buying imports. In this sense, the ICU was no different from the Bretton Woods system of pegged exchange rates. But Keynes wanted to restrain surplus countries too. He noted that historically one country's trade deficit was often more the fault of other countries' intentional currency undervaluation, export subsidies, or other foreign trade restrictions than of the deficit country's excessive consumption or government debt. He did not think it was fair that the system ultimately adopted at Bretton Woods would punish only deficit countries for their trade imbalances. Keynes thus proposed limits on how many bancors a country could accumulate in its ICU account as a result of overseas sales by its exporters. These limits would be enforced by having the ICU tax a rising percentage of the bancors that exceeded the limits. In short, both deficit and surplus countries would be motivated to balance their trade.

Keynes's proposal went nowhere at Bretton Woods because the United States was strongly opposed to the ICU and the bancor. Harry Dexter White responded to the British proposal as follows: "[W]e have been perfectly adamant on that point. We have taken the position of absolutely no." White instead proposed what he called the International Stabilization Fund, which would become the International Monetary Fund by the end of the conference. The United States wanted the dollar to be the reserve currency and the center of the international economy. White and the U.S. delegation were able to discourage Keynes from insisting on his proposal, and the British delegation agreed to support the creation of the IMF instead. The IMF would still operate as a lender of last resort to central banks faced with having to support their currencies in the foreign exchange market, but there would be no explicit restrictions on international financial flows, current account imbalances, or the accumulation of private and public foreign debt. The burden of correcting a trade deficit would fall largely on the deficit country. Under Keynes's proposal, China would not have been able to accumulate nearly US$3 trillion in foreign reserves.

Various components of Keynes's plan have been put forward in recent years as possible solutions to the large imbalances in trade and assets and the huge accumulations of reserves by some countries. Zhou Xiaochuan, the governor of the People's Bank of China (the Chinese central bank), in 2009 urged the world to adopt a new international reserve currency "that is disconnected from individual nations and is able to remain stable in the long run, thus removing the inherent deficiencies caused by using credit-based national currencies."[6] Zhou's speech was interpreted as an indication of China's concern about the future value of its huge stock of U.S. dollar reserves. Interestingly, Zhou mentioned Keynes as the source for his idea, although he made no mention of Keynes's parallel proposal to limit the accumulation of foreign reserves. China today holds nearly US$3 trillion in foreign reserves.

In 2010, the IMF brought up Keynes's full plan for an international reserve currency administered by an international institution that would also have the means to limit both trade surpluses and trade deficits. However, the IMF report (2010, p. 15) does not suggest limiting international financial flows to the extent that Keynes proposed:

> A multilateral framework would recognize the benefits of capital account liberalization under appropriate circumstances, while acknowledging a role for certain measures, such as capital controls, to dampen excessive movement when necessary. The emphasis should be on making sure that measures on cross-border flows motivated by domestic economy considerations actually help reduce global volatility and do not have adverse effects on others.

It is not clear whether the IMF report proposes another Plaza Accord, which we detailed in Chapter 16, or the creation of a new permanent institution. In any case, it will be difficult to introduce serious restrictions on international financial flows or to explicitly prevent countries from running persistent trade surpluses or deficits. The IMF report (ibid.) recognizes that "achieving consistency between a new multilateral framework and existing arrangements would need to be considered, and may be difficult."

Two weeks before the meeting of the leaders of the world's twenty largest economies, the so-called **G20**, in November 2010, the United States officially proposed explicit limits on trade surpluses at 4 percent of a country's GDP. One week before the meeting, China officially responded to the U.S. plan. China argued that the plan would take the world back "to the days of planned economies."[7] It was not clear how the limits proposed by the United States would be enforced, given that there is no international institution that controls international financial flows. It may be that another agreement, perhaps similar to the Plaza Accord in 1985, is more realistic; of course, it would not be likely to reduce future trade surpluses or further accumulation of reserves.

Given the extent of international economic integration and the dominant role of the private financial industry in the global economy, not to mention that industry's political clout in the United States and Europe, it is unlikely we will see Keynes's International Clearing Union, his taxation of accumulated surpluses, or a full substitution of bancors for dollars.

Not Only Keynes Was Ignored

In the late 1990s, as various financial crises in developing economies battered per capita incomes, there were frequent calls for new international meetings to design a new order that could prevent repeated crises. Economists Barry Eichengreen and Richard Portes (1995), Jeffrey Sachs (1995), and Anne O. Krueger (2001) called for discussions to create an international sovereign bankruptcy court. Banking CEO Henry Kaufman (1998) advocated the creation of a global financial regulatory agency to coordinate the activities of the fragmented network of national regulatory agencies. The currency speculator who became a billionaire betting against the British pound and French franc in 1992, George Soros, became a financial pundit and advocated for, among other things, the creation of an international deposit insurance corporation to protect small consumer bank deposits throughout the world (Soros 1998). There were also the usual calls for reforming the existing international institutions such as the World Bank, the IMF, and the Bank for International Settlements.

Little has come of these suggestions, however, even as further financial crises in Russia, Argentina, and Turkey continued to plague the international monetary system in the early 2000s. Many East Asian countries took matters into their own hands and accelerated the accumulation of foreign reserves by undervaluing their currencies and generating huge trade surpluses. In late 2010, the IMF announced plans to discuss shifting voting rights and giving developing countries more say in the institution. This may have been a ploy to reduce pressure for more substantive reforms; voting rights have been under discussion for many years.

Some New Proposals

Perhaps it was the false impression that financial crises occur only in developing economies and countries transitioning from communism to capitalism that prevented serious reform of the international financial order. But now it is clear that no country is immune to financial crises. In fact, the events since 2008 suggest that a financial crisis originating in a developed country's private financial industry is much more devastating than a foreign exchange rate crises in a developing economy.

Joseph Stiglitz et al. (2010) argue for a strong global response to the economic downturn. National responses are inevitably less accurate and weaker than what is needed because they do not take their effects on other countries into consideration. A case in point is the fiscal stimuli, which are often criticized because some of the increase in aggregate demand "spills over" into other countries and weakens the domestic benefits. When every country takes such a view, argues Stiglitz, the sum of national fiscal stimulus measures is likely to be too small to address the global slowdown.

Stiglitz chaired a United Nations commission that was given the task of preparing an interim report on what went wrong in 2008 and how to prevent another, similar economic crisis from developing. The report was presented at the G20 meeting in London in June 2009. The United Nations commission concluded that:

1. The 2008 crisis was caused by deregulation.
2. Self-regulation does not work.
3. Regulation must deal with the spread of financial failures across borders.
4. Transparency alone will not always eliminate the failures of complex financial markets and products.
5. Incentives in the private financial industry encourage excessive risk-taking and prevent accurate risk assessment.
6. Individual incentives in the private financial industry further encourage risky strategic choices that undermine individual financial firms.
7. Financial firms have grown too big, making government bailouts more likely and, thus, giving those firms an incentive to take on excessive risk.
8. Regulation should be comprehensive and global in order to avoid a "race to the bottom" across types of institutions, types of instruments, and borders.
9. If a race to the bottom develops, countries must be permitted to take defensive measures to protect their regulatory structures.

10. The precautionary principle should be applied where uncertainty is great; some financial innovations and products should simply be prohibited.

These recommendations are straightforward, but the politically powerful private financial industry has lobbied aggressively to prevent their implementation.

The United Nations commission report also addresses the concerns of developing nations. For example, the report recommends that the G20 nations agree to immediately implement:

1. Strong fiscal stimulus policies in developed countries
2. Additional funding for developing countries to stimulate their economies
3. Funding in the form of grants, not loans, to avoid creating more long-run debt
4. Developed countries committing 1 percent of their stimulus packages to funding projects and programs in developing countries
5. More freedom for developing economies to carry out diverse economic policies that diverge from the mainstream consensus
6. Avoiding developed-country protectionism
7. Further opening developed-country markets to developing countries' exports
8. Eliminating developed-country agricultural subsidies that distort international trade

These measures were included in the report by Stiglitz's United Nations commission in order to prevent developed countries from using the Great Recession as an excuse to renege on their earlier promises to increase development aid and open their markets. The commission's fear was justified in part by the fact that the stimulus packages enacted by developed economies almost all contained "buy domestic" clauses for recipients of the stimulus funds, a clear violation of earlier promises to keep their markets open to imports from developing countries.

The **Bank for International Settlements (BIS)**, an institution created after World War I along with the League of Nations, still operates to promote international financial integration. Located in Basel, Switzerland, the BIS maintains a large staff of economists and bankers, many supplied on a temporary basis by central banks from around the world, and it routinely brings together the heads of the world's central banks to discuss global financial issues. The BIS recently also set forth a number of recommendations for reform ahead of the 2009 G20 meeting.[8] Given the staffing and financial support of the BIS, these recommendations can be taken as a consensus view of the world's central banks. Among the BIS proposals were:

1. Over-the-counter markets and interbank transactions should be replaced by open exchanges where all market participants can observe bids, prices, and volumes.
2. Financial institutions that pose a greater risk to the international financial system should be required to hold larger reserves against future crises.
3. Financial institutions should be classified according to their risk, and each type of institution should be restricted to customers that can handle the risk and complexities.

The BIS report also scolded national governments for their indiscriminate bailouts of their financial firms, which it feared would increase moral hazard in the future because government interventions have often consolidated the financial industry into fewer but larger financial conglomerates that inevitably prove to be "too big to fail" in the next financial crisis.

There have been many more proposals by individual economists, the financial industry, pundits, and private and public organizations and agencies. Eventually some consensus may develop. Whatever specific consensus that develops will tend to reflect the models that are used to analyze and explain the causes of the crisis and the consequences of proposed new regulations and institutions.

Whether policy makers listen to heterodox or orthodox economists will make a huge difference. The financial crisis was generated by a complex process that can only be understood from a holistic perspective.

Alternative Monetary Regimes: Islamic Finance

In discussions on reforming the international monetary system, most economists and policy makers proceed as if the entire international financial system is integrated and operates on the same principles. The integration of the international financial industry is not yet complete, however. The fact that not all national banking systems were affected by the U.S. subprime mortgage debacle suggests that there are still some firewalls between national financial systems. Furthermore, not all financial systems operate on the same principles. For example, **Islamic finance**, or **sharia-compliant finance**, is very different from the Western system we have been discussing. Neither the power of the international financial firms nor the strength of the dollar has been able to prevent the growth of Islamic finance. This specialized segment of the banking industry is driven by religious preferences and is concentrated in several Islamic countries. In recent years, a number of private international banks based in the major baking centers have begun offering sharia-compliant banking services.

Sharia law has been interpreted by Islamic scholars as prohibiting the charging of predetermined, guaranteed interest rates. Islamic finance deals with this prohibition in various ways.[9] The belief that predetermined and guaranteed rates of interest go against Islamic principles is based on the prophet Muhammad's prohibition of *riba,* or "an excess"; the charging of a fixed rate of interest is said to be the type of *riba* that the prophet had in mind. Many Muslims believe that social justice requires borrowers and lenders to share rewards as well as losses. Such equal sharing of risk prohibits the exchange of risk common to Western finance, in which the borrower commonly has to pay interest regardless of the success or failure of the project for which the money was borrowed. Thus, Islamic finance does not offer savings accounts that pay a predetermined rate. Mutual funds in stocks that pay dividends according to company performance are acceptable according to most Islamic scholars. It should be pointed out that Islam is not the only religion to see fixed interest rates as potentially exploitative; until recently, the Roman Catholic Church banned interest entirely, even if rates varied according to the fortunes of the borrower.

In some ways, Islamic finance is no different from most financial markets. Islamic finance seeks to efficiently allocate savings to the highest-return projects, as that would be the preference of both lenders and borrowers. The recent expansion of Islamic mutual funds that invest in stocks, commodities, or leasing contracts suggests that these funds have not been severely constrained in providing liquidity while still meeting Islamic finance rules. The securitization of investments permits the pooling of risk while still, in principle, following Islamic law.

Interestingly, the equal sharing of risk can prevent some of the instability that has plagued Western financial sectors because savers and investors are more likely to share the same concerns and interests. Also, the closer synchronization of payoff periods and holding periods reduces the likelihood that financial institutions will suffer cash flow problems and default on their short-run obligations. The sharing of profits and losses by lenders and borrowers is quite appropriate for financing new entrepreneurs, as well. For example, the **venture capital** funds that have been so important in promoting new enterprises in the United States behave much as Islamic finance requires: if a new entrepreneur fails, the venture capital fund writes the project off, but if the venture succeeds, the lender takes a large portion of the profits. For ventures that have a high probability of failure, but which pay handsome rewards in the case of success, the standard fixed-interest loan is not very efficient: the lender suffers the loss of most if not all of the principal if the project fails, but gains only the stated interest return while the entrepreneur captures most of the large gain in the case of success. This may be why banks traditionally favor well-established firms and individuals for loans over riskier entrepreneurs with new projects. Just as the venture capital firm does, the Islamic financial institution may be more likely to favor riskier but potentially highly profitable projects because it will share in the profits.

Islamic banks face a unique adverse selection problem: according to Timur Kuran (1995, p. 162) Islamic banks fear "that industrialists with high expected returns will borrow from conventional banks (to maximize their returns in the likely event of success), while those with low expected returns will favor profit and loss sharing (to minimize their losses in the likely event of failure.)" This is why, Kuran says, Islamic banks go to great lengths to devise ways to identify poor credit risks.

Islamic finance has also not been able to solve the difficulty of engaging in transactions between Muslims and non-Muslims. For example, Islamic banks find it difficult to lend to firms that also carry some conventional debt, and Islamic stock funds must decide whether they can include stock in companies that have issued conventional fixed-interest bonds. Compounding these problems is the fact that religious principles are not consistently interpreted or applied in different Islamic countries. Finally, there is the interesting question of how Islamic finance handles government borrowing: How do savers "share risk" with a government? How does one define a government's profits? Of course, the Western model of finance has not dealt with the sharing of risk very effectively either, as has become all too clear in recent years.

After the global financial meltdown in 2008, the shift toward sharia-compliant financial activity continued, albeit at a modest pace. Despite official support, Indonesia's sharia banking industry still accounted for less than 2 percent of the Indonesian banking industry's total assets in 2009. In Malaysia, on the other hand, sharia-compliant banks held 17 percent of total bank sector assets in 2009.[10] In early 2009, after the global financial markets had been frozen by the Western financial crisis, the Indonesian government was able to sell $462 million in sharia-compliant bonds to retail investors. It will be interesting to see whether the global slowdown in investment, trade, and economic activity in general will slow all forms of banking, or whether the obvious failures of Western finance will lead more investors, savers, and governments to take advantage of Islamic finance's more equal sharing of risks and its inherent requirement for greater transparency.

SOME CONCLUSIONS AND PREDICTIONS

We mentioned earlier that many economists admitted that they were surprised by the severity of the 2008 financial crisis and subsequent global economic recession. The reason for their surprise was that their orthodox models had not predicted such an outcome. Recall from the discussion of the difference between orthodox and heterodox economics, as well as Chapter 13's discussion of financial markets, that mainstream orthodox macroeconomics had come to embrace the neoclassical paradigm of continuous functions, stable equilibria, rational people, and complete and competitive markets. At the start of the twenty-first century, macroeconomics had linked its aggregate model to **microfoundations**, which are microeconomic models that logically generate aggregate outcomes. As discussed in Chapter 2, these systems of microeconomic models were neither accurate nor realistic.

Among the microfoundations of aggregate economic outcomes, discussed in Chapter 13, was Eugene F. Fama's (1970) model of efficient markets that built all available information into asset prices, Friedman's (1953) hypothesis that speculation always stabilizes financial markets, the Coase theorem (Ronald Coase, 1960) that eliminated the problem of externalities, Robert E. Lucas, Jr. (1972, 1973) and John F. Muth's (1961) rational expectations hypothesis, and blind faith in the efficiency of markets to channel not only goods and services but also financial assets to their most productive applications. Underlying the whole paradigm is Kenneth Arrow and Gerard Debreu's (1954) and Debreu's (1959) elaborate general equilibrium models that included competitive markets in contingent commodities. These markets, combined with the microfoundations just described and other convenient assumptions such as stable and separable individual preferences and stable and separable production and cost functions, effectively eliminated risk and uncertainty from neoclassical analysis. Therefore, the possibility of crises and sudden reversals of economic activity was ignored by most orthodox economists.

Mainstream economists did not foresee the 2007–2008 recession because their smooth, continuous equilibrium models did not include the possibility of such an event. Even the large imbalances that economists observed, such as the government deficits in many developed countries, the huge trade deficits and surpluses, the accumulation of seemingly unsustainable debt by governments and entire countries, and the unrealistic asset prices in the stock market in 2000 and housing markets in the early 2000s, did not ring alarm bells. The neoclassical equilibrium models were deemed to be realistic, which meant markets would somehow correct the imbalances. Under the assumption of rational expectations, rational investors would surely cause the markets to plunge and correct the imbalances if they were indeed unsustainable.

An equally relevant question for macroeconomics and international finance is: why are so many orthodox macroeconomists and financial economists still reluctant to lay their neoclassical models aside and embrace alternative models? There might be more enthusiasm for reforming the international monetary system if economists embraced the ideas of Keynes and Minsky. For a possible answer to this question, Chapter 2's sociological justification for heterodox economics provides some useful insight. A sociological analysis of economic thought since 2007 reveals that the strength of the neoclassical paradigm is still limiting mainstream economists' perspective.

Recall from the section titled "A Sociological Justification for Heterodoxy" in Chapter 2 that the French sociologist Pierre Bourdieu defined culture as a combination of a **habitus** and a **doxa**, which humans create in order to deal with the reality of the **field** they must live and work in. The habitus of mainstream economics includes using the neoclassical paradigm to address all economic questions. It is inherently difficult for a thinking person to deal with the combination of an *objective* field of economics and a *subjective* habitus that mandates the use of an unrealistic model in order to be able to function. The mainstream economists, therefore, embraced a doxa, which Bourdieu defined as a complex set of beliefs that at least superficially justify the habitus and its relationship to the reality of the field of economics. The economists' doxa includes the assumptions of the neoclassical models, such as perfect competition, rational decisions, separable preferences, et cetera, all "believed" by economists to be reasonable approximations of reality and, therefore, justifications for using the neoclassical models in addressing economic issues. Together, the doxa and habitus create a culture that tends to make economists reject policies that call for active macroeconomic policies, the regulation of the financial sector, or restrictions on profit-motivated financial innovation. These are, of course, precisely the policies that Keynes and Minsky would prescribe. Given the power of culture to stop political change, it may take more than a few years of recession to change the culture of economics. After all, it took the collapse of the gold standard and a decade-long Great Depression with 25 percent unemployment to bring Keynes to prominence in the 1930s.

Heterodox economists are not tied to the neoclassical culture, which means they are more willing to accept alternative paradigms and models. Heterodox economics is, therefore, also more ready to accept the research from other fields of science and social science that supports Keynes's view of uncertainty and Minsky's financial instability hypothesis. When these are combined, the proposals by Stiglitz's United Nations commission are perfectly straightforward. Why would policy makers not agree?

The neoclassical paradigm fits the interests of the private international financial firms much more closely. A return to high levels of regulation, prohibitions on certain types of banking and financial innovation, restrictions on international financial flows, and above all international regulatory institutions that are not controlled by governments sympathetic to business and finance are all outcomes that the wealthy and aggressive lobbyists will resist. If the first two years following the start of the

Great Recession in 2007 are any indication, few of the Stiglitz commission's recommendations will be implemented. Thus, heterodox economists are likely to follow Minsky and predict that there will be another financial crisis in the future.

By the way, the Mount Washington Hotel in Bretton Woods is still open. The beautiful old hotel was entirely refurbished just a few years ago, and a new conference wing was opened in 2008. As long as they ban the thousands of lobbyists that would no doubt try to take over the vast grounds, there is plenty of room at the hotel for delegates from all 150 countries that are members of the IMF.

In the meantime, it is interesting to think about what a new Bretton Woods conference would look like at this point in history. The position of the United States now is similar to that of Great Britain at the original Bretton Woods conference, since it is the most recent owner of the world's reserve currency. On the other hand, while the British pound had already lost its position to the U.S. dollar in 1944, today the demise of the dollar has not yet occurred. It may not occur for a long time. China, Brazil, and Russia, among other countries, are increasingly arguing for a new reserve currency; countries that have accumulated large amounts of dollars, like China, South Korea, Japan, and Taiwan, are justifiably concerned about the future value of their cache of dollars and dollar-denominated assets.

The United States does not relish the prospect of borrowing in something other than dollars. With dollar loans converted to, say, bancor loans the United States would be exposed to exchange risk. Like Greece, the U.S. government would be forced to reduce its current account deficit and its government budget deficit in order to prevent the ratings agencies from sharply downgrading its bonds. U.S. consumption would have to fall in order to generate more internal savings, which is not an attractive policy for an economy mired in recession. But while the U.S. delegation at a new Bretton Woods conference would resist the creation of an international reserve currency like the bancor, it would be likely to push other countries to agree to limit their trade surpluses.

If there is no progress at a new Bretton Woods conference, China and others could simply begin accumulating other currencies as reserves, which they certainly have the option to do under today's order. But they would cause their huge accumulated stocks of dollar reserves to depreciate in value as they sell dollars and purchase other currencies in which to hold their reserves. Therefore, China wants to exchange its dollars for a new reserve currency before the dollar falls in value.

Finally, it is fun to imagine who might make up the delegations at a new Bretton Woods conference. Treasury Secretary Timothy Geithner would probably head the U.S. delegation. But who would play the role of Keynes? Is there someone today of his stature—the elder statesman who had correctly predicted the difficulty in restoring the gold standard after World War I and created the field of macroeconomics to explain the Great Depression? And if there is a person of Keynes's stature today, would he be invited to take a prominent seat at the table of a new Bretton Woods conference?

CHAPTER SUMMARY

1. Many economists have admitted that they were surprised by the severity of the 2008 financial crisis and the Great Recession. The reason for their surprise was that their orthodox models had not predicted such outcomes.

2. At the start of the twenty-first century, macroeconomics had linked its aggregate models to *microfoundations,* which are microeconomic models that logically generate the hypothesized aggregate outcomes.

3. The microfoundations have turned out to be overly simplistic, a requirement for mathematical tractability, in that they hypothesized smooth adjustments to stable equilibria. That is, in order to generate solutions to their models, economists had to assume microfoundations that effectively ruled out the possibility of sudden large shifts and economic crises.

4. Most of the post–World War II period, which includes the Bretton Woods order and the post–

Bretton Woods mixture of orders, was characterized by various failures, including inflation, balance of payments crises, and financial instability.

5. Recently, the 2008 financial crisis and, in 2009, the first global decline in GDP since World War II put a strain on the euro area, which in 2010 began to face the real possibility of disintegration.

6. Discussion of the current international monetary order's weaknesses invariably returns to the question of whether a government should seek to peg or float its currency.

7. The response to the 2008 financial crisis and economic recession was quick, but the fragmented international monetary system, in which every country sets their own policies, made the national responses inconsistent and inefficient.

8. In most countries, the policy response to the 2008 financial crash and economic recession consisted of some combination of (a) fiscal expansion in the form of increased government spending and cuts in taxes, (b) monetary expansion, (c) direct infusions of cash into the private banking system in order reverse its sudden seizure in 2008, and (d) beginning discussions on how to change the regulations and government agencies responsible for overseeing the financial sector.

9. John Maynard Keynes (1936) explained that during a deep economic recession, the economy tends to become stuck in a *liquidity trap,* in which further monetary expansion will not lower interest rates any further because when the interest rate approaches zero percent no one will acquire long-term assets and banks will not lend for fear of suffering capital losses when the interest rate goes back up in the future.

10. As Keynes (1936) pointed out, creating the conditions under which prospective investors are willing to borrow and invest again is, by itself, not enough to end a financial crisis. We must also take into account the other facet of the state of confidence, namely the confidence of the lending institutions in those who seek to borrow from them, sometimes described as the state of credit.

11. In their review of Carmen Reinhart and Kenneth Rogoff's conclusion that financial crises provoke exceptionally long recessions, Yeva Nersisyan and Randall Wray (2010a, 2010b) found no cases of such recessions in countries that let their currencies float and issued debt only in their own currency. In short, financial crises occur only when exchange rates are fixed and foreign borrowing is denominated in foreign currencies.

12. Two ideas that have been recently revived are Keynes's bancor and International Clearing Union. The ICU would regulate the exchange of currencies, act as a lender of last resort to national central banks, and force countries to keep their international accounts in balance. The bancor would be a neutral international reserve currency that takes the place of the U.S. dollar in the current international monetary system.

13. Keynes correctly saw foreign debt as the fundamental reason why large exchange rate adjustments cause financial crises and economic recessions, and he wanted the Bretton Woods order to include rules and institutions to prevent such financial crises.

14. Not only would Keynes's ICU have limited countries' trade deficits by restricting foreign borrowing; he also proposed limiting trade surpluses by having the ICU tax a rising percentage of the accumulated bancors. In short, he wanted incentives for both deficit and surplus countries to balance their trade.

15. One different financial network that has been developing for quite a few years is *Islamic,* or *sharia-compliant,* finance.

16. Sharia law has been interpreted by Islamic scholars as prohibiting the charging of predetermined, guaranteed interest rates; many Muslims believe that social justice requires borrowers and lenders to share rewards as well as losses.

17. Islamic finance's insistence on an equal sharing of risk prohibits the exchange of risk common to Western finance; this limits the benefits of financial transactions, but it adds to the stability of the financial system and prevents defaults that require oppressive repayment schemes.

18. Unlike the microfoundations-based mainstream financial mind-set that has prevented orthodox economists from anticipating the inevitable and frequent financial crises, heterodox economists such as Hyman Minsky not only accept the possibility of crises, but they also understand that specific measures are needed to prevent them.

KEY TERMS AND CONCEPTS

anchor
bancor
Bank for International Settlements (BIS)
beggar-thy-neighbor policy
confidence
convention
doxa
European central bank
field
habitus

International Clearing Union (ICU)
International Monetary Fund (IMF)
Islamic finance
liquidity trap
microfoundations
primary budget surplus
Sharia-compliant finance
Stability and Growth Pact
Triffin paradox

PROBLEMS AND QUESTIONS

1. Do you think it is fair that the taxpayers of one country bail out a bank with customers in other countries? Discuss.
2. Why have so many emerging economies intentionally devalued their currencies to accumulate reserves? Discuss and explain.
3. Discuss the various causes of financial crises. How can they be prevented? How should the international financial system be reformed to reduce the chances that a financial sector in one or more countries is forced to curtail lending?
4. Does the globalization of financial services imply that regulation and oversight should be conducted by international institutions rather than national institutions, as is currently the case? Discuss.
5. Explain John Maynard Keynes's proposal for the International Clearing Union. Do you think it could have worked? How different would the world be today if the ICU had been put in place and maintained up to now?
6. Explain the Triffin paradox and how it applies to today's international economic system. Could it have been avoided with the use of the bancor in place of the dollar as the world's reserve currency?
7. Do we need another Bretton Woods conference? If yes, what should the agenda be? If no, then how should the recent financial failures be addressed?
8. Explain the Keynesian liquidity trap. How does the existence of a liquidity trap limit policy makers' options for dealing with high unemployment?
9. Speculate on how likely it is that the BIS's suggestions for dealing with the global financial crisis will be carried out. What could block their implementation? Explain.
10. What are some of the concerns of developing countries during the 2007–2008 financial crisis and economic slowdown? Discuss how the Stiglitz (2010) report for the United Nations deals with these concerns.
11. Explain why Islamic finance might be more appropriate for directing funding toward new entrepreneurs than the traditional fixed-interest loans given by banks in most countries of the world. Base your explanation on the example of a banker facing a prospective entrepreneur with a project costing $100 that has a 75 percent chance of earning a 200 percent return on investment and a 25 percent chance of losing all the money invested. Would you give the loan at, say, 10 percent interest? What if you could split the actual return evenly with the entrepreneur?
12. Discuss the advantages and disadvantages of Islamic finance, making specific references to the traditional banking problems of risk, adverse selection, and moral hazard.

13. Through 2011, most governments had relied on economic advisors that tended to view the world through orthodox economic models for solutions to the global economic slowdown. Discusss how orthodox and heterodox economists differ in their prescriptions for analyzing the economic situation and implementing economic policies to deal with the crisis.

NOTES

1. *Wall Street Journal* (2011), "Greek Economy Shrinks by 6.9%," August 12.

2. Maurice Obstfeld and Alan M. Taylor (2001).

3. Atish R. Ghosh, Ann-Marie Gulde, Jonathan D. Ostry, and Holger Wolf (1996).

4. Tony Barber (2008), "EU Calls for Tighter Financial Controls," *Financial Times,* November 5. Keynes's speeches and articles on the issue can be found in John Maynard Keynes (1980), *The Collected Writings,* vol. 25, *Activities, 1940–44, Shaping the Post-war World: The Clearing Union,* editors Donald E. Moggridge and Elizabeth S. Johnson, New York: Cambridge University Press for the Royal Economic Society.

5. Described in detail in Armand van Dormael (1978), *Bretton Woods: Birth of a Monetary System,* London: Macmillan.

6. Quoted in Jami Anderlini (2009), "China Calls for a New Reserve Currency," *Financial Times,* March 23.

7. Quoted in Alan Beattie, Geoff Dyer, and Chris Giles (2010), "China Tees Up G20 Showdown with Snub for U.S. Plan to Limit Surpluses," *Financial Times,* November 6.

8. Chris Giles (2009), "BIS Calls for Wide Global Financial Reforms," *Financial Times,* June 30.

9. For an introduction to Islamic finance, see Zamir Iqbal (1997) or Timur Kuran (1995).

10. John Aglionby (2009), "Indonesian Bond Success Bodes Well," *Financial Times,* March 2.

PART SIX

IMMIGRATION

Like all components of the international economic integration, immigration is a very complex phenomenon that is related to all other forms of international economic integration across the economic, social, and natural spheres. This complexity is reflected in a comment by the Swiss novelist Max Frisch: "We wanted workers, and people came." During the 1960s, Swiss policy makers created programs to attract foreign workers to work in Switzerland for a limited period of time. However, the arrival of foreign people, and their families, quickly brought many unexpected social and economic changes. The complexity of immigration was also illustrated in the example given earlier in this textbook of how the flow of Mexican immigrants to the Untied States, and the social upheaval this caused in both Mexico and the United States, was driven in part by the opening of the Mexican border to the inflow of subsidized U.S. corn after Mexico signed the North American Free Trade Agreement. This phenomenon could be described as: "We just wanted to export more corn, and people came."

Part Six of this book is divided into two chapters. Chapter 18 introduces the subject of immigration by providing some important definitions and a brief general history of international migration. Immigration is the international economic activity that most directly brings people into contact. Therefore it influences, and is influenced by, events in the social sphere, which means purely economic models of immigration cannot capture all the causes and consequences of immigration. This chapter augments the orthodox labor supply and demand model of immigration by analyzing many further causes and consequences of the international movement of people. Also discussed are illegal immigration and the social conflicts that seem to drive many disputes over immigration policy.

Chapter 19 discusses immigration policy. Immigration policies reflect a complex and often contradictory set of political and social, as well as economic, factors. As these factors change, policy can take sudden and unpredictable turns. Most of the chapter is devoted to describing the history of immigration policy in the United States and Canada. These countries have, over the past two hundred years, moved from placing few restrictions on the entry of foreigners toward imposing tight limits, and then, most recently, back again to more open immigration policies. In short, these countries provide two very important and interesting case studies of how immigration policy evolves in the face of changing economic conditions and within the parameters of the economic, social, and natural spheres.

These chapters on immigration and immigration policy are the appropriate concluding part of international economics. The human experience with immigration underscores the many difficulties government policy makers and people in general have in dealing with strangers who seek to live among us in our communities. To date, even societies that we would regard as progressive and humanitarian have been unable to collectively design and enact immigration policies that are, at the same time, economically efficient, socially stabilizing, and just. Given the importance of immigration as an economic and political issue in so many countries, you will find these two chapters most interesting. Hopefully, you will also find them helpful in making sense out of the often emotional and increasingly bitter arguments about immigration.

CHAPTER 18

Immigration: The International Movement of People

> We wanted workers, and people came.
>
> —Max Frisch

The rate of growth of the world's population is the difference between the rate at which people are born and at which they die. For an individual country, however, population may also change because people migrate from one country to another. International migration, or **immigration**, has grown rapidly over the past half century, and it is now a major determinant of population growth in many countries.

International migration is an important determinant of income, economic growth, and social change in countries at both ends of the migration flows. For developing economies as a whole, remittances of income back home by migrants exceed 10 percent of gross domestic product (GDP). And in some developed economies, Canada and Switzerland, for example, 20 percent or more of the labor force is foreign born. Of course, immigration is itself a result of income differences across countries, and economic phenomena such as income growth, technological change, and employment have been shown to strongly influence immigration. Countries also have put in place many laws, regulations, and institutions to promote, restrict, and in other ways deal with the movement of people into and out of their territory.

Like all aspects of the international economic integration, immigration is a very complex phenomenon that is intimately related to many other aspects of the economic, social, and natural spheres. This complexity is reflected in the quote above from the Swiss novelist Max Frisch.[1] During the 1960s, Swiss policy makers created programs to attract foreign workers to work for a limited period of time. However, the arrival of these people, and their families, quickly brought many unexpected social and economic changes. Immigration is the international economic activity that most directly brings people into contact. It therefore influences, and is influenced by, the social sphere. Purely economic models of immigration cannot capture all the causes and consequences of immigration. This chapter augments the labor market model of immigration by analyzing many further causes and consequences of the international movement of people.

INTERNATIONAL MIGRATION

Scientific evidence suggests that the human species originated in eastern Africa some two hundred thousand years ago. We also know that humans eventually spread across the face of the earth. Migrations are one of the features of humanity. Unlike most animal species, which have tended to reside in fairly specific natural regions and climates, humans have adapted to a great variety of natural environments. Starting about sixty thousand years ago, humans walked or sailed out of Africa and eventually settled in all of the world's climates, landscapes, and altitudes. Human beings can be found living in the frigid northern regions of Canada and Russia, as well as in the tropical regions of Southeast Asia and the Brazilian Amazon.

Early Migrations

A description of early human migrations can be constructed using genealogical markers in DNA that permit scientists to trace the spread of humans backward in time. When people move, they take their genes along and pass them on to their descendants in their new homes. Thus, every present-day population retains clues as to who its predecessors were. When this type of scientific analysis is combined with evidence found by anthropologists, archeologists, paleontologists, and linguists, a fascinating story of human migration emerges. The research suggests that all humans alive today descended from earlier *homo sapiens* who lived in Africa two hundred thousand years ago.[2]

People moved from one location to another, probably for a variety of reasons such as climate changes, glaciation, natural disasters, depletion of game, the growth of population relative to available resources, and threats from other humans or animals. Because there were no political boundaries, these movements of people are usually referred to as **migrations** rather than *immigration*. Natural barriers such as oceans, deserts, and mountain ranges slowed the spread of humans across the earth. Humans were living in all corners of the world twenty thousand years ago, which implies there were no natural barriers that could permanently block humans from migrating.

The very earliest human migration was probably over land on foot, although human ancestors no doubt also learned to make boats millions of years ago. Human seafaring must have taken place well over forty thousand years ago, because human remains that old have been found in Australia and on islands far from any mainland. The migration of people to the Western Hemisphere occurred in several waves between ten thousand and thirty thousand years ago, probably across what we now call the Bering Strait from Asia to North America. Given humans' capacity for traveling on water, migration to the Western Hemisphere did not necessarily have to coincide with the often-mentioned land bridge that existed between present-day Russia and Alaska during the glaciation of the last ice age. People could have sailed their primitive boats across the narrow Bering Strait at any time. Nomadic groups occupied Europe over forty thousand years ago.

Population growth increased when the new technologies of farming, irrigation, animal husbandry, specialization, exchange, and urbanization enabled humans to use the earth's resources more efficiently. Permanent settlements also led to well-defined economies, subject to uniform sets of institutions and surrounded by political boundaries that, at least to some degree, restricted the movement of people. Citizenship and national origin became characteristics by which to identify people. A new term was used to describe the migration of people across political boundaries: **immigration**. The new political and social boundaries have not entirely restricted human migration. Viewed holistically, the same economic and social development that accompanied the permanent settlements and the creation of political boundaries also ended up, eventually, spurring the technological change that improved communications and built the means of transportation that integrated the individual national societies into an internationally integrated global community.

Recent Immigration

The movement of people from Europe and Africa to the Western Hemisphere between 1500 and the present stands out as the greatest migration of modern times. It is estimated that about 75 million Europeans left their native countries and immigrated to what are now Canada, the United States, Argentina, Brazil, and many smaller countries in Latin America and the Caribbean. More than 10 million Africans were taken as slaves to the Western Hemisphere during the period from 1500 to 1900. The greatest number went to the Caribbean (4 million) and Brazil (3.6 million).

The largest single migration of people in the twentieth century took place between India and Pakistan in 1947. The partitioning of India after independence from Great Britain caused about 7 million Muslims to move from what is today India into that portion of the former British colony of India that became Pakistan, and about an equal number of Hindus were moved in the opposite direction from what is now Pakistan into India. At the close of World War II, almost 6 million Japanese moved back to Japan from China (Manchuria), Korea, and Formosa (today's Taiwan), areas occupied by Japan during the first half of the twentieth century.

Immigration increased rapidly toward the end of the twentieth century. Canada, Australia, New Zealand, and the United States received large inflows of immigrants from Europe throughout the post–World War II period. Australia and Canada each received more than 2 million immigrants between 1946 and 1964. A number of Western European countries, which had supplied so many people to the rest of the world from 1600 to 1900, themselves began to receive large inflows of immigrants from elsewhere in Europe and, after 1960, from North Africa. Even Ireland, which sent over 4 million immigrants to the Western Hemisphere in the second half of the nineteenth century, began receiving large inflows of immigrants toward the end of the twentieth. Because of this immigration, in 2004 Ireland's population again exceeded 4 million, which had not happened since 1871.[3] Some 8 million Germans expelled from Eastern Europe after World War II settled in West Germany, and over 1 million ethnic French moved to France during Algeria's war of independence in the late 1950s. The collapse of the Soviet Union and the other communist governments in Eastern Europe has, since 1990, resulted in immigration from Eastern Europe to the high-income Western European economies. Over 1 million immigrants legally enter European countries each year, and perhaps another five hundred thousand asylum seekers and unauthorized immigrants enter each year as well.[4] Immigration has greatly changed many European societies, as suggested by the high percentages of foreigners living in each country, shown in Table 18.1. Switzerland's population and labor force are about 25 percent foreign, and Luxembourg's labor force is over one-third foreign born.

People do not immigrate only to the developed countries of Europe and North America. There are an estimated 7 million Pakistanis, Filipinos, Indians, Palestinians, Egyptians, and other foreigners working in Saudi Arabia. Perhaps another 5 million foreigners live and work as construction workers, domestics, and day laborers in the other oil-rich Gulf states on the Arabian Peninsula.[5] The rapidly growing Asian economies of Singapore, Malaysia, and Thailand also have attracted many immigrants from populous countries such as Indonesia, Bangladesh, the Philippines, Pakistan, and India. An estimated one in four factory workers in Malaysia are foreigners.[6] Jordan has the highest percentage of foreign-born residents of any country in the world.

Why Do People Immigrate?

The most important determinant of immigration generally appears to be the difference in income levels and economic opportunities between countries. The relationship between relative income levels and immigration is not linear, however. Migration from the very poorest countries of the world is actually quite small; most of the immigration to rich countries comes from the group of intermediate-income developing countries. There clearly are other determinants of immigration, some of which may outweigh the differences in income between countries. Immigration from very poor countries may be limited by the cost of the long journey to another country. Also, people from very poor countries may understand that they lack the education or job skills necessary to be successful in higher-income countries. There are also language and cultural barriers to immigration,

Table 18.1

Foreign-Born Population and Labor Force: 2004

	% of Population	% of Labor Force
Europe:		
Austria	13.0	15.3
Belgium	11.5	11.4
Denmark	6.3	5.9
France	10.0	11.3
Germany	13.0	12.2
Ireland	11.0	10.0
Italy	2.5	5.9
Luxembourg	33.1	45.0
Netherlands	10.6	11.1
Spain	5.3	11.2
Sweden	12.2	13.3
Switzerland	23.5	25.3
United Kingdom	9.3	9.6
Japan	1.2	1.0
Traditional Immigrant Destinations:		
Australia	23.6	24.9
Canada	18.0	17.8
United States	12.8	15.1

Source: OECD (2006), *International Migration Outlook,* Paris: OECD, Chart 1.4 and Table 1.8.

and, of course, humans' own psychological resistance to change. Also, many high-income countries severely restrict the entrance of immigrants. This latter determinant of immigration is so important that we devote an entire chapter to immigration policy.

Immigration directly affects a country's rate of population growth, although population growth through immigration differs from natural population growth in several important ways. First of all, immigrants are generally different from the native citizens of the country in terms of their culture, education, skills, and social behavior. The willingness of immigrants to encounter the hardships entailed in moving from one country to another suggests that they are not like the average citizens of the countries they emigrate from. They almost never are like the average citizens of the countries they immigrate to. Second, immigrants are less often infants or very old people; most of the world's immigrants today are adults of working age. Therefore, immigration has different social and economic effects on the source and destination countries than does natural population growth. This is an important point; many pundits have suggested that immigration can compensate for the declines in birth rates and the aging of populations in most high-income countries.

Many Types of Immigrants

A common image of immigrants is that they are **settlers**, that is, people who permanently move to another country. Many immigrants today fit this description, but among the millions of people who move across borders each year, many fall into other categories.

Many people go to live and work in foreign countries temporarily. These immigrants are often referred to as **contract workers** if they move on a temporary basis in order to perform a specific type of work. Contract workers may work just for a harvest season or a tourist season, such as Italian hotel workers in Switzerland and Mexican agricultural workers in the United States. Or, they may remain in the country for a number of years, such as the factory workers from southern Europe and Turkey in Germany, the Netherlands, and Belgium in the 1960s and the Egyptian, Indian, and Pakistani workers working in the oil-producing Middle Eastern states today.

Many immigrants today are **professionals** who move to another country to perform specialized technical or management jobs. Professionals include the managers and other employees of the transnational corporations that were described in Chapter 4. Other professionals work for the growing number of international nonprofit organizations and institutions, such as the United Nations, the World Bank, and regional development banks, that carry out a variety of functions in foreign countries. They also work for firms that supply the growing international trade in services, such as financial services, retailing, and communications.

A fourth category of immigrants is **asylum seekers** and **refugees**, which includes those people who leave their home countries to escape political, religious, and various other threats to their personal safety or forms of oppression. According to the United Nations High Commission for Refugees, there were 11–12 million refugees in the world at the end of 2011, most of whom were fleeing war and ethnic strife in the many African countries that were suffering civil wars and Iraq and Afghanistan, attacked by the United States in the first decade of the 2000s. Wars in the Balkans and the disintegration of the Soviet Union pushed many people to seek asylum in Western Europe.

A fifth category of immigrants is **unauthorized** or **illegal immigrants**. These are people who cross the border in violation of the laws of the **destination country** and without the required documentation. The United States Immigration and Naturalization Service and various research groups have estimated that there were over 10 million undocumented, and presumably unauthorized, workers in the United States in 2005.[7] The International Labour Organization (ILO) estimated that in 1991 there were 2.6 million immigrants living illegally in Western Europe, and that number had about doubled by the year 2000.[8] It may have doubled once again by 2010. However, these numbers are very imprecise because unauthorized immigrants seldom openly identify themselves for fear of being deported or punished.

Another category is made up of **temporary immigrants** who do not fall easily into any of the categories listed so far. For example, there are about 2 million students in foreign countries in any one year—nearly five hundred thousand in the United States alone. Other temporary residents of foreign countries are diplomats, employees of nonprofit organizations, researchers, employees of transportation firms, visiting professors and teachers, religious workers, et cetera.

Finally, there are **involuntary immigrants**. Historically this category included the millions caught in the world slave trade that flourished until well into the nineteenth century. Today, people are still forced to migrate, such as when families in one country sell their children into indentured servitude in another country. In fact, there is a fuzzy line between involuntary immigration and the desperate attempts by people to better their circumstances by agreeing to very oppressive working conditions in other countries. As long as there are desperate people, we will continue to see the inhuman trafficking of humans who have no other way to improve their dismal conditions than to "accept" exploitation across borders, unless more coordinated international action to stop it is agreed upon.

Many immigrants fall into more than one of the above categories. For example, **emigrants** may leave very poor countries to escape hunger or oppression and also to seek higher wages. Temporary workers may become permanent residents, as in the case of the **guest workers** in the fast-growing Western European economies in the 1960s. Many guest workers eventually sought and gained permanent residency in their host countries.

A LABOR MARKET MODEL OF IMMIGRATION

To analyze the economic causes and consequences of immigration, we begin with the mainstream neoclassical labor market supply and demand model of immigration. In this model, immigrants were viewed only as workers. We purposely present a simple two-country labor market model of immigration in Figure 18.1. Because of different economic conditions in the two countries, Nativo and Destino, the supply and demand curves for labor are different in each country. As a result, wages are ten dollars in Destino and four pesos in Nativo. If we know that the exchange rate between Destino dollars and Nativo pesos is one dollar = two pesos, we can translate the peso wage into dollars. Thus, in terms of dollars, wages are five times higher in Destino than in Nativo, ten dollars compared to two dollars. If people find ways to move between the two countries, the wage difference will cause some Nativan labor to move to Destino. The immigration will cause the supply curve for labor to shift to the left in Nativo and to the right Destino.

Figure 18.1 depicts the case where immigration causes the supply curves to shift to where wages rise to the peso equivalent of $3 in Nativo and fall to $8 in Destino. Figure 18.1 thus depicts the realistic situation where labor migration tends to reduce, but not eliminate, the difference in wages between two countries. Only partial arbitrage of wages is likely because there are restrictions and costs of immigration.

Who Gains from Immigration?

Figure 18.1 illustrates why labor migration is a controversial issue in many countries: Even though the overall worldwide output increases and total gains outweigh the losses, some well-defined groups suffer welfare losses when people immigrate. In the Destino-Nativo case, the immigrants from Nativo gain higher wages. Nativan workers remaining in their home country also gain from immigration because the decline in labor supply causes wages to rise to six pesos from four pesos when the migrants leave. The owners of other factors of production in Nativo suffer a loss in income, however, because the other factors have fewer units of labor to work with. In Destino, on the other hand, the wage of the native-born Destino workers falls with the influx of Nativan immigrants. Employers and other factor owners gain from the availability of more workers who complement the factors they own. The capital-labor ratio rises in Nativo and it falls in Destino.

Recall from Chapter 3 that the area under the demand curve represents the value of total output. In the case of total demand for labor, the area under the curve represents total output in the economy. In Figure 18.1, this total area is split between the return to labor and the return to the owners of the other factors (capital, land) of production. Table 18.2 summarizes the various gains and losses to labor and the other factors of production following the migration of workers from Nativo to Destino as shown in Figure 18.1.

Immigrants' income increases from h in the left-hand diagram in Figure 18.1 to H in the right-hand diagram, a fourfold increase; wages in Destino end up at eight dollars, four times the Nativo wage equivalent to two dollars that the workers earned before immigrating. This increased income is generally assumed to be the cause of the immigration.

Immigration thus increases world output and income because the gain in output in Destino, H&G, is greater than the loss of output g&h, in Nativo. This rise in the value of total world output makes perfect sense if you keep in mind that labor moves from a country where its marginal contribution to the real value of output is low, somewhere between two and three dollars, to a country where its marginal contribution to the real value of output is higher, between ten dollars before immigration began and eight dollars after immigration occurs.

Max Frisch's comment quoted at the start of this chapter reminds us that immigrants are not just workers. Immigrants perform many other functions: they innovate and start businesses, they have

Figure 18.1 **The Labor Markets after Immigration**

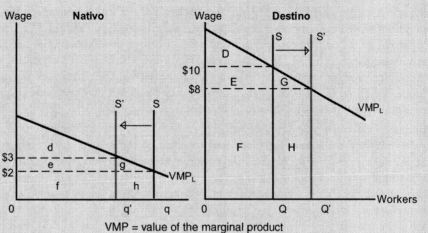

VMP = value of the marginal product

Table 18.2

Summary of Gains and Losses from Figure 18.1

1. Nativo:	
Owners of other (nonlabor) factors:	loss of e + g
Remaining workers:	gain of e
Net change in real income:	loss of g
2. Destino:	
Workers originally in Destino:	loss of E
Owners of other (nonlabor) factors:	gain of E + G
Net change in real income:	gain of G
3. Immigrants:	
Wages in Nativo:	loss of h
Wages in Destino:	gain of H
Net change in real income:	gain of H − h
4. World (1 + 2 + 3):	
Net change in Nativo real income:	loss of g
Net change in Destino real income:	gain of G
Net gains for immigrants:	gain of H − h
Net change in world income:	gain of (H + G) − (h + g) > 0

children, they consume products, they congest limited infrastructure and collectively owned facilities, they use up resources, and they change society in the destination country. The simple supply and demand labor market model of immigration does not capture these additional effects.

The Effect of Immigration on Domestic Product Demand

The simple labor market model of immigration does not recognize that an increase in the quantity of labor employed also increases income in the destination country, which increases aggregate demand and, hence, the demand for labor. Newly arrived immigrants acquire housing, food, and other goods and services produced in the economy, thus effectively demanding some of their own labor and causing the value of the marginal product (VMP) of labor curve to shift up when they take up residence in a country. Also, Figure 18.1 shows that as total output rises in the country that receives immigrants, some of the rise in income is captured by the native owners of the other factors, who also increase their demand for products that require labor input. This rise in income will cause the demand curve for labor, the VMP curve in Figure 18.2, to rise. Therefore, immigrants do not cause the wage to fall to B, as Figure 18.1 would suggest, but only to C, because immigrants cause the demand for labor to increase along with the supply of labor.

Note that this **demand effect** of immigration depends on the degree to which a person's demand spreads between the local economy and the rest of the world. In general, not everything can be transported without cost across borders, and consumption is biased toward local products. In this case, it matters where consumers are located, and thus, the movement of people from one country to another also shifts demand for factors, like labor, from one economy to another.

In the source country, the labor demand effect of immigration has the opposite effects. There, the departure of a substantial number of workers implies that there are fewer consumers. Thus, all other things equal, migration reduces labor demand in the source country. In this case, shown in Figure 18.3, the demand curve for labor will shift downward as the supply curve of labor shifts leftward, and the net positive effect of the departure of some of the country's workers will be smaller. For example, after immigrants leave the country, wages rise only from A to C, not to B as would be the case in Figure 18.3 if only the supply curve shifted.

As an illustration of the demand effect of immigration, Örn Bodvarsson and your author (2003, 2006) describe the economic impact of the arrival of about four thousand Hispanic immigrants in the small city of Lexington, Nebraska, to take jobs at a new meat packing plant. Because nearly all the immigrants were employed in what was effectively an export industry and very few initially worked in businesses that served the local economy, it was relatively easy to measure the local demand effect of the immigration surge. As a result of the arrival of the immigrants, Lexington's population grew from 6,600 in 1990 to just over 10,000 by 2000. Census data and other evidence on county employment, the unemployment rate, local retail sales, industrial employment, tax revenue, school attendance, housing prices, and new business creation suggest that the immigration brought a strong rebound in overall employment and economic growth in Lexington.

Bodvarsson and Van den Berg (2008) use data from the well-known Mariel Boatlift that brought a hundred thousand Cuban immigrants to greater Miami in 1980 over a period of just a few months after the Cuban government suddenly permitted people to leave the country. We specifically examined whether immigrant demand effects can explain David Card's (1990) earlier finding that the surge in immigration did not appear to have any adverse effect on the unemployment rate or wages in Miami. Our statistical analysis shows, as we found for Lexington, that immigration's demand effects are highly and significantly positive. Immigrants in effect demand some of their own labor when they move to a new country.

Income Remittances

The simple labor market model of immigration also does not incorporate the possibility that immigrants send some of their income to relatives back in their native countries. Such international transfers of money by immigrants are called **remittances**.

An Inter-American Development Bank survey (2004) of immigrants living in the United States revealed that more than 60 percent of Latin American immigrants in the United States send some money to relatives in their native countries. The World Bank (2007) estimated that total remittances by Latin American immigrants in the United States were equal to over $50 billion in 2005.

Figure 18.2 **Immigration and Demand for Labor**

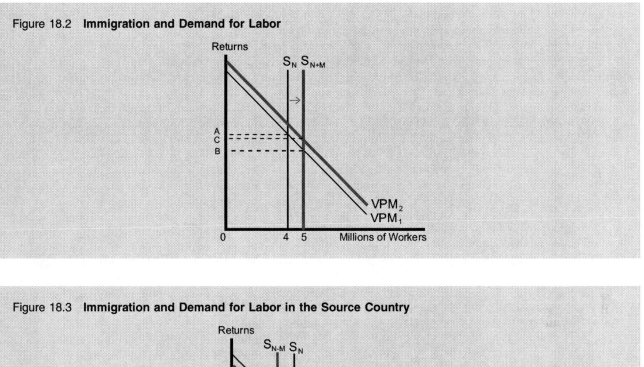

Figure 18.3 **Immigration and Demand for Labor in the Source Country**

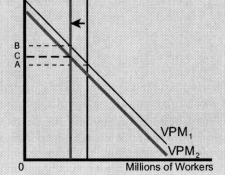

Perhaps another $10 billion in remittances were sent by Asian immigrants to their native lands. Other researchers have estimated that temporary Mexican workers in the United States send about half of their income home, while permanent Mexican immigrants to the United States send about 15 percent of their U.S. income to family in Mexico.[9] Immigrant remittances are very important to developing countries' total income, accounting for more than 1 percent of GDP in most developing economies and exceeding 5 percent of GDP in some. Table 18.3 summarizes recent estimates of immigrant remittances.

The growth of immigrant remittances shown in Table 18.3 is not an unexpected by-product of immigration. Immigration from poor countries to rich countries is often motivated specifically by the need to earn money to support the family that remains behind. According to a 2003 poll of Ecuadorian families who have members working abroad:

> The majority of Ecuadorian emigrants were motivated for reasons other than personal economic problems. Instead, their decision to emigrate is the product of a family consensus, in which the younger, healthier, and best-equipped family members were chosen to make the journey.[10]

Table 18.3

Immigrant Remittance Payments Received by Developing Countries, by Region, 2000–2006
(billions of U.S. dollars)

	2000	2001	2002	2003	2004	2005[a]	2006
East Asia and Pacific	17	29	29	35	39	43	47
Europe and Central Asia	13	13	14	17	23	31	32
Latin America & Caribbean	20	24	28	35	41	48	53
Middle East and North Africa	13	15	16	20	23	24	25
South Asia	17	19	24	31	31	36	41
Sub-Saharan Africa	5	5	5	6	8	9	9
Total	*85*	*96*	*117*	*143*	*165*	*193*	*206*

[a] Estimated.

Source: World Bank (2007), *Global Development Finance 2007,* Washington, DC: World Bank, Box 2.2, p. 54. Numbers are the sum of the categories Workers' Remittances, Compensation of Employees, and Migrant Transfers from the *Balance of Payments Statistics Yearbook 2007,* Washington DC: International Monetary Fund.

The poll also found that the cost of emigration was often financed with the help of the family remaining behind.

The decision to immigrate in search of income to remit back to family and relatives is, fundamentally, no different from decisions made by hunter/gatherer tribes tens of thousands of years ago. Local food supplies were running out, it would have been normal to send people on long journeys to find food or to locate better living conditions. Such journeys were often more dangerous than crossing political borders without authorization today. Hostile tribes had to be confronted, there were physical dangers crossing oceans and large land masses inhabited by predators and where food and water sources were unknown, and there was no guarantee life would be any easier elsewhere.

Critics of immigration in destination countries often suggest that their country does not gain from immigration precisely because immigrants send their earnings back to the source countries. However, it is doubtful that immigrant remittances are large enough to substantially reduce aggregate demand in high-income destination countries. On the other hand, because income is low in many immigrant source countries, remittances can more easily convert source-country losses from the departure of immigrants into net gains. For example, suppose that immigration causes the total income of the workers and owners of other factors of production remaining in a source country to decrease by the area g, as illustrated in Figure 18.4. As long as remittances exceed g, income rises in Source. The difference in wages shown in Figure 18.4, $2 in Source and $8 after immigrants arrive in Destination, means that the area g is only about one-sixteenth the size of the area H, the total earnings of immigrants in Destination. If immigrants send home to Source more than $2.50 for every $8 they earn, the source country's total income increases. There will, most likely, be an increase in labor demand, shown as a shift from VMP_1 to VMP_2 in the source country in Figure 18.4. The destination country still experiences a net gain in total income after the immigration as long as the area G plus the gains in real output caused by the demand effect discussed above, the areas J + K, are greater than the g + h remitted. In

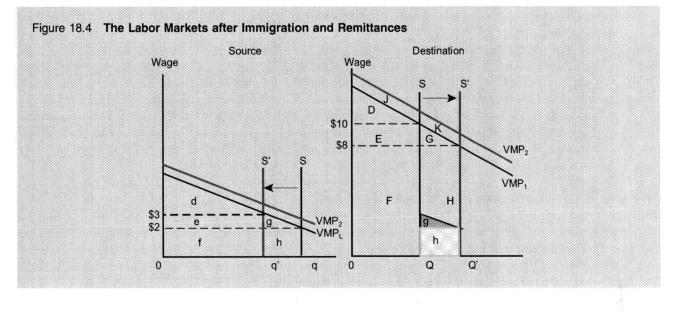

Figure 18.4 The Labor Markets after Immigration and Remittances

sum, remittances by immigrants can result in total income increasing in both the source and destination countries.

The potentially positive impact of remittances on the source country's overall welfare is well understood by many source-country policy makers. Governments in some labor-abundant countries have even adopted policies that effectively encourage people to immigrate to countries where incomes are much higher. The Philippines, for example, has a state-sponsored program to send workers abroad.

Because immigrants' remittances tend to decline the longer they live abroad, source-country governments have taken measures to maintain the allegiance of former citizens to their native countries. Some source countries have recently changed their national laws to encourage permanent immigrants to keep their native-country citizenship even if they acquire foreign citizenship. Mexico now even allows former citizens to reclaim Mexican citizenship after losing it by becoming citizens in the United States. In 2004, Mexico began permitting millions of Mexican citizens living in the United States to vote in Mexican elections, even if they held dual U.S./Mexican citizenship.[11] The Mexican state of Zacatecas passed a law in 2003 to let the eight hundred thousand Zacatecans who now live in the United States return to run for local political office.[12] The main motive for these legal changes was, no doubt, to maintain ties with the people who left the country and to encourage their continued remittances to relatives back home.

Externalities in the Destination Country

Immigration generates a variety of **externalities** that result in gains or losses to the destination country. For example, the arrival of immigrants can increase productivity throughout the economy by increasing the size of the market and thereby raising the level of competition. Also, by increasing the total size of the economy, immigrants permit the economy to operate more efficiently, because producers are better able to exploit **economies of scale**. Economic historian Nathan Rosenberg (1994, p. 113) attributes the rapid economic growth of the United States in the 1800s to "rapid growth in demand and circumstances conducive to a high degree of product standardization." Rosenberg goes on to explain why the U.S. market grew so large: "Probably the most pervasive force of all was the extremely rapid rate of population growth . . . with immigration assuming a role of some significance in the 1840s." By 1900, U.S. per capita income exceeded Britain's.

Immigration may also generate negative externalities. For example, immigration may cause congestion in public services such as schools, roads, sewers, electric power systems, and parks. More complex are externalities that alter social conditions and culture in the destination country. Some residents in the destination country welcome the diversity that immigrants bring to their communities, but some of the loudest opponents of immigration in destination countries clearly view the effects of immigrants on the national culture negatively. Not only do immigrants often struggle to adapt in their new communities, but the communities often have trouble adapting to the immigrants. The costs of these adjustments must be added to the analysis of immigration.

The Costs of Government Services for Immigrants

Another weakness of the simple labor market model of immigration is that it does not capture government-intermediated transfers between immigrants and native citizens. Public discussions of immigration in destination countries often focus on immigrants' use of public services and their receipts of government assistance. In most developed economies, which are the principal destination countries for immigrants, such services and transfers are certainly much larger than the net effects of immigration measured in most studies of immigration. The estimated net gains can quickly disappear if immigrants pay just a little less in taxes or use slightly more government services than natives do.

The evidence does not support the popular belief that immigrants are a fiscal burden in the United States, however. Except for refugees and elderly immigrants, immigrants to the United States in fact use government services to a lesser degree than natives. And even if we include refugees, who are often more frequent users of government services than other immigrants, as a group immigrants use government services only slightly more often and receive only slightly more welfare payments than natives on average. For example, according to the 1990 census, 9 percent of immigrant families received welfare payments, a percentage that was only slightly more than the 7.4 percent of U.S.-born families that received welfare payments. After the Great Recession, the percentages have become more similar.

Joseph Kirchner and Stephen E. Baldwin (1992) found that pre-1982 legal immigrants to the United States living in the six states with the largest immigrant populations paid more in total taxes than they received in government-provided benefits. Madeline Zavodny (1997) showed that immigrants do not make settlement decisions based on the availability of welfare and social services; they settle where there are jobs and where they have close family. That is, immigrants use state and local government services, but they do not seem to immigrate just to take advantage of those services.[13]

Kirchner and Baldwin (1992) also calculated that the fiscal burden of immigrants fell mostly on state and local governments, and the federal government actually increased its income tax and social security tax revenues from the arrival of immigrants. The average immigrant is less educated and has a larger family compared to natives, so immigrants were more likely to use state and local government-provided education. But because immigrants are younger than natives, they are large contributors to Social Security, a federal program, while they receive much less from Social Security than natives, on average.

A special report by the Texas Comptroller of Public Accounts (2006) analyzes the financial impact of unauthorized immigrants on the Texas state budget and economy. Table 18.4 shows which major Texas government-sponsored social and educational programs unauthorized immigrants are denied access to and which ones they can qualify for. In addition to the programs listed in Table 18.4, children of unauthorized immigrants in Texas can attend college at in-state tuition rates if they graduate from a Texas high school. The special report also considered the law enforcement

Table 18.4

Major Government-Sponsored Programs and Their Availability to Undocumented Immigrants

Unavailable	Available
Medicare	K–12 Education, some Higher Education
Medicaid	Emergency Medicaid Care
Children's Health Insurance (CHIP)	Substance Abuse Services
Food Stamps	Mental Health Services
Supplemental Security Income (SSI)	Immunizations
Public Housing Assistance	Women and Children's Health Services
Job Opportunity for Low Income Individuals	Public Health
Child Care and Development	EMS

Source: United States Department of Health and Human Services; published as Exhibit 1 in Texas Comptroller of Public Accounts (2006), "Undocumented Immigrants in Texas: A Financial Analysis of the Impact to the State Budget and Economy," special report, Austin: Texas Comptroller of Public Accounts, December.

Table 18.5

Costs, Revenues, and Economic Impact of Undocumented Immigrants in Texas, 2005

Costs		Revenues	
Education	– $967.8	State Tax Revenue	$999.0
Health care	– 58.0	School Property Tax	582.1
Incarceration	– 130.6		
Total	**– 1,156.4**	**Total**	**1,581.1**

Source: Exhibit 18 in Texas Comptroller of Public Accounts (2006), "Undocumented Immigrants in Texas: A Financial Analysis of the Impact to the State Budget and Economy," special report, Austin: Texas Comptroller of Public Accounts, December.

and criminal justice system costs of the estimated 1.4 million unauthorized immigrants in Texas in 2004–2005. Total state expenditures for unauthorized immigrants in Texas were estimated to be $1,156 million.

The study uses a standard macroeconomic model (that the state comptroller's office uses to forecast revenue) to estimate total taxes and fees paid by the unauthorized immigrants. It finds the fiscal income from the immigrants by assuming they suddenly disappear and concludes that their presence increased the gross state product by $17.7 billion, which increased property taxes, sales taxes, fees for services, et cetera by $1,581 million. Therefore, the state government gained $425 million from the presence of 1.4 million unauthorized immigrants. Table 18.5 summarizes the study's results. The conclusion from this study from Texas is that unauthorized immigrants are certainly not the large drain on state government coffers that many critics of illegal immigration suggest.

The longer immigrants, both authorized and unauthorized, are in the country, the less onerous the situation for state and local governments, however. The children of immigrants pay more taxes and receive fewer transfers, and their increased incomes make them even greater net contributors to the social security fund. Adam M. Zeretsky (1997) of the Federal Reserve Bank of St. Louis concludes: "When it's all added up . . . most long-run calculations show that immigrants make a net positive contribution to public coffers."

Assaf Razin, Efraim Sadka, and Phillip Swagel (1998) found that in Europe the tax-transfers ratio for immigrants has become less onerous because governments adjusted both taxes and transfer programs in order to improve the balance for native workers. They found that for eleven European countries, both taxes on workers and transfers to the poor were reduced as immigrants came to represent a higher percentage of the population. The 1990s welfare reforms in the United States, which reduced benefits to noncitizens, are further evidence that the political process adjusts immigrants' access to welfare benefits as immigration rises.

Are U.S. Immigrants More Costly Today Than in the Past?

Many Americans are descendants of turn-of-the-century immigrants, and a myth of self-reliant nineteenth-century immigrants is enthusiastically nurtured in American culture. As for today's immigrants, polls show Americans think that today's immigrants often come just for the welfare benefits and tax-supported public schools. The evidence paints different pictures of immigrants today and 100 years ago.

In fact, in 1909, about half of all public welfare recipients nationwide were immigrant families, even though immigrants made up about 15 percent of the total population. At about the same time in Chicago, two-thirds of people receiving public assistance were foreign-born.[14] In the early 1900s, nearly three-quarters of all students in New York City's public schools were children of immigrants; over half of all students in the public schools of the thirty largest U.S. cities were children of immigrant families. The so-called fiscal burden of immigrants, if there is one at all, is clearly not a new phenomenon. As we will see in the next chapter, on immigration policy, the United States began to restrict immigration in the 1920s.

Tentative Conclusions from the Static Supply and Demand Model

This section shows that the simple labor market model of immigration does not provide an accurate picture of immigration's consequences, because it ignores immigration's demand effects, remittances, and externalities. These extensions of the static labor market model are not enough to capture the full economic effects of immigration, however. Immigration also needs to be viewed holistically from dynamic, systemic, and inter-disciplinary perspectives. The next section begins developing these broader perspectives by examining the relationship between immigration and long-term economic growth and development.

IMMIGRATION'S LONG-RUN EFFECTS ON ECONOMIC GROWTH

Immigration is likely to have long-run effects that are very different from the immediate changes that occur when immigrants first leave their native societies and continue life in another society. In this section, we examine what economists and other social scientists understand about the long-run effects of immigration on countries' economic growth and social development.

Immigration's Dynamic Effects

There are several reasons why the relationship between immigration and long-run economic growth may be positive in the destination and source countries. Immigrants bring new ideas, knowledge, and technologies to the destination country. The importance of technology and ideas carried by immigrants was recognized by the U.S. government back in the early 1800s when it offered special incentives for British engineers and managers to bring British industrial technologies to the

United States. More generally, immigrants often have talents and personalities that are especially appropriate for innovation; after all, immigrants seem to be people who are willing to take risks, and make short-term sacrifices for longer-term gains Also, immigrants are willing to be different! The arrival of new people can also reduce the economic and political power of vested interests that have been obstructing the efforts of some members of society to innovate or reform the economic and political systems.

The Schumpeterian model of innovation can help to distinguish the potential effects of immigration on technological change and long-run economic growth. Recall from Chapter 6 that this model recognizes innovation as a costly activity that requires scarce resources. Recall, also, that the basic logic of the Schumpeterian model leads to the conclusion that, in general, innovation is a positive function of (1) the total amount of productive resources available in the economy, (2) the gains that innovation is expected to generate, (3) the efficiency with which innovative resources can generate beneficial innovations, and (4) how readily a society and its firms are willing to sacrifice current income for future income.

Joseph Schumpeter (1934) emphasized the role of entrepreneurs in the process of creative destruction. The entrepreneur is the person who sees the opportunities for introducing a new product, changing a firm's management organization, exploiting a new market, finding a new source of raw materials, cutting the costs of production, or motivating the labor force. Schumpeter (1934, p. 155) considered the entrepreneur as something of a social deviant because his or her attitude is different from that of the average member of society:

> The reaction of the social environment against one who wishes to do something new . . . manifests itself first of all in the existence of legal and political impediments. But neglecting this, any deviating conduct by a member of a social group is condemned, though in greatly varying degrees according as the social group is used to such conduct or not.

Schumpeter singled out immigrants as a group that is especially likely to be entrepreneurial. He argued that immigrants were usually less attached to the traditions of society and, therefore, less reluctant to innovate.

Barry R. Chiswick (2000) found that immigrants exhibit personal characteristics favorable to economic growth, and those characteristics are more pronounced "the greater the out of pocket (direct) costs of migration and return migration, the greater the effect of ability on lowering the costs of migration, and the smaller are the wage differences by skill in the lower income origin than in the higher income destination." Chiswick's data confirms that immigrants are less *risk averse,* more adaptable, and more ambitious than the average person in their countries of origin.

The Schumpeterian model suggests that the increase in population from immigration can benefit innovation for the simple reason that there are more people, and more people are available to engage in innovative activity as opposed to production. To the extent that immigrants are *better* entrepreneurs, not just additional entrepreneurs and workers, the efficiency of innovation improves. That is, the resource cost of generating innovations and new ideas falls.

That immigrants carry ideas and technologies with them to their destination countries is interestingly documented by Carlo Cipolla (1978) in his account of how immigrants in the 1500s helped to develop the Swiss clock and watch industry that played such an important role in developing Switzerland's comparative advantage in technology and precision engineering. That the clock industry came to be centered in Geneva, Switzerland, is a historical accident of immigration. Cipolla found that many early clock makers were French, not Swiss. Also, a large percentage of the early French clock makers, who were both highly literate and, often, interested in various aspects of science, were also active in the Protestant Reformation movement. When the Roman Catholic monarch of

France expelled the *Huguenots,* as French Protestants were called, some Protestant French clock makers went to Geneva, a Calvinist city. According to Cipolla (p. 64), the Swiss watch industry was founded by "the inflow of a handful of refugees—to the injection of a small but precious amount of human skills."

The Brain Drain

In a source country, migration may alleviate unemployment, resource shortages, and overpopulation. On the other hand, to the extent that the destination country gains knowledgeable and ambitious immigrants, the source country loses those people. Therefore, immigration may rob source countries of important resources for economic development.[15] As in fact the United States hoped in the early 1800s, immigrants may bring ideas with them that create foreign competition for source-country businesses.

More serious, the Schumpeterian perspective suggests that immigration robs source countries of their most prized resources, resources that are necessary for economic growth and development. During the past three decades, over 70 percent of newly trained physicians in Pakistan left the country, and over 60 percent of Ghana's doctors emigrated to other, usually more developed, countries. There are more Haitian physicians practicing medicine in the United States than in Haiti. Twenty-five years ago, about 30 percent of sub-Saharan Africa's educated population had immigrated to other parts of the world.[16] The departure of developing countries' most talented and educated natives has been referred to as the **brain drain**.

The brain drain has been encouraged by immigration policies in destination countries. Canada and Australia, for example, award immigrant visas according to point systems that strongly reward education and skills. Political leaders in the United States have called for similar measures.

Education and skills are what economists call human capital. Like physical capital, human capital is the result of investment—in education, training, and the trial-and-error process of learning by doing. Physical capital is generally location specific, and it cannot be easily transferred from one country to another. That is, it must remain where it was created. Human capital, on the other hand, travels with people. Immigrants carry human capital with them when they move to another country. The brain drain may be a problem for source countries because educated and skilled immigrants leave with human capital that was partially paid for by people remaining in the source country. This means poor countries bear the burden of providing immigrants with the human capital needed to function efficiently in high-income economies, but the richer destination economies enjoy the increase in output.

The principal cause of the brain drain is that professional and technical skills are not fully exploited in the emigrants' home countries. Often, technology is so much less developed in poor economies that the returns to all factors, even the scarce ones, are lower. Human capital needs more and better factors to work with if it is to earn the returns that it can earn in developed economies. For example, physicians are very scarce in Equatorial Guinea, but if a doctor has no hospital or no medicines to dispense, she cannot be very productive. That same doctor, in a well-equipped hospital and with pharmacies stocked with the latest medicines, adds much more to human health in a developed country. And of course, her income is much, much higher in a more developed economy. One solution to the brain drain is higher incomes in the source countries, but how does a country raise incomes without talented and educated people? The brain drain is thus a vicious cycle, in which low incomes drive educated people abroad, which makes increasing investment in education seem futile, and so incomes remain low.

Can Remittances Mitigate the Brain Drain?

Some economists have suggested that the brain drain's negative effect on source countries' long-run economic growth can be neutralized if the immigrants remit a substantial portion of their earnings. But the growth effects of remittances depend critically on how they are used. If remittances are used to improve infrastructure, housing, and, perhaps most important, increase education, they can raise long-run welfare. Indeed, a study by Alexandra Cox Edwards and Manuelita Ureta (2003) finds that in El Salvador remittances have had a large impact on whether children remain in school. However, in their statistical study for a large sample of countries over the period 1970–1998, Ralph Chami, Connel Fullenkamp, and Samir Jahjah (2003, abstract) uncover serious **moral hazard** problems with remittances:

> The dependency on these transfers induces recipients to use remittances as a substitute for labor income, and to lower their work effort. . . . The aggregate impact of moral hazard can be quite significant, and our empirical results suggest that this particular moral hazard problem does affect economic activity in many economies.

To deal with moral hazard, the government of the state of Zacatecas in Mexico offers three dollars in government funds toward specific infrastructure projects in migrants' native towns and villages for every dollar migrants contribute to the investment funds. The migrants can monitor the progress of community projects through online progress reports.

Brain Drain or Service Exports?

The Indian government has in recent years actively promoted the outflow of its educated workers, in part because the Indian software industry views the work permits for Indian programmers as necessary for expanding its global business. Exporting services such as software development often requires a physical presence in the export market, and that requires the movement of people. When, after the terrorist attacks in the United States in 2001, it became more difficult for Indian firms supplying information technology services to the United States to obtain work permits for their employees, they lobbied hard to make the visa process less cumbersome.

In general, as international trade in services expands, immigration and international trade become more closely linked. When services are personally delivered, the temporary migration of people and international trade are one and the same thing. In the case of India's information service industry, the movement of highly talented people is clearly not a brain drain in the traditional sense. Of course, there have been suggestions that Indian service firms could provide their services abroad by hiring people locally, and that the immigrant visas permit Indian firms to operate in the United States with lower-cost labor.

Fundamental to this whole debate is the lack of evidence on whether the United States really has a shortage of labor in high-technology sectors of the economy. All other things equal, the arrival of highly educated workers from abroad depresses the wages of educated U.S. workers. This, in turn, reduces the incentives for Americans to acquire education, which diminishes the apparent need to maintain educational institutions in the United States. Hence, the brain drain may not promote long-run welfare in the United States either.

UNAUTHORIZED (ILLEGAL) IMMIGRATION

The incentives for people to emigrate from low-income countries to high-income countries clash with the restrictive immigration policies of the high-income countries. (The next chapter details immigration policies in the United States and Canada.) This clash between policies and economic incentives results in what is popularly referred to as *illegal immigration* or what we will more appropriately call *unauthorized immigration.* There is no accurate data on unauthorized immigration because, obviously, unauthorized immigrants generally prefer to hide their status for fear of being detected and deported back to their native countries. Estimates do exist, though. For example, the ILO estimated that in 1991 there were 2.6 million immigrants living illegally in Western Europe. That number was estimated to have doubled by the end of the decade.[17] Official estimates suggested there were about 5 million undocumented workers in the United States in 1996, and that the number had risen to 6 million by 2000.[18] Census data for 2000 put the number closer to 9 million.[19] Table 18.6 provides more recent estimates.

The United States has attracted unauthorized immigrants ever since it instituted its first restrictions on immigration. For example, passage of the Chinese Exclusion Act of 1882 quickly resulted in Chinese immigrants finding ways to circumvent the restrictions. Strict ethnic quotas for immigration established in 1924 also induced people to walk into the United States across the unguarded northern and southern borders. The U.S. Congress then established stronger border enforcement, and the *United States Border Patrol* was established to guard the Mexican and Canadian borders against unauthorized entry. Unauthorized immigration grew whenever there were work opportunities in the United States. With rising unauthorized immigration in the early 2000s, the United States has started a multibillion-dollar project to construct a bigger fence along the U.S.-Mexican border.

Europe also has many unauthorized immigrants. For example, despite extremely high unemployment, Spain has attracted many unauthorized immigrants from North and Central Africa and Latin America, perhaps over 1 million in total, to fill lower-wage jobs. Latin Americans are attracted to Spain by the common culture and language, and they are able to assimilate into Spanish society relatively easily.

Unauthorized immigration occurs in less developed economies too. There are several million unauthorized immigrants in South Africa, which is not a wealthy country but does offer higher wages than most of its neighbors. Even though wages are even higher in developed countries in Europe, another destination for African immigrants, it is usually much easier to get to South Africa. According to a report on immigration to South Africa in *The Economist* (2000): "There are no oceans to cross. From anywhere below the Sahara, anyone with a few grand for the truck-driver can hitch a ride south. South Africa's land border is roughly 4,000 km long and extremely porous."[20] Foreign workers in South Africa remit income back to their native countries. Remittances account for about 10 percent of Lesotho's GDP, for example.

Unauthorized Immigration as Labor Market Segmentation

An interesting question is why destination countries so often seem to implicitly accept unauthorized immigration, even though their formal laws and regulations call for strict punishment and expulsion of unauthorized immigrants. The labor market supply and demand model of immigration can be combined with political science to explain the *implicit* tolerance of unauthorized immigrants in countries that *explicitly* have enacted laws and regulations to restrict immigration.

In terms of the static labor market model shown in Figure 18.5, immigration would be less objectionable to native labor in the destination country if somehow the employers in the destination country could gain the area G without native workers having to transfer part of their labor income, equal to area E, to employers. In Figure 18.5, government policies that keep wages for native French workers at €10 but let immigrants work for €8 so that employers would only increase their welfare by area G from employing immigrants. Such wage differentials would imply discrimination between

Table 18.6

Estimates of the Unauthorized Immigrant Population: Selected OECD Countries

Country	Number	% of Population	Year
Australia	50,000	0.2	2005
Japan	210,000	0.2	2005
United States	10,300,000	3.6	2004
Netherlands[1]	125,000–230,000	0.8–1.4	2004
Switzerland[1]	80,000–100,000	1.1–1.5	2005
Spain	690,000	1.6	2005
Italy	700,000	1.2	2002
Portugal	185,000	1.8	2001
Greece	370,000	3.4	2001

[1] The original studies from the Netherlands and Switzerland provide ranges rather than point estimates.
Source: Table 1.6 from OECD (2006), *International Migration Outlook,* Paris: OECD, p. 46.

native and immigrant workers, of course. Note that unauthorized immigration in effect enables such discrimination: by not giving immigrants full legal status in the labor market, they can be treated differently from other workers.

Figure 18.5 illustrates how such a discriminatory scheme enabled by the illegal status of foreign workers distributes economic welfare. Suppose that unauthorized immigrants are arrested and deported back to their native countries if they are caught working in jobs that the native workers in the destination country seek, but they are left alone if they work in jobs along the labor demand curve between a and b in Figure 18.5. The unauthorized immigrants from Cameroon, under competitive labor market conditions, earn €8, and their total earnings equal the area H. The jobs that generate labor returns of at least €10 are open only to authorized workers with legal status because unauthorized workers are arrested and deported if they take one of those jobs at €10. Thus, total wage income for the 0Q native workers remains equal to the area E + F despite the arrival of unauthorized immigrants from Cameroon. Legal workers can earn €10, so they do not seek employment in the €8 segment of the labor market. The labor market is thus **segmented** into two separate markets with wages of €10 and €8, respectively. French employers gain income equal to area G from employing unauthorized immigrant workers.

Thus, schemes whereby immigrants are allowed to work only in sectors of the economy where native workers earning pre-immigration wages would not be employed will prove beneficial to immigrants and employers without lowering the welfare of native French workers. French workers, therefore, may not object much to unauthorized immigration from Cameroon, especially if natives can use their higher wages to consume the products or services provided by the immigrants.[21]

In most countries that attract large numbers of unauthorized immigrants, undocumented foreign workers indeed tend to occupy jobs that pay lower wages. These are also usually jobs that employers claim they would not offer if wages were high. At the same time, unauthorized immigrants are often barred from applying for work in the higher-wage segments of the market either through government enforcement or through the control of employment by labor unions.

There is ample evidence that employers use the threat of deportation to push the wage for unauthorized immigrants below the competitive market wage. In such a case, the employer surplus of G is larger than in Figure 18.5. Restrictions on unauthorized immigrants' use of taxpayer-funded

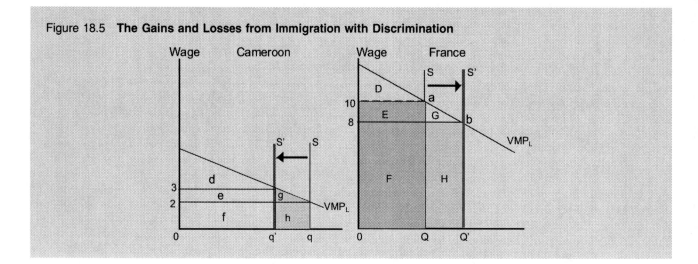

Figure 18.5 **The Gains and Losses from Immigration with Discrimination**

public services, such as those passed by the federal and various state governments in the United States during the 1990s and copied in many other high-income countries in Europe, further serve to keep the inflow of unauthorized foreign workers from having a negative impact on the welfare of native workers. The gains from immigration accruing to developing countries are, therefore, diminished if a large percentage of immigrants are unable to gain legal status in the destination countries.

Unauthorized Immigration Can Be Deadly

In June 2000, Europe was stunned by the deaths by suffocation of fifty-eight Chinese migrants locked in an airtight cargo truck during a ferry crossing of the English Channel from France to the United Kingdom. Only two of the passengers survived to tell the story of their ill-fated trip from China. It seems the sixty passengers had spent four months traveling from China's Fujian province via Moscow and Eastern Europe. They had paid traffickers to carry them to London, where they had been promised jobs that would pay wages well above what they could earn in their native China. However, the passengers would have been placed in jobs in which they would have effectively been indentured servants until they paid off their debts of £15,000 to £20,000 (US$22,500 to US$30,000).

The suffocation incident was not an isolated event. The umbrella organization for a group of multicultural advocacy organizations in Europe, United for Intercultural Action, reports that since 1988 more than 14,000 immigrants have died trying to reach Europe.[22] Drowning was the most common cause of death. Similar numbers of deaths have been documented for immigrants seeking to reach the United States.[23]

The increased role of gangs in the trafficking of unauthorized workers results from the tightening of restrictions on immigration. The Chinese workers could not even get to Europe legally; airlines will not let passengers board without valid entry visas because they are responsible for the return trip if the passengers are refused entry in the destination country. European embassies and consulates in China give tourist or student visas only to Chinese who can prove they have sufficiently high incomes to be tourists or overseas students. Poor people from poor countries must, therefore, resort to human traffickers for help if they decide to seek work in another country.

Increased spending on border patrols has made it more difficult for Mexicans and Central Americans to cross the Mexico-U.S. border. In the past, it was easy for an individual to walk across the border, but now traffickers are more often employed to help immigrants cross the 2,000-mile-long border in more remote areas. Hundreds of people have died of hunger or thirst trying to cross remote deserts between the United States and Mexico. In an odd case of one country's government helping immigrants overcome barriers paid for by another country's government, the Mexican government maintains a program to equip unauthorized immigrants with survival kits containing water, medicines, bandages, and anti-dehydration powder.[24] Also, U.S. charities have provided assistance to Mexicans stranded in the border desert region.

CONCLUSIONS

This chapter began with the labor market model of immigration, which is standard in the mainstream immigration economics literature. This model is biased toward viewing immigrants exclusively as workers, not consumers, investors, or innovators. It describes the effects of immigration entirely in terms of changes in wages for human labor. It obviously does not give a complete picture of a phenomenon as complex as the movement of people between countries. People move for a variety or reasons, with higher wages just one of those.

We showed in this chapter that the model can easily be extended to incorporate other reactions to immigration beyond the simple effect of the labor supply shift. For example, studies have shown that the arrival of immigrants increases both the demand and supply curves of labor. Immigrants are consumers as well as workers, and they effectively demand part of the output they produce as workers, starting a multiplier process that increases the income of others throughout the economy. Immigrants generate a variety of externalities, some positive and some negative. This chapter also discussed how immigration may increase the overall growth of the destination economy. Economists have so far developed few dynamic models of immigration beyond the ad hoc approach of inserting immigration into existing models. Economists have generated very little statistical evidence linking immigration to economic growth.

The Economic Significance of Immigration

Relative to international trade, immigration seems rather insignificant. The value of world exports is over 25 percent of total world gross domestic product (GDP), but only about 3 percent of the world's population has immigrated to another country. However, sheer numbers or percentages may not give us an accurate measure of immigration's economic importance. Richard B. Freeman (2006) suggests we compare the impact of the different components of international economic integration in terms of how well they have arbitraged price differences across countries. Specifically, Freeman judges the impact of immigration, international trade, and international investment, respectively, by comparing the variations in wages, product prices, and asset returns across countries. Purchasing power parity ratios are usually used to compare real wage differences across countries, but immigration can be motivated even by nominal price differences if migrants expect to return to their native lands. Where incomes are very high and the gain from crossing the border is on the order of multiples of five or more, large numbers of people do usually immigrate. In many high-income countries, immigrants make up close to 10 percent of the population. Over 20 percent of Swiss residents are foreign born, and the percentage of immigrants is high in some other countries, such as Canada, as well. In the case of purchasing power parity wages, adjusted to be more comparable in terms of their purchasing power, the difference in incomes vary from ratios of over 3 to as much as 7. In nominal terms, the ratios are as high as 15.6. Therefore, by crossing the border, a physician from a poor country can increase her real wages by a factor of 15. A sample of the data Freeman compiled with Remco H. Oostendorp is shown in Table 18.7.[25]

Freeman then compares product prices using *The Economist*'s well-known Big Mac price index, which compares the price of the identical McDonald's Big Mac hamburger across sixty-five coun-

Table 18.7

Monthly Earnings by Occupation and by Country Ranking: 1998–2002

Occupation	US$ using exchange rates			US$ using purchasing power parity		
	Top 20%	Bottom 20%	Ratio	Top 20%	Bottom 20%	Ratio
Physician	2,856	183	15.6	3,815	753	5.1
Insurance Agent	1,668	205	8.1	2,214	684	3.2
Computer Programmer	2,114	166	12.7	2,693	774	3.5
Logger	1,040	77	13.5	1,547	213	7.2

Source: Table 2 in Richard B. Freeman (2006), "People Flows in Globalization," *Journal of Economic Perspectives,* 20(2), pp. 145–170.

tries. He finds, in 2007, the Big Mac index varies by a ratio of 2:1 between the lowest and highest price groups. Obviously, Big Macs are not tradable goods, but most of the inputs are directly or indirectly tradable. Finally, Freeman also shows that the variation across asset returns in countries in the highest 20 percent and those in the bottom 20 percent is only 1:1.43.

These numbers suggest that international trade and international investment are much more effective arbitragers than immigration. Apparently, immigration has much further to expand before the arbitrage opportunities for workers are exhausted.

A More Holistic Perspective on Immigration

As the Swiss writer Max Frisch noted, immigrants are people, not commodities or mere inputs in the production function. People migrate, or not, for many reasons, not only income differences. Further more, immigration is an integral part of the evolving process of economic and social development. Ever since humans abandoned the lifestyle of a hunter-gatherer society, in which they interacted with relatively small numbers of other people, the number of strangers people deal with on a regular basis has expanded. And people have increasingly concentrated in certain centralized locations. The economic term for this is *agglomeration,* which is a natural result when there are economies of scale in production and innovation. If the production and innovative activities also generate positive externalities that require proximity for their exploitation, then agglomeration is further encouraged. In our internationally integrated economy, the forces of agglomeration now also cross borders. Rising immigration is the likely result. In 2008, for the first time in history, over half of all people on earth lived in urban regions. And people with talents that are in high demand in the most dynamic centers of production and innovation will be attracted from wherever they may be.

It is also important to note that the process of economic change and agglomeration is largely driven by the business strategies of transnational corporations. These corporations dominate production, innovation, international trade, and international investment in most countries. This fact, combined with the inherent disruptiveness of economic change and international economic integration, make immigration a controversial and easily maligned phenomenon. Immigrants are blamed for changes and conflicts that are caused by a complex mixture of forces. It seems that people still prefer to put a face on things, and immigrants, by their very presence in the midst of other people's countries, cultures, and labor markets, attract attention. The political rhetoric from anti-immigrant groups in countries ranging from the Netherlands and the United States to South Africa and Indonesia can be appalling. People still have real trouble dealing with strangers.

This chapter provided many reasons why a country might consider restricting immigration. Some of these reasons are purely economic, others are more holistic in that they seek a less conflict-prone process of economic change, and others are just plain ugly. Restrictions abound, as they have throughout history. The next chapter examines the history of immigration policy in the United States and elsewhere. You are encouraged to use the models and analysis from this chapter to explain the shifts in immigration policy detailed in the next chapter.

CHAPTER SUMMARY

1. Immigration is one of the four categories of international economic activity that comprise international economic integration, or what the press often refers to as globalization.

2. People have always migrated across the earth; migration is the earliest form of international economic integration.

3. Income differences between countries explain a great part of the variation in immigration, but the relationship between relative income levels and immigration is not linear. Migration from the very poorest countries of the world is actually quite small and most of the immigration to rich countries comes from the group of intermediate-income developing countries.

4. Immigrants fall into different categories: settlers, contract workers, professionals, asylum seekers and refugees, unauthorized immigrants, temporary immigrants, involuntary immigrants, and guest workers.

5. Most economic models assume that immigrants move from one country to another because they expect to improve their well-being, but there are many other reasons why immigrants move to another country or, on the other hand, decide to stay at home.

6. The labor supply and demand model of immigration, which holds labor demand constant in both the source and destinations countries, shows that immigration causes wages to rise in the source country and fall in the destination country.

7. The labor supply and demand model of immigration also shows that in the destination country wages decline for native workers who are similar to the immigrants, and increases the returns to factors that complement immigrant labor.

8. The labor supply and demand model of immigration shows that immigration causes the overall welfare of the destination country and total world income to rise; it causes total welfare to decline in the source country; and immigrants reap large gains.

9. The labor supply and demand model perhaps gives a fairly accurate picture of the immediate effects of immigration as people perceive them, which means the model can be useful for explaining immigration policy.

10. All other things do not remain equal when immigrants arrive, however, as the labor supply and demand model effectively assumes; among other things, immigrants generate both positive and negative externalities.

11. Immigrants also affect aggregate demand for output in both the source and destination countries because immigrants are consumers as well as workers.

12. The gains and losses from immigration are also affected by the size of immigrant remittances to their source countries.

13. Immigrants may affect the rate of economic growth in the source and destination countries because they may have human capital that is especially important for R&D activity, they are especially entrepreneurial, they facilitate the spread of technology and knowledge, and they reduce the economic and political power of vested interests who have been obstructing the efforts of some members of society to innovate or reform the economic and political systems.

14. Unauthorized immigrants are not as large a drain on state government coffers as many critics of illegal immigration suggest for the simple reason that unauthorized immigrants do not have access to as many government services and programs as legal immigrants do.

15. Unauthorized immigration is often tolerated in high-income countries because employers reap the benefits of cheaper labor, and they use immigrants' lack of legal status to exploit them. Illegal status effectively segments the labor market.

16. The immigration by educated people from developing economies, where education is scarce, is sometimes referred to as the brain drain.
17. There are few easy policies for dealing with the brain drain since it is usually the result of failing institutions in the source country.
18. Of all the types of international economic activities, immigration seems to be the one that still has the most to grow. Government policies continue to restrict immigration.

KEY TERMS AND CONCEPTS

asylum seekers
brain drain
contract workers
demand effect
economies of scale
emigrant
externalities
guest workers
human capital
illegal immigrants
immigration

involuntary immigrants
migrations
moral hazard
professionals
refugees
remittances
segmented (labor market)
settlers
temporary immigrants
unauthorized (immigrants)

PROBLEMS AND QUESTIONS

1. Suppose that there are two countries, Guatemala and Mexico. Suppose also that Guatemala's 100 workers earn a wage of 4 pesos, and Mexico's 40 workers earn a wage of 14 pesos.
   a. Assume that 40 Guatemalan workers immigrate to Mexico, and the wage falls to 10 pesos in Mexico and rises to 7 pesos in Guatemala. Use the labor supply model of immigration to illustrate the supply effects of this immigration from Guatemala to Mexico, assuming the demand curves for labor are linear and the supply curve of labor is perfectly vertical.
   b. Calculate the exact gains and losses to workers, immigrants, and other factor owners in Guatemala and Mexico, just as in Table 18.2.
   c. Now, draw a new set of diagrams, repeating the shift in supply from part a of this problem, but also include a shift in the demand curves to reflect the fact that immigrants are consumers as well as workers. Specifically, assume that with the simultaneous shifting of both the supply and demand curves for labor the wage rises to 5.5 pesos in Guatemala and falls to 12 pesos in Mexico. Also, assume that the demand curves for labor shift in such a way that they remain perfectly parallel to the original demand curves (this assumption enables you to find the y-intercept of the new demand curve).
   d. Calculate the gains and losses from immigration in Guatemala and Mexico from the diagram for part c above.
   e. Finally, suppose that the Guatemalan immigrants in Mexico live very frugally and remit a large part of their Mexican income back to family in Guatemala. This makes the demand curves rise in both Mexico and Guatemala; assume that in this case immigration causes the wage to fall to 11 pesos in Mexico and rise to 8 pesos in Guatemala. Draw the curves to reflect these changes.
   f. Calculate the gains and losses from immigration as drawn in part e above.
2. Show how it is possible for the source country to increase its per capita income after a group of workers immigrates to another economy even if the per capita income of the workers and other factor owners remaining in the country falls.

3. The noted nineteenth-century economist John Stuart Mill wrote: "[I]t is vain to say, that all mouths which the increase of mankind calls into existence, bring with them hands. The new mouths require as much food as the old ones, and the hands do not produce as much" (*Principles of Political Economy* [1848]).
   a. Use the labor market model of immigration to show what Mill meant by his remark.
   b. What did Mill leave out in his analysis, and how did these omissions bias his conclusion?
4. Is the brain drain a problem for developing countries? How should the brain drain be dealt with?
5. Do you think that international migrants self-select in a way that results in migrants having, on average, different personal characteristics than people who do not migrate? Why, and what consequences would such differences or similarities have on the source and destination countries?
6. Investigate the likely demographic trends in the United States, Germany, Japan, or another country that you might be interested in and for which population forecasts are available. What effect would an increase in immigration of foreign workers have on the ratio of retired people to working people in the short run? What effect would it have in the long run?
7. Given the income differences across countries and the improvements in transportation and communications, why do so few people immigrate? Discuss the possible reasons for the remaining huge differences in wages across countries despite growing immigration.
8. Use Figure 18.5 to explain why unauthorized immigration is often permitted to continue despite strong laws against it. Do you think there are further reasons why unauthorized immigration is so large in so many countries?
9. Each year hundreds of people from poor countries die trying to immigrate to high-income countries without authorization. Why would so many people risk their lives to violate the law and cross borders without the required documents and permissions?
10. Explain the brain drain. Is the brain drain really a serious economic problem for developing countries? Explain.

NOTES

1. Quoted in Colin Nickerson (2006), "A Lesson in Immigration: Guest Worker Experiments Transformed Europe," *Boston Globe,* April 19.
2. See, for example, Spencer Wells (2003), Nicholas Wade (2003), Katy Owens and Mary-Claire King (1999), and Carl Zimmer (2005).
3. Tom Hundley (2004), "Booming Ireland Sees Population Swell to 130-Year High," *Chicago Tribune,* December 4.
4. "Millions Want to Come" (1998), *The Economist,* April 4.
5. Robin Allen (2000), "A Time Bomb in the Desert," *Financial Times,* June 10–11.
6. Peter Waldman (1998), "Grim Farewell for Asia's Foreign Workers," *Wall Street Journal,* January 9.
7. Reported in OECD (2006).
8. "Millions Want to Come" (1998), *The Economist,* April 4.
9. From a Federal Reserve Bank conference presentation summarized in Elizabeth Handlin, Margerethe Krontoft, and William Testa (2002).
10. Reported in Charo Quesada (2003).
11. Tim Weiner (2004), "Fox Seeks to Allow Mexicans Living Abroad to Vote in 2006," *Wall Street Journal,* June 16.
12. John Authers (2004), "Tomato King Looks to Make Mark for Mexican Migrants," *Financial Times,* July 1.
13. Zavodny's conclusions were confirmed by Richard Vedder, Lowell Gallaway, and Stephen Moore (2000).
14. See, for example, Frederick Rose (1995), "Muddled Masses: The Growing Backlash Against Immigrants Includes Many Myths," *Wall Street Journal,* April 26.
15. K. Miyagiwa (1991), N.U. Haque and S.-J. Kim (1995), and K.-Y. Wong and C.K. Yip (1999) present some statistical evidence that immigration slows growth, all other things equal, in source countries.
16. Aaron Siegel (1993), *An Atlas of International Migration,* London: Hans Zell.
17. "Millions Want to Come" (1998), *The Economist,* April 4.

18. Data from the Immigration and Naturalization Service, Office of Policy and Planning, www.ins.gov, January 21, 2001.

19. Christopher Parks and Henry Tricks (2000), "Illicit Angels of America's Economic Miracle," *Financial Times,* February 23; Everett Ehrlich (2001), "The Mystery of the Missing Millions," *Financial Times,* March 7; and Paul Magnusson (2001), "The Border Is More Porous than You Think," *Business Week,* April 9.

20. "South Africa's Migrant Workers: A Ticket to Prosperity" (2000), *The Economist,* September 2.

21. Our model reflects Hillman and Weiss (1999).

22. United for Intercultural Action (2011), "Fortress Europe: A Deadly Exodus," downloaded from OWNI.eu, the online news site, on August 14, 2011: http://owni.eu/2011/03/04/app-fortress-europe-a-deadly-exodus/.

23. John Bowe (2010), "Bound for America," *Mother Jones,* May–June, pp. 61–65.

24. "Sex, Death and Desert Snafus" (2001), *The Economist,* May 24.

25. Richard B. Freeman and Remco H. Oostendorp (2003), "Occupational Wages Around the World Database," http://www.nber.org/oww/.

CHAPTER 19

Immigration Policy

"Give me your tired, your poor,
Your huddled masses yearning to breathe free,
The wretched refuse of your teeming shore.
Send these, the homeless, tempest-tost to me,
I lift my lamp beside the golden door!"

—Emma Lazarus (from "The New Colossus" [1883]
inscribed on the base of the Statue of Liberty in New York Harbor)

Despite huge income differences, wars, and the natural desire of people to better themselves, nearly all humans in the world live in their native country. Even in the global economy of today, only about 200 million, or about 3 percent, of the world's 7.5 billion people are living outside the country they were born in. These numbers suggest that we should not ask why people immigrate, but why most people do *not* immigrate.

This chapter examines one of the main reasons why people do not immigrate: nearly all countries restrict the entry of foreigners seeking to take up residence and find employment within their borders and require immigrants to obtain visas before they can legally enter. A country's **immigration policy** specifies the criteria under which immigrant visas can be issued or refused. Some countries tie immigrant visas to specific employment. In the case of most job-specific immigrant visas, when the employment ends, the immigrant must leave the country. Many immigrant destination countries limit immigrant visas to people with family or ethnic ties to the destination country. For example, Israel permits only people of Jewish heritage to immigrate. The United States gives people with family connections and with high levels of education priority in awarding immigrant visas. Poorly educated foreigners with no family ties to anyone already in the country have little chance of gaining legal entry into the United States. Most countries place numerical limits on the number of immigrant visas issued, regardless of immigrant qualifications and characteristics.

Immigration policy is more than just a set of regulations, visa criteria, and border control measures, however. This chapter details U.S. and Canadian immigration policies over the past two centuries. This interesting historical survey makes it clear that a country's immigration policy tends to reflect a complex combination of social, economic, and political factors. Immigration policy reflects both the good and the bad of a country's national culture, and the power of its special interests, its relationship with the rest of the world, and its historical path of economic development.

The Purpose of Immigration Policy

The analysis of government policies tends to focus on welfare, both overall national welfare and the distribution of welfare across a population. In the previous chapter, we analyzed the economic effects of immigration on native workers in the destination country, the workers remaining behind in the source country, the owners of other productive factors and resources in both the source and destination countries, and on different generations over time. In the case of immigration policy, therefore, economists must address some interesting questions, such as: Whose welfare should immigration policy seek to maximize? And, if it is not just economic welfare that matters: What exactly do we want our countries' immigration policies to accomplish?

Individual Rights and Community

Immigration policy, like so much government policy, reflects a conflict between two fundamental values: individual rights and community interests. If the pursuit of individual freedom is foremost, then countries should avoid imposing barriers on the free exit and entry of people. On the other hand, if policy makers seek to preserve a community with a specific culture, a particular distribution of responsibilities and rewards, or a vested set of economic interests, then restrictions on the entry of foreigners and the departure of natives may be called for.

The classic liberalism that underlies Western political systems, at least in principle, appears to give individuals stature in society. To the political scientist Joseph Carens (1987, p. 251), the liberal view offers "little basis for drawing fundamental distinctions between citizens and aliens who seek to become citizens." **Libertarians** like Robert Nozick (1974) give national governments few roles beyond the protection of property and of individuals from abuse or intimidation by others. **Objectivists** like Ayn Rand (1967) would limit government to supporting a free-market capitalist system, which would seem to restrict government to providing for the protection of all persons and property against theft, fraud, intimidation, and restrictions on ownership or movement.

Another strand of classic liberalism, however, leads to the **social-contractionist** philosophy of John A. Rawls (1971), which was discussed in Chapter 7. Rawls argues that an unbiased definition of social justice can only be determined from behind a "veil of ignorance" where individuals know nothing about their own particular circumstances. According to this perspective, a *just society* would be the one people would choose to be born into if they did not know what their class, race, gender, sexual orientation, level of wealth, education, talent, and other personal and social characteristics would be. Under this scenario, people would be most concerned about the conditions in which the least well-off people would live, because they themselves could end up in that situation. Governments would have the role of not only providing people with personal freedom and equal opportunity to acquire education, wealth, and social status, but also helping the unfortunate and the poorly endowed. At first glance, Rawls's concept of social justice seems similar to libertarianism and objectivism, and points to keeping the borders open for immigrants. Wouldn't people behind a veil of ignorance choose to have a right to emigrate in case they found themselves living in a country with civil war, widespread poverty, or oppression according to race, gender, or ethnic group?

A third strand of classic liberalism led to the type of **utilitarian** thinking that lies behind the labor market supply and demand models of immigration we have presented in this book. These models suggest that the net gains from immigration are positive under specific assumptions, but they also show why some people and groups oppose open immigration. Utilitarian models often make assumptions about social welfare that lead to the conclusion that open borders are the welfare-maximizing immigration policy. Therefore, all the major schools of liberal thought suggest that governments should not restrict immigration.

Contrary to the classic liberal perspective, the **community perspective** often points to restrictions on immigration. The sense of community is fundamental to human behavior. After all, humans evolved as members of small hunter-gatherer groups that survived in the ever-changing natural environments they inhabited because they were protective of each other and fearful of outsiders. In modern societies, the nation is the basic political unit for making group rules to govern human activity. If we view the nation as our community, then it becomes perfectly reasonable to restrict the movement of people across our nation's borders.

In sum, immigration policy is likely to reflect a compromise, or according to many historians, a temporary armistice between the human sense of community and individualist tendencies. Historically, immigration policies have been shaped both by people's support of freedom of movement and their equally strong demands for protection from potentially objectionable new members of their community. These political and philosophical preferences are often exploited by business and other interest groups to shape immigration policies in destination countries toward keeping borders open to foreign labor. The determinants of immigration policy are many and complex, and often seemingly contradictory, which makes immigration policy difficult to explain or predict.

Classifying Immigration Policies

To compare immigration policies across countries and over time, it is useful to classify them according to a small set of important goals that they are intended to accomplish. A nation's immigration policy consists of a set of laws, regulations, and bureaucratic procedures that address the following questions:

1. Is immigration to be restricted?
2. If immigration is to be restricted, how many immigrants will be allowed to enter the country?
3. If the number of foreigners seeking to immigrate exceeds the number of immigrants to be allowed into the country, what criteria will be used to ration the scarce entry permits?
4. How strongly will the immigration restrictions be enforced?
5. What methods will be used to enforce immigration restrictions?
6. How are immigrants to be treated compared to citizens of the country?
7. Will all immigrants be treated the same, or will some categories of immigrants be favored over others?

Countries seem to be very unsure about how to answer these questions. A country's immigration policies can vary greatly from one period of time to another, and lawmakers and government authorities often issue laws and regulations that seem to reflect conflicting goals. We will look at how these questions were answered at different times in U.S. history in the next section.

UNITED STATES IMMIGRATION POLICY IN THE NINETEENTH CENTURY

The historian Oscar Handlin (1951) wrote that the history of the United States is fundamentally "the history of immigration." Over the past two centuries, the United States has received more immigrants than any other country, and it continues to receive more immigrants than any other country today. However, the United States did not always welcome immigrants. In fact, immigration inflows fluctuated widely over the past two centuries, and these fluctuations were, in part, due to very substantial shifts in U.S. immigration policy.

Table 19.1 shows how immigration to the United States grew throughout the nineteenth and twentieth centuries. From just fifty thousand or so immigrants per year during the early 1900s,

Table 19.1

Immigration to the United States

Decade	Number (thousands)	Rate[1]
1820–1830	152	1.3
1831–1840	599	3.9
1841–1850	1,713	8.3
1851–1860	2,598	9.4
1861–1870	2,315	6.4
1871–1880	2,812	6.2
1881–1890	5,247	9.2
1891–1900	3,688	5.4
1901–1910	8,795	10.4
1911–1920	5,736	5.7
1921–1930	4,107	3.5
1931–1940	528	0.4
1941–1950	1,035	0.7
1951–1960	2,515	1.5
1961–1970	3,322	1.7
1971–1980	4,493	2.1
1981–1990	7,256	3.0
1991–2000	9,081	3.4
2001–2010	10,501	3.4

[1] Number of immigrants per thousand residents of the United States.
Source: United States Department of Commerce, Bureau of the Census (2009), *Statistical Abstract of the United States 2009,* Washington, DC; 2001–2010 from the Office of Immigration Statistics (2010), *2010 Yearbook of Immigration Statistics,* U.S. Department of Homeland Security.

immigration grew persistently and rapidly throughout that century. By its end, annual inflows of immigrants had reached nearly 1 million per year. During the first decade of the twentieth century, over 10 million permanent legal immigrants arrived in the United States. In seven of those individual years, annual arrivals exceeded 1 million people, which at the time exceeded 1 percent of the U.S. population. About 15 percent of the U.S. population was foreign born.

In 1924, for the first time, U.S. policy broadly restricted the entry of new immigrants. Then, in the latter half of the twentieth century, immigration to the United States again grew. Immigration reached nearly 1 million persons per year by the year 2000 and 1.3 million per year by 2006, although net figures, adjusted for emigration by U.S. residents, was closer to 1 million. This growth in U.S. immigration reflects, in part, the United States' increasingly accommodating immigration policies. They were not entirely open, however, and economic forces stimulated the growth of unauthorized immigration to the United States during the latter half of the twentieth century. The U.S. government estimated there were 11.6 million unauthorized immigrants in the United States in 2008. In 2010, the Pew Center estimated that about 1 million unauthorized immigrants had gone back to their native countries because of high U.S. unemployment. It is safe to say that in 2010 there were still at least 10 million unauthorized immigrants living in the United States.

Not shown in Table 19.1 are the variations in the source countries of U.S. immigrants. During the 1800s, most immigrants to the United States came from the British Isles and northern Europe. During the early 1900s, many immigrants came from southern and eastern Europe. Today, most U.S. immigrants come from developing countries in Latin America and Asia.

The table also does not show that many immigrants to the United States eventually returned to their native countries. Toward the end of the 1800s, as international transportation became less dan-

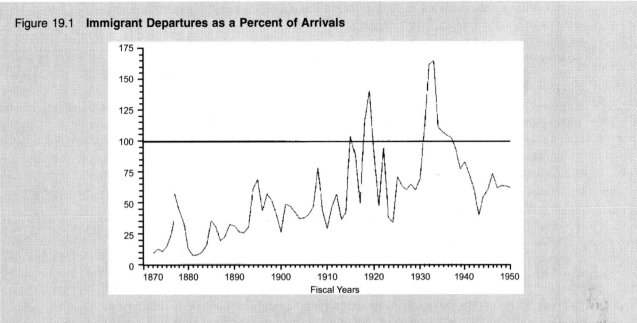

Figure 19.1 Immigrant Departures as a Percent of Arrivals

Source: Table 11, Susan B. Carter and Richard Sutch (1997), "Historical Perspective on the Economic Conse-quences of Immigration to the United States," in C. Hirschman, P. Kasinitz, and J. DeWind (eds.), *The Hardbook of International Migration: The American Experience*, New York: Russell Sage Foundation, pp. 319–341.

gerous and much less expensive, immigrants moved in both directions more frequently, with returns reflecting economic conditions in the United States and abroad. As Figure 19.1 clearly shows, in the Great Depression, many more people left the United States than arrived.

Early Immigration Policy

After its establishment, the U.S. government openly encouraged immigration from Europe, an understandable policy for a geographically large country controlled by a small ethnically Euro-pean population. Americans of European background were outnumbered by African American slaves and Native Americans. In a speech on December 2, 1783, not long after he led the defini-tive defeat of the British forces in the Battle of Yorktown, George Washington told an audience of Irish immigrants:

> The bosom of America is open to receive not only the opulent and respectable stranger, but the oppressed and persecuted of all nations and religions, whom we shall welcome to participate in all of our rights and privileges, if by decency and propriety of conduct they appear to merit the enjoyment.[1]

Nearly sixty years later, President John Tyler would openly invite foreigners "to come and settle among us as members of our rapidly growing family."[2]

In 1787, the drafters of the U.S. Constitution included provisions giving Congress the power to "establish a uniform Rule of Naturalization." The Constitution also stated that once they gained citizenship, foreign-born citizens were eligible to hold all government offices except the presidency. It also explicitly permitted forced immigration, that is, the slave trade, from Africa for twenty more years, until 1808.

In 1790, Congress passed its first immigration legislation. Among other things, this legislation set a period of two years for "free white persons" to become eligible for citizenship. In 1795, the number of years of residency required before citizenship could be applied for was increased to five. Then, the **Alien and Sedition Acts** passed during the John Adams administration restricted the entry of some "free white persons," which seemed to refer to people who prominent members of Adams's political party thought might be inclined to vote for Thomas Jefferson. In 1798, the period of residency required before citizenship could be applied for was increased to fourteen years. In 1802, during the Jefferson administration, it was changed back to five years, where it remains today.

The Constitution no longer authorized the "importation" of African slaves after 1808. There is evidence, however, that close to fifty thousand Africans may have been brought into the country illegally after 1808. It would take the Civil War, further Constitutional amendments, and many additional laws in the latter half of the next century for the descendants of African slaves to gain the same political and legal status as white citizens.

The 1790 immigration law establishing unrestricted immigration for "free white people" would eventually be used against Asian immigrants later in the century. Racial discrimination was a prominent characteristic of nineteenth-century U.S. culture, and it was clearly reflected in immigration law and policy.

The Latter Half of the Nineteenth Century

During the 1830s about sixty thousand immigrants arrived in the United States each year, and by the 1850s, the number of annual arrivals had increased almost fivefold to over 250,000 per year. Toward the end of the 1840s and into the 1850s, each year nearly ten new immigrants arrived for every thousand residents. The U.S. population was growing by about 1 percent per year just from immigration. Many of these immigrants were Irish escaping their native country's potato famine.

The Irish immigrants were often disparaged because they were Roman Catholics. Increasing numbers of Germans were also arriving by mid-century, and the majority of them were Catholic too. The anti-Catholic sentiment was easily transformed into anti-immigrant sentiment. An exclusive and secret society of white Protestant men called the **Order of the Star-Spangled Banner** arose in the 1850s to protest the rise of Roman Catholicism in the United States. Because they would always reply "I know nothing" when questioned about their organization, members of the order were referred to as the **Know-Nothings**. By the mid-1850s, the Order of the Star-Spangled Banner had over a million white males as members, or about one-eighth of all eligible white voters in the country. Remember, only men could vote in the nineteenth century, and in the Southern states, only white men could vote. The order formed a political party, the *American Party,* whose candidate, the former President Millard Fillmore, captured 20 percent of the vote in 1856. The Civil War, in which many recent immigrants fought, reduced the anti-Catholic fervor, and the Know-Nothings gradually faded away.

Opposition to immigration did not entirely go away after the Civil War, however. Congress began debating legislation to modify the Naturalization Act of 1790, which still limited immigration to "free white persons." The proposed legislation came under attack, and not only because it provided for the full naturalization of African Americans. Many Americans had found a new scapegoat for their economic and social problems: Chinese immigrants. In the 1860s, thousands of Chinese had come to work on the transcontinental railroad, and by 1870 there were some sixty-three thousand Chinese in the United States, almost all males and almost all living in California. By the 1880 census, further arrivals increased the number to over 100,000.

Anti-Chinese sentiment was initially confined to California. But when, in 1870, a shoe factory in North Adams, Massachusetts, brought in seventy-five Chinese people from California to replace striking workers, labor organizations were quick to depict Chinese immigrants as a threat to American workers. When labor groups targeted Chinese immigrants, they effectively provided economic cover for various racist and cultural-supremacist groups. Congress passed several laws restricting Chinese immigration during the 1870s; however, the White House vetoed them because established trade treaties between the United States and China prohibited restrictions on Chinese immigration. Recall from Chapter 9 that U.S. trade policy included the forced opening of the Chinese market to foreign goods, and it would have been awkward for the United States to violate treaties it effectively had forced on China. More important was the political pressure from private business interests to keep borders open to all immigration. Chinese immigrants were convenient for breaking strikes by the newly formed labor unions in the late 1800s.

The Chinese Exclusion Act

In 1876, Congress again passed legislation banning Chinese immigration, and although President Rutherford B. Hayes again vetoed it, he did promise to renegotiate the treaties so as to permit the restriction of Chinese immigration. In 1882, after a new trade treaty with China was negotiated, Congress passed a bill entitled "To Execute Certain Treaty Stipulations Relating to Chinese," popularly referred to as the **Chinese Exclusion Act**. This law banned immigration from China for ten years, except for immediate family members of Chinese already in the country. Anti-Chinese sentiment was bolstered by the high unemployment of the recessionary years of the late 1880s and early 1890s, and in 1892 the **Geary Act** not only extended the ban on Chinese immigration for another ten years, but added restrictions on Chinese already living in the United States. The act denied the right of bail to Chinese in habeas corpus proceedings, and all Chinese immigrants were required to carry an identification document called a *certificate of residence*. Most Chinese refused to acquire the certificates in a passive form of protest.

These initial immigration laws and court decisions still affect immigration laws and regulations today. L. Salyer (1995, p. 247) argues that "the doctrines providing the foundation for immigration law arose out of the struggles on the West Coast among Chinese immigrants, government officials, and federal judges over the enforcement of the Chinese exclusion laws." Chinese immigrants often challenged the U.S. government in court after the Chinese Exclusion Act. One case was taken to the Supreme Court in 1893 in an attempt to overturn the Geary Act, but, by a 5–3 vote, the Court ruled that the act was constitutional. Amazingly, the five judges against the appeal justified their votes by arguing in the majority brief that Congress had the power to monitor and deport resident aliens if "their removal is necessary or expedient for the public interest" (quote from *Fong Yue Ting* v. *United States* provided in Salyer, p. 247). This Supreme Court decision effectively established that unnaturalized immigrants were at the mercy of Congress and did not enjoy the full rights accorded citizens. Furthermore, at the insistence of some government officials, the Court majority also explicitly wrote that "the nation's gates could be effectively guarded only if they [government officials] were allowed full authority and discretion over immigration policy without interference from the federal courts" (quoted in Salyer, p. 248). The Supreme Court's support of the centralization of immigration procedures in Congress not only resulted in increasingly arbitrary processes, but it effectively made the final decisions of the U.S. immigration authorities uncontestable in the courts. The recent arbitrary and seemingly unconstitutional procedures used by the government in dealing with suspected terrorists and their alleged supporters in the United States, who are generally non-naturalized foreigners, are not as radical a departure as commentators make them out to be; post–9/11 treatment of foreigners is legally supported by the nineteenth-century drift of U.S. law toward recognizing substantially fewer rights for immigrants than for native-born Americans.

Securing the Border to Keep the Riffraff Out

In 1875, a law was passed that prohibited the entry of foreigners who were "destitute," engaged in "immoral activities," or suffered from obvious health or physical problems. This law was not very explicit, and little money was allocated for enforcement. In 1882, a law was passed that authorized the creation of a bureaucracy to process immigrants; the same law required the government to deny entry to "paupers or persons likely to become a public charge." During the 1880s Congress formally created the *Office of Immigration*. This agency later came to be called the **Immigration and Naturalization Service (INS)**, the name it maintained for nearly a century until the recent reorganization of national security following the September 11, 2001, terrorist attacks. The purpose of the new agency was to enforce the immigration laws, and, bolstered by the court decisions mentioned above, Congress gave the agency the power to instantly deport noncitizens without giving them access to the due process of law mandated by the Constitution. Immigrant processing centers were established on Ellis Island in New York City and in San Francisco to check that people met the health and moral conditions mandated by the laws. In 1892, a commissioner general of immigration was appointed by the president to run the immigration bureaucracy with its newly hired inspectors, examiners, translators, border guards, and administrators.

The establishment of the immigrant-processing center on Ellis Island is a landmark in U.S. immigration policy. It represents the beginning of serious control of immigrant inflows. Beginning in 1892, over 12 million immigrants would pass through Ellis Island (since 1924, immigrants have been processed abroad at U.S. embassies and consulates). Despite Ellis Island's reputation, however, the screening was not very rigorous. First, not everyone was required to pass through Ellis Island. Ships bringing immigrants to New York City would routinely dock at one of the piers on Manhattan Island, and first- and second-class passengers were immediately passed through customs and granted entry to the United States, "the theory being that if a person could afford to purchase a first or second class ticket, they were unlikely to become a public charge in America."[3] Most immigrants traveled in third class or were steerage (deck) passengers, however, and these passengers were ferried to Ellis Island after the ship docked in Manhattan. There they were given a quick physical exam (often lasting a mere 5 or 6 seconds) consisting of a quick check of immigrants' eyes and skin. Then inspectors briefly questioned them in order to ascertain whether they were likely to become a burden on society. They were often returned to Manhattan within a few hours and permitted to travel on to their final destinations in the United States.

Records show that around 1900, fewer than two out of every 100 arrivals were refused entry. The low percentage of rejections was, no doubt, due to careful prescreening by the steamship lines. U.S. authorities required the shipping lines to carry passengers who were refused entry back to their original ports of embarkation.

Not as well known as Ellis Island is its counterpart on the West Coast, Angel Island in San Francisco Bay. Angel Island processed several hundred thousand immigrants between 1910 and 1940. Similar to the practice in New York, first- and second-class passengers disembarked in San Francisco, and the remainder were ferried to Angel Island for processing. This took much longer than at Ellis Island, however, because Angel Island was set up to prevent unauthorized Chinese immigrants from gaining entry to the United States. The Chinese Exclusion Act was generally interpreted as banning all Asian immigrants except immediate relatives of persons already living in the United States. Chinese immigrants were, therefore, kept in detention on Angel Island for a month or more while immigration officials subjected both them and their American relatives to extensive, and often abusive, questioning. If the detainees and their relatives on shore did not give identical answers to the officials' questions, that would "prove" the immigrants were lying about their kinship. There are many stories of personnel on Angel Island passing information to on-shore relatives about the questions being asked so that they could coordinate their answers.

Some Chinese and Japanese immigrants took advantage of an existing treaty between China and the United States that was interpreted by immigration officials to allow Asian businessmen to enter the country; they pretended to be high-level business representatives or merchants. However, to do this required the purchase of first-class passage, which was beyond the financial capacity of most immigrants. Also, several thousand Japanese "mail-order brides" were quickly admitted into the United States under special arrangements between immigration brokers and immigration inspectors. After the 1906 San Francisco earthquake destroyed all immigration records, all Chinese in the country, whether they had entered fraudulently or legally, were effectively accepted as legal residents for lack of evidence to the contrary.

Pro-Immigration Forces Kept Immigration Open

European immigration continued to grow during the 1880s and into the twentieth century. As the U.S. foreign-born population approached 15 percent of the total, political pressure for curbs on immigration gained strength. High unemployment during the financial panics and economic recessions that were common in the United States' unregulated capitalist economy led many Americans to blame their hardships on immigrants. Many politicians were only too happy to demonize the nonvoting new arrivals. Just as Roman Catholic immigrants from Ireland and Germany had spooked many natives earlier in the nineteenth century, the even more diverse ethnic backgrounds of immigrants at the turn of the century rekindled religious, racial, and ethnic biases. Opponents of immigration lamented the deteriorating "quality" of new immigrants, a clear code word for discussing immigrants from Italy, Russia, Greece, and other countries of southern and eastern Europe.

Legislation placing strict limits on all immigration came within a few votes of passing in 1897 and again in 1898, but no major restrictions on immigration actually passed during the first two decades of the twentieth century. Claudia Goldin (1994) argues that immigrants themselves were a decisive political force that was crucial in shaping legislation and preventing immigration restrictions from gaining enough votes for passage. The growing numbers of naturalized, and thus voting, immigrants in the large urban areas were such a political force that urban politicians remained solidly pro-immigrant. In cities like New York and Chicago, immigrants made up as much as half the population. The political machines in the large cities looked at arriving immigrants as future voters whose loyalty could be guaranteed by an openly pro-immigrant stance. Also critical to keeping the borders largely open to immigration was U.S. industry's interest in keeping labor costs low.

Assessing the Early Policies

In terms of the policy questions listed in the first section of this chapter, by the end of the nineteenth century U.S. immigration policies had shifted to where some foreigners were no longer permitted to freely immigrate to the United States, but white Europeans continued to have almost unrestricted entry. There were no numerical limits to immigration; nonetheless, Asians without close family ties and other nonwhites were effectively prohibited from entering the United States. The United States devoted very few resources to enforce the restrictions on immigration, although an immigration bureaucracy was created and processing centers were built. Immigrants continued to enjoy most of the rights of native-born Americans under the Constitution, but court decisions determined that the Congress had the power to limit the rights of non-naturalized residents.

THE SHIFT IN U.S. POLICY IN THE EARLY TWENTIETH CENTURY

The first decade of the twentieth century saw the largest-ever numbers of immigrants arriving annually in the United States, and immigrants made up a much larger percentage of the country's population than they do today. Annual immigrant arrivals exceeded 1 percent of the total U.S. population; that is, immigration accounted for over one full percentage point of total annual U.S. population growth in the early 1900s. This was also a period of rapid industrialization and technological progress in the United States, and many people were uncomfortable with the many changes to their way of life. The increasing numbers of foreign immigrants were a convenient scapegoat for all kinds of problems that people did not understand.

The Major Shift in U.S. Immigration Policy

Legislation was introduced in Congress to require literacy tests for immigrants in 1903 and 1907, and laws were passed in 1913 and 1915 but vetoed by President Woodrow Wilson. In 1917, Congress again passed the literacy test, and this time it mustered the necessary two-thirds majority in both the House of Representatives and the Senate to override President Wilson's veto. The ease with which the presidential veto was overridden in 1917 reflected the change in Americans' feelings about immigration.

Several trends converged to shift U.S. immigration policy after the close of the First World War. The horrific experience of the war made many Americans look more inward and support more isolationist policies. Also, conservative economic policies with the aim of putting the U.S. dollar back on the gold standard included tight monetary policy and lower government spending, both of which sharply increased unemployment. Anti-immigration groups used the communist revolution in Russia as proof that foreign immigrants could bring dangerous political ideas to the United States. Anti-Semitism no doubt also played a role. Finally, the election of a Republican president in 1920, Warren Harding, eliminated the threat of a veto.

In 1921, Congress passed the **Emergency Quota Act**, which for the first time set strict limits on immigration. It restricted immigration from outside the Western Hemisphere to about 350,000 people. It was enacted for one year only, but in 1922 Congress renewed it for two more years. After opponents to open immigration gained strength in both the House and the Senate in 1924, the **Immigration Act of 1924** was passed. This act mandated that annual immigration from each foreign country be limited to 2 percent of the total number of descendants of immigrants of that national origin residing in the United States, with an overall limit of 150,000 people per year. Immediate family members and other close relatives were exempt from the overall limits, and about 300,000 immigrants still entered the United States each year during the remaining 1920s.

Leading up to the Immigration Act, there was considerable debate on how to calculate national origins and determine the quotas for immigration from each foreign country. Congress approved carrying out a "scientific" study on the ethnic composition of the U.S. population, but during the long deliberations leading up to the final bill the House ended up siding with its most nativist members and agreed to use the 1890 census, the first to ask people about their ethnic and national origins. Using the 1890 census appealed to those people who felt that the post-1890 immigration from southern and eastern Europe upset the "traditional" ethnic makeup of the United States. Critics of the bill sarcastically referred to the 1890 census as the "Anglo-Saxon census." In 1929, the quotas were adjusted to reflect the results found by a panel of experts that had worked under the auspices of a group called the *American Council of Learned Societies*. This panel somehow came to the conclusion that 43.4 percent of Americans traced their origins back to people who were in the country at the time of the American Revolution and, presumably, of Anglo-Saxon descent. This revision reduced the quotas for most immigrants except those from the United Kingdom.

One of the predictable consequences of the new quotas was the beginning of unauthorized immigration. If anything, the economic incentives to immigrate to the United States were stronger during the 1920s because, as discussed in Chapter 15, many European economies suffered severe economic downturns after World War I while the U.S. economy appeared to perform somewhat better during its Roaring Twenties, at least if you focused only on the stock and bond markets. As immigrants began evading the new restrictions, Congress reacted in a way that has become familiar in the latter half of the twentieth century: It allocated more funds for enforcement of the immigration laws and protection of the border. The Bureau of Immigration was expanded, and the **United**

States Border Patrol was established to guard the Mexican and Canadian borders against the unauthorized entry of foreigners.

In sum, U.S. immigration policy was completely changed, and by the end of the 1920s, immigration was tightly limited. There was an overall limit of 150,000 immigrants plus exceptions for, among others, family members and residents of the Western Hemisphere. Country quotas were not to exceed 2 percent of total number of that national origin already in the United States. Deportations became more frequent, and border controls were strengthened. Nevertheless, unauthorized immigration from Canada, Mexico, and elsewhere became more common as it proved very difficult to close the thousands of miles of U.S. border to determined immigrants.

Some Immigration Horror Stories during the Great Depression

The Great Depression and its high unemployment of over 20 percent reduced the economic incentives for foreigners to come to the United States during the 1930s. In many of the Great Depression years, the number of people leaving the country exceeded the number of new arrivals. The restrictions of the *Immigration Act of 1924* were seldom tested for most nationalities. On the other hand, the "likely to become a public charge" clause that appeared in 1882 immigration legislation was increasingly applied to restrict specific categories of immigrants. In 1930, perhaps as a reaction to the rising unemployment, President Herbert H. Hoover explicitly instructed consular offices to refuse an immigrant visa to anyone thought likely to become a public charge. The clause was most often used to bar prospective Mexican immigrants in the 1920s and 1930s.

The discretionary power of American consulates in granting immigrant visas, derived from the nineteenth-century court decisions described earlier, was used inconsistently. For example, during the 1930s some consuls granted as many visas as they could to persecuted Jews and intellectuals in Nazi Germany, but most granted very few. Overall, U.S. consuls in Germany granted only half as many immigrant visas as were allowed under the quota system during the Nazi government. Attempts by some legislators to pass bills allowing more refugees to enter the United States failed, and the administration of Franklin D. Roosevelt did not push the issue. Many would-be refugees died in German concentration camps after failing to gain visas to enter the United States.

The most shameful example of U.S. indifference to the plight of Jews in Nazi Germany is its handling of one group of 933 Jewish refugees. The refugees had been on the quota list at various U.S. consulates in Germany, but the final documents were delayed for reasons never made clear. Fearing for their lives, the refugees boarded a Hamburg-Amerika Line ship bound for Havana, Cuba. They hoped to wait for their documents in the Western Hemisphere, far from Hitler's police. But Cuba already had over two thousand refugees waiting in Havana, and U.S. authorities pressured the Cuban government to refuse entry to the 933 passengers. The ship then sailed for Miami, hoping to find sympathetic U.S. authorities. Instead, the ship was ordered to leave U.S. waters, and a Coast Guard cutter was assigned to follow the ship to make sure no passengers tried to swim ashore. Eventually the ship returned to Europe, where France, Belgium, the Netherlands, and Great Britain each agreed to take a portion of the passengers. Unfortunately, a few months later, Germany invaded the first three of those countries, and many of these Jewish refugees eventually still perished at the hands of the Nazis.

Immigration Policy during World War II

The start of World War II saw the internment of some 125,000 Japanese Americans in the American version of concentration camps, an act that was officially recognized only by President Bill Clinton's apology in the late 1990s. U.S. law permits the government to imprison persons 14 years old or older who are citizens of countries that the United States is at war with. However, the Japanese Americans imprisoned during World War II were almost all American citizens, and the great majority were born in the United States. They were held in ten internment camps, most of which were in desolate areas, and provided the most rudimentary living conditions. Even though this action by the U.S. government was not sanctioned under U.S. law, a Supreme Court decision approved the government's actions retroactively much later.

Another interesting development during the war was a new temporary worker program for Mexicans. While Mexican immigration was strongly discouraged during the Great Depression, Mexican workers were actively sought during World War II. The so-called **Bracero Program** authorized temporary work permits for Mexicans working in agriculture and performing jobs formerly held by Americans who were drafted into the armed forces.

POST–WORLD WAR II IMMIGRATION POLICY

Economic and political conditions were much changed after World War II, and immigration policy began to shift again. In 1945 the War Brides Act permitted the spouses and children of U.S. citizens to immigrate to the United States outside the established quotas. The Bracero Program was continued. And the presence of large numbers of refugees, or what were then called **displaced persons**, following the war motivated special legislation authorizing the United States to accept about four hundred thousand immigrants outside the usual quotas. Included under these special provisions were people who had been imprisoned and persecuted in the Axis countries, many of whom were still housed in various refugee camps in Europe. The 1948 **Displaced Persons Act** introduced the concept of **immigrant sponsorship**, under which a person or group in the United States assumed responsibility for immigrants' welfare after their arrival. Sponsorship enabled immigration authorities to satisfy earlier immigration legislation requiring them to refuse visas to persons "likely to become public charges." The **Refugee Relief Act of 1953** authorized another 200,000 visas for refugees outside the quota.

Slow Shifts in Immigration Law

The small openings for more immigrants to enter the United States after World War II did not imply an end to the anti-immigrant and nativist sentiments that had closed the country to immigration two decades earlier, however. In fact, anti-immigrant feeling was also fueled by Cold War paranoia about communist infiltrators in the United States, a sentiment that peaked during the McCarthy Senate hearings in the early 1950s. The Republican-controlled House and Senate began work on a new immigration bill that both strengthened the existing system of ethnic quotas and added explicit restrictions on the immigration of suspected subversives. The *Immigration and Nationality Act of 1952,* drafted by Senator Patrick McCarran of Nevada, the head of the Senate Judiciary Committee, kept most quotas in place, increased border patrols, and mandated new entry restrictions for persons with political philosophies deemed un-American. This latter provision would keep noted intellectuals such as Jean-Paul Sartre from coming to the United States to give even a single lecture. On the other hand, McCarran's legislation required quite a few compromises with politicians who favored various openings to immigration, and some provisions of the act ended up permitting more immigrants to come to the United States. Specifically, it eliminated the anti-Asian bias in the quota system, and it explicitly reinforced the provision in the 1924 legislation that implied immigrants from the Western Hemisphere and spouses and minor children of U.S. citizens did not fall under the quota system. The act also included the unlimited authorization of immigrant visas for spouses and children of Americans and authorized immigrants. This "family reunion" criterion for awarding visas caused an immediate increase in immigration during the 1950s.

A New Immigration Law in 1965

Under pressure in the early 1960s from many liberal senators and congressmen, President John F. Kennedy proposed to replace the 1924 Immigration Act and its quota system by a system based on (1) skills and national labor requirements, (2) family reunion, and (3) the first come, first served principle. No action had yet been taken by Congress when Kennedy was assassinated in the fall of 1963, but after President Lyndon B. Johnson signed the **Civil Rights Act of 1964**, the blatantly racist and discriminatory 1924 immigration statutes seemed completely out of touch with contemporary political sentiments. In 1965, the Johnson administration pushed through new legislation to replace the discriminatory ethnic quota system.

The **Immigration and Nationality Act of 1965**, which amended the earlier act of that name, prescribed that 80 percent of the numerical limits were to be allocated to relatives of persons already living in the United States, and the remaining were to be allocated to those with desirable skills and their family members. Immediate family, that is, spouses and children, of U.S. citizens were no longer subject to numerical limits at all.

The new immigration law led to sharp increases in the number of immigrants, as Table 19.1 shows. Also not foreseen was the sharp change in the mix of nationalities of immigrants. By the 1960s, Europe had recovered from World War II and, by the 1960s and 1970s, reached standards of living comparable to those in the United States. Thus, the incentives for Europeans to immigrate to the United States were weaker than they had been. Also, the emphasis on family ties tended to favor the more recent immigrants, who were more likely to be from Latin America and Asia; most European immigrants from the nineteenth and early twentieth centuries had long since cut their ties to Europe. Immigration from Europe, therefore, declined sharply relative to immigration from Latin America and Asia.

The change in the sources of U.S. immigrants has attracted the attention of economists. According to George Borjas (1985, 1994), the skill levels of successive immigrant waves to the United States have declined over the post–World War II period. He concluded that the lower-skilled immigrants will never become as productive as the average U.S. native worker. Other studies dispute Borjas's conclusions. Guillermina Jasso and Mark R. Rosenzweig (1988) use data that track individuals over time rather than the standard census data that Borjas and most other researchers use, which in effect lets researchers compare only distinct groups at ten-year intervals. Jasso and Rosenzweig found a faster occupational mobility than the census data suggest. Also, there clearly is an improvement in income from one generation of Hispanic immigrants to another; the census data show that the children of Hispanic immigrants born in the United States earn much more than their parents, even if they remain under the U.S. average.[4] Upward social and economic mobility is closely related to English-language skills, according to Barry R. Chiswick and Paul W. Miller (1999), and second-generation Hispanics are nearly all fluent in English. This debate seems strangely reminiscent of the debate about the "quality" of immigrants at the start of the twentieth century.

Other economists have brought up concerns about immigration's effect on the distribution of income in the United States. Immigration after the 1960s had contributed, at least statistically, to the growing wage spread between low-income and high-income workers in recent years. Also, some categories of U.S. workers, such as those without a high school degree, who compete directly with immigrants have seen their wages fall between 5 and 10 percent. Social mobility in the United States, in general, has slowed down in recent decades, but it is not clear how much immigration has contributed to this phenomenon.

Unauthorized Immigration Grows Rapidly

The Bracero Program was permitted to expire in 1964, which reduced the possibilities for Mexicans without advanced education levels or special skills to get visas to work legally in the United States.

The 1,500-mile border was largely unguarded, however, and many former braceros continued to enter the United States to work illegally in the same jobs they had held when the program operated. U.S. employers were willing accomplices, as were American landlords, retailers, and many other economic interests that stood to gain from the presence of foreign workers and consumers. Also, rapid population growth in Mexico and many other Latin American countries further increased the supply of immigrants to the United States.

RECENT UNITED STATES IMMIGRATION POLICY

Both legal and unauthorized immigration grew during the 1970s and 1980s. In 1979, Congress authorized the creation of the Select Commission on Immigration and Refugee Policy (SCIRP) to report by 1981 on how best to deal with immigration. The commission concluded that unauthorized immigration was the major problem, and it recommended (1) increased border patrols, (2) forgery-proof identification cards for legal immigrants, (3) holding employers responsible for hiring unauthorized workers, and (4) amnesty for unauthorized immigrants who had been in the country for a long time. In 1981, President Ronald Reagan established a task force to study immigration, and it came to nearly identical conclusions.

Immigration Reform and Control Act

After several years of debate, new legislation was passed. The **Immigration Reform and Control Act of 1986 (IRCA)** generally followed the recommendations of SCIRP and President Reagan's task force. The combination of amnesty, improved identification, holding employers responsible for hiring unauthorized immigrants, and tougher border controls was a compromise between those who emphasized tougher enforcement and those who sought a humanitarian way of dealing with longtime unauthorized immigrants. The legislation both welcomed past unauthorized immigrants and threatened potential new unauthorized immigrants.

IRCA's one-time amnesty for unauthorized immigrants resulted in about 2.7 million unauthorized aliens already living in the United States gaining legal residence status. Lobbied by business and agricultural interests, Congress subsequently failed to fund the border and employer enforcement measures in IRCA, and twenty years later measures to require forgery-proof identification documents for immigrants and to enforce employer responsibility had still not been put into effect.

In a study of unauthorized immigration during the decade after IRCA, Gordon H. Hansen, Raymond Robertson, and Antonio Spilimbergo (2002) find that increased border patrols had no noticeable effect on the number of people entering the United States illegally. Nor did the threatened punishment of employers slow the hiring of unauthorized immigrants. Even though the new law prohibited employers from "knowingly hiring, recruiting, or referring for a fee aliens not authorized to work in the United States," punishment was almost never applied. The requirement for employers to verify citizenship did little more than create a new industry in supplying forged copies of the social security cards, driver's licenses, and birth certificates.

Some politicians have recently claimed that the amnesty actually increased unauthorized immigration to the United States. Even though the amnesty was advertised as a one-time event, never to be repeated, some prospective immigrants could also have interpreted it as a signal that if enough new unauthorized aliens enter the United States, eventually their status will have to be legalized with yet another "one-time" amnesty. However, Pia Orrenius and Madeline Zavodny (2003) examine immigration data and conclude that flows of unauthorized immigrants after 1986 merely followed long-run trends and were, therefore, unaffected by the amnesty. At the same time, predictions that there would be further amnesties were not entirely without merit: In 2000, President Clinton called for new legislation authorizing the legalization of the status of some additional unauthorized aliens living in the United States. In 2006, amnesty for some or all of the approximately 10 million unauthorized immigrants in the United States was a central piece of the George W. Bush administration's proposals for new immigration legislation.

There are several obvious reasons for the continued growth of illegal immigration after the passage of IRCA. First, the 1994 financial crisis in Mexico and the relatively slow economic growth after that pushed many Mexican workers to seek work north of the border. Also, there was the effect of the North American Free Trade Agreement on the rural sector in Mexico. Recall from the discussion of the links between trade and immigration in Chapter 7 that the inflow of subsidized U.S. grains made farming in Mexico unprofitable, and rising rural unemployment further pushed many Mexicans to seek work in the United States. Finally, U.S. manufacturers and construction firms were happy to employ immigrant workers willing to accept lower wages. Unauthorized immigration was, therefore, the result of several factors beyond the intentional failure of U.S. policy makers to enforce all the provisions of IRCA.

After IRCA

The Immigration Act of 1990 again altered the mix of immigrants permitted to enter the United States. This act acknowledged the arguments of those who lamented the decline in the average skill and education levels of U.S. immigrants by reducing residence visas for unskilled labor and increasing visas for "priority workers" and professionals with job offers from U.S. employers in hand. The 1990 act also specified that 10,000 permanent residence visas be made available to foreigners who invest more than $1 million in the United States and create new jobs for at least ten U.S. residents.

The **Illegal Immigration Reform and Immigrant Responsibility Act of 1996** authorized a clearinghouse that employers can call to verify the status of prospective immigrant employees. This measure was in response to the proliferation of forged documents, which made employer checks of standard documents almost meaningless. (Such a clearinghouse had, in fact, been authorized in IRCA, but had never been funded.) Funds for the border patrol were increased. A second law from 1996, the Personal Responsibility and Work Opportunity Reconciliation Act, which reduced the scope of public welfare and other public assistance programs, also had a direct effect on immigration: noncitizens were barred from some types public assistance, and eligibility for some other types of assistance was made more difficult.

And still, there were an estimated 6 million unauthorized immigrants in the United States in 2000, and over 10 million by 2010. Employers continued to hire unauthorized immigrants, landlords continued to rent houses to them, stores continued to sell to them, banks continued to send their wages home, legal citizens married some of them, schools educated their children, and churches welcomed them into their congregations. There was little will to stop unauthorized immigrants from coming to the United States, working there, living there, and settling there.

Temporary Work Visas

The United States issues a variety of temporary work visas. These visas permit a worker to work and the worker's family to live in the United States for a specified period, after which the foreigners must depart the country. In some instances, these visas can be extended or converted to permanent residence visas. These visas are easier to obtain than permanent residence visas, and it normally takes forty-five days or less to complete the application process.

In this category are visas that fall under the H-1B program for business and H-2A for agriculture. The American Competitiveness in the Twenty-First Century Act of 2000 about doubled the number of temporary H-1B work visas that can be issued. Before 2000, there was a ceiling of 65,000 H-1B visas per year. This was raised to 115,000 in 2000, and 195,000 for 2001, 2002, and 2003.

Universities and nonprofit research organizations are exempt from the numerical limits, and thus the 2000 act actually expanded the number of temporary work-related visas by even more than the explicit numbers suggest. In 2001, 384,200 H-1B visas were issued, well above the stated ceiling.[5] However, beginning in 2004 the ceiling for the number of H-1B visas was again lowered to 65,000 per year. In 2009, 60,000 temporary workers entered the United States to work in agriculture with H-2A visas.

Another important category of temporary work visas is L1 visas for "intracompany transfers." In 2001, 328,500 L1 visas were issued, about double the number from five years earlier. The large rise in L1 visas has stimulated some debate, with suggestions that both U.S. multinational firms and foreign multinationals operating in the United States are abusing the category in order to bring less expensive workers from abroad. On the other hand, the large increase in foreign direct investment in the United States by foreign multinational firms over the past ten years would naturally tend to increase the number of L1 visa requests as the foreign owners of U.S. businesses shuffle in employees from foreign branches. As firms become increasingly oriented to the global economy, this category of visas is destined to continue growing. In 2002, new legislation reduced the former requirement that recipients of L1 visas have been employed by the multinational company for a full year to just six months.

Summarizing Recent U.S. Policy

At the start of the twenty-first century, the United States restricted immigration using a complex set of criteria for allocating permanent residence visas and temporary work visas. There were numerical limits for many categories of immigrants defined by family relationships, skills, education, et cetera, and for the specially legislated, such as the H-1B and H-2A work visas. Huge backlogs, confusing regulations, inconsistent treatment of applicants, lax enforcement of immigration laws, the widespread presence of unauthorized immigrants, and the rapid expansion of the non-native population in the United States left few people satisfied. But momentum toward reforming immigration policy was interrupted by the attack on the World Trade Center on September 11, 2001.

Post–9/11 Immigration Policy

The Patriot Act of 2001 gave the government increased powers to control, apprehend, and deport foreign citizens in the United States. Foreigners who had legal permanent residence status in the country effectively lost civil and political rights. The Patriot Act even has provisions that allow the government to revoke citizenship previously awarded to foreigners if ties to terrorists are proven. Applications for temporary student visas have been subject to more extensive security checks, and these visas have effectively become more restricted.

In 2003, the Immigration and Naturalization Service (INS) was moved into the new **Department of Homeland Security** and split into two separate agencies. One is the **U.S. Citizenship and Immigration Services (USCIS)**, which handles citizenship issues, applications for permanent residence, nonimmigrant visitor and student applications, asylum, and refugees. The other is the Bureau of **Immigration and Customs Enforcement (ICE)**, which consolidates all border enforcement activities. The police force of the U.S. Border Patrol is now part of ICE.

The new split of the old Immigration and Naturalization Service (INS) into two separate agencies makes sense. The old INS faced contradictory goals. On the one hand, it was charged with processing new immigrant applications and welcoming immigrants to the country, but on the other hand it was also charged with keeping unwanted foreigners out of the country. Was the INS supposed to make it difficult for someone to immigrate, or was it supposed to facilitate the process? Today, USCIS employs about eighteen thousand people, and the staffs at U.S. embassies and consulates augment the USCIS staff. ICE employs 40,000 police, investigators, and administrative staff. In recent years, National Guard troops have occasionally been used to reinforce the Border Patrol, although the deployment of the military on domestic U.S. soil runs afoul of the U.S. Constitution.

Immigration Reform Stalls

With growing unauthorized immigration and foreign-born residents reaching 12 percent of the total U.S. population, immigration became a serious issue that was taken up by both the Senate and the House. In 2006, the Senate approved a comprehensive immigration bill that combined an amnesty of many unauthorized immigrants living in the country, a new program of temporary work visas, workplace enforcement of documentation, a new border fence, and sharply increased border security personnel. The House of Representatives, on the other hand, passed a bill that included only increased border security and increased punishment of unauthorized immigrants already in the country. An initial version of the House bill even included a provision charging all unauthorized immigrants, and any Americans who assisted unauthorized immigrants, as felons. Reconciliation between the two bills was not pursued, and no legislation was passed in 2006.

By 2011, no new immigration legislation has been passed other than further authorizations for building a border fence and funding border enforcement. In practice, the government has greatly stepped up arrests and deportations of unauthorized immigrants. Also, immigration judges are increasingly charging and convicting unauthorized immigrants with felonies such as the use of a fake social security number and lying to obtain employment, forcing them to serve a prison term before they are deported. These convictions are often decided at trials where immigrants' "day in court" lasts only a few seconds as hundreds of apprehended immigrant workers are charged, allowed to make a plea, and convicted in a matter of a just a few hours. With their felony convictions, the immigrants effectively forego any chance of future amnesty, and they would be arrested immediately if they came back to the United States after their deportation. Some four hundred thousand unauthorized immigrants were deported in 2010. It is estimated that over three hundred thousand immigrants are imprisoned in the United States at any one time, many in privately operated prisons under contract to ICE.

In sum, by 2010, U.S. immigration policy had veered sharply toward more enforcement, both on the border and within the country. A comprehensive reform such as the 1965 Immigration Act or the 1986 IRCA is unlikely given the anti-immigrant rhetoric of many Americans and the lukewarm support for serious reform by interest groups.

IMMIGRATION POLICY IN CANADA

Canada is another country that became a major destination for immigrants over the past two centuries. Its immigration policy changed frequently during this period, following a pattern not unlike that of its large neighbor to the south, the United States. Canada did not actively restrict immigration during the 1800s, but at the start of the twentieth century it explicitly limited immigrant flows according to the national origin of the immigrants. More recently, Canada has issued proportionately more immigrant visas than the United States. Nearly 20 percent of Canada's population was foreign born in 2010.

There are some major differences between Canadian and U.S. immigration policies. Canada remained a British colony during the 1800s, and this meant its sources of immigrants were more closely linked to Great Britain and its empire. Today, Canada has diverged from U.S. immigration policy by skewing its visa criteria much more toward admitting immigrants based on skills rather than the principle of family reunion that dominates U.S. policy.

On a per capita basis, immigration has been more important as a source of population growth in Canada. Table 19.2 shows that in the most recent decade, immigration contributed more to Canadian population growth than the difference between natural births and deaths. Table 19.2 also reveals another important difference between the U.S. and Canadian experiences, namely that Canada often lost as many people to emigration as it gained from immigration. Emigration from Canada was predominantly to the United States, which suggests many immigrants have used Canada as a way station to the United States.

The Early Years

Beginning with the French explorer Jacques Cartier in the early 1500s, the earliest European modern-day immigrants to Canada were French traders and adventurers. The first permanent settlement by French colonizers was in 1604, when a group led by Samuel de Champlain established a colony at Port Royal, on the Bay of Fundy in what is today Nova Scotia. British explorers also entered territory that would later become Canada, beginning a rivalry between the French and British for control of the area. European immigrants suffered attacks by the natives, disease, hunger, and setbacks from the harsh climate. But the most important factor that limited immigration to Canada was the proximity of the thirteen British colonies to the south that would become the Untied States. These colonies were more attractive to most British immigrants. French colonists likewise found French colonies in other parts of the world more attractive than the forested lands of Canada. In 1763, when all of the French territory in what is now Canada was ceded to the British, there were just sixty-five thousand European colonists in the combined territory.[6]

At the end of the American Revolution many loyalists (those who had sided with the British) moved to the British territory of Canada rather than return to Britain. In addition, at the close of the War of 1812 between Britain and the United States, British soldiers were encouraged to stay in Canada in order to boost the number of English-speaking colonists to counter the influence of the French-speaking residents of Quebec. The Irish potato famine of 1846–1849 brought hundreds of thousands of Irish to Canada. Notably, more than half of these Irish immigrants to Canada eventually moved to the United States; for many, Canada was viewed as a route to the United States from the start.

Canada's Treatment of Chinese Immigrants

Canada's first Chinese immigrants came in the late 1870s and early 1880s to build the western section of the Canadian Pacific Railway. This railway was a very important development in Canada's history, and the country probably would not exist in its current form without it. The colony of British Columbia agreed to join the Canadian Confederation on the condition that a transcontinental railway be built to link British Columbia to the rest of Britain's Canadian colonies. The railroad was a huge enterprise for the sparsely populated territory, and the Canadian Confederation's first prime minister, John MacDonald, sought to make the building of the railroad as attractive as possible to investors and as inexpensive as possible for the government. When objections arose to the recruitment of Chinese labor to build the railroad, he argued in Parliament: "It is simply a question of alternatives: either you must have this labour or you can't have the railway."[7]

At first, thousands of Chinese workers were attracted from California, where they had finished work on the U.S. transcontinental railroad. However, they quickly tired of the hard work and low pay offered by the Canadian railroad, and most left for the goldfields in British Columbia. Additional workers were brought directly from Guangdong Province in China, but many of these underpaid and overworked laborers also soon left for the goldfields. Yet more Chinese immigrants were contracted. By the time the Canadian Pacific Railway was completed, twenty thousand to thirty thousand Chinese men were in Canada.

Table 19.2

Canadian Population Growth and Immigration

	Total population at the end of period	Population added during period	Births	Deaths	Immigration	Emigration
Decades:						
1851–1861	3,230,000	793,000	1,281,000	670,000	352,000	170,000
1861–1871	3,689,000	459,000	1,370,000	760,000	260,000	410,000
1871–1881	4,325,000	636,000	1,480,000	790,000	350,000	404,000
1881–1891	4,833,000	508,000	1,524,000	870,000	680,000	826,000
1891–1901	5,371,000	538,000	1,548,000	880,000	250,000	380,000
1901–1911	7,207,000	1,836,000	1,925,000	900,000	1,550,000	740,000
1911–1921	8,788,000	1,581,000	2,340,000	1,070,000	1,400,000	1,089,000
1921–1931	10,377,000	1,589,000	2,415,000	1,055,000	1,200,000	970,000
1931–1941	11,507,000	1,130,000	2,294,000	1,072,000	149,000	241,000
1941–1951	13,648,000	2,141,000	3,186,000	1,214,000	548,000	379,000
5-Year Periods:						
1951–1956	16,081,000	2,433,000	2,106,000	633,000	783,000	185,000
1956–1961	18,238,000	2,157,000	2,362,000	687,000	760,000	278,000
1961–1966	20,015,000	1,777,000	2,249,000	731,000	539,000	280,000
1966–1971	21,568,000	1,553,000	1,856,000	766,000	890,000	427,000
1971–1976	23,450,000	1,488,000	1,760,000	824,000	1,053,000	358,000
1976–1981	24,820,000	1,371,000	1,820,000	843,000	771,000	278,000
1981–1986	26,101,000	1,281,000	1,872,000	885,000	678,000	278,000
1986–1991	28,031,000	1,930,000	1,933,000	946,000	1,164,000	213,000
1991–1996	29,611,000	1,580,000	1,936,000	1,024,000	1,118,000	338,000
1996–2001	31,021,000	1,410,000	1,705,000	1,089,000	1,217,000	376,000
2001–2006	32,723,000	1,702,000	2,006,000	1,130,000	1,446,080	237,000
2007–2010	34,500,000	1,777,000	1,505,000	972,000	1,017,000	214,000

Source: Statistics Canada (2005), "Population and Growth Components (1851–2001 Censuses)," Data for 2006 downloaded December 9, 2007, from Statistics Canada site; 2007–2010 four-year period taken from: Statistics Canada (2011) Quarterly Demographic Estimates, January to March 2011, Report 91–002–X, downloaded from www.stat.com.gc.ca/91–002–X/91–002–X2011001–eng.pdf.

At this point, the Canadian government sought to curtail further immigration from China, first by levying a head tax of $50 on Chinese immigrants in 1885. (The parallel with the United States' *Chinese Exclusion Act* of 1882 is obvious.) It is difficult to stop immigration between countries once a substantial number of immigrants have paved the way, and more Chinese immigrants continued to arrive despite the head tax. The head tax was increased from $50 to $100 in 1900 and to $500 (equivalent to $8,000 today) in 1903. Indicative of the strong anti-Chinese bias in Canadian immigration policy was the fact, as reported by Janet Dench (2007) of the Canadian Council for Refugees, that between 1901 and 1918 the Canadian government collected CAN$18 million from Chinese immigrants and spent about CAN$10 million to encourage immigration from Europe.

Around the turn of the century, when immigration was surging in the United States, increasing numbers of European immigrants began to arrive in Canada as well. As in the United States, where the 1862 Homestead Act simply assumed that the U.S. government owned the land and could thus assign ownership to European immigrants, the British government of Canada ignored native Americans' land rights and awarded large tracts to immigrants from Europe. The Canadian Pacific Railway actively promoted settlement on lands bordering their rights of way in order to generate traffic. A second transcontinental railway that ran to the north of the Canadian Pacific, the Grand Trunk Pacific, did the same around the turn of the century. Table 19.2 shows that during the first decade of the twentieth century, immigration exceeded 1.5 million.

Summary of Nineteenth-Century Policy

Canada was British territory throughout the nineteenth century, which meant immigration policies reflected British interests as much as they reflected local Canadian interests. Britain was interested in shifting Canada's population balance away from French-speaking Quebec and toward the English-speaking areas of the country. According to N. Kelley and M. Trebilcock (2000, p. 107):

> The location of immigration agents and the focus of financial incentives indicated the groups of immigrants which the government preferred. Throughout these years, Britons, northern Europeans, and Americans received the most attention and the most generous offers of assistance in emigrating to Canada. And while formal barriers to entry on the basis of race did not exist until the passing of the Chinese Immigration Act in 1885, the manner in which promotional activities and incentives were distributed exhibited strong racial preferences.

British citizens remained British citizens when they immigrated to Canada, since Canada was British territory. Other immigrants could become British subjects after three years' residency in Canada. Only in the twentieth century would the question of whether Canadians were Canadian or British citizens be definitively settled.

The Twentieth-Century Shift in Policy

After substantial inflows of immigrants in the latter half of the nineteenth century, there was a growing sentiment to limit immigration to Canada. These sentiments often manifest themselves in the form of explicit racial bias, not unlike what we described for the United States in the previous chapter. There was strong support for continued immigration from business interests in Canada. The Canadian mining industry, the railroads, and new manufacturers sought to lower labor costs in their sparsely populated country. Nevertheless, Canada began to explicitly limit all immigration at the beginning of the twentieth century.

The **1910 Immigration Act** gave Canadian authorities considerable discretionary power over who could enter Canada. According to one provision in the law, the government could prohibit immigrants "belonging to any race deemed unsuited to the climate or requirements of Canada." The "climate" criterion was, obviously, intended to be applied in the case of nonwhite applicants.[8] In early 1923, the government issued an order limiting Chinese immigration to "agriculturalists, farm labourers, female domestic servants, and wife and children of a person legally in Canada." This measure was quickly attacked as too weak by opponents of Chinese immigration, and was followed a few months later by a new Chinese Immigration Act, which banned Chinese immigrants altogether. The law went into effect on July 1, a day known as Canada Day to most Canadians but called "Humiliation Day" by Chinese Canadians. This exclusion remained in effect until 1947. In 2006, Canada issued an official apology and compensation for having discriminated against Chinese immigrants.

While Canada did not establish a rigorous quota system as the United States did in 1924, the Canadian government effectively kept the border open only to British subjects, Americans, and citizens of "preferred countries." These were explicitly defined as Norway, Sweden, Denmark, Finland, Luxembourg, Germany, Switzerland, Holland, Belgium, and France. Only agriculturalists, farm laborers, female domestic servants, and sponsored family members would be admitted from "non-preferred countries." These countries were on another limited list consisting of Austria, Hungary, Poland, Romania, Lithuania, Estonia, Latvia, Bulgaria, Yugoslavia, and Czechoslovakia. Immigrants from southern European countries or non-European countries were not on either list.

The economic conditions during the 1930s had a very detrimental effect on how Canadian immigrants were treated. Between 1930 and 1935, about twenty-eight thousand immigrants were deported from Canada for becoming a "public charge."[9] In effect, the consequences of the Great Depression became grounds for deportation. Canada admitted only about five thousand Jewish refugees during the 1930s because it had never formulated a policy toward refugees, leaving them to deal with the existing immigration bureaucracy and procedures that were largely shaped by ethnic biases and the high unemployment rate during the Great Depression.[10] In comparison, Argentina, a country with a fascist-leaning military government during the 1930s, admitted 63,000 Jewish refugees.

Canadian Policy Shifts after World War II

After the close of World War II, Canada took many steps to become a fully independent nation. This shift in national focus included a new emphasis on immigration. Prime Minister William Lyon Mackenzie King outlined his vision for postwar Canadian immigration policy as follows in 1947:

> The policy of the government is to foster the growth of the population of Canada by the encouragement of immigration. The government will seek by legislation, regulation, and vigorous administration, to ensure the careful selection and permanent settlement of such numbers of immigrants as can advantageously be absorbed in our national economy.[11]

In this speech, Mackenzie King explicitly noted that "objectionable discrimination" in earlier legislation and administration of immigration should be removed. But he then seemed to suggest that not all discrimination was necessarily "objectionable":

> [T]he people of Canada do not wish, as a result of mass immigration, to make a fundamental alteration in the character of our population. Large-scale immigration from the orient would change the fundamental composition of the Canadian population.[12]

Little by little, however, additional legislation began to eliminate most, if not all, discriminatory provisions in Canadian immigration law.

There were several reasons why Canada opened its borders to more people from a much larger number of foreign countries. First, World War II directly changed Canadian public opinion on human and civil rights. The Canadian government had actively promoted the idea that Canada fought the war against racial bias and totalitarianism; after the war, it would be pressed by its citizens to reflect those ideas more broadly. There may also have been some sense of guilt about Canada's failure to accept Jewish immigrants fleeing Nazi Germany before the war. Anti-communist sentiment also increased Canada's acceptance of refugees from countries that were not the traditional sources of Canadian immigrants. And as mentioned, after the war Canadians were increasingly interested in the long-run development of "their country." Immigrants were, therefore, viewed less as threats to Canadians' well-being and more as contributors to Canadian economic growth. Perhaps even more important was the view that immigration could increase the size of the Canadian economy relative to its huge southern neighbor. Finally, with the **1946 Canadian Citizenship Act**, Canada became the first Commonwealth country to establish citizenship distinct from British citizenship. All in all, as Table 19.2 shows, Canadian immigration rose sharply after World War II, and it has continued growing to where today most of Canada's population growth is due to immigration, not natural increases.

In the following few decades, Canada's policy shifted toward more openness to immigration. This shift can be best grasped by comparing the language in its immigration laws from 1910, 1952, and 1976. For example, the *1910 Immigration Act* states that the government may block the entry of:

1. Those belonging to nationalities unlikely to assimilate and who consequently prevent the building up of a united nation of people of similar customs and ideals.
2. Those who from the mode of life and occupations are likely to crowd into urban centers and bring about a state of congestion which might result in unemployment and a lowering of the standards of our national life.

Not long after World War II, the Immigration Act of 1952 still defined a number of criteria that may be used to exclude certain immigrants:

1. Nationality, citizenship, ethnic group, occupation, class or geographical area of origin.
2. Peculiar customs, habits, modes of life, or methods of holding property.
3. Unsuitability with regard to climatic, economic, social conditions.
4. Probable inability to become readily assimilated or to assume the duties or responsibilities of citizenship.

But a quarter of a century later, the 1976 Immigration Act established new objectives for immigration policy:

1. To enrich and strengthen the cultural and social fabric of Canada, taking into account the federal and bilingual character of Canada.
2. To ensure that any person who seeks admission to Canada in either a permanent or temporary basis is subject to standards of admission that do not discriminate on grounds of race, national or ethnic origin, colour or sex.[13]

Canadian immigration law thus shifted from an explicit bias against nonwhite immigrants from regions other than northern Europe to an explicit ban on any discrimination on the basis of ethnic or racial origins. Arguably, however, the full text of the 1976 legislation still leaves some openings for the government to discriminate against people who are judged to be less likely to assimilate quickly into Canadian society.

Canada's Immigration Policy in the Twenty-first Century

Canadian immigration law recognizes three categories of immigrants: (1) family and closely related persons; (2) independent immigrants admitted on the basis of skill, capital, and labor market requirements; and (3) refugees. Canadian government officials have considerable discretion in how they award immigrant visas, especially for people who fall into the latter two categories. To minimize the arbitrariness of their decisions for immigrants admitted on the basis of skills and labor market needs, Canadian authorities have established an objective point system to rate prospective immigrants.

The Canadian point system is heavily biased toward immigrants with skills and high levels of education. Family ties also add points. Canada's immigration website (www.cic.gc.ca) has an interactive test that lets foreigners calculate the number of points they are likely to be awarded by immigration authorities. In a matter of minutes a person can tell whether they exceed the number of points required, which is subject to change, for a permanent residence visa. Points are awarded for education, English and French language skills, age, occupation, and a job offer from a Canadian employer. Essentially, if you are under 40, have a university degree or ample experience in a profession, and are fluent in English or French, you will most likely qualify for a permanent residence visa.

Canada's active promotion of immigration has been linked to the fear that the slowdown of the natural rate of population growth and the resulting rapid aging of the Canadian population will put severe pressure on the future provision of social services and retirement benefits. For example, when population projections suggested in 2000 that by 2021 there would be only two working Canadians for each retiree, compared to the current 6-to-1 ratio, Canada's immigration minister vowed to increase immigration by 50 percent. She stated, "We know we start having demographic problems in 2010."[14] Richard N. Cooper (2002) convincingly argues that immigration cannot serve as a permanent solution to the burden of population aging, however. In 2010, the Conservative government was beginning to consider measures to reduce immigration. No doubt, the worldwide economic recession had much to do with the waning enthusiasm for accepting more foreign workers.

In sum, Canada restricts immigration, and would-be immigrants must qualify for an immigrant visa. But there are no strict numerical limits on immigration; rather, Canada uses a point system to qualify immigrants for a visa. This point system is flexible in that the authorities can adjust the points awarded for various personal and professional characteristics as the Canadian labor market changes and economic conditions vary. The point system has been calibrated to allow quite a few immigrants to enter Canada, as evidenced by the fact that in 2010, over 20 percent of the people living in Canada were born elsewhere. This high proportion of foreigners has led to increased opposition to immigration, a movement that seems to be taking its cue from rising anti-immigrant sentiment in the United States and Western Europe. New policy shifts may be forthcoming.

CONCLUSIONS

The United States provides an interesting case study on immigration policy because it has traditionally attracted so many immigrants and its policies on immigration have varied so much over the years. Immigration policies reflect a complex and often contradictory set of political, social, and economic factors. As these factors change, policy can take sudden and unpredictable turns.

At the start of the first decade of twenty-first century, with the U.S. economy seemingly growing rapidly and unemployment low, the surge in U.S. immigration was not creating much political pressure for new laws to sharply curtail immigration. But by 2010, after nearly a decade of obsession with foreign terrorism and a recession that drove unemployment to 10 percent of the official labor force and 18 percent of the true labor force, anti-immigrant rhetoric has become louder and less compromising. Meanwhile, enabled by two hundred years of contradictory legislation and regulation, the government was legally able to push U.S. immigration policy and enforcement toward becoming more restrictive, greatly increasing arrests, incarcerations, and deportations.

Recall from above that in the United States opposition to immigration festered for decades in the nineteenth and early twentieth centuries, but efforts to sharply restrict immigration were thwarted with the passage of weaker laws enhancing border controls, creating more rigorous bureaucratic procedures, and placing discriminatory bans on Chinese immigrants, a minority most Americans did not identify themselves with. But this latent, easily diverted opposition suddenly came together to cause a massive reversal of immigration policy in the form of the 1924 Immigration Reform Act that established tight ethnic quotas. After half a century of immigration liberalization after World War II, it is increasingly likely that there may be yet another reversal in the making.

Canadian immigration has also varied greatly over the years, with both economics and politics contributing to the variation. And even though Canada receives, as a percentage of its population, a much larger number of immigrants than the United States, this does not mean there is complete agreement among all Canadians for keeping the borders open to immigrants. For example, the columnist Daniel Stoffman argued in 2006, well before the 2007–2008 global recession slowed economic growth, that Canada should slow down immigration because immigrants were not assimilating: "The solution is not more ESL [English as a second language] teachers. Kids don't learn English from teachers. They learn it from other kids. But they can't if the other kids don't speak English. If the flow of new immigrants were more moderate, this problem would disappear."[15]

The history of immigration policy is not encouraging. The only consistent feature of immigration policy is the presence of blatant contradictions. For example, not long after George Washington welcomed the "oppressed and persecuted of all nations and religions" in 1783, the Constitution negotiated among the thirteen colonies and ratified in 1788 authorized the continued importation of African slaves until 1808. And at the same time that the United States proudly erected the French-donated Statue of Liberty in New York Harbor, with Emma Lazarus's poem engraved on its base famously welcoming *your tired, your poor, Your huddled masses yearning to breathe free,*" Congress was busy banning Chinese and any other immigrants that authorities deemed likely to become a "public charge," and the Supreme Court allowed Congress's racist ban to stand by stating that noncitizen residents of the United States did not enjoy the rights laid out in the U.S. Constitution.

To understand the contradictions of immigration policy, it is useful to return to the Chapter 1 discussion of Paul Seabright's (2010) point about how humanity struggles to understand its complex existence and to build the institutions necessary to deal with the complex global interdependence it has created. Clearly, the human capacity for abstract thought has not yet enabled us to avoid mass genocides, world wars, and economic depressions. This chapter's history of immigration policy shows that we have not always dealt well with the conflicting human urges to engage with strangers and to shun them.

Given its complexity, immigration policy serves as a measure of the human capacity for dealing with difficult systemic issues. Humanity occasionally achieves enlightened outcomes, such as the Canadian and U.S. shifts in policy during the 1960s and 1970s. But such moments of human progress usually followed earlier periods of more blatant discrimination and bias, and they have almost always been followed by less enlightened collective decisions. In any case, nearly all countries have continued to restrict, exploit, and brutally punish those strangers who seek to move into their midst. As the American poet Walt Whitman wrote in the late 1800s:

> Do I contradict myself?
> Very well then I contradict myself,
> (I am large, I contain multitudes.)[16]

Indeed, it is difficult to avoid contradictions when dealing with complex systems while also having to coordinate many conflicting personal and group interests driven by basic human instincts.

In the case of immigration, we need even more than sophisticated abstract thinking and institutions that guide collective decisions toward achieving a better balance between the mutual gains from direct human interaction and the potential conflicts that such interaction creates. Immigration policy must also take into consideration that people are happiest when, in the words of John A. Rawls (1971, pp. 4–5), "a society . . . is not only designed to advance the good of its members but when it is also effectively regulated by a public conception of justice." To date, even the allegedly most progressive societies have been unable to collectively design and enact immigration policies that objectively can be judged to be economically efficient, socially stabilizing, and just.

CHAPTER SUMMARY

1. Only about 200 million, or little more than 3 percent, of the world's 6.5 billion people are living outside the country they were born in. These numbers suggest that the most important question is not why people immigrate, but why nearly all people do *not* immigrate.

2. Government restrictions on immigration, or what we generally refer to as immigration policy, are the main reason more people do not immigrate from poor to wealthy countries.

3. This chapter details the history of U.S. and Canadian immigration policy, which shows that immigration

policies have fluctuated between supporting people's freedom of movement and acting on their equally strong demands for protection from potentially objectionable new members of their community.

4. Immigration policy is likely to be a compromise between the human sense of community and individualist tendencies. Also, business and other interest groups often exploit fundamental political and philosophical differences to shape immigration policies in destination countries.

5. After its independence from Britain, the U.S. government openly encouraged immigration from Europe, a policy that reflected the fact that the United States was a geographically large country with a small European population outnumbered by African American slaves and Native Americans.

6. By the mid-1800s, however, resentment in the United States against Irish and Catholic immigrants grew into the Know-Nothing political movement.

7. In the 1880s immigration procedures in the United States were tightened, and in 1882 the blatantly discriminatory Chinese Exclusion Act was passed.

8. There was increased political support for curbs on immigration in the late 1800s and early 1900s in the United States, but it took until the 1920s before legislation was passed to sharply limit immigration by means of a quota system designed to keep the ethnic composition of the U.S. population similar to what it had been in 1890, before the surge in immigration from southern and eastern Europe.

9. The Great Depression meant that the immigration restrictions of the *Immigration Act of 1924* were seldom tested for most nationalities, but the "likely to become a public charge" clause in 1882 immigration legislation was increasingly applied to restrict specific categories of immigrants.

10. The 1965 Immigration and Nationality Act effectively replaced the U.S. quota system with a set of general criteria permitting essentially unlimited immigrant visas for close relatives of persons already living in the United States as well as people with special skills. The 1965 law ended up permitting immigration to the United States to grow rapidly.

11. By 2000, about 1 million persons were immigrating legally to the United States each year, and many more foreign workers entered the country illegally.

12. *The Immigration Reform and Control Act of 1986* (IRCA) sought to stop unauthorized immigration to the United States by providing amnesty for past unauthorized immigrants, improving identification of people working in the United States, holding employers responsible for hiring unauthorized immigrants, and establishing tougher border controls.

13. By 2010, the United States was managing immigration according to a large set of criteria for allocating permanent residence visas and temporary work visas.

14. Huge backlogs, confusing regulations, inconsistent treatment of applicants, lax enforcement of immigration laws, the widespread presence of unauthorized immigrants, and the rapid expansion of the non-native population in the United States have left few Americans satisfied with immigration policy, but by 2010 reform of the system had become hopelessly bogged down in a contentious political process.

15. Canada's immigration policy also changed frequently over the past two hundred years, following a pattern somewhat similar to that of the United States.

16. Canada did not actively restrict European immigration during the 1800s, but it did explicitly discriminate against Asian immigrants in the late 1800s.

17. Canadian immigration policy gradually became more liberal and less discriminatory during the twentieth century.

18. In the latter part of the twentieth century, Canada's immigration policy began to differ from that of the United States in that it issues proportionately many more immigrant visas, and it issues more visas according to a point system that adjusts the number of points awarded for various personal and professional characteristics as the Canadian labor market and economic conditions change.

19. Immigration policy serves as a measure of the human capacity for dealing with difficult systemic issues. Humanity occasionally achieves enlightened outcomes, such as the Canadian and U.S. shifts in policy during the 1960s and 1970s, but such moments of human progress have almost always been followed by less enlightened collective decisions.

20. Immigration policy remains a contentious issue in nearly all high-income countries in the world today, and policies continue to restrict, exploit, and punish those strangers who seek to move into others' midst.

KEY TERMS AND CONCEPTS

1910 Immigration Act
1946 Canadian Citizenship Act
Alien and Sedition Acts
Bracero Program
Bureau of Immigration and Customs
    Enforcement (ICE)
Chinese Exclusion Act
Civil Rights Act of 1964
community perspective
department of homeland Security
displaced persons
Displaced Persons Act
Emergency Quota Act
Geary Act
Illegal Immigration Reform and Immigrant
    Responsibility Act of 1996 (IRCA)

immigrant sponsorship
Immigration Act of 1924
Immigration and Nationality Act of 1965
Immigration and Naturalization Service (INS)
immigration policy
Immigration Reform and Control Act of
    1986 (IRCA)
Know-Nothings
libertarians
objectivists
Order of the Star-Spangled Banner
Refugee Relief Act of 1953
Social contractionists
U.S. Citizenship and Immigration Services (USCIS)
United States Border Patrol
utilitarian

PROBLEMS AND QUESTIONS

1. U.S. immigration policy was quite favorable toward European immigrants right after independence. Explain why.
2. Should society maximize the welfare of natives? Or should we be concerned primarily about the welfare of immigrants? Explain how immigration policy will affect natives and immigrants differently. How do you think that your country's current immigration policies affect the welfare of natives and immigrants?
3. The labor market model of immigration in fact assumes that it is the difference in wages that drives immigration. Yet, the highest flows of immigrants are not from the very poorest countries; the largest flows seem to be from medium-income countries such as Mexico and the Philippines. What might cause such differences in immigrant inflows?
4. The Statue of Liberty in New York harbor carries a well-known poem whose last lines are:

> *"Give me your tired, your poor,*
> *Your huddled masses yearning to breathe free,*
> *The wretched refuse of your teeming shore.*
> *Send these, the homeless, tempest-tost to me,*
> *I lift my lamp beside the golden door!"*

Do these lines give an accurate picture of immigration to the United States? Do they give an accurate picture of immigration in general? Why or why not?
5. How did the United States answer the "six policy questions" during the early twentieth century? During the early twenty-first century?
6. Discuss the economic consequences of the Immigration and Nationality Act of 1965, which abolished the national quota system in favor of a new set of criteria for the granting of permanent residence visas.

7. Whose welfare should immigration policy seek to maximize? And if it is not just economic welfare, what do we want our countries' immigration policies to accomplish?
8. Given the large income differences across countries and the improvements in transportation and communications, why do so few people emigrate?
9. Immigration has been a major factor in the economic growth of the United States. Use the data in Table 19.1 and draw a graph that shows the level of immigration for each decade since 1850. Interpret the graph, suggesting reasons for the ups and downs in immigration flows. Were the variations in immigrant inflows largely driven by shifts in economic conditions, or did other factors play a role?
10. This chapter describes both U.S. and Canadian immigration policy over the past two centuries. How were the countries' policies similar? What might explain the similarities?
11. Compare today's immigration policies in the United States and Canada. Should the United States shift its policy more toward Canada's point system that favors talented and educated immigrants? Explain. (Hint: You could examine how the shift in U.S. policy would affect the alternative goals of economic growth and social justice.)

NOTES

1. Quoted in John C. Fitzpatrick, ed. (1931), p. 254.
2. Quoted in James D. Richardson, ed. (1903), p. 41.
3. National Park Service (2001), "Ellis Island History," www.nps.gov/stli/serv02.htm, March 7.
4. See Eduardo Porter (2001), "U.S. Hispanics Show Increasing Upward Mobility," *Wall Street Journal*, February 15.
5. Table IV.33, OECD (2004), *Trends in International Migration 2003*, Paris: OECD.
6. William A. Carrothers (1948).
7. Quoted in Ian Macdonald, and Betty O'Keefe (2000), *Canadian Holy War: A Story of Clans, Tongs, Murder, and Bigotry,* Surrey, BC: Heritage House Publishing Company Ltd.
8. Janet Dench (2007).
9. C. Bélanger (2006).
10. Ibid.
11. Quoted in Dench (2007).
12. Ibid.
13. These excerpts of past laws are from "Contrasting Canadian Immigration Regulations (1910, 1952, 1970s)," Marianopolis College website on Quebec History, Documents of Canadian History, http://faculty.marianopolis. edu/c.belanger/QuebecHistory/readings/CanadianImmigrationRegulations/, downloaded on December 8, 2007.
14. Quoted in Julian Beltrame (2000), "Canada Is Taking Steps to Boost Immigration," *Wall Street Journal*, July 10.
15. Daniel Stoffman (2006), "Too Much, Too Soon," *Globe and Mail,* July 26.
16. Excerpt from Walt Whitman (1881), "Song of Myself," in Whitman, *Leaves of Grass,* at http://www. whitmanarchive.org.

PART SEVEN

CONCLUSIONS

CHAPTER 20

The Evolving International Economy

> Changing paradigms is not easy. Too many have invested too much in the wrong models.
>
> —Joseph Stiglitz (2010)

Economists tend to look favorably on the rapid growth of international trade, international investment, international finance, and international migration and, therefore, to advocate for open borders. If challenged, most would probably reply that they base their advocacy on solid, proven analysis carried out by economists for three centuries. Their view is, no doubt, also influenced by the fact that growing international economic integration has coincided with the rapid growth of material wealth over the past two hundred years. For example, while world trade expanded from less than 1 percent of output to about one quarter of all goods produced, the world's average per capita gross domestic product (GDP) increased by a factor of ten.[1] Of course, GDP does not accurately reflect human well-being, but many alternative measures of human welfare also point to a clear improvement. For example, life expectancy in the world has tripled since 1800, infant mortality has become rarer in most countries, education levels have risen almost everywhere, nutrition has become more constant, more people have access to safe water than ever before, and labor-saving technologies have been developed to reduce physical toil in almost all types of human work. Should we not, therefore, be celebrating our good fortune to be living in today's economically integrated global economy?

There is little evidence that humans are much happier today than they were in the past. Happiness surveys, behavioral economics, psychological experiments, and neuroscience all have produced evidence that individual happiness is largely determined by one's relative status in society rather than absolute wealth. Therefore, it is likely that the growth of income disparities within countries and across countries over the past two hundred years has, at least in part, offset the welfare-enhancing effect of the growth of average per capita material well-being. The growing discrepancies in incomes are commonly measured in terms of such indicators as poverty rates, health crises, hunger, oppression, discrimination, and unemployment. The 2007–2008 Great Recession, discussed in Chapters 13 and 17, is a most vivid reminder that financial instability, unemployment, and income losses remain serious problems in all economies because international economic integration enables economic shocks in any country to batter all economies. Many people may be inclined to see the international economic integration that coincided with increased economic inequality and instability as the immediate cause of the latter problems.

This heterodox textbook has, hopefully, bridged this gap in perceptions by taking a much more holistic approach to international economics. It should be obvious to all perceptive observers that international economic integration is an integral part of the continuous, and evolving, process of human social development within the natural environment. To many, the growth of economic activity, its geographic spread across all continents, and humans' ability to exploit available resources to their advantage make up an evolutionary success story. Humanity has done very well for itself. But the process of evolution is not linear, stable, or easily predictable, and the future may not be as kind. Economic development is not an automatic process.

Orthodox economics cannot deal with nonlinearity, instability, and the inherent uncertainty of complex systems. Its smooth, continuous functions based on assumptions of stable market systems bias mainstream economists toward an optimistic view of international economic integration. It also leads mainstream economists to ignore the many potential dangers of continued rapid economic growth and international economic integration.

Heterodox economists, who accept and, one would hope, understand the implications of complexity and uncertainty thus have a very important role to play: economists and policy makers' understanding of international economics will determine how they deal with the many economic, social, and environmental problems human society has to face. International trade, investment, finance, and migration have made these problems global rather than purely national. Since earlier chapters have already focused on financial instability, debt accumulation, trade imbalances, and inequality, this chapter focuses on, arguably, the most devastating consequence of the rapid growth of human society on earth: the conflict between humanity's expanding economic activity and the health of the natural environment. This conflict is global, and solutions require global cooperation, yet orthodox international economists devote very little attention to this most international of all economic issues. Heterodox analysis is comfortably positioned to deal with the interactions between economic activity and the natural environment.

ECONOMIC GROWTH AND THE ECOSYSTEM

Neoclassical models almost invariably limit their analysis to purely economic variables. Furthermore, neoclassical models often accept scientific reductionism and avoid even the many linkages among economic variables. Recall from Chapter 1 Herman Daly's (2001) suggestion that the economy should be analyzed as being embedded within human society, which in turn is embedded within the natural environment. Figure 20.1 depicts Daly's ideas in terms of what we called the *spheres of human existence.* Human social institutions do not deal well with all interactions between economic activity and nature, such as when industrial pollution is hidden from public sight or the full consequences of economic growth are not understood. This is why in Figure 20.1 we show the economic sphere not entirely within social sphere.

This holistic perspective of international economic activities as firmly linked to the society and the natural environment in many complex ways explains why economists have so many problems explaining economic phenomena or predicting economic outcomes accurately. Statistical analysis based on neoclassical relationships is similarly hampered; a statistical model that does not include all the explanatory variables is said to suffer from **omitted variable bias** and **specification error**.

Earth's ecosystem is under severe pressure from the past and present growth of the human population and each human's expanding environmental footprint. In the section of Chapter 1 titled "The Natural Environment," we summarized the evidence on humanity's exploitation of earth's natural services. We quoted a study by Mathis Wackernagel and a group of associates (2002) that estimated that humanity's exploitation of earth's resources grew from 70 percent of capacity in 1961 to 120 percent in 1999. The World Wildlife Fund (WWF) estimated that in 2005, "humanity's demand on the planet's living resources . . . exceeds the planet's regenerative capacity by about 30 percent" (WWF 2008, p. 2). We repeat a diagram from Chapter 1 as Figure 20.2 here to illustrate the estimated path of humanity's demand for nature's renewable resources since 1960. Sometime during the 1980s, the human population began using nature's renewable resources at a rate that exceeded the capacity of earth's ecological system to sustain its capacity to supply them.

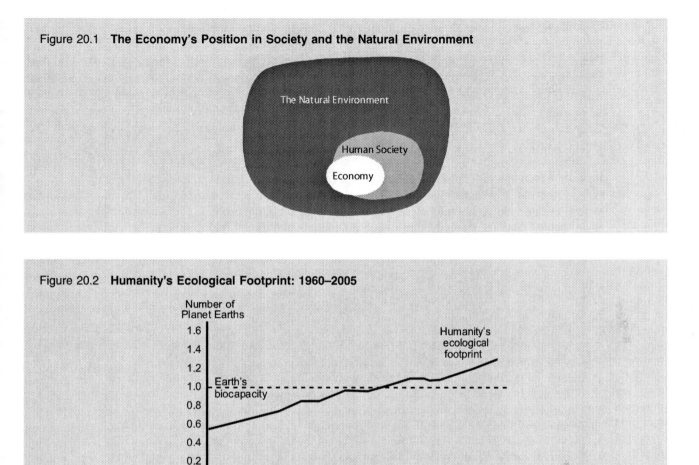

Figure 20.1 The Economy's Position in Society and the Natural Environment

The Natural Environment

Human Society

Economy

Figure 20.2 Humanity's Ecological Footprint: 1960–2005

Number of
Planet Earths

Humanity's
ecological
footprint

Earth's
biocapacity

The World Wildlife Fund defines humanity's global **ecological footprint** in terms of global hectares (gha). A gha is the average capacity of one hectare of the planet's surface to produce services and absorb waste, and an ecological footprint is effectively the sum of (1) all forest, grazing land, cropland, and fishing grounds required to produce the food, fiber, and timber humanity consumes, (2) all land and water to absorb the wastes emitted when humans use energy, and (3) all land and water required for humanity's living space, production, transportation, and storage. According to the World Wildlife Fund (2008), the total productive area of the earth is equal to 13.6 billion global hectares, or 2.1 gha per person in 2005. In that year, however, the global ecological footprint was estimated to be 17.5 billion gha, or 2.7 gha per person. Hence the WWF's conclusion that exploitation of the earth's resources exceeds the planet's regenerative capacity by about 30 percent.

At the same time, technological advances do not seem to be sustaining the effective resource stocks of nonrenewable natural resources. In the case of petroleum, evidence suggests that humanity is approaching peak extraction, and future supply of crude oil will prove increasingly difficult to find and more costly to exploit. Of course, technological progress can make new energy sources available, but, to date, there are few convenient alternatives to petroleum. The world's fastest growing emerging economies, including Brazil, China, India, and Russia, are building infrastructures that rapidly increase the use of petroleum products.

Global Warming

There is broad consensus among scientists that the earth's atmosphere is warming, and that **global warming** is caused by human economic activity. *Greenhouse gas (GHG) emissions* come from industry, transport, power generation, and agricultural production. Global warming is the result of (a) human activity that releases GHGs into the atmosphere, which then (b) cause the atmosphere's temperatures to rise. Global warming exposes humanity to potentially very large changes in the earth's climate.

There is some uncertainty over what the consequences of global warming will be for humanity, although scientists do agree that there is a very real possibility that a continuation of current trends in the growth of GHG emissions will, over the next century, jeopardize human life and many other forms of life on earth. There is considerable uncertainty as to exactly how much warming will occur as a result of past and current human activity. This uncertainty is due to the likelihood of delayed **feedback effects** from the initial increase in temperatures caused by the growth of GHG emissions from human industrial and agricultural activities. Scientists are gathering evidence of the release of methane gases from increased melting of the Arctic tundra. There is the fear that there will be less reflection of the sun's heat with the melting of polar ice. Any of these feedback effects could cause a sudden, steep upward spiral of atmospheric temperatures, which could then reach a *tipping point* beyond which stopping global warming will be nearly impossible. The fact that the full consequences of the clearly observable phenomenon of global warming are uncertain is often used by policy makers to justify inaction.

The complexity of global warming is described in many reports by, among others, the OECD (2002), the European Union (2008), and the Intergovernmental Panel on Climate Change (IPCC; 2007). Nicholas Stern, who was commissioned by the British government to report on global warming, describes the process as follows:

> Greenhouse gas emissions are externalities and represent the biggest market failure the world has seen. We all produce emissions, people around the world are already suffering from past emissions, and current emissions will have potentially catastrophic impacts in the future. Thus, these emissions are not ordinary, localized externalities. Risk on a global scale is at the core of the issue. (2008, p. 1)

Global warming is a very troublesome phenomenon for a variety of reasons: it is a global phenomenon whose consequences no country can escape, there is a real possibility that it will have extremely costly, even catastrophic, consequences, and it constitutes an extraordinary failure not only of markets but of humanity in general. Secondary effects from the warming of the atmosphere include rising ocean levels because of the melting of ice in the Arctic, the Antarctic, and mountain glaciers. Entire countries, such as Bangladesh, the Netherlands, and many small island countries, could be submerged. The tropical regions of the earth will become uninhabitable, and droughts and massive flooding will further push millions of people to relocate to other countries and continents. Such population shifts have never occurred without considerable conflict. And if the feedback effects cause an exponential rise in global warming beyond anything experienced on earth for the last 70 million or more years, most living species could perish.

A timely response to the potentially disastrous consequences of global warming has been hindered by the fact that global warming is a very slow process with a great deal of momentum. Scientists attribute the greatest portion of current GHGs to post–World War II industrial production, agricultural expansion, and transportation activities—in short, the past sixty years of economic growth—but this acceleration of GHG emissions is only now beginning to raise atmospheric temperatures. The slow reaction of the climate to GHG accumulation also means that current GHG emissions will not have a noticeable effect on atmospheric temperatures for many years. Therefore, people currently engaged in the activities that cause the release of GHGs into the atmosphere do not see or feel the full consequences of their actions. Their children and grandchildren will experience the full effects of the warming of the atmosphere. A second implication of the long lag between GHG emissions and atmospheric warming is that the warming process will not stop, much less reverse itself, for decades even if humans were to sharply cut their GHG emissions today. Finally, there is still uncertainty about the long-run effects of global warming. These characteristics of **anthropogenic**, or human-made, climate change combine to make it difficult for us to take collective action to mitigate global warming. For these reasons, even though scientific evidence is certain that anthropogenic GHG emissions are rising and atmospheric temperatures have definitely begun increasing, these phenomena are not obvious to most people. And if the difficulty of engaging in abstract thinking is not enough, the fact that measures to stop global warming require very substantial changes in the way industry produces and people live also makes people reluctant to accept the scientific evidence.

Scientific Evidence of Global Warming

Scientists have been aware of the potential for human activity to change the earth's climate for at least 100 years. Joseph Fourier (1827) described how the atmosphere trapped heat from the sun. John Tyndall (1861) identified the types of gases that trapped heat. Svante Arrhenius (1896) calculated the possible effects of a doubling of GHGs. Among the various GHGs is carbon dioxide, which today accounts for between two-thirds and three-fourths of all GHGs in the atmosphere. GHGs include methane, nitrous oxide, and hydrofluorocarbons. These GHGs accumulate in the atmosphere for many years. The length of time that emissions remain in the atmosphere depends on a variety of factors, and some GHGs remain in the air longer than others.

Evidence that the earth's atmosphere is becoming warmer was quite convincing by the early 1980s, and many scientists began to actively urge action to mitigate the consequences of global warming. Furthermore, the evidence on global warming left little doubt that the economic activity of humans was responsible. In 1990, the IPCC, a United Nations–sponsored working group of hundreds of scientists from around the world, issued a report that predicted that the continued growth of carbon emissions from human activities such as industry, coal-fired power plants, automobiles, aircraft, and agricultural development would raise temperatures by 1°C by the year 2030. The report also predicted that current trends would probably double the concentration of carbon in the atmosphere in less than a century, perhaps as early as 2050. It was estimated that such a doubling would eventually raise average temperatures in the world between 1.5 and 4.5°C (3–8°F). Such a rise in temperatures would be unprecedented. Evidence on atmospheric temperatures over the past 800,000 years shows that humanity has never experienced such temperatures. The IPCC's forecasts were based on computer simulation models called *General Circulation Models* (GCMs), which quantify the complex climate system.

The IPCC's 1990 conclusions echoed the warnings issued by James Hansen of NASA's Goddard Institute for Space in testimony before a U.S. Senate committee in 1988. Hansen's testimony before a packed room received widespread coverage in the press and ignited a debate about global warming. Interestingly, twenty years later, Hansen was invited to speak before the House of Representatives' Select Committee on Energy Independence and Global Warming to provide an update on available knowledge about global warming. This time, only one member of the House of Representatives was present, most of the audience consisted of invited guests, and the news media largely ignored the testimony. And yet, our knowledge about global warming is more complete and alarming than it was twenty years ago. Hansen's 2008 testimony followed the 2000 and 2007 updates of the IPCC report on global warming, and presented the latest compilations of research results on climate change. The 2007 IPCC report notes that, since 1987, carbon dioxide emissions have risen by one-third. The report also confirms earlier projections of global warming:

> There is now "visible and unequivocal" evidence of the impacts of climate change, and consensus that human activities have been decisive in the warming observed so far: global average temperatures have risen by about 0.74°C since 1906, and the rise this century is projected to be between 1.8°C and 4°C.

Over the past fifty years, temperatures have risen by 0.13°C per decade, about twice the rate over the fifty years before that. The rate has increased even faster over the past twenty years, and is now estimated to be rising by 0.25°C (0.45°F) per decade. Concentrations of GHGs in the atmosphere are approaching 400 parts per million (ppm), up from less than 280 ppm throughout the past 800,000 years. Concentrations are rising by about 2.5 to 3.0 ppm (carbon equivalent) per year. Methane concentrations, which are many times more potent in capturing the sun's heat in the atmosphere, have more than doubled over the past century. This powerful GHG is still much less prevalent than carbon in the atmosphere, and carbon emissions account for about two-thirds of all GHG emissions globally. The new technique of fracturing shale formations to recover natural gas, which is commonly referred to as fracking, will release much more methane into the atmosphere.[2]

The 2007 IPCC report also discusses potential feedback mechanisms that are likely to accompany the rise in temperatures. For example, the report mentions that some scientists have conducted experiments suggesting that a 2°C rise in temperatures is likely to cause some melting of the permafrost in the Arctic, which would release large amounts of carbon and methane now stored in the frozen ground. Such feedback could, under quite plausible assumptions, accelerate global warming toward an uncontrollable vicious cycle in which warming breeds more warming. Under such a scenario, which was not included in the probabilities in the IPCC report, temperatures could rise by 10°C (18°F) or more. Carbon is also stored in the ocean bottom, and it is not yet clear how much of this carbon will be released into the atmosphere if water temperatures rise, but research suggests that there would be an increase in the amount of carbon released into the water and, eventually, the atmosphere.

The feedback processes are the most difficult to predict, which is why most reports of global warming, such as the IPCC reports and Stern's report, have focused only on the direct consequences of rising GHG emissions. But the possibility of feedback effects certainly increases the risk of permitting the continued growth of GHG emissions.

Stern (2008, p. 5) summarizes the many estimates of global warming and its consequences as follows:

> There seems little doubt that, under BAU [business as usual], the annual increments to stocks would average somewhere well above 3ppm CO_2e [carbon dioxide equivalent], perhaps 4 or more, over the next century. That is likely to take us to around, or well beyond, 750ppm CO_2e by the end of the century. If we manage to stabilize there, that would give us around a 50–50 chance of a stabilization temperature increase above 5°C [9°F].

To stabilize temperatures, the stock of GHGs has to be stabilized. Since current emissions are adding to the stock by nearly 3 ppm per year, GHG emissions have to be reduced. According to Stern (2008), scientific consensus suggests that to stabilize the stock of GHGs at 450 ppm, carbon-equivalent emissions of GHGs will have to be reduced gradually and consistently, starting now, until they reach a level in 2050 that is 70 percent less than their 2007 level. Since the world's population is expected to rise by nearly 50 percent over this period, per capita emissions will have to fall to just 20 percent of today's levels. And if current rates of economic growth continue, emissions per dollar of GDP will have to fall by over 90 percent. This will require large changes in technology and the way humans live. The possibility of uncontrollable global warming triggered by feedback mechanisms has prompted some climatologists and environmentalists to call for a target of 350 ppm by 2050. Even that level would still be above 280 ppm, which was never exceeded by the GHG stock during all of human history until this past century.

Nature's Services: Essential to Economies

According to ecologist Gretchen Daily, "Nature's services are the conditions and processes through which natural ecosystems support and fulfill human life."[3] Because this definition covers essentially all renewable natural resources as well as the great variety of supports nature provides on an ongoing basis, such as soil replenishment and waste recycling, it is useful to categorize these services. Nature's services include:

Provisioning Services. Provisions are the products that nature provides to us directly, such as food, spices, water, air, warmth, vitamin D through sunlight, firewood, and myriad other things that humans usually take for granted. When humans were hunters and gatherers, their existence largely depended directly on nature's services. Today, we still depend on the direct provisions of nature, although our high degree of industrialization and urbanization has separated us at least one stage from most of nature's provisions. Yet even our industrial societies depend on climate, raw materials, energy, scenery, land, and other directly supplied natural products. For example, nine of the top ten pharmaceutical products originated from natural plant species. Most people in poor countries depend directly on nature for fresh food, water, shelter, fuel, and most other products critical to their sustenance.

Regulating Services. Nature regulates our climate, recycles our waste, and maintains our relationships with all other living species. For example, natural forests, oceans, and soils sequester much of the carbon that humans emit into the air with our campfires, automobiles, and power plants. Human waste is converted into fertile soil, minerals, and other organic materials that are again recycled through the ecosystem. Forests and other vegetation help to absorb rain into the ground for storage and later use; they also prevent flooding and soil erosion.

Supporting Services. Nature itself helps to maintain the ecosystem. For example, nature purifies water through evaporation and precipitation; it cleans the air through wind, gravity, precipitation, and carbon capture. Over 100,000 different animal species, such as bats, bees, flies, moths, birds, and butterflies, provide pollination services for foods that comprise one-third of the human diet. Living organisms in nature maintain a diversity and balance that usually (but not always) prevents one species from destroying all others, including humans. For example, nature provides effective pest and disease control by regulating the relative quantities of bacteria, viruses, and other carriers that might infect humans.

Cultural Services. Nature provides the environment in which humans live and create their cultures. In fact, nature helps to shape and preserve those cultures by providing the settings, the natural locations, that groups revere. Natural scenery, warm beaches, and mountains to climb are integral parts of human social and spiritual life. Nature also provides the inspiration for scientific discoveries.

Preserving Services. The diversity and redundancy of the ecosystem provides insurance against future uncertainties.[4] If one species fails, it does not imply an immediate threat to humans because there are many other species that provide similar services and can take up the slack. Some biologists have highlighted the portfolio effect of this diversity; the great variety of living organisms in the ecosystem reduces the risk of instability in the natural environment.[5] It also gives humans more options to live the way they prefer in terms of climate, scenery, and food consumption, for example.

This short set of examples certainly does not exhaust the very broad range of services that nature provides humanity. Since humanity came into being after the ecosystem, or nature, had been providing these and similar services for hundreds of millions, even billions, of years, we tend to take nature's services for granted.

Robert Costanza et al. (1997) estimated that in 1997 the value of the goods and services provided by our natural environment fell somewhere between US$16 trillion and $54 trillion, or a median of $33 trillion, per year. Since measured world GDP for 1997 was about $18 trillion, we can conclude that a full accounting of the value of what nature provides us every year is, on average, perhaps double current measures of world GDP. According to this estimate, the services of the ecosystem are worth more to humans than everything that we produce on earth. Humans provide for only 25 to 50 percent of the goods and services we consume. Our most popular economic measures, such as GDP, do not recognize this, which means that economists, policy makers, and everyone else who has been taught that GDP measures total economic output do not recognize the importance of the ecosystem for human welfare.

These estimates of the value of nature's services are, at best, very rough approximations, and researchers have used a variety of practical methods to calculate them.[6] In some cases, researchers can calculate the cost of services that humans would have to incur in order to provide nature's services, such as waste treatment or water purification, ourselves. In other cases, where the loss of biodiversity (see the following section) has already occurred, researchers can directly calculate the loss of benefits, such as the decline in the catch of ocean fish or the loss of tourist revenue when natural scenery is destroyed. Economists can also indirectly calculate the value of scenery, good climate, and soil quality by looking at how much more people pay for land located in scenic areas, warm climates, and fertile regions than for land in less attractive areas. Health costs associated with deteriorating environments also provide useful information. However, it is very difficult to account for every single natural service that sustains human life.

Economic Activity and the Acceleration of Biodiversity Loss

Global warming is not the only adverse natural phenomenon caused by the growing material consumption of our increasing population. Humanity's growing footprint has also caused an accelerating loss of **biodiversity**. *Biodiversity* refers to the variety of species of plants, animals, and micro-organisms on earth, the genetic variations and differing traits within species, and the way these species coexist within ecosystems.

The process of evolution continually results in species becoming extinct, but economic and population growth over the past century have caused the rate at which individual species are becoming extinct to accelerate precipitously. According to the most conservative estimates, the rate of extinction in the last 100 years was at least 100 times as fast as the long-run rate over the past few million years. Harvard University biologist Edward O. Wilson (2002) estimates the true rate is probably 1,000 to 10,000 times the historical rate. Andrew Balmford and William Bond (2005) survey the entire scientific literature on species loss, and they conclude that extinctions are occurring at rates several hundred times as fast as in the past. They also conclude that the cause of the acceleration is the growth of the human population to 7 billion as well as its per capita increase in consumption and, therefore, in its use of nature's services.

Wilson's estimate varies so much because scientists have distinguished only about 1.5 million species of living organisms, while educated guesses suggest there are probably as many as 100 million species on our planet. We can only tabulate the extinctions of those species that we monitor carefully, which are just a very small fraction of the 1.5 million species that scientists have identified and classified. Scientific estimates of the loss of biodiversity, therefore, are based on a minute sample of the unknown total number of species living on earth. As is the case for all sampling methods, the full picture can be presented only as broad ranges of possible outcomes.

Humanity's growing footprint is altering the populations of many other living organisms on earth. More space for humans means less space for other animals and plants. For example, the development of agriculture, which played such a large role in the growth of the human population, necessarily replaced diverse natural forests, grasslands, and wetlands with areas devoted to growing a small number of food crops. Modern agricultural enterprises have extended the practice of **monoculture** to most countries of the world. Monoculture, also referred to as *industrial farming,* is the practice of planting single crops across extensive regions in order to make the use of large equipment economical and to exploit the use of certain species of crops and animals. Most of the world now grows the same small number of varieties of corn, wheat, rice, fruits, and vegetables and raises the same small number of species of cows, pigs, chickens, and sheep.

The benefits of monoculture are, allegedly, that the most efficient plants and animals are grown and raised. This suggested gain in efficiency has been widely referred to as the *Green Revolution,* and it has been credited for humanity's ability to avoid starvation despite the growth of world population from 2.5 billion in 1950 to about 7 billion in 2010. The benefits of monoculture have been greatly overstated, however. There is evidence that in developing countries, small farms are at least as efficient as large farms. More intensive small-scale farming achieves the highest levels of productivity, all other things equal.[7] At the same time, the efficiency gains from genetic engineering have, in fact, been shown to be negative. Genetically engineered crops have certain advantages, such as increased resistance to certain pests or to drought, but, overall, their output per acre has not been larger than that of conventional crops. Also, a number of crops produced on large-scale farms have less nutritional value than their natural counterparts.[8]

In addition to making life more difficult for many other living species, the human destruction of biodiversity endangers our own existence. Despite the impressive technologies humans have developed, we are still dependent on nature's many services for our existence. Biodiversity provides a type of insurance against the future extinctions of individual species. A good example of how the loss of biodiversity endangers humans is the Irish potato blight of 1846. One evolved pest destroyed the Irish potato crop, which consisted entirely of a few very closely related species of potatoes, the only major source of nutrition. Over 1 million Irish died of starvation. Today, genetic engineering and cloning could make animal species so nearly identical across the world that one type of new bacteria or virus could wipe out a huge portion of the world's meat or dairy supplies. Specially bred or engineered animals and crops increasingly provide critical inputs for industrial products or the raw materials for pharmaceutical products. The loss of biodiversity means that, like nineteenth-century Ireland, human society is again putting most of its eggs in one basket.

No Sense of Urgency among Policy Makers

As with global warming, specific estimates of the acceleration of the rate of the decline in biodiversity are uncertain. But also as with global warming, scientists are almost certain that the process is real and that it will have adverse effects on humanity's well-being. The trends in climate change and biodiversity are truly alarming. Yet, the world's leaders failed to reach an agreement to take action at the United Nations' Copenhagen climate conference at the end of 2009. In fact, President Barack Obama of the United States, the country that has contributed more CO_2 emissions than any other country, explicitly refused to agree to specific country goals for reducing emissions. He pushed through a much weaker proposal under which each country remained free to shape its own response to climate change. The collective action needed to stop or mitigate climate change did not happen. This conference was expected to bring the signing of a new international agreement to replace the Kyoto Protocol that had specified countries' actions to reduce carbon emissions only through 2012. Apparently, the global economic recession and the slow economic recovery seemed to have pushed long-run issues such as global warming to the back of the queue. In 2010, a United Nations–sponsored meeting on species depletion brought agreement on some specific goals, but they were relatively modest. The question is why it is so difficult for national governments to cooperate on these very large issues.

POLICY MAKING UNDER UNCERTAINTY

Designing policies to stop global warming or to mitigate its effects is complicated by the uncertainty of how much the higher greenhouse gas (GHG) concentrations in the atmosphere will actually change the climate. The direction of change is clear, but there is still debate over how the rest of the natural environment, and humanity in particular, will be affected in the future. Also, we are not sure how humans will cope with the warmer climate and their altered natural environment. Similarly, in the case of biodiversity losses, we can clearly see the direction of the trends, but since we monitor only a small percentage of all living species, we do not know exactly how many are affected by the human footprint or how their future fate will interact with the rest of the ecosystem. Economist and statistician Robert Pindyck (2007, abstract) states the situation faced by economists analyzing environmental issues as follows:

> In a world of certainty, the design of environmental policy is relatively straightforward, and boils down to maximizing the present value of the flow of social benefits minus costs. But the real world is one of considerable uncertainty—over the physical and ecological impact of pollution, over the economic costs and benefits of reducing it, and over the discount rates that should be used to compute present values. The implications of uncertainty are complicated by the fact that most environmental policy problems involve highly nonlinear damage functions, important reversibilities, and long time horizons.

So, what should policy be in the case of a certainly damaging but potentially catastrophic natural outcome?

Risk versus Uncertainty

First, recall the difference between **risk** and **uncertainty**, discussed in Chapter 13 in the context of financial uncertainty. Risk is what insurance companies normally deal with, namely a set of potential outcomes with well-defined probabilities that permit us to calculate expected values and state the likelihood that a future outcome will fall within a specific range of possible outcomes. Uncertainty is what we face with global warming and the loss of biodiversity: we are not sure of the probabilities with which each of the possible outcomes will occur in the future. Uncertainty also implies that we do not even have a reasonable grasp of all the possible outcomes. Many policy makers seem to be saying, perhaps not in their words but certainly in their actions, that uncertainty mandates that we wait to act until we learn more. That is probably not the right decision in the cases of global warming and biodiversity loss.

Martin L. Weitzman (2007) notes that when there is uncertainty about the probability distribution of some possible outcome, the estimated probability distribution becomes flatter and with "fatter" tails. To understand what Weitzman means, look first at Figure 20.3. This diagram shows a distribution of outcomes characterized by the standard normal distribution function $f(x)$, a function you will be familiar with if you have taken an elementary statistics course. The normal distribution is centered on the mean outcome μ, and nearly all outcomes fall between the mean and plus or minus three standard deviations, σ, from the mean. The standard deviation is simply the average difference between the average outcome and an actual observed outcome.

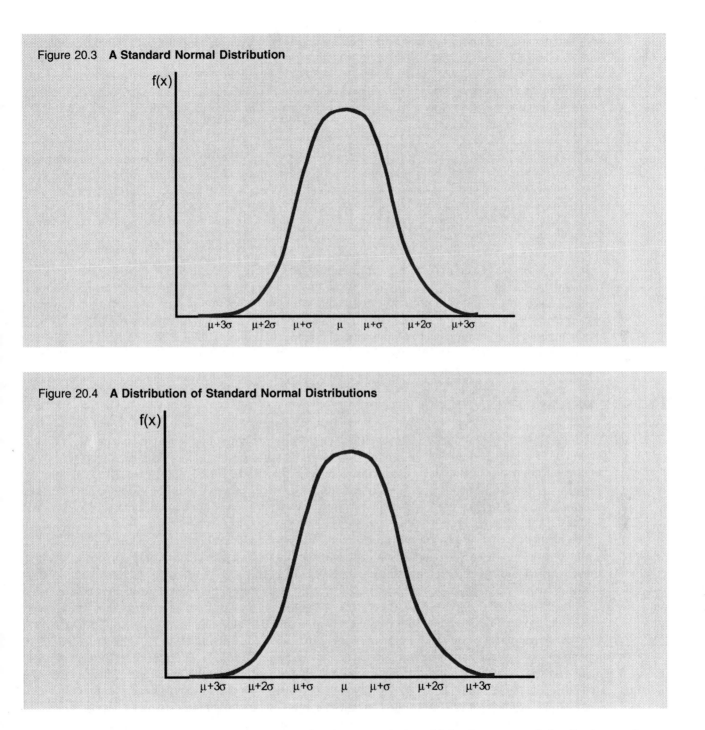

Figure 20.3   **A Standard Normal Distribution**

Figure 20.4   **A Distribution of Standard Normal Distributions**

Now suppose that we are not certain about precisely which of a group of distributions a future outcome will lie on. Figure 20.4 shows a "distribution of distributions" as well as an "aggregate distribution" that includes all possible outcomes across all of the possible distributions. Notice how the aggregate distribution has "fatter" tails than any individual normal distribution. That means that extreme outcomes are relatively more likely when there is uncertainty about the precise location of the distribution. For example, for the normal distribution centered on μ, there is virtually no chance that an outcome lying more than three standard deviations from the expected mean will occur. But with the uncertainty about the exact location of the distribution of outcomes, an outcome that lies four standard deviations from the expected mean clearly has a substantial likelihood of occurring, as evidenced by the distance between the thicker aggregate distribution and the horizontal axis at $\mu+4\sigma$ and $\mu4\sigma$. In short, as the Oxford University economist Paul Klemperer writes, "The continuing scientific uncertainty about the pace of climate change should make us more concerned, not less."[9] According to Weitzman (2007):

> The tiny probabilities of nightmare impacts of climate change are all such crude ballpark estimates that there is a tendency . . . to dismiss them on the "scientific" grounds that they are much too highly speculative to be taken seriously because they are statistically indistinguishable from zero. . . . [T]he exact opposite is in fact true . . . the more speculative and fuzzy are the tiny tail probabilities of high-impact extreme events, the less ignorable and the more serious is the situation for an agent whose welfare is measured by present discounted expected utility.

In his study, Weitzman assumes a common intertemporal welfare function to show that, under a variety of plausible discount rates, catastrophic environmental events with very small likelihoods should be actively avoided so long as abatement costs are no more than a few percent of the value of human life. Current estimates are that the costs of lowering carbon emissions back to historical levels are not more than 2 percent of annual global GDP, which is just a small fraction of any reasonable estimate of the value of all human life on earth. This leads Weitzman to reject the wait-and-see approach to global warming.

The Cost of Controlling Global Warming

The Intergovernmental Panel on Climate Change (2007) estimated that it would cost between 1 and 2 percent of world GDP to reduce greenhouse gas emissions enough to avoid global warming, and the Stern Report (2007) also suggests a cost of 1 percent of GDP for mitigating the effects of global warming. In 2008, Stern increased his cost estimate to closer to 2 percent of global GDP because updated evidence suggested that global warming was progressing more rapidly than scientists had thought a few years earlier.

The costs of stopping global warming include a variety of changes to human activity on earth. About two-thirds of the GHGs that we put into the atmosphere are from energy use in industry, transportation, agriculture, and heating and cooling our homes and buildings. The remaining GHGs are the result of waste management and the destruction of forests and other natural environments as we convert more land to our needs. Therefore, switching to new sources of energy that emit fewer GHGs can reduce GHGs. For example, we can replace coal-fueled electricity generation with solar, wind, water, and less-polluting natural gas. The ultimate costs of reducing GHG emissions will also depend on how well humans develop new technologies that improve the ratio of output relative to GHG-emitting inputs in generating energy, powering transportation, and producing industrial output. Part of the cost of reducing GHG emissions consists of shifting demand to products that require less energy input, such as more energy-efficient homes, more efficient appliances, more vegetarian diets, smaller and more efficient automobiles, and public transportation. Costs also include conservation, such as maintaining forests that absorb carbon, storing water, and protecting living species that provide valuable services to humanity or form critical links in the ecological system. Of course, any serious plan to reduce GHG emissions must also include changes in lifestyles and some reductions in material consumption. These measures will not be easy, which suggests that, in economic terms, they will be costly. But given the evidence that in the long run people are not much happier with more material consumption, welfare may not be much affected by modest changes in material consumption, especially if it is offset with more leisure and social activities.

Figure 20.5 The McKinsey Report Diagram of Global Warming Abatement Costs

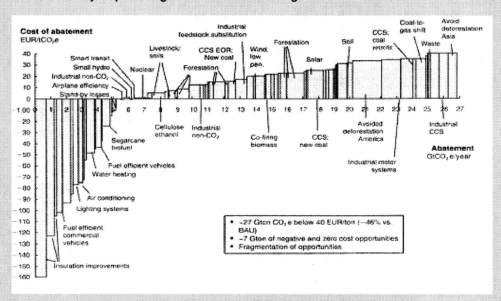

Source: Per-Anders Enkvist, Tomas Nauclér, and Jerker Rosander (2007), "A Cost Curve for Greenhouse Gas Reduction," the *McKinsey Quarterly*, 2007, no. 1, pp. 35–45.

Not all of the measures to reduce GHG emissions will have an economic cost, however. For example, raising the efficiency of automobile engines, improving insulation in buildings and homes, and replacing incandescent lightbulbs save us much more than the initial purchase cost. It seems that humans are locked into many habits that make no economic sense at all. Figure 20.5 presents a diagram that shows that a substantial portion of the measures needed to reduce GHG emissions to levels that will stabilize GHGs at 550 ppm (parts per million) are not net costs. The gains from measures that actually reduce costs and the positive costs related to other necessary measures sum to about 1 percent of world GDP.

As you contemplate Figure 20.5, keep in mind that it assumes the optimal mitigation strategy is to limit the rise in GHGs in the atmosphere to 550 ppm. Bill McKibben (2008) argues for bringing the concentration of GHGs back to 350 ppm in order to avoid triggering potential feedback mechanisms. Figure 20.5 assumes that we need to reduce average annual emissions by 27 carbon-equivalent gigatons in order to stabilize emissions at 550 ppm by 2050. The prospective projects and measures are shown from left to right from the least costly (most profitable) to the most costly. The cost of each project or measure is given on the vertical axis on the left. If we wanted to stabilize carbon emissions at a lower level, obviously we would have to move to more costly projects, and total costs would rise, possibly at an increasing rate. Again, it is very difficult to predict the future course of technological change and, therefore, the precise costs of stabilizing the earth's temperatures at any given level, but it seems reasonable at this point that mitigating global warming will cost us about 2 percent of annual GDP. The safer goals of GHG stabilization at 350 ppm or 250 ppm will cost somewhat more than that.

The Cost of Stopping Biodiversity Loss

Biodiversity loss is not any easier to deal with than anthropogenic climate change. Protection of biodiversity seems to clash directly with economic and population growth. Most of the damage to the ecosystem comes from modern agriculture, but agriculture is fundamental to human existence. Most people, and their governments, are reluctant to restrict the production of food. This is why most governments, in fact, subsidize agriculture. Yet, the environmental costs of monoculture, chemical fertilizers and pesticides, and contained animal-feeding operations are certainly large.

Agriculture's carbon and methane emissions and the substantial reductions in earth's biodiversity are now recognized. GHG emissions from other sources, and the global warming they cause, also contribute to the loss of plant and animal species. Carbon directly affects living organisms because global warming affects the earth's climate, which in turn affects the survival, or demise, of living organisms. When carbon dioxide is released into the air, about a third soon ends up in the oceans. When the CO_2 dissolves in water, it forms a weak acid and increases the acidity of the oceans. If the current growth of carbon emissions continues, the acidity of the oceans will increase enough to push many marine organisms into extinction before the end of this century. The earth will lose its reef-building corals, for example. Stern (2007), the *Stern Report,* projects a loss of 1 million species over the next fifty years if global warming progresses as predicted under "business as usual."

At the same time, the loss of plant and animal species affects global warming. Forests, prairies, and oceans are important carbon sinks, and their decline will increase the amount of carbon released into the atmosphere. In other words, biodiversity loss and global warming are each other's feedback effects. In short, the cost of losing biodiversity could be very large. But the cost of stopping this loss is perceived to be rather high. It will be interesting to see how governments balance the economic importance of food production with the future costs of the loss of biodiversity.

Why Is It So Hard to Insure Against Environmental Disaster?

How much should humans be willing to pay to insure our future existence or the existence of our grandchildren? To estimate such a number, we first need to define the value of our existence. As Kip Viscusi's (1993) survey of various studies of the value of life concludes, economists and the courts have put the value of a human life in the United States at about $7 million, on average, in 2010 dollars. Since average per capita GDP in the United States is about $45,000, a human life there is worth about $150 per dollar of per capita GDP. We can extend this value to the whole world if we recognize that global average per capita GDP in 2010 was about $10,000 and there were nearly 7 billion people. Therefore, the total value of human life on earth is equal to 7 billion people x $10,000 x $150, or about $10 quadrillion (that is 10 million billion). This amount is 7,500 times annual world GDP of $67 trillion. Hence, if we must spend 1–2 percent of GDP per year to stop global warming, individuals are effectively being asked to make a payment between $13 and $25 to insure an asset of $100,000 against an uncertain possibility of total loss. People spend much more than that to insure their homes and cars, the losses of which would not threaten their survival. So far, however, people seem reluctant to demand their governments spend such a small premium to insure the future of humanity. Why is that?

The following quote from F. Scott Fitzgerald's novel *The Great Gatsby* (1925, pp. 187–188) may provide one clue:

> I couldn't forgive him or like him but I saw that what he had done was, to him, entirely justified. It was all very careless and confused. They were careless people . . . they smashed up things and creatures and then retreated back into their money or their vast carelessness, or whatever it was that kept them together, and let other people clean up the mess they had made.

That is, the wealthy, who wield power in most societies, are disproportionately responsible for damaging the ecosystem because of their excessive consumption. But they can use their wealth to protect themselves from this damage, and to shield themselves from seeing the suffering they have caused to others. The poor, who consume much less, do suffer the consequences. Says a representative for the Maasai tribe in Kenya, who lost 5 million cattle to drought in the first decade of the twenty-first century: "The Maasai community does not drive 4x4s or fly off on holidays in airplanes. We have not caused climate change, yet we are the ones suffering."[10] The French journalist Hervé Kempf (2007) invokes Thorstein Veblen's *Theory of the Leisure Class* (1899) to point out that the high levels of consumption, and environmental damage, by the wealthy are multiplied by middle-class consumers who seek to emulate the wealthy class's resource-using consumption patterns. Can the wealthy United States, which produces the greatest share of the GHGs in the atmosphere and whose culture and corporations stimulate mass consumption around the world, continue its consumption while refusing to contribute to the costs of mitigating the global warming and species depletion its behavior helped to cause?

ECONOMIC GROWTH AND THE ENVIRONMENT

Solow's neoclassical model of economic growth, presented in Chapter 6, predicts that, over the long run, economic growth can continue only as long as there is technological progress to offset the diminishing returns to capital. Indeed, over the past two hundred years, an acceleration of technological change overcame diminishing returns to capital. This apparent victory of human ingenuity over diminishing returns has led many economists, social scientists, and political leaders, and most everyone else, to expect GDP to continue growing in the future. After all, there is no obvious limit to the human mind's ability to develop new ideas.

Financial Times feature writer Richard Tomkins (2003) looks back further than two hundred years, however, and suggests that some skepticism may be in order:

> In the industrialized west, we assume that the "normal" rate of economic growth is 2–3 per cent a year because it is what we have experienced in our lifetimes. For most of human history, however, "normal"—in terms of per capita growth—has meant more or less zero.

Are the past two hundred years indeed nothing more than a brief exception, a special episode that will soon end? Or is humanity now on a new, permanently steeper growth path?

To answer such questions, we must first analyze how we have been able to generate the recent technological advances that have enabled human society to avoid diminishing returns to the expansion of factories, farms, and cities. As suggested by Schumpeter's model of technological change, the fact that we overcame diminishing returns to capital means that humans were somehow motivated to employ enough resources toward research and development activities to generate the necessary productivity gains. Second, we have to understand the potential barriers to continued output growth in the future. Below we develop an augmented Solow model that illustrates the environmental obstacles humans face in continuing twentieth-century growth rates.

Nature as the Next Source of Diminishing Returns

Recall the Solow growth model introduced in Chapter 6, which related output to investment in capital. There are, of course, other productive variables that go into the economy's aggregate production function. For example, natural resources are inputs in most productive processes. If natural resources cannot be expanded, then there will be diminishing returns to increases in the other productive factors like capital.

Natural resources consist of both *nonrenewable,* or **exhaustible**, resources and *renewable* resources, or what we are calling *nature's services.* Humanity's exploitation of renewable natural resources is not unrelated to its exploitation of exhaustible resources. In fact, Jeffrey Krautkraemer

(1998) argues that nature's capacity to supply services such as carbon sinks, clean water, and fertile soils is directly endangered by the use of polluting exhaustible resources such as carbon fuels. The finite nature of exhaustible resources like carbon fuels may thus be a less pressing issue than the deterioration of the ecosystem that provides nature's renewable resources. Krautkraemer suggests we are likely to destroy ourselves with climate change long before the oil runs out. In short, the capacity of the ecosystem to supply its services and finite exhaustible resources is likely to be a source of diminishing returns in the economy. In the following section, by expanding the Solow model to explicitly include both nature and the economy that the Solow model traditionally represents, we illustrate how the limited capacity of nature affects the economy.

A Two-Sector Solow Growth Model

Suppose that the economy, or in terms of Figure 20.1, the economic sphere of human existence, is represented in the Solow model by the production function

$$(20.1) \qquad\qquad Y = f(K \times E_K, S \times E_S)$$

in which output is produced using capital, K, and renewable resources, S. The E's represent factor-specific technologies, so that the production function shows the *effective* stock of physical capital, $K \times E_K$, and nature's *effective* capacity to generate its services, $S \times E_S$. We explicitly include technologies in our model in order to be able, potentially, to generate the economic growth illustrated in Figure 6.6 of Chapter 6. The effective supply of a resource is equal to the ultimate benefit its use in production yields, so that an improvement in technology increases the effective stock of a physical resource. Also, we assume that the quantities of other resources, like labor, are fixed. Ominously, this extension of the Solow model will make it clear that despite including technology, the limits in the natural sphere of human existence can prevent even technological progress in the economy from sustaining economic growth.

We can illustrate this version of the Solow model in a three-dimensional diagram, with Y on one axis and K and S on the other two axes. Or, we can break our analysis down into two parts, each consisting of two dimensions. The latter approach is more convenient given that we are limited to two dimensions on the pages of this book. We begin with the *natural* dimension of the model, in which output Y is related to the amount of nature's services S. Then we will also show the Solow model with its traditional *economic* dimension, in which output Y is related to the stock of capital K. Both physical capital and the ecosystem are subject to depreciation, but the depreciation function in the ecosystem is clearly not linear as we assumed for the orthodox Solow model.

The services that the ecosystem provides are gradually replenished after humans make use of them. Therefore, the quantity of nature's services is limited by nature's capacity to replenish. For example, if humanity's economic output puts CO_2 into the air faster than the natural system can dissipate it, then the atmosphere deteriorates and the benefits provided by the natural climatic conditions diminish. Similarly, if human production uses water faster than natural processes replenish the water, then less water will be available in the future. A notable example is the shrinking of the Aral Sea in Central Asia to one-third its original size after irrigation projects diverted too much water.

The more intensively humans use renewable resources, the more likely that nature will not be able to keep up and humans will need to carry out costly conservation efforts to support and restore nature's capacity to provide its services. Conservation involves such things as planting trees, stocking rivers with fish, repairing shorelines and beaches, filtering waste water, using catalytic converters on automobile exhaust systems, et cetera. If humanity increasingly stresses nature without engaging in the necessary conservation efforts to sustain the ecosystem, the ecosystem's capacity to provide services declines.

Figure 20.6 shows the natural sphere of the economy. The production function in the natural sphere has a diminishing slope under the assumption that there are diminishing returns to inputs of

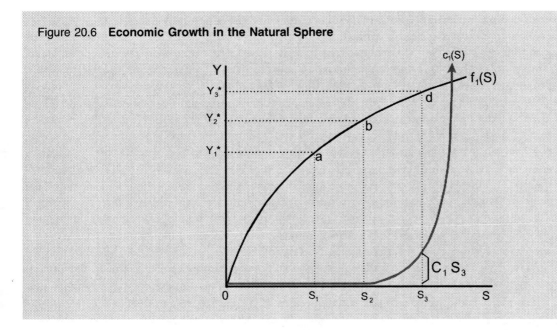

Figure 20.6 **Economic Growth in the Natural Sphere**

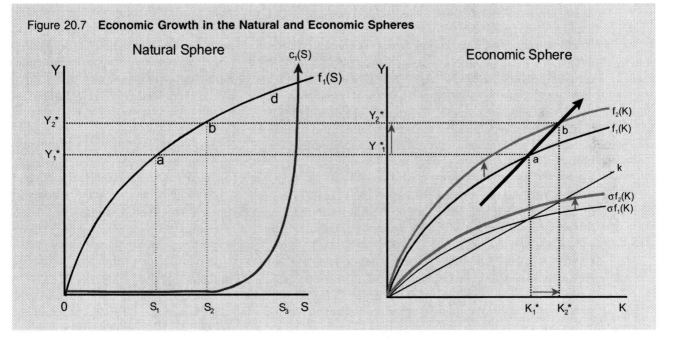

Figure 20.7 **Economic Growth in the Natural and Economic Spheres**

natural resources, all other inputs remaining the same. There is also a "depreciation" function, which we call the **conservation function**, in recognition of the need to engage in explicit conservation activities to prevent a reduction in nature's capacity to provide renewable services. For example, if a farmer does not rotate his crops to restore nutrients to the soil, the soil will lose its fertility and the effective supply of soil will decline.

The conservation function is not a linear function, as Solow assumed for physical capital. Nature's capacity to provide its services may not be stressed at all at low levels of use, say between the levels of human economic output between Y_1 and Y_2 in Figure 20.6. Nature can increase its services from S_1 to S_2 at virtually zero marginal cost. However, when human society increases its economic output to Y_3, there is a noticeable stress on the natural ecosystem. Conservation activities with an economic cost of $c(S_3) > 0$ are required to sustain such resource use. There is an obvious maximization problem here: if the marginal cost of conservation is greater than the marginal gain in output, then human production is not welfare maximizing.

Figure 20.7 presents the complete "holistic" Solow model with the natural and economic spheres depicted side by side. First, suppose that in the economic sphere technological progress increases output from Y_1 to Y_2 by moving the economy to a new steady state that requires an increase in the capital stock from K_1 to K_2. This holistic version of the Solow model in Figure 20.7 shows that such an increase in output also requires increased inputs of natural services such as rainfall, oxygen, dissipation of air pollutants, absorption of water runoff, et cetera. Specifically, in the left-hand diagram, the rise in output from Y_1 to Y_2 requires no additional conservation costs because the conservation cost curve is horizontal. The ecosystem's capacity has not been reached, and sufficient services of nature are forthcoming for economic output to rise to Y_2.

Now, suppose that the incentives for innovation in the economic sphere are high and humanity develops new technologies that push the economy to an even higher steady state. But suppose, also, that humanity does not see the sharply rising conservation cost curve in the left-hand-side diagram. Figure 20.8 illustrates what the consequences of further growth in the economic dimension will be.

Another shift in the production function to $f_3(K)$ increases output from Y_2 to Y_3, and, ignorant of the environmental consequences, the economy implicitly assumes that the required natural services will be available for the taking as usual. The conservation cost curve shows, however, that sustaining the use of nature's services when exploitation rises above S_2 requires costly conservation activities—air pollution controls, water purification plants, soil conservation, irrigation projects, recycling, et cetera. Since output Y_3 requires nature's services equal to S_3, if the conservation efforts costing $c_1(S_3)$ are not undertaken, the higher use of resources will destroy some of nature's capacity to provide its services in the future. In this case, at output Y_3 the net domestic product (NDP), which is the economic output minus the loss of natural resources, is less than Y_3.

Suppose that, indeed, the required expenditures of $c_1(S_3)$ are not undertaken because humanity prefers to ignore the required conservation costs. This causes the conservation curve, which reflects the cost of nature's services, to shift to the left, as shown in Figure 20.9. The decline in nature's capacity to provide its renewable resources also causes the production function shown in the economic dimension to decline, since any reduction in one of the inputs not shown in the two dimensions of the economic sphere shifts the economic production function downward.

Notice, however, that the decline in production is not a one-time phenomenon if decisions in the economic sphere continue to ignore the consequences of economic activity on the natural sphere. Because of the deterioration of nature's productive capacity and the leftward shift of the conservation curve, costly conservation activities are now necessary at levels of exploitation of nature's services below S_2, the level at which nature used to be able to replenish itself without human help. If human society now engages in real conservation activities costing $c_2(S_2)$, there will be further deterioration of nature's capacity to provide water, air, solar heat, carbon sinks, flood control, et cetera. But to restore the ecosystem back to its former capacity, conservation in excess of $c_2(S_2)$ will be necessary. Of course, if the natural sphere is still ignored, perhaps because there is no price on nature's services or governments do not regulate the use of nature's services, then the downward spiral of environmental deterioration will continue.

In this latter case, the environmental devastation in the natural sphere causes the production function in the economic sphere to fall back to $f_2(K)$, and output thus falls back to Y_2. And unless society begins to engage in conservation activities equal to $c_2(S_2)$, there will be further decline in nature's services, reflected in the leftward shift in the conservation cost curve to $c_3(S_3)$. Output

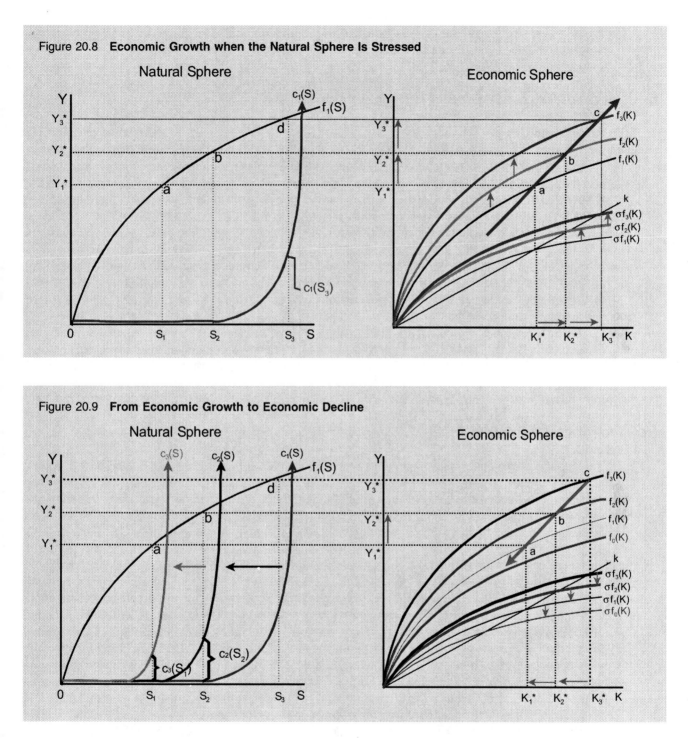

Figure 20.8   Economic Growth when the Natural Sphere Is Stressed

Natural Sphere

Economic Sphere

Figure 20.9   From Economic Growth to Economic Decline

Natural Sphere

Economic Sphere

in the economic sphere will fall further, perhaps back to Y_1. When the economic decline reduces society's use of nature's services to S_1, even that formerly sustainable level of exploitation of nature's services now requires costly conservation in order to prevent the ecosystem's capacity from deteriorating further. If only society had left "good enough" alone at Y_2! It now takes a considerable effort to reverse the damage and resume a sustainable rate of economic development. The lesson here is that the decline in nature's services diminishes the production function in the economic sphere. Investment falls because the environmental disaster reduces the production function, income, and saving. The capital stock in the economic sphere thus declines to a lower steady state.

The Need for Technological Change in Both Spheres

Recall from Chapter 6 how the Solow model made it very clear that, in the face of diminishing returns and real costs to maintain constantly depreciating capital stocks, continued growth in output is possible only if there is technological progress that enables producers to get more output out of a given set of inputs. This conclusion also holds when the natural environment is included in the Solow model. Figure 20.10 illustrates that, had there been improvements in how human society transforms nature's renewable resources into output, output could have increased to Y_3 without triggering a devastating collapse of output. Specifically, if technological progress had shifted nature's effective production function out from $f_1(S)$ to $f_2(S)$ in the natural sphere in tandem with the shift from $f_2(K)$ to $f_3(K)$ in the economic sphere, then output could have increased to Y_3 without requiring any additional use of nature's services beyond S_2. Hence, the two-dimensional Solow model shows that technological change in both spheres can keep society's stress on the ecosystem at levels where nature can sustain its services.

The Solow model's concepts of diminishing returns, balanced growth of effective resources, the existence of a steady state, the need to maintain society's stocks of productive resources, and technological change are quite appropriate within the holistic multisphere perspective. The model has much to say about sustainable development when it is applied to all spheres of human existence rather than just the economic sphere.

The Two-Sector Model's Insights

The enhanced two-sphere Solow model suggests that when economic activity pressures the natural environment, the cost of maintaining nature's services accelerates in nonlinear fashion. First, up to a certain level, economic growth does not damage the ecosystem's capacity to provide its crucial services to humanity. Nature is strong and resilient, but at some point the human footprint becomes large enough to do damage and explicit conservation activities are called for. Or, as Figure 20.10 suggests, humanity can do things differently and find better technologies for producing what it needs and wants more efficiently. But such changes will not happen if humanity ignores the damage it is doing.

Humanity's social and economic institutions, everything from its informal culture to its formal legal institutions, are not set up to induce its investors, producers, and consumers to take account of what happens in the natural sphere. The slow-moving changes in biodiversity and the lagging momentum of climate change only make it more likely that humans will not recognize the damage their economic growth is doing to the natural environment. In fact, humans are indeed failing to either make the investments in conservation to prevent a deterioration in the ecosystem's capacity to provide its services or to generate the necessary new ideas, new knowledge, or new technologies that increase the efficiency with which the economies of the world use natural resources and nature's services. Recall the estimate by Mathis Wackernagel et al. (2002) and the more recent update from the World Wildlife Fund (2008) that humanity's use of the nature's services has grown to 130 percent of capacity. The advance of climate change and the loss of biodiversity discussed in the previous sections describe in more detail two areas where the growing number of humans and the rise in our per capita production of material goods and services are damaging the ecosystem that provides natural services that we need for our existence. The worst-case scenario illustrated above with the enhanced two-sphere Solow model is now actually being played out. Does humanity,

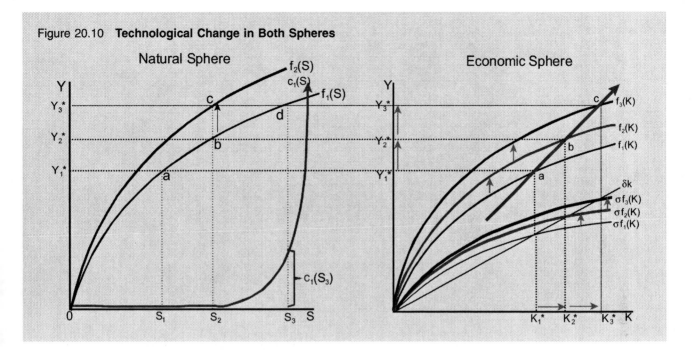

Figure 20.10   **Technological Change in Both Spheres**

therefore, face the prospect of declining real incomes, a complete reversal of the human experience over the past two hundred years?

Environmental Costs and Economic Growth

Business leaders often argue that environmental regulations, restrictions on carbon emissions, pollution controls, protection of endangered species, and other environmental regulations will slow economic growth. These arguments can be understood using the logic of the two-dimensional Solow model above, which suggests that sustainable growth across all three spheres of human existence will likely result in slower growth in the economic sphere. Therefore, those who look only at the economic sphere are indeed correct in fearing that efforts to deal with environmental damage will cause the growth of material output to decline. The narrow economic focus also suggests there is little cause for alarm about the future sustainability of economic growth. In most high-income countries, GDP growth seems to have been sufficient to cover the depreciation of the physical capital stock in the economic sphere. Also, the potential for future profits seems to have motivated enough costly research and development to continually shift the production function higher in economic sphere. But the narrow focus on the economic sphere ignores the environmental and social costs.

Figure 20.11 illustrates a potential path of sustainable development. The economy moves to an equilibrium at output Y_4, which is greater than Y_2 but smaller than Y_3. Y_4 is the result of a slower rate of technological change in the economic sphere, where the production function shifts only as far as $f_4(K)$. It is also the result of a lower rate of saving applied in the economic sphere, one that supports only the level of capital investment K_2^*. This lower production and investment in the economic sphere frees up savings to generate enough innovation in the natural sphere either to shift the production function down from $f_2(S)$ to $f_4(S)$ in the economic sphere or to cover the conservation cost $c_1(S)$ in the natural sphere. In sum, by diverting resources toward actions that mitigate environmental degradation, GDP grows more slowly. But this slower rate of growth in the economic sphere is sustainable because costs in both the economic and natural spheres are covered.

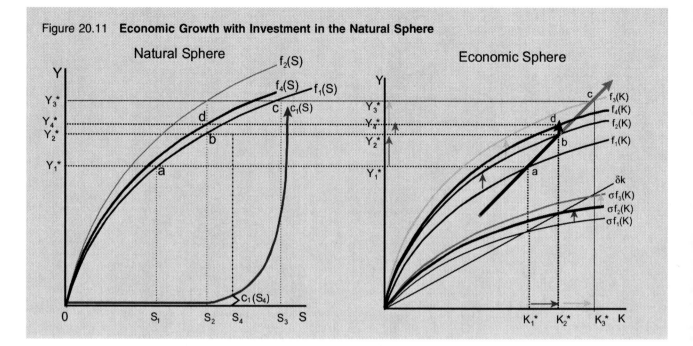

Figure 20.11 **Economic Growth with Investment in the Natural Sphere**

Will humanity indeed save more, consume less, conserve the ecosystem, and innovate in both spheres in order to achieve sustainable growth to Y_4? There may be resistance by those who view their existence as taking place exclusively in the economic sphere because the growth of output in the economic sphere will not be as fast. Because business culture focuses only on a bottom line that depends on outcomes in the economic sphere, such shortsighted business opposition to environmental policies is to be expected. Holism suggests that, for the well-being of humanity, such resistance must be overcome; otherwise, there will be a collapse in economic output as in the example of Figure 20.9.

The Political Economy of Environmental Policy

In 2010, the United States remained one of just two countries that had not ratified the Kyoto Protocol. It had failed to pass even a modest law, known as the Lieberman-Warner Climate Security Act, that provided for a mere 4 to 6 percent reduction in 2020 GHG emissions from 1990 levels. This contrasts with the European Union and individual European countries, which committed to much greater reductions.

There seems to be a political consensus across countries that, if carbon emissions are to be restricted, such restrictions should use a scheme called **cap and trade**. Such schemes consist of setting a specific emissions limit and then issuing permits to emit that can be freely traded. Under cap and trade, those emitters who can find cheaper alternatives to purchasing carbon permits will thus be motivated to invest in those alternative technologies. Only those who find it most costly to convert to other methods and technologies would be willing to pay for the permits. Many environmentalists oppose cap and trade schemes, however.

First of all, cap and trade establishes an effective property right over the atmosphere, and human nature suggests such property rights will not be easily surrendered once granted. If the rights to emit carbon are awarded to firms and countries according to current emissions, as has been the case for those few cap and trade schemes that have been implemented, then a cap and trade system effectively constitutes what the environmental organization Rising Tide calls a "massive resource grab." The commons would be privatized, and it would be unequally distributed to those with the greatest wealth. And since the wealthy nations emit the most carbon, such a privatization would benefit the rich countries most.[11]

Another fear about cap and trade is that the market for carbon permits would be unstable and, therefore, fail to provide clear incentives for firms to invest in alternative energy systems, conservation, and new products. Also, if prices fluctuate unpredictably, as they are likely to do for the same reasons that financial markets in general fluctuate in unpredictable ways, consumers will be less decisive in changing their consumption patterns.

Furthermore, there are fears about how the carbon markets will be operated. Will they turn into typical financial markets, where speculators and gamblers dominate short-term trading, much like they do in stock and foreign exchange markets? Will the world's financial firms run the carbon markets as over-the-counter markets that they manipulate for their own profit?

Most worrisome is how carbon permits would be allocated and their overall quantities determined. The recent experience of the European Union is sobering. Early in the 2000s, the EU initiated a cap and trade scheme and promptly issued so many permits that their price fell to near zero, thus failing to motivate any change in behavior by producers or consumers. Also, the issuing of carbon permits requires a rather elaborate monitoring system to keep track of who emits how much carbon, reconciles the emissions with the permits issued, and punishes violations. Critics of cap and trade correctly foresee massive violations, corruption, and large-scale failures in government oversight.

Overall, a **carbon tax** is much simpler than a cap and trade scheme. Most carbon fuels are already taxed, and providers of carbon fuels are concentrated and easily identified. Much like the way transport costs are shared by exporters and importers, explained in Chapter 5, the carbon tax is effectively shared by users and producers as prices paid by end users rise, prices received by suppliers fall, and the quantity transacted falls. Also, a tax can be more easily adjusted in the face of shifts in supply and demand in order to maintain the long-run target prices needed to motivate innovation and conservation.

There is another very important reason why economists prefer carbon taxes to cap and trade schemes: where the latter largely reward current polluters, the former are a source of revenue for the government while actually correcting for costly market failures in the economy. According to David Roodman (1999, p. 173):

> [T]ax burdens are already substantial in most countries. So there are plenty of taxes that could be cut with the money raised from environmental taxes. A tax shift would result—not a tax increase. Today, nearly 95 percent of the $7.5 trillion in tax revenues raised each year worldwide comes from levies on payrolls, personal income, corporate profits, capital gains, trade, and built property—all of which are essentially penalties for work and investment. It violates common sense to tax heavily the activities societies generally want while taxing lightly the activities they do not want.

Carbon taxes are essentially a benefit for society because they move the price of carbon fuels closer to their true opportunity costs. This differentiates them from most other taxes that cause prices to diverge from underlying opportunity costs. Carbon taxes explicitly set the socially optimal price that society implicitly paid in the form of lost future output and living standards. These "free" carbon taxes offer an efficient substitute for other taxes that do distort and create deadweight losses. Perhaps the revenue from a carbon tax can be directly allocated toward conservation projects and innovative new technologies that shift up the production function in the natural sphere.

SOME TENTATIVE THOUGHTS

This chapter concludes the study of international economics with a detailed discussion of two important environmental issues, global warming and the rapid loss of biodiversity. Recall that Chapter 1 began with the story of Jinfeng, China, the city to which a former German steel mill, environmental pollution and all, had been relocated. These clashes between economic growth and the ecosystem, and in which international trade, investment, finance, and migration play key roles, exemplify the increasing complexity that humanity must deal with for its survival.

The inclusion of environmental issues in an international economics textbook is compatible with our heterodox approach to international economics. At the start of this textbook, we wrote:

> [T]he international economic activities normally studied in the field of international economics, such as international trade, international investment, international finance, and immigration, are interrelated and have broad economic, social, and environmental consequences. The interdependencies created among countries by trade, investment, finance, and migration imply that countries are no longer in complete control of their own destinies, and the effects of economic change in one country inevitably spill over into other economies. The purpose of this textbook is to extend the traditional analysis of international economics in order to recognize the complexity of international economic activity, provide the perspectives from which we can make sense of these complexities, and arrive at more accurate assessments of how international economic activity affects human well-being.

Fundamentally, international economic integration implies an increase in human interactions over greater distances, across more borders, and between more and more varied countries. This process of international economic integration is an integral component of the much broader process of human economic and social development.

Overall, international economic integration has been good for human well-being. But this textbook has also explained why the growing interdependence among greater numbers of people can be problematic. The clash between the continued growth of human economic activity and the life-supporting capacity of the ecosystem is perhaps humanity's greatest challenge today. The holistic approach of this textbook, in contrast to the mainstream neoclassical paradigm, naturally brings this issue to the forefront.

It is ironic that orthodox international economics, which has so enthusiastically urged economists to widen their perspective by thinking internationally rather than nationally, now constrains itself within the economic sphere when in fact human life evolves through interaction with the economic, social, and natural spheres. For example, orthodox international financial economists were so convinced financial market deregulation was necessary that when the financial crisis hit, they could not understand what went wrong. Orthodox international trade economists argued for years that all tariffs and quotas were detrimental to human welfare, so now they struggle to explain why governments are reluctant to complete the Doha Round of multilateral trade negotiations. And international business economists continue to advocate deregulation and unrestricted international economic integration while closing their eyes to how growth in the economic sphere causes environmental disasters like global warming and the loss of biodiversity.

Orthodox mainstream economists effectively remain blinded by the neoclassical model that assumes the world consists of 7 billion socially isolated but somehow fully informed individuals that interact with each other every moment of the day in a massive set of efficient and competitive markets. Sociologists may be able to explain why this doxa helps economists succeed in their field, but the neoclassical paradigm certainly does not bring forth the knowledge the world needs to solve its looming crises. Unfortunately, Joseph Stiglitz's remark quoted at the start of this chapter seems to be correct: "Changing paradigms is not easy. Too many have invested too much in the wrong models."[12] Despite the recent Great Recession, repeated financial instability, growing social inequality, and pending environmental disasters, mainstream economists are still clinging to their neoclassical models. This is a shame because the world needs enlightened intellectual leadership to deal with systemic problems such as we face. Heterodox economics can help chart a more fruitful course.

Heterodox perspectives reveal overwhelming evidence, from the distant past's archeological finds to current neuroscientific experiments, that shows clearly how humans survived and flourished by cooperating with each other. Humans are social animals. This suggests that group behavior provides the best course of action for dealing with our pending global crises. As pointed out in Chapter 1, the past two hundred years' economic growth is testimony to humans' ability, however limited, to design institutions that permit strangers to cooperate. Judging from today's political discussions of global warming, species depletion, financial instability, and social inequality, humanity seems to have forgotten about its past success in cooperating and acting collectively to deal with difficult systemic issues. Instead, we see political leaders focusing on special interests to the detriment of the interests of vast numbers of the world's people. Orthodox international economics feeds this competitive world view. Heterodox economics, on the other hand, points humanity toward cooperation because its holistic perspective sees humanity residing in the natural sphere of human existence, where humanity must cooperate to survive.

A heterodox approach to international economics improves the odds of dealing with future events successfully. Heterodox economists are less likely to be constrained by institutions and policies that conflict with nature and with social stability. Heterodox economics' broader perspectives are more likely to discover the changes humanity must make in its society in order to remain compatible with its changing economic, social, and natural environments.

In sum, humanity urgently needs a massive dose of collective abstract thinking that enables a more cooperative global response to the problems all 7 billion people face. And humanity needs international economists to lead this exercise in abstract thinking and cooperative behavior because our greatest challenges, and the necessary responses, are all international.

CHAPTER SUMMARY

1. The growth of international trade, investment, finance, and migration has integrated the world economically and socially and also has increased the stress on the natural environment. Economists' and policy makers' understanding of international economics will, therefore, determine how national policies address the many economic, social, and environmental problems human society has to face.

2. Heterodox international economists, who seek to understand the implications of complexity and uncertainty, have a very important role to play in economics. Orthodox economics' smooth, continuous functions, based on assumptions of stable markets, bias mainstream economic analysis and blind it to the many potential environmental dangers of continued rapid economic growth and international economic integration.

3. Environmental issues are increasingly international in nature, and they are becoming more urgent.

4. Humanity's demand for nature's renewable resources, or nature's services, now exceeds the planet's regenerative capacity by about 30 percent.

5. Global warming is an especially clear example of humanity's overuse of nature's services; greenhouse gas emissions now exceed the atmosphere's capacity to absorb them without triggering changes in the climate.

6. Global warming is a major policy problem because the exact channels of causality are not well understood by individual consumers and producers and the uncertain consequences of current human activity will be felt mostly in the future.

7. Environmental problems are difficult not only because they require high levels of abstract thinking, but because the solutions to environmental problems like global warming require very substantial changes in the way industry produces and how people live. Therefore, people are predisposed to distrust even the most clear scientific evidence. Of course, special interests linked to the status quo lobby hard to avoid the costs of the needed adjustments.

8. This chapter also explains why the free rider problem makes it so difficult for national governments—faced by internal political pressures from consumers, producers, and business lobbies—to cooperate on very critical international economic and environmental issues.

9. Some critics of environmental policies have argued that uncertainty about the true costs and benefits mandate a wait-and-see approach. Martin L. Weitzman shows, however, that under reasonable discount rates, uncertain but potentially catastrophic environmental events with a very small likelihood should be actively avoided so long as

abatement costs are no more than a few percent of the value of human life.

10. The cost of prevention of environmental catastrophe is not high: if we must spend 2 percent of GDP per year to stop global warming, we are effectively being asked to make a payment of about $25 to insure an asset of $100,000 against possibility of total loss. People spend much more than this to insure their homes and cars, the losses of which would not threaten their survival.

11. This chapter uses a two-sector Solow growth model to illustrate how economic activity in the economic sphere is related to the natural sphere where the ecosystem produces its services. Economic growth requires that growth be sustainable in both spheres.

12. The natural sphere also calls for investment to compensate for depreciation and innovation to maintain growth of real human economic activity, just as the Solow model suggests for the economic sphere.

13. The two-sector Solow model illustrates the effects of growth in the economic sphere that has been much too fast given humanity's failure to cover the depreciation of the ecosystem and its capacity to continue supplying nature's services needed in the economic sphere.

14. The two-sector Solow growth model shows how the failure to account for environmental damage can trigger an actual decline in output in the economic sphere.

15. The two-sector Solow growth model, just like the single-sector version of the model, shows that technological change is necessary to sustain economic growth, and the two-sector model shows clearly that technological change must occur in both spheres.

16. Humanity's social and economic institutions, including everything from informal culture to formal legal institutions, are not set up to induce its investors, producers, and consumers to take account of what happens in the natural sphere. There are few effective signals and institutions that lead to innovation and technological change in the natural sphere.

17. It is apparent from the two-sector Solow model that, when the full costs of all the investment and innovation needed to achieve sustainable economic growth are recognized, growth will be much slower than humanity has experienced over the past two hundred years. Further growth of many types of human economic activity may simply not be possible anymore, but low-resource activities can take their place.

18. The past two hundred years' growth not only occurred when environmental costs were not as great because the human footprint was still small, but much environmental damage was simply ignored and its costs implicitly pushed into the future that rising atmospheric temperatures and rapid losses of species suggest we have now reached.

19. Because business culture focuses only on a bottom line that depends on outcomes in the economic sphere, business opposition to environmental policies is to be expected. For the sake of long-run human well-being, such resistance must be overcome.

20. A number of alternative policies have been suggested to provide incentives for producers and consumers to reduce greenhouse gas emissions or change behavior that causes other environmental damage. Included are schemes such as carbon taxes, and cap and trade.

KEY TERMS AND CONCEPTS

anthropogenic climate change
biodiversity
cap and trade
carbon tax
conservation function
cultural services
ecological footprint
effective resource supply
exhaustible (resources)
feedback effects
global hectares (gha)
global warming

monoculture
nature's services
nonrenewable natural resources
omitted variable bias
preserving services of nature
provisioning services of nature
regulating services of nature
risk
specification error
supporting services of nature
uncertainty

PROBLEMS AND QUESTIONS

1. How might economists redefine economic development in order to take into account nature's services and the depletion of nonrenewable resources? Will such a measure increase or decrease the level of real income? Will it increase or decrease the rate of growth of economic output? (Hint: Discuss the definitions of real income and economic output, and then take nature's production into consideration.)
2. Provide your intuitive explanation of Martin Weitzman's point that uncertainty actually raises the estimate of the potential cost of global warming relative to a risky event with known outcomes. Do you agree with Weitzman's analysis of uncertainty?
3. In light of Martin Weitzman's analysis and the difficulty of assessing the potential costs of uncertain events, assess the logic of the phrase "What you don't know won't hurt you."
4. Explain why biodiversity serves as an insurance policy for human survival. Provide examples of how biodiversity protects humanity from future disaster.
5. Explain precisely how the orthodox Solow model, which links investment and GDP, is biased in its conclusions. What does the model omit, and how does this omission distort the model's conclusions?
6. Does a law that forces private industry to pay the full costs of its negative externalities on the environment slow economic development? Explain why or why not.
7. After analyzing economic growth using the two-sector Solow model, do you still think economies can grow forever? Why or why not? Explain your answer.
8. What policies are needed to guarantee technological innovation in the natural sphere of the two-sector Solow model? Describe explicitly how innovators can be motivated to shift the production function of the biosystem.
9. What kind of trade policies could improve the likelihood of human society avoiding a disastrous clash with nature? Should governments prohibit all international trade, or should it be restricted in some more detailed manner? Explain precisely what your suggested policies would accomplish.
10. Do you think humanity will overcome the diminishing returns caused by the limited capacity of the ecosystem to provide nature's services? Why or why not?
11. Why, according to many scientists who observe global warming, is it urgent to act now to restrict greenhouse gas emissions? Why should we not wait until we are absolutely sure that private industry cannot find a technological solution to the problem? Discuss using the material from this chapter and any other analysis that might be relevant to the question.
12. *Financial Times* feature writer Richard Tomkins (2003) looks back further than two hundred years, and notes:

> In the industrialized west, we assume that the "normal" rate of economic growth is 2–3 per cent a year because it is what we have experienced in our lifetimes. For most of human history, however, "normal"—in terms of per capita growth—has meant more or less zero.

Are the past two hundred years indeed nothing more than a brief exception, a special episode that will soon end? Or, is humanity now on a new permanently steeper growth path? Why is the growth of international trade, finance, investment, and migration important for answering this question?

NOTES

1. Angus Maddison (2006).
2. See, for example, Howarth et al. (2001).

3. Quoted in a news release from Stanford University, Stanford, CA, February 6, 1997.

4. See, for example, B.H. Walker (1992) and S. Naeem (1998).

5. See, for example, David Tilman, Clarence L. Lehman, and Charles E. Bristow (1998).

6. Many of these methods are detailed in S.C. Farber, Robert Costanza, and M.A. Wilson (2002).

7. See, for example, Willis L. Peterson (1997); Fatma Gül Ünal (2008); Colin Tudge (2005); L.E. Drinkwater, P. Wagoner, and M. Sarrantonio (1998); and Jules Pretty and Rachel Hine (2001).

8. See, for example, Union of Concerned Scientists (2009), George Monbiot (2000), and Donald R. Davis, Melvin D. Epp, and Hugh D. Riordan (2004).

9. Paul Klemperer (2008), "If Climate Sceptics Are Right, It Is Time to Worry," *Financial Times,* February 29.

10. Quoted in Naomi Klein (2009), "Climate Rage," *Rolling Stone,* November 11.

11. For more on this issue, see Larry Lohman (2006).

12. Joseph Stiglitz (2010), "Needed: A New Economic Paradigm," *Financial Times (USA),* August 20.

Appendix

WILLIAM JENNINGS BRYAN'S "CROSS OF GOLD" SPEECH, JULY 9, 1896

This speech was given during the 1896 Democratic National Convention. It was Bryan's contribution to a planned convention-wide debate over monetary policy. A moderately well-known delegate before he gave the speech, Bryan immediately became one of the front-runners for the party's nomination for president. When none of the previous front-runners could muster a majority among the delegates, after numerous votes Bryan was eventually chosen as the Democratic Party's presidential candidate.

Mr. Chairman and Gentlemen of the Convention:

I would be presumptuous, indeed, to present myself against the distinguished gentlemen to whom you have listened if this were a mere measuring of abilities; but this is not a contest between persons. The humblest citizen in all the land, when clad in the armor of a righteous cause, is stronger than all the hosts of error. I come to speak to you in defence of a cause as holy as the cause of liberty—the cause of humanity.

When this debate is concluded, a motion will be made to lay upon the table the resolution offered in commendation of the Administration, and also the resolution offered in condemnation of the Administration. We object to bringing this question down to the level of persons. The individual is but an atom; he is born, he acts, he dies; but principles are eternal; and this has been a contest over a principle.

Never before in the history of this country has there been witnessed such a contest as that through which we have just passed. Never before in the history of American politics has a great issue been fought out as this issue has been, by the voters of a great party. On the fourth of March, 1895, a few Democrats, most of them members of Congress, issued an address to the Democrats of the nation, asserting that the money question was the paramount issue of the hour; declaring that a majority of the Democratic party had the right to control the action of the party on this paramount issue; and concluding with the request that the believers in the free coinage of silver in the Democratic party should organize, take charge of, and control the policy of the Democratic party. Three months later, at Memphis, an organization was perfected, and the silver Democrats went forth openly and courageously proclaiming their belief, and declaring that, if successful, they would crystallize into a platform the declaration which they had made. Then began the conflict. With a zeal approaching the zeal which inspired the Crusaders who followed Peter the Hermit, our silver Democrats went forth from victory unto victory until they are now assembled, not to discuss, not to debate, but to enter up the judgment already rendered by the plain people of this country. In this contest brother has been arrayed against brother, father against son. The warmest ties of love, acquaintance, and association have been disregarded; old leaders have been cast aside when they have refused to give expression to the sentiments of those whom they would lead, and new leaders have sprung up to give direction to this cause of truth. Thus has the contest been waged, and we have assembled here under as binding and solemn instructions as were ever imposed upon representatives of the people.

We do not come as individuals. As individuals we might have been glad to compliment the gentleman from New York [Senator Hill], but we know that the people for whom we speak would never be willing to put him in a position where he could thwart the will of the Democratic party. I say it was not a question of persons; it was a question of principle, and it is not with gladness, my friends, that we find ourselves brought into conflict with those who are now arrayed on the other side.

The gentleman who preceded me [ex-Governor Russell] spoke of the state of Massachusetts; let me assure him that not one present in all this Convention entertains the least hostility to the people of the state of Massachusetts, but we stand here representing people who are the equals, before the law, of the greatest citizens in the state of Massachusetts. When you [turning to the gold delegates] come before us and tell us that we are about to disturb your business interests, we reply that you have disturbed our business interests by your course.

We say to you that you have made the definition of a business man too limited in its application. The man who is employed for wages is as much a business man as his employer; the attorney in a country town is as much a business man as the corporation counsel in a great metropolis; the merchant at the cross-roads store is as much a business man as the merchant of New York; the farmer who goes forth in the morning and toils all day, who begins in spring and toils all summer, and who by the application of brain and muscle to the natural resources of the country creates wealth, is as much a business man as the man who goes upon the Board of Trade and bets upon the price of grain; the miners who go down a thousand feet into the earth, or climb two thousand feet upon the cliffs, and bring forth from their hiding places the precious metals to be poured into the channels of trade are as much businessmen as the few financial magnates who, in a back room, corner the money of the world. We come to speak of this broader class of business men.

Ah, my friends, we say not one word against those who live upon the Atlantic Coast, but the hardy pioneers who have braved all the dangers of the wilderness, who have made the desert to blossom as the rose—the pioneers away out there [pointing to the West], who rear their children near to Nature's heart, where they can mingle their voices with the voices of the birds—out there where they have erected schoolhouses for the education of their young, churches where they praise their creator, and cemeteries where rest the ashes of their dead—these people, we say, are as deserving of the consideration of our party as any people in this country. It is for these that we speak. We do not come as aggressors. Our war is not a war of conquest; we are fighting in the defence of our homes, our families, and posterity. We have petitioned, and our petitions have been scorned; we have entreated, and our entreaties have been disregarded; we have begged, and they have mocked when our calamity came. We beg no longer; we entreat no more; we petition no more. We defy them!

The gentleman from Wisconsin has said that he fears a Robespierre. My friends, in this land of the free you need not fear that a tyrant will spring up from among the people. What we need is an Andrew Jackson to stand, as Jackson stood, against the encroachments of organized wealth.

They tell us that this platform was made to catch votes. We reply to them that changing conditions make new issues; that the principles upon which Democracy rests are as everlasting as the hills, but that they must be applied to new conditions as they arise. Conditions have arisen, and we are here to meet those conditions. They tell us that the income tax ought not to be brought in here; that it is a new idea. They criticise us for our criticism of the Supreme Court of the United States. My friends, we have not criticised; we have simply called attention to what you already know. If you want criticisms, read the dissenting opinions of the court. There you will find criticisms. They say that we passed an unconstitutional law; we deny it. The income tax law was not unconstitutional when it was passed; it was not unconstitutional when it went before the Supreme Court for the first time; it did not become unconstitutional until one of the judges changed his mind, and we cannot be expected to know when a judge will change his mind. The income tax is just. It simply intends to put the burdens of government justly upon the backs of the people. I am in favor of an income tax. When I find a man who is not willing to bear his share of the burdens of the government which protects him, I find a man who is unworthy to enjoy the blessings of a government like ours.

They say that we are opposing national bank currency; it is true. If you will read what Thomas Benton said, you will find he said that, in searching history, he could find but one parallel to Andrew Jackson; that was Cicero, who destroyed the conspiracy of Catiline and saved Rome. Benton said that Cicero only did for Rome what Jackson did for us when he destroyed the bank conspiracy and saved America. We say in our platform that we believe that the right to coin and issue money is a function of government. We believe it. We believe that it is a part of sovereignty, and can no more with safety be delegated to private individuals than we could afford to delegate to private individuals the power to make penal statutes or levy taxes. Mr. Jefferson, who was once regarded as good Democratic authority, seems to have differed in opinion from the gentleman who has addressed us on the part of the minority. Those who are opposed to this proposition tell us that the issue of paper money is a function of the bank, and that the government ought to go out of the banking business. I stand with Jefferson rather than with them, and tell them, as he did that the issue of money is a function of government, and that the banks ought to go out of the governing business.

They complain about the plank which declares against life tenure in office. They have tried to strain it to mean that which it does not mean. What we oppose by that plank is the life tenure which is being built up in Washington and which excludes from participation in official benefits the humbler members of society.

Let me call your attention to two or three important things. The gentleman from New York says that he will propose an amendment to the platform providing that the proposed change in our monetary system shall not affect contracts already made. Let me remind you that there is no intention of affecting those contracts which, according to present laws, are made payable in gold; but if he means to say that we cannot change our monetary system without protecting those who have loaned money before the change was made, I desire to ask him where, in law or in morals, he can find justification for not protecting the debtors when the act of 1873 was passed, if he now insists that we must protect the creditors.

He says he will also propose an amendment which will provide for the suspension of free coinage if we fail to maintain a parity within a year. We reply that when we advocate a policy which we believe will be successful we are not compelled to raise a doubt as to our own sincerity by suggesting what we shall do if we fail. I ask him, if he would apply his logic to us, why he does not apply it to himself. He says he wants this country to try to secure an international agreement. Why does he not tell us what he is going to do if he fails to secure an international agreement? There is more reason for him to do that than there is for us to provide against the failure to maintain the parity. Our opponents have tried for twenty years to secure an international agreement, and those are waiting for it most patiently who does not want it at all.

And now, my friends, let me come to the paramount issue. If they ask us why it is that we say more on the money question than we say upon the tariff question, I reply that, if protection has slain its thousands, the gold standard has slain its tens of thousands. If they ask us why we do not embody in our platform all the things that we believe in, we reply that when we have restored the money of the Constitution all other necessary reforms will be possible; but that until this is done there is no other reform that can be accomplished.

Why is it that within three months such a change has come over the country? Three months ago when it was confidently asserted that those who believe in the gold standard would frame our platform and nominate our candidates, even the advocates of the gold standard did not think that we could elect a President. And they had good reason for their doubt, because there is scarcely a state here to-day asking for the gold standard which is not in the absolute control of the Republican party. But note the change. Mr. McKinley was nominated at St. Louis upon a platform which declared for the maintenance of the gold standard until it can be changed into bimetallism by international agreement. Mr. McKinley was the most popular man among the Republicans, and three months ago everybody in the Republican party prophesied his election. How is it to-day? Why, the man who was once pleased to think that he looked like Napoleon—that man shudders to-day when he remembers that he was nominated on the anniversary of the battle of Waterloo. Not only that, but as he listens he can hear with ever-increasing distinctness the sound of the waves as they beat upon the lonely shores of St. Helena.

Why this change? Ah, my friends, is not the reason for the change evident to any one who will look at the matter? No private character, however pure, no personal popularity, however great, can protect from the avenging wrath of an indignant people a man who will declare that he is in favor of fastening the gold standard upon this country, or who is willing to surrender the right of self-government and place the legislative control of our affairs in the hands of foreign potentates and powers.

We go forth confident that we shall win. Why? Because upon the paramount issue of this campaign there is not a spot of ground upon which the enemy will dare to challenge battle. If they tell us that the gold standard is a good thing, we shall point to their platform and tell them that their platform pledges the party to get rid of the gold standard and substitute bimetallism. If the gold standard is a good thing, why try to get rid of it? I call your attention to the fact that some of the very people who are in this Convention to-day and who tell us that we ought to declare in favor of international bimetallism—thereby declaring that the gold standard is wrong and that the principle of bimetallism is better—these very people four months ago were open and avowed advocates of the gold standard, and were then telling us that we could not legislate two metals together, even with the aid of all the world. If the gold standard is a good thing, we ought to declare in favor of its retention and not in favor of abandoning it; and if the gold standard is a bad thing why should we wait until other nations are willing to help us to let go? Here is the line of battle, and we care not upon which issue they force the fight; we are prepared to meet them on either issue or on both. If they tell us that the gold standard is the standard of civilization, we reply to them that this, the most enlightened of all the nations of the earth, has never declared for a gold standard and that both the great parties this year are declaring against it. If the gold standard is the standard of civilization, why, my friends, should we not have it? If they come to meet us on that issue we can present the history of our nation. More than that; we can tell them that they will search the pages of history in vain to find a single instance where the common people of any land have ever declared themselves in favor of the gold standard. They can find where the holders of fixed investments have declared for a gold standard, but not where the masses have.

Mr. Carlisle said in 1878 that this was a struggle between "the idle holders of idle capital" and "the struggling masses, who produce the wealth and pay the taxes of the country"; and, my friends, the question we are to decide is: Upon which side will the Democratic party fight; upon the side of "the idle holders of idle capital" or upon the side of "the struggling masses"? That is the question which the party must answer first, and then it must be answered by each individual hereafter. The sympathies of the Democratic party, as shown by the platform, are on the side of the struggling masses who have ever been the foundation of the Democratic party. There are two ideas of government. There are those who believe that, if you will only legislate to make the well-to-do prosperous, their prosperity will leak through on those below. The Democratic idea, however, has been that if you legislate to make the masses prosperous, their prosperity will find its way up through every class which rests upon them.

You come to us and tell us that the great cities are in favor of the gold standard; we reply that the great cities rest upon our broad and fertile prairies. Burn down your cities and leave our farms, and your cities will spring up again as if by magic; but destroy our farms and the grass will grow in the streets of every city in the country.

My friends, we declare that this nation is able to legislate for its own people on every question, without waiting for the aid or consent of any other nation on earth; and upon that issue we expect to carry every state in the Union. I shall not slander the inhabitants of the fair state of Massachusetts nor the inhabitants of the state of New York by saying that, when they are confronted with the proposition, they will declare that this nation is not able to attend to its own business. It is the issue of 1776 over again. Our ancestors, when but three millions in number had the courage to declare their political independence of every other nation; shall we, their descendants, when we have grown to seventy millions, declare that we are less independent than our forefathers?

No, my friends, that will never be the verdict of our people. Therefore, we care not upon what lines the battle is fought. If they say bimetallism is good, but that we cannot have it until other nations help us, we reply that, instead of having a gold standard because England has, we will restore bimetallism, and then let England have bimetallism because the United States has it. If they dare to come out in the open field and defend the gold standard as a good thing, we will fight them to the uttermost. Having behind us the producing masses of this nation and the world, supported by the commercial interests, the laboring interests and the toilers everywhere, we will answer their demand for a gold standard by saying to them: You shall not press down upon the brow of labor this crown of thorns, you shall not crucify mankind upon a cross of gold.

Source: Official Proceedings of the Democratic National Convention Held in Chicago, Illinois, July 7, 8, 9, 10, and 11, 1896 (Logansport, Indiana, 1896).

Glossary

Terms in *italic* refer to glossary entries.

– A –

absolute advantage – The principle of absolute advantage reflects the idea, popularized by Adam Smith (1776), that countries should specialize in producing what they can produce more cheaply and importing those things others produce more cheaply.

absorption – A country's total domestic expenditures on final goods and services, which is equal to total output minus net exports.

abstract reasoning – The process of thinking logically about some complex issue or problem.

ad valorem tariff – A tax on imports specified as a percentage of the value of the product being taxed. See also *specific tariff*.

adding machine model – The political economy model that links the likelihood of an economic policy being enacted to the absolute number of people directly affected by the policy.

adjustable exchange rate peg – The exchange rate arrangement under the *Bretton Woods order* and the *European Monetary System*, which required central banks to intervene in the foreign exchange market in order to keep currencies within a 1 percent band around an openly stated target exchange rate, except in the case of a fundamental disequilibrium that clashed with the long-run policy objectives of full employment and economic growth.

adverse selection – A market failure caused by the fact that the market price changes the types of people who seek to transact in a market. For example, a high rate of interest may lead only the riskiest borrowers to seek loans, or a high price of insurance may result in only those with very high probabilities of experiencing the insured event purchasing insurance.

agglomeration – The dynamic process whereby economic activity is increasingly concentrated in specific geographic regions. The process is hypothesized to occur because (1) industrial activity is subject to increasing returns to scale and (2) long-run growth depends on the combinatorial process of technological change, which is highly path dependent and dependent on human interactions.

aggregate demand (AD) curve – The curve that depicts the economy's total demand for output, including consumption, investment, government, and net foreign demand, as a function of the overall price level.

aggregate indifference curves – Often referred to as the social indifference curves or community indifference curves, this is the set of indifference curves often used in general equilibrium models to represent a population's tastes and preferences. The aggregate indifference curves are assumed by orthodox economic theory to be the sum or some other functional aggregate of individual indifference curves. *Heterodox economics* does not accept that such an aggregate measure of welfare or preferences can be depicted by a stable, unchanging set of individual welfare functions when dynamic economic processes continually change incomes, the distribution of incomes, and all other types of economic outcomes that influence individual well-being.

aggregate supply (AS) curve – The curve that depicts the economy's total supply of output as a function of the overall price level; the long-run AS curve is usually drawn as a vertical line under the assumption that supply in the long run is purely a real phenomenon related to the economy's total resources and its level of technology and, therefore, unaffected by the overall price level.

Alien and Sedition Acts – Discriminatory and arbitrary immigration laws of the 1790s that targeted individuals with specific political and social viewpoints; among other things, these laws restricted the entry of people that prominent members of President John Adams's political party thought might be inclined to vote for Thomas Jefferson.

American depositary receipts (ADRs) – Receipts for foreign equity shares deposited with a U.S. financial firm, which are then traded on U.S. stock markets, thus enabling U.S. wealth holders to acquire foreign assets without having to buy them on foreign exchanges using foreign exchange.

anchor – In finance, the term for a reference price that guides expectations and beliefs in the case of uncertainty and the absence of complete knowledge.

Andean Group – A five-country common market that includes Bolivia, Colombia, Ecuador, Peru, and Venezuela.

anthropogenic – Human made. Phenomena such as *global warming* or *biodiversity* loss are said to be anthropogenic because they are caused by the growth of human society.

antidumping duty – A *tariff* imposed by an importing country that believes it is the target of foreign dumping in order to offset the margin of dumping and raise the domestic price to where it would fall if the foreign supplier charged a price that reflected true costs and a "fair" profit.

appreciation – See *currency appreciation.*

arbitrage – The process that effectively combines distinct markets into a single integrated market by means of profit-seekers buying goods or assets in those segments of the market where prices are low and selling where prices are high.

Articles of Agreement – See *Bretton Woods order.*

ASEAN – Association of Southeast Asian Nations. This is a *trade bloc* that is attempting to establish a free *trade area* among Brunei, Cambodia, Indonesia, Laos, Malaysia, Myanmar, Philippines, Singapore, Thailand, and Vietnam.

Asian Tigers – The group of East Asian countries consisting of Hong Kong, South Korea, Singapore, and Taiwan that grew very rapidly during the second half of the twentieth century. Many authors have designated other fast-growing East Asian countries such as Indonesia, Malaysia, the Philippines, and Thailand as the "new Asian tigers."

asset diversification – Spreading one's wealth among a variety of assets in order to reduce the overall risk of the asset portfolio. See also *portfolio diversification.*

asset risk – The uncertainty surrounding an asset's future returns and residual value.

asylum seekers – People who request permission to take up residence in another country to escape serious threats to their safety and well-being.

asymmetric information – The situation where those on one side of a transaction have a different information set than those on the other side of the transaction. Asymmetric information can result in *adverse selection* and *moral hazard,* both of which cause financial markets to fail to efficiently allocate savings to investment projects.

auction quota – An import quota for which import permits are auctioned to the highest bidders; at the margin, an auction quota provides the government with the same revenue as an equivalent tariff.

automatic processes – The processes of the human brain that occur with little or no awareness or feeling of effort. Reactions to pain, danger, and physical trauma, for example, are mostly automatic; these evolved brain processes, and the behavior they trigger, do not follow normative axioms of inference and choice. See also *deliberative processes* and *emotional processes.*

– B –

Bagehot's rule – One of the implicit rules that central banks were urged to follow under the *gold standard.*

Specifically, the rule stated that if the central bank must serve as a lender of last resort in the case of short-term credit crises in the domestic banking sector, it should always charge interest rates well above those charged in the markets in order to keep such lending to a minimum.

balance of payments (BoP) – The account, compiled by nearly all countries, that records all of a country's international transactions according to a standard format.

bancor – The international reserve currency suggested by John Maynard Keynes in a series of speeches in the early 1940s. The bancor would be managed by an *International Clearing Union (ICU),* which would be a type of global central bank through which all international payments were cleared.

Bank for International Settlements (BIS) – One of the international institutions that emerged from the Paris Peace Conference after World War I; located in Basel, Switzerland, the BIS was intended to serve as an international clearinghouse for central banks, a type of central bank for central banks.

bank run – The sudden panic among bank depositors that leads them all to attempt to withdraw their money at the same time, with the result that the bank cannot satisfy the depositors' requests. The bank may have to declare insolvency if it cannot find the funds to pay depositors. See also *deposit insurance.*

bank secrecy laws – Laws enacted by governments to prevent banks from revealing the identities of owners of bank accounts. Bank secrecy laws allegedly protect depositors, but they also serve to hide tax evasion, fraud, and various illegal activities. Switzerland is well known for its bank secrecy laws; they are being disputed by the tax authorities in the United States and various European countries seeking to uncover tax evasion.

Bastable test – The criterion that an infant industry must eventually generate welfare gains that exceed the costs of protection, all properly discounted. See also the *infant industry argument for protection.*

beggar-thy-neighbor policy – An economic policy, such as an intentional devaluation of a currency, intended to boost the domestic economy at the expense of a foreign economy. Specifically, this is a policy that shifts economic variables in ways that improve economic indica-

tors, such as economic growth or employment at home but worsen such indicators overseas.

bills of exchange – These are invoices issued by sellers to buyers that could be transferred to others, which allowed them to circulate as a type of paper *money.* These were common in international trade in Europe several hundred years ago, and they are often given as an example of early paper money.

bimetallism – The simultaneous circulation of coins made of silver and gold as well as paper money convertible to both silver and gold.

biodiversity – The number of different species of plants, animals, and micro-organisms on earth, the genetic variations and traits within species, and the way these species coexist within ecosystems.

biological leash – Most of the observed behavior of nonhuman living creatures was passed on through genes, so that changes in the way they live, how they interact with each other, and how they deal with their natural environment occur through the slow process of evolution. Thus, the advance of knowledge is constrained by the slow pace of evolution.

bourgeoisie – Karl Marx's term for the capitalist class, the owners of the means of production. See also *proletariat.*

Bracero Program – Instituted during World War II, this program permitted U.S. employers to employ Mexican workers on a temporary basis in the United States. This program was intended to provide labor to take the place of U.S. workers drafted into the military. It remained in effect until the early 1960s at the behest of U.S. agricultural firms, but was finally terminated at the insistence of U.S. labor groups.

Brady bonds – Bonds issued by developing-country governments in the late 1980s and early 1990s under the *Brady Plan;* these effectively constituted a rescheduling and partial write-off of earlier loan obligations, and they were guaranteed by developed-country governments to make them attractive to private purchasers.

Brady Plan – The framework that ultimately provided solutions to the 1982 debt crisis, it consisted of a combination of debt write-offs by creditors, substantial policy changes to improve the likelihood of debt repayment by debtor governments, lending and oversight of *Washington consensus* policy changes by the *International Monetary Fund,* and subsidies by developed-country governments in the form of loan guarantees for the private creditor banks.

brain drain – The common phenomenon in which professional and university-educated people leave their native developing country, where they received their training, and migrate to more developed economies. The causes of the brain drain are many, but among the most obvious are unattractive working conditions at home, economic and political problems at home, and higher incomes in more developed economies.

Bretton Woods – A small town in northern New Hampshire in the United States, the location of the Mount Washington Hotel where the July 1944 *Bretton Woods Monetary Conference* was held.

Bretton Woods agreement – The final agreement among the nation attending the July, 1944, Bretton Woods International Monetary Conference. The agreement provided for the post-World War II monetary order of pegged exchange rates, dollar dominance, and the *International Monetary Fund (IMF).* See also Bretton Woods Conference.

Bretton Woods Monetary Conference – The July 1944 meeting that brought together the financial and economic leadership of the Allied countries with the intent of designing the post–World War II international monetary order that would serve to promote economic recovery and world peace.

Bretton Woods order – The set of rules specified under the Articles of Agreement established at the 1944 *Bretton Woods Monetary Conference,* which effectively created a system of *pegged exchange rates* in which the dollar became the reserve currency and U.S. monetary policy anchored the global monetary system. The articles also created the *International Monetary Fund (IMF).* The order functioned until the early 1970s, when it was replaced with a mixture of exchange rate regimes applied by individual governments, as formalized by the *Second Amendment to the Articles of Agreement* in 1978.

Bretton Woods system – The international financial system that evolved from the *order* established at the *Bretton Woods Monetary Conference,* consisting of exchange rates *pegged* by means of central bank *intervention* and assistance from the *International Monetary Fund (IMF),* currency convertibility to facilitate international trade, and emphasis on sound domestic economic policies to promote full employment and economic growth.

Bureau of Immigration and Customs Enforcement (ICE) – One of the two agencies created after September 11, 2001, to replace the *U.S. Immigration and Naturalization Service (INS).* ICE focuses on enforcement and border protection. See also *U.S. Citizenship and Immigration Services (USCIS).*

"buy domestic" regulations – Rules or laws that require government agencies and others in the economy to buy from domestic sources rather than from the lowest-cost domestic or foreign supplier.

– C –

cabotage – Also known as trans-shipment costs, these are the costs incurred when goods have to be transferred from one mode of transportation to another for them to reach their destination, as from ship to train in a port city or aircraft to truck at the airport.

CACM (Central American Common Market) – One of the oldest trade blocs, the CACM is a customs union that was formed in 1960 among Costa Rica, El Salvador, Guatemala, Honduras, and Nicaragua. It was inactive during the civil wars and other conflicts of the 1980s and 1990s, but is again becoming a viable trade bloc in the early 2000s; it recently signed a free trade agreement with Mexico.

Cairns Group – A coalition of developed and developing countries that export agricultural commodities, it was formed during the 1985–1994 Uruguay Round of multilateral trade negotiations to push for liberalization of agricultural trade.

cap and trade – A scheme consisting of setting specific emissions limits and then issuing a corresponding number of permits to emit that can be freely traded. Under cap and trade, those emitters who can find cheaper alternatives to purchasing carbon permits will thus be motivated to invest in those alternative technologies.

capital account – This is a very small category of adjustments to a country's foreign assets and of little importance in the overall *balance of payments*. The continued use of the term is confusing, however, because prior to the *International Monetary Fund*'s revision of balance of payments accounting rules in 1996 what we now call the *financial account* was called the capital account.

capital controls – Legal restrictions on the purchase of foreign assets or the sale of domestic assets to foreigners.

capital flight – The movement of a large amount of wealth out of a country, usually against the laws or wishes of the country's government, because wealth holders fear confiscation, inflation, or just poor economic conditions. Capital flight is common in developing economies with poorly functioning financial sectors, arbitrary economic policies, high levels of inflation, or poor protection of property rights.

capital mobility – The ease with which assets are exchanged across borders.

carbon tax – A tax levied on a product or directly on a producer in order to internalize the external costs of climate change caused by the emission of *greenhouse gases* like carbon dioxide into the atmosphere.

CARICOM (Caribbean Community) – A *free trade area* formed by many of the small Caribbean island states.

carry trade – This is the practice of carrying assets denominated in currencies in which interest rates are high and paying for them by borrowing currencies with low interest rates. The carry trade effectively gambles that the *interest parity condition* will not hold and that the interest differential will not be *arbitraged* away through *exchange rate* shifts.

cartel – A collusive arrangement among suppliers (firms or governments of supplying countries) to fix prices, control supply, or in some other way limit competition among suppliers in order to raise supplier profits at the expense of consumers.

cash instruments – Financial assets whose values are determined in markets where these instruments can be easily bought and sold for cash.

Central American Free Trade Agreement (CAFTA) – The free trade agreement, which went into effect in 2010, between the Dominican Republic, Costa Rica, El Salvador, Guatemala, Honduras, Nicaragua, and the United States. The members of CAFTA agreed to open their borders to the free flow of goods and most services, but immigration was explicitly not addressed in the agreement.

centralized exchange – Centralized markets where large numbers of buyers and sellers interact directly and set asset prices through some process in which buyers and sellers, that is, those who demand and those who supply, balance total supply and demand. Examples of exchanges are stock markets, livestock auctions, and *foreign exchange futures*.

ceteris paribus – The Latin words meaning "all other things equal," and used to state the well-known assumption of partial equilibrium analysis in microeconomics.

Chinese Exclusion Act – The first U.S. legislation to explicitly limit immigration, this law was blatantly racist since it specifically banned only Chinese immigrants.

circular flow diagram – An often-used textbook diagram that depicts the economy as consisting of a flow of payments that circulate from households to producers and back again, effectively showing how total demand and total supply must be in balance for the economy to remain stable.

Civil Rights Act of 1964 – The milestone U.S. law that banned racial and ethnic discrimination.

Coase theorem – Attributed to Ronald Coase (1960), this hypothesis states that *externalities* will not necessarily cause markets to fail, because people and firms are motivated to find ways to negotiate some mutually beneficial sharing of the external costs or benefits.

Cocagne – The mythical, utopian place that existed in the minds of medieval European writers and artists.

Cognitive processes – See *deliberative processes*.

Coinage Act of 1816 – The act by British Parliament to tie the pound to specific weight and purity of gold. With this law and several others, it was hoped that the full backing of the pound by gold would prevent the inflationary printing of money by the government.

collateralized debt obligations (CDOs) – These are derivatives consisting of claims to shares of large bundles of financial instruments. For example, a CDO is created when a bank originates mortgages, puts them together into one large bundle, and then sells shares in the earnings from the mortgages or auto loans to investors, pension funds, hedge funds, and other banks.

colonialism – The conquest and military and administrative occupation of foreign lands by a country for its own economic gain. European colonialism between the fifteenth and nineteenth centuries usually involved the active participation of private capital from the colonizing country, a joint public/private activity that was part of the system of *mercantilism* that blurred the lines between government and business.

combinatorial process – A process in which new outcomes are the result of combinations of previous outcomes. Many economists claim that technological progress is a combinatorial process because new ideas are combinations of old ideas. A combinatorial process exhibits very rapidly accelerating growth.

Common Agriculture Policy (CAP) – A policy adopted jointly in the 1960s by the six members of the *European Economic Community*. The CAP is the earliest example of community-wide economic policies among European countries and marked the beginning of their path toward a greater economic union. The program has been continued by the European Parliament as more members were added and the current *European Union* took form.

common market (CM) – A *trade bloc* that establishes completely free trade among member countries, sets common *tariffs* and other trade restrictions against outside countries, and permits the free movement of factors of production such as capital and labor.

community – A social group of any size that shares certain geographic, cultural, and/or institutional characteristics. We speak of a city or town as a community, but we also use the term as in the academic community, the religious community, or the immigrant community to define a permanent cultural or social group.

community indifference curves – See *aggregate indifference curves.*

community perspective – The philosophical view that analyzes immigration by how it affects a community. The community view is not always favorable to immigration because it explicitly recognizes immigrants' effect on culture, income distribution, employment, congestion, and other social outcomes.

comparative advantage – The activity or activities for which the economy's *opportunity costs* are the lowest and, therefore, the activities the economy should specialize in and whose products it should export. The principle of comparative advantage prescribes that economies and individuals should concentrate on doing what they do relatively well rather than seeking to do a little bit of everything for themselves. It is a fundamental principle the leads international economics to conclude that international trade is always welfare enhancing.

competitive advantage – A firm's advantage in providing customers with a greater *value* of goods or services than its competitors. The term is sometimes used to describe the entire business sector of a country, in which case it must be differentiated from *comparative advantage.*

compound growth process – The general formula for a compound growth process shows that, if per capita real GDP grows at an annual rate of R, then after T years the level of per capita real GDP will be: $GDP_T = GDP_{t=0}(1 + R)^T$.

compounding – The process by which a constant rate of growth of a variable causes ever-larger absolute increases in the variable; an exponential process.

conduit – A newly created entity that was specifically designed to house a new financial asset or set of assets so that they would not appear on the books of the financial firm that created or structured the asset(s). The widespread use of conduits made it very difficult to gauge the financial weaknesses of financial firms after the 2007–2008 Great Recession and the financial collapse in 2008. Many financial economists believe that conduits were intentionally designed to deceive regulators and market participants.

conservation function – The relationship between the use of *nature's services* and the damage to nature from using the services. This function is used in the natural sphere of the two-sector *Solow growth model*, and it plays the same role in the natural sphere as the *depreciation* function plays in the economic sphere of the *model.*

consumer surplus – The net gains for consumers of a product, equal to the sum of all successive marginal gains minus the market price paid for the products.

consumption possibilities line (CPL) – The line that extends from the production point on the *production possibilities frontier* at a slope equal to the terms of trade in the general equilibrium diagram of an economy. According to the *Heckscher-Ohlin model,* the economy's most efficient consumption point lies on the consumption possibilities line where it is tangent with an *indifference curve.*

contingent commodities – Commodities and assets that are available to be purchased or sold only when certain pre-specified conditions are met. The assumption of the existence of contingent commodities for all risky or uncertain outcomes enabled Kenneth Arrow and Gerard Debreu (1954) and Debreu (1959) to construct *general equilibrium models* of the economy without the complicating factor of *risk or uncertainty.*

contract workers – People who go to another country for some limited period of time to perform a specific job under an agreed-to advance arrangement or contract.

convention – A term used by John Maynard Keynes to describe the rough understanding or beliefs of how things work in *markets* and the economy, which Keynes said enabled people to make long-term decisions under the prevailing state of *uncertainty* about the future.

Convention on International Civil Aviation – A 1944 agreement that, among other things, established that fuel for international air travel and transport of goods, including food, is exempt from national taxes.

convertibility – The freedom to exchange a currency for any other.

copyright – A legal instrument that assigns the ownership of original works—novels, movies, plays, textbooks, et cetera—to the creators of the works and protects them against unauthorized use and copying for some defined period of time.

core competencies – Those activities that provide a firm with its highest markup and profit margins. Modern management theory advocates that firms *outsource* to other suppliers all activities except for their core competencies in order to maximize profits.

Corn Laws – British seventeenth and eighteenth-century laws that kept wheat prices artificially high in Great Britain. Only the landed gentry had voting rights at the time these laws were enacted. The landed gentry lost their political clout with the Reform Act of 1832 and were no longer able to resist calls for liberalizing wheat imports; in 1846 the Corn Laws were repealed for good, enabling Britain to become a truly free-trading country for most of the remainder of the nineteenth century.

countervailing duty – A tariff levied on imports of goods or services that have benefitted from government subsidies in order to cancel the advantage that such subsidies give the foreign exporter.

covered interest parity condition – The *interest parity condition* in which the *forward exchange rate* is used in place of the expected future exchange rate, in effect "covering" the exchange risk of the *intertemporal arbitrage.*

crawling peg – An exchange rate that is gradually changed according to a predetermined or mechanically determined schedule to reflect relative changes in currencies' purchasing power.

creative destruction – Joseph Schumpeter's term for the process in which firms continually seek profits by means of gaining an advantage in the marketplace through innovation. As a result of "creative" activity, a firm "destroys" the monopoly power that its competitors had gained as a result of earlier innovations. But the gain is only temporary because the creative innovation of its competitors will, in turn, eventually destroy its monopoly. This continued creative destruction prevents permanent monopolies from developing and enables society to experience continued *technological progress.*

credit – A payment inflow into the country from abroad according to standard *balance of payments* accounting.

credit default swaps (CDSs) – Options that pay out the full value of an asset in the case of *default.* These *derivative instruments* are sometimes purchased by owners of the insured assets, but also by hedge funds, speculators, and plain old gamblers who do not own any of the insured assets and only seek to gamble on the asset's default.

crony capitalism – This term describes the close relationship between the *financial sector* and a familiar set of borrowers in industry and commerce. Crony capitalism is almost inevitable given that it is easier for banks to lend to familiar customers than to unknown borrowers, but it can seriously bias the flow of financing in the economy toward established firms, to the detriment of innovative new firms.

cross-section data – A set of observations made at a given point in time of a set of diverse people, firms, countries, et cetera. See also *time-series data.*

cultural capital – The acquired behavioral characteristics, material goods, and formal institutional certifications that give a person status in a specific field or in society in general. See also *inherited cultural capital, objectified cultural capital,* and *institutionalized cultural capital.*

cultural services of nature – Nature provides the environment in which humans live and create their cultures. In fact, nature helps to shape and preserve those cultures by providing the setting, the scenery, and the natural locations that are revered by cultures.

culture – A set of informal ideas, beliefs, conventions, habits, and customs that dominates the thinking of a specific group of people. Culture is often classified as an informal institution. Humans create these symbolic belief structures to give their activities significance. Culture helps humans deal with life in their complex social and natural environments by supplementing their evolved instincts and their limited amount of rationally acquired knowledge. There are many cultures, and individuals may adhere to more than one; that is, they identify themselves with various different groups of people with whom they share beliefs, traditions, and customs. See also *institutions.*

currency appreciation (depreciation) – An increase (a decrease) in the value of a currency relative to other currencies.

currency board – An exchange rate arrangement under which domestic currency is issued by the monetary authorities only when foreign currency is presented in exchange, which guarantees that the government holds foreign reserves to back up all newly issued currency. This system is similar to a commodity standard in that it links the domestic money supply to the inflow or outflow of foreign exchange.

current account – The part of the *balance of payments* that records the value of a country's international trade of goods and services, factor payments, and asset returns.

customs union (CU) – A *trade bloc* in which the member countries agree not only to allow the free trade of goods between their economies, but also to maintain a set of common *tariffs* and other trade restrictions against nonmember countries.

– D –

Dawes Plan – The 1924–1929 U.S. plan to provide loans to the German Weimar Republic in order to enable it to meet its World War I *reparations payments* as demanded in the Treaty of Versailles.

deadweight loss – The welfare losses due to a price distortion that prevents a market from reaching an efficient equilibrium, such as when a tariff is imposed on an import market and domestic prices no longer reflect worldwide *opportunity costs.*

deadweight loss of imperfect competition – The difference between the value of additional output and the opportunity costs to society of producing the additional output caused by producers' ability to set prices above marginal costs.

debased money – This term describes the loss of *purchasing power of money,* and dates from the times when people would scrape small slivers of gold or silver from coins before using them in transactions.

debits – Payment outflows to foreigners in the *balance of payments.*

debt burden – The size of debt relative to some other variable that represents the ability to service that debt. For example, a government's debt burden is often stated as total debt relative to the size of the economy in terms of *gross domestic product.*

debt crisis – The serious, real economic consequences resulting from a case where scheduled debt servicing cannot be maintained and borrowers and/or lenders have to make adjustments to the scheduled flow of future payments. Debt crises have occurred with frequency since the early 1980s.

debt crisis of 1982 – In 1982, a sudden shift in international financial flows caused some forty developing economies to *default* on or seek a renegotiation of their foreign debt obligations. The *exchange rate crises* and *financial crises* that followed triggered economic crises that effectively marked the end of an unprecedented period of economic growth in most developing countries in Africa, Asia, and Latin America that had stretched over the 1950s, 1960s, and 1970s. The debt crisis followed a period when international financial firms had sharply increased loans to developing economies.

debt repudiation – The intentional decision not to honor debt obligations.

debt service – The interest and principal payments due on a debt.

default – The failure to meet the terms of an *intertemporal transaction*. For example, a firm's inability to meet interest payments on a loan is a default on the loan. A firm's failure to deliver already-paid-for goods on the date agreed to is a default on the delivery.

deliberative processes – The processes of the human brain that are closest to human thought processes hypothesized by neoclassical economic theory. The deliberative processes are capable of abstract thought as well as logical reasoning. The deliberative processes originate in the prefrontal cortex area of the human brain. See also *automatic processes* and *emotional processes*.

demand effect – Though this is often left out of mainstream economics discussions of the costs and benefits of immigration for a national economy, immigrants are consumers as well as workers, who spend part or all of their income in the destination country and, therefore, boost aggregate demand as well as aggregate supply.

demand side – In macroeconomic modeling, the demand side of the economy refers to the structure of aggregate demand for the economy's production. Neoclassical analysis normally represents the demand side of the economy with a set of *indifference curves*, where each curve shows people's preferences among the various products that the economy can produce and the level of the curve represents the overall level of satisfaction.

Department of Homeland Security – The new cabinet-level U.S. department that was created after the September 11, 2001, terrorist attacks to carry out the nonmilitary aspects of national security.

dependency theory – A school of thought that interpreted *colonialism* and postcolonial experiences as suggesting that developing countries should sever all economic ties with their former colonial masters or current neocolonial economic powers. This school of thought was especially strong in Latin America, where the United States was seen as a dominant neocolonial power.

deposit insurance – Usually a government-supported scheme whereby bank depositors are protected against losses in the case of bank failure. Deposit insurance was instituted in the United States in the 1930s to ward off threats of *bank runs*. But unless banks and other intermediaries are closely regulated, such insurance can worsen the principal-agent problem because principals have less motivation to monitor agent activity. See also *bank run* and *principal-agent problem*.

depreciation – The wearing out or using up of the stock of capital. The proportion of capital that "wears out" in each period of time is the rate of depreciation. See also *currency appreciation (depreciation)*.

derivative instruments – Often referred to as derivatives, these are options, futures, swaps, and other financial instruments whose values are derived from other assets such as cash and real assets such as real estate. Derivative instruments may be acquired to hedge risk, to provide insurance against specific losses and negative events, or simply to gamble or speculate.

derivatives – See *derivative instruments* above.

destination country – The country where international migrants settle and find employment.

devaluation – A change in the *fixed exchange rate* that causes the national currency to decline in value relative to other currencies.

development economics – The field of economics that studies how an economy develops, that is, improves the well-being of the people living in the economy.

diminishing returns – The decline in marginal returns to consecutive increments of variable inputs as they are combined with other fixed inputs.

direct technology transfer – When ideas and knowledge are transferred in the form of designs, directions, instructions, blueprints, or diagrams that are used directly by people in other countries to learn, understand, and apply the ideas and knowledge. See also *indirect technology transfer.*

dirty float – An exchange rate arrangement where market forces are permitted to exercise considerable influence but government continues to intervene in the market as well. Also referred to as a *managed float.*

displaced persons – A term often used to describe *refugees.*

Displaced Persons Act – This special act to admit *refugees* after World War I introduced the concept of *immigrant sponsorship,* under which some person or group in the United States assumed responsibility for immigrants' welfare after their arrival.

diversification – The basic principle of acquiring a variety of assets in order to reduce overall risk, effectively "not putting all your eggs in one basket."

Doha Round – The latest round of multilateral trade negotiations, initiated in 2001 in Doha, Qatar. Scheduled to be completed in 2005, the round lay dormant and unfinished in 2011 as difficult issues remained unsolved and some countries had doubts about some of the portions of the agreement already negotiated.

doxa – A term adopted by French sociologist Pierre Bourdieu to describe the complex set of beliefs and narratives that effectively explain the reality of one's *field.* Doxa are the fundamental, deep-seated, but mostly unproven set of beliefs that a person comes to rely on for survival within a particular *field.*

drawback – A border tax refund to compensate for *tariffs* paid on imports when those imports are re-exported or incorporated in products that are exported; tariff drawbacks are intended to prevent import tariffs from reducing exports as the *Lerner symmetry theorem* predicts.

dumping – Depending on the context in which this term is used, dumping refers to either selling below cost, selling at a lower price in one market compared to other markets, or the lowering of prices in order to drive the competition out of business. The *World Trade Organiza-* *tion* provides its own definition of dumping: either selling below cost or selling at a lower price abroad than at home. See also *predatory dumping.*

Dutch East India Company – The English name for the *Verenigde Oost-Indische Compagnie (VOC),* one of the first *transnational corporations.* In 1602, the company was granted a charter by the Dutch monarch to conduct colonial activities in Asia, and it financed itself by selling stock to wealthy merchants as well as on the Amsterdam Stock Exchange.

dynamic model – A model that describes the complete path of changes of variables over time as a result of either a one-time change or continued changes in policies or external circumstances.

– E –

ecological footprint – The sum of (1) all forest, grazing land, cropland, and fishing grounds required to produce the food, fiber, and timber humanity consumes, (2) all land and water to absorb the wastes emitted when humans use energy, and (3) all land, water, air, and other natural resources required for humanity's living space, production, transportation, and storage.

economic growth – A sustained improvement in individual welfare, brought about by an increase in the economy's stock of productive resources or by an improvement in the way the economy transforms resources into welfare-enhancing output. The growth of real per capita GDP is often used as a proxy for economic growth, although many other measures have been suggested.

economic integration – The degree to which separate national economies are linked and approximate the behavior of a single economy. Economies are said to be fully integrated if they behave more as one single economy. International trade, finance, investment, and migration tend to increase the amount of economic integration.

economic miracle – A term often used to describe an economy that suddenly grew at a very fast rate and permits it to catch up to higher-income countries. The rapid recoveries of Japan and Germany after World War II, the growth of the *Asian Tigers,* and most recently, China's rapid growth are often called miracles, even though there are clear economic explanations for them.

economic model – A simplified, logical representation of the real economy that highlights key relationships that are important to understanding and analyzing certain economic issues. A model intentionally omits many details deemed to be irrelevant to the problem at hand, thereby permitting the user of the model to focus on relationships among variables that *are* deemed to be important.

economic problem – The fundamental problem addressed by neoclassical economics, namely that the economy has limited resources with which to satisfy unlimited wants. In the *Heckscher-Ohlin model,* this is a maximization problem that is illustrated by the *production possibilities frontier* curve on the supply side and a set of *indifference curves* on the demand side.

economic union (EU) – A regional trade area that has all the characteristics of a *common market* plus members agree to a uniform set of macroeconomic and microeconomic policies. This is the highest form of regional economic integration.

economically significant – The interpretation of statistical results that suggests a certain coefficient is sufficiently large that the effect of the variable will generate a change in an outcome that substantially affects the situation being analyzed. Economic significance differs from *statistical significance*; a variable can be statistically significant in the sense that there is substantial probability that it indeed influences the dependent variable in a regression, but the size of the coefficient may still be so small that the variable's effect is not economically significant.

economies of scale – See *increasing returns to scale.*

ecosystem – The earth's ecological system, consisting of all the organisms and nonliving physical components that the organisms interact with such as water, the atmosphere, and solar rays.

effective exchange rate – A weighted average of a set of *foreign exchange rates* that provides a more realistic indication of the value of an overall currency in the global economy.

effective resource stock – The physical stock of natural resources measured in terms of the goods and services that can be produced with the resources; if technology enables producers to get more output out of the same resources, the effective stock rises.

effective tariff – A tariff is stated as a percentage of the value added of an industry's production rather than the percentage of the imported product's nominal value. An effective tariff gives a better measure of the amount of protection that a tariff provides to a specific industry.

elasticity of demand – See *income elasticity of demand.*

Emergency Quota Act – This 1921 legislation was a major shift in U.S. immigration policy as it set strict limits on immigration of all foreigners seeking to enter the United States. It established only a one-year restriction, but was extended in 1922 for two more years, and followed in 1924 by a permanent quota system that severely limited immigration from southern and eastern Europe.

emerging economies – A name often used to describe developing economies that have achieved consistent economic growth in recent decades.

emerging markets – A term often used to describe developing economies that offer potentially profitable business and investment opportunities; frequently used as a synonym for developing countries or less-developed countries.

emotional processes – The processes that occur in a part of the human brain that is of relatively recent evolution. The word *instinct* is often used to describe emotional behaviors. See also *automatic processes* and *deliberative processes.*

empirical analysis – The systematic analysis of empirical evidence. Usually statistical methods are used to interpret economic data.

empirical evidence – Actual observations and quantitative data representing real-world activity. Such observations can be used to create scientific *hypotheses* or test those hypotheses.

enclosure – The breaking up of communal lands into separate private land holdings in Britain during the seventeenth and eighteenth centuries, which effectively drove those without the means to secure ownership of enclosed land out of rural areas and into cities and towns to seek work in England's new industries.

endogenous tariff model – A political economy model in which trade policies are the result of the trade-off between politicians' need to raise campaign funds to influence uninformed voters and their need to minimize the politically unpopular welfare losses from trade restrictions enacted to satisfy campaign contributors seeking protection.

Engel's law – A relationship between demand and income, popularized by Ernst Engel, a nineteenth-century statistician, which states that the income elasticity of food is quite low and therefore the proportion of a country's income spent on food declines as per capita income rises.

entrepreneur – A person who innovates by applying new ideas and knowledge in ways never before done. An entrepreneur sees the opportunities for introducing a new product, changing a firm's management organization, exploiting a new market, finding a new source of raw materials, cutting the costs of production, or finding a better way of motivating the labor force. Entrepreneurs are often managers more than inventors; they are the ones who see the commercial potential of inventions.

equal opportunity – Most people agree that, in the abstract, fairness or justice requires that all people have an equal opportunity to pursue their interests and, thus, have an equal chance to improve their own and their families' well-being. In practice, there is little agreement on what conditions are necessary to guarantee equal opportunity.

equity market – Another name for a stock market where shares in corporations are bought and sold.

equivalent tariffs and quotas – *Tariffs* and *quotas* are said to be equivalent if they cause the same price increases, protection of *producer surplus*, and quantitative reductions in trade.

escape clause – A clause in a legal document or agreement that allows for a temporary exception to the agreement's basic principles under certain prescribed circumstances.

euro – The name of the single currency managed by the *European Central Bank* and used by over half of the members of the European Union. In 2010, the excessive borrowing of several euro country governments began to put into doubt the viability of the single currency area.

Eurocurrency – A time deposit of money in, or a loan from, a bank located in a country other than the country that issues the money.

Eurocurrency market – The largely unregulated worldwide market for lending and borrowing Eurocurrencies.

Eurodollars – The precursor to the more general term *Eurocurrency,* from the 1950s and 1960s when U.S. dollars were almost exclusively used for non-national currency accounts in the major money center banks.

European Atomic Energy Community (Euratom) – One of the early agencies created by what would become the six initial members of the *European Economic Community (EEC)*. Euratom was to bring the nuclear industries of the six countries under one roof, a measure designed to reduce fears that former World War II adversaries would develop competing nuclear arsenals as a by-product of broader nuclear research.

European Central Bank (ECB) – Located in Frankfurt, Germany, this is the central bank for the euro-area countries. The ECB is modeled on the former German Central Bank, which maintained a strict focus on price stability.

European Coal and Steel Community (ECSC) – The first step toward European economic integration, this agency sought in 1950 to reduce fears of Germany's industrial recovery among other European countries.

European Economic Community (EEC) – The *common market* formed in 1958 by France, Germany, Italy, and the Benelux countries. Designed as a *customs union*, the EEC gradually expanded in terms of numbers and economically, first into a common market; by 2010 it had become the *European Union (EU)*.

European Free Trade Area (EFTA) – The economic integration scheme that joined most European countries not in the *European Economic Community (EEC)* and, later, the *European Union (EU)*, this remained essentially a *free trade area* in contrast to the much more integrated *European Union*.

European Monetary System (EMS) – A formal system of *fixed exchange rates* agreed to in 1979 by Germany, Italy, France, Belgium, Holland, Ireland, and Luxembourg. Other *European Union (EU)* members eventually joined, and after five years of exchange rate stability in the late 1980s, the system collapsed in the early 1990s when policy inconsistencies made fixed rates impossible to maintain.

European Monetary Union (EMU) – The framework that covered a set of policies intended to establish a single currency for European countries. The framework was initiated in the late 1980s, and it culminated with the substitution of the *euro* for the national currencies of 12 European countries in 2002, and expanded to 17 countries by 2011. Debt problems of some member countries threatened the EMU after 2009.

European Union (EU) – The economic union currently consisting of twenty-seven European countries. The EU began as the six-nation *European Economic Community (EEC)* in 1958, and has evolved into a large union with many common economic policies. In the first decade of the twenty-first century, sixteen of the EU's members had adopted a single currency called the *euro*.

evolutionary model of economic change – See *Schumpeter model* and *creative destruction*.

exchange control – Restrictions on the exchange of currencies imposed in order to prevent certain international transactions or to influence the equilibrium exchange rate.

exchange rate – The price of one currency in terms of another, usually stated as the domestic currency price of one unit of foreign currency, but can be equally well stated in foreign terms, that is, in terms of the amount of foreign currency needed to purchase one unit of domestic currency.

exchange rate crisis – A sudden fall in the international price of a country's currency that causes widespread bankruptcies and a deep recession as that country's debtors are forced to *default* on their foreign currency debt.

exchange rate stabilization fund – An agency or office that was often established by governments during the Great Depression to use accumulated foreign exchange reserves to intervene in the foreign exchange market. These funds were officially designated to smooth out seasonal and speculative fluctuations in exchange rates, but many governments used the stabilization funds to actively undervalue their currencies in order to give their exporters an advantage in international markets and thus boost aggregate demand and reduce unemployment in the domestic economy.

excludable good – A good whose use can be limited to a certain person or certain people. In effect, an excludable good can become private property whose ownership can be enforced. Patents and copyrights are an attempt to exclude users from using ideas, concepts, technology, and knowledge so that their private ownership can be established and enforced.

exhaustible resources – Natural resources that are fixed in supply and, therefore, exhausted when used. They are sometimes called *nonrenewable natural resources*.

export orientation – After the *World Bank* (1993) attributed the economic success of East Asian countries to their "outward orientation," in contrast to most other developing regions' adoption of import substitution industrialization, many mainstream economists and economic advisors advocated export-oriented economic policies. These policies consisted of competitive exchange rates, free trade, free domestic markets, and less government involvement in the economy.

export quota – A quantitative restriction on exports, usually implemented to keep domestic prices artificially low or to guarantee the domestic supply of products deemed critical to society's survival.

externality – An economic consequence of one person's or firm's activity that raises or decreases others' welfare but is not taken into consideration by those undertaking the activity; externalities occur because markets do not exist to accurately price the costs and benefits of all economic activity.

– F –

factor accumulation – The growth of the economy's stocks of factors of production. An economy can grow either (1) because the economy's factors of production are increased or (2) because technology improvements permit the economy to produce more output for a given set of resources. The former is sometimes referred to as growth through factor accumulation. This type of growth is examined by means of a model developed by Robert Solow around the middle of the twentieth century.

factor payments – Wage payments, dividend payments, interest payments, and other payments to the factors of production. In the *balance of payments*, factor payments are recorded in the *current account*.

factor price equalization theorem – By combining the *Heckscher-Ohlin (HO) theorem* and the *Stolper-Samuel-*

son theorem in a two-country, two-good, and two-factor model under the assumptions of identical preferences and technologies, free trade, no transport costs, and perfect competition, the HO model of international trade predicts that not only will the price of each of the final products be equalized across countries, but the price of each factor of production will also be the same in every country.

factory system – The concentration of production in large-scale production units, such as factories or, today, extensive *monoculture* agriculture.

fallacy of composition – The choices that improve an individual's well-being, all other things equal, may not improve anyone's welfare if everyone makes the same decision. In macroeconomics, the example of personal saving is often given as an example of the fallacy of composition: Personal saving is good for every individual, but if everyone saves more, the economy may end up with higher unemployment and lower real savings in the long run.

fast-track authority – The commitment by the U.S. legislature to quickly vote yes or no on the ratification of a trade treaty brought to it by the country's negotiators without altering the treaty in any way. Because of the controversial nature of fast-track authority, in 2001 President George W. Bush gave it a new name: *trade promotion authority*.

feedback effects – In general, any secondary effects of some phenomenon that end up strengthening the initial effects. An example of a feedback effect is the additional *global warming* caused by the release of the greenhouse gas methane from the melting Arctic tundra caused by an initial phase of *global warming* caused by *anthropogenic* carbon emissions.

fiat money – Currency that is designated as legal tender by law, or by fiat, but is not redeemable into other stores of value with intrinsic value, such as gold or silver.

field – French sociologist Pierre Bourdieu defines a field as the social or intellectual arena within which people spend much of their working hours and within which they focus their efforts to advance their primary social interests. Even though people identify with a broad national or ethnic culture, in going about their daily activities they tend to pay attention mostly to their immediate professional or social environment.

financial account (of the balance of payments) – The section of the *balance of payments* that lists a country's international payments generated by the sale and purchase of assets.

financial assets – Financial obligations such as loans, bonds, or even simple IOUs written on the back of an envelope and agreed to by a handshake. Financial assets differ from *real assets* that have an inherent value of their own or the direct capability of generating real output, such as real estate, commodities, or a piece of machinery.

financial crisis – A disruption of the normal functioning of a nation's financial system during which savings no longer flow smoothly to investment opportunities, often with severe negative effects on overall economic activity and economic growth; a period when intertemporal transactions are difficult to carry out.

financial depth – The greater the variety of assets exchanged and the more efficiently the financial sector is able to channel purchasing power from a diverse set of savers to a diverse set of investors, the "deeper" is the financial sector.

financial exchanges – Centralized exchanges where large numbers of buyers and sellers exchange standardized (uniform) *financial assets*, in contrast to *over-the-counter markets* that provide customized financial assets designed to meet the particular needs of buyers and sellers. Centralized financial exchanges are seen as more transparent and *liquid*, and therefore less prone to *financial crises*.

financial industry – The sum total of stock and bond markets, banks, pension funds, insurance companies, and *over-the-counter markets* for financial instruments and *derivatives*. This term is generally used to describe the *financial markets* and intermediaries, but not the central bank or government-run banking entities and regulatory agencies.

financial innovation – The creation of new financial institutions and instruments. An economy that has experienced a large amount of financial innovation and thus has a variety of intermediaries and markets is said to have a "deep" financial sector. Not all financial innovations improve the performance of the financial sector, however. Profit-motivated financial innovation has in recent years increased financial complexity to where it actually endangers the economy by hiding malfeasance and obscuring necessary market information.

financial instability hypothesis – Hyman P. Minsky's (1979) hypothesis that predicted that in a capitalist system every extended economic boom will inevitably be followed by a financial crash.

financial intermediary – An institution such as a bank, a mutual fund, or a pension fund that acquires money from savers and channels it to assets or investments. Often, intermediaries issue savers a financial asset, such as a deposit or an account, and then use the money to acquire other assets, real or financial. Some intermediaries act more like *brokers* in that they assume no direct obligations to savers and investors. The intermediary, by pooling risk and acquiring expertise in evaluating investments, permits savers to indirectly earn returns from assets they would, by themselves, have difficulty in evaluating and acquiring.

financial investment – The acquisition of financial instruments such as cash, checking accounts, corporate stock, government and private bonds, foreign exchange, bank deposits, and other forms of loans to financial firms, businesses, organizations, and individuals.

financial markets – Markets where financial and real assets are exchanged, such as stock markets, bond markets, and real estate markets. Financial markets can be centralized exchanges or *over-the-counter markets*.

financial sector – The sector of the economy where assets are exchanged and savings are channeled to investments and borrowers.

firewall – A term often used in the financial industry to refer to regulatory barriers between different segments of the industry. For example, the 1933 *Glass-Steagall Act* in the United States banned commercial banks from engaging in investment banking, that is, placed a firewall between the two types of banking with very different risk structures.

fiscal policy – In macroeconomics, fiscal policy refers to government expenditures and taxation, and how this affects *aggregate demand* in the economy.

fixed exchange rate – An exchange rate that is intentionally prevented from changing by means of specific government policies that intervene in the *foreign exchange markets*. See also *pegged exchange rate*.

fixed-rate dollar standard – A term sometimes used to describe the *Bretton Woods* monetary order, under which all members, except the United States, pegged their currencies to the U.S. dollar through *foreign exchange market* intervention.

fixed-factors model – A modified version of the *Heckscher-Ohlin model* of international trade in which not all resources can be shifted between industries in response to changes in relative product prices. The model shows that when not all factors of production are "mobile" across industries, the gains from free trade are not as great as when all factors can be shifted between industries. Also, the gains and losses from trade are distributed differently when some factors are not mobile across industries.

floating exchange rate – An exchange rate that is determined exclusively by the unhindered forces of supply and demand, and which tends to change whenever demand and supply change.

f.o.b. (free on board) – The price of a good that includes the cost of the product plus the cost of loading it on a truck, ship, or aircraft, but does not include the actual transportation cost, insurance, tariffs, or any other costs involved in actually moving the product to its final destination.

Fordney-McCumber Tariff – The 1922 U.S. law that nearly doubled U.S. import tariffs.

foreign aid – The direct government-to-government transfers and aid provided by government-funded development banks and other international agencies. Foreign aid is usually intended to deal with short-run emergencies and long-run programs to promote economic growth and development.

foreign direct investment (FDI) – Investment by businesses and firms in factories, warehouses, sales offices, stores, and other permanent facilities located abroad in which the investing firm has a controlling interest. For a foreign investment to be classified as FDI, the rule of thumb used most often is that the foreign firm own at least 10 percent of the foreign project or enterprise.

foreign exchange dealer – A firm, usually a major commercial bank, that buys and sells foreign exchange and earns a profit from the spread between the buying and selling prices.

foreign exchange broker – A firm or individual who, for a commission, arranges foreign exchange transactions between interested parties.

foreign exchange futures – Like forward exchange transactions, futures are contractual agreements to exchange currencies at some future date, except that futures are bought and sold in uniform amounts for specific future dates on centralized financial exchanges. Futures are convenient for small buyers and sellers who do not have access to the over-the-counter market.

foreign exchange market – The worldwide set of markets where the many different national currencies are exchanged.

foreign exchange market intervention – The buying and selling of foreign exchange by a government agency, usually the central bank, to keep the intersection of supply and demand from deviating from the targeted exchange rate.

foreign exchange rate – See *exchange rate.*

foreign exchange risk – The risk that is inherent to all assets denominated in foreign currencies, which is that exchange rate changes will alter the domestic currency value of foreign products and assets.

foreign mergers and acquisitions (M&A) – The part of *foreign direct investment* that consists of the acquisition of existing foreign firms, as opposed to *greenfield investment,* which consists of establishing new businesses and factories from scratch.

foreign sales corporation (FSC) – A foreign corporation established as an affiliate of a U.S. corporation for the purpose of sheltering foreign profits from U.S. taxation; FSCs are openly encouraged by U.S. law, but in 2001 the *World Trade Organization* ruled that they were an unfair method of export promotion.

forward exchange market – The market where currencies are currently traded for future delivery or receipt.

forward exchange rate – The price of one currency in terms of another currency for an exchange that is contractually agreed on today but will be carried out at a determined future date.

forward transactions – In the *over-the-counter* market for *foreign exchange,* forward transactions are contracts to buy or sell currencies at specified exchange rates for delivery at some specific future date or dates.

free rider problem – A common problem for voluntary organizations, where individuals or groups who stand to benefit from the activities of the organization do not contribute to its operating costs because they figure everyone else will contribute and they will still get to enjoy the benefits.

free trade area (FTA) – A trade bloc within which member states completely liberalize trade among themselves but maintain their own trade barriers against outside countries.

Free Trade Area of the Americas (FTAA) – A free trade area covering the entire Western Hemisphere, proposed by President George W. Bush in 2001 and for which negotiations were to get underway after he gained *fast-track authority* from Congress in 2002.

fundamental disequilibrium – An exchange rate that is not compatible with the monetary and fiscal policies necessary to maintain full employment, promote economic growth, or satisfy other important domestic policy objectives.

futures market for foreign exchange – Similar to the forward exchange transactions in that futures contracts set the price, date, and exchange rate for a transaction scheduled to take place in the future. But futures contracts differ from the forward market in that they are standard contracts traded on centralized exchanges. Futures contracts for foreign exchange are traded in uniform amounts and for certain future dates. Futures markets are very small compared to the huge *over-the-counter* forward market.

– G –

G7 – A group of seven countries, Canada, France, Germany, Italy, Japan, the United Kingdom, and the United States, that have met annually since 1976 to discuss economic and political issues.

G8 – The G7 plus Russia; the G8 replaced the G7 after 1998.

G20 – An international forum of finance ministers and central bankers from nineteen industrial countries plus the *European Union* to discuss and study policy issues among industrial and emerging economies. The G-20 includes several emerging economies, including Brazil, China, and India.

G77 – A coalition of developing countries intended to promote the interests of developing countries; the group had grown to 133 countries by 2002, but it is still called the G77.

GATS – The General Agreement on Trade in Services Negotiated during the *Uruguay Round,* it guides ongoing negotiation on the liberalization of world trade in services.

GDP – Gross domestic product, which is the total value added of production that occurs within a country's borders, regardless of who owns the factors of production used in the production process.

GNP – Gross national product, which is the total value added produced by a nation's factors of production, regardless of where they are located.

Gaia hypothesis – James E. Lovelock's (1972) famous hypothesis states that the planet Earth functions as a large homeostatic organism that actively adjusts its "internal" natural conditions. The Greek goddess Gaia personified "Mother Earth." The Gaia hypothesis seems to suggest that somehow the system will adjust and restore stability to the overall ecological environment. See also *Medea hypothesis.*

gain from specialization – The gain in welfare that results from shifting an economy's resources in order to reflect worldwide *opportunity costs.*

gain from trade – The gain in welfare from being able to export and import rather than being limited to selling and buying in the domestic market.

Geary Act – Extended the ban on Chinese immigration for another ten years after 1892, and added restrictions on Chinese already living in the United States For example, the Geary Act denied the right of bail to Chinese in habeas corpus proceedings, and all Chinese immigrants were required to carry an identification document called a certificate of residence.

General Agreement on Tariffs and Trade (GATT) – The agreement reached by the major economies after World War II (1947) that established the legal framework within which international trade policy was to be set and trade negotiations were to be conducted. It provides the fundamental rules that govern the *World Trade Organization (WTO)* today.

general equilibrium model – A model that describes an equilibrium relationship between certain economic variables taking into consideration the need to simultaneously maintain equilibrium across all sectors and markets in the economy. General equilibrium models differ fundamentally from *partial equilibrium models,* which describe an equilibrium relationship between certain variables in just one market or one sector of the economy while assuming that all other things elsewhere in the economy remain unchanged.

General Theory of Employment, Interest, and Money – John Maynard Keynes's 1936 work that showed policy makers how to design economic policies aimed at specific groups and sectors of the economy in order to most effectively push the economy back toward full employment. See also *Keynes.*

geographic arbitrage – The purchase in one location and sale in another in order to profit from differences in prices for identical products or assets. Also known as *spatial arbitrage.*

Gini coefficient – A convenient numerical measure of income inequality derived from the *Lorenz curve.*

Glass-Steagall Act – Enacted in the United States in 1933, this law banned commercial banks from engaging in investment banking. That is, the act placed a *firewall* between the two types of banking with very different risk structures. The repeal of this act in 1999 was followed by the financial meltdown in 2007, which caused the first decline in worldwide economic activity since World War II.

global Gini coefficient – A *Gini coefficient* calculated using a data set that combines income data by income group for all the world's countries.

global hectares (gha) – The average capacity of one hectare of the earth's surface to produce services and absorb waste.

global warming – The unprecedented warming of the earth's atmosphere that scientists trace to the growth in *greenhouse gas emissions* generated by the increased economic activity over the past two centuries.

globalization – The popular term for the increase in international trade as a percentage of world output, the increase in international investment as a percentage of total world investment, and the increase in the proportion of people living and working in countries other than their country of birth.

gold-exchange standard – Established in 1926, this was a type of fractional reserve monetary system that increased the world money supply relative to the gold base, a convenient result given the difficulties of deflating prices to the point where money supplies could be fully backed by gold. However, it also meant that changes in the availability of reserve currencies would affect the world's money supply.

gold parity – The rate at which a currency could be converted to gold under the 1880–1913 *gold standard,* set in terms of ounces of gold per unit of currency.

gold standard – The international monetary order that prevailed over the period 1880–1913, under which countries made their currencies fully *convertible* to gold at fixed *gold parities* so that all exchange rates were effectively *fixed.* The system worked for as long as it did because governments engaged in relatively little economic policy making that could have undermined confidence in the permanence of the fixed exchange rates.

gravity model of trade – As its name suggests, this model is based on the equation for gravity from physics, and it thus hypothesizes that the volume of trade between a pair of countries is a negative function of the distance between the countries and a positive function of the "mass," or size, of the two economies.

gray market – The selling of branded products by persons and firms that are not approved by the producers of the branded products.

Green Revolution – The name often given to the post-1960s rapid introduction of new agricultural technologies that is credited for enabling the world to avoid famine in the face of accelerating population growth. By the end of the twentieth century it was apparent that the new technologies introduced new stresses in society and the natural environment, however.

greenfield investment – The establishment of new businesses and production facilities, as opposed to *mergers and acquisitions*, which consist of absorbing existing businesses into a new firm. See also *mergers and acquisitions.*

greenhouse gases (GHGs) – The chemical gases that contribute to the atmosphere's ability absorb the heat of the sun. When GHGs rise, atmospheric temperatures tend to rise over time. Carbon gases are the most common GHG, although methane is also significant. Methane is much more potent than carbon in heating the atmosphere, although it does not remain suspended as long as carbon. Other GHGs include water vapor, nitrous acid, and ozone.

greenhouse gas (GHG) emissions – The emissions by industry, power plants, autos, and various other producers and users of fuels that contribute to the greenhouse effect in the earth's atmosphere.

growth theory – The field of economics that is concerned with how economies grow. Traditional growth theory has been part of the broader field of macroeconomics and has focused on developed economies, in contrast to *development economics,* which traditionally focused on the growth of developing economies. This textbook avoids this dichotomy and treats all economic growth as a common field of study.

guest worker – A temporary immigrant attracted to a destination country in order to work at a specific job for some limited length of time.

– H –

habitus – A term popularized by French sociologist Pierre Bourdieu to define the beliefs and ideas that are widely held in the subculture, or *field*, that people most directly identify with as they go about their daily lives. Habitus specifically consists of a set of attitudes and dispositions that identifies a person as belonging to a specific subculture.

Hanseatic League – Also known as the *Hansa* in German, this was an informal network of cities along the Baltic and North Seas and throughout northern Germany during the fourteenth, fifteenth, and sixteenth centuries that established a type of *free trade* area.

happiness studies – A wide variety of statistical and analytical studies of the state of human happiness or satisfaction with life using data from surveys that directly ask people to express their opinion on their perceived well-being. See also *happiness surveys.*

happiness surveys – Opinion surveys that ask people how happy or satisfied they are with their lives. Such surveys have been carried out for many years in many countries, so it is now possible to compare happiness across countries and over time.

hard currency – A common term used to describe a convertible currency that is expected to maintain its value in the future; in other words, a currency that serves as a relatively safe store of value.

Heart of Darkness – Joseph Conrad's short novel about an English captain hired by a colonial enterprise to navigate a river boat to an ivory-trading post deep in the Belgian Congo in the late nineteenth century. The novel is a harsh condemnation of *colonialism*, the myth of its benevolence, and its true brutality. The novel contains vivid descriptions of the hopelessness in societies destroyed by colonial exploitation of colonies' natural resources.

Heckscher-Ohlin (HO) model – The general equilibrium model of trade (explained in Chapter 3) consisting of the *production possibilities frontier* and *indifference curves,* which was first developed by two Swedish economists, Eli Heckscher and Bertil Ohlin, in the 1920s. The model shows that, in the case of free trade, countries export the goods for which they enjoy a *comparative advantage* and import goods in which they do not enjoy a comparative advantage. The HO model also shows that all countries gain from free trade, regardless of their levels of income or development.

Heckscher-Ohlin (HO) theorem – In the case of two countries, two products, and two factors, plus a large set of other simplifying assumptions, free trade will result in each country exporting the product whose industry intensively uses the country's relatively abundant factor.

hedge finance – The term used by Hyman Minsky to describe the case where revenues and cash inflows are more than sufficient to meet debt service, including principal payments when they are scheduled to come due. See also *speculative finance* and *Ponzi finance.*

hedging – The use of various techniques to reduce exposure to future price fluctuations; the potential for foreign exchange rate fluctuations lead many international traders and investors to *hedge* foreign exchange rate risk. The word *hedge* for financial instruments that aim to contain future price volatility probably is derived from the practice common in Britain of growing hedges around the edges of one's property to delineate a boundary and to keep animals contained.

heterodox economics – An approach to economic analysis that advocates the use of a wide range of *paradigms* and *models*, and fundamentally embraces the principle of *holism.* See also *orthodox economics.*

heterodoxy – The prefix *hetero* has its origins in ancient Greek, where it means "other" or "different." The word *doxy* refers to a doctrine, a framework of analysis, or what many social scientists would call a *paradigm.* Heterodoxy thus suggests a set of ideas, perspectives, and models that are different from the *orthodox* perspective or approach to economic analysis. See also *orthodoxy.*

heuristics – Useful life rules and other behavioral guidelines that have proven beneficial for humanity in the past and are widely advocated even though their accuracy has not been scientifically proven. Stereotyping and rules of thumb are heuristics. Cultures are characterized by large sets of heuristics.

HIPC (highly indebted poor countries) – The countries that can participate in an agreement among governments and international agencies such as the *World Bank* and *International Monetary Fund (IMF)* to unilaterally reduce foreign debt owed by very poor developing countries. Under an HIPC agreement, poor countries have to meet specific economic, political, and social conditions and formulate policies approved by the IMF and World Bank, which limited participation.

hold-up problem – A potential market failure in the situation in which a purchasing firm has a real incentive to induce a supplier to make substantial investment in building capacity and know-how for supplying specialized products, and then to renegotiate the terms of the contract once the supplier is locked into this new supplier capacity. Suppliers leery of opening themselves to such pressure can strengthen their hand by holding up their investments until the *outsourcing* firm agrees to contractual terms more favorable to the supplier.

holism – The term *holism* is derived from the Greek word *holos,* meaning entire, total, whole. Holism is the explicit recognition that the component parts of a whole cannot be understood in isolation and their functions cannot be predicted without knowing the whole environment in which they exist. In the case of international economic activity, the overall economic, social, and natural outcomes are seen as a function of both the international economic system's parts and their interactions. Holism tends to focus on systems within a dynamic process that impacts, and is impacted by, the broad social and natural environments that humans inhabit. See also *scientific reductionism.*

holistic science – The application of the *scientific method* within a framework of analysis that recognizes the need to view the world as a complex system that encompasses human society and the entire *ecosystem*, and in which the parts and the interactions among the parts continually evolve. See also *holism.*

home bias puzzle – Also known as the international diversification puzzle, this refers to the seemingly small amount of international asset diversification that actually occurs despite the many opportunities for people to acquire foreign assets.

homeostasis – This term is credited to Claude Bernard, who used it in 1865 to describe a living organism that automatically or instinctively regulates its internal environment so as to survive within variable external environments. A typical example of homeostatic adjustment is the maintenance of constant body temperature by endothermic animals, such as mammals and birds, in response to changes in external temperatures.

homeostatic brain behavior – *Homeostasis* in the human brain's processes explains why humans react intensely to changes in their circumstances, and it also explains why humans are very adaptable in the long run. See also the more general concept of *homeostasis.*

horizontal foreign direct investment – *Foreign direct investment (FDI)* that duplicates facilities and operations that a *transnational corporation* already owns and operates in other countries. The huge French retailer Carrefour, for example, operates distribution centers and chains of retail stores in a number of countries, and its investment in distribution, warehousing, and retail facilities is similar in every country. See also *foreign direct investment* and *vertical foreign direct investment.*

hot potato process – The large number of transactions needed to rebalance the inventories of foreign currencies by the dealers in the *over-the-counter market* for *foreign exchange* following a purchase by or sale to an outside customer.

human capital – The knowledge acquired by workers, often the result of specific investments in education, training, and self-learning. Human capital involves investment just as does the creation of physical capital. Like physical capital, human capital is subject to *depreciation.*

human technology – Holistically, this term refers to the set of knowledge, methods, procedures, and techniques that humans have accumulated and can store outside their bodies, and which they use to go about their daily lives, including their economic activities. Human knowledge, as opposed to biologically transmitted knowledge, is transferred from one generation to another by a process known as intergenerational communicative learning.

hyperinflation – Very high inflation that is usually characterized by a general unwillingness to hold a currency as a way to store wealth. The velocity of money thus accelerates, and as everyone seeks to buy other goods that hold their value better than money, inflation is further accelerated.

hypothesis – In the *scientific method*, an idea is a hypothesis until it is proven by an objectively obtained set of data, direct observations of real phenomena, or a carefully designed test, at which point it becomes a *theory*. A hypothesis is a carefully thought-out probe into the space between what we know and what we don't know.

– I –

illegal immigrants – People who immigrate without following the required formal, legal procedures to gain entry to another country. A less derogatory name for illegal immigrants is *unauthorized immigrants.*

Illegal Immigration Reform and Immigrant Responsibility Act of 1996 – This U.S. law authorized a clearinghouse where employers can verify the status of prospective *immigrant* employees. This measure was in response to the proliferation of forged documents, which made employer checks of standard documents almost meaningless. Such a clearinghouse had, in fact, been authorized by earlier legislation, but had never been funded by the U.S. Congress.

immigrant remittances – Payments by immigrants to their family, relatives, friends, and other groups back in their native countries. These are technically designated as private transfers in the *current account* of the *balance of payments*.

immigrant sponsorship – The pledge by an American relative or organization to support an immigrant financially should they need assistance; the procedure of sponsorship was instituted to avoid having immigrants become a "charge of the state."

immigration – The migration of people across political boundaries.

Immigration Act of 1924 – This act limited U.S. immigration from any particular country to 2 percent of the number of descendants of immigrants of that nationality residing in the United States thirty-five years earlier in 1890. These blatantly discriminatory and racist immigration quotas appealed to the many Americans who feared that recent immigration from southern and eastern Europe was upsetting the country's racial and ethnic balance.

Immigration and Customs Enforcement (ICE) – The agency of the U.S. *Department of Homeland Security* charged with enforcing immigration laws and regulations.

Immigration and Nationality Act of 1952 – Drafted by Senator Patrick McCarran of Nevada, this act fit the McCarthy era of anti-communist paranoia by keeping most quotas from the *1924 Immigration Act* in place, increasing border patrols, and setting much tighter entry restrictions for persons with "un-American political philosophies." This latter provision would end up keeping noted intellectuals such as Jean-Paul Sartre from ever coming to the United States to give even a single lecture.

Immigration and Nationality Act of 1965 – This act abolished the United States' ethnic quotas on immigration in favor of a new set of criteria for the granting of permanent resident visas; 80 percent of the numerical limits were to be allocated to relatives of persons already living in the United States, the remaining were to be allocated to those with desirable skills and their family members,

and spouses and children of U.S. citizens were no longer subject to numerical limits at all.

Immigration and Naturalization Service (INS) – The bureaucracy set up to administer the U.S. immigration laws and procedures. The agency faced conflicting incentives, charged with welcoming foreign immigrants legally admitted into the country as well as closing the border to unauthorized immigrants and deporting those caught inside the country.

immigration policy – A country's laws, regulations, and procedures that govern the entry of immigrants and the conditions under which they are permitted to reside and work.

Immigration Reform and Control Act of 1986 (IRCA) – This U.S. legislation strengthened the *U.S. Border Patrol*, which is the federal police force that seeks to prevent *unauthorized immigrants* from crossing the border, and, for the first time, established penalties on employers who knowingly employ illegal aliens. The act also provided a one-time pardon for illegal immigrants who had lived in the United States for many years, and offered them the opportunity to gain legal permanent residence status. About 2.5 million *unauthorized immigrants* legalized their status under the act. The act is comprehensive in scope, but enforcement and funding has limited its effectiveness in curbing *unauthorized immigration*.

immiserizing growth – The special case where investment increases a country's export capacity to such an extent that its rising exports reduce its terms of trade to such an extent that the gains from output growth are more than offset by the terms of trade loss. Brazil, which expanded coffee planting rapidly in the early twentieth century only to suffer sharp changes in its terms of trade, is often given as an example.

import substitution industrialization (ISI) – A policy strategy that consists of promoting the substitution of domestic production to replace imports by using protectionist trade policies and domestic policies to target selected industries. Import substitution policies are often referred to as import substitution industrialization (ISI) policies to emphasize that the main goal of the policies was to create a domestic manufacturing industry.

income elasticity of demand – A measure of the responsiveness of the quantity demanded of some good to the change in income of those persons demanding the good. Specifically, it is the proportional or percentage change in the quantity demanded relative to the percentage change in income.

increasing costs – The case of rising per unit production costs as production expands. This case is also referred to as rising *opportunity costs*—the more of a certain product is produced, the greater the value of other products that must be foregone.

increasing returns to scale – The phenomenon in which average costs fall as the volume of production increases. *Economies of scale* tend to lead to a concentration of production in a small number of large production facilities or, from an economy-wide perspective, to international specialization and trade rather than national self-sufficiency.

indifference curve – A set of all combinations of available products that leave a welfare-maximizing consumer equally well off and, therefore, indifferent in choosing among them.

indirect production – When a product is obtained by the two-step process of first producing some other product for export and then using the foreign revenue to acquire the desired product abroad.

indirect technology transfer – *Technology* improvements that are embodied in the products that are imported from abroad. International trade is required for such transfers. See also *direct technology transfer.*

infant industry argument for protection – One of the most-often-used arguments to justify restrictions on foreign imports. The idea is that some industries require a period of time to learn or develop before they become competitive; without protection from foreign competition, it is claimed, such industries would never develop, to the alleged long-run detriment of the economy.

inherited cultural capital – Those parts of *culture* that can take considerable time for parents and communities to transfer to new members, such as habits developed during years of training and education, specific terminology and models, social behavior and professional procedures, and, of course, personal relationships.

innovation – The process of creating new technology, new ideas, new institutions, new business structures,

and any other changes in the way people live, work, and engage in economic and social activity.

institutionalism – A broad category of economic *paradigms* that focus on human institutions and how they influence human economic behavior and economic outcomes. Institutionalists are more aware than neoclassical economists of the many alternative mechanisms that are in place along with markets for allocating production, resources, incomes.

institutionalized cultural capital – Institutional symbols and certifications of *cultural capital* held by individuals, such as diplomas, titles, awards, certifications, and other official credentials.

institutions – The laws, social norms, traditions, religious beliefs, and many other established rules of behavior that provide the incentives that guide behavior. Institutions determine how promptly a society takes advantage of the many opportunities to raise human welfare. Economic failures such as hunger, poverty, war, and unemployment are almost always the result of faulty institutions that give rational people incentives to behave in a destructive rather than a constructive manner. Institutions are often categorized as formal institutions, such as laws, government regulatory agencies, and permanent organizations, or informal institutions, such as culture and social mores.

intellectual property rights – Legal rights of ownership to ideas, knowledge, writing, art, and other creations; *patents* and *copyrights* are common forms of intellectual property rights. From an economic perspective there is no difference, for example, between a physical piece of machinery, over which property rights can be established in most societies, and the software that controls the machine, for which many countries have been reluctant to grant property rights. This issue is extremely important in the modern world economy, where ideas are often more valuable than physical property.

interest parity condition – The relationship between the *spot exchange rate* and the expected future exchange rates under the assumption of perfect *intertemporal arbitrage*. The difference between the spot and future exchange rates depends on the rates of return on assets.

intermediate goods – The goods and services a producer acquires from other producers that are incorporated into the goods that the first producer, in turn, sells to consumers or other producers for further processing. The trend for businesses to increasingly focus on their core competencies and to *outsource* more stages of production to other producers means that the exchange of intermediate goods among producers is growing in proportion to final production.

intermodalism – The integration of different modes of shipping by a single provider, eliminating the need for producers to have to deal with a variety of shippers to get their goods to their customers.

internalized transactions – Transactions that occur within an organization such as a firm rather than through external markets that are open to other suppliers and demanders.

International Bank for Reconstruction and Development – See *World Bank.*

International Clearing Union (ICU) – Proposed by John Maynard Keynes at the *Bretton Woods Monetary Conference,* this would be a type of global central bank through which all international payments would be cleared. Keynes saw the ICU as an institution for enforcing balanced trade, which it would do by limiting deficit countries' ability to run persistent trade deficits and by confiscating accumulated reserves of countries that ran persistent surpluses.

international economic integration – The expansion of human interactions, such as trade, investment, financing, and migration, over greater distances, and among more countries.

international finance – The various forms of international borrowing and lending, including bank lending, foreign bond sales and purchases, and other forms of *portfolio investment*. International finance differs from *international investment*, which in economic terms involves the actual creation of capital. Sometimes the term *international financial investment* is used to differentiate finance from investment.

international investment – The purchase of financial and real assets by individuals, firms, financial organizations, or government agencies in one country from people, firms, financial organizations, or government agencies in other countries.

international investment position – See *net international position*. The net value of (1) foreign assets that are owned by a country's own citizens, firms, and government agencies and (2) domestic assets that are owned by foreign citizens, firms, and governments.

international marketing – The marketing of a product in a foreign country or countries; a firm that engages in international marketing focuses on global marketing opportunities and threats rather than limiting itself to a single national market.

international migration – The movement of people across borders with the intent of taking up residence and seeking employment in another country permanently or for an extended period of time.

International Monetary Fund (IMF) – One of the institutions created at the 1944 *Bretton Woods Monetary Conference,* the IMF was initially intended to serve as the central banks' central banker and provide international liquidity and foreign reserves to help national central banks keep exchange rates pegged. Since the abandonment of the Bretton Woods *international monetary order,* the IMF has gained new functions, such as enforcing the *Brady plans,* arranging emergency financing for countries confronting financial panics, and pushing for *Washington consensus* economic reforms in poor economies.

international monetary order – The rules, laws, and regulations that govern international transactions and the foreign exchange markets. Together with the public and private institutions that carry out, regulate, and control international financial transactions, the international monetary order defines the international financial system.

International Trade Organization (ITO) – An institution proposed at the *Bretton Woods Monetary Conference* that was intended to serve as a permanent international organization to promote trade liberalization and set the rules for international trade. The idea was never put into effect because the United States, among others, opposed it for fear that it would impose on national sovereignty. It would not be until 1994 that a similar organization, the *World Trade Organization (WTO),* would come into being.

intertemporal arbitrage – Arbitrage between the *spot* and *forward foreign exchange markets,* usually stated as the *interest parity condition.*

intertemporal comparative advantage – The advantage that a country has in producing today versus investing today and producing tomorrow, relative to that trade-off in other countries. A country with an intertemporal comparative advantage in investing must run a trade deficit in order to exploit this advantage.

intertemporal consumption possibilities frontier (ICPF) – A two-dimensional illustration of the set of points that represent the trade-off that must be made between first-period consumption and second-period consumption. The curvature of the *consumption possibilities frontier* illustrates a variable trade-off that may reflect *diminishing returns* to investment.

intertemporal transaction – A transaction that involves payments or the delivery of goods today for goods or payments in the future. Intertemporal markets are problematic because they must deal with the risk of default and the lack of perfect information about transactors and future economic conditions.

intervention – See *foreign exchange market intervention.*

intra-firm trade – Goods and services traded between domestic and foreign affiliates of the same transnational firm. About one third of world trade in manufactures is intra-firm trade; that is, the products cross borders but never leave the firm

intra-industry trade – A pattern of international trade that shows products from the same industry being both imported and exported.

investment houses – A name given to London's investment banks during the eighteenth and nineteenth centuries.

involuntary immigrant – Included in this category of immigrants are the millions of people caught in the world slave trade; modern cases of involuntary immigration often involve human trafficking in child labor or sex workers.

Islamic finance – Financial intermediaries, markets, and instruments that are consistent with *Sharia law.* In general, Islamic finance differs from conventional Western finance in that it eschews fixed interest rates and requires some equal sharing of *risk* and returns between borrowers and lenders.

– J –

J-curve effect – The j-shaped path of a country's trade balance that reflects the initial deterioration and eventual improvement of the trade balance that often follows a sharp *depreciation* of a country's currency.

joint venture – A firm that is jointly owned by two or more other firms, and is usually formally structured to specify how control, operation, and profits are shared.

just-in-time supply systems – The inventory and supply system developed by Japanese manufacturers to reduce manufacturing costs. Production of parts and final assembly are closely coordinated so that parts supplies do not pile up at any point in the overall manufacturing process, causing needless inventory expenses.

– K –

Kennedy Round – The *GATT* trade round held in Geneva from 1964 through 1967, which reinvigorated post–World War II trade negotiations by successfully concluding with a lowering of most industrial goods *tariffs* by, on average, over 30 percent.

Keynes, John Maynard – The noted twentieth-century macroeconomist, best known for having pioneered the field of macroeconomics with his 1936 work, *The General Theory of Employment, Interest, and Money.*

Know-Nothings – See the *Order of the Star-Spangled Banner.*

– L –

Latin Monetary Union – A monetary union among France, Belgium, and Switzerland, and Italy during the 1870s, in which each of the four countries was authorized to issue identical silver and gold coins that were legal means of payment throughout the region.

law of similars – A law, often enacted as part of *import substitution industrialization (ISI)* policies, that explicitly authorized a complete ban of all imports of similar products as soon as any domestic firm could show it was capable of supplying any specific product to the domestic market.

leader-follower models – Growth models that explain the differential growth experienced by developed and developing economies over the past two hundred years. These models generally hypothesize that *innovation* is concentrated in the more developed economies and that *technology* flows slowly or with a lag from so-called technology leaders to follower countries.

learning by doing – The concept that the longer one performs a task, the more productive one gets at performing it. *Learning by doing* may pertain to individuals, factories, entire firms, entire economies, or the whole world economy. The classic example of learning by doing, which shows how accumulated production lowered costs, is the Liberty Ship program in the United States during World War II.

learning curve – A curve that relates a product's per unit costs of production to its cumulative production. For example, the *learning-by-doing* process suggests a declining learning curve.

Lerner symmetry theorem – Named in honor of Abba Lerner, who first rigorously proved it, this theorem states that any restraint on imports also effectively acts as a restraint on exports. The converse is also true: If a government acts to expand exports, the shift in resources causes imports to increase as well. The symmetry is caused by two mechanisms: (1) a reduction in imports and increased domestic production raises the cost of domestic inputs and resources, thus making production for exports more expensive, and (2) reduced imports appreciate the *exchange rate*, thus reducing the international competitiveness of exporters.

libertarianism – The philosophy that gives government few roles beyond the protection of property and of individuals from abuse or intimidation by others.

linear regression equation – The equation of the line or multidimensional plane of the form $y = a + b_1X_1 + b_2X_2 + b_3X_3 + \ldots + b_nX_n$ where the X's are a set of n different independent or explanatory variables thought to explain the dependent variable y. Estimates of the coefficients, b_1 through b_n, are usually calculated by the method of least squares. See also *regression analysis*.

liquidity trap – The situation faced by a central bank during a severe economic recession, when increasing the money supply has no effect on the interest rate and, therefore, does not stimulate *aggregate demand*.

London interbank offered rate (LIBOR) – The interest rate Eurocurrency banks offer to pay on deposits.

Long-Term Arrangement (LTA) on Cotton Textiles – A *voluntary export restraint* (VER) arrangement limiting exports of cotton textiles and clothing from developing countries to the United States that went into effect in 1962.

Lorenz curve – The curve connecting points showing the cumulative shares of national income listed from the lowest-income groups to the highest. The Lorenz curve is used to calculate the *Gini coefficient*, a common measure of income inequality.

loss aversion – People who will fight harder to hold on to what they have than to acquire something new are said to be loss averse.

Louvre Accord – An agreement among major economies of the world to stop the depreciation of the U.S. dollar in 1987.

– M –

MNE – The abbreviation for multinational enterprise. In this textbook we use an alternative term, *transnational corporation (TNC)*.

Maastricht Treaty – The treaty signed in 1991 by members of the European Union in which they agreed to establish a single currency to replace members' individual currencies.

Maghribi traders – A network of Jewish traders that connected the commercial cities around the Mediterranean Sea for several centuries after the fall of the Roman Empire. The network of personal contacts developed because: (1) the legal systems across the large region were not useful for enforcing agreements and contracts from a long distance, (2) it was inefficient for merchants to travel with their cargoes to distant locations, and (3) the variability of market conditions around the Mediterranean required on-the-spot decisions about when to buy and sell at prices that could not be predicted.

managed exchange rates – An exchange rate regime characterized by widespread government interference with *exchange rates*, from exchange market intervention to direct restrictions on international trade and financial flows. See also *dirty float*.

maquiladora – A type of industrial park that functions as a duty-free zone that permits producers to import components, parts, and raw materials free of tariffs and to export the finished products without incurring trade taxes. First established by Mexico along its border with the United States, these industrial zones were designed to attract foreign firms to employ Mexican labor. Similar industrial zones have since been established in many developing countries throughout the world.

market liquidity – This term usually refers to the size and volume of a *financial market*; the more liquid a market, the easier it is for buyers and sellers to exchange their assets in a timely manner.

market maker – A dealer that has sufficient inventory and financial reserves to satisfy the needs of prospective buyers and sellers upon demand.

market segmentation – A common marketing practice of charging different prices in different markets, depending on the elasticity of demand in each market. Market segmentation can bring charges of *price discrimination*.

marketing – The set of business activities consisting of sales promotion, advertising, and market research. The field of marketing itself views marketing much more broadly as the entire range of activities beginning with the conceptualization of goods and services, continuing through the research and development stage, the design of the manufacturing process, the distribution network, and culminating with promotion and sales activities. This book adopts the definition of marketing as consisting of all activities that enhance the perceived value of a product to customers. See also *value*.

Marshall Plan – Named after U.S. Secretary of State George Marshall, this was a huge assistance program initiated in 1948 to provide the financial means for European countries to recover from World War II.

measurement error – The inaccuracies and biases introduced into statistical analysis by the fact that data are inaccurate and incomplete.

Medea hypothesis – Peter Ward's (2009) hypothesis to counter the *Gaia hypothesis*, named in honor of the mythological Greek sorceress who killed her own children in a fit of rage against her husband. Ward points out that the paleontological record suggests that Mother Earth occasionally drives a very large proportion of species into extinction at the same time. That is, just like complex economic and social systems, the ecosystem is also subject to booms and busts. Ward contends that because humanity evolved in a relatively stable natural environment over the past few million years, the recent unprecedented growth of the human population and its economic activity will cause the ecosystem to adjust in ways that could overwhelm humans' own *homeostatic* adjustment mechanisms. The Medea hypothesis states that earth will survive with or without humans, whereas the *Gaia hypothesis* suggests that earth's stabilizing forces will likely allow the continuation of human existence.

median voter model – A political economy model that predicts the candidate who proposes policies that favor slightly more than half of the voters, regardless of the size of the gains or losses for each of those votes associated with those policies, will win the election.

medium of exchange – One of the three functions of *money*.

medium-run economic growth – A term often used to describe the transitional growth that occurs when a shift in parameters in the *Solow model* changes the *steady state equilibrium* in the absence of any *technological progress*.

mercantilism – A holistic definition of mercantilism is: all the devices—legislative, administrative, and regulatory—by which societies still predominantly agrarian sought to transform themselves into trading and industrial societies. In practice, mercantilism generally implied the active use of government power to further the interests of private commercial interests, including protection from foreign competition, colonial conquest of foreign resources and markets, and the issuance of *patents* and other exclusive permits to support *cartels* and favored business groups. Mercantilism flourished in Europe during the sixteenth, seventeenth, and eighteenth centuries. When mercantilism was projected internationally, it became *colonialism*.

merchandise trade balance – The net value of merchandise exports and imports, where merchandise means physical goods only.

MERCOSUR – Known as MERCOSUL in Portuguese, this is a *common market* consisting of Argentina, Brazil,

Paraguay, and Uruguay formed in 1992; Chile and Bolivia are associate members that conduct free trade with MERCOSUR countries but have not adopted their (high) common *tariffs* on outside countries.

mergers and acquisitions (M&A) – *Foreign direct investment* that involves acquiring controlling interests in existing foreign firms. See also *greenfield investment*.

meta-ideas – A name that Paul M. Romer (1993) gives to those new ideas, innovations, inventions, and abstract concepts that set society on a path to an exceptionally large number of new ideas, inventions, and concepts.

microfoundations – Neoclassical analysis followed in the footsteps of Léon Walras by seeking a consistent model that systematically links the economy's individual consumers, workers, producers, bankers, and investors to the economy's aggregate performance. Neoclassical economists spearheaded the search in macroeconomics for microfoundations that could explain how individual units brought about the observed macroeconomic outcomes. Strong simplifying assumptions are necessary in order to build practical macroeconomic models that are logically compatible with simple models of individual and firm behavior. The result of the quest for microfoundations was that neither the microeconomic models used to represent individuals and firms, nor the macroeconomic models of the aggregate behavior, were realistic or general.

migration – The act of moving geographically from one place to another permanently or for an extended period of time.

Mill test – The criterion that an infant industry must be able to eventually operate successfully without trade protection and government support.

model – A simplified representation of a hypothesized or proven real phenomenon that is specific enough to be scientifically tested using real observations, experiments, or empirical data. Economics uses a wide variety of models, each based on a set of assumptions and techniques associated with the many economic *paradigms*. Economic models can be graphic, mathematical, or verbal.

money – Anything that is readily accepted in exchange for goods and services, because it can serve as a *store of value* until it is used as a *medium of exchange* and passed on in exchange for something else of value. Monetary transactions are often recorded in terms of their money value, in which case money also serves as a unit of account.

monetary order – See *international monetary order*.

monetary policy – The activities of the central bank that impact the supply of money in circulation.

monoculture – The large-scale, capital-intense production of single crops covering vast tracts of land formerly divided into much smaller-scale and more varied agricultural production. Monoculture is motivated by *economies of scale*, which are derived from the substitution of large equipment for labor, the heavy application of chemical fertilizers and insecticides in place of more labor-intensive and varied exploitation of the land, and industrial food processing operations in which machinery and assembly-line methods require uniform products. Monoculture is accused of causing the sharp rate of species depletion the world is experiencing.

moral hazard – The likelihood that a borrower will engage in more risky or less productive behavior.

most favored nation (MFN) principle – A key principle included in most trade agreements, which mandates that nations refrain from discriminating in how they treat different trade partners.

Multifiber Agreement (MFA) – The elaborate system of *import quotas* on clothing and textiles formally established during the 1970s, under which nearly all importers and exporters agreed to nontransferable product-by-product and country-by-country quantitative limits. The MFA was phased out in 2005 and replaced by equivalent tariffs that could in the future be negotiated down.

multilateral trade negotiations – Trade negotiations among a large number of countries simultaneously, as opposed to bilateral negotiations between two countries. Multilateral negotiations were enabled under the *General Agreement on Tariffs and Trade (GATT)* after World War II.

multinational enterprise (MNE) – A multinational enterprise, also referred to as a multinational corporation (MNC), is a firm that operates or controls business activities in more than one country. In this textbook we use the term *transnational corporation (TNC)* to describe private firms that operate internationally.

multi-paradigmatic approach – This term applies to *heterodox economics*, which intentionally seeks to examine issues using more than one *paradigm* or modeling framework in recognition of the biases that are likely to hamper analysis that is confined by one paradigm.

– N –

NAFTA – See *North American Free Trade Agreement* and *North American Free Trade Area*.

naked CDSs – Credit default swaps purchased by buyers who did not actually own the covered assets. Naked CDSs are essentially a form of gambling. There are many cases where the purchasers or sellers of naked CDSs actually have some influence over the likelihood that the insured assets would fail, which constitutes a very serious conflict of interest in the financial industry.

national treatment – The principle that foreign products, once they have entered the country, have paid required tariffs, and have met other border requirements, should be treated exactly the same way as domestic products.

natural resource curse – The name given to the common finding that countries that export only natural resources do not develop economically. Many explanations have been given for the natural resource curse: (1) the transnational firms who dominate trade have the power to suppress prices of natural resources, (2) the elasticity of demand for natural resources is low, and (3) the concentration of ownership of resources keeps export earnings in the hands of local elite business and resource groups that use their earnings to control political institutions that restrict economic and social change.

nature's services – Natural production of resources and the continual processes that help to maintain the ecosystem. For example, nature supplies fresh air, water, and trees for lumber. It also supplies services, such as flood control by absorbing water in soil and spreading seeds with its winds. Technically, nature's production should be divided into products and services. But, perhaps as a sign of humanity's imagined superiority over nature, the literature often refers to all natural products as nature's services rather than nature's production.

neoclassical growth model – See *Solow growth model*.

neoclassical paradigm – A framework of economic analysis that fits with the thinking of the neoclassical school. The neoclassical paradigm generally sees the economic sphere as consisting of a complete set of stable markets that efficiently set prices in a competitive environment so that prices provide accurate signals that lead rational individuals to behave in ways that, when all actions are summed, result in socially optimal economic outcomes. Heterodox economists argue that the neoclassical paradigm has blinded mainstream economics to the reality of life in the economic, social, and natural spheres, where markets are missing, complexity creates *externalities* to all individual actions, and human welfare cannot be determined purely by output in the economic sphere.

neoclassical school – The school of economic thought associated with Alfred Marshall and other late-nineteenth-century economists, who we described as having implicitly accepted the unsound strategy of *scientific reductionism* in order to focus their analytical attention on individual producers, consumers, and the markets. The principal feature of neoclassical thinking is that it views the economy from the static perspective of a fixed set of resources, which implies that the economy's principal problem is to seek the optimal allocation of that set of scarce resources that maximizes consumers' welfare. Neoclassical analysis is also characterized by marginal analysis and cost-benefit analysis. The neoclassical school has been criticized for making rather unrealistic assumptions about how product markets operate, rational behavior on the part of consumers, the separability of individual preference functions, the efficiency of financial markets, and the pervasiveness of markets to cover all exchanges and contingencies.

net international investment position – An estimate of the net sum of all foreign assets owned by a country's own citizens, businesses, organizations, financial firms, and governments, and all domestic assets owned by foreign citizens, businesses, organizations, financial firms, and governments. A country's net investment position at a given point in time is a stock variable determined, in large part, by the flows on the *balance of payments* in all previous years.

neuroscience – The scientific study of the functions of the brain. Neuroscience has discovered that the human brain does not operate in ways that would bring about human behavior as it is described by neoclassical models.

neutral technological change – The special case where technology changes the marginal productivities of all factors of production by the exact same proportion.

news – The arrival of new information and knowledge that was not previously known or predictable from previously known facts and models.

1910 Immigration Act – This law gave Canadian authorities considerable discretionary power over who could enter Canada. According to one provision in the law, the government could prohibit immigrants "belonging to any race deemed unsuited to the climate or requirements of Canada." The climate criterion was obviously intended to be applied in the case of nonwhite applicants.

1946 Canadian Citizenship Act – With this law in 1946, Canada became the first Commonwealth country to establish citizenship distinct from British citizenship.

1982 debt crisis – The simultaneous *default* or renegotiation of debts by over forty developing economies in 1982 occurred after world interest rates rose sharply following the tightening of monetary policies by a number of developed economies to slow rising inflation.

nonrenewable natural resources – Resources that exist in nature in a fixed amount. They are sometimes referred to as *exhaustible resources.*

nonrival good – The opposite of a *rival good* in that one person's use of the good does not prevent another from using it. Technology is often described as a nonrival good; if one person uses it, others are not prevented from using the same ideas or knowledge. After the nonrival good has been produced, the marginal cost of supplying the nonrival good to one more user is therefore zero, meaning that competitive market forces will tend to drive the price of a nonrival good to zero unless the supplier can somehow make the good excludable or restrict its use.

nontariff barrier (NTB) – A catchall name for all trade barriers other than *tariffs*, such as *quotas*, *voluntary export restraints*, government procurement rules, et cetera.

normative economics – This term refers to analysis by economists that includes judgments about the fair-ness, sustainability, or social desirability of economic outcomes or policies.

North American Free Trade Agreement (NAFTA) – The free trade agreement that went into effect in 1994 between Canada, Mexico, and the United States. Under NAFTA, the three countries agreed to open their borders to the free flow of goods and most services, but immigration was explicitly not addressed in the agreement.

The North American Free Trade Area (NAFTA) – Consisting of Canada, Mexico, and the United States, this trade bloc became a true free trade area at the end of the first decade of the 2000s, when virtually all remaining tariffs and trade barriers on goods were eliminated. Some barriers on services remained in 2010, however, and the agreement has not been explicitly extended to immigration, as some suggested would happen, even though the displacement of Mexican farmers by rising grain imports indirectly contributed to rising immigrant flows.

–O–

objectified cultural capital – Tools, equipment, clothing, and other objects whose possession define a member of a subculture or field, such as a musical instrument, an office, a wardrobe, or an intellectual's library of books.

objectivism – The philosophy centered on the idea that all answers to human problems can be found through reason and objective thought.

official transactions – Those *balance of payments* transactions that involve official assets, which are currencies and assets bought and sold by central banks for the purpose of influencing the *foreign exchange rate.*

offshore bank – A bank located in one country that is organized to provide business predominantly for depositors and borrowers in other countries.

off-shoring – Outsourcing that crosses borders. See *outsourcing.*

omitted variable bias – The inaccuracy of regression estimates when a statistical regression model does not include all the variables or explicitly model all the true relationships between all the relevant variables. The error occurs because, when causal variables are omitted, statistical methods attribute some causality to one or more of the included variables that are partially correlated with the omitted true causal variables.

open economy – An economy that does not severely restrict international trade, international investment, and international migration and permits these international economic activities to interact with domestic economic activity.

open market operations – The central bank purchases and sales of assets such as government bonds in open asset markets with the express purpose of changing the supply of money in circulation. A recent form of open market operation that involves the purchase of longer-term government securities and nongovernment securities in order to lower interest rates of specific maturities of lending or specific categories of financing is referred to as *quantitative easing.*

open position – A term used to describe a one-sided commitment in the foreign exchange market, such as when someone commits to buying or selling a currency at a predetermined price without hedging that commitment, thus leaving himself or herself open to potential losses from foreign exchange rate fluctuations.

opportunity cost – The most fundamental concept in economics: states the cost of doing one thing in terms of the other things that could have been done had the economy's resources not been employed to perform the first task.

optimal currency area – This term was coined by Robert Mundell in the 1960s, when he examined whether a group of countries could benefit from substituting a single currency for the individual national currencies. He argued that the size of an optimal currency area depends on the mobility of resources, the sharing of political *institutions* and social *cultures*, and the flexibility of *markets*.

Order of the Star-Spangled Banner – Also known as the Know-Nothings because they replied "I know nothing" when questioned about their movement, this group opposed immigration by Irish and other Roman Catholics they deemed to be a threat to the culture of the United States.

orthodox economics – The mainstream economics paradigm embraced by the majority of economists. In current economics textbooks, the orthodox paradigm is clearly the *neoclassical paradigm.* See also *neoclassical school.*

orthodoxy – The word element *ortho,* which comes from Greek, means straight, right, or correct. The word *doxy* refers to a doctrine, a framework of analysis, or what many social scientists would call a *paradigm.* Thus, orthodoxy refers to mainstream or culturally sanctioned thinking, as opposed to *heterodoxy,* which refers to alternative viewpoints that fall outside the accepted mainstream culture.

outsourcing – The process of contracting business services and manufacturing services out to other businesses in order to focus a firm's activities on its most profitable activities. When outsourcing is to foreign factories, it is often referred to as *off-shoring.*

over-the-counter market – A market made up of individual dealers who maintain stocks of merchandise or assets, and who stand ready to sell or buy upon demand. Bonds, foreign exchange, and financial derivatives are most often traded in over-the-counter markets. These are less transparent than exchanges because they reveal little information about prices and trading volumes; buyers and sellers see the price of only one particular transaction. The *foreign exchange market* is an over-the-counter market.

overvalued currency – A currency whose value is greater than it would be at its true market equilibrium. Overvalued currencies often depreciate in value, which can cause exchange rate crises and financial crises. It is difficult to determine the correct value of a currency, and many suggestions of currency overvaluations are not borne out by subsequent exchange rate behavior.

–P–

panel studies – Statistical regressions that simultaneously apply *time-series* and *cross-section* data, say ten years of annual observations for a set of 100 countries.

paradigm – A consistent, logical conceptual framework of beliefs, philosophies, practices, and accepted patterns for organizing thought in an intellectual discipline. Economic models are usually based on a set of assumptions that reflect some specific paradigm, such as the *neoclassical paradigm* in mainstream economics today.

Paris Peace Conference – The conference of world leaders that met for six months in 1919 to negotiate a peace agreement, establish international institutions such as the League of Nations and the *Bank for International Settlements*, and redraw national boundaries in favor of nations and nationalist groups that effectively defined themselves as the winners of World War I.

partial equilibrium model – A model that describes an equilibrium relationship between certain variables in just one market or one sector of the economy while assuming that all other things elsewhere in the economy remain unchanged.

patent – A right of ownership granted to the inventor or creator of a technique, process, or idea. A patent is intended to exclude others from producing or marketing the technique, process, or idea for some limited period of time without the explicit permission of the inventor.

path-dependent process – A process that continuously builds on prior outcomes so that later outcomes depend on previous outcomes along a clear progression of outcomes that appears as a continuous path. Innovation is such a process, since new ideas are combinations of previous ideas; hence, current *technology* depends on the prior accumulation of technology. A path-dependent process need not be smooth and steady; the path can have sharp turns and declines, but it is continuous.

pegged exchange rate – A term often used synonymously with *fixed exchange rate* but is also used to refer specifically to the arrangement under the *Bretton Woods order,* which required central banks to intervene in the *foreign exchange market* in order to keep currencies within a 1 percent band around an openly stated target exchange rate except in the case of a fundamental disequilibrium that clashed with the long-run aims of full employment and economic growth.

petrodollars – The current account surpluses of oil exporting countries that were deposited in the *Eurocurrency* market during the 1970s. These deposits were largely recycled as loans to oil-importing countries.

Plaza Accord – The agreement signed in 1985 by France, Germany, Japan, and the United States at the Plaza Hotel in New York, which specified the national policies each country would adopt in order to push the value of the U.S. dollar down and enable the United States to balance its trade. The accord showed that countries could still co-operate and formulate joint economic policies, although the effectiveness of the agreement in accomplishing its goals is open to debate.

policy flexibility – A term used in this book to describe the leeway that government policy makers have to pursue various policy objectives before they run up against the implicit constraints imposed by effects of their economic policies on the performance of the economy. For example, a government may desire to print money in order to fund a pet project, but it may not be able to because printing money would cause an undesirable increase in inflation. Another example is the *trilemma*, which states that *globalization* and *fixed exchange rates* restrict a government's domestic *monetary* and *fiscal policies.*

political economy – The field of study that combines economics and political science in order to explain the relationship between political activity and its economic effects.

Ponzi finance – A term used by Hyman P. Minsky to describe any project that requires new borrowing to service its interest and principal.

Ponzi scheme – A finance scheme in which new borrowing or investment is required just to meet interest or dividend payments; essentially a project with negative cash flow, whose existence depends on new investors providing finds in order to maintain the appearance of viability.

portfolio diversification – The reduction of *risk* by combining different assets whose returns are not perfectly correlated.

portfolio investment – The acquisition of financial assets in quantities too small to give the owners any controlling interest in the firms and enterprises who issued the stock, bonds, or other financial instruments.

positive economics – This term refers to analysis by economists that alleges to be free from value judgments and cultural bias. Positive economics focuses on facts and observed behavioral relationships, and it includes the development and testing of *hypotheses*. Sociologists and behavioral economists have argued that it is impossible to escape *culture* and human nature in the framing of economic analyses and the setting of hypotheses, and only by explicitly recognizing the power of culture and human nature can major inaccuracies and biases be avoided.

positive-sum game – This generally refers to a form of human interaction that results in all parties becoming better off. This contrasts with a zero-sum game, in which one side of the transaction gains at the expense of the other, and a negative-sum game, in which all participants would have been better off never entering into the transaction or interaction.

power of compounding – The results of a *compound growth process* tend to surprise people, as small periodic changes eventually cause very large absolute changes.

precautionary principle – In a complex process where some of the possible outcomes are truly catastrophic, but the complexity does not permit a precise calculation of probabilities for such outcomes, it can be prudent to take action to minimize the chances of having to face such outcomes. For example, the precautionary principle suggests that the world's governments should take strong action to limit *greenhouse gas emissions* that cause *global warming* precisely because we do not know exactly how likely it is that a rise in temperatures of several degrees will do substantial damage to humanity.

predatory dumping – Similar to predatory pricing, the intentional selling of foreign goods below cost with the intent of eliminating domestic competition so that, in the future, the dumping firm(s) can exploit their greater market power to the long-run detriment of the importing nation.

predatory pricing – Action by a firm to lower prices in order to drive its competition out of business, with the intent of exploiting its monopoly power once the competition has been eliminated.

preferential trade area (PTA) – A regional trade area in which the member countries agree to lower trade barriers within the group to levels below those erected against outside economies. They do not establish complete free trade within their area. PTAs are illegal under GATT/WTO rules, although developing countries have been permitted to form PTAs.

preserving services of nature – The insurance provided by the diversity and redundancy of the *ecosystem*. The failure of one species does not immediately threaten humans because there are many other species that provide similar services and can take up the slack. The *ecosystem* is over-engineered, but the redundancy serves an important insurance, or preserving, function.

price discrimination – The practice of charging different customers different prices for the same product in order to increase overall *producer surplus* at the expense of *consumer surplus*.

primary budget surplus – Government receipts minus all expenditures except for interest payments on accumulated debt. In order for an undebted government to balance its total receipts and expenditures and avoid accumulating new debt, it would have to generate a primary budget surplus equal to the interest payments on its debt.

principal-agent problem – Banks, money managers, and hedge funds (the agents), among other intermediaries, effectively play with other people's (the principals) money, and they may have incentives that lead them to treat funds differently from how financial investors would prefer. For example, a profit-maximizing bank finds it advantageous to invest in excessively risky assets because if things work out, then the bank owners enjoy high profits, but if things do not work out, it is the depositors who suffer most of the losses.

producer surplus – The net gains to producers of a product, equal to the total revenue minus the sum of marginal (variable) costs.

product cycle model – A model developed by Raymond Vernon that describes how production shifts from developed to developing economies over the life of a product. The resources needed to develop and produce new products are different from the resources needed to produce mature products; hence, production gradually shifts from where R&D is carried out to where routine production costs, especially labor costs, are cheapest. Later in the product cycle, labor costs matter more because the routinization of production makes inputs like human capital less important.

product value – A product's *value,* V, is often defined by the value equation $V = B/P$, where B and P are the product's benefits and price, respectively. Product benefits are the perceived characteristics of a product, which are influenced by tastes, culture, traditions, habits, and active marketing activities such as advertising, public relations, pricing strategies, market positioning, distribution strategies, and sales organizations.

production function – The relationship between productive inputs and the level of output, usually written in mathematical form as $Y = f(K, H, L, R, ...)$ where Y is output and K, H, L, R, et cetera are the productive inputs such as physical capital, human capital, labor, natural resources, and so forth.

production possibilities frontier (PPF) – A graphic representation of the set of all combinations of products that an economy can produce given its resources and *technology*.

professional immigrant – An immigrant who moves to another country to perform a specialized technical or management job. Professional immigrants include the managers and other employees of the transnational corporations.

prohibitive tariff – A tax on imports that is set so high that trade is no longer attractive and imports fall to zero.

proletariat – According to Karl Marx, the social class made up of workers, both employed and unemployed, as well as bankrupt former members of the *bourgeoisie*.

provisioning services of nature – These are the products that nature provides to us directly, such as food, spices, water, air, warmth, vitamin D through sunlight, firewood, and myriad other things.

purchasing power – Effectively, the real amount of goods and services that can be acquired for something such as income, money, or wages, for example.

purchasing power parity (PPP) – A *theory* that states that the *exchange rate* reflects the differences in the general price levels between countries, based on the idea that trade, as a process of *arbitrage*, will cause the prices of goods to be the same everywhere. The explicit relationship between the *exchange rate* and national price levels is $e = P/P^*$, where e is the nominal exchange rate, P is the domestic price index, and P^* is the foreign price index. PPP is also a term that is used to describe any

adjustment of national and foreign measures for their real *purchasing power*.

– Q –

quantitative easing – A recent form of open market operation that involves the purchase of longer-term government securities and nongovernment securities in order to lower interest rates of specific maturities of lending or specific categories of financing. See also *open market operations*.

quantitative trade restrictions – Commonly referred to as import *quotas*, quantitative trade restrictions set specific limits on the quantity of foreign goods or services that may enter the country.

quota – See *quantitative trade restrictions*.

quota rent – The arbitrage profit that accrues to importers when a *quantitative trade restriction*, or quota, keeps the quantity imported below its free-market equilibrium level.

– R –

Rambouillet Summit – In 1975, the *Bretton Woods* countries met in France to work out a new international monetary order to create a "stable system" of exchange rates, but not a "system of stable exchange rates," as some countries had urged. The word play shows how far apart countries were in trying to design a successor to the collapsed *Bretton Woods order* in the early 1970s.

rational expectations – The expectations that people are assumed to hold when they use (1) all available information plus (2) their best understanding of how markets and the economy function, and they also use (3) logical reasoning to reach their conclusions about the future. Rational expectations is a popular assumption in modern macroeconomics, even though evidence shows people do not consistently act according to the three rules listed above.

real assets – Physical, tangible assets such as buildings, land, and factories.

real exchange rate – The nominal exchange rate adjusted for price levels; specifically, where e is defined as the nominal exchange rate, the real exchange rate is

$R = eP^*/P$, where P and P* are the domestic and foreign price levels, respectively.

Reciprocal Trade Agreements Act (RTAA) – The 1934 U.S. law giving the president *fast-track authority* to negotiate tariff reductions with other countries, marking the first time that Congress, which has the constitutional power to determine trade policy, gave the executive branch of government the authority to negotiate tariffs without direct Congressional involvement. The RTAA was a strong reaction to the disastrous trade war that followed the United States' *1930 Smoot-Hawley tariffs.*

recycled petrodollars – Most oil-exporting countries deposited their *petrodollars* in the *Eurocurrency* market during the 1970s, and this money was, in turn, lent to oil-importing countries, who thus gained access to the dollars needed to pay for the more expensive oil without reducing economic growth.

Refugee Relief Act of 1953 – This 1953 act of the U.S. Congress authorized an extra 200,000 permanent resident visas outside the quota system established under the restrictive *Immigration Act of 1924*. This act replaced the *Displaced Persons Act of 1948*, which expired in 1953.

refugees – People who flee serious threats to their safety and well-being; refugees often end up migrating to other countries in order to seek better economic, political, or social conditions. Most countries treat political refugees differently from economic refugees, with certain political refugees usually getting more sympathetic treatment.

regional economics – The domestic equivalent of the field of international economics, which studies trade, investment, finance, and migration between regions within a single country.

regional trade bloc – A group of countries that agree to reduce or eliminate trade barriers between them while maintaining barriers to trade with countries outside the group; there are different types of regional trade areas, such as *free trade areas, customs unions, common markets,* and *economic unions.*

regression analysis – A statistical method that tries to uncover the relationship between a variable to be explained and some set of explanatory or independent variables. Usually using the least-squares method, regres-
sion analysis is essentially the process of determining the linear function that is most likely to have generated a scatter of observed data points. Regression programs generate coefficient values, which are like the slope of the fitted line, and these describe the relationship between the variables. See also *linear regression equation.*

regulating services of nature – Nature's services that regulate our climate, recycle our waste, and maintain our relationships with all other living species. Examples are the forests and grasslands that absorb rain into the ground for storage and later use and prevent flooding and soil erosion.

remittances – See *immigrant remittances.*

renewable resources – Natural resources that are continuously replenished and restored by nature, such as fresh water or oxygen. They are included among the services of nature or *nature's services*. Excessive exploitation of nature's services reduces the ecosystem's capacity to provide its services in the future.

rent – The return to a factor that exceeds its opportunity cost, or what is necessary to keep that factor employed in its current function as opposed to some other application.

rent-evading activity – An attempt to carry out mutually beneficial transactions in violation of rules, laws, or other institutions that restrict them. Rent-evading activities, such as smuggling or black markets, differ from *rent-seeking activities,* which are attempts to get policy makers to create restrictions on mutually beneficial transactions.

rent-seeking activities – Activities that use costly (scarce) resources to obtain transfers but which do not add to output or overall welfare. Included among rent-seeking activities are things like lobbying, bribery, public relations, and political campaign contributions.

reparations payments – Transfer payments as compensation for damage caused. Specifically, Germany was required to pay reparations payments after World War I.

reserve currency – This is internationally recognized and negotiable money that central banks hold as a store of value to meet future international payments, and as an asset to actively *intervene* in the foreign exchange markets. Currently, the U.S. dollar, the *euro*, the Japanese yen, and the Swiss franc are the most-held reserve currencies.

retaliation – The raising of trade barriers in response to another country's increase in trade barriers.

retaliatory tariffs – Import taxes imposed by an exporting country in retaliation for other countries' imposition of import taxes on those exports. The imposition of retaliatory tariffs can escalate into the *trade war*.

revaluation – A change in a currency peg that increases its value relative to other currencies. See also *devaluation* and *pegged exchange rate*.

reversal of financial flows – The case where a country's *financial account* suddenly shifts from positive to negative, or vice-versa. Financial flow reversals require difficult real adjustments on the *current account* or other policy shifts to compensate for the financial account changes.

risk – The variation in outcomes that can be described with a known distribution function, so that the mean, median, and spread of outcomes are reasonably well understood. See also *uncertainty*.

risk aversion – The desire to avoid risk and increase certainty. Risk aversion is why risky assets must pay higher rates of return in order to induce buyers to hold them.

risk premium – The amount that the expected yield of an asset (including a currency) exceeds that of a risk-free asset because of the perceived risk of the asset.

rollover – This essentially refers to the new financing required in the cases that Hyman P. Minsky calls *speculative* or *Ponzi financing*, in which cash inflows do not fully cover debt servicing and principle repayment.

round – In the context of the *GATT* and *WTO*, a multilateral trade negotiation process; nine rounds have been completed since the *GATT*'s founding in 1947, and the current *Doha Round* is the tenth.

rules of the game – The term often used for the *order* that guides the international monetary system.

– S –

sanctions – See *trade sanction*.

scarcity – In economics, the situation in which limited resources are available to satisfy seemingly unlimited wants. Scarcity is the reason we study economics, because if there were no scarcity and if everyone had more than he or she wanted, we would not have to concern ourselves with how to allocate our resources and how to raise per capita output. Scarcity mandates that we make decisions as to what to produce, how to produce it, who should receive the output, and when they should receive it.

Schumpeterian growth models – A set of growth models recently developed by a number of economists based on Joseph Schumpeter's model showing *technological progress* as the result of a *creative destruction* process whereby entrepreneurs intentionally apply resources to develop new products and processes in order to better their competitors and gain monopoly profits.

Schumpeter model – Joseph Schumpeter described the capitalist economy as a "perennial gale of creative destruction," and he constructed a model that specifies innovation as a costly process that uses scarce resources, which are paid for out of expected future profits from creatively destroying current technologies. Schumpeter's model is a truly dynamic one that specifies an ongoing process. His model also captures another important characteristic of economic growth, which is that the creation of something new requires that resources be reallocated, and often some existing economic activity must be eliminated. See also *creative destruction*.

science – The practice of following the scientific method.

scientific hypothesis – A falsifiable construct or model that accurately and logically explains the facts you observe. A hypothesis must be confronted with objectively obtained evidence or objectively designed experiments in order to verify its accuracy.

scientific method – The set of procedures, or steps, that must be followed if one is to be a scientist. *Science* is defined as a set of phenomena that are studied in accordance with the scientific method.

scientific observation – An objectively observed and described phenomenon or fact, which is then built into a *scientific hypothesis*.

scientific reductionism – The analytical approach that assumes that we can understand the whole by learning about its parts, one part at a time. In effect, scientific reductionism accepts that the whole is the straightforward sum of its parts. *Holistic scientists*, on the other hand, argue that to understand a complex process or system, one must understand not just the parts, but also how the parts interact. Scientific reductionism is not scientific if there are good reasons to suspect that the interactions between the components of the system determine the outcomes of the overall system. See also *holism*.

Second Amendment to the Bretton Woods Articles of Agreement – In 1978, the member countries of the *International Monetary Fund (IMF)* agreed on the Second Amendment to the original Bretton Woods Articles of Agreement, which officially legalized the *floating exchange rates* that had been a fact since 1973. This amendment also committed countries to maintaining stable economic policies in order to minimize exchange rate volatility and authorized the IMF to monitor and critique countries' economic policies on a continual basis.

Securities and Exchange Commission (SEC) – An agency created in the United States during the 1930s to oversee financial markets such as the stock and bond markets.

securitization – The bundling of a large number of assets into a single security, in which shares can then be sold. Securitization effectively spreads the risk of the individual underlying assets among the purchasers of shares. Some securities are *tranched*, which reduces the risk to some buyers of shares and increases the risk to others. See also *tranche, subprime mortgage, structured financial product*.

segmented labor market – A labor market in which *arbitrage* is restricted and different wages are paid for similar types of work. Segmentation may occur across different industries, distinct geographic locations, or different groups of people. Segmentation is a form of discrimination.

seignorage – The gains to the government from its monopoly on creating money, which are equal to the difference between the real purchasing power of newly created money and the cost of creating the new money. In the case of gold coins, seignorage is equal to the difference between the purchasing power of the coin and the costs of the gold, other raw materials, and the manufacturing process of stamping the coin. *Fiat money* produces the highest seignorage earnings.

services of nature – See *nature's services*.

settlers – International migrants who become permanent residents in the destination country.

Sharia-compliant finance – See *Islamic finance*.

shrinkage – A term used in transport and distribution activity to represent pilferage, theft, spoilage, or deterioration of products in transit or storage.

Silk Road – The land trade route through central Asia linking China and the Middle East and Europe at the time of the Roman Empire, over which innovative Chinese products were brought to the Mediterranean region.

Single European Act – In 1985, a widely publicized white paper by a commission headed by European Commission President Jacques Delors proposed creating a true single market serving more than 300 million consumers by eliminating remaining obstacles to trade. In 1986 this idea was realized in this act, which set out a precise timetable for completing 275 steps necessary to establish the single market by the start of 1993.

small country assumption – The assumption that a country is so small that it has no noticeable effect on prices in the rest of the world. The assumption is convenient because it lets the analyst assume that the *terms of trade* remain constant as a country expands or contracts exports or imports.

Smithsonian Agreement – The 1971 financial agreement that President Richard M. Nixon described as "the most significant monetary agreement in the history of the world," and under which countries agreed to repeg exchange rates and continue with the *Bretton Woods order*. It was abandoned after less than two years when exchange rates were set free to float.

Smoot-Hawley Tariff Act – The sharp increase in U.S. tariffs authorized by Congress in 1930 and signed into law by President Herbert H. Hoover after a year of lobbying by special interests and political maneuvering; this tariff triggered a *trade war* that quickly reduced world trade and helped to push the world into the depression that was developing.

smuggling – The illegal evasion of tariffs and other import restrictions.

snake in the tunnel – The tighter bands for exchange rates that were maintained between European currencies while the whole group of currencies was permitted to fluctuate more widely against the rest of the world's currencies.

social climate – As used by Joseph Schumpeter, the environment within which the *entrepreneur* has to operate. Schumpeter focused on the *institutions* that guide the activity of the special group of people he called entrepreneurs. He included among the critical institutions society's attitude toward business success, how well the education system prepares potential entrepreneurs, and how much freedom mavericks have to pursue their ambitions.

social-contractionism – The view that unbiased definition of social justice can only be determined from behind a *veil of ignorance* where individuals know nothing about their own particular circumstances. This philosophical view recognizes that people's viewpoints are never entirely objective because culture, economic conditions, and limited perspectives always cause bias.

social indifference curves – See *aggregate indifference curves*.

social scientist – Someone who follows the scientific method in order to further knowledge and understanding of human society.

Solow growth model – Robert Solow's (1956) constant-returns-to-scale model with several variable inputs, each subject to *diminishing returns*. The most important conclusion of the Solow model is that permanent economic growth is possible only if there is continued *technological progress*; mere *factor accumulation* eventually results in stagnation, no matter how high the rate of savings and investment. This textbook presents a two-section version of the Solow model to illustrate the relationship between the natural and economic sectors.

source country – The term used to describe the country that international migrants left when they moved to another country to seek residence and employment.

sovereign risk – The risk that an autonomous foreign government will *default* on its contractual obligations, leaving the creditor with limited legal recourse.

spatial arbitrage – See *geographic arbitrage*.

specialization – The process whereby people increasingly concentrate on a few tasks rather than performing every job necessary for their existence, which, when combined with exchange, permits them to produce greater amounts of real output. Referred to as the *division of labor* by Adam Smith.

specie – A term used to describe precious metals such as gold and silver that are used as *money*.

specific tariff – A tax on imports specified as a specific money amount per unit, unlike an *ad valorem tariff*, which is linked to the price of the product being taxed.

specification error – In statistics, a specification error refers to any case where the statistical model inaccurately represents the true process being modeled. Specification errors are commonly due to the failure to include all relevant variables, the use of linear relationships when the true relationship is nonlinear, and the use of a single equation when the relationship is part of a more complex multi-equation system.

speculation – The intention of earning a profit by buying (selling) an asset at one point in time in order to sell (buy) an asset at a later date when prices are expected to be higher (lower).

speculative attack – A massive surge in buying or selling precipitated by a change in expectations about future price movements, which causes an immediate large price change.

speculative finance – A term used by Hyman P. Minsky to describe the case in which, explicitly or implicitly, earnings and other revenues cover interest payments but not the full repayment of principle when it comes due. Thus, speculative finance effectively assumes that lenders will be able to *roll over* their debts when they come due in order to gain more time to pay them off. See also *hedge finance* and *Ponzi finance*.

speculator – Any person or organization that attempts gain from future price changes by taking an open position in a market, such as when someone contracts to buy foreign exchange in the forward market at a price that they estimate to be below the price that will actually prevail in the future. A speculator willingly assumes *risk*, unlike a hedger, who covers all risks.

spillover – See *technology spillover.*

spot exchange rate – The price set in the *spot market* for *foreign exchange*, it represents the current price for foreign exchange.

spot market – The segment of the foreign exchange market where currencies are traded for immediate delivery.

Spread Index – Calculated by the United Nations Conference on Trade and Development, this index measures the *globalization* of a corporation as the square root of the ratio of foreign affiliates to all affiliates, multiplied by the number of host countries.

Stability and Growth Pact – In 1997 European Union members established the accession criteria, and in 2002 these criteria were formally extended into a set of ongoing rules of behavior. These rules were not adhered to, and the euro area's difficulties after 2010 were caused by the excessive accumulation of foreign debt by the governments of Greece, Ireland, Portugal, Spain, and other European Union countries.

stable equilibrium – An equilibrium in which economic decision makers have no incentive to change their economic behavior, and if some shock pushes the economy away from the equilibrium, actions will be automatically triggered to bring the economy back to equilibrium.

standardized product – A product whose production technology is widely understood, for which equipment can be easily acquired, and for which not much specialized labor is required.

static economic model – An economic model that describes how key variables will eventually change as a result of a one-time change in policy or economic circumstances, *all other things equal (ceteris paribus)*, but it does not show how long it takes the economy to achieve its final equilibrium or how the variables change during the transition period.

statistical discrepancy – This is the balancing item in the *balance of payments* designed to capture the missing transactions that prevent the balance of payments from balancing. Globally, the sum of all countries' statistical discrepancies usually exceeds US$100 billion, which suggests that data on international trade and finance are not quite accurate.

statistical significance – A technical term that describes the probability that statistical analysis will accept as proof that the data confirm a hypothesized relationship.

steady state equilibrium – The stable equilibrium levels of output and the capital stock described by the *Solow growth model*. Specifically, it is the level of output where the capital stock suffers depreciation exactly equal to the economy's level of saving. See also the *Solow growth model.*

Stolper-Samuelson theorem – An important theorem from international economics that states that for a simple two-factor, two-good general equilibrium model of trade, when the economy moves to free trade the return to the factor used intensively in the growing export industry rises and the return to the factor used intensively in the shrinking import-competing industry falls. This finding depends on a number of strong assumptions, but its intuitive logic sheds some light on why certain groups would be opposed to free trade even though the total availability of welfare-enhancing goods and services increases with free trade.

store of value – One of the functions of money, namely, its ability to hold value until it is passed on in exchange for something else.

strategic trade policy – Government policies that interfere with the free flow of trade in order to protect or promote industries that are deemed to have exceptional growth prospects or beneficial effects on the country's economic performance.

structural change – The condition that certain sectors grow relative to others, and thus the relative contributions of each sector change. For example, the Industrial Revolution is characterized by a gradual increase in manufacturing activity relative to agricultural activities. Today, the more developed economies of the world are undergoing structural change toward services and away from agriculture and manufacturing.

structuralism – A school of economic thought related to the French philosophical movement led by, among others, anthropologist Claude Lévi-Strauss. Structuralism replaced existentialism as the most popular philosophical concept in the late 1940s and 1950s among French philosophers and their followers. Structuralists hypothesized that human behavior is determined by various structures or systems. They therefore concluded that human economic behavior could be explained and predicted only if the basic social, political, natural, and economic structures were understood.

structuralist school of economics – Like the philosophical structuralists, who rejected the idea that humans make choices according to their free will, structuralist economists explicitly rejected mainstream economics' fundamental assumption that economic outcomes were the result of free choices made by individuals who sought, rationally, to maximize their individual welfare. Thus, where modern economic analysis assumes smooth functions and continuous marginal adjustments to price signals, structuralist economists during the 1950s and 1960s argued that developing economies were plagued by structural rigidities, such as culture and institutions, which prevented smooth adjustments.

structured financial product – This term generally refers to financial instruments such as *collateralized debt obligations (CDOs)*, which are divided into tranches in order to make the underlying set of assets more attractive to the specific needs of potential buyers. See also *securitization* and *tranche.*

subprime mortgage – A mortgage given to a customer with a below-average probability of servicing the debt according to the contractual terms. Subprime mortgages normally charge above-average interest rates.

subsidy – Any type of payment, tax reduction, or other financial benefit given by government for some specific economic activity, such as an export subsidy, a production subsidy, or a consumption subsidy. A subsidy has been referred to as a negative tax.

Super 301 – A U.S. law that permits the government to impose up to 100 percent *tariffs* on imports of individual foreign suppliers that are deemed to trade unfairly. The United States has applied such arbitrary tariffs on imports of steel, food products, and lumber in response to lobbying by domestic industries.

supply side – In macroeconomic analysis, the supply side of the economy represents the economy's total capacity, assumed to be determined by the available factors of production, natural resources, and the level of *technology* with which factors and resources can be transformed into products. In mainstream microeconomics, the supply side is normally represented by a *production possibilities frontier*.

supporting services of nature – The services of nature that are inputs into the processes of human production. For example, the pollination provided by insects and birds that enable a farmer to grow fruit, the solar rays that enable crops to grow, and the water that seeps into a farmer's well are supporting services, or more specifically intermediate inputs, provided by nature.

swap transaction – In the foreign exchange market, the simultaneous spot sale (purchase) and forward purchase (sale) of an asset.

symbolic violence – This term, coined by the French sociologist Pierre Bourdieu, refers to the use of cultural capital to impose on others. Instead of actual physical violence to oppress or steal from others, cultural symbols such as formal degrees, learned behaviors such as speech and body language, and inherited material objects such as tools and clothes give people an advantage over others in human interactions.

– T –

tacit knowledge – Knowledge that is transferred by example rather than learned through explicit instructions. Michael Polanyi argued that the tacit nature of most knowledge and *technology* means adoption requires costly and time-consuming person-to-person interactions.

tariff – A tax on imports.

tariff escalation – The practice of levying higher tariffs for manufactured products than for raw materials, and increasingly higher tariffs the greater the value added by the industry.

tariffication – The conversion of nontariff barriers into their equivalent tariffs. It is generally thought to be easier to negotiate reductions in tariffs than reductions in a varied assortment of trade barriers whose effects are more difficult to quantify, which is why tariffication is often part of a trade liberalization process.

tax haven – A sovereign country that attracts foreign firms to locate certain activities within its borders because it offers to tax those activities less than other countries do.

technical barrier to trade – A mandatory requirement or technical standard that imports must meet before they are permitted to enter the country.

technological change – A change in the relationship between production and inputs. Technology improves when output increases for the same set of inputs, in which case technological change is often referred to as *technological progress.*

technological follower – A firm or country that is not able to profitably innovate and lead in producing new products that use the most advanced technologies, and instead waits for new technologies to become standardized before adopting them for its own use.

technological leader – The firm or nation with the most advanced technology that enjoys a comparative advantage in developing and producing new products.

technological progress – The specific type of technological change that expands humans' ability to convert resources into welfare-enhancing production.

technology – The relationship between productive inputs and output, which neoclassical economics usually models as a *production function.* In practice, technology in an economy can have a very broad meaning, and it can include ideas, methods, habits, economic and social institutions, business organization, et cetera. See also *human technology.*

technology spillover – When technology is obtained at less than the original cost to the inventor, then there is said to be a *spillover* of technology. Whether international trade enhances the spread of *technology* often comes down to whether it generates international technology spillovers.

technology transfers – The passing on of ideas, techniques, methods, designs, and other forms of knowledge from one person, organization, or firm to others. Because of technology's special role in enabling continuous economic growth, and given the high costs of creating new knowledge from scratch, the international transfer of technology is very important for the growth of human well-being.

temporary immigrants – Immigrants who remain in the destination country for only a limited amount of time, such as students, professionals hired to perform a specific task, or employees of transnational firms who shift among the firm's branches in different countries.

terms of trade (ToT) – The amount of exports that a country needs to supply to the international market in order to obtain a given amount of imports; the rate at which countries can exchange exports for imports in the world market.

territoriality – The fundamental emotional attachment to their possessions and geographic territory that people, and many other living species, exhibit. Territoriality implies that people are loss averse, and will fight harder to hold on to what they have than to acquire something new.

theory – In science, a theory is a precise conceptual framework that consistently explains existing facts and accurately predicts future facts. The *scientific method* says that a *hypothesis* becomes a theory only after it is proven by an objectively obtained set of data, direct observations of real phenomena, or carefully designed tests. The popular definition of the word *theory* does not match the scientific definition of a *theory;* most people think of a theory as a vague or abstract idea.

three-person game – A game in which three players compete, which makes it substantially more complex than a two-person game because coalitions are possible. The 1982 debt crisis turned into a three-person game when the governments of the world's major developed economies realized that total loans to foreign governments exceeded the capital of most of their major commercial banks.

time-series data – A set of observations of a specific phenomenon taken at a series of consecutive points in time or periods of time. See also *cross-section data.*

tipping point – A term often used in the field of ecology and environmental sciences to designate a point in time when a certain complex process suddenly shifts to a different evolutionary path. For example, the gradual rise in atmospheric temperatures attributable to *anthropogenic* carbon emissions causes the Arctic permafrost to melt and release huge amounts of stored methane, with the result that *global warming* accelerates sharply.

Tokyo Round – The round of *GATT* trade negotiations that took place between1974 and 1979, which lowered *tariffs* for most manufactured goods and some other products by about one-third.

total factor productivity (TFP) – A measure of output relative to the quantity of inputs used in producing the output; TFP is often given as a growth rate, measuring the increase in output relative to the increase in real inputs, in which case it can be used as a measure of *technological change.*

trade adjustment assistance – Justified by standard trade theory that shows that free trade causes a net increase in economic welfare, trade adjustment assistance is intended to have those who gain from free trade compensate those who suffer welfare losses or job losses.

trade bloc – A common name for a regional free trade area, such as a *free trade area,* a *customs union,* a *common market,* or an *economic union.*

trade creation – The increase in trade that results from a shift in trade policy and is, all other things equal, welfare enhancing.

trade credit – Credit given to cover the costs of trade, most often to cover the short-term period that goods are in transit or to permit exporters to offer foreign buyers competitive terms of payment.

trade diversion – The redirection of a country's foreign trade away from the world's low cost suppliers and high-priced markets as a result of a discriminatory regional trade agreement, which, all other things equal, reduces the welfare gains from trade.

trade policy – A nation's set of laws, regulations, rules, and procedures that apply to international trade.

trade promotion authority – See *fast-track authority.*

trade sanction – A trade restriction imposed by one country in order to punish another country or persuade another country to change objectionable policies or behavior.

trade triangle – The graphic depiction of international trade in the two-dimensional graphic *Heckscher-Ohlin model,* which shows how much domestically produced production, measured along one axis, is exported in exchange for imports of a product measured along the

other axis. The slope of the hypotenuse measures the *terms of trade (ToT).*

trade war – The escalation of trade restrictions across many countries when one country's increased trade barriers cause other countries to retaliate and increase their tariffs and other forms of protection on many products.

tranche – A share of a *collateralized debt obligation* backed by a large set of assets, where each share is given a rank for being paid a promised return. The top tranche is paid first, then, if there are returns left, the next tranche is paid, and so forth.

transactions costs – These are all the explicit costs, the time, and the preparation necessary in order to carry out the exchange of goods and services. Transactions costs include business activities such as marketing.

transfer payments – Payments that are not in exchange for any good or service, but are more like gifts. *Foreign aid* and *immigrant remittances* are examples of international transfer payments.

transfer price – The internal price that transnational firms use to record an exchange between branches of the same firm located in different countries.

transitional economic growth – See *medium-run economic growth* and the *Solow growth model.*

transnational corporation (TNC) – A firm or corporation that manages and owns production and distribution facilities in more than one country. By definition, TNCs carry out all of the world's *foreign direct investment (FDI).*

transparency – Refers to the clarity, openness, predictability, and comprehensibility of policies, procedures, and regulations.

Treaty of Rome – The 1957 treaty that established the European Economic Community (EEC), originally signed by Belgium, France, West Germany, Italy, Luxembourg, and the Netherlands.

Treaty of Versailles – The treaty that formally ended World War I in 1919, which among other things determined that Germany and its allies had to compensate the Allied countries for their war losses, a measure that John

Maynard Keynes argued would create resentment that could lead to another war. The treaty also redrew many European borders and created several new countries.

triangular arbitrage – *Arbitrage* consisting of at least two exchanges of currency to exploit inconsistencies across different bilateral exchange rates.

Triffin paradox – Robert Triffin (1960) warned that there was a fundamental inconsistency in the *Bretton Woods order:* As the owner of the world's *reserve currency*, the United States was obligated to run trade deficits so that the rest of the world could "earn" dollar reserves, but the more dollars were held by foreigners, the more likely that the dollar could come under speculative attack and the less foreigners would want to hold dollars as reserves.

trilemma – Policy makers cannot simultaneously fix the exchange rate, set economic policies with only domestic goals in mind, and permit the free flow of goods and assets across national borders; they can pursue only two of those options simultaneously. The trilemma explains the failures of most *fixed exchange rate* systems.

Tripartite Monetary Agreement – The agreement signed by the United States, Great Britain, and France in 1936 that established a new financial order consisting of *fixed exchange rates* maintained through continual central bank *intervention*. This agreement was a model for the *Bretton Woods international monetary order* established in 1944.

TRIPs – The acronym used by the WTO to refer to its Agreement on Trade-Related Intellectual Property Rights.

–U–

unauthorized immigrant – a person who cross the border in violation of the immigration laws of the destination country and without the required documentation.

uncertainty – The situation where future outcomes cannot be predicted, nor is the distribution of possible outcomes understood well enough to be able to attribute probabilities to the potential outcomes. In many cases of uncertainty, all possible outcomes are not even known. See also *risk*.

underdevelopment – The term used by some 1950s and 1960s structuralist and dependency theorists to describe the unique situation of contemporary poor countries. In their view, the developed countries of the day had never been underdeveloped, only undeveloped, because they had never passed through a stage where they had had to coexist with much wealthier and more highly industrialized countries and, thus, be forced to play the role of subservient provider of the wealthy countries' economic needs, as the current poor countries do today.

undervalued currency – A currency whose value is less than it would be at the true market equilibrium.

uninformed voter model – A political economy model that suggests that small special interest groups will have a disproportionately large influence on government policies because most voters have little information on most issues that do not directly affect them.

unit of account – One of the three functions of money, namely money's purpose as the commodity in which all other things are valued. See also *money*.

United States Border Patrol – The agency charged with guarding the U.S. border. The Constitution does not permit the active use of military forces within the United States, hence the creation of a special police organization to enforce immigration laws at the border was required.

U.S. Citizenship and Immigration Services (USCIS) – The second agency, along with ICE, created out of the original INS after the reorganization of U.S. security agencies after the 2001 terrorist attacks. USCIS is the bureaucratic organization that processes immigration visas and naturalization requests.

Uruguay Round – The ambitious *GATT* round of trade negotiations that took place from 1987 through 1994, and which attempted to negotiate trade restrictions that had theretofore been ignored, such as those on agricultural trade, clothing trade, services trade, and intellectual property rights. The round achieved some success in most areas, although much work remained at its conclusion, some of which was taken up in the *Doha Round* that began in 2002.

utilitarianism – The philosophical approach to human well-being that most closely resembles the simple tallying of gains and losses as is done in the supply and demand models of trade and immigration.

– V –

value – The net sum of a product's perceived benefits, such as quality, convenience, and prestige, relative to its price. See also *value equation*.

value added – The value that a producer adds to the labor, capital, raw materials, and other parts, components, and inputs acquired from other producer. The sum of producer values added equals *gross domestic product (GDP)*.

value equation – An equation that defines the value of a product as the ratio of the product's benefits to its cost, or $V = B/P$, where V = value, B = benefits, and P = price.

value of the marginal product (VMP) of labor – The price of output times the real marginal product of labor, which is the price that demanders of labor are willing to pay, at the margin, for the use of labor; the VMP curve is effectively the demand curve for a productive resource such as labor.

vehicle currency – The currency that individuals, firms, and financial firms use to conduct international transactions.

veil of ignorance – A principle with which to judge how just a society is, developed by John Harsanyi and John Rawls. Their idea is the following: Imagine that you are somehow transported into space while everyone's roles on Earth are completely reorganized and restructured. Given that from behind your "veil of ignorance" you do not know in what role you will be returned to Earth, how would you like to see society organized? Rawls argued that people would prefer a very egalitarian society in which they minimize their chances of ending up poor, unhealthy, and oppressed. He thus defined justice in terms of equality.

velocity of money – The frequency with which money exchanges hands, usually measured per year.

venture capital – Part *foreign direct investment*, part *portfolio investment*, and part bank financing, venture capital is a creative form of financing that tries to deal with the difficulties of *intertemporal transactions* involving risky start-up businesses.

Verenigde Oost-Indische Compagnie (VOC) – See *Dutch East India Company*.

Vernon's model – See *product cycle model*.

vertical foreign direct investment – FDI that occurs when a transnational corporation builds or acquires foreign facilities that comprise one stage of its complete production process. An example of a vertical foreign direct investment is Ford Motor Company's engine plant in Brazil, which supplies engine blocks to Ford assembly plants in Brazil, Europe, and the United States. See also *horizontal FDI*.

vertical specialization – The breakdown of the productive process in which producers specialize in just one level of the overall production process. Vertically specialized firms acquire materials, parts, components, et cetera from other firms, and they sell their production on to other firms in the final stages of the production process. Vertical specialization is related to the increasing trend for firms to engage in *outsourcing* of certain parts of their production process.

voluntary export restraint (VER) – A voluntary limit on exports that looks just like an import quota except that it is administered by the exporting country and the exporters are usually allowed to capture the associated quota rents.

– W –

WTO – See *World Trade Organization*.

Washington consensus – The set of economic reforms pushed by the *IMF* and *World Bank* after the *1982 debt crisis*, which included free trade, reduced government involvement in the economy, a realistic foreign exchange rate, conservative monetary policies to reduce inflation, balanced government budgets, privatization of government assets, reduced labor market regulation, and diminished financial regulation. Many heterodox economists argue that the Washington consensus has enabled the spread of *transnational corporations* and transnational financial corporations, which is described by some as a modern form of *colonialism*, others as modern *mercantilism*. See also *dependency theory, colonialism*, and *mercantilism*.

Wealth of Nations – The shortened title of Adam Smith's monumental 1776 work, *An Inquiry into the Nature and Causes of the Wealth of Nations*, which is often regarded as the first economics textbook. In its three volumes, Smith explained what enables an economy to provide its citizens with a high standard of living. He also laid out the gains from trade and international *specialization*, as well as the principle of *absolute advantage*, the intellectual precursor to the very important concept of *comparative advantage* popularized by David Ricardo in 1817.

welfare function – A function widely used in economics that relates human well-being to some set of material goods and services. Conceptually, nonmaterial things could be added to the welfare function, but this has seldom been done in practice. Welfare functions are also commonly specified as separable and additive across humans so that they can be aggregated into *social welfare functions*, but this assumption ignores the obvious welfare effects of status, human interactions, and income distribution.

World Bank – The common name for the *International Bank for Reconstruction and Development*, the sister institution to the *International Monetary Fund* that was proposed during the *Bretton Woods Monetary Conference* in 1944 to anchor the post–World War II *international monetary system*.

World Trade Organization (WTO) – The permanent organization established in 1994 to succeed the *General Agreement on Tariffs and Trade (GATT)*, to administer the rules established under the GATT and its successive negotiating rounds, and to administer formal trade dispute settlement procedures agreed on during the Uruguay Round.

– X –

X-Efficiency – Harvey Leibenstein's concept that efficiency in production is a variable that is determined by competitive conditions, not a constant rigidly defined by a *production function*.

– Z –

Zero-sum game – See *positive-sum game*.

Bibliography

Abramovitz, Moses (1986), "Catching Up, Forging Ahead, and Falling Behind," *Journal of Economic History* 46(2):385–406.

Acemoglu, D., S. Johnson, and R. Robinson (2002), "Reversal of Fortune: Geography and Institutions in the Making of the Modern World Income Distribution," *Quarterly Journal of Economics* 107(4):1231–1294.

Ades, Alberto F., and Edward L. Glaeser (1999), "Evidence on Growth, Increasing Returns, and the Extent of the Market," *Quarterly Journal of Economics* 114(3):1025–1045.

Aghion, Philippe, and Jeffrey G. Williamson (1998), *Growth, Inequality and Globalization,* Cambridge, U.K.: Cambridge University Press.

Aghion, Philippe, and Peter Howitt (1992), "A Model of Growth through Creative Destruction," *Econometrica* 60:323–351.

Agrawal, Ajay, Iain Cackburn, and John McHale (2006), "Gone But Not Forgotten: Labor Flows, Knowledge Spillovers, and Enduring Social Capital," *Journal of Economic Geography* 6:571–591.

Akerlof, George A. (2007), "The Missing Motivation in Macroeconomics," *American Economic Review* 97(1):5–36.

Akerlof, George A., and Janet L. Yellen (1987), "Rational Models of Irrational Behavior," *American Economic Review* 77(2):197–217.

Alden, Edward (2001), "WTO Ruling Raises Trade Tensions," *Financial Times,* June 23–24.

Alesina, Alberto, Enrico Spolaore, and Romain Waczciarg (2000), "Economic Integration and Political Disintegration," *American Economic Review* 90(5):1276–1296.

Altshuler, Roseanne, Harry Grubert, and T. Scott Newlon (2001), "Has U.S. Investment Abroad Become More Sensitive to Tax Rates?" in *International Taxation and Multinational Activity,* James Hines, Jr. (ed.), Chicago: University of Chicago Press, pp. 9–32.

Amsden, Alice, and Wan-wen Chu (2003), *Beyond Late Development: Taiwan's Upgrading Policies,* Cambridge, MA: MIT Press.

Anand, Sudhir, and Paul Segal (2008), "What Do We Know about Global Income Inequality?" *Journal of Economic Perspectives* 46(1):57–94.

Anderson, James E. (1979), "A Theoretical Foundation for the Gravity Equation," *American Economic Review* 69(1):106–116.

Anderson, James E., and Douglas Marcouiller (2002), "Insecurity and the Pattern of Trade: An Empirical Investigation," *Review of Economics and Statistics* 84(2):345–352.

Angell, James W. (1933), "Exchange Depreciation, Foreign Trade and National Welfare," *Proceedings of the Academy of Political Science* 15:290–291.

Appleyard, Dennis, Alfred Field, and Steven Cobb (2010), *International Economics,* New York: McGraw-Hill/Irwin.

Aristotle (350 BCE [2010]), *Rhetoric,* trans. W. Rhys Roberts, University Park, PA: Penn State Electronic Classics Series.

Arndt, H.W. (1978), *The Rise and Fall of Economic Growth,* Chicago: University of Chicago Press.

Arrhenius, Svante (1896), "On the Influence of Carbonic Acid and Air upon the Temperature of the Ground," *Philosophical Magazine* 41(2):237–272.

Arrow, Kenneth J. (1963), *Social Choice and Individual Values,* 2d ed., New Haven, CT: Yale University Press.

Arrow, Kenneth, and Gerard Debreu (1954), "Existence of an Equilibrium for a Competitive Economy," *Econometrica* 22:265–290.

Aurbach, A.J., K.A. Hassett, and S.D. Oliner (1994), "Reassessing the Social Returns to Equipment Investment," *Quarterly Journal of Economics* 109:789–802.

Bachetta, Phillippe, and Eric van Wincoop (2000), "Does Exchange Rate Stability Increase Trade and Welfare?" *American Economic Review* 90:1093–1109.

Baer, Werner (2008), *The Brazilian Economy: Growth and Development,* 6th ed., Boulder, CO: Lynne Reinner.

Bairoch, Paul (1993), *Economics and World History: Myths and Paradoxes,* Chicago: University of Chicago Press.

Balassa, Bela (1986), "Intra-Industry Specialization: A Cross-Country Analysis," *European Economic Review* 30(1):27–42.

Baldwin, Robert E. (1970), *Nontariff Distortions of International Trade*, Washington, DC: Brookings Institution.

———— (1985), *The Political Economy of U.S. Import Policy*, Cambridge, MA: The MIT Press.

———— (1992), "Measuring Dynamic Gains from Trade," *Journal of Political Economy* 100(11):162–174.

———— (2001), "Regulatory Protectionism, Developing Nations, and a Two-Tier World Trade System," in Susan M. Collins and Dani Rodrik (eds.), *Brookings Trade Forum 2000*, Washington, DC: Brookings Institution, pp. 237–293.

———— (2003), "Openness and Growth: What's the Empirical Relationship?" in Robert E. Baldwin, and L. Alan Winters (eds.), *Challenges to Globalization*, Chicago: University of Chicago Press.

Balmford, Andrew, and William Bond (2005), "Trends in the State of Nature and their Implications for Human Well-being," *Ecology Letters* 8:1218–1234.

Banerjee, Abhijit, and Esther Duflo (2007), "The Economic Lives of the Poor," *Journal of Economic Perspectives* 21(1):141–167.

Barabási, A-L. (2002), *Linked: The New Science of Networks,* Cambridge, MA: Perseus Press.

Baran, Paul (1957), *The Political Economy of Growth,* New York: Monthly Review Press.

Barro, Robert J. (2001), "Economic Growth in East Asia Before and After the Financial Crisis," NBER Working Paper W8330, June.

Basevi, Giorgio (1966), "The United States Tariff Structure: Estimates of Effective Rates of Protection of United States Industries and Industrial Labor," *The Review of Economics and Statistics* 48(2):147–170.

Baumol, William J., Sue Anne Batey Blackman, and Edward N. Wolff (1989), *Productivity and American Leadership: The Long View,* Cambridge, MA: MIT Press.

Baysinger, Barry, Robert B. Eckelund, Jr., and Robert D. Tollison (1980), "Mercantilism as a Rent-Seeking Society," chapter 14 in James M. Buchanan, Robert D. Tollison, and Gordon Tullock (eds.), *Toward a Theory of the Rent-Seeking Society,* College Station: Texas A&M University Press.

Beine, M., F. Docquier, and F. Rapoport (2003), "Brain Drain and Human Capital Formation in Developing Countries: Winners and Losers," *Economic Journal* 118(528):631–652.

Bélanger, C. (2006), *L'Encyclopédie de l'histoire du Québec,* Marionapolis College (downloaded from the website http://faculty.marianopolis.edu/c.belanger/QuebecHistory/readings/).

Ben-David, Dan, and Michael B. Loewy (1998), "Free Trade, Growth, and Convergence," *Journal of Economic Growth* 3:143–170.

Bernanke, Ben (2000), "A Crash Course for Central Bankers," *Foreign Policy,* September–October.

Bhagwati, Jagdish (1958), "Immiserizing Growth: A Geometrical Note," *Review of Economic Studies* 25:201–205.

———— (1998), "The Capital Myth," *Foreign Affairs* 77(3):7–13.

Bhalla, Surjit S. (2002), *Imagine There's No Country,* Washington, DC: Institute for International Economics.

Biggs, Tyler S. (1991), "Heterogeneous Firms and Efficient Financial Intermediation in Taiwan," in Michael Roemer and Christine Jones (eds.), *Markets in Developing Countries,* San Francisco: ICS Press.

Birdsall, Nancy, David Ross, and Richard Sabot (1995), "Inequality and Growth Reconsidered: Lessons from East Asia," *World Bank Economic Review* 9(3):477–508.

BIS (2010), "Triennial Central Bank Survey of Foreign Exchange and Derivatives Market Activity in April 2010," Basel, Switzerland: Bank for International Settlements, September.

Blanc, Hélène, and Cristophe Sierra (1999), "The Internationalization of R&D by Multinationals: A Trade-off between External and Internal Proximity," *Cambridge Journal of Economics* 23:187–206.

Blanchard, Olivier J., and Francesco Giavazzi (2002), "Current Account Deficits in the Euro Area: The End of the Feldstein Horioka Puzzle?" *Brooking Papers on Economic Activity* 2002(2):147–182.

Blanchard, Olivier J., and Michael Kremer (1997), "Disorganization," *Quarterly Journal of Economics* 112(4):1091–1126.

Blanchflower, David, and Andrew J. Oswald (2004), "Well-Being Over Time in Britain and the USA," *Journal of Public Economics* 88:1359–1386.

Blattman, Christopher, Jason Hwang, and Jeffrey Williamson (2004), "The Impact of the Terms of Trade on Economic Development in the Periphery, 1870–1939: Volatility and Secular Change," NBER Working Paper 10600, July.

Blau, F. (1980), "Immigration and Labor Earnings in Early Twentieth-Century America," *Research in Population Economics* 2:21–41.

Blendon, Robert J., et al. (1997), "Bridging the Gap between the Public's and Economists' Views of the Economy," *Journal of Economic Perspectives* 11(3):105–118.

Blinder, Alan (2006), "Offshoring: The Latest Industrial Revolution?" *Foreign Affairs,* March.

Blomström, Magnus, and Ari Kokko (1998), "Multinational Corporations and Spillovers," *Journal of Economic Surveys* 12(3):247–277.

Bodvarsson, Örn, and Hendrik Van den Berg (2003), "The Impact of Immigration on a Local Economy: The Case of Dawson County, Nebraska." *Great Plains Research* 13(2):291–309.

——— (2006), "Does Immigration Affect Labor Demand? Model and Test," in S. Polachek, C. Chiswwick, and H. Rapoport (eds.), *Research in Labor Economics,* vol. 24, New York: Elsevier.

Bodvarsson, Örn, Hendrik Van den Berg, and Joshua Lewer (2008), "Measuring Immigration's Effects on Labor Demand: A Reconsideration of the Miami Boatlift," *Labour Economics* 15(4):560–574.

Bordo, Michael, Thomas Helbing, and Harold James (2007), "Swiss Exchange Rate Policy in the 1930s: Was the Delay in Devaluation Too High a Price to Pay for Conservatism?" *Open Economies Review* 18(1):1–25.

Bords, Michael D., John Landon Lane, and Angela Redish (2004), "Good versus Bad Deflation: Lessons for the Gold Standard Era," NBER Working Papers 10329, National Bureau of Economic Research, Inc.

Borensztein, E., J. De Gregorio, and J-W. Lee (1998), "How Does Foreign Direct Investment Affect Economic Growth?" *Journal of International Economics* 45:115–135.

Borga, Maria, and Raymond J. Mataloni, Jr. (2001), "Direct Investment Positions for 2000, Country and Industry Detail," *Survey of Current Business,* July:16–29.

Borjas, George J. (1985), "Assimilation, Changes in Cohort Quality, and the Earnings of Immigrants," *Journal of Labor Economics* 3(4):463–489.

——— (1994), "The Economics of Immigration," *Journal of Economic Literature* 32(4).

——— (1995), "The Economic Benefits from Immigration," *Journal of Economic Perspectives* 9(2):3–22.

Bouchard, T.J. Jr., D.T. Lykken, M. McGue, N.L. Segal, and A. Tellegen (1990), "Sources of Human Psychological Differences: The Minnesota Study of Twins Reared Apart," *Science* 250(4978):223–228.

Boughton, James M. (1994), "Harry Dexter White and the International Monetary Fund," downloaded from www.imf.org/external/pubs/ft/fandd/1998/09/boughton.htm, August 20, 2005.

Boulding, Kenneth (1956), "General Systems Theory: The Skeleton of Science," *Management Science* 2,3:197–208.

——— (1966), "The Economics of the Coming Spaceship Earth," in H. Jarrett (ed.), *Environmental Quality in a Growing Economy,* Resources for the Future, Baltimore, MD: Johns Hopkins University Press.

Bourdieu, Pierre (1977), *Outline of a Theory of Practice,* Cambridge, U.K.: Cambridge University Press.

——— (1988), *Homo Academicus,* Cambridge, U.K.: Polity Press.

——— (2000), *Pascallian Meditations,* Cambridge, U.K.: Cambridge University Press.

——— (2001), *Masculine Domination,* Cambridge, U.K.: Polity Press.

——— (2005), *Science of Science and Reflexivity,* Chicago: University of Chicago Press.

Brainard, S. Lael (1997), "An Empirical Assessment of the Proximity-Concentration Trade-off Between Multinational Sales and Trade," *American Economic Review* 87(4):520–544.

Brezis, Elise, Paul Krugman, and Daniel Tsiddon (1993), "Leapfrogging in International Competition: A Theory of Cycles in National Technological Leadership." *American Economic Review* 83(5):1211–1219.

Brook, Timothy (2008), *Vermeer's Hat: The Seventeenth Century and the Dawn of the Global World,* New York: Bloomsbury Press.

Brown, John Murray (2000), "Ireland Fine-Tunes Software with Ear to Cultural Nuisance," *Financial Times,* November 29.

Bruton, Henry J. (1989), "Import Substitution," chapter 30 in Hollis Chenery and T.N. Srinivasan (eds.), *Handbook of Development Economics,* vol. 2, Amsterdam: Elsevier.

——— (1998), "A Reconsideration of Import Substitution," *Journal of Economic Literature* 31:903–936.

Buchanan, James M., and Gordon Tullock (1962), *The Calculus of Consent,* Ann Arbor: University of Michigan Press.

Burtless, Gary (1995), "International Trade and the Rise in Earnings Inequality," *Journal of Economic Literature* 33(2):800–816.

Cai, Fang, and Francis E. Warnock (2004), "International Diversification at Home and Abroad," Board of Governors of the Federal Reserve System, discussion paper 793, Washington, DC, February.

Cameron, Rondo (1993), *A Concise Economic History of the World: From Paleolithic Times to the Present,* 2d ed., New York: Oxford University Press.

——— (1997), *A Concise Economic History of the World,* 3d ed., Oxford: Oxford University Press.

Card, David (1990), "The Impact of the Mariel Boatlift on the Miami Labor Market," *Industrial and Labor Relations Review* 43(2):245–257.

Carens, Joseph (1987), "Aliens and Citizens: The Case for Open Borders," *Review of Politics* 49:251–273.

Carrington, William J., and Enrica Detragiache (1998), "How Big Is the Brain Drain?" IMF working paper WP/98/102, July.

Carrothers, William A. (1948), "Immigration," in Wallace, W.S. (ed.), *The Encyclopedia of Canada,* vol. 3, Toronto: University Associates of Canada, pp. 239–249.

Carter, Susan B., and Richard Sutch (1997), "Historical Perspective on the Economic Consequences of Immigration into the United States," in C. Hirschman, P. Kasinitz, and J. DeWind (eds.), *The Handbook of International Migration: The American Experience,* New York: Russell Sage Foundation, 1999:319–341.

Caves, Richard E. (1976), "Economic Models of Political Choice: Canada's Tariff Structure, *Canadian Journal of Economics* 9(2):278–300.

——— (1996), *Multinational Enterprise and Economic Analysis,* Cambridge, U.K.: Cambridge University Press.

Chacholiades, Miltiades (1990), *International Economics,* New York: McGraw-Hill.

Chami, Ralph, Connel Fullenkamp, and Samir Jahjah (2003), "Are Immigrant Remittance Flows a Source of Capital for Development?" IMF Working Paper 03/189, International Monetary Fund.

Champernowne, D.G., and F.A. Cowell (1998), *Economic Inequality and Income Distribution,* Cambridge, U.K.: Cambridge University Press.

Champion, Marc, and Matthew Kaminski (2000), "Availability of Work in London Lures Chinese Migrants," *Wall Street Journal,* June 21.

Chinn, Menzie D., and Guy Merideth (2004), "Monetary Policy and Long-Horizon Uncovered Interest Parity, *IMF Staff Papers* 51(3):409–430.

Chiodo, Abbigail J., and Michael T. Owyang (2002), "A Case Study of a Currency Crisis: The Russian Default of 1998," *Federal Reserve Bank of St. Louis Review* 84(6)7–17.

Chiswick, Barry R. (1978), "The Effect of Americanization on the Earnings of Foreign-born Men," *Journal of Political Economy* 86:897–921.

——— (2000), "Are Immigrants Favorably Self-Selected? An Economic Analysis," in Caroline D. Brettell and James F. Hollifield (eds.), *Migration Theory: Talking Across Disciplines,* New York: Routledge, pp. 61–76.

Chiswick, Barry R., and Paul W. Miller (1999), "Immigrant Earnings: Language Skills, Linguistic Concentrations and the Business Cycle," *Journal of Population Economics* 15(1):31–57.

Chu, Wan-wen (1997), "Causes of Growth: A Study of Taiwan's Bicycle Industry," *Cambridge Journal of Economics* 21:55–72.

Cipolla, Carlo (1978), *Clocks and Culture, 1300–1700,* New York: W.W. Norton.

Clarida, Richard H. (1997), "Dumping: In Theory, in Policy, and in Practice," in Jagdish Bhagwati and Robert E. Hudec (eds.), *Fair Trade and Harmonization, Prerequisites for Trade?* vol. 1, Cambridge, MA: MIT Press.

Clover, Charles (2002), "Warlords Take Their Toll on Afghanistan Truckers," *Financial Times,* May 28.

Coase, Ronald (1960), "The Problem of Social Costs," *Journal of Law and Economics* 3:1–44.

Cobb-Clark, Deborah (2004), "Selection Policy and the Labour Market Outcomes of New Immigrants," IZA Discussion Paper no. 1380, November.

Cohn, Steven Mark (2007), *Reintroducing Macroeconomics: A Critical Approach,* Armonk, NY: M.E. Sharpe.

Conrad, Joseph (1899 [2003]), *Heart of Darkness,* New York: Barnes and Noble Classics.

Cooper, Richard N. (1992), "Fettered to Gold? Economic Policy in the Interwar Period," *Journal of Economic Literature* 30(4):2120–2128.

——— (2002), "The Economic Impact of Demographic Change: A Case for More Immigration," in Jane Sneddon Little and Robert K. Triest (eds.), *Seismic Shifts: The Economic Impact of Demographic Change,* Boston: Federal Reserve Bank of Boston.

Costanza, Robert, et al. (1997), "The Value of the World's Ecosystem Services and Natural Capital," *Nature* 387:253–260.

Crafts, Nicholas, and Anthony J. Venables (2001), "Globalization and Geography: An Historical Perspective," in Michael Bordo, Alan Taylor, and Jeffrey G. Williamson (eds.), *Globalization in Historical Perspective,* Chicago: University of Chicago Press.

Craig, J. Bruce (2004), *Treasonable Doubt, The Harry Dexter White Spy Case,* Lawrence: University of Kansas Press.

Cross, Sam Y. (1998), *All About the Foreign Exchange Market in the United States,* New York: Federal Reserve Bank of New York.

Daly, Herman E. (1999), "Uneconomic Growth, in Theory, in Fact, in History, and in Relation to Globalization," Clemens Lecture 11, St. John's University, October 25.

Daniels, Roger (2004), *Guarding the Golden Door,* New York: Hill and Wang.

Davies, Glyn (1996), *A History of Money,* rev. ed., Cardiff: University of Wales Press.

Davis, David, and David E. Weinstein (2001), "Market Size, Linkages, and Productivity: A Study of Japanese Regions," in Ravi Kanbur, and Anthony Venables (eds.), *Spatial Inequality and Development,* Oxford: Oxford University Press.

Davis, Donald R., Melvin D. Epp, and Hugh D. Riordan (2004), "Changes in USDA Food Composition Data for 43 Garden Crops, 1950 to 1999," *Journal of the American College of Nutrition* 23(6):669–682.

Davis, Lance E., and Robert Gallman (1999), *Waves, Tides, and Sandcastles: The Impact of Foreign Capital Flows on Evolving Financial Markets in the New World, 1865–1914,* New York: Cambridge University Press.

Davis, Lucas W., and Matthew E. Kahn (2008), "International Trade in Used Durable Goods: The Environmental Consequences of NAFTA," NBER Working Paper 14565, December.

——— (2010), "International Trade in Used Vehicles: The Environmental Consequences of NAFTA," *American Economic Journal: Economic Policy* 2(4):58–82.

Davisson, William L., and James E. Harper (1972), *European Economic History,* vol. 1: *The Ancient World,* New York: Appleton-Century-Crofts.

De Grauwe, Paul (1989), *International Money: Postwar Trends and Theories,* Oxford: Oxford University Press.

——— (2009), "Warring Economists Are Carried Along by the Crowd," *Financial Times,* July 22.

De Long, J. Bradford, and Lawrence H. Summers (1991), "Equipment Investment and Economic Growth," *Quarterly Journal of Economics* 106(2):445–502.

——— (1992), "Equipment Investment and Economic Growth: How Strong Is the Nexus?" *Brookings Papers on Economic Activity* (1):57–199.

De Roover, Raymond (1948), *Money, Banking and Credit in Medieval Bruges,* Cambridge, MA: The Medieval Academy of America.

Deaton, Angus (1999), "Commodity Prices and Growth in Africa," *Journal of Economic Perspectives* 13(3):23–40.

Debreu, Gerard (1959), *Theory of Value,* New Haven, CT: Yale University Press.

Decenty, Jean, and Claus Lamm (2006), "Human Empathy through the Lens of Social Neuroscience," *Scientific World Journal* 6:1146–1163.

Dench, Janet (2007), "A Hundred Years of Immigration to Canada, 1900–1999: A Chronology Focusing on Refugees and Discrimination," Canadian Council for Refugees; downloaded on December 9, 2007, from www.ccrweb.ca//history.html.

Dernberg, Thomas F. (1989), *Global Macroeconomics,* New York: Harper & Row.

Di Tella, Rafael, and Robert MacCulloch (2008), "Happiness Adaption to Income beyond 'Basic Needs,'" NBER Working Paper 14539, December.

Dolan, Paul, Tessa Peasgood, and Matthew White (2008), "Do We Really Know What Makes Us Happy? A Review of Economics Literature on the Factors Associated with Subjective Well-Being," *Journal of Economic Psychology* 29:94–122.

Dolinskaya, Irina (2002), "Explaining Russia's Output Collapse," *IMF Staff Papers* 40(2):155–174.

Dominguez, Kathryn M., and Jeffrey A. Frankel (1993), *Does Foreign Exchange Intervention Work?* Washington, DC: Institute for International Economics.

van Dormael, Armand (1978), *Bretton Woods: Birth of a Monetary System,* London: Macmillan.

Drinkwater, L.E., P. Wagoner, and M. Sarrantonio (1998), "Legume-Based Cropping Systems Have Reduced Carbon and Nitrogen Losses," *Nature* 396(19 November):262–265.

Drucker, Peter F. (1987), "From World Trade to World Investment," *Wall Street Journal,* May 26.

Easterlin, Richard A. (2003a), "Explaining Happiness," *Proceedings of the National Academy of Sciences* 100(19):11176–11183.

——— (2003b), "Building a Better Theory of Well-Being," IZA Discussion Paper no. 742, March.

Eckelund, Robert B., and Robert Tollison (1981), *Mercantilism as a Rent Seeking Society,* College Station: Texas A&M University Press.

Economic Commission for Latin America and the Caribbean (2009), *Historical Statistics for Latin America: 1950–2008.* Santiago: ECLAC.

Edelstein, Michael (1982), *Overseas Investment in the Age of High Imperialism: The United Kingdom, 1850–1914,* New York: Columbia University Press.

Edwards, Alexandra Cox, and Manuelita Ureta (2003), "International Migration, Remittances, and Schooling: Evidence From El Salvador," *Journal of Development Economics* 72(2):429–461.

Edwards, Sebastian (1998), "Openness, Productivity and Growth: What Do We Really Know?" *Economic Journal* 108(1):383–398.

Ehrlich, Paul (1972), in Sue Titus Reid and David L. Lyon (eds.), *Population Crisis—An Interdisciplinary Perspective,* Glenview, IL: Foresman.

Eichengreen, Barry (1992), *Gold Fetters: The Gold Standard and the Great Depression, 1919–1939,* New York: Oxford University Press.

——— (1996), *Globalizing Capital: A History of the International Monetary System,* Princeton, NJ: Princeton University Press.

Eichengreen, Barry, and Richard Portes (1995), *Crisis? What Crisis? Orderly Workouts for Sovereign Debtors,* London: Centre for Economic Policy Research.

Eichengreen, Barry, and Peter Temin (2000), "The Gold Standard and the Great Depression," *Contemporary European History* 9(2):183–207.

Elías, Victor J. *Sources of Growth: A Study of Seven Latin American Economies.* San Francisco: ICS Press, 1989.

Engel, Charles, and John Rogers (1996), "How Wide Is the Border?" *American Economic Review* 86(5):1112–1125.

Enkvist, Per-Anders, Tomas Nauclér, and Jerker Rosander (2007), "A Cost Curve for Greenhouse Gas Reduction," *McKinsey Quarterly* 2007(1):35–45.

Ensminger, J. (1997), "Transaction Costs and Islam: Explaining Conversion in Africa," *Journal of Institutional and Theoretical Economics* 153(1):4–29.

Espenshade, T., J. Baraka, and J. Huber (1997), "Implications of the 1996 Welfare and Immigration Reform Acts for U.S. immigration," *Population and Development Review* 23(4):769–801.

European Union (2005), "Do Currency Markets Absorb News Quickly?" *Journal of International Money and Finance* 24(2):197–217.

—— (2006), "Understanding Order Flow," *International Journal of Finance and Economics* 11(1):3–23.

—— (2008), *The Economics of Ecosystems and Biodiversity: An Interim Report,* downloaded from http://ec.europa.eu/environment/nature/biodiversity/economics/pdf/teeb_report.pdf.

Evans, Martin D., and Richard K. Lyons (2002), "Order Flow and Exchange Rate Dynamics," *Journal of Political Economy* 110:170–180.

—— (2005), "Do Currency Markets Absorb News Quickly?" *Journal of International Money and Finance* 24(2):197–217.

—— (2006), "Understanding Order Flow," *International Journal of Finance and Economics* 11(1):3–23.

Fama, Eugene F. (1970), "Efficient Capital Markets: A Review of Theory and Empirical Work," *Journal of Finance* 25(2):383–417.

Farber, S.C., Robert Costanza, and M.A. Wilson (2002), "Economic and Ecological Concepts for Valuing Ecosystem Services," *Ecological Economics* 41:375–392.

Feenstra, Robert (1992), "How Costly Is Protectionism?" *Journal of Economic Perspectives* 6(3):159–178.

Fehr, Hans, Sabine Jokisch, and Laurence Kotlikoff (2004), "The Role of Immigration in Dealing with the Developed World's Demographic Transition, *Finanzarchiv* 60:296–324.

Fei, John C.H., and Gustav Ranis (1964), *Development of the Labor Surplus Economy,* Homewood, IL: Irwin.

Fields, Gary S. (1980), *Poverty, Inequality, and Development,* Cambridge, U.K.: Cambridge University Press.

Fisman, Raymond, and Shang-Jin Wei (2004), "Tax Rates and Tax Evasion: Evidence from 'Missing Imports' in China," *Journal of Political Economy* 112(2):471–496.

Fitzgerald, F. Scott (1925[1992]), *The Great Gatsby,* New York: Collier Books.

Fitzpatrick, John C., ed. (1931), *The Writings of George Washington,* Washington, DC: Government Printing Office.

Flood, Robert P. (1994), "Collapsing Exchange Rate Regimes: Another Linear Example," *Journal of International Economics* 41(3–4):223–234.

Flood, Robert P., and Andrew K. Rose (2002), Uncovered Interest Parity in Crisis," *IMF Staff Papers* 49(2):252–266.

Flood, Robert P., and Mark P. Taylor (1996), "Exchange Rate Economics: What's Wrong with the Conventional Macro Approach?" in Jeffrey A. Frankel, Giampaolo Galli, and Alberto Giovannini (eds.), *The Microstructure of Foreign Exchange Markets,* Chicago: University of Chicago Press, 261–301.

Florida, Richard (2005), "The World Is Spiky," *Atlantic Monthly,* October.

Fourier, Joseph (1827), "Mémoire sur les températures du globe terrestre et des espaces planétaires," *Mémoires de l'académie royale des sciences* 7:569–604.

Frank, Andre Gunder (1967), *Dependent Accumulation and Under-Development.* London: Macmillan.

Frankel, Jeffrey A. (1999), "Comments" to Michael D. Bordo, Barry Eichengreen, and Douglas A. Irwin, "Is Globalization Today Really Different than Globalization a Hunderd Years Ago?" in Susan M. Collins and Robert Z. Lawwrence (eds.), *Brookings Trade Policy Forum 1999,* Washington, DC: Brookings Institution Press, pp. 51–55.

—— (2008), "Everything You Always Wanted to Know about the Carry Trade, and Perhaps Much More," *Milken Institute Review,* 1st quarter, 2008.

—— (2010), "The Natural Resource Curse: A Survey," NBER Working Paper 15836, March.

Frankel, Jeffrey, and Andrew K. Rose (2002), "An Estimate of the Effect of Common Currencies on Trade and Income," *Quarterly Journal of Economics* 116(2):437–466.

Frankel, Jeffrey, and Nouriel Roubini (2002), "The Role of Industrial Country Policies in Emerging Market Crises," in Martin Feldstein (ed.), *Financial and Currency Crises in Emerging Market Economies,* Chicago: University of Chicago Press.

Frankel, Jeffrey, and Sergio Schmukler (1996), "Country Fund Discounts and the Mexican Crisis of December 1994: Did Local Residents Turn Pessimistic Before International Investors?" *Open Economies Review* 7:511–534.

Frederick, Shane (2005), "Cognitive Reflection and Decision Making," *Journal of Economic Perspectives,*19(4):25–42.

Freeman, Richard B. (2006), "People Flows in Globalization," *Journal of Economic Perspectives* 20(2):145–170.

Frenkel, Jacob (1983), "Flexible Exchange Rates, Prices, and the Role of 'News': Lessons from the 1970s," in Jagdeep S. Bhandari and Bluford H. Putnam (eds.), *Economic Interdependence and Flexible Exchange Rates,* Cambridge, MA: MIT Press.

Friedman, Milton (1953), "The Case for Flexible Exchange Rates," in Milton Friedman (ed.), *Essays on Positive Economics,* Chicago: University of Chicago Press, pp. 157–203.

——— (1957), *A Theory of the Consumption Function,* Princeton, NJ: Princeton University Press.

——— (1968), "The Role of Monetary Policy," *American Economic Review* 58(1):1–17.

——— (1990a), "Bimetallism Revisited," *Journal of Economic Perspectives* 4(4):85–104.

——— (1990b), "The Crime of 1873," *Journal of Political Economy* 98(4):1154–1194.

——— (1992), "Déjà Vu in the Currency Markets," *Wall Street Journal,* September 22.

Friedman, Milton, and Anna Jacobson Schwartz (1963), *A Monetary History of the United States 1867–1960,* Princeton, NJ: Princeton University Press.

Fuess, Scott M., Jr., and Hendrik Van den Berg (1997), "Transactions Activities and Productivity Growth in Mexico," *Journal of Developing Areas* 31(1):387–398.

Funabashi, Yoichi (1988), *Managing the Dollar: From the Plaza to the Louvre,* Washington, DC: Institute for International Economics.

Furtado, Celso (1963), *The Economic Growth of Brazil: A Survey from Colonial Times to Modern Times.* Berkeley: University of California Press.

Garrett, Geoffrey (2000), "The Causes of Globalization," *Comparative Political Studies* 33(6–7):941–991.

General Agreement on Tariffs and Trade (1994), *The Results of the Uruguay Round of Multilateral Trade Negotiations,* Geneva: GATT Secretariat (available on the World Trade Organization website, www.wto.org).

Ghosh, Atish R., Ann-Marie Gulde, Jonathan D. Ostry, and Holger Wolf (1996), *Does the Exchange Rate Regime Matter for Inflation and Growth?* Washington, DC: International Monetary Fund.

Glade, William P. (1969), *The Latin American Economies: A Study of Their Institutional Evolution.* New York: American Book.

Gladwell, Malcolm (2008), "In the Air: Who Says Big Ideas Are Rare?" *New Yorker,* May 12.

Glaeser, Edward, H.D. Kallal, José A. Scheinkman, and Andre Schleifer (1992), "Growth in Cities," *Journal of Political Economy* 100(6):1126–1152.

Goldfajn, Ilan, and Eduardo Refinetti Guardia (2003), "Fiscal Rules and Debt Sustainability in Brazil," *Technical Notes* 39(July), Central Bank of Brazil.

Goldin, Claudia (1994), "The Political Economy of Immigration Restriction in the United States, 1890 to 1921," in Claudia Goldin and Gary Libecap (eds.), *The Regulated Economy: An Historical Analysis of Political Economy,* Chicago: University of Chicago Press, pp. 223–258.

Grampp, William D. (1987), "Britain and Free Trade: In Whose Interest?" *Public Choice* 55:245–256.

Greenlaw, D., J. Hatzins, A. Kashyap, and Y.S. Shin (2008), "Leveraged Losses: Lessons from the Mortgage Market Meltdown," Proceedings of the U.S. Monetary Policy Forum.

Greenpeace International (2009), "Reality Check on Carbon Storage," policy paper posted on www.greenpeace.org.

Greenspan, Alan (2001), Testimony of Chairman Alan Greenspan Before the Committee on Finance, U.S. Senate, April 4.

Greif, Avner (1989), "Reputation and Coalitions in Medieval Trade: Evidence on the Maghribi," *Journal of Economic History* 49(4):857–882.

——— (1994), "Cultural Beliefs and the Organization of Society: A Historical and Theoretical Reflection on Collectivist and Individualist Societies," *Journal of Political Economy* 102(5):912–950.

Gresik, Thomas A. (2001), "The Taxing Task of Taxing Multinationals," *Journal of Economic Literature* 39(3):800–838.

Gribbin, John (2002), *Science: A History,* London: Penguin Press.

Griliches, Zvi (1957), "Hybrid Corn: An Exploration of the Economics of Technical Change," *Econometrica* 25(4):501–522.

Grimwade, Nigel (1989), *International Trade: New Patterns of Trade, Production and Investment,* London: Routledge.

Grossman, Gene M., and Elhanan Helpman (1991), *Innovation and Growth in the Global Economy,* Cambridge, MA: MIT Press.

Gül Ünal, Fatma (2008), "Small Is Beautiful: Evidence of an Inverse Relationship between Farm Size and Yield in Turkey," working paper 551, Annandale-on-Hudson, NY: Levi Institute of Bard College, December.

Haberler, Gottfried (1937), *Prosperity and Depression: A Theoretical Analysis of Cyclical Movements,* London: George Allen and Unwin.

Haidt, Jonathan (2006), *The Happiness Hypothesis,* New York: Basic Books.

Handlin, Elizabeth, Margerethe Krontoft, and William Testa (2002), "Remittances and the Unbanked," *Chicago Fed Letter,* no. 175a, March.

Handlin, Oscar (1951), *The Uprooted,* Boston: Little, Brown.

Hansen, Gordon H., Raymond Robertson, and Antonio Spilimbergo (2002), "Does Border Enforcement Protect U.S. Workers From Illegal Immigration?" *Review of Economics and Statistics* 84:73–92.

Haque, N.U., and S.-J. Kim (1995), "Human Capital Flight: Impact of Migration on Income and Growth, *IMF Staff Papers* 42(3):577–607.

Harley, C.K. (1988), "Ocean Freight Rates and Productivity, 1840–1913: The Primacy of Mechanical Invention Confirmed," *Journal of Economic History* 48:851–876.

Harris, Seymour (1936), *Exchange Depreciation,* Cambridge, MA: Harvard University Press.

Hartley, C.Knick (1988), "Ocean Freight Rates and Productivity, 1840–1913: The Primacy of Mechanical Invention Reaffirmed," *Journal of Economic History* 48:851–876.

Hatton, Timothy, and John Williamson (1998), *The Age of Mass Migration: Causes and Economic Consequences,* New York: Oxford University Press.

——— (2005), *Global Migration and the World Economy: Two Centuries of Policy and Performance,* Cambridge, MA: MIT Press.

Hausman, Ricardo, and Frederico Sturtzenegger (2006), "U.S. and Global Imbalances: Can Dark Matter Prevent a Big Bang?" Working Paper, Cambridge, MA: Harvard University.

Henning, Randall (1994), *Currencies and Politics in the United States, Germany and Japan,* Washington, DC: Institute for International Economics.

Herlihy, David V. (2004), *Bicycle: The History,* New Haven, CT: Yale University Press.

Higgins, Patrick C., and Owen F. Humpage (2004), "Walking on a Fence: Brazil's Public-Sector Debt," Federal Reserve Bank of Cleveland Policy Discussion Paper no. 6, February.

Hill, Peter J. (1971), "The Economic Impact of Immigration into the United States," *Journal of Economic History* 31(1):260–263.

Hillman, Ayre, and Avi Weiss (1999), "A Theory of Permissible Illegal Immigration," *European Journal of Political Economy* 15(4):585–604.

Hipple, F. Steb (1990), "The Measurement of International Trade Related to Multinational Companies," *American Economic Review* 80(5):1263–1270.

Holmes, Thomas J., and James A. Schmitz, Jr. (1995), "Resistance to New Technology and Trade between Areas," *Quarterly Review* (Federal Reserve Bank of Minneapolis) 19(1):1–14.

——— (1998), "A Gain from Trade: More Research, Less Obstruction," Research Department Staff Report 245, March, Federal Reserve Bank of Minneapolis.

Hoover, Edgar M., and Frank Giarratani (1984), *An Introduction to Regional Economics,* New York: Alfred A. Knopf.

Howarth, Robert W., Renee Santoro, and Anthony Ingraffea (2011), "Methane and the Greenhouse-Gas Footprint of Natural Gas from Shale Formations: A letter," *Climatic Change* 106(4):679–690.

Hufbauer, Gary Clyde, and Kimberly Ann Elliott (1994), *Measuring the Costs of Protection in the United States,* Washington, DC: Institute for International Economics.

Hummels, David (1999), "Have International Transportation Costs Declined?" working paper, University of Chicago, September.

Hummels, David, Jun Ishii, and Kei-Mu Yi (2000), "The Nature and Growth of Vertical Specialization in World Trade," *Journal of International Economics* 54(1):75–96.

Humpage, Owen F., and William P. Osterberg (2000), "Why Intervention Rarely Works," *Economic Commentary,* Federal Reserve Bank of Cleveland, February 1.

Hunter, Linda, and James R. Markusen (1988), "Per-Capita Income as a Determinant of Trade," in Robert Feenstra (ed.), *Empirical Methods for International Economics,* Cambridge: MIT Press, pp. 89–109.

Hymans, Saul H., and Frank P. Stafford (1995), "Divergence, Convergence, and the Gains from Trade," *Review of International Economics* 3(1):118–123.

Inter-American Development Bank (2004), "Latin American Immigrants in the United States Send $30 Billion to Homelands in 2004," news release, May 17.

Intergovernmental Panel on Climate Change (2007), *IPCC Report on Global Warming,* New York: United Nations.

International Monetary Fund (2010), "Reserve Accumulation and International Monetary Stability," paper prepared by the Strategy, Policy, and Review Department, April 13.

Iqbal, Zamir (1997), "Islamic Financial System," *Finance & Development,* pp. 42–45, June.

Irwin, Douglas A. (2000), "Tariffs and Growth in Late Nineteenth Century America," *World Economy* 24:15–30.

Isard, Walter (1975), *Introduction to Regional Science,* Englewood Cliffs, NJ: Prentice-Hall.

——— (2006), "Uncovered Interest Parity," IMF Working Paper WP/06/96, April.

Jackson, John H. (1992), *The World Trading System,* Cambridge, MA: MIT Press.

——— (1997), *The World Trading System: Law and Policy of International Relations,* 2d ed., Cambridge, MA: MIT Press.

Jaffe, Adam B., Manuel Trajtenberg, and Rebecca Henderson (1993), "Geographic Localization of Knowledge Spillovers as Evidenced by Patent Citations," *Quarterly Journal of Economics* 117(3):577–598.

Jasso, Guillermina, and Mark R. Rosenzweig (1988), "How Well Do U.S. Immigrants Do? Vintage Effects, Emigration Selectivity, and Occupational Mobility," *Research in Population Economics* 6:229–253.

Jensen, Michael C., and William H. Meckling (1976), "Theory of the Firm: Managerial Behavior, Agency Costs and Ownership Structure," *Journal of Financial Economics* 3(4):305–360.

Johnson, Harry G. (1960), "The Cost of Protection and the Scientific Tariff," *Journal of Political Economy* 68(4):327–345.

Johnson, Leland L. (1967), "Problems of Import Substitution: The Chilean Automobile Industry," *Economic Development and Cultural Change* 16(1):202–216.

Kahneman, Daniel, and Amos Tversky (2000), *Choices, Values and Frames,* Cambridge, U.K.: Cambridge University Press.

Kane, Mary (2008), "How Fraud Fueled the Mortgage Crisis," *Washington Independent,* May 1.

Kaufman, Henry (1998), "Preventing the Next Global Financial Crisis," *Washington Post,* January 28.

Kelley, N., and M. Trebilcock (2000), *The Making of the Mosaic,* Toronto: University of Toronto Press.

Kempf, Hervé (2007), *How the Rich Are Destroying the Earth,* White River Junction, VT: Chelsea Green.

Kenen, Peter B. (1967), *International Economics,* 2d ed., Engelwood Cliffs, NJ: Prentice-Hall.

Kenwood, A.G., and A.L. Lougheed (1992), *The Growth of the International Economy 1820–1990,* 3rd ed., London: Routledge.

Keynes, John Maynard (1920), *The Economic Consequences of the Peace,* London: Harcourt, Brace and Howe.

——— (1923), *A Tract on Monetary Reform,* London: Macmillan.

——— (1936), *The General Theory of Employment, Interest, and Money,* London: Macmillan.

——— (1943 [1969]), "Proposals for an International Clearing Union," reprinted in International Monetary Fund (1969), *1945–65,* vol. 3, "Documents," Washington, DC

——— (1980), *The Collected Writings,* vol. 25, *Activities, 1940–44, Shaping the Post-War World: The Clearing Union,* ed. Donald E. Moggridge and Elizabeth S. Johnson, New York: Cambridge University Press for the Royal Economic Society.

Kindleberger, Charles P. (1973), *The World Depression, 1929–1939,* London: Allen Lane Penguin Press.

King, Harlan W. (2001), "The International Investment Position of the United States at Yearend 2000," *Survey of Current Business,* July:7–15.

Kirchner, Joseph, and Stephen E. Baldwin (1992), "The Fiscal Impact of Eligible Legalized Aliens," a study performed under a contract between the KRA Corporation and the U.S. Department of Health and Human Services (unpublished).

Kleinknecht, Alfred, and Jan ter Wengel (1998), "The Myth of Economic Globalisation," *Cambridge Journal of Economics* 22:637–647.

Kopchuk, Wojciech, Joel B. Slemrod, and Shlomo Yitzaki (2002), "Why World Distribution Fails," *European Economic Review* 49(4):1051–1079.

Kouparitsas, Michael (2005), "Is There Evidence of the New Economy in U.S. GDP Data?" Federal Reserve Bank of Chicago, *Economic Perspectives* 29(1):12–29.

Krautkraemer, Jeffrey A. (1998), "Nonrenewable Resource Scarcity," *Journal of Economic Literature* 36(4):2065–2107.

Kravis, Irving B. (1970), "Trade as a Handmaiden of Growth: Similarities between the Nineteenth and Twentieth Centuries," *Economic Journal* 80(32):850–872.

Kremer, Michael (1993), "Population Growth and Technological Change: One Million B.C. to 1990," *Quarterly Journal of Economics* 108(3):681–716.

Krueger, Anne O. (1974), "The Political Economy of the Rent-Seeking Society," *American Economic Review* 64:291–303.

——— (1980), "Trade Policy as an Input to Development," *American Economic Review* 70(2):288–292.

——— (2001), "International Financial Architecture for 2002: A New Approach to Sovereign Debt Restructuring," address at the National Economists' Club, American Enterprise Institute, Washington, DC, November 26.

Krueger, Anne O., and Junho Yoo (2001), "Chaebol Capitalism and the Currency-Financial Crisis in Korea," chapter 13 in Sebastain Edwards and Jeffrey Frankel (eds.), *Preventing Currency Crises in Emerging Markets*, Chicago: University of Chicago Press.

Krugman, Paul R. (1979), "Increasing Returns, Monopolistic Competition, and International Trade," *Journal of International Economics* 9(4):469–479.

——— (1987), "Is Free Trade Passé?" *Journal of Economic Perspectives* 1(2):131–144.

——— (1991), *Geography and Trade,* Cambridge, MA: MIT Press.

——— (1994), "Does Third World Growth Hurt First World Prosperity?" *Harvard Business Review,* July–August:113–121; reprinted in Paul Krugman (1996), *Pop Internationalism,* chapter 4, Cambridge, MA: MIT Press.

——— (2000), "Introduction," in Paul Krugman (ed.), *Currency Crises,* Chicago: University of Chicago Press.

——— (2008), "Trade and Wages, Reconsidered," *Brookings Papers on Economic Activity* 2:103–154.

Kuran, Timur (1995), "Islamic Economics and the Islamic Subeconomy," *Journal of Economic Literature* 9(4):155–173.

Kuttner, Robert (1999), *Everything For Sale: The Virtues and Limits of Markets,* Chicago: University of Chicago Press.

Kynge, James (2006), *China Shakes the World,* Boston: Houghton Mifflin.

Laird, Sam, and Alexander Yeats (1990), "Trends in Nontariff Barriers of Developed Countries," *Weltwirtschaftliches Archiv* 126(2):299–325.

Lal, Deepak (1998), *Unintended Consequences,* Cambridge, MA: MIT Press.

Lanchester, John (2009), "It's Finished," *London Review of Books,* May 28.

Leboeuf, Robyn Aimee (2002), "Alternating Selves and Conflicting Choices: Identity Salience and Preference Inconsistency," *Dissertation Abstracts International* 63(2–B):1088.

Lebreton, Maël, et al. (2009), "The Brain Structural Disposition to Social Interaction," *European Journal of Neuroscience* 29(11):2247–2252.

LeDoux, Joseph E. (1996), *The Emotional Brain: The Mysterious Underpinnings of Emotional Life,* New York: Simon and Schuster.

Leggett, Karby (2000), "Protectionism May Still Hamper China Trade," *Wall Street Journal,* May 26.

Lerner, Abba P. (1934), "The Symmetry between Import and Export Taxes," *Economica* 3:306–313.

Levine, Ross (1997), "Financial Development and Economic Growth: Views and Agenda," *Journal of Economic Literature* 35(2):688–726.

Levinson, Arik, and Scott Taylor (2008), "Unmasking the Pollution Haven Effect," *International Economic Review* 49(1):223–254.

Levy, Philip I. (1999), "Sanctions on South Africa: What Did They Do?" *American Economic Review* 89(2):415–420.

Lewer, Joshua J., and Hendrik Van den Berg (2003a), "Does Trade Composition Matter for Medium-Run Growth? Time-Series Evidence for 28 Countries," *Journal of International Trade and Economic Growth* 2(1):39–96.

———— (2003b), "How Large Is International Trade's Effect on Economic Growth?" *Journal of Economic Surveys* 17(3):363–396.

Lewis, W. Arthur (1954), "Economic Development with Unlimited Supplies of Labor," *Manchester School* 22(2):139–191.

Linnemann, H. (1966), *An Econometric Study of International Trade Flows,* Amsterdam, Netherlands: North-Holland Pub Co.

Lipsey, Robert E. (2001), "Home and Host Country Effects of FDI," NBER Working Paper 9293, October.

———— (2004), "Foreign Direct Investment and the Operations of Multinational Firms: Concepts, History, and Data," in Robert E. Baldwin and L. Alan Winters (eds.), *Challenges to Globalization,* Chicago: University of Chicago Press, pp. 333–379.

Lohman, Larry (2006), "Carbon Trading: A Critical Conversation on Climate Change, Privatization, and Power," *Development Dialogue* 48, September.

Lopez, Rigoberto A. (1989), "Political Economy of U.S. Sugar Policies," *American Journal of Agricultural Economics* 71:19–31.

Lopez-Cordova, J. Ernesto, and Christopher Meissner (2003), "Exchange Rate Regimes and International Trade: Evidence from the Classical Gold Standard Era," *American Economic Review* 93(1):344–353.

———— (2005), "The Globalization of Trade and Democracy, 1870–2000," NBER Working Paper 11117, February.

Lovelock, James E. (1972), "Gaia as Seen through the Atmosphere," *Atmospheric Environment* 6(8):579–580.

Lowenberg, Anton D., and William H. Kaempfer (1998), *The Origins and Demise of South African Apartheid: A Public Choice Analysis,* Ann Arbor: University of Michigan Press.

Lowenstein, Roger (2008), "Triple-A Failure," *New York Times Magazine,* April 27.

Lucas, Robert E., Jr. (1972), "Expectations and the Neutrality of Money," *Journal of Economic Theory* 4:103–124.

———— (1973), "Some International Evidence on Output-Inflation Tradeoffs," *American Economic Review* 68:326–334.

———— (1990), "Why Doesn't Capital Flow from Rich to Poor Countries?" *American Economic Review* 80(2):92–96.

Lykken, David T. (1999), *Happiness: What Sudies on Twins Show Us About Nature, Nurture, and the Happiness Set Point,* New York: Golden Books.

Lyons, Richard K. (1996), "Foreign Exchange Volume: Sound and Fury Signifying Nothing?" in Jeffrey A. Frankel, Giampaolo Galli, and Alberto Giovannini (eds.), *The Microstructure of Foreign Exchange Markets,* Chicago: University of Chicago Press, pp. 183–206.

———— (1998), Profits and Position Control: A Week of FX Dealing," *Journal of International Money and Finance* 17:97–115.

———— (2001), *The Microstructure Approach to Exchange Rates,* Cambridge, MA: MIT Press.

Macdonald, Ian, and Betty O'Keefe (2000), *Canadian Holy War: A Story of Clans, Tongs, Murder, and Bigotry,* Surrey, BC: Heritage House Publishing Company Ltd.

MacMillan, Margaret (2001), *Paris 1919,* New York: Random House.

Maddison, Angus (1991), *Dynamic Forces in Capitalist Development, A Long-Run Comparative View,* New York: Oxford University Press.

———— (1995), *Monitoring the World Economy 1820–1992,* Paris: OECD.

———— (2001), *The World Economy: A Millennial Perspective,* Paris: OECD.

———— (2006), *Historical Statistics for the World Economy: 1–2003 AD,* Statistical Appendix; downloaded from http://ggdc.net/maddison/. Maintained by the Groningen Growth & Development Centre at the University of Groningen, Netherlands.

Magee, Stephen P., William A. Brock, and Leslie Young (1989), *Black Hole Tariffs and Endogenous Policy Theory,* Cambridge: Cambridge University Press.

Mahalanobis, P.C. (1955), "The Approach of Operational Research to Planning in India," *Sankahya* 16(1,2):3–120.

Mahatir Bin Mohamad (1997), "Highwaymen of the Global Economy," *Wall Street Journal,* September 23.

Malabre, Alfred L., Jr. (2003), *Lost Prophets: An Insider's History of the Modern Economists,* Frederick, MD: Beard Books.

Mandeville, Bernard (1732 [1714]), *The Fable of the Bees or Private Vices, Publick Benefits, vol. 1.* Indianapolis: Liberty Fund.

Mansfield, Edwin (1961), "Technical Change and the Rate of Imitation," *Econometrica* 29(4):741–766.

Mansfield, Edwin, Mark Schwartz, and Samuel Wagner (1981), "Imitation Costs and Patents: An Empirical Study," *Economic Journal* 91(364):907–918.

Marcal, Leah E. (2001), "Does Trade Adjustment Assistance Help Trade-Displaced Workers?" *Contemporary Economic Policy,* 19(1):59–72.

Markusen, James (1986), "Explaining the Volume of Trade: An Eclectic Approach," *American Economic Review* 76(5):1002–1011.

Marshall, Alfred (1920 [1959]), *Principles of Economics,* 8th ed., London: Macmillan.

Maskus, Keith E. (1987), "The International Political Economy of U.S. Sugar Policy in the 1980's," Working Paper no. 1, U.S. Department of State, Bureau of Economic and Business Affairs, September.

Massachusetts Institute of Technology Energy Laboratory (2000), "On the Road in 2020: A Lifecycle Analysis of New Automobile Technologies," MIT Working Paper EL 00–003.

Mataloni, Raymond J., Jr. (2005), "U.S. Multinational Companies: Operations in 2003," *Survey of Current Business* (July): 9–15.

May, Robert M. (2010), "Ecological Science and Tomorrow's World," *Philosophical Transactions of the Royal Society* 365:41–47.

Mayda, Anna Maria, and Dani Rodrik (2005), "Why Are Some People (And Countries) More Protectionist Than Others?" *European Economic Review* 49(6):1393–1430.

McClintock, John (2009), *The Uniting of Nations: An Essay on Global Governance,* 3d ed. Brussels: Peter Lang.

McGee, Robert W. (1993), "The Case to Repeal Antidumping Laws," *Northwestern Journal of International Law and Business* 13(3):491–562.

McGraham, Ellen R., and Richard Rogerson (1998), "Changes in Hours Worked Since 1950," Federal Reserve Bank of Minneapolis, *Quarterly Review* 22(1):2–19.

McKenzie, M.D. (1999), "The Impact of Exchange Rate Volatility on International Trade Flows," *Journal of Economic Surveys* 13(1):71–106.

McKibben, Bill (2008), *Deep Economy: The Wealth of Communities and the Durable Future,* New York: St. Martin's.

McKinnon, Ronald I. (1993), "The Rules of the Game: International Money in Historical Perspective," *Journal of Economic Literature* 31(1):1–44.

Meadows, Donella H., Dennis L. Meadows, Jörgen Ronders, and William Behrens (1972), *The Limits to Growth,* New York: Universe Books.

Medin, Douglas, and Max H. Bazerman (1999), "Broadening Behavioral Decision Research: Multiple Levels of Cognitive Processing," *Psychonomic Bulletin and Review* 6(4):533–546.

Meese, Richard, and Kenneth Rogoff (1983), "Empirical Exchange Rate Models of the Seventies," *Journal of International Economics* 14:3–24.

Meissner, Christopher M. (2005), "A New World Order: Explaining the Emergence of the Classical Gold Standard," *Journal of International Economics* 66(2):385–406.

Messerlin, Patrick A. (2001), *Measuring the Costs of Protection in Europe: European Commercial Policy in the 2000s,* Washington, DC: Institute for International Economics.

Michalos, A.C. (1985), "Multiple Discrepancy Theory (MDT)," *Social Indicators Research* 16:347–413.

Milanovic, Branko (2006), "An Estimate of Average Income and Inequality in Byzantium around Year 1000," *Review of Income and Wealth* 52(2):449–470.

Milanovic, Branko, Peter H. Lindert, and Jeffrey G. Williamson (2007), "Measuring Ancient Inequality," NBER Working Paper 13550, October.

Mill, John Stuart (1848), *Principles of Political Economy,* online at www.econlib.org/library/Mill/mlP.html.

Minsky, Hyman P. (1982), *Can "It" Happen Again? Essays in Instability and Finance,* Armonk, NY: M.E. Sharpe.

Miyagiwa, K. (1991), "Scale Economies in Education and the Brain Drain Problem, *International Economic Review* 32(3):743–759.

Monbiot, George (2000), "Biotech Has Bamboozled Us All," *Guardian,* August 24.

Moran, Theodore H. (1998), *Foreign Direct Investment and Development,* Washington, DC: Institute for International Economics.

Morgenson, Gretchen (2008), "Behind Insurer's Crisis, Blind Eye to a Web of Risk," *New York Times,* September 28.

Morisset, Jacques (1998), "Unfair Trade? The Increasing Gap between World and Domestic Prices in Commodity Markets during the Past 25 Years," *World Bank Economic Review* 12(3):503–523.

Mountford, A. (1997), "Can a Brain Drain Be Good for Growth in the Source Economy?" *Journal of Development Economics* 58(2):287–303.

Mun, Thomas (1664 [1986]), *England's Treasure by Forraign Trade,* London (printed by J.G. for Thomas Clark [reprint by Augustus M. Kelley, Fairfield, NJ].

Mundell, Robert A. (1979), *The Future of the International Finance System,* in A.L.K. Acheson, L.K. Chart, and M.F.J. Prachowny, Bretton Woods Revisited, Toronto: University of Toronto Press, p. 92.

——— (2000), "A Reconsideration of the Twentieth Century," *American Economic Review* 90(3):317–340.

Mussa, Michael (2000), "Factors Driving Global Economic Integration," paper presented at the Federal Reserve Bank of Kansas City symposium, Jackson Hole, WY, August 25.

Muth, John F. (1961), "Rational Expectations and the Theory of Price Movements," *Econometrica* 29:315–335.

Myrdal, Gunnar (1956), *Economic Theory and the Underdeveloped Regions,* London: G. Duckworth.

Naeem, S. (1998), "Species Redundancy and Ecosystem Reliability," *Conservation Biology* 12:39–45.

National Futures Association (2004), *Trading in the Retail Off-Exchange Foreign Currency Market: What Investors Need to Know,* Chicago: NFA.

Neely, Christopher J., and Paul A. Weller (2001), "Intraday Technical Trading in the Foreign Exchange Market," working paper, Federal Reserve Bank of St. Louis, January 10.

Nelson, Katherine, and Richard R. Nelson (2002), "On the Nature and Evolution of Human Know-How," *Research Policy* 31:719–733.

Nersisyan, Yeva, and Randall Wray (2010a), "Does Excessive Sovereign Debt Really Hurt Growth? A Critique of This Time Is Different, by Reinhart and Rogoff," Working Paper no. 603, Levy Economics Institute of Bard College, June.

——— (2010b), "Deficit Hysteria Redux? Why We Should Stop Worrying About U.S. Government Deficits," Public Policy Brief no. 111, Levi Economics Institute of Bard College.

Nixon, Edgar B. (1969), *Franklin D. Roosevelt and Foreign Affairs,* vol. 1 *January 1933–February 1934,* Cambridge, MA: Harvard University Press.

Norris, Floyd (2009), "Tax Break for Profits Went Awry," *New York Times,* June 4.

North, Douglass C. (1958), "Ocean Freight Rates and Economic Development 1750–1913," *Journal of Economic History* 18:556–573.

——— (2005), *Understanding the Process of Economic Change,* Princeton, NJ: Princeton University Press.

Nozick, Robert (1974), *Anarchy, State, and Utopia,* New York: Basic Books.

Nurkse, Ragnar (1944), *International Currency Experience,* Geneva: League of Nations.

Obstfeld, Maurice (1998), "The Global Capital Market: Benefactor or Menace?" *Journal of Economic Perspectives* 12(4):9–30.

Obstfeld, Maurice, and Alan M. Taylor (1998), "The Great Depression as a Watershed: International Capital Mobility over the Long Run," in Michael D. Bordo, Claudia D. Goldin, and Eugene N. White (eds.), *The Defining Moment: The Great Depression and the American Economy in the Twentieth Century,* Chicago: University of Chicago Press, pp. 353–402.

——— (2001), "Globalization and Capital Markets," in Michael D. Bordo, Alan M. Taylor and Jeffrey G. Williamson (eds.), *Globalization in Historical Perspective,* Chicago: University of Chicago Press, pp. 121–188.

——— (2002), "Sovereign Risk, Credibility and the Gold Standard: 1870–1913 versus 1925–31," *Economic Journal* 113(487):241–275.

——— (2004), *Global Capital Markets, Integration, Crisis, and Growth,* Cambridge: Cambridge University Press.

Obstfeld, Maurice, and Kenneth Rogoff (1995), "The Mirage of Fixed Exchange Rates," *Journal of Economic Perspectives* 9(4):73–96.

Obstfeld, Maurice, Jay C. Shambaugh, and Alan M. Taylor (2004), "Monetary Sovereignty, Exchange Rates, and Capital Controls: The Trilemma in the Interwar Period," *IMF Staff Papers* 51:75–108.

——— (2005), "The Trilemma in History: Tradeoffs among Exchange Rates, Monetary Policies, and Capital Mobility," *Review of Economics and Statistics* 87(3):423–438.

OECD (2002), *Working Together Towards Sustainable Development,* Paris: OECD.

——— (2004a), "Migration During 1820–1920, The First Global Century," chap. 1 in *World Economic Survey 2004,* Paris: OECD.

——— (2004b), *Trends in International Migration,* Paris: OECD.

——— (2006), *International Migration Outlook,* Paris: OECD.

Ofer, Gur (1987), "Soviet Economic Growth: 1928–1985," *Journal of Economic Literature* 25:1767–1833.

Olson, Mancur (1965), *The Logic of Collective Action: Public Goods and the Theory of Groups,* Cambridge, MA: Harvard University Press.

O'Rourke, Kevin H., and Jeffrey G. Williamson (1999), *Globalization and History: The Evolution of a Nineteenth Century Atlantic Economy,* Cambridge, MA: MIT Press.

Orrenius, Pia M., and Madeline Zavodny (2003), "Do Amnesty Programs Encourage Illegal Immigration? Evidence from IRCA," *Demography* 40(3):437–450.

Oswald, A.J., and N. Powdthavee (2008), "Does Happiness Adapt? A Longitudinal Study of Disability with Implications for Economists and Judges," *Journal of Public Economics* 92:1061–1077.

Owens, Katy, and Mary-Claire King (1999), "Genomic Views of Human History," *Science* 286(October 15).

Palley, Thomas (1998), *Plenty of Nothing: The Downsizing of the American Dream and the Case for Structural Keynesianism.* Princeton, NJ: Princeton University Press.

——— (2006), "Rethinking Trade and Trade Policy: Gomory, Baumol, and Samuelson on Comparative Advantage," Public Policy Brief no. 86, Levy Economics Institute of Bard College.

Park, Yung Chul, and Jong-Wha Lee (2001), "Recovery and Sustainability in East Asia," NBER Working Paper W8373, July.

Passel, Jeffrey S. (2006), "The Size and Characteristics of the Unauthorized Migrant Population in the U.S., Estimates Based on the March 2005 Current Population Survey, *Research Report,* Pew Hispanic Center, March 7.

Patinkin, Don (1965), *Money, Interest, and Prices,* New York: Harper & Row.

Persson, Torsten, and Guido Tabellini (1994), "Is Inequality Harmful for Growth?" *Economic Review* 57:787–806.

Petty, William (1682), *Another Essay in Political Arithmetic. Also referenced as: Political Arithmetic: Or Discourse Concerning the Extent and Value of Lands, People, Buildings.* London 1683, repr. Hull 1899; Dusseldorf 1992; downloadable from http://www.efm.bris.ac.uk/het/petty/poliarit.htm, accessed December 22, 2008.

Phelps, Edmund (1968), "Money-Wage Dynamics and Labor-Market Equilibrium," *Journal of Political Economy* 76(3, Part 2):678–711.

Phillips, A.W. (1958), "The Relation between Unemployment and the Rate of Change of Money Wage Rates in the United Kingdom, 1861–1957," *Economica* 25:283–300.

Pigou, Arthur Cecil (1917–1918), "The Value of Money," *Quarterly Journal of Economics* 32(1):38–65.

Pindyck, Robert S. (2007), "Uncertainty in Environmental Economics," *Review of Environmental Economics and Policy* 1(1):26–44.

Pleij, Herman (2001), *Dreaming of Cockaigne,* New York: Columbia University Press; translation by Diane Webb; original title: *Dromen Van Cocagne,* Amsterdam: Uitgeverij Prometheus, 1997.

Plender, John (2010), "Rules of Engagement," *Financial Times,* July 12.

Poincaré, Jules Henri (1908), "Mathematical Creation," reprinted in Brewster Ghiselin (ed.), 1952, *The Creative Process,* Berkeley: University of California Press, pp. 42–63.

Polanyi, Michael (1958), *Personal Knowledge: Towards a Post Critical Philosophy,* London: Routledge.

Popp, David (2002), "Induced Innovation and Energy Prices," *American Economic Review* 92:160–180.

——— (2004), "R&D Subsidies and Climate Policy: Is There a Free Lunch?" NBER Working Paper 10880, October.

Prebisch, Raúl (1950), *The Economic Development of Latin America and Its Principal Problems,* Lake Success, NY: United Nations Department of Social Affairs.

——— (1959), "Commercial Policy in the Underdeveloped Countries," *American Economic Review* 49(2):251–273.

Pretty, Jules, and Rachel Hine (2001), *Reducing Food Poverty with Sustainable Agriculture: A Summary of New Evidence,* Centre for Environment and Society, University of Essex, February.

Pritchett, Lant (1997), "Divergence, Big Time," *Journal of Economic Perspectives* 11(3):3–17.

Prowse, Michael (2003), "Why Capitalism Will Never Permit Us to Live a Life of Leisure," *Financial Times,* August 9–10.

Prusa, Thomas J., and Susan Skeath (2001), "The Economic and Strategic Motives for Antidumping Filings," *Weltwirtschaftliches Archiv* 138(3):389–413.

Psacharopoulos, George, and Patrinos, Harry (2004), "Returns to Investment in Education: A Further Update," *Education Economics* 2(2):111–134.

Quesada, Charo (2003), "Why Emigrate?" *IDB América,* Inter-American Development Bank, October 28.

Rand, Ayn (1967), *Capitalism: The Unknown Ideal,* NewYork: Signet Books.

Rauch, James E. (1999), "Networks versus Markets in International Trade," *Journal of International Economics* 48(1):7–35.

——— (2001), "Business and Social Networks," *Journal of Economic Literature* 39(4):1177–1203.

Rauch, James, and A. Casella (2003), "Overcoming Informational Barriers to International Resource Allocation: Prices and Group Ties," *Economic Journal* 113(1):21–42.

Ravetz, Jerry (1995), "Economics as an Elite Folk Science: The Suppression of Uncertainty," *Journal of Post Keynesian Economics* 17(2):165–184.

Rawls, John A. (1971), *A Theory of Justice,* Cambridge, MA: Harvard University Press.

Razin, Assaf, Efraim Sadka, and Phillip Swagel (1998), "Tax Burden and Migration: A Political Economy Theory and Evidence," *Journal of Public Economics* 85(2):167–190.

Rees, Martin (2005), *Our Final Hour: A Scientist's Warning,* New York: Basic Books.

Reinhart, Carmen, and Kenneth Rogoff (2009), *This Time Is Different: Eight Centuries of Financial Folly,* Princeton, NJ: Princeton University Press.

Richardson, James D., ed. (1903), *Messages and Papers of the Presidents,* Washington, DC: Bureau of National Literature and Art.

Richtel, Matt (2008), "Edison . . . Wasn't He the Guy Who Invented Everything?" *New York Times,* March 30.

Rigobon, Roberto, and Dani Rodrik (2005), "Rule of Law, Democracy, Openness, and Income: Estimating the Interrelationships," *Economics of Transition* 13(3):533–564.

Rising Tide North America (2009), "Hoodwinked in the Hothouse: False Solutions to Climate Change," pamphlet downloaded from www.risingtide.org in November 2009.

Robertson, D.H. (1938), "The Future of International Trade," *The Economic Journal* 48(189):1–14.

Rodriguez, Francisco, and Dani Rodrik (1999), "Trade Policy and Economic Growth: A Skeptics Guide to the Cross-National Evidence." NBER Working Paper, no. 7081.

——— (2001), "Trade Policy and Economic Growth: A Skeptics Guide to the Cross-National Evidence," in Ben Bernanke and Kenneth S. Rogoff (eds.), *NBER Macroeconomics Annual 2000,* Cambridge, MA: MIT Press, pp. 261–338.

Rodrik, Dani (1998), "Symposium on Globalization in Perspective: An Introduction," *Journal of Economic Perspectives* 12(4):3–8.

Rodrik, Dani, Arvind Subramanian, and Francesco Trebbi (2004), "Institutions Rule: The Primacy of Institutions over Geography and Integration in Economic Development," *Journal of Economic Growth* 9(2):131–165.

Rogoff, Kenneth (1999), "International Institutions for Reducing Global Financial Instability," *Journal of Economic Perspectives* 13(4):21–42.

Romer, Paul M. (1990), "Endogenous Technological Change," *Journal of Political Economy* 98(5), Part II:S71–S102.

——— (1993), "Idea Gaps and Object Gaps in Economic Development," *Journal of Monetary Economics* 32:543–573.

Roodman, David Malin (1999), "Building a Sustainable Society," in Lester R. Brown, Christopher Flavin, and Hillary French (eds.), *State of the World 1999, a Worldwatch Institute Report on Progress toward a Sustainable Society,* New York: W.W. Norton.

Rose, Andrew K. (2005), "One Reason Countries Pay Their Debts: Renegotiation and International Trade," *Journal of Development Economics* 77(1):189–206.

Rose, Andrew K., and Eric van Wincoop (2001), "National Money as a Barrier to International Trade: The Real Case for Currency Union," *American Economic Review* 91(2):383–390.

Rosenberg, Nathan (1994), *Exploring the Black Box: Technology, Economics, and History,* Cambridge, U.K.: Cambridge University Press.

Rosenthal, Elisabeth (2008), "Environmental Cost of Shipping Groceries Around the World," *New York Times,* April 26, downloaded from www.nytimes.com/2008/04/26/business/worldbusiness/26food.html.

Sachs, Jeffrey, and Andrew Warner (1995), "Natural Resource Abundance and Economic Growth," NBER Working Paper no. 5398.

——— (2001), "The Curse of Natural Resources," *European Economic Review* 45(4–6):827–838.

Salyer, L. (1995), *Laws Harsh as Tigers: Chinese Immigrants and the Shaping of Modern Immigration Law.* Chapel Hill: University of North Carolina Press.

Samuelson, Paul A. (2004), "Where Ricardo and Mill Rebut and Confirm Arguments of Mainstream Economists Supporting Globalization," *Journal of Economic Perspectives* 18(3):135–146.

Sanati, Cyrus (2009), "As Regulator Watched, A.I.G. Unit Piled on Risk," *New York Times,* March 5.

Sarno, Lucio, and Mark P. Taylor (2001), "Official Intervention in the Foreign Exchange Market: Is It Effective and, If So, How Does It Work?" *Journal of Economic Literature* 39(3):839–868.

Saxenian, AnnaLee (2002) "Silicon Valley's New Immigrant High-Growth Entrepreneurs," *Economic Development Quarterly* 16(1):20–31.

Scheve, K., and M. Slaughter (2001), *Globalization and the Perceptions of American Workers,* Washington, DC: Institute for International Economics.

Schiff, M. (2004), "When Migrants Overstay Their Legal Welcome: A Proposed Solution to the Guest-Worker Program," IZA Discussion Paper 1401, November.

Schonhardt-Bailey, Cheryl (1991), "Specific Factors, Capital Markets, Portfolio Diversification, and Free Trade: Domestic Determinants of the Repeal of the Corn Laws," *World Politics* 43:545–569.

Schumpeter, Joseph (1934), *The Theory of Economic Development,* Cambridge, MA: Harvard University Press.

Scott, Robert (2008), "The China Trade Toll: Widespread Wage Suppression, 2 Million Jobs Lost in the U.S.," EPI Briefing Paper no. 219, July 30, Economic Policy Institute.

Seabright, Paul (2010), *The Company of Strangers: A Natural History of Economic Life,* 2d ed., Princeton, NJ: Princeton University Press.

Sebastian Edwards (1998), "Openness, Productivity, and Growth: What Do We Really Know?" *Economic Journal* 108:383–398.

Seib, Gerald F. (1998), "Sanctions Here, Sanctions There: Time to Pause?" *Wall Street Journal,* June 17.

Shambaugh, Jay C. (2004), "The Effect of Fixed Exchange Rates on Monetary Policy," *Quarterly Journal of Economics* 114(1):301–352.

Shapiro, Mark (2010), "Conning the Climate," *Harper's Magazine,* February:31–39.

Shatz, Howard J., and Anthony J. Venables (2000), "The Geography of International Investment," in G.L. Clark, M. Feldman, and M.S. Gertler (eds.), *The Oxford Handbook of Economic Geography,* Oxford, U.K.: Oxford University Press.

Shiller, Robert J. (1997), "Why Do People Dislike Inflation?" in Christina D. Romer and David H. Romer (eds.), *Reducing Inflation: Motivation and Strategy,* Chicago: University of Chicago Press, pp. 13–70.

Siegel, Aaron (1993), *An Atlas of International Migration,* London: Hans Zell Publishers.

Silverman, Rachel Emma (1999), "Rich and Richer: Fifty of the Wealthiest People of the Past 1,000 Years," *The Wall Street Journal,* January 11, p. R6.

Simonian, Haig (2009), "Swiss Meet U.S. Government over Defence of Bank Secrecy," *Financial Times,* March 2.

Skidmore, Thomas E., and Peter H. Smith. *Modern Latin America,* 3d ed. New York: Oxford University Press, 1992.

Smith, Adam (1776 [1976]), *An Inquiry into the Nature and Causes of the Wealth of Nations,* Chicago: University of Chicago Press.

Solow, Robert (1956), "A Contribution to the Theory of Economic Growth," *Quarterly Journal of Economics* 70(1):65–94.

——— (1957), "Technical Change and the Aggregate Production Function," *Review of Economics and Statistics* 39:312–320.

——— (1960), "Investment and Technological Progress," in Kenneth Arrow, Samuel Karlin, and Patrick Suppes (eds.), *Mathematical Models in the Social Sciences,* Stanford, CA: Stanford University Press, pp. 89–104.

Soros, George (1998), *The Crisis of Global Capitalism,* New York: Public Affairs Press.

Stark, O., C. Helmenstein, and A. Prskawetz (1998), "Human Capital Depletion, Human Capital Formation, and Migration: A Blessing or a 'Curse'?" *Economics Letters* 60(3):363–367.

Stein, Stanley J. (1974), *Vassouras: A Brazilian Coffee County 1850–1890.* New York: Atheneum.

Stern, Nicholas (2007), *The Economics of Climate Change [The Stern Report],* Cambridge, U.K.: Cambridge University Press.

Stiglitz, Joseph (2008), "The Economics of Climate Change," *American Economic Review* 98(2):1–37.

——— (2009), "A Global Recovery for a Global Recession," *Nation,* June 24.

——— (2010), "Needed: A New Economic Paradism," *Financial Times*, August 20.

Stiglitz, Joseph, et al. (2010), *The Stiglitz Report: Reforming the International Monetary and Financial Systems in the Wake of the Global Crisis,* New York: New Press.

Stiglitz, Joseph, and Andrew Weiss (1981), "Credit Rationing in Markets with Imperfect Information," *American Economic Review* 71:393–410.

Stolper, Wolfgang, and Paul A. Samuelson (1941), "Protection and Real Wages," *Review of Economic Studies* 9(1):58–73.

Stulz, René M. (2005), "The Limits of Financial Globalization," *Journal of Finance* 60(4):1595–1638.

Summerhill, William R. (1999), "Railroads in Imperial Brazil, 1854–1889," In *Latin America and the World Economy Since 1800,* John H. Coatsworth and Alan M. Taylor (eds.), Cambridge, MA: Harvard University Press, pp. 383–405.

Sutthiphisal, Dhanoos (2006), "The Geography of Invention in High- and Low-Technology Industries: Evidence from the Second Industrial Revolution," *Journal of Economic History* 66(2):492–496.

Svensson, Peter (1998), "Strategic Trade Policy and Endogenous R&D-Subsidies: An Empirical Study," *Kyklos* 51(2):259–275.

Tanner, Helen Hornbeck (1995), *The Settling of North America,* New York: Macmillan.

Tanzi, Vito (2006), "Things Will Fall Apart But It Is the Aftermath that Matters," *Financial Times,* February 24.

Tarr, David G., and Morris E. Morkre (1984), *Aggregate Costs to the United States of Tariffs and Quotas on Imports: General Tariff Cuts and Removal of Quotas on Automobiles, Steel, Sugar, and Textiles,* Bureau of Economics Staff Report to the Federal Trade Commission, February.

Teece, David J. (1977), "Technology Transfer by Multinational Firms: The Resource Cost of Transferring Technological Know-How," *Economic Journal* 77(1):49–57.

Temple, Jonathan (1998), "Equipment Investment and the Solow Model," *Oxford Economic Papers* 50:39–62.

Tenreyro, Silvana, and Robert J. Barro (2007), "Economic Effects of Currency Unions," *Economic Inquiry* 45(1):1–23.

Teresi, Dick (2002), *Lost Discoveries,* New York: Simon and Schuster.

Texas Comptroller of Public Accounts (2006), "Undocumented Immigrants in Texas: A Financial Analysis of the Impact to the State Budget and Economy," special report, Austin: Texas Comptroller of Public Accounts, December.

Thaler, Richard, and Henrik Conqvist (2004), "Design Choices in Privatized Social-Security Systems: Learning from the Swedish Experience," *American Economic Review* 94(2):424–428.

Thaler, Richard, and Cass Sunstein (2008), *Nudge: Improving Decisions about Health, Wealth, and Happiness*, New Haven: Yale University Press.

Thorp, Rosemary (1998), *Progress, Poverty, and Exclusion: An Economic History of Latin America in the 20th Century.* Washington, DC: Inter-American Development Bank.

Tilman, David, Clarence L. Lehman, and Charles E. Bristow (1998), "Diversity-Stability Relationships: Statistical Inevitability or Ecological Consequence?" *American Naturalist* 151:177–282.

Tinbergen, Jan (1962), *Shaping the World Economy.* New York: Twentieth Century Fund.

Tomkins, Richard (2003), "Economic Progress Was Quite Nice While It Lasted," *Financial Times,* January 24.

Trefler, Daniel (1995), "The Case of the Missing Trade and Other Mysteries," *American Economic Review* 85(5):1029–1046.

Triffin, Robert (1960), *Gold and the Dollar Crisis,* New Haven: Yale University Press.

Tudge, Colin (2005), "Feeding People Is Easy: But We Have to Re-think the World from First Principles," *Public Health Nutrition* 8(6A):716–723.

Tullock, Gordon (1967), "The Welfare Costs of Tariffs, Monopolies, and Theft," *Western Economic Journal* 5:224–232.

——— (1993), *Rent Seeking,* Brookfield, VT: Edward Elgar.

Turner, R.K., J. Paavola, P. Cooper, S. Farber, V. Jessamy, and S. Georgio (2003), "Valuing Nature: Lessons Learned and Future Directions," *Ecological Economics* 46:493–510.

Tyndall, John (1861), "On the Absorption and Radiation of Heat by Gases and Vapours," *Philosophical Magazine* 22:169–194, 273–285.

UNCTAD (2007), *World Investment Report 2007,* New York: United Nations Conference on Trade and Development.

——— (2008), *Handbook of Statistics 2008,* New York: United Nations.

Union of Concerned Scientists (2009), "Failure to Yield," report downloaded from ucsusa.org/food_and_agriculture/.

U.S. Department of Commerce (1988), *United States Sugar Policy–An Analysis,* Washington, DC: U.S. Government Printing Office.

Van den Berg, Hendrik, and Lewer, Joshua J. (2001), "Do Capital-Importing Countries Really Grow Faster: An Empirical Test Using Panel Data for 27 Countries," *Global Economy Quarterly* 2(1):1–36.

——— (2007), *International Trade and Economic Growth,* Armonk, NY: M.E. Sharpe.

van Wincoop, Eric, and Kei-Mu Yi (2000), "Asia Crisis Postmortem: Where Did the Money Go and Did the United States Benefit?" Federal Reserve Bank of New York *Economic Policy Review,* September:51–70.

Veblen, Thorstein (1899), *The Theory of the Leisure Class,* New York: Modern Library.

Vedder, Richard, Lowell Gallaway, and Stephen Moore (2000), "The Immigration Problem: Then and Now," *Independent Review* 4(3):347–364.

Velde, François (2002), "The Crime of 1873: Back to the Scene," Federal Reserve Bank of Chicago Working Paper No. 2002–29.

Vernon, Raymond (1966), "International Investment and International Trade in the Product Cycle," *Quarterly Journal of Economics* 80(2):190–207.

Vidal J.-P. (1998), "The Effect of Emigration on Human Capital Formation," *Journal of Population Economics* 11(4):589–600.

Viscusi, Kip (1993), "The Value of Risks to Life and Health," *Journal of Economics Literature* 31(4):1912–1946.

Volcker, Paul A. (1999), "A Perspective on Financial Crises," in Jane Sneddon Little and Giovanni P. Olivei (eds.), *Rethinking the International Monetary System,* Conference Series no. 43, Federal Reserve Bank of Boston, June.

Wackernagel, Mathis, et al. (2002), "Tracking the Ecological Overshoot of the Human Economy," *Proceedings of the National Academy of Sciences* 99:9266–9271.

Wade, Nicholas (2003), "Dating of Australian Remains Backs Theory of Early Migration of Humans," *New York Times,* February 19.

Walker, B.H. (1992), "Biodiversity and Ecological Redundancy," *Conservation Biology* 6:18–23.

Wallich, Henry C. (1972), "The Monetary Crisis of 1971: The Lessons to Be Learned," lecture, Per Jacobsson Foundation, Washington, DC, September 24.

Ward, Peter (2009), *The Medea Hypothesis,* Princeton, NJ: Princeton University Press.

Weber, Max (1978), *Economy and Society,* Berkeley: University of California Press.

Wei, S. (1996), "Intra-national versus International Trade: How Stubborn Are Nations in Global Integration?" NBER Working Paper 5531.

Weil, David N. (2002), "Demographic Shocks: The View from History," in Jane Sneddon Little and Robert K. Triest (eds.), *Seismic Shifts: The Economic Impact of Demographic Change,* Boston: Federal Reserve Bank of Boston.

Weitzman, Martin L. (1996), "Hybridizing Growth Theory," *American Economic Review* 86(2):207–212.

——— (1998), "Recombinant Growth," *Quarterly Journal of Economics* 113(2):331–360.

—— (1999), "Pricing the Limits to Growth from Minerals Depletion," *Quarterly Journal of Economics* 114(2):691–706.

—— (2007), "Structural Uncertainty and the Value of Statistical Life in the Economics of Catastrophic Climate Change," NBER Working Paper No. 13490, October.

Wells, Spencer (2003), *The Journey of Man: A Genetic Odyssey,* New York: Random House.

Wenders, John T. (1987), *The Economics of Telecommunications*, Cambridge, MA: Ballinger Publishing Co.

Wessel, David, and Bob Davis (2007), "Pain from Free Trade Spurs Second Thoughts," *Wall Street Journal,* March 28.

Whalley, John, and Colleen Hamilton (1996), *The Trading System after the Uruguay Round,* Washington, DC: Institute for International Economics.

Wiedman, T., R. Wood, M. Lenzen, J. Minx, D. Guan, and J. Barrett (2008), *Development of an Embedded Carbon Emissions Indicator,* Report to the U.K. Department for Environment, Food and Rural Affairs (DEFRA) by Stockholm Environment Institute at the University of York and Centre for Integrated Sustainability Analysis at the University of Sydney, June, DEFRA, London, U.K.

Wilkins, Mira (1970), *The Emergence of Multinational Enterprise: American Business Abroad from the Colonial Era to 1914,* Cambridge, MA: Harvard University Press.

Williams, Frances, and Guy de Jonqières (2002), "Stalled in Geneva," *Financial Times,* June 19.

Williamson, John (1977), *The Failure of World Monetary Reform, 1971–1974,* London: Thomas Nelson and Sons.

Willis L. Peterson (1997), "Are Large Farms More Efficient?" Working Paper, Staff Paper P97–2. University of Minnesota, Department of Applied Economics, January 1997.

Wilson, Charles (1963), *Mercantilism,* London: Routledge & Kegan Paul.

Wilson, Edward O. (1975), *Sociobiology: The New Synthesis,* Cambridge, MA: Harvard University Press.

—— (2002), *The Future of Life,* New York: Alfred A. Knopf.

van Wincoop, Eric, and Kei-Mu Yi (2000), "Asia Crisis Postmortem: Where Did the Money Go and Did the United States Benefit?" *Economic Policy Review*, Federal Reserve Bank of New York, September, pp. 51–70.

Wong, K.-Y., and C.K. Yip (1999), "Education, Economic Growth, and the Brain Drain," *Journal of Economic Dynamics and Control* 23(5–6):699–726.

World Bank (1993), *The East Asian Miracle.* New York: Oxford University Press.

—— (2002), *World Development Report 2002,* Washington, DC: World Bank.

—— (2007), *Global Development Finance 2007,* Washington, DC: World Bank.

World Trade Organization (2010), *Annual Report of the WTO,* Geneva: WTO.

World Wildlife Fund (2008), *Living Planet Report 2008,* Gland, Switzerland: World Wildlife Fund for Nature.

Yeager, Leland (1976), *International Monetary Relations: Theory, History, and Policy,* New York: Harper & Row.

Zavodny, Madeline (1997), "Welfare and the Locational Choices of New Immigrants," *Economic Review,* Federal Reserve Bank of Dallas, 2nd Quarter: 2–10.

Zeile, William J. (2005), "U.S. Affiliates of Foreign Countries, Operations in 2003," *Survey of Current Business,* August:198–210.

Zeretsky, Adam M. (1997), "A Burden on the Economy? Immigration and the Economy," *Regional Economist,* Federal Reserve Bank of St. Louis, October.

Zhang, Shuguang, Yansheng Zhang, and Zhongxin Wan (1998), *Measuring the Costs of Protection in China,* Washington, DC: Institute for International Economics.

Zhu, Susan Chun (2005), "Can Product Cycles Explain Skill Upgrades?" *Journal of International Economics* 66:131–155.

Zimmer, Carl (2005), *Smithsonian Intimate Guide to Human Origins,* New York: HarperCollins.

Zukav, Gary (1979), *The Dancing Wu Li Masters: An Overview of the New Physics*, New York: William Morrow.

Index

Italic page references indicate tables, charts, and graphs.

Pegged exchange rates, 344, 415–416, 449, 453, 481
PepsiCo, 128
Perceived value of product, 127
Perfect competition, assumption of, 112, 118, 156, 268
Peril point, 251
Permanent economic growth, 148–151
Perón, Juan, 279
Perry, Matthew, 246
Personal Responsibility and Work Opportunity Reconciliation Act (1996), 541
Petrodollars, recycling, 392–394
Petty, William, 7, 161
Phelps, Edmund, 375
Phillips, A.W., 375
Phillips curve, 375
Physical science theory, 29
Pindyck, Robert, 566
Pizza Hut, 128
Plaza Accord (1985), 458–459, 488
Pleij, Herman, 96
Plutarch, 3
Poincaré, Jules Henri, 160
Polanyi, Michael, 186
Policy. *See* Economic policy; Immigration policy
Political economy of international trade, 235–241
Politics, 138, 235–241
Ponzi finance, 379
Ponzi schemes/ventures, 379
Portes, Richard, 488–489
Portfolio effect, 563
Portfolio investment, 317, 365–368
Portugal, 270
Poverty, 486
Powdthavee, N., 102
Power of compounding, 139
PPF. *See* Production possibilities frontier
Prebisch, Raúl, 277–279
Precautionary principle, 43
Preferential trade area (PTA), 260–261
Premium, 369
Preserving services, 563
Price discrimination and, 226
Price elasticity, 222
Price gap, 85–86
Pricing, 127, *128*
Primary budget surplus, 406–407, 477
Principal-agent problem, 311
Producer surplus, 73–74, *74*, 92–95
Product cycle model, 181–183, *183*, 193
Production, 156
Production function, 138, 146, *147*, 158

Production possibilities frontier (PPF)
adjustments to free trade and, 89–90
curve, 56, *57*, 58–59, *59*
defining, 56
differences in, 61–62, 66–67
economic growth and, 136, *137*
Heckscher-Ohlin model and, 56–59, *57*, 61–62, *62*, 66–67, 136, *137*
increasing returns to scale and, 113–115, *115*
Samuelson's argument and, example of, 190, *191*
two-country model and, 61–63, *63*, *64*, 75, *76*
Products, 127, 129, 182
Professional workers, 505
Profit, 156
Proletariat, 175
Promotion, 127, *128*
Provisioning services, 563
Prusa, Thomas, 225–226
Psacharopoulos, George, 69
Psychology, 96, 102–103, 178–179
PTA, 260–261
Ptolemy, 34
Public sector debt, 406–408
Purchasing power, 329, 421

Q

Quantitative trade restrictions, 208. *See also* Quotas
Quintiles of households, 167
Quota rent, 211–213
Quotas
auction, 215
defining, 208–209
equivalent, 216–217
numerical example of, 213–214
quota rent and, 211–213
sugar, U.S., 237–239, *239*
in supply and demand model of trade, 209–212, *211*
tariffs and, 215–217, *217*
voluntary export restraints and, 214–215
welfare effects of, *211*, 212, *214*
worth of, 241, *241*
QWERTY keyboard layout, 155

R

R&D activities, 125, 158
Radioactivity theory, 29
Rambouillet Summit (1975), 456
Rand, Ayn, 528

Ranis, Gustav, 277
Rational expectations, 375, 387
Ravetz, Jerry, 47
Rawls, John A., 166, 177–179, 528, 550
Razin, Assaf, 514
RBS, 363
Real assets, 313
Reciprocal Trade Agreements Act (RTAA) (1934), 249, 251
Recycling petrodollars, 392–394
Redish, Angela, 429
Redundancy of ecosystem, 563
Reform Act (1832), 244
Reform after Great Recession, 482–486
Refugee Relief Act (1953), 538
Refugees, 505, 537
Regional economic integration, 260–262, *261*
Regulating services, 563
Regulations, 125, 485–486. *See also specific law*
Reinhart, Carmen, 483
Relativity theory, 29
Remittances, 508–511, *510*, 517
Rent, 211–212
Rent-evading activity, 241
Rent-seeking behavior, 240–241, 270
Reparations payments, 434
Reputations of firms, 124
Retail currency exchange, 333–335
Retaliatory tariffs, 258
Returns to capital, 317–318
Revaluation of currency, 453
Reversal of international financial flows, 387, 395
Ricardo, David, 16, 65, 244
Rigobon, Roberto, 144
Risk, 316–317, 325, 344, 353, 566–568
Risk reduction, 6, 8
Robertson, Raymond, 540
Rodriguez, Francisco, 142, 144
Rodrik, Dani, 16, 77, 142, 144
Rogers, John, 14
Rogoff, Kenneth, 397, 483
Rollovers, 395
Roman Catholic Church, 421, 491
Romer, Paul, 138–139, 152, 160
Roodman, David, 579
Roosevelt, Franklin D., 180, 249, 251, 440–441, 447, 537
Rose, Andrew K., 397–398, 467
Rosenberg, Nathan, 511–512, 516
Rosenthal, Elizabeth, 106
Rosenzweig, Mark R., 539
Roubini, Nouriel, 479
Royal Bank of Scotland (RBS), 363

About the Author

Hendrik Van den Berg is professor of economics at the University of Nebraska–Lincoln, where since 1989 he has taught classes in economic growth and development, international economics, international finance, and the economics of immigration. He received B.A. and M.A. degrees in economics from the State University of New York at Albany in 1971 and 1973, respectively, and M.S. and Ph.D. degrees in economics from the University of Wisconsin–Madison in 1987 and 1989. After graduating from SUNY at Albany, he joined the U.S. Department of State and served as commercial attaché at the U.S. Embassy in Managua, Nicaragua, and the U.S. Trade Center in São Paulo, Brazil. In 1979, Hendrik left the foreign service to manage the Brazilian office of Marsteller, an advertising/public relations subsidiary of Young and Rubicam, and in 1980, he became planning manager of Singer do Brasil, the Brazilian subsidiary of the U.S.-based Singer Company. In 1985, he returned to economics and enrolled in the Ph.D. program at the University of Wisconsin. In 1989, after graduating with a Ph.D. in economics, Hendrik accepted the position of assistant professor of economics at Nebraska.

Hendrik's broad background in diplomacy, business, academia, and overseas living have helped to shape his adoption of the heterodox approach to economics. He has published numerous articles on exchange rates, international trade, alternative estimates of economic growth, the relationship between international trade and economic growth, the economics of immigration, and other topics in economic development. He has written a number of economics textbooks, among which are: *Economic Growth and Development* (2001), *International Economics* (2004), and *International Finance and Open-Economy Macroeconomics* (2010). He jointly wrote graduate-level economics textbooks: *The Economics of Immigration* (2009) with Orn Borvarsson and *International Trade and Economic Growth* with Joshua Lewer. The latter was published by M.E. Sharpe in 2007.